Major Foreign Powers

SIXTH EDITION

MAJOR

GWENDOLEN M. CARTER Northwestern University

JOHN H. HERZ The City College,
The City University of New York

FOREIGN POWERS

SIXTH EDITION

HARCOURT BRACE JOVANOVICH, INC.

NEW YORK   CHICAGO
SAN FRANCISCO   ATLANTA

Preface to the Sixth Edition

"To write a book on comparative government at a time like the present is, in many respects, a foolhardy enterprise": thus began the preface to the first edition, and the statement remains equally true today. The speed with which events develop makes difficult the long observation and mature analysis so important to the evaluation of institutions and policies. If the political systems of the two postwar Germanies have proven more stable than many people predicted, that of postwar France has changed radically in response to internal and external pressures. Although the facilities for careful observation are still somewhat restricted in the Soviet Union, the transition from Stalin to post-Stalinist and, subsequently, to post-Khrushchev leadership has exhibited significant developments within the one-party system. And Great Britain is now engaged, under its new Conservative government, in re-evaluating the results of the extensive experimentation at the end of World War II. Thus, in this sixth edition, as in earlier editions, extensive changes have been necessary in every section of the work. Moreover, these changes often reflect processes that subsequent policies and events are certain to affect.

Yet the conditions that make the writing and rewriting of this book difficult are the very ones that make it most important for Americans to understand the politics of major foreign powers. The pleasant times of peace and stability, when it is easier to prepare such studies, are also the times when foreign events have less effect on American life. But these times seem to have gone forever. We live in permanent crisis, and it is in such times that it becomes essential for Americans to have the widest possible knowledge of conditions and developments in important countries abroad.

MAJOR FOREIGN POWERS

The four countries dealt with in this book are of unquestionable importance to the United States. The Soviet Union and the United States are the world's two "superpowers." Great Britain and France still retain both influence and prestige, despite their diminished power. The fourth country, Germany, has been a great power and even the two parts of a divided Germany each play a significant role in international affairs. All four countries afford a wealth of political material of profound significance for the study of government.

To concentrate on these countries is not to suggest that others are lacking in political interest. Sweden and Switzerland, for example, have engaged in political and economic experiments of great interest for the Western democracies; so too have such overseas members of the Commonwealth of Nations as Canada, Australia, and New Zealand. India's courageous experiment with political democracy, Japan's attempt to build free government, the changing political forms of Africa's newly independent countries, and developments in the long-established states of Latin America demand our attention. So do conditions in Communist countries outside the Soviet Union, especially China and particularly since it has entered the United Nations. Both in the extended introduction and in the conclusion we shall refer to such countries, as well as to our major powers, in order to develop a broad framework of government and politics in the twentieth century. But such a framework needs to be combined with a thorough study of the institutions and politics of the four countries we deem most significant to Americans both as factors in international politics and as political laboratories.

APPROACH TO THE SUBJECT

Any book on comparative politics and government—whether it uses, as this one does, the country-by-country method or the method of comparing political processes and governmental institutions as such—needs to say something about the comparative method favored by the authors. The intellectual tools the authors use in their approach should be clearly described, especially at a time when the behavioralist revolution has overturned most of the traditional methods and concepts of political science. We applaud some of the scholarly innovation of the last fifteen or twenty years, much of which has considerable merit. By drawing attention to the behavior patterns of human beings as determining events in politics as well as in other areas of social life, behavioralism has been a healthy corrective for studies and approaches too exclusively concerned with the products of these behavior patterns: institutions, constitutions, and so forth. Similarly, there is value to the new emphasis on the study of elites, of political "socialization" of the young, of political "mobilization," of "integration" of groups into national units. In many of these studies the use of the quantitative method, increasingly refined statistical tools, and more careful conceptualization have proven valuable.

We welcome all of this. We have never accepted either the strictly legalistic or the descriptive institutional approach that behavioralists rightly criticize. From the first edition of this book we have utilized structural functionalism. Even before this term was widely adopted, we used this approach to analyze the way in which the institutions of government and the processes of politics in the four countries of our study have functioned, or failed to function, and why. Subsequently, we have added new types of data taken from wherever we have found them illuminating, as, for example, from survey research and opinion polls.

We have, however, not found it useful to change our basic terminology. It seemed clearer

to continue to write of the activities and functions of parties, movements, interest groups, rather than to describe them in terms of "interest aggregation." We describe the process of decision- and policy-making precisely in those words rather than in such terms as "authoritative allocation of values." In our description of law-making and the execution or implementation of the laws, we retain simple language rather than refer to "rule-making" and "rule application." Instead of using such terms as "inputs" and "outputs" or the curious phrase "within-puts," we have continued to write about the processes influencing government or the results of governmental action.

Moreover, this book continues to emphasize the historical approach to the evolution of institutions and the ways in which they have been used, reflecting our belief that it is an essential concomitant to the analysis of contemporary government and politics. We have continued to present in some detail the political ideas that have had the most impact on the thought and action of people in the countries with which we have been chiefly concerned. At the same time we have given greater attention to "political culture." Our overriding purpose is to analyze and compare in an understandable and meaningful fashion the key features of the political life and institutions of the four countries in our study. For this reason we have not attempted to theorize abstractly or to build models, but to derive our judgments directly from our material.

We hold comparison to be a major tool for understanding. We have therefore attempted from the very beginning, in our discussion of British politics, to draw comparisons with those American organs and procedures with which the reader may be expected to be familiar. Similarly, in the section on France, we make comparisons between the presidential-parliamentary government of its Fifth Republic and the parliamentary system of Great Britain. West Germany offers still a third variant in parliamentary and executive practice. The Soviet Union, of course, provides the most striking contrasts to the other three major powers. Naturally, there are marked similarities as well as differences between the Soviet Union and the Communist-controlled German Democratic Republic, which is treated in the German section.

Throughout, we have tried to depict governments not as casual or arbitrary collections of institutions in a vacuum apart from the people who have produced them, but as living complexes of activities and arrangements that change and develop in response to the character, needs, desires, and purposes of human beings. Although there is general uniformity in the arrangements of material within the treatment of each country, there are differences in places where clarity suggests them. Thus, while the first chapter in the British, French, and German sections discusses land and people, social structure, education, and organs of public opinion, the first chapter for the Soviet Union deals with ideology, history, and the constitution. The second chapters for Great Britain, France, and Germany handle the most significant historical events and influences that have molded the institutions of the respective governments, whereas the parallel chapter for the Soviet Union deals with land, people, society, and the processes of mass communication. The third chapters in all sections turn to political parties and elections. The fourth chapters are devoted to representative bodies. The fifth in all sections is concerned with the executive and the nature of political leadership (in the section on Germany, also with the administration). The sixth (except for Germany) is concerned with national and local administration. The seventh chapter (for Germany, the sixth) turns to the administration of justice. The seventh chapter of the German section deals with Berlin, both West and East, and with the German Democratic Republic, thereby facilitating comparisons with the Federal Republic and providing a unified treatment of a Communist regime outside the Soviet Union. The eighth chapter in each section considers the position of the country in the world today.

The book opens with a consideration of the most significant issues for modern government and points up the contrast between democratic and totalitarian forms. The conclusion picks up general issues raised in the introduction and seeks to extend the comparisons of structure and function handled in the body of the work. It is our hope that together they will serve both as a synthesizing review and as an aid to understanding the most significant forces and problems affecting contemporary politics and government.

In writing *Major Foreign Powers* we have had in mind the reader who is seeking an introduction to politics rather than the scholar who has already specialized in the field. Wherever possible, therefore, we have dispensed with the top-heavy apparatus of scholarship that requires a footnote for every statement and thus diverts the reader from the principal train of thought. The source of specialized statistical data, however, is generally provided. The reader who wishes to pursue subjects further will be able to do so by using the comprehensive bibliography of relevant books and articles in English, prepared by Professor Louise W. Holborn of the Radcliffe Institute, who has contributed helpfully to all editions of the book.

The first edition of this book was the result of close collaboration between Gwendolen M. Carter and John C. Ranney. Following Mr. Ranney's untimely death, the subsequent editions were prepared by Miss Carter and John H. Herz. Miss Carter is responsible for the sections on Great Britain, France, and the Soviet Union and Mr. Herz for the section on Germany, which was added in the second edition. The two authors jointly prepared the introduction and the conclusion and at all times have worked closely together to maintain the unity of the work.

THE AUTHORS' PERSONAL POSITION

Each of the major foreign powers today is the focus of great controversy, and an author inevitably finds himself involved in questions that go beyond a mere description of political institutions and processes. Once one has ascertained as accurately as possible how an institution works, how power is exercised, how rulers are chosen, how elections are arranged, or which interests rule, the further question arises: Does the institution work well or badly, is the system good or bad?

In many cases, the answer to this question

will depend on one's personal set of values or standard of judgment. The person who thinks of poverty or unemployment as the greatest evil may well come to a different conclusion from the person who hates political tyranny above all else; the person who worships efficiency will look at the same institution in a very different light from the person who thinks it most important that men should base all their institutions on voluntary consent.

It has therefore seemed well to the authors to do two things. First, we have tried to explain in our discussion of the politics of each country the nature of the ideas the aims, and the traditions that have had a dominating political influence, so that it will be possible to judge the institutions of each country in the light of its own standards and beliefs. But we have also thought it important, on issues that are controversial, to make our own point of view perfectly clear—both because it should be more stimulating for the reader to see the issues discussed frankly, even when he might himself disagree, and because it would be deceptive in any case to evade value judgments at a time when even to avoid an issue is to take a position. We therefore have not tried to conceal the fact that we share the political beliefs of liberal Americans. To us a society is bad that lacks the traditional democratic freedoms of thought, speech, press, and association. But a society is not good that is marked by poverty, ignorance, unemployment, or social and racial discrimination. Like most Americans, we would like to make the best of both worlds: to see the good political and spiritual life combined with the good material life. And it has seemed to us important to discover to what extent any one of these major foreign powers has succeeded in combining these ideals.

ACKNOWLEDGMENTS

At the conclusion of so extended a survey, the authors are bound to think with special gratitude of the many people who have given them assistance in reading and criticizing parts of the manuscript, in providing information, and in helping with the innumerable technical jobs involved in the preparation of a book. None of them, of course, bears any responsibility for any faults in the book, but they are largely responsible for whatever merit the book has.

Although lack of space prevents us from again mentioning individually those who gave both advice and criticism in the preparation of earlier editions, our sense of gratitude to them remains keen. For helpful suggestions and counsel in preparing the sixth edition, the authors extend their special appreciation to Professor Jeremy R. Azrael of the University of Chicago; Professor Severyn Bialer of Columbia University; Professor Gerard Braunthal of the University of Massachusetts; Professor Remi Clignet of Northwestern University; Professor Bernard Crick of Birkbeck College, University of London; Professor Alfred Diamant of Indiana University; Professor Ira Katznelson of Columbia University; Professor Mark Kesselman of Columbia University; Dr. Donald Schwartz of the Center for Russian and East European Studies, University of Toronto; and to Professor Lawrence Wylie of Harvard University. We also thank the British, French, and German Information Services for their help.

GWENDOLEN M. CARTER
JOHN H. HERZ

Contents

III

The Government of Germany, by John H. Herz

IV

The Government of the Soviet Union, by Gwendolen M. Carter

Charts
and
Maps

GREAT BRITAIN

FRANCE

GERMANY

SOVIET UNION

Introduction

CONTEMPORARY GOVERNMENT AND POLITICS

Any contemporary study of government and politics must begin from one, all-important perspective: the rapid increase of population and the effects of technology have placed in jeopardy the very existence of mankind on this planet of limited size and finite resources. They may lead toward doom through the destruction of the world's environment or through suicidal nuclear conflict, or they may spur solutions to the world's problems through peaceful cooperation. In either case, man's future has become a common venture. For better or worse, the fate of this country is now tied to that of the rest of the world. At no time, therefore, has it been more critical for Americans to understand the governments and politics of other nations.

RANGE AND UNITS OF GOVERNMENT

Previous editions of this book could justly begin by explaining the role of big government as primarily a consequence of traditional industrialism. We could still say of the great environmental issues created by what is sometimes called the second industrial revolution or, somewhat more fancifully, "the technotronic age," that "only gradually do the problems of the preservation of resources, natural as well as human, of land and landscape, of purity of water and air, of the protection of physical health (endangered as it is by pollution and chemicals) and of mental health (threatened by the new mechanized way of life) enter our consciousness." A mere five years after the last edition of this book, these problems have entered with a vengeance.

It has also become increasingly clear that the most urgent tasks facing the human race, whether they are ecological or political, are worldwide in scope, requiring global policies and planning for their accomplishment. We cannot say for sure whether the obvious conclusion—formation of global patterns of government—will be reached in time for man to survive. What is abundantly clear, however, is that the traditional units of government will have to face problems in environmental planning and in political ordering that will surpass anything they have confronted in the past.

The primary unit of government, for the foreseeable future, will still be the nation-state. Not too long ago, many students of government and international relations thought that nuclear weapon systems had made the state obsolete because these systems had rendered the nation so penetrable that the state had lost its essential function of protection. Environmental problems might well have added to that doubt. But it appears that the traditional unit is hardier than many had assumed. One reason for this is that nuclear deterrence, by rendering nuclear war less likely, has given the state a new lease on life, under the wings, to use a metaphor, of the superpowers. The latter have divided the world, or much of it, into mutually agreed on zones of noninterference. This protects the smaller states, in the respective spheres at least, from annihilation by the other side. As someone has put it, a bit flippantly, the only country a superpower can still attack with impunity is one of its allies (e.g., the Soviet Union's invasion of Czechoslovakia). This comment somewhat overstates the case because it ignores the "gray areas" where superpowers still vie for influence or for control. But on the whole, the system of deterrence so far has prevented nuclear war and has enabled states to continue existing and conducting themselves as more or less independent entities.

Several divergent trends currently affect the nation-state system by bolstering it up or else by weakening it. After the immediate postwar era, when the emergence of the superpowers and their expansionism made the fate of nations questionable, there had been a strong reassertion of the spirit of national collectivity. This reassertion seems to reflect the increasing sense of loneliness and alienation human beings experience in a mechanized, dehumanized world. They tend to look for reassurance and reinforcement to those "natural" groupings that for centuries or millennia have been their chief rallying points: tribe, ethnic group, and so forth. In some cases this has even meant challenging the integration of long-established states by an insistence on the distinctiveness of some linguistic, cultural, or similar entity existing within them (e.g., Scots and Welsh in Britain, Bretons in France, Basques in Spain, or Quebecois in Canada). In the developing world this trend is apparent in the persistence with which ethnic and similar groups resist national integration (e.g., Eritrea or centrifugal trends in India). Yet nationalism also has reasserted itself both in Eastern and in Western Europe against the tendencies of the superpowers to dominate their spheres and in the Third World through "national liberation" movements, whether under Communist guidance or not.

A contrary trend has been toward supranational regional integration. This process has made some progress in the area of the older states, particularly in Western Europe. We shall return to this process and what it has meant to some of the European countries in the sections devoted to individual countries. How it is taking place, and why, will be analyzed in detail.

DIVERSITY AND UNIFORMITY

In studying states, we encounter, first, the problem of their increasing number and diversity. Half a century ago there were fewer than fifty sovereign countries. Today there are about one hundred and thirty, with more to come. No one can hope to study them all. Nor are their numbers the only difficulty. When Aristotle prepared the first great treatise on government and politics, he is said to have put his students to work analyzing some hundred and fifty constitutions. But their task was easier than ours. Compared to the systems within the relatively close world of the ancient polis, the present variety of the world's political units is vastly broader. Not only is there a sharp contrast between the systems, usually referred to as "East" and "West," but also there are important differences among the countries within each group. Nor is this all. In the Middle and the Far East, Africa, and Latin America, we are confronted with a diversity that is constantly increasing as more and more countries acquire their independence.

Among the newer states, we find some with advanced forms of organization patterned on Western models, as are India and Jamaica, or conducted as "one-party democracies" like Tanzania and the Ivory Coast, or, increasingly, governed under army rule as in the Congo, Pakistan, and Nigeria. We also find a continuing heritage of the "premodern" age. Some developing countries, in fact, are still in the primitive stage of civilization, with nomadic forms of life and feudal or absolutist institutions. Even within one region such as the Middle East, countries of this type, like Oman and Arabia, lie close to advanced states such as Lebanon and Israel. Moreover, the degree of governmental control may range all the way from the regulation and organization of almost all aspects of life to a bare minimum of government and administration.

But we should not exaggerate the degree of diversity. Beneath the surface appearance of great variety lie trends toward rapidly increasing uniformity. The outlook of traditional man is yielding almost everywhere to that of modernity. Traditionalism is bound to give way with the "revolution of rising expectations." The universal desire for the better life that can be expected from scientific thought and industrial technology inevitably penetrates into areas in which the traditional, fatalistic outlook used to make people shun the very idea of change. Once the expectation of rapid advance becomes prevalent, it cannot be stopped by inherited political institutions or processes. Nothing distinguishes our age more sharply from preceding ages than the rate at which change is taking place. Thus the technological-scientific process that sweeps the planet may result in a more homogeneous mankind, with its previous, abundantly diverse forms of culture and civilization and its widely varied stages of development merged into a controlled, organized, and largely man-made cosmos.

Before this happens, however, the developing world will be faced with tremendous problems of transformation and adjustment. There are three dominant reasons why this is so. The first is the rapid rate of development. Whereas most of the so-called developed countries of the West had centuries in which to achieve the transition from premodern to modern society, the new countries strain to achieve it in a matter of decades. Second, the radical nature of the change compels the developing countries to leap from primitive conditions to the jet age. The third is the urgency of some of the basic problems, particularly the problem of raising living standards for an exploding population.

Hence, in order to achieve political modernization, it is likely and understandable that the new countries will often use forms of government, administration, and law that are different from standard Western models. (Western in this context refers to communism as well as to democracy, since both owe their basic principles to Western civilization.) The African version of the one-party state, for instance, may turn out to be equidistant from the two-party or multiparty model of democracy and the Communist state-party model. Nonetheless, it may well fulfill the needs of a transitional, developing society. These new African states may also develop quite unorthodox procedures and institutions to achieve such familiar results as the protection of individual or family rights and interests.

In one respect, however, it is very likely that the modernized world of the future will become increasingly uniform. We can already observe the growth of a degree of equality through the impact of science and technology, because these are based on common experience and common talent. Technologically trained man is exchangeable. With the technological approach it makes little difference whether a problem is researched in the United States, Argentina, or Japan. The technical rules for establishing an up-to-date atomic pile or a system of pest control or a computer programming system are the same, whether applied by people of white, black, or oriental extraction, living under communism, fascism, or liberal democracy.

Hence, a degree of egalitarianism underlies modernity. This fact is not denied, but, on the contrary, it is strongly emphasized in doctrine and in practice even by those political systems that otherwise fail to meet the requirements of democracy: that is, the Communist ones. And even in South Africa, which so exceptionally illustrates the countertrend, that is, the counterpolicy of inequality, the technological facts of life have rendered complete apartheid (racial separation) impossible in practice because of the need for African workers in industry.

Generally, of course, egalitarian aspirations have had their strongest effects in the last decades in Africa, Asia, and in other parts of the world where the vast majority of mankind had been living under colonial systems. The process of emancipation, in the sense of eliminating what the modern mind sees as irrational inequalities based on group, class, caste (as of slaves or serfs), religious or racial differentiation (as of Jews or Muslims), or on sex, seems to follow the same curve of acceleration that characterizes other developments.

Apart from this, however, it is far from certain that what emerges from the process of political modernization will turn out to be democratic in the sense of Western democracy. There was a time, at the turn of the century, when one took for granted that an advanced industrial country would be a democracy. Experience since the end of World War I, however, has shattered this belief. Since that time, totalitarianism, both fascist and communist, has made deep inroads into regions where democracy seemed at least to have a chance. Moreover, communism has emerged as *the* great alternative to liberal democracy in the transformation of "backward" societies into modern or "advanced" ones. The trend toward uniformity, then, is not toward a single model of political organization; it is primarily toward two opposing models, the liberal-democratic and the communist-totalitarian, if it is not toward something distinctively different from both.

BASIC CONCEPTS AND PATTERNS OF GOVERNMENT

One cause of the misunderstanding and confusion so often found in the study of politics is the lack of rigorous and clear-cut definitions of basic terms. In the foregoing discussion we have spoken a bit loosely about democracy and totalitarianism, liberalism and authoritarianism. Therefore, before proceeding further into the study of our four major countries, we propose to define more clearly these four basic political concepts.

We shall cast our definitions in terms of a twofold dichotomy, depending upon which one of two fundamental political questions is posed. The first of these questions concerns the bearer of political power, that is, the subject of policy- or decision-making: Who governs? To this the answer may be: the many or the few. If the totality of the adult members of a particular political community—that is, the people—hold ultimate political power, we call this form of government *democracy*. The rule of a minority —whether an aristocratic elite, or another oligarchy, or, in the extreme event, a one-man absolutist monarchy or a one-man dictatorship —we call *authoritarianism*.

The second, quite different, basic question concerns the sphere controlled by political authority (whether or not it be organized in democratic or in authoritarian fashion): How wide is this sphere? How much of the life of society and of its members falls under government direction? If political authority extends in principle over everything in the life of the people, the regime is *totalitarian*. If government is limited, leaving certain, often large, spheres of individual and group life protected by convention or law against government intervention, we call the regime *liberal*.

Definitions such as these, of course, are subject to historical change and qualification. The definition of *democracy*, for instance, depends greatly on what, at a particular point of historical development, is defined as *the people*. Athenian democracy would today be considered

oligarchy, since its citizens lorded it over a majority of slaves, noncitizens, and women who at that time were not included in *the people*. By the same token, the rule of the white minority in South Africa cannot be characterized as democratic. In reference to the other dichotomy, a laissez-faire liberal of the mid-nineteenth century might have termed *totalitarian* the degree of government regulation and government intervention, especially in the fields of economy and industrial relations, which obtains today in "liberal," democratic countries such as the United States. Today those countries, with their broad areas of protected individual and group liberties and freedoms, appear genuinely liberal in contrast to totalitarian dictatorships.

The natural correlates among these four concepts are liberal democracy and totalitarian authoritarianism, or totalitarian dictatorship. Indeed, when talking before of *democracy* and *totalitarianism*, we used these two terms as shorthand versions of the above. However, it is also possible to correlate the concepts crosswise—that is, democracy with totalitarianism, and authoritarianism with liberalism. There have been examples of these latter types in history. In the initial stages of a popular revolution (as in the French Revolution), democracy may tend to disregard limitations on popular control and thus become totalitarian. And conversely, a ruling minority may accept limitations on its authoritarian rule, as witness the early nineteenth-century monarchical-aristocratic "constitutionalism" of continental European countries, out of which grew the German *Rechtsstaat*, or England before it became fully democratic.

Much more common, however, are the other pairings. In fact, experience suggests that totalitarian democracy, as in the French Revolution, turns into small-group or one-man rule, whereas liberal authoritarianism tends to give way to full-fledged liberal democracy. The combination of liberalism and democracy characterized political developments in the Western countries in the era of the rising middle classes and the first industrial revolution. In the twentieth century, however, the impact of unsolved social and international problems created a reaction that turned many societies into totalitarian ones, a development that reached its acme in the fascism of the German-Nazi variety and the Stalinist and Maoist versions of Communism. In some of the new states, the trend has similarly been away from democracy (to the degree this existed) toward the authoritarianism of military regimes.

Thus between the polar systems there are many gradations. Regimes characterized by oligarchic or dictatorial controls may lack some or most of the characteristics of totalitarianism. In fact, the standard, traditional forms of "rule from above," as they are inherited from the predemocratic, more or less authoritarian past, still prevail in many countries of the not-yet-modernized variety, as, for example, in traditional Latin American junta rule. Even fascist dictatorships showed significant variation, ranging from the extreme of Nazi totalitarianism over less complete Italian fascist control to such protofascist regimes as those in Spain and Portugal, which in fact are quite similar to traditional predemocratic authoritarian regimes based on social and economic conservatism. One problem facing such regimes is whether their political conservatism can withstand the winds of change that modernization—the aim of all or most countries—carries with it. A predemocratic climate of attitudes, especially in the relationship of governors to governed, is ill-suited to the antipaternalistic tendencies of modern man in the modernized, technically oriented world.

Communist regimes, on the other hand, make social change a major objective. Thus they are more in line with the trend toward modernization. But even they (as China, the Soviet Union, Yugoslavia, and such former satellites as Poland clearly indicate) differ markedly in revolutionary fervor, in type of leadership, in organization of social and economic structures, and, as has become increasingly clear in recent years, in the range of their controls. Indeed, the latter variation may be the most significant one. In some cases there appears to be a transformation from totalitarianism to a more or less liberal authoritarianism. In some Eastern European countries, the "thaw" in the realm of culture has inaugurated a degree of experimentation in literature, in art, and in related fields that almost equals the cultural freedom in the West. If such trends should in due course be accompanied by more liberalism in the area of the political rights of individuals and group freedoms, the development might even presage a moderation of dictatorship and authoritarian controls. In the light of the trend in liberal democracies toward the concentration of power in the executive and the increasing difficulty of maintaining popular control over such power, some foresee an era of "convergence" in which democracy and totalitarianism might no longer form such polar contrasts. However, as the ill-fated attempt of the Czechs to give "socialism" a more human, that is, more liberal face has shown, there are limits beyond which Communist polities are not permitted by their superpower to stray.

In recent years the dichotomy of totalitarianism and democracy has been attacked by some as involving a "cold war" spirit of equating *all* Communist regimes with the most excessive of the fascist regimes, in particular, with Nazism. This, needless to say, has not been our intention when suggesting the dichotomy. We mean the distinction of regimes rather as a conceptual tool for the analysis of systems, where concepts serve as "ideal types," in Max Weber's sense; that is, as standards to which real systems and actual regimes may approximate. While we believe the totalitarianism-democracy dichotomy is still a useful one for purposes of clarification, we fully recognize that concepts and definitions like these must be applied with extreme care. Thus not all Communist systems but, perhaps, Stalinism at its height (and corresponding stages of regimes in satellite countries) came close to exhibiting the symptomatic features of totalitarianism, whereas pre- and post-Stalinist stages in the development of the Soviet system (not to mention such stages in other Communist systems, such as the Dubček period in Czechoslovakia) veered away from it. By the same token not all systems commonly referred to as democratic are equally close to the ideal of liberal democracy, as defined above. The American political system, for instance, has exhibited certain trends (at one point under the label of "McCarthyism") toward authoritarianism, if not totalitarianism.

Keeping these qualifications in mind, we turn to actual "democracies" and observe that they vary in practice perhaps more than "totalitarian" regimes. Three major types seem to prevail: the parliamentary democracy, of which

Great Britain can serve as the prototype; the presidential-congressional system of the United States; and the presidential-parliamentary system of the French Fifth Republic. These will be briefly dealt with before we enter into a more detailed discussion of specific political systems.

The prime characteristic of a parliamentary system is the fusion of the executive and the legislature. The executive becomes the governing group not as the result of a direct and separate vote by the electorate, as in the presidential system, but because it comprises the leaders of one or several parties represented in the legislature who command sufficient support within that body to pass the legislation they desire. Technically, this system is based on the institution of expressing or denying confidence in the executive. Where parliament can force the government (in the sense of the executive) to resign by voting "nonconfidence" in it—or at least by compelling the executive to dissolve parliament in such a case and appeal to the electorate—the parliamentary system is operating in its classical form. It should be pointed out, however, that party discipline, coupled with the two-party system in the United Kingdom, has meant that in practice the power of dissolution gives the executive a powerful influence on parliament rather than the other way around.

The presidential pattern of government is another major type of representative democracy. Its distinctive feature, in contrast to parliamentary government, is that the chief executive holds office whether or not he is supported by the majority in the legislature. In the United States, the voters may elect a president from one party and give the majority in Congress to the other. Even when the president's party dominates the legislature, the president has less assured control over the passage of laws than has even a weak British prime minister. Yet at the same time, there are great resources at the disposal of an American president. In guaranteed possession of office for four years, he is leader of his party, controls the administration, and can appeal directly to the people to support his program.

On the other hand, the presidential system is one of built-in restraints. The constitutional provisions for dividing and balancing authority —the bicameralism of two more or less equally powerful chambers, federalism, judicial review, staggered elections, the presidential veto, and the power inhering in the necessities for legislative consent—all combine to prevent or to impede major changes in policy until public pressures have built up on a broad scale. Where the parliamentary system responds quickly to popular majorities, the American presidential system reinforces the position of powerful minorities, and especially those that traditionally have been most strongly represented in the committees of the legislature.

With France under the Fifth Republic, there is a unique combination of parliamentary and presidential institutions. The president cannot be replaced during his seven years of office unless he resigns (as Charles de Gaulle did in 1969) or dies. Moreover, the president selects the premier, who retains office only as long as he possesses the president's confidence. But the Assembly still possesses the power to pass a vote of censure or to reject a vote of confidence. Such action led to the resignation of the premier and his ministers in 1962 and to new elections. This hybrid of presidential and parliamentary institutions has brought France an executive equal in dominance to that in Great Britain, while maintaining closer interaction between ministry and legislature than in the United States.

FOUR MAJOR POWERS AND SYSTEMS

Having sketched some basic concepts and patterns of government, we are now ready to apply the definitions to the study of the four countries we have chosen. There are strong reasons for approaching comparative government through studying Great Britain, France, Germany, and the Soviet Union, while keeping in mind the United States both for comparison and for contrast. These countries are selected not because they are "the great" foreign powers. (Today the United States and the Soviet Union are, of course, the dominant nation-states in terms of power; countries such as Great Britain, France, Germany, Japan, and China can no longer, or not yet, measure up to them in these terms.) Great Britain, the Soviet Union, Germany, and France have been selected for study because they offer a variety of political experience and a range of governmental institutions that are representative of many other countries. In one way or another, these four powers (or five, with the United States) have influenced governmental forms and practices throughout the world.

Great Britain, of course, developed earliest and perhaps most successfully that form of representative democracy, the parliamentary system, whose close interrelationship and coordination of legislative and executive contrast most vividly with the American pattern of separation of powers. The impact of British parliamentary institutions on the independent states that were formerly its colonies has indeed been remarkable. Rarely have institutions resembled so closely the parent stock as those of Canada, Australia, and New Zealand. While it is perhaps not so surprising to find British institutions and traditions operating in the older parts of the Commonwealth, it is remarkable to find some of its newer members, such as India, Malaysia, Zambia, Jamaica, and Trinidad, experimenting with British-type representative and parliamentary institutions despite their differences from older Commonwealth members in historical background and tradition, standards of living, degree of literacy, size of the middle class, and other economic and social conditions.

But the parliamentary variant of democracy is infinitely flexible. France, in its rather tortuous constitutional history, has presented us in the past with an unstable, multiparty parliamentarism that has had variants in other continental European countries. (The Italian system evinces this instability.) France's systems of administration and of local government and its codes of law have been widely copied. More recently, French experience has illustrated one of the supreme problems with which nontotalitarian countries are faced: how to combine democracy with stability. Executive dominance of the Fifth Republic is not only a new form for French "democracy," but it has been widely copied—although with less successful results— in France's former African colonies.

Germany is represented chiefly because of the range and variety of its political experience. The person from the West who studies the varied regimes that Germany has had can never again feel complacent about the universal applicability, even to countries of basically Western background, of the political principles and institutions to which he, as a Westerner, is accustomed. German experience illustrates one great problem of modern government: how to establish liberal democracy in a society that, although highly developed economically and educationally, has strong nondemocratic traits and traditions. As Germany's recent history shows, such an environment is open to the double perils of rightist and leftist totalitarianism. As a matter of fact, the present division of Germany into two units—one exhibiting the toils of a liberal democracy trying to outgrow the remnants of authoritarianism, the other representing one variant of Soviet-type Communism—symbolizes the age-old German dilemma deriving from so many contrary trends and experiences.

In contrast to Great Britain and France, there is little in Germany (except for a professional and expert civil service) that has been an influence on or a model for other nations. It is the problematic character of the German experience that is interesting to students of comparative government and politics. Thus a country such as Japan, with some basically similar problems, has exhibited surprising similarities to Germany in its political development and governmental institutions.

As for the Soviet Union, the American who studies Soviet government and politics inevitably becomes acquainted with a new set of standards for judging political principles and political action. The Soviet Union is, of course, the current prototype of the *other*, the nondemocratic trend. To be sure, China, Yugoslavia, and even Poland are in some respects markedly different from the Soviet Union; but the latter, although no longer recognized officially by other Communist countries as the "leader," is still the model for most socialist countries, as we see in the description of the East German system (the German Democratic Republic), which is included in the section on Germany.

When studying these four countries and their systems, we shall not be interested exclusively in their uniqueness and individuality. All organized society is today confronted with certain fundamental, overall problems, and it is one of the rewards of studying comparative politics to observe how different systems cope with them. In the following pages, therefore, the most important among these problems will be considered under four headings: the

increasing role of government among the institutions of society; the impact of a new international environment on domestic governmental and political systems; the impact of constant emergency or crisis on domestic governments; and the impact of doctrine or "ideology."

THE INCREASING ROLE OF GOVERNMENT

The distinguishing feature of modern government is that it is universally recognized and accepted as an active force in the shaping of economic, social, and, increasingly, ecological conditions. Indeed, government is looked on as a major, and even the dominant, organizing power in society.

THE ACCELERATION PROCESS

What characterizes our world above everything else, as we have said before, is not merely change or transformation as such, but the speed of developments, the rate of change. The curve that reflects this rate of change rises slowly at first and then ever more rapidly and steeply; it also applies to more and more areas of human affairs. At the turn of the century, Henry Adams, in one of his prophetic moods, suggested a law or a "rule of phase," according to which mankind goes through various "energizing" stages—a long religious stage, a somewhat shorter but still centuries-long mechanical one, followed by an even shorter but more high-powered electrical phase, and, finally, an "ethereal" (perhaps we should say nuclear) phase. Adams' exponential curve has proved more or less correct in the most varied areas of life: in the demographic history of mankind, where the rise was at first imperceptible and has now arrived at a population explosion; in the discovery, exploitation, and now, often, threatening exhaustion of mineral resources and even water; in the development of the weapons of war and the increase in their destructiveness, from bow and arrow through gunpowder to H-bomb; in scientific discoveries and technological inventions; and in the means of communication and transportation (the so-called

annihilation of time and space, or, better, of time and distance).

This is a change, moreover, that is one-directional. Throughout most of history, the technological process did not vitally interfere with other processes—for example, the cultural, social, political ones—and thus left the world varied and diverse. Now it tends to swallow everything up that is not yet under its control, in favor of worldwide "modernization." Man's more or less natural habitat is being replaced by a completely man-made, synthetic environment. It took man thousands of years to gain insight into the nature of his environment and to evolve means of survival in his struggle with hostile forces. It took hundreds of years to discover and explore the distant stretches of the globe. Now the whole surface of the earth is being transformed into a cultivated area, a "second nature" that serves exclusively to maintain human beings and provide the necessities of their life. At the same time, man is propelling himself into the universe. In a great paradox this process of radical transformation is rendering the diverse ever more rigid and conforming. We rush into conformity. This cannot but have a profound impact on the functioning of government and on the relation of man to his government.

THE EMERGENCE OF BIG GOVERNMENT

We have become so accustomed to government as an active, positive agent in the direction of our affairs that we often fail to realize the significance of the change this represents. Even autocratic government in the age of European absolutism was never as big and comprehensive as that of present times. It *could* not be so pervasive (even had it wanted to be), because the range of its activities was restricted by relatively undeveloped means of communication, transportation, and the like; the lord of a manor could therefore be more autonomous, even in a political sense, than the individual member of the "sovereign" people in a modern, integrated, mass society. The government did not *need* to be so encompassing because of the less complicated nature of a numerically smaller society.

Numbers are all-important. In a small community most affairs can be regulated by the voluntary cooperation of its members without the machinery of government—that is, administration, bureaucracy, and similar institutions. Larger units require much more organization. A school of thirty or fifty pupils can be run by a few teachers aided by a mother or two. One with thousands of students requires a higher proportion of teachers, a school board, and a school administration, including personnel services, a payroll office, and so forth.

In society at large the emergence of big government has been in essence a by-product of changes that were themselves of a revolutionary character; primarily it has been a by-product of the industrial revolutions since the beginning of the nineteenth century. The French Revolution and the first industrial revolution gave rise to a profound change in attitudes toward the individual and his place within the community. The French Revolution preached the equality of individuals, a doctrine that directly challenged the long-existent, rigid social hierarchies of Europe; at the same time it aroused the sentiment of nationalism that exalts the community. Thus the individual was freed only to be merged into the group. But if the French Revolution provided much of the ideology and spur for social change, it was the industrial revolution that provided the new circumstances in which change became inevitable. The new industrialism with its new modes of production opened the way for individual activity and permitted social mobility to a degree never before seen. Yet while industrialism stimulated individualism, particularly in its early stages, its own inner logic was toward mass production, standardization, and vast economic units. Thus with industrialization, as with the French Revolution, the tendency was to free the individual from the restrictions of the past only to fit him into new and larger entities. Inevitably, the breakdown of traditional social and economic groupings produced the mass society characteristic of our time.

In the mass society created by the first industrial revolution the role of government by necessity changed. The state had to adjust conflicting demands of different groups and classes. And it had to establish certain minimum standards of living and social well-being that were demanded by the new doctrine of equality. Thus government, as the agent of the state, was compelled to assume more and more responsibility for the creation and distribution of wealth. In so doing, government almost universally became big government, both in the scope of its activities and responsibilities and in the numbers of those it directly employed. Paradoxically, the two chief theories produced during, and in consequence of, this first age of industrialization—Marxism and liberalism— were both based on political expectations that were contradicted by what ensued in practice. The one forecast the "withering away" of the state, that is, of the coercive means of society; the other forecast that the state would be reduced to insignificance under conditions of laissez faire. What actually emerged was either totalitarianism or the rise of the giant welfare— and all too often warfare—state.

In our century government confronts new and diverse responsibilities as a result of the process of acceleration we outlined above and as a result of the second industrial revolution produced by that process. From the nineteenth century on, with the first industrial revolution, the state had to intervene to protect labor from exploitation, provide for social security, and so forth. Obviously, these goals are still important (and, in many societies, still unachieved) today. But these functions must now be coupled with the "community" tasks that the technological process and ensuing modernity impose. If, for reasons of environmental pollution or of threatening exhaustion of resources, the use of certain chemicals must be licensed or the use of a resource restricted, this inevitably means new bureaucracy. With its creation the problem arises of whether it will be independent in its judgment or influenced by extraneous "interests." In capitalist countries there is the danger that officialdom will be influenced or even controlled by those interests *against* which it is supposed to protect either the weaker groups or the community at large.

Other problems lead beyond the confines of the nation. If, for example, one nation is ready to launch a program of pollution control while others are not, the latter enjoy the undue "advantage" of being able to continue polluting not only their own domain but the air or the oceans of the world. Population control poses particularly delicate problems, domestically and internationally, where numbers are measures of political influence, as with certain ethnic or religious groups. Yet all of us are now in the same (overcrowded) boat; therefore, we need to develop global policies and agreements.

Left alone, technological advance tends to become free-wheeling and unconcerned about community interests. By a kind of iron law of "technological conformism," man tends to be dragged by the scientific-technological development wherever the latter leads him. Without controls, there will be no limits on the speed of cars or planes (whatever the utility, or even profitability, of, say, supersonic planes) or the use of insecticides; no concern for priorities in the allocation of funds and resources for space exploration or highway building or for the production of luxury goods versus slum clearance or mass educational facilities. Especially in a competitive system, rival big interests feel compelled to follow the trend of bigness, speed, and so forth, so long as it is profitable to do so. Hence organized society must intervene to protect the public sector against the private sector and to oppose technological advance that is unconcerned with or even injurious to human interests. It must stop waste; it must establish priorities. In short, it must become the conscience of the community at large and the guardian of its long-range interests, as opposed to special and short-range interests.

But it is not only in competitive societies that the law of technological conformism applies. Conservationists in the Soviet Union, for example, also fight the advance of industry, which threatens to pollute the lakes and the rivers. Soviet scientists, artists, and writers have called for government intervention to halt this process. All over the world, regardless of the system, there is some reversal of basic attitudes toward economic growth at the expense of the environment. Organized protests and action alert us to those outgrowths of the technological process that endanger the continuity of mankind.

The new ecological challenge confronts the main variants of political systems with new and as yet unsolved difficulties. First, the developing countries: How, in addition to their tasks of nation-building and modernization, can they hope to cope successfully with problems that seem to baffle the resources of the most advanced countries? The problem of urbanization, for instance, and its concomitant slums, pollution, inadequate transportation facilities, overcrowding, raise issues that are as threatening to many of them as they are to the developed states. Second, the very freedom of developed, Western-type nations presents them with a major problem of how to reconcile a "free-for-all" competitive style with the planning needed to cope with the exigencies of environmental control. Will people voluntarily give up using passenger cars in favor of mass transportation? Will anything short of a near-totalitarian system be able to cope with such problems in opposition to the respective private "interests" and to deeply ingrained cultural habits and attitude patterns? Third, the Communist countries, which seem to have the advantage in possessing the overall planning machinery the new situation calls for, are likely to encounter a major difficulty of how to overcome the bureaucratic waste and rigidities inherent in a vast "dirigist" system. And, as in the Western industrial nations, the Communist countries feel impelled to expand economic growth even at the expense of the environment. Much of the future of individual nations and of the human race itself will depend on how these challenges are met by the variants of political systems.

Finally, as we have seen, government today cannot refrain from coming to grips with what, in the past, has rarely been a matter for public policy: the population problem. For government to interfere in this most intimate of human matters is distasteful to many, and yet it may have become government's most basic task. Where almost everything in the production and consumption of things becomes plannable and planned, the size of the underlying stratum of humans, for whom the planning and organizing are done, cannot remain uncontrolled. If it remains so, it tends to nullify the other efforts. The fact that population has so far not been controlled except in rare cases, such as Japan, accounts for many of the political and general ills of the present-day world. Both types of government functions already identified—the social welfare and the environmental tasks—can be rendered fruitless when the number of people to whom they apply increases without control. Where population continues to explode, all efforts to aid the developing majority of mankind can assume the Alice-in-Wonderland character of running faster and faster only to stay in the same spot. All the efforts of the free world to extend its own ideals and institutions to the Third World will remain illusory so long as billions of uprooted people fall prey to extremism or anarchy. In the modernized world the wars against poverty and discrimination must come to naught unless this problem is tackled. Thus governmental means are likely to be used more and more to extend human control over this last and most fundamental social frontier.

THE NEED TO LIMIT BIG GOVERNMENT

Will the increasing functions of government lead to something like Orwell's "Big Brother," an all-powerful, all-encompassing state? The very listing of its powers shows the need for restraint. If the state is needed to restrain the technological process and those inclined to exploit this process to the utmost, the state in turn must be restrained from using its powers in an arbitrary and uncontrolled fashion. Even the earlier industrial society and its government led to some misuse of power. Any large-scale organization tends toward pervasive control, whether the organization is a large business corporation, a labor union, a farmers' association, or a government. This is because a huge and complex agency can function only through coordination from one central place. But the power to control involves the danger of irresponsibility. Unchecked power of interference and regulation is the essence of totalitarianism, and large-scale mass society thus bears within itself a totalitarian trend.

The possibilities of domination have been vastly increased by the technological potentialities of the twentieth century. Hitler's and Stalin's setups for the exploitation and annihilation of millions of humans were only spectacular examples of what can be "technically" achieved through the modern means of organizing and controlling society and the human beings it includes. Nuclear weapons are merely ultimates in a vast range of powers and capabilities. There are others. Science reveals more and more the social and mental malleability of man, and even the feasibility of biological transformation, opening up vistas of psychological manipulation and eugenic determination of inheritance that might change the very nature of mankind. Add to this the almost incredible intrusions that can now be made into the most intimate spheres of one's personal life—"bugging" a home or a place of work with electronic devices, for example—and one perceives the need for protection not only *by* government against private groups but no less for protection *against* governmental abuse. If the state does—and must—control such actions, who or what controls or restrains the state?

It is here above all that democracy and totalitarianism part ways. The distinctive feature of liberal democracy is that it is "limited government." What counts is not only the rule of the majority but even more the right, or at least the chance, for individuals and minorities freely to develop themselves. But any genuine freedom in the personal and group spheres presupposes the placing of limits upon political power. It is only when there are limits on what government may do and on the way in which it may do it that citizens are free. Particularly in our mass societies, where the people at large can exercise at best only a limited control over crucial matters of domestic and foreign policy, the difference between free and totalitarian countries seems to reduce itself ultimately to two questions: can the citizen force a review of governmental decisions either through judicial processes or through the use of the ballot; and can there be meaningful protection of an inviolable sphere of privacy in which the otherwise organized, mechanized, ordered, and oftentimes bullied individual may yet proceed according to his will, whim, or fantasy, his beliefs or disbeliefs, in a socially useful and adjusted or an entirely useless and unadjusted fashion.

REQUIREMENTS FOR
LIMITED GOVERNMENT

But how is it possible to establish and maintain limitations when the technological and organizational trends of modern society—by their own force of gravity, so to speak—pull in the opposite direction? It seems so much easier and so much more effective to confer on those responsible for decisions the unhampered authority to do what they see fit to do. But the history of this century stands as a solemn record of warning that such handing over of authority may lead to the cruelest tyranny and the most inhuman abuse.

To ensure limited government requires a number of technical devices that, while seemingly of secondary importance as compared with general objectives and major principles, yet are vital for the successful operation of liberal democracy. To the person who is dazzled by the more dramatic conflicts in ultimate aim and aspiration among the world's leading political systems, the issue of political mechanics may appear drab and unimportant. Yet it is upon such "wretched technicalities" (to borrow the phrase of Ortega y Gasset) that the noblest political principles and aspirations depend. If the machinery is bad, the end, however magnificent, is bound to suffer.

What counts, however, in assessing these more technical devices and institutions is not simply their existence in the provisions of constitutions or statutes, nor their presence on organization charts. Indeed, the organization chart of the government in a country controlled by Communism or some non-Communist version of authoritarianism may look quite similar to that of a Western-type democracy. What it usually does not show is the all-pervasive power exercised by the top level of the single party. Similarly, the written constitution of such a country may sound liberal and democratic, since it can contain, for instance, provisions safeguarding the freedom of the press or rules concerning debating and voting in an elected parliament. What these provisions do not tell us is that all media are owned and controlled by the state, the party, or by the party-domi-nated organizations and therefore cannot voice independent opinions; or that genuine opposition, or even criticism, can hardly be expected from members of a parliament elected from a list of candidates all of whom were chosen or approved by the ruling party, or from a "parliament" of hand-picked stooges of a military junta.

While one must not mistake a system operating behind a totalitarian or authoritarian façade for limited government, one must also be aware of the criticism often made of what we consider genuine liberal-democratic institutions and procedures. These criticisms are often mirror images of the ones we have just leveled against nondemocratic make-beliefs. Marxism and fascism, for instance, both claim that what we call freedom of opinion and of opinion-formation in the democracies disregards the fact that most of the mass media are controlled by powerful business and financial interests. Seemingly free elections can mean little where the voters have only a choice between two candidates whose positions are so alike that it means voting between tweedledee and tweedledum or when candidates or parties are disadvantaged by steeply rising campaign expenses. We should not take such criticism lightly. In all big society there is the constant threat of "oligarchism," of concentration or petrification of power, and of manipulation of controls. Free institutions are constantly liable to be corrupted, and the façades of democratic institutions must be pierced to find out whether or not they serve genuinely liberal purposes.

There are four groups of questions to keep in mind when asking how, and to what extent, limited government functions in a specific instance. One set of questions concerns the instruments and channels of political information and expression; another asks whether and how the channels of political action are kept open and untrammeled; a third group is concerned with the influence of pressure groups on governmental and political life; and the last centers on how to keep the executive as well as the bureaucracy "responsible."

Freedom of information and expression

If the people, as voters, are to give meaningful direction to politics—that is, to choose between genuine alternatives—they must first of all have a chance to inform themselves freely about conditions and, in particular, about the various alternatives that exist. This implies, of course, that anyone with an idea or a policy to offer is given a chance to put it before the people and to have it freely discussed. For this reason, democratic government can be little better than its sources of information. Freedom of information and expression of opinion require not only the absence of political intimidation but also a minimal economic chance to compete in the "market place of ideas." We have referred to the charge that even in liberal democracies the facilities for informing citizens and for expressing different opinions are often inadequate and even perverted. Owners of newspapers, for instance, may want to concentrate on sensational features that will attract readers at the expense of the task of providing political information. Party- or government-controlled papers may present only their own slanted points of view. Moreover, where the press, the radio, and television have become big business, those who control them may use their influence to promote the interests of wealthy advertisers or the ideology of the ruling "Establishment," leaving the mass of the people, or groups advocating different ideas, without adequate channels of expression. Especially when it comes to elections or similar expressions of "the will of the people," the effectiveness of the media with smaller circulation, such as "journals of opinion" or opposition pamphlets, reaching at best only thousands, hardly counts in comparison with the impact of the mass media reaching tens of millions.

The free expression of opinion, however, is more than a question of formal channels of communication, serious though this question may become through the increasing control of such channels by ever fewer people. Equally important is the broader question of education, both of the young and of adults, and of creating and maintaining an interest in the great issues of the times. An educational system that—for fear of raising controversial issues, whether in the field of religion, the arts, or in domestic and international affairs—limits itself to the merely technical, dulls the mind and eventually creates the selfsame conformity that is the hallmark of indoctrination under totalitarianism. Per-

sons who hardly look at the headlines of articles on political news will not benefit from the most informative coverage of such news in the best papers in the world.

In this respect the growing complexity of issues makes more difficult the adequate dissemination of information for democratic opinion-formation. In our highly specialized society, most people are laymen except in their own areas of expertise, and there is an increasing complexity in technical matters: How many people, for instance, understand or even know the technicalities of military defense and defense systems? Or in the economic sphere: How many feel at home with the technicalities of a large-scale budget or of the international payments problems? Or in matters of organization: How many understand the structure and functioning of even one of the large executive agencies of the United States government, let alone the overlapping setups in totalitarian countries? Moreover, the public is daily confronted with an increasing number of issues, all competing for its attention. And if a big scandal does arouse its interest, the public's ire tends to be fleeting and the issue to be forgotten with the next scandal. Periodically recurring "revelations," whether of conditions in prisons or insane asylums, or of the plight of migratory workers, of organized crime, or of police brutality (the list could be extended ad infinitum), testify to the difficulty of arousing the public to such an extent that it will insist on action. Finally, there is the steady increase in the size of the audience whose views should be taken into consideration by the policymakers who are supposed to be responsive to the public. Policymakers are tempted to disregard opponents or critics who are few in number as long as they can control or assuage the millions whose apathy they easily identify with consensus.

One should not forget, however, that as long as freedom of the press (in the broad sense given it through the interpretation of the courts in the United States) exists in principle, there are times and ways in which the media can assert themselves as institutions of criticism or complaint. Technological innovations such as television may work in their favor, sometimes by simply allowing the facts to be presented in all their crude immediacy. No one who saw it at the time will forget the damning effect television exposure had on Senator Joseph McCarthy at the height of "McCarthyism." And a few courageous newsmen, despite the threat of being damned by the Establishment as "nervous nellies" or "effete snobs," have dared to bring to the dinner table the atrocities of a war, with the effect that a disturbed nation is compelling the government to reverse itself and to try to terminate it.

Freedom of political action

By freedom of political action we mean political activity beyond the reception of information and the expression of opinion. Even to voice opinion, or at least to make such voicing effective, people must be able to rally together and to organize themselves in movements, parties, or similar ways to exercise that influence, which, in the mass age, can be exerted only by the many acting jointly. Here, again, it is frequently asserted that the channels of action are seriously limited. To cast a ballot once in two or four years seems to some critics a not very meaningful form of political participation. The voter is free to join a political party; but the parties themselves, according to the charge, are far from democratic in their internal organization. A small elite of bosses or bureaucrats allegedly chooses the candidates and dictates policy. This tends to create apathy in the voter or party member outside the clique. Moreover, parties in representative systems are primarily used to elect the people's representatives to parliamentary assemblies. And here, again, charges are frequently made against the allegedly unrepresentative nature or the ineffective ways of using such instruments of representation. Thus it is held that the parliaments in a democracy are a far from accurate reproduction of the sentiments of the voters, both in the strength of party representation and in the reflection of the economic interests and social divisions of the country as a whole. In those countries that have a two-party system, the strength of the larger party is likely to be greatly exaggerated; in those that have a multiparty system, parliamentary manipulation may result in a government very different from the one the citizens thought they were voting for.

Moreover, the development of party discipline may oblige members of the legislature to vote in accordance with the orders of a small group of leaders, sometimes against their own convictions and the desires of the people who elected them. The popular impression of representative assemblies may, indeed, be one of a group of spokesmen of special interests battling and wrangling without thought of the common welfare of the country. Some observers talk of the "decline of parliaments" and suggest that the chosen representatives of the people in practice delegate their authority to the executive and to the civil servants. Regarding continental European systems, it has also become popular to talk of the "waning of the opposition," in the sense of the vanishing of parties offering meaningful alternatives.

These are charges to which we will be returning; until then it is important to keep in mind that parties and representative assemblies, as in Great Britain, can still be alert to the needs of individuals and groups or, as in Italy—with a vengeance—can even determine the political fate of the executive.

Freedom from nongovernmental pressures

We have just referred to the charge that in some situations special interests appear to dominate the battles of seemingly representative assemblies. Such interests may also exercise undue and disproportionate influence in other spheres of government and politics. They may control the press or other instruments of information or culture and stifle the free development of entertainment; they may inhibit open discussion of issues in the schools or in the churches; and they may affect the policies of the government through their influence over the parties, over the choice of party candidates and their representatives, or through lobbies in parliament.

Moreover, interest groups may influence the executive and the administration by bringing pressure to bear on officeholders and by staffing key positions with people who think that what is good for their respective group or class is good for the country. One of the decisive tests of a democratic regime is whether it can oppose such pressures, not only through the counter-pressure of another interest group, but also through the "countervailing force" of the general public interest (of consumers, for example, or through a public agency that forces competition).

Limiting executive power

Power in modern society may be too concentrated either within or outside the realm of government. In contrast to totalitarian regimes, with their characteristic concentration of power in party and government, democracies may appear particularly open to the dangers of nongovernmental, especially economic, influences and controls. Yet in an age of big and comprehensive government the opposite danger—of government itself growing too powerful—cannot be overlooked. We have seen how technological developments may provide the executive with powers of domination; we shall see below how international developments tend to strengthen the executive even more. Thus to place restraints on the use of executive power is the fourth important task of limited government.

The problem here is how to restrain the executive without crippling it. Restraint at the top level might lead merely to enhancing the power and influence of that other portion of the executive branch, the bureaucracy, which, although legally and organizationally subordinate, yet possesses large and varied possibilities of independent action because of the vast and complex functions entrusted to it. President Truman was once quoted as remarking when his successor was about to begin his job: "Poor Ike! He will sit there, and he will say: 'Do this, do that.' And nothing will happen." However exaggerated the comment, there are situations that render the top executive inefficient and leave the rest of the administration irresponsible. They lend themselves to the often heard charges that, at a time when government requires prompt, vigorous, imaginative, and decisive action, the democratic executive may be slow and bumbling, weakened by systems of checks and balances, handicapped by wranglings over jurisdictions, subjected to the pressures of special interests, corrupted by the requirements of partisan politics, and too in-

expert to know the solution to the increasingly complex problems of modern political life. Equally it is suggested that the top executive is forced to delegate authority to a dominant and expert bureaucracy that was not chosen by the voter and that cannot be controlled by him; as a result, because of the immense complexities of modern politics and the infinitely varied devices for confusing and misleading the public, the voter cannot tell whom to blame for policies that he dislikes.

At the same time, the top level of government has greatly increased responsibilities in such fields as defense and foreign policy. And even in free-enterprise countries, there is an ever increasing degree of planning and regulation of more and more areas in the domestic field. It is often argued, therefore, that to subject the expert planners to control by the inexpert public would destroy the value of their plans. The problem here is how to combine effective, long-range planning, which requires firm and stable government, with that minimum of popular control that inhibits arbitrariness and prevents lack of responsiveness.

But the test of limited government here, as elsewhere, is whether controls, popular or other, are available and how they are used. It is intriguing to study how different democracies have developed various procedures in this connection. To keep the bureaucracy responsible, such political devices as parliamentary control and criticism, ministerial and cabinet responsibility, and specific consent to appointments by parliament are commonly used. Other major devices to restrain the bureaucracy are through judicial means—such as appeals to ordinary or to special administrative courts staffed with independent judges—by persons claiming injury or violation of rights and interests by administrative action, or through the ombudsman, who investigates private complaints against official actions. Indeed, it is this same roster of devices and procedures that lends itself to the enforcement of responsibility at the top level of government. Beyond this, of course, one chief means of keeping both the executive and the legislature limited in power is by limiting their tenure of office—that is, by holding periodic elections. In this way, the job of limitation reverts to the people.

THE IMPACT OF THE INTERNATIONAL ENVIRONMENT

Big governments within the nation-states, as we have seen, are increasingly faced with global tasks and the strains that arise from the international environment in which they must operate. Due to developments in science and technology (e.g., nuclear weapons, the exploration of space, and the exploitability of the ocean bed), and also due to the emergence of new nations and new power groupings, this environment has been changing rapidly. The increase in the number of independent states suggests, again, the Adams' curve of acceleration. International cooperation, global planning, development of standards of internation behavior ("international law") are needed for coexistence in this turbulent era. But the internationalism indicated by the growing interdependence of nations and their common tasks has run into the age-old bloc of power politics and national separatism. The ingrained habits of international actors are to conduct international affairs as "foreign" affairs of their respective "independent" units. We still lack what a German has called *Weltinnenpolitik*, a global domestic policy, as it were. Or, to put the same problem in the words of an American scholar: "If the continuance of the system of sovereign national states implies that we shall live on algae in caverns, then I say, 'To hell with it'. . . . If the price of national sovereignty is a nuclear war every generation or so, again I say, 'To hell with it,' for the loyalties upon which national sovereignty depends will not stand up under these circumstances." [1]

FROM SELF-SUFFICIENCY
TO INTERDEPENDENCE

For some centuries after the modern nation-state emerged, domestic affairs were relatively autonomous. Political institutions grew out of native soil, and changes, even revolutionary ones, were due to indigenous forces and indigenous movements. Foreign influences were not themselves without effect, but they were commonly transformed and shaped to fit the needs of the nation itself. Thus liberal democracy would change in character or meaning when exported from one country to another. Indeed, throughout this period domestic political forces and movements were less influenced by foreign affairs than they were themselves influences on foreign policies, as, for example, when Britain sided with liberal-democratic forces or when tsarist Russia backed the cause of absolutism on the Continent for its own internal political reasons.

That era has long ended. Today, world affairs have a tremendous impact on internal politics and institutions. This is due not only to the reduced effect of distance and increased effectiveness of communications, but also, and very basically, to the diminished security of the nation-state. In the past, when weapons of defense still matched weapons of offense, the territorial state was a more or less self-contained unit that, surrounded with defensible boundaries, could provide its citizens with protection from outside control. Since then not only has industrialization transformed economic self-sufficiency into dependence on the world market, thereby conjuring up the danger of defeat in war through blockade, but the nature of war has changed fundamentally. Air war and now nuclear war, by circumventing the defensive wall and by opening the way to vertical penetration, have put an end to the frontier in its traditional function of protecting and safeguarding "sovereignty."

Out of this strategic development has come the emergence of superpowers and their blocs, compared with which even former big powers now occupy inferior status. There is a whole new status-ordering of nations. Bipolarization has meant the growing influence of superpowers on the affairs of lesser nations and a competition, intensified by ideological conflict, for influence, if not control, between the two leading powers.

[1] Kenneth E. Boulding, "A Pure Theory of Death," *Beyond Economics: Essays on Society, Religion, and Ethics* (Ann Arbor, University of Michigan Press, 1968), pp. 125–26.

RELATIONS BETWEEN STRONGER AND LESSER POWERS

Inclusion in one or the other power bloc or defense system means adjustments of policy and sometimes of governmental institutions as well. The latter are most obvious in the relations of the lesser members to their "Big Brother" in the Soviet bloc. The initial copying by these once correctly called satellites of Soviet institutions and their ensuing subservience to Soviet policies—domestic as well as foreign—was primarily due to their common system of political belief. There have also been continuing pressures on them to conform to Soviet demands, especially under Stalin, but sporadically renewed under succeeding Soviet leaders, as in Hungary and Czechoslovakia.

In the West, political ideals are sometimes less influential on institutions than one might wish them to be. Dictatorships, or otherwise authoritarian regimes, such as in Spain, in Greece, and in Latin America, are not excluded from Western alliances. But even so, the political impact of the alignment is frequently powerful. This impact is felt first of all in the determination of objectives and in the conduct of foreign policy. Once a Western orientation has been decided upon, anything but this orientation may appear as "defection"; major groups and parties must thus agree on one and the same foreign policy. Such pressure toward foreign policy conformity may in due course affect matters of internal policy and domestic institutions as well. The United States, as the leading power, is constantly tempted—for what it may consider bonafide security reasons—to make sure that only "reliable" persons and groups are in control of its ally's government. It may then place pressure on that government not only to exclude Communists and affiliated groups from political power, but also to keep out of positions of influence other parties and individuals suspected of, for instance, "neutralist" leanings. It may try to influence elections (as the United States did in the fifties in West Germany and Italy) or election systems (as in Greece at that time). It may even go so far as to intervene, more or less overtly, by military means, as the United States did in Guatemala and the Dominican Republic to force their realignment, in a manner all too similar to the Soviets' use of force in Hungary and Czechoslovakia.

Sometimes interventions, while overtly presented as a means to counteract Communist, Castroite, or similar "subversion," are motivated instead by an urge to protect business holdings and investments from attempts of nationalist regimes to free themselves from outside economic controls. Policies like these have led to strong objections by some allies.

But attempts to influence the affairs of less powerful countries may backfire. In the 1960s, "allies"—such as China in the East and France in the West—have often asserted their autonomy so forcefully that there has been a decline of bipolar power concentration in favor of an emerging multipolarity. In consequence, the influence exercised by the superpowers has tended to become more subtle. Soviet control of Eastern European allies, formerly exercised over the respective governments through Soviet army and Communist party control, lessened after Stalin's death. Some of the Eastern European countries began experimenting with their own processes and institutions, especially in the cultural and economic fields. However, the basic decision in favor of Communism is still imposed from outside the country. The abortiveness of the Hungarian revolution of 1956, as well as the frost that killed the "Prague Spring" of 1968, indicate the limits set on the freedom of action enjoyed by the members of the Soviet bloc. What is usually referred to as the "Brezhnev Doctrine" (which was formulated following the Soviet-bloc invasion of Czechoslovakia in 1968) has spelled out these limits. These limits are reached when the Soviets perceive a "threat" to the "cause of socialism" and to "the common interests of the socialist camp"; in other words, when they fear defection of the respective unit from the sphere of "socialism" into that of the "capitalist order," the common enemy. In the case of Hungary it was the denunciation of Hungary's membership in the Warsaw Pact organization that brought about Soviet military intervention. In the Czechoslovak case it seems to have been the internal liberalization of policies and of the regime (especially permitting intraparty "factional" opposition in place of "democratic centralism") that was the "unforgivable" sin.

In the West, interference such as that mentioned above has become rarer. Indeed, relations between the United States and its European (NATO) allies are on a more or less equal plane. De Gaulle would not stand for less, and his example encouraged others. It still remains to be seen whether basic foreign policy orientations will be left unimpaired. For example, the bold attempt in 1970 by the Brandt government in West Germany to open new lines to the East has met an uncertain reception in Washington, notwithstanding the fact that *détente* had been the announced policy line of the West for many years, and despite the clear intention of all major political forces in the Federal Republic to stay in the Western sphere.

In the case of the uncommitted countries, neither East nor West has generally tried to influence developments through open control or intervention. Both sides have been satisfied with any kind of system and type of government so long as they could hope to sway the respective unit to their side or at least to keep it out of the opponent's camp. As we have pointed out, modified Western-type systems are found in many of the newly independent countries as an outgrowth of their colonial heritage, but because of their strong nationalism this has not necessarily meant a Western orientation or a Western influence over domestic politics. Big power influence is due rather to economic, cultural, or even military ties, either continued by former colonial powers or newly established by others; or it is due to economic-financial, technical, or educational assistance. An example of the former is France's continued ties to most of its former African colonies, based on strong cultural, economic, educational, and linguistic links ("francophone countries"), which on occasion have been forcefully supplemented by military intervention when a friendly regime is threatened from within. Some former British dependencies similarly retain close relations with the United Kingdom, aided by the mutual bond that exists through the Commonwealth. Influence based on development aid is drastically illustrated by Egypt, where the sudden withdrawal of a United States offer to help build the Aswan Dam gave the Soviet Union a golden opportunity to move in, so well used to this day. Even countries much occupied with their own affairs

(including their own development), such as China or Israel, have tried to make political use of foreign aid.

In these various ways, superpower competition and conflict may be transferred to the Third World. In addition, developments at home may have an impact on developments abroad. Soviet successes in space or industry may help to pull a small country's elite in an Easterly direction. The West, in as far as it implements its claims to eliminate poverty and to establish racial equality and genuine freedom of expression, may attract these elites to the West. Beyond this, much depends, as we have observed before, on whether these countries will be able to cope with their pressing economic, social, and demographic problems. Political and governmental chaos, or rapid succession of dictatorial regimes, might ensue if these countries fail to cope effectively.

THE IMPACT OF
INTERNATIONAL ORGANIZATION

As we have just discussed, a world of self-sufficient, separate nations has been moving toward interdependence. Nevertheless, national powers have not seen fit so far to yield correspondingly large portions of their sovereignty to any world government. Direct governmental functions of international organizations are restricted to activities such as those of the United Nations' peace-keeping forces, as in the Congo; or the legal protection and resettlement of the Office of the High Commissioner for Refugees (UNHCR), or economic and social planning and aid to developing countries through the United Nations Development Program (UNDP). Indirectly, of course, such agencies and their activities can influence countries and their policies in many ways. Foreign policies may be affected through pressures exerted by the Security Council or the General Assembly (as in the pressures on Great Britain and France, not to mention Israel, during the Suez crisis of 1956 or, although with little success, on countries still practicing "colonialist" racial policies, such as South Africa or Rhodesia). Even the development of domestic institutions and habits may be affected by outside influences. The newer countries, in particular, can learn much about the practices of more mature ones through contacts in the United Nations and elsewhere. Thus, for example, while equality of rights for women is not yet fully recognized in some Latin American, Asian, and African countries, it is difficult for them to withstand pressures at home to extend such rights when the latter are promoted on the international level. International cooperation can be expected to become more vital as well as more encompassing with the increasing urgency of those community tasks resulting from the sweep of technology and modernization that make the preservation of a common domain of mankind a common interest of mankind. Thus it has been suggested that the control and exploitation of the resources of the oceanic sea bed should be entrusted to a United Nations' agency.

Regionally, there has been more progress. Some nations have transferred to supranational institutions considerable portions of what used to be under "exclusive domestic jurisdiction." In this regard Western Europe, with its manifold array of joint organizations, has set the pace, particularly with the influential "Commission" of the Common Market, which affects the positions and the policies of interest groups in the six member countries and to some extent also those of their political parties and executive departments. The domestic politics of member states cannot remain as they were before, when basic economic, labor, and related affairs are decided through regional arrangements. There are the beginnings of cross-national party relationships, although the jurisdiction of regional parliamentary institutions is still very limited. On the other hand, the "European" bureaucracy at Brussels, the seat of the Commission, already shows the tendency of all bureaucracy to extend its influence. In this respect the existence of a court of the European Communities is important to protect interests, like those of business corporations, that come under the rule of the Communities. The new arrangements of the Common Market may turn out to be of great significance for the future of government and politics. Their example may prove that gradual development toward genuine world government is possible through a process of step-by-step devolution of national sovereignty. And the example may be followed ultimately by groupings of the newly independent countries, many of which seem scarcely viable, economically and otherwise, as separate entities.

THE IMPACT OF CONSTANT EMERGENCY

Despite some trends toward integration, which we have just discussed, international relations are still fundamentally characterized by antagonism. The split of a technically integrated world, with its opposed power blocs, ideological conflicts, and possible danger of even minor confrontations heating up into a nuclear holocaust has created a sense of constant crisis never experienced during the relatively secure periods of "peace" in former times. Whereas totalitarian regimes are equipped to cope with crises and emergencies (one might almost define totalitarian rule as a perpetual state of emergency, or martial law), democracies, as limited governments, cannot but encounter serious problems in these situations. We have already spoken of the need for concentrating much power at the top for immediate and far-reaching decisions, in order to cope with international crises. Another need is for secrecy, which may be abused by limiting the flow of public information to prefabricated official news handouts. An intelligence organization, such as the CIA or FBI, may engage in activities and actions far beyond the collection of information without knowledge of the public. All of this may reduce the area in which the people at large, or even their representatives, can effectively participate in political decisions.

There are still more serious threats to liberal democracy. Apparent danger to national security may give rise to emotionalism or hysteria, which, as in the United States at the time of McCarthyism in the fifties, tends to endanger free institutions. Many recall how during that period the power of legislative investigation, which for a time was almost unlimited and unchecked, not only affected personal rights and liberties but also such constitutional principles as the separation of powers within the government itself. More recently, a protracted war has divided this nation, causing neglect of urgent domestic needs, again threatening basic liberties. Using the slogan of "law and order," the executive, confronted by crime waves and civil unrest created by this very neglect, has been tempted to circumvent fundamental law and traditional constitutional order. There have been instances of "preventive detention" of mere suspects (the Nazis had another name for it), "no-knock" entry into homes, police surveillance of persons through wiretapping, and the maintenance of files on "undesirables" without legal safeguards for the individual's

reputation. Even West Germany, at a time of unequaled domestic tranquillity in the 1960s, saw fit to enact "emergency legislation" providing for the transfer of vast powers to small executive-cum-parliamentary bodies during "states of internal or international tension" (legislation that, of itself, rallied the radical left and led to disorders). The effect of such policies may be conformity or else political polarization, either of which is conducive to the erosion of free institutions.

There is, however, no inevitability in such developments. The British, for instance, did not yield to the frenzy of fear and suspicion that leads to the invasion of vital personal interests with far-fetched charges, "faceless" accusers, and ostracism; they have usually approached problems of internal security with both official and public restraints.

THE IMPACT OF IDEOLOGY

Deeper than some of the challenges to liberal democracy already mentioned is another that is intimately connected with our constant state of emergency. The question is whether—in this time of international crises and internal strain, when the burdens of governments become complex almost beyond comprehension—human beings have the mental and moral qualities necessary for self-government. Democracy, to be successful, must stand on the assumption that men can think calmly, adjust their differences peaceably, consider other people's interests and ideas, make concessions and compromises, tolerate opposition and disagreement, and refrain from violence and the temptation to impose their will by force. Men suffering from anxiety, whether it is inspired by the dangers of nuclear holocaust or by the desperation of hunger or unemployment, find it hard to put public duty before private interest and to refrain from violence when it appears that violence will be effective.

What, then, in such situations, can give people standards of stable and sober behavior in society? We are apt to forget, if we are living in relatively normal conditions, how large is the

incidence of strain and emergency in this century. What percentages of populations had to flee from persecution or became victims of domestic strife or foreign war? How many tried to escape rural starvation only to vegetate in overcrowded shanty towns? How many became victims of military or police brutality, or, out of dire need, criminals, bums, "dregs of society"? How many have been condemned to a lifetime sentence served in slums or ghettos? What, under such conditions, holds a community together?

THE APPEAL OF FASCISM

We in the West have tended to assume that political units like nation-states are founded on, or could and should be founded on, the free and voluntary association of self-determining, rational, enlightened human beings. We have tended to overlook the impact of sheer coercion, as well as irrational, emotional attitude patterns, born of frustration and despair, that may lead to the rule of the few and the subjection of the many. We also have tended to overlook the impact of tradition and custom, especially in the "socialization" of the new generations—that is, the way in which the young are adjusted to the "establishment" into which they are born, whether it be through formal education or through the influence of the family. The attempt to render the individual autonomous and to make him the foundation of free communities has been rare and recent. For most of history, political communities have been kept together by an unquestioning, tradition-bound allegiance of the ruled to the rulers. Generally, there was no conscious effort to indoctrinate the people, nor even to mold their attitudes and opinions through formal education; this was not necessary. It was the prevailing atmosphere, the transmitted value and belief systems that provided these standards. And it was in large part religion that provided whatever institutional and organizational apparatus was required to ensure their hold.

With the era of the Enlightenment came a change in attitude. It now seemed possible and desirable to conduct human affairs on the basis of conscious, deliberate, and free acceptance of value standards. Loyalty freely given provides a stronger and more democratic foundation of nations than does an enforced allegiance—or even a less consciously and more traditionally established allegiance. Such loyalty has become the democratic ideal.

Frequently, however, it was a new, emotional belief pattern that took the place of traditionalism, rather than the rational, liberal-democratic approach. In our century collective emotionalism became the basis of fascism, which in turn was based on extreme nationalism. When nationalism is simply a moderate and relatively calm feeling of belonging to that group that constitutes the nation, it can be reconciled with a liberal-democratic attitude pattern. But to the extent that nationalism becomes a substitute religion for those who need or are instilled with more extreme and fervent feelings of attachment, it becomes a focal point for emphatic identification with one group and for antagonism, even hatred, toward all others. Thus nationalism, in many parts of the world, became identical with exclusivism. Whether in the form of theories of racial superiorities and in-feriorities, of Social Darwinism and imperialism, or of other doctrines, it became the ideological foundation of various movements of what, in a broad sense, may be called the "fascist" variety of totalitarianism.

The frustration of the individual in a society that has lost its grip and makes him look for new allegiance and identification through common hatred and enmity may terminate in fascism. The friend-foe relationship then becomes the underlying basis of all political attitudes and action. The foe may be within, or without, or both. What particular group serves as a focal point matters little: it may be Jews, considered as a racial group, in the Nazi-type of anti-Semitism; it may be Africans, as in the racism of potential poor whites in South Africa, or blacks in American southern states; it may be an ultra-nationalist syndicalism directed against both foreigners and domestic "exploiters," as in the earlier stages of Mussolini's or Franco's fascism or Peronism in Argentina; or, more frequently in our time, it may be simply anticommunism of the McCarthy or Birchite variety. The masses supporting such movements are usually people lost in the maze of modern society who have become alienated from traditional ways of life and who have tried to find safe and absorbing new ones in movements and belief systems of this nature. The leaders frequently are those fearful of being harmed in their vested interests by new economic trends (e.g., small businessmen afraid of being wiped out by corporate concentration) or those scared by threats —imagined or real—of revolutionary upheaval. Thus, where socialism, communism, or an even newer left seems to threaten, the "backlash" easily despairs of democratic processes to counter the threat and turns to the person or group promising stern reaction and strong leadership.

THE APPEAL OF COMMUNISM

Fascism provides one kind of modern totalitarian ideology, Marxism another. Appealing to intellectuals with its view of world history and exploitation of labor, which seemed particularly credible in the conditions of nineteenth-century industrialization, Marxism sought to rouse the proletariat to revolt against the classes that were exploiting it. In Russia, tsarist autocracy, coupled with a small but advanced industrial structure whose workers lived within a milieu of social and cultural backwardness, provided an extreme example of the conditions Lenin's organizational genius sought to destroy. In the more industrialized European countries, especially in Germany, the rapidly forming proletariat at first was also strongly influenced by Marxism, constituting an entirely new "subculture" on the basis of socialist views and interpretations. Subsequently, however, amelioration of working conditions and the integration of the proletariat into a milieu transformed by ever more highly developing industrialism led to the weakening or attenuation of radical Marxist doctrine or to its replacement by social reformism—an attitude that has always characterized noncontinental countries such as Britain (with its "gradualist" or "Fabian" labor ideology) or the United States (with its primarily nonideological labor movement). Thus in the developed countries of the West, the appeal of communism has lessened, due to rising standards of living and the fact that the working classes and their leaders could seek their ends by utilizing the processes of liberal democracy.

Yet the rational or quasi-rational Marxist explanation of historical evolution and current conditions continues to draw many in the West as well as in the East who reject the irrational mysticism and racial or nationalist dogmas of fascism. By interrelating the station and fate of exploited individuals with the future destiny of mankind, Marxism answers their yearning for a coherent philosophy of government and politics. Although the driving force of ideology is now less evident in the Soviet Union than are the instruments of development and authority, the "cultural revolution" in China demonstrates the power of contemporary versions of the Marxist creed.

In its self-interpretation, Communism is very different from simple rule by force. Concentration of power appears as the means necessary to attain an ultimate and fixed end toward which history is moving. Everything that now happens is merely a transitional stage on history's inexorable path toward human emancipation and freedom. If opinion has to be controlled, it is only because portions of the public are still "backward" and have therefore to be educated by a vanguard that possesses full consciousness of what is historically necessary. If the members of this same vanguard have to exercise dictatorial powers, they do so as agents of a movement that fulfills the deepest yearnings of the masses; they thus act democratically, it is said, in a more profound way than do the "people's representatives" in the West who, according to this view, are mere self-seeking agents or stooges of business or other interests.

This Communist self-interpretation affects not only the regimes under its control but also many outside its immediate sphere of influence. In the non-Communist world, what often impresses the half-starved, miserable individual affected by the "revolution of rising expectations" is the example of societies that have been able to pull themselves up by their own efforts from similarly miserable beginnings to their current levels of economic development and political power. If this can only be had at the price of a temporary sacrifice of liberties (whose value, in any event, is unknown to many of them), it may seem to them not too highly priced. The West can here hardly hope to compete successfully by merely opposing its own ideology of freedom; it must be able to promise, credibly, a better material future as well.

IDEOLOGY TODAY

What role are ideologies likely to play in the future? Looking from the vantage point of the early seventies, one is tempted to say that the heyday of opposing ideologies and clashing systems is over; that it was reached in the thirties, forties, and early fifties of this century and has since yielded to less doctrinal antagonism, what some have called "deideologization." Fascism, at least in its extreme, Nazi-type variety, lost its appeal after the defeat of the Axis powers and the postwar revelations of its atrocities. Communism of the Stalinist variety also lost some of its attraction with revelations of the abuse of personal power that came with de-Stalinization. Moreover, for those living under totalitarian regimes, there seems to be a law of diminishing returns through indoctrination. Although individuals in mass society may long for safe beliefs, they become confused when doctrines are too frantically advanced or when, in the conflict of regimes and ideologies, one replaces another in bewildering sequence. Individuals become cynical or apathetic and tend to avoid taking sides or positions of responsibility—a disease common not only in Communist regimes but also in places where democracy has replaced totalitarianism, as in West Germany or Italy.

There is still more to "deideologization." Regimes once founded on the doctrinal-revolutionary fervor of their leaders can turn into "Establishments," where a technologically motivated managerial elite rules bureaucratically rather than ideologically. The doctrine is used to induce conformity, but as a tool rather than a master. The genuinely motivating ideology becomes technological progress, which the capitalist and Third Worlds also seek. In this sense there is some "convergence" between the Soviet Union and the West. But there remains the doctrinal radicalism of younger Communist regimes, such as China and Cuba. Indeed, in China the "cultural revolution" seems to have been instigated from above because of Mao's fear lest the original spirit of the revolution be replaced by bureaucratism.

Finally, there is the new phenomenon of the political extremism and ideological commitments that affect the younger generations and, in particular, their elites—the students—all over the world. If these movements constitute a revival of political ideology, it is not, generally, a revival of traditional Communist doctrine and movement. To be sure, Mao and Castro (or, rather, Che Guevara) figure among the heroes of the New Left. But they do so not as representatives of certain regimes (which, as "Establishments," inevitably exhibit Establishment features of bureaucratism and, more generally, of societal "repression" and manipulation), but because (mistakenly or not) they are considered to be symbols of the struggle against *any* kind of established regime or government. In other words, a doctrine of anarchism, rather than of communism, imbues the new radicals. Anarchists may agree on what to attack and destroy. They usually disagree on what to put in place of the "old," and they disintegrate into warring factions. Thus, instead of an age

where doctrines wane and people agree on "practical" ways of life, or where specific doctrines oppose each other, this may become an age that is marked by fuzziness in standards, values, doctrines, and objectives.

When Communism, as a clear-cut doctrine, opposed democracy as an equally unambiguous set of principles, one at least knew who opposed whom. Now everything seems to become uncertain. The Communist elite, at least in the older regimes, is no longer wedded to the original doctrine and is thus unsure of the future. In the West, the elites' old belief in progress, economic growth, and in increasing affluence yields to doubt when confronted with the new problems posed by a deteriorating environment. The deterioration of the environment, as well as the apparently intractable nature of many of the social problems, such as poverty and racial inequality, makes many, especially the young, despair of solving the world's problems, "cop out" of society, or vent their frustration in resorting to violence.

But this dismal picture is not necessarily indicative of the future. On the contrary, one could well imagine a merging of the different dissatisfied or critical groups in a common approach. The "cop-outs," for instance, could become actively interested in the problems of social justice, and the critics from the New Left, as well as "older" liberals, could become involved in ways to solve the ecological problems. A response to some demands *can* go hand in hand with the solution to others: for instance, decent housing, with ample air, space, playgrounds, and parks would save or restore the environment *and* at the same time provide jobs for the "underclass." If such priorities are made the basis for social and political action, a new ideology of "conservative" (in the sense of value-conserving) progress might evolve. Hopefully, we might then enter an age characterized by a more positive approach and by a more cooperative policy than is visible now.

Keeping in mind the challenge of clashing ideologies or "deideologization," the dangers of an increasingly lethal world environment, as well as the older (and partly more technical) challenges to government, we shall now turn to the individual political systems of the four countries we have selected. In doing so, we have not thought of arguing a case or presenting a defense of one or another system; rather, we have tried to present the facts objectively, and, in selecting and assessing them, to be as fair and accurate as possible. Let the reader draw his conclusion. This, in itself, is an exercise in liberal democracy that would be hard to perform under totalitarian or authoritarian controls. To this extent, but only to this extent, does the study of government and politics involve commitment to a cause.

I The government of the United Kingdom of Great Britain and Northern Ireland

Introduction

Throughout the twentieth century Great Britain has been the strongest and most reliable ally of the United States; equally, the United States has been Britain's most powerful support. Whatever differences in attitude and approach have existed—and there have been many—the bonds of self-interest, history, and sentiment have been too strong to allow the rupture of their often cited "special relationship." As Great Britain now moves to assume a place within the European Common Market, however, new questions arise about the character and strength of that relationship. How much did it depend on Great Britain's position as a world power rather than a European one? Will the Atlantic alliance be complementary to or be replaced by a British orientation that looks south and east rather than west? What will be the effect on foreign affairs of Britain's inevitable concentration on adjusting its economic and political alignments to a more Continental role?

Bismarck said long ago that the most significant fact for the twentieth century would be that Americans speak English. British institutions, English literature, law, and education have had a deep and persistent effect on American life. The advanced British social welfare system and radical approaches to the care of the environment have unfortunately had less impact in this country. The old stereotype of the British as a highly conservative people perpetuating the past through their lords and castles and their colorful royal ceremonies is a technicolor screen, which tends to conceal the active experimentation by means of which the British are seeking new ways to cope with the manifold problems of a highly industrial, urbanized society. There is much for Americans to learn from British attempts and even failures to master the most pressing problems of our day—such as poverty, pollution, color prejudice, and discrimination—for it is in these areas that we, too, are struggling to find solutions.

In the chapters that follow there is abundant material on the British heritage of history and ideas; the explanation of why one of the two major political parties of supposedly staid Britain is called Labor and was founded on a socialist creed; the ways in which the British are seeking to make the workings of their legislative body more efficient and responsible; how powerful the prime minister is in practice in comparison with the president of the United States; the structure and operation of the nationalized enterprises, which manage one-fifth of British economic life; the character of English law and courts, which have so direct a relationship to our own legal system; and the changing orientations of British foreign policy. In all these areas, the British have raised basic questions as to whether institutions and policies are fulfilling the purposes of the British people and adhering to the high standards of democracy they prize. In learning about contemporary Britain, its problems and its efforts to wrestle with them, we not only can learn about a great country, which in the nineteenth century was the world's leading power, but also can gain constructive perspective on our own current issues and how to tackle them.

1

The
British people
and
their politics

1 THE CHALLENGE TO GREAT BRITAIN

The British [1] people today face great challenges: to revitalize their economy; to adjust to their changed position in world affairs; to devise new political techniques in response to defects in traditional institutions; to respond constructively to increasing regional self-consciousness in Scotland and Wales and to the strains caused by postwar colored immigration; and to find new ways, as they have in the past, to resolve the conflicts and tensions that are endemic in a mobile industrial society. The external reputation of the British people for steadiness and sanity tends to conceal from outsiders the widespread questioning of standard values and of institutionalized ways of acting that pervades British society. The British are making persistent, although occasionally

contradictory, efforts to cope with these challenges. But the process is a painful one, and the tensions manifest themselves in angry outbursts from time to time at the character or the slowness of change.

Great Britain was long one of the world's great powers and is the one whose institutions have been most widely copied in other countries. Both the Conservative and Labor parties have been reluctant, therefore, to restrict their country's international role despite its unstable balance of payments and lessening influence in international crises. Both parties sought when in office during the sixties to secure entry to the Common Market, although both contain sharp internal divisions of opinion on this European orientation. Labor has led in stressing the need to reduce the outlay on military expenditures and to concentrate more on the welfare of the people of the British Isles. The Conservatives have also reluctantly conceded the need for retrenchments in overseas commitments, especially east of Suez. Thus it is the extent and timing of withdrawals, rather than fundamental orientations, that divide the parties in the field of international relations.

The second great issue in British politics—which revolves around the dimensions and character of what is called "the welfare state"—creates more clear-cut differences between the parties. At issue is the degree to which the power and resources of the government should be used to create a more egalitarian society. In

[1] *British* in this section refers to the inhabitants of the United Kingdom, although properly the term can be used also to refer to persons in other parts of the British Commonwealth and empire. *Great Britain* and the *United Kingdom* will be used interchangeably, although, strictly speaking, Great Britain includes only England, Wales, and Scotland.

Northern Ireland, it should be noted, differs from the other parts of the United Kingdom in that its population is represented in a legislature of its own in Belfast, as well as in the British Parliament. The partition of Ireland, which dates from 1921, divides the island between the homogeneous Catholic Irish Republic, which occupies most of its territory, and Protestant-dominated Northern Ireland in its northeastern corner, which has home rule inside the United Kingdom. Sporadic violence between Protestants and Catholics in Northern Ireland, particularly since 1969, has led to the presence of British troops to maintain order. (For more details on this situation, see Chapter 8, Section 1.)

part the approach to securing this objective has been through state-supported institutions like schools and hospitals, but it involves also a more equitable distribution of wealth, largely through taxation. The Conservatives, who place primary emphasis on individual initiative and the enterprise of the capitalist class, believe that economic health requires trade union reform and restraint in wage increases. Although they are committed to extend aid to those groups in society who cannot provide for themselves—that is, the aged, ill, infirm, children, and unemployed—they also aim at lower taxation to encourage active entrepreneurship inside and outside the country. The Labor party, as an article of faith, is primarily committed, on the other hand, to the well-being of the working class and to a basic egalitarianism to be secured through using state instrumentalities to create conditions for its realization. Although in practice the orientation and behavior of the leaders of both parties are less far apart than these contrasts might suggest, there are distinctive differences in policy decisions, depending on which party is in office.

Both British parties believe strongly in personal rights and the rule of law. They believe that individual freedom must be combined, however, with effective government, and that open discussion should be organized through channels that protect minority rights but facilitate majority action. Although class, regional, and, now, color distinctions complicate the process of reaching decisions and responding to them, both parties are dedicated to the effective use of parliamentary institutions (although possibly reformed and revitalized) in their search for constructive answers to complicated and delicate issues. With all the ferment of change, convention still maintains its hold. Although Britain's future is difficult to calculate, the ways in which it has surmounted crises in the past lends support to the faith that it will do so again.

THE IMPORTANCE OF BRITAIN FOR OTHER COUNTRIES

British political machinery and experience have long had unusual importance for other countries, for no people in modern times have

been more fertile in the invention and adaptation of political institutions. Wherever men of British descent founded new governments in the last century and a half—in Canada, Australia, and New Zealand—they carried British institutions with them. Moreover, such countries as India, Kenya, and Jamaica, when they became independent, adapted British forms and institutions. On the continent of Europe almost every democracy has been strongly, if not always happily, influenced by the British example. The person who understands British government has a standard, therefore, by which to measure many of the world's democracies.

SIMILARITIES WITH AND DIFFERENCES FROM THE UNITED STATES

The British government, moreover, is sometimes held up as an example for Americans to imitate. Some of its more ardent admirers, it must be confessed, value it for different and even conflicting reasons, and some of them seriously misunderstand its character. Yet not infrequently the American people are urged to scrap some part of their constitutional machinery or political practices in favor of the British equivalent.

It is all the more important, therefore, to understand the extent to which the two countries are comparable. The sharing of a common language and of common cultural, legal, and political traditions often encourages the assumption that the political outlook and conduct of the two countries must also be similar. Both nations take it for granted that peoples who are not "Anglo-Saxon" will differ from them in attitude and policy, but each is subject to a peculiar irritation when it finds its standards disregarded by the other. There is shrewdness in the comment that Great Britain and the United States are divided by their common language.

There are, in actuality, important political differences between the two countries, differences that stem in large measure from dissimilarities in geography, economic structure, class divisions, way of life, and inherited political ideas and institutions. Anyone who is to understand British politics, therefore, must first of all know something about these differences.

2 THE ISLAND AND THE PEOPLE

THE ISLAND

The fact that Britain is an island has long conditioned British attitudes. Only twenty-two miles of water separate the southeast shore of England from the European continent—and plans are under consideration to build a connecting tunnel—but for many generations those few miles gave the British people the feeling of security that the Atlantic and the Pacific, until recently, gave Americans. Today, air warfare and nuclear armaments have destroyed any such idea. If the Channel helped to prevent Hitler's armies from conquering Great Britain, it could not keep the Allies from successfully invading occupied France, and it could not keep German planes and rockets from devastating many heavily populated centers on the British island.

Yet there are certain ways in which the earlier protective role of the Channel still influences British politics. During the critical centuries when Continental states developed great standing armies that became instruments of autocratic government, the British were relatively free from any corresponding threat. The British army, as the saying goes, was a navy; and a navy was hardly an asset in putting down popular resistance to royal authority on land. Security from invasion made it possible, in the seventeenth and eighteenth centuries, for the British to develop and consolidate free institutions of government at the very time that their neighbors across the Channel were submitting to absolute monarchy. Thus, although the Channel today has lost much of its defensive importance, the free institutions that it protected continue to exist.

Commercial and military position

Great Britain's geographical position has been important in another respect. So long as the Mediterranean was the chief path of trade, the island suffered commercially from its location on the fringe of the European world. But once America was discovered, the new trade routes turned the island into a center of world commerce. Great Britain pioneered the industrial revolution. Favorable conditions for importing raw materials and exporting manufactured goods made it the workshop of the world. Partly through the resulting capital accumulation, Great Britain became, too, the world's greatest banking center. If the island had remained purely agricultural, its population would necessarily have been small; but the profits from its industry, shipping, and worldwide investments made it easy to import the food and resources necessary to support a population larger than that of more self-sufficient France.

Great Britain's dependence on sea power encouraged its acquisition of key points on the world's trade routes: Gibraltar, at the mouth of the Mediterranean; the Falkland Islands, off the southern tip of South America; Cape Town, in southern Africa; and Singapore, dominating the route around Southeast Asia. Overseas settlement in areas that became Canada, Australia, New Zealand, and South Africa formed the core from which developed the modern British Commonwealth of Nations. During the nineteenth century the British navy, unmatched in strength, provided a condition of security that is often called the "Pax Britannica," which made possible an exchange of goods and services that helped both these overseas areas and Great Britain itself. Widely scattered other countries, like India, Malaysia, and Nigeria, where the British once governed diverse peoples very different from themselves in race, traditions, and conditions of life, have moved through self-government to independence since World War II but still associate themselves with Great Britain through the Commonwealth. These vast international connections brought Great Britain power, prestige, and wealth, and stretched its communication lines around the world.

Today this very dependence on foreign trade constitutes both a military and an economic liability. Because of its relative poverty in raw materials other than coal, Great Britain relies heavily on outside sources to maintain its factories; it needs oil from the Middle East, rubber from Malaysia, nickel from Canada, iron ore to make the steel with which to produce the locomotives and heavy machinery that form so substantial a part of its exports, and much besides. Although a proportion of its foreign investments have been reestablished since the days they were liquidated to pay the costs of two world wars, Great Britain must earn most of the money for food and raw materials by selling in foreign markets—often, as in the United States, in the face of protective tariffs. Fourteen to twenty percent of its gross national product (GNP) is exported, compared to 4 percent for the United States.

Since Great Britain remains predominantly a processing economy, failure to maintain its imports and exports can be disastrous. Both the United States and the Soviet Union have vast resources and markets at home; in an emergency they could support themselves to a considerable extent. But to Great Britain such an emergency might mean strangulation. Thus, whereas the United States and the Soviet Union, in military terms, think first of all of security from attack against the homeland, Great Britain must also think of the equally fatal effect of any serious interference with its commerce with distant lands. Moreover, failure to compete economically could also mean a kind of death by attrition.

Climate and size

Another geographical consideration of great political importance is the smallness of the British island and the evenness of its climate. Great Britain (not including Northern Ireland, which has an area of 5,244 square miles) has an area of only 89,041 square miles, as compared with 3,022,387 for the continental United States. The island is twice the size of Pennsylvania but a little smaller than Oregon. Moreover, the major portion of its population (which by mid-1971 was about 55.5 million) is concentrated in a relatively small area, since in the north and west (including most of Scotland and Wales) the country is hilly or mountainous. The climate, however, is remarkably even. There is somewhat more rain in the west than in the east and somewhat more sun in the east, but the winters tend to be mild, the summers cool,

and the rainfall fairly well distributed throughout the year. There is nothing to compare with the great range of climate and the vast distances that encourage the distinctive outlook and individuality of different American regions. On the contrary, the great bulk of the people live within a few hours' train or motor ride of London, and the same newspapers can be read on the same morning throughout the island.

As a result, the Englishman is more likely than the American to think in exclusively national terms. Both in Scotland and in Wales there is a strong local consciousness, recently reflected in regional parties (see Chapter 3, Section 2), although the national parties win the seats in general elections. However, less than one-sixth of the British population is Scottish or Welsh. In England itself, where the overwhelming majority of the people live, there is little particularist feeling. There is considerable interest in local history and in regional variations in landscape, architecture, and dialect, but this interest is not reflected in a distinctive political feeling. Political parties can use the same literature and emphasize the same principles in Somerset as in London or Norfolk or Yorkshire.

Great Britain's relative homogeneity and compactness have an important political consequence. In American politics little is more significant than the extent of political decentralization. Not only do sections of the country have distinct characters of their own, but each state has a complete government. The most important political organizations in the United States are state and local rather than national. No American party can win a national election unless it carries several of the great sections, and every party platform represents a compromise of rival sectional interests. Votes in Congress often run along sectional rather than party lines, and even the nominations for national office must take geography into account: if the presidential nominee comes from the West, the vice-presidential nominee must come from the East or the South.

In England, in contrast, no one cares whether a party's leaders come from Durham or Devon or Essex. Unlike American practice, candidates for the legislature do not need to be residents of the constituencies for which they stand. Historically, the smallness of the island simpli-

THE UNITED KINGDOM OF GREAT BRITAIN AND NORTHERN IRELAND

fied the task of centralizing the government; and governmental centralization, reinforced by ease of transportation and communication, has fostered a well-integrated political and economic life. Apart from the strong sectionalism in Northern Ireland (accentuated by recent violence) and the marked self-consciousness in Scotland and Wales (which leads to demands for some devolution of governmental responsibilities), the most important political issues in Great Britain are not primarily regional in character; parties are free to plan in national rather than local terms.

THE PEOPLE: NATIONALITY

In origin the inhabitants of Great Britain are both ancient and diverse, for the early history of the island is, almost to the point of monotony, one of invasion, conquest, and settlement by different peoples coming from a great variety of geographical areas. In later years Shakespeare could hail the "silver sea" surrounding the British isle and serving it

          . . . in the office of a wall,
     Or as a moat defensive to a house
     Against the envy of less happier lands.

But in prehistoric and early historic times, the seas often acted as a highroad bringing invaders and visitors from far places as the airways do today.

The first historical knowledge we have of the inhabitants of the island comes from a time when most of Great Britain was inhabited by Celts. By reputation they were a folk of imagination and quick intelligence, though somewhat lacking in discipline and emotional restraint; and even today there is an amusing tendency to attribute any marked strain of individuality or lyricism in English writing, or any "un-English" political excitement among the masses of the people, to a survival of this Celtic element in the national character.

For a time, from the first to the fifth centuries, England and a part of Scotland were under the control of the Romans; but apart from their famous roads, a number of ruins, and some place names, few direct traces of Roman influence have survived. With the withdrawal of their legions early in the fifth century, the island was left open to the inroads of various Germanic peoples: Angles, Saxons, Jutes, and, later, Danes. As the invaders penetrated westward, it was only on the fringes of Wales, Cornwall, Cumberland, and western Scotland that the Celts continued to predominate.

The last great invasion of England took place in 1066, when the Normans gave the country, for a time, a ruling class which was French in customs, language, and manners, but which was not numerous enough to make fundamental changes in the composition of the population. Since that time there has been no successful invasion of the country. Moreover, except for the Celtic fringes of Wales (where about 30 percent of the people speak Welsh) and of Scotland (where a few Highlanders speak Gaelic), the Irish immigrants in a few large cities, and a wartime infiltration of Poles and central Europeans, the population of Britain was long exceptionally uniform in language, religion, and way of life.

Since World War II, however, the British have confronted a color and immigration problem that bears on their Commonwealth relations and their economic situation, as well as on their population structure. Immigrants from the West Indies and the Indian subcontinent had brought Great Britain's colored population to an estimated 1.2 million by mid-1969. (By 1985, the specialized British Runnymede Trust estimates, there will be fewer than 3 million colored people in Britain, two-fifths of them born there.) Although the 1969 figures represent only 2.7 percent of the population—compared to the black 11 percent in the United States—the same problems of discrimination in housing and employment have been apparent in the urban areas, where they are most numerous. So, too, has the intensity of local bitterness against them, reflected in or whipped up by the inflammatory speeches of Enoch Powell, a Conservative, who has been termed "a George C. Wallace with an Oxford accent."

In 1962, for the first time in British history, restrictions were placed on immigration from Commonwealth countries—a move that roused ill feeling in some of the new countries of that association (see Chapter 8, Section 1). Moreover, progressively tightened restrictions have followed under both Labor and Conservative governments. Although parallel acts have been passed prohibiting racial discrimination in "places of public resort" (comparable to the public accommodations section of the Civil Rights Act of 1964) and establishing a Race Relations Board that can investigate cases of discrimination, the problems remain. But whereas color was an election issue in a few local areas in 1964, despite strong official party disapproval, it has played only a minor role in scattered constituencies in subsequent elections.

Immigration into Great Britain needs to be considered in a broader context than the color issue suggests. The present population includes an unusually high proportion of young people up to fifteen years of age and older ones over sixty-five. Because of lower birth rates in the early 1950s (repeated from 1964 to 1969), no net growth in the labor force can be foreseen before 1975, particularly since there will be a sharp drop in 1972 when the school-leaving age is raised. In contrast, because of the different American postwar pattern in births, there will be 35 percent more eighteen-to-twenty-four-year-olds in the United States in 1975 than in 1965. Moreover, according to the Organization for Economic Cooperation and Development (OECD) estimates in 1969, the likely growth, including immigration, in the active population in the United States between 1965 and 1980 will be nearly 30 percent, with comparable increases in France and Switzerland. In Britain, West Germany, Italy, and Sweden the active population, in contrast, will probably be not much, if at all, larger in 1980 than in 1965.

On balance, net postwar emigration from Great Britain—which varied between nineteen thousand and sixty-three thousand during the five years from 1965 to 1970—has balanced net immigration (now limited to under thirty-five thousand a year). On these projections, the British population may appear to be reaching stabilization, which will comfort those who have been alarmed about overcrowding Britain's available land space. But those concerned to expand production may look with envy on the annual intake into economically prosperous West Germany of hundreds of thousands of temporary foreign workers from its European partners and perhaps one hundred and fifty thousand into France. Britain, too, will face comparable inflows when it joins the Common Market, for although Commonwealth immi-gration need not be affected, Britain will have to provide free entry to workers from its new European partners. Thus the population issue is far from settled. Much more study is needed of the relation between size of population, extent of skills, industrial expansion, housing, and the other services for its people to which Great Britain is committed.

THE PEOPLE: RELIGION

Religion has had a greater influence on British politics than most of the British themselves realize. It is politically important, for example, that there is no great religious division and that, as a whole, the island's people are overwhelmingly Protestant. A few of the oldest and noblest families are Catholic, and recent immigration from Ireland has added significantly to this church's adherents in the poorest and least influential sections of society; but altogether under 10 percent of the population in the United Kingdom are Catholic (compared with 20 percent of the population in the United States). Thus there is no basis whatsoever for a Catholic political party such as those that have existed in France, Italy, and other countries.

Of greater political significance is the division that exists within the Protestant church. At present, about 70 percent of the people of England are, at least nominally, adherents of the Church of England, that is, the Anglican Church, which corresponds to the Episcopal church in the United States; about 20 percent are so-called Nonconformists, who are generally Methodists (700,000), Baptists, Congregationalists, or Presbyterians. In Scotland, however, the mass of the people belong to the Presbyterian church, which is the Church of Scotland, and in Wales most belong to Nonconformist denominations.

The Church of England

Because it is an established church, the Church of England is to a certain extent involved in politics. Its head is the monarch, and representatives of the Church sit in the House of Lords and help to make the law of the land. Anglican clergy performed the ceremony of crowning the present queen; it is they who open Parliament with prayer. The highest members of the clergy are, in effect, appointed by the Crown, on the nomination of the prime minister. Despite numerous Church commissions set up since 1870, of which the latest reported in December 1970, they have not found ways for the Church to have more freedom in determining its own affairs. The greatest concern is that the creed of the Church of England is established by parliamentary statute and may be changed only by parliamentary action.[2]

More important than the present state of the establishment, however, is the historical influence of the opposition between the Church of England and Nonconformity. Authority in the Church of England, as just noted, traditionally has come from above, and it was natural for those accustomed to authority in the Church to support it in the state. Thus there has been a marked tendency for at least those of the upper class who are Anglicans in religion to be Conservatives in politics. And the Conservative party still considers itself, to some extent, the special defender of religion and the interests of the Church.

Nonconformist influence

English Nonconformists, in contrast, have tended to be critical of state authority ever since their persecution in the seventeenth century.[3] The Congregationalists (who still call themselves "Independents") and Baptists practiced a peculiarly loose and individualistic form of church organization. Authority rested in the congregation, not in a clerical hierarchy, and members were free at any time to withdraw and

form new churches. Such ideas, when applied in the political sphere, are closely related to those in the American Declaration of Independence (both denominations, of course, colonized New England) and provide grounds for questioning the legitimacy of any authority not based upon consent. Throughout the nineteenth century the Liberal party, with its emphasis on personal liberty and the limitation of state authority, drew its strongest support from these churches. Today there remains a large Nonconformist element in the Labor party.

It is still possible, in several important respects, to trace the influence of Nonconformity upon British politics. In the first place, the Nonconformists' demand for toleration of different religious ideas and organizations led naturally to insistence on respect for different political ideas and parties. In addition, Nonconformity is the source of the "Nonconformist conscience" (a first cousin of the "New England conscience"), which has come to be shared by a large section of the Anglican Church and which expects the conduct of the government, in foreign as in domestic policy, to be moral and Christian. For example, there was a vast outpouring of indignation within Great Britain itself against Eden's use of force in the 1956 Suez crisis and deep concern at the Conservative decision in 1971 to sell arms to South Africa.

Yet if the Nonconformist heritage has had an idealistic influence upon British politics, it has also had an intensely practical one. In some Continental Protestant churches, political action has always been suspect, but the British churches have encouraged a general interest and participation in politics. It used to be said in the nineteenth century that every Nonconformist chapel was a recruiting station for the Liberal party. When the Labor party was founded, it was no accident that its party organization combined local democracy with a high degree of centralization, for many of its early leaders were themselves Methodist or Baptist lay preachers who could place both their eloquence and their practical knowledge of organization at the disposal of the new party.

In addition, the Nonconformist churches made their chief appeal to people in the lower

---

[2] Since it often happens that the prime minister is not himself an Anglican, there results an odd situation (and one which many Anglicans dislike) under which the highest clergy of the Church may be nominated by a Welsh Nonconformist like Lloyd George, a Presbyterian like Balfour or Bonar Law, or even—to achieve the ultimate in doctrinal incongruity—by a Unitarian like Neville Chamberlain. Moreover, many members of Parliament are Nonconformists, Jews, Catholics, or members of no church at all. In 1927 and 1928, changes in the Prayer Book of the Church of England, requested by the representative bodies of the Church, were refused by Parliament partly because of the votes of Nonconformists and even—to the scandal of the devout—of one Parsee.

[3] Although the Methodists, whose religious activity began in the eighteenth century, preached a doctrine of obedience and submission to state authority, they organized vigorous political action on such issues as prison reform and abolition of the slave trade.

classes whom the established Church failed to reach. In countries such as Russia or France or Germany, where the church tended to identify its interests with those of the upper classes, it was natural to regard the church as an ally or tool of an oppressive state, an instrument for keeping the exploited in subjection. But in England the lower classes had a church of their own that was itself to some extent oppressed by and critical of state authority. Accordingly, there was no need, in attacking political injustice, to attack religion as well. On the contrary, religion played an important part in fostering both the trade union and the socialist movement in Great Britain. And since it is difficult to be both a Christian and a believer in the extreme doctrine of class war, religion contributed to the moderation as well as to the idealism of the Labor party.

Today all the British churches cooperate in programs of social betterment, and some of their most eminent members are advocates of radical economic reform. The vote on church union between the Anglicans and the Methodists failed in mid-1969 only because the Anglican lower clergy did not support it to the necessary 75 percent, but the efforts go on both in England and Wales. Moreover, by his formal visit to the Pope in 1965, the Archbishop of Canterbury supported the idea of wider associations, which are one of Britain's greatest needs.

POLITICAL CULTURE

In way of life, as in nationality and religion, the British people are exceptionally homogeneous. The sentimental American still likes to think of England as a "green and pleasant land" of villages, churches, and country houses, and the tourist still prefers a visit to the Lake Country or Stratford-on-Avon to an acquaintance with Manchester or Glasgow. But the unromantic fact is that Great Britain is heavily urbanized and industrialized; its population is one of the densest of any Western country. Whereas the United States has some 57 people to the square mile, the United Kingdom as a whole has 607, more than ten times as many, and England and Wales have 837, that is, nearly fifteen times as many. This density, coupled with intense industrialization in certain centers like Birmingham, Manchester, and indeed the whole of the "black country," and of other urban conglomerations, has led to a high degree of urbanization, reaching 80 percent in England and Wales and 70 percent in Scotland (the latter the same degree as in the United States). The British stress on industry has resulted in a very heavy proportion of urban workers compared to those still on the land. Only 3.2 percent of the British working force is in agriculture (in the United States it is 6.7 percent), while 46 percent work in industry, mining, and the like (compared to 40.9 percent in the United States). Thus, whereas the proportion of urban workers to farmers in the United States is six-and-a-half to one, in Great Britain there are fourteen urban workers to every farmer. This latter situation, as we shall see, has a massive impact on the class and party systems.

But while occupation, urbanization, and industrialization are strong conditioners of political attitudes, they are not the only ones. The British class structure, which has long been the basic fact of British society, also reflects other factors such as tradition, education, behavior, manner of living, and, although to a decreasing extent, accent. Above all, the class structure and its impact rest on social self-perception.

Traditionally, the British class structure made its sharpest line of demarcation not between the aristocracy [4] and the middle class (as has so often been the case on the Continent) but between the upper middle and the lower middle class. The most important factor in determining who fell on which side of the line used to be education, which in turn was determined not only by financial standing but also by inherited traditions, sense of values, and habit.

EDUCATION

Prior to the Education Act of 1944, fees were imposed for secondary school education, and most children dropped out at fourteen, at the

---

[4] In Great Britain, a title ordinarily descends only to the eldest son, while the rest of the children of a nobleman become "commoners." Thus a person may be closely related to a number of peers without having a title himself, and the distinction between the aristocracy and the upper middle class is blurred.

end of elementary education, with no chance to enter schools that would prepare them for college and relatively little preparation for a job. The educational system thus tended not only to perpetuate the class structure but also to stratify the opportunities for employment.

Moreover, educational opportunities were further limited by the predominant position of the private preparatory schools (comparable to the private elementary schools in the United States), which had a virtual monopoly over entry to the great public boarding schools such as Eton and Harrow (called "public" because they are not run for private profit, though they are entirely or mainly independent of state aid or control, and are, in fact, like the American private preparatory schools), to which students normally go at thirteen. Only 5 to 10 percent of the schoolboy population entered the preparatory schools and the great public boarding schools, but the great majority of this group went on to a university, particularly to the most ancient and distinguished British universities, Oxford and Cambridge. Although Oxford and Cambridge accounted for about one-quarter of all the university students in England and Wales before the war, only a small percentage of their prewar undergraduates had attended the state elementary schools, although half of the students at other British universities were trained at such schools.

Moreover, in contrast to the United States only a relatively small proportion of British youth attended college. With a population three times as large, the United States had twenty times as many students in colleges and universities in 1939 as had Great Britain (1 million as compared with 50 thousand). It is true that socially and intellectually the American college, at least in the first two years, is more akin to a British secondary school than to a British university and that vocational and professional training in Great Britain is handled in other types of institutions. Also, in proportion to the total population, the number of university students in Great Britain had doubled since 1900. Nonetheless, only a relatively small minority of one in a thousand enjoyed higher education in prewar Britain.

Britain extended free compulsory education up to the age of fifteen with the 1944 Education Act. But the gap between the children of the middle-class and working-class families tended to be perpetuated by the division between the academically oriented grammar schools, which required success in the eleven-plus examinations for entry, and the modern schools to which went the children who did not achieve this standard. Labor bitterly attacked this division and urged its replacement by a system of comprehensive schools combining grammar, technical, and modern school sections. These schools thus include a broad range of courses that provide much the same educational base for all and thus aid social mobility. The Conservatives, traditionally protective of the middle class and also concerned for academic excellence, resisted the change during their period of office from 1951 to 1964; Labor attempted to institute it on a national scale in 1965. Since the responsibilities for public education are divided between local authorities and the national government, the issue has been a complex and often divisive one. Local authorities could choose between six major types of organization for comprehensive education, and the choice and implementation of the plans have been affected by local conditions, the party orientation of the particular local council, and the pressures of teachers' groups.[5] The end result in many areas, however, has been a widespread transformation of British secondary education.

A unified, free system now extends through age sixteen (raised from fifteen in 1972), and free tuition and mandatory grants (average £276 [$622] a year) are provided for all students taking first degree (undergraduate) courses, high-level nondegree courses, and teacher-training courses. Introduction of testing for aptitudes in place of the eleven-plus examinations, much more coeducation, use of team teaching and of educational television are comparable to the more creative innovations in American secondary education. At the same time, a much higher proportion of those educated at public schools, followed by those who graduate from grammar schools, continue to go to the university than is the case for those attending comprehensive schools.

[5] Paul E. Peterson, "British Interest Group Theory Reexamined: The Politics of Comprehensive Education in Three British Cities," *Comparative Politics* (April 1971), pp. 381–402.

The number of universities has expanded to forty-five, all of which are privately run but receive block five-year government grants (paid in annual installments) through an independent body, the University Grants Committee, on the basis of their requirements and plans. Prospective candidates for most universities apply through the University Central Council on Admissions instead of directly to individual universities, so their applications can be passed on to their second choice if they fail to be accepted at their first. (Just under sixty thousand were admitted in 1971 out of over one hundred and fifteen thousand candidates.) Moreover, local technical colleges draw an increasing number of those graduating from secondary schools.

To widen opportunities for higher education, the Labor government instituted an educational experiment known as the Open University, which is a unique blend of a correspondence course, television and radio broadcasts, individual tutoring, and additional facilities at 250 study centers throughout the country. Founded by Royal Charter in June 1969, the Open University's first academic year started in January 1971 with 25,000 students enrolled in its basic course, thereby doubling Britain's university enrollment of first-year students. The Open University has its own center in Milton Keynes in North Buckinghamshire, with a staff of some 350 academics and administrators, while other staff members are located in different parts of the country. It concentrates its efforts on preparation for the B.A. degree in arts or in science, which can be taken through its facilities in a minimum of three years, although most students will take longer. Each student has a tutor, must take an annual written examination, and must attend a two-week summer school. Costs, both to the students and the government, are low compared to conventional study. Thus the Open University vastly enlarges the possibilities for pursuing higher education in Britain, capitalizing on the relative smallness of the country's area in comparison to population and bringing high-quality training within much easier reach of those already employed or otherwise prevented from pursuing regular, full-time study.

British higher education in conventional institutions was evaluated in 1971 by the University Central Council on Admissions as well as by the Department of Education and Science and the local associations that provide the students' grants. Arguments in support of raising grants are that the drop-out rate among British students is one of the lowest in the world, that graduates are produced rapidly, gauged by international standards, that the cost per graduate student is among the least expensive anywhere, and that a high proportion of students are studying science and technology. Over 40 percent of those admitted to the university still come, however, from the top 15 percent of professional homes in Britain. As a consequence, the children of unskilled and skilled workers have somewhat less chance of a university education in Britain than in most other Western European countries. Nonetheless the educational changes that have been instituted in the postwar period have brought the system considerably closer to the goal of equality.

SOCIAL SECURITY

Another striking change in British life has resulted from the extension of "welfare state" responsibilities, which rest on the premise that the weaker members of society must be protected from the worst effects of economic pressures in integrated, industrialized, modern society. Between 1906 and 1911, almost thirty years before comparable American action (although not as early as in Germany), the British government had instituted a "New Deal" that provided national health and unemployment insurance for some groups, noncontributory old age pensions, a national system of unemployment exchanges, and free meals for school children. Piecemeal extensions after World War I failed, however, to overcome the basic causes of urban poverty: interruption or loss of earning power due to unemployment or illness and more children than families could support on meager incomes. Following the famous Beveridge Plan to establish a "national minimum standard" for all, comprehensive social security schemes based on insurance were established by 1948 that covered everyone "from the cradle to the grave" (or, more jocularly, "from the womb to the tomb").

This social security program, supported by individual and employer contributions and government funds,[6] provides benefits on retirement for women at sixty and men at sixty-five, special benefits for those suffering industrial injuries, for widows, orphans, and for maternity periods and, most controversial and costly, virtually free medical and hospital care.

The British National Health Service pays doctors salaries according to certain prescribed scales (whose levels have been determined by a variety of bodies, including a special review board, but remain unsatisfactory to many doctors). Patients enroll with the doctors of their choice, who treat them without charge when they are in need. The permissible limit for a doctor's list is 3,500 patients (or 5,500 for a doctor with an assistant), but doctors claim, not surprisingly, that even national average lists of over 2,000 are much too large. Hospitals are nationalized and free (private paid care is also available) but are under decentralized control; medical and dental clinics and health centers are directed by local government authorities and executive councils whose members are nominated by the latter and by local practitioners and the department responsible for health. Prescription costs are a source of contention between Labor and the Conservatives, the former keeping them low and the latter imposing higher charges. There are also charges for eyeglasses, dentures, and wigs.

Despite the comprehensiveness of these programs, there were still half a million families with a million and a half children in serious need in 1966 and possibly as many as 5 million in 1970 below the poverty line. Trade union leaders called that year for an increase in family allowances and asserted that inadequate wages were a major cause of this poverty. Other proposals have been for minimum wage legislation, a negative income tax, or minimum income guarantees. On the other side of the ledger is the fact that the cost of social services is increasing more rapidly than is national wealth. Although a considerable percentage of the support for social security, including national health care, comes from employers and employees (contributions from both were in-creased under the 1967 National Insurance Act), the costs of family allowances, and particularly of the health services, heavily tax the Exchequer.

Five-and-a-third percent of the national income is spent on health services, which is far more than originally anticipated. These growing costs are partly because people live longer, there are more chronic illnesses, and there are new sources of illness that are more expensive to treat. Some criticisms of the present health service maintain that costs could be reduced through structural changes that would overcome the present overlapping between the roles of general practitioners, the hospitals, and local community services. Others stress the need for more doctors.[7] Inadequacies in current standards of subsidized care are said to be the reason why a million to a million and a half people still prefer to contribute to private health schemes. Yet infant mortality rates have been brought down from 46 per 1,000 live births in 1945 to 18 in 1969 (20.7 in the United States), and the maternity death rate from 1,260 per 100,000 births to 19 (27.4 in the United States). A 1968 survey indicated that 95 percent of the people were satisfied with the present health system, including doctors.

Inadequate housing also creates pressing social problems. Although both the Conservatives and Labor have set targets for new houses to meet the demands of an increasing population and to replace the buildings destroyed during the war or made unsafe by time, slums and overcrowding still persist. Two million existing houses have been declared unfit for human habitation, and there are even some persons who remain homeless. The two political parties have approached this problem from different perspectives. Labor has emphasized security for tenants through rent control, which it reimposed in 1964, and favors public building by local authorities for rental purposes. The Conservatives lifted most rent controls in 1957, but extensive property speculation culminating in a well-publicized scandal, and undue concentration on office and luxury building were unpalatable effects that they are unlikely to permit again. They have rescinded Labor's ban

---

[6] The small weekly family allowances for all children after the first and also war pensions are a direct charge on the Exchequer.

[7] One-half of all junior doctors in Great Britain now come from overseas, many of them from India or the West Indies—so do the nurses—and an average of four hundred doctors and ninety dentists leave Britain every year.

on selling council-built houses, however, and are once again encouraging private builders to construct houses for home ownership.

Housing relates not only to urban renewal and building but also, especially in a densely populated country like Great Britain, to the siting of industry, the building of new towns, and land use and values. Some impressive advances have been made regarding constructive land use. Fifteen new towns had been built by 1960, and a number of new national and forest parks and nature reserves have been established. Problems of compensation and of taxing increased values have bedeviled arrangements, however, with the Conservatives placing premiums on sales to private interests and Labor favoring purchases for public purposes and development charges for other interests.

Conservatives and Labor also differ in their general approaches to social welfare. Labor's egalitarianism leads it to favor across-the-board benefits and to have special concern for the needs of the working class. Labor sees social welfare as part of the vast redistribution of wealth in Britain, which it favors. The Conservatives, in contrast, believe that pensions should provide only a basic income floor below which people cannot fall; that any higher or "second floor" should be dependent on people's own income levels or on employers' insurance plans. Their special concern is for the obviously disadvantaged, the disabled, widows, and the aged, for whom higher pensions were included in their first budget. Their perspective on other social services is strongly influenced by the fact that the costs of social welfare place a very heavy charge on the national budget as well as on employers on whom they depend to improve Britain's economic position.

THE CLASS STRUCTURE IN A
PERIOD OF CHANGE

What is apparent from the foregoing survey is that the British people have moved a long way since World War II in overcoming the most pressing sources of poverty and inequality. In many ways, British society has become more egalitarian than American society. Regional differences in standards of living, although they exist especially in Wales and Scot-

land, are less marked than in areas of the United States. Education is now provided on a more egalitarian basis, particularly since all schools must meet national standards. Social welfare extends much further than in the United States, especially in the field of health. What impact, we must ask, have these developments had on the British class structure, particularly in a time when the distinctions between classes have been under heavy attack as unwarranted and, of course, undemocratic?

Perhaps the most surprising result of recent surveys of the working and middle classes is that despite the major changes that have occurred in their conditions of life, there has been so little change in their self-perception and attitudes. A series of articles in *The Times* (September 28 through October 2, 1969) by Roy Lewis and Angus Maude, who had previously made a significant study of the British middle class,[8] coupled with the data from public surveys made in 1948 and 1969, show that approximately the same percentages regarded themselves as working class or as belonging to different sections of the middle class in 1969 as in 1948. Specifically, whereas 46 percent of the sample in 1948 rated themselves as working class, 50 percent did so in 1969; and whereas the 1948 divisions into upper middle, middle, and lower middle class found 6 percent, 28 percent, and 13 percent placing themselves respectively in those categories, 1969 found 4 percent, 31 percent, and 14 percent doing the same. The change from 2 to 1 percent of those rating themselves upper class seems generally insignificant. What is striking is that if the 5 percent who did not answer in 1948 are divided statistically between the working class and the middle class, there has been no significant change in the social self-assessment of the population during the twenty-one years in which Great Britain has been going through what most people regard as a peaceful social revolution.

This paradox suggests that far from becoming a "classless" society in which the affluent working class has merged with the middle class, British society retains most of the same class distinctions it used to have. In other words, the once popular theory of *embourgeoisement*, that

[8] Roy Lewis and Angus Maude, *The English Middle Classes.*

Survey of Self-Assessment on Class Basis

	SOCIAL CLASS SELF-DEFINITION	TOTAL	WORKING	LOWER MIDDLE	MIDDLE	UPPER MIDDLE	UPPER
	BASE: ALL INFORMANTS HAVING JOB	623	309	85	192	35	2
How satisfied are you with the sort of job you have?		%	%	%	%	%	No.
	Very satisfied	52	45	56	59	66	(1)
	Fairly satisfied	38	42	38	32	26	(1)
	Fairly dissatisfied	6	8	1	7	8	(–)
	Very dissatisfied	4	5	5	2	—	(–)
	BASE: ALL INFORMANTS	948	471	129	292	50	6
How satisfied are you with the sort of house you live in?		%	%	%	%	%	No.
	Very satisfied	47	44	44	54	52	(1)
	Fairly satisfied	34	35	37	30	32	(4)
	Fairly dissatisfied	10	10	12	8	10	(–)
	Very dissatisfied	9	11	7	8	6	(1)
	BASE: ALL INFORMANTS	948	471	129	292	50	6
How satisfied are you with the people you make friends with?		%	%	%	%	%	No.
	Very satisfied	75	73	75	81	78	(3)
	Fairly satisfied	22	24	24	18	18	(3)
	Fairly dissatisfied	2	2	1	1	4	(–)
	Very dissatisfied	1	1	—	*	—	(–)
	BASE: ALL INFORMANTS	948	471	129	292	50	6
How satisfied are you with the kind of neighborhood you live in?		%	%	%	%	%	No.
	Very satisfied	53	49	49	61	56	(1)
	Fairly satisfied	30	32	33	26	24	(3)
	Fairly dissatisfied	9	9	9	7	14	(1)
	Very dissatisfied	8	10	9	6	6	(1)

Source: Marplan Ltd., Market Research, *The Times*, September 29, 1969.

is, of all being merged into an amorphous middle class, does not hold. Even though youth from the working class may complete their advanced education, the appeal of habitual association may well counterbalance the new stimuli of academic training and a white-collar job. Moreover, since working-class families rarely have the same desire as middle-class families to have their children pursue higher education, the numbers of those who turn their back on possibilities for scholarships and university training and prefer manual labor remains considerable. Upward mobility is not difficult, although it is probably less common than generally supposed. In the Marplan survey, half of those describing themselves as lower middle class said their parents had been working class, and one-fifth of the self-styled middle class said

the same. But despite the far-reaching changes in education, housing, and the rise in material standards of living, no more people appear to *feel* middle class than immediately after the war.

The strongest influence on what people feel about their "class" appears to be associations. The social pressures of the work place and trade unionism commonly counterbalance the middle-class influences operating through education and rising standards of living. A 1968 study [9] of the political attitudes and voting practices of a sample of highly paid manual workers in Luton, a prosperous and growing industrial center somewhat removed from the older industrial areas of the country, indicated

[9] John E. Goldthorpe et al., *The Affluent Worker: Political Attitudes and Behaviour.*

both a strong retention of working-class perceptions and steadfast loyalty to the Labor party.

Nonetheless, despite the high proportion of urban workers in Britain's industrial society and the 50 percent of its population whose self-perception places them in the working-class category, not all of them support the Labor party, or it would always be in office. There has always been a percentage of manual laborers who support the Conservatives, originally because of a deference pattern of behavior but more recently because they accept the Conservatives as a national, not a class party. Women are more inclined to vote Conservative than are men from the working and lower middle classes. Young people usually follow the same voting patterns as their families. Where Labor party allegiance is consistent, however, it often embodies an intensity not found among Conservatives.

The prevailing fact in British political life is the remarkable consistency with which a high proportion of constituencies return the same party to Parliament election after election and the no less consistently small margins that separate the percentage totals of votes cast for the two major parties in general elections (see Chapter 3, Section 3). Although it is obvious that governments change, the swing of the electoral pendulum may be due more to nonvoting than to changing party allegiances or the impact of new voters. British political alignments appear extraordinarily fixed.

At the same time there is no sense of a "class war." David E. Butler and Donald E. Stokes, in their comprehensive study of political change in Britain, point out that "the image of politics as the representation of opposing class interests," which was increasingly accepted in the interwar and immediate postwar periods, is not common among newer Labor voters.[10] The need for Labor to be concerned with national interests when in office or seeking it has drawn its leaders away from primary identification with class goals. Moreover, the spread of affluence into large segments of the population and the leveling effect of the mass media, especially television, has inevitably ameliorated much of the bitterness of the past

and made it common to consider that the interests of all classes are compatible. Such political and social controversy as exists is largely within and between the middle classes. Its perhaps oversensitive conscience has been torn both by its sense of guilt over privilege and enforced conformity of standards and no less by its concern at the new permissiveness decreed by middle-class representatives in Parliament in such matters as homosexual practices, divorce, abortion, pornography, gambling, censorship, and the abolition of capital punishment. In addition, the character of middle-class life has changed materially, for this is the first generation to be almost wholly without regular paid domestic service, especially on a live-in basis. The horizons of middle-class mothers have necessarily shrunk; they have less time to devote to "good works," and, in particular, much less time for local government activities.

Probably the most noticeable impact of social change on occupation has been the replacement of the independent entrepreneur by the salaried professional manager. Family businesses and new small businesses appear to be on the way out due to heavy taxation and to the ability of big business to absorb promising concerns. Owner-occupied farms are similarly being sold or sometimes fragmented to pay the bills on the rest. It is easier to leave securities to one's children than to pass on a business or a professional partnership, although even the former process suffers from heavy estate and capital gains taxes. Nonetheless, the middle class seems satisfied with its prospects for increased salaries and higher standards of living. Since there has been no noticeable shortening of professional training courses, the waiting period for ultimate prosperity is often considerable, but those in the professions, such as doctors, teachers, airline pilots, have turned, and generally effectively, to trade union techniques in bargaining with the government, which provides their livelihood.

INTEREST GROUPS

It once was thought that interest or pressure groups scarcely existed in Great Britain, and certainly not to the degree they do in the

[10] David E. Butler and Donald E. Stokes, *Political Change in Britain: Factors Shaping Electoral Choice*, pp. 115–17.

United States. The crucial difference between the operation of pressure groups in the two countries, however, is neither their numbers nor their effectiveness, but the way they operate. The purpose of an interest group is obviously to secure the most favorable conditions possible for its members by urging their case where support may be decisive. In the United States, it is natural, therefore, for interest groups to exert pressure directly on individual congressmen, who are far less bound by party discipline than their opposite numbers in Great Britain. American pressure groups also work on and with the administration at every level from the president through the bureaus, but because Congress has control over appropriations, they naturally focus a great deal of their attention there.

In Great Britain, the distribution of effective power within the political system leads to different tactics. Pressure is focused on the executive and administrative departments, because they are the locus of decision-making. Disciplined parties mean that it is not the individual members of Parliament but the Cabinet and Shadow Cabinet who are the effective molders of policy. In as far as interest groups focus their attention on political parties, it is rather on their central offices than on the parliamentary parties. But above all, as we shall see in Chapter 6, interest groups work with and through the administration, which to a very large degree is entrusted with instituting and supervising the broad social and economic policies that have been transforming much of the character of British life. The British are neither so concerned about delegated legislation nor so suspicious of organized group pressures as are Americans. On the contrary, they welcome an open relationship between the representatives of special interests and the government bureaucracy, making provisions in numerous instances for official representation of such interests in advisory committees or for engaging them in formal negotiations, as with the National Farmers' Union in the government's annual price review.

A striking illustration of the operations of group politics is provided by Harry Eckstein's detailed study, *Pressure Group Politics: The Case of the British Medical Association.* Whereas less than half those eligible belong to a British trade union, 80 percent of all doctors are members of the British Medical Association (BMA). Although it has undertaken more of a broad public relations campaign since his study (which was first published in 1960), the BMA has followed the general pattern of exerting its chief influence on whatever administrative department is responsible for health. Unlike some other British pressure groups, like the National Farmers' Union itself, the National Union of Manufacturers, and the Federation of British Industries, all of which were long (and rather too obviously for their own initial effectiveness with Labor) aligned to the Conservative party, the BMA has studiously avoided identification with either political party. As far as Parliament is concerned, the BMA can depend on presenting its point of view through those MP's who are doctors, a normal way in the British system (see Chapter 4, Section 1) for voicing the views of special interests. Occasionally, as when the government had decided to ban the manufacture of heroin, the BMA managed to create enough back-bench pressure to have the measure withdrawn. Its chief activities, however, are concentrated in the administration, where, by mutual consent, the BMA is consulted on almost every departmental decision. Only on the very tricky issue of doctors' salary ranges has the government been forced to take the matter out of the range of departmental decisions, but its review bodies' recommendations have not avoided more or less open public negotiations.

The fact that the government and the BMA have disagreed sharply on the issue of doctors' pay does not obviate the accepted value for the political process of pressure group activities. The BMA, like other interest groups, provides a wealth of information both on practical details and on desires. Moreover, pressure groups, as Eckstein points out,[11] perform two significant general and in a sense divergent functions: both an integrative function, by organizing objectives into "manageable ranges of alternatives for action"; and "a 'disjunctive' function,"

[11] Harry Eckstein, *Pressure Group Politics: The Case of the British Medical Association,* p. 162. For an important reexamination of Eckstein's thesis on group politics, see Peterson, "British Interest Group Theory Reexamined," *Comparative Politics* (April 1971), pp. 381–402.

by keeping specific needs and demands visible within what might otherwise be too low a common denominator of aggregated interests that have been sieved through the funnels of two disciplined political parties.

The growing participation of government in economic life, with the concomitant closeness of its relations with organized producers, has also helped to stimulate industrial and trade associations. Concentration has gone further in industry than in commerce, the two being organized separately. By the 1950s, 90 percent of the larger firms and 76 percent of the smaller ones belonged to one or another of the thirteen hundred industrial trade associations. World War I had seen the formation of the Federation of British Industries (FBI, British style) and the National Union of Manufacturers (NUM). Another "peak" organization is the Confederation of British Industry, whose two hundred and seventy affiliates negotiate with 70 percent of the worker population. The FBI now represents six-sevenths of all industrial concerns employing more than ten workers. Some thirty or forty associations, each covering a total industry, seek with varying success to coordinate their interests when they consult with the relevant government department. Where there are a number of big producers, as in chemicals and motor cars, coordination is much easier to secure than when many small firms are involved. In comparison with industry, commerce is more dispersed, although the Association of British Chambers of Commerce (ABCC), founded in 1860, now has over a hundred constituent chambers, with some sixty thousand members. Many retail merchants who are not within the ABCC belong to the National Chamber of Trade.

Concentration of trade unions is no less striking. The Trades Union Congress (TUC), founded in 1868, has never had a rival, nor has it ever experienced a split such as that between the CIO and the AFL. By 1894, the TUC already represented 65 percent of all unionists and had a million members; by 1970, it represented almost all the more than nine million registered trade unionists. It should be noted, however, that the TUC can rarely act effectively as a unitary body. Its members are divided among over six hundred unions, but two-thirds of these are in the eighteen largest unions, just over half in eight unions, each of which has over a quarter of a million members, while the Transport and General Workers Union has just over a million and a half members.

Because of the special relation of the unions to the Labor party, both as constituent members and through their own sponsored MP's, much of their influence is exerted through the party. Even so, the TUC, like the big trade and producers' associations, maintains constant and close relations with the executive, both ministers and civil servants. Like other organized producers, trade unions share in the rough structure of functional representation that exists side by side with parliamentary representation, mainly through advisory committees. In addition, however, an almost constant series of less formal contacts goes on through visits and phone calls. What Samuel Beer calls "an intricate system of bidding and bargaining" proceeds constantly, linking parties and administration to the major interest groups of the country.

3 THE ECONOMY AND THE STATE

THE ECONOMIC PROBLEM

The most serious problems facing the British today are economic. Wage inflation, a plethora of strikes, low output per man compared, for example, to the United States, the lowest increase in industrial production of any highly industrialized country, and a sharp decline in Britain's share of manufactured exports are sources of worry to whatever government is in office. Great Britain remains heavily dependent on its overseas trade, which amounted in the mid-1960s to about 14 percent of the GNP. There was substantial growth in its share of world trade thereafter, and a large invisible surplus continued from the carrying trade, services abroad, and investments overseas. Moreover, the Labor government transformed what had been an annual deficit rate of £800 million in the balance of payments into an annual £600 million surplus, largely as a result of the 1967 devaluation of the pound. But the devaluation in itself, although essential and probably overdue, created internal strains from which Britain is still suffering.

The impact of devaluation on the British people was sharply to check the growth in their personal standard of living, since the immediate effect was to raise prices. Temporarily, demands for comparable increases in wages were restrained by the wage freeze Labor had imposed, but as soon as these restrictions were removed, there were widespread demands for rises in pay. At the same time, however, firms were suffering from decreases in profits and therefore reluctant either to expand production or to increase pay. Unemployment grew, wage demands and strikes, both official and unofficial, took place, and inflation was stimulated by the interaction of rising prices and increased wages.

The special dilemma that the Conservatives confront is that their program of checking trade union wage demands, which they see as the major cause of Britain's galloping inflation, accelerated unemployment, particularly in certain areas of the economy, to a degree that threatened explosive social and political pressures. The Conservatives oppose wage and price freezes (such as the Labor government imposed in 1966 but subsequently modified radically under trade union pressure) and have tried, by psychological and other pressures, to keep wage increases, especially in nationalized industries, to progressively lower percentage advances. (Wages rose 7.5 percent in 1969 and 13 percent during the year ending August 1971.) But following prolonged strikes by the dock workers, electrical workers, and postal workers (the latter patiently endured by the public), the government found itself confronted with recommendations by independent boards that exceeded the levels it had set. Moreover, moral pressure on private industry to hold down wage increases failed in the main because employers in capital-intensive industries preferred to yield substantial wage increases rather than risk strikes. At the same

time that this process was continuing, unemployment was mounting to nearly one million by the end of 1971, by far the highest total since 1940. Although calculations vary as to relative levels of unemployment in Great Britain and the United States, it appears that they have been approximately the same, varying between 4.5 and 5 percent of the working population.

The Conservatives' projected "hard line" with business inefficiency has, in practice, also been bent. Although bankruptcy at Rolls-Royce met an initial cold response, the government quickly nationalized part of the huge concern and subsequently offered substantial underpinning of costs to enable Rolls-Royce to fulfill its American contract for TriStar engines. The United States Congress in August 1971 approved a government guarantee of 250 million dollars in bank loans for the Lockheed Aircraft Corporation, the American company concerned, thereby rescuing the TriStar contract for Rolls-Royce engines.

The Conservative government puts particular emphasis on individual initiative to stimulate the economy. It has reduced the corporation tax and the standard rate of income tax (after deductions and exemptions), the latter in such a way as to benefit those with higher incomes. It eliminated the selective employment tax (SET) in 1971. This tax was introduced in 1966 to raise revenue, particularly from the construction and service occupations, which previously paid lower taxes than did industry, and by this means also to induce workers to shift to manufacturing. The SET was particularly disliked by business because of the extensive paper work involved. Its removal led to claims of some lowering of prices, but on the whole it appeared that the benefits were not passed on to the consumers. Subsequently, the purchase tax was reduced. The Conservative government plans ultimately to shift much of its indirect taxation to the value-added tax (VAT), which is used widely in Common Market countries. The base of VAT is the total income originating from the enterprise and its profits but without reference to the cost of the raw materials it uses. The theory is that VAT is imposed on the contribution a firm makes to the national income, and it is left to the individual firm to determine on what basis the tax shall be estimated. If the product is exported, the tax is returnable, making it a way of subsidizing exports. Like SET, VAT requires complicated administration both by business and by the government.

The Conservatives have also sought to save money by cutting subsidies and increasing charges for health and welfare services, except for the very poor and for cultural facilities. Prescriptions and dental work cost more, free milk is now provided in schools for a smaller age group, museums must charge admission fees, and food costs will rise if and when agricultural subsidies are reduced. These policies have naturally led to sharp criticisms from Labor.

Many British economists believed that more drastic cutting of indirect taxation, coupled with government pump-priming to achieve a 5 percent growth rate within two years, was necessary to break, or at least much reduce, the interacting cycle of price and wage increases that was stimulating the disturbingly high rate of inflation. The Trades Union Congress, although worried about unemployment, was not prepared to hold back wage demands unless the economy improved. Moreover, although the Conservative government was ready in 1971 to enter the Common Market, there were obvious disadvantages to doing so in a period of recession. But confronted with a still more serious problem of how to turn recession into growth without unduly adding to the inflationary spiral, the Conservatives chose not to institute a wage and price freeze such as President Nixon imposed in August 1971 but to depend on appeals for wage restraint and tax cuts to stimulate consumer spending, investment, and employment.

It is commonly believed by the British that they are the most heavily taxed people in the world. According to a report of the Organization for Economic Cooperation and Development (OECD), however, Britain came only sixth in 1968 among OECD's fourteen member states, which are the most developed outside the Communist world. But if social security contributions are omitted, Britain moves into third place, along with the Scandinavian countries, and is one of four in which taxes take more than one-third of the national income. Britain is also one of five OECD countries

in which private individuals contribute more than 30 percent of the national income in taxes. Moreover, indirect taxes in 1968 were taking 19 percent of the British national income. Most interesting is the fact that British companies are among the most lightly taxed in the world, if social security taxes are taken into account, paying less than half what companies are taxed in France, Holland, and Japan, and not much more than half what American companies pay. In addition, British companies get considerable sums returned in investment grants. It seems difficult to maintain, therefore, that the tax burden on British companies is what has been holding them back.

The crucial problem appears to be the productivity of labor. A hundred years ago Britain's real product per head was the highest in the world. Up to 1939, it was second only to the United States. By late 1970, however, Britain had slipped to thirteenth place among Western countries, with the United States at the top, followed by the three Scandinavian countries, Canada, Australia, New Zealand, Germany, France, the Netherlands, Belgium, and Switzerland. The reason is that, although Britain's postwar rate of growth was higher than in earlier periods, it has not used modern technology and improved productivity to the degree that Germany, France, Italy, and Japan have. Labor tried to stimulate industrial training and encourage more mobility of workers, but the problems still remain.

There appear to be many reasons for this development. Trade unions have resisted modernization, soft Commonwealth markets offered easy access after the war but expanded less quickly as these countries industrialized, management has been less aggressive than in other countries and less skillful in handling fast growth where it has occurred, technical education has still lagged behind classical studies, the "brain drain" has robbed Britain of some of its best talent, and taxation, with its heavy burden on higher income groups, may have been discouraging. Moreover, concern for the balance of payments has led to stop-and-go government policies and deflationary programs that have acted as a curb on growth from time to time.

There are different ways of evaluating a satisfactory economic situation in any given country.

Growth in GNP is commonly regarded as the norm. But to ensure that all people live well above the poverty level may be still more desirable. Britain's welfare state seeks to ensure a basic standard of living that will not be dragged down by sudden emergencies such as illness, unemployment, or industrial injuries. Social and economic stability may be preferable to rapid growth. Yet it is also clear both from the industrial ferment in Britain in the last few years and from the general sense of malaise in regard to British institutions and performance, internally as well as externally, that the British are not satisfied with conditions as they are. Yet the obvious signs of dissatisfaction such as strikes, slowdowns, and the bitterness caused by the provisions of the Conservatives' Industrial Relations Act (not unlike the American Taft-Hartley Act), which seeks to regulate collective bargaining and union behavior, may in themselves impede whatever efforts are made to tackle the causes of inflation and of Britain's relatively slow industrial growth. Thus the need to break out of the cycle of largely self-defeating efforts to improve conditions, to find more constructive ways to restore mutual confidence, and to stimulate cooperative efforts to work toward broadly accepted goals.

4 ORGANS OF POLITICAL OPINION

POLITICS AND PUBLIC OPINION

In studying the politics of any country, it is important not only to understand the nature of the social, economic, and other divisions of the population but to discover what organs of public and political opinion are available for the expression of these interests.

Experts still disagree about the exact meaning of *public opinion*, but no one today challenges the fact of its importance. In democracies it has long been assumed that governments ought, in general, to do what their people want them to do. And even in dictatorships the rulers, far from ignoring public opinion, have become proficient in the art of molding and manipulating it. In every modern country, regardless of form of government, the press, radio, and television are political weapons of tremendous power, and few things are so indicative of the nature of a government as the way in which that power is exercised.

THE PRESS

In a democracy like Great Britain's, the press has three major political functions: to provide channels of communication for news and views; to inquire into and criticize governmental and privately run affairs, so as to keep the public informed and alert (a role that gives it the title of "the fourth estate"); and to represent different positions on public issues of the day, so that citizens have the necessary facts and arguments out of which to form opinions. To perform these functions, it is necessary to have a variety of publications reflecting different points of view but, hopefully, with a common commitment to presenting the news as cogently and impartially as possible.

The assumption behind the special role the press is expected to play is that information and arguments represent power. Later on in Chapter 4 we shall discuss the way in which debates in Parliament are presented to the public, for only if these debates receive publicity will they fulfill the role of public education for which political representation is designed, and only if the public is prepared for new issues and new problems will it be able to influence its representatives before it is too late. There is a very special responsibility on the media, not only the press but also radio and television, to keep the public continuously alerted to all aspects of public issues.

In some countries the government interferes with the press to such a degree that news is immediately suspect. On this score, the British have had little ground for complaint. In the years before World War II, when the Conservatives were in power, there were occasional complaints that certain officials had tried to

influence the press, the radio, and even news-reels in an attempt to prevent the publication of inconvenient news items or distasteful opinions. There was no open censorship, but tactful suggestions might be made to editors, reporters, or proprietors; and since proprietors often were Conservative in sympathy, and since editors and reporters might conceivably be reluctant to antagonize officials upon whom they were dependent for information, the suggestions may have had some influence.

During the war, the government acquired extraordinary authority under the Emergency Powers (Defence) Act of 1939 (not unlike its predecessor, the Defence of the Realm Act, 1914) to prohibit publications that were likely to cause serious public disorder or to promote disaffection. But these powers were exercised, on the whole, with laudable restraint and ended soon after the war.

The structure of the British press

Both the 1947–49 and 1961–62 Royal Commissions on the Press were concerned not with the influence of government on the press but with the growing concentration of private ownership. The few vast publishing empires, it was suggested, might use their power to control the ideas and information reaching a large section of the British public or to influence the government itself. Unlike newspapers in the United States, the typical large morning newspaper in Great Britain has a national as well as a local circulation, which combined is far larger than that of any single American newspaper. This is partly because of the differences in size of the two countries but also because the British read more newspapers proportionately than any other people in the world.

Although the consensus now is that there are no longer "press barons" who act as Lord Beaverbrook and Lord Northcliffe did in the 1920s and 1930s when they used their papers to further their own strong political views, it is important to take a careful look at the contemporary structure and trends in the British newspaper world. A recent study [12] points out

[12] Colin Seymour-Ure, *The Press, Politics and the Public: An Essay on the Role of the National Press in the British Political System.*

that the total circulation of national newspapers has slipped from a peak in the 1950s, but that the number of daily newspapers has increased from nine to ten, although the number of Sunday newspapers went down from eleven in 1937 to eight since 1961. Total circulation figures for both types of papers, however, remained constant in the 1960s. So have those of provincial morning papers (eighteen in number) and evening ones (down from seventy-four to seventy-one) and Sunday newspapers (constant at five), but these now sell below the 1947 level. London evening papers shrank from three in 1947 to two by 1961, and their combined circulation continues to fall.

These gross statistics should be broken down into a distinction between "quality" papers— *The Daily Telegraph, The Guardian, The Times,* and *The Financial Times*—and "popular" papers—*Daily Mirror, Daily Mail, Sun* (formerly the *Daily Herald*), *Daily Sketch* (which closed in 1971), and *Morning Star* (until 1966, the *Daily Worker*). It becomes apparent, then, that the shrinkage in circulation is in the popular papers. In contrast, the quality papers have increased dramatically in sales, although, of course, their circulation totals are much smaller. Five out of every six adults in Britain reads one or more newspapers. Readership is generally counted as three times circulation.

Within this complex, the increasing concentration of ownership is evident—the total sank from fourteen in 1947 to ten in 1967. Moreover, the Daily Mirror group (International Publishing Company, IPC) increased its holdings of national dailies and Sunday papers from nineteen in 1947 to forty-three papers in 1966; Beaverbrook Newspapers, from sixteen to twenty; News of the World Organization reduced its number from nineteen to sixteen; Daily Mail and General Trust rose from thirteen to twenty-five. This trend is also understandable. It costs a prohibitive amount to start a newspaper, and many do not run at a profit. Indeed, only three national newspapers were making a profit in 1967. Revenue comes from sales and from advertisements. Quality newspapers get more than twice as much from the latter (especially classified advertisements) as from sales; popular papers make a third to a half times as much from sales as from advertisements. It is not surprising that the trend is toward the ownership of papers of both types in a single hand or concern, so as to balance revenues and costs against each other. More important is the question: Does this concentration of control provide the public with only slanted or partial presentation of the news?

The most important issue here is one of political partisanship. Those newspapers showing a Conservative bias in the 1966 election included six dailies—*The Times, The Daily Telegraph, The Financial Times, Daily Express, Daily Mail,* and *Daily Sketch* (merged into the *Daily Mail* in 1971)—and four Sunday papers—*The Sunday Times, Sunday Telegraph, Sunday Express,* and *News of the World*—with a joint estimated readership of 31.5 million. Those that had an anti-Conservative bias were four dailies—*The Guardian, Daily Mirror, Sun,* and *Daily Worker*—and four Sunday papers—*Sunday Mirror, The Observer, Sunday Citizen,* and *People*—with an estimated readership of approximately 33 million. In the event, of course, the Conservatives were handsomely defeated in that election.

It may be assumed that most readers take the newspaper that corresponds to their own political preferences. In general this seemed the case in 1966 except in regard to the *Daily Sketch,* which Seymour-Ure suggests would be "the natural paper of that electorally important person, the Working Class Tory,"[13] whereas, in practice, the voting intentions of its readers registered in 1964 were heavily Labor and Liberal. What seems obvious in any case is that partisanships tended to cancel each other out or, to put it in other terms, that there was a very wide range of publications pointing out the merits of each side and equally publicizing flaws in the other.

All those persons with large press holdings necessarily look on them as ways of making a profit. Lord Beaverbrook asserted in 1947, however, that his prime objective was a political rather than a commercial one. Lord Thomson maintains he is mainly interested in making money, and he appears to be much more typical than Beaverbrook of most proprietors today. The Monopolies Commission reported in 1966 that "the Thomson Organisation has in practice given its editors a great deal of freedom."[14] The Economist Intelligence Unit, after a searching investigation the same year, concluded that *The Sunday Times* and the *Daily Mirror,* both of which had proprietors who were more politically committed than Lord Thomson, were models of "efficient management," whose proprietors set the general lines of policy for editors but left details to them. It is also noticeable that well-known columnists and cartoonists seem to enjoy complete liberty in expressing their own positions on issues, regardless of whether or not they conflict with those of management.

In 1970, the press provided adequate, if rather dull, coverage of the election. Although the campaign generated much less excitement than in 1966, the wavering course of the public opinion polls introduced a helpful element of suspense (see Chapter 3, Section 3). Those papers supporting the Conservatives, in particular the *Daily Mail, Daily Sketch, The Daily Telegraph, Daily Express, The Sunday Times, Sunday Express,* and *Sunday Telegraph,* indicated their positions rather earlier than did the Labor supporters, the *Daily Mirror, Sun, The Guardian, Sunday Mirror, News of the World,* and the *People,* but neither group was as uncritical either of the policies or of the leaders on its preferred side as in previous elections. *The Times* ultimately came out for the Conservatives; *The Observer* endorsed neither. Problems with the economy received greatest attention, with the Tory-supporting press exploiting it fully, while those endorsing Labor were more defensive. From June 10 to 13, less than a week before polling day, there was a newspaper blackout as a strike stopped the publication of all national newspapers. Thus the dependence on television coverage became even greater than usual, but unlike 1966, when the press tended to regard television as a competitor, this time it saw television as complementary to itself.

The press had gone through some significant changes in ownership and approach between the

---

[13] Seymour-Ure, *The Press, Politics and the Public,* pp. 54–55.

[14] Seymour-Ure, *The Press, Politics and the Public,* pp. 115–

1966 and 1970 elections. *The Times* had passed into Lord Thomson's organization in 1967, been redesigned, and had increased its circulation 60 percent, although it was still not making a profit. The *Sun* (formerly the strongly Labor oriented *Daily Herald*) had been sold to the Murdoch interests and transformed into a popular tabloid without any apparent ideological commitment, although it was strongly pro-Labor and anti-Powell in 1970. The most striking changes affected the IPC publications. Their colorful and opinionated chairman, Cecil King, had been ousted in 1968, and two years later the *Daily Mirror*, with the rest of the huge IPC publications, was taken over by the Reed paper and publishing group. Thus concentration continued but with some shifts in personnel, which emphasized the business aspects of newspaper publishing.

Evaluating the effect of press coverage in the 1970 election, Colin Seymour-Ure suggests that it helped to "integrate" the campaign by providing a national focus.[15] In its search for an issue, the press tended to focus on the difficulties of the British economy, thereby attacking Labor at its weakest point. Overall, the press was pro-Conservative, even though not optimistic. But since the press almost universally expected a Tory defeat, it can hardly be said that it contributed much to the Conservative victory.

To safeguard the freedom of the press and to combat abuses of it, the first Royal Commission on the Press had recommended the establishment of a General Council of the Press. In July 1953, a council of twenty-five members, nominated by editors, journalists, and managers, began to respond to specific complaints against newspapers and tried to determine standards in controversial issues. Its annual reports show a keen concern for public as well as professional interests. In response to urging from the press for more publicity on local government affairs, the council succeeded in securing an act sponsored by a member of Parliament, which went into effect in June 1961. In 1963, it strongly criticized the imprisonment of two journalists who had refused

to reveal their source of information in the Vassall spy case. In 1971, it censured Lord Arran for the intemperate language he used in the *Evening News* toward the Arabs in commenting on the Middle East. Publicity is its best means of exerting influence.

The influential press

Of particular importance, as we have suggested, is the influence wielded by several national dailies of quality. Among these papers are the Conservative *The Daily Telegraph*; *The Financial Times*, which is widely read by business people; and the liberal *Guardian*, formerly *The Manchester Guardian*, which has an international reputation for the excellence of its news and editorial comment that is ably supported by its weekly airmail edition for overseas.

The Times of London, however, is the most powerful of the island's newspapers. Its readers include the most eminent people in Great Britain: government officials, politicians, judges, diplomats, scholars, clergymen, officers of the army and navy, and the well-educated classes in general. Its reporting is noted for reliability and completeness, if not for liveliness; and, especially in foreign affairs, its reputation for reflecting or even anticipating government policy gives it an almost official tone. One of its most famous features is "Letters to *The Times*," which may provoke a national debate as effectively as might a speech in the House of Commons.

In addition to these daily papers and to *The Sunday Times* and *The Observer*, certain weekly periodicals wield great influence. This is particularly true of *The Economist* (nonpartisan and widely read abroad as at home), the *Spectator* (moderately Conservative in tendency), and the *New Statesman and Nation* and the *Tribune* (which speak for Labor groups). Such publications indulge in discussions of ideas and issues, and it is in these periodicals, rather than in the daily press, that new and unorthodox ideas can best win a hearing. Their readers are, as in the case of *The Times* and *The Guardian*, men and women who themselves influence opinion and legislation; such publications, therefore, often

---

[15] Seymour-Ure, "Fleet Street," in *The British Election of 1970*, by David E. Butler and Michael Pinto-Duschinsky, pp. 231–58.

Elite Response to Importance of Press
(In Percentages)

READ REGULARLY	
The Times	67
The Daily Telegraph	43
Financial Times	26
The Guardian	20
Daily Express	19
Daily Mail	12
Daily Mirror	4
The Sun	2
None of these	3
Not answered	1
Wrote in others	1

Usefulness of Daily Newspapers
(In Percentages)

	INTERNATIONAL NEWS	PARLIAMENT	COMMENT	THE ARTS	COMMERCE/ INDUSTRY
The Times	61	62	51	46	39
Daily Telegraph	32	30	30	20	17
The Sun	*	*	1	*	—
Daily Mirror	*	1	2	*	*
Daily Mail	1	2	5	*	1
The Guardian	14	17	21	16	5
Financial Times	10	6	11	12	44
Daily Express	2	3	7	*	1
None of these	1	1	2	5	2
Not answered	9	9	10	19	16

* Less than 0.5%.

Where Influence Lies
(In Percentages)

"VERY INFLUENTIAL"	
BBC	52
Parliament	42
The Press	40
Trade Unions	33
Civil Service	23
The Monarchy	15
The Church	2

	VERY INFLUENTIAL	FAIRLY INFLUENTIAL	NOT VERY INFLUENTIAL	NOT AT ALL INFLUENTIAL	UNDECIDED	NO ANSWER
The Church	2	18	55	23	1	2
The Monarchy	15	39	30	13	1	2
Parliament	42	40	12	1	1	3
BBC	52	39	6	1	1	1
The Press	40	47	9	1	1	1
Trade Unions	33	42	18	3	2	2
Civil Service	23	30	24	15	4	3

Source: The Times, October 1, 1971.

exert a greater influence on politics than do newspapers with many times their circulation.

RADIO AND TELEVISION

Important as the press is in providing news and discussion, the growth of radio and particularly of television provides powerful means of capturing public attention. But while private enterprise predominates in the publishing field in Great Britain, radio broadcasting remained a government monopoly until the Conservatives introduced commercial broadcasting in 1971. Television followed the same path until late in 1955.

The British Broadcasting Corporation (BBC), a public corporation established in 1927 and financed by individual license fees, still provides most radio programs, but it has long since been outstripped in the television field by commercial television. The latter is organized in a very different way in Great Britain from the way it is organized in the United States. In 1954, the Independent Television Authority (ITA) was established for an initial ten-year period—subsequently extended to 1976—to own and operate transmitting stations; the cost is met by private companies that provide programs, own the production studios and equipment, and reap the profits of advertising. The role of ITA is to see that programs report the news accurately (in practice they have done so more attractively than has the BBC), preserve reasonable impartiality in controversial issues, and do not violate good taste.

As a channel of communication, television has particular importance as "the most pervasive, most trusted, and . . . most potent" of the mass media.[16] Its use raises special questions: Should journalists and producers be free to direct public attention to the issues *they* feel are politically important? If so, how can a balanced presentation of different points of view be secured? If not, what controls or safeguards should be instituted and by what bodies? For if it is vital for the press to provide a wide variety of approaches to the news it purveys, is it not still more important that television does the same? And whereas television in the United States operates through a variety of networks and local stations (which, however, may all be insensitive to minority and radical positions), British television has a far more limited range of programs and thus, one might feel, a more concentrated political impact.

The most careful study of these issues, particularly as they are related to a general election, has been made in the book *Television in Politics: Its Uses and Influence*, whose authors, Jay G. Blumler and Denis McQuail, deliberately set out to analyze their findings for the 1964 election in the perspective of an earlier study of the effect of television in the election of 1959. The latter study had concluded that its impact was relatively negligible. Major changes had occurred, however, between the two elections in the attitudes of political parties, and especially of the Labor party, regarding the use that could be made of television to secure voter support. As Richard Rose has commented, the 1964 general election saw "in duration, expense, and expertise the biggest propaganda campaign in twentieth-century British politics."[17] It was in that election that television came into its own as the most important of all means of political communication.

The principle of providing free radio and television time to political parties at election time is well established. In 1964, and again in 1966 and 1970, the ratio of free time allotted to the Labor, Conservative, and Liberal parties was five to five to three, respectively. Originally provided in fifteen minute doses, party broadcasts were limited in 1970 to ten minutes in response to viewer reactions, and thirteen broadcasts were held: five Labor, five Tory, and three Liberal. (Minor parties feel, legitimately, that they are discriminated against.) The parties were similarly given these allocations of time on radio. In 1970, the same general rules imposed by the parties were adhered to as in earlier post–1959 elections: no live audiences (because of rowdiness at speeches in 1959), no Sunday programs, and full consultation as to speakers and choice of constituencies for surveys. Television is also expected to main-

---

[16] Jay G. Blumler and Denis McQuail, *Television in Politics: Its Uses and Influence,* p. 3.

[17] Richard Rose, *Influencing Voters: A Study of Campaign Rationality,* p. 14. (See especially Chapter 1.)

tain impartiality in matters of party controversy and to refrain from editorializings.

In 1964, Harold Wilson had sought a face-to-face debate, but the Conservatives had refused; in 1966, Heath sought such a debate but Wilson refused unless the Liberal leader was included as an equal participant, which the Tories rejected because it appeared to put them on the same plane as the Liberals; in 1970, Wilson again ruled out a confrontation with Heath. Although the three leaders appeared once on the same broadcast, there was no debate. But despite the absence of this dramatic approach, the leaders of the two major parties inevitably attract the greatest attention in every election, and necessarily at the expense of coverage for other parties.

Although the 1970 election caught television unawares, with ITA, in particular, already booked on prime time with presenting the World Cup series, the general conclusions reached by Blumler and McQuail in their study of the impact of television in the 1964 election appear to hold. Their findings indicated that the high levels of political viewing in 1964 were chiefly motivated by a desire for information, particularly the desire to learn more about political developments that might affect the viewers' own lives. The Blumler-McQuail study also showed that only a few sought help in deciding how to vote, and that most had already made up their mind on this issue before campaigning began and did not change. If viewing during the 1970 campaign did have an effect, it was probably to the advantage of the Conservatives, who had worked out an integrated and attractive campaign series, whereas Labor, conscious of how much of its film prepared for the 1964 election campaign had not been used, decided on virtually impromptu appearances, whose effects were often messy.

It is not only in politics, however, that the impact of radio and television is felt. Widespread public demand for an external agency somewhat comparable to the Press Council to review specific complaints against BBC radio or television programs led to the appointment early in 1972 of three distinguished independent individuals to form the Programmes Complaints Commission. Its jurisdiction is limited to complaints where "a viewer, listener or or-

ganization continues to feel aggrieved after receiving a BBC explanation." The effect of its judgments, which must be publicized by the BBC in print or on the air, depends on public and agency reactions. Many people hope, therefore, that in the long run the commission will acquire more authority, both to review standards of taste for programs (e.g., violence on the screen) and to recommend restitution where damage has been proved.

ADEQUACY OF THE ORGANS OF INFORMATION AND OPINION

The press, radio, and television in Great Britain offer suggestive contrasts both with each other and with the corresponding institutions in the United States.

If one takes as a standard the number of channels for different views, for free discussion, and for reliable information, then the great American advantage is that there are many more such channels. While British national newspapers have tended to drive local papers out of business, most American cities still have daily newspapers of their own, making it easier for different regional views to be expressed. Yet even in the United States the growth of the chain newspaper has restricted this independence, while the decline in the number of cities with competing dailies is even more serious. Thus, while there are more daily newspapers in the United States than in Britain, there are many towns where the reader cannot choose among papers that reflect differing political outlooks.

In contrast, the great advantage of the British press is that the major—and even some minor (e.g., the Communist)—political movements in the country have their views expressed in organs of national circulation and that anyone on the island can choose among several, widely different national newspapers. The great disadvantage, shared in the United States, is that the extraordinary expense of starting and maintaining a newspaper means that the presentation of rival views in daily and Sunday papers depends on proprietors and a limited number of editors.

In theory, radio and television should in both countries provide notable instruments for political information and expression. Yet in the United States, although there is more independence and diversity of ownership and a freer expression of opinion on controversial issues, the influence of advertising agencies and sponsors restricts the amount of time devoted to public affairs, while political comment tends to be one-sided and conservative. Yet the British have also not found the way to take full advantage of these media.

To make the organs of information and opinion contribute helpfully to an enlightened public opinion is, in fact, no simple task. To place control in the hands of private owners is often to give a disproportionate voice to conservative political groups. To place control in such public organizations as political parties, cooperatives, trade unions, or business associations may give a wider representation to divergent views, but such organizations are likely to be even more one-sided than private owners

in their presentation of the news. To place supervision and control in the government, quite apart from any danger inherent in official control of the sources of information, may be to achieve impartiality in reporting at the expense of the most fertile kind of political discussion and argument. To place control in the sort of trusteeship under which *The Times*, *The Guardian*, and *The Observer* used to be published provides greater personal freedom for editors and writers, but there was a possibility (happily avoided) of deterioration through lack of competition.

Increasingly it is suggested that the best solution lies in the simultaneous existence of a variety of forms. Thus the competition of privately owned publications and commercial television can act as a spur to those owned by public bodies or by trusteeships, while the existence of the latter can provide a check on the accuracy and completeness of the former.

5　BRITAIN IN A PERIOD OF CHANGE

In almost every aspect of life the British are seeking new relationships and forms of action. This process of change reflects an oppressive sense of dissatisfaction with a society that is falling short of its ideals of justice, humanism, fraternity, and beauty. The aim of those who promote change is to reawaken a sense of destiny in Britain and determination to achieve it. World War II had called forth almost superhuman efforts to withstand bombing and the threat of invasion. The immediate postwar period saw the creation of the welfare state. But there are now questions in some quarters as to whether welfare aid is not more of a burden than a benefit, and whether efforts to achieve social harmony have not sapped initiative. Conversely, there is fear that a concentration on individual self-interest may undermine personal standards of conduct and divide society more sharply into the well-to-do and the less favored. To some degree these opposed positions reflect the philosophies of the Conservatives and Labor, but the issues go more deeply than in party politics. These issues, as in the

United States, revolve around the basic question: What are the overriding values that society and government should use as guides in making their decisions?

The chapter that follows gives a more complete picture of the historic foundations of British institutions, ways of acting, and formative political ideas. Thereafter, the dynamic element in British government, the political parties, will be analyzed, as well as the ways in which they operate within the legislature and the functioning and power of the executive. In the sections on the national and local administration, law and the courts, and finally foreign affairs an account will be given of government in action seeking to promote the public good internally and externally in response to the political actions of the elected representatives of the people. After this broad survey we will return again to the issues raised in this chapter and in the Introduction to the study of Great Britain, in an effort to provide some clearer guidelines to the likely course of British politics and life.

2

The British political heritage

1 HISTORICAL BACKGROUND

Few things are more perplexing to the outside observer than the British habit of preserving the form of inherited institutions while modifying their spirit and their function. Other great countries, such as France, Germany, and Russia, have altered their political systems openly, deliberately, and violently. But in Great Britain, with only one important interruption, political innovation has taken place within a framework of continuity. In some instances, notably the evolution of the Cabinet system, change came about gradually through the blend of chance and expediency. The essential background to this development, however, the assertion of Parliament's power vis-à-vis the monarchy, required a civil war and the Revolution of 1688. Thereafter, inside this structural balance there grew up not only a Cabinet government exercising the still existing powers of the Royal Prerogative but also the modern two-party system, which steadily tilted the balance of power between the two chambers toward that one, the House of Commons, which is popularly elected. At the same time, the process of evolution that curbed its power left virtually untouched the membership of the so-called upper house. Thus the anachronism of a second chamber based largely on the hereditary principle continues to exist in Great Britain's highly structured and socially minded modern democracy. In a period like the present when calculated change is being proposed in almost every aspect of British life, it is particularly important to be aware of how change has taken place in the past and of the framework within which it is being sought for the future.

ORIGINS OF THE PARLIAMENTARY SYSTEM

The origins of the British Parliament often are traced to ancient Anglo-Saxon times when a council known as the Witenagemot (or Witan), whose composition and powers are still a matter of debate, used to be called together to advise the English kings. With the Norman Conquest in 1066 the Witan disappeared; but William the Conqueror, while concentrating greater power in his own hands than the Saxon kings had known, summoned a *Magnum Concilium* (Great Council) at regular intervals. At such times, according to *The Anglo-Saxon Chronicle*, the greatest men in England were with him: "archbishops, bishops, and abbots, earls, thegns, and knights." In the intervals between these meetings, a smaller *Curia Regis* (King's Court, or Little Council) remained to advise the king. The practical work of administration was carried on by the royal household.

In contrast to the kings of France, whose

authority continued to be challenged and limited by powerful nobles who commanded the allegiance of their tenants, William instituted a system of land tenure according to which the first loyalty of every landholder was to the king and not to a local lord. From an early period, therefore, England attained a degree of political centralization far greater than that on the Continent. Yet institutions of local government which had originated before the Conquest continued in existence and provided a limited experience in self-government.

It was William's great-grandson, Henry II (1154–89), whose reign (which followed a period of anarchy) marked the next great advance in English government. Traveling or itinerant justices now fostered the growth of a law common to all the land. Moreover, the grand jury was used for accusation and was followed by the jury of verdict, which replaced the earlier methods of trial by ordeal, battle, or compurgation.

EARLY LIMITATIONS ON
ROYAL AUTHORITY

If it was due to the strength of Henry II that an orderly and firm governmental authority was established, it was due to the weakness of his son John (1199–1216) that this authority was limited by Magna Charta (the Great Charter), the most famous if not the most effective of those restraints on political authority that are the essence of constitutionalism. Subsequent tradition has transformed into a charter of English liberty what was primarily a guarantee of the specific rights of English barons. Yet certain articles—such as the famous provision (Article 39) that no free man might be arrested, imprisoned, dispossessed, outlawed or exiled, or harassed in any other way save by the lawful judgment of his peers or the law of the land—lent themselves to a far broader interpretation and application than their sponsors imagined. The document was not democratic in any modern sense, but it reiterated the principle that the king was not unlimited in power and that abuses of power might be resisted. The legend that was subsequently attached to Magna Charta made it a powerful instrument for liberty.

THE GROWING SPECIALIZATION
OF FUNCTION

With the passage of time, there was a tendency for judicial or administrative business, which required the continuous attention of some governmental body, to fall to the lot of the *Curia Regis*. As the amount of business increased and the members of the *Curia Regis* became more highly skilled and specialized, such subdivisions as the Courts of Exchequer, Common Pleas, King's Bench, and Chancery, which were the forerunners of the modern court system, split off from it. More purely administrative work was left to the royal household, to such institutions as the Exchequer and the Secretary of State, which developed out of it, and to the main core of the *Curia Regis*.

Somewhat later the *Curia Regis* itself developed into what was known as the Permanent Council; it was within this body that, in the fifteenth century, the Privy Council, a smaller and more efficient body, grew up and eventually assumed the powers of its larger and more unwieldy parent. In turn, a still smaller entity never defined in law, the Cabinet, grew up within the Privy Council in the eighteenth century. Today the Cabinet still formally legitimizes its acts through the Privy Council, although in practice it is the Cabinet that makes executive decisions.

THE RISE OF PARLIAMENT

The *Magnum Concilium* (Great Council) of the kings of England was a meeting of the great nobles and ecclesiastics of the kingdom, somewhat resembling a modern House of Lords. From time to time, however, and generally for the purpose of winning popular consent to the levying of new taxes, kings would summon representatives of the lesser gentry, who were too numerous to attend in person. In 1213, King John, in need of money, commanded the presence of four "discreet knights" from each county, and in 1254 (at a time when the Great Council was coming to be known as Parliament) Henry III, also in need of money, summoned two knights from each county. In 1265, Simon de Montfort, who had led the barons in a temporarily successful revolt against the king, summoned a Parliament to which were invited not only two knights from each shire but two burgesses from each of those boroughs (towns) known to be friendly to his party. And although, with the reestablishment of King Henry's power, this practice was temporarily abandoned, the famous Model Parliament, held in 1295 by Henry's son, Edward I, included burgesses as well as knights, clergy, and barons.

At this time the privilege of attending Parliament was commonly regarded as a mixed blessing. Far from demanding the privilege as a right, people looked upon it with understandable apprehension, both because the journey to Parliament was expensive, uncomfortable, time-consuming, and, on occasion, dangerous, and because those summoned to Parliament were summoned to increase their own taxes. Thus attendance at Parliament was compulsory rather than the result of any demand for the right of representation. The lesser gentry and the burgesses were ordered to attend when they became prosperous enough to attract the attention of a government ever eager for new sources of revenue.

For a time Parliament met in three groups or estates: one for the nobility, one for the clergy, and one for the commoners. The lesser clergy, however, eventually withdrew; the higher clergy (who were themselves great nobles) met with the nobility; and the lesser barons or knights (who often were the younger sons of the nobility) sat with the commons, thereby helping to prevent the growth of a sharp political cleavage between the nobles and the middle classes, such as occurred in France. By the end of the fourteenth century, the system of two chambers, one for the lords and one for the commons, had taken shape. Moreover, early in the fifteenth century it came to be understood that proposals for grants of money should originate in the House of Commons and then win the approval of the Lords, an arrangement which, by centering the power of the purse in the House of Commons, enormously enhanced its authority.

During this period Parliament also acquired certain legislative powers. Earlier, individual commoners had had the right to present petitions to the king asking for redress of griev-ances, and eventually the Commons presented such petitions as a body. Successive kings discovered that it was easier to persuade Parliament to grant new taxes if the petitions were granted first, and laws began to be enacted by the king at the request of the Commons and with the assent of the Lords. However, not until early in the fifteenth century did the laws always coincide with the terms of the petitions. Henry V (1413–22) agreed that nothing should be enacted that changed the substance of the petitions; and during the reign of his successor, Henry VI (1422–61), the formula came into use which is still followed: statutes are made "by the King's most excellent majesty by and with the consent of the Lords Spiritual and Temporal, and Commons, in this present Parliament assembled, and by the authority of the same."

TUDOR ABSOLUTISM

Much of the fifteenth century was occupied by those struggles between rival factions of the nobility known as the Wars of the Roses. The ultimate victor in this conflict, Henry VII (1485–1509), was the first of the Tudor dynasty, a line of energetic monarchs who gave the country the firm and orderly government it wanted and so enhanced the authority of the king that the period is often referred to as that of "Tudor absolutism." Partly because of the effectiveness of the great nobles in killing one another off, Henry succeeded in concentrating great power in his own hands. Parliament during his reign was the servant of the king rather than an independent force, and the real center of governmental activity was the Privy Council, a group of advisers chosen by the king and drawn from the middle classes rather than from the great nobility. Under the Tudors, too, greater authority in local government was given to country gentlemen (rather than nobles), who served without pay as justices of the peace and acquired both the political experience and the sense of public service that have been outstanding virtues of the British upper classes.

Although the power of Parliament declined under Henry VII, the struggle between Henry VIII (1509–47) and the Roman Catholic

Church increased Parliament's prestige, not because Parliament failed to act as a docile instrument of the king but because the king made so much use of it as an ally in the struggle. Thus the "Reformation Parliament," which sat from 1529 to 1536, acquired a political experience and importance and enjoyed a degree of freedom of speech that set powerful precedents for later times. It was this Parliament that passed the legislation completing the breach with the Church of Rome and making the king the supreme head of the Church of England.

During the dozen years that intervened between the governments of Henry VIII and his daughter Elizabeth I (1558–1603), Edward VI (1547–53), a Protestant, and Mary (1553–58), an ardent Catholic, reigned over a country torn by religious controversy and plagued by bad government. Elizabeth, however, reestablished the Anglican Church of her father, with a ritual resembling that of the Catholic Church but with a creed that was more definitely Protestant than that of the church of Henry VIII. During her reign England came to identify itself with Protestantism in opposition to the Catholicism of its bitter enemy, Spain.

Elizabeth's government, like that of her father and grandfather, was firm and orderly, and it commanded the overwhelming support of public opinion. By this time members of the House of Commons, far from considering their duties a burden, had come to take pride in their growing political influence and to act with greater independence. Toward the end of Elizabeth's reign, the members (particularly those who were Puritans, that is, belonged to the extreme Protestant wing of the Church of England) increasingly indulged in criticism; it was evident that, although the devotion of the Parliament to the queen was very great, a tactless successor might find this body a source of serious opposition to his will.

THE LIMITATION OF ROYAL AUTHORITY

Elizabeth's successor, James I (1603–25), the first of the Stuart kings, was sufficiently tactless to precipitate precisely such opposition. Already king of Scotland, James I became ruler of the entire British island, although it was not until 1707, under Queen Anne, that the Act of Union formally united the two countries.[1]

In his native Scotland, James had already found the Calvinistic (Presbyterian) form of Protestantism far too democratic for his tastes; and the rapid growth of Puritanism in England provoked his opposition for similar reasons. His firm belief in the divine right of kings conflicted sharply with Parliament's conception of its own authority. From 1611 to 1621, with the exception of a few weeks in 1614, James actually ruled without any Parliament at all; and, when finally he was obliged to summon a new Parliament, its vigorous criticism led him quickly to dissolve it.

Far from ending with James's death, royal quarrels with Parliament grew more bitter. Charles I (1625–49) dissolved his first two Parliaments in rapid succession and resorted to highly unpopular forced loans in the absence of financial grants from that body. When Parliament was again summoned, in 1628, a Petition of Right (which ranks with Magna Charta as a charter of British freedom) was drawn up, asserting the ancient liberties of the kingdom and denouncing royal abuses of power. Charles was forced to accept this document.

Eventually, however, quarrels between the king and Parliament's Puritan members resulted in the Civil War which lasted from 1642 to 1649. In this struggle, which reflected a social as well as a political and religious cleavage, the majority of the peers, the Anglicans, and the Catholics supported the king; the majority of the townspeople and the Puritans supported Parliament; and the landlords and country gentry divided themselves between the two parties. In 1649 the defeated king was executed, and in 1653 Oliver Cromwell, who as leader of the victorious parliamentary armies already held effective power, assumed the title of Lord Protector under the only two written constitutions England has ever had, the Instrument of Government (1653) and the Humble Petition and Advice (1656). Yet Cromwell, like his royal

[1] Wales had been added to the Crown by Edward I in 1284, and the fact that the Tudor dynasty was Welsh in origin later helped to reconcile Wales to this union. But Scottish and Welsh nationalism are still political forces (see Chapter 3, Section 3).

predecessor, repeatedly disagreed with and dissolved Parliament, and his death in 1658 led quickly to the restoration of the monarchy with Charles II (1660–85) as king. The Instrument of Government vanished, the Anglican Church was reestablished, and all Nonconformists suffered serious restrictions upon their religious and civil rights.

In appearance Charles accepted the supremacy of Parliament; and although he disagreed with it from time to time and secretly longed for absolute power, controversy was never pushed to the point of endangering the throne. Charles's brother and successor, James II (1685–88), was less discreet. Even before his accession large numbers of "Petitioners" asked that he be barred from the throne because of his adherence to Catholicism, while "Abhorrers" of the petition upheld his right to the succession. Once he had become king, however, James's efforts to restore the Catholic Church enraged both Nonconformists and Anglicans (including many of the Abhorrers), and his quarrels with Parliament precipitated the Glorious Revolution of 1688, which drove him from the throne and transferred the crown to his daughter Mary and her husband William, Prince of Orange.

At the time of their accession, the quarrel between king and Parliament was finally settled. Parliament, in the famous Bill of Rights of 1689, listed the practices that had caused trouble during the previous half-century and forbade their revival in clear and unequivocal language. The legislative authority of Parliament was assured, the king was forbidden to levy any tax or impost without parliamentary consent, the regular convening of Parliament was guaranteed, and certain individual liberties were specifically confirmed. A few years later, in 1701, the authority of Parliament over the Crown was established beyond all doubt when the Act of Settlement deliberately changed the order of succession to the throne, passing over the Catholic descendants of James II and providing that James's daughter Anne (1702–14) should be succeeded by the German, but Protestant, House of Hanover. British sovereigns, unlike those in certain Continental states where the official religion was that of the ruler, henceforth had to belong to the established church of their people.

THE RISE OF THE CABINET

The reigns of the first two Hanoverian kings, George I (1714–27) and George II (1727–60), marked a further, if less dramatic, decline in the royal power as authority passed into the hands of the Cabinet, a small group of leading ministers who advised the king.

It had long been apparent that the Privy Council was too large and unwieldy a body to conduct public business, and smaller groups had already been used for the purpose of guiding legislation through Parliament. However, so long as the Stuart monarchs remained on the throne, they maintained their right to choose their own ministers and to change them at will. Both William and Anne continued to choose their Cabinet ministers and to meet with them regularly, but it was obvious that their relations with Parliament were better when the Cabinet had the confidence of Parliament. Thus began the practice of choosing ministers who shared the same general views—and the views of the majority of the members of Parliament. There was no change in the law, but the dependence of the ministry upon the king lessened; at the same time, its dependence upon Parliament increased.

The first two Georges took a greater interest in Hanoverian affairs than in British. Far from trying to expand the Royal Prerogative, they let slip some of the powers that William and Anne had been careful to maintain. And since they had trouble understanding both the English language and English politics, they gave up the practice of presiding over meetings of Cabinet ministers.

From 1721 to 1742, both Cabinet and Parliament accepted the leadership of Sir Robert Walpole, who was First Lord of the Treasury and Chancellor of the Exchequer and who was in fact the first British "prime minister," a title that did not come into general use until much later.[2] When, in 1742, Walpole lost the support of the House of Commons, he resigned his office, an act which implied that the survival of a ministry depended not upon the favor of the king but upon the acquiescence of Parliament. George III (1760–1820) tried, with some success, to recover the lost ground; but growing

---

[2] This title was first used officially in the Treaty of Berlin, 1878, but not in a statute until 1917.

opposition in Parliament (as indicated by its famous resolution of 1780 that "the influence of the Crown has increased, is increasing, and ought to be diminished") and the insanity of the king during the last decades of his reign put an end to the effort.

THE RISE OF PARTIES
AND OF DEMOCRACY

The growth of political parties in England was as gradual and unintentional as other changes in the government, but no change was of greater importance. Before the seventeenth century rival groups of nobles might contend for power, as in the Wars of the Roses, and there were adherents of different religious principles, but there were no political parties in the modern sense. The division in the Civil War, however, between the aristocratic, Anglican Cavaliers who fought for King Charles and the middle-class, Puritan Roundheads who supported Parliament reflected a difference in religious and political principles as well as economic interests that prepared the way for future party alignments. With the Restoration of Charles II there appeared a clearer difference between the greater part of the land-owning gentry (the Tory squires), who upheld the authority of the king and the Anglican Church, and the alliance of powerful Whig nobles with the Nonconformists and the mercantile classes —a difference paralleling that between Abhorrers and Petitioners. When James II opened his attack on the Anglican Church, however, the Tories were torn between loyalty to the king and loyalty to the Church; some joined the Whigs in inviting William and Mary to take power, while others remained unreconciled to the change. Thus the Glorious Revolution, for a time, had the curious effect of making Whigs rather than Tories the chief support of the monarch on the throne, although not of monarchy as an institution.

The eighteenth and early nineteenth centuries witnessed almost incredibly long periods of office, first for the Whigs under the first two Georges and later, with one brief interruption, from 1783 to 1830, for the Tories. But it is still more important to be aware that these two nascent political parties represented virtually the same interests. As feudal restrictions on economic development were swept away during the seventeenth century, the way was opened for vast economic expansion. Capitalist agriculture, leading to the enclosure movement and the loss of independence of the English peasant, produced efficient and rich returns from the land. Parallel to this development went economic expansion overseas by commercial interests. Each process worked to the other's advantage and drew both land-owning and commercial classes into each other's spheres. The result was a massive interpenetration that has stamped their character ever since.

Reform of the suffrage

Although the principle of the supremacy of the House of Commons had been clearly established, that house was far from being a widely representative body. Property qualifications fixed in the fifteenth century still determined the vote in many areas, while the failure to redistribute seats in accordance with movements of population resulted in the growth of "rotten boroughs" (which had lost most of their population but retained their original representation) and "pocket boroughs" (which were under the control of landed proprietors who frequently sold the right to represent the borough in Parliament). Thus, in the Scottish constituency of Bute, only one of the fourteen thousand inhabitants had the right to vote, and he was therefore in a position to elect himself unanimously to Parliament. The constituency of Old Sarum had no residents at all, and Dunwich had sunk beneath the sea, but each was still represented in Parliament. In contrast, large towns grew up that had no representation.[3]

As the industrial revolution created a large class of well-to-do businessmen who were eager for a greater share of political power, agitation for reform increased. Yet those in Parliament clung tenaciously to power; and it was not until a Whig government came into office, late in 1830, that popular agitation met with a favor-

[3] When Americans, in the years before their Revolution, complained of "taxation without representation," it was pointed out that English communities too were taxed without having any parliamentary representation. The argument that relevant interests were represented, that is, of merchants, hardly appealed to either side.

able parliamentary response. Even then it was necessary to dissolve the House of Commons and hold a new election before a safe majority could be found for the bill reforming Parliament. The House of Lords continued its resistance until the king threatened to appoint enough new peers to assure a majority for the bill.

The Great Reform Act of 1832 did not increase the electorate drastically (about half a million men, mostly drawn from the upper half of the middle class, gained the right to vote), but it did away with the worst inequalities of the old system. Most of the rotten and pocket boroughs were eliminated; the representation of the smaller communities was consolidated or lowered; and new or increased representation was given to the large ones. But the climax of the evolution begun in 1832 was only reached in 1885 with the series of acts on representation (1867 and 1884), corrupt and illegal practices (1883), and redistribution and registration (1885) that established the constitutional principle that representation must approximate population. In 1918, the decisive advance in this regard was made when the vote was finally given to all male citizens age twenty-one and over and, with important qualifications, to women of thirty and over. In 1928, the suffrage was extended to women on the same basis as men. Thus by stages reaching over nearly a century, the British achieved universal adult suffrage.

Change in party character

The original increase in the number of voters had relatively little effect upon the political system. During the first part of the nineteenth century, both parties continued to draw their support from the well-to-do classes, and many members of these relatively informal groupings were intimately related through family and social ties. Even in policy, lines tended to be blurred. The Whigs were somewhat more willing to accept mild electoral reform; but many Tories were in agreement with them, and in 1867 they "dished the Whigs" by themselves, introducing the legislation that extended the right to vote. In fact, the Tories (who were, at this time, identified with the land-owning rather than the manufacturing element) were somewhat more willing than the Whigs to support measures of social reform, such as restrictions on the exploitation of women and children in industry.

In the meantime, however, the working class, bitter at the hardships of rapidly growing industrialization, had made its own efforts to create change and failed. In 1819, it mounted a nascent national political campaign and was repressed. Working-class agitation was part of the ferment that led to the reform movement in 1831–32, but labor failed to share its returns. For a decade Chartism sought ineffectually to extend the franchise. Thereafter, while Continental socialist parties were taking form under the spur of Marxist philosophy, a period of profound disillusionment and even apathy marked the British working class. The British Social Democratic Federation, formed in 1884, had no appreciable effect in extending its Marxist concepts to labor. When the latter began seriously to organize at the turn of the century, it was to protect itself against the restrictions on trade union organization implicit in the Taff-Vale decision. Once the Labor party began to penetrate into Parliament, however, it grew rapidly to become the predominant representative of the working class.

The Labor party formed a distinctively new feature in the British party system. Both the Conservatives (as the Tories were now called) and the Liberal party (as the Whigs were now named) had grown up *inside* Parliament and subsequently reached out for extraparliamentary organization following the 1867 electoral act. The Labor party sprang from the grassroots *outside* Parliament and used its extraparliamentary organization to reach into the legislature to influence the uses of political power.

Even before the Labor party emerged as a political force, however, the established parties had developed all the characteristic features of the modern political party: representative constituency associations coordinated by a national organization; an annual conference; a central party headquarters, destined to become ever more powerful; party election manifestos; and the special role of the party leader in an electoral campaign. The latter factor was accelerated in the last quarter of the nineteenth century by the fact that both the Conservatives and Liberals possessed exceptionally able and popular leaders, Disraeli and Gladstone, who in themselves came to symbolize to the voters the spirit of their respective parties. As voters were increasingly influenced in choosing their representatives by party leaders, policies, and organization, the party began to assume its modern role of link through Parliament between people and government.

By the time the Labor party became a factor in the political scene, sharp divisions over Irish home rule led the Conservative and Liberal parties to draw apart once more into more distinctive groupings. The old nobility had moved, almost without exception, into the Conservative party. The latter became more stamped by land-owning interests. While it had the support of some urban middle and working classes, as it has today, its backbone was in the rural areas where the local squire and the Anglican parson exercised dominant political influence. The Liberals attracted the new and wealthy industrialists who opposed high tariffs (it had been the growing industrial middle class that successfully secured the abolition of the Corn Laws in 1846) and also government interference in industry. It was also supported in the main by the Nonconformist middle classes and the majority of those workers who had the right to vote.

But with Labor's rapid growth in working-class popularity, the Liberals increasingly lost members at both ends. Although there were periods in the nineteen twenties when none of the three parties could win a parliamentary majority, there was a strong tendency for the wealthy industrialists and merchants to switch their allegiance to the Conservatives, while the working class found the Labor party the most effective advocate of its interests. Thus the Liberals became a minor party, and the British political scene resumed its traditional form of a two-party system: Conservatives and Labor.

Reform of the House of Lords

The successive extensions of the franchise also brought a fundamental change in the position of the House of Lords. So long as the House of Commons remained unreformed, the influence of the Lords was very great, and it was not unusual for the majority of the members of the Cabinet, including the prime minister himself, to be members of that chamber. But as the right to vote was widened, so grew the prestige of the House of Commons as the spokesman of the electorate. Leadership in the Cabinet came to rest with men who could win elections and who were likely to be members of the House of Commons. Moreover, the opposition of the Lords to many of the political, social, and economic reforms accepted by the House of Commons led to increasing irritation; and when, in 1909, a struggle broke out over the Lords' financial powers, the way was prepared for the Parliament Act of 1911, which enabled the House of Commons, by complying with fairly rigorous conditions, to pass even nonfinancial legislation over the Lords' veto.

Thus, through a series of changes that worked themselves out over long periods of time, the British government developed from a highly centralized monarchy into one of the most advanced democracies in the world.

2   THE BRITISH CONSTITUTION

FORM AND FACT

The gradualness of this evolution, and the British habit of retaining traditional forms despite radical changes in the position of power, produced two characteristics of the British constitution that confuse most Americans: there is no single place in which the constitution as a whole is clearly and definitely written down, and those provisions of the constitution that do exist in writing often differ markedly from actual constitutional practice. A foreigner who reads the American Constitution will be misled about certain political practices (he will find, for example, no mention of judicial review, the cabinet, or political parties, and the electoral college will seem much more important than in fact it is), but in general he will find a not too inaccurate outline of the structure of the American government. In Great Britain, however, the form and the fact of the constitution sometimes seem to have very little to do with each other. Walter Bagehot could write, for example, in the introduction to the 1872 edition of his classic book *The English Constitution*, that Queen Victoria possessed the constitutional power to:

> . . . disband the army . . . ; she could dismiss all the officers, from the General Commander-in-Chief downwards; she could dismiss all the sailors too; she could sell off all our ships of war and all our naval stores; she could make a peace by the sacrifice of Cornwall, and begin a war for the conquest of Brittany. She could make every citizen in the United Kingdom, male or female, a peer; she could make every parish in the United Kingdom a "university"; she could dismiss most of the civil servants; she could pardon all offenders.

Yet any ruler who used his constitutional powers in this way, contrary to the advice of his prime minister and Cabinet, would find the entire country denouncing him for the unconstitutionality of his action. Nor is the confusion lessened by the fact that no law provides either for a prime minister or for a Cabinet. The fact is that, unlike the American, the British constitution is not a definable body of fundamental and mostly written rules. Rather, it is, as a parliamentarian has said, "a blend of formal law, precedent, and tradition." It is similar to the American Constitution, however, in that it consists of the rules that affect the working of governmental institutions. These rules are found in part in statutes but can be fully understood only through an examination of the institutions and procedures to be described in the following chapters.

CONSTITUTIONAL SOURCES

Great documents

Among the sources from which the constitution is drawn are, in the first place, certain great charters, petitions, and statutes such as Magna Charta, the Petition of Right, the Bill of Rights, the Act of Settlement, the Reform Act of 1832, and the Parliament Act of 1911. Most of these were acts passed by Parliament, but a document such as Magna Charta is considered to be part of the constitution simply because it represents a great landmark in national history, much as though Americans considered the Declaration of Independence and the Emancipation Proclamation to be part of their Constitution—as, indeed, they are part of the living tradition of American government.

The distinguishing thing about most of these charters and statutes is that they were the products of constitutional crisis and that they contain the terms of settlement of those crises. In the life of any great country certain issues arise that, like the controversy over slavery in the United States, cut to the foundations of the political system. In Britain, once such an issue has been definitely settled, either by the victory of one party or by a definitive compromise, the British consider that settlement part of their constitution. In spirit this practice is not unlike the addition of the Thirteenth, Fourteenth, and Fifteenth Amendments to the American Constitution at the end of the Civil War. But in Great Britain, since there is no written constitution to amend, the settlement generally takes the form of a law that looks like any other law passed by Parliament. What makes it a part of the constitution is the context of constitutional struggle within which it originated, as in the case of the Great Reform Act of 1832 or the Parliament Act of 1911, and the fact that it shapes the character of some part of the governmental machinery.

Important statutes

In addition to these more spectacular charters and statutes, there are certain other statutes that are significant, not because they mark the conclusion of a great constitutional struggle but because they deal with subjects of such intrinsic importance as to place them automatically in a category above ordinary law. Into this category, for example, fall the laws extending the right to vote.

None of these laws aroused the excitement that characterized the Reform Act of 1832, but any attempt to repeal them would now be regarded as an attack upon the basic constitutional principle of universal suffrage. Yet, whereas in the United States the granting of the suffrage to women was embodied in a formal amendment to the Constitution, electoral reforms in Great Britain have been made through the process of ordinary legislation.

While electoral laws have a particular relevance to the extension of political democracy, it is worth noting at this point that two significant areas of British government that have been completely transformed by statute are local administration and the public service. The former agencies of local administration, the justices of the peace and corporations of long established towns, became obsolete in the early nineteenth century. They were originally replaced by *ad hoc* agencies, but subsequently a structure of elected councils was set up that was more suitable for the period of representative government. Since then, many local services, like the provision of education and hospitals, have become part of integrated national systems.

The development of the British public service, which plays a vital role in government, was similarly the result of legislation. In sharp contrast to Continental countries, especially France and Prussia, where a highly centralized bureaucracy became the instrument of monarchical power, the supremacy of Parliament over the king kept the British public service in a disorganized and ineffective state until the mid-nineteenth century. Thereafter, it was shaped into a career service, steadily assuming more and more functions with the growth of "big government."

The long-range impact of these two developments has been great. The elective character of local institutions and recruitment by merit in the civil service may be ranked with electoral reform as basic principles of the constitution. But it is important to be aware at the same time that the growth of government functions, the far-reaching impact of administrative decisions, and the discretion inevitably vested in the hands of members of the bureaucracy have made it difficult to maintain the supremacy of Parliament and Great Britain's cherished "rule of law." Many of the new devices introduced in recent times, like the parliamentary commissioner (the ombudsman, see Chapter 4,

Section 3), are efforts to safeguard the rights of individuals in the face of the ever-growing role of government and of fears lest it abuse its power.

Judicial decisions

A third important source of constitutional principles is to be found in court decisions. In interpreting the provisions of the charters and statutes that are part of the British constitution, judges have, to some extent, defined and developed its meaning much as the Supreme Court has clarified and expanded the provisions of the American Constitution. Even more significant, however, is the fact that some of the most important principles of the British constitution are principles of the common law —that is, principles not established by any law passed by Parliament or ordained by the king but rather established in the courts through the use of decisions in individual cases as precedents for decisions in later cases. The first decisions often were based on common customs or usages; as these decisions "broadened down from precedent to precedent," there grew up a body of principles of general application that is looked on as a bulwark of British freedom and an essential part of the constitution. The right to trial by jury and the writ of habeas corpus (which prevents a person being held in prison without trial) both developed in the courts of common law.

Today, according to the common law, the British subject has full freedom to say or write anything he pleases so long as it is not slanderous, libelous, seditious, obscene, or blasphemous; and public meetings may be disbanded only if the assembly becomes riotous or seems likely to commit a breach of the peace or a crime of violence. For the most part, such limitations do not constitute a serious interference with political liberty. *Blasphemy* and *obscenity* have little application to politics, and considerable latitude is given to strong political language before *libel* or *slander* can be invoked. *Sedition*, however, has at times received an unpleasantly broad and vague application, and the leeway that the police enjoy in determining what is a "breach of the peace" has aroused considerable concern. Indeed, as we shall see, there have been proposals that the civil rights that are embodied in the American Bill of Rights should receive statutory reinforcement in Britain.

The conventions of the British constitution

Fourth, and most difficult for Americans to understand, is that part of the British constitution that depends on custom or convention. These conventions ordinarily are not embodied in written laws and thus are not enforceable in the courts. Moreover, since they constantly grow and change and adapt themselves to new circumstances, it is difficult to say at any moment exactly what they are. As our study of the growth of Parliament and the Cabinet has shown, such conventions usually originate in practices that are followed for the sake of convenience. But if such practices are followed for a long enough time, the person who departs from them will be denounced for the "unconstitutionality" of his action.

One of the accepted conventions of the unwritten constitution is that if a government resigns, the monarch shall ask the leader of the opposition to form a new government. Another (as the Preamble to the Statute of Westminster, 1931, declares) is that a law affecting the succession to the throne or the royal title shall require the assent of the Parliaments of the overseas members of the Commonwealth as well as of the United Kingdom. Although there is no recourse to law if these conventions are disregarded, such an action would be a profound shock to the public. Similarly, if a minister publicly disagreed with governmental policy and yet refused to resign his portfolio, or if the monarch refused to dissolve the House of Commons on the request of the prime minister or refused to sign a particular law, there would be a popular reaction at least as strong as that which greeted President Roosevelt's plan to modify the composition of the Supreme Court. So pervasive is the loyalty to constitutional practices, that such a course of action seems unthinkable. In this sense, the protection of the constitution is in the hearts and minds of the people.

There are, however, more practical sanctions. The conventions of the constitution exist because they serve a real purpose. To violate them is often to make the government itself unworkable. If, for example, the queen began to act independently of the Cabinet, the Cabinet itself would resign, and the House of Commons would undoubtedly refuse to give its support to any new Cabinet—if, indeed, any members could be found to join such a Cabinet. The British government works only if the Cabinet and the House of Commons are in accord and if the queen follows the advice of the Cabinet. To depart from these rules in any important respect is to interfere with the whole machinery of government.

If a convention of the constitution is violated, it can, of course, be enacted into law. For example, it was long assumed that, through lack of use, the House of Lords had lost its power to reject any financial measure passed by the House of Commons. In 1909, however, the House of Lords rejected the famous Lloyd George budget that threatened the economic interests of many of the peers by placing heavy taxes on land. The Liberal party, which controlled the House of Commons at this time, denounced the Lords' action as a breach of the constitution and succeeded, after a bitter struggle, in winning the passage of the Parliament Act of 1911. This act made it impossible for the Lords to delay money bills for more than one month. In this way, the written law restored a violated constitutional convention.

Such developments should not be difficult for Americans to understand. In the United States few constitutional practices are more important than the action of the Supreme Court in holding acts of Congress unconstitutional when they conflict with the Court's interpretation of the Constitution. Yet one may read the American Constitution through without finding any statement granting this power to the Court. Nonetheless, it has by now become so established a part of the American form of government that only the most extreme reactionaries would think of challenging it. The practice has become part of the living constitution if not of the written one. Similarly, it was once maintained that the custom of having no president serve for more than two consecutive terms had become an unbreakable precedent. In 1940, in fact, when President Roosevelt ran for a third term, his opponent, Wendell Willkie, actually charged that he was acting unconstitutionally

—thereby using the word in its British rather than its American sense. The subsequent Twenty-second Amendment to the American Constitution, which limits the president to two terms, indicated that the convention was more firmly rooted than it at first seemed to be.

Sometimes a practice may be a matter of usage rather than of convention. During the greater part of the nineteenth century the prime minister was at least as likely to be a member of the House of Lords as of the House of Commons. However, as the House of Commons gained prestige with the extension of the right to vote and with the curtailment of the power of the House of Lords, it became increasingly inconvenient to have the chief spokesman of the Cabinet in the House of Lords when the Cabinet's fate was being decided in the House of Commons. From 1902 on, prime ministers were regularly chosen from the House of Commons. What may well be the decisive precedent was established in 1923 when the king, in appointing a new prime minister, passed over the most prominent Conservative, Lord Curzon, and appointed Mr. Stanley Baldwin.[4]

Later it was suggested that the same development was taking place in connection with the important post of Foreign Secretary. Here, too, there was a disadvantage in having a subordinate official explain and defend foreign policy in the House of Commons; the precedent seemed to be building up that only a member of the House of Commons might hold the post. In this case, the expectation proved premature, for Prime Minister Chamberlain appointed Lord Halifax to the position, and in 1960, despite protests, Prime Minister Macmillan chose Lord Home as Foreign Secretary. In 1970, Prime Minister Heath also chose him to be Foreign Secretary, but since he had renounced his peerage in the meantime, Alec Douglas-Home is now in the House of Commons.

Because British government is party government—that is, carried on by whatever organized group has received majority support at the polls—it has been increasingly felt that the election returns should not only designate

[4] The fact that Mr. Baldwin was more acceptable to the rank-and-file of his party than Lord Curzon and the lack of representation of the Labor party—the official opposition —in the House of Lords may well have been the decisive reasons for the action; popular belief in the official interpretation, however, soundly established the precedent.

which party shall assume the responsibilities of governing but should also control, both negatively and positively, the program that it undertakes while in office. This view has given rise to what is called the "mandate convention," which assumes that the government should institute radical changes only if the electorate has passed on them at a general election. This view was a matter of considerable controversy after the Labor party's victory at the polls in 1945. It was noticeable, however, that the Conservative majority in the House of Lords, in the years immediately following 1945, approved bills instituting such measures as nationalization, with which it was out of sympathy, on the ground that Labor had received a mandate from the electorate. Moreover, when the Labor government decided in 1947 to reduce the length of time the Lords could hold up legislation, its action was bitterly attacked as a violation of the mandate convention, since this measure altered the balance of power between Lords and Commons and had not been submitted to the electorate. It is clear from subsequent developments that the mandate convention is not yet finally established. The frequency of references to it, however, indicates a growing effort to establish some voters' control over major governmental decisions.

CONSTITUTIONAL PRINCIPLES

We can now sum up the most important principles of the constitution.

The first of these is the *fusion of powers*, which means that the monarch must always take the advice of the Cabinet, and the Cabinet must always have the support of the House of Commons. According to this principle there can never be in Great Britain the kind of prolonged disagreement between the executive and the legislature that has occurred so often in the United States. In the latter, as we well know, it is not at all unusual for the president to veto legislation passed by Congress or for Congress to refuse to pass legislation recommended by the president. This is particularly the case when, as in President Nixon's first term, the president belongs to one party and the majority of congressmen to the other.

In Great Britain, such disagreements are impossible. Before the days of disciplined parties, it might have been a debatable point whether Parliament controlled the prime minister and Cabinet, or whether the prime minister and Cabinet controlled Parliament. No one contested, however, the principle that they must work in agreement. Today there is no chance that the House of Commons would vote against an important measure sponsored by the Cabinet or pass a bill opposed by the Cabinet. Thus, in sharp contrast to the United States, the executive and the legislature in Great Britain never follow conflicting policies.

It is easy to misunderstand the nature of this fusion of powers. Even Bagehot suggested that it meant that the Cabinet is merely a committee of the working majority of the House of Commons. On the contrary, although there is no formal separation of executive and legislative powers in the British parliamentary system corresponding to the somewhat artificial division in the American system, there is a very real distinction between the Cabinet and Parliament. In fact, the key to the British system of government is the continuously maintained balance between the Cabinet's executive and legislative initiative and the consideration of legislation by Parliament. The Cabinet, or "government," makes appointments, summons Parliament, initiates and organizes the legislative program, decides on dissolutions, all without consulting Parliament. In so doing, it uses the inherent power of the Crown (which it represents), a power vast in extent and still not wholly defined in scope. Through this power, and the strength resulting from a well-disciplined party, the Cabinet provides positive and effective direction of affairs. The function of Parliament is not to weaken or supersede this leadership but to make sure that there is full consideration by the public, as well as by its own members, of all the issues introduced by the government before it gives them its formal consent.

A second and closely related principle is the *supremacy of Parliament*. Supreme legal power in Great Britain is exercised by Parliament (the House of Commons, the House of Lords, and the sovereign), which according to the old saying can do everything but make a woman a man and a man a woman. In contrast to American practice, there is no judicial review in the sense of testing the constitutional validity of laws, and there is no complicated process of constitutional amendment. The veto power of the titular executive has lapsed through nonuse, and the king will accept any measure passed by the two houses of Parliament. No court would dare to hold an act of Parliament unconstitutional, and, theoretically, Parliament itself can change the constitution at any time simply by passing an ordinary law. Thus, it is sometimes pointed out that Parliament could, quite legally, extend its own term of office forever, depose the king (who would have to sign the warrant), turn England into a republic, make Buddhism the established religion, or restrict the right to vote to women of seventy years old and over.

Yet merely to say this is to point to the absurdity of the idea. Parliamentary supremacy is exercised in the spirit of responsibility, and responsibility is to the nation as a whole, not just to the majority in Parliament. There is a strong sense of "the rules of the game." Profound psychological checks and self-restraints commonly come into operation when substantial changes affecting the functions and balance of institutions are under consideration. Devices such as all-party conferences and royal commissions, which will be considered in Chapter 4, can be used to analyze proposals introducing legislation. Thus, although Parliament is legally supreme, it acts with responsible self-restraint.

Theoretically, there is a major difference between the American concept that legal authority vests ultimately in the citizens, who confer it temporarily on the president and on Congress, and the British concept that legal authority inheres in Parliament and in the Crown (whose authority is now exercised by the Cabinet). According to the British concept the British Parliament and Cabinet are two co-equal, interrelated elements, each possessing and exercising an independent authority, not, as in the United States, an authority merely delegated by the voters.

But the distinction should not be pushed too far. Although *legal authority* rests in the Cabinet (using the authority of the Crown) and in Parliament, *political power* resides in the British people as it does in the American people through their right to vote for the representatives and government of their choice. Perhaps the greatest practical importance of the distinction regarding the ultimate seat of legal authority in the two countries, therefore, is in the attitude of the elected representatives: in the United States, members of the House of Representatives are likely to look on themselves as delegates from their constituencies; thus only the president and, to a lesser degree, the Senate represent the whole country. In Great Britain, on the other hand, members of Parliament, particularly the ministers, accept a primary loyalty to act on behalf of the country as a whole.

A third important principle is the distinction between the king as a person and *the Crown as an institution.* Regardless of the personal qualities of the individual, the institution of monarchy is the object of great respect, both because of its antiquity and because of the ceremony and pageantry of which it is the focus. Whatever changes may take place behind the governmental façade, the Crown continues to symbolize the stability and durability of British institutions and to command the loyalty of the British people.

In form, the powers of the Crown are very great. Every action of the government is carried out in its name. It is the Crown that makes appointments and assents to laws, that makes treaties and commands the armed forces. The not wholly defined prerogative powers inhering in the Crown can be used during emergencies. Moreover, as noted, *legally* the ministers derive their authority from the Crown and in this sense are responsible to it. But to say that the Crown has these powers and position is very different from saying that the monarch can make use of them independently. On the contrary, as we have been pointing out, the ruler may exercise these powers only on the advice of his ministers, who, of course, are responsible *politically* to Parliament and the electorate. In short, the powers of the Crown are always used as the Cabinet, supported by Parliament, wants them to be used.

Finally, one of the fundamental principles of the constitution is the *rule of law,* according to which the government and its agents, as well as individual citizens, are subject to laws that are definite and known in advance and that can be modified only by act of Parliament.

Thus, no citizen may be punished unless he has been found guilty of violating the law in a trial before a regular court whose procedure safeguards him against arbitrary conviction. Similarly, the courts will protect the citizen against government officials who interfere with his rights contrary to law. Thus both government officials and private citizens are equally subject to one body of law and one system of courts.

As in the United States, the courts are the primary protectors in Great Britain of what we call "civil liberties": freedom of speech, freedom of association, freedom of assembly, and freedom from arrest and imprisonment "except," as Magna Charta stated it, "by judgment of his peers or by the law of the land." Historically, the common-law courts have been vigilant to stop the government from exercising arbitrary power. As noted, the courts devised the writ of habeas corpus centuries before Parliament passed the Habeas Corpus Act in 1679. They are still entrusted with the task of seeing that executive authorities do not exceed the powers entrusted to them and do not deviate from the strict procedures under which they should act. Yet it is no longer accepted unquestioningly that they are adequate to this task.

ARE CIVIL LIBERTIES ADEQUATELY PROTECTED?

There are two special reasons for doubts regarding the adequacy of current procedures for protecting civil liberties in the United Kingdom. The first is that while most people continue to act within the known and traditional boundaries of freedom of opinion, speech, and action, there are an increasing number of individuals and groups that operate out of a different cultural context and feel that they have rights that are inadequately or condescendingly protected. Many students and "hippies" obviously feel outside the established consensus but so also do radicals on the right, such as working-class Powellites.

This universal problem, experienced also in the United States and on the continent of Europe, is felt with particular sensitivity in Great Britain because of its long history of expanding liberties through eliminating restrictive laws, like those hampering trade union activity, and illiberal institutions, like the Lord Chamberlain's theater censorship. Indeed, a series of liberalizing statutes was passed under the Labor government in the late 1960s relating to abortion, homosexuality, and divorce, while capital punishment was abolished. Yet there are still nonconforming groups that feel restricted. A particular problem caused by some of those outside the present consensus is, of course, that their freedom to act impinges at certain points—as with the Powellites—on the rights and even safety of others.

The second and more widespread concern focuses on the steady encroachment on individual liberties by big government and by the administration in implementing parliamentary statutes. In a debate on the subject in the House of Lords on June 18, 1969, cogent reasons were given why human rights now need more protection in Britain than in the past: the concentration of power in the central government, especially in the executive; the growth of the administrative structure and the need for remedies in case of administrative abuse; the increasing invasion of privacy and use of computors to store information about individuals (a practice recently challenged in the United States when it was disclosed that army sources had been collecting such material concerning some distinguished political figures as well as dissidents).

A perennial cause of concern has been the executive discretion of the Home Secretary. Its use early in 1970 to deport Rudi Dutschke, a radical student leader who had been active in West Berlin but was then studying at Cambridge University after convalescing from a bullet wound suffered two years before, was hotly criticized. So, too, was the fact that the evidence on which the decision was based was presented to the tribunal in secret.

Probably the most serious abridgment of human rights by a British statute was the Commonwealth Immigration Act 1968, which, in response to fear of a massive population movement, withdrew the right of entry to the United Kingdom from citizens of Asian origin living in Africa. In response, one of the rights proposed for legislation is the right to a valid passport, and another is the right of all citizens to entry to and residence in the country.

As an alternative to the Right of Privacy Bill, which had been introduced in Parliament, the Labor government at the beginning of 1970 appointed a committee, under the chairmanship of the Right Honorable Kenneth Younger, to "consider whether legislation is needed to give further protection to the individual citizen and to commercial and industrial interests against intrusions into privacy by private persons and organizations or by companies and to make recommendations." Legislation for this purpose and to safeguard specific civil rights might be like our Bill of Rights, which simply states rights possessed by the American people and leaves it to the courts to determine in a particular case how to test whether the relevant law violates them or not, or the rights might be defined in the legislation. Such a statute could be entrenched—that is, given a superior status that demands a special procedure for amendment or rescinding—but in the light of the long-established British practice of regarding certain legislation as of constitutional importance, it seems unlikely that such an unusual step would be taken.

However the British settle this problem, it is clear from American experience that legislation can perform only part of the task of protecting civil liberties and human rights. What remains crucial is the attitude of ordinary citizens, and of the police, toward civil liberties. Anyone who has listened to the explosive utterances of orators at Hyde Park Corner and watched their orderly audiences realizes the value of such safety valves. The story of the London bobby listening to a particularly inflammatory speech and finally drawling, "All them as is going to burn down Buckingham Palace make a line on this side," is fortunately also not untypical. Such an atmosphere, where it exists, remains the best protection of civil liberties, although it may well be aided by written guarantees.

THE VALUE OF THE CONSTITUTION

Admirable as are the principles of the British constitution, Americans, and occasionally the

British themselves, may be troubled by a number of questions that are variations on a single theme: with a constitution that is, in part, so vague and that can be changed so easily, either through the imperceptible development of custom or by the passage of an ordinary act of Parliament, how can anyone be sure that constitutional principles really will be maintained in times of special stress? In the United States the Constitution can be formally amended only by a long and complicated process, and Americans occasionally question the usefulness of the much-heralded rule of law if Parliament can change that law at any time.

As already pointed out, however, Parliament does not change the law lightly or without careful consideration. There is, in fact, a very real restraint upon its authority, although a different kind of restraint from that to which Americans are accustomed. The first defense of the constitution lies in the force of tradition and public opinion rather than in a court or a difficult process of amendment. The members of Parliament, like most Englishmen, have been brought up to believe in discussion, in the rights of individuals and minorities, and in the need to preserve the essential character of the constitution. It is true that the same forces act in defense of the American Constitution, but in the United States there is more of an inclination to leave this defense to the Supreme Court. Yet there is something to be said for a system that makes it clear that the maintenance of the constitution is the responsibility of the people themselves.

Despite the current concern in Great Britain regarding the protection of civil rights, it would be hard to prove that they are any less secure in Great Britain than in the United States. If the Supreme Court of the United States has an excellent record for the protection of civil liberties, there have been times when, by its own confession, it has lapsed. Moreover, it takes a long time and a good deal of money to carry a case to the Supreme Court, and by the time a decision is rendered it may be too late to remedy the damage. Humble people, who are the most likely to be oppressed, may not even be able to raise the necessary money.

One advantage of a written constitution, it is sometimes said, is the greater ease with which the ordinary citizen may detect an infraction of its provisions. The lines are more distinctly drawn; it is not so hard to tell when someone steps over the boundary of constitutional prohibition; and there is a tangible statement around which public opinion can rally. Yet in fact many issues touching civil rights seem far from clear until after the judges have ruled on them.

Another claim is as debatable. The difficult process of amendment, in the case of the American Constitution, may give the public a longer warning about a contemplated change, a greater opportunity to think matters through, and even a margin of time in which to change their minds and recover from transitory hysteria. But the very difficulty and complexity of the process constitute an invitation to circumvention. It is so hard to get an extremely controversial amendment adopted that constitutional flexibility—particularly in the extension of the government's economic powers—has come to depend on the willingness of the Supreme Court to render a broad interpretation of constitutional wording rather than upon a deliberate decision of the electorate to change these words. Here, too, there is something to be said for a method of change whereby amendments may be made in a straightforward manner in sufficient time to meet the essential needs of a changing society, yet without sacrificing the considerable thought and discussion of their implications.

In any event, the ultimate defense of any constitution, whether written or unwritten, whether equipped with elaborate defense mechanisms or with none at all, must lie in the watchful concern of its people. In their alertness and use of constructive imagination, the British have at least as good a record as Americans.

3 BRITISH POLITICAL IDEAS

To understand the attitudes of a people as well as the political programs of particular groups, it is necessary to know the political ideas that have claimed their allegiance, for nowhere is it more true than in politics that ideas are both the forerunners and the outcome of action. In the course of the past hundred years, three great currents of ideas have competed for the political allegiance of British citizens. In the middle of the nineteenth century the principal contenders were conservatism and liberalism. Today they are conservatism and socialism. But although liberalism has declined as an independent force, its successful rivals have absorbed a significant portion of its content. As a result, it is impossible to understand contemporary politics in Great Britain without some familiarity with all three currents of thought.

BRITISH CONSERVATISM

In Great Britain, as in every other country, the natural tendency of conservatives is to like traditional institutions and political principles and to regard any far-reaching innovation with suspicion, if not distaste. Established institutions, they think, rest upon the safest of all foundations: that of experience. To desert them is to abandon oneself to the uncharted seas of theorizing and speculation. Although change may be necessary at certain times, it is not necessarily a good thing in itself, and thus it should be carried out in such a way as to preserve as many as possible of the inherited institutions.

There are certain differences between British and American conservatives, however, that result from differences in the institutions they have inherited. Where American conservatives are devoted to a constitutional system that places strong restraints upon the government, British Conservatives trace their descent from the Tory party, which once stood for the authority of the Crown against parliamentary limitation. Although British Conservatives have

long since come to accept the supremacy of Parliament, the fact that for so many generations the upper classes controlled Parliament encouraged a greater willingness to uphold the authority of the state than seems natural to American conservatives.

The influence of Burke

Somewhat paradoxically, the man who has had the greatest influence on Conservative thought, Edmund Burke (1729–97), considered himself a Whig. He defended the rights of the American colonists at the time of the Revolution, and he was devoted to the principles of the Glorious Revolution of 1688. To Burke, however, these revolutions had been fought in defense of the established constitution and the inherited rights of Englishmen. This was a very different view from the affirmation of natural rights of the American Declaration of Independence, for Burke believed that men possessed only those rights that had evolved through history; thus Englishmen, wherever they were, had rights not possessed, for example, by Frenchmen.

The French Revolution of 1789 seemed to Burke to have an entirely different character. Its leaders frankly proclaimed their intention of destroying or remolding such time-honored institutions as the monarchy, the aristocracy, and the established church; they proclaimed their belief in the power of reason to create new institutions and to remedy ancient injustices. To Burke, human reason seemed but a weak and fallible guide in comparison with the lessons of tradition and experience. If new circumstances required changes in the inherited constitution, Burke wanted them to be made within the spirit of that constitution and with as little modification as possible of its inherited form.

Burke viewed society as living and growing well beyond the lifetime of any individual or generation and linking the past, the present, and the future. Society, he said, is a contract, not to be lightly entered into like "a partnership agreement in a trade of pepper and coffee, calico or tobacco . . . and to be dissolved by the fancy of the parties." And he added: "It is to be looked on with other reverence. . . . It is a partnership in all science; a partnership in all art; a partnership in every virtue, and in all perfection. As the end of such a partnership cannot be obtained in many generations, it becomes a partnership not only between those who are living, but between those who are living, those who are dead, and those who are to be born." In such a perspective, whose essential character is accepted by most conservatives today, the purpose of change is to preserve the balance of institutions, both public and private. The way in which the British constitution has adapted itself to new conditions meets the conservative ideal of continuity, which embodies distrust of changes based on "theory" but also forceful and often creative responses to circumstance.

Modern conservatism

It has been typical of the best of Conservative leaders, such as Benjamin Disraeli (later Earl of Beaconsfield, 1804–81) and Winston Churchill (later Sir Winston, 1874–1964), that they have known when to yield to the demands of a democratic and industrial age. By making concessions before the accumulated pressure and irritation became too great, they not only retained a strong popular following but were able to make reforms in their own way, thus preserving much of the traditional order. Further, they were often able to determine the direction and the extent of the changes.

This adaptability to new circumstances has been easier for British than American conservatives, because the former have had no objection to state activity and have rejected both the doctrine of the right of the individual against the state and any belief in inalienable natural rights. Today, Conservative spokesmen regard certain principles, sacrosanct to American free-enterprise conservatives, as the core of the "liberal heresy." Partly because of this adaptability, partly because of the long, slow development of the British constitution, partly perhaps because the British tend to be empiricists rather than theorists, much of the conservative approach has deeply permeated British thinking and ways of action, even those of the Labor party.

Imperialism

In the late nineteenth century, Conservatives became identified with another doctrine: imperialism. Earlier in the century many Englishmen, disillusioned by the loss of the American colonies and preoccupied with the industrial transformation at home, took little interest in the nation's overseas possessions. Disraeli himself could say in 1852 that "these wretched colonies will all be independent too in a few years and are a millstone around our necks." The empire continued to grow, but it grew, according to the famous phrase, "in a fit of absence of mind."

During the last third of the century, however, there was a remarkable change in the attitude both of statesmen and of the people as a whole. It was Disraeli who made Queen Victoria Empress of India and, with farsighted shrewdness, acquired for Britain the predominant control of the new Suez Canal, which so greatly shortened the route to India, Australia, and Hong Kong. As the economic competition of other countries developed, the possession of empire markets gained in significance. Moreover, the idea of empire began to appeal to those leading monotonous lives in bleak industrial cities. The acquisition of an empire became a source of pride.

The doctrine of imperialism, justified by its supporters as embodying a sense of responsibility for the development and welfare of subject peoples, was at its best a benevolent paternalism, but all too often took the form of exploitation. Most imperialists thought of national profit and power before they thought of colonial welfare. Even when most responsible for those they governed, imperialists enjoyed a feeling of superiority that could not easily be reconciled with a spirit of democracy.

At first there were many Liberal as well as Conservative imperialists, but with the passage of time Liberals increasingly denounced the acquisition of territory by conquest and demanded greater rights for colonial peoples—a stand in which they were joined by the new Labor party. In contrast, Conservatives tended to resist the transfer of imperial power and the postwar transformation of the dependent Asian and African empire into part of a multiracial Commonwealth, but here, as elsewhere, they ultimately yielded to circumstances and helped to direct its final stages.

BRITISH LIBERALISM

The influence of Locke

To the average American, the most familiar ideas in British politics are those associated with some of the early Whig thinkers. In particular the writings of John Locke (1632–1704), who wrote in defense of the Glorious Revolution of 1688, influenced the leaders of the American Revolution and found their way into the popular political vocabulary of the time. Thus, much of the American Declaration of Independence is simply a restatement of Locke's principles.

Locke taught that all men are naturally equal; that they possess a natural right to life, liberty, and property; that governments are voluntary associations formed to protect these rights; and that governments should be so organized and limited as to prevent an abuse of their powers. To that end Locke advocated a separation of powers between the executive and the legislative branches of government, and he denied the right of a government to injure the lives or property of its subjects, to tax or take property without consent, to delegate to other agencies powers granted it by the people, or to rule by arbitrary decree instead of by laws duly enacted by Parliament. If a government violated these principles, Locke believed that the people had the right to recall their grant of power and to set up a new government.

Much of the divergence between political thinking in Great Britain and the United States today can be understood in terms of the degree of rejection or acceptance of Locke's ideas. In the United States the success of a government founded upon these principles has seemed sufficient proof of their validity; but in late eighteenth-century Great Britain, Locke's belief in natural rights and the right of revolution came to be identified with the excesses of the French Revolution and the Reign of Terror. While British Liberals (and, today, many British Conservatives) continue to believe in limited government, Liberal reforms would have been long in coming to Great Britain if they had had no other intellectual foundation than a belief in natural rights.

The Utilitarians

The man who, more than any other, provided a fresh basis for Liberal political action, Jeremy Bentham (1748–1833), was a Tory in origin. He had even less use than Burke for the doctrine of natural rights, for in his view the aim of government was not to protect men's "rights" but to promote "the greatest happiness of the greatest number," with each individual counting like every other. Every governmental policy was to be judged by its "utility," that is, by its tendency to increase human pleasure and to decrease human pain. Bentham worked out elaborate tables by which such utility could be judged; the policy that resulted in the greatest happiness was the policy to be followed.

There was nothing intrinsically democratic in this theory, except its emphasis on equality: but since Bentham was convinced that men are fundamentally selfish, he felt that only a government of the people would look out for the interests of the people.

The result was that Bentham, for reasons very different from those of Locke, came to some of the same conclusions. He did not think that men are equal because of a law of nature, but he did think that each man's happiness is as important as that of any other. Using this criterion, he subjected the inherited institutions of his time to a devastating rational analysis and advocated sweeping changes in such institutions as the electoral system, the law, the penal system, and the poor law.

Bentham's influence on the course of British Liberalism was prodigious. In place of the discredited school of natural rights, he offered a new program of practical political reforms that made a strong appeal to the common sense of the British people and that, it is sometimes said, helped to save Great Britain from the kind of violent revolution that afflicted the Continent. His influence, however, also helped to separate the main current of British Liberalism from the main current of American democratic thought. Whereas Americans continued to believe in the existence of individual rights beyond the power of government and in the necessity of separating and balancing powers in order to control the government, Bentham saw no need to check government so long as it was promoting the happiness of the majority of the people. His "greatest happiness" principle provided a strong basis for popular government and majority rule, even at the expense of minority rights. Moreover, where many American liberals long clung to the idea that that government is best that governs least, Bentham and his followers (the Utilitarians or Philosophical Radicals) logically were bound to uphold governmental action aimed at the elimination of human misery. Thus Benthamite Liberals welcomed social welfare programs long before such programs became part of the creed of American liberals.

Economic liberalism

Bentham himself did not foresee to what extent his ideas could be used to justify governmental action. In economic affairs, paradoxically, he accepted the teaching of Adam Smith (1723–90), who believed that there is a natural harmony of economic interests, and that men, if not interfered with by the government, will unconsciously promote the interests of the community at the same time that they consciously promote their own.

According to Smith, the community pays its highest rewards to those who provide the services it most desires; and, since each individual wishes to earn as much money as possible, he will do exactly those things that the community wishes him to do. As a result, the government does not need to, and indeed ought not to, interfere with the economy but should limit itself to national defense, the protection of life and property, and the building of certain public works too costly for private individuals to undertake.

In the early part of the nineteenth century there was no apparent conflict between the ideas of Bentham and those of Smith. Merchants and industrialists supported the Liberal party as the agent of laissez faire and free enterprise at the same time that radicals supported it as the advocate of a broader suffrage

and other democratic reforms. The advance of the industrial revolution and the growing demand for economic reform strained this happy partnership. Factory owners were bitterly opposed to many of the reforms that other Liberals advocated enthusiastically as the most effective way of promoting human happiness and eliminating human misery.

The influence of Mill

To some extent this conflict in Liberal ideas was personified in the life of John Stuart Mill (1806–73). Mill's father, James Mill, had been one of Bentham's most able and intimate disciples, and John Stuart Mill himself grew up in the citadel of Benthamite ideas. As a young man, however, he began to question certain of Bentham's teachings. In particular, he placed greater emphasis upon the worth of the individual personality, and he thought the great objective of society to be not the happiness of the individual but his growth and development. Better, he thought, to be Socrates dissatisfied than a satisfied pig. Thus society should aim at the cultivation of those qualities that are peculiarly human and that distinguish men from animals: before all else the power to think well and to think for oneself.

Such a goal led Mill to be suspicious of any state activity that would limit the freedom of the citizen or reduce his self-reliance. At the same time, however, Mill was well aware of the existence of economic abuses that only the state could remedy. In his famous essay *On Liberty* (1859) he tried to draw a distinction between those actions of the individual that concern only himself, with which the state ought not to interfere, and those actions likely to affect or harm others, which the state may control or prohibit. Thus the state might intervene to prevent the adulteration of goods or to force employers to provide healthful working conditions.

Mill also came to believe that political reforms of the sort advocated by many Liberals —the extension of the suffrage, and the reform of the law and of Parliament—although desirable in themselves would not produce a good society unless accompanied by far-reaching economic reforms. The fundamental problem of society, he wrote in his *Autobiography*, was "to unite the greatest individual liberty of action with a common ownership in the raw material of the globe and an equal participation of all in the benefits of combined labor." Thus Mill had, in fact, become a socialist in ideal—although a reluctant socialist who believed intensely in individual self-reliance and in freedom of thought and expression and who wished to combine this freedom with social and economic equality. He did not try to say in any detail how this change was to come about, but apparently it was his hope that through education and experience men might come voluntarily to "dig and weave" for their country as well as to fight for it.

Today British Liberalism is still struggling with the problem of how to reconcile individual liberty with social welfare. Many of the merchants and industrialists, who used to provide the party with its financial strength, have gone over to the Conservatives, and Conservative leaders often appeal to the rest of the Liberals to follow that example. Yet it is increasingly common today to hear Conservatives using the old Liberal slogans of individual freedom from government control.

Many Liberal voters have also turned to Labor—in some instances not because they approved of socialism in principle but because Labor's concrete program of social reform appealed to idealistic elements within the Liberal party. Moreover, as the Liberal party itself weakened, a vote for Labor often seemed the most effective way of voting against Conservatism and imperialism.

Today the Liberals, more than any other party, concern themselves with the protection of individual liberty. But they combine this devotion to liberty with what they call "a radical programme of practical reform." Thus it is characteristic of the present attitude of the party that Lord Beveridge, the sponsor of the famous Beveridge Plan for security "from the cradle to the grave," was one of its conspicuous leaders.

BRITISH SOCIALISM

Toward the end of the nineteenth century, as we have seen, the issue of economic reform was replacing political reform as the subject of great-est political controversy. To many reformers the obvious way of bringing about change was direct economic action by trade unions and consumers' cooperatives. But there were also those who believed that only political action could remedy economic and social injustice. Among them some, like H. M. Hyndman and the Social Democratic Federation, were under the influence of Karl Marx and believed that reform would come through class warfare and revolution. Others, like the members of the Independent Labor party, placed greater emphasis on winning seats in Parliament and local councils and concentrated on an ethical and democratic appeal which, in the Nonconformist tradition, had great influence on the British workingman.

The Fabians

Some of the most influential ideas, however, were those of the Fabian Society, which was founded in 1884. Unlike Marxist socialists, the Fabians opposed the doctrine of class warfare and advocated a policy of planned gradualism. As the saying went, they substituted evolution for revolution. But evolution must be urged along the correct path. Their motto was, "For the right moment you must wait, as Fabius did most patiently when warring against Hannibal, though many censured his delays; but when the time comes you must strike hard, as Fabius did, or your waiting will be in vain, and fruitless."

The membership of the Fabian Society has never exceeded a few thousand, but among its members have been men and women of the greatest ability and influence: George Bernard Shaw, Sidney and Beatrice Webb, H. G. Wells, Graham Wallas, Ramsay MacDonald; and in more recent years, Harold Laski, G. D. H. and Margaret Cole, R. H. Tawney, Leonard Woolf, Clement Attlee, and Hugh Gaitskell. When the Labor party came into power in 1945 and introduced its massive program of nationalization, the Fabian membership included 229 members of Parliament, several Cabinet ministers, and the prime minister himself. And if one hears little of the Fabians these days, and much more of the antidoctrinaire attitudes and impact of Harold Wilson, this fact does not undercut the long-term, creative effects of the Fabian Society.

The aim of the Society, as stated in 1896, was "to persuade the English people to make their political constitution thoroughly democratic and so to socialize their industries as to make the livelihood of the people entirely independent of private Capitalism." Its method, in Shaw's words, was to give up "the delightful ease of revolutionary heroics" for the "hard work of practical reform on ordinary parliamentary lines." By raising wages, shortening hours of work, providing security in old age, ill health, and unemployment, and promoting public health and safety, they hoped to destroy or to reduce some of the worst evils of modern industrial society. By taxing inheritance, ground rents, and income from investments, they hoped to reduce the outstanding economic inequalities. And by increasing public ownership, local as well as national, of public utilities such as gas, water, electricity, and public transport, they hoped gradually to extend the amount of public ownership, to gain experience in the public management of property, and to prove the efficiency and practicability of such management. What was at first done on a small scale and in individual instances could eventually be expanded, they thought, into a completely socialized society.

The outstanding achievement of the Fabian Society was its influence on public opinion inside and outside the Labor party. The brilliant scholars, writers, and speakers who served the Society presented the results of their research and experience in a vivid and effective way. Fabian pamphlets and Fabian lectures reached and influenced large numbers of people, especially in the middle classes, who would have been antagonized by talk of revolution and bored by theory but who could be convinced by hard facts and common sense. The Labor party itself had particular need of these clear and penetrating analyses of domestic, colonial, and foreign affairs with their farsighted proposals for policies to achieve the ends the party sought. Coming late to the political scene and into a milieu shaped for centuries by others, Labor would have remained at a serious disadvantage both inside and outside Parliament without the intellectual resources the Fabians provided. More than any other group, it was the Fabian Society that gave the practical cast to British socialism that distinguishes it from the more doctrinaire socialism of the Continent.

In 1900, some of the trade unions, the Social Democratic Federation, the Independent Labor party, and the Fabians formed the organization that later became the Labor party and is today the political arm of British socialism. As a result, it is characteristic of British socialism that there is no one orthodox school of thought. Rather, a variety of ideas and many types of people are found within its ranks. Instead of formulating a rigid ideological program to which all must adhere, there has been a willingness, in a typically British way, to avoid ultimate theoretical issues while agreeing upon and striving for immediate concrete goals.

The notable achievements of the post–World War II Labor government in making Great Britain more "socialist"—the nationalization of major industries, the creation of the national health service, and the reconversion of the economy from war to peace—left fewer specific goals around which to formulate programs. Hugh Gaitskell, whose optimistic rationality envisaged social evolution proceeding by stages, held the party to a middle way that attracted a wide spectrum of middle-class as well as working-class support. Although the Harold Wilson administration has been criticized for not moving Britain to a more egalitarian society, it must be admitted that socialist thinking these days appears more characteristic of certain intellectual and upper middle-class groups than of its traditional working-class base. The New Left of Trotskyites, Maoists, anarchists, and student "radicals" is looked on askance by the Old Left, which divides its energies between its traditional role inside the party and specific outside issues, like child poverty, saving the environment, or antiapartheid movements. Some of this energy rubs off on the Labor party, which remains more "progressive" in objectives than the Conservatives and more effective than the Liberals.

In a period of relative affluence, the similarities between political parties tend to become more prominent than the differences. Yet British Conservatives under Edward Heath are raising questions about the scope of public ownership and of social services that no Labor administration would consider. It is to Labor's advantage that the Powellites' center is within the Tories. The class base of each of the two major parties has not noticeably shifted. None of these differences is so great as to provoke more than sharp debate within a political system equally accepted by both. Yet however marginal the differences between the two major parties may appear to be, each under pressure still reflects the ideas and forces out of which it came.

3

British
parties
and
elections

1 THE CHARACTER OF THE BRITISH PARTY SYSTEM

Without an understanding of the character and functions of British parties, the most important aspects of British politics would seem inexplicable. It is the parties that aggregate the vast variety of aspirations and demands of every section of the British populace. It is the parties that articulate these demands in understandable principles and programs and that recruit teams of potential officeholders that are pledged to support these principles and programs. At all times, the voluntary associations that we call parties serve as links between individuals and groups on the one hand and the processes of government on the other, focusing and even creating demands through their promises and performance, as well as responding to government actions or opposition demands.

Thus in the infinitely complex and continuous interactions of interests and pressures within modern Britain, political parties play an indispensable role. They reduce alternatives to manageable dimensions. Moreover, through identification and discipline, they support the fusion of authority in the hands of persons who are at one and the same time Cabinet, parliamentary, and party leaders. By these means, political decision-making is kept visible and responsive as well as effective.

Let us now take a few steps back to some simpler statements on the purpose and role of political parties. Everyone agrees that in a democracy the government ought in general to do what the people want it to do, and everyone agrees that the government should be led by men whom the people themselves have chosen. But it is easier to say this than to discover a workable way of determining what the people want. The ordinary citizen, acting alone, is comparatively helpless when it comes to drawing up a complete program for his government. He lacks the time, the information, and the practical experience to work out the solution to political problems for himself, and as an individual he is too unimportant for the government to care very much what he may think. If he wants to influence the policy of his government, his best resort is to join with others who share his general views, to work out a common program with their help, and to run candidates for office who are pledged to put this program into effect.

This work of uniting, of organizing, and of agreeing on candidates is characteristic of political parties in all democracies. For those citizens who want to participate actively in politics, parties provide the natural channel for action. For the rest of the community, they offer a choice of candidates and policies. The ordinary voter, instead of having to determine his personal attitude on every issue, has the far easier task of deciding which of two or three broad programs suits him best. And the party

77

that wins the favor of the largest number of voters, ideally at least, proceeds to carry out the program the voters have approved.

But if this is the ideal function of political parties, it must be admitted that it is a function often performed half-heartedly or badly. Many men in any country join and work for a political party not so much because of their devotion to its public aims as because of their desire for personal power and the material advantages of office. Some parties may even be so organized as to impede rather than encourage political action by the ordinary voter. Thus, in judging the degree of democracy in and the effectiveness of any party system, it is necessary to ask several questions:

Does it offer the mass of the people a meaningful and an adequate choice both of policies and of leaders?

Do the parties respond to the needs of the people and the country, are they flexible enough to allow for change, and are they responsive to new ideas, programs, and groups?

Is the internal organization of the parties sufficiently democratic to provide a channel for active political participation by the rank-and-file of the membership, not just in promoting the victory of the party, but in determining its policies and choosing its leadership?

Does the party system assist the process of arriving peacefully at a settlement of controversial issues, or does it exacerbate the differences among the different elements in the community?

Is the party system an effective instrument for carrying out the judgment of the voters once they have made a choice of parties?

SIMILARITIES IN TWO-PARTY SYSTEMS: GREAT BRITAIN AND THE UNITED STATES

In more ways than is commonly believed, the British party system is like the American. In both countries political parties are large, popular organizations that try to win public office in order to promote policies in which they believe and also to enjoy the material privileges that go along with office. In both countries, ordinarily, there are two large parties. Although in Britain the Liberals have managed to maintain a foothold of representation in Parliament

since their decline after World War I, and regional parties occasionally emerge, there is no such division of votes and representation as is common in France and in Germany. Thus British and American voters can generally count that their votes will result in a clear-cut majority in the legislature for one major party or the other, although coalition and even minority governments have not been unusual in Great Britain in this century.

It would ordinarily be argued, however, that the division between parties in Great Britain has a different class basis from that in the United States. It is true that party loyalties in Great Britain have deep historical, social, and family links that do much to explain the persistence of party allegiances. But it is also true that the ultimate purpose of a party is to win an election. Thus when there are only two major contestants for office, each must strive to command as wide a spectrum of support throughout the country as possible. Thus while Labor maintains its dominance in mining, steel, and the docks, the Conservatives attract not only the fast-disappearing traditional working-class Tory, with his tradition of deference, but also the workers in new industries and in white-overall and white-collar industrial occupations.[1] These facts support the notion that the social solidarity of the working class is no longer necessarily reflected in its patterns of voting. Conservatives remain relatively strong in rural areas, but Labor has bitten into some of them. Labor's social-welfare emphasis appeals to most of those in need, but Conservative support among retired persons is particularly strong. Labor commands a strong hold on the professional classes, but both Conservatives and Liberals take their share.

It is thus becoming less true that it is easier to guess a man's political allegiance in Great

[1] In a 1960 sample of five hundred working-class men and women, who by industry, trade union membership, sex, age, and membership in employer-run superannuation schemes matched the total adult working-class population of Great Britain, only 56 percent said they were working class, 40 percent described themselves as a middle class, and the remaining 4 percent refused to consider themselves part of any class group. Thirty-eight percent of those describing themselves as working class, and 16 percent of those calling themselves middle class, supported Labor. Twenty-two percent of those who described themselves as working class, and 24 percent of those calling themselves middle class, supported the Conservatives.

Britain from his social status than it is in the United States. The Conservatives have a built-in base of support among the upper classes and the wealthy, but it is clear that in the United States the Republican party also secures a disproportionate share of the votes of the more prosperous. Organized labor and minority groups generally support the Democrats, although the trade unions have no such organic relation to either party in the United States as they have to Labor in Britain. The less prosperous professional groups in the United States tend to be as staunchly loyal to the Democrats as they are to Labor in Britain.

A close examination of British parties reveals that, in practice, there may be as wide differences *within* a particular political party as there are *between* them. The stereotypes of both British and American political parties tend to stress the differences between the extreme wings of each of the contestants—right-wing Conservatives or Republicans contrasted with left-wing Laborites or Democrats—but the degree of consensus on policy in the middle or median points of the major parties on both sides of the Atlantic is often no less striking. It may even be the case that over such issues as the welfare state or international involvements, the differences in the basic positions of the Democratic and Republican parties have been wider apart than those of Conservatives and Labor. In further trans-Atlantic comparisons, Labor is more egalitarian in philosophy than the Democrats; the Conservatives have a more philosophical basis for their commitment to hierarchy than have the Republicans. Thus Labor is more oriented to the interests of the working classes than are the Democrats, although less so under Wilson than in previous periods; while the Conservatives are probably only rarely more to the right than the Republicans. What is essential in evaluating both British and American parties—and particularly the former, since British parties have so long been pictured in the United States as being poles apart—is that in both countries the parties are different coalitions of ideas and interests, that neither of these parties is nearly as homogeneous as ordinarily supposed, and that there is more overlap in their spectrum of opinions, support, and policies than is generally realized.

DIFFERENCES BETWEEN BRITISH AND AMERICAN PARTIES

The differences that exist between British and American parties are largely organizational and relate to structural factors in the two countries: the single-member districts, the unitary as compared to federal form of government, and the parliamentary in contrast to the presidential system. A noticeable result is in the degree of *centralization*. In the United States, power rests (if at all) with state and local party organizations, and no man can remain a leader of a national party unless he has the support of these organizations. Between elections, in the United States, the national party organizations almost disappear. Furthermore, the turnover at all levels of the American party organization is high. Thus diffuse organization characterizes the American party system, whereas there is much greater permanence in British party organization. A further striking difference is that in the United States, the congressional and presidential parties are far from being the same, while in Great Britain the national organization of each party is concerned only with a single election which determines both the representation in Parliament and the executive. Moreover, although American parties are increasingly concerned with national issues and personalities, the British have a much longer tradition in this regard.

This tendency is encouraged by the smallness of the country and the relative homogeneity of its population. In the United States, as we know, parties must appeal to a great variety of clashing sectional, class, and social interests, and they cannot appeal too wholeheartedly to one without antagonizing the rest. The party that concentrates on the labor vote, for example, may lose the farmer and the middle classes. The party that devotes itself to the industrial East will irritate the West and the South. Any precise commitment to one group may mean a loss of votes from others. No party can win unless it has the support of a combination of groups and sections, and party programs tend to reflect this diversity. It is true that the Republicans emphasize business interests and the value of a balanced budget and are suspicious of the expansion of federal control, while the Democrats identify themselves with social-welfare programs and do not hesitate to use national powers, financial and other, to aid underprivileged groups. This difference between the American parties has at times been sharper than that between the British, all of which accept the social welfare state. Nonetheless, both Republicans and Democrats attempt to appeal to all groups in the community, a factor in the somewhat surprising coalitions that occasionally appear.

British parties are as eager for victory as are American, but their job is somewhat simpler. Sectionalism is less important, although the Scots and the Welsh have distinctive needs and demands and so do certain areas in the north of England. In general, however, the focusing of national life in and around London is paralleled in party organization.

DISCIPLINE

In Great Britain, the attitude and voting of members in Parliament is largely predictable from their party alignment, but this is not the case in Congress. Americans are accustomed to the idea that politics makes strange bedfellows, and in the past they have accepted without much question the alliance of conservative southerners with urban radicals in the Democratic party and the combination of eastern captains of industry with midwestern farmers in the Republican. But one of the recurrent patterns of American politics has been the alignment in Congress of Republican and Democratic conservatives against Republican and Democratic liberals. In neither party have party leaders been able to impose discipline in congressional voting on their nominal followers.

There was a time, during the first part of the nineteenth century, when British parties also were strange and somewhat loose alliances and when advocates and opponents of free trade, imperialism, and progressive social legislation could be found within the ranks of both the Conservative and Liberal parties. This was a time, however, when comparatively few citizens had the right to vote and when, although the sources of their wealth might be different, all voters were drawn from the same well-to-do class. Members of Parliament could be acquainted personally with a large proportion of their electors and hold their seats on the basis of personal rather than party loyalties. There was little need for elaborate political organization.

Even after the Reform Act of 1832, many seats continued, to all intents and purposes, to be pocket boroughs of wealthy landholding or commercial families; and although some attempt was made to organize parties on a more popular scale, they continued to be somewhat unstable alliances of members of Parliament united on personal grounds rather than mass organizations of people bent on promoting some common policy.

It was the extension of the right to vote in 1867 and later years that sharply modified the system. Once the mass of the people could participate in elections, it was no longer possible for the parliamentary candidate to know most of the electors personally. He needed an organization to reach them, and he had to have money to pay for it. But he had no patronage of his own at his disposal, and, unless he was a very wealthy man in his own right, he inevitably turned to the national party for help. In the years after 1867, therefore, both of the large parties were obliged to build up organizations, and by the time of the Conservative electoral victory of 1874 it was clear that political success largely depended on the appeal of the party's program and leader and the effectiveness of the party organization. This was particularly true for Labor when it entered the party arena, for only by solidarity could it hope to match the greater resources of the older parties.

The building of effective party organizations had a far-reaching if unintentional consequence. Once the candidate for Parliament became more dependent for his success on the work and money of the organization than on his own efforts, his personal independence was restricted. If he voted frequently against the party's leaders on important issues, he could hardly expect their organization to support him in the next election. Yet he could not win the election, in most instances, without such support. The result is that the ordinary member of Parliament does not vote against the leaders of his party with the casualness that characterizes much congressional cross-voting in the United States. The member of Congress is mainly dependent on local support and represents local interest, and these interests may disagree with the national leaders or be indifferent to certain national issues. Although there have always been elements of disaffection in each of the major political parties in Great Britain, and split voting on issues of conscience or conviction, members of Parliament commonly vote in support of positions assumed by their leaders.

To follow so closely their party's leaders and program, as British MP's commonly do, would appear intolerable to the average member of the American Congress. The latter likes to think of himself as capable of making up his mind on each issue as it arises and of voting as he thinks right, regardless of his party leader or even of his party platform. To him the behavior of British MP's destroys an element of personal freedom essential to democracy.

Some members of Parliament would agree with this analysis. But others among them would undoubtedly point out that the freedom of the member of Congress is sometimes purchased at the price of party irresponsibility. The president may well find that he uses votes from the opposition party in order to carry through a program or policy on which his own party is split. Thus it is more difficult to place responsibility for particular decisions, at least

as far as Congress is concerned. But in Great Britain the voter knows that if the Conservative party is successful in an election, it will have the power to carry out its program; and the same is true of a Labor victory.

Moreover, as we well know, it is quite possible to have a Republican president at the same time that Congress contains more Democrats than Republicans. Not only was this the situation in 1968 when Richard Nixon was first elected president, but it remained so after the congressional elections in 1970. Such a situation is, of course, impossible in Great Britain where the prime minister achieves the country's highest office not because votes have been cast for him directly, or through a special electoral college as in the United States, but because his party has more members in the House of Commons than has any other party. The prime minister and his parliamentary party are thus tied together in Great Britain in a way unknown in the United States. Congressional candidates may be elected "on the coat-tails" of a popular president but this fact may make little difference to how faithfully the congressman votes for "his" president's policies. In Great Britain, as we have noted several times, it is the exception for the MP to break party lines, since he knows that his party's appeal and leaders have been major factors in securing his election, and that future elections may depend on party solidarity.

2 HOW THE PARTIES ARE ORGANIZED

British political parties are among the largest in the world. Nearly one-quarter of all those eligible for the franchise belong to one or another of the political parties. The Labor party can boast of by far the largest number, something over seven million, most of them affiliated trade union members, but in the early 1960s some eight hundred thousand in constituency organizations. The Conservatives count nearly three million, an unusually high total for a right-wing party. One-fifth to one-quarter of those who customarily vote Conservative are members of the party's organization, whereas

only about one-thirteenth or one-fourteenth of those who normally vote Labor are enrolled as individual members. Many Labor supporters, of course, are enrolled through the unions. The big increase in the number of individual Labor members came at the end of the war, just before and after the major electoral success of 1945. The Conservatives with a mammoth effort trebled their membership in the late forties and early fifties.

The next section describes the formal extra-parliamentary structure of individual British parties and also indicates organizational developments between the elections of 1966 and 1970. In this way it will be possible to gain a better understanding of the character of the parties, how they work in and out of office, and what is involved in preparing for an election.

THE CONSERVATIVE PARTY

The Conservatives pride themselves on being a national party, drawing support, as they do, from all segments of society, and standing for social order, modernity, and individual initiative. For the past century, they have distinguished themselves in promoting compromises and concessions in response to changing conditions that have eased and helped to reconcile the conflicts of different classes in British society. The party is not based on dogma but on principles so broad as to be capable of the widest possible interpretation. A clear indication of this breadth of principle is that Enoch Powell, whom Heath expelled from the Conservative shadow cabinet (the party leadership while in opposition) in 1968 for an inflammatory speech on immigration, still campaigned for the Tories in 1970.

Although committed to social welfare—which they differentiate sharply from socialism—Conservatives maintain that the state should only do for individuals what they cannot do adequately for themselves. Thus the party is dedicated to limited government to the degree that is possible in a complex industrial world. Its leaders believe that while the state can establish the framework for a good life, individuals and groups should develop their own ways to realize it.

Conservatives take special pride in traditional institutions—the monarchy, Parliament, and law—but they also look on them as efficient instruments of modern society that should constantly be subjected to scrutiny and open to change. They accept public ownership (as with BBC) when convinced it is the most practical expedient to meet a specific need. Edward Heath's particular concern for efficient administration is rooted in the Toryism of Disraeli, Pitt, and Peel. Never "little Englanders," Conservatives view foreign policy primarily as a means of advancing and protecting British interests. Policies toward the Soviet Union or South Africa are looked on, therefore, from the perspective of aiding trade or ensuring peace rather than of standards derived from the character of their regimes. This explains the Heath government's attitude to the sale of arms to South Africa.

The Conservatives thus combine breadth of philosophy with some hard-headed notions about government and policies. They appeal nationally but continue to believe in a natural hierarchy of ability, if no longer officially in a hierarchy of birth and status. Thus they counterpoise to Labor's emphasis on egalitarianism what they believe to be a more natural, and therefore more lasting, view of society based on the differences in men's capacities, energies, and achievements.

The party structure

Historically, the Conservative party came into existence *inside* Parliament and only subsequently reached outside for electoral organization. This is the reason why the constituency units are known as associations. These associations tend to function like clubs. In middle-class districts, where the Conservatives are strongest, it is often "the thing to do" to belong to the local Conservative party organization, just as it is to belong to other accepted social groups. While the associations are open to all who care to participate, their middle-class leadership provides a flavor, which may not appeal to the less well-to-do in the community.

Active constituencies have a hierarchy of leaders, a few at the top in the constituency offices and others holding posts in the association's component sections, the ward branches, and women's and youth groups. Formal decisions are taken in the constituency's Executive Committee, which includes representatives of all such groups, but since that body includes about fifty or more members, it elects a smaller group known as the General Purposes Committee, which generally makes the decisions. The key decision, of course, is the selection of the candidate, and it is this small group that exercises paramount influence in this matter as well as all others.

Manual workers are almost entirely absent from local Conservative leadership—as, indeed, they are also from Conservative benches in

Parliament—although they will form a substantial proportion of the voters in a constituency. In Greenwich, for example, a 1950 survey found that lower-income groups formed 60 percent of the voters but only 9 percent of the leaders. National headquarters deplores the over-representation of the middle class in constituency organizations and their general apathy in performing an integrating role within their segments of society. It made strong, but relatively unsuccessful, efforts between the two elections to persuade constituency associations to become more representative and also to modernize their organization, particularly in the cities. It had more effect in getting the local associations to raise more money and to pay higher salaries to the professional party agents who carry much of the responsibility for organizing campaigns. It is largely due to these efforts that the number of agents remained as high in 1970 as in 1966.

In the past, local Conservative associations had tended to choose candidates who could pay their own campaign expenses and contribute heavily to party funds. In 1948, however, sensitive to the charge of being the party of wealth, the Conservatives had accepted the far-reaching recommendations of the Maxwell Fyfe Committee on Party Organization that candidates should be relieved of all election expenses and that contributions to party funds by the local MP or a candidate should be restricted to £50 or £25, respectively. Although Conservatives commonly spend twice as much on a campaign as Labor does, financial resources, paradoxically, now play a less important role in the selection of Conservative candidates than of Labor candidates.

Despite their potentially greater resources, the Conservatives found themselves in urgent need of raising funds after the 1966 election. Through a national appeal from the autumn of 1967 to early 1969, they succeeded in raising £2.25 million ($6 million), over £.75 million ($1.8 million) of it from local associations. Nonetheless, although this response once again balanced the Conservative budget, it did not permit spending in the 1970 election on the scale of 1964. Thus while the Conservatives had some financial advantage in the election, they had to depend heavily for success on efficiency, morale, and intraparty communications.

Party machinery

The Conservative party machinery is divided into two almost autonomous structures: one of them is democratic, the other autocratic. The *democratic* organization is the National Union of Conservative and Unionist Associations, which is a federation of the constituency associations and the eleven areas and Scotland into which they are grouped. The *autocratic* organization is that of the party proper, which the party leader controls. He appoints the party chairman (from 1967 to 1970, Anthony Barber, subsequently Chancellor of the Exchequer), the officers, the honorary treasurers, the deputy chairman, who is the chief professional executive and is responsible for the coordination of the work of the Central Office and the Research Department, and the two vice-chairmen, who are responsible for candidates and the women's organization, respectively. The two organizations, although retaining separate identities, interact continuously at both national and area level, a situation epitomized by the fact that the director of organization, the senior of the three directors of Central Office departments, is honorary secretary to the National Union and directly in charge of the Area Offices of the Central Office.

THE NATIONAL UNION   The most prized reward for an ardent volunteer worker in the Conservative party is to be chosen as a delegate to the annual conference of the National Union. Conservatives often claim that their organization is more democratic than that of the Labor party because their constituency units have more autonomy, because each constituency organization has equal representation at the annual conference, and because their representatives to the conference are "free to speak and vote according to their consciences." But the corollary to this equality and freedom is the relative lack of influence, let alone power of the conference and, indeed, of the National Union as a whole. The conference, in particular, with its four thousand or more participants is a rally of the faithful, more concerned with politics than administration. In the past, its hundreds of resolutions and wide-ranging discussions had not even been attended by the party leader until they were over, and he then appeared to give a prepared speech often un-related to what the delegates had been discuss-ing. Since 1965, however, Heath has made it a practice to attend during the debates of the conference, answering even sharp comments from the floor, and speaking to those points most at issue in the minds of conference mem-bers.

The official top decision-making organ of the National Union, the Central Council, with its 3,000 members, who are mainly appointed by constituency associations, is much too large to be effective, and so, in practice, is the Execu-tive Committee, which has 150 members. Thus the real work is done by the General Purposes Committee of 54 members chosen from the executive. Both these latter organizations are primarily elected from below, but the leader and chief whip sit ex officio in both, and some seats are reserved for representatives of the parliamentary party and the party organization and for a few selected members. A further link between the National Union and the party organization is the Advisory Committee on Policy, which similarly includes representatives from the National Union, the parliamentary party, the party organization, and selected members. Technically, the Advisory Committee on Policy, at present under the chairmanship of the deputy leader of the party, is directly responsible to the leader of the party and is serviced by the Research Department, whose director is ex-officio secretary.

The smaller and higher the organ, the lower the percentage of party workers. Jean Blondel reported in 1963 that while party workers held 80 percent of the seats on the Executive Com-mittee, allocated carefully to represent the variety of interests in the constituency asso-ciations, and 67 percent on the General Pur-poses Committee, only 36 percent—that is, eight out of twenty-two—of those on the Ad-visory Committee on Policy.[2] Parliamentary members held their highest proportion of members on the latter body, and the chairman of the 1922 Committee of Backbenchers sits on all three bodies. Selected members were held to strengthen the party bureaucracy on

the Advisory Committee on Policy and the party workers on the two chief National Union committees.

The selected members provide the closest approach to representation of supporting in-terests within the Conservative structure, mak-ing a sharp contrast to the Labor party or-ganization's heavy official representation of associated groups, especially the trade unions. At the same time, all those on national organs of the Conservative party are looked on as representing groups or bodies with distinctive interests: the hierarchy of the National Union, the parliamentary party, and Central Office at one level, and also a wide variety of sub-groups representing different areas of the coun-try as well as women, young Conservatives, trade unionists, frontbenchers and backbench-ers. Thus, whatever their power, they provide the means by which the leader can keep in touch with all sections of the party and through them learn the currents of opinion in their constituencies.

THE CENTRAL OFFICE   The party leader, as we have seen, controls the Conservative Cen-tral Office (32 Smith Square) and appoints the chief officials of the party bureaucracy. This centralization of authority within the party proper provides the leader of the Conservative party with great power and also great responsi-bility. Confronted with a decline in organiza-tion and a generally dispirited party after the electoral defeats of 1964 and 1966, Heath and his officials had three major organizational tasks: to bridge the divisions that had de-veloped between the shadow cabinet and the backbenchers, between MP's and the constitu-ency associations, and between local standard bearers and the electorate. In addition, there was great need to meet a threatening financial situation and to adopt more modern elec-tioneering techniques, particularly those using market research.

Their "quiet revolution," even though not fully realized, met a number of visible needs. New top officials, particularly with the appoint-ment in 1967 of Anthony Barber as party chair-man, stimulated Central Office efficiency and forged closer bonds with the centrally ap-pointed area chairmen and some eighty key or

[2] Jean Blondel, *Voters, Parties, and Leaders: The Social Fabric of British Politics*, p. 118.

Structure of the Conservative Party

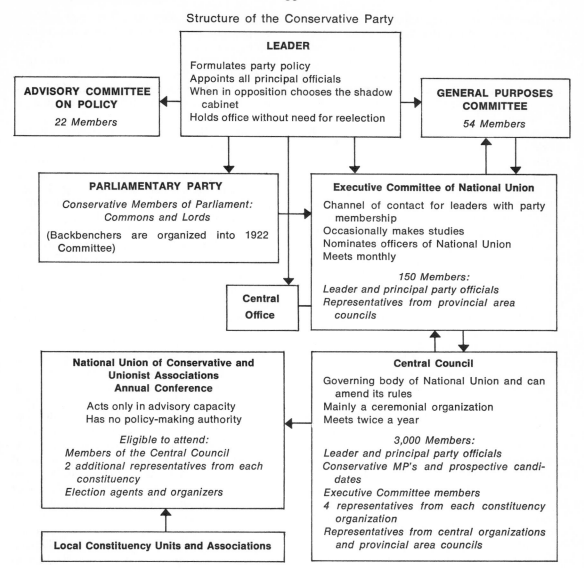

LEADER

Formulates party policy
Appoints all principal officials
When in opposition chooses the shadow
  cabinet
Holds office without need for reelection

**ADVISORY COMMITTEE
ON POLICY**

22 Members

**GENERAL PURPOSES
COMMITTEE**

54 Members

PARLIAMENTARY PARTY

*Conservative Members of Parliament:
Commons and Lords*

(Backbenchers are organized into 1922
Committee)

Executive Committee of National Union

Channel of contact for leaders with party
  membership
Occasionally makes studies
Nominates officers of National Union
Meets monthly

*150 Members:
Leader and principal party officials
Representatives from provincial area
  councils*

**Central
Office**

**National Union of Conservative and
Unionist Associations
Annual Conference**

Acts only in advisory capacity
Has no policy-making authority

*Eligible to attend:
Members of the Central Council
2 additional representatives from each
  constituency
Election agents and organizers*

Central Council

Governing body of National Union and can
  amend its rules
Mainly a ceremonial organization
Meets twice a year

*3,000 Members:
Leader and principal party officials
Conservative MP's and prospective candidates
Executive Committee members
4 representatives from each constituency
  organization
Representatives from central organizations
  and provincial area councils*

Local Constituency Units and Associations

"critical" constituencies where the electoral outcome might not be sure. There was a major expansion of the Research Department, which is particularly important when a party is in opposition and thus without civil service help. Bureaucratic expenses were cut and moderately successful financial campaigns carried out. Confronted with the possibility of reduced business contributions under new Labor legislation requiring their disclosure, special appeals were made to the constituencies, and regional teams toured the country in search of support—"eighteen months of eating for the Party," one participant called it.[3] Moreover, party accounts were published for the first time. A redrawn Central Office list of recommended parliamentary candidates (customarily prepared after each election) was openly aimed at bringing younger, more broadly representative members into Parliament, a party objec-

[3] David E. Butler and Michael Pinto-Duschinsky, *The British General Election of 1970*, p. 97.

tive since Maxwell Fyfe's reforms, proposed in 1948. A special committee examined all aspects of the profession of party agents and recommended higher salaries for these key figures in electoral activities. Technical advice was sought on how best to capitalize on the free radio and television time allowed parties. Moreover, market research techniques were heavily drawn on, particularly, as we shall see, during the 1970 election campaign to keep Mr. Heath constantly abreast of the impact of particular issues upon the voters.

THE PARLIAMENTARY CONSERVATIVE PARTY Within the parliamentary Conservative party, the leader commonly has the same overriding personal power that the formal organizatio.1 of the party provides him, but he is subject to much more ultimate restraint. Unlike the Labor leader, the Conservative leader chooses his own shadow cabinet when out of office. When the party is in power, Conservative ministers do not even attend the meetings of Conservative backbenchers. The leader alone determines how the party whip is to be used or whether a member is to be expelled from the party. Moreover, the formulation of party policy is officially the leader's prerogative.

Yet the name given to the meeting of Conservative backbenchers, the "1922 Committee," carries a moral that few Conservative leaders can overlook. It was the famous Carlton Club meeting of Conservative MP's in October 1922 that led to the downfall of Austen Chamberlain, leader of the Conservative party in the House of Commons. The organization of private (that is, non-officeholding) Conservative MP's into the 1922 Committee followed almost immediately thereafter. Contrary to Labor party practice, ministers may attend the meetings of this group only by invitation. This is true also of the specialized committees of the Conservative parliamentary party, which have no fixed personnel, as is common with Labor. Thus there is a significant degree of organization among the Conservative private members that exists apart from ministerial direction and influence. And while the 1922 Committee is the parliamentary equivalent of the National Union—that is, it is a sounding board of sentiment, not a policymaker—the leader can remain such only if he retains the confidence of

his parliamentary members. This fact explains the apparent paradox that three Conservative leaders, Austen Chamberlain, Neville Chamberlain (to make way for Winston Churchill's leadership in 1940), and, although less obviously, Sir Alec Douglas-Home in 1965 have found themselves compelled to give up their office.

Although Sir Alec Douglas-Home lost the basic confidence of his party in his ability to win a future election, he established two important innovations: the presence of the leader throughout the annual conference (although, as we have seen, Heath was the first to implement the practice); and a formalized procedure for the selection of the Conservative leader. Secrecy and agreement on a particular individual by certain Conservative "notables" (sometimes called "the magic circle" or "country house politics" or, more elegantly, the "customary processes of consultation") had played a disproportionate and subsequently bitterly criticized role in the selection of both Macmillan in 1957 and Douglas-Home in 1963.

The new procedure, approved by the national Union Executive and other relevant agencies, was formally announced in February 1965 and was thus available, after Douglas-Home's subsequent resignation, for the election of Edward Heath later that year. It is similar, although not identical, to the procedure used by the Labor party. In the event that there are more than two candidates, although this has never yet happened, Labor has an eliminating ballot in which all members of the parliamentary Labor party can vote. The decisive contest is between two names, as in Wilson's hard-fought and closely won battle with George Brown for the election in October 1963.

The Conservative procedure, followed only when a new leader is needed, provides for three ballots, with the voting limited to Conservative MP's in the Commons. The chairman of the 1922 Committee of backbenchers directs the process. Nominations are published, although the names of proposers and seconders remain secret; to win on the first ballot a candidate needs to get both an overall majority and 15 percent more of the votes than any other candidate, a stiff hurdle. On the second ballot, fresh nominations are required (providing scope for further consultative processes), but an overall majority is sufficient. If a third ballot is needed, a preferential voting system is used to bring the new leader a decisive majority. Once this crucial stage of selection has been completed, the choice is presented to the traditional party meeting in Church House, numbering 1,076 persons in 1965, made up of Conservative members of the Commons and Lords, candidates for election, and the non-parliamentary members of the National Union Executive. Although in a fifty-year period the name proposed to this final party meeting has never been challenged, the process would begin all over again if such were to happen.

In practice, the new Conservative process for selecting the leader worked smoothly and quickly following Home's resignation on July 22, 1965. The first ballot results were as follows: Heath, 150 votes; Maudling, 133; and Powell, 15. Both Maudling and Powell withdrew, and Heath was unanimously accepted at the traditional meeting on August 2, 1965. Not only had the Conservatives used a new and open process for choosing their leader, but Heath was the first Conservative in over forty years not to become both party leader and prime minister at virtually the same moment. The subsequent defeat of his party in 1966 and its opposition role in Parliament confronted him with greater difficulties in re-knitting the party's unity and developing its forward look than faced his predecessors. Only with the Conservative victory in 1970 did Heath come fully into his own.

THE LABOR PARTY

The Labor party, founded to advance the purposes of the working class and still committed to its interests, also thinks of itself as a national party. Harold Wilson's goal has been to establish Labor as the dominant ruling party in Great Britain in place of the Conservatives. By edging Labor's policies into the middle, he sought to continue the combination of working- and middle-class support that had brought the party its dramatic victory in 1966.

Although both Labor and the Conservatives strive to appeal to a broad spectrum of support, there remain basic differences between them in philosophy and approach. These differences revolve around egalitarianism versus hierarchy. Labor believes in equality of treatment, equality of respect, and the equal right of each person to happiness, security, and fulfillment. Where the Conservatives believe men should be free to rise to the limits of their abilities and opportunities, and are suspicious of attempts to legislate greater social equality, Labor's objectives are to abolish gross inequalities in the distribution of wealth, the continuing and pervasive inequalities in the treatment of persons resulting from class (identified by accent, schooling, occupation, and type of home), and inequalities in power. The Conservatives resist the extension of government intervention both because it results in an unwieldy bureaucracy and because it tampers with the existing order of society and thus appears to them harmful and inherently likely to fail. Labor, in contrast, calls on the power of the state to levy taxation in the interests of the masses, to provide services for all, especially through public expenditures on schools, hospitals, and welfare, to control prices, and to regulate commerce. In particular, the two parties may not differ as widely when in office as these distinctions suggest, but their basic impulses are different as are the motives behind their calculated policies.

Confronting the electorate in 1970, Labor had the advantages of office and the choice of a precise date at which to test their fortunes but the handicap of a succession of economic and political difficulties since its 1966 electoral victory. The continuing and worsening balance-of-payment crisis, unsolved by increased taxation, had led in November 1967 to the devaluation of the pound against which the Labor government had struggled, probably for too long. Rhodesia's unconstitutional, unilateral declaration of independence, solved neither by bargaining nor by sanctions, had damaged Britain's reputation in the Commonwealth and the United Nations. Labor's application to join the Common Market had been even more peremptorily refused by President de Gaulle than the earlier application by the Conservatives. There was continued and severe tension between the Labor government and the trade unions over prices, wages, income policies, and formal and informal strikes. The effort to solve the situation through the Trade Disputes Bill of 1969 had roused such strong party and trade union opposition that it had to be abandoned. But on the more positive side, and probably the cause of Labor's much improved standing in opinion polls and the borough (town) elections in the spring of 1970, a healthy balance-of-payments surplus had appeared at last and, less desirable, a round of wage increases to balance continued heavy taxation and the rising cost of goods.

The Labor party's fortunes in the constituencies had followed fairly closely the national situation. From 1966 to 1969, there was a sharp decline in party membership in the constituencies, which brought the membership probably as low as 300,000 by the spring of 1970, well under half of what it had been several years before. The number of constituency parties with more than 2,000 members fell from 68 in 1966 to 23 in 1969. The number of full-time party agents sank in the same period from 204 to 146. In all these respects, improvement was noticeable as national morale rose, but Labor's organization, never so efficient as that of the Conservatives, was still lagging far behind by the time of the election campaign. In part, this was also due to Harold Wilson's playing down of the electoral role of Labor's national organization and to the party's extraordinarily complex, not to say cumbersome, structure.

Party structure

The Labor party's organization is one of the most complicated designed by the mind of man. From the time of its foundation the party has been composed of a number of autonomous organizations that have allied themselves for political purposes; in allotting each organization its appropriate representation in the general framework and in balancing the different, and sometimes jealous, groups against one another, simplicity and clarity of structure were early casualties.

Four types of organization have combined to make the Labor party: socialist and other societies composed for the most part of intellectuals and professional men; trade unions; cooperatives; and local and regional organizations of the Labor party.

SOCIALIST AND OTHER SOCIETIES   In the first group are the Fabian Society, the Socialist Medical Association, the Jewish Socialist Labor party, and the National Association of Labor Teachers. In numbers these organizations are very small, and the terms of membership in the party now make it impossible for them to develop programs and policies of their own. In the past, however, as the history of the Fabian Society has indicated, they had a distinguished part in the development of the party's philosophy, and their research facilities and professional services still contribute new ideas and useful reports.

TRADE UNIONS   The most striking feature of Labor party membership, at least to an American, is the predominance of trade unionists. The long alliance between the Labor party and the bulk of British trade unions traditionally rested on a deeply felt identity of interest and on mutual confidence. Trade union participation in politics has always been looked on as subsidiary to collective bargaining, and its importance to the unions varies in proportion to the effectiveness of the party in furthering their interests.

As long as Ernest Bevin and Arthur Deakin controlled the mammoth Transport and General Workers' Union (TGWU), which casts one-sixth of the votes at Labor party conferences, the three major unions acted as a homogeneous and loyal group, automatically supporting the policies of the National Executive Committee (NEC). But beginning in the late fifties, trade unions have become much more divided in their allegiances. Frank Cousins of the Transport and General Workers' Union and Jack Jones, who succeeded him in 1968, are well to the left in political orientation and have not hesitated on occasions to throw their weight against Harold Wilson and other parliamentary leaders in the annual conference and in the National Executive Committee. Moreover, the struggle between the Labor government and the unions over the Trade Disputes Bill of 1969 brought their relations to a low point.

This has been a matter for great concern because the unions furnish the bulk of the Labor party's membership and also more than 80 percent of its annual income. Faced with a substantial deficit after the 1970 election, the Labor party naturally turned to its surest source of financial support, the trade unions. Through a curious, partly personal, partly union arrangement, a so-called political levy goes automatically from each worker's wages into his union's political fund unless the worker signs a statement opposing the contribution. (In 1927, following the general strike of the year before, the Trades Dispute Act required workers to volunteer to pay the political levy. The Labor government reversed the process in 1946.) The fee up to 1971 (amounting to seven and a half pence or ten cents) is less than half that paid by individual constituency members. The Labor party hopes to double or even nearly triple the size of the political levy to enable it to maintain a healthy financial situation in the years to come. The process for approval, however, is as complex as are most changes within the Labor party structure. The National Executive had already taken the necessary first step by March 1971 in approving talks with the unions; the latter must then be approached individually by party leaders; and whatever figure is agreed upon is then taken to the party's annual conference.[4] Thereafter, many of the unions themselves will require constitutional changes before the levy can be raised, and this process requires a rules revision conference. Labor's need for more funds, therefore, will not be met quickly.

Oddly enough, each union can decide the number of its members on whom to pay affiliation fees to the party. Since votes at the annual party conference depend on how many affiliation fees are paid (one vote for every five thousand paid-up members), union leaders must decide between their desire for votes and for funds for their own election budgets.

Union election budgets are particularly important for those unions that sponsor their own parliamentary candidates. Union candidates[5] generally stand for relatively safe seats, and in 1970, 112 of their candidates won out of the 137 seats they contested. (In 1966, they had elected 132 out of 138 candidates.) The Mineworkers secured the largest share, 20, but the Transport and General Workers' Union took 19, and the Amalgamated Union of Engineers and Foundrymen (AEF), 16. Twenty other unions shared in union-sponsored parliamentary representation. Trade unionists have only rarely been influential MP's, because they are often selected more as a reward for past services than for their brilliance or eloquence. The left-wing leadership of the TGWU and AEF had little effect on their choice of candidates. The Wilson Report after Labor's defeat in 1955 criticized the unions for not contesting or at least supporting campaigns in marginal seats, but the smaller number of union-sponsored MP's resulted from the general decline in Labor's representation, not from particularly difficult constituencies.

THE COOPERATIVES   The cooperatives have been a disappointment to Labor. Nearly two out of every three families belong to societies engaged in cooperative trading and manufacturing. Their active support could represent an enormous addition to the party's strength, both in money and in membership. But only the Royal Arsenal Cooperative Society, one of the oldest and largest of cooperative societies, has affiliated with the Labor party at the national level, though the London Cooperative Society (LCS), urged by their left-wing Young Chartist group, was considering affiliation in 1971. The cooperatives have had a political party of their own since 1917—the Cooperative party—and the LCS is its largest society. Although this party has refused to affiliate nationally with the Labor party, it has an electoral arrangement with it to run candidates as "Cooperative and Labor" in thirty constituencies. Although this limit is maintained, the National Executive of the Labor party has agreed that in addition to the fifteen seats won in 1970, the Cooperative party in the future can contest three Labor-held seats "if vacancies occur," and four in "favorable constituencies," if it will also

---

[4] Affiliation fees amounted to £306,939 ($736,653) in 1970, of which the trade unions had contributed £272,145 ($653,148) and local Labor parties only £33,729 ($70,949). Faced with an estimated deficit by mid-1971 of £153,000 ($357,200) and a projected deficit of £398,000 ($955,200) by 1975, the NEC requested the annual conference in September 1971 to provide substantial increases in both membership and affiliation fees to increase the income of Transport House to £1,000,000 ($2,400,000) over the next five years, so as to wipe out the deficit and greatly improve central party organization.

[5] It is a party rule that every Labor candidate must belong to a union appropriate to his occupation, if there is one, but this affiliation is often merely nominal.

fight eight in "difficult constituencies." With these concessions, the Cooperative party hopes to increase its representation in the House of Commons to twenty-two. MP's who carry this designation normally vote with the Labor party, although they did not do so over SET (see Chapter 1, Section 3). Although the arrangement does not seem conducive to an enthusiastic relationship, it appears to be the best possible for both sides under present circumstances.

LOCAL ORGANIZATION: THE CONSTITUENCY PARTIES   If the trade unions provide most of the membership and the money, the Labor party's local organizations provide most of the energy and do most of the work. Membership in these organizations is open to anyone who formally accepts the party's program by signing a membership card and paying a small monthly fee. Some people who already belong to the party by virtue of their membership in trade unions or socialist societies also enroll as individual members of the constituency organizations.

The most energetic, the most sincere, and the most ideologically inclined are likely to be found within the constituency members. It is the party militants who collect the party's dues, sell and distribute its literature, organize entertainments and bazaars in order to raise money, and do the hard work of electioneering. Perhaps two-fifths of those enrolled in Labor party organizations can be termed activists, a considerably higher proportion than in Conservative associations. At the same time, far from all Labor party members are left-wing socialists, although there are proportionately more of that disposition among party members than among Labor voters. The proportion of manual workers among Labor voters and Labor party members appears about the same.

Like the Conservatives, the structure of local parties (which are broadly grouped into eleven regions) includes both a large organization that technically makes the decisions and a much smaller body that actually does so. The larger body, called by Labor the General Management Committee, not only has representatives of the wards and women's and youth groups but also of the trade unions and other affiliated organizations. The more effective Executive Committee is composed, as with the Conservatives, of members elected by the larger body. The leaders of local Labor organizations are drawn more from the middle class than this class's proportion among members would indicate, and the same is now true of representation in Parliament. But there is much less of a gap in attitude between these leaders and those members who are manual workers than is found in Conservative associations, for the principles of equality and solidarity still extend throughout local Labor organizations. The old alliance between workers and intelligentsia is reflected in most Labor constituencies, with those white-collar workers who have not renounced their ties with manual workers acting as a bridge between the latter and the teachers who form a heavy proportion of Labor's local middle-class activists.

It used to be said that a major source of tension within the Labor party was between the socialist radicals in the constituency parties and the basically conservative trade union. Since left-wingers took over two of the largest unions, the TGWU and AEF, some of the resolutions and apparently also the voting at the annual conference have been as much to the left from these sources as from the constituencies. The sharpest differences in policies, in fact, have been between those backed by the parliamentary leadership, or by the NEC, on the one hand, and those of left-wing elements from whatever source. Wilson, in particular, has felt that the party should not only be loyal to the broad interests of the masses but also appeal to the middle class with a moderate outlook characteristic of a prosperous society. The militants, in contrast, wish to keep more of the socialist dogma to the fore. In foreign policy the moderates support the special relationship with the United States, while the militants are openly critical of what they term American capitalist imperialism and the American involvement in Vietnam. But while both groups wish to keep all channels open with the Soviet Union and Eastern Europe, neither side endorses Communist dictatorships, and there has been no disposition to join forces with the Communists in the kind of left-wing alignments experimented with in France.

Party machinery

Federal structures are always complicated and that of the Labor party is particularly so. In theory its ruling body is the annual conference, which leads to the claim that policies endorsed by the conference and by the NEC, which the conference elects, should be binding on the parliamentary party. This claim results from the historical evolution of the party, which, unlike that of the Conservative party, originated *outside* of Parliament and extended its activities into that body to secure the power to implement its policies. (Strictly speaking, the name "Labor party" belongs to the mass membership outside Parliament but includes those inside who are correctly entitled "The Parliamentary Labor party.") But, in practice, all the conventions of the parliamentary system thrust the ultimate decision-making authority into the hands of the parliamentary party and its leader whom Labor MP's, and not the conference, elect. Thus the leader of the parliamentary party becomes automatically leader of the party. There is also a National Council of Labor with trade unions, cooperatives, NEC, and MP representation, but it plays only a minor advisory role.

The conference and the NEC have certain powers, however, that have never been challenged. A two-thirds majority of a card vote at the annual conference can determine "what specific proposals of legislative, financial or administrative reform shall be included in the Party programme" (Clause V of the Labor party constitution). In November 1968, the NEC decided that when government policies differed substantially from conference resolutions, the relevant ministers should be requested to explain why. Moreover, the Parliamentary Committee of Labor MP's must meet with the NEC to decide what items are to be included in the election manifesto. This interaction assures expression of views of the membership party and transmittal of information, but the decision-making remains firmly in the hands of the parliamentary party as long as it is in office.

THE ANNUAL CONFERENCE Labor's annual conference is considerably smaller in size than its Conservative counterpart, since only about twelve hundred attend, compared to the three or four thousand at the Conservative conference. The conference lasts five days, longer than the Conservatives' annual gathering, and constitutes a serious drain on the resources of the delegates.

The Labor conference has changed its role since the party has become an effective contestant for supreme political power. Prior to that time, the conference could expect to be a major factor in molding the party's national policies. Once the parliamentary Labor party became the government, however, this situation necessarily changed. Decisions on policy and tactics became the prerogatives of the party *in* Parliament, and the conference became more of a sounding board to gauge party opinion *outside* Parliament. Transport House (Labor's head office) has never been reconciled to this development, inevitable though it is when Labor is in office. After Labor lost the election in 1970 and confronted the crucial decision of whether or not to support entry into the Common Market, there was sharp disagreement as to whether it would be the conference, called into an almost unprecedented special session in July 1971, that would make that decision or the parliamentary leaders of the party. Wilson insisted, however, in preserving his own ultimate freedom of action on this issue.

The most distinctive feature of Labor's annual conference is the special position of the trade unions. They have the right to send more than half the delegates—a right rarely exercised —and to control five-sixths of the vote. This is because each of the affiliated organizations has one voting card for every five thousand paid-up members or fraction thereof, and there are seventy-nine trade unions, five socialist societies, and one cooperative society affiliated. Each organization, including the constituencies, may propose one resolution (and, later, one amendment to a proposed resolution) for discussion. The organizations know before the conference is held which issues will be taken up, and they may discuss them in advance and instruct their delegates; in this way discussion of issues in local meetings may contribute significantly to the political education of the members.

Structure of the Labor Party

LEADER

When prime minister, selects the Cabinet

CENTRAL OFFICE

Transport House

PARLIAMENTARY LABOR PARTY

Labor Members of Parliament: Commons and Lords

When in opposition, selects the shadow cabinet and annually elects leader

National Executive Committee

Directs and controls the activity of the Labor party *outside* Parliament

28 Members:
Leader and deputy leader, ex officio
12 chosen by trade union delegates
* 7 by local party organizations*
* 3 by socialists, professional, and cooperative delegates*
* 5 women and treasurer chosen by the whole conference*

National Council of Labor

Acts largely in advisory capacity

21 Members:
7 members chosen by Trades Union Congress
7 chosen by Cooperative Union
3 chosen by National Executive Committee
4 chosen by parliamentary Labor party

Annual Party Conference

Considers the broad outlines of party policy

Can amend the constitution of the Labor party

Eligible to attend but no votes unless they are delegates:
Labor MP's and peers and prospective candidates
Agents
Party officials
Eligible to vote:
Delegates from trade unions, constituency and borough parties, societies affiliated with the Labor party, and federations of labor parties

Trade Unions

Local Party Organizations

Socialist and Professional Societies and Royal Arsenal Cooperative Society

It used to be that the party leadership could count on the trade union vote to swing decisions in the conference the way it wished, but, as already suggested, the large unions with left-wing leadership have used their votes several times to defeat policies that party leaders have endorsed. In 1960, the TGWU, AEF, and two other unions voted down the leaders' defense policies, a sharp indication that when the party is in opposition the support of the unions should not be taken for granted. More disturbing were two defeats in conference while the party was in office: the first in 1967 opposing the government's stand on American policy in Vietnam; and the second, and more serious since a matter of domestic policy, a demand in 1968 for the repeal of the prices and incomes legislation. While no party in office will necessarily feel bound to react to a negative vote in conference, the leaders are anxious to avoid such a public rebuff and may well temper their policies to avoid it.

THE NATIONAL EXECUTIVE COMMITTEE   The National Executive Committee, whose members are chosen annually by the conference, provides leadership for the latter and also manages party affairs between conferences and directs its head office. The committee is the most powerful organ in the Labor party, outside of Parliament, and potentially it might challenge the decision-making power of the parliamentary party. In practice, however, its composition makes such a challenge extremely unlikely. Of its twenty-eight members (the parliamentary leader and deputy leader are ex officio), twelve are elected by the trade union delegates, seven by the constituency parties and federation delegates, one by the delegates of the socialist, cooperative, and professional associations, and six—five women and the treasurer—by the conference as a whole. Since the General Council of the Trades Union Congress will not allow its members to stand for the NEC, the trade union members are rarely of high distinction or influence. Most important, however, is the fact that the delegates' choices are so frequently MP's that the latter generally form a majority of the members of the NEC. Especially when the party is in office, they are naturally reluctant

to put any impediments in the government's way.

The NEC is responsible for discipline within the party. It can withdraw or refuse endorsement of candidates and, in contrast to the Conservatives, Labor runs an official candidate against an unendorsed one. It can expel individuals, but on several occasions it has also welcomed back errant members it had formerly ejected. It can disaffiliate an organization, a severe penalty that results in a branch losing the financial support of the local trade unions. The NEC, working through subcommittees, also develops policy statements to be submitted to the annual conference and, as already noted, shares decisions with the relevant committee of the parliamentary party as to what goes into the party's manifesto. Beyond these specific powers, the NEC controls Labor's head office, Transport House, whereas it is the Conservative leader who has that authority within his party. Transport House is chiefly responsible for organizing and coordinating Labor party activities throughout the country, and its lack of effectiveness prior to the 1970 election was a severe handicap to Labor's electoral campaign.

THE HEAD OFFICE   Not particularly good even at the time of the previous election, Labor party organization deteriorated steadily between 1966 and the end of 1968. Many old-line Labor stalwarts resisted modernization, and little had been done to respond to the highly critical 1955 report on party organization by Wilson himself. Moreover, there were tensions between Wilson and Transport House, since the latter wished to publicize the socialist principles on which the party had been founded while the prime minister preferred to emphasize specific programs in wooing the electorate. A further source of division resulted from the choice in 1968 as general secretary of the TGWU's second in command, Harry Nicholas, instead of Wilson's nominee. Moreover, while Nicholas inspired some much needed constituency enthusiasm, he never gained much reputation in his role as administrator. A scheme to recruit more constituency agents did not get under way until mid-1969 and did little more than stop the decline that had been occurring in their numbers. Despite agonized complaints about lack of money, this latter issue was less significant than the stultifying caution that kept publicity and organizational efforts at a low and unimaginative level. Not until August 1969 was a campaign committee formed. Although warned by Wilson in general terms to keep its options open, this committee appears, like Transport House itself, to have geared its program to an October election. When the June date was announced, it became, indeed, the "do-it-yourself" campaign that had been prophesied.

THE PARLIAMENTARY LABOR PARTY   Although the extraparliamentary organization of the Labor party is the major channel through which the opinions of its members can be expressed, it is the parliamentary Labor party that is the real center of power within the party. This is because only the parliamentary members of the Labor party can directly affect national policy. Moreover, it is the parliamentary Labor party that elects the party leader; if the party is out of office, it reelects him annually, commonly by acclamation.

It is worth noting that the Labor party has displayed more loyalty to its leaders and less ruthlessness than the Conservative party. Despite widespread dissatisfaction with Ramsay MacDonald's attitude toward socialist goals, it was his decision to form a national government in 1931 that precipitated the break. (The Labor party maintained a solid front against participation.) When George Lansbury in 1935 confronted an irreconcilable conflict between his party's support of sanctions over Italy's attack on Ethiopia and his own pacifism, it was his decision to resign. Despite Gaitskell's unpopular attacks on Clause IV of the party's constitution, which pledged the party to try to establish a society based on "the common ownership of the means of production, distribution and exchange . . . ," and despite his opposition to unilateral nuclear disarmament, which the party conference approved by a narrow margin in 1960, Gaitskell was reelected party leader in the unprecedented contest with Wilson later the same year.

The fact that when the party is in power its leader is the most powerful political figure in Great Britain gives him at all times an extraor-dinary degree of influence and authority throughout the whole party. At the same time, Labor leaders are expected to listen to criticism, both within the party as a whole and within the parliamentary Labor party, and to provide personal leadership on all occasions. Thus party leaders always attend the sessions of the annual party conference, direct discussions, and reply directly to questions. When the parliamentary Labor party is in a minority in Parliament, meetings of caucus—which is made up of all Labor members in both the Commons and the Lords—are held at least once a week to discuss and decide party policy, and these members elect the shadow cabinet that occupies the front opposition benches.

Even when the Labor party is in power, however, special care is taken to consult party members outside the Cabinet. A liaison committee composed of some backbenchers, the chief whip, the Lord President of the Council, and one representative of the Labor peers acts as intermediary between the Cabinet and the party. The parliamentary party as a whole continues to meet at least once every two weeks for policy discussions in which the prime minister and Cabinet members frequently participate.

The parliamentary Labor party can expel MP's from the parliamentary caucus (the technical expression is "to withdraw the whip" —that is, not to send notices of party meetings). The most notable dissident, Aneurin Bevan, was temporarily expelled on several occasions. But, under normal circumstances, whether the party is in office or out, unity is maintained in the parliamentary Labor party less by rewards and punishments than by the awareness that only a united party can hope to gain and maintain parliamentary power. When so serious a source of division appeared, however, as whether or not to support entry into the Common Market, differences of approach emerged to complicate, as in the early 1960s, the maintenance of unity in the parliamentary party.

THE MINOR PARTIES

In a parliamentary situation in which it is a foregone conclusion that one or the other of the two major parties will form the next government, the prospects for minor parties are depressing. Yet rarely have there seemed such good opportunities for them to command attention as after 1966. The drastic fall in Labor support in the country was reflected in their plummeting in the polls from 47 percent in 1966 to 26 percent in 1968. Among the Conservatives, dispirited by two defeats, the new leader was still largely an unknown figure.

The Liberals could be expected to be the chief beneficiaries from the apparent decline of the two major parties. Prior to the rise of Labor, the Liberals themselves had formed one of Great Britain's two major parties, and they were still capable of securing a substantial number of votes throughout the country as "the party of principle." In more limited areas, Welsh and Scottish nationalism had spawned distinctive political parties that were feeding on local discontents. On the extreme left was the perennial Communist party, although, rather surprisingly, no Maoist or New Left political movements comparable to those on the Continent. On the extreme right were dissident groups, the National Front, the British National party, and a small Labor break-away, the National Democratic party. Yet in the event, none of these parties or groups did well in the 1970 election.

The Liberal party

The Liberal party had made its best showings in the 1964 and 1966 elections with 3 million and then almost 2.5 million votes in 1966 and 12 MP's (later raised to 13). On the other hand, despite Labor's tenuous majority from 1964 to 1966, that party had made no overtures to the Liberals, and Wilson's favored middle-of-the-road stance in policies undercut the Liberal claim that the electorate should turn to them to provide a radical, nonsocialist alternative to the Conservatives. Faced with this dilemma, the Liberal leader and its best-known figure, Jo Grimond, decided to turn the party over to other hands, and in January 1967, on a badly split vote, Jeremy Thorpe, a vigorous, flamboyant, left-leaning, and opportunistic Etonian, was chosen leader.

But the party had reached the height of its limited effectiveness. It was split between its traditional semiconservative, if anti-Tory, right, its down-to-earth center, and its radical left,

within which the Young Liberals' antiapartheid demonstrations against the visit of the South African cricket team earned more publicity than votes. Although the party received enough money before the election to pay off its huge overdraft and to make small contributions to some of its constituency organizations, these funds came almost exclusively from a very few donors. (The party, normally less open about its accounts than either Labor or Conservatives, let it be known after the 1970 election that 85 percent of the contributions in the previous eight months had come from fewer than twenty-five people.) Perhaps above all, their program for dispersed political power through regional assemblies, more standing select committees, a revised tax structure favoring VAT (value-added tax), workers' councils, and 50 percent of votes for workers at annual company meetings failed to provide the attractive middle ground that might have enabled the Liberals to capitalize on public discontent. The electoral returns in 1970 resulted in the loss of a large number of deposits and seven seats, and penned the Liberal victories into the narrowest areas up to that date. Although they still polled over 2 million votes, the total number continued the downward trend from the 1964 pinnacle. This trend boded ill for their future as a party with nation-wide support.

Scottish and Welsh national parties

While the Liberal party failed to capitalize on discontent with Labor policies and Conservative promises, the Scottish National party (SNP) and, to a much lesser extent, Plaid Cymru in Wales, gave dramatic political evidence of the reality of Scottish and Welsh national consciousness. The two regions differ most noticeably in the fact that the linguistic base that is so important in Welsh nationalism is not a significant feature in Scotland. In the latter region it is socio-economic arguments based on the lower standards of living there than in England and the desire for some political devolution that appear to have the strongest effect. Temporarily, the response to these parties raised doubts as to the validity of the assumption that the British party system adequately aggregates the interests of these areas with the interests of England.

Both Scotland and Wales are traditional Labor strongholds, although the Liberals have long been able to elect a few MP's in both areas. In 1966, the Labor party had reached its highest level of support in Scotland, virtually 50 percent of the vote and 46 MP's elected. The Conservatives were markedly in decline with only 20 seats and 37.7 percent of the vote. The SNP came second in the poll in only three seats, while its average vote represented under 15 percent of the total. But thereafter the SNP rapidly increased its number of local branches, which rose from 40 in 1963 to 515 in 1970. It recruited large numbers of young people, who flaunted its distinctive emblem, to reach a total of over 100,000 members in all, and it built a sound financial base largely through running lotteries. In March 1967, the SNP's American-style electioneering brought its percentage of the vote in a Glasgow by-election to 28.2; in November, it captured a presumedly safe Labor seat at Hamilton (Lanarkshire) with a voluble and attractive candidate, Winifred Ewing. The traditional parties were stunned. Labor launched a bitter attack in 1968; the Conservatives finally came out in favor of devolution; the Liberals and SNP mutually rejected the notion of electoral cooperation. In 1970, the SNP fought sixty-five constituencies but, although it polled twice as many votes as in 1966, it was already in decline. Forty-three of its candidates lost their deposits (forfeited if a candidate does not poll one-eighth of the votes cast, see Section 3), and the one seat it won was in the Western Isles. The swing to the Conservatives in Scotland exactly matched that in England.

In Wales, Plaid Cymru, with three hundred branches and a claimed membership of over forty thousand, put forward candidates in all the thirty-six Welsh constituencies. Its chief support was among teachers, professionals, and traditional religious groups, but it extended for the first time beyond Welsh-speaking groups. Plaid Cymru had greater difficulties than SNP, however, in securing wide support. The violent tactics of its extremist wing alienated many Welshmen, and the linguistic, geographical, and other divisions within Wales handicapped it in presenting a nationalist appeal. Its failures at the polls were not unexpected.

Developments in both areas and particularly in Scotland pose problems for the Conservatives and, indeed, for the British people. Should the distinctive Scottish legal system, the Scottish Office, and the Scottish Grand Committee of the House of Commons be preludes to far-reaching constitutional devolutions of power? Is their nationalism rising or diminishing? The recommendations of the Crowther Commission on the Constitution will be watched with special attention in areas increasingly self-conscious but not presently separatist in sentiment.

Extreme left- and right-wing parties

The Communist party in Great Britain has followed so opportunistic and shifting a policy that it has disillusioned many of its former supporters and remains in a weak position. It is chiefly of interest because of its efforts to infiltrate the leadership of certain unions and to place a few "crypto-Communists" among Labor MP's. In its relations with the Labor party, the Communist party has alternated between scurrilous attacks and efforts to affiliate. These efforts have invariably been rejected, and under present party rules they cannot even be considered.

The Communist party, by itself, is extremely weak numerically, although its members to some extent make up in enthusiasm and unquestioning devotion what they lack in numbers. Since the 1945 election, when the party won two seats, the Communists have not succeeded in placing a candidate in Parliament. They put up a hundred candidates in 1950, in their first and only attempt to fight an election on a national scale, between ten and eighteen in 1951–59, thirty-six in 1964, fifty-seven in 1966, and fifty-eight in 1970. All their candidates lost their deposits in 1951, 1964, 1966, and 1970, and virtually all in the intervening elections. Their percentage of votes is so small, therefore, as hardly to be worth noticing, except as an indication of discontent in one or two industrial districts.

The right-wing National Front, the British National party, and the National Democratic party, with its rightist program of national regeneration, also showed little evidence of electoral strength. The former put up ten candidates but nothing substantial in the way of a constituency campaign. Among them, these parties and a few isolated others polled just under 200,000 votes—a more substantial showing than the 38,400 of the Communists, but a bare 7 percent of the total votes cast. When the time comes to exercise their franchise, the overwhelming majority of electors in Great Britain prefer to put their votes where they may have some chance of influencing the outcome.

3 ELECTIONS

Elections are the testing points of democracy. They determine who shall govern, and they thus provide a supreme test of party appeal, fervor, and efficiency. If the party is already in office, the electorate is passing on its record. If it is in opposition, the electorate is gauging its promise. A wide variety of external factors may affect an electoral situation: the balance of payments, foreign affairs, a pay dispute, a strike, even, as in 1970, the potential disruptions during a South African cricket tour (which was canceled through government intervention to prevent disorders). There are no sure ways, it seems, of determining which of the major parties will win. And this, in itself, is what makes parties, candidates, constituencies, and central offices focus on the moment when the vote is cast, for the result, whatever the reason may be, will determine their role until the next general election.

In Great Britain, postwar elections have been decided by relatively small changes in the proportion of votes received by the two major parties. Only once in this period has the gap between these two parties been more than 7 percent. The "swing," that is, the percentage of votes moving from one major party to the other in the next election, had ranged prior to 1970 from as little as 1.1 percent to the Conservatives in 1951 to 3.1 percent to Labor in 1964. In 1970, the swing to the Conservatives, reckoned as a percentage of the two-party vote, was 5.3, the highest since the war; as a percentage of the total vote cast the swing was 4.8; and as a percentage of the registered electorate, 3.6. Yet the total percentage of the votes cast for the Tories was 46.1, whereas those for Labor amounted to 43.8, a difference of only 2.3 percent.

If one examines election returns on a constituency basis, there is even more striking evidence for the consistency of party allegiance by the overwhelming proportion of voters. A study of 453 constituencies during the four elections of the 1950s disclosed the fact that 87.2 percent of them returned the same party each time. Only 58 constituencies changed party hands at all and, still more striking, only 7 of these changed twice. Another study including the 1964 election concluded that 71 percent of all seats in the House of Commons could be regarded as "safe" for the party holding them.[6] Thus, even more than in the United States, a high proportion of elections are foregone conclusions as far as their party outcome is concerned. The determination of which party shall govern is made within one-quarter of the seats contested.

This marked stability in party voting seems to undercut the importance of party policies, programs, and leaders, and to some degree it does. Yet there are other ways than switching votes by which electors signify their dissatisfaction. Low levels of constituency activity, difficulty in securing adequate funds, and failure to go to the polls are effective means of indicating lack of enthusiasm for proposals and performance. Labor's defeat in 1970 was probably due more to diminished enthusiasm for its program, particularly after the abortive Trade Disputes Bill of 1969, than to positive efforts by the Conservatives.

ELECTION DATE

Elections in Great Britain may occur with very little warning, and British parties are therefore obliged to adopt a strategy quite different

6 Jorgen Rasmussen, "The Implications of Safe Seats for British Democracy," *Western Political Quarterly* (1966), pp. 516–29.

GEOGRAPHY OF A TYPICAL BRITISH ELECTION, 1959

PERCENTAGE OF VOTES CAST FOR
CONSERVATIVE CANDIDATES

PERCENTAGE OF VOTES CAST FOR
LABOR CANDIDATES

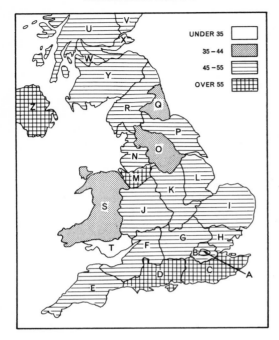

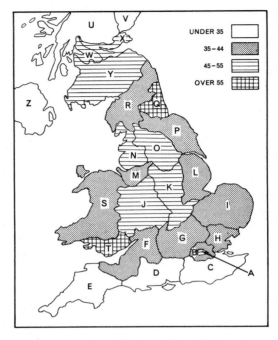

Source: The areas are those used by David E. Butler and Richard Rose. *The British General Election of 1959,* p. 190. By permission of Macmillan and Co., Ltd. and St. Martin's Press.

Important cities are in parentheses. **A** County of London **B** Suburban Boroughs
C Southeast **D** Wessex (*Portsmouth*) **E** West of England (*Plymouth*) **F** Severn
(*Bristol*) **G** South Central **H** Outer Essex **I** East Anglia **J** West Midlands (*Birmingham,
Coventry*) **K** Northeast Midlands (*Nottingham, Leicester*) **L** Lincolnshire **M** Cheshire
N Lancashire (*Liverpool, Manchester*) **O** West Riding (*Sheffield, Leeds, Bradford*) **P** East
& North Riding (*York, Hull*) **Q** Northeast England (*Newcastle*) **R** Border **S** Rural Wales
T Industrial Wales (*Cardiff, Swansea*)
SCOTLAND **U** Highlands **V** Northeast **W** Clyde (*Glasgow*) **X** Forth (*Edinburgh*)
Y Lowlands
NORTHERN IRELAND **Z** (*Belfast*)

from that of American parties. In the United States, of course, anyone can predict the date of presidential elections for generations to come. The Constitution requires that the election be held every four years, whether it is convenient or not: candidates may announce their availability a year or more in advance, and there is active competition for delegates to national conventions in the winter and spring preceding an election. The nominating conventions themselves are held during the summer; September and October are dedicated to campaign addresses; by the time the voters make their decision early in November, they have been exposed to many months of electioneering.

In Great Britain, in contrast, the prime minister may advise the monarch to dissolve Parliament and ask for new elections any time he desires. Elections are supposed to be not more than five years apart (although because of the war there was no election in Great Britain between 1935 and 1945), but within this five-year period the prime minister has complete freedom to set the time of voting. Thus it would be perfectly possible for several elections to take place within a single year, although the cost, inconvenience, and public irritation work strongly against overfrequent elections. A prime minister with a strong majority in the House of Commons will probably wait four years. In the course of the fourth year of office, however, he and his colleagues will begin to look for favorable issues on which they can "go to the country," and when they have found such an issue and when the time seems appropriate, the monarch, on the prime minister's advice, will dissolve Parliament. Naturally, the prime minister attempts to select a moment favorable to his own party's electoral chances, but, as the 1950, 1951, 1964, and 1970 elections demonstrated, it is difficult in a complex political situation to be sure to whose advantage the time will work. In any case, except in extraordinary circumstances, the power to dissolve has only a marginal effect on the outcome of the election.

The time between dissolution and election is very short. On the eighth day (not counting Sundays and holidays) after the Royal Proclamation of Dissolution, candidates must have filed their nomination papers, and nine days after that (again excluding Sundays and holidays) the vote is taken. It is common, however, to give between twenty-eight and thirty-five days of notice of the exact date of the coming election. In 1970, Prime Minister Wilson conformed to precedent and gave thirty-one days of notice.

On May 18, Wilson went to Buckingham Palace to inform the queen of his decision to hold the election in June; that evening 10 Downing Street issued the announcement. The election date was set for June 18, 1970. Parliament would be dissolved on May 29. The official campaign would lie between those two dates.

Why did Wilson choose a June rather than an October date for the election? Was he wise to do so? Was the upswing in Labor's standing in the country, which began with the vastly improved balance of trade figures in September 1969, sufficient to reverse Labor's public image of inefficient handling of the economy? Would the rise in wage settlements in January and February 1970 result in popularity or criticism? Was the widespread public approval of Roy Jenkins' cautious, moderate budget in April 1970 the key to continued momentum toward Labor? The common belief is that Wilson finally decided on June because the opinion polls, starting with the Harris Poll of April 22, 1970, began at long last to show a Labor lead.

Wilson himself discounts this factor. He maintains that his decision resulted from the fact that the severe downswing in Labor's showing in the borough elections from 1967 through 1969 had been reversed in the spring of 1970. Labor's surprising success in the spring polls, followed by the municipal voting, were only decisive, he declares, in carrying others along with him in his decision.[7] In fact, it appears there was general agreement in the Cabinet and party that a June election was almost sure to yield a small majority whereas waiting until October might well jeopardize Labor's chance.

Opinion polls

Whatever effect the polls may have had on Prime Minister Wilson's decision on the election date—and it was widely commented at the time that if the polls became an infallible way of choosing an election date, they placed a devastating weapon in the hands of a prime minister—their failure to predict the electoral result correctly in 1970 raised many questions regarding their reliability. In earlier postwar elections they had accurately predicted the winning party even though their estimates of the percentage of votes varied considerably from the final result. Particularly after 1959, they shot into prominence as the best, indeed the only continuously available, evidence of public sentiment. From 1961 on, National Opinion Polls (NOP), a subsidiary of Associated Newspapers, had added its regular political polling to that of the Gallup Polls. Poll watching had considerable impact on both the style of the election campaigns in 1964 and 1966 as well as on the morale of the candidates. What happened in 1970?

The best experts on opinion polls, known as psephologists, agree that polling techniques were not to blame for the debacle in 1970. National Opinion Polls distributed their efforts among a stratified sample of two hundred constituencies and at two sampling points in each. Its degree of dispersion was double that used in the 1966 election. Marplan, which had the greatest errors, selected its interviewees by recognized random sampling methods. Opinion Research Center (ORC), which in the end

[7] Harold Wilson in *The Observer*, March 21, 1971, and *Britannica Book of the Year*, 1971.

Accuracy of the Polls, 1945–64
(Winner and Percentage Margin of Victory)

YEAR	ACTUAL RESULT (G.B. ONLY)*	GALLUP PERCENT	DAILY EXPRESS PERCENT	RESEARCH SERVICES PERCENT	NATIONAL OPINION POLLS PERCENT	AVERAGE ERROR PERCENT
1945	Lab. 9.8	Lab. 6.0	—	—	—	3.8
1950	Lab. 3.3	Lab. 1.5	Lab. 0.5	—	—	2.3
1951	—	C. 2.5	C. 4.0	C. 7.0	—	6.0
1955	C. 1.9	C. 3.5	C. 2.7	—	—	1.2
1959	C. 4.2	C. 2.0	C. 3.7	—	C. 3.9	1.0
1964	Lab. 1.9	Lab. 3.5	C. 0.8	Lab. 1.0	Lab. 3.1	1.6
Average error		2.5	2.5	4.7	0.8	2.5

* In 1951 Labor won 1.5 percent more votes in Great Britain, but the Conservatives won a parliamentary majority.

Source: The Times (London), March 9, 1966.

Accuracy of the Polls, 1966
(In Percentages)

OPINION POLL FORECASTS	ACTUAL RESULTS G.B. ONLY	GALLUP	NOP	RESEARCH SERVICES	DAILY EXPRESS
Conservative	41.4	−1.4	+0.2	+0.2	−4.0
Labor	48.7	+2.3	+1.9	+1.0	+5.9
Liberal	8.6	−0.6	−1.2	−0.3	−0.9
Average error on major parties	—	1.4	1.1	0.5	3.4
Error in forecast of Labor lead	—	3.7	1.7	0.8	9.9

Source: Adapted from David E. Butler and Anthony King, *The British General Election of 1966*, p. 175.

Accuracy of the Polls, 1970
(In Percentages)

	ORC G.B.	HARRIS G.B.	NOP G.B.	GALLUP G.B.	MARPLAN U.K.	AVERAGE OF 5 POLLS	ACTUAL RESULTS G.B.
Conservative	46.5	46	44.0	42	41.5	44.0	46.2
Labor	45.5	48	48.1	49	50.2	48.2	43.8
Liberal	6.5	5	6.4	7.5	7.0	6.7	7.6
Misc.	1.5	1	1.3	1.5	1.3	1.3	2.4
Labor lead	−1.0	2.0	4.1	7.0	8.7	4.3	−2.4
Average error on 3 parties share	1.0	2.3	2.6	3.2	3.9	2.6	—
Error on lead	1.4	4.4	6.5	9.4	12.0	7.1	—

Source: David E. Butler and Michael Pinto-Duschinsky, *The British General Election of 1970*, p. 179.

indicated a Tory victory, and Gallup Poll, which predicated a final Labor lead of 7 percent, both used quota-sampling techniques. What seems to have made the difference in reliability were how close the polls were taken to the actual date of the election—Opinion Research Center and the Louis Harris Organization, which took the latest samples, both indicated evidence of a Conservative recovery —and the kind of judgment used in adjusting the "raw" returns. The director of Opinion Research Center correctly judged that Conservative supporters were more likely to vote on election day than Labor supporters and adjusted returns in the light of this expectation. In making this judgment, he was aided by the results of 300 re-interviews, in addition to their 1,583 earlier interviews.[8]

In the future, the public may be more wary in its expectations from public opinion polls. Polls can demonstrate trends but not precise results. The polls themselves will no doubt continue their sampling of registered voters as close as possible to election day, use re-interviews more extensively, and inquire if the respondent plans to vote.

More important, however, is the evidence that the campaign itself was a crucial factor in the outcome of the election. The most intense use of polls was not by the press, although it was overloaded with their results, but by the Conservatives and particularly by Mr. Heath. Three times a day, in fact, private poll results from Opinion Research Center provided him with information on the electorate's reactions to particular issues. His confidence in the ultimate result must have been much bolstered by what he heard. For it seems apparent that there was a late swingback to the Tories in the last days

of the campaign, partly perhaps because earlier doubts about Labor's ability to cope with Britain's disturbing economic situation were cemented by the announcement three days before the election of a trade deficit of 3 million pounds, a figure subsequently found to be inaccurate, partly, perhaps, because Heath's last television performance outshone the one by Wilson, or because Powell introduced the racial issue at the last moment, or maybe for some deeper reasons.

But if some factors aided the Conservatives, what caused the abstentions, presumably mainly by Laborites, that brought the voting down to 72 percent of the electorate, the lowest turnout since 1935? To gain more perspective, it is essential to examine other factors and, in particular, the party programs, the national campaigning, the constituencies, how they had chosen their candidates, who the candidates were, who could vote, how the constituency organizations marshaled their efforts to persuade and get out the voters, and what the electoral results were that put the Conservatives into power on June 18, 1970.

Party programs and national campaigning

Party programs are commonly bland documents that blur distinctions and stress generalities. Yet in 1970, there were distinctive differences between the Conservatives' well produced *A Better Tomorrow*, issued on May 26, 1970, and Labor's hastily put together *Now Britain's Strong—Let's Make Her Great to Live in*, which appeared the following day. Stressing their intention to "hand back responsibilities wherever we can to the individual, to the family, to private initiative, to the local authority, to the people," the Tories restated in contemporary terms the traditional Conservative view of a free and orderly society in which initiative, competition, and effort can maximize production to the advantage of individuals and society. In contrast, Labor maintained its emphasis on an egalitarianism in which society "must be ready to meet the basic needs of all its members," and all are protected against "economic forces they cannot control."

These differences were reflected concretely in their contrasting attitudes on national controls and supervision and on taxation. Labor

[8] The number of interviews used by Opinion Research Center was the smallest sample of all the polls, indicating that care in the selection of respondents is more important than their numbers, but it also proves the key role of interpretation. The size of samples in 1970 ranged from that of the ORC to *The Sunday Times* "Poll of Polls," which sampled twelve thousand people, although only relatively small increases in accuracy can be expected from samples higher than one thousand. Because of the intense public interest in polling techniques and results, the five major polls—Harris, Gallup, Marplan, ORC, and NOP—agreed in May 1970 to a new Code of Practice for opinion polls, under which each pledged to reveal full details of its methods and the composition of its samples to journalists, academics, students, other polling organizations, and political parties.

heralded a National Port Authority under which to reorganize ports and docks, a new National Freight Corporation "to cut out the old and wasteful competition between road and rail," and an Airways Board to plan for both the BOAC and BEA. The Tories declared they would "stop further nationalization and create a climate for free enterprise to expand." Further, they rejected "the detailed intervention of Socialism," which they maintained "usurps the functions of management and seeks to dictate prices and earnings in industry." Moreover, where Labor declared that "we shall ensure . . . that there is a greater contribution to the National Revenue from the rich" (a mild formulation of the wealth tax specified in their 1969 *Agenda for a Generation*), the Conservatives hinted at the introduction of the VAT, which makes goods more expensive for average consumers by adding a related tax at each point in production. And while both emphasized their commitment to social security and pensions, particularly for the elderly, the Tories maintained that "in contrast to the Labour Party, our view is that, for the great majority of people, this can and should be achieved through the expansion and improvement of occupational schemes."

Neither of these manifestos, and even less the Liberal manifesto *What a Life!*, appears to have had much impact on the electorate. What is noticeable, however, is that the Conservatives in office have moved stolidly through item after item on their program. It would have been better, therefore, if the public had paid it more attention.

In addition to the manifestos, there were national speeches in person and on television. It is conventional wisdom to believe it is national rather than local campaigns that swing elections—if, indeed, their results are determined at so late a date. More than in previous postwar elections, the national campaigns in 1970 were built around the two party leaders, Wilson and Heath. Wilson was more informal in his campaigning, but Heath loosened up as time went on and obviously also enjoyed responding to heckling. Wilson made twenty-three appearances in different parts of the country between May 29, when Parliament was dissolved, and June 17, the day before the polling; Heath made nineteen, three of them

in Bexley, his home constituency. Both appeared three times on television, the first time together with Thorpe, the Liberal leader, on the BBC forum. Both Heath and Wilson held daily press conferences. Wilson's "walkabouts," making off-the-cuff speeches, achieved short-term successes, but Heath's more carefully staged public meetings had a stronger cumulative effect. Wilson appeared chiefly in the role of cheerleader, encouraging the electorate to leave problems to him and to enjoy the unprecedentedly beautiful June weather; Heath tried to awaken the public to impending dangers. Wilson said, in effect, "Trust me"; Heath said, "Change is essential." And as evidence accumulated of the rising costs of living and an unstable economic picture, these issues apparently had great impact in the constituencies, where the final decisions were to be made.

THE CONSTITUENCIES

Constituency boundaries can have a major, and perhaps decisive, influence on the outcome of an election. The British have avoided legislative "gerrymandering" by requiring periodic redrawing of constituency boundaries for England, Scotland, Wales, and Northern Ireland, each handled separately by a permanent Boundary Commission, composed of five members, mostly civil servants, and presided over by the Speaker. The objective is to provide geographical areas roughly equal in population. To an American, the prescribed number of voters in a British constituency (59,825) is remarkably small.

General reviews of constituency boundaries have taken place in 1918, 1948, 1954, and 1969. Labor is particularly sensitive to redistribution because its supporters tend to be massed in urban areas where their majorities include "wasted" votes, although, in fact, other reasons like levels of voting are probably more influential in elections. It was commonly accepted, however, that the 1948 redistribution hurt Labor's electoral prospects, and fear of this effect, coupled with the fact that it was sponsoring substantial changes in local government boundaries (see Chapter 6, Section 3) are probably reasons why the Labor government did not implement the alterations in boundaries proposed in 1969 by the Boundary Commission.

The 1948 Representation of the People Act (amended slightly in 1949) had resulted in an almost new electoral map. The total number of seats for the House of Commons dropped from 640 to 625 (largely due to the abolition of the two remaining forms of plural voting: the business premises vote and the university graduates vote [9]); only 80 constituencies retained their former boundaries; and many of the rest were so extensively redrawn as to be new in fact, if not always in name. A further review of constituency boundaries in 1954 was less drastic in results, but it led to the abolishing of 6 constituencies and the creation of 11 new ones (all in England) and brought the membership of the House up to 630.

The proposals of the 1969 Boundary Commission envisaged no less radical changes in the electoral map. They provide for 5 additional constituencies, major alterations in the boundaries of 322 of the existing 630 constituencies, and minor changes in another 38. In Greater London, it recommended reducing the 104 seats to 92, while Birmingham, Manchester, and Liverpool each lost a seat. Responding to the movement of population from the cities to suburban areas, 16 counties were to gain 22 seats in all. It was commonly believed that the effect of amalgamating city constituencies, where Labor is strong, and creating new seats in country areas, where the Conservatives get their best results, would give the latter an advantage of 10 to 20 seats.

Justifying their lack of action on the need to wait for implementation of the Redcliffe-Maud proposals for local government boundaries, which would necessarily also change those for constituencies, the Labor government only proposed changes for the London districts and nine others. Efforts by the Lords to force the government to implement the Boundary Commission's proposals met with blocking tactics that resulted in the 1970 election being fought with the old boundaries. The Conservatives,

not surprisingly, passed the Boundary Commission's proposals into law in November 1970.

THE VOTER

The Labor government introduced one major change in the franchise prior to the 1970 election by lowering the voting age from twenty-one to eighteen through the 1969 Representation of the People Act. This change, which met in practice with far less enthusiasm by the group enfranchised than had been hoped, added more than three and a half years to the age span for voting, since cumbersome procedures had led in the past to a four- to seven-month delay for new voters to be enrolled on the voting register. Although the new provisions made it possible for anyone to vote from the day of his or her eighteenth birthday, new constituency registers (which the government, not the voter, as in the United States, is responsible for keeping up to date), compiled October 10, 1969, probably listed only about 70 percent of the new voters. In any case, the new voters seem not to have affected the outcome in any particular constituency. Those turning eighteen subsequent to February 16, 1970, when the new register came into effect, will be registered automatically.

THE CANDIDATE

British constituencies vary their choice of candidates between local figures, ex-MP's, or other party figures urged discreetly by the party's central office, or occasionally outsiders, since they are not required by law or custom, as in the United States, to select candidates only from their own district. Sitting MP's rarely have difficulty in being endorsed again, although private pressure may be exerted to persuade a few of the older and less desirable ones to stand down voluntarily.[10] Others may

---

[9] The business premises vote was relatively insignificant except in the City of London and a few other constituencies in the larger cities, where it has traditionally been a Conservative asset. There were 12 university seats, however, of which about half were generally held by distinguished Independents, such as Sir A. P. Herbert and Sir Arthur Salter. None of the university seats was ever held by Labor.

[10] Only seven candidates for the 1970 election—two Conservatives and five Labor—were over seventy years old (there had been nineteen in 1966, twenty-three in 1964, and thirty in 1955); one of these, S. O. Davies of Merthyr Tydfil, who was eighty-three years old, was repudiated by his local Labor party on grounds of age but won as an Independent.

seek a safer seat than available locally, a process that sometimes entails trying for acceptance in a number of places before being selected. Party members in a constituency usually favor local figures, however, and the most frequent cause of complaint against local selection committee choices in 1970 centered around this issue.

According to British election law, any citizen who is twenty-one years old or over—unless he or she falls in the oddly juxtaposed categories of peers, clergymen of the Roman or established Church, lunatics, criminals, or bankrupts—may become a candidate for Parliament by filing papers on nomination day signed by two registered voters (who are called nominators) and by eight other registered electors who "assent" to the nomination. There are no primaries, as in the United States. In practice, the decision on the candidate is made by the constituency organizations. A small subcommittee canvasses available candidates, often seeking central office advice in the process, for national endorsement of a candidate is required by the central offices for all those carrying the official party label. The two to five most promising persons are then brought before the twenty- to sixty-member selection committee—the Executive Council of the Conservative constituency association, or for the Labor party the General Management Committee—to speak briefly and answer questions. After their choice is made by ballot it is subsequently considered by a general party meeting which rarely dissents.

In 1970, most of the selection procedures within the two major parties were for Conservatives since Labor had brought in large groups of young members both in 1964 and 1966. In many cases selection of the candidate was tantamount to election, for in the five previous general elections and ensuing by-elections fought on the 1955 constituency boundaries, 470 seats had been won invariably by the same party, leaving only 160 which had changed hands. Moreover, the outcome in a number of these latter seats also seemed fairly likely. Thus, in practice, it was the selection committees rather than the electorate that chose most of the members of the 1970 Parliament, a fact that poses the same problem for British democracy as the "solid South" has done for the representative system in the United States.

Every candidate must deposit the sum of £150, the money to be forfeited if he or she does not receive one-eighth of the total number of votes cast in the election. This financial provision is intended to restrict frivolous candidacies; its effect is to place a heavy burden on the smaller parties that have relatively little chance either of electing their candidate or even saving their deposit. It may be asked, in fact, why parties and candidates facing hopeless odds continue to contest elections. The Liberals, for example, put up 332 candidates of whom 182 lost their deposits, costing the party £27,000 ($64,800).[11] But the excitement of campaigning and the sheer zest of putting forward their ideas seems enough to keep a constant supply of candidates for hopeless efforts and parties feel the need to keep their supporters alert and encouraged. Indeed, an election may be the only time that the party platform and slogans are paraded locally, and those who believe firmly in their cause find this justification enough for the effort.

Long before he files his nomination papers, an official party candidate begins to "nurse" his constituency, showing himself in public as much as possible, joining local clubs, meeting the voters, and generally making himself well known and popular. Conservative candidates, who often have considerable personal wealth, discover that every charitable organization in the constituency expects a financial contribution; and although Labor's less affluent candidates can hardly hope to win popularity in this fashion, they compensate for their handicap by the assiduity with which they visit, advise, and help the residents of the district, often becoming a combination of errand boy and father confessor whose time and services are expected to be at the disposal of every voter.

The impact of a "familiar" candidate may be considerable over a period of time. If, as has been estimated, a well-known and popular candidate may make a difference of 1 to 3 percent in the vote, this margin may be enough to swing the election. Careful observers of variations in regional or local swings from the national pattern suggest that a candidate's

[11] In 1970, 406 of the 1,837 candidates lost their deposits: 6 Labor, 11 Conservative, 182 Liberal, 58 Communist, 42 Scottish Nationalist, 25 Welsh Nationalist, and 82 others.

personal following is the most likely source of the difference.

THE AGENT

In addition to a candidate, a well-organized constituency has an agent, whose job it is to know the intricacies of the election law and to see that his party does not violate it, to direct the work of fighting a campaign, and, between campaigns, to build an organization and prepare the strategy for victory. During an election he is the nerve center of the party organization, assigning workers to the places where they can do the most good, watching the plans and activities of the opposing parties, sensing the feelings of the voters, discovering the greatest threats to victory in time to meet them, and generally keeping all the threads of party organization and activity in his hands. The agents are really professionals, trained by their parties and having their own professional associations. A successful agent may be promoted to a job in a better-paying constituency or in the party's central office. Candidates are dependent upon agents for advice on their campaign activities (although an occasional candidate attributes his political success to the flouting of his agent's instructions), and it is the agent who must plan meetings and arrange and supervise the collecting of signatures and the filing of nomination papers, the securing of committee rooms and meeting places, and the printing and distribution of publicity and advertising.

The extensive use of trained constituency agents has been a striking development in party organization since the war. The Conservative party has by far the largest and best-trained group of agents. In 1970, they had 439 certified agents, some of whom acted for more than one constituency. Only a small proportion of their constituency organizations, mostly in Scotland and Lancashire, had to depend on volunteers. In contrast, the number of Labor's full-time constituency agents had dropped from 204 in 1966 to 149 in June 1970. In the remaining constituencies, Labor had to depend on volunteers, a number of whom had acted as election agents in previous elections but some who were recruited at the last moment. Most Labor constituency organizations appear to have counted on the summer to prepare for the election and were thus less ready for the election campaign than were Conservative constituency organizations.

ELECTION EXPENSES

The amount of money that can be spent *in the election period* by any candidate in any constituency is limited by law, the exact figure depending on whether the constituency is rural or urban and on the number of voters it contains. Limits of expenditure were raised in 1969 from £450 to £750 ($1,800) plus 2d. per elector in county seats and 1½d. in boroughs. These limits result in astonishingly low expenditures by American standards (e.g., Edward Heath spent only $2,590 during the election period).[12] It must be noted, however, that no limit is placed on the amount of money that can be spent *before* an election is called.

In addition to the limitation on actual election expenses, there are heavy penalties, including forfeiture of election, for bribery, "treating," exerting undue influence, declaring false election expenses, and incurring expenses without the authority of the candidate or election agent (a device that prevents private persons from spending money to help their candidate, thus evading the restrictions). There are lighter penalties for paying to convey voters to the polls, publishing propaganda without an imprint, paying for music, banners, ribbons, and other marks of distinction, paying private electors for advertising, publishing false personal statements about a candidate, and disturbing election meetings. Party agents receive elaborate instructions from headquarters warning them of all the pitfalls. The services of bands may be accepted only as a free gift, and even a cup of tea at campaign headquarters must be paid for to avoid a charge of "treating."

These restrictions are intended to equalize electoral opportunities, but it is doubtful whether they serve much purpose. The funds spent by constituencies and central offices, and

---

[12] Total election expenses in 1970 for the 1,837 candidates were listed as $3,342,710, and personal expenses of candidates, like hotels and traveling, which are not subject to limitation, as $175,641. The larger electorate, due to the lower voting age plus the increase in permissible spending, increased the totals over those in 1966.

by the candidate himself outside the three weeks of the formal election period, are far more important. It is clear that the Conservatives will always have an advantage in the money at their disposal, and this cannot be removed by such rigid provisions governing expenditures in the last stages of the election. Probably only a bipartisan political fund distributed according to votes cast in the election would do so. What is more important than immediate pre-election spending is the quality of research at central headquarters and the organization and activity in the constituencies, and it was here that the disparity between the resources of the two major parties was most telling.

THE LOCAL CAMPAIGN

The foundation of the local parliamentary campaign is the canvass. It is the aim of each party to call on every voter in the district, both to give out literature and to learn, if possible, how he will vote. Elaborate and secret records are then compiled, on which the party bases its campaign. No party wastes its time on those who are going to vote for its opponent, but the parties do need to know who their supporters are so that they can be sure to get them to the polls; and they want to know who is doubtful so that they can tell where to concentrate their energy.

Much of the work of canvassing and compiling records is done by women. The Conservatives profit from the leisure of women in the upper classes; but even in the Labor party women often have more time than their husbands and are better able to find a free hour or two in the afternoon to attend meetings, work at headquarters, canvass, or collect dues. Regular meetings are held to keep them informed of current events, and such meetings may perform a social as well as an educational and political service. It is noteworthy that all parties have large women's organizations and that Labor has five seats reserved for women on its National Executive Committee, two of them in the constituency section.

The most effective events in a campaign used to be the formal meetings addressed by candidates and prominent party leaders. Political use of television and other forms of national propaganda have added a new and powerful dimension to campaigning. What has surprised both parties, however, is that far from reducing interest in meetings, television appears to strengthen it, although the older type of formal session is much less popular than more spontaneous street meetings. And if at such meetings there are fewer bands and less ornate decorations than at American party rallies, in one sense the meetings are livelier than their American counterpart. Heckling has been turned into a fine art, and the candidate must expect to be harried and interrupted by sharp, witty, and inconvenient questions. The test is often one of his good humor and presence of mind rather than of his principles, and a quick and clever response can sometimes do the candidate more good than the most carefully prepared speech.

The best picture the voter receives of the candidate's position is contained in the "election address," a pamphlet of three or four pages mailed to the voters post free. The pamphlet usually contains a picture of the candidate, a statement of the principles and issues in which he is interested, and the events that have distinguished his career. According to the post-election Gallup survey, 53 percent of the 1970 electorate said they had read at least one election address, the highest percentage since 1959. Although centrally produced literature and posters were ordered, their bulk was three times less than in the peak year of 1951 and even then had been relatively small compared to the flood of local material.

No issue appeared to dominate the campaign. Those most often mentioned were high prices, taxes, unemployment, and the Common Market (although it figured little in national campaigning). Although race relations had become more tense since 1966, and Enoch Powell provided the most striking speeches of the 1970 campaign, there were none of the racial slogans, obscenities, or bitterness that had marred the 1964 campaign. This was largely because of the determination on both sides to play down the divisive and potentially explosive immigration issue. Housing and abuse of the social services were mentioned occasionally to canvassers but few purely local issues. One candidate declared the campaign had been

MAP OF THE GENERAL ELECTION, 1970

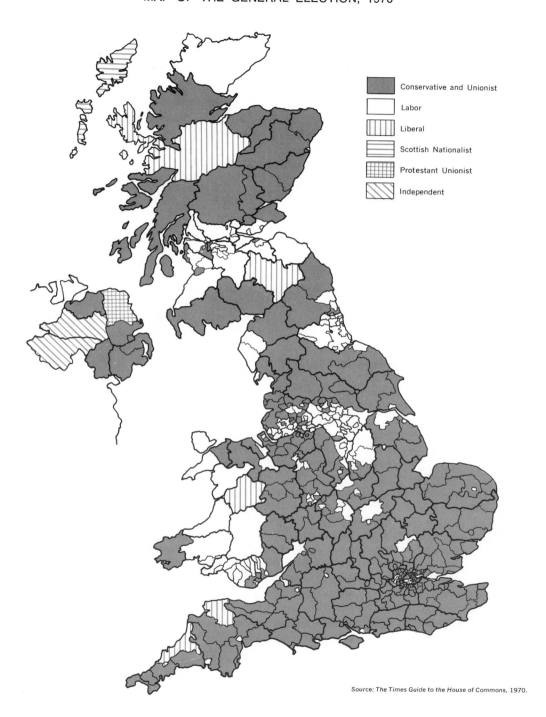

Conservative and Unionist

Labor

Liberal

Scottish Nationalist

Protestant Unionist

Independent

Source: The Times Guide to the House of Commons, 1970.

"without issues." Heath awakened only mild feelings on both sides whereas Wilson, although hated bitterly by some Conservatives, was almost universally admired for his "cleverness." One acute observer remarked: "The people wanted Wilson but not Labour, the Conservatives but not Heath." But it was Heath they got, perhaps particularly because the Conservatives had the superior organization and brought out the vote.

One place where organization had a potent influence was on the postal vote, which may have determined the outcome in at least six to eight constituencies. A wide source of dissatisfaction over the June election among Conservative voters revolved around plans for holidays abroad at that time, not in itself an adequate justification for voting by mail. Moreover, more people were eligible for postal votes in 1970 than in 1966 because the register was three months older and because the 1969 Representation of the People Act permitted postal voting for people moving within the same urban area. Although the proportion of voting by mail only rose from 1.9 to 2.1 percent, 730,000 persons were enrolled on the absent voters register, and 84 percent of these voted, 2 percent less than in 1966, but an average of 973 per constituency. Estimates are that the postal vote divided 75:25 down to 60:40 in favor of the Conservatives. In 32 seats the number of postal votes exceeded the Conservative majority, but it was probably decisive only in about one-quarter of them. Nonetheless, 6 to 8 seats form a considerable proportion of the Conservative majority of 30. Whether publicity, canvassing, and organization determined the outcome in the other 12 to 14 constituencies in which the Conversatives had the narrowest majorities is more debatable, particularly in the light of the significance of Labor abstentions.

ELECTION RETURNS

Eighty-eight constituencies changed hands in 1970, and the Conservatives made a net gain of 66 seats, both records for any postwar

The National Results, 1945–70

	ELECTORATE AND TURNOUT	VOTES CAST	CONSERVATIVE	LABOR	LIBERAL	NATIONALIST †	COMMUNIST	OTHERS
1945 *	73.3%	100%	39.8%	48.3%	9.1%	0.6%	0.4%	1.8%
	32,836,419	24,082,612	9,577,667	11,632,891	2,197,191	138,415	102,760	433,688
1950	84.0%	100%	43.5%	46.1%	9.1%	0.6%	0.3%	0.4%
	34,269,770	28,772,671	12,502,567	13,266,592	2,621,548	173,161	91,746	117,057
1951	82.5%	100%	48.0%	48.8%	2.5%	0.5%	0.1%	0.1%
	34,645,573	28,595,668	13,717,538	13,948,605	730,556	145,521	21,640	31,808
1955	76.8%	100%	49.7%	46.4%	2.7%	0.9%	0.1%	0.2%
	34,858,263	26,760,493	13,311,936	12,404,970	722,405	225,591	33,144	62,447
1959	78.7%	100%	49.4%	43.8%	5.9%	0.6%	0.1%	0.2%
	35,397,080	27,859,241	13,749,830	12,215,538	1,638,571	182,788	30,897	61,619
1964	77.1%	100%	43.4%	44.1%	11.2%	0.9%	0.2%	0.2%
	35,892,572	27,655,374	12,001,396	12,205,814	3,092,878	249,866	45,932	53,116
1966	75.8%	100%	41.9%	47.9%	8.5%	1.2%	0.2%	0.3%
	35,964,684	27,263,606	11,418,433	13,064,951	2,327,533	315,431	62,112	75,146
1970	72.0%	100%	46.4%	43.0%	7.5%	2.4%	0.1%	0.7%
	39,364,297	28,345,678	13,145,082	12,179,573	2,117,659	672,356	38,431	192,577

* University seats are excluded: other 1945 figures are adjusted to eliminate the distortions introduced by double voting in the 15 two-member seats then existing.
† Including all types of Irish Nationalist.

Source: David E. Butler and Michael Pinto-Duschinsky, *The British General Election of 1970,* p. 353.

election. The Conservatives won 1 seat from the National Democrats, 5 from the Liberals, and the rest from Labor. Labor won 6 seats from the Conservatives, half of the latter's 12 by-election gains between 1966 and 1970, 2 from the Liberals, and 2 from Scottish and Welsh Nationalists. They lost 1 to Independent Labor (the elderly gentleman who refused to withdraw), and 1 to the Scottish Nationalists. Ulster Unionists lost 2 seats, 1 to a Protestant Unionist, and 1 to a Catholic Unity candidate. In sum, 542 constituencies returned the same party as in 1966, but the changes provided a Tory victory that was both surprising and decisive.

The swing in voting, even in marginal seats, showed an equally striking degree of national uniformity. No section of England and Scotland showed less than a 2.6 percent swing to the Tories. The swing was most marked in the Midlands and Leicester; lowest in rural Wales, ship-building Merseyside, Humberside, Tyneside, and most of Scotland. The Liberals, whose vote sank almost everywhere, for the first time won no seat outside the West Country, Wales, and Scotland. The Communists did worse even than usual. The Scottish and Welsh Nationalists made gains in votes only in the most remote rural areas.

On a longer-range projection, the change in the political balance between the cities and the rest of the country became still more apparent. Of the eighteen seats the Conservatives won for the first time since 1945, none were in London and only one, Leicester, was in a big city. Labor, on the other hand, held on to twenty seats— fifteen of them in London or another big city —which they had never won in the 1950s. But as in the past, both parties polled substantial percentages of votes in most constituencies.

In general, the pattern of party support continued. The Conservatives continued to secure more support from older citizens than from the young; women also tended to be more Conservative than men but by the same degree as in 1966. The middle class, including white-collar workers, continued to vote either Conservative or Liberal. But while manual workers, however affluent, remained staunchly Labor, their activists were sufficiently disgruntled as a result of Barbara Castle's 1969 Trade Disputes Bill to cut down their efforts to get out that vote.

If the defeat of a party that was ahead in the polls at the moment of dissolution was unprecedented, so had been Labor's recovery from its 20 percent deficit in the polls a year before. However much the Conservatives could cheer their victory and, in particular, their leader, the only one among them who had never lost confidence in a Tory victory, the electoral result seemed less a positive than a negative one: the lesser of two evils. The electoral future can be expected to depend even more than usual, therefore, on the voters' reactions to the Conservative record in office.

4   EFFECTIVENESS OF THE BRITISH PARTY SYSTEM

By now it should be possible to hazard certain answers to the questions asked at the beginning of this chapter.

CHOICE OF CANDIDATES AND POLICIES

In the first place, certain critics charge that the choices offered by the major British parties are narrow and unnatural. Human interests and human desires, they point out, are almost infinite in their diversity; to force them all into one of two molds is to destroy the representativeness of the system and to oblige people to vote, not in favor of a program for which they feel genuine enthusiasm, but against the program they dislike the more.

Paradoxically, other critics make exactly the opposite complaint. Extreme Conservatives and Laborites protest that the programs of the two parties, in appealing to the uncommitted voter in the middle, have become so similar that each has sacrificed its essential beliefs and made any real choice impossible. Left-wing Laborites feel that their party is too lukewarm in its socialism and makes too many concessions to the middle-class element. Thus they charge that left-wingers are compelled to vote, on election day, not for the radical program they would prefer but for a milk-and-water reformism that completely misrepresents their attitude. Similarly, many an old-line Tory of the Colonel Blimp vintage finds himself horrified at the Conservative party's acceptance of many features of a collectivist society. Yet, since there is no way in which he can vote clearly and unmistakably for the old England of the ruling classes and the vested interests, he votes reluctantly for a program in which he does not believe. Both of these groups would charge, in short, that everybody in England is obliged to accept the kind of program that appeals, in particular, to the lower middle classes.

Party representativeness

Another paradox arises when one questions the representativeness of the parties. It is the extremists and the militants—that is, voters who are not typical of the electorate as a whole—who are most likely to join a party organization. Thus the party that is most representative of its rank-and-file faces difficulties in working out a program that is representative of the community in general. In this sense, extreme democracy inside the party may be a handicap to democracy outside, and the giving of authority to a party's leaders may actually increase the representativeness of the party's program. For it is the extremists who find it most difficult to compromise and who are most willing to take a noble, unyielding, and doctrinaire stand. But the responsibilities of the party's leaders are considerably broader. They are expected to lead the party to victory, and for this they have to win the support of those who are not party members. The party members will vote for them anyway: they have nowhere else to go. It is the uncommitted voter who must be won. Thus the party's leadership is more concerned with finding a program that can attract the support of the community in general; it will stop only at that point where a loss of enthusiasm on the part of party workers will provide a counterbalancing threat to success in the election.

Intraparty organization

It is natural, however, for members of both great parties to complain about the lack of democracy in party organization: in the Conservative party, it is charged, the leader and his chosen associates make the crucial decisions, and the rank-and-file are free only to cheer and to "recommend"; in the Labor party, it is charged, trade union votes dominate the party conference. In any case, the parliamentary leader may refuse to accept its decisions. No system, say the complainants, so undemocratic in its foundations can possibly be democratic in its results.

To some extent, the Labor party has worked out more democratic procedures that the Conservative. There is more participation in local organizations. Moreover, through the mechanism of the party conference the rank-and-file have an opportunity to challenge party policy, to cross-examine party leaders, and to take part in a vigorous debate that has a powerful psychological influence. At the same time, through its predominance in the NEC, the leadership can usually prevent the party from taking action that would alienate a large number of uncommitted voters. Thus the leadership is held responsible to the rank-and-file of the party not in the sense that it is subject to their dictation but in the sense that it is forced to listen to criticism and to justify its policies. This is the case also within the parliamentary party, where backbenchers discuss issues freely and often critically with their leaders, though less so when the latter are in office.

In the Conservative party the balance is different: the personal power of the party leader is greater, and the prestige of the party conference is less, although the leadership now undergoes the kind of cross-examination and participates in the kind of debate that characterize a Labor conference. Yet, as we have seen, the parliamentary party can be ruthless in deposing a leader if he appears out of step or ineffective. Thus if immediate checks on the leader are less obvious in the Conservative party, the ultimate controls tend to be more drastic.

PARTY EFFECTIVENESS

One last paradox concerns the effectiveness of each party in responding to public demands and needs, for here too a restriction on democracy within the party may be said to contribute to democracy on a national plane. The high degree of party discipline exercised over members of Parliament and sometimes over constituency organizations can cause charges of intraparty dictatorship; yet it is only a disciplined party that can ensure the execution of the policies for which the party was put into office. Freedom for each party representative to follow his own conscience or whim may mean the failure of the party as "an effective instrument for carrying out the judgment of the voters once they have made a choice of parties."

In making the parties such an effective instrument, the two-party system performs an essential function. The voter might make a more accurate choice and one closer to his own ideas if there were a greater variety of major parties representing each gradation from reaction to revolution. But there would be no guarantee, and in fact the probabilities would be all against the possibility, that any one party would receive a majority of the seats in the House of Commons and thus be in a position to carry out its program. If no party exercises control, no party can be blamed or praised for what results. Under a two-party system, however, so long as a party is well disciplined, responsibility cannot be evaded. If a party has a clear majority, it has no excuse for not governing effectively.

PARTIES AS AGGREGATES OF GROUP DEMANDS

While it is clear that in a democratic society parties compete in the market place for consumers' votes, it should be equally clear that in what is so largely a managed economy, they also act to aggregate the demands of producers' groups and to arbitrate between their claims. We have already noted how parties may themselves create future demands through their policies, particularly since those policies are likely to create environments within which some groups fare better than others. The system thus works in a circular fashion, with parties and interest groups interacting constantly with each other. Thus parties are sometimes called "switchboards with a bias."

Interest groups are themselves significant channels of communication, without which the political system could not be truly representative or, indeed, democratic. At the same time, interest groups have different aims, objectives, and membership from political parties. Interest groups are concerned to exert pressure, not to take power; their objectives are usually sharply focused; and their membership is limited to one section of society. In the intricately constructed industrial society of the day, there are vast industrial complexes, which serve as their own pressure groups; protective organizations concerned with the interests of their members, whether these be business or labor or the professions or sport or motoring; promotional groups urging a particular cause; informal groupings such as churches, which may on occasions take an active role in a national issue like arms for South Africa; and interests that cut across these more sharply defined concerns. In focusing so directly upon party organizations and votes in this chapter, there is a danger of appearing to suggest that only parties and election time are important in the representative system, whereas the interaction between government and interest groups and between opposition parties and interest groups is continuous and essential to the health of the system. Paradoxically, the more such channels of communication bring their information and their special positions to the parties and react to their programs and policies, the more broadly representative the latter are likely to be.

CONCLUSION

By this time it should be evident that many of the criticisms made of the British party system cancel one another out and that it is impossible for this system, or any system, to meet some of the criteria of an effective and democratic system without simultaneously departing from others. In achieving a balance of the various desiderata, however, the British have not been unsuccessful. The choice presented to the voter, even if a moderate one, is clear and real, for there are significant differences between the policies and performance of the two major parties, similar though they may be in many respects. Special groups and interests, like those of the colored immigrants, however, often find it difficult to get adequate presentation of their needs, although they are increasingly calling attention to themselves. Since parties and programs attempt to attract as many voters as possible, they inevitably seek to appeal as broadly as they can, rather than to express the positions of their most militant party members. This watering-down process necessarily leads to dissatisfaction but is a consequence of broad representativeness. In neither party do the rank-and-file have direct control over the decisions of their leaders; but in both parties, channels have been developed for applying great pressure upon the leaders. And finally, the two-party system, by virtually ensuring that one party will win a majority of the seats in the House of Commons, provides that party with the effective power to govern responsibly.

4

The
British
Parliament

The functioning of Parliament, and especially of the House of Commons, is crucial to the relation between the British public and their government. Once an election is over, the leaders of the majority party assume responsibility as the government, become vested with vast independent powers, and are aided by a vast bureaucracy. The purpose of Parliament is to analyze the character and likely effect of the legislation it is called upon to consider, to serve as a public forum for debate on matters of national concern, and to protect individual liberties by investigating cases of injustice caused by governmental action. Through these activities, Parliament not only seeks, or should seek, to make the government defend its policies in public, but it also seeks to inform and alert the public to the implications of government policies. For the House of Commons must prepare public opinion as well as represent it. In both senses it is the essential hinge of democracy.

The working of the British political system, and particularly of the "mother of Parliaments," has long been held up as a model to other countries and, indeed, widely copied by countries of the Commonwealth of Nations. But increasingly, and especially in the past few years, both the system and the operations of Parliament have been sharply criticized. As the business of government has grown in scope and complexity, the Cabinet's control over the timetable and subject matter of parliamentary business has vastly increased. Formal opportunities for criticism have been taken over almost entirely by the opposition frontbench.

Under these circumstances, there have been limited opportunities for the active backbenchers of either party to participate effectively in the parliamentary process. Their frustration and that of those who have elected them is part of the malaise that has been affecting British political life.

Much of the focus of recent attention has been on parliamentary procedures and on the need for more aid and better facilities for MP's. There has been a wealth of proposals from inside and outside Parliament that have aimed at providing more scope for individual members and more support for their efforts. More measures of reform have been introduced recently, in fact, than for scores of years. This process is far from concluded. For this reason and because it is not yet sure that all the reforms which have been introduced will be maintained, the description in this chapter of institutions like specialized committees, and even of legislative procedures must be seen to record a particular stage of change and not some assured resolution of the difficulties that caused the reform movement. Indeed, it is clear that there remains much still to change.

The efforts to reform the workings of Parliament are not unlike those that have attempted—so far without success—to crack the seniority system in the United States Congress. Both seek to make procedures more flexible and to provide younger members who have new ideas and experience with opportunities to break through traditional procedures so as to have their own direct impact on the formulation of policies. In the United States, the problem centers on the tenacious hold on the powerful committee structure by those, mostly from the South, who have succeeded in securing reelection over and over again. In Great Britain, the problem is not only the procedures as such but their reflection of the rigidities of party government and party discipline. In both countries, economic problems overshadow debates on the allocation of resources. In both, the press, radio, and, above all, television skim the cream of controversy and highlight "hot" issues before they reach the floor of the legislature. But in both countries, the legislature is the institutional center of the continuing democratic process.

It is particularly important, therefore, for Americans to understand not only the major differences between their own and British representative institutions but also the common problems that afflict them. On the one hand, the problem may be one of deadlocks, on the other that of railroading, but common to both is the sense that neither the elected member nor the electorate is having the impact on decisions that democracy assumes. The steps of change are often slow, and taken individually they may appear minute. But they represent continuing creative efforts to make the institutions of government correspond to the assumptions and purposes of democracy. As such they are vital to the health of the political process.

1   THE HOUSE OF COMMONS: ITS MEMBERS

In light of the critical comments heard so often about the "decline of Parliament" as an effective factor in the determination of policy, it might be expected that the caliber of its members would steadily decline. But such, in practice, is not the case. The prestige of being an MP in Great Britain is far higher than that of being a member of the House of Representatives in the United States. For one thing, the term of office is commonly much longer; for another, the House of Commons is the obvious center within which the drama of political action and power is played out. And although, in practice, certain committees of the House of Representatives exercise far more independent power than does any group in the British Parliament apart from the Cabinet, there is still a sense of collective importance that continues to attract to the Commons men and women of wide experience and impressive ability.

There have been many specific studies of the social, educational, and occupational characteristics of MP's in particular Parliaments. These studies tend to show that, on the whole, the representation of Labor is more diverse and, in this sense, more representative than that of the Conservatives, who continue to draw from a fairly narrow social group. The crucial feature for both is that the representative is a *party* man. Samuel Beer in *British Policies in the Collectivist Age* [1] has differentiated between four types of representation that have been characteristic at different periods: what he calls the "old Whig theory" of representing particular interests, ranks, orders, and estates; the mid-nineteenth century "Liberal" theory that representatives should be individuals who are independent of interests; the "Radical" theory of representing the people as a whole as against either individuals or interests; and the "collectivist" theory of contests between two major parties. Clearly it is the latter which now predominates.

The 630 members of Parliament elected in June 1970 nearly all came into politics after World War II, for 78 of those holding seats (49 Labor, 27 Conservatives, and 2 Liberals) had decided not to stand.[2] The age balance of

---

[1] Beer's "collectivist" theory also highlights the impact on policy of the functional representation of producers' and consumers' groups, an impact exercised very largely on the administration, which is responsible for the execution of what he sees as widely accepted general policy.

[2] On average there is a turnover of one-fifth of the membership of the House of Commons through deaths and retirements in any five-year term. Tory MP's average age forty when they enter the House, and retire about age sixty-three, after twenty-three years in Parliament; Labor MP's enter on average at forty-five years of age and remain until sixty-six, that is, twenty-one years in the House. Sixty-three MP's retired at the end of the 1966 Parliament. Only 5

The House of Commons, 1945–70

	1945	1950	1951	1955	1959	1964	1966	1970
Conservative	213	298	321	345	365	304	253	330
Labor	393	315	295	277	258	317	363	287
Liberal	12	9	6	6	6	9	12	6
Others	22	3	3	2	1	0	2	7
Total	640	625	625	630	630	630	630	630

Source: David E. Butler and Michael Pinto-Duschinsky, *The British General Election of 1970*, p. 354.

the new House did not change perceptibly, however, and its youngest member is still Bernadette Devlin, twenty-three in 1970. For the first time, no Conservative under thirty was elected, although five Labor candidates under thirty won seats. The most surprising feature of the 1970 House is the large number of MP's, 150, who had been elected for the first time—83 Conservatives, and 64 Labor, and 3 others—the largest number of new members since 1945. Twenty-one of the 48 Conservatives who had been defeated in 1966 (of whom 6 had been returned in by-elections thereafter) and 6 of those who had lost their seats in 1964 secured election.

The social profile of the Tory MP in the 1970 Parliament does not differ materially from the earlier stereotype of male, public school, and Oxford or Cambridge, comfortably well-off, and in the professions or business, although some commentators have called them a more socially minded and politically sophisticated parliamentary group. Thirty-eight members of its left-wing ginger group, the Bow Group, were elected instead of 17 in the former Parliament. They are balanced, however, by 30 members of the right-wing Monday Group, 10 elected for the first time. Moreover, a spot check after the election suggested that 33 of the new MP's were sympathetic to Enoch Powell's position on immigration.

One hundred and sixty-seven Conservative MP's have been to public school and university, and 80 to public school alone. Eton continued to provide 18 percent of all Tory MP's, only slightly less than the 24 percent in 1951, and

1970 MP's had served continuously since before the war; 7 others had experience in prewar Parliaments; and 4 had entered in wartime by-elections.

Oxford and Cambridge 52 percent, the same figure as in 1951. Forty-five percent of all Tory members are in the professions, with barristers far in the lead with 60 MP's, followed by the armed services with 24. Eighty Tory MP's are company directors and 101 in all in business, compared to 140 in the professions. Thirty-one are said to be farmers (but not whether they have large or small holdings) and 30 journalists. The working classes remain virtually invisible, with only the 2 same trade unionists (the one elected 1955 and the other in 1964) holding Conservative parliamentary seats. Among the 330 Tory MP's, 15 are women and 9 are Jews (an increase in both cases from earlier Parliaments). The vast majority of Tory members are nominal Anglicans (Episcopalians in American parlance); 13 are Catholic.

Labor representation in the 1970 Parliament, particularly among its new members, is increasingly similar to that of the Conservatives. Labor is also heavily male (only 10 women members, the smallest number since the war); 53 percent are university educated (although with a higher percentage at other universities than at Oxford or Cambridge), and 60 have been to public schools, although only 7 of these had not also gone to the university. The majority seem nominal Anglicans, although 40 Labor MP's declared they are agnostics, atheists, or humanists (designations to which no Conservative MP would admit), 31 are Jews, and 22 Catholics. Forty percent are in the professions, including 56 teachers (school through university, whereas the Conservatives number only 6), 34 barristers, and only 3 from the armed services. Only 10 percent are in business, 28 in all, among whom only 4 MP's are company directors and 10 company executives. Most notable, working-class representation has sunk from 37 percent in 1951 to 26 percent in 1970. While 112 of those elected were sponsored by trade

unions, and 17 by the Cooperative party, the actual number of workingmen among Labor MP's has steadily diminished.

Of the new Labor MP's, 32 are from the professions, 11 from business, and 1 a housewife. Of the 10 who might be termed workers, 2 are railroad clerks in administrative positions and 2 are draughtsmen. Only 2 miners, 1 construction worker, and 1 seaman can genuinely be looked on as manual workers.

It is worth noting what a change in the composition of the House of Commons these similarities indicate. The rise of Labor had introduced into Parliament something of the class division that prevailed in the rest of the country. While the Conservative benches continued to look like those of the nineteenth-century House, that is, gentlemen of means who were the product of similar education and ways of life, those on the Labor benches were often manual workers who had themselves known economic hardships. Trade union representatives long continued to be drawn from such a group, but even they now display more middle-class characteristics. Thus the House has once more acquired a relative similarity in the background, training, and professions of the members on both sides, although there remain distinctively different attitudes on most issues.

PRACTICAL EXPERIENCE

The House continues to include a wide occupational distribution, which means that many of its members have some direct personal experience with particular social institutions and aspects of the economy discussed by that body. In the American Congress most of the members are lawyers, and it is obvious that the duties of a lawyer and legislator are easily combined; but in the House of Commons less than one-fifth of the members are lawyers. Organized interests in Great Britain are not limited to attempts to *influence* members of Parliament; some of their own group *become* members of Parliament. Ronald Butt quotes the Chancellor of the Exchequer at the time, James Callaghan, in a speech of July 3, 1965, as saying he did not think of Conservative MP's in the Finance Bill debate as representing particular constituencies but "I look at them

Occupation of Elected MP's, 1970

	CONSERVATIVE	LABOR
	Elected	Elected
Professions		
Barrister	60	34
Solicitor	14	13
Doctor/Dentist	6	7
Architect/Surveyor	3	2
Civil Engineer	1	2
Chartered Secretary/ Accountant	6	6
Civil Servant/Local Government	12	3
Armed Services	24	—
Teaching		
University	1	13
Adult	2	10
School	6	33
Other Consultants	14	9
Scientific Research	0	5
Total	149	137
Business		
Company Director	80	4
Company Executive	14	10
Commerce/Insurance	3	5
Management/Clerical	1	7
Small Business	3	2
Total	101	28
Misc. White Collar	1	3
Private Means	4	—
Politician/Political Organizer	10	11
Publisher/Journalist	30	27
Farmer	31	1
Housewife	1	1
Student	—	—
Local Administrator	1	3
Total	78	46
Clerk	—	4
Miner	—	22
Skilled Worker	2	33
Semi/Unskilled	—	17
Total	2	76
Grand Total	330	287

Source: Adapted from Butler and Pinto-Duschinsky, *British General Election of 1970,* p. 302.

and say, 'investment trusts,' 'capital specula-
tors,' or 'that is the fellow who is the Stock
Exchange man who makes a profit on gilt-
edged.' " [3] Labor has its miners and metal workers. Both sides, although in varying numbers,
have teachers, doctors, engineers, and farmers.
And many of these persons belong to special
interest groups like the Federation of British
Industries, the National Farmers' Union, the
British Medical Association, and so forth. It is
generally known to what interest a particular
member belongs, but formal disclosure has
been proposed. It does not appear, however,
that the existence of such interests runs counter to party allegiance and leads to cross-voting.
On the contrary, as the chancellor's comment
was intended to suggest, the presence in the
House of persons with special expertise and
experience is welcomed. The Commons gives
special attention to speeches based on such
knowledge and experience, and the presence of
such persons is looked on as added strength to
intelligent discussion.

THE ROLE OF AN MP

Since the House of Commons is the visible
expression of the principle of representation,
it is important to examine the role of the MP
from this angle. An MP is first and foremost
a member of a party. He also has special responsibilities to his constituency. In the third
place, his personal conscience may impel him
to take certain stands. A British MP, therefore,
must balance these three roles.

No one doubts that in the eyes of those who
elected him, as well as of his party leaders, the
party label predominates. To a considerable
degree this involves obedience to the party
whip. It may also, however, involve opportunities to influence the policies of a party behind
the scenes (see Section 5). Backbench influence
is commonly greater when a party is in opposition than when it is in office, but in its later
years of office Labor Cabinet members, and
often the prime minister, met on a regular
weekly basis with the parliamentary party both
to secure constituency reactions and to engage
in discussions on policy. Moreover, during the

same period there was increasing leniency by
those in charge of party discipline, especially
in the Labor party where it used to be extremely
rigorous.

Increasing attention is now being given also
to the role of an MP in relation to his constituency. In the first place it has been suggested by
data drawn from 1955 to 1959 [4] that the nature
of a constituency can be correlated more closely
than formerly believed with policy positions
taken by MP's on certain issues. On the sensitive question of attitudes to immigration, however, responses to a questionnaire sent in March
and April 1969, when correlated with voting in
February 1969 on the Sandys' motion for a
stricter immigration bill, seem to suggest that
party position rather than constituency racial
composition determine attitudes.[5]

A more important question—the role of the
MP in mobilizing consent within his constituency—has been highlighted by Samuel Beer.[6]
Mobilizing consent means educating constituents on those matters that are not publicized
during the general election but which come up
subsequently in response to changing conditions and new needs. Although unlike an American congressman a British MP is not bound
by the rule of residence, it is common for him
to maintain at least a center within the constituency, to perform numerous services for its
members, and to keep them informed on the
progress of parliamentary business, a process
simpler in Great Britain because constituencies
have many less members than in the
United States. Beer believes, however, that the
MP could do much more than he does now
to provide what he calls "a more continuous,
intimate interchange between authority and
those subject to authority." This requires not
only access by members of the governing party
to the discussions on which policy is based, but
also, as is continually pointed out, better facilities for understanding, explaining, and thus
criticizing what government is doing. In a time

---

[3] Ronald Butt, *The Power of Parliament*, p. 461.

[4] Samuel E. Finer, H. B. Berrington, and D. V. Bartholomew,
Backbench Opinion in the House of Commons, 1955–1959.

[5] Robert C. Frasure, "Constituency Racial Composition and
the Attitudes of British M.P.'s," *Comparative Politics*, 3
(2) (January 1971), pp. 201–10.

[6] Samuel H. Beer, "The British Legislature and the Problem
of Mobilizing Consent," *Essays on Reform, 1967,* ed. by
Bernard Crick, pp. 81–100.

like the present when so much depends on the public's response to governmental decisions, this role of stimulating awareness of the purposes to which action is directed may well be one of the most important functions of the MP.

The third issue, of individual conscience, is far from unimportant. There are issues, like the attitude of Labor members to nuclear disarmament, which are accepted as matters of conscience. But there is also a broader range of matters, as discussed later, which is now seen to have implications for conscience. This is suf-

ficiently sensitive both from the side of the individual member and of the whips to make it more difficult to generalize than in regard to the two other aspects of the MP's role. It should be noted, however, that the opportunity to raise questions related to civil liberties, to provoke investigations in particular cases, and to vote on such decisions as whether to return Dr. Robert A. Soblen to the United States, to which he was being extradited at the time he sought asylum in Britain, are related to personal convictions that differentiate them from more general issues of national policy.

2   THE HOUSE OF COMMONS: ORGANIZATION

CEREMONIES

The average visitor is likely to be deeply impressed by the amount of ceremonial in the House of Commons. Most afternoons at 2:30 and Friday mornings at 11:00, as the House convenes, the Speaker in wig and gown marches in solemn procession through the central hall to the chamber to the shout of "Hats off, Strangers!" With him go the chaplain in his robes and the sergeant-at-arms bearing a sword. The Speaker ascends his canopied throne, the chaplain reads the 67th Psalm and three short prayers, the doorkeeper shouts, "Mr. Speaker at the Chair," and while those members who feel less need of divine guidance stream into the room, the House of Commons begins the business of the day.[7]

This procedure is a daily event. When a new session of Parliament opens (generally once a year), there are additional ceremonies. The peers in their crimson robes and their wives in satins and tiaras assemble in their chamber, the Earl Marshal and the Lord Great Chamberlain stepping backwards precede the black and gold sword of state and the dusty red cap of state held aloft on a little stick, and the reigning monarch and royal family enter and take their seats. The Commons is then summoned to the bar of the Lords' chamber by the "Gentleman Usher of the Black Rod," an officer bear-

ing an ebony rod with a golden tip. Here it listens to the queen read "the speech from the throne," outlining the policies for the coming session and what legislative action will be taken. In reality, of course, the speech has been prepared by the Cabinet. Nonetheless, when the Commons returns to its own chamber, it promptly passes a motion returning "humble thanks" to "Her Majesty" for her "Gracious Speech."

Before the discussion begins, one more tradition must be complied with: the House must listen to the first reading of a bill "for the more effectual preventing of Clandestine Outlawries" —not because the danger of clandestine outlawries is so great that action must be taken before the queen's message can be attended to, but as a sign that the Commons has the power in its own right to proceed with legislation without the queen's recommendation. In fact, so slight is the pressure for the bill that it is then and there abandoned, to be introduced again in identical form at the beginning of the next session. The House in the meantime moves on to debate the reply to the "Gracious Speech."

Customs of debate

During its debates the House observes certain characteristic customs. Members never address one another directly or call one another by name. All remarks are addressed to the Speaker,

---

[7] While Parliament is in session, the flag flies from the tower, and at night a light shows.

and other members are referred to as "the honorable Member for South Hackney" or the "honorable Member for Bootle" or whatever the member's constituency happens to be—unless, indeed, there is some additional distinction. Thus members of the Cabinet and of the Privy Council are referred to as "the right honorable gentleman, the Member for Limehouse," or Woodford, or Warwick and Leamington. Lawyers are "honorable and learned" gentlemen, officers are "honorable and gallant," and the sons and daughters of peers are addressed as "the noble lord" or "the noble lady."

Whenever a new member makes his maiden speech in Parliament, he humbly asks the forbearance of the House, and at the close of his speech the next speaker (who is generally a member of the opposing party) congratulates him on the success of his effort, assures him that, although he does not necessarily agree with all of it, he has listened with great interest, and expresses the hope that there will be many times in the future when the House may have the pleasure of hearing him on subjects in regard to which he has special competence. Similarly, when a new Cabinet minister makes his first speech, the next speaker for the opposition congratulates him on his appointment and on the success of his speech before he proceeds to attack the points that the minister has just made.

When the debate is over, the House of Commons also has its peculiar way of taking votes. If there is any doubt in the Speaker's mind as to where the majority lies, or if the minority demands a "division," bells are rung and the policemen in the lobbies and corridors shout, "Division." After two minutes the Speaker puts the question again, two tellers come forward from each side, and the members rise from their places and march into the lobbies. Those who vote "aye" go into one lobby, and those who vote "no" go into another. Six minutes are allowed for late arrivals from smoking room, writing room, restaurant, and corridor. Then the doors are locked, the members are identified and counted, and the tellers come forward to report the result to the Speaker, those representing the majority standing on the right facing the Speaker and those representing the minority on the left.

The case for "quaintness"

To foreigners the daily ceremonial, the pageantry of the opening session, the response to the summons of Black Rod or to the cry of "Division," the fictions concerning the "queen's speech," the exaggerated courtesy with which members are referred to may appear either quaint or ridiculous, and in either case useless. Nothing could be further from the truth. No parliament can retain the respect of its people—and indeed no parliament can transact business—if it is in constant turmoil. The ceremonial and the exaggerated deference and courtesy help to produce an atmosphere of mutual respect.

On the first day of a new Parliament, new members are warned of the conduct expected from them in the House. Ordinarily, a gesture from the Speaker is enough to quiet the House. If a disturbance breaks out, the Speaker simply rises from his seat, and the bickering members usually subside. If one of them continues to be obstreperous, the Speaker as a last resort can "name" him, and the House (including his own party) votes immediately for his suspension. But an apt comment, humor, and ensuing laughter are more common ways of keeping the House on an even keel.

This does not mean that the discussion is a lukewarm, milk-and-water affair. Courtesy and formality are thoroughly compatible with aggressiveness, sharpness, and vigor; and understatement can be as telling as overstatement. The art of the graceful taunt has been highly developed, together with the art of the witty but cutting rejoinder. Moreover, members are aware that the eyes, if not of the country, at least of the press are upon them, and when they wish to hit, they hit hard. The fact that they call one another "honorable" and congratulate one another on their delivery does not prevent the most vigorous criticism—yet it helps to keep the debate on the level of rational discussion and good humor and to prevent it from degenerating into a purposeless row.

THE SPEAKER

The smooth functioning of the House depends on the Speaker. Once the spokesman of the Commons before the monarch, the Speaker is now the regulator of debate. A major part of his function is to ensure the government efficient handling of its business. This role dates back to a famous occasion in January 1881 when the Irish members were attempting to bring all parliamentary business to a halt (not unlike a filibuster), and the Speaker on his own authority moved a closure. The following year, Gladstone introduced procedural changes that mark a watershed in the management of parliamentary affairs. Members henceforth lost their cherished right of moving the adjournment of the House in order to discuss any issue and this procedure was restricted to only those matters accepted by the Speaker as of urgent public importance. Government control of the House was assured. Other forms of closure followed, to which, however, the Speaker must agree. Since 1918, the Speaker has been empowered to select the amendments on which a vote will be taken, and in other ways he sees that government business proceeds smoothly, although with due attention to the most serious objections raised to a particular measure.

But the Speaker is also the protector of the rights of the opposition, the private member, and the public. In a recent far-reaching relaxation of restrictions, the Speaker was empowered in 1967 to determine when there is "a specific and important matter which should have urgent consideration." This provision enables the House to debate at short notice urgent foreign or domestic situations whether or not they involve ministerial responsibility.

Not only does the Speaker make such far-reaching decisions, on which he is not required to justify himself, but together with the whips he also determines who participates in a debate. The leaders of both major parties and representatives of minor parties can be expected to speak, but opportunities for backbenchers are apt to be slim. In one explanation of the order of debate the Speaker announced that:

> I have worked out a list of about 30 names covering, I hope, most interests and, geographically, most areas, but that leaves something over 70 who will be disappointed. Naturally, in these circumstances, I have had to disregard, to a great extent, the claims of maiden speeches, and I am sorry to say, too, that I have had to

disregard many old Members who have not spoken yet in this Parliament, but I really could not work them in under the scheme that I have adopted.

At the same time, backbenchers naturally look to the Speaker to give them as substantial opportunities as possible. They cherish the words of Colonel Douglas Clifton Brown in 1945: "As Speaker, I am not the Government's man, nor the Opposition's man. I am the House of Commons man and I believe, above all, the backbenchers' man."

It is this view of the role of the Speaker that led to backbencher protests over the selection of Selwyn Lloyd as Speaker in January 1971 to replace Horace King, Labor's first Speaker, who had resigned because of age after performing superbly in the position from 1965 through 1970. Agreed upon mutually by both the Cabinet and the shadow cabinet, Lloyd brought a wealth of experience to the office, including continuous representation of the same constituency since 1945, Lord Privy Seal, and Leader of the House, in which latter role he showed particular sensitivity to the interests of backbenchers. But Labor backbenchers resented their own lack of consultation in the nomination, and some went so far as to nominate a startled and unwilling candidate at the last moment and finally to vote against Lloyd. He was overwhelmingly confirmed, but in the future a more open method of selection is assured.

Once selected, the Speaker rises above the parliamentary battle and breaks his ties with his own party. If a new election results in a victory for the opposition, he continues in office (in the United States he would be replaced); and he is proposed for reappointment by the leaders of the party to which he does not belong. In fact, once chosen, the Speaker retains his office until death or voluntary retirement.

For a long time, there was also a tradition that the Speaker of the House of Commons should be reelected without opposition. In 1935, 1945, and 1964, however, the Labor party, to maintain the vitality of its local constituency organization, contested the reelection of the Conservative Speaker in his own district, but with notable lack of success. The Conservatives did not contest King's seat either in 1966 or in 1970, although representatives of minor groups did so unsuccessfully. It seems, therefore, that the electorate is as determined to maintain the tradition that the Speaker should be reelected to the House as the parties have been to maintain the tradition of reappointment within the chamber.

THE WHIPS

The effectiveness of the parliamentary system is almost as dependent on the party whips as on the Speaker. It is the business of the whips of each party to keep in touch with party members, to inform them what business is coming up and when a vote is going to be taken, and to see to it that they are present to vote as their leaders want them to. The chief whip of the majority party is the parliamentary secretary to the treasury (sometimes still referred to as the "patronage secretary," although patronage is not what it once was or what it still is in the United States). Three or more lords commissioners of the treasury assist him, as do the comptroller and the vice-chamberlain of the royal household. All these officials draw a salary from the government, and there may, in addition, be a number of unpaid whips. Opposition whips work without official pay.

Reputation to the contrary, it is more important for the whips to be tactful, sympathetic, observant, and likeable than to be fierce. They must know what the private members are thinking, for the whips are the principal channel through which the party's leaders learn of the feeling of the rank-and-file. They must identify the rising young members of their party. They try to keep the members in line through good temper and reasonable appeals rather than threats and a display of force; but they also know how to suggest to the erring member the perils of party unorthodoxy. They must know what the opposition is likely to do next and what tactics will be most successful in getting business through the House with the least expenditure of energy and risk of embarrassment.

The word *whip* is also used for the notice sent to each party member listing Parliament's business for the week. If an item in this list is not underlined, there is no special reason for the member to be present; and if it is underlined only once, the matter is not very pressing. A *two-line whip,* however, means that the business is really important; and if an item is underscored three times, nothing should keep the member from voting.

Informal agreements

Gladstone once commented that the British constitution "presumes more boldly than any other, the good faith of those who work it." And it is, in fact, chiefly through voluntary and informal agreements, based on this good faith, that the House decides on its business and gets it done. What efficiency the House has is mainly the result of the ease with which the opposing parties enter into arrangements "behind the Speaker's chair" and "through the usual channels" to determine what shall be discussed, when it shall be discussed, and how much time shall be allotted to the discussion. A breakdown of this system of voluntary agreement, such as occurred over the use of closures to push through the Industrial Relations Bill early in 1971, vastly complicates the working of the parliamentary system as a whole.

Under the normal method of arranging matters informally, the whips of the opposing parties (who are the "usual channels") consult with the leaders of their parties and then with one another "behind the Speaker's chair." The opposition whips may agree to speed the debate on certain measures if the majority's leaders in turn agree to discuss certain topics in which the opposition is especially interested. Without arrangements of this sort, Parliament might have the best rules of procedure in the world and still be an outstanding failure. When a select committee of Parliament investigated the procedure on public business in 1931, the prime minister at the time, Ramsay MacDonald, told its members: "I must pay my tribute to the 'usual channels.' They are simply admirable. Whenever a reasonable arrangement can be made it is made. . . . I do not know how you could do your work in this House without the 'usual channels.' "

THE CHAMBER

If the House of Commons in action is ceremonious, it is also extremely intimate. The room in which it meets is a small one: there are seats for only 346 members on the floor, although in normal times there are somewhat more than 600 members; there is no space even for desks. At one end of the room is the Speaker's throne, and in front of the throne sit three clerks, in wig and gown, at the head of a long table holding books, documents, and two dispatch boxes. Five benches run along either side of the Speaker, the table, and the center aisle. On the Speaker's right sit the members of the majority party, with their leaders (the Cabinet ministers) occupying the front bench, which is called the Front Treasury Bench. Directly opposite them, on the other side of the table, the shadow cabinet (the leaders of the opposition) occupies the front opposition bench. There is no gradation or middle ground. One's position must be taken frankly, for or against the Cabinet.

On ordinary occasions there may be only forty or fifty members in the House (a quorum is only forty), and the front benches may be relatively empty; but at question period and for

Floor of the House of Commons

great debates members flock into the chamber, fill the seats, overflow into the gallery, and stand about the sides, lending a feeling of excitement and drama, of history in the making. This is most impressive and tends to make the speakers themselves eager to rise to the occasion.

The smallness of the House has an important influence on the nature of the debate. In such a chamber it would be foolish to engage in oratorical pyrotechnics. The members are on the same level with one another—there is no rostrum from which to harangue the assembly. If they speak from the front benches, half of their audience is behind them. If they speak from the back benches, half of the audience has its back toward them. The opposition sits only a few feet away: there is no need to shout in order to make it hear. Indeed, the leaders of either party can address one another almost in conversational tones across the table. They may, upon occasion, strike the table or the dispatch box for emphasis, or indulge in a restrained gesture, but there is little temptation to play to the grandstand. It is easy for members to make interjections, ask questions, and carry on a running debate that is serious, intimate, and not devoid of flashes of wit.

There is, in fact, a much admired and carefully cultivated "House of Commons style"— easy, casual, conversational, characterized by presence of mind and equability of temper. Occasionally, as in the case of Lloyd George or Winston Churchill, brilliance in speech will win great admiration; but in general the House prides itself on giving its attention to men who may be clumsy in their expression but who are deeply sincere or thoroughly competent to speak on the subject in hand. The rules of debate revolve around the three "r's": relevance, repetition (to be avoided), and reading (which is not permitted). The members themselves know the tricks of addressing crowds in their own constituencies, and they have no desire to listen to an eloquent windbag. The man who can impress them is the man who knows his business. No audience, in short, is a better judge of capacity and of character.

3 THE HOUSE OF COMMONS: ITS WORK

It used to be said that the principal job of the House of Commons is to make, to support, and to overthrow ministries. Strictly speaking, a ministry consists of about ninety or more offices of ministerial rank filled by members of the party that has the confidence of the House of Commons. About twenty of the most important ministers comprise the Cabinet, and the decisions of the Cabinet are binding on all ministers. The British also use the word *government* much as Americans use the word *administration* when they speak of "the Nixon administration" or a "Democratic administration." Thus, in practice, the terms *Cabinet*, *ministry*, and *government* tend to be used interchangeably.

According to Bagehot's classic work on the English constitution, "The House of Commons lives in a state of perpetual potential choice: at any moment it can choose a ruler and dismiss a ruler." Today, however, this statement has lost its meaning. With the extension of the suffrage from 1867 on and the growth of party organization and party discipline, the occasions on which the House of Commons is in a position to expel a majority government are virtually nonexistent. Only in those exceptional cases when no party controls a majority of the seats in Parliament (as in 1923–24 and 1929–31) is the ministry unstable; and even then it is not necessarily unstable, for divided opponents are unlikely to wish to force an election. Labor's slim majority between 1964 and 1966 placed its members under great strain but did not prevent it from executing major and extensive legislation. It takes a major crisis, and, indeed, a deep split within the party itself, to force the resignation of a government composed of the leaders of a party with a majority.

But this is not to say that the task of the opposition is futile. In the first place, the opposition exists to demonstrate that there is an alternative government. It must also seek to demonstrate that it is a credible alternative and that if it were in office it would be more effective, more intelligent, and more concerned for the interests of the public than the government in power. This is difficult. Action is always more newsworthy than criticism. In the crucial areas of foreign policy, defense, and the state of the pound, the opposition will be reluctant to lay itself open to the charge of "irresponsibility" by making criticisms that might damage the interests of the country as a whole. Nonetheless, Labor's attack on British policy in Suez in 1956 created a great national debate with far-reaching consequences for both parties and the allegiance of the electorate. Moreover, the opposition, if sufficiently sensitive, can capitalize on swings in public opinion, such as the discontent with austerity, which the Conservatives exploited in 1951, and the social-democratic appeal to the frustrated middle class, which helped to bring Labor into power in 1964.

The second major function of the opposition is to keep to the fore a sense of alternatives. Its criticisms may sometimes sound like caricatures of what the government considers its honest efforts to seek worthy national policies, but its role is to attack. The adversary procedure of the law courts, with its deliberate exaggeration of the strong points of both the prosecution and the defense, is also characteristic of Parliament. Indeed, one of the useful results of the need to oppose is sometimes the production of an alternative plan, as for example on immigration, that may lead to modifications in what the government decides to propose. There is no doubt that the role of the opposition is an arduous and, if long sustained, a frustrating one, but it remains at the core of what Parliament has been designed to do.

PROCEDURES FOR CRITICISM
IN THE HOUSE

The organized opposition has its best opportunity to criticize governmental policy as a whole when it raises the amendment to the queen's "Gracious Speech," which is, of course, a review of the Cabinet's position and legislative plans. But it also has a further twenty-nine Opposition Days (technically called Supply Days but always used to raise questions of

policy rather than the appropriation) that may now be scattered through the session and, as always, focused on any topic it wishes. Moreover, traditionally there are three two-day debates on the Consolidated Fund (of which one, by convention, is at the disposal of backbenchers to raise any subject they like). In response to appeals for more topicality of such debates, four half-days can be earmarked for debates on pressing subjects raised at no more than forty-eight hours' notice.

These guaranteed opportunities provide the opposition with 25 to 30 percent of parliamentary time. In addition, the opposition may ask for special facilities to attack the Cabinet's policy in general or to discuss some especially important issue. If the opposition "demands a day" for a *motion of censure*, the Cabinet will find time for a debate in the near future. On such occasions each side brings forth its biggest guns. The prime minister and the man seeking to take his place, the leader of the opposition, face each other in a type of direct contest for which there is no equivalent in the American system. The press and the public are both watching to render their verdicts on the relative competence of the two parties. The Speaker's power to authorize a debate on "a specific and important matter which should have urgent consideration" is yet another means of providing the dramatic spectacle of verbal thrust and counterthrust by two opposing forces, which rivets attention upon the House.

Backbenchers have their particular opportunities to raise issues on the *motion for adjournment*, commonly debated during the last half hour (10 to 10:30 P.M.) of the day's business. Originally the Speaker allocated the subjects for debate from a list submitted to him, giving preference to an individual or constituency grievance, but more recently members have balloted for all but one of these sessions.

THE QUESTION PERIOD

The most famous of parliamentary devices for securing information, publicizing government errors or omissions, safeguarding civil liberties, and keeping the administration alert and responsive are questions. A former clerk of the House has called them "the one procedural invention of the democratic age." [8] They have no counterpart in the American or in Continental legislative systems.

Four afternoons a week for the first hour (apart from prayers) of the sitting of the House of Commons, ministers give oral answers to questions that have been submitted to them in writing and in advance by a member of the House from any party, including the one in power. If he wishes, the questioner or, if called upon by the Speaker, any other member may then ask one or occasionally two supplementary questions on the spur of the moment for the minister to answer. There is thus this added element of suspense for the minister and his advisers as well as for the spectators.

Due to the great increase in the number of oral questions without any corresponding increase in the total time allocated, the only person who answers questions every week is the prime minister, who always does so at 3:15 P.M. on Tuesdays and Thursdays. These are naturally the high points of most weeks, and the press and public galleries are usually crowded at those times. Ministers have been placed on a known rotation system that brings them to the top of the list about once in five weeks.

To prevent clogging the period allocated to a particular minister, no starred question (that is, one for oral answer) can be requested more than twenty-one days ahead of his turn to answer. Even so, it is far from certain that a questioner will succeed in getting an oral answer. In 1959, there was an average of 131 questions a day on the order paper (which is printed each day and distributed to the members and visitors) of which 41 and 52 supplementaries were answered.[9] Members can also get written answers to their unstarred questions, but there is no obligation to answer a written parliamentary question on the day for which it is requested. Moreover, question time is unique in its opportunities for publicity. It comes at the start of the day's business when the House is fullest, and a striking comment may even be reported in the evening papers.

While oral answers are still by far the most desired, the cumulative effect of vast numbers of unstarred questions (for example, Ernest Marples requested sixty-eight on a single day, July 14, 1969, asking about procurement arrangements in eight different departments) can also be great. Another technique for making a special impact is for a number of members to put in approximately the same question on a particular matter. Since the answers are printed and circulated, they have considerable political impact as well as ability to shake the department concerned.

To evaluate the total effect of oral and written questions is difficult. They are, naturally, only a "spot check" on government operations. Since, however, no minister or civil servant can guess what questions will be asked during a session, the questions keep a certain tension in the administration that is useful. It is always possible for a minister in a sensitive area like foreign affairs to reply that it is not in the public interest to disclose the information requested, but this is rare. It is also possible, and indeed common, for departments like the Treasury to resist the most pointed inquiries, a good reason for the more searching investigations through the ombudsman and select committees, of which more will be said later. But with all caveats, the spectacle of the prime minister and his ministers appearing on the floor of the House to answer specific questions put by members for their own information or to publicize a complaint by one of their constituents is an impressive one. It is a major way of demonstrating the sense of public responsibility of the leaders of the government, and it is a sharp testing time for ministers, particularly new ones.

THE PARLIAMENTARY COMMISSIONER FOR ADMINISTRATION: THE OMBUDSMAN

A parliamentary question is the traditional and obvious way in which an individual can appeal through his MP against what he considers unfair or improper handling of his interests by a government department. The volume of such complaints means, in practice, however, that only those that are of genuine political importance either to individual rights or to

[8] Lord Campion quoted in D. N. Chester and Nona Bowring, *Questions in Parliament*, p. 269.

[9] D. N. Chester, "Questions in Parliament," *The Commons in Transition*, ed. by A. H. Hanson and Bernard Crick, p. 98.

public policy can be considered by this means. There are also other problems besides lack of time connected with questions. A minister may be uncommunicative; only the department itself has access to the files related to a particular case. The famous Crichel Down case in 1954 (described in Chapter 5, Section 1) of an arbitrary departmental action was only made the subject of an independent inquiry leading to a reversal of the decision after long and persistent nagging of the government both inside and outside Parliament.

To provide a further flexible instrument for investigating complaints against the operations of central government departments, Parliament in 1967 adapted a widely publicized Scandinavian institution known commonly as the ombudsman and officially named the Parliamentary Commissioner for Administration. The particular British form of this institution is careful not to remove from the MP the primary responsibility of seeing that his constituents do not suffer injustice at the hands of the administration. On the contrary, it is for the MP alone to decide whether the complaint is appropriate for reference to the parliamentary commissioner. Moreover, in order not to overlap with existing parliamentary powers of investigation, complaints against local government, the police, and public corporations (see discussion of select committees below) are excluded from the commissioner's purview.

As with so many British institutions, the full range of the commissioner's responsibilities and powers is still being worked out. He reports to the MP on each case referred to him and provides an annual report to Parliament on the scope of his activities. The Select Committee on Parliamentary Privilege, set up in November 1967 to examine these reports, provides a significant reinforcement of his role. Major questions regarding the exercise of his functions are whether he has the right to criticize a ministerial decision, and whether he should indicate publicly in his reports where the blame and responsibility lie for particular maladministration within a department. Both actions were originally criticized on the ground that they could undermine ministerial responsibility, and both were upheld by the select committee as being the purpose of the act which established

the commissioner's office. In other words, the committee rejected the notion that ministerial accountability involves the complete anonymity of civil servants. It also implied that a thoroughly bad rule, as well as a bad decision about how to implement it, falls within the definition of maladministration, which the commissioner is empowered to investigate and determine. Yet the acceptable limits of the commissioner's decisions are still being worked out in relation to the wide range of practical situations he is called upon to investigate.

By the end of 1968, 542 MP's had referred complaints to the commissioner's office, 374 cases had been examined and the MP's provided with reports, while 727 complaints had been rejected as outside the commissioner's jurisdiction. So too were 808 written complaints received direct from the public.[10] Some of the cases, like delay with tax refunds and permission to remain in the country, resulted in the relevant department's providing compensation or finding alternative ways of meeting the request. In other words, the type of decision appears generally to be related to alleviating an individual hardship. But the fact that the resolution of such cases is made at all reflects a loosening of inflexibility in departmental rulings, which is precisely what is desired. What seems still needed is a more precise definition of what an "aggrieved person" means in terms of the statute, more freedom for the commissioner to make his own investigations without waiting for a specific complaint to be referred to him, and better reporting to the press of the investigations in particular cases. Some critics would maintain that what is needed most of all is a thoroughgoing system of administrative law on the French model (see Chapter 7, Section 4), but that seems a far from likely possibility.

THE MOVEMENT FOR
PARLIAMENTARY REFORM

The establishment of the office of the parliamentary commissioner was one response to the pressure for parliamentary reform that was

[10] Geoffrey Marshall, "Parliament and the Ombudsman," *The Commons in Transition,* ed. by Hanson and Crick, pp. 123–24.

swelling during the early 1960s and reached a peak in 1966 when Labor was returned with a comfortable majority and Richard Crossman became the innovative but realistic Leader of the House. The Labor members of the 1960s were of a new type, strongly committed to the Labor movement as such but much more professionally trained and experienced than had been common in the past. Many of them had been engaged in decision-making at the local level and felt frustrated by their lack of power within Parliament. Committed to improvements in administration, education, social services, taxation, they found themselves without effective instruments of inquiry into the actual working of government machinery.

In 1966, the Cabinet approved in principle the establishment of specialized committees but on one condition: that the departments whose work they would examine should agree. In what was emphasized as "a sessional experiment," two new specialist committees were set up, one on agriculture and one on science and technology. They received the traditional power of select committees "to send for persons, papers, and records"; in addition they were given the specific authority to examine witnesses in public and, at least the second of the two committees, to employ some outside consultants. Although the "usual channels" appear to have suggested noncontroversial subjects for them to examine, in practice they plunged into highly significant issues: the nuclear reactor program, and the Ministry of Agriculture's plans for studying the effect of joining the Common Market on the British subsidy and price review system.

The pacemaker for these two specialized committees was the Nationalized Industries Committee, set up in 1955 as a result of backbench Conservative pressure to examine the reports, accounts, policies, and practices of the nationalized industries (see the fuller description of nationalized industries in Chapter 6, Section 2). The committee had proved its usefulness and become a permanent part of parliamentary machinery, but its value as a precedent was somewhat limited by the fact that it was largely confined to considering technical matters on which the government kept its hands off, and not the general issues of policy affecting nationalized industries on which the parties so sharply disagree.

Select committees have long been a means of investigating and reporting on a particular problem. In the nineteenth century, much important legislation resulted from their reports. With the growth of party divisions, the investigation of controversial subjects like the coal mines, social security, local government, population, and the civil service has been generally handed over by common consent to prestigious if often ponderous *Royal Commissions* composed of outside experts or to more flexible executive-controlled departmental committees. As with other innovative proposals of parliamentary reform, the whips have been nervous that select committees dealing with matters of public policy may undercut the responsibility and authority of the government. Thus in an era of specialization, there still remains official pressure to keep parliamentary procedure unspecialized.

The argument in support of more specialized examination of the detail of administration is, however, that under modern conditions it is no longer possible, if it ever was, to conduct government by general rules. The more government becomes involved in social and economic policies—and in Great Britain it is highly involved in the management of both—the more the citizen is affected by specific decisions. If Parliament is to scrutinize effectively the performance of government, its members must be equipped with better tools for securing information and for evaluating the specific impact of general policies. The use and disuse of select committees, and also the facilities available for MP's to secure and make use of their own information, are relevant to these facts. So also are they to Parliament's special role of keeping public opinion alert, informed, and energized, for it is not enough to have the data without the techniques of communication. The most penetrating report in the world will have no public impact if it remains buried in the files. The number of those who read the daily Hansard (the published record of parliamentary debates) is infinitesimal. If Parliament is to compete with more spectacular but less important news, it needs to use the media more effectively.

Specialized committees after 1966

The experiment of using specialized committees had a somewhat checkered but quite impressive history after 1966. A third Committee on Education and Science was set up in 1967; and subsequently committees on overseas aid and development, Scottish affairs, and race relations and immigration; the Committee on Agriculture, despite its protests, was terminated, however, in February 1969, with indications that such departmental investigations would shift fairly often; the Committee on Science and Technology has survived the change of government, and the Conservative leadership appears to have accepted the value of investigations by select committees in fields that are "noncontroversial," in the party sense. Its Green Paper of October 1970 (Cmnd. 4507) suggests retaining the subject matter of specialized committees on the nationalized industries, science and technology, race relations and immigration, and Scottish affairs, along with a Select Committee on Expenditure that would have a wider role than the former Estimates Committee, enabling it to examine the policies behind expenditures and even to question ministers on them. This is a substantial advance on the pre–1966 situation.

On balance, it seems fair to say the new specialized committees provided a more radical advance in parliamentary scrutiny of administration between 1966 and 1970 than had been anticipated or was, perhaps, appreciated. A number of useful reports were written. To a certain degree, backbenchers came into their own through this new type of check on the executive.

Yet there have also been problems to take into account. Backbenchers have complained about the heavy load placed upon them by committee assignments, with those in the new, specialized committees added to the eight standing committees to which bills are referred (see below), the committees on nationalized industries and the parliamentary commissioner, the Scottish and Welsh committees, and those dealing with the internal affairs of the House.[11] When the Finance Bill was also moved to committee instead of being taken on the floor of the House, it made a total of 629 committee assignments in 1969 being carried by about one-half the members of the House (one hundred or so government members and about forty opposition frontbench members do not serve on specialist committees, and another two hundred members rarely make themselves available). Thus the possibility exists that there will not be enough MP's available for work in the House or that attention will be drawn away from the latter.

In the second place, the committees have been inadequately staffed. The Agriculture Committee, for example, had less than half the time of a senior clerk. As Boyd-Carpenter, a prominent Conservative, pointed out in the debate on the Green Paper on select committees, November 6, 1970, the effective working of a committee depends on the provision of adequate and substantial staff.

The most disturbing problems that have developed are that the expert knowledge acquired by the members of the specialist committees has not had much impact on the House as a whole, and that the government has paid very little, if any, attention to their recommendations. Most of the committees have not had their reports debated and when the one on science and technology came to the floor in May 1968, there were only seventeen MP's present, including eleven committee members! Moreover, the government did not accept its recommendation on the organization for nuclear reactors.

Two more positive conclusions, however, can be put forward. A certain number of MP's have gained expert knowledge of the workings of departments, which they can contribute to subsequent debates. Even more important, perhaps, is the awareness within the departments of the possibilities of searching parliamentary scrutiny. In the 1970 session, the Committee on Nationalized Industries fought its way through a thicket of Treasury objections to the Bank of England itself, a striking demonstration that much more is possible than may yet have been achieved. While specialized committees may not have either the role or the potentialities their backers originally suggested

---

11 Some perennial select committees—the Committee on Privilege and, on a more mundane level, the Kitchen and   Refreshment Rooms Committee—deal with procedural or domestic matters of concern to the House itself.

and are certainly never intended to challenge the authority of the Cabinet, they have demonstrated capacities that have won respect as useful tools of parliamentary inquiry in a time of highly specialized governmental activity.

Facilities for MP's

The specialized committees have provided an institutionalized means for probing the workings of the administration, but many members, particularly of the Labor party, feel that it is even more important to provide more adequate reimbursement and facilities to enhance their competence in their jobs. Particularly surprising features of the position of a British MP as compared with an American congressman are the extraordinarily inadequate conditions of service that still persist. Only since 1964 have some small allowances for secretarial assistance been introduced; none of the two hundred odd desks for members and seventy for secretaries that are scattered around the buildings are private; there are few private rooms within the House itself where constituents can talk quietly with their members; there are no private telephones; and messages are conveyed only when the House is sitting. Travel is paid only between the MP's home or constituency and London during the session.

Above and beyond these major inconveniences is the lack of research aids in any sense comparable to those provided for Congress by the 243 (in 1966) persons employed by the Legislative Reference Service of the Congressional Library, one-half of whom are senior specialists engaged in research that is directly related to the needs and requests of members of Congress. In the Library of the House of Commons, there were only 19 graduate library clerks in 1970 who would "look things up" for MP's, of whom 12 concentrated on written replies to specific questions. The latter often arise because parliamentary questions have been returned with a note that the information is available in print; sometimes the parliamentary answer is found inadequate for the MP's needs. To a limited extent the library's research staff has also helped specialist committees, although in rare situations, as we have seen, there have been limited funds for outside experts.

These lacks of almost everything that an American tends to take for granted as necessary supports for efficient operations throw an almost unbearable burden upon those MP's who have no other means of securing them. And this, in turn, brings up the issue of compensation. MP's received no pay at all until 1911. Their salary has moved up by slow stages from the original £400 (about $1,000) to £3,250 ($7,800), the level existing since 1964. (In comparison, congressmen receive a base salary of $42,500, plus substantial allowances for assistance, and Canadian MP's, who may offer a more realistic base for comparison, receive $12,000 a year and a nontaxable $6,000 for expenses.) Thus British MP's must either have private resources, or hold another job in addition to their parliamentary work, or skimp the latter, or continuously overtax themselves. It is no wonder that most Labor and some Conservative members complain.

There is much to be said for making the job of MP a full-time one, particularly if committee work is to be increased. There is even more to be said for relating salary and expense accounts to services and facilities. Both should be linked to costs, either on a cost-of-living basis or by relating the salaries of MP's to those of some other group (in Norway they are tied to those of a sector of senior civil servants), so that Parliament is not placed in the embarrassing position, particularly in a time of financial stringency, of voting itself more money. The key point is to direct radical attention to meeting the reasonable needs of an MP to perform his function effectively. Only so can the work of Parliament itself be efficiently performed.

Publicity for the work of Parliament

But no matter how much more efficient the parliamentary instruments of investigation become, and no matter how effective the individual MP, Parliament will not perform a major part of its function unless it transmits to the public its own sense of urgency about public problems. It should also be able to identify for the public the issues around which controversy will subsequently center, which means before policy has already been determined. The great debates and, to a lesser degree, question period help to perform these functions. But as Parliament becomes more specialized in its attention to the detail of administration, there is need for carefully designed publicity that will catch the attention of the public and both alert and inform it. This is essential for "mobilizing consent" to the continuing operations of government as well as for raising necessary questions and problems likely to arise from legislation before it is too late.

The press is still probably the best forum through which such publicity can be handled. The press gallery is too small, but at least it exists.[12] But more could be done to identify in popular terms the issues being debated or analyzed if reporters were provided with reports well ahead of time, and "tipped off" on key issues. The Select Committee on Parliamentary Privilege, in its 1967–68 report, proposed that the House should take a more pragmatic view of alleged "contempts" in reporting matters under advisement. The current move to relax the operations of the Official Secrets Act, of which a British attorney general once said only half jokingly that it could cover "the number of cups of tea consumed per week in a Government department," is long overdue. This sixty-year-old law makes no distinction between security material and anything else and prohibits the receipt or publication of a government document unless an official has authorized dissemination. In the biggest Secrets case in years, however, in which *The Daily Telegraph*, its editor, and two others were prosecuted for issuing a report on the Nigerian

civil war that by its critical comment on federal leadership embarrassed the Labor government, although it disclosed no matter of security, the judge in a surprise decision in early February 1971 not only cleared the defendants and ordered the government to pay costs but urged the latter to consider whether the Secrets Act had not "reached retirement age and should be pensioned off." Thus it may well be that Parliament will gradually become free of the antipublicity strait jacket that it has riveted on itself. It remains one of the cherished and legitimate boasts of the British that "secret" discussions remain secret (quite unlike those in Washington that usually hit the press almost immediately thereafter), but it seems unnecessary, and detrimental to its role of public information, that such reports and, indeed, many discussions, such as those on party policies, are kept from the public.

Television, a seemingly obvious means of linking the Commons to the public, has encountered much skepticism that is probably legitimate. If debates are to be televised, they would need to be edited for showing. Oddly enough the Lords agreed in 1967 to closed circuit television. The Commons, after more than a decade of discussion, finally resolved in December 1967 "to approve the making of sound recordings of its proceedings for an experimental period for the purpose of providing for Members specimen programmes." But there seems little disposition to expand the use of this media. Its cumulative effect might well blunt the edge of interest, except on rare occasions, rather than enhance it.

4 THE HOUSE OF COMMONS: LAWMAKING

The House of Commons has so long enjoyed the reputation of being the world's greatest lawmaking body that it may be disconcerting to most people to have given prior consideration in this chapter to Parliament's role as critic and public educator. But it is of the essence of the parliamentary system that

[12] As late as 1771 it was illegal to report debates in the House of Commons; to evade punishment, editors disguised their parliamentary reports under such titles as "Proceedings of the Lower Room of the Robin Hood Society" or the "Report of the Senate of Lilliputia." Early in the nineteenth century, however, William Cobbett began to print parliamentary debates as a supplement to his *Political Register;* in 1811 the work was taken over

by his printer, T. C. Hansard, who published *Hansard's Parliamentary Debates;* and today, although the government itself now publishes the text of the debates, this record still goes by the popular name of Hansard. It is an interesting commentary on British practice that the 1762 motion forbidding reports was only formally repealed in 1968.

legislation is a function of government. The positive force exercised by government, that is, by the Cabinet, is through the making of laws. Since the Cabinet controls the votes of the majority of the members of the Commons, there is no basis for doubting that public bills will be passed if the government so determines. The crucial role in public of the opposition, therefore, and in private of the government's own backbenchers, is as far as possible to use the techniques of inquiry, discussion, and opinion-forming *before* the Cabinet has fully committed itself not only to the principle but also to the details of a measure.

On average, the House of Commons spends about half its time examining bills. The Study of Parliament Group, a private group of university professors and officers of both houses, which has been making a serious analysis of the working of Parliament since mid-1964, maintains that the Commons spends too much time on legislation and too little on general debate and scrutiny of the administration. The Procedure Committee, which devoted its 1966–67 report to public bill procedure, did not agree. It did suggest, however, that more use could be made of ways in which the Commons could get into the legislative act earlier: for example, by government publishing a White Paper (i.e., a statement of proposals on a given subject) to be debated before the bill on that subject is introduced; White Papers on all major items in the "queen's speech" and special days set aside to debate them; *ad hoc* committees to consider the form of future legislation; and a willing ear to proposals by specialized committees, as with the recommendations of the Committee on Nationalized Industries regarding the form of the public corporation for the Post Office. The Procedure Committee also foresaw a further use of select committees to consider technical measures after their second reading.

In response to these dual stimuli and his own vigorous sense of realistic innovation, Leader of the House Richard Crossman introduced in the fall of 1967 a series of procedural changes in the handling of public bills (i.e., those of general importance to the country as a whole) to "streamline" the passage of legislation. Traditionally, all legislation has moved through five stages before going to the Lords for comparable stages, resolving any differences, and receiving the royal assent: a nominal *first reading*; a crucial *second reading* on the principles and purposes of the bill; a *committee stage* that deals with detailed provisions related to the agreed purpose, unlike the process in the United States where it is the crucial stage for analysis, redrafting, and even pigeonholing; a *report* stage that reviews amendments proposed in committee; and *third reading* as a whole, in which only verbal changes can be made and the bill is either passed or rejected. Under the Crossman reforms, bills can now go straight to committee for second reading and report stages unless twenty members rise in the House to object; and third readings are formal unless six members demand a debate. Since under those provisions so much can be done through committees (which will consist of between twenty and eighty members), voluntary time-tabling and use of the guillotine (see below) are now permitted.

It remains to be seen how far the Conservative government will make use of these new provisions. Contrary to the expectations of the Labor opposition, Prime Minister Heath decided to refer the controversial Industrial Relations Bill to *Committee of the Whole House*, which is the House of Commons itself sitting under a different name, with a chairman instead of the Speaker presiding, and a more flexible procedure in which motions do not need to be seconded and the same person can speak repeatedly. Formerly, all revenue and appropriation measures were considered in the Committee of the Whole, but because this procedure is so time consuming (an average of up to one-fifth of the working time of the House was spent in this procedure over a recent ten-year period), its role as the Committee of Supply was abolished in 1966, and as the Committee of Ways and Means in 1967. At the end of the latter year, Crossman forced through on a party vote the possibility of sending the Finance Bill "upstairs," that is, to a standing committee. The Conservatives bitterly opposed this procedure, however, as removing a fundamental right of individual members to criticize so vital a measure. In practice, when the "technical" aspects of the Finance Bill were sent to a standing committee in the 1968–69 session, that procedure appeared to work so smoothly as to restrict still further the publicity the Finance Bill generally secures through providing opportunities for general debate. Thus it is far from sure that in the future the Finance Bill will go to a standing committee rather than be considered in detail by the House as a whole.

SOME FURTHER LEGISLATIVE MATTERS

In considering the process of legislation, we have already described both the traditional stages for the passage of a bill and the Crossman procedural changes. In order to make the British legislative system quite clear, it will be useful at this point to differentiate between public and private bills, to describe the standing committees to which most measures are referred, to define the forms of closure that can be used to accelerate the progress of a bill, and to describe the process of delegated legislation.

Public and private bills

Public bills, as we have noted, are those of general importance; *private bills* concern a special locality or person or body of persons. A public bill can be introduced by any member of Parliament except that only a minister can introduce a money bill. If the bill is introduced by a minister it is called a *government bill;* if by a private member, it is called a *private member's bill* (not to be confused with a private bill, which has its own special procedure). Relatively few private members' bills become law, commonly not more than one major and several minor such measures in a session.

The first problem for private members' bills is to find time not already secured by the government and official opposition. Members must ballot for the privilege of introducing their bill; even if they succeed in the draw there are further problems. The member must somehow or other manage the technical job of draftsmanship, and he must act as his own floor manager—persuading enough members to attend the discussion of his bill, both on the floor and in committee, to maintain a quorum, and persuading enough members to vote in favor of it so that there will be a majority. Finally, he

must be assured of the approval—or at least the benevolent neutrality—of the leaders of the majority party, for only those bills are likely to receive the approval of the House that the leaders are willing to see approved.[13]

The procedure for a private bill is quite different. Individuals or groups who desire its enactment simply file petitions with an official in each House called the "Examiner of Petitions for Private Bills" and with the government department most directly concerned. Persons whose interests are affected by the bill are notified, and when these conditions have been complied with, the bill is read a first time and ordered to be read a second time. Following the second reading, those bills that are unopposed go to a committee on unopposed bills, while the others are sent to a private-bills committee that holds elaborate hearings in which each side is represented by paid counsel, and witnesses with an interest in the bill are brought in to testify. The committee members act as impartial judges, and their report to the House of Commons is almost invariably adopted without discussion.

Regardless of whether it is opposed or not, the passage of a private bill is an expensive proposition. Both houses impose high fees related to the amount of money the bill proposes to raise or expend, and it is necessary to pay fixed parliamentary agent's fees as well as printing bills for the draft statute and the eight advertisements that must run in the local press and London *Gazette* before consideration. Thus, even if the procedure is straightforward, the cost may give a local authority pause.

Standing committees

Earlier in this chapter attention was focused on select and specialized committees, and mention has been made of the use of the Committee of the Whole House. The normal procedure

---

[13] These are only the major pitfalls that the private member must avoid. One can find an elaborate and grimly amusing description of the others in Sir A. P. Herbert's book, *The Ayes Have It,* which recounts the author's own difficulties in winning acceptance of a bill for divorce reform. In spite of his exceptionally good luck, it is worth noting that even one so blessed in friends and ability could not get his bill accepted without considerable assistance from the government of the day.

for legislation, however, is to go to one of the eight *standing committees*, which, to quote Bernard Crick, "are thought of as the House of Commons in miniature and not as a gathering of specialists or special interests." [14] Since 1960, there has not even been a core of members appointed to each committee. The Speaker appoints a chairman and, as required, anything from twenty to fifty members roughly in proportion to the strength of the parties in the House. Apart from the Scottish Standing Committee,[15] to which any measure exclusively concerned with Scotland is referred, and one reserved for private members' bills, there is no specialization of subject matter, although some regard is given to the interests of the members when they are assigned. Bills are referred quite arbitrarily in accordance with their position on the parliamentary timetable to whichever standing committee is ready to receive them.

Standing committees fulfill a very different role from their American counterparts. The latter each have a particular focus, for example, agriculture, education, and ways-and-means. As indicated, they provided a crucial stage in the legislative process. In Great Britain, however, a standing committee must accept the general purpose of the bill as defined in second reading and concentrate on the detailed provisions for implementing this purpose. Thus, unlike standing committees in the American system, those in Parliament are not supposed to undertake a creative consideration of the broader issues related to a particular measure, and hence they cannot call for witnesses or papers and have no research staffs. Not surprisingly, service on parliamentary standing committees is unpopular because it is time consuming and devoted to details. At the same time, the work these committees do is essential and occasionally decisive in producing a constructively framed measure.

Periodically, in the course of considering more effective means for MP's to supervise the executive, proposals are made for strengthening the committee system by making it more spe-

cialized and functional. We have seen how specialized committees have been used creatively in limited "nonpolitical" fields, but there seems little chance they would be allowed to go deeply into such topics as defense, foreign affairs, or even social security. To allow standing committees to do so is also unlikely since the executive jealously guards its prerogative in the former fields and its control over legislation in general. Some observers also feel that a proliferation of parliamentary committees to examine government work in progress, however appropriate to the separation of powers in the American system, would be dysfunctional in the homogeneous British political system in which the Cabinet and majority party are mutually supportive under normal conditions and not intended to check each other. Under these circumstances, the most constructive proposals appear to be to lower the size of committee quorums so as to provide more flexible movement of specially interested MP's from committee to committee as their subjects change. Standing committees could also usefully have more facilities, and perhaps adopt greater flexibility in concentrating on the more important provisions of a measure rather than taking up its clauses in order.

LIMITATIONS ON DEBATE

Since the demands on parliamentary time are so numerous and pressing, a variety of means have been developed to prevent filibusters and other time-consuming attempts to delay or obstruct business and thus to concentrate attention on the most important aspects of legislation. In one way or another, these means depend on the impartiality and good judgment of the Speaker, who, as we have seen, first instigated the closure, and here, as elsewhere, is the supreme regulator of the work of the House.

Of the formal devices used by the House of Commons, the most important are various forms of *closure*. Any member may at any time move that "the question be now put," and if the Speaker is willing to entertain the motion, the House of Commons must vote immediately and without further debate on the question of whether or not it desires an immediate vote on

[14] Bernard Crick, *The Reform of Parliament*, p. 85.

[15] There is also the Scottish Grand Committee, consisting of all members from Scottish constituencies plus ten to fifteen other members as needed to preserve the balance of parties, which pays prior attention to all matters referring to Scotland.

the subject under discussion. If at least one hundred members vote in favor of the motion, and if they constitute a majority of those present and voting, debate is halted and a final vote taken. Of course, a majority party always has one hundred votes at its disposal, and the provision would be open to serious abuse were it not for the fact that the Speaker refuses to accept such a motion until the opposition has had a fair chance to present its case.

There are several refinements of the closure procedure. A *guillotine* resolution may be adopted, as with the Industrial Relations Bill of 1971, assigning a certain amount of time in advance for the debate on a specific measure. At the conclusion of that time, regardless of where the debate stands, the guillotine falls and a vote is taken. In order to prevent such a procedure from concentrating debate on the opening provisions of a bill, the device of *closure by compartments* may be used to divide a bill into a number of sections, assign a certain amount of time to each, and arrange for the guillotine to fall as each subperiod of time elapses. In addition, through the use of the *kangaroo*, the Speaker may arrange to concentrate the debate upon those proposed amendments that are most important or most controversial, hopping over those that are of less consequence. Such restrictions are loudly deplored by ordinary members of Parliament, but the whips and the leaders of the great parties insist that only through such limitations can the parliamentary machine be made to work.

DELEGATED LEGISLATION

A further way of providing time and expertness is for Parliament to pass bills in general outline, at the same time delegating the power (in theory to a minister or ministers, in practice to government officials) to make rulings and regulations that will achieve the intent of the bill in specific cases. Thus Parliament sets the general purposes of the legislation, but expert administrators work out the technical details that Parliament has neither the time, the information, nor the skill to anticipate. If changing circumstances or unpredictable developments make certain rules inappropriate or obsolete, the administrators are free to make

new regulations to carry out Parliament's original purpose, and Parliament itself need not be troubled to pass new legislation.

Such a delegation of legislative authority has obvious advantages in achieving expertness and flexibility, and every advanced industrialized country has had to resort to delegated legislation in order to prevent the legislative machinery from breaking down in the face of the volume and technicality of laws demanded by the public. The question is how to maintain adequate parliamentary control.

Since June 1944, a select committee of Parliament called the Statutory Instruments or Scrutiny Committee has considered all statutory rules and orders to decide whether they violate any of the limitations of the relevant act. Only some 3 or 4 percent of administrative rules and orders must be affirmed by Parliament; about half the others lie before the House for forty days and are then considered approved if there has been no negative prayer (that is, appeal) against them. Sometimes the House is not even aware an administrative rule is on the table unless the Scrutiny Committee makes one of its rare special reports on it. In order to determine whether it should do so, the Scrutiny Committee can call departmental witnesses to explain what has been done, but it is sharply limited in checking or criticizing such action and in asking why it has been done. Moreover, despite the fact that the committee is expected to investigate "unexpected" or "unusual" use of powers, it is not allowed to question the relevant minister, on the grounds that this is the prerogative of the House as a whole: a curiously rigid and restrictive view of ministerial responsibility.

In light of the large and probably growing use of delegated legislation, these procedures seem strikingly inadequate. There is at present no clear way of determining the extent of the rights being assigned to ministers or their departments rather than to Parliament or the courts of law. The volume of orders is so great that it is almost impossible to provide adequate scrutiny in the committee's fortnightly meetings. Moreover, delegated legislation may well affect matters of principle but the Scrutiny Committee is not allowed to discuss the merits of the matters before them. Even when it makes a report to the House, there is no automatic debate on the matter, so it is left to some individual member to raise the issue—if he wants to do so.

The distinctive American answer to delegated legislation is the regulatory commission, but in the United Kingdom it is felt that such institutions would violate the close relation between the executive and the legislature. Congress itself has no procedure for reviewing administrative orders unless special provisions are written into legislation such as the Administrative Reorganization Act of 1946, which authorizes the president to propose plans for reorganization of administrative departments or agencies. In those cases the plans are transmitted to Congress and go into effect if not rejected within a prescribed period of time. Another approach is for administrative orders to be challenged in court—a practice more common in the United States than in Great Britain—to determine whether the rule is within the delegation of power and whether proper procedures have been observed. None of these practices in either country provides adequate supervision of the use of delegated legislation, but the complexity and technicality of so much of contemporary government activity make such use inevitable.

5 THE HOUSE OF COMMONS AND FINANCE

Control over the public purse strings is the great traditional weapon of popular defense against executive tyranny, and according to constitutional custom, as reinforced by statute, this power belongs exclusively to the House of Commons. All money bills must be introduced in this House, and since the constitutional crisis of 1911 the House of Lords has had no power to reject a money bill passed by the Commons.

In practice, however, the House of Commons has yielded its financial power to the Cabinet. According to the Standing Orders of the House of Commons, the House may consider no proposal for the expenditure of money that is not recommended by the Crown (that is, the Cabinet); and any proposal to reduce expenditures is considered an indication of lack of confidence. (The so-called Supply Days, formerly hitched to proposals to cut a department's grant by some infinitesimal sum, are now openly given over to general debates on subjects chosen by the opposition.) Thus, unless the Cabinet itself is willing to propose an increase in expenditure or to accept a proposal to reduce appropriations, the budget as originally proposed is adopted unchanged. So strong is the presumption that the budget will be approved in the form presented by the Chancellor of the Exchequer that the provisions are put into effect immediately following the speech in which the chancellor "opens his budget." The chancellor and his colleagues are bound by so strong an obligation of secrecy before the delivery of the speech (in order to prevent the possibility that someone might profit from the possession of inside information) that, in the fall of 1947, even the inadvertent revealing of certain budgetary proposals a few minutes before the speech entailed the prompt resignation of the chancellor, Hugh Dalton. A graver indiscretion by James Thomas, Chancellor of the Exchequer in 1936, abruptly and permanently terminated his parliamentary career.

The consequence of this system is to ensure the enactment of an expertly prepared budget that can easily arouse considerable envy in the breasts of American officials. In the United States, as in the United Kingdom, the executive may prepare a careful plan for balancing revenue and expenditure, but the United States Congress is its own master in budgetary as in other matters. Once the president's financial proposals have been set adrift on the legislative sea, they are at the mercy of the winds of congressional prejudice and special interests. Unpopular taxes may be cut; special expenditures demanded by powerful pressure groups may be added; executive departments that have incurred congressional wrath may find their appropriations drastically reduced; and the most carefully laid plans of the administration may be disrupted. During the debates on the budget many an executive agency lives in a condition of the tensest anxiety, wondering whether it may be eliminated entirely through the loss of its appropriations—a situation that is hardly calculated to encourage able men to enter public service. And there are times when any resemblance between plans for expenditure and plans for revenue seems to be little more than coincidental.

But if Americans sometimes look at the British system with envy, it leaves open many questions about how parliamentary scrutiny and public information can be provided. These are questions to which much attention has been given in recent years. The Plowden Report (Cmnd. 1432, 1961) pointed out that as far as is politically feasible debates on finance should deal with major issues affecting the formulation of government policies. The annual economic survey presented at the same time as the budget, and debated together with the chancellor's taxation proposals, is far more useful for this purpose than the annual estimates, whose form remains confusing to most persons outside the Treasury. Moreover, White Papers in 1963 and 1966 attempted to forecast expenditures over a five-year period, and this has now become customary. Many grants, of course, like those for defense, local authorities, universities, social welfare, are already determined well in advance of the presentation of estimates. Only changes in legislation are likely to affect such areas of expenditure, and these naturally are debated in Parliament.

The use of a select committee to focus attention on public expenditure has so far been disappointing. First appointed in 1912, the Select Committee on Estimates, with its six or more subcommittees, mainly occupied itself with spot checks on administrative efficiency. It was replaced in 1971 by a Select Committee on Expenditure (as recommended by the Select Committee on Procedure in December 1968) that is "to consider public expenditure and to examine the form of the papers relating to public expenditure presented to this House." In so doing, it can also question ministers, a new development. The Expenditure Committee has a general subcommittee (sixteen members) and eight further subcommittees (nine members each) that examine the activities, estimates of expenditures, and efficiency of selected functional fields of administration dealt with by government departments, such as power, trans-

port and communication, and housing, health and welfare. The total operations of the Committee on Expenditure are being evaluated side by side with those of other select committees to prevent both overlaps and omissions. Thus the whole structure of investigation is still in a mobile state.

While the purpose of the Estimates, and now of the Expenditure Committee, is to consider current expenditures and where possible to seek economies, that of the powerful Public Accounts Committee is to ensure that public money has neither been wasted nor used for purposes for which it was not intended. In this task, the Committee is immensely aided by the Comptroller and Auditor General with his large and expert staff, who are unique among administrative officials in being directly responsible to Parliament and not to the executive. Not only can the committee draw on the results of the continuous checking of departmental accounts by the five to six hundred members of the Exchequer and Audit Department of the Comptroller and Auditor General, but it can also examine its own witnesses. If the Expenditure Committee were provided with equal facilities, it might be able to catch some mistakes before rather than after they are committed. For example, in 1964 the Public Accounts Committee discovered that due to an underestimate of development costs of the "Bloodhound" missile, the company developing its guidance system had made what were termed "excessive" profits. Subsequently arrangements were made for repayment of substantial portions of the undue profits, but much trouble and expense would have been saved if the error had been discovered earlier. Here, as in so many places in Parliament's work, better facilities are needed to cope with the pressures of work and time.

Even if the process of parliamentary supervision of finance is so considerably improved, there still remain overriding problems connected with overall expenditures and investment and the relation of one form of expenditure to another (e.g., of social welfare and defense). In many ways these are the most important decisions a government makes, for they have a crucial impact on the country's rate of growth, level of employment, ratio of public and private advance, and, probably, international standing. Projections and economic analyses are helpful, and these are being increasingly provided. But it is debatable whether Parliament can be equipped to oversee these all-important issues, or whether any existing legislative body adequately does so.

6 THE PRIVATE MEMBER'S INFLUENCE

The combination of party discipline and effective rules of closure makes Parliament a remarkably efficient body in the sense of getting work done. And the most vaunted advantage of the British parliamentary system is its freedom from the sort of deadlock between executive and legislature that occurs so frequently in the United States. A good many Englishmen, however, maintain that the efficiency of Parliament is purchased at a high price. It is possible—as it is not in the United States—for the government to draw up a coherent and well-planned program of legislation in the knowledge that it will pass through the legislature without serious mutilation. But the immunity of such legislative proposals is possible, they say, only because the ordinary member of Parliament accepts his party's leadership and discipline.

Because of limitations on time, the average member only occasionally can introduce a bill of his own, and his chances of participating in an important debate are slim indeed. Moreover, only under exceptional circumstances does a member disregard the prescription of the party whips, and it is the exceptional issue on which the party whips have nothing to prescribe. One of those rare occasions came in 1964 when the House of Commons, on a free vote on a private member's bill to abolish capital punishment, demonstrated, as it had already done in 1956 under similar circumstances, its opposition to the death penalty. (The House of Lords, which had vetoed the measure in 1956, finally acceded in mid-1965.) Free votes were subsequently allowed on liberalizing the laws governing abortion and homosexuality between consenting adults (both introduced by private members). Only on such issues are parties apt to welcome the full exercise of individual conscience. The unprecedented Conservative party decision in mid-October 1971 to permit its members a free vote over entry to the Common Market, on which both major parties were seriously split, was made largely for tactical reasons.

THE BASES OF PARTY DISCIPLINE

There are several reasons why members normally respond to discipline. In the first place, the party member who regularly and intentionally defied the leadership of his party would almost certainly lose the support of both his local and the national party organization in the next election. Here it must be remembered that the ordinary member secures election only partially because of his own qualities and more particularly because he belongs to a particular party.

Behind the cruder weapons of party discipline, however, there are certain psychological considerations that exert a strong influence upon the private member. Thus he knows that if he votes against the policy of his party when it is in power, its chances of being returned to office at the next election will have been impaired. Nothing is more likely to shake the confidence of the electorate than a serious split in the forces of a party in Parliament. The Liberal party lost its power largely because of repeated splits in its ranks, and Labor's disastrous defeat of 1931 followed a similar cleavage in the party.

A member of a party may disagree bitterly with his leaders on one issue or even on four or five, but that is a very different thing from wanting the opposition to take over the government. If he disagrees with his own party on even 20 percent of its policies, he probably disagrees with the opposition on 90 or 95 percent. The discontented members of a party are usually those who are on the extremes furthest away from the principal opposition. Thus the most disgruntled members of the Conservative party are generally the reactionary Tories who may dislike the moderation of their own party but who turn apoplectic at the thought of bringing Labor into power; and the most dissatisfied of Labor's followers are the ones who are most radical and who would die before they would help to establish a Conservative government. Even if they disagree with their party leadership on an important issue, the knowledge that a serious defection will undermine its appeal and threaten to bring the enemy into power is enough to make most of them swallow their scruples and go into the correct lobby.

If there is an important amount of resentment in party ranks, however, concessions are likely to be made. Naturally, leaders are even more anxious to avoid an open party split than are their followers, and they will do much to avoid so dangerous a situation. Ronald Butt in his impressive study of *The Power of Parliament* has given a detailed and careful analysis of the situations between 1945 and 1969 in which Labor and Conservative backbenchers have tried to influence their parties' policies and even voted against them. While a government may feel that political advantage or sheer necessity impels it to go ahead in the face of strong backbench opposition, as with the "wage-freeze" provisions in Labor's Income Bill in 1966, it will only do so after the most serious consideration and efforts to persuade their followers to accede.

Butt maintains that Labor backbenchers have been "more ferociously insubordinate" [16] but at the same time less effective than Conservative backbenchers in influencing the policies of their leaders when the latter are in power. The Labor backbench rebellions between 1945 and 1951 were almost entirely over foreign policy, opposing the close alignment with the United States against the Soviet Union and urging a mediating role between the two. Twenty-three Labor members voted in December 1945 against taking an American loan, while forty-four abstained. In 1948, thirty of them voted against the government's Palestine Bill. Still more serious was the open opposition to the retention of conscription in 1946. On this occasion, as again in 1966 on Wilson's decision to maintain Britain's position east of Suez, the

prime minister went to the unusual length of calling for a virtual vote of confidence within the parliamentary Labor party, although in general party leaders maintain that their responsibility is to the House as a whole, not simply to their own party.

Labor's open divisions over foreign and defense policies undermined public confidence in 1951 and thus contributed markedly to the Conservative victory in that year just as its divisions in the late 1950s and early 1960s over both defense and the traditional commitment to complete public ownership contributed to keeping it out of office until Hugh Gaitskell and Harold Wilson managed to reunite the party by 1963. But the backbench opposition to its foreign and defense policies from 1945 to 1951 had relatively little effect on Labor's policies. This is partly because the domestic policy of nationalization was eminently satisfactory to the rank-and-file, and because the "rebellions" were localized in a special group of Labor members. It was also because in the most serious of the revolts, that over conscription, Labor leaders had not only the support of the Conservatives but also of the bulk of public opinion.

Conservatives came into office in 1951 as a party of "national unity," but almost immediately pressures developed among their backbenchers for a more distinctively Tory policy of a free market and private enterprise. Already in April 1952, thirty-nine Conservative members signed an Early Day motion criticizing the government's delay in denationalizing steel and road haulage; within a week Prime Minister Churchill announced the intention to proceed with both. Butt attributes the establishment of the Select Committee on Nationalized Industries in 1955 to Conservative backbench pressure to secure more effective parliamentary supervision of state-owned industries.[17] Conservative backbenchers, supported by powerful industrial interests, also secured the breakup of the BBC's television monopoly and the establishment of commercial television.[18] These successes were achieved mainly, however, be-

---

[16] Butt, *Power of Parliament*, p. 187.

[17] Butt, *Power of Parliament*, pp. 207–08.

[18] See H. H. Wilson, "Pressures on Parliament: The Commercial TV Affair," *Politics in Europe: Five Cases in European Government*, ed. by Gwendolen M. Carter and Alan F. Westin.

cause they were limited and specific objectives that did not run counter to their leaders' major program.

The Suez crisis of 1956 demonstrates both the effect of earlier persistent right-wing nagging at Conservative leaders to preserve British interests in Egypt and the relatively slight effect of those who opposed the forcible British and French action aimed at keeping Suez an international waterway. Only eight Conservative backbenchers abstained in the crucial vote of confidence on November 8, 1956 (it may be noted that none of the eight won seats again as Conservative members), but the obvious divisions within the party both over the action itself and subsequently the withdrawal from it (principally motivated by American and Commonwealth opposition and the impact on the balance of payments) seriously shook the party. Anthony Eden's resignation due to ill health may have avoided a more forcible ouster. Butt attributes Harold Macmillan's succession as party leader and thus prime minister instead of R. A. Butler's to the fact that the latter's opposition to the Suez venture made him unacceptable to a wide spectrum of the Conservative party.

The Macmillan government proved so sensitive to backbench opinion that in 1957 it made substantial concessions to delay the impact of its Rent Bill and even withdrew its Shops Bill. In its original form the Rent Bill would have removed at the end of six months rent control, which affected some eight hundred thousand tenants. Although they favored the principle of freeing landlords from restrictions, many Conservative backbenchers feared the potential impact on their constituents of rent hikes and tabled a series of amendments at the committee stage. The press also took up the issue. Although the period of reducing rent control was then extended to fifteen months, eleven Conservatives openly abstained when the bill came to a vote.

The withdrawal of the Shops Bill is an even better instance of the effect of backbench opposition. Although organized retail interests and the unions supported the proposed lowering of the general closing hour from 8 P.M. to 7 P.M. and late closing once a week from 9 to 8 P.M., Conservative backbenchers rushed into the fray on behalf of the "small man" whose best means of competition with large chains seemed to be to stay open longer hours. Faced with their continued opposition, the bill was ultimately withdrawn. In another case, the backbench revolt in 1964 against the Conservative government's decision to abolish resale price maintenance (the climax to a long debate within the party) was marked by its unprecedented motion for rejection of the bill on February 16, 1964, and a final, somewhat unsatisfactory resolution of the issue through compromise amendments.

Yet there were also issues over which the Macmillan government refused to budge. One hundred backbenchers tabled a motion on February 9, 1961, criticizing the government's Central African policies as too much determined by African interests, but since Labor favored still more progressive policies the government persisted. A rebellion aimed at restoring corporal punishment failed for the same reason, although sixty-nine Conservatives voted against their leaders. More serious issues dividing the Conservatives were entry into the Common Market, nuclear defense (in which the party leaders accepted heavier expenditures than they would have done without backbench pressure), and the Profumo scandal, which nearly cost Macmillan the leadership of his party. Although he survived the test, he might not have done so if there had been an obvious alternative leader.

The opposition to British entry into the Common Market was powered by older Conservative backbenchers who feared it would infringe on British sovereignty and damage British and Commonwealth agriculture. They pursued a campaign inside and outside Parliament to thwart Macmillan's effort to join the EEC. On March 21, 1962, more than thirty Conservatives moved in the Commons that the government should make it clear to Common Market countries that Britain would not join without "special arrangements to protect the vital interests in the countries of our own Commonwealth partnership." There was another comparable motion on July 30, 1962. In the end, of course, it was President de Gaulle's veto that stopped negotiations, but the division on the issue within the Conservative parliamentary party ran deep. (The Party Conference voted in support both in 1961 and 1962.) Only a substantial indoctrination process under Macmillan prepared the way for the parliamentary party to later accept Heath's position on Common Market membership.

During Labor's second substantial period of office, from 1964 to 1970, the influence of its backbenchers continued, in Butt's view, to establish broad limits within which government policy could be carried on. Backbench pressure appears to have forced the renationalization of steel on which Wilson was never very keen. Effective crossbench pressure helped to shape the 1965 Race Relations Bill, while Labor backbench influence led to dropping a proposed provision for deportation of Commonwealth citizens if "public interest" so required. The Cabinet's decision in February 1968 to limit the entry of Kenya Asians through the new Commonwealth Immigrants Bill led to a storm of protest and 62 votes against it, including 35 Labor votes, and 180 abstentions. When the new Race Relations Bill extending prohibitions on discrimination in housing, employment, and insurance was proposed in April, it was at a time of considerable tension, due to a disturbing speech by Enoch Powell. But the two front benches, although pressed by their own backbenchers, maintained a tenuous accommodation with each other and with their own more extreme followers that kept the issue from becoming the subject of a party fight.

Wilson had to meet stiff criticism from his own party on maintaining Britain's position east of Suez, and he subsequently modified the policy. Another bone of contention was American policy in Vietnam, from which nearly a third of the Labor parliamentary party demanded in a formal motion that the government disassociate itself, as did the annual conference. On appeal Wilson was upheld both in the parliamentary party and in the House, although there were thirty-two Labor abstentions. Milder methods of discipline were introduced to cover more than the traditional ones of conscience, such as religion, pacifism, and so forth. On two issues in which conscience clearly was involved—the response to Rhodesia's unconstitutional declaration of independence and maintenance of the arms

embargo against South Africa—many Labor backbenchers felt intensely and helped to stiffen the government's position.

The most serious quarrel between the Labor Cabinet and its followers and their union supporters came in 1969 over the bill to reform industrial relations and limit the scope and number of unofficial strikes. Fifty-three Labor members voted against Barbara Castle's White Paper "In Place of Strife" (Cmnd. 3888) and forty abstained. The Cabinet split. The government then decided on a much revised short bill to impose a conciliation period, dropping in the process a bill to reform the House of Lords, which was meeting strong opposition from backbenchers on both sides of the House. After substantial negotiations with the unions, Wilson decided in June 1969 to drop the Industrial Relations Bill in return for an undertaking by the Trades Union Congress to deal with unofficial strikes. The issue was thus left to the Conservative government, which assumed office in June 1970 with a clear mandate for an industrial relations measure that, paradoxically, was to be subjected to bitter frontbench as well as backbench objections by the Labor opposition and considerable nonofficial obstructionism.

This data on backbench influence and efforts helps to modify the traditional picture of backbenchers as "brute votes" herded into the division lobbies by the whips. It indicates the degree to which party leaders, particularly the whips, and the Leader of the House must keep in continuous touch with backbench currents of opinion and take them into account before launching a bill and even during its progress. Certain other features of the parliamentary scene should be added. When a party is in office, it must be concerned much of the time with a national as compared to a party approach to issues—hence the Conservative government's nationalization of Rolls-Royce—and its sharpest criticism may well come, therefore, from those of its own followers who cling most rigidly to party dogma. In general, backbenchers are much less likely to embarrass their leaders if the party has a slim majority, as Labor had between 1964 and 1966, than when it has a safe majority; at the same time, party leaders have to watch their votes as Wilson did in withholding the called-for measure on steel renationalization during that period because of the open opposition of two of the members of his tiny majority. Thus it is apparent that party government is not always dominant. But ordinarily there are strong resources at the command of party leaders that, as we suggested at the start of this section, commonly assure them success if they remain firm in their determination to push through a measure or a policy.

7 THE HOUSE OF LORDS

The efforts to make parliamentary procedures and the supervision of the administration more effective do not stop short with the House of Commons; they have relevance also in regard to Great Britain's anachronistic second chamber, the House of Lords. Everyone agrees that a second chamber is needed to perform certain functions, and most people would agree that the House of Lords now undertakes some useful tasks. What is not settled, however, is exactly what functions it should perform in order to complement but in no way challenge the functioning of the House of Commons and, still more difficult, what should be the membership of a reconstituted second chamber.

In November 1968, a White Paper on House of Lords reform (Cmnd. 3799) [19] proposed comprehensive and radical changes that suggest ways of ultimately resolving both issues. These proposals seek to eliminate the hereditary basis of membership; to prevent any one party from having a permanent majority, as the Conservatives have always had, and also to assure the government of the day a "reasonable" working majority; to further restrict the power of the House of Lords to delay public legislation; and to abolish the Lords' "absolute power to withhold consent to subordinate legislation against the will of the Commons." The proposed composition of the Lords for securing these objectives is a two-tier house in which there would be both "voting" and "nonvoting" members, the latter with the right to ask questions, move motions, and serve on committees but not to vote; restriction of voting and of future membership to peers of the first creation; existing peers by succession to remain nonvoting members for life (unless created life peers), but no subsequent succession to carry the right to a seat; the number of bishops to be gradually reduced from twenty-six to sixteen; and the Law Lords to be retained.

PRESENT COMPOSITION OF THE HOUSE OF LORDS

How different this body would be from the present House can easily be seen by describing its composition at the time the White Paper was issued. The overwhelming majority of its 1,062 members hold their seats not because of any popular demand for their services, nor because of any marked capacity for legislative work, nor even because of any outstanding personal achievement or intelligence (although some of the peers are extremely able and intelligent). Rather, most of the members hold their seats as the result of chance: the typical peer, who represents 90 percent of the membership, simply happens to be the eldest son of the eldest son in a chain reaching back to an ancestor who was first created a nobleman.[20]

In addition to 736 hereditary peers by succession and 122 of first creation, the House of Lords in August 1968 included 26 lords spiritual of the Church of England; 23 serving or retired lords of appeal in ordinary (the "Law Lords," whose seats are held for life and may not be

---

[19] The White Paper drew on discussions on reform of the Lords in the Joint Party Conference on the subject. Parliament No. 2 Bill, 1969, which was intended to implement the reforms, was ultimately withdrawn due to backbench opposition and obstruction from both parties and to make way for Labor's Industrial Relations Bill, which, in turn, was withdrawn due to Labor backbench and union pressure.

[20] This is less far back in many instances than commonly believed. Almost half of the peerages have been created since 1906; only one in fifteen dates from 1689; and only one in fifty from 1485. Moreover, a "boom in barons"—forty-six new peers in the last six months of 1964 to increase Labor and Liberal representation in the Lords—created an unprecedently rapid increase in numbers, although Pitt had created fifty in five years, Lloyd George a hundred and fifteen in six years, and Attlee ninety-eight in six years.

inherited); and 155 life peers and peeresses appointed under the Life Peerage Act of 1958. (Since 1963, peeresses in their own right also sit in the House of Lords.)

The greatest outcry in the past against the inevitability of hereditary succession came from rising young politicians, like Quintin Hogg and, even more strenuously, Anthony Wedgwood Benn, who long sought the right to hold a seat in the House of Commons. Finally, in 1963 the Peerage Act permitted the disclaimer of peerages, an opportunity seized by Hogg, who, somewhat paradoxically, has now returned to his peerage as Lord Chancellor. The measure also permitted the Earl of Home to become Sir Alec Douglas-Home, for a short while leader of the Conservative party and prime minister after Macmillan's resignation.

The 1958 and 1963 Peerage Acts introduced two new principles into the composition of the House of Lords, the one of additions for life only (a principle previously restricted to the Law Lords), the other of possible renunciation of peerages. Since only a relatively small minority attend regularly, a Standing Order of 1963 added the provision that if a peer or peeress did not respond to the writ of summons and take the oath within a month of the opening of the session, he or she would be considered to have applied for leave of absence and would not, therefore, be able to take part in proceedings. None of these provisions, however, has satisfactorily met the problem of designing an acceptable second chamber. The Conservatives are reluctant to give up the hereditary principle as the dominant basis for its composition, while Labor has termed the social privilege embodied in the present House an affront to democracy. Yet both parties have come to agree in general about the legitimate and desired functions of the second chamber, an approach that may ultimately result in agreement about its composition.

THE POWERS OF THE HOUSE OF LORDS

Over the years, the House of Lords has steadily lost its coordinate power with that of the House of Commons. It was early accepted that no defeat in the House of Lords could force out a Cabinet. It was also long under-

stood that the peers should not reject or modify financial legislation contrary to the wishes of the House of Commons. When, in 1909, the House of Lords did reject the Lloyd George budget with its heavy land taxes, the resulting constitutional crisis led to the Parliament Act of 1911, which removed the Lords' power of rejecting a money bill. This act also substituted for the Lords' previous power of defeating legislation a power of delay. Henceforth the House of Commons could pass any measure over the Lords' opposition if it did so three times in three successive sessions within a period of two years. This procedure was further cut by the postwar Labor government through the Parliament Act of 1949 to two successive sessions and one year between the original second reading and the date on which the bill passed the second time. More important than these restrictions, however, is the awareness that no elected government will ever permit the nonelected Lords to throw out an important measure of legislation. As Lord Carrington, Conservative Leader in the House of Lords, said on February 16, 1967: "It has always been my view that the House of Lords will only be able to use its delaying power once"—meaning that power would be abolished forthwith.

One coequal power that the House of Lords still retains is the power to withhold consent to subordinate legislation (i.e., orders in council or ministerial order or regulation), private bills, and bills to confirm provisional orders, none of which comes within the limitations of the Parliament Acts. Although in practice this power has been a theoretical rather than practical check on the overall control of the House of Commons, Labor has proposed that it should be abolished.

THE FUNCTIONS OF THE
HOUSE OF LORDS

More important to consider than its still remaining powers are those functions that are inadequately performed by the Commons and that the Lords can perform well. As early as 1918, Lord Bryce made the classic statement on such functions, of which two have become even more important today because of the pressures of time on the Commons. These two are to examine and revise bills coming from the Commons and to initiate bills on noncontroversial subjects so they are in shape for Commons' consideration. A further important function is to provide a forum for wide-ranging debate on significant, nonpartisan issues.

By far the most important part of the Lords' work concerns the task of examination and revision, for that chamber has both the time and the expertise to catch flaws and ambiguities resulting either from clumsy drafting or from the many amendments that have been inserted in a particular measure during its passage through the Commons and that the Parliamentary Counsel's Office has not had time to catch. In the unusually badly drafted Transport Bill of 1947, for example, the Lords proposed 242 amendments, 200 of which were purely drafting or agreed amendments and accepted by the Commons, while the other amendments that were forced through by the Conservative majority in the Lords were rejected in the Commons—a good indication both of the usefulness of the reviewing function and of the restraints on the power of the Lords.

In the second range of activities identified by Lord Bryce, the Lords have been particularly effective in highly technical matters, especially those concerning such subjects as law, patents, and accountancy, and in examining the existing situation in matters in which the government does not wish to become directly involved like abortion, homosexuality, and artificial insemination. The Lords also perform a sterling task in handling noncontroversial government measures, reviewing obsolete statutes, contributing to the Joint Standing Committee on Consolidated Bills, which seeks to bring into a single measure related provisions scattered through many statutes, and reviewing private bills, about half of which start in the Lords. It must also be noted that for historical reasons the House of Lords is the highest court of appeal in the kingdom (a fact considered further in Chapter 7). During its sittings as a court, however, only the nine Law Lords, the Lord Chancellor, and any members who hold or have held high judicial office take part in the proceedings.

Although, as we have pointed out, the membership of the House of Lords is so large, about fifty to eighty of those members do most of the hard, routine work that is so valuable. Perhaps another fifty join in when their special field of competence is under consideration. The life peers have added some unusually intelligent and experienced individuals to the personnel of the House (although the patronage, so common with new peerages, has also not been absent to the degree anticipated). There have also been distinguished "Lords of the first creation," like Lord Attlee, Lord Beveridge, author of the famous social insurance report, and Lord Lindsay, political philosopher and Master of Balliol College, Oxford. Some of the most useful members of the Lords are crossbench, that is, they do not take the party whip.[21] While any British government is likely to feel more at ease when it has a working majority in the House of Lords as well as the Commons, what is most needed are composition and functions that can most adequately supplement the Commons in performing those tasks to which the movement of parliamentary reform has been dedicated.

[21] In support of its proposal to abolish the hereditary basis for membership of the Lords and break its permanent Conservative majority, the 1968 White Paper pointed out that in August 1968 there were 350 peers who took the Conservative whip, compared to 115 who took the Labor whip, and 40 the Liberal whip. Taking into account attendance at more than one-third of the sittings up to August in the 1967–68 session, however, the ratios were closer with 125 taking the Conservative whip, 95 the Labor whip, 20 the Liberal whip, and about 50 no whip at all. The ratios swung the other way when the party designation and attendance of created peers—that is, life peers and those of the first creation—were considered. Figures for this group of 326 members indicated 95 Labor, 77 Conservative, 8 Liberal, and 141 without a party whip; and for those 153 who attended more than one-third of the sittings, 81 Labor, 38 Conservatives, 8 Liberal, and 26 without the party whip.

8   THE FUTURE OF PARLIAMENTARY REFORM

To implement the movement for parliamentary reform may well require much more articulation of the work of the two Houses than has been attempted so far. Such articulation would proceed from a determination of what the Lords could do to relieve the Commons of some of its current, time-consuming legislative work so the latter could devote more attention to developing informed criticism of ministerial and departmental conduct of affairs and to looking ahead to impending social and economic problems. Bernard Crick, a member of the Study of Parliament Group, in his revised second edition of *The Reform of Parliament*, has outlined a series of functions the Lords could perform in these regards. While the most active member of the House of Lords might well find that his proposals relegate them to further obscurity and a dull program, the functions build on much of their present work but carry the logic still further.

Professor Crick proposes removing all power of delay and restricting the legislative function of the House of Lords to determining the internal consistency and points of law and administration in a measure, thus making it "an upper house to and for the Commons of scrutiny and investigation" on the pattern of select committees. Standing committees of the Lords should concentrate, in his view, on subordinate legislation (which, as we have seen, gets far too little

scrutiny under present circumstances), statutory powers (where the same problem exists), and the machinery of government (as proposed by Jo Grimond, then parliamentary leader of the Liberal party in a debate on the subject on November 19, 1964). In addition to having its Law Lords provide the final court of appeal, Crick suggests that the Lords have a standing committee on administrative justice, which could supplement the rather circumscribed work of the parliamentary commissioner. As far as debates are concerned, he endorses, as do all observers, the widest possible latitude to consider any subject under the sun.

Crick envisages a highly competent and experienced body of men and women working on the agreed understanding that they are taking nonpartisan tasks off the shoulders of the Commons without in any way challenging the latter's control of decisions. (He also suggests adding some salaried short-term members for particular fields.) With the basic work of inquiry and scrutiny being done on their behalf in the Lords, the Commons could concentrate on basic social and economic problems. Some movement in these directions has already been made. It is hard to deny that the end result could meet many of the criticisms that have been raised throughout this chapter *if*—and it remains a big *if*—the knotty problem of the composition of the Lords can be settled.

5

The British Cabinet, prime minister, and monarch

1   THE CABINET

The Cabinet is the apex of party government. It is invested with power through the electoral decision, which has provided its party with the majority of seats in the Commons, and it maintains its authority because of the support of that majority. It provides legislative and administrative initiative to the House of Commons, whose role, as we have seen, is to consider, criticize, and legitimize these initiatives.

Although the Cabinet is the central instrument of government, one can search the law without finding more than incidental reference to it or to its leader, the prime minister. The Cabinet, in fact, is one of the typical anomalies of British politics. Its power arises not from any formal delegation of authority but from its dominance over those who do possess legal power: the Parliament, the monarch, the Privy Council, and the permanent administrative staff.

In form the Cabinet is a group of royal advisers that grew out of the royal household and the Privy Council, much as the Privy Council itself descended from the Great Council of the Norman kings by way of the *Curia Regis* and the Permanent Council. Every Cabinet minister is appointed to the Privy Council. Since membership in the Council is for life, the Privy Council is a very large body that includes both former and incumbent Cabinet members,

together with certain public servants from the civil service and military forces. In its name are issued "orders in Council," a great variety of executive orders many of which are a form of delegated legislation representing an exercise of general authority granted by act of Parliament.

HOW THE CABINET IS CHOSEN AND ACTS

If in form the Cabinet is a group of royal advisers, in practice it operates very differently. Far from having a free hand in appointing its members, the monarch must choose as prime minister the leader of the party that secures a majority in the House of Commons and the prime minister himself selects the remaining members of the Cabinet. The Cabinet exercises the prerogative powers of the Crown, such as summoning and dissolving Parliament, although the writs are issued in the name of the monarch. The speech the monarch reads at the opening of Parliament is written by the prime minister and his associates. In short, the monarchy has no independent involvement in the political process—quite likely the requirement for its continued existence.

Not only in form, but also in composition, powers, and relationship to the legislature, the British Cabinet is obviously very different from the American cabinet. In the United States, the president may choose whomever he pleases, subject to confirmation by the Senate. He may even select a member of the opposite party, as when President Nixon appointed a Democrat, John Connally, to be Secretary of Commerce in 1971, while earlier Presidents Kennedy and Johnson had a Republican, Robert McNamara, as Secretary of Defense. Few cabinet members are ever chosen from Congress, and those who are must resign their seats in Congress. While the president may pick whom he wishes to head the great departments of government, he can as easily dismiss them or ignore their advice. Moreover, no one expects the members of the American cabinet to have one common position on all issues. It is also evident that neither the president nor the relevant cabinet member can count on all members of the president's party to vote in support of the measures they recommend.

In Great Britain, however, the prime minister not only chooses all the members of his Cabinet from his own party but each must hold a seat in Parliament to be eligible for office. When Patrick Gordon Walker failed to win a seat in a specially staged by-election in 1964, he had to forfeit his appointment as Secretary of State for Foreign Affairs. Moreover, while technically the prime minister is at liberty to offer posts in his government to anyone he likes, in practice there are a considerable number of prominent party figures who virtually choose themselves. Making a Cabinet is a matter of delicately balancing the important and influential but also differing points of view and political outlooks. In this sense, the Cabinet becomes a microcosm of the party.

Despite the variety of opinions within a Cabinet, the essence of Cabinet responsibility is that, after a matter has been thoroughly explored, all shall agree to support the same policy in public. Indeed, if one Cabinet member feels strongly enough that the policy approved by the majority of his colleagues is wrong, he is honor bound to resign. If he does not do so—and it is a startling and rare occasion when such a resignation takes place—the minister is duty bound to speak in support of the collective decision and to vote in favor of it in the House. And this credo of collective responsibility ex-

tends not only to the fifteen or twenty Cabinet members who made the final decision but to all those holding one office or another through to the unpaid parliamentary secretaries, which, in practice, means nearly one-third of the total parliamentary party. The principle received concrete enforcement in 1967 when seven parliamentary private secretaries were dismissed for abstaining on May 10 on a motion to authorize British entry into the Common Market.

The convention of collective responsibility was intended originally as a means of making the Cabinet responsible to Parliament. It has become, in practice, a device for isolating and to a degree neutralizing dissatisfaction with generally agreed upon Cabinet policies, and it thus helps to keep backbenchers in check by denying them influential leadership.

Since the dogma of collective responsibility acts so forcefully to reinforce the position of the Cabinet, it is not surprising that the opposition should also attempt to secure similar solidarity behind the decisions of the shadow cabinet. While the pressures are not quite so strong when a party is in opposition, it is noteworthy that Enoch Powell was expelled from the Conservative shadow cabinet in 1968 because of a provocative speech on colored immigration.

Since a Cabinet minister is not only a member of a governing collectivity but also the head of an administrative department, he is held responsible in Parliament for its administration as well as for general policy. Parliamentary questions, the investigations of the parliamentary commissioner (ombudsman), specialized committees and debates on Opposition days, or motions for adjournment can all focus on the ill-functioning of a department or a harmful decision it has made. High civil servants cannot be cross-examined in Parliament on departmental decisions (although occasionally they are by the commissioner or a committee) and the approach must be through the relevant minister, for he is in Parliament and therefore "get-at-able." Whether evidence of departmental mismanagement leads to the resignation of a minister generally depends on whether the party is ready to stand behind the minister or to sacrifice him. In the Crichel Down case, the relevant minister, Sir Thomas

Dugdale, resigned.[1] But others have not done so. Ministerial resignations may also take place for broader reasons, for example, when the Cabinet wishes to disavow a policy, as with the Hoare-Laval Pact during League of Nations sanctions against Italy's aggression in Ethiopia, or for personal behavior, as with the unhappy Profumo case.

THE MEMBERSHIP OF THE CABINET

The prime minister decides the size of his Cabinet and, within certain limits, determines which departments shall be represented in it. Since World War II, Cabinets have averaged between eighteen and twenty-three members, much larger than the Churchill war Cabinet of six to eight members, who were freed of departmental duties and met almost daily. Despite subsequent appeals to separate planning and administrative functions in the interests of efficiency, postwar Cabinets continue to include both. Thus, in addition to the prime minister, the central figure, a normal Cabinet includes the Chancellor of the Exchequer, the Foreign and Home Secretaries, Lord Chancellor, the Ministers of Defense, Labor, and Agriculture, and other key figures. Other ministers may be moved in and out of the formal Cabinet depending on how much focus there is on their sphere of activity. For example, the Minister for Fuel and Power was dropped from the Cabinet in 1947 after the nationalization of the coal mines had been carried through.

Another feature of Cabinet formation is the frequent reshuffling of offices, a practice that reflects the prime minister's sense for gaining effective teamwork but also tends to increase the influence in government departments of the top permanent officials. Only twelve of the twenty-three members of the Cabinet that fought the election in 1966 still held places in Wilson's 1970 Cabinet. Only four, including the prime minister, still held the same offices as in 1964. Nine of the new members had worked their way up from junior ministerial posts, and only two had been drawn from the backbenches. The first Heath Cabinet in 1970 included only nine members of the previous Conservative Cabinet.

It is uncommon for a parliamentary newcomer to be brought immediately into the Cabinet. A Wilson experiment in this regard made Frank Cousins, General Secretary of the Transport and General Workers' Union, Minister of Technology in 1964 on entering the Commons. Cousins subsequently voted against the government's prices and incomes policies and soon resigned. The Heath equivalent to the Cousins appointment was that of John Davies, who was made Secretary of State for Trade and Industry. Heath also appointed Peter Walker, a self-made millionaire, Secretary of State for the Environment, although he had no previous ministerial experience. In addition, he appointed a somewhat obscure backbencher who is a transportation expert, John Peyton, as senior minister responsible for transportation in the Department for the Environment. Thus Heath demonstrated his concern for technical experience and efficiency. It appears, however, that the general practice holds of drawing Cabinet members from among those with experience in Parliament and as a junior minister.

THE FUNCTIONS OF THE CABINET AND THEIR COORDINATION

The Cabinet has three major functions: to make the final determination on policy to be submitted to Parliament; to control the national executive in accordance with policies approved by Parliament; and to maintain continuous coordination and delimitation of the work of the many departments of state.

To fulfill these vast responsibilities, various organizational arrangements have been attempted. Prime Minister Churchill introduced the practice of coordinating ministers or "overlords" who supervised the work of several min-

[1] The Crichel Down case, which became a by-word throughout Great Britain, concerned an estate in Dorset that had been requisitioned by the government in 1937 as a bombing site. When it was no longer needed for this purpose, its hereditary owners tried to buy it back, but their offer was curtly rejected by the Ministry of Agriculture, which planned to use the area as a model farm. Only because of remarkable persistence and vigor were the former owners finally able to secure a public hearing of the issue, and only thereafter were they allowed to regain their land. See R. Douglas Brown, *The Battle of Crichel Down*.

istries, but sharp Labor criticism that such a development undercut ministerial responsibility led to the end of the experiment in 1953. From 1947 to 1964, however, the Admiralty, War Office, and Air Ministry were coordinated under the Minister of Defense who, unlike the "overlords," had statutory authority. More successful has been the regrouping of ministries, the use of Cabinet committees, and the expansion of the staff and role of the Cabinet Secretariat.

Regrouping of ministries

The Wilson government undertook a systematic regrouping of ministries. The separate defense departments were replaced in 1964 by a single Ministry of Defense, the Ministries of Pensions and National Insurance were merged in 1966 into the Ministry of Social Security, the Department of Foreign and Commonwealth Affairs combined in 1968 the responsibilities of the Foreign Office and Commonwealth Relations Office (which had previously taken over those of the Colonial Office), and several other mergers were undertaken. In this period, however, a somewhat controversial new Department of Economic Affairs (DEA) was set up to act as a balance to the traditional coordination of the Treasury, the rationale being that while the latter continued to be responsible for controlling expenditures and for monetary management, the DEA would plan for economic expansion, regional development, and industrial productivity. In 1969, the department was abolished, however, and its planning function was returned to the Treasury (see Chapter 6, Section 2).

The Heath government plans still further reorganization of government departments and offices. A unified Department of Trade and Industry was early established to combine the traditional functions of the Board of Trade (including those for civil aviation) with those of the Ministry of Technology (except for its aerospace functions). It operates under a secretary of state supported by two ministers who are not in the Cabinet. The Ministries of Housing and Local Government, Public Buildings and Works and Transport were grouped under the Ministry for the Environment. (The Scottish and Welsh Offices continue to play the major roles in these fields for their areas.) In the words of the White Paper on the reorganization of the central government (Cmnd. 4506) of October 1970, the objective of these and subsequent reorganizations is to match "the field of responsibility of government departments to coherent fields of policy and administration," which would be determined functionally.

Cabinet committees

Cabinet or interdepartmental committees, a second major means of coordination and preparation for final decisions, aid the process of collective responsibility by formalizing the interaction of different views held by ministers in overlapping segments of government business. Some of these committees are *ad hoc* to deal with particular problems and others are standing committees concerned with major areas of governmental activity such as foreign affairs, social welfare, public expenditure, and economic policy. Harold Wilson, who greatly expanded the use of Cabinet committees, described them in 1967 as "the Cabinet in microcosm," representative not only in numbers but in "opinions and shades of opinion, so that everyone who is really departmentally concerned and one or two who are not will be involved." [2]

The power of the chairmen of Cabinet committees was also increased under Wilson. He himself chaired the committees on defense and overseas policy, and on economic policy, while other senior ministers chaired those particularly relevant to their concerns. The Wilson view was that if the committee reached a clear decision that satisfied its chairman, the matter was then settled. Thus, the older system under which a junior minister could "reserve his position" and have the matter referred to the full Cabinet was replaced by the much more ticklish process of a possible appeal to the prime minister, who then decided at his own discretion whether or not to refer the matter to the Cabinet as a whole.

Side by side with this decentralization of many decisions to lower Cabinet levels, Wilson introduced in 1968 a necessary complementary

[2] See Louise W. Holborn, John H. Herz, and Gwendolen M. Carter, *Documents of Major Foreign Powers*, p. 72.

organ called the Parliamentary Committee, which was, in effect, an inner Cabinet. Composed of the prime minister and seven to nine senior Cabinet ministers, this committee met twice a week to consider all issues of genuine political importance. Unlike all other Cabinet committees, each of which is paralleled by an interdepartmental civil service committee representing the same fields, the Parliamentary Committee received its briefings from the Cabinet Secretariat. The decisions of the Parliamentary Committee were referred to the full Cabinet, which usually met every week for coordination.

It appears that Prime Minister Heath returned to the practice of using the larger Cabinet for consideration of policy issues, although he also streamlined the ministry as a whole. By grouping previous departments into one, their numbers have been somewhat reduced. It is noteworthy, however, that the October 1970 White Paper on reorganization of the central government specifically endorsed the flexibility of the existing system of interdepartmental committees.

The Cabinet Secretariat

Underpinning the work of Cabinet committees, of the full Cabinet, and of the prime minister himself is the Cabinet Secretariat, or Cabinet Office. As with the House of Commons, effective staff support is crucial for bringing together the most relevant material on which decisions are to be based. Wilson doubled the numbers in the Cabinet Secretariat to about a hundred civil servants, drawn from regular departments and organized functionally under the Cabinet Secretary and several assistant secretaries into broad divisions to deal with economic affairs, social policy, and overseas policies. He also brought in a number of experts from the universities, including economists, and made the chief scientific adviser to the government a full-time member of the Cabinet Office and chairman of an advisory committee drawn from the universities, industry, and the Royal Society to plan the science and technology budget for government-sponsored research. Moreover, in 1967 the Central Statistical Office, which has always been a part of the Cabinet Office, was reorganized to give it greater scope in monitoring the data-gathering of the departments and to provide long-range projections.

The chief Heath innovation in the Cabinet Office has been to establish a small multidisciplinary central policy review staff. This body, which is designed to aid the Cabinet as a whole, concentrates on aiding ministers in defining the relative priorities in their areas, the strategies for carrying out these priorities, and also in considering possible alternatives where choice exists.

In the light of its importance today, it is hard to realize that the Cabinet acquired a secretariat so late. The effective breakthrough was made at the end of 1916 when Lloyd George took office as prime minister and established the War Cabinet Secretariat. At the end of the war, this precedent led to the establishment of the Cabinet Secretariat as we now know it. Before that time, there was scant preparation for the meetings, no agenda, and inadequate records. In some cases Cabinet members could not even remember what had been decided. Thus Lord Hartington's private secretary once wrote to Gladstone's secretary: "There must have been some decision. . . . My chief has told me to ask you what the devil *was* decided, for he be damned if he knows."

Today, activities are highly organized. The Cabinet Secretariat, or Cabinet Office, under the direction of the relevant chairman or of the prime minister, organizes the agenda for meetings, keeps a careful record of the conclusions, and circulates them to the ministers. A few days before each meeting the agenda must be sent around so that each member will know what is to be discussed. Careful memoranda describing and explaining the measures under consideration are circulated at least two days before proposals are discussed. A short summary familiarizes the minister who is bogged down in departmental duties with the major points in the argument. In addition, copies of Foreign Office telegrams and dispatches are sent to the members of the Cabinet to keep them informed of day-to-day developments in foreign policy. All departments directly concerned in a measure (including the Treasury, if there are financial provisions) are expected to consult with one another and to work out an agreement for presentation to the relevant committee before the matter is placed on the agenda and the memorandum circulated. Once the relevant Cabinet committee has come to an agreement, the matter is settled, as we have seen, or if of special importance, the Cabinet can often dispose of it with comparatively little discussion.

Not only does the Cabinet Secretariat service the Cabinet and its committees, it also acts as the prime minister's personal staff. The permanent secretary of the Cabinet, the Cabinet Secretary, is at the same time the permanent secretary for the prime minister. Each minister, of course, has a permanent secretary as chief adviser as well as head of the civil service of his department. The permanent secretary of the Cabinet provides the same kind of informational and coordinating service for the prime minister in regard to all policy matters related to the general running of the government. Equally, the Cabinet Secretariat's chief scientific adviser is also the prime minister's scientific adviser.

Under Wilson, the Cabinet Secretariat greatly extended its supervision of the workings of the administration. Whereas formerly Treasury or perhaps Foreign Office officials would chair the interdepartmental committees (paralleling those of the Cabinet committees) through which high-ranking civil servants coordinate policies at their own level, the Cabinet Office took over the function of providing most of these chairmen. Thus the Cabinet Secretariat has become a very high-level and high-powered instrument at the disposal of the Cabinet, and particularly of the prime minister, not only for the preparation of the legislative agenda but also for the management of executive business and supervision of the administration.

As far as the staffing of the Cabinet Secretariat is concerned, the tenure of the permanent secretary tends to be very long: Lord Hankey served for twenty-two years and Tom Jones, his deputy, for a substantial period. Since 1963 the office has been held by Sir Burke Trend (sometimes termed, therefore, "the second most powerful man in England"). But Wilson followed his predecessor's example in keeping the tenure of most other members of the Cabinet Secretariat fairly short. In his words: "There is too much danger of their

becoming 'ivory tower'; they come from departments and go back to departments."[3]

THE ORGANIZATION OF THE MINISTRY

The Cabinet naturally carries the ultimate responsibility for policy decisions and initiatives, but it is the apex of the very much larger ministry, numbering between eighty-five and over a hundred. Heath pruned the number of ministers below Cabinet rank when he acquired office so that they totaled about twenty less than those serving under Wilson. Questions have been raised, however, both regarding the appropriate numbers for a ministry under modern conditions and the most efficient organization of those below Cabinet rank. The issue is not only one of maintaining traditional Cabinet authority but also of spreading responsibilities for junior ministers down the line. Backbenchers, as we have seen, can play a role in the discussion of party policy but this is far less prized than participation in the actual exercise of governmental responsibilities. Moreover, with the vast scale and complexity of modern government, the range of fields and responsibilities is so great as to demand a substantial spreading of these responsibilities. These responsibilities include not only the massive volume of legislation but also the steady increase in parliamentary questions, the response to the growth of select committees, increasing interaction with constituents, which throws an ever-growing burden on the departments to respond to questions and problems, the persistent activities of "lobbies," and demands of international organizations, all of which in one way or another must be coped with by the ministry in office.

There are currently what approximate to four tiers of ministers: the ministers in the Cabinet; the ministers with Cabinet rank (and salaries) heading departments but not regularly in the Cabinet; the ministers of state (whose salaries vary); and the parliamentary secretaries. The numbers in each rank, and the gap between them, have varied over the years. Where Attlee in 1950 had thirteen depart-

[3] Holborn, Herz, Carter, *Documents of Major Foreign Powers*, p. 64.

mental ministers outside the Cabinet, Wilson in 1970 had only three. But conversely, in place of Attlee's three ministers of state, Wilson ended up with twenty-two, only six less than the number of parliamentary secretaries. Wilson also adopted the unusual practice of publicly specifying responsibilities for certain parliamentary secretaries (e.g., the ebullient Jennie Lee was given the arts, and even before she was raised to the rank of minister of state, she operated directly under the prime minister rather than the Secretary of State for Education). Traditionally, however, parliamentary secretaries are workhorses, serving their minister in the House and in his department but acknowledging the superiority within the latter of the permanent secretary.

There is also another rank, that of parliamentary private secretary (PPS), whose members serve without pay and at the invitation of ministers, but only with the approval of the chief whip's office. Their function has been described as "calculated to lighten the ministerial load," or, more facetiously, as "either to open the door, or if the minister is dry to see that the necessary stimulant is provided." There are twenty-nine private secretaries in the Heath government: there were thirty-seven under Prime Minister Macmillan, but only fifteen prior to World War I. In 1922, Winston Churchill became the first minister to have two PPS's.

This office has both advantages and disadvantages. It provides the first step on the long and uncertain road to promotion. Between 1918 and 1955, 60 percent of parliamentary private secretaries achieved ministerial office: of the Heath Cabinet, only five out of eighteen had been PPS's, but these included Sir Alec Douglas-Home, Anthony Barber, and Peter Walker. A PPS has a ring-side seat to the working of the government. He sits on standing committees; he attends conferences at his ministry. He has become a participant, however lowly, in the making of policy.

The disadvantage of being a PPS is that it inhibits parliamentary performance. A PPS is expected to refrain from requesting a question or speaking on his minister's subject, not to sign Early Day motions or show hostility of any kind to government measures. The dismissal of seven PPS's in 1967 for abstaining on the motion to enter the Common Market has already been mentioned and had an earlier precedent in the dismissal of four PPS's in 1949 for voting against the Labor government.

Every administration works out its own allocation of ministerial responsibilities, and these seem likely to change with experience. Shortly after Heath assumed office, a Labor MP, William Rodgers, proposed a five-tier structure that has interest as a possible model.[4] Recommending that the Cabinet itself be no larger than Wilson's Parliamentary Committee, Rodgers suggested that there also be twelve to fifteen functional departments with clearly defined fields and ministers who were responsible to Parliament, and a new category of "mini-ministers" who work within federally organized departments and should also be answerable to Parliament even though coordinated by a secretary of state. Below them again but recognized as the key middle rank, he put the ministers of state, of whom he thought Wilson's twenty-two were more appropriate than Heath's original twelve. Finally, he suggested using the rank of parliamentary secretary as a probationary grade from which prospects could be moved in and out without disfavor to their chance of later becoming a minister of state. Whether or not such a plan or some of its aspects are adopted, it provides a rational scheme of organization against which existing practices can be tested.

CABINET DICTATORSHIP?

Americans, who endorse the checks and balances of their own system, and who see the legislation that the Cabinet supports being passed by the House of Commons, while legislation that it opposes has no chance to do so, sometimes charge that Great Britain lives under a system of "Cabinet dictatorship." Such a charge is a gross oversimplification, however, for it overlooks the fact that a British government is under constant pressure from the opposition, from its own backbenchers, from the

---

[4] William Rodgers, "The Case for an Even Smaller Cabinet," *The Times* (July 1, 1970).

press, and from the public when a major issue is under consideration. It is true that at a moment of emergency, as with the bankruptcy of Rolls-Royce, the British Cabinet can move with extraordinary speed to force a decision through Parliament, but such occasions are fortunately rare. While no one can claim that the public is adequately alerted most of the time to the implications of issues that develop after an election campaign has been held, there is normally a process of public information through debates in the House and other means of analyzing and investigating issues that can be exploited.

It is clear that the government may disregard public opinion on a few issues so long as it knows that the public approves its record in general. But if there is widespread public revulsion and heavy backbench pressure the government will almost inevitably make concessions. In addition to all these reasons why the charge of Cabinet "dictatorship" is not justified, the British executive has traditionally acted with admirable restraint in its use of power, recognizing that the key to the successful functioning of the parliamentary system is that the House of Commons should have ample opportunity to criticize its policies, and that, in this sense, the House should be the mouthpiece of public opinion.

In any event, there is a certain superficiality in speaking of responsibility only as the ability of the people to prevent the government from doing what the people do not want it to do. At least as important is the government's ability positively to do what the people want it to do. And here the difference between the two systems is more clearly marked. If the British and the American executives were equally bent on pushing through a policy desired by the majority of the people, the British executive would be far more likely to succeed. Under the American system of separating governmental powers —and checking and balancing them—and with the laxness of party discipline, Congress often responds to the efforts not of a majority of the people, but of a minority. All that a minority group need do to check legislation is to control a single house of Congress or, in some cases, a single committee, in particular the Rules Committee, of the House of Representa-

tives. In Great Britain such a situation would be inconceivable.

The issue may be summarized thus: Is it better to have a government capable of carrying out the will of the people—but also capable of carrying through something the people do not will? Or is it better to have a government so checked and balanced that it is not likely to push through an unpopular program simply because it cannot overcome even minor opposition? In a period of relative calm there may be something to be said for the second alternative as a way of forcing divergent groups to compose their differences and work out a generally acceptable program. But in times of crisis, which these days seem omnipresent, the government that cannot take decisive and prompt action is in danger of losing important opportunities. Ordinarily, when need is great, the American Congress has been willing to support many of the president's measures. The British executive, however, has the great advantage of being able to plan a comprehensive and coherent program and to ensure its enactment under virtually all circumstances, while the American executive not infrequently has his proposals rejected by a Congress unable to develop an integrated and consistent policy of its own.

It used to be thought that the British and American situations were so different, particularly regarding the presence of minorities, race prejudice, discrimination, and regional disparities, that the power of the majority under the British system to push through its program did not offer the kind of threat to minority rights that it would in the United States. In Northern Ireland, however, the Protestant majority has used its dominance in the local legislature to maintain discriminatory provisions adversely affecting the Catholics (see Chapter 8, Section 1). The Parliament at Westminster has been restrained, on the whole, in exercising its power to the disadvantage of minority groups, although some would claim that both Labor and the Conservatives have yielded too much in their immigration legislation to majority pressures. It is apparent, however, that there is an inherent danger in the British system in the lack of effective safeguards for minority and regional interests, which may pose more serious problems in the future.

2 THE PRIME MINISTER

THE PRIME MINISTER AND THE CABINET

It is sometimes charged, particularly by British observers, that if there is no "Cabinet dictatorship" in Great Britain, there is a dictatorship by the prime minister within his Cabinet and even within his party. This too seems a gross exaggeration. While technically the prime minister chooses his associates, many of them choose themselves. Neither Macmillan nor Douglas-Home, for example, could have maintained an administration without the support of R. A. Butler, whom they outdistanced for the prime ministership but with whom they could not dispense. Demands for the resignation of influential Cabinet members, such as Macmillan made in 1962, seriously shake confidence in the party leader. Although Wilson's use of Cabinet committees might have seemed to undercut the authority of the full Cabinet, it permitted thorough discussion of issues by those ministers most affected by them and the association of the senior ministers with the prime minister in decisions on policy. Labor and Conservative backbenchers, as we have seen, are insistent upon being kept informed regarding policy plans and vocal in reacting to them. Even the prime minister's ultimate threat of calling for a dissolution is hedged with practical restraints because it is at least as likely, if not more so, that he will be turned out of office as that his party's MP's with "safe" seats will lose them at the next election.

Although there is no doubt that the prime minister is the most important member of his Cabinet and party, he only remains so as long as he retains the confidence and support of his associates. There are many factors that contribute to such confidence and support: his leadership and particularly, perhaps, his handling of dissension; the caliber and effectiveness of his principal associates in the Cabinet; the situations with which he has to deal, and his policies regarding them; his timing in crises; his ability to infuse public confidence

at the right moments. Labor is more constant than are the Tories in support of its leaders, as we have already indicated, but the debates and voting in Labor's annual conferences give indications of continued or lessening popularity. In the end, the success of a party leader depends most of all on his persuasiveness, on confidence in his judgment, and on the sense of cohesion he transmits to those with whom he works.

If one compares the position of the prime minister to that of the president, there are obvious strong features on both sides. The prime minister is far more likely to secure his program intact, although there are instances, as with Labor's Industrial Relations Bill, where it becomes necessary to drop a highly controversial measure. A prime minister never faces the situation of President Nixon's first term in which there was a Democratic majority in Congress, for the essence of Cabinet government, of course, is that the Cabinet and the majority in Parliament are of the same party. On the other hand, the president is master of his cabinet to a degree that no prime minister is. Moreover, the president's guaranteed term of office is something on which no prime minister can depend, even though most of them stay in office at least four years. But both Eden and Macmillan felt obliged to resign because of ill health, although neither had as serious an illness as that which incapacitated Woodrow Wilson without forcing his removal, and no president could have been removed from office as Neville Chamberlain was in 1940. The opposite side of a guaranteed term, however, is that the prime minister can choose the moment at which he wishes to fight the election, which gives him some, although, as Harold Wilson discovered, not enough advantage to win.

In terms of personal staff, the president has a big advantage, for no prime minister can draw on anything like the resources of the White House staff. The prime minister depends on the expert but relatively small Cabinet Secretariat, as we have seen, and also has a still smaller private staff at 10 Downing Street composed of official and political aides. Wilson, who declared that he attached "enormous importance" to his private political secretariat to maintain links with the parliamentary party, the party in the country, and to answer "the thousands of people who write to me," drew into it officials with "earthy" experience, that is, from departments concerned with industry, agriculture, labor, and so forth, as well as the traditional Foreign Office and Treasury personnel.[5] One additional sharp contrast here with the American White House staff is that apart from his press officer and personal secretaries, all the prime minister's aides are drawn from the civil service.

Conservative prime ministers have always been able to draw also on the resources of the Conservative Party Research Department. This body is more professionally staffed than is the research office of the Labor party and is directly responsible to the leader of the Conservative party, who personally appoints the top officials of the Conservative Central Office.

Richard Crossman once declared that the British have "the worst informed government in the world." That it could benefit from a better flow of information and from more coordinated long-range thinking and planning is not unique. The dependence on staff from the departments may well tend to create an overemphasis on particular problems to the detriment of a general overview on current issues and future possibilities. The shadow of impending general elections tends to shorten the perspective of planning, particularly in the latter years of an administration. Some of these difficulties in planning seem inherent in the nature of democratic government but improved sources and use of information and long-range projections would be helpful.

In one other respect, that of training for the job, the prime minister normally has the advantage. No man can step into the post of prime minister who has not served a long apprenticeship in Parliament and in the councils of his party. The man who can sustain the crossfire of parliamentary debate for many

years and maintain a leading role before one of the most exacting audiences in the world, who can convince his colleagues, many of whom are no less brilliant and efficient, that his strategy for the party is the best possible one, and who can also appeal effectively to the public is likely to be extremely versatile, as well as able and experienced. In the United States there is no comparable device for the testing and winnowing out of the ablest leaders.

British prime ministers have varied greatly in their presence, characteristics, and ways of acting. Winston Churchill, of course, was forceful, eloquent, and thrived on action and danger. Neville Chamberlain, in contrast, had far less popular appeal and failed the test of wartime organization. Chamberlain's two predecessors, Stanley Baldwin and Ramsay MacDonald, were also very different: Baldwin being less energetic in pushing his personal views and loyal to his associates; MacDonald's brilliance and ambition leading him to break with his party in 1931, an act for which he has never been forgiven by some Laborites. Clement R. Attlee as prime minister aimed to win agreement among his colleagues rather than to impose his own will, but in his sincere, unspectacular way he was usually decisive and, on occasions, ruthless. Macmillan dominated his Cabinet by sheer intellectual capacity but encouraged discussions and yielded gracefully when necessary. Douglas-Home was not an effective prime minister. Wilson's ready tongue (sometimes too sharp for his party's comfort), his energy, ebullience, and forcefulness made him an effective if not always popular leader. Heath's quiet persistence, developing parliamentary flair, and obstinacy under pressure make him yet another type of prime minister. To some degree, as with the presidency, the role of prime minister brings out unexpected qualities and capacities in a man. Both offices keep their holders in a constant blaze of publicity that highlights weaknesses and failures to a degree that might break less confident personalities.

If this concentration on the qualities and role of the prime minister appears to place him in a very special position within the governing structure of Great Britain, it is perhaps necessary to conclude by reemphasizing the fact that British government is party government. A party gains the majority of seats in

---

[5] Holborn, Herz, Carter, *Documents of Major Foreign Powers*, pp. 63–64.

an election less because of the personality and appeal of its leader than because the public prefers its program and potential. Leadership is inevitably a highly significant part of how the party conducts itself. Among the greatest services a party leader can perform is to persuade its members that they must adopt more forward-looking policies, as Macmillan did in educating the Conservatives to the need for Britain to enter the Common Market, and as Gaitskell did in showing the Labor party that it must give up its former rigid emphasis on nationalization. But the character of those elected to a party is an equally important part of its profile as well as of its appeal. Maintaining the confidence and support of the party's elected members is essential to effective government. In the end, party government, whatever its limitations, requires the interrelationship of the electorate, the leadership, and the backbenchers in the working of British government.

3 THE MONARCH

The British monarch is far more conspicuous than powerful. The coronation is an unparalleled public spectacle; and the monarch's drive to the Houses of Parliament to open a new session is lined with throngs of spectators. Indeed, crowds of people will gather to watch any member of the royal family who would scarcely turn their heads (save in time of grave national crisis or during a bitter political campaign) to catch a view of the prime minister. Newspapers and magazines chronicle in detail the activities of royalty: Prince Charles has a birthday, Princess Anne visits the theater, or Queen Elizabeth opens a flower show, and the evening papers give as much room to pictures and descriptions of the event as they would to most political developments abroad. A prime minister may make a significant political decision without one-half the fanfare that accompanies a royal visit to a Welsh or Scottish village.

Yet in spite of the ceremonial and the excitement, the prime minister and the Cabinet rule. The monarch is not devoid of influence, but it tends to be informal, contingent, and often highly speculative. What influence the monarch has, in short, depends on personality rather than on formal power. He has the right to be informed and to be consulted. The prime minister must always tell him of Cabinet decisions and must be ready to explain the reasons for any policy. The monarch can, in the words of Bagehot, encourage and warn; and if he is intelligent, these opportunities may be important.

The monarch has the advantage of continuity. In the course of a normal reign many governments come and go, and there are close contacts with the leading statesmen of the age. It is not difficult as a result to acquire considerable political knowledge and experience. And since the prime minister must discuss his policies with the monarch, speak of new developments, and listen to what he has to say, the latter is in a position to influence the man who is most deeply concerned with policy.

Few people really know, until long after the monarch has died, how much of a part he or she has played in politics. Queen Victoria, for example, was a woman of decided opinions. In the great rivalry between Gladstone and Disraeli, she was heart and soul with Disraeli. Repeatedly she took action behind the scenes to help her political friends and to impede her enemies. Again, in the reign of Edward VII, the king's support of the French alliance was a factor in cementing the *entente cordiale*. George V is reported to have acted as something of a brake on the Liberal government that was in office when he succeeded to the throne. More important, George V, as we know from Harold Nicolson's biography, urged Prime Minister MacDonald, following his resignation in 1931, to form a new Cabinet made up of leaders of the other parties and persuaded the leaders of the other parties to concur. But there is still complaint, particularly from Labor, that the monarch in so doing exceeded his constitutional powers.

It is now difficult to imagine a situation in

which the monarch would exercise independent initiative in a political matter. As long as one party has a clear majority, and that party has an accepted leader, the monarch must ask him to become prime minister. The situation is more difficult if no party has a clear majority in Parliament. In this case the way might seem to be open to the exercise of some discretion by the monarch as to which party leader he should turn to first. The likelihood is, however, that the parties would decide the matter between them.

The recent past has witnessed the awkward situation of Conservative prime ministers resigning through ill health—first Anthony Eden in 1957, and subsequently Harold Macmillan in 1964—without leaving an assured succession. Queen Elizabeth used conventional channels in seeking the advice of elder Conservative statesmen before turning to Macmillan in 1957, and again in 1964 in requesting Douglas-Home to assume the prime ministership. Particularly in the latter case, however, there was sharp criticism of even this degree of royal initiative. Already in 1957 the Labor party had declared publicly that if it were in a similar situation, the monarch should take no action until the parliamentary Labor party had made its own choice of leader. The Conservatives have also now established their own formal method for selecting a new leader, as we have seen (Chapter 3, Section 2), so the monarch will never again be placed in the equivocal position of appearing to favor one person over another.

CONTRIBUTIONS OF THE MONARCHY

What, then, are the contributions of the monarchy to Great Britain? It is apparent that the monarchy can be and is used to further specific national goals, both economic and political. Recently the royal family, particularly its younger members, has been sent abroad as ambassadors of trade. Prince Philip's visit to the United States in 1966 coincided with a new drive for exports; Princess Margaret and her husband appeared at a series of British weeks in American department stores in 1967, and she went to a comparable occasion in

Tokyo in 1969; Princess Alexandra performed the same service in Vienna the same year.

More important, constitutional monarchy can help to provide cohesion to a country which is not free from racial or regional strains. The brilliantly staged and strikingly successful installation of Charles as Prince of Wales in 1969 was not unrelated to the rise of Welsh nationalism. Some feel the government might also have made use of royal influence and even presence to try to ameliorate the strained and now explosive situation in Northern Ireland, although the latter's local government may well be reluctant since a brick was thrown at the queen in 1966, the last time she visited that part of the United Kingdom. Another suggestion is that a royal example of racial and color tolerance inside (as so frequently outside) Great Britain might influence those most affected not only by prejudice but also by loyalty and snobbery.

It is noticeable that the more the powers of the monarchy have atrophied, the greater its symbolic significance has become. The open republicanism of the nineteenth century finds no echo today. On the contrary, the monarchy has a special appeal to mass democracy, both as a symbol of national unity and as a source of constant interest. It answers a need for color and drama, for the personification of principles, that is all too often left unsatisfied in modern society. Especially in a time of strain and unsatisfied hopes, the need for diversion and for emotional outlets is a significant one.

The life of the royal family, moreover, provides an element of human interest and warmth that has a wide appeal. The skillfully made moving picture of the everyday affairs of the queen and her family was as popular as the film of the coronation itself. Indeed, there is an insatiable curiosity about the routines as well as the diversions of the royal family, their clothes, their trips, and their romances. Moreover, the queen's close family relations, her charm, and her deep sense of responsibility, paralleled as they are by those of Prince Charles, provide a pattern of life that many seek to emulate.

It is sometimes suggested that in an age of leader-worshipping cults, monarchy may divert potentially dangerous inclinations into harmless channels. Those irrational feelings that occasionally menace democracy may be focused on the monarch to the people's hearts content, for their trust cannot be abused—because the monarch lacks the power as well as the inclination to abuse it.

Above all, perhaps, the fact that the monarch reigns but does not rule means that loyalty is common to both government and opposition. Such a personal focus of loyalty as the Crown provides in a real sense puts and keeps politicians in their proper places not only as rulers but also as public servants.

THE MONARCH AND THE COMMONWEALTH

Whatever one may say of the role of the monarch within Great Britain, there can be no question of its value for the Commonwealth of Nations. For the Crown is the symbol of the reality of that association.

Colonies, of course, can be governed as effectively by a republic as by a monarchy. But the evolution of British colonies from a position of dependence on Great Britain to one of independence within the Commonwealth was greatly facilitated by the fact that there was a monarchy to act both as a formal and a sentimental link between them; for thus, although they had no common parliament or cabinet, they had a common sovereign.

Today the queen of the United Kingdom is at the same time the queen of Canada, Australia, and New Zealand of the older Commonwealth, and, among its postwar members, Ceylon, Sierra Leone, Jamaica, Trinidad and Tobago, Malta, Mauritius, Fiji, and Barbados. Although the other members of the Commonwealth are republics, they acknowledge the Crown as the symbol of the free association of the Commonwealth nations and, in a similarly symbolic sense, the queen as "head of the Commonwealth."

Particularly among some of those of Anglo-Saxon descent in the overseas parts of the Commonwealth, there is a somewhat romantic and emotional, but patriotic and powerful, loyalty to the king or queen that helps to hold these areas close to the people of the United Kingdom. Thus George VI's visit to Canada in 1939 helped to consolidate the sentiment that brought that country united into World War II. The royal tours of unprecedented extent that Elizabeth II and her husband, Prince Philip, have taken to overseas parts of the Commonwealth help to affirm the reality of the relationship. Although much of the attraction is through the pageantry in these visits, they also enhance the still existing sense of loyalty to the monarchy, particularly among older people. The decision to omit the queen's Christmas broadcast one year gave rise to widespread protest overseas and to its reinstatement the following year. The integrative symbolic and personal effect of the monarchy may have a steadily diminishing impact throughout the Commonwealth, but it is far from having vanished.

6

The British administration: national and local

1 THE RANGE OF PUBLIC RESPONSIBILITIES

In the past century no development the world over has been more spectacular than the increase in the scope of government activity. In the early nineteenth century the major responsibilities of government were to provide peace and order and to make it easy for private enterprise to do the rest. But the growth of heavy industry and crowded cities following the industrial revolution created problems of health and exploitation that individual efforts could not solve. One after another, each group in the community turned to the state to provide protection or aid, and each new demand added to the work of government.

Thus in the early nineteenth century the danger of disease and epidemics in Great Britain's overcrowded communities brought a demand for compulsory rules of sanitation and for the establishment of public health services. Public outcry against the widespread use of child labor in cotton mills and coal mines resulted in restrictive legislation while, more positively, the state also assumed responsibility for providing public education. Labor sought protection against dangerous work conditions and later won the right to organize and bargain collectively. Industry, in turn, as it came to be challenged by the competition of other countries, asked protection through tariffs and sought positive public aid in reequipping itself for greater productivity. British farmers, long neglected in the national concentration on industry, ultimately secured benefits of government-sponsored research and price supports. Individuals, at first the aged, the destitute, and the unemployed, and since World War II also the sick, families with more than one dependent child, and, in fact, all those who have exceptional need, receive government support in one form or another. Most recently, and most far-reaching are the responsibilities for the national economy, which involve measures to stimulate growth, ameliorate unemployment, ease regional inequities, and sustain the balance of trade. In all these fields, the state through its central, regional, and local agents increasingly intervenes in the affairs of the community and the lives of individuals.

2 THE STRUCTURE OF ADMINISTRATION

In undertaking such widespread responsibilities, the government has used a variety of instrumentalities. At the center are the regular departments whose structure reflects the growth of functions but whose changing pattern indicates never-ceasing efforts to respond both to concepts of rational organization and to political and personal pressures. The Treasury services and keeps a watchful eye on the departments, maintaining a check on all expenditures and a central policymaking role pervasive throughout the whole administration. Its concern for economic planning will be dealt with in conjunction with other agencies used in that somewhat problematic field. In addition, the relatively new Civil Service Department now exercises overall supervision and direction of staffing, especially at the top levels.

On a somewhat different level, the nationalized industries run by public corporations, which provide services that once were furnished by private enterprise, now account for about one-fifth of all economic activity in Great Britain. Finally, there is a confusing wealth of advisory and *ad hoc* agencies.

These types of instrumentalities will be described one after the other, but it is important to keep in mind that they necessarily and constantly interact. Public administration is not a settled and static series of bureaus, departments, corporations, and agencies but a vast number of functions being carried on by a very large number of persons, almost all of whom belong to the public or civil service. Exactly where within the overall structure of administration these persons carry on their required functions may be less important than the fact that the functions are handled. There have been and continue to be many different ways in which different British governments have tackled the omnipresent problem of administrative organization. It is also true that a variety of factors influence these decisions: coherence of function, response to immediate as compared to long-range needs, coordination, political philosophy, personal prestige and pressures. As the chapter on Parliament pointed out, administration is a highly significant and also highly political activity, as well as one in which popular control is particularly difficult to maintain.

THE MINISTRIES OR DEPARTMENTS

The most important and largest number of functions within the British administration are performed by the regular ministries or departments. The distinctive feature of a ministry is that it is organized hierarchically under a minister who is responsible for answering in Parliament both for the general aspects of departmental policy and for the detailed actions of his subordinates. Most of these ministers hold Cabinet rank, but those in charge of departments who are outside the Cabinet are equally answerable to Parliament. We have already indicated some of the difficulties for parliamentary control that are involved in the doctrines of ministerial and collective responsibility, and we will discuss this issue further below.

The considerable variety in the titles both of the ministries and of those who head them is sometimes confusing. In the United States all administrative departments are created by act of Congress, and each is under a single head known as the secretary (except in the Department of Justice). In Great Britain the ministries have had a variety of origins that is reflected in the variety of their names. Some ministries, such as the Treasury (the descendant of the Exchequer, which evolved from the royal household), stem from great offices of an earlier time; others, such as the Foreign Office, War Office, and Home Office, have evolved from the ancient office of secretary of state (for which reason each is capable legally of performing the duties of all the others, except in cases where special responsibilities have been defined in legislation); only the more recent ministries were created by act of Parliament. In addition, some ministries were established under boards or commissions, as in the cases of the Treasury and the Board of Trade. However, it was discovered in time that such ministries were more efficient if authority were concentrated in a single person. Although there is still a Treasury Board, it never meets; the real head of the Treasury is the Chancellor of the Exchequer (not the prime minister, although he has the title of First Lord of the Treasury). The real head of the Board of Trade, now incorporated in the Department of Trade and Industry (1970), was the president of the Board of Trade, a title now added to that of Secretary of Trade and Industry. Thus, despite seeming differences in organization, each of the British ministries has a single head, although "federal" ministries like the Department of the Environment have ministers in charge of special areas of work under the overall responsibility of the Secretary of State for the Environment.

Because of the frequent changes in areas of responsibility and titles, which can be made smoothly by order-in-council, subject only to negative prayer or appeal against them (see Chapter 4, Section 4), no effort will be made to be exhaustive in listing the central ministries of the British government. They fall into four main categories: defense and external affairs; internal order; economic and social matters; and finance and economic planning. In considering these different fields (as of 1970), only the most striking or broadly characteristic aspects will be described.

The two fields of *defense and external affairs* have been subject in recent times to a consolidation and fusion process. The three former service departments—the Admiralty (traditionally given precedence because of the age-old dependence on the Navy), the War Office (Army), and the Air Ministry—were made integral parts of a single Ministry of Defense in 1964, instead of merely being coordinated by it. In a pattern common to several integrated departments, the Secretary of State for Defense has two ministers of defense under him, one for administration and one for equipment, and three undersecretaries, one for each of the services.

In external affairs, four former departments have been combined: the Colonial Office, which up to 1966 was responsible for Britain's remaining colonies, mostly islands and ministates; the Commonwealth Relations Office, which until 1968 handled relations with members of the Commonwealth and, for historical reasons, those with Ireland and South Africa, although these countries left the Commonwealth in 1949 and 1961, respectively (see Chapter 8, Section 1); the Ministry for Overseas Development, which until 1970 administered Britain's aid program; and the Foreign Office, renamed the Foreign and Commonwealth Office.

The Home Office, which is primarily responsible for *internal law and order*, in as far as these fields are not controlled by local authorities, has been subject to the process both of fusion and of fission. Since all administrative responsibilities that have not been assigned by law or convention to another minister fall under the Home Secretary, it has been common to add new responsibilities to the Home Office as they arose but also to take them away as these functions became large and urgent enough to require separate departments of their own.

At the present time (1970), the Home Office has jurisdiction over the metropolitan police of London, and because of the practice of grants-in-aid the right to establish standards of organization, discipline, and equipment for the police elsewhere; it supervises the treatment of offenders, including juveniles, and the probation service, administers immigration and naturalization legislation, and regulates the conduct of elections, civil defense, and fire services. The Home Office is responsible for the organization of the magistrates' courts, while the Lord Chancellor, an eminent judicial figure who is also Speaker of the House of Lords, controls the personnel and machinery of the courts of law, appoints the justices of the peace, and recommends other appointments to the judiciary in England and Wales. (For a thorough consideration of the courts, see Chapter 7, Section 2.)

The ministries concerned with *economic and social matters* are the most numerous, as can be expected, and the most changeable. The economic ministries, however organized, deal chiefly with industrial and income policies, regional policies, local government, housing, public buildings and works, power, transport, natural resources, technology, relations with the trade unions, and social service payments. Social ministries deal with such subjects as insurance and welfare, health, education, and the arts. We have already described how the Ministries of Housing and Local Government, of Public Building and Works, and of Transport were unified by the Heath government into a single Department of the Environment (see Chapter 5, Section 1). Previously, the Ministry of Housing and Local Government had split off from the Ministry of Health, and much earlier the latter had taken over the powers of the old Local Government Board. While the Department of the Environment was given major responsibility for developing regional policy, industrial development in the regions was vested in the newly fused Department of Trade and Industry. Thus the process of fusion and of fission goes on with its attendant problems of potential overloading, coordination, and parliamentary control.

The most important department responsible for *finance* and *economic planning* and the key administrative agency for *interministerial coordination* is the Treasury. The Treasury was also responsible up to 1968 for the supervision of the civil service, but this function on the advice of the Fulton Committee (see Section 4) was then transferred to a new Civil Service Department. This development left the Treasury still more concentrated than before on its policymaking functions, which lie at the heart of administration organization and coordination. The central role of the Treasury is to control the spending of all government and other public bodies. It is also in charge of international financial negotiations, and it deals with economic management and, since 1969, again with economic planning in the sense of forecasts. It should be noted also that Treasury personnel does not spend all its time in a single office but moves around to other bodies like the Cabinet Office, interdepartmental committees (for which it provided all the chairmen until Wilson inserted more Cabinet Office personnel), the specialized departments, the Bank of England, and so forth, to secure information, give advice, and maintain coordination.

The coordination and control by the Treasury are exercised at every stage of departmental policy. No ministry may make a proposal involving expenditures or present a financial estimate to the Cabinet without first receiving Treasury authorization. Thus, if a ministry wishes to expand its activities, it must persuade the Treasury that such an expansion is necessary and that it does not involve duplication of a task already performed by another agency. Since the Treasury is likely to be far more open to a projected expenditure if the reasons have been carefully explained in advance and if it has been consulted early in the development of the project, there is a strong incentive for representatives of other ministries to keep in constant touch with the Treasury in order to win a sympathetic comprehension of departmental needs. In this way, Treasury officials acquire an overall picture of the plans and activities of all ministries, which is of the greatest assistance in integrating and reconciling their multifarious activities.

All sections of the Treasury are represented, of course, on the top-level committee that prepares the budget, described by Sir Stafford Cripps, Chancellor of the Exchequer in 1950, as "the most important control and the most important instrument for influencing economic policy that is available to the Government." [1] As long as there are no general controls on wages, prices, and flow of goods (rationing), the budget is the major instrument for regulating the operation of the economy through raising or lowering taxes and through checking or expanding government spending. In the United States the president proposes the budget but the Congress disposes of the money, often in a fundamentally different way from what the administration had planned. In Great Britain there is never any doubt that the major recommendations of the budget, which is a closely knit financial plan, will be accepted exactly as proposed. In any case, no estimate for a ministry may be increased by Parliament.

The Treasury also controls the collection and expenditure of public money. All government revenue, which is collected for the Treasury by the Board of Inland Revenue, the Board of Customs and Excise, the Post Office, and the Commissioners of Crown Lands, goes directly into the Consolidated Fund, which is deposited in the Bank of England. About 15 percent of national expenditures fall in the category of permanent charges, which are not voted annually. These include the interest on the national debt, the salaries of judges, and the Civil List, which covers the expenditures of the royal family—all matters that are normally kept out of politics. All other matters, including the expenditures of all ministries, must be authorized by annual statutes, the parliamentary check upon the financial system. This check is reinforced by the semi-independent Exchequer and Audit Department under the Comptroller and Auditor General, an important nonpolitical officer, who is quite independent of the Treasury (although he works closely with it in checking expenditures by the ministries) and who makes an annual report on withdrawals of

[1] Quoted in Samuel Brittan, *Steering the Economy: The Role of the Treasury*, p. 38.

public money directly to the highly important parliamentary Public Accounts Committee.

Even after their estimates have been voted, ministries are not free to spend their appropriations as they wish. They can draw their money from the Consolidated Fund only through a requisition by the Treasury, countersigned by the Comptroller and Auditor General, and this is normally issued for only one-quarter of their appropriations at a time. Moreover, any increase in the number or salaries of officials in a ministry has to receive Treasury approval, even if the ministry has enough money on hand to provide for it.

Not surprisingly, such great concentration of power in the hands of a relatively small department—comprising perhaps a thousand members as compared to others, like Defense, which employs well over a hundred thousand—has led to sharp criticism. This criticism was principally leveled at the Treasury's responsibilities for the civil service and for economic planning. The civil service function was finally removed, as already indicated, to a new Civil Service Department established in 1968. A more complicated path was followed in regard to Treasury responsibilities for economic planning.

ECONOMIC PLANNING

The British, in practice, have never wholeheartedly adopted a notion of economic planning to the degree that the French, for example, did after World War II. Nonetheless, the combination of Keynesian economics, that is, the use of fiscal policies to limit trade cycles and unemployment, and to stimulate desirable economic activities, coupled with the experience during World War II of government control over all aspects of economic life led to new commitments to undertake government intervention in the economy on behalf of public welfare. It was a coalition government, headed by Prime Minister Churchill, which declared in a famous 1944 White Paper that "the Government accepts as one of their primary aims and responsibilities the maintenance of a high and stable level of employment after the war." How this objective, which requires economic

growth as well as a high and stable balance of payments, is to be secured, however, has led to much discussion and experimentation both in regard to policies and to instrumentalities.

Labor's commitment to democratic socialism naturally made it sympathetic to the extension of public ownership—reflected in large-scale nationalization projects immediately after the war (see below)—economic planning (where it made tentative but not very far-reaching efforts in its first period of office), and controls. The Conservatives, supported by public weariness of postwar restrictions, continued until the late 1950s to believe that competition could be an adequate stimulus to the economy. Faced, however, with the dismal evidence of economic sluggishness, balance-of-payments crises, inadequate infrastructure, and regional imbalances, they established a body in 1962 that was to concern itself with economic planning and longer-range projections: the National Economic Development Council (NEDC, commonly known as "Neddy"), whose developing organization was somewhat patterned on the effective machinery for economic planning that had been set up in France after the war. Thus, as in France, a series of bodies, known as "Little Neddies," were established in 1963 in which representatives of employers, trade unions, and relevant government departments worked out estimates of growth to be combined into a broad plan.

What is called "indicative planning," that is, a projection of what will happen to selected industries and sectors, including the public sector, if certain targets for overall growth are set, was embodied in the NEDC Plan for 1961–66, published by the Conservative government in 1963, and in Labor's National Plan of September 1963, covering the years 1966–70 and mainly prepared by the new Ministry of Economic Affairs. It must be admitted, however, that the expectation that the planning institutions would stimulate the economic growth at which they aimed—for example, the 1961–66 plan specified 4 percent growth—was not realized. The fundamental disequilibrium affecting the British balance of payments, and ultimately forcing (rather too late) the devaluation of the pound in November 1967, spelled the end of the effort at indicative planning. The

Green Paper published early in 1969 on "Economic Assessment to 1972" made its projections as forecasts rather than as instruments of policy.

In the meantime, the controversial Ministry of Economic Affairs had risen and was about to fall. It was established in 1964 to provide for more forceful planning for growth than was expected from "Neddy's" essentially advisory functions and those of the reorganized Treasury. This ministry took over much of the staff of the National Economy Group established in 1962 inside the Treasury, in response to Plowden recommendations to concentrate on economic planning, forecasting, and advising. In 1969, however, the Ministry of Economic Affairs was abolished and the economic planning functions were restored to the Treasury.

The Heath government introduced yet another addition to economic planning. It noted in its October 1970 White Paper on the reorganization of central government (see Chapter 5, Section 1) that the Treasury's "detailed and comprehensive" annual Public Expenditure Surveys, linked as they were to "medium-term economic assessments," provided "one of the basic elements in the information ministers' need to enable them to balance the claims of competing blocks of public expenditure." To fill two remaining gaps, however, it drew on the team of businessmen based in the Civil Service Department to help identify alternative policy options before final decisions were taken. This team now examines the objectives of expenditure against general government strategy and analyzes existing programs and the major policy options on them. Thus the government gains a better notion of desirable objectives in programs expressed as far as possible "in output terms," and it can examine alternative programs before making its final decisions. Considering the tradition of budget secrecy, it remains to be seen whether this information will be transmitted to Parliament for prior debate.

CIVIL SERVANTS AND MINISTERIAL RESPONSIBILITY

The vast responsibilities carried by the administration in any modern state naturally lead to fears that, in practice, it is the nonelected public personnel that operates government, whereas the elected representatives of the people, whether in Parliament or in the ministry, have relatively little influence on ultimate decisions. This concern, as we have seen, underlies much of the malaise in Parliament, and there can be no doubt that the relation between those formally responsible for the political aspects of government and those who are supposed to be apolitical—and hence, civil—is a sensitive but crucial one. More will be said on this issue in the course of the chapter.

Organization of a department

British departments are organized on a hierarchical principle. Immediately below the minister is the permanent secretary, who is both chief adviser to the minister and chief administrative officer of the department. In an American department, the top offices nearly always change hands when a new administration comes into office, but not in the United Kingdom, where experience and continuity are weighted more heavily than is sympathy with a particular political program.

The permanent secretary and the undersecretary, if there is one, must be constantly available for consultation with the minister, particularly when Parliament is in session; thus, the detailed control of administration is mainly in the hands of the assistant secretaries who head the several divisions into which a ministry is divided. Each of these divisions deals with a particular activity or area, and their work is coordinated through the higher officials in the ministry and by use of intra- and interdepartmental committees.

The permanent secretary, as the link between the rest of the ministry and the minister, inevitably has a great deal of discretion, of course, in determining what material to lay before the minister. Even more important is the fact that he may have a much wider range of experience than the minister himself in the subject matter of the ministry, particularly when the minister has recently come into office. In practice, however, the relative importance of the minister and the permanent secretary is likely to be a matter of personality. Inexperienced, weak, and overtaxed ministers may be swayed consistently by their advisers; but a minister who has a definite conception of what he wishes to accomplish can carry it through. A high civil servant may, and should, put before a minister his best arguments in favor of one course of action. If he is overruled, the ethics of the service demand that he carry out his minister's policy loyally and as effectively as possible. And in the end, since it is the minister who must stand before Parliament and assume responsibility for what his department has done, the minister will want to be convinced of the soundness of an important policy before he undertakes to support it publicly.

The minister and his political associates will also want to consider the public reaction to a particular way of handling a problem. If the permanent officials are the experts on the most efficient way of securing a particular purpose, the minister is, or should be, the expert on public opinion in his own party, in Parliament, and in the country. Moreover, a minister may have a broader view of the totality of an issue. R. A. Butler, who for four years was Chancellor of the Exchequer, was not an expert on technical Treasury operations, but Samuel Brittan suggests that it was his "hunches as a political animal that on occasion enabled him to separate bad advice from good"[2] and choose the wiser policy.

Ministerial and collective responsibility

What concerns MP's, however, is that the policies they can debate in Parliament are likely to have been largely settled already or else deal with generalities, whereas policy and administration are made up of vast numbers of specific decisions. It is this problem that has led to the pressure for more specialized committees, for more White Papers that lay out plans before they are formulated in legislation, for the parliamentary commissioner to get inside the workings of a department and identify which particular civil servant has been responsible for an error of judgment or for an inflexible decision that does not take particular human needs into account, and in this and other ways to remove some of the anonymity that shields civil servants.

This raises issues that are hotly debated. Brittan, for example, favors more open government, with the chance for civil servants to explain and defend their policy advice before parliamentary committees, as in the United States, rather than to have to filter it through a ministerial voice. He points out that the convention of a single minister being responsible for all departmental policy hardly stands up in the light of the constant interaction within interdepartmental committees, not to mention those in the Cabinet. He also feels that for the public to know that a variety of opinions has been canvassed before a final decision is reached would strengthen, rather than weaken, the case.[3]

The Fulton Committee on the Civil Service, which made no radical proposals on this issue, admitted that the assumption that a minister has "full detailed knowledge and control of all the activities of his department" is "no longer tenable." The special problem, as A. H. Hanson and Malcolm Wallace point out in *Governing Britain*,[4] is not, in fact, that greater openness and less anonymity are not compatible with ministerial responsibility as long as the principle of obedience is maintained, but that the equally important principle of political neutrality might be impaired. The more individual civil servants are identified with particular lines of policy, the more likely it might be that they would be caught up in actual political strife. And since the permanent tenure of civil servants rests on the assumption that they will not only serve faithfully whatever administration is in office but also not use their privileged position to the detriment of either side, the issue remains a sensitive one, not likely to be resolved in the immediate future.

THE NATIONALIZED ENTERPRISES

Public enterprise is a long-established feature of all modern governments. But its scope, justification, management, pay scales, relation to private enterprise, and articulation with the British representative system of government are once more somewhat in flux. No one could

[2] Brittan, *Steering the Economy*, p. 115.

[3] Brittan, *Steering the Economy*, pp. 34–35.

[4] A. H. Hanson and Malcolm Wallace, *Governing Britain*, pp. 145–47.

have anticipated when the Heath government came into office in June 1970 that, despite its broad commitment to stimulating competition and private enterprise, it would have felt impelled in February 1971 to nationalize a major part of Rolls-Royce because of the latter's bankruptcy, and that it would have pushed the nationalization measure through with unprecedented speed in a single evening. Less surprising, although with far-reaching consequences, have been the pressures on nationalized enterprises to divest themselves of at least some of the profitable sidelines they had developed. Wage disputes and strikes against the Electricity Board and the Post Office, the latter newly turned from a government department into a public corporation, strained government, union, and public patience and ingenuity early in 1971. Thus what had come to be thought of as a fairly settled aspect of governmental responsibilities since World War II has once more become a source of debate and controversy.

Labor's nationalization program after World War II had extended public ownership to just under one-fifth of the country's enterprises. To some degree this program, with its strong Fabian overtones, built upon earlier measures, in particular the four large-scale public enterprises that had been established in the interwar period (by Conservative or predominantly Conservative governments): the British Broadcasting Corporation (BBC), which provided British radio and now part of television broadcasting; the Central Electricity Board (now absorbed in the general nationalization of electricity), which built and operated four thousand miles of high-voltage transmission wires, known as the Grid, that cover Great Britain with a network of power; the London Passenger Transport Board (now under the Transport Commission), which operates various forms of transportation in the vast London area; and British Imperial Airways.

Most of the present nationalized enterprises date from the Labor government's first session when it nationalized the Bank of England, the coal mines, and telecommunications and consolidated national control over civil aviation. All electric power supply and transmission were nationalized in 1947. The railroads, road transport, all London transport, docks, and inland waterways came under national control at the beginning of 1948. The nationalization of gas supply and some parts of the iron and steel industry rounded out the program.

The most controversial aspects of the nationalization program were long-distance road haulage and iron and steel, the only two enterprises that were profitable and had not previously been under at least quasi-governmental control. Both were denationalized subsequently by the Conservatives—a process that creates its own confusions—but most of road transport was left under the Transport Commission, and a large measure of public control was retained over the production of iron and steel despite the sale back to private hands by 1955 of more than half of the steel producing concerns. Labor again nationalized steel under the Iron and Steel Corporation in 1967, and the Heath government has not moved to denationalize it again.

The characteristic form of organization for a nationalized enterprise is the *public corporation*,[5] which is designed to combine commercial flexibility with public accountability. Except for public ownership and the consequent necessity of ensuring ultimate ministerial and parliamentary responsibility, such a corporation is organized like a privately owned corporation or joint-stock company. It is a legal entity that can sue and be sued, sell goods and services, make a profit if possible, enter into contracts, and acquire property of its own. Since it is established by statute, however, it is not subject to company law. Although it is owned by the government, up to 49 percent of its equity could be acquired by the public, as is the case with British Petroleum, although in practice few nationalized enterprises are so attractive to private capital.

The public corporation stands outside the departmental structure and is responsible in

[5] Public corporations may be said to fall into three types: the industrial or commercial corporation that runs an industry or public utility; the social service corporation, such as the National Assistance Board or the New Town Development Corporation; and the supervisory public corporation, such as the Iron and Steel Board. Only the industrial or commercial corporation is described here, although the BBC is sometimes said to stand in "a sort of no-man's land" between the social service corporations and the nationalized industries. The ordinary social service corporation has less independence than the industrial corporation from ministerial control, because its purpose is to provide a particular social service on behalf of a government department.

its day-to-day operations not to a minister or to Parliament but to a board whose responsibilities are broadly suggested in the statute. Within these limits, this board is empowered to recruit staff and plan the operations of the corporation. The board is appointed, however, by the minister to whom the enterprise is assigned, who also has further significant powers to determine conditions of service, approve raising capital from appropriate sources, be provided with whatever information he requests, and, potentially most far reaching, give "directions of a general character as to the exercise of performance by the Board of their functions in relation to matters appearing to the Minister to affect public interest."

This mating of commercial initiative with ministerial and parliamentary responsibilities is a constructive way of extending public control without bringing public enterprises into the sphere of party politics. But it involves issues that have not yet been satisfactorily resolved. What should be the boundary between commercial autonomy and public supervision and direction? Is ministerial supervision compatible with strong and imaginative direction by the chief operating figure of the corporation, the chairman of its board? Can parliamentary supervision be secured without impairing the drive of the particular enterprise? For while the successful operation of a nationalized industry is dependent to a large degree on the forcefulness and insight of the man placed in charge, the maintenance of public control involves investigation, supervision, and a measure of official direction.

Each of the nationalized industries has been endowed with a somewhat different structure and function. The National Coal Board was established in 1946 to reorganize, consolidate, and modernize one of the largest, oldest, and most depressed of British industries and to run it as a single centralized enterprise. The Gas Council, in contrast, which was set up two years later, merely coordinates a number of area boards that, in turn, took over numerous existing concerns, some of which were municipally owned. The Gas Council concentrates, therefore, on general policy, research, and industrial relations. It is noteworthy that the gas industry is almost unique among nationalized industries in continuing with its original form, whereas coal, inland transport, and electricity have all been subject to subsequent reorganizations seeking more efficient and responsible structures.

To make clear-cut separation of the functions of the boards and their chairmen, on the one hand, and the responsible minister on the other has been found, in practice, to be virtually impossible. In theory, as we have seen, the separation is between day-to-day management and policy, but these spheres interact too much to fit into separate boxes. Moreover, although apart from the Coal Board, which was financed from the start by the Exchequer, the other three industries mentioned were expected originally to secure their finance from the issue of stock; their failure to secure adequate credit led them also to dependence on the Treasury.

The Conservatives tried to make a distinction between "commercial" and "public" responsibilities but with equal lack of success. As the White Paper of 1961 on the financial and economic obligations of the nationalized industries (Cmnd. 1337) pointed out, nationalized concerns have "wider obligations than commercial concerns in the private sector." Setting targets for the returns on their assets, which also take into account their social contribution, was proposed as a means to combine "the maximum contribution to their own development and the well-being of the community as a whole." More sophisticated techniques were added by the 1967 White Paper on the nationalized industries (Cmnd. 3437). But these, like earlier efforts, tended to make the relation between the board and the minister even closer than before.

As long as there is a common, basic philosophy and agreement on long-range plans between the chairman of the board and the minister and, indeed, the government in power, this close association can work well. But when Lord Robens, for ten years the distinguished, effective, and popular chairman of the Coal Board, resigned in January 1971, it was because the Heath government refused to let his nationalized industry decide for itself what fields it should enter. Nationalized industries, in fact, have branched into many lucrative supplementary fields. The Coal Board, for example, makes houses for its employees, leases time on its computers, has developed mining by-products that brings it into the chemical business, and has a share in rich-looking prospects for North Sea gas and oil. British Rail runs a profitable chain of hotels and operates ferries to the Continent. It appears that the Heath government feels that some of these ancillary businesses should be returned to private hands, and that the nationalized industries should not be allowed to cover deficits in one aspect of their work with such profitable ventures. From the other side it is open to question whether a superb and forceful manager of an industrialized enterprise should be prevented from engaging in such imaginative expansion. Lord Robens obviously felt that he did not wish to continue as chairman of the Coal Board if his freedom of initiative was curbed in this fashion.

There appears to be a basic issue of principle involved in this issue that goes deep into the roles of nationalized industries within the national economy and their management. The Conservative Minister of Industry, who has special responsibilities for the nationalized industries, has maintained that "by and large the public sector should be concerned primarily with those activities which cannot sensibly be done by the private sector." Lord Robens, in contrast, stressed the responsibility of nationalized enterprises both to the public and to their own workers. Taking over a depressed industry with a history of severe labor troubles, the Coal Board, under Lord Robens' leadership, managed to preserve the miners' morale in a period of contraction. His resignation indicated his fear that restrictive government policies would impair morale at all levels, as well as possibilities of a viable and independent existence for a public corporation such as he directed.

On another level, the Iron and Steel Corporation, which faced both overall losses and an impending rise in steel prices in 1971 when it was in the process of carrying out a major five-year modernization plan, was threatened with either losing some of its specialized and profitable steel and construction branches or facing the competition of government-financed steel imports from cheaper sources. A proposal by its chairman, Lord Melchett, who was formerly a leading banker, to sell shares to the public up to 49 percent of the equity, is another possible alternative approach to improving the corporation's position in the eyes of the government.

One persistent question regarding the relation between the minister and the chairman of a nationalized enterprise is whether it would not be better to remove the power of appointment from the former and vest it in a small permanent board with its own staff. This committee could examine the whole field of potential candidates, keep permanent records, and thus be better equipped to make proposals for chairmen and board members of particular enterprises. Whether the board should also have the power to review proposals for dismissals—as in the case of Lord Hall, who lost his post as chairman of the new Post Office public corporation in November 1970 on ground of inadequate management of its operations, and at an earlier date the chairmen of British Overseas Airways Corporation and of British Rail for failure to meet their targets—is another question. But lack of any guaranteed term of office, coupled with current inadequate pension arrangements, may make it difficult to recruit the best men for the job.

Not only ministerial but also parliamentary supervision of nationalized enterprises has been a matter of continuing concern. Questions on day-to-day management are clearly ruled out, while opportunities for discussion in Parliament of the annual reports of nationalized industries were found inadequate, when they were held at all. Largely due to backbench pressure, the Select Committee on Nationalized Industries was finally given broad scope in 1956 to examine their reports and accounts and has since produced a series of excellent analyses of both the policy and administration of particular industries. Working in a nonpartisan fashion, taking evidence from related ministries and outside experts, and checking back at intervals to see how its recommendations have been implemented, this select committee has in many ways provided a model for such parliamentary investigations. It is worth noting, however, that Lord Robens favors setting up an independent public accountability commission to ensure that public enterprises are run in the best interests of the public, leaving it to their own chairmen to decide how best to run them in their own interest.

ADVISORY COUNCILS AND GROUP ACTIVITY

Advisory councils and group activity are often two sides of the same interaction between private concerns and the administration. The former operate through formal channels of advice by producers or consumers, for which provision is made in the law; the latter springs from the activities of a group that are directed toward its own interest. But in either case, the interaction is likely to be rewarding from both sides. The public administration, like political parties and, indeed, MP's, needs the specialized, detailed information that interest groups can provide, the more so since so much of their work is concerned these days with highly specific matters. Moreover, administration, like the representative system itself, needs to keep as much aware of public reactions to its measures as is possible. While it may be argued that particular interest groups present very partial views of public concern, their combined impact and illumination can be considerable.

A wide range of advisory committees—of which some five hundred include representatives of producer groups—dot the departments. Some of these committees are highly specialized; others are of more general character. Some have grown up out of convenience; many are required by law. A large complement of advisory committees was established, for example, under the 1947 Agricultural Act, which obliged the minister to "consult with such bodies of persons" as appear to represent "the interests of producers." The purpose of group representation is to assure those who are to be affected by the implementation of legislation that they will be consulted and, if possible, to associate them with the forms adopted. Thus the Ministry of Agriculture not only has its network of advisory committees (both to receive and to give advice), but also may consult the National Farmers' Union either officially or unofficially. Indeed, since the war, agricultural price-fixing has involved annual negotiations with the National Farmers' Union, and these levels are endorsed by that body, although officially announced by the government.

There is also much detailed information of which a department can make use and which it can secure more easily and cheaply through a trade association than by doing its own research. The Ministry of Transport, for example, can secure useful technical information, particularly on minutiae, from the Society of Motor Manufacturers and Traders, as well as through the National Advisory Council for the Motor Manufacturing Industry. The latter has the advantage, however, of including not only representatives of government and employers but also of relevant unions, as well as an independent member. It acts officially as a means of regular consultation on such subjects as "the location of industry, exports, imports, research, design and progress" of the motor industry.

This integration of interest groups into the process of government is not an abdication of responsibility by representative and administrative agencies. It is, rather, a sensible accommodation between those agencies that are responsible for formulating and carrying out public policy and those most intimately affected by such action. As Samuel H. Beer points out in his *British Politics in the Collectivist Age*, interest groups in Great Britain are "domesticated" and tied into normal operations of government, particularly those of the administration. In the United States, the degree of independence in voting of a congressman leads most interest groups to focus their pressures upon the legislature; in Great Britain, party allegiance and discipline are not overriden by group pressures. It is natural, therefore, for interest groups to concentrate on the administration with what is normally mutual advantage.

3 LOCAL AND REGIONAL GOVERNMENT

"Apoplexy at the center; anaemia at the extremities": this is the picture of an over-centralized administration, all too characteristic of modern governments. It is a picture that has given rise to proposals for local government reform ever since World War II. Moreover, the renewed interest in economic planning in the sixties coupled with expressions of Welsh and Scottish nationalism have stimulated thinking about regional decentralization and deconcentration of the functions of government. The urge for reform has even led to the setting up of the Crowther Commission on Constitutional Reform, which is to report in 1972. But in the meantime, the constantly increasing pressures for centralization that are reflected in the vast scope of the responsibilities possessed by the British central administration need to be counterbalanced more adequately by functions that are locally stimulated and performed.

The movement for reform is spurred by both the noticeable apathy regarding local self-government, once the pride of English democracy, and an awareness of how out of date its units, functions, and finances have become. But while most people agree that there is need to relieve the burdens and balance the powers and responsibilities of the central administration, there has been considerable disagreement over what plans should be implemented. The Royal Commission, which met from 1966 to 1969 under the chairmanship of Lord Redcliffe-Maud, carried out the most comprehensive modern scrutiny of local government in England (the area to which its mandate was restricted) and proposed a radical series of changes; the Conservatives produced no less radical but very different proposals in February 1971. Both sets of proposals seek in their different ways to reconcile the twin demands of efficiency and popular participation in such a way that they fit modern conditions, since the existing local government system no longer does.

Local autonomy was established early in England and Wales,[6] but local self-government is relatively recent. From the time of the Tudors, justices of the peace, appointed by the Crown and selected from the local gentry, exercised a benevolent direction as judges, legislators, and executives in county areas, while local oligarchies ruled in the ancient but antiquated boroughs or towns. The dominance of both groups was not undercut until the nineteenth century, when the industrial revolution and the resulting increase in governmental activities laid responsibilities on local areas that they were obviously incapable of handling. The first shift in authority, however, was to a series of boards and commissioners, established one by one as local areas assumed new tasks in regard to public health, highways, public assistance to the poor, and elementary education. Since each of the new authorities was usually provided with a new set of areas within which to carry out its work, England and Wales became a bewildering network of sanitary districts, poor law districts, conservation districts, and so forth, whose boundaries rarely coincided. Only through a series of local government acts, extending to 1894, was order brought out of this chaos. In a parallel development, governing power was transferred gradually to elected councils, first in the boroughs or towns (1835), then in the counties and the newly created county boroughs or cities (1888), and finally in the subdivisions of the counties, the districts and parishes (1894). Thus by the end of the nineteenth century, local self-government had been established as the rule throughout England and Wales.

It has become more difficult, however, to speak of a separate sphere of local action clearly set off from national government. Certain services once looked on as purely local have steadily taken on more national significance. The local school is part of a national educational system; public assistance is no longer

[6] There were slight, although not essential, variations in the forms of local government in Scotland and Northern Ireland. The institutions described are those of England and Wales.

a community task but a national responsibility; even gas and electricity, once characteristically municipal services, have now been nationalized. It remains true that there is still considerable local flexibility in these spheres, and that there are possibilities of a local veto or restraint on certain key policy issues, as with Labor's program for comprehensive schools (see Chapter 1, Section 2). But the great expansion in what are essentially local personal services—education, child care, old people's welfare, mental health, and so forth—has necessarily resulted in the establishment of national standards and the need for national financial support.

Facilitating the rapidity of this change is the fact that in Great Britain there is no constitutional division of powers such as that existing between the national and state governments in the United States. There are only two levels of government in Great Britain—national and local—instead of the three levels of government in the United States—national, state, and local. And the British Parliament has authority over both the organization and the powers of local governments in the same way as American state governments have authority over the local governments, like cities and counties, within their boundaries. Thus reform of local government and arrangements for regional deconcentration will be carried through by national legislation.

PROJECTS FOR REFORM

The Redcliffe-Maud Commission proposed replacing the present fragmented system of 1,210 local authorities [7] (not including 7,000 parish councils and London), which reflect a town-country division outmoded by modern means of communication, by a system of metropolitan areas and 58 unitary authorities integrated by 8 new provincial councils and based on continuing local councils at the borough, district, and parish levels, if the people want them. The commission picked out three metropolitan areas, besides Greater London, as satisfactory planning units for which it sug-

gested two-tier systems with services divided between the metropolitan authority and the metropolitan district councils. The most radical part of the proposals was that the existing relations in functions and finance [8] were to be replaced by giving the new authorities freedom to set their own priorities inside broad, national policies, local sources of funding (to flow from gasoline and motor taxes and driving license fees), and general power and discretion in spending these funds.

The elective principle and regionalism both had a place in the Redcliffe-Maud proposals. The commission believed that the authorities for the unitary areas combining town and country districts should consist of up to 75 elected members who would be free to choose their own organization as well as being responsible for decentralizing and consulting about activities within their area. These areas, the commission suggested, would vary widely in size and population, all the way from 195,-000 to a million, since it found no appropriate formula for delimiting them.

The eight provincial councils, which would replace the existing regional economic councils, were to be indirectly elected through the directly elected local authorities. Their special responsibility would be to undertake physical and economic planning within their area in consultation with central authorities and to decide the location of special services, like schools for handicapped children. The commission proposed no services for them to run on their own but that they have their own staffs (unlike the existing planning councils) and power to spend money for special projects.

---

[7] The system existing in 1971 included 45 countries, 79 county boroughs (which include all the important cities in the country except London), 227 noncounty boroughs (consisting of towns not big or important enough to rank as county boroughs), 449 urban districts, and 410 rural districts.

[8] The central government contributed 57 percent of all local expenditures in 1970–71. These funds came in the form of *grants-in-aid*, which meet, for example, about half the cost of local police forces and 20 to 75 percent of the cost of roads, and *Exchequer equalization grants*, which are provided on the basis of need to poor areas so that the services they provide do not fall too short of those established by wealthier communities that can afford to add to prescribed standards.

The chief source of local government finance has traditionally been *rates*, or taxes, in proportion to the annual rental value of property in the area; revenue is also gained from rental of municipal property, some license fees, and so forth. It was estimated that if the Redcliffe-Maud proposals for independent sources of income were adopted, the proportion of central government financing would drop to about 14 percent, which would necessarily make a great change in the relation between central and local government.

LOCAL GOVERNMENT AREAS AS PROPOSED BY THE
REDCLIFFE-MAUD COMMISSION, 1966–69

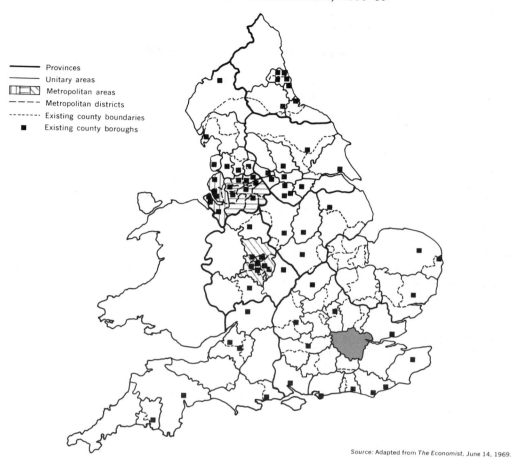

Provinces
Unitary areas
Metropolitan areas
Metropolitan districts
Existing county boundaries
■   Existing county boroughs

Source: Adapted from The Economist, June 14, 1969.

Their form, however, was left otherwise blank in anticipation of whatever proposals, if any, will be made on regional government by the Crowther Commission, which reports in 1972. Local councils, as indicated, would exist only where they were wanted. In the words of the report: "The only *duty* of the local council would be to represent local opinion, but it would have the *right* to be consulted on matters of special interest to its inhabitants, and it would have the *power* to do for the local community a number of things done locally."

These proposals were approved with modifications by the Labor government. It suggested, in its February 1970 White Paper, fifty-one instead of fifty-eight unitary authorities, increasing the number of metropolitan au-

thorities to five, and making local councils more effective by some joint memberships between district and unitary authority committees. It rejected the notion, however, that the larger local councils should provide some of the major services such as education. The Wilson administration also refused to commit itself to the suggestion of provincial councils to provide the framework for regional decentralization, preferring to wait for the recommendations of the Crowther Commission on Constitutional Reform.

Although the Heath government is equally committed to local government reform, the pattern proposed by its new Ministry of the Environment is quite a different one. In February 1971, it issued three White Papers on local government reform in Scotland (Cmnd. 4583), Wales (no Cmnd.), and England (Cmnd. 4584). These White Papers outline the major features of what was embodied in legislation in the fall of 1971. On April 1, 1974, 380 new councils in England and 43 in Wales will begin work under the new arrangements. The changeover in Scotland will come a year later.

The Conservative government's plan provided for yet a smaller number of what are still called counties. Thus in place of the existing sixty-two administrative counties (which were often, but not always, identical with historic counties like Devon and Hampshire) and eighty-three county boroughs or the Royal Commission's proposed fifty-eight unitary authorities, there are only thirty counties, some of whose boundaries are necessarily new. To compensate for such large and somewhat remote units, there is a second tier of boroughs and districts. But apart from the six most densely populated areas that are named metropolitan counties and patterned on the structure of Greater London (see below), metropolitan districts, county and municipal boroughs have lost their major powers to the counties, which, as with the Redcliffe-Maud proposals, include town and country areas. While Scotland, which has been provided with eight "regional" authorities, and Wales, with seven new counties, were assigned their numbers and areas of second-tier districts in their White Papers, the exact demarcation of the 360-odd county districts for England, that is, those outside of the metropolitan areas, were determined by a Boundary Commission set up after the legislation was passed. In general, large towns have become districts in their own right but without their previously enjoyed independent status and with reduced functions, while outside of such urban centers, districts include between 40,000 and 100,000 people.

Two much debated features of the White Paper proposals were the allocation of functions between the counties and districts outside the metropolitan areas and the boundaries of the latter. Towns that had enjoyed the status and extended functions of county boroughs protested vigorously. The change, as originally proposed, was indeed radical. Whereas towns had previously had their own schools and libraries, settled their own traffic and highway arrangements, run their own buses and the full range of social services, and done their own planning, they were confronted with the prospect of becoming responsible only for housing, neighborhood improvement, rubbish collection, and local development. Moreover, the inhabitants of those towns not fortunate enough to be selected as the county seat confronted the prospect of having to travel to another town to check administrative policy, for example, with the social-service director, or to lobby the council. Subsequent provision for the delegation of authority by the county to the district, where this did not interfere with county functions, ameliorated the situation somewhat, but it did not wholly ease the strained feelings involved.

The issue of metropolitan boundaries and division of functions was a further source of debate. Some felt that the boundaries of the six metropolitan counties (outside of London) were drawn too tight around their built-up areas to permit a reasonable interaction with their adjoining regions. Others argued, however, that these boundaries were necessary to prevent the unfortunate consequences of "urban sprawl." The metropolitan counties, it should be noted, have fewer powers than those possessed by other counties. Education and social services inside the metropolitan counties are left to the metropolitan districts into which they are divided, which, in some cases—for example, Birmingham, Newcastle, Manchester—are cities in their own right. Strategic planning and transportation, naturally, are metropolitan county functions, but some have felt that housing, which is not, should also be included because of its urgency and close relation to general planning.

The Redcliffe-Maud proposals for a few large all-purpose areas, particularly as formulated by the Labor government, offered a good possibility of strengthening local government by giving it a stronger base and making lines of responsibility clearer. The Conservative two-tier system retains both the overlapping responsibilities and small authorities that weakened local government in the past. Moreover, this system will diminish both the status and responsibility of the cities, the units which were most likely to be able to share power with the central government if their functions had been expanded rather than decreased. The

LOCAL GOVERNMENT AREAS PROPOSED BY
CONSERVATIVE GOVERNMENT, FEBRUARY 1971

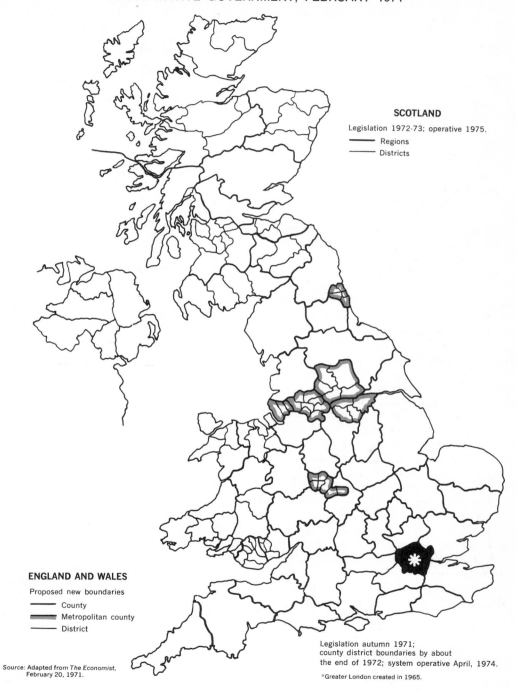

SCOTLAND

Legislation 1972-73; operative 1975.

——— Regions
——— Districts

ENGLAND AND WALES

Proposed new boundaries

——— County
▬▬▬ Metropolitan county
——— District

Source: Adapted from *The Economist*,
February 20, 1971.

Legislation autumn 1971;
county district boundaries by about
the end of 1972; system operative April, 1974.

*Greater London created in 1965.

county councils, on the other hand, which will become the chief local authority areas, seem unlikely to offer such a workable possibility for effective decentralization of functions and decision-making. The likelihood, therefore, is that the present reorganization of units will do little, if anything, to strengthen the role played by local government or, indeed, to halt its decline.

The whole issue of regional planning is still debated. The closest the British have moved to establishing specific machinery for regional planning is the structure set up by the Labor government in 1964. It consisted of both an executive Planning Board, made up of departmental officials entrusted by central ministries with control of relevant functions in their regions, and an advisory Planning Council, whose members are appointed by the relevant ministry from persons qualified either through expert knowledge or because they represent particular regional interest groups, like businessmen, trade unionists, and members of local government councils. The Conservative White Paper places the responsibility for policy planning on the counties, but the districts are to provide planning permissions, a division that may complicate effective action, as it has tended to do in the past. Districts will be expected to conform to general plans drawn up by their county, but there may be some tensions when the political persuasion of the two bodies is different. Another problem is that some counties, at least, may not provide broad enough areas for planning large-scale development, physical communications, and major land use. Not surprisingly, the government wishes to await the recommendations of the Crowther Commission (as indeed Labor did when in power) before proposing provincial divisions, if it follows the Redcliffe-Maud Royal Commission in that regard. But this hiatus leaves the major units below the central government level with unsuitable boundaries for planning purposes.

THE COUNCILS

Traditionally, the organ of self-government in every unit of local government has been the council, and this continues to be the case for the units of the new scheme. Not only is there far less diversity in the structure of local government in England than in the United States (where county and city governments differ widely in form, and where there are a number of different types of city government), but there is also no separation of powers in English local government such as is common in American city government. Thus the local government council in England has both executive and legislative powers, decides matters of policy, passes ordinances, fixes the budget, considers the way in which programs should be carried out in detail, and selects and works with the permanent officials who run the local services.

Members of a local government council have traditionally been elected for three-year terms; some, called aldermen, were chosen (or, to use a more technical term, co-opted) by the councilors themselves. Since property qualifications for voting in local government elections were swept away in 1945, anyone who can vote in a parliamentary election also has the local franchise. One result is that local elections took on the character of miniature national elections, with Conservatives and Labor working hard to gain control of local councils, both to demonstrate their political strength throughout the country and to consolidate their influence in the organs that administer so many national programs. In general, Labor is strong in urban areas and the Conservatives outside of them, which Labor charged had some bearing on Conservative government proposals for local government reform. On the other hand, England is so strongly urbanized that in practice the new counties, unlike the old ones, may be dominated by townsfolk and not the rural gentry. There will at least have to be a wholly new orientation of party machines to these levels with consequences not yet predictable.

In the past, in any case, once councils had been elected, party politics were less dominant than in the national sphere. Labor has claimed that there is more drive behind programs for social welfare, recreation centers, and housing when Laborites control a council, and the Conservatives have maintained that they are more efficient and financially responsible. Confronted with major responsibilities for most of the public arrangements molding the conditions of life in our complicated and crowded environments, the overriding issue is to get on with the job.

While the council as a whole determines the general outlines of a local program, most council work is administrative and is carried out by committees. These committees function wherever local government has responsibilities. They inspect schools, hire teachers, work on plans for roads, parks, and sewerage systems, or discuss specifications for the units in new housing developments, working closely at all times with the members of their permanent administrative staff. As a result, members of the council acquire a practical experience in governmental problems and administrative work for which members of Parliament have no equivalent. The fact that so much of the work of local government is administrative leads to great dependence on the advice of the local civil service. Moreover, local administration must fit within the overall pattern of central administration. Local government reform seeks to provide some genuine local autonomy within this system.

Local government autonomy, however, depends on more local control of sources of funding and of how these funds are spent. So far the central government has not provided much scope for local judgment. Unless it does so, local authorities will continue to be chiefly agents of the central government rather than of their communities. If this is the case, the hopes of the reformers for more decentralization of decision-making and more citizen participation in local institutions will not be realized.

4 THE PUBLIC SERVICE

The success of any organization depends on the people who do its work. This fact is particularly true of the public service, which demands of its members not only efficiency but also devotion to public purposes. To the extent that the public servant acts in an official capacity, he must be neutral toward the aims of the government. He must be willing to serve with equal energy and devotion the purposes of a Conservative government when it is in power and of a Labor government when it is in power. If his private opinions are opposed to public policy, it is the public policy that he must serve, conscientiously and wholeheartedly.

To state this principle, however, is to open up a whole series of supplementary questions on the best ways of realizing it in practice. Both Great Britain and the United States have had to find practical answers to issues like these: What training and what qualities are most important for the public servant who is to be both expert and responsible? To what extent can public servants be allowed, in private life, to engage in partisan political activity? To what extent may they enjoy the right to strike or (especially in business enterprises run by the government) the right to a closed shop? How representative should the public service be in the sense of having its personnel typify a cross section of the people whom it serves? Is it more desirable for the highest public servants to be professional in the sense of having permanency of tenure or to be active supporters of, and to change office with, the government of the day?

THE CIVIL SERVICE

Great Britain developed one set of answers to these questions in the middle of the nineteenth century that still influences the character of its administration. Reform of its government service arose out of Great Britain's own particular type of spoils system: not, as in the United States, one in which new administrations regularly replaced government officials with their own appointees, but one in which government offices had become the preserve of the sons of noble families who could not make a living elsewhere. Thus the principal need was not, as in the United States, for permanence of tenure, but to secure people of ability and appropriate training.

At that time most government work was paper work—that is, it consisted mainly of collecting material, keeping records, and writing reports for the use of ministers. The work of the public service seemed to fall, therefore, into a great number of routine jobs that could be done by people of average ability, as long as they were careful and well supervised, and a very much smaller number of positions at the top that demanded great insight and judgment. When Lord Macaulay undertook the task of "housecleaning" the service, it was decided that recruitment for both lower and upper positions should be by merit. For the top key group of officials Macaulay had the example of the training instituted somewhat earlier at Haileybury for the recruitment and selection of young men for the Indian service, a selection avowedly designed to secure the type of able, cultured English gentleman who would best maintain British prestige abroad. Such men were the products of the English universities of the day; it was therefore not surprising that the tests designed for recruiting the home civil service were likewise geared to the educational system. Those who wished to become high administrators had to demonstrate their ability through tests similar to comprehensive final examinations at a university, while the army of clerks was recruited on the basis of examinations similar to those in secondary school.

To make sure that the tests were administered fairly, a Civil Service Commission [9] was established in 1855, and, since 1870, open competitions have been the normal means of entry to the British civil service (as contrasted with the political service, i.e., ministers responsible to Parliament). Success in these competitive tests is now necessary both for positions within the United Kingdom and outside. Those who receive a certificate of qualification from the Civil Service Commission are ranked as part of the established civil service and have long enjoyed permanent tenure.

Up to World War I, departments maintained their autonomy in recruitment and promotion, and during the war a vast number of able people were called in to service the war effort. It was only thereafter that decisive changes took place. The civil service became centralized and unified under the Treasury. The permanent secretary of the Treasury was declared to be head of the civil service. The Treasury thus acquired not only effective control over appointments to the departments but by virtue of this strategic position also over promotions. The minister retained a right of veto but not of selection. Along with this decisive change went the long-prized establishment of "general" classes, of which the top administrative class was the one of vital importance for policymaking. The class of technical specialists, which was created later, was looked on as inferior in status and pay to the "generalists," for whom promotion to higher ranks was far better assured. Not surprisingly the nonindustrial service expanded rapidly in response to the increase in duties being assumed by the state. In 1901, it included 116,713 members; in 1939, 374,300; in 1965, 676,900; and, even excluding the transformation of the Post Office into a public corporation, about 475,000 in 1968. The dominant administrative class remained small, although it too grew between 1939 and 1965 from 2,100 to 3,500.

As elsewhere within British government, scrutiny and change are now the order of the day in the civil service. Although changes had been made in recruitment procedures, notably in increased use of the interview for selection and in moving from one grade to another through promotion, the Fulton Report,[10] the most extensive and critical review of the civil service in generations, prefaced its proposals in June 1968 with the somewhat unhistorical comment: "The Home Civil Service today is still fundamentally the product of the nineteenth-century philosophy of the Northcote-Trevelyan Report. [As noted previously, it dates from about 1919.] The tasks it faces are those of the second half of the twentieth century.

---

[9] The British Civil Service Commission is composed of three members who are appointed by the Cabinet. Unlike the United States Civil Service Commission, whose three members are generally chosen from outside the service, the British commissioners are nearly always persons of long experience in the British civil service and hold office until eligible for retirement under regular civil service rules. Since the British commissioners almost never have had active political experience before appointment, there is no rule in Great Britain (in contrast to the United States) that only two of the three members of the commission may belong to the same political party.

[10] The Fulton Committee was appointed by Prime Minister Wilson on February 8, 1966, to examine "the structure, recruitment and management, including training, of the Home Civil Service." The chairman, Lord Fulton, was then vice-chancellor of Sussex University.

This is what we have found; it is what we seek to remedy." Several of the committee's detailed proposals have been already adopted, and the British civil service today is involved in a long process of adjusting to these changes and the new reform philosophy.

The change that may have the most long-range impact is to remove the responsibility for the central management of the civil service from the Treasury to a new Civil Service Department directly under the prime minister. The Fulton Committee rejected the view that "under concentrated control the two functions of controlling expenditure and managing the Service can each be more effectively discharged" and argued that a new system requires a new instrumentality. By making an outstanding and strongly reformist civil servant, Sir William Armstrong, head of the Home Civil Service, and of the Civil Service Department in 1968, and thus giving him supervision of all departments and a decisive voice in all senior appointments, the process of change stimulated by the Fulton Report has been provided with effective leadership.

Regrading the civil service

The Fulton Committee struck hard at the multiplicity of divisions—47 general classes and 1,400 departmental classes—which it felt limited flexibility and movement within the civil service. "All classes," it stated, "should be abolished and replaced by a single, unified grading structure covering all civil servants from top to bottom in the nonindustrial part of the Service," with different levels of pay matching different levels of skill and responsibility. Job classification was looked on as the key to this regrouping, which resembles the personnel divisions of the American civil service with its twenty or so grades regardless of the particular area of operation. This reconstitution of the service was instituted on January 1, 1971, with interim mergers of a number of classes covering about 250,000 of the nonindustrial civil service, and changes affecting some 560 members of the top echelons.

The top division or class of the British civil service prior to January 1, 1971, was called the *administrative class*, sometimes known as "the

permanent brain trust" or "mandarins," who carry heavy responsibilities for formulating policy, advising ministers, and controlling and directing departments. Under any scheme of organization these civil servants inevitably have a strong political influence, since ministers, particularly when they come into office but to some extent at all times, depend on them both for information and for the advice that is basic to political decisions and debate. Sir William Armstrong once commented: "The chief danger to which politicians and Ministers are open is not, as is often supposed, that obstructive bureaucrats will drag their feet in implementing their schemes, but that their own optimism will carry them into schemes and policies which will subsequently be seen to fail and which attention to the experience and information available from the Civil Service might have avoided." It is the responsibility of top administrators, and particularly the permanent secretary of a department, to advise and, where necessary, to warn his minister.

The next level used to be known as the *executive class*. It was responsible for specialization in fields like taxation and accountancy, preliminary investigations, answers to parliamentary questions, and, with experience, for important decisions. Mobility from the executive to the administrative class had been considerable well before the Fulton Report and also an indication of the fact that the two might well be merged.

Below these two classes traditionally were the *subclerical* and *clerical services*, comprising more than three-quarters of the established nonindustrial civil service and performing repetitive tasks like typing and working under orders. Little change can occur here.

Selecting the upper civil servants

The characteristics and selection of those clearly destined for top roles in the civil service have been the most controversial aspects of recruitment. A social survey prepared under the direction of two social scientists for the Fulton Committee indicated that the administrative class was disproportionately composed of individuals from "privileged" social and educational backgrounds, two-thirds of them graduates of Oxford or Cambridge, and 56 percent privately educated.[11] The similarity of this background to that of a large number of MP's, particularly in the Conservative party, and to highly placed executives in commercial and industrial enterprises has often led to accusations that, in practice, Great Britain is dominated by a relatively small elite whose associations in the same schools, universities, and clubs have formed them into a self-perpetuating clique with class-centered interests rather than directed for the national good. This accusation, however unjustified, has been a major factor in the demands for a change in the selection procedures for the administrative class.

The focus of criticism in the selection process was placed on the so-called country-house technique of a whole battery of tests conducted over two or three days for a group of about twenty candidates who had already been winnowed from other contestants by their demonstrated academic excellence and achievements in the prescribed qualifying written examination. This technique had already been sharply castigated as early as 1959 in an essay entitled "The Apotheosis of the Dilettante" by Dr. Thomas Balogh (who was subsequently, from 1964 to 1967, economic adviser to the Cabinet). His charge was that by giving greater weight to the interview, "the safeguards against class-prejudice and nepotism established by the anonymity of the written examination were considerably weakened." [12]

To investigate whether the "country-house" technique—known as Method II—unduly weighted the selection process toward those from a particular background and educational stream, the Labor government established yet another committee, this time under J. G. W. Davies, assistant to the governor of the Bank of England.[13] This committee, which also examined the Halsey-Crewe survey, concentrated its attention on current selection procedures rather than on those persons already in the service, noted a broadening in the pattern of recruitment in the previous five years, but con-

cluded that the social background of those who applied still remained too narrow. In general, however, the committee concluded that the main method for recruiting the hundred future policymakers who are chosen annually from the seven hundred contestants was "something to which the public service can point with pride" for achieving a more complete picture of the individual at the moment of selection than either the American or the French civil services secure. At the same time it recommended—and the government approved—lessening the rigidity of academic requirements (by substituting an honors degree for the first- or second-class honors previously demanded) enroute to ultimately dropping formal academic qualifications for eligibility. Moreover, all candidates, including those with first-class honors, who had previously been exempted, were henceforth to take the written qualifying examination, which was recast in 1971 to prevent any undue advantage to candidates with arts degrees.

The Fulton Committee had proposed either to abolish the final selection board that conducts the "country-house" tests or to instruct the board only to add a fixed mark to those received from the two previous stages of examination. The government decided on the Davies Committee recommendation to retain the board but to increase its representation of outside interests by including two non-civil service examiners instead of one.

The effect on the composition of Britain's top civil servants of these changes will only be perceptible a long time hence. It will become apparent first at the level of assistant secretary, where most civil servants achieve their highest rank. This rank is crucial for the effective administration of the department, but it is not involved directly in policymaking. Only relatively few are promoted to the level above assistant secretary to that of undersecretary, which marks the decisive move into the upper civil service. It is these persons that the Civil Service Department watches carefully for the talent to fill top jobs in ministries throughout the service.

One of the major differences between the British and American civil services lies in the fact that the former is a career service in which the members of the administrative class have a

---

[11] A. H. Halsey and I. M. Crewe, "The Civil Service," *Social Survey of the Civil Service*, 3 (1) (1969).

[12] Reprinted in *Crisis in the Civil Service*, ed. by Hugh Thomas, p. 19.

[13] *Report of the Committee of Inquiry into the Method II System of Selection*, 1969.

chance for promotion to the highest administrative positions in the department, whereas in
the United States the top departmental offices
nearly always change hands when a new administration comes into office—not simply, as
critics sometimes suggest, in order to provide
political spoils for the electoral victor, but because of the belief that the policies of the new
administration will be carried out most effectively if those responsible for their administration are actively in sympathy with them. The
vigor and imagination with which some political appointees tackle their jobs give support to
this view, and some observers have suggested
that the British system, by forcing a high civil
servant to subject his own political beliefs and
prejudices to those of the government that
happens to be in power at a given time, may
well substitute experience for a dynamic enthusiasm. The British view, however, is that
men of the highest caliber will not enter the
civil service unless they can look forward to
positions of great responsibility in which they
will share in the making of policy.

It is worth noting the training and experience of the thirty top civil servants who were
permanent secretaries in 1971. Twenty-six of
them had gone to Oxford or Cambridge; two
to the London School of Economics; one to
Glasgow University; and one, exceptionally,
had not gone to the university at all. Only
eleven had gone to public schools (i.e., to one
of the great private boarding schools), one of
them to Eton and one to Harrow; the rest
came from grammar schools, except for one
educated in New Zealand. Most of them had
worked their way up through the service, but
a few had also had experience outside Whitehall: Sir Arnold France, the one permanent
secretary who did not go to the university,
spent eleven years in the District Bank; another
worked in a large brokerage firm; a third in
Transport House. Their changes of career, however, were due to the war and, as the Fulton
Committee pointed out, it had become very
difficult for a man of experience to enter the
service in middle age, one of the particular
advantages of the American system.

The Fulton Committee had also criticized
what it considered an exaggerated stress on the
"generalist," and felt that scientists, engineers,
and other specialists had not been given either
the opportunities for advancement or the authority they should possess. The Committee
charged as well that too few civil servants were
"skilled managers," that there was too little
career planning and management and not
enough contact between the civil service and
the community it exists to serve. In general, it
felt there should be "greater professionalism,"
with the specialists getting more training in
management and the administrators more
specialized training in either social administration or economic and financial administration.
All civil servants, it urged, should have some
knowledge of and experience with quantitative
techniques (not yet widely taught in the English educational system).

Some of these criticisms, particularly the
lack of "professionalism," were much resented
by the civil service and, indeed, were probably
based on lack of understanding of the in-
tricacy of the tasks of the upper civil service
and the competence with which it carries its
responsibilities. It was also felt that the committee had an inadequate appreciation of the
service's ability to accommodate and even promote change. But some of its suggestions—for
example, the proposals for more flexible interchange with outside professions—have been endorsed by Sir William Armstrong himself. As
early as 1965 in giving evidence to the Estimates Committee, Sir William had stressed
the value of young administrators—in his
words, "the top end of the assistant principals
and the junior principals, people round about
28 to 30"—going into industry or banking for
about a year, so they would get the "feel" of
how these enterprises work as well as the experience of another type of administration. He
also urged continued training and research on
the special problems of government administration.

Neither Wilson nor Heath, however, was
satisfied to depend wholly on the resources of
the civil service for implementing their policies.
Wilson turned in 1964 to two economists,
Thomas Balogh and Nicholas Kaldor. The
latter was brought into the Treasury as special
adviser to the chancellor on taxation and introduced corporation, capital gains, and selective employment taxes—not all of which

were welcomed by that department. Heath brought into the same role F. A. Cockfield, who had become Commissioner of Internal Revenue in 1951 at age thirty-one, and moved in 1953 to be finance director, and subsequently managing director of Boots Pure Drugs (a massive concern spread throughout England). After resigning in 1967 he had become president of the Royal Statistical Society and a tax adviser to the Conservative party. An advocate of low tax rates and low government expenditures, his advice, like that of Kaldor, seemed likely to conflict with orthodox Treasury views with unpredictable effects on budgetmaking.

More widely publicized, although possibly less influential, were the fifteen or so businessmen, including a top executive from Britain's most efficiently run chain store, Marks and Spencer, who were brought in to advise on civil service management. They were recruited with the objective of securing the massive economies in both men and money to which the Conservatives are dedicated. Whether they succeed in transforming the bureaucratic process or are swallowed up by it is as yet uncertain.

Training civil servants

The third, and easiest, Fulton reform to adopt was to establish a Civil Service College. In the past the civil service had done relatively little to provide systematic training for its members, a very serious lack because in general, as we have seen, recruitment has been based on ability rather than experience. The French have a well-planned three-year course for those wishing to enter the public service, a course that includes both study, with a heavy legal emphasis, and experience in different branches of the administration. The new British Civil Service College concentrates on postentry training and builds on the experience of the Center for Administrative Studies (established in 1963), which provided training for specialists and administrators in their third year of service. It is too early to evaluate as yet the role and effect of the Civil Service College and of the recommendations regarding opportunities for specialists and for better career planning. In general, however, there has appeared to be

some disillusionment among specialists regarding the effect of Fulton recommendations on their behalf.

Redundancy and pay scales

Not only is the civil service sensitive regarding the recent spate of criticism to which it has been subjected, but it has also been alarmed over plans for reductions in its numbers and the impact on its pay scales of the new grading system. At the opening of the Civil Service College in June 1970 shortly after the general election, Prime Minister Heath warned of his plans to reduce the total number and cost of civil servants, following reduction in their functions and commitments, for he admitted that savings by rationalization and improved organization were limited. A major step in streamlining the government superstructure was taken early in January 1971 by eliminating more than three hundred advisory committees providing services to farmers, and cutting the number of civil servants in the Ministry of Agriculture by fifteen hundred persons, that is, by 10 percent of its staff (Cmnd. 4564, 1971). The impact is most likely to fall on small farmers who make up about 70 percent of the holdings and to lead to demands for increased prices. Not surprisingly, it also led to protests by the Institution of Professional Civil Service hoping to deter other ministers from similar cuts.

As Heath had warned, however, the civil service is likely to face continued reduction in size. The Labor government had added sixty-five thousand civil servants between 1964 and June 1970, and theoretically these could all have been in danger. The greatest risk, however, was faced by senior civil servants, particularly the three hundred undersecretaries, of whom sixty-five were combined in the merger of the Board of Trade and the Ministry of Technology into the Department of Trade and Industry. Redundancy discussions between the government and civil service staff unions and associations suggested premature retirement as "desirable in the public interest" for a considerable number at the top. Such a development would be watched with particular interest by the younger members of the First Division Association, which represents the top ranks at

Whitehall, since it might reduce their otherwise long waits for promotion.

At least the Conservative government decided in August 1970 to implement the recommendations of the Plowden Committee on pay levels in the higher civil service. These involved paying the balance of salary increases recommended a year before and accepted in principle by the Labor government. As of January 1, 1971, permanent secretaries received £14,000 ($33,600); the top three, £15,000 ($36,000), much more than the Cabinet ministers they serve, who get £8,500 ($20,400); deputy secretaries, £9,000 ($21,600); undersecretaries, £6,750 ($14,200); and assistant secretaries from £4,390 to £5,640 ($10,536 to $13,536), the latter comprising 8.5 percent increases. Other pay requests are being pressed through established channels.

EMPLOYER-EMPLOYEE RELATIONS

As an employer, government faces many of the same issues in labor relations that private business confronts. Government employees below the administrative rank have never been restricted either in Great Britain or the United States in their right to form unions. Moreover, in both countries, civil service unions have been allowed to affiliate with ordinary industrial unions since 1946, when Labor repealed the ban on affiliation which had been imposed by the Conservatives following the General Strike of 1926.

Traditionally, however, strikes by civil servants, although not illegal (they are punishable in the United States under the Taft-Hartley Act, 1947), have not been considered an acceptable form of pressure. But the National Union of Teachers and the National Local Government Officers' Association early in 1970 both approved the first strikes since their formation, a possible harbinger of things to come.

Moreover, it was not clear in the early stages of the Industrial Relations Bill whether it would include the civil service in its provisions. The service was not specifically excluded, as were members of the armed forces and the police, nor included in the consultative document, but the subsequent bill appeared to cover them. If it were made subject to the legislation, the staff side of the National Whitley Council declared in November 1970 that it would not hesitate to sue the government as employer for any breach of contract. From the side of the government, it might be difficult to ignore government employees when it was trying to enforce legal requirements elsewhere. But in the light of the successes of the Whitley method of negotiating, evolved over half a century, it seems unlikely that it will be superceded by a more legalistic framework.

Whitley Councils

The normal channel for consideration of all questions affecting employment in the civil service is the Whitley Council, a joint negotiation board on which members of the higher civil service and representatives of civil service unions are represented equally. Their joint considerations are expected to end with a general agreement acceptable to both sides.

Organized on every level of the civil service, Whitley Councils act on problems appropriate to their various spheres. The National Whitley Council consists of fifty-four members, of whom the twenty-seven official members are appointed by the Chancellor of the Exchequer (evidence of Treasury financial control), while the twenty-seven staff members include leading officials of various civil service associations, many of them professional, full-time trade union workers. It lays down the general principles governing conditions of service and proposes legislation affecting the conditions of civil servants. About seventy autonomous councils operate on the department level and are concerned with the application of particular rules. In some cases there are also district and local Whitley Councils, and every ministry with a large number of industrial employees, like the Ministry of the Environment, has a Joint Industrial Council that deals with any matters outside wages and trade questions.

Some of the most important reports on which changes in the civil service have been based (including recruitment after World War II and equal pay for men and women in the nonindustrial civil service) have been drafted by the National Whitley Council. Nonetheless, many staff members feel that they have too little influence on decisions at the national level. This is hardly surprising, for the official members of the National Whitley Council can only meet staff demands within the limits established by the Treasury and ministers. A public recommendation by the National Whitley Council means in fact a policy already approved by the Cabinet.

Whitley Councils have much to commend them. They regularize contacts between higher and lower civil servants and provide for frank exchanges of views; they help employees to see the purpose of new plans and training programs; and they help employers to understand better the effect of what they do. The councils cannot provide for joint management of the ministries, for the latter are not business enterprises but the staffs of politically responsible ministers. But the councils do a great deal to fit rules to individual situations and to stimulate good relations.

As far as salaries and wages are concerned, the Treasury negotiates with the staff associations, or trade unions, to try to find a settlement satisfactory to both sides. If this is not possible, however, the government long ago committed itself to the principle of arbitration. For non-industrial civil servants, the Civil Service Arbitration Tribunal (of which the Treasury names one member, the unions another, and the Minister of Labor the chairman) provides awards that the government accepts as binding under normal circumstances. But when during 1949–50, the tribunal, despite its sympathy with the claims presented to it, refused to adjudicate because the government had declared a national wage freeze, both the service and many outside considered the principle of arbitration had been seriously violated. In 1961, a pay pause, involving a pay standstill in the public sector and alteration of terms under which disputed claims could be taken to arbitration, evoked widespread protests and ultimately forced restoration of normal arbitration procedures. But in a period of staff reductions, rampant inflation, and widespread strikes in industry and nationalized enterprises to force pay increases, the Civil Service Arbitration Tribunal will be under very heavy pressure to satisfy the demands placed upon it. The same is true for the Industrial Court, which is made up in a comparable manner to the Civil Service Arbitration Board and deals with disputes affecting industrial personnel. The best that can be said for both is that they provide a primary court of reference for pay disputes, which, unlike the Whitley Councils, stands higher than either the staff or the government.

Employer-employee relations in the nationalized industries

No such provisions for arbitration over wage disputes exist for the nationalized industries. This lack was particularly serious in the prolonged strike early in 1971 by postal workers, whose recent transfer from civil service rules and facilities to those of a nationalized enterprise left them, they maintained, with no other means to exert pressure on the government. In the slightly earlier strike by workers in the nationalized electrical industry, the Heath government had subsequently turned to a court of inquiry set up especially to consider the wage dispute and this precedent was also adopted after the postmen went back to work, despite the public dismay at the size of the pay increase the earlier tribunal had proposed. Thus it appears that each nationalized enterprise will have to work out its own procedures in attempting to forestall or deal with such serious interruptions of vital public services and the government will have to continue to confront wage pressures.

Workers in nationalized industries occupy a half-way position between those in the civil service and in private industry. They are not recruited under civil service provisions nor have the nationalized industries yet developed their own formal merit systems as, for example, has the American TVA. The preponderance of technical personnel in some public enterprises, plus the similarity of their work to that of private industry, makes it necessary, according to their officials, to compete flexibly for staff with pay rates and working conditions comparable to those of the market place. But since the government is better able to control the budgets and pay scales of public enterprises than those of private industry and commerce, there remain serious strains that are felt most acutely in a period of governmental retrenchment.

Employees in nationalized industries must belong to a union, in accordance with the insistence of the Trades Union Congress, but not necessarily a single one for the whole industry, for such a ruling might have destroyed certain existing unions. From the side of the government, however, it is much more satisfactory if it can negotiate with a single union rather than several.

The position of unions inside nationalized enterprises is a complicated one. Restrictive practices (such as limiting the production of any single worker, requiring the employment of a minimum number of workers on certain types of jobs, or rigidly imposing limitations on the work a particular employee may perform) that developed to prevent employers from exploiting their workers and to spread employment around seem much less justified when the employer is the government and the service is for the community. But the habits of many years are hard to change, and inflation bites as hard on the workers in public as in private enterprises.

THE OVERSEAS SERVICE

What has been written so far has been concerned mainly with the Home Civil Service, but comparable scrutiny, criticism, and recommendations for adjustments and cuts have also been made in regard to the British Diplomatic Service. As did the Fulton Report, the Duncan Review Committee on Overseas Representation [14] recommended merging the administrative and executive classes and also proposed freer and permanent movement between the Diplomatic Service and other professions, including the Home Civil Service. This proposal, not yet fully implemented, aimed at reversing, in the interests of rationalization and reduced personnel, the earlier process of separation between the overseas and home services.

While it had not been until 1943 that the official separation of the Foreign Service and the Home Civil Service had been decreed, the two had long possessed different channels of recruitment and thus characteristics. With its emphasis on competitive examinations, the Home Civil Service had never been the preserve of the wealthy and aristocratic, while the opposite had been true for the Foreign Service. Not until the consolidation in 1943 of the four overseas services—the Foreign Office, the Diplomatic Service, the Commercial Diplomatic Service, and the Consular Service—were the requirements dropped that a candidate had to satisfy a board of selection before being allowed to sit for the written examinations (greatly curbing henceforth the Secretary of State's age-long power of patronage), and also possess a private income. The next step in consolidation followed the 1964 report of the Plowden Committee,[15] which recommended amalgamating the Foreign Office and Commonwealth Relations Office (finally consummated in 1968) and bringing their staffs into a comparable system of organization to that of the Home Civil Service. From there the proposals of the Duncan Committee for steps to integrate these two services would seem to follow logically.

Some of the more policy-oriented proposals of the Duncan Committee, however, were greeted with severe criticism, in particular its proposed division of British representation abroad between "comprehensive" missions with full political and commercial staffs—to be restricted, in its view, to Great Britain's "area of concentration": Western Europe, North America, the Soviet bloc, China, and "certain other countries in the outer area"—and "selective" missions in the rest that would normally have only a basic strength of three "United Kingdom-based officers." The committee also envisaged commercial work as the most urgent task of British overseas representatives. Finally, it wounded many sensibilities by declaring brusquely that "information services should project Britain as a trading partner with a great culture and democratic tradition, rather than as a world power of the first order." Not surprisingly, the Labor government's response to the report was noncommittal and included only an assurance that no area of the world would be diplomatically neglected. As Great Britain progressively withdraws from active involvement in different parts of the world (see Chap-

---

[14] *Report of the Review Committee on Overseas Representation 1968–1969* (Cmnd. 4107), 1969.

[15] *Report of the Committee on Representational Services Overseas, 1962–63* (Cmnd. 2276), 1964.

ter 8, Section 2), however, the impact on the overseas service will not be unlike what the Duncan Report recommended.

INTERNAL SECURITY IN THE CIVIL SERVICE

Perhaps the most difficult and certainly the most delicate problem faced in recent years within the British civil service has been to establish an adequate program of internal security in a climate of opinion that abhorred the excesses of McCarthyism in the United States. It has been the misfortune of both the Labor and the Conservative governments to find out too late that valuable information had been transmitted to the Soviet Union by supposedly responsible government servants. The Profumo case that rocked the Macmillan government had strong implications for security as well as morality. Thus, a progressively tighter security program has been instituted within the service, although without changing its essential features.

The British security program aims at excluding possibly disloyal persons (that is, with either Communist or fascist associations) from sensitive areas; it operates without publicity; and as far as possible people are transferred within the service rather than discharged. All civil servants engaged in work related to defense contracts are required to state specifically whether they fall within the purview of the security program, and they are automatically disqualified for security posts if they acknowledge having had such connections. Moreover, in certain sensitive areas investigation is automatic. Although the investigations of the security services necessarily remain confidential, a civil servant under suspicion receives full opportunity to reply to the charges of unreliability and, if he so desires, to have a personal interview with his immediate superior, with the minister, and with a specially constituted advisory body of three eminent retired civil servants known as the Three Advisers.

The British have handled their security program with quietness and without disrupting the morale of the service. But periodically cases have arisen, such as the Vassall spy case in 1962 or the still more serious case of Maclean and Burgess in 1951. Both Maclean and Burgess were members of the British Foreign Service who had been under surveillance by security services but who nonetheless were able to flee to Moscow after transmitting secret information to the Soviet Union. Such cases have raised grave questions regarding the adequacy of security arrangements.

The series of bodies that have investigated security arrangements in the civil service have focused on a number of different points for concern. The Conference of seven Privy Councillors set up in 1955 following the Maclean-Burgess affair warned particularly about the risks presented by Communists and by those subject to Communist influence or possessing character defects such as drunkenness, addiction of drugs, homosexuality, or "any loose living that may seriously affect a man's reliability." [16] Contrary to general practice, it advised in these "borderline cases" to "continue tilting the balance in favour of offering greater protection to the security of the State rather than in the direction of safeguarding the rights of the individual." In 1962, the Redcliffe-Maud Commission [17] warned about the number of Communists and Communist sympathizers who held positions in staff associations and trade unions. In 1964, following the Vassall case of espionage by an admiralty clerk at the Naval Attache's Office in Moscow, a Standing Security Commission was set up, under the chairmanship of a High Court judge, that, in addition to its investigation of specific cases,[18] recommended an educational campaign to stimulate awareness among middle and lower grades of their responsibilities in regard to security matters. The Duncan Report, however, suggested there could be savings in overseas security arrangements.

As the Profumo case illustrated, laxness in security-mindedness is not restricted to the civil service. Yet there are inevitably so many matters of importance to security in such agencies as the Foreign and Commonwealth Office, the Defense Department, and the Atomic Energy

[16] *Statement on the Findings of the Conference of Privy Councillors on Security* (Cmnd. 9715), 1956.

[17] White Paper, *Security Procedures in the Public Service* (Cmnd. 1681), 1962.

[18] *Report of the Standing Security Commission, June, 1965* (Cmnd. 2722), 1965.

Organization that it is natural for attention to center upon their members. No system can be wholly assured against security leaks, but on the whole both the handling of such issues and their infrequency are tributes to the service.

LOCAL GOVERNMENT OFFICIALS

Local government, as we have seen, has long carried a substantial part of the responsibility for administration at the local level and will continue to do so under the new structure. In their work, the local councils depend not on nationally appointed public servants but on officials selected and paid for by themselves. In fact, local government authorities in normal times employ more people than the national government, about one-quarter of whom are teachers, and a considerable proportion do administrative, technical, and clerical work. Much of the importance of local governments, in their day-to-day working with the national government, arises from this control of their own officials. If local councils gain more independent sources of finance to underpin their functions, these officials may find themselves under new strains between their local masters and national plans.

On the whole, the highest local officials are of outstanding ability, partly because the national government has established standards for most professional positions, and partly because of the high professional ideals maintained by the National Association of Local Government Officers, a voluntary organization with steadily increasing influence, particularly after its successful 1970 strike. In contrast to the general practice in the national administration, the permanent heads of departments in local governments are chosen because of their special training in health, housing, road building, and so forth, and are trained doctors, engineers, or other experts, not general administrators. Some observers consider this unfortunate, believing that it often turns a good doctor into a bad administrator, and that local government would be better advised to recruit general administrators from the universities, as is done in the national government. But there are others who feel that local government could teach the national government a good deal about the administrative usefulness of the expert. Newcastle's innovation in 1965 in making a former Ford executive Britain's first city manager (thereby adopting an American device) may also carry useful lessons.

At least there is general self-congratulation that the English local government service escaped the spoils system that has haunted so many American cities and counties. Nor have there been experiments in electing local government officials, and thus there has been no counterweight to the authority of the council. In fact, English government officials, on the whole, are loyal to their councils to a fault, even when their own farsighted plans are crippled by too parsimonious councilors.

The major problems in local government service are found at the lower levels. Emphasis on professional qualifications for high officials means that opportunities for promotion from lower (and less specialized) levels are much more restricted than in the national civil service. In addition, local councils often try to balance the cost of hiring well-trained professional men by employing inadequately trained people in lower positions. Until after World War II, junior clerks were sometimes brought into the service at an immature age and without good records in secondary education. Training plans were lacking. Only recently have Whitley Councils become common at every level of local government service. Thus there is still much to be done to develop the uniformly high standards in the service on which the excellence of local government programs must depend.

HOW SATISFACTORY IS THE CIVIL SERVICE?

Although the British have engaged recently in an unprecedented spate of criticisms of their civil service, on the whole it commands respect and possesses far higher prestige than the American civil service. The average member of the upper civil service is neither a "philosopher king" nor a daring innovator, but he is competent, wide awake, and responsible. He enters the service through tests that emphasize clear, logical thinking and expression and ability to view situations objectively. In the service he works on important problems during most of his life. Moreover, he is schooled throughout his career in its professional ethics, according to which he must put public interest above personal advantage.

The civil servant is expressly forbidden to put himself in a position where duty and interests conflict. "The public expects from them a standard of integrity and conduct not only inflexible but fastidious," stated a report of 1928. The permanent secretary of the Air Ministry was dismissed in 1936 for using his knowledge of public negotiations for his own private advantage, a rare example of violation of the primary rule of the civil service code.

The second major rule in the civil service code of ethics is the ban on direct political activity. "The step from the civil service politician to the politicized civil servant is but a short one," a Royal Commission warned. Although other elements of the code are embodied in Treasury minutes or departmental codes or enshrined in custom, this prohibition is embodied in legislation.

Yet while ministers and the Cabinet must assume the formal responsibility for policy, there can be little doubt that high civil servants inevitably have a significant influence on its formation. In a period when issues are vastly complicated and the flow of information overwhelming, the resources and experience of top civil servants and the financial advice, not to say warnings, of the Treasury are apt to be weighted heavily and be possibly conclusive.

It is this realization that has spurred proposals for more use of technical personnel and especially of trained and experienced economists to analyze the many issues impinging on their expertise. It has even been proposed that ministers should bring with them into the departments their own personal staffs, as French ministers do, not only to reinforce their positions but also to make it unnecessary for high civil servants to appear to be supporting policies that, in fact, they oppose. Under such conditions it might be possible to remove some of the cloaks of anonymity that most high civil servants wrap around themselves in accordance with constitutional principles and allow Parliament and the public to gain better perspectives on the reasons for and against a particular policy.

High civil servants are sometimes spoken of as "statesmen in disguise." But in addition to their sophistication and smooth handling of day-to-day affairs (in which the most searching questions and sharpest controversies are all too often smothered in generalities and good fellowship) is the need for energetic innovation. The machinery is in process of reorganization, the pressing issues of a time of crisis are constantly to the fore. No one doubts the almost uniquely high standards of probity, impressive neutrality, and ability of the British civil service. But much will depend in the future on whether it also brings imagination, originality, and perception to bear on the tasks of government.

7

English
law
and
courts

1 ENGLISH COMMON LAW

The traditional association of law and liberty is so intimate that, particularly in Anglo-Saxon countries, what is called "the rule of law" is looked on as the essence of free government (see Chapter 2, Section 2). According to this concept, every individual in the community has certain rights that should not be infringed upon by other individuals or by government officials. Independent courts are available to which he may appeal if there is any interference with these rights. The rule of law means too that if an individual is accused of failing to do his duty or of committing an injustice, he cannot be punished until after he has had a public hearing in the courts and a formal verdict, based on a specific and known body of law, has been made against him.

Certain additional features of the rule of law are equally important as safeguards of individual liberty. Thus the rule of law (sometimes spoken of as "government under law") implies that the powers of the government can be extended or changed only through regular and accepted political processes that result in publicly known legislation. This is particularly important at a time when government is assuming so many new responsibilities that directly affect the community, for otherwise people might not know rights that they possess or might be punished under rules of which they

were unaware, as was true in Nazi Germany and has been so in the Soviet Union. In Anglo-Saxon countries the rights and duties of the government and the relations between the government and private individuals within the state are defined in what is called *public law*. Because the powers of government are defined, government officials are limited to those actions for which they have specific authority, and a private individual can check a particular action by asking the courts to determine whether it is justified by the provisions of the law under which the official is acting.

The law (which may be defined broadly as a known body of rules related to general principles that the courts use in deciding specific cases referred to them) and independent, impartial courts are as important in ordinary social relations within the community as they are in preventing arbitrary action by the government and its agents. By defining individual rights and duties the law removes uncertainties regarding the rules governing daily conduct and renders unnecessary recourse to violence to settle disputes. *Private law* is concerned with the relations between private persons (for example, husband and wife or partners) and with questions relating to private property or to one's own person, such as contracts and torts (for example, slander, trespass, and assault).

Most of private law falls into the category of *civil law*,[1] which concerns itself with the rights of individuals looked on merely as individuals. In civil law, individuals have to take the responsibility for bringing cases before the courts. But if the violation of the rights of one individual by another is considered to be a threat to public order the case comes under *criminal law*, which is public law and for which the government assumes responsibility. While trespass, for example, is a civil offense because it affects only the person whose property has been interfered with, murder is a criminal offense because it robs the community of one of its members and, by example, may threaten the security of others. Other acts that violate certain standards or rules established by the government may also be prosecuted under criminal law.

The exact content and relationship of the various bodies of law change and develop with changing conditions. Otherwise they would put society in a strait jacket. The economic and social needs of society have been affected so vastly by industrialization, for example, that what was once considered to be a matter that only affected the individuals immediately concerned (for example, child labor) has become a matter of concern to society as a whole. Moreover, as some individual rights are curtailed (for example, that of employers to determine the conditions of work for their employees), new rights, such as the right to benefits under social security and workmen's compensation for injuries, are extended.

Ideally, therefore, the law should meet two criteria. It should be certain and precise so that it provides known standards for action. At the same time, it should be flexible enough to meet new conditions.

The peculiar pride of the Anglo-American legal system lies in its ability to combine a high degree of certainty as to legal rules with striking adaptability to changing conditions. This characteristic has been demonstrated in the long continuity of the English common law, extending over eight hundred years. During this time the English have developed a national

system of law characterized by a complex interweaving of written statutes and unwritten custom and precedent. The adaptability of this system of law has been demonstrated not only in England but, under different conditions, in most English-speaking countries, including many of the newer members of the Commonwealth.[2] While the United States diverged sharply from English practices in establishing its political institutions, the American legal system was built directly on English legal rules, practices, and institutions. And although American law and courts have developed their own distinctive features, it is still true that precedents are occasionally exchanged across the Atlantic.

THE STRANDS OF ENGLISH LAW

The characteristic features of the English common law system were molded by experience and can scarcely be understood apart from their historical development. The legal system of England and Wales,[3] although well integrated, developed historically out of three strands: *common law*, *equity*, and *statute law*. Although all three have long merged to form a single system of law, common law, equity, and statute have had separate roots and arose out of particular circumstances and needs.

Common law and equity are sometimes, although inaccurately, spoken of as "unwritten law," because they developed out of the decisions of judges; statute law is thought of as "written law," because it results from the legislative process. Many of the rules that developed from the historic common law and equity have been embodied in legislation, but there are also certain customary procedures and rights that come from the past and are valid in courts of law without legislative formulation.

Historically, the *common law* dates back to

---

[1] The term *civil law* is also used in quite a different sense to distinguish jurisprudence based on Roman sources from the jurisprudence of Anglo-American countries, which has its roots in common law. For the former, see Chapter 7 in the section on France and Chapter 6 in the section on Germany.

[2] Ceylon has Roman-Dutch law, for historical reasons, as do Rhodesia and South Africa, formerly in the Commonwealth.

[3] Scotland and Northern Ireland have their own legal rules and institutions, which differ in part from those of England and Wales. Scottish law, in particular, has been more strongly affected by Roman law than has English law. They also have separate court systems and slight differences in their legal professions. Everything in this chapter, therefore, refers only to England and Wales.

the twelfth and thirteenth centuries when traveling royal judges, sent out in the interests of centralizing authority, forged a law "common" to the whole kingdom out of the cases and customs of local communities and their own knowledge and judgment. This "common" law was then used as the basis for decisions in the new royal courts at Westminster: King's Bench, Exchequer, and Common Pleas. This law was both stable and adaptable. It was stable because the rule of precedent was soon adopted that ensured that once a decision has been reached in a particular type of case, subsequent cases of a similar kind should be decided by the same rule. It was adaptable because every case has individual features, and there were, and are usually, a number of precedents on which to draw. Even so, as feudalism gave place to a moneyed economy, and new needs developed, the common law was found inadequate to deal with all cases. Thus developed the second historical strand in English law: equity.

Equity was rooted not in custom but in conscience. Where the common law courts did not provide a just redress of grievances, an appeal could be made through the king to the chancellor, "the keeper of the King's conscience," who after investigation could issue a special writ ordering performance of the act necessary to secure justice. Equity, for example, could force performance of a contract, whereas common law could only give damages for its breach. Moreover the chancellor, like a modern court, could issue a writ of equity to prevent a house from being destroyed to make way for a public road until after the need for the action had been investigated, whereas common law could only provide damages if the destruction were proved unnecessary.

Another characteristic and important provision of equity was, and is, the "trust." Under common law, property transferred to another person became his own, even though he might be administering it for the benefit of a third person—for example, the infant child of the original owner. Under equity the chancellor could not take away the right of ownership from the person to whom the property had been transferred, but he could order that person to use it for the purpose for which it had been given to him—that is, for the benefit of the child. Thus equity did not abolish rights that existed under common law but insisted that they be used in a just or equitable way. This notion of a trust has had many applications. In the form of settlements under wills or of charitable organizations the trust became a central institution of English and American property law.

Common law and equity were shaped by judges to fit the needs of the periods in which they were formed. Common law provided a basic system of law that built on local customs but shaped them in terms of the new centralized royal authority. Equity supplemented its rules to add what one authority has called "the practice of the 'good citizen,' i.e., the really upright and conscientious person." Gradually equity, too, became a system bound by precedent. In the eighteenth century, a great chancellor declared that the doctrines of equity "ought to be as well settled and made as uniform as those of the Common Law."

The third, and now most important as well as massive, strand in English law is "written" or *statute* law—that is, legislation passed by Parliament or statutory instruments enacted by any one of the subordinate bodies to which Parliament has delegated lawmaking powers. Until the nineteenth century, however, almost all private law, as well as almost all criminal law, was common law or equity. Even when the criminal law was embodied in statutes in the nineteenth and twentieth centuries, as was most of the law governing trusts, partnerships, bills of exchange, and sales of goods and lands, it retained some principles of common law. In this sense, in the fields of private and criminal law, statute law, like equity, is complementary to common law.

There is a fundamental difference, however, between the relation of common law and equity and that between common law and statute law. Equity does not contradict common law but mitigates it or meets its deficiencies. Statute law overrides common law. In fact, the main reason for passing statutes in the field of private law has been to alter rules that had become established by judicial decision but no longer fitted community standards, such as regulating the relations between parent and child. When common law and equity are inadequate or do not meet contemporary needs, recourse must be made to statute.

SHOULD CIVIL LIBERTIES BE PROTECTED BY STATUTE LAW?

The English are seriously considering today whether they should have recourse to statute law to protect their cherished civil liberties more adequately. Historically, their right to personal liberty (although ensured in one important regard by the writ of habeas corpus), or to hold public meetings, engage in free speech, maintain a free press, and otherwise to act independently outside of government regulations could be said, as did A. V. Dicey in his classic statement of the rule of law, to depend on judicial decisions in particular cases brought by private persons. It is true that there are, in practice, legal and parliamentary safeguards for civil liberties, and that the Bill of Rights of 1689 is not only important historically but has also been quoted in modern courts of law in cases concerned with freedom of speech. At the same time, there is not a single modern document listing these rights that would be comparable to the Bill of Rights that amends the Constitution of the United States or to those adopted by members of the Commonwealth of Nations, including India, Malaysia, and, through a postwar addition to its constitution, Canada. Great Britain is a party, however, to the European Convention of Human Rights of 1950, and has accepted the jurisdiction of the European Court of Human Rights, to which individuals can take well-authenticated cases in which a state has violated their rights.

Delivering the Haldane Lecture at London University in December 1970, Lord Justice Salmon extended his support to the widespread demands for a modern bill of rights to provide judges with the power to declare certain repressive measures illegal and thus help to check the ever-increasing number of restrictions to which individuals are subjected. He thus called attention to the crucial point that judges are circumscribed in what they can achieve by the law that they administer. Suggesting that a modern bill of rights might be entrenched by requiring a 75 percent majority of both Houses of Parliament for its repeal, Lord Justice Salmon endorsed yet a more radical break from the traditional practice of passing measures of constitutional significance by simple legislation (see Chapter 2, .Section 2). But whether entrenched or not, a British bill of rights might have a major impact, both in reinforcing the ability of the courts to defend individual rights from encroachments and by turning the focus of public attention upon the significance of civil liberties and the potential danger to them.

2 JUDGES, JURIES, AND OFFICIALS

No one can overlook the importance of the judge for the development of the English common law system. Courts are judges sitting in their official capacities to consider and pass judgment in particular cases that have been referred to them. On the judges' knowledge, judgment, integrity, and independence depends the quality of the legal decisions that not only settle particular cases but also decide precedents for the future.

One of the great struggles for individual liberty in England centered upon the independence of the judiciary. The royal courts were originally set up by order of the king, but they quickly acquired a large measure of autonomy.

Nonetheless, since the judges were appointed and dismissed at royal pleasure, the king possessed powerful weapons if he wished to bend the administration of justice to his purposes. Moreover, the king was the ultimate "fount of justice," and Stuart kings maintained that this gave them the right to override the customary rules of law. As great a Lord Chancellor as Francis Bacon declared that judges should be "lions under the throne." But the judges of the seventeenth century resisted royal efforts to make their decisions serve royal purposes. The Act of Settlement, 1701, put the judiciary beyond fear of government pressure. Accordingly, English judges, although appointed by the government, came to hold office for life or until retirement, in the same way as do American federal judges.[4]

In addition to safeguarding the independence of their judiciary, the English put a high premium on specialized legal knowledge and experience. All English judges are drawn from the legal profession, so that, unlike the Continental system in which judges and lawyers belong to two separate, although similar, professions, English judges have a long background as practicing members of the Bar. Americans, too, draw their judges mainly from the legal profession; but in England there has long been a further restriction on the selection of judges unknown in the United States: English judges have come traditionally from that part of the legal profession whose members are known as barristers.

THE LEGAL PROFESSION

The distinctive feature of the English legal profession has long been its division into two separate groups: solicitors and barristers. Insofar as this division finds a parallel in the United States, it is in the distinction between the office lawyer who prepares cases and the court lawyer who argues them. But in England the distinction has been so great that solicitors and barristers receive their credentials from their own separate societies and until recently solicitors could not easily qualify for admission to the Bar.

Solicitors are the workhorses of the legal profession. They deal directly with clients, undertake all routine legal office work, and work on the briefs to be argued by barristers in the higher courts. The preparation for this profession does not necessarily involve university training (although nearly half of the seventeen thousand or so solicitors have university de-

grees), but the ability and knowledge to pass a number of special professional examinations. It is also necessary to be "articled," that is, apprenticed, to a solicitor for a specified length of time: five years if without a university degree; three years if the degree is in a subject other than law; and two years if a law degree is possessed. Once accepted as a "Solicitor of the Supreme Court," a solicitor begins his career, probably also joining the Law Society, which is a voluntary association of solicitors that possesses certain statutory powers.

Barristers, in contrast, possess a high degree of legal specialization and their under twenty-five hundred members comprise the country's best-known legal talent. Their chief functions are to provide solicitors with legal advice, either in general or in preparation for a trial, and to conduct cases, particularly before the higher courts. They depend on solicitors for their work rather than dealing directly with clients.

All barristers are members of one of the four Inns of Court, which are long-established, self-governing voluntary organizations providing a corporate life for their members in historic buildings. The Inns of Court combine the training and examination functions of a law school with the perpetual upholding of standards of a professional association. Acting together, the Inns of Court form the Bar.

Barristers are themselves divided between "Junior Barristers" and "Queen's Counsel" (QC's), the latter known colloquially as "Silks," since they, unlike the Juniors, are entitled to wear silk gowns. QC's become such on recommendation of the Lord Chancellor, a distinction usually extended when a barrister reaches the top of his profession. They are limited by rules to certain types of work, mainly pleading in open court, and cannot appear without a Junior, but they get higher fees than do the latter. It is from the ranks of the QC's that judges are commonly chosen.

The English court system, however, is badly clogged with cases, and barristers' fees are high. For these reasons, and because solicitors have long desired a larger role in the English legal system, proposals have been made that there should be fewer restrictions on their right to plead in the new circuit crown courts set up under the 1971 Court Act and, more novel,

[4] Most American states, in contrast to the British system of appointment, select the judges for the state judiciaries through direct election or election by the legislature. One argument in support of election is that the practice of judicial review gives the judges a political function, and that therefore they should be kept responsive to public opinion. It is generally acknowledged, however, that the caliber of elected judges is less high than that of appointed judges.

that they should be eligible for judicial appointments. Prior to the new act, solicitors were allowed to sit as the chairman and deputy chairman of county quarter sessions (see below), and some who have so acted might be promoted. In any case, to remove the ban on appointing a solicitor to a judicial position would provide the Lord Chancellor with some flexibility in filling openings at the high court level.

Moreover, in the long run (and perhaps some barristers fear this), more solicitors might be appointed to the bench if more were allowed the experience of pleading in court. Solicitors have long been allowed to appear in magistrates' and county courts, and the Lord Chief Justice supported a proposal in the House of Lords during discussion of the Court Bill that they be allowed to plead in the circuit courts when a case comes for sentencing after being tried in a lower court.

Proposals have been made for radical changes in the English legal system aimed at unification both of training and functions. The Committee on Legal Education composed of judges and lawyers under the chairmanship of Justice Ormrod made the controversial recommendation in March 1971 (Cmnd. 4595) that both branches of the profession should be brought together and trained through the universities instead of their own professional bodies. Following an obligatory university law degree, all aspirants would join legal firms for practical experience before taking qualifying examinations to admit them to the Bar or as solicitors. Subsequently, a solicitor would work for three years as an assistant solicitor under a practicing one. Barristers would serve a period as pupils in chambers to secure their experience. In working out the details of training, the committee recommended establishing an advisory committee on legal education to give advice on setting up the necessary courses at the universities, and it also proposed setting up an institute of professional legal studies.

Such a major change, which is dependent on the agreement of the existing professional institutions, may well not be accepted. Yet the situation confronting the court system is an urgent one. Solicitors charged, even before the new Court Act was implemented, that they were facing intolerable difficulties in assuring their clients adequate legal support in court. Since barristers are paid by the number of cases in which they appear, it has been to their interest to handle as many as possible in the same place and on the same day to the consequent neglect of more isolated cases. The restrictions regarding the roles of QC's and Juniors add further complications. But what has been the most forceful spur to reconsideration of the situation of the legal profession has been the new demand under the 1971 Court Act that established a new crown court in place of quarter sessions and assizes (see below) and required some forty additional judges immediately, and ultimately another thirty. The majority of the Royal Commission on Quarter Sessions and Assizes under Lord Beeching's chairmanship, whose 1969 report led to the 1971 Court Bill, had rather hesitatingly recommended that appointments to "circuit judges" be open to solicitors; the Court Bill restricted them to barristers of at least ten years' experience. But something will have to give.

THE QUALITIES OF THE JUDICIARY

Drawing the English judiciary solely from among barristers has had certain consequences. For one, it has meant that English judges combined great ability and experience in interpreting the law with high standards of personal integrity. No suspicion of corruption touches even the lower levels of the judiciary, and much of the innate respect for the law in England comes from the distinguished service of generations of judges.

At the same time, judges have traditionally been drawn from the wealthy and privileged classes of society; as a result, the judicial system in England is occasionally stigmatized as a class system. Young barristers, since they depend on the work that solicitors give them, often have difficulty in earning enough to support themselves in their early years of practice. Thus, few enter the profession unless they have some outside support. But once they start earning, successful barristers receive some of the largest incomes in England. Thus the barrister is likely to belong to a well-to-do family and to have acquired large personal means and social prestige before he is invited to become a judge.

The old socialist charges that as long as English judges were drawn from the ruling class, labor would find that the courts, far from protecting their liberties, would in practice connive against them, have fallen away. The class character of the English judiciary, in fact, is far less marked now than in the past. Yet it would seem that there is much to be said for extending the range of choice far more widely. The Beeching Commission found that nearly 70 percent of people awaiting trial at the central criminal court (commonly known as Old Bailey) had to wait longer than the eight weeks recommended as a maximum by the Streatfield Committee in 1961. Public sentiment is clearly behind swifter justice, and the bottleneck is due to the lack of an adequate number of judges.

THE JUSTICES OF THE PEACE

At one place in the English judicial system professional judges give way for the most part to "amateurs," the justices of the peace. Apart from the full-time, paid judges who hold court in larger towns, the justices of the peace staff the local petty sessions courts of criminal jurisdiction, where all but 2 or 3 percent of criminal cases are settled. Justices are selected on the basis of personal qualities from among the local inhabitants of a district, receive a short course of training before starting their work, and serve without pay. The justices of the peace were originally (under an act of 1361) the king's agents in maintaining peace in the counties and were usually drawn from "the gentry." Their responsibilities are now limited to minor criminal cases, but having J.P. after one's name still carries considerable prestige.

Throughout England and Wales there were 19,250 persons staffing the lowest criminal courts in 1971, of whom only the 47 stipendiary magistrates (37 of whom are in London) can sit alone in trying a case. (In matrimonial cases, the magistrates sit with two lay justices of the peace.) J.P.'s never act alone, except in granting minor appeals for bail. Because younger people can rarely afford to give so much time

without pay,[5] most of the justices of the peace are well over fifty. Following the recommendation of a Royal Commission in 1948, there is now an age limit of seventy-five (sixty-five on the juvenile court bench), which is gradually being reduced. It is sometimes charged that the privileged position of J.P.'s makes them unsympathetic to those whose offenses they judge and that they depend too much on the testimony of the local police. But the system has many advantages. The use of so many unpaid officials keeps the costs of criminal jurisdiction low. In the small cases with which they are mainly concerned, the local knowledge of the justices may enable them to impose particularly appropriate penalties or to temper justice with mercy. Perhaps the best feature of the system is that it strengthens the tradition that justice belongs to the people and is their responsibility.

THE JURY

Another use of amateurs in the judicial process is the jury. Traditionally, one of the most important rights of an Englishman or an American is trial by his peers. Taken together with the writ of habeas corpus, under which a person accused of a crime must be brought to trial or released within a limited period of time, the right to demand jury trial has long been looked on in Anglo-Saxon countries as a basic safeguard of individual liberty.

Jury trial has become far less common, however, than it was in the past. This is particularly the case in England, although it is also happening in the United States. The grand jury, still used in the United States to determine whether the prosecution has enough evidence to proceed with a trial, was abolished in England in 1933. The petty, or ordinary, jury

[5] The Heath government approved loss-of-earnings allowances and new subsistence payments to justices of the peace starting early in 1971–72. It also agreed to pay subsistence allowances to magistrates within three miles of their homes, thereby eliminating an earlier irritating restriction. The ten stipendiary magistrates outside London serve in cities like Birmingham and Manchester and one or two smaller centers. While their power to decide cases by themselves is called "indefensible," it is too popular to change. They correspond to the police magistrates found in every American city.

of "twelve good men and true" is still used invariably in both countries in trying the most serious criminal offenses, such as rape, kidnaping, and murder. The jury makes the vital decision whether the defendant is guilty or innocent, and under the 1967 Criminal Justice Act, majority verdicts—ten to two, eleven to one, or ten to one—are permitted, although unanimity is required if the jury numbers nine or fewer. The judge, of course, decides the actual sentence. But jury trial is rare in English civil cases, much less common than in American courts. Still more surprising is the relatively small use by the English of juries in minor criminal cases. Barely 10 percent of those who could have a jury trial choose to do so.

Part of the reason for not using juries in civil cases is that the litigants must pay the jury's fees. Defendants may decide against jury trial in lesser criminal cases because jury service, in practice, is mainly restricted to the well-to-do, who cannot be expected to have great insight into the problems of the poor. The most important reasons for the decline in the use of juries, however, seem to be the desire for speedy trials and the belief that—apart from cases involving public morality, such as libel— the jury's injection of its own sense of justice into a case is not needed as a safeguard for the rights of the defendant.

THE JUDICIAL ADMINISTRATIVE SYSTEM

English judges have traditionally had a very large degree of independence in running the courts, for there is no central administrative department such as the Ministry of Justice in France. The Lord Chancellor is largely responsible for ensuring a smoothly working judicial system. The power to make appointments, draft rules, direct cases from one court to another, and maintain general supervision of all court business provides considerable authority, but there is a strong feeling that a more efficient structure is now needed. The Lord Chancellor, who is always chosen by the prime minister from among distinguished senior barristers of his party, has only a small office, which is heavily overburdened and ill equipped to oversee the reorganization of the courts. The Beeching Commission had proposed that the Lord Chancellor be given responsibility for the whole judicial system— except for magistrates' courts—and that a senior officer, to be called circuit administrator, be appointed for each geographical group of courts. The natural corollary would seem to be the establishment of a government department that the Lord Chancellor would head.

No one person in the United States combines so many judicial offices and functions as does the Lord Chancellor. He presides over the House of Lords,[6] and is a member of the Cabinet. He appoints all the justices of the peace, county court justices, and judges to the central courts, except for two—the Lord Chief Justice and the Master of the Rolls—who are appointed by the prime minister. He is expected to keep the court structure efficient, up to date, and abreast of its work, a task for which he obviously needs more administrative support.

Most judges have life tenure (county court judges retire at seventy-two or may be dismissed, but this is very rare), and many remain in the same post to which they were originally appointed. Most administrative officials hold office under civil service rulings. Most court rules are traditional. But in a time of change when a basic reorganization of the court system is taking place, the old assumption that it can be mainly self-operating no longer holds.

There is no real parallel in England to the American offices of federal and state district attorneys. The Director of Public Prosecutions in Britain only intervenes in cases where the detailed services of his office are required, for example, because of complexity or national interest. In 1969, for instance, he undertook prosecutions in only 2,014 cases, of which 1,255 concerned indictable offenses and 759 nonindictable ones. All these interventions were at the request of a public agency although private individuals could also have appealed to him. Otherwise criminal prosecutions are conducted by private barristers retained by the state for

---

[6] The attorney general and his chief assistant, the solicitor general, who give legal advice to ministries and represent the Crown in cases in which its interests are concerned, are members of the House of Commons.

that purpose or in the magistrates courts by police officers who are usually assigned full time to this responsibility. As far as the records of the case are concerned, the policeman appears in his private capacity, e.g., Smith v. X. Any individual has the right to prosecute personally but few do so.

Although the number of serious crimes in England has increased substantially over the past few years, it is still considerably lower than in the United States. Thus the burden on the English court system, particularly above the lowest level of criminal courts, is proportionately smaller than in this country. But the same problems of over-crowded dockets and long delays exist in both countries. Thus neither in England nor in the United States does the court system fulfill its function of providing swift impartial justice in defense of public order and individual or group rights.

3   THE COURTS

The central institutions of the judicial system are the courts. Courts can decide only those cases that are brought before them either by a private individual or a public officer. No matter how unjust a situation may be, the courts have no means of interfering unless a specific complaint is filed. But the character and accessibility of the courts have a good deal to do with the frequency with which they are used. If justice is to be easily available to all people, there must be local courts as well as national, their procedures must not be too technical, and the cost must be within the reach of persons of average means.

A century ago the English court system was a bewildering collection of separate courts. The royal central courts had been superimposed on the local courts. Different sets of courts administered common law and equity, and there was a constant struggle among and within the systems to acquire cases and thus the fees that litigants paid. Conflicts of jurisdiction were frequent, and the litigant who made a mistake about the court in which to start his case might find himself forced to begin all over again in another court after a long and expensive process in the first one. In addition, there was little uniformity of procedure. The complexity of court organization defeated the purpose of making justice easily available.

A determined effort to tackle this problem and bring uniformity into the court structure was made through the Judicature Acts between 1873 and 1876. The distinction between common law and equity courts was swept away, and all courts received the right, where necessary, to use both kinds of law. The central courts were combined technically into the High Court of Justice and the Supreme Court of Judicature, which, although they are only symbols of unity and not courts that ever meet, serve the purpose of preventing conflicts of jurisdiction among the separate central courts of which they are composed. As the chart on page 196 makes clear, each of the three divisions of the High Court of Justice specializes in a particular subject matter (rearranged under the Administration of Justice Act of 1970), but the fiction of maintaining that they are part of the High Court of Justice simplifies the transfer of cases from one to another if necessary.

The Court Act of 1971 instituted the second major reorganization of the courts. It was based on the recommendations of the Royal Commission on Quarter Sessions and Assizes, under Lord Beeching, which extended its originally narrow terms of reference to take in the whole court system. The rationalization and decentralization of the court structure it proposed sought to rearrange the whole judicial system under effective and responsible administration so as to make the courts more geographically and functionally suited to their tasks.

The specific proposal for the higher courts, implemented in the Court Act, was to set up a new type of court, the Crown Court, to sit in a large number of urban centers to deal with all the more serious criminal cases. The Crown Court absorbed the criminal jurisdiction of the previously existing fifty-eight courts of quarter session, and the ninety-three borough sessions,

Court System of England and Wales

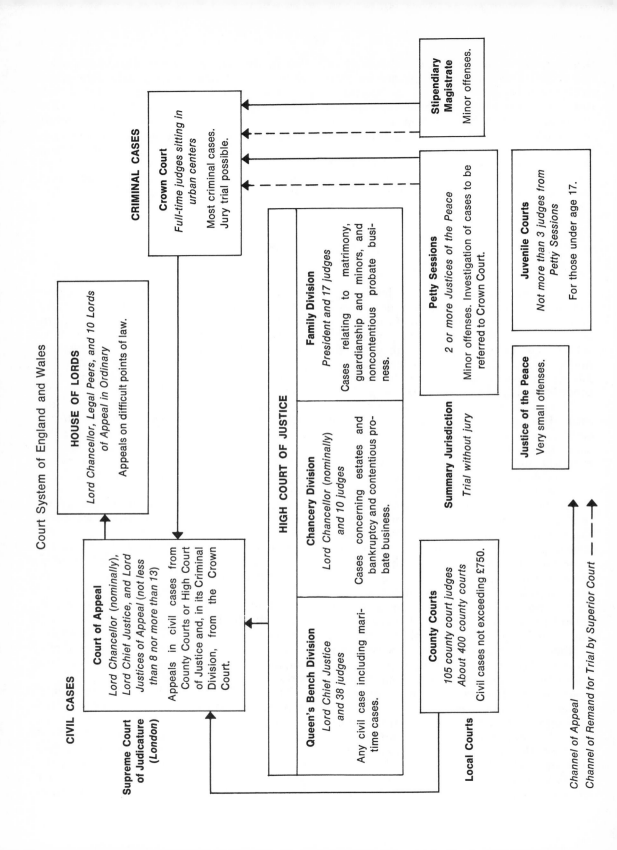

CIVIL CASES

Supreme Court of Judicature (London)

Court of Appeal
Lord Chancellor (nominally), Lord Chief Justice, and Lord Justices of Appeal (not less than 8 nor more than 13)

Appeals in civil cases from County Courts or High Court of Justice and, in its Criminal Division, from the Crown Court.

HOUSE OF LORDS
Lord Chancellor, Legal Peers, and 10 Lords of Appeal in Ordinary

Appeals on difficult points of law.

CRIMINAL CASES

Crown Court
Full-time judges sitting in urban centers

Most criminal cases. Jury trial possible.

Stipendiary Magistrate
Minor offenses.

HIGH COURT OF JUSTICE

Chancery Division
Lord Chancellor (nominally) and 10 judges

Cases concerning estates and bankruptcy and contentious probate business.

Family Division
President and 17 judges

Cases relating to matrimony, guardianship and minors, and noncontentious probate business.

Queen's Bench Division
Lord Chief Justice and 38 judges

Any civil case including maritime cases.

Summary Jurisdiction
Trial without jury

Petty Sessions
2 or more Justices of the Peace

Minor offenses. Investigation of cases to be referred to Crown Court.

Local Courts

County Courts
105 county court judges About 400 county courts
Civil cases not exceeding £750.

Justice of the Peace
Very small offenses.

Juvenile Courts
Not more than 3 judges from Petty Sessions

For those under age 17.

Channel of Appeal ⟶
Channel of Remand for Trial by Superior Court – – –

the central criminal court (i.e., Old Bailey), and the assize courts. Courts of quarter session dealt with cases like assault, stealing, or housebreaking where specialized judicial knowledge was not essential. The traveling assize judge, who periodically held court in at least one assize town in every county, could handle serious offenses, including murder and treason, and also had civil jurisdiction. In place of these two sets of courts, the Beeching Commission suggested that about twenty towns outside of London should be centers for both the High Court—to deal with civil cases that the assize courts had inadequately handled—and the most serious criminal cases in the Crown Court, and another eighty towns should be centers for the Crown Court alone. Even this latter number, it believed, could be sharply reduced as soon as more courts are established in the main towns.

To staff the new structure, the Beeching Commission's report envisaged a new bench of judges known as "circuit judges," consisting of the 105 county court judges and all full-time judges, other than High Court judges, who were in the higher criminal courts. These circuit judges would be expected to specialize, for while most county court judges could handle criminal cases, judges who are experienced only with criminal cases rarely are capable of dealing with civil cases. A special problem involved in the reorganization was that a large proportion, about three hundred members of the criminal judiciary, were part-time judges who also carried on their professions as barristers and would thus be eliminated. The change meant, therefore, the appointment of about forty new judges, as discussed above, with probably another thirty to follow.

The commission further recommended reducing the civil work of the High Court by increasing the jurisdiction of the county courts in both contract and tort cases from its existing limit of £700 to £1,000. Moreover, the jurisdiction of county court registrars, whose courts provide the only reasonably inexpensive remedies for small claims, should be raised, it felt, from £30 to £100.

While the 1971 Court Act did not implement the full range of proposals of the Beeching Commission, it established the Crown Court in place of quarter sessions and assizes, and introduced the process of reorganization to

which the commission's report had pointed. By thus decentralizing the structure, the Court Act moved the English judicial system close to a simple hierarchy of courts within which there is no duplication of work. Such a degree of unification fills American observers with envy.[7]

DIFFERENCES BETWEEN CIVIL AND CRIMINAL CASES

The basic division in the English court system between civil and criminal cases builds on the distinction made in the first section of this chapter. Civil law, as we have seen, is concerned with the relations between individuals when no element of public security is involved. Disputes over contracts, boundaries, wills, the payment of debts, or suits for divorce are all typical subjects for civil courts. The person seeking redress institutes an *action* to right whatever wrong has been committed and often, in addition, to force the payment of a fine to the injured person.

Civil cases are expensive, especially for the loser. Since they are for the benefit of individuals, the government takes no responsibility for paying their cost, apart from the salary of the judge and the basic maintenance of the court. To meet the additional expenses of running the courts, litigants pay fees that are often quite high. Frequently these costs are added to the damages imposed, thereby making unsuccessful litigation an extremely costly process.

There are a number of ways in which criminal cases differ from civil cases. Since criminal cases involve acts that affect public order, they begin through *prosecutions*, instituted in the name of the Crown.

Further, because criminal jurisdiction is concerned with acts that affect society as a whole, the costs of a criminal trial may be borne by

[7] There are fifty-two hierarchies of courts in the United States, since each state and the District of Columbia has one, and there is also the federal structure. The federal courts are well unified, much better than most state court systems. In general, there is little overlapping between the two systems, since the federal courts handle cases involving federal laws and the state courts those involving state laws. If the litigants are from two different states, however, they have the choice of bringing the case before a state court or a federal court, the latter being permitted on ground of "diversity of citizenship."

the public, although the defendant in a criminal case can be made to pay all or part of what are sometimes very high costs of the proceedings, if the court thinks fit. Any fines imposed go into the public treasury. In such cases as assault, damages may also be awarded to an injured person; those damages are, however, usually collected through a civil suit conducted parallel to the criminal prosecution.

In both civil and criminal cases it is possible to appeal from the judgment of a lower court if permission is granted by the higher court. Only in exceptional cases, however, are appeals permitted on the ground that the facts elucidated by the lower court are in question—a rather common practice in the United States. In England, appeals are generally restricted to cases where the interpretation of law by the lower court is challenged.

THE STRUCTURE OF THE COURTS

The separation between the civil and the criminal courts is most clearly marked at the local level. There are two sets of courts and no exchange of personnel between them.[8] The county courts deal only with civil cases. The magistrates' courts and petty sessions, staffed by justices of the peace, deal with minor criminal cases, juvenile hearings, and matrimonial disputes (but not divorce). Appeals in family matters go, however, to the Family Division of the High Court.

The higher courts are also clearly separated between those that handle civil and those that handle criminal cases. Their personnel, however, is not separated so distinctly. Judges for the higher criminal courts are drawn from courts in the civil hierarchy. The only place where hierarchies of civil and criminal courts officially merge is at the very apex, where the Court of Appeal and the House of Lords provide the final source of appeal for both.

---

[8] This practice of having separate courts for civil and criminal cases finds no parallel in the United States. American county courts, for example, have extensive criminal as well as civil jurisdiction and are found in almost every one of the 3,050 counties into which the United States is divided. Many American states have a maze of local courts, in none of which is there so clear a separation of function as between the English county courts and courts of the justices of the peace.

The House of Lords

It may seem odd that the highest court of appeal in England is the House of Lords. This court is a classic example of the continuity of English institutions: the historic right of the House of Lords to hear appeals dates back to the days of the *Magnum Concilium* of Norman times. But no less is this a classic example of the ability of the English to alter practice while retaining form: for more than a century it has not been the House of Lords as a whole that acts as a court but a very select group of its members, a group, in fact, that is elevated to the peerage for the sole purpose of performing this judicial function. In 1876, provision was made for the appointment of seven (now nine) Lords of Appeal in Ordinary (commonly known as Law Lords) who are paid professional judges with life peerages. Together with the Lord Chancellor and those peers who hold or have held high judicial office (such as former Lord Chancellors), they form the actual court of appeal. Thus, as other peers are excluded from participation, the appellate jurisdiction of the House of Lords in practice is that of a small group of highly trained legal experts. In a surprising "practice direction" of July 1966, these judges declared they would not be bound by precedent if it hampered them in taking contemporary conditions into account in making a judgment. In only one instance, however, have they overruled an earlier decision.

The existence of this second appeal court is an expensive anomaly and its value and conservative orientation have been challenged. At least it is used sparingly. Its chief function is to elucidate particularly difficult points of law, and it rarely hears more than fifty cases a year, of which very few are criminal cases. The House of Lords is the highest court not only for England and Wales but for Scotland and Northern Ireland as well; in this way it performs a distinctive function by providing a certain unification for the three judicial systems.

The Judicial Committee of the Privy Council

There is one other appeal body, the Judicial Committee of the Privy Council, which, strictly speaking, does not belong in the English judicial hierarchy, because it reviews cases appealed from courts in various parts of the British Commonwealth and empire outside Great Britain itself. Technically the Judicial Committee is not a court that renders decisions but a body that gives advice to the monarch on cases referred to it; in practice, however, the distinction is unimportant. Although the jurisdiction of the Judicial Committee of the Privy Council is very different from that of the House of Lords, its personnel is almost identical because, at the time when the Law Lords were created as salaried life peers, it was decided that they could carry the bulk of work in both bodies. Moreover, whoever else participates in the judicial work of the House of Lords is almost always a privy councilor and thus entitled to be a member of the Judicial Committee of the Privy Council. The main difference in the membership of the two bodies is due to the practice of adding, on occasion, one or more judges from the Commonwealth overseas to the Judicial Committee, particularly when a case affecting a particular area is under consideration. Any independent Commonwealth country may eliminate or restrict the right of appeal to the Judicial Committee of the Privy Council, and several of them, including Canada, have done so. It still serves, however, as the final source of appeal for British territories that have not acquired full rights of self-government.

EVALUATION OF THE ENGLISH COURT SYSTEM

The court system in England and Wales is well organized to handle different types of cases according to their degree of severity and to permit appeals so that there can be a check on the judgment and reasoning of the judges in lower courts. The independence of the judiciary and the courts ensures freedom from political influence. But there are other questions that must be raised in determining whether or not English courts are adequate to their responsibilities. What is the atmosphere of the courts? Do the courts provide an opportunity for all aspects of a situation to be explored? Do they give private persons adequate protection in criminal cases when the resources of the government are behind the prosecution? Do the courts provide speedy, effective means of settling disputes? Is justice, in practice, open to all on equal terms?

Visitors to English courts are impressed by the solemnity of the proceedings. Even lower courts have a dignity and formality that in the United States is almost wholly confined to the higher courts. Arrayed in wig and gown, the judge or judges sit above and apart from the rest of the court. The lawyers, also gowned, present the circumstances of the case and reply to each other's arguments in a restrained way that contrasts with the vehemence so often displayed by American lawyers. Witnesses are brought forward and questioned as to the facts, but there is no "bullying." The defendant and plaintiff may present their views. The judge listens attentively, giving the impression that every fact is important in making his final decision. Spectators are not permitted to make a noise or to indicate their sympathies. The atmosphere is that of a learned debate. There may be drama in a great lawyer's brilliant presentation of a case or in the manner in which he draws the facts from an unwilling witness. But the appeal is not to the spectators in the courtroom: it is to the judge, or jury and judge, who will make the decision. The presentation may be eloquent but to be effective it must be logical and based on a wide knowledge of legal practices.

The distinctive feature of a trial in an English or an American court, as compared with a trial in a Continental court, is that in the Anglo-Saxon system the judge looks on himself as an umpire before whom a case is argued, not as an investigator seeking to determine guilt or innocence. The English or American judge makes little effort to speed the proceedings. He leaves the major responsibility for bringing out the facts to the interested parties. During the trial the judge does not assume an active role in cross-questioning, as does a Continental judge, although English judges are apt to play a more decisive part in bringing out relevant facts than are American judges. The English judge makes sure that irrelevant material is excluded from consideration and that full opportunity is given to all sides to present their case. It is left to the parties, at least in a civil case, to make use of their chance.

The notion that a trial is a contest in which both sides should have an equal chance is maintained also in criminal cases, although here the prosecution, with the resources of the government behind it, has an obvious advantage. Much is done, therefore, to afford protection to the defendant. A person accused by the police of a breach of law must be immediately warned that anything he says may be taken down and used in evidence. Furthermore, in the trial, witnesses may not be asked leading questions (for example, not "Did you see a revolver in his hand?" but "Did you see anything in his hand?" and "What was it?"). Nor may evidence be introduced of previous misdoing calculated to prejudice opinion against the defendant.

Other safeguards guarantee that there can be no arrest without a warrant; crimes must be known to the law, that is, there can be no prosecution for an act that had not been declared to be a crime at the time it was committed; ignorance of fact is a complete defense—for example, in a case for bigamy, ignorance of the fact of a previous marriage. By these means the individual is given protection from arbitrary state action.

The Criminal Justice Act of 1967 sought to make criminal procedures more efficient and quicker and finally to replace the old concept of retribution with the modern view that criminal jurisdiction aims not only at protecting the community from its dangerous members but also to reform the latter. Written testimony now has equal validity with spoken evidence; juries can give weighted majority verdicts (a controversial move aimed at securing more convictions); suspended sentences were introduced for less serious crimes, although not those involving personal violence, and the Home Secretary was empowered to release all except lifers after serving one-third of their sentences if no public danger was involved; and increasingly severe fines are used with greater frequency in place of imprisonment as another approach to lowering the prison population. Beating of delinquent prisoners was finally abolished. Strict licensing of pistols and rifles already existed before the 1967 act, but tighter controls on shotguns now require securing a license from the police for this weapon.

The problem of overcrowded dockets and jails still remained in 1969, however, as evidenced by the strictures of the Beeching Commission. The 1971 Court Act is obviously directed toward streamlining the structure for criminal justice and increasing the number of judges. The 1972 Criminal Justice Act permits some form of community service to be substituted for a prison sentence. To curb the rising crime rate, the government has invested heavily in new equipment and raised police rates of pay, but crime detection is still plagued by short-handedness, which is intensified by difficulty in recruiting and by the numbers of men leaving the police force. Although the upper ranks of the police support the abolition of the death penalty, the lower ranks understandably would like it reinstated for murdering a policeman. But despite slogans of "law and order," and concern at certain inadequacies in law enforcement, the courts maintain their elaborate protection of the rights of the accused to give him the maximum chance to defend himself.

On the whole, English legal procedures are not encumbered by technicalities, as happens so often in the United States where the rules are generally the result of legislative activity and frequently unsuited to their avowed purpose of aiding the execution of justice. English rules governing the giving of evidence, pleading, and so forth are drafted by the Rules Committee under the Lord Chancellor, and are so simple, straightforward, and effective that it is rare to have a decision reversed in England on a question of procedure, in marked contrast to the frequency with which this happens in the United States.

The high cost of legal aid and the centralization of the appeal courts for civil cases are the most serious inadequacies of the English court system. Technically, of course, the courts are open to all on equal terms. But in practice it is like saying that everyone has a right to buy a Cadillac. Court and lawyers' fees are so high in England (as well as in the United States) that people of moderate means cannot view the prospect of civil litigation without concern. Moreover, although court fees are not necessarily imposed in criminal cases, legal aid is as expensive in this field as in civil cases.

The most substantial attempt in English legal history to meet the charge that the court system unduly handicaps poor litigants was made by the Legal Aid Act of 1949. Although since 1926 there had been an enlarged program of free legal aid for people who were entirely without means, the system had suffered from various defects, such as lack of publicity, no provision of aid in the county courts, and lack of relevance to the problems confronting those of moderate income. The Legal Aid Act of 1949 covers representation in all the regular courts and, in effect, provides that the very poor pay nothing for legal aid and that those of moderate income pay what they can afford. The Law Society and Bar Council administer the system of legal aid; the Ministry of Social Security investigates the question of means (a fact that restrains many people from applying for aid); and the Treasury finances the plan. Certain types of action, notably those that are open to abuse, such as suits for libel, are not covered by the act.

Many people feel, however, that provisions of the 1949 act do not sufficiently meet the criticism that the English court system unduly favors the wealthy. They advocate a national legal service, comparable to the National Health Service, under which lawyers would be organized for the service of the community. As in the United States, it is doubtful whether the poor have an adequate awareness of those provisions of the law that could be used to their advantage. The next step, therefore, would seem to be to approach the problems of legal aid from that perspective, to make justice a positive benefit to all.

4 JUDICIAL CONTROL OF GOVERNMENT OFFICIALS

To judge the acts of government officials by the same rules of law and by the same courts as the acts of ordinary citizens has long been considered a major safeguard of liberty in Anglo-Saxon countries. One of the characteristic features of the "rule of law," declared A. V. Dicey, a great nineteenth-century commentator on the British constitution, is that "every man, whatever be his rank or condition, is subject to the ordinary law of the realm and amenable to the jurisdiction of the ordinary tribunals"; and he drove this point home by declaring that "every official, from the Prime Minister down to a constable or a collector of taxes, is under the same responsibility for every act done without legal justification as any other citizen." Thus an official is no more above the law than anyone else and is equally responsible for justifying his actions in regular court proceedings.

Great Britain and the United States both continue to uphold the general rule expressed by Dicey and, in consequence, despite considerable contemporary urging of its necessity, do not follow the Continental practice of having a separate system of administrative law to cover the relations between government officials and private individuals and a separate system of administrative courts for such cases. Nevertheless, there have been certain modifications of the rigid interpretation of the view expressed by Dicey. Thus in both the United States and Great Britain today there are a number of administrative tribunals that deal with certain types of complaints against official actions. Moreover, in the interest both of forceful governmental action and of effective recompense to individuals injured by the action of state officials, there have also been gradual modifications of the rule that government officials are personally liable for acts committed without legal authority.

Part of the reason for this latter development lies in the danger that an official may not perform his duty according to his best judgment for fear of a personal suit for damages as the result of a decision taken in an official capacity. Or it could happen that the citizen who had been injured might well find himself unable to collect adequate recompense from the official personally.

Take, for example, the case of a sanitary inspector who believes he detects foot-and-mouth disease in a cow at the stockyards. He orders the animal to be killed at once. Subsequently it is found that the animal was not suffering from the disease. The owner attempts to get redress through the courts. If the judge agrees that the action of the inspector did not fall under the authority of the law, the inspector becomes personally liable for damages. On the other hand, if the judge finds the inspector justified in his action because the law provides him with a wide range of discretion, the owner of the cow is left without redress, so long as the state refuses to assume responsibility.

To meet such problems, both the courts and the government have gradually modified their stands. English and American courts usually uphold a government official in a private damage suit as long as there is no proof of negligence. In addition, both the British and American governments have made it easier to enter suit against the government itself in many types of cases.

It is still true that when the government is providing its basic services, such as maintenance of order, conduct of foreign affairs, and operations of the army and navy, it is not subject to suit. (But a bystander injured by a policeman in pursuit of a murderer may seek compensation from the Criminal Injuries Compensation Board.) Since the Crown Proceedings Act of 1947, it has been relatively easy to get redress for injuries suffered by individuals in the course of the non-law-enforcing operations of government.

The Crown Proceedings Act enables ordinary citizens for the first time to bring suit against the government in the same courts (for example, the county court) and in the same way "as if the Crown were a fellow citizen." Thus in the case of the sanitary inspector mentioned above, the owner of the cow could now collect damages from the state, while the inspector himself would be free from responsibility as long as there was no negligence involved. Moreover, the act makes government departments responsible not only for statutory duties but also for the common law duties imposed on ordinary employers, owners, and so forth.

At a time when the state is acquiring such extended functions of regulation, control, and operation of services, little could be more important than to establish the right of individuals freely to sue government agencies in case of injuries. In the words of an attorney general, this act ensures that "the rights of the little man are just as mighty, and are entitled to just the same protection, as the rights of the mighty state." What it recognizes, in fact, is that the principle of equality before the law

requires new procedures to protect the citizen in his relations with the modern administrative state.

Still a further means of safeguarding the interests of the citizen in relation to administrative actions is provided by the Parliamentary Commissioner for Administration (see Chapter 4, Section 4), to whom MP's can refer complaints of personal injustice or misuse of power for his investigation. Although this office is far from achieving the range of activities of the Scandinavian ombudsman, on which it was supposed to be modeled, it adds one more instrument for investigating complaints against administrative arbitrariness or incompetence.

ADMINISTRATIVE TRIBUNALS

Although supporters of the Anglo-American system oppose setting up a separate system of administrative courts for dealing with official acts, it has been found useful, both in the United States and Great Britain, to set up what are called administrative tribunals. These tribunals share the characteristic features of courts of law: independence of the executive, the application of known rules, a certain formality in procedure, and binding decisions not subject to ministerial review or rejection. They are administrative only in that they are composed of administrators, not judges, and that they handle cases and questions arising out of administrative regulations.

In both countries there have long been commissions to consider railway rates and tax and patent appeals. Great Britain has special tribunals, both regular and *ad hoc* (that is, set up for a particular case), to which employers and employees may by agreement refer industrial disputes. Moreover, several British ministries have special bodies to deal with appeals on their handling of their particular responsibilities, among the most valuable of which are the local appeals tribunals on social insurance legislation and benefits, which are representative of the public, employers, and employees, and which provide a much needed human touch in a complex system.

There are several justifications for this development. In the first place, procedure in these administrative tribunals is direct, speedy, cheap, and easy for a layman to understand. Workmen's compensation cases, for example, used to be referred in England to the county courts where the procedure was time-consuming, tedious, and costly; now they are handled by an administrative tribunal that can adjust its procedure to the particular case, is not bound by rigid precedents, and yet strives to provide uniform rulings. In fact, just because there is a single central tribunal, there is more apt to be consistency of treatment and coordination of results. Further, administrative tribunals are staffed by experts who deal with subjects, for example, patents, that require technical knowledge. Administrative tribunals can be particularly useful in setting up new standards in a previously unexplored field, for example, town and country planning, which challenge private property rights, traditionally protected by the common law.

Following the Franks Committee Report on Administrative Tribunals and Procedures, the Tribunals and Inquiries Act of 1958 set up the Council on Tribunals, which is charged with general supervision of all British administrative tribunals and with presenting an annual report to Parliament on their workings. Moreover, the decisions of administrative tribunals can be examined by the law courts through appeal on a point of law and through the general right of review by higher courts over the decisions of all lower courts, including administrative tribunals. While administrative tribunals are likely to be the best judges of the relevant facts, for example, the safety devices in a factory in a workmen's compensation case, the courts make the final decision on whether the tribunal was acting within its powers as defined by statute and following prescribed procedures.

Courts, as we have seen, do not provide the only restraint on the public administration. The Cabinet, individual ministers, and parliamentary instruments, in particular the specialized committees and the parliamentary commissioner, attempt to supervise the functioning of the administration. But the task is an overwhelming one and beyond the capacity of political figures. It is for this reason that there have recently been proposals in Great Britain to establish a comprehensive system of administrative law and courts comparable to that which operates so smoothly and efficiently in France. To do so would be to break finally with a historic tradition, but the need is pressing for more comprehensive, swift, and inexpensive means of dealing with complaints of administrative abuse or excessive use of power. By providing such means, the British might also relieve some of the pressures both on the law courts and on Parliament to safeguard the interests of individual citizens.

8

Great Britain
and
the world

By geography, Great Britain is a European country; through history it became a world power. In the nineteenth century it held a dominant international position by virtue of its industrial leadership, financial power, and naval supremacy. But today Great Britain is no longer preeminent in any of these fields. Moreover, as we have seen, its domestic economic problems are of grave dimensions. Thus the British face agonizing dilemmas over how far their international commitments should still extend and what role they should now pursue in world affairs.

In each of the three great intersecting spheres of the Western world—the Atlantic community, Western Europe, and the Commonwealth of Nations—Great Britain possesses or seeks a distinctive position. The Commonwealth group of thirty-one independent states, with some forty dependencies (twenty-two of them a British responsibility), scattered throughout the continents of the world, total 900 million people, one-quarter of the world's population, occupying 19 percent of its surface.

Within this group, Great Britain, as the senior partner, enjoys a unique relationship based on history, interest, and a common acceptance of the Crown as the symbol of their unity. In the Atlantic community, Great Britain and the United States have an unshakable, although not uncritical alignment. Only in Western Europe had the British failed to achieve the integrated role that many felt should form the core of its economic relationships and political associations. Although British entry into the Common Market is now assured, divisions of opinion within Britain over the advisability of this move complicate the adjustments that are necessarily involved. Moreover, the British have still to work out in practice how best to interrelate their new position in Western Europe with their other associations.

Before we attempt to analyze more fully the competing claims of Britain's relationship to the Commonwealth, to the United States, and to Western Europe, we must consider in more detail the characteristics of the Commonwealth.

1   THE COMMONWEALTH OF NATIONS

The Commonwealth of Nations [1] has long been a remarkable and unique international grouping. Although France has remained even more influential in most of its former African colonies than Britain is in any Commonwealth country, a result in the main of the extent of

[1] The older name "British Commonwealth of Nations" has generally been replaced by "Commonwealth of Nations" since 1949, when it was formally recognized that the accession of the Asian Dominions meant that the proportion of British within the Commonwealth was, in fact, small. French-Canadians and Afrikaners always resented the prefix "British." It is still used in Great Britain, however, and also in Australia and New Zealand.

French aid programs, control of trade and tariffs, and educational and technical experts abroad, it was unable to sustain the Franco-African Community for which the constitution of the Fifth Republic provided in 1958. But in a much earlier period, Great Britain succeeded in transforming the colonial relation of those overseas areas that contained predominantly white populations into a distinctive international relation without any intervening stage of separation. Moreover, it subsequently fostered the same transition for other colonies in Africa, Asia, and the Caribbean. Since the Commonwealth of Nations thus provides an example of close cooperation between countries of equal status but widely differing strength, some observers have called it a model for international associations.

The Commonwealth of Nations consists of Great Britain and those former members of the British empire that have acquired full control over every aspect of their internal and external policies but choose to retain a special relationship with Great Britain and other members of the Commonwealth. The relationship was developed historically by Canada, Australia, New Zealand, and South Africa; it was extended in 1947 and 1948 to India, Pakistan (the Muslim part of the Indian subcontinent), and Ceylon; and from 1957 on it was extended to Ghana, Malaysia, Nigeria, Cyprus, Sierra Leone, Tanzania (the union of Tanganyika and Zanzibar), Kenya, Uganda, Jamaica, Malawi, Zambia, Gambia, Malta, Singapore, Trinidad and Tobago, Guyana, Botswana (formerly Bechuanaland), Lesotho (formerly Basutoland), Barbados, Swaziland, Fiji, Mauritius, Tonga, and Western Samoa. In a time when the international trend has been toward nationalism and separatism, these countries of widely differing geographical position, size, natural environment, racial composition, and political power have distinctive political and economic relations within the Commonwealth of Nations.

The strength of the Commonwealth is the strength of the relationship existing between these countries and Great Britain. To understand the present bonds uniting the Commonwealth, we must see how Canada, Australia, New Zealand, and South Africa passed from a position of dependence to one of equality of status with Great Britain without an intervening stage of separation. It is necessary, also, to see why the other countries chose to be members of the Commonwealth when they acquired independence of Great Britain. The bonds of the Commonwealth come not only out of history but also out of present circumstances.

THE EVOLUTION OF COMMONWEALTH STATUS

The original overseas members of the Commonwealth, Canada, Australia, New Zealand, and South Africa, were British "colonies of settlement," although the original settlers in Canada were French and in South Africa (until 1961 a Commonwealth member) they were Afrikaners. (The Afrikaners outnumber those of British extraction, and both are far outnumbered by the local Africans, Indians, and Colored.) But British institutions and traditions had a strong formative influence in these countries, leading to a feeling of loyalty and common purpose with Great Britain, at least among those of British descent. Moreover, in its era of undisputed naval, economic, and financial dominance, Great Britain provided them with notable benefits. The British Navy (to which the colonies contributed nothing except port facilities) ensured their defense. Free of the crippling burdens of armaments, the small populations of these huge areas could concentrate on developing their own resources. Great Britain was both their major market and source of capital.

But loyalty and material benefit would not have been enough to maintain the British connection if political aspirations had been disregarded. The reason the second British empire did not go the way of the first British empire, which split asunder in the American War of Independence, was that a way was found to enable colonies to develop self-government without ceasing to be British. This way was called *responsible government*, which stemmed from the famous report of Lord Durham who was sent to Canada following a rebellion in 1837. Durham recommended that locally elected representatives be empowered to make their own decisions in matters of internal policy, a right soon stretched to include tariffs and immigration regulations. When small scattered colonies

THE COMMONWEALTH OF NATIONS

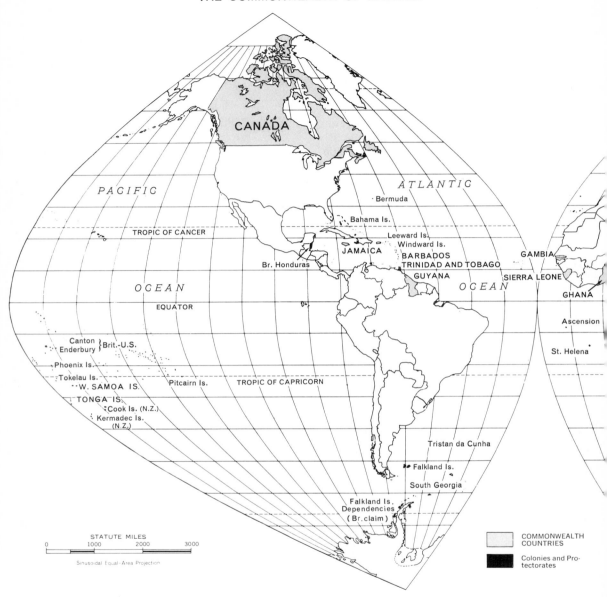

CANADA

PACIFIC   ATLANTIC

· Bermuda

· Bahama Is.

TROPIC OF CANCER   Leeward Is.
                                    Windward Is.   GAMBIA
                        JAMAICA   BARBADOS
                    Br. Honduras   TRINIDAD AND TOBAGO SIERRA LEONE
                                    GUYANA

OCEAN   OCEAN   GHANA

EQUATOR   Ascension

Canton } Brit.-U.S.   St. Helena
Enderbury }
Phoenix Is.
Tokelau Is.
W. SAMOA IS.   Pitcairn Is.   TROPIC OF CAPRICORN
TONGA IS.
Cook Is. (N.Z.)
Kermadec Is.
(N.Z.)
                                  Tristan da Cunha

                                  · Falkland Is.

                                  South Georgia

                        Falkland Is.
                        Dependencies
                        (Br. claim)

STATUTE MILES
0   1000   2000   3000

Sinusoidal Equal-Area Projection

COMMONWEALTH
COUNTRIES

Colonies and Pro-
tectorates

were consolidated into the larger units of Canada, Australia, New Zealand, and South Africa, the constitutional right to control their own affairs was called "dominion status." [2]

Before 1914 Great Britain maintained ultimate control of foreign relations, and in World War I it declared war for the Dominions as well as for the empire. But the great wartime

[2] The name "dominion" was first used at the time of Canada's Confederation in 1867. It was derived from the Biblical phrase, "Thy dominion shall stretch from sea to sea." It was long used to refer to any of the self-governing overseas members of the Commonwealth and took its mean-

ing from whatever status Canada or Australia possessed at a given time. Thus it had no fixed connotation that could limit their development to full independence. Except for New Zealand, "dominion" is not an official part of the name of any Commonwealth country.

contributions freely made by Canada (which with only eight and a half million people lost more soldiers in the war than did the United States) and by Australia, New Zealand, and South Africa justified their claims to independence of action in this sphere as well as in internal matters.

In the interwar period, traditional forms were brought into line with political realities. The Dominions became separate members of the League of Nations. Equality of status was recognized in the Balfour Report of the Imperial Conference of 1926, which declared Great Britain and the Dominions to be "autonomous communities within the British empire, equal in status, in no way subordinate one to another in any aspect of their domestic or external affairs, though united by a common allegiance to the Crown, and freely associated as members of the British Commonwealth of Nations." The Statute of Westminster, 1931, drafted after consideration by political leaders from all parts of the Commonwealth, brought legal forms into harmony with long-existing constitutional conventions by opening the way for Dominion parliaments to become formally supreme in their own jurisdictions.

The Statute of Westminster, 1931

The Statute of Westminster declares that no British law shall henceforth have effect in a Commonwealth country except on request of that country, that British laws already having effect within it can be repealed by the legislature of that country, and that no power to disallow a statute inheres in the British government. The Statute of Westminster thus made it possible to abolish appeals to the Judicial Committee of the Privy Council (see Chapter 7, Section 3), which traditionally had been the final court of appeal of all British subjects outside Great Britain. Ireland and Canada began the process of abolishing the right to appeal to the Judicial Committee, and appeals now come only from dependent territories and a few Commonwealth countries. The Statute of Westminster also made it possible for the legislation of overseas Commonwealth members to have extraterritorial effect, that is, outside the particular country, for example, over its own merchant shipping.

The Statute of Westminster is often termed the Magna Charta of the Commonwealth. Although informal constitutional arrangements had long approximated the legal position made possible by the Statute, it was welcomed enthusiastically by Ireland, South Africa, and Canada. The latter was able to adopt it, however, only after provisions were inserted at the insistence of its provinces to make sure that the act could not be used to change the balance of the federal system without their consent. Australia and New Zealand were more reluctant to bring the provisions of the act into effect, and they did not do so until 1942 and 1947, respectively. Subsequent members of the **Commonwealth** inherited it automatically.

Independent policies and ultimate unity

During the interwar period, legal and constitutional issues within the Commonwealth were satisfactorily solved. It was less easy to evolve a workable basis for policy that would harmonize the strictly limited interests of individual Dominions with the worldwide commitments of Great Britain. The basis finally reached combined a constant flow of information and much informal consultation among the different members of the Commonwealth with ultimate freedom of action on the part of each individual member. Such freedom of action was limited in practice by the recognition that, should trouble arise, only popular policies would be supported by other members of the Commonwealth. In the 1920s, for instance, Canada and South Africa disassociated themselves from British Middle East policies and at all times were less ready for commitments to Great Britain than were Australia and New Zealand. The Irish Free State, or Eire, comprising twenty-six of the thirty-two counties of Ireland,[3] a reluctant postwar addition, withdrew from the Commonwealth in 1936. But from 1937 on, the threat of Germany and Japan drew the remaining members of the Commonwealth together. When war broke out in September 1939, Canada, Australia, New Zealand, and South Africa by their own acts entered the conflict in support of Great Britain and in opposition to aggression.

At the end of the war many people expected that the weakened position of Great Britain

[3] The partition of Ireland took place in 1921 following a civil war in which its predominantly Catholic and Gaelic areas sought independence. In the island's six northeastern counties, known as Ulster, however, the predominantly Protestant descendants of the Scottish and English settlers who had colonized that area in the seventeenth century clung to their union with Britain. Ulster was provided, therefore, with its own local parliament in Belfast as well as representation in the British Parliament. This status was further guaranteed in the Ireland Act of 1949. But Protestant discrimination against the large Catholic minority in Ulster has intensified the pressures for a united Ireland. Communal violence broke out in Belfast in August 1969, and British troops have patrolled disturbed areas since. The illegal Irish Republican Army continues to press terrorist attacks across the border. Although the Belfast government, under urging from London, has introduced an extensive program of social and political reform to reduce segregation and discrimination, the situation in Ulster remains tense and a particular source of concern to the British government.

would lead to the breakup of the Commonwealth. On the contrary, the association has steadily expanded. As Great Britain's numerous colonies have achieved independence, most of them have chosen to be members of the Commonwealth. Burma and Sudan decided not to do so when they became independent in 1948 and 1956, respectively. British and Italian Somaliland joined to form the Somali Republic in 1960 and the Southern Cameroons became part of the Cameroon Republic in 1961. (Northern Cameroons became part of Nigeria.) Otherwise, as the dependent empire has diminished in size, so the Commonwealth has grown.

Republics in the Commonwealth

The importance of the Crown for the Commonwealth has already been emphasized. Yet beginning with India in 1949, many Commonwealth countries have decided to become republics. Nothing illustrates better the pragmatic flexibility of the association than the ease with which a satisfactory resolution of this situation was devised. When a state becomes a republic it must make a formal request to a Commonwealth conference to be allowed to remain within the Commonwealth and, except in regard to South Africa, no objection has ever been raised. The latter, smarting from criticism of its discriminatory racial policies, withdrew its 1961 request to be accepted as a republic and left the Commonwealth. All the others have been welcomed as members of the Commonwealth and have accepted the Crown "as the symbol of the free association" of the independent countries that compose it and, in a similarly symbolic spirit, the queen as "the head of the Commonwealth."

Commonwealth institutions

The Commonwealth has relatively little political machinery. As recently as 1965, the first Commonwealth secretariat was set up in London under a Canadian secretary general, Arnold Smith. Since then the agenda and arrangements for the Commonwealth's most important institution for formal exchange of views, the *Conference of Prime Ministers* (or Imperial Conference, as it used to be called),

are in the hands of a body that is drawn not only from the British civil service, as used to be the case, but from the Commonwealth at large. Moreover, increasingly, meetings of the conference are held in different parts of the Commonwealth, such as Lagos, Nigeria, in 1965, and Singapore, Malaysia, in 1971.

Numerous other Commonwealth meetings have dealt with subjects such as trade, the convertibility of sterling, and economic aid to developing countries. There are also *ad hoc* conferences in many other fields of mutual interest, such as welfare, agriculture, and technology; constant exchanges among "opposite numbers" in particular Commonwealth countries; and meetings of Commonwealth representatives to the United Nations and other international gatherings.

THE BONDS AND STRAINS IN THE COMMONWEALTH

It may well be asked: Why does the Commonwealth hold together? The machinery it has evolved for purposes of consultation does not bind individual members to a particular course of action. The symbol of a common Crown is not enough to determine policy. In practice, its members quite often differ from each other in international conferences.

That the Commonwealth is not an exclusive group is demonstrated by the close defensive arrangements existing between Canada and the United States. But this very lack of exclusiveness is itself a source of strength to the Commonwealth. Membership in that body does not prevent a country from pursuing policies conducive to its particular interests. The only agreed-upon limitation is that it shall notify the other members before it undertakes such action. Thus Commonwealth membership involves few sacrifices except in moments of supreme crisis. On the other hand, it provides a number of advantages both to Great Britain and to its partners.

Strategic ties

For Great Britain, the most important consideration is that twice in a generation the prompt and voluntary support of the **older**

Commonwealth members has been a major element in supporting a British struggle for survival. During the year from the fall of France to the Nazi attack on the Soviet Union, Canada was Great Britain's strongest ally.

For the Commonwealth at large, however, there is no longer a defensive unity. Since World War II, the defense of the North Atlantic has become an international responsibility (safeguarded by the North Atlantic Treaty Organization) and no longer, as before World War II, chiefly a British responsibility. In the Pacific and Southeast Asia it is the United States on which Commonwealth members— particularly Australia and New Zealand—must depend, a fact reflected in Australia's token participation in Vietnam.

It must not be forgotten, however, that there were some two hundred thousand Commonwealth troops, mostly British, fighting guerrillas in Malaya from 1948 to 1960 when the crisis ended. The Wilson government began the substantial withdrawal of British troops from Singapore and Malaysia, which left only thirty-five thousand there in 1971, and the Heath government can be expected to continue the reduction. Nonetheless, it has agreed to be an equal partner with Australia and New Zealand in the five-member Southeast Asia Treaty Organization, which also includes Singapore and Malaysia. Reluctantly, other British military responsibilities "east of Suez" are being phased out so the western Indian Ocean, long looked on as "a British lake," now lacks defensive strength. In this situation, the factors that have strategic significance are chiefly Britain's willingness to make arms available to Commonwealth members under external attack (as, for example, to India in 1962 when it was attacked by China and to Malaysia against Indonesia), the potentialities of the scattered staging posts of the Royal Navy and Air Force, and the sense of responsibility toward Britain itself that the older Commonwealth members have. Yet it is not unimportant that the Declaration of Principles of the 1971 Prime Minister's Conference asserted that "the security of each member state from external aggression is a matter of concern to all members."

Economic relations

The most important material advantages of the Commonwealth relation have been economic. Except for Canada, whose dollar is linked to the American, all the members of the Commonwealth are part (and by far the most important part) of the *sterling area*, made up of those countries within which the pound sterling rather than the dollar is the principal unit of exchange. The thirty-one Commonwealth countries apart from Canada, and eight non-Commonwealth countries including South Africa and Jordan, keep their foreign currency assets, private and public, in London. In January 1971, these assets totaled more than £3.5 billion, of which more than 1 billion are held as official reserves. It is through these funds that Commonwealth members, other than Canada, largely finance their international trade and float their loans. In 1968, members contracted through the Basle agreement to keep a certain proportion of their reserves in London in return for a dollar guarantee of their worth. Even should a Commonwealth member decide to withdraw from the association, it is hardly likely to withdraw its reserves, particularly since Britain pays high interest rates on them, unless for punitive reasons. Normally, financial policies are closely coordinated between Commonwealth members. One of the most important annual Commonwealth conferences is the gathering of their finance ministers before the meeting of the International Monetary Fund (IMF). For the developing countries there is special urgency to the use of IMF special drawing rights to increase the flow of development aid.

Intra-Commonwealth trade was long encouraged by *imperial preference* under which Commonwealth countries extended to each other lower tariff rates than most favored-nation agreements provided. Such preferences were originally extended by the older overseas Commonwealth members in return for defense. In 1932, when they were formalized, Britain was taking a third of Commonwealth exports, and Commonwealth countries bought a third of British exports. But the Commonwealth was never used to develop the kind of closed trading units the French, Dutch, and

Belgium empires established. Moreover, since changes in the global tariff structure—the General Agreement on Tariffs and Trade and the Kennedy round cuts—preference continues largely only through bilateral agreements initiated by Britain itself.

The Commonwealth is thus no longer a *trading block*, for although its members and their associated states account for one-fifth of the world's trade, only one-quarter of it is among themselves. For some Commonwealth countries, however, like New Zealand, Tanzania, and Malawi, intra-Commonwealth trade is more than half their total, most of it either directly with Great Britain or with immediate neighbors.

Great Britain's Common Market negotiations take these facts into consideration. Two of the most difficult situations were those of New Zealand's dairy products, of which 80 to 90 percent of exports go to Great Britain, and Britain's guaranteed market for sugar from the major Commonwealth producing countries in the West Indies, Fiji, Mauritius, Australia, Swaziland, and a few others. But mutually satisfactory agreements were reached in mid-1971.

The European Economic Community has offered associate status to nine African Commonwealth members, comparable to that enjoyed by the eighteen African countries (mostly former French colonies or trust territories) already securing both favorable conditions for their exports and financial aid through the Yaoundé Convention. The EEC is also considering associate membership for the three Commonwealth members in southern Africa—Botswana, Lesotho, and Swaziland—despite their customs union with South Africa. Two other possibilities for the latter countries would be to adopt a more limited arrangement such as Kenya, Uganda, and Tanzania secured with the Common Market in 1970, or simply to conclude a trade agreement.

There may be advantages, therefore, as well as problems for Commonwealth countries due to Britain's membership in the Common Market. In 1971, the Common Market countries were only taking 5 percent of their imports from the Commonwealth, apart from Great Britain and Canada. British entry might encourage greater access for Commonwealth goods, except from Canada. The latter is seeking market diversification and, in the process, is increasing its sales to Great Britain and the EEC countries. Canada is somewhat apprehensive, therefore, lest an enlarged Common Market might become a more exclusive trading block, with current Canadian exports of minerals to the Continent edged out by the advantages extended to African Commonwealth countries through associate status. No one can tell at this point, in fact, what the trends will be or their ultimate impact on Commonwealth countries and the economic ties of that association.

British overseas *aid*, particularly but not exclusively to its own former colonies, has at last come close to the 1 percent of its gross national product that it had pledged. (American foreign aid is well below this percentage of GNP.) In 1950, a special Commonwealth program of economic aid and technical assistance for India, Pakistan, and Ceylon was launched under the name of the *Colombo Plan*. Subsequently extended to other southern and southeast Asian countries and with substantial support from the United States (now larger than Commonwealth contributions) and Japan, the Colombo Plan has achieved excellent results. Great Britain and Canada have provided financial, economic, technical, and educational aid to developing African and West Indian Commonwealth countries. In 1970, Britain gave £157 million (approximately $376.8 million) in bilateral aid to developing countries in the Commonwealth, approximately 90 percent of its aid total. Canada gave $350 million in aid, 80 percent to Commonwealth countries, in particular India and the West Indies.

Seventeen thousand Commonwealth students were studying in Britain in 1971, forty-five hundred of them postgraduates. Both Britain and Canada, it may be noted, also have programs for volunteers overseas somewhat comparable to the Peace Corps, although concentrating on more specialized personnel. There are also two general Commonwealth aid agencies, the Commonwealth Development Corporation, with borrowing powers of £225 million ($540 million), and the Commonwealth Development Finance Company, with funds of £40 million ($96 million), which particularly but not exclusively service developing Commonwealth countries. The 1971 Commonwealth Development Fund is intended to supplement multilateral aid. The special interest of these and other British aid programs in the developing Commonwealth countries makes them an additional reinforcement of the Commonwealth relation.

Citizenship and immigration

A serious blow to the Commonwealth relationship has resulted from the use made in recent years by Asian and Caribbean citizens of the historic right of entry and settlement in Britain of persons from Commonwealth countries and the resulting restrictions which now differ little from those imposed on aliens. As recently as 1948, the British Nationality Act had declared that any citizen of the United Kingdom, its colonies, or a Commonwealth country was a "British subject" or "Commonwealth citizen" (the terms being interchangeable) and thereby possessed the right to enter Great Britain at any time, to qualify for the franchise, to be a member of Parliament or of the civil service (except in wartime). But accelerated immigration from the newer Commonwealth countries, notably India, Pakistan, and the West Indies, led to local internal tensions (see Chapter 1, Section 1) and progressively restrictive measures.

The first of these measures, the Commonwealth Immigrants Act, passed by the Conservative government in 1962, set no specific limits to Commonwealth immigration but required labor permits for entry, thereby facilitating administrative control. Labor, initially hostile to this legislation, found itself forced by public opinion to renew the act's provisions in 1964. The following year, as we have seen, it introduced an act prohibiting racial discrimination in "places of public resort," but it also formally reduced the number of labor vouchers to 8,500 (of which 1,000 were reserved for Malta), abolished entry of unskilled workers, and extended the power of the Home Secretary to repatriate. In 1968, panic over the possibility of massive emigration of Kenya Asians squeezed out by Africanization and pos-

sessing British citizenship led to the openly discriminatory Commonwealth Immigrants Act providing controls over their entry into Great Britain. This measure was only partially counterbalanced by a somewhat strengthened Race Relations Act supervised by the Race Relations Board and a select committee.

In 1971, the Conservative government introduced yet another Immigration Bill, which placed all persons seeking work on the same footing, whether they come from a Commonwealth country or not, and required renewal of the original work permit after a year.

The 1971 legislation also introduced the controversial distinction of "patriality," limiting full freedom to come and go as desired to citizens of the United Kingdom and colonies who had themselves or their parents or grandparents been born in Great Britain or who had settled in Great Britain for five years, as well as Commonwealth citizens whose father, mother, or grandparent had been born in Great Britain. Commonwealth citizens resident in Great Britain for five years remain free to stay unconditionally, to vote, and to participate freely in political life. Citizenship is necessary, however, for a complete safeguard against deportation, and the provisions for aiding voluntary repatriation have also caused some alarm.

These progressive restrictions on the earlier right of entry to Great Britain from Commonwealth countries and of securing work on the same terms as local residents only bring British provisions to a situation comparable to those long existing in most other Commonwealth countries. Moreover, British emigration, especially to the older Commonwealth members, is in fact considerably more substantial than immigration to Britain from them. But since many of the British now associate the Commonwealth with Britain's "color problem," the latter has caused considerable revulsion against the association. Moreover, in the Caribbean, in particular, and among West Indians and Asians resident in Britain, the immigration restrictions so clearly slanted against the colored from the Commonwealth have aroused apprehensions and bitterness. Thus, this particular "bond of Commonwealth" has turned into a source of strain.

The Commonwealth stance on southern Africa

There is yet one further issue that strains the Commonwealth relationship, that is, its policies toward southern Africa. Until 1961, when it withdrew from the Commonwealth, South Africa's legislatively enforced color discrimination was a constant affront to the Commonwealth's multiracialism and particularly to its Asian, African, and West Indian members. Fortunately for its continued cohesion, the sharp criticism of South Africa's racial policies that led it to leave the Commonwealth came from Canada as much as from newer Commonwealth members. Moreover, when Rhodesia made its unilateral and unconstitutional declaration of independence in 1965, the Commonwealth as a whole united behind Prime Minister Wilson's request for United Nations sanctions, which attempted, although unsuccessfully, to force Rhodesia's small, white, ruling minority to agree to the progressive extension of the franchise to the African majority. But Prime Minister Heath's decision to sell arms to South Africa, despite the forceful opposition of Prime Minister Trudeau of Canada and leaders of the postwar Commonwealth countries at the Singapore Conference of Prime Ministers in January 1971, threatened the association as no previous British external action had done. Although Heath maintained that Britain had an obligation to supply seven Wasp helicopters under the Simonstown agreement, which provides berths in South Africa for the British Navy, the fact that he announced the decision to send them without waiting for the first meeting of the Commonwealth committee of eight, set up at Singapore to consider the issue, added yet another source of friction.

WILL THE COMMONWEALTH CONTINUE?

Cooperation in the Commonwealth rests on the willingness to work for and the understanding of common purposes. Sentiment, traditional ties, a common heritage of laws and institutions, shared experiences, all play their role in maintaining the relationship, particularly among the old Commonwealth members. Prac-

tical economic advantages are influential with the newer members and their Commonwealth relation will help them to secure associate membership in the Common Market. Technical and professional cooperation extended on a broad scale is of particular importance to the developing members of the Commonwealth. Although the first drafts of the Declaration of Principles at Singapore strongly and directly condemned South African apartheid practices, the final statement, drafted by President Kenneth Kaunda of Zambia, did so by implication. The Declaration of Principles adopted on January 22, 1971, by the leaders of the thirty-one Commonwealth states at the Singapore Conference of Prime Ministers [4] begins:

> The Commonwealth of Nations is a voluntary association of independent sovereign states, each responsible for its own policies, consulting and cooperating in the common interests of their peoples and in the promotion of international understanding and world peace.

It asserts that "the Commonwealth is one of the most fruitful associations" for removing the causes of war, promoting toleration, combating injustice, and securing development. It also includes, as a distinct innovation in Commonwealth statements, a formulation of "certain principles" held "in common." These principles include "the liberty of the individual," "equal rights for all citizens regardless of race, colour, creed or political belief," and "their inalienable right to participate by means of free

[4] The member countries of the Commonwealth at the Singapore meeting were: Australia, Barbados, Botswana, Canada, Ceylon, Cyprus, Fiji, Gambia, Ghana, Guyana, India, Jamaica, Kenya, Lesotho, Malawi, Malaysia, Malta, Mauritius, New Zealand, Nigeria, Pakistan, Sierra Leone, Singapore, Swaziland, Tanzania, Tonga, Trinidad and Tobago, Uganda, United Kingdom, Western Samoa, Zambia. Additionally, the Republic of Nauru in the Pacific is a special member, and the Associated States of the Eastern Caribbean participate in Commonwealth meetings, but not in the heads-of-government sessions. The West Indies Associated States, which are self-governing but for which Great Britain retains responsibility for foreign affairs and defense, are as follows: Antigua, Dominica, Grenada, St. Christopher-Nevis-Anguilla, St. Lucia, and St. Vincent. These and other small unviable islands scattered throughout the oceans of the world (see map in this chapter) provide a continuing problem for Great Britain because no special status has been evolved for them short of an unrealistic independence, and many are now proving to be significant strategically in the light of Soviet and Chinese expansion.

and democratic processes in framing the society in which they live."

More distinctive and directly related to the concerns of the newer Commonwealth members are the paragraphs referring to racial prejudice and discrimination that start: "We recognize racial prejudice as a dangerous sickness threatening the healthy development of the human race and racial discrimination as an unmitigated evil of society." Then in a sentence obviously meant to relate to the British inten-

tion of selling arms to South Africa, it added: "No country will afford to regimes which practise racial discrimination assistance which in its own judgment directly contributes to the pursuit or consolidation of this evil policy."

Well before South Africa left the Commonwealth, nonracial policies were said to be the key to the continued existence of the multiracial Commonwealth. This could still be the case.

2　INTERNATIONAL RELATIONS

The Commonwealth was long considered the inner area of British international relations, providing built-in opportunities for influence and trade. But Great Britain's foreign policy is concerned more deeply now with its relations with the United States and Western Europe. In addition, Britain seeks good economic and political relations with the Soviet Union and Eastern Europe and has tried to retain its influence with the Arab countries, without impairing its links with Israel.

If all these areas were friendly with one another, the historic position of the British in regard to each might provide them with unparalleled opportunities to act as a center of unity. But the harsh fact is that jealousy, rivalries, divisions, and even aggression between and within blocs have been more common in the postwar world than have friendship and cooperation. Moreover, Britain has sometimes exacerbated its own problem by dealing with each of its associations separately and failing to fit the different parts of its foreign policy into a coherent whole.

Britain's most difficult problem has been its relation with Western Europe. It is drawn impellingly to that area by geography, military strategy, and, increasingly, by economic interest. Yet there are barriers of culture, language, and, most fundamentally, attitude that have made association difficult for both sides. The French, particularly under de Gaulle, sought a dominant position in Western Europe that they could hardly maintain if Britain were an active participant in all its programs. Moreover,

they were suspicious of the role and intentions of the United States in Europe. The British, in contrast, wished to associate the Atlantic alliance wherever possible with any strategic commitments they made on the Continent. In addition, as far as economic relations are concerned, influential groups within Great Britain pressed the possibility that either the older Atlantic Commonwealth relation or a pan-European one would be more to British interests than merging itself in a purely Western European group. Thus, although the French and British have now agreed on British entry into the Common Market, there remain sharp divisions in Great Britain itself over whether the move will be to the country's own advantage.

In the field of strategy and defense the British early committed themselves to a solely European grouping, but with the ultimate objective of associating the United States and Canada with it. Thus the British gave the lead to the Brussels Treaty of 1948 that pledged political, economic, and cultural cooperation among Great Britain, France, and the Low Countries—Belgium, Holland, and Luxembourg—and joint military action in case of attack. The consummation of Britain's general strategic objectives, however, was the North Atlantic Treaty Organization (NATO), established in 1949, in which the United States and Canada associated themselves in a vast system of mutual defense with the five Brussels Treaty powers, as well as Norway, Denmark, Iceland, Portugal, and Italy, and, after 1951, Greece and

Turkey. NATO achieved two major British strategic objectives; a continued United States military presence in Europe, and, after further British guarantees through the Assembly of Western European Union to allay French apprehensions, the admission into NATO of newly sovereign and rearmed West Germany.

But NATO was organized in a period when the Soviet Union lacked nuclear weapons, and thereafter de Gaulle grew increasingly dissatisfied with what he considered a static strategic concept (instead of a more mobile nuclear-powered one) and with the integrated military command under an American commander. Thus in the late 1960s de Gaulle forced American troops and installations out of France, thereby impairing what unity NATO had achieved.

By the early 1970s, new situations were evolving. The American military presence in Europe, at least in its current dimensions, was being questioned by Americans themselves as well as by many Europeans. The new *Ostpolitik* of seeking a *détente* with the Soviet Union had been inaugurated by Chancellor Willy Brandt. While not seeking to take West Germany out of its Western alignment, this policy opened avenues for progressive and constructive interactions between East and West. At the same time, the focus of attention for Great Britain had settled firmly upon its economic relations with Western Europe.

In the immediate postwar period, the British had taken the lead in organizing the plans for European self-help incorporated in the requests for American aid under the Marshall Plan. They strongly backed the European Payments Union, established in 1950, to aid the freer flow of trade and payments throughout the portion of Europe not dominated by the Soviet Union. They participated vigorously in the Organization for European Economic Cooperation (OEEC) and its 1962 successor, the Organization for Economic Cooperation and Development (OECD), both concerned with development aid and trade policies, and they did so more enthusiastically after 1951 when both the United States and Canada became associated. But the British stood aloof from the process of Western European integration that began that latter year with the establishment of the European Coal and Steel Community (ECSC).

The Conservative government felt at that time that the ECSC free trade market for coal, iron ore, steel, and scrap, under an institutional structure, would not last long. They justified their refusal to participate by maintaining that membership would encroach on their sovereignty and be incompatible with Commonwealth arrangements. They viewed with considerable suspicion, as a possible threat to their own interests, the second of the specialized Western European agencies, Euratom, which established an atomic energy pool and shared the costs of nuclear research among its members. Most significant was the initial refusal to sign the Rome Treaty, which envisaged gradual removal of restrictions on trade between its six members—France, West Germany, Italy, Holland, Belgium, and Luxembourg—and the establishment of a common external tariff. Thus Great Britain stood outside the European Economic Community, generally known as the Common Market, which came into existence on January 1, 1958, and missed the opportunity to mold the character of that association in liberal directions during its most formative years.

The British made proposals shortly thereafter for a wider free trade area in Europe, and even for one that would also include the Commonwealth, but these plans would clearly have brought Great Britain itself into the key position within whatever grouping was established, and they were rejected as threats to the nascent EEC. Embittered by this failure, the British took the lead in establishing in 1959, largely as a bargaining counter, the much less promising association known as the European Free Trade Association (EFTA), which included Norway, Sweden, Denmark, Switzerland, Austria, and Portugal. But by 1961, the Conservative government decided to seek membership in the increasingly prosperous Common Market, a process that, despite two intervening vetos on British membership by President de Gaulle in 1963 and again in 1967, began once again in 1970, and seemed assured by late 1971.

Many issues are raised by British membership in the Common Market and in the two other Communities, Coal and Steel, and Euratom. The initial hurdle that dominated the first period of negotiations was the financial contributions the British government was willing to make both in the interim period of adjustment and thereafter. But there were still more serious problems. The potential impact of Common Market membership on its Commonwealth partners has already been indicated. Internally, agriculture offers a delicate and controversial issue. The common agricultural policy of the Six has been hammered out with particular difficulty and exactness. Its key feature is to maintain farmers' incomes out of market sales and to manipulate the market by high price guarantees and a system of variable levies to keep the cost of agricultural imports at a comparable or higher level. The British, in contrast, permit the relatively free importation of agricultural produce and maintain farmers' incomes through a deficiency payments scheme for farmers and annual price reviews. Participation in the Common Market means that the cost of British food will rise substantially, probably the most effective argument used by anti-Marketeers. The British also give subsidies to specialized groups like the hillsheep farmers and to sensitive sections of British farming, like horticulture, as a means of maintaining their competitiveness.

British participation in the Common Market, on the other hand, opens industrial opportunities in a market of nearly 300 million people, larger than that of the United States. This circumstance was cited frequently in favor of entry. Closer technological cooperation may well help to overcome the "technological gap" between European (including British) and American production. Whether economic planning for so large and diverse a grouping is feasible is open to question, but its importance for exploiting the advantages of so large a market is obvious.

Other special issues have included the persistent British balance-of-payments problem, with its relation to the position of sterling either as a reserve currency or absorbed in a possibly stronger European reserve currency; the necessity for Great Britain to accept the EEC's value-added tax (i.e., a production tax that is applied successively to each stage of a product at which "value" is added) as the major form of indirect taxation; and the impact on social security benefits of higher food prices and the value-added tax. The White Paper, "Britain and the European Communities: An Economic

Assessment" (Cmnd. 4289, 1970), distinguished between the "impact effects" and the "dynamic effects" of entry into the Communities, suggesting that the latter could be expected in the long run to offset the obvious cost of such changes as would be involved in the new agricultural policies and their financing. Heath said in February 1971 that "we must find arrangements for our entry into the Community which are tolerable in the short run and clearly and visibly beneficial in the long run." That negotiations on all these points had been concluded satisfactorily by late June 1971 was a tribute to all parties concerned.

British membership in the European Economic Community has political as well as economic consequences. There are at present four rather little-known European parliamentary institutions, in the first three of which the British already participated: the semiofficial NATO conference of parliamentarians who debate but do not decide policy; the Assembly of Western European Union, whose members are appointed by national governments and which discusses defense issues in its meetings twice a year, although it has no executive powers; the Council of Europe, set up by treaty in 1949 with eighteen European member states, which can discuss anything except defense, but also has no executive powers; and the European parliament, called officially the Assembly of European Communities, one of the integral institutions set up under the Treaty of Rome for the six members of the Common Market, which is also advisory in functions and without executive powers. The last named institution commonly meets in Strasbourg for five-day sessions about ten times a year (its secretariat, however, is in Luxembourg). Its 142 members are appointed by their respective governments on the basis of proportional strength (except for the Communists) in their own assemblies, and they sit in Strasbourg by parties, not by national groupings. One question is: With what parties will the British Labor party associate itself? More importantly: Will the European parliament become more clearly representative and effective with British membership in the EEC?

Meeting with members of European parliaments in February 1971, Prime Minister Heath declared that the argument between federation and confederation was "sterile and unworthy" and called for new institutions to suit the needs of the European community. President Pompidou has spoken of advancing "step by step, toward a union, which when it has sufficiently become so, both in fact and in the minds of the peoples—and only then—will be able to have its own policy, its own independence, its own role in the world." The parliamentarians to whom Heath spoke went so far as to declare it "essential to accelerate the creation of an economically and politically united Europe, embracing all European countries which accept the obligations involved," and to propose that the functions of the European Economic Community be extended "and should in particular embrace foreign policy and defence." Whatever the road and the speed, political implications are involved.

These political implications were used by opponents of entry to bolster their case. Enoch Powell exploited the concerns of the Tory rightist anti-Marketeers who, as we have seen (Chapter 4, Section 6), had used parliamentary tactics in 1962 to express their concern over British terms for entry into the Common Market. Richard Crossman used the *New Statesman*, which he edits, to suggest that Labor had no commitment to entry and printed cogent warnings by Nicholas Kaldor. Jo Grimond, former leader of the Liberal party, had also reversed his former stand in favor of entry.

Harold Wilson determined his stand on entry by his sense for how best to maintain the unity of the Labor party, whose trade union affiliates, in particular, were almost unanimously opposed to membership in the EEC on grounds of higher costs of food and stiff industrial competition. Although the parliamentary Conservative party also split on the issue of entry, its constituency organizations strongly backed membership. Late in 1971, Parliament approved entering the Common Market by a decisive majority that cut across party lines, but there remain grave doubts and opposition among substantial portions of the population.

Much remains in flux in Great Britain's role in international affairs. The adjustments to its membership in the European Economic Community and European parliament will absorb much of its attention in the coming years. Yet Britain must also work out how best to interrelate this new association with its historic, although much weakened, ties with the Commonwealth and with its traditional alignment with the United States in a time when the latter is reconsidering its international commitments. Since Britain is still eager to maintain a significant role in other areas, there are also strains to face in its Middle East policies and relations with the Soviet Union. How successfully Britain deals with these complex issues will determine its future standing and influence on the world scene.

Conclusion

The British are at a particularly difficult point in their history. They are torn between their desire to maintain themselves as a world power and their more inward-looking, and perhaps more constructive, awareness of the pressing nature of the many needs at home. This overriding issue of priorities is bound up with the basic questioning of values as well as possibilities that pervade so many aspects of British life today. So too is the more detailed consideration of the implications of diverse approaches to pressing internal and external problems.

Although Great Britain has decided to join the European Economic Community and its associated organizations and thus has moved decisively toward a Western European orientation, its people and government are determined to maintain their distinctiveness in character and policies within this entity as they have done in the past with other relationships. This distinctiveness arises from a blend of tradition and modernity. Thus it builds on the past, and often retains those forms, but is responsive in action to the perceived needs of the present and the future.

The British cherish their parliamentary procedures, but they also seek to make them more responsive and responsible to those inside as well as outside the chambers. They are attacking some of the last traditional strongholds of privilege in education, the civil service, and the administration of the law, to make them more democratic in membership and function. They are expanding the range of social services to meet more adequately the needs of the disabled and the elderly. They are making belated but far-reaching efforts to improve the environment of cities and countryside alike, efforts such as those virtually eliminating fog from London, refurbishing formerly grimy Midland towns, and landscaping highways, which go far beyond what has yet been accomplished in the United States.

Britain's economic problems, however, remain pervasive and worrisome. Its membership in the Common Market raises new and difficult questions. Will this participation provide the necessary stimulus to challenge both British workers and management to more effective efforts and a new awareness of their mutual dependence? Or will the efficiency of Continental enterprises and the lower pay of many Continental workers obviate the advantages of the larger market for British manufactures? Will the cost-of-living rise much higher because of guaranteed agricultural prices within the Common Market? And will this rise more than offset what additional prosperity can be expected from industrial expansion? These issues are crucial whatever general lines of policy are followed, for they cut to the heart of what Britain is able to provide for its people.

Whatever developments take place in Great Britain, they will be of great importance to the United States. Membership in the Common Market may somewhat change but will not in any sense destroy their close relations of the past. It is possible that far from drawing Britain away from the United States, the effect of its membership in the EEC may be to associate our country more closely with Western Europe. Moreover, a more prosperous Britain would be a more effective ally. As the United States itself begins to diminish the scope of its international activities and responsibilities and turn more attention to what needs to be done at home, there is much it can learn from how the British are adjusting to their changed role in international affairs. Although Great Britain is far from having found solutions to its "color" problems or to many of the other ills of a modern industrial society, the efforts it is making are well worth our careful consideration, as we too try to find solutions for these omnipresent and demanding problems.

II The government of France

Introduction

More than any other country in Europe, France both attracts and irritates Americans. For generations, American writers and artists have found a spiritual home in Paris. The floods of tourists who make their way to and through France every summer bear witness to the continued attraction of French urban and rural life, French food and wines, and the distinctiveness of the French people. French and American soldiers have fought side by side in France itself in two world wars. Yet along with these reasons for closeness goes a nagging awareness of how little Americans understand France and the French. The basic aloofness of the French, their ill-veiled air of superiority, their latent and sometimes obvious antipathy to the American stamp that accompanies the spread of American business and commerce, puzzle and disturb Americans. The latter rarely feel themselves to be the kind of people the French seem to assume they are. The French, from their side, anticipate a lack of American understanding of their culture, their history, and their preferred ways of life.

France is indeed a highly distinctive country, one that fits neither the accustomed patterns of American nor of British life and institutions.

Great elements of strength as well as weakness characterize France. No other culture has been so much admired or been so pervasive historically as has French culture. Yet no mature people has appeared to be more volatile. Although now apparently stable, French political institutions have changed so frequently in the past as to provide in themselves a study in comparative government. The French, in fact, traditionally regard their politicians with suspicion as prone to corruption and even treason. Plots and scandals are relished with enthusiasm. President Charles de Gaulle once called the French "the most fickle and unmanageable people on earth." Yet there are more serious sources of dissatisfaction that erupt from time to time, as evidenced by the student-sparked revolt of 1968. Basic to much of the current dissension, as well as to the management of French life, is France's overcentralized bureaucratic administration, inherited from Napoleonic times. France is complex, and so are the French. All the more reason, therefore, to examine at some length those factors that have made the French what they are and alert ourselves to their contemporary role in Europe and beyond.

1

The
French
people
and their
politics

1 PARADOX AND PROSPECTS

France, an old and proud nation-state, has reasserted its prewar position of prominence in Western Europe and is playing an important world role, politically and culturally. Its distinctive combination of presidential and parliamentary institutions is underpinned by an experienced, highly centralized administration. Moreover, a remarkable postwar economic development has enabled France not only to overcome earlier periods of stagnation and the devastation of World War II but also to become one of the most highly industrialized countries of its area. Thus its per capita gross national product (GNP) is only slightly below that of Germany and well ahead of the United Kingdom's. That much still needs changing was highlighted by the near revolution led by students in 1968. Further evidence for the need of change is given by the continued economic and social disparities between Paris and the rest of the country, and between the industrialized northeast and east and the still stagnating west and southwest. But President Georges Pompidou is consolidating many of the gains made under de Gaulle and trying, if somewhat tentatively, to infuse the more static sections of French life with the dynamism so obvious elsewhere.

FRANCE AND THE WORLD

Developments in France have a significant influence on the rest of the world. Its well-established postwar association with West Germany and its key position in the Common Market provide stability for an area that long resembled a cockpit. Its economic, military, and cultural relations with the African territories that were once part of its empire are far stronger than those of Britain with its former colonies. The former have also adopted the de Gaulle model of presidential dominance, while English-speaking Africa has almost entirely abandoned classical parliamentary forms. France early recognized Communist China and was followed in doing so by many Francophone African states. At the United Nations and in the tangled Middle East and Southeast Asian situations, France pursues policies that are often opposed to those of the United States and Britain. Moreover, its statesmen do not hesitate to criticize forcefully American and British policies with which they do not agree. Thus France sometimes forms the center of a third grouping, or bloc, between the Anglo-American and Soviet alignments.

2   THE LAND AND THE PEOPLE

THE LAND

Geographical influences

In comparison with the United States or the Soviet Union, France is small in area; yet it is larger than any other Western or central European country. Its territory of 213,000 square miles (somewhat smaller than the state of Texas but almost two and one-half times the size of Great Britain) contains a population (in 1970) of just over 50 million people (in comparison with Great Britain's 54 million). Its climate is temperate, its landscape for the most part is gentle though varied, and its beauty and fertility have long been proverbial.

A variety of geographical influences have contributed to French national unity. At its farthest extremes the country is not much more than six hundred miles across, and most of France lies within a few hours' train travel from Paris. With the exception of the Vosges Mountains (which separate Alsace from the rest of France) there are no barriers dividing one section of the country from another. On the contrary, the great river systems—the Seine, the Loire, the Rhône, the Gironde, the Garonne—link the coast with the interior regions and the different parts of the interior with one another. Certain uplands exist, as in Brittany and the *Massif Central* of south-central France, but they do not interfere with easy communication from south to north and west to east.

France's sense of national unity has also been encouraged by the existence of natural boundaries that cut it off from other lands. Of its six sides, three are bounded by water (the English Channel on the north, the Atlantic Ocean on the west, and the Mediterranean Sea on the south), and two by mountains (the Pyrénées in the south, and the Alps and the Jura Mountains in the east). Only on the northeastern frontier is there an absence of natural barriers. French history for centuries has been dominated by the struggle first to establish a northeastern boundary and then to maintain it

against attack. On this frontier France has had to meet invasion three times in the last century. It is only in recent years that firm cooperation between Western European countries has eliminated the fear of aggression.

Regional variations

Despite its compactness, France is a land of many distinct regions and attitudes. Far more than in England, differences have survived in costume, dialect, and way of life. According to popular stereotypes, the dark-haired son of the Midi (the south of France) is noted for his eloquence, his excitability, his religious indifference, and his political radicalism; the blond Norman for his reticence, shrewdness, and conservatism; the Breton, for his mystical piety; and the Lorrainer for his steadfast patriotism.

More important are the political and economic contrasts. The north and northeast, where some 80 percent of French industry is concentrated, are politically conservative but economically progressive. The west, center, and southwest are politically to the left but slow in introducing economic innovations. But France's economic revolution is bringing new industry to these latter areas, often under government stimulus, with a consequent lessening of the old restrictive influence of small landholders and businessmen.

THE PEOPLE

Nationality

As in Great Britain, the earliest inhabitants of France of whom we have historical record (the Gauls) were Celts. As early as 600 B.C., however, the Greeks had founded a colony at Marseilles on the Mediterranean coast, and in the second and first centuries B.C. this region (whose modern name, Provence, is derived from the Latin word *provincia*) opened the way first to Roman influence and then to Roman conquest of all Gaul. But in contrast

FRANCE

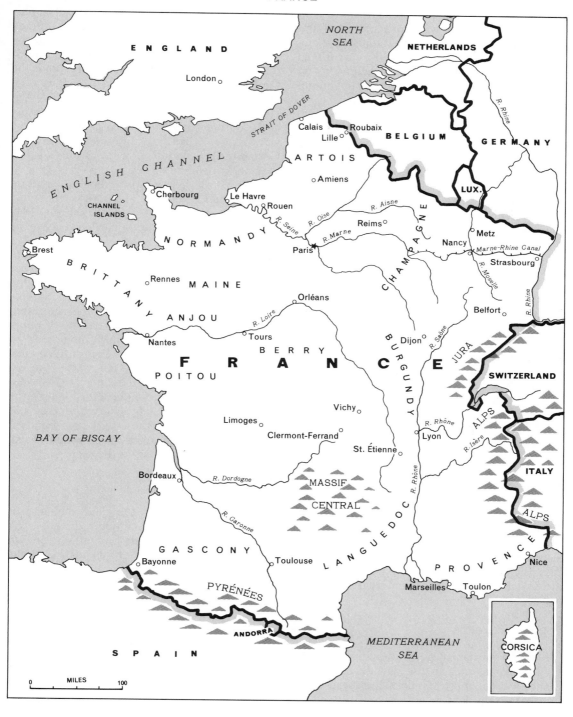

ENGLAND

NORTH
SEA

NETHERLANDS

London

STRAIT OF DOVER

ENGLISH CHANNEL

Calais
Roubaix
Lille
BELGIUM
GERMANY

R. Rhine

ARTOIS

Amiens

LUX.

Cherbourg
Le Havre
Rouen

R. Aisne

CHANNEL
ISLANDS

NORMANDY

R. Seine
R. Oise
Reims
Metz
Nancy

Paris
R. Marne
Marne-Rhine Canal

Brest

R. Moselle

Strasbourg

BRITTANY

Rennes
MAINE

CHAMPAGNE

R. Rhine

Belfort

ANJOU
Orléans
R. Loire

Nantes
Tours
BERRY

Dijon
JURA

SWITZERLAND

F R A N C E

BURGUNDY

POITOU

R. Saône

BAY OF BISCAY

Limoges
Vichy
R. Rhône

ALPS

Clermont-Ferrand
Lyon

R. Isère

St. Étienne

ITALY

Bordeaux
R. Dordogne
MASSIF

CENTRAL

ALPS

R. Garonne

GASCONY

LANGUEDOC
R. Rhône

PROVENCE

Bayonne
Toulouse
Nice

PYRÉNÉES
Marseilles
Toulon

ANDORRA

S P A I N
MEDITERRANEAN
SEA

CORSICA

0   MILES   100

to Great Britain, where the Roman influence was neither profound nor permanent, Roman influence on France was both powerful and continuous. The Gallic peoples adjusted themselves to their conquerors with exceptional ease, and the impact of Roman language and law is still apparent. As a result, it is common to speak of France as a "Latin" country.

Early in the fifth century A.D. France was invaded and conquered by a succession of Germanic tribes—the Visigoths, the Burgundians, and the Franks—but the Teutonic conquerors did not, as in England, destroy the earlier way of life. The fighting in France between Celt and Teuton was less bitter than in England, and particularly in the southern half of the country the conquerors tended to accept the language, law, and religion of the people they conquered.

In the centuries that followed there were few infiltrations or additions of new blood. The Northmen who invaded Normandy quickly adopted the language and institutions of the natives, and only Brittany (which offered a haven to Celtic refugees from the British Isles) and Alsace (which was not acquired until the seventeenth century) contain a significant number of people who speak a language other than French. There are, however, a small Basque-speaking minority in the south and a small Flemish-speaking minority in the north. With the possible exceptions of Alsace (where the inhabitants, although generally loyal to France, continue to speak a Germanic dialect and at times press for a degree of autonomy) and of Brittany (with its small "liberation" front), there is no problem in continental France of national minorities. The tension between people of different nationalities, which has complicated the political life of such countries as Belgium, Czechoslovakia, Canada, and the Soviet Union, has no counterpart in French politics.

Population trends

France's particular population problem has been its birth rate. In the days of Napoleon, France was the most populous European country apart from Russia. It was outstripped by Germany in 1870, by Great Britain at about the turn of the century, and even by Italy in 1930. While the rest of Europe experienced a phenomenal population increase, France suffered a steady decline in its birth rate throughout the nineteenth century. To translate the end result into military terms: France, which had the same number of men of military age as Germany at the time of the Franco-Prussian War (1870), had less than half as many as Germany at the outbreak of World War II. Since France was also less urbanized and industrialized than Germany, its economic power was much below that of its neighbor.

After World War II, the French population made a sudden increase at a rate considerably higher than that of its neighbors. From 1949 to 1954 it grew by 5 million, almost as many as during the whole nineteenth century. But in the 1960s, the birth rate fell again. Also, since the proportion of the young is high, the working population totaled by 1970 only the same number, 20.5 million, as it had in 1900, although the total population had increased from 40 to 50 million. Its low density of population, 91 per square kilometer compared to between 200 and 300 for the British, Germans, Dutch, and Belgians, is seen to be one of France's most serious economic weaknesses. But whether government plans for higher baby bonuses, increased paid maternity leave, and housing priorities for those with four children will overcome the characteristic French dislike of large families remains to be seen.

Religion

France, traditionally "the eldest daughter of the Church," is overwhelmingly Catholic. Of its 50 million inhabitants, 40 million are, in some degree, attached to the Roman Catholic faith; fewer than a million are Protestant; some 300,000 are Jews; the rest are atheists or free thinkers. Catholic ideals and interests might seem a unifying factor in French life.

Yet if eight out of ten Frenchmen are Catholic in form, fewer than three in ten are deeply devoted to the interests of the Church. Most Frenchmen are Catholic in the sense that many Americans are Protestant: they attend the great church festivals, and they use their churches for baptisms, weddings, and funerals. But they resent the interference of the Church in politics, and it is not unusual for a Frenchman to be both Catholic and anticlerical.

Indeed, the position of the Catholic Church in France was until quite recently a subject of bitter political controversy, in contrast to Great Britain, where religion has not been a major political issue for several generations past. Before the French Revolution, the Catholic Church was closely allied with the monarchical regime, which vigorously persecuted heresy (notably Protestantism) and religious and philosophical speculation. But this very persecution aroused the enmity of liberal intellectuals against the monarchy and against the Church as well. This enmity was slow to die. Restrictive proclerical measures under the Bourbon monarchy (1815–30), a reaction to the excesses against the Church during the French Revolution, convinced many nineteenth-century Frenchmen that no one could be both a devout Catholic and a good republican. Although the latter years of that century saw a lessening of tension between the Church and the Republic, the Dreyfus affair (see Chapter 2, Section 2) and legislation separating church and state revived the earlier bitterness. Thereafter and until World War II, the Church avoided overt political action. The fact, however, that Marshal Henri Pétain's Vichy regime, which appeared to collaborate with the Nazis, bestowed special privileges on the Church and received support from some of the highest Church officials again aroused republican suspicions. On the other hand, there was also notable Catholic resistance to the Nazis, which helps to explain the strength of liberal political Catholicism at the end of the war (see Chapter 3, Section 2).

The sharpest controversy affecting the Roman Catholic Church in postwar France has centered on education. Republican statesmen were long convinced that children educated by the Church grow up to be supporters of clerical and antirepublican groups and that only a school system that is republican politically and "neutral" theologically would produce citizens devoted to the Republic. But state facilities are badly overtaxed. Private schools, attended by one child in six at the primary level and one in three at the secondary level, are largely denominational and indispensable, particularly in the west of France. Essential state support extended grudgingly to private schools from 1951 to 1959, and on a more comprehensive basis from 1959 on, was fought bitterly in the earlier period, however, by the anticlerical Radicals and Socialists and provided one of the more divisive issues that racked the Fourth Republic.

FRENCH POLITICAL CULTURE

French political culture contains contradictory elements. A supreme individualism, suspicious of authority, exists side by side with an awareness of the need for strong and centralized government; a passionate prizing of individual achievements is combined with an overriding value placed on equality; a basically well-knit social fabric yet includes violent antagonisms over symbols such as flags, the basis of political legitimacy (royalist versus republican), attitudes toward property (conservative versus socialist), and foreign alignments (especially relations with the United States and the Soviet Union). A desire for change, especially in this time of rapid social and economic developments, is coupled with the lack of a pragmatic approach to politics that often relegates effective action to moments of crisis. In his book *The Bureaucratic Phenomenon*, Michel Crozier shows perceptively that France is organized in such a way that decisive change in the French system must be total and that, in consequence, change does not occur. Hence, far more than in Britain or the United States, French politics include pressures and sometimes violent action by the extreme right or the extreme left, which herd more moderate groups into center and often ineffective positions on touchy issues.

Pervasive elements in French political culture are the result of France's long history as a peasant nation whose small landowners clung to their plots with passionate attachment. Ownership created an intense individualism and suspicion of government lest it endorse dispossession. At the same time, government was seen as a factor to be manipulated for the farmers' self-interest. This mentality is slow to change, although movement to the cities is constant and inexorable. Whereas 35 percent of the French were peasant landowners prior to World War II, the percentage had sunk to 18 percent by the end of the 1960s. Per capita farm incomes are still 30 percent lower than those of industrial workers, despite recent increases resulting from advances in agricultural technology, consolidation of farms, and Common Market privileges, including subsidies for food exports. Thus the exodus from the farms, which forms France's most striking social and economic change, may well bring that country closer to the British and American models, in which only 5 percent and 6 percent of the people respectively are farmers.

Small and often inefficient family businesses are also being challenged in the retail trade. Although their number has dropped somewhat due to the growing competition of chain stores and supermarkets, there are still more than seven hundred thousand privately owned shops (i.e., one per fifty-six inhabitants as compared with one per hundred in the United States), 80 percent of which are family businesses with no employees. High prices have scarcely been curbed by a 1965 law penalizing firms with large profit margins, and there are no effective consumers' associations. But government reforms, foreign influences, and new ways of living are perceptibly changing the pattern of distribution of goods, as happened earlier in both Britain and the United States.

Although France is being transformed from a semirural to an urbanized society, this process has accentuated the dominant position of Paris, which is not only the hub of a highly centralized administrative system but also contains an overpowering share of the country's private companies and activities. One-quarter of all industrial workers, one-third of college and graduate students, and two-thirds of France's writers and artists live and work in Paris. No other city in France begins to approach Paris in population, prestige, and functions. In fact, where Paris has nearly 9 million people, the next largest cities in France have fewer than a million. Thus there is no urban counterpoise to the concentration in Paris comparable to that provided by the great provincial cities of Britain. This fact provokes resentment in other areas and magnifies the national impact of outbreaks in Paris like that of 1968.

A marked feature of the uneven distribution of wealth and activity in France lies in regional disparities: in particular, between the heavily industrialized northeast and the well-developed east on the one hand and the much less industrially advanced west, center, and south on the other. The northeast has two advantages: its coal and iron deposits, and its proximity to the heavily populated region around Paris. Within the northeast, which covers only 20 percent of the nation's territory, 38 percent of the population produces 46 percent of the country's industrial and agricultural output, and at a 25 percent higher productivity rate than the national average. In comparison, the western part of the country (the area west of a line drawn from Le Havre to Marseilles) is falling behind in agriculture and is experiencing relatively slight industrial development. The most recent French plans (see Chapter 6, Section 1) seek to reduce this serious imbalance, but it will be a long-term process, and it must take into account the strains of Common Market competition.

3   CRISIS, 1968, AND ITS AFTERMATH

Compounding these persistent sources of strain is a nation-wide, one may almost say a worldwide, crisis of civilization that strikes at the roots of all traditional institutions. It is of the essence of modern industrialized society that this crisis is most apparent in the area of communication, particularly in education and the mass media. These major means of transmitting the values of society have come under attack in France and in the United States both from inside and outside the relevant institutions.

The immediate genesis of the near-revolution of 1968 in France lay in the perennial educational problems of highly centralized educational structures, the outmoded and rigid traditional curriculum, overcrowded classrooms and quarters, and the slowness and inadequacies of educational and social change. Education and social change are intimately related in France, for the educational system has long been a source of class division. Those from the working class customarily sent their children to free municipal nurseries and primary schools (similar to American grade schools) until compulsory education ended at age fourteen. The bourgeoisie, in contrast, commonly sent their children to the kindergarten and junior departments of the secondary schools (like American private day schools). These latter institutions concentrated on the examinations taken at age eleven for the secondary schools, the sole route to the *baccalauréat* examination that, in turn, provides the sole route to the university. Thus the educational channel virtually decided future occupations and position in life.

The *baccalauréat* examination was reduced in 1966 to a single set of papers, but it retained much of its old concentration on the classics as compared to science and the social sciences. By noticeably lowering standards, this change accelerated the flood of students in the university system, which reached the total of 602,000 in 1967–68 compared to 170,000 in 1958. Yet the teaching profession opposed even the slight concessions that a relatively weak Ministry of National Education proposed to make to broader social groups. Thus little was done to meet growing protests except by creating new campuses: four regional universities at Rouen, Amiens, and Orléans, and two residential campuses in suburbs outside of Paris—Orsay and Nanterre.

The location of some of these institutions created additional tensions. At Nanterre, where the first outburst occurred, the campus lay between cheap housing and an industrial wasteland remote from the life of the city. Its students, who were almost exclusively middle class and who specialized in social science, fueled the demand for student influence within the educational system and increased relevance of subject matter to contemporary needs. The open protests began, as in many American universities, with a challenge to the strict segregation imposed between the boys' and girls' residential blocks. Demonstrations and further demands by activists and the students' union,

Union Nationale des Étudiants Français (UNEF), were met by inaction or by calling in the police. Both responses enraged the students, who were already aroused by anti-American Vietnam protests. They turned shortly from challenging the archaic and unwieldy university system to challenging the state that controlled it.

The explosion came in May, but there had been petty guerrilla actions in the Latin Quarter and outlying universities that warned of what was impending. Nonetheless, Prime Minister Pompidou took off for Iran and Afghanistan on May 2; the next day the revolt erupted. For ten days de Gaulle and his administration did virtually nothing. What Crozier calls the *société bloquée* ("blocked society") lived up to its name, making no change for fear it meant total change. During that time police arrests had led to rock throwing, to barricades, and to widespread solidarity among thousands of previously unorganized students. On May 10, infuriated by government intransigence and massed police, the students threw up barricades throughout the Latin Quarter. The police charged and bloody fighting ensued. The revolt was turned to insurrection.

Pompidou returned the following day, but his conciliatory gestures came too late. The fever had spread to the workers, who had a host of grievances and demands for more representation in industrial decisions. Moreover, there was widespread unemployment among the employable youth under age twenty, who quickly joined the movement. A strike and demonstration on May 13 was called by France's most powerful unions, the Communist-led *Confédération Générale du Travail* (CGT), with some eight hundred thousand members and the *Confédération Française et Démocratique du Travail* (CFDT), a militant non-Communist breakaway from the Catholic-oriented *Confédération Française des Travailleurs Chrétiens* (CFTC), together with the *Fédération de l'Éducation Nationale* (FEN), which unites anticlerical left-wing teachers from radicals to Communists. The date was the tenth anniversary of the Algerian putsch, which had brought de Gaulle to power (see Chapter 2, Section 3). The parade across Paris of eight hundred thousand workers led by student activists was intended as a political challenge to the regime.

Event led to event. From mid-May to mid-June 1968, France was immobilized in the grip of a nation-wide strike. More than 10 million workers and students seized and occupied buildings and factories. The ferment spread to professional men, especially to doctors in hospitals that were dominated by rigid seniority systems and to the young priests of the Catholic Church. Most of the personnel of the *Office de Radiodiffusion-Télévision Française* (ORTF) resigned in protest against strict government directives on how to handle news of the strike. Their action dramatized the nagging bureaucratic interference with the dissemination of news. It also reflected the upsurge of feeling against overcentralization, the complex, often overlapping and pervasive administrative machinery of state, the lack of effect of protests against unjustifiable administrative decisions, and the slowness of change.

The crisis highlighted more than the widespread desire for reform. It pointed up the impotence of parliament, whose debates and votes had no effect on the situation. But even more important at that juncture was that the Communist party and the CGT were not ready nor did they try to take advantage of this opportunity to overthrow the government or to force radical change. On the contrary, both split early with the student movement. Moreover, the CGT, in particular, found difficulty in establishing control over its own left-wing and Maoist elements. What influence the unions had, and it was not great, tended to be thrown against the wildcat occupation of factories. A further factor influencing the situation was that the farmers, who on other occasions had erupted in protests, remained out of sympathy with the urban-induced revolt, and their leading organization, the *Fédération Nationale des Syndicats d'Exploitants Agricoles* (FNSEA), counseled calm.

These facts do much to explain the public *volte-face* from basic sympathy with the students and workers to widespread enthusiasm when de Gaulle, returned from a lightning visit to army units on the Rhine, announced his decision to dissolve the National Assembly and call for new elections. These elections in 1968 reflected far more sweeping support for Gaullism, including some from the working class, than had those of 1962 and 1967. Yet the votes were essentially negative ones, against disorder rather than for any positive program. The dissatisfactions that had created the crisis remained.

THE SLOWNESS OF REFORM
AFTER THE ELECTIONS

The crisis of 1968 had provoked widespread proposals for reform in every aspect of life, especially education, housing, social security, and workers' participation in decision-making. But it proved far easier to design new structures than to implement them. Some of the useful proposals in education to reduce class divisiveness included raising the school-leaving age to sixteen (continuously postponed until more teachers and classrooms are available), delaying the fateful decision between lycée and technical school until age fifteen, and making this decision on the basis of the student's overall record. For the universities, Edgar Faure, de Gaulle's Minister of Education, proposed comprehensive changes in the fall of 1969, including the delegation of power to consider curricular and administrative matters to regional rectors and newly created parity commissions, elected in each university by students and professors; the reduction in size of individual universities; and the lessening of the dominant influence of senior professors. This program was approved almost unanimously by the National Assembly. But the necessary drive to put these changes into effect has so far been less than the stubborn resistance of the educational establishment.

For labor, it was decided that a profit-sharing law passed in 1967 but not designed to go into effect before 1972 should be implemented earlier, and that legal status should be given to unions inside each firm. But two major issues of special importance to the working class—housing and social security—are caught in the bind between demand and funds. The housing shortage is a major domestic problem. A smaller proportion of France's GNP is spent on housing than in most other Western European countries; the number of new apartments being built annually is far fewer than in Britain or

Germany; there is a serious lack of cheap state housing; and there is flagrant speculation in land and property that has skyrocketed rents and prices in urban areas. Comprehensive plans for meeting the needs of Paris' ever growing population have changed from decentralization, which was found inefficient, to redirecting concentrations of population away from the center of the city to self-contained adjoining towns; but the pressures go on.

In social security the fault is less the government's lack of effective policies, as is the case with housing, than the dilemma faced by all industrialized countries: the enormous expense and equally great attractiveness of comprehensive welfare coverage, especially in health. France adopted a cradle-to-grave social security system after World War II that operates in a unique fashion through three financially autonomous funds—one for health, one for old-age pensions, and one for family allowances—that are administered by management boards with worker, employer, and, at the national level, civil service representation. The family allowance fund, designed particularly to encourage the French birth rate, was the only one of the three showing a surplus in 1970, while the health fund, through which up to 90 percent of the cost of drugs and all hospital expenses are covered, was not only seriously in deficit but appeared likely to plunge rapidly into vastly greater debt. Proposals to increase contributions, amounting to 10 percent of the wage bill by employers and 6 percent by employees, have met with violent protests. Plans to modernize the nation's hospitals, one-third of which are private, and to curb excessive prescription costs have met resistance from hospital administrations and doctors. Hence, in this field, as in many others, self-interest in protecting existing structures and privileges handicaps government efforts to meet national needs and thereby bridge national divisions.

THE FRENCH ECONOMY AND CONTINUED UNREST

France's economy is still expanding in response to modernization programs; its balance-of-payments problems caused by the great strike of 1968 had given way to a healthy trade balance by mid-1970. Pompidou's mild restrictions on government spending and consumer credit and his 1969 devaluation of the franc have been enough to restore the economy to its previous state of health. But his government must still move cautiously with its deflationary measures to curb still rising prices, lest these measures stimulate further social unrest.

The persistence of strikes gives evidence that the malaise reflected in the crisis of 1968 is still festering. In November 1969, demonstrations by farmers in many parts of France reflected their uneasiness over government policies favoring consolidation of farms. In the same month there were strikes by workers in the French electrical industries and nuclear centers, and by medical students protesting limits on the number of entries to medical school. Two months earlier it had been the turn of small tradesmen to protest with violence against taxes, competition from supermarkets, and controls on increased prices. In April 1970, secondary school teachers followed parents in striking to publicize demands for better schools and equipment, better working conditions for both teachers and pupils, and more grants to aid wider participation in educational opportunities.

In the summer of 1970, left-wing youth added to the ferment by daubing expensive cars, yachts, and villas in holiday resorts with slogans like "Down with money!" and "No vacation for the rich!" The government had already outlawed extremist organizations, seized their publications, and arrested their militants (in particular, Alain Geismar, head of the banned Proletarian Left), following highly planned guerrillalike riots in June 1970 in Paris, Grenoble, Rouen, and Marseilles. Although the riot police countered these raids, the police are in general unhappy at being forced into a repressive role against students and extremists. Moreover, they have pay and work grievances of their own. These feelings were given dramatic expression in June 1970 when the police union, *Fédération Autonome des Syndicats de Police* (FASP), which includes about 80 percent of ordinary city and riot police, threatened that its members would report sick en masse unless the government dealt with their complaints and also changed its policies toward the universities and public order.

Despite these strains, the French national economy continues to expand, although still unevenly. This expansion is the more striking because the economy had been virtually static in the years before World War II. The original credit for the improvement must be given to Marshall aid. Subsequently, government planning for modernization and economic growth has been supported by judicious injections of capital into selected areas of the economy. More recently, Common Market arrangements have provided considerable stimulus to certain regions and industries, although others, like textiles, have suffered disastrously through external competition. The results have been that overall industrial production has risen decisively, diversification has become more common, and many French products can now compete on favorable terms with those of France's neighbors.

France's large measure of self-sufficiency has made it easier for its government to plan for economic growth than it has been for the British government. The French economy benefits from an unusual balance between industry and agriculture. In addition, France is rich in certain resources: it produces 9.7 percent of the world's supply of bauxite (the principal ore of aluminum); it is the world's third-largest producer of iron ore (after the Soviet Union and the United States); and it is the world's leading exporter of potash.

Despite these advantages and advances in production and distribution, there are still problems for its economy. A larger and better-trained labor force is needed. It is still proving difficult to persuade backward areas of the country to accept new techniques and the dislocations that accompany them. What has already been accomplished, however, makes it clear that France's economic growth is sound and that French prosperity is likely to become more evenly distributed as industrialization proceeds.

4   ORGANIZED INTEREST GROUPS

In 1968, workers and students had taken matters into their own hands in their violent protests against the inadequacies of French social policies. It is particularly significant that after the initial outbursts the organized interest groups in their fields had neither led nor approved the worker-student actions. This fact reflected not only the unwillingness of the Communist party and the major unions to use the opportunity to undermine the government but also a considerable weakness in their overall control of labor. This lack, which contrasts with the strength and scope of British trade unions, had already been demonstrated in 1947 and 1948 when the Communist party had called first a general strike to force a change of government and subsequently one aimed at crippling the coal mines, but had failed in its objective due to the opposition of many workers and the forceful action of the ministry. The earlier strike also caused a split in CGT ranks by what became the *Force Ouvrière* (FO).

The growth and influence of French interest groups is handicapped by what to Americans is a surprising lack of faith in voluntary associations as means of achieving their ends. The majority of such organizations include a relatively small percentage of those who are eligible. Not more than one-quarter of the farmers belong to any of the numerous agricultural groups; and probably less than one-fifth of the eligible wage earners belong to trade unions. Despite the intense activity of student groups in 1968, including those in high schools as well as universities, no more than one-fifth belong to one of the recognized youth organizations that extend left from UNEF to *Jeunesses Communistes Révolutionaires* (JCR), which, under Alain Krivine, powered the radical Proletarian Left. Only parent-teachers' associations and pressure groups for and against parochial schools number over a million members, as, characteristically, do the home distillers of tax-free liquor (whose effect on chronic alcoholism has been a major, and not easily controlled, social problem).

ORGANIZED LABOR

Organized interest groups, especially among labor, have also suffered from fragmentation. The French trade union movement is divided into one major, two minor, and several smaller groups. The CGT is still by far the largest, with more members than all French political parties put together. The much smaller Catholic trade unions are strongest among white-collar workers in private industry. Originally united in the CFTC, they are now split between a very small union that keeps the original name to preserve the reference to Christianity and a larger union that has replaced the word *Christian* by *Democratic* (CFDT). Still smaller is the *Confédération Générale du Travail—Force Ouvrière* (FO), which includes most unionized civil servants and state-employed workers (see Chapter 6, Section 4).

Strains between employers and workers, and workers and their unions complicate the process of industrial bargaining. Moreover, many issues of special importance to workers like social security and family allowances are out of the range of employer or worker control. Most problems of discipline and working conditions are settled by the employers so that only basic wages are left to be settled by collective bargaining, and even in this field the state plays a role. In mid-1970, the French employers' association, the *Confédération Nationale du Patronat Français* (CNPF), and four unions, the CGT, FO, CFDT, and the union of supervisory personnel signed a nation-wide agreement to set up a job-training fund through which wage earners could improve their skills or learn new ones; but even this useful step to promote industrial development has joint financing by employers and the state. It is hardly surprising, therefore, that unlike workers in Great Britain and the United States, French workers tend to exert their pressures directly on the state. Knowing that the interrelatedness of all aspects of French life and the pervasiveness of central control give the national government the key to most problems, trade unions are almost inevitably allied directly or indirectly to political parties, the CGT to the Communists, the FO to the Socialists, and the CFDT, with its new militancy and democratic-socialist philosophy, to the non-Communist left in general. Under the Fifth Republic these associations have brought few returns, which is part of the reason for the nation-wide rash of wildcat strikes during the crisis of 1968.

ORGANIZED FARMERS

In agriculture, traditionally a far more individualistic occupation, attempts have been made to produce a counterpart to the organization of industrial workers. The Vichy regime speeded the emergence of an indigenous peasant elite. The originally clandestine *Confédération Générale d'Agriculture* (CGA) came from the underground. After the Liberation, the CGA included seven segments, of which only the FNSEA, its one syndicalist component, was open to all active farm operators: owners, cash-farmers, and share-tenants. By 1950, old or Vichy leadership had replaced the more left-wing, the FNSEA was superceding the CGA, and in 1951 the FNSEA surged into politics with the unexpected success of the Peasant party, two-thirds of whose members the FNSEA had endorsed. From 1951 to 1956, the alliance of the Republican Independents and Peasant party controlled over a hundred seats in the Assembly, and every Minister of Agriculture was selected from this group.

The basic weakness of the syndicalist and traditional rural leadership was its failure to wrestle with the fundamental causes of peasant discontent, such as the marginality of many peasants, disparity between farm prices and costs, and the drift to the cities. The cause of agricultural modernization was taken up by a transformed Catholic organization, the *Jeunesse Agricole Chrétienne* (JAC), which became the most dynamic influence for change in rural France. Taking over the moribund syndicalist youth organization with FNSEA approval, the Jacistes formed and powered the *Cercle National des Jeunes Agriculteurs* (CNJA). It stood almost alone among agricultural interests in giving a qualified approval to Michel Debré's Agricultural Charter, which was finally forced through the Senate by combined executive and Assembly action. When the government failed to implement its provisions, rural dissatisfaction erupted into widespread and prolonged violence, leading to the 1962 Pisani Charter. CNJA leaders welcomed the charter as a genuinely constructive program for speeding rural structural change by subsidizing purchase of small plots to be grouped into workable farms, protecting professional farmers from speculative purchase of farming land, and giving producers' groups power to negotiate collective marketing agreements. Although the relatively conservative FNSEA still holds a leading role among agricultural associations, the CNJA has effectively thrown its weight behind the transformation taking place in rural France.

ORGANIZED BUSINESS

French employers are more united than French farmers or than French labor. But the progression to the present efficiently organized employers' association, the CNPF, was a slow one. The original employers' association, the *Confédération Générale de la Production Française* (CGPF), established in 1919 in response to government urging, was forced in June 1936 to conclude the humiliating "Matignon Agreement" with the CGT. This agreement provided genuine freedom for workers to organize and bargain collectively, minimum wages, the forty-hour week, and holidays with pay.

The French business community as a whole supported the Vichy regime, particularly in its early stages, and approved its emphasis on labor discipline and a government-directed economy. This cohesion aided them in organizing the CNPF in the first half of 1946. The CNPF remains a loose, decentralized federation of trade associations, but its executive body is capable of swift and decisive action in the interests of employers. The CNPF has not demonstrated, however, such forward-looking attitudes as have British or American employers' associations and tends to act defensively and in short- rather than long-range terms.

This fact gave rise early in 1970 to the creation of a new employers' association, *Entreprise et Progrès*, by more than a hundred of France's younger and more progressive industrialists. This group hopes to achieve more dynamic

modernization through exchanges of views and information every two months and by drawing on the graduates of the *Institut Supérieur d'Affaires* (ISA), patterned on the Harvard Business School. In so doing, it has the tacit blessing of the Pompidou government, which is more aware than was the de Gaulle regime of the need not only to develop a sounder infrastructure but also to concentrate French industry within narrower limits. Above all, French industry and business need to break away from outmoded patterns of thought, and it is in regard to this objective that Pompidou and the members of this new association are most in agreement.

TACTICS

French interest groups differ from their British and American counterparts in two ways: the French make less use of professionals (found almost exclusively in business associations) and of propaganda and public relations tactics. In part the latter situation arises from uncertainties regarding the legitimacy of group activities, which the government watches warily and on occasion bans. Partly it results from slowness to adopt modern organizational methods and partly from French expectations that it is from government that action results. Hence many voluntary associations have constitutional links to the administration (see Chapter 6, Section 2), a different means of achieving their purposes than is followed in Britain and the United States, but quite an effective one.

Where formerly interest groups put their demands directly to parliamentary candidates, the weakening of parliamentary influence under the Fifth Republic has led them to concentrate most of their attention on the administration and on the political executive, the major source of action. Most French ministries have a wide range of advisory committees composed of representatives from special interests, and sometimes a government bureau will not make a decision without the agreement of the relevant committee to share the responsibility. Interest groups have also sought influence through members of ministerial *cabinets* (the close aides with which each minister surrounds himself) and tried to capitalize on divisions within the administrative corps. Both the president and premier now seek to close these avenues of influence through closer administrative control.

Although direct influence on and connections with the state may appear to be the most effective means of securing their objectives, interest groups must also maintain their membership. Sometimes, especially among the peasantry and the students, who feel they have little influence within the Fifth Republic, this drive to attract support leads to radical plans, inflated demands, and militant action. Hence the curious paradox of some interest group behavior, oscillating between violent manifestations of discontent and active interaction with political forces and the bureaucracy.

THE ARMY

By one set of criteria, the army is part of the administration, military not civil, but equally remote from either pressure or party politics. But in France, this aloofness has alternated with action directly related to particular policies. The new national army of the Republic protected the nation from invasion, brought Napoleon I to power, and under his command marched across Europe imbued with ideological zeal. But during the Restoration and throughout the nineteenth century, the army was used

to suppress social upheavals and became the guardian of order rather than the defender of freedom. Like Marshal Pétain, the remnant of the army after defeat in 1940 was obsessed by the fear of an internal Communist takeover, although it took no active steps to affect policy. In 1958, the army's open support of General de Gaulle was a major contribution to the demise of the Fourth Republic.

Humiliated and defeated in Indochina by 1954, the army struggled for seven years to keep Algeria French. When senior army officers realized that de Gaulle, far from advancing the purpose for which they had supported him, intended to give Algeria independence, they mutinied in April 1961. Later, other officers attempted de Gaulle's assassination.

Although he reacted swiftly, sternly, and decisively to punish those responsible for the mutiny, de Gaulle saw the vital need to reintegrate an alienated army into France while insulating it from politics. Much reduced in numbers to about a third of a million, but equipped with modern weapons, the French professional army became once more isolated from society. In the fateful days of May 1968, it is believed that it was assurance of army support, if need arose, that gave de Gaulle confidence to reassert himself in the threatening strike-induced crisis. But even if true, there has been no aftermath to suggest a more active role for the army in the political life of France.

5 CHANNELS OF COMMUNICATION

In the absence of strong national political parties, a special responsibility for communication falls on the French mass media. Despite the high standards of literacy and education, however, the media have never had the influence that the British press, radio, and television, and some American broadcasters do, because they lack public confidence. It is well known that much of the French press is used by partisan political or commercial interests to further their own purposes, and that the government keeps a constant scrutiny over the dissemination of news lest it encourage some type of political takeover. Hence, whereas news-

papers in Great Britain and the United States are commercial enterprises that depend heavily on advertisements (whose revenues in France are low), the press in France, with few exceptions, represents special interests and is subject to excessive political control.

The wartime Resistance movement aimed to transform the press so that it reflected only "the consciences of journalists and readers." These high standards did not long persist, although special interests seem now less influential. While France has no big press lords in the British sense, most French newspapers get support from commercial or political interests.

Paris-Soir, a Gaullist-oriented paper with the highest daily circulation of any French daily, is associated with Hachette, the dominant distributor of papers and books, while the textile industry helps to support two other major Paris dailies, *Le Figaro,* and *L'Aurore,* respectively independent and moderate rightist. The sponsorship of newspapers by political parties is more surprising to an American. These papers have suffered sharp drops in circulation since World War II. The sharpest drops in circulation have been suffered by the official Communist newspaper, *L'Humanité,* and the Socialist paper, *Le Populaire.*

Only strong newspapers can survive in France today, a factor leading to a number of fusions since the end of World War II. The total number of Paris papers dropped from twenty-eight at the end of the war to fourteen by the mid-1960s. The provincial press, which holds up well in competition with Paris newspapers, has been marked by the same trends of consolidation, greater uniformity, and often blandness of approach.

By far the most outstanding paper in France (some say in Europe) is *Le Monde,* the nearest equivalent to *The Times* of London. The completeness and accuracy of its news, its brilliant, sometimes witty political analyses, its hospitality to nonconformist views, its restrained reporting of unpalatable realities, and the excellence of its foreign correspondents result in a readership of many professional men, businessmen, high administrators, and political figures. Alone among Paris dailies, *Le Monde,* whose circulation doubled in ten years to over four hundred thousand in 1970, has a substantial readership outside the capital, both in the provinces and in North Africa. In 1969, it introduced a weekly selection of its news in English that was subsequently incorporated as a separate section in the *Manchester Guardian Weekly.*

Le Monde fought successfully the efforts of a group of businessmen to take it over and, under an arrangement whereby its editorial staff owns 49 percent of the shares, its editor is assured tenure as long as his staff supports him. Following *Le Monde's* example, several other French papers set up journalists' associations with a blocking vote in management decisions. *Le Figaro's* journalists even went on strike in May 1969, seeking guarantees that the textile and sugar concerns that hold its controlling interest will not interfere with the way they run the paper. Thus journalists attempt to keep the news they purvey from being distorted by the interests on whose money they depend.

No less serious a source of pressures on news and the press is the government itself. During the Algerian war de Gaulle's government frequently seized issues of dailies and weeklies that contained unpalatable news or comments. Subsequently, use was made of an old law providing punishment for certain kinds of attacks on the head of state. In May 1970, the Pompidou government arrested two editors of the small Maoist tabloid *La Cause du Peuple* and made them vulnerable to prosecution by outlawing their Proletarian Left group the morning of the trial. In the meantime, Jean Paul Sartre had technically assumed the editorship of the paper and, after the two editors were sentenced to mild terms in prison, sought arrest, but unsuccessfully, to dramatize what he considered the government's repressive measures.

RADIO AND TELEVISION

French radio and television fulfill the purpose of nation-wide communication, which the press, with the possible exception of *Le Monde,* does not. But radio and television are far more susceptible to manipulation and control by the government. Television is a complete government monopoly, as is French radio, but a high proportion of radio listeners tune in to broadcasts from Luxembourg, Monte Carlo, the Saar, and Britain, since these present more varied news and points of view and often more entertainment.

The government has never concealed its belief that both radio and television should be used to advance the purposes of the regime, particularly since much of the press is deemed hostile. General de Gaulle's masterful use of these media swung public opinion against threatening revolts during the Algerian war. His carefully stage-managed presidential conferences particularly suited his lofty approach to national issues. Until the presidential campaign of 1965, the speeches of opposition leaders were often ignored. In 1965, however, use of radio and television by all candidates during the two weeks before the election led to brilliant exchanges and forced de Gaulle to appear far more than he had intended. In 1969, each of the eight candidates for president received one hundred minutes of prime time on both radio and television, although the contest was clearly between only two of them: Georges Pompidou and interim President (following de Gaulle's resignation) Alain Poher.

The government's structure for radio and broadcasting has long been under strong attack. The *Office de Radiodiffusion-Télévision Française* (ORTF) was set up in 1964, not as an autonomous agency, like the BBC, but under a board of directors composed of high civil servants, and representatives of the public, press, and ORTF personnel. The Minister of Information retained supervision, and the government appointed, and could dismiss, the director general and his chief assistants. Evidence that this system offers little of the independence sought was provided when members of the ORTF staff were severely penalized for their 1968 strike in protest at government directives on how to handle the crisis. Despite assurances to the contrary, and a reorganization under which the board was enlarged by more staff representation and given more powers, one-third of the broadcasting journalists (all of them among the strikers) were declared superfluous. Subsequently, despite assurances by the Pompidou regime of noninterference with news handling, Premier Jacques Chaban-Delmas infuriated liberals by refusing in June 1970 to allow a television production of a sequence from the 1965 film *The Battle of Algiers* (which had never been shown in France) lest the army and former Algerian settlers be outraged by scenes of French brutality. The French left, which prides itself on the superiority of French liberalness and intellectual distinction as compared with the United States, has been particularly disturbed by the obvious contrast between these restrictions and the openness of the American media in its devastating exposure of American actions in Vietnam.

Although several influential deputies had pressed for an independent television network, this effort received a severe setback when a nine-man commission, set up in October 1969 by the premier to recommend modifications in the ORTF's statute, reported in July 1970 against such competition with the state monopoly. The commission suggested instead that there should be three television channels, each run by a separate state-owned company, and that the ORTF should become only a financial holding company to distribute resources among them. The third television channel now scheduled to begin operating in the summer of 1972 will be run jointly with regional and local radio services. The commission also proposed merging the offices of chairman and managing director of ORTF, providing him with a fixed term of three or four years, reducing government nominees to a minority, and raising trade union and public representatives to a majority on the board of directors. For funds, the commission proposed an increase in license fees but no more than the eight minutes of advertising a day currently permitted. Even this small concession to commercial interests, it may be noted, had aroused heated protests when introduced in 1968!

THE EFFECTIVENESS OF THE MASS MEDIA

The French press suffers from many of the contradictions of French life. Excessive centralization exists side by side with a high degree of partisanship. Controls based on fear that news will acerbate conflicts interact with the suspicions of a public that anticipates the existence of plots, corruption, and bias. Resentment that news is scanty has also furthered a decline in circulation well below what could be expected of so literate and intellectual a people.

The Fifth Republic has been far more pathological about secrecy than was the Fourth Republic. Under the earlier regime, parliament debated the important issues, debate ran high, and out-of-office ministers could be counted on to provide "leaks" that gave special insight into the workings of the political scene. Under the Fifth Republic, parliament is limited in time and functions, and government officials concentrate on "handouts" that throw little light on the most significant developments of the day. Under such circumstances the press is hard put to keep the public abreast even of current news.

Radio and television, as government monopolies, have generally been little more revealing. Only during the lively 1965 presidential campaign, and the still more open contest in 1969, has there been a genuine plumbing of issues and enlightening disputation. The widespread interest and enthusiasm these events engendered are evidence that the media could be playing a much more effective role in communication if news were allowed to sell itself as it does in Great Britain and the United States. Until such a transformation takes place, however, the mass media will play a much less important part in spreading knowledge, understanding, and some sense of cohesion in France than they do in the other two countries.

2

The French political heritage

The most paradoxical and, in many ways, confusing feature of the French political heritage is that deep-rooted conservatism and continuity in tradition and administration underlie exceptionally frequent constitutional changes. Since the Glorious Revolution of 1688, Great Britain has made no violent change in its government. Since 1789, the United States has had only one constitution and has had no successful rebellions. In contrast to Anglo-American political continuity, France has had eleven constitutions since 1789: three constitutional monarchies, two empires, one semidictatorship, and five republics. Moreover, most of these changes have been effected by violence. But if as a result the French take their political institutions far less for granted than do Americans and British, it must also be said that most constitutional changes have had far less impact on their individual lives.

In the course of this and succeeding chapters, more will be said not only about the nature of French politics but also about French political ideas and institutions. The dual themes of basic continuity and revolutionary change will be explored. First, however, it is essential to have some knowledge of the characteristics of earlier regimes.

1 ANTECEDENTS OF THE REPUBLIC

THE HERITAGE OF
THE ANCIEN RÉGIME

Modern France's chief inheritance from the ancient monarchy is the tradition of a highly centralized, hierarchical administration, a tradition that is all the stronger because of the long and painful struggle required for its establishment. The power of the medieval kings of France was far more severely restricted than that of their English counterparts. For many years the frequent wars with England (culminating in the Hundred Years' War, from 1337 to 1453) divided the country; and even after the invaders had been expelled, the French kings were unable to exercise effective authority over such powerful nobles as the Dukes of Burgundy and Brittany. Louis XI (1461–83), through the skillful, Machiavellian use of his power, reduced their authority substantially. Throughout the sixteenth century great nobles intrigued and fought against the royal authority. But in the seventeenth century a succession of great ministers of the king—Richelieu (who crushed the last vestiges of Protestant military power and political autonomy), Mazarin, and

Colbert—unified the country politically and established a centralized administrative hierarchy that was dependent solely on the authority of the king. Despite all subsequent constitutional changes in France, the system of monarchical administration is still recognizable, although transformed under the Fourth and Fifth Republics into a modern, efficient technocracy (see Chapter 6).

The Middle Ages had seen the growth of an embryonic French parliament, the Estates General, representing the nobility, the clergy, and the growing middle class. This body, however, met only when summoned by the king, and from 1614 to 1789 it was not summoned at all. In the absence of organs for the representation and defense of their economic and political interests, the growing middle class regarded with ever increasing animus the high taxes (from which the nobility were exempt), the financial ineptitude of the government, the class barriers to high-ranking positions in the army and administration, the restrictions on industry and trade, the arbitrary exercise of the royal authority, and the limitations on freedom of thought, expression, and political action. The great French Revolution started out in 1789 to abolish privilege and reform the monarchy. But the very violence of change led inexorably to abolishing the monarchy and executing the king and those associated with him.

As the Revolution advanced, it was marked not only by foreign war and by civil strife between Royalists and Revolutionists but by a struggle among the Revolutionists themselves. A Reign of Terror followed in which the Revolution destroyed many of its own supporters—first those who had been more moderate and finally the terrorists themselves. In 1795, in reaction against both the excesses and the idealism of the preceding years, power was entrusted to the five-man Directory, a government characterized by weakness, mediocrity, and corruption. There was little popular desire to defend so uninspiring a regime when Napoleon Bonaparte, one of the distinguished generals of the Revolutionary armies, attacked it, proclaimed the Consulate (with himself as First Consul) in 1799, made himself Consul for life in 1802, and established an empire (with himself as emperor) in 1804.

THE REVOLUTIONARY HERITAGE

The life of the First French Republic was thus short, agitated, and bloody, but it had enduring consequences. The work of unifying the country was completed by sweeping away all internal economic barriers and by proclaiming the French Republic to be, in the famous phrase, "one and indivisible." Moreover, this unity found a powerful spiritual reinforcement in the growth of a fervent sentiment of national patriotism, symbolized in the national anthem, *La Marseillaise*, and the deep attachment to the tricolored flag, which, at least until the Popular Front of the mid-1930s, overrode the divisions of religion, class, political outlook, and economic interest.

In addition, the Revolution abolished the reign of privilege and established, as an enduring principle of French government, the "career open to talent." The partial destruction and division of the great estates of the nobility and the Church helped to create the powerful, property-owning rural middle class in which the Republic, in later generations, was to find its strongest support. And the noble aspiration toward political liberty and self-government expounded in the Declaration of the Rights of Man and of the Citizen provided an ideal and a precedent for subsequent, and more successful, struggles for human freedom.

FROM NAPOLEON TO
THE THIRD REPUBLIC

Napoleon maintained and consolidated many of the social and economic gains of the Revolution: the elimination of privileges based on class, the destruction of provincial barriers to trade, the freeing of the people from feudal tithes and duties, and the distribution of property among the peasants. Moreover, he added significant contributions of his own. His codification of the law and reorganization of the administration determined the form of two institutions that have remained essentially unchanged through all the political vicissitudes of the coming generations and have had a profound effect on French political life.

At the same time, Napoleon's success in destroying the Republic led many Frenchmen to fear strong leadership and to distrust the people as a bulwark of democracy. Each of Napoleon's successive usurpations was ratified in plebiscites by an overwhelming majority of the people, and it was evident that the masses were ready to exchange a perilous liberty for personal security, political order, and military glory.

The defeat of Napoleon in 1814 and 1815 and the restoration of the Bourbon monarchy under Louis XVIII provided France with a second opportunity to develop constitutional monarchy and parliamentary government. The remnants of the ancient nobility and the higher clergy were reluctant, however, to adjust themselves to the new political code. The accession of Charles X in 1824 inaugurated an era of reaction that precipitated the revolution of July 1830 and the substitution of a new monarch, Louis Philippe of the House of Orléans, who was pledged to constitutional government and to moderate policies. However, there was no clear acceptance of the principle of ministerial responsibility and, therefore, of popular supremacy, and the Orleanist monarchy's prosecution of its political opponents suggested that monarchy could not be reconciled, as in Great Britain, with political liberty or with democratic government. In 1848, with surprising ease, the king was dethroned and France began its second republican experiment.

The life of the Second Republic was short and agitated. From the start there appeared a cleavage between the moderate men of the middle class who favored republican government but feared social upheaval, and the radical working class of Paris, which had been primarily responsible for the Revolution. The two elements came to blows in the bloody "June days" of 1848. The moderates, who controlled the government and were supported by the provinces (which looked upon "red Paris" with great distrust), triumphed over their opponents.

Their victory, however, was short-lived. In the presidential election of December 1848, the candidates of both moderate and radical republicans were overwhelmed by a tremendous popular vote for Louis Napoleon Bonaparte, the nephew of the great Napoleon whose orderly and glorious government appeared in retrospect as something of a golden age. Imitating his uncle, "Napoleon the Little" in December 1851 dissolved the legislative assembly, seized its leaders, and won the consent of the people (in each case by an overwhelming vote), first to an extension of the presidential term of office to ten years and then to the establishment of an empire, in 1852, to be ruled by Louis Napoleon under the title of Napoleon III. Thus for a second time a Republic that lacked internal cohesion was overthrown by a strong, popular leader with monarchical ambitions.

The first years of imperial government were marked by the vigorous persecution of political opponents and the concentration of great power in the person of the emperor. Yet it was symbolic of the cleavage between those who were interested primarily in political liberty and those who were chiefly devoted to social justice that certain socialists supported the empire in its early years in the hope that it would introduce economic and social reforms.

As popular dissatisfaction with the imperial government increased, an attempt was made to transform the regime into a "liberal empire," although the problem of whether a ministry's first responsibility was to the legislature or to the emperor was never clearly resolved. The disastrous Franco-Prussian War of 1870 intervened before the new constitutional experiment could be carried very far. In September a new revolt in Paris overthrew the government and established the Third Republic.

Thus the agitated years between 1815 and 1870 had brought no clear agreement on fundamental political principles and institutions; if anything, the political problem had grown more complicated. Frenchmen were divided into supporters of Bourbons, Orléans, and Bonapartes, those who favored a moderate republic, and those who favored radical social reform. Yet there was one gain: each of the different regimes had experimented with some form of parliament. Thus, even though the problem of the relation of executive to legislature had never been worked out, a considerable degree of familiarity with parliamentary institutions had been gained, and the new Republic could draw on a valuable store of political and parliamentary experience.

2 THE POLITICAL HERITAGE OF THE THIRD AND FOURTH REPUBLICS

THE THIRD REPUBLIC

For many years after the collapse of the empire, the life of the Republic was anything but secure. The first elections actually resulted in the victory of a royalist majority, and it was only because the monarchists could not agree which king to restore that the Republic, more or less by default, was permitted to survive. In addition, in 1871 the city of Paris, which had precipitated every successful revolution since 1789, again revolted and established a government known as the Commune. This time, however, the revolt was mercilessly crushed, and the very vigor with which the provisional government suppressed the Communards reassured the mass of non-Parisian voters that a republican government could also be conservative and stable. Yet the new prestige of the Republic was purchased at the price of bitter hatred, and the memory of the martyrs of the Commune is still cherished by Paris workers.

It was not until 1875 that France acquired the makeshift constitution under which the country lived, somewhat to its own surprise, until 1940—a far longer period of existence than any other French constitution. The new constitution was really a series of three laws: on the organization of public powers; on the relations among the public powers; and on the organization of the Senate. It was passed by a combination of republicans and of moderate royalists who were tired of long delay, eager for some kind of definite political order, and willing to compromise on a set of laws that could easily be adapted to a restored monarchy. According to these laws, a bicameral parliament was set up consisting of a Chamber of Deputies to be elected by universal suffrage and a Senate chosen by indirect election. The two chambers meeting in joint session (under the title of National Assembly) had the power to elect a president of the Republic for a term of seven years. The National Assembly could amend the constitutional laws by a majority vote after each chamber had adopted a resolution to that effect. Ministers were collectively responsible to the chambers for the general policy of the government and individually responsible for their personal acts. With the consent of the Senate, the president could dissolve the Chamber of Deputies before the expiration of its term of office (four years) and call new elections.

The Sixteenth of May

It was not long before these laws met their first severe test. The president of the Republic, Marshal Marie de MacMahon, was a royalist and a strong partisan of the Church. When the Chamber of Deputies (of which the republicans had control) passed an anticlerical resolution, MacMahon rebuked the chamber. On the famous Sixteenth of May 1877, Premier Jules Simon resigned in protest, as MacMahon had hoped he would. The president then appointed a proclerical ministry that lacked the confidence of the Chamber of Deputies and proceeded to dissolve the chamber with the consent of a bare majority of the Senate. Many feared that the Republic was in extreme danger. MacMahon's supporters were decisively beaten, and in 1879 the president resigned his office.

The episode had an enduring effect on the Third Republic. From that time on, the dissolution of parliament in case of disagreement between the ministry and the parliamentary majority was not considered a normal part of the parliamentary process, as it has been in Great Britain, but rather as a weapon that would be used only by a potential destroyer of the Republic.

MacMahon's successor, Jules Grévy (1879–87), was authentically republican and sufficiently colorless to prevent any fear of his aspirations. During his period of office, the Republic further strengthened itself by instituting a system of universal, free, and lay education that was intended to be secular and neutral toward religion. In practice, however, the teaching was ardently republican, and the survival of the Republic was often attributed to its prowess in the battle for the minds of the children.

The Boulanger episode

The colorlessness as well as the corruption of the Grévy administration explain to some extent the phenomenal growth in popularity, in 1886, of General Georges Boulanger, the Minister of War, a young man of dashing appearance but questionable character. Having won dramatic expressions of support in different parts of France, Boulanger finally succeeded in sweeping the city of Paris, the old stronghold of radical republicanism. When his friends urged him to overthrow the government by force, however, his nerve failed; he fled the country, and in 1891 he committed suicide on the grave of his mistress. While this fiasco made royalists and clericals appear absurd, good republicans shuddered at the thought of what an able adversary might have done with the opportunities Boulanger had squandered.

The Dreyfus affair

In 1892, Pope Leo XIII called on French Catholics to accept the republican government, but unfortunately such efforts at reconciliation (which might have simplified French politics by eliminating the religious issue) were doomed by the crisis known as the Dreyfus affair.

A financial scandal involving high government officials and Jewish bankers had shaken the Republic and raised the issue of anti-Semitism. To this fire, fuel was added by word that a young Jewish army captain, Alfred Dreyfus, had been found guilty of selling military information to Germany and had been condemned to imprisonment on Devil's Island. By an extraordinary series of coincidences and accidents, however, Dreyfus' family and friends learned that top officers of the French army knew that the real culprit was not Dreyfus but probably a cosmopolitan adventurer, Major Charles Esterhazy, the nephew of a highly placed military figure, General Walsin. Largely to conceal the corruption, intrigues, and chaos that ruled in the Ministry of War, officers had connived to suppress facts and ultimately to forge evidence against Dreyfus.

The charges against the army created a national crisis. Most royalists, clericals, militarists, and superpatriots, as well as those who hated Jews, Protestants, and foreigners, felt that an attack on the army was an attack on France itself, and that it was far better that an innocent Jew should suffer than that the integrity of military commanders should be questioned. Most of the staunch republicans, the anticlericals, and the socialists saw the struggle as one between intolerance and reaction on the one side, and justice and liberty on the other. Intellectuals, like the writers Émile Zola and Anatole France and the painter Claude Monet, together with many scholars and teachers, deserted their studies and studios and joined with such practical politicians as Georges Clemenceau and Jean Jaurès to clear Dreyfus' name.

Esterhazy and the forger, Colonel Henry, ultimately confessed, and Dreyfus was liberated and restored to the army. Even so, many anti-Dreyfusards refused to believe the evidence or insisted quite frankly that justice was less important than order and national power. Thus the case intensified divisions that had seemed on the point of lessening.

The anticlerical reaction

Some of the republicans who triumphed in the struggle over Dreyfus were as fanatical as their most reactionary opponents, and they now turned their fury against the Church. The Combes Ministry, which came into office in 1902 (Combes himself had been trained for the priesthood), led the attack. Government officials and army officers were discriminated against if they went to Mass or sent their children to Church schools; and in 1905 the famous *Separation Law* not only revoked the government's power over the appointment of bishops (a change that the Church welcomed) but deprived the Church of all financial support from the government. It also vested ownership of all churches in the government, although religious congregations were permitted to continue to use them without payment. Although the government soon relaxed its rigid enforcement, faithful Catholics bitterly resented and resisted the provisions of this law.

The interwar period

World War I did not shake the stability of the Republic. Although the country passed through a series of financial crises from 1924 to 1928, it was the economic depression of the early 1930s, coinciding with the rise of fascism in Germany and with new financial scandals, that brought the Republic again into danger. In January 1934, the suicide of Serge Alexandre Stavisky, a Jew of Russian origin (and therefore an apt subject for anti-Semitic and nationalist propaganda), disclosed financial malpractices that could only have been carried on with the friendly tolerance of high government officials. The cabinet of Premier Camille Chautemps, by trying to hush up the scandal, gave ammunition to those who charged that the government was corrupt from top to bottom and was conniving with swindlers and thieves. Early in February 1934, two mobs—one predominantly fascist, with a sprinkling of royalists, and subsequently one largely Communist —attacked the Chamber of Deputies. The police, with great difficulty, held the mobs in check, but the cabinet resigned.

The Popular Front

In the face of the depression and the menace of fascism, the three great parties and organizations of the left—the Radicals (the moderate lower–middle-class party, often called the Radical Socialists), the Socialists, and the Communists—drew together in the Popular Front of 1935. Forming a common front, they won a substantial, although not overwhelming, victory in the election of 1936, and Léon Blum, the leader of the Socialist party and a Jew, became premier (a fact that gave further encouragement to anti-Semitism among the rightists).

The Blum government, concentrating at first on social reform, passed a series of laws providing for collective bargaining, the raising of wages, nationalization of the munitions industry, the forty-hour week, aid to farmers, and the reorganization of the Bank of France. In economic and social life, it created a veritable watershed in French development.

But Popular Front reforms took place in an atmosphere of great social tension. Moreover, the outbreak of the Spanish Civil War (1936) intensified the bitterness between the right and the left and to some extent revived the clerical issue. Despite its far-reaching program, the Popular Front developed serious cracks within a relatively short time and was obliged to resign after one year in office.

The end of the Third Republic

In the following years no government provided the firmness and leadership needed to meet the ensuing succession of crises. Communist infiltration of labor and other groups, polarization of sentiment over the Spanish Civil War, and the dismemberment of Czechoslovakia under the Munich Agreement of September 1938, created widespread division and unrest. There was an increasing tendency for emergency powers to become a regular and necessary part of the political order. The outbreak of conflict in 1939, coupled with the Nazi-Soviet nonaggression pact, left French leaders stunned and incapable of unified action. The most shattering evidence of cabinet instability was the parliamentary crisis in March 1940 (the month Hitler's armies invaded Norway). The country was on the verge of a second parliamentary crisis when the Germans invaded the Low Countries in May. Thus the government had neither the confidence nor the support of the country at the time of its greatest trial. France's subsequent disaster was intensified by the absence of effective political leadership.

On June 16, 1940, a new cabinet was formed under the leadership of Marshal Henri Pétain, a hero of World War I, who was looked on, even by the left, as a model military man. Only when in power did he display his clerical and authoritarian sympathies. Pétain promptly opened negotiations for an armistice with the Nazis. Signed on June 22, it divided France between an occupied northern zone and an unoccupied southern zone. The National Assembly (the Chamber of Deputies and Senate in joint session) convened at Vichy, the capital of the unoccupied zone, and by 569 votes to 80 gave "all power to the Government of the Republic under the authority and signature of Marshal Pétain." The Third Republic was at an end.

THE VICHY REGIME

Until November 1942 (when the entire country was occupied by German troops) France was divided. The German army occupied the northern half of the country and a strip along the Atlantic coast, while the remainder of the southern half (unoccupied, or Vichy France) retained a semblance of independence under Marshal Pétain.

Pétain was supposed to frame a new constitution (to be ratified by popular vote) guaranteeing the rights of "work, family, and native country"—a vague but significant substitution for the traditional republican trinity of liberty, equality, and fraternity. But the constitution was never promulgated. Throughout the life of his government its only legal basis was in the provisional grant of powers. Pétain did, however, issue a series of "constitutional instruments" that repealed the constitutional provision for the election of a president, abolished the responsibility of the government to the legislature, and ended the latter's legislative powers. From this time on Pétain himself held all legislative power, and the ministers were responsible to him.

The announced aim of the Pétain government was to bring about regeneration and to free the nation of the vices that were thought to have destroyed France under the Third Republic. Masonic lodges (which were regarded as a republican political machine) were dissolved and their members deprived of government office. Organizations of workers and employers were disbanded, and state organization of industry was introduced under organizing committees, which rapidly fell under the control of big business. Attempts were made to introduce religious education into the schools, and subsidies were given to Catholic schools. In addition, under pressure from the Nazis, the government introduced anti-Semitic policies of such severity as to evoke formal protests from both Catholic and Protestant leaders.

THE RESISTANCE AND THE LIBERATION

From the moment France fell, General de Gaulle, at the time relatively unknown to the masses of the French people, rallied a group of "Free French" in London and appealed to the people of his country to resist. At first he had little popular support, but as the Pétain government revealed its undemocratic character, as the Germans drafted labor for work in Germany, and as the stubborn British defense showed that the war was not over, the Resistance movement became stronger. Many young men escaped to join de Gaulle's army, and many more joined in the work of the underground. After the German attack on the Soviet Union in the summer of 1941, the French Communists took an outstanding part in the Resistance movement. The movement always included men and women of all political opinions, however, from extreme rightists to liberal Catholics and Socialists. Workers and members of the professions provided the most recruits.

The political and economic program of the National Council of Resistance (which combined all the leading resistance groups) called for a provisional republican government headed by General de Gaulle; the reestablishment of democracy with full freedom of thought, conscience, and expression; full equality of all citizens before the law; and the institution of social and economic democracy through the destruction of the great "feudal" economic and financial interests and through a planned economy under which private interests would be subordinated to the general interest. About the political ideas of General de Gaulle himself, there was considerable uncertainty. It was known that he was a pious Catholic, and as an army officer he was naturally suspect to many good republicans. Yet he proclaimed his loyalty to the Republic, and as the day of liberation approached he came personally to symbolize the spirit of the Resistance.

With the liberation of France in 1944, General de Gaulle became head of the provisional government. An assembly existed, but it was purely consultative. The cabinet was chosen by de Gaulle and was responsible to him alone. Thus the regime in the first fourteen months following the Liberation was rightly called a "dictatorship by consent." This situation was probably inevitable, for the political balance at the time of liberation was seriously distorted, as future instability and uncertainty were to demonstrate.

THE FORMATION OF
THE FOURTH REPUBLIC

It was obvious that France must have a new constitution, and when the first legislative assembly was elected in October 1945, the people, by a vote of 18.5 million to 700,000, decided that one of its tasks should be to frame such a document. Thus France was governed for several months by a combined legislature and constitutional convention known as the "Constituent Assembly."

But although the people were agreed on the need for a new constitution, they were not agreed on its nature. Conservative quarters called for a strengthening of the executive according to a somewhat incongruous blend of American and British practices. Most leftists, however, were opposed to any strengthening of the president or premier and maintained that parliament alone should represent the national sovereignty.

The first version

As a result, the first version of the constitution, a leftist draft that was presented to the voters in May 1946, placed almost complete authority in the hands of a single chamber called the National Assembly. General de Gaulle, who had resigned as president in January 1946 following a series of controversies with the left, maintained silence on the issue of ratification. But a new party, the Catholic *Mouvement Républicain Populaire* (MRP), and the few remaining Radicals, as well as the rightist political organizations, urged a negative vote. The Communists and Socialists naturally urged ratification, as did the Communist-controlled CGT. To the general surprise, however, the constitution was rejected by a narrow margin—10,584,539 votes to 9,454,034.

The second try

In the new Constituent Assembly, elected in June 1946, the MRP replaced the Communists as the largest party, but the Communists and Socialists, when supported by deputies from Overseas France, were still able by a very slight margin to outvote their opponents. As a result, the second version of the constitution was very much like the first. Although a second chamber, the Council of the Republic, was added, power continued to be concentrated in the National Assembly, and the executive remained weak. Nonetheless, the MRP (even while announcing its intention to seek amendments) decided to join with the Communists and Socialists in urging the voters to accept the constitution. General de Gaulle, however, demanded that it be rejected, and in this attitude he was supported by the Radicals and the parties of the right.

The results of the election were curiously indecisive. In the referendum of October 1946, 9,297,470 voters supported the constitution; 8,165,459 voted against it; and 7,775,893 eligible voters stayed away from the polls. Thus the constitution of the Fourth Republic came into being with what General de Gaulle and his supporters claimed was the support of only a little more than a third of the population.

THE BALANCE SHEET OF
THE FOURTH REPUBLIC

The paradox of the Fourth Republic is that despite the slim margin with which it came into existence, and the almost universal opprobrium with which it ended thirteen years later, it encompassed a period in which a newly vigorous France came into being. By 1958, France had its highest birth rate in a century; much of its industry had been modernized, and its industrial production had expanded since 1953, as quickly as that of Germany and far faster than that of either Great Britain or the United States. The French standard of living had improved markedly, partly because of economic growth and partly because of the advanced social security system established after the Liberation. Moreover, France under the Fourth Republic undertook a farsighted and generally successful policy of closer relations with its Western European neighbors, culminating in the acceptance of the Common Market and Euratom in mid-1957.

Why, then, was the Fourth Republic written off as a failure in 1958, both at home and abroad? Partly, it was because France's parliamentary regime had found itself increasingly handicapped by the presence on both the extreme left and the extreme right of large groups that rejected the parliamentary system in the form in which it existed and thus forced the moderate parties that lay between them into a constant series of expedients to maintain effective government. Because of this handicap, the Fourth Republic never succeeded in enforcing a genuinely equitable social distribution of the national income; it proved incapable of resisting the pressures of special groups (such as those producing alcohol); it failed to cope with the problems posed by the poverty of the Catholic schools, in which one-fifth of the children of France were being educated; and it could not tackle effectively the urgent needs of tax reform and improved housing. But beyond this, the Fourth Republic was weakened irreparably by the dismal succession of defeats in France's overseas possessions and the costly and long, drawn-out war in Algeria. It was the crisis in Algeria that brought de Gaulle to power once more in 1958 and led to the Fifth Republic.

The twelve-and-a-half-year period of de Gaulle's political semi-isolation had seen shifting party alignments as confusing as those of the Third Republic. When de Gaulle resigned from office in January 1946, he had left the political field to three large, well-disciplined, but ill-mated political parties: the Communists, the Socialists, and the new socially progressive Catholic MRP. Their uneasy partnership lasted less than a year. In May 1947, the Communists voted against the government and were ejected from it; an ensuing wave of revolutionary strikes led by the CGT was ruthlessly broken. De Gaulle's new political organization, the *Rassemblement du Peuple Française* (RPF), had already appeared on the right. He intended the RPF to be above parties, but its legislative representatives were soon playing the parliamentary game. Paradoxically, RPF votes combined with Communist votes to thwart the Socialist-MRP alignment, and the latter was forced to rely increasingly on the Radicals and Independents.

The new electoral law of 1951, by aiding electoral alliances, weakened the proportionate strength of the Communists and RPF in the Assembly. Coveting a share in power, many former Radicals and Independents, who had gained their seats as representatives of the RPF, now moved into the central coalition. In 1952, the RPF split openly; in 1953, de Gaulle renounced it. In 1954, a new alignment of Radicals and Socialists helped Pierre Mendès-France displace the MRP and Independents. He replaced the latter's do-nothing policies with a whirlwind attack on France's major external issues. He made a settlement in, and withdrew from, Indochina; he gave internal autonomy to Tunisia; and he forced the project for the European Defense Community to a vote, in which, however, it was rejected. In the election of 1956, Mendès-France's new Left gained strength, the MRP and Independents held their own, and a new antidemocratic rightist group, the Poujadists, a protest movement of small shopkeepers and backward farmers against the dislocations of modernization, appeared in the chamber. But despite his apparent electoral success, Mendès-France was gradually isolated, and the Socialists and MRP combined under the former's leader, Guy Mollet. On February 6, 1956, however, Mollet capitulated to riots organized by French *colons* (settlers) against a liberal settlement of the Algerian question. By so doing, he made it virtually impossible for any other leader of the Fourth Republic to work out an acceptable solution in Algeria.

3 THE FIFTH REPUBLIC

THE FOUNDING OF THE FIFTH REPUBLIC

The Fifth Republic was born out of violence and the need to reestablish political unity and stability. It has rightly been called the de Gaulle Republic, for de Gaulle molded its constitution and its policies to his own view of the country's needs in a way no other Frenchman had been able to do since the days of Napoleon I. Whether in so doing de Gaulle provided the permanent base of stability in France that he sought is not yet certain. What is certain is that he forced French politics and institutions into radically new patterns.

The war that destroyed the Fourth Republic was a colonial-type struggle, the Algerian revolt. Guy Mollet's swing to the side of the *colons* led to the pitting of 350,000 French soldiers against some 15,000 active Arab rebels. But as warfare descended into barbarism on both sides, the French became increasingly sick of the sacrifices, uneasy about the tactics, and insecure at home. In the autumn of 1957, there was no government for five weeks because none could secure a majority. When the government fell again in April 1958, it took a month to patch another one together. As Pierre Pflimlin prepared to present his cabinet to the Assembly on May 13, the extremist Europeans in Algeria, fearful that he would propose negotiations with the rebels, broke into a frenzy. A self-elected revolutionary committee took office in Algiers under the benevolent eye of the army. Ten days later the extremists had seized control of Corsica. France itself appeared imperiled.

In fact, a stalemate had set in. Whatever the leaders of the army might have desired, it was questionable if the young conscripts would have marched on Paris. But the politicians in Paris were paralyzed. Only de Gaulle was clear about what should be done.

On May 15, de Gaulle publicly announced his readiness, if he was called upon, to assume power. After a tense period of waiting, President René Coty acted. Pflimlin resigned and de Gaulle was appointed premier. On June 1, the Assembly accepted him by a majority of about a hundred, mainly from the right but including Radicals and Socialists. The Communists voted solidly against him. De Gaulle's condition for accepting office was the power to rule by decree for six months, at the end of which time he promised to propose a new constitution for the country's vote.

Those who supported de Gaulle in this time of crisis were motivated by various expectations. The Gaullists saw the chance at last for strong executive leadership; many who disliked de Gaulle's principles and personal authority saw them as the only way out of France's current impasse but looked on them as a temporary evil; those leading the revolt, especially the "colonels," could not believe that a general

did not share their view of how to maintain the glory of France. Only the Gaullists were to be satisfied.

De Gaulle used the six-month period of decree power to push through a host of reforms. A new constitution was formulated, under the direction of Michel Debré. This constitution changed the balance of French political life. It vested legislative leadership in the executive and played down the role of the Assembly. It made a post in the cabinet incompatible with membership in the Assembly. The choice of premier henceforth rested with the president. The presidency, clearly designed for de Gaulle himself, emerged as the balance wheel in the constitutional system. Although the presidency was not yet the popularly elected office de Gaulle ultimately made it, the president in the Fifth Republic was clearly intended from the start to stand out as the representative of the nation, selected, as he was, by a strikingly large and broad electoral college of local government representatives.

In September 1958, in a referendum in which the French territories in Africa and elsewhere as well as metropolitan France voted, the constitution of the Fifth Republic was accepted by an overwhelming majority of the voters—30,708,438 to 5,394,970. Metropolitan France voted 17,688,790 to 4,624,511. The constitution of the Fourth Republic, as we have seen, had been greeted by marked lack of enthusiasm; that of the Fifth Republic, for all its novelty, or perhaps because of it, was launched on a wave of overwhelming approval.

THE POLITICAL SYSTEM OF
THE FIFTH REPUBLIC

The most striking characteristics of the Fifth Republic have been the length of time that de Gaulle's dominant leadership received overwhelming support from the French electorate (from June 1958, when de Gaulle took over power, to December 1965, when he was forced to participate in a second ballot to win the first direct election for the presidency of France); the use of the referendum as an institution and source of authority; the emergence and apparent persistence of a Gaullist coalition or association that produced a dominant, even majority party, the *Union pour la Nouvelle République* (UNR), in the National Assembly for the first time in the history of republican France; the smoothness of transition to Pompidou's presidency following de Gaulle's abrupt resignation in 1969; the new political personnel that has carried on and added to the technical revolution that has been transforming France; and the widespread character of social and economic change.

It is these facts, spelled out in detail in succeeding chapters, rather than the constitution itself, that are the significant factors in the making of the new France. Yet it has been the de Gaulle constitution, as modified at his own insistence, that has provided the framework within which the forces of contemporary France have been at work. It is necessary, therefore, to look at the constitution of the Fifth Republic, particularly in the perspective of those of the Third and Fourth Republics, to understand the France of today.

THE CONSTITUTION OF THE FIFTH REPUBLIC

Partly by design, but partly also because of its dual parentage, the constitution of the Fifth Republic is a hybrid of presidential and parliamentary government. De Gaulle saw strong executive leadership as the primary objective and insisted that the president, far from being the choice of the legislative chambers, as he had been under the Fourth Republic, and with no legislative role, should be a national figure both in manner of choice and in authority. But Michel Debré, with his training in law and political science and his experience in the Fourth Republic's second chamber, possessed the perspective of a parliamentarian and the temperament of a reformer. The structure he designed, therefore, is a reformed parliamentary system in which the former excessive power of the National Assembly and the consequent instability of the cabinet are curbed by constitutional restrictions.

The power to dissolve the legislature has always been looked on as a major means of maintaining executive leadership in a parliamentary system. It was determined that there should be a major change in the Fifth Republic

in regard to the use of this power. We have seen that after the MacMahon intervention on the famous Sixteenth of May, the use of dissolution had lapsed in the Third Republic; it was so hedged with restrictions under the Fourth Republic that it was virtually useless. Thus the premier was left at the mercy of the competing interests and ambitions of the members of the lower house, who, in contrast to the relatively clear-cut divisions characteristic of British and American politics, were divided into a spectrum of political ideologies and groups extending from the far left to the far right. French governments in the Third and Fourth Republics were always coalitions, therefore, that depended on the support of several parties, and often the withdrawal of a single parliamentary group would mean the fall of the ministry. Whereas British prime ministers could commonly count on being in office for four or five years and could thus make long-range plans, a French premier was lucky if he could survive for a year. While the same person often retained a ministry through several governments, top leadership was subject to frequent changes. Sometimes, as we have seen, the country was left for weeks on end without a cabinet in office.

Under the Fifth Republic, the power of dissolution, as a reinforcement of executive leadership, was specifically written into the constitution. But rather than being at the disposal of the premier, as in effect it is in Great Britain, the right to dissolve the French legislature is vested in the president, and in practice it has been exercised at his discretion. Thus when Debré wanted the chambers dissolved at the end of the Algerian war in mid-1962, at a time when de Gaulle's prestige was particularly high, his request was refused. It was Debré himself who lost his position, being replaced as premier in April 1962 by Georges Pompidou, who had never been even a member of parliament or of a political party.

This illustration of how de Gaulle as president overrode the advice of his premier is characteristic of the way in which he systematically eroded the parliamentary features of the constitution in favor of presidential leadership. The constitution declares that the president is responsible for "the regular functioning of the governmental authorities, as well as the continuance of the state," and also for "national independence, the integrity of the territory, respect for . . . treaties." Under the Fourth Republic, the premier and cabinet were in control of foreign affairs, but from the start de Gaulle, as president, insisted on determining foreign policy. On May 15, 1962, for example, he publicly described his European policy even before informing the cabinet, five of whose members, those from the MRP, promptly resigned.

Indeed, de Gaulle maintained an important role in regard to all major policy decisions. He referred those concerning Algeria directly to the people through referendums rather than to the legislature. Despite charges of unconstitutionality, he also insisted on a referendum on the issue of direct election of the president. Beyond these specific issues, de Gaulle also molded those economic and social decisions, particularly of an unpopular character, for which the cabinet had to take public responsibility. Moreover, when the military putsch in Algiers took place in April 1961, he used his emergency powers to govern the country until the autumn, preventing the two chambers either from legislating or introducing motions of censure against the government.

The greatest change in the functioning of the political system under the Fifth Republic has been the relative powerlessness of the legislature. For this situation there were many reasons. One dominant reason was the personality and towering presence of de Gaulle, particularly in contrast to the transitory, often fumbling leadership of the Fourth Republic. The other was the awareness of the tightrope to be walked if the army was to be made to accept Algerian independence (which was not proclaimed until July 1962). Throughout his eleven years of office, de Gaulle's position was buttressed not only by the unswerving personal loyalty first of Debré, then of Pompidou, and finally of Couve de Murville, but also by the limited time—five and a half months in the year—in which the legislature can be in session and by the remarkable strength of the Gaullist alignment in the lower chamber.

One cause of the instability of the cabinet during the Third and Fourth Republics had been the divided and shifting character of the party system. On the left were three large parties: the Radicals (the loosely organized party of the anticlerical lower middle class—that is, the small shopkeepers, the less successful professional men, and the small farmers); the better organized Socialists; and the tightly controlled Communists. In the Fourth Republic, as we have seen, there was also a new socially minded Catholic party, the MRP, which, except for its Catholicism, often seemed more to the left than the Radicals. On the right the political situation was less clear, for there the groupings were looser and the organizations less highly developed. In general, the right was conservative in economic matters but was divided between those who were anticlerical and strongly republican and those who were proclerical and socially conservative.

Under the Fifth Republic, the number of parties has been no less than previously (indeed a small new party, the *Parti Socialiste Unifié* [PSU], appeared in 1958 between the Communists and the Socialists). But there was a decisive difference: until 1969 the parties aligned themselves either for or against de Gaulle's policies instead of trying to devise policies of their own around which to organize enough support to control the chambers. The Communists were always bitterly opposed to de Gaulle, but their numbers in the National Assembly were reduced by a return to voting through single-member constituencies. The Socialists supported de Gaulle's accession to office in 1958 and endorsed the Algerian settlement, but they criticized almost everything else. The Radicals, the "vital center" in the Third Republic and a balance wheel in the Fourth, were decimated in the November 1958 Assembly elections, although they retained strength in the Senate and in particular areas of France. The MRP supported de Gaulle during the Algerian war but broke with him over his European policy and his authoritarian attitudes toward parliament. The Independents (the term in France is synonymous with conservative) in the Assembly opposed the Algerian settlement, although their ministers reluctantly accepted it. Most significant, however, the amorphous UNR, despite its slight organization and program, began to bring France some semblance of a three-party system: the UNR (since 1968 renamed UDR, *Union pour la Défense de la République*), ordinarily in coalition with some other support; the rest of the non-Communist parties; and the Communists, who formed a bloc of their own.

The National Assembly has not been acquiescent in the reduction of its status and authority. Even during the Algerian war, its deputies tried to resurrect the process of interpellation that had been used with deadly effect under the Fourth Republic to destroy ministries. The deputies were only stopped in this effort by the action of the Constitutional Council, the official guardian of the functioning of the constitution. Debré had to force bills through parliament four times by staking the life of his government on the outcome. In 1961, all parties except the UNR walked out of the Assembly in protest against the curbing of their legislative powers during de Gaulle's assumption of emergency powers. In 1962, the "old parties" battled fiercely with de Gaulle, who not only overrode both the Assembly and the Senate but also ignored the advice of the Constitutional Council and the Council of State (see Chapter 6, Section 2) in his determination to take his own route to establishing the direct election of the president. Thus the opposition deputies tried, repeatedly but unsuccessfully, to recapture the role the Assembly played in the past.

Basic to the realignment of executive-legislative relations under the Fifth Republic is the fact that the president, and not the premier, controls the executive power. And the only way in which the Assembly can influence the president is through the premier and the cabinet. As Debré envisaged the government of the Fifth Republic, and indeed as it appears in the constitution, executive-legislative relations would be those of a traditional parliamentary system, except that the rulemaking functions of the Assembly were restricted and those of the premier and his cabinet specified. Under those circumstances, the president would have remained above the political battle, in the role de Gaulle once described as "a national arbiter far removed from political struggles." But circumstances—in particular, the Algerian struggle and the dangers posed by an alienated army and de Gaulle's determination to dominate policy—led the political system of the Fifth Republic to operate much more in presidential than in parliamentary terms.

It was long thought that the provisions of the constitution, the ill-concealed impatience of the deputies over their subordinate role, and the renewal of political concern throughout the country might tilt the balance between president and parliament once de Gaulle retired. Indeed, the fact that de Gaulle had to enter a second ballot in the first direct election for president, in December 1965, seemed to indicate that his prestige was weakening. Moreover, in the crisis of 1968, as we have seen, de Gaulle lacked effectiveness until the last moment when the announcement of an election swung the balance—a feat reflected in the uniquely high total of votes and seats won by the UDR in the election late that year. Nonetheless, de Gaulle failed to win his referendum on regionalism and Senate reorganization in 1969 and promptly resigned.

The smooth transition to Pompidou late that year suggests that the Fifth Republic has in fact developed a moderately stable method of decision-making with a strong president and a premier subordinate to him. That this relationship may be challenged from time to time, depending on the personalities of the incumbents, is possible, although the president's power to dismiss the premier, demonstrated so ruthlessly toward Pompidou by de Gaulle after the crisis of 1968, provides a powerful trump card in the president's hand. At the same time, no president can govern effectively without a party base in parliament, for which he must depend either on the premier or on his own prestige. Thus the Fifth Republic's unique combination of presidential and parliamentary institutions must either tilt toward the British or the American system or else enshrine a working partnership between dual centers of power.

Emergency powers: Article 16

The most controversial clause in the constitution of the Fifth Republic is Article 16, under which the president can assume emergency powers at his own discretion. The constitution provides that he shall consult the premier, the chairmen of the two chambers, and the Constitutional Council before declaring such a state of emergency. It defines the conditions that constitute a state of emergency as a threat to the institutions of the Republic, the country's independence, or the fulfillment of its international commitments. Nonetheless, the clause leaves the president full freedom to make the ultimate decision on his own judgment and thereby legalizes his use of full powers.

Behind de Gaulle's insistence on the insertion of this provision in the constitution was the break in the continuity of the French political system in 1940, with the Nazi invasion. It was not another war, however, but an ill-planned coup on the part of certain French officers in Algeria that gave rise to the declaration of an emergency in April 1961. No one in France disputed the need for and the use of these powers at that moment, but the deputies of the older political parties grew restive and bitter over being kept so long from exercising their normal legislative functions.

The referendum

While Article 16 permits the executive to by-pass parliamentary procedures in times of extreme crisis, the process of referendum throws certain crucial decisions to popular vote. The constitutions of both the Fourth and the Fifth Republics were legitimized by being accepted by majority vote in a referendum. Indeed, the first draft of the constitution of the Fourth Republic was rejected by the voters on May 5, 1946, and the second draft was accepted five months later. The constitution of the Fifth Republic was accepted by referendum on September 28, 1958.

Whether other types of decisions should be made by referendum has been a matter of controversy. The referendum was a favorite means for General de Gaulle to capitalize on his popularity and on the widespread belief, particularly in the early days of the Fifth Republic, that he was indispensable. His use of the referendum to win support for Algerian independence was widely accepted as the best way of keeping this controversial issue out of the party arena. But there was great hostility on the part of the "old parties," and tacit, if not explicit, opposition

from the Constitutional Council and the Council of State to his use of the referendum, rather than the regular amendment procedure, to institute the choice of the president by direct election.

The effectiveness of the referendum as a decision-making or ratifying device rapidly diminished thereafter. De Gaulle's proposal to hold a referendum in the crisis of 1968 had no effect either in stopping the strikes or in restoring public confidence. Only his announcement of an election had these desired effects. In 1969, de Gaulle's characteristic threat to resign if the referendum were defeated (immediately implemented after the results were known) failed to have the effect it had had on earlier occasions of securing the ratification of a policy on which he had already decided. In fact, de Gaulle's use of the referendum in each of the situations in which he was supported was plebiscitary rather than a choice between alternatives. Once the overshadowing issues of France's postwar politics—Algeria and the stability of its constitutional system—were settled, decisions could better be made through political action. Thus it seems likely that the referendum will not be used again unless some new major issue of national well-being should develop.

The Constitutional Council

The Constitutional Council of the Fifth Republic and the Constitutional Committee of the Fourth Republic were established to ensure that constitutional provisions would possess a certain superiority over ordinary laws. (There was no comparable body under the Third Republic.) To an American, who is used to judicial review by the Supreme Court, neither of these French institutions may seem to have much constitutional effect. Indeed, the Constitutional Committee convened only once during the twelve years of the Fourth Republic and then only to resolve a question of legislative procedure in its role of protecting the Council of the Republic in its relation with the far stronger National Assembly.

The Constitutional Council of the Fifth Republic, however, plays quite an important role in the constitutional life of France, particularly since parliament is restricted to defined activities by the constitution of 1958. Thus it passes on the standing orders of parliament and, on request of the government (but not of a minority in parliament), it can determine the boundaries of executive and legislative competence and whether laws (other than organic laws) or treaties are in conformity with the constitution. Moreover, it passes on the validity of elections for the president and parliament, and of a referendum, and it must be consulted by the president before he calls a referendum. What advice the council gave de Gaulle in 1962 when he formulated the referendum question on direct election of the president can never be known for sure, since the deliberations and advice of the council are bound by the rule of secrecy, but it is believed that it counseled, although unsuccessfully, against the use of this procedure. Thus ultimately, despite the many decisions and considerable number of advisory opinions the Constitutional Council provides, its constitutional role is limited. The constitution, in practice, is balanced politically rather than through legal verdicts.

The process of amendment

The 1958 constitution, like that of 1946, has a relatively simple formula for amendment. Article 89 specifies that the president, on the request of the premier or a deputy, makes the initial proposal. The proposal must then be adopted in identical terms by both chambers and ratified either by a referendum or, if the president so decides, by a three-fifths majority of the two chambers sitting together. (Under the Fourth Republic, the Assembly could dispense with the consent of the second chamber if it had a two-thirds majority among its own members.) It seems unlikely, however, that the amendment procedure will be used in the Fifth Republic. This is partly because de Gaulle bypassed this procedure when making the most decisive change in the constitutional balance of power—that is, the direct election of the president—and because the sphere of the executive is already so great that efforts to curb it by this means are unlikely to have success.

4   FRENCH POLITICAL IDEAS

Far more than in Anglo-Saxon countries, political ideas in France have remained the fighting words of political action. The Jacobins coined the phrase "enemies of the people"; the Dreyfus case precipitated long-standing differences over political and moral values. What sometimes seem hairsplitting differences of interpretation lead to bitter outbursts. At least some of these verbal divisions do little more than ruffle the surface, but others go deep into the social fabric. Basically, there remains a fundamental difference between those who support traditional representative government and those who favor the plebiscitary tradition. Each can claim to be more democratic than the other, thereby producing an endless source of controversy.

RIGHTS AND THE GENERAL WILL

One of the most influential French philosophers of the eighteenth century, Jean Jacques Rousseau (1712–78), had a passionate hatred of tyranny. Rousseau envisaged the direct participation of all citizens in the political process. He made a vital distinction, however, between responding to one's own selfish interest and seeking the well-being of the whole group. In his famous formulation of the concept of the "general will," [1] Rousseau denounced the dangers inherent in representative institutions as a mere balancing of selfish interests against each other. To be governed by the general will, in contrast, was best not only for the community but also for every individual. This view led to

---

[1] In Rousseau's *Social Contract* the "general will" is presented as an expression of the best interests of all the members of a community. Rousseau distinguished between the will of all the people in a community and the "general will." The "will of all," in his view, is the sum of all private interests. Private interest, however, can be divided into two parts: self-interest that is peculiar to each individual and self-interest that each individual shares with other members of the community. If the conflicting self-interests of individuals are subtracted then the shared or common self-interest of the community will remain. This shared interest approximates the "general will."

the notion that once the general will is identified, the individual should "be forced to be free." The problem is how to identify the general will, and in the end the doctrine inclines to establishing a supreme lawmaker, selected by a kind of plebiscitary democracy. Bonapartist plebiscites were so identified both by those who endorsed them as expressions of popular will and by those who castigated them as despotisms.

The eighteenth-century philosophers of the Enlightenment were equally antagonized by political tyranny and religious superstition. But they believed in inalienable human rights, which the government could not abrogate, the rule of reason, limited government, and human progress. They influenced the American Declaration of Independence and the Virginia Declaration of Rights. Essentially, their credo led them to a notion of representative government to which men, who were basically rational, would contribute both as responsible leaders and as intelligent followers. Montesquieu, who had so strong an influence on the framers of the American Constitution, believed the political and the social features of a society interacted with each other so that the character of government affected the nature of society. Thus, establishing limits on government powers would aid the growth of a self-reliant society. The philosophers of the Enlightenment concerned themselves with political liberty and its protection against the government, whereas Rousseau was chiefly concerned with political equality and the right of all men to participate in their government.

THE DECLARATION OF THE RIGHTS OF MAN AND OF THE CITIZEN

The French Declaration of the Rights of Man and of the Citizen (1789)—the counterpart of the American Declaration of Independence—contained elements of both philosophies. The preamble, following the doctrine of natural rights, proclaimed that "forgetfulness or scorn for the rights of man are the only causes of public misfortunes and the corruption of governments." The first two articles maintained that "men are born and remain free and equal in rights; social distinctions can only be founded upon common utility," and that "the aim of every political association is the conservation of the natural and imprescriptible rights of man; these rights are liberty, property, security, and resistance to oppression." Article 3, however, introduced a Rousseau-like element: "The principle of all sovereignty resides essentially in the Nation; no body, no individual can exercise authority which does not expressly emanate from it."

Article 6 (apart from its provision for representative government) declared: "Law is the expression of the general will; all citizens have the right to participate personally, or by their representatives, in its formation; it should be the same for all, whether it protects or punishes. All citizens, being equal in its eyes, are equally eligible for all dignities, positions, and public offices, according to their capacity, and without other distinction than that of their virtues and of their talents."

Other articles in the Declaration protected men from arbitrary arrest, imprisonment, and punishment; guaranteed freedom of thought, including religious thought; proclaimed "the free communication of ideas and opinions" to be "one of the most precious rights of man"; guaranteed to each citizen the right to "speak, write, and print freely"; and proclaimed property to be "an inviolable and sacred right." Except for the guarantee of property and of the "career open to talent" and a provision calling for popular consent to taxation, the framers of the Declaration were more concerned with political than with economic rights.

At various periods of French history many of these rights have been violated. But the "ideas of 1789"—equality, popular sovereignty, liberty, the career open to talent, and government under law—remain the heart of traditional republican doctrine in France.

THE CONSERVATIVE REACTION

The French Revolution, with its culmination in the Reign of Terror, brought shock and disillusionment to many of the French people, and it was natural for a school of thinkers to appear who defended the monarchical tradition and challenged the political assumptions on which the Revolution had been based. Never very influential so far as the mass of the French people were concerned, certain of their ideas have nevertheless continued to dominate the thinking of leaders of the upper classes and of literary and intellectual circles.

The earlier post-Revolutionary traditionalists centered their loyalty on a hereditary monarchy, an aristocratic order, and an established church. The Vicomte de Bonald (1754–1840) denied the equality of men and maintained that the happiest society is one in which each person remains in the place determined by tradition and inheritance. The Comte de Maistre (1753–1821), like Burke, maintained that inherited institutions and even inherited prejudices reflected more wisdom than human reason could attain and favored an unlimited rule by the able and energetic few.

Later traditionalists (while not necessarily rejecting these ideas) added an extreme nationalism to the conservative faith. Maurice Barrès (1862–1923), a popular novelist who was devoted to his much-invaded province of Lorraine, wrote that "every question must be solved in sole relation to the interests of France." Charles Maurras (1868–1952), whose area of Provence was imbued with the classical tradition of Greece and Rome, saw France as the representative and defender of that tradition against the "barbarians" of the Teutonic and Anglo-Saxon world. On the side of public order in the Dreyfus case, Maurras denied the concept of universal justice and upheld what he termed "integral nationalism," that is, "the exclusive pursuit of national policies, the absolute maintenance of national integrity, and the steady increase of national power," for, in his view, "a nation declines when it loses military might."

Maurras lived long enough to be one of the supporters of the antirepublican and antidemocratic government of Marshal Pétain, paradoxically preferring to have Pétain overthrow the Republic than to see republican France victorious in the war. Maurras was imprisoned for his collaborationist activities. The successors of Maurras long retained their bitterness toward General de Gaulle for his opposition to Marshal Pétain, whom they regarded as the symbol of religious orthodoxy, political order, and authority.

SOCIALISM AND COMMUNISM

Yet another influential strain among French political ideas is that of socialism. The early French socialists, like Comte Claude Henri de Saint-Simon (1760–1825), Charles Fourier (1772–1837), Louis Blanc (1811–82), Louis Auguste Blanqui (1805–81), and Pierre-Joseph Proudhon (1809–65), were true children of the Enlightenment, believing in man's capacity for reason and progress and that social evils result from the institutions and not from any wickedness of man. With the exception of Blanqui, they envisaged a peaceful, not violent reformation of society.

There continued to be a strong humanitarian and reformist current in French socialist thinking, even after Marxism had come to be the predominant type of socialism in France toward the end of the nineteenth century. Jean Jaurès (1859–1914), who more than anyone else personified French socialism, was ready to acknowledge in orthodox Marxist fashion that political developments were dependent on economic ones, but he rejected the inevitability of class warfare. On the contrary, he believed that capitalists and workers shared certain interests in common that could be made the basis of a peaceful evolution toward the socialist society.

Jaurès was assassinated at the outbreak of World War I in 1914; in the later years of that great struggle the socialist movement was seriously divided. An increasingly large minority became disillusioned and turned either to pacifism or, more significantly, to the belief, propagated by Lenin, that the international war must be turned into a civil war, a class struggle between the bourgeoisie and the proletariat. In 1920, the left wing of the Socialists adopted the name of "Communists" and joined the Moscow-led Third International.

Most of the leaders of the Socialist party, however, remained loyal to the old name and the old program. Their following included not only workers but also a large part of the population of the small towns and countryside, as well as many members of the white-collar middle class, including a high proportion of government employees. As a result, there were several different "chapels," or what the French often call *tendances*, within the Socialist party: one devoted to radical social change and the interests of the working class, and commonly called the "doctrinaires"; one that was strongly pacifistic; and one that represented the progressive middle classes who desired moderate social reform within the framework of constitutional democracy.

Christian socialism

Throughout the nineteenth century there had been some more or less isolated individuals in France who preached a doctrine of Christian socialism, believing that democracy and social reform should be achieved through the application of Christian principles. Early in the twentieth century the movement known as the *Sillon*, led by Marc Sangnier, a young Catholic who believed devoutly in the Church's social mission, attempted "to place the social forces of Catholicism at the service of democracy." The group was condemned and silenced by the Vatican in 1910 for its claim to independence from the authority of the Church. But in the interwar period, a small party known as the Popular Democrats represented a continuation of the doctrine of a democratic and social Catholicism. Its leaders were prominent in the Resistance, and under the new name of the *Mouvement Républicain Populaire* (MRP), the group emerged as one of the strongest, and for a time most influential, parties of postwar France.

FRENCH POLITICAL IDEAS
IN THE INTERWAR PERIOD

Hitler came to power in 1933 in Germany at the very time when a disastrous economic depression had aroused a demand for sweeping social reform in France. A few rightists maintained the position of traditional French nationalism: Germany, whether monarchist, democratic, or fascist, must be kept powerless. A somewhat greater number, however, felt that France had been too corrupted by Marxism, anticlericalism, and lack of discipline to be able to fight successfully against the fascist powers.

Disunity on the left was just as serious as that on the right. The majority of Radical Socialists and Socialists reluctantly came to the conclusion that it was necessary to fight German aggression in order to save French democracy. But many Radicals were leaders in the effort to appease Hitler. And while at least half the Socialists resolutely opposed appeasement, most of their deputies voted for Marshal Pétain, although there were forty among them who refused to swing with the majority. The leaders of the Catholic progressives, the Popular Democrats, stood firmly against appeasement. But the Communists, after being most vocal in the demand for resistance to Hitler, reversed their position in August 1939 when they received word of the Hitler-Stalin pact and actively opposed French participation in the war. The state of bewilderment and the lack of conviction of the ordinary Frenchman in 1939 and 1940 undoubtedly were important elements in the German triumph.

THE RESISTANCE

In its first months the Resistance movement lacked any clear political philosophy. Its leader, General de Gaulle, a devout Catholic, seemed to some to symbolize the militarism, nationalism, and clericalism that, at least to an earlier generation, marked an enemy of the Republic. However, as the Vichy government revealed its antirepublican and antitrade union character, and as leading representatives of the Church and of big business collaborated with it, the Resistance movement became increasingly leftist in composition. Those Catholics who participated in the Resistance generally represented the Christian socialist element in the Church. And in 1941, particularly after the invasion of the Soviet Union, the Communists took a conspicuous part in Resistance activities. The program of the National Council of Resistance, which after 1943 combined all the major parties and organizations of the Resistance, called for radical social and economic reform. When a new constitution for the Fourth Republic was drawn up and ratified, its preamble, after reaffirming "the rights and freedoms of man and of the citizen consecrated by the Declaration of Rights of 1789," set forth a long list of social and economic guarantees.

POLITICAL TRENDS OF
THE POSTWAR PERIOD

Although the constitution represented a victory for the socialist parties—Christian, reformist, and Communist—the political representatives of these ideologies failed to maintain the tenuous alliance forged during the Resistance and while temporarily in power in the postwar coalition of the Socialists, Communists, and MRP. When this association broke asunder in 1947, traditionalism and conservatism began to regain ground. Badly discredited at first by their association with the Vichy regime, the conservatives steadily won new strength, partly as a reaction against Communist-induced strikes, partly by exploiting General de Gaulle to his disgust, and partly as a result of the natural swing of the political pendulum.

In the Fourth Republic, France was plagued both by colonial and by Communist problems. In many ways ideology was subordinated to the day-to-day efforts to deal with these persistent threats to stability. No other nation in Europe, it may be noted, was faced with both problems at once. Great Britain had the colonial problem, Italy had the Communist problem, but neither had to battle simultaneously on two fronts. The Fourth Republic was able to cope with the Communist problem but not with the colonial one. In Indochina and in Algeria, the by-products of colonialism racked the country, split parties, and humiliated the army. In black Africa, events were less tumultuous, but there was no lack of bitterness over the manipulations through which colonial officials kept their power.

The Fifth Republic was also haunted by the specter of colonialism. The long, drawn-out struggle for control that ended in defeat in Indochina was succeeded by a no less bitter and costly struggle from 1954 to 1962 to maintain control in Algeria, a struggle made much more bitter by the presence there of over a million *colons*. Their intransigence and threat brought de Gaulle to power. His first years in office were overshadowed by this disastrous situation from which France only emerged with difficulty with acceptance of Algerian inde-

pendence in 1962. In the meantime, decolonization in black Africa had proceeded more smoothly, although the much heralded French Community proved largely stillborn (see Chapter 8, Section 1). But France continued in the sixties to act as paymaster and also as protector of shaky regimes in its former African colonies. Late in 1971, French soldiers were still aiding the regime in Chad to crush a long-standing rebellion by northern Muslim tribesmen—despite vigorous criticism in France of this continued involvement.

In domestic affairs, de Gaulle's return to power in 1958 was heralded by Gaullists as foreshadowing a "new France," devoid of the political squabbling that had marked, and sometimes disgraced, the Fourth Republic. De Gaulle himself, once free of the Algerian dilemma, preached a new self-assured nationalism that would restore France to its "rightful place" in the concert of nations: that of a leader. To achieve that place France would organize a "Third World" in foreign affairs between the power groupings of the United States and the Soviet Union; at home it would evolve a society governed in an ultramodern fashion, and united by faith in its "exalted destiny."

Among the major strands of thought that are found in "Gaullism"—its authoritarianism, its monarchical tendency, and its cult of personality—an acute analyst, Henry Ehrmann, author of *Politics in France*, believes that Bonapartism is the strongest. De Gaulle's own preference for plebiscitary democracy through the use of referendums, instead of procedures involving elected representatives in the legislative body, and his fusion of this "direct democracy" with nationalism possess similarities to practices under the two Napoleons. Yet de Gaulle was clearly never a dictator. Moreover, his identification of France with himself led him to seek policies of unity rather than deliberately to favor the right or the left. His legacy to Pompidou was a political, economic, and social structure that still needed radical reform to achieve his high ideals for a France once more in the front rank of international society. But de Gaulle maintained at least an overall unity in France as it went through the traumatic experience of disengagement from Algeria; he sponsored social reform; and he demonstrated that even the most authoritarian of France's modern leaders was responsive to evidence that he had lost the massive personal support throughout France that to him had been the essential justification of his rule.

Pompidou does not possess the aura of de Gaulle. His pragmatism is basically conservative, but a modernized conservatism that appreciates the need for economic modernization and social change at the same time that he insists on "law and order," even at the price of repression. He is also apparently less concerned with the glory of France than with effective action in a more limited sphere than de Gaulle envisaged. His forte is not in being heroic but efficient.

In the face of this modernized conservatism, the forces of the left, divided over colonial situations and their own relations, have attempted to find bonds of unity. But, in practice, even the Communists have been hard put to maintain their adherents in the face of differences between pro- and anti-Stalinists, between those who supported and those who opposed the Soviet invasion of Czechoslovakia, and between those espousing the Russian brand of Communism and those more attracted by Trotskyism or Maoism. The Socialists have found difficulty in retaining overall unity between their different *tendances* (which split badly over Algeria) and even more in deciding whether their ideological commitment to socialism should lead them to work with the Communists in a common front against Gaullism, or whether such an association might not lead to their absorption, or at least domination by the more highly organized Communists. The Christian socialists, as represented by the MRP, steadily disintegrated during the Fifth Republic and were ultimately merged in the center.

Today, then, as in the past, there is a conflict of ideas in France that is represented by organized political movements or parties. To understand their appeal and comprehend their strength, it is necessary to look at these organizations in more detail.

3

French
parties
and
elections

1   THE CHARACTER OF THE FRENCH PARTY SYSTEM

The French party system has long challenged the generalizations about political parties that Englishmen and Americans are tempted to make. To them it seems natural that there should be two large parties, that one should rule and the other oppose, and that every once in a while they should exchange positions. The rise of a third party has usually been regarded as a disrupting influence that upsets the entire system. Particularly in Great Britain, government seems possible and comprehensible only when one party is able to take the responsibility for political leadership and when there is a united and forceful opposition prepared to take power whenever that party is defeated.

In France, the alignment of parties has traditionally been far more complex. It was not until the Fifth Republic that France possessed a majority party, the UNR-UDR. This party combines a spectrum of varied interests, attitudes, and social groups, making it more comparable to one of the major American political parties than to the political organizations with which France has been familiar in the past. These latter parties had, and those in opposition to the Gaullists still possess, an ideological, historical, or social base that has made it almost impossible for them to coalesce into an effective working partnership. The two crucial strands in the history of political organizations in the Fifth Republic are the evolution of the

Gaullist majority on the right, and the political maneuvering concerned with largely abortive efforts to establish a cohesive alignment in the center, or center-left, or left that could effectively challenge this majority.

Much of the background to this party history has already been sketched in the section on the balance sheet of the Fourth Republic in Chapter 2. The wavering progression of the RPF from de Gaulle's ideal of a grouping above party to its intimate involvement in party politics, its split in 1952, de Gaulle's renunciation of any association with the RPF the following year, and, finally, its disappearance along with most of those who had been swept into the Assembly under its banner in 1951, make a strange prelude to the dominant position the UNR-UDR ultimately achieved in the Fifth Republic. The division in the left, which split the Communists and Socialists in 1947 after a year and a quarter of coalition government with the MRP, did not disappear during the Fourth Republic nor, despite substantial efforts from both sides, was it ever fully overcome during the Fifth Republic. The center was no more successful in its efforts to recapture the key position it held tenuously but persistently throughout much of the Fourth Republic. A detailed account of the successes and failures of these political parties and their shifting alignments will be presented in the later sections of this chapter. First, however, it is essential to indicate certain significant changes that have been taking place in relation to political organizations since 1958 and to describe the character of the membership and organization of the political parties that have appealed to the electorate since the Fifth Republic came into being.

2   THE PARTY SPECTRUM

The social and economic changes in France since World War II have inevitably affected French political allegiances and forms. The growth of urbanization and some lessening in regional variations have affected traditional patterns of regional voting. The religious issue, which long injected sharp divisions into the party system, has become somewhat muted. Institutionalized political extremism appears to be diminishing both on the right (the Poujadists, for example, soon disappeared) and on the left (witness the Communist party's efforts to promote order rather than to capitalize on the outbreaks of 1968, although the Maoists are prone to violence). The popular election of the president, which forces a clear-cut alternative between two candidates, has tended to promote alliances that, however impermanent, may indicate a long-range trend toward fewer parties.

It is important to be aware, however, that no French party, including the Communists and the UNR-UDR, has a mass membership like that of the British Labor party. All are what is known as *cadres parties*, with a smaller number of registered members and a much smaller number of effective molders of policy than their electoral totals would seem to indicate. Indeed, most Frenchmen are probably more tenuously connected to the political parties for which they vote than are American voters and certainly much more so than are British voters. Hence significant swings in support of particular parties or leaders can occur fairly easily, although some stability in French voting patterns has been noticeable. Apart from the consistency of Communist voting and the steady advance of the UNR-UDR in electoral support, following and ultimately outstripping that given to de Gaulle himself in referendums through 1962 and in the presidential election of 1965, most parties have not shown long-term electoral consistency. A major

question facing all political alignments, however, is posed by the flood of young voters who will be eligible to influence political objectives and organizations when the next Assembly elections are held in 1973.

THE UNR-UDR

There is a strange paradox in the current party system of France. General Charles de Gaulle, the man behind whom developed the only majority party in France's history, one that has drawn electoral support from all elements in the population, never believed in political parties nor, perhaps, even in the representative system within which they play an essential role. As we have seen, the UNR's predecessor, the RPF, had a very checkered history under the Fourth Republic. But the UNR, thrown together so hastily after de Gaulle's return to political power in 1958, has proved a new phenomenon in French political life: a party, united at first only in its allegiance to an outstanding personality, that has steadily grown in its vote-getting capacity throughout the Fifth Republic. Unlike the Radicals, which occupied a somewhat comparable position of dominance within the Third Republic at the turn of the century, the UNR-UDR is a strictly disciplined organization, despite the disparate groups that it holds together.

The UNR-UDR is commonly looked on as a party of the right, but it has steadily increased the variety of its national constituency, including somewhat wavering but substantial working-class support. In 1958, the UNR took 1.5 million votes away from the Communist party; in 1968, the UDR regained much of what the Communists had won back in the meantime. Paradoxically, although the Gaullists and the Communist party appear the great antagonists of the Fifth Republic, there have been many similarities in their policies, particularly under de Gaulle. De Gaulle's attacks on American involvement in Vietnam; his cooperation with Eastern Europe; the withdrawal from NATO; his refusal to admit Great Britain to the Common Market; the condemnation of Israel in 1967 and subsequent refusal of arms are all in line with the Communist party's own objectives. Moreover, the Communist party's main practical objective domestically is to improve wages and working conditions; many workers, especially in the industrial north, felt that de Gaulle, and now feel that Pompidou, could accomplish more in this regard than can Communist-approved tactics. While Pompidou is more of a conservative than was de Gaulle, he is a modernizing conservative who believes in improving workers' conditions within a dynamic economy.

Fear arising from the 1968 disorders, and probably antagonism toward Paris, the seat of the student uprisings, helped to extend UDR support among peasants, even from backward areas of the country, as well as among small shopkeepers and those in traditionally "left" areas of the south. In the election of that year, the UDR received the votes of between 40 and 55 percent of farmers, industrial and commercial interests, professional men, higher and middle management, employees, women, older people, and, more surprising, unemployed. Geographically, the support was proportionally highest in rural communes, then in towns with populations under twenty thousand, and in those over one hundred thousand; the support was lowest—30 percent—in Paris. Thus the UDR displayed more uniform political support throughout the country than any other party.

The party activists, including party officials, are much more solidly middle class than is the UDR's electoral support. They are mainly businessmen, technicians, and professional personnel, including a few *notables*. Rather more varied backgrounds are found among the top figures in the party, almost all of whom at one time or another have had a special personal link with de Gaulle himself. A rigidly orthodox group that calls itself the *Présence et Action du Gaullisme* was formed immediately after Pompidou's election as president for the purpose of upholding the strict essence of what they

regard as de Gaulle's heritage. Proponents of more rapid social change, the *Union Démocratique du Travail* (UDT), have been critical of Pompidou for exactly opposite reasons. UDR party members, who number between eighty and ninety thousand, are clearly divided between right and left wings, each with important figures like Debré on the right and Faure on the left.

Nonetheless, party discipline has been maintained throughout the lifetime of the UNR. Some of its strongest adherents broke with de Gaulle over his Algerian policies, but they were ejected from the party and failed to secure election thereafter, providing a salutary warning to others. Apart from education policies, over which UNR-UDR deputies have often differed from the government, they support government measures solidly down the line.

The party itself inherited the tightly knit organization developed for the RPF that combined workshop organizations (not unlike Communist cells) and units in local divisions down to the *cantons*. On this base was erected a regional and national structure that included a national congress and council but was directed in practice by an executive committee. Members of this executive were hand-picked and controlled by de Gaulle in his period of leadership, although toward the end they were increasingly drawn from parliament.

The UDR uses the electoral district as its basic unit; these are grouped into department units; and the national organization includes a congress, council, central committee, political committee, and a secretariat. In practice, the UNR has no real power at the regional level. Moreover, while in theory the congress is the supreme policymaker with the council acting during its sessions, the political committee is the dominant organ. The central committee deals with discipline and approves the selection of candidates and such political alliances as are entered into. Whereas the secretariat handles information, propaganda, and electoral advice to candidates quite efficiently, it is the political committee that makes important party policy decisions and determines party strategy in conjunction with the president. The political committee is now composed largely of the chairmen of party groups in the National Assembly and UDR cabinet members.

The major questions related to the UDR's future are whether it will retain its unity during the present Assembly and how well it will fare in the elections of 1973. Despite prophesies that the party would not hold together once de Gaulle left office, the 700 national and local officials forming the National Council, meeting in November 1969, closed ranks behind Pompidou. Nonetheless, there have been rumblings of discontent over the choice of ministers for the cabinet (see Chapter 5) and over what is charged to be inadequate consultation with the parliamentary party before legislation is introduced into the Assembly. Such grievances are likely to develop when so substantial a parliamentary majority exists, but there seems little likelihood of their resulting in splits in the party as a whole or among its parliamentary representatives. The more serious questions are whether these strains will lessen local enthusiasm for the UDR and what effect this might have during the next election.

THE INDEPENDENT REPUBLICANS

With minimal party organization and spotty local support, the *Républicains Indépendents* (RI) form more truly a party of the right than does the UNR-UDR with its broad national constituency. Since the election of 1962, the RI have been chiefly important because of their close association with the larger Gaullist party and because of their leader, Giscard d'Estaing, who served under de Gaulle (except from 1967 to 1968) and again under Pompidou as Minister of Finance and Economic Affairs. RI votes provided the UNR with its majority in the Assembly after the 1962 and 1967 elections and, indeed, were essential after 1967 to keep government control firmly in Gaullist hands. In return for RI support, UNR-UDR strategists insisted in 1967 and 1968 that only one candidate be chosen from the two parties to stand in the first ballot, thereby assuring a considerable RI representation in the Assembly.

The precursors of the RI had a fragmented and checkered history. They consisted of several rather ill-defined parties in the Fourth Republic, which were known by several different and changing names in the first, second, and third Assemblies. Under one designation or another,

these groups held between seventy-five and one hundred seats.

Broadly speaking, these rightist groups all stood for the traditional institutions of the family and the church, urged support for church schools, and opposed nationalization and economic *dirigisme* (planning). Although they inclined toward the right-wing Radicals on economic policy, they were divided from them on the clerical issue. Despite, or perhaps because of, their lack of a precise program, they attracted considerable support. They provided (in March 1952) one of the Fourth Republic's most popular premiers, Antoine Pinay, subsequently the formulator of the first programs of economic liberalism under de Gaulle. In the 1956 Assembly, however, their opposition to the economic programs of the left and center, and their hostility to concessions on Algeria, caused the fall of ministry after ministry and greatly contributed to the collapse of the Fourth Republic.

Nonetheless, in 1958 the Independents emerged as the second largest party of the Assembly. For a brief span, it appeared that they might realize their ambition of becoming the great conservative party of France. The Independents drew strength from small or large, rather than middle-sized communities. They appealed to persons of moderate but comfortable means, and they had the support of local *notables*. But they were also associated with the discredited Fourth Republic and with the values of a rurally oriented society that was rapidly becoming obsolete.

Moreover, the Independents soon split over de Gaulle's leadership and policies. By 1962 they had disintegrated into three distinct groups: an anti-Gaullist but constitutional group that campaigned against de Gaulle's decision to have the president selected by direct election, suffered disastrously in the process, and ultimately merged with the center; an anti-Gaullist extremist movement that bore some faint resemblance to the Poujadists, but soon vanished; and the pro-Gaullist Independents, who linked themselves with the UNR to form a parliamentary majority after the 1962 elections.

Giscard d'Estaing insists that his pro-Gaullist group, the RI, maintain a separate existence. He opposed de Gaulle's decision to hold a referendum in 1969 and campaigned against it. After de Gaulle's resignation, however, d'Estaing swung his support to Pompidou, although he, himself, had cherished ambitions for the presidency. D'Estaing's marked talents (he is one of the most brilliant graduates of the *École Nationale d'Administration* and has long combined a career in the Inspectorate of Finance with elected office) and forward-looking economic views (which accord so little with traditional conservative policies) make him useful to Pompidou as Minister of Finance, but his wavering political allegiances in the past have come under attack by more consistent Gaullists in the cabinet. His own political future and that of his Independent Republicans seem increasingly inseparable from what happens to the UDR, for only if the latter organization disintegrates could his basically rightist conservative party play an independent role in French politics.

THE CENTER

Center parties in France have oscillated between placing ministers in key positions in governing coalitions and growing impotence as their political support is drained off to others. Of no group has this been more true than the *Mouvement Républicain Populaire* (MRP), the bright hope of the social-minded Catholic left at the end of World War II. After steadily diminishing returns, the MRP revived briefly as part of the Democratic Center under Jean Lecanuet, whose spectacular performance in the 1965 presidential race had brought him temporary national prominence, although not a place in the runoff. The remnants of the old MRP appear to be dwindling in their new form, the *Progrès et Démocratie Moderne* (PDM), which secured only just over 10 percent of the votes and twenty-nine seats in the 1968 election.

While the MRP shared a checkered history with the Independents, it suffered a much steadier decline in popular support after its spectacular debut in 1946 when it polled more than one-quarter of the votes and became part of the governing coalition together with the Socialist and Communist parties. Its appearance constituted a double phenomenon: the emergence of a large and well-organized party apparently capable of balancing the great parties that traditionally constituted the French left; and the creation of a party able to combine friendliness to the Catholic Church with a democratic and semisocialist policy. But by the time of the 1951 election, much of MRP support had been drawn off to the RPF and conservative parties and never returned. It thus became all too apparent that its initial popular response had resulted from fear of communism or admiration of de Gaulle, a Catholic, and not from enthusiasm for social reform. Even with reduced numbers the party was plagued by the fact that its electorate was so much more conservative than its leaders, who continued to play significant roles in the Fourth Republic, furnishing it with five prime ministers and a number of bright and vigorous young ministers.

Initially supportive of de Gaulle in 1958, the five MRP ministers in the cabinet resigned in protest at his sharp words in 1962 against European integration. But this opposition by the leadership to de Gaulle's European policy further alienated the party's followers. In May 1963, the annual congress voted in support of merging its identity in a new opposition party; in 1965 this happened in effect; and in 1967, the party voted to "efface itself."

Lecanuet himself had also misjudged public opinion. He took the 3.7 million votes he received in 1965 as an indication of enthusiasm for a non-Gaullist center. But the returns in 1967 and 1968 contained only minimal evidence of such sentiment. Lecanuet now cherishes hopes of a center-oriented "third core" in conjunction with the Radical party, but its electoral future is not promising.

THE RADICAL SOCIALIST PARTY

Whereas the MRP and Democratic Center have passed off the political stage, another, far older center-left party, the Radical Socialists, may be reentering from the wings. Meeting in extraordinary congress in February 1970, the Radicals, spurred by their dynamic new secretary general, Jean-Jacques Servan-Schreiber, voted a program embodying far-reaching changes designed to offer an alternative both to Gaullism and to the Communists. Aiming to make the French economy egalitarian, democratic, and progressive, their manifesto proposes an end to state subsidies to private industrial and agricultural enterprises so as to liberate the state from domination by economic interests; educational opportunities for low-income families; ultimate abolition of competitive examinations for entry to major schools; an end to taxes on inheritances under $60,000 but steeply rising rates thereafter; and redistribution of political power so it is diffused all the way from municipalities to a federated United States of Europe. The most attractive feature of the program is probably its stress on the region and its opposition to the dominance of Paris.

This striking program springs not from traditional Radical Socialism, which has rarely been either radical or socialist, but from Servan-Schreiber, owner and editor of the popular *L'Express* and author of the best seller *The American Challenge*. He temporarily became the most spectacular figure in French politics after he assumed leadership of the virtually moribund Radical party and began to shape it into his model of an effective center party that would be capable, ultimately, of being once again a major force in French political life. In order to do so, Servan-Schreiber turned not to the party's headquarters but to potential supporters, to whom he appealed through the pages of his newspaper. The response was instructive. Farmers and workers greeted the appeal with indifference, industrial and commercial employees showed only a little more interest, but engineers, architects, administrators, company directors, and other executives responded with unbounded enthusiasm. Yet the traditional base of Radical power has been the middle class of small towns and villages that possesses an ingrained fear of the growing industrial and urbanized society of France. So Servan-Schreiber's reconstructed Radical Socialists must stress the appeal of decentralization as well as modernization.

A retrospective look at the history of the Radical party up to 1969 will explain the general surprise when Servan-Schreiber assumed the position of secretary general. In the Third Republic, the Radicals had already manifested both its faults and its virtues. Powered by anticlericalism and a belief in the sanctity of private property, infinitely adjustable to circumstance and possible alliances, the Radicals

had been almost perpetually in the government and the promoters of some of France's most progressive legislation: abolition of government censorship, separation of church and state, compulsory primary education. At first discredited by their identification with the inefficiency, corruption, and collapse of the Third Republic, the Radicals had reestablished their local electoral machines by 1950, steadily increased their representation in the Assembly, and became part of the center governing coalitions. One of their top figures, Henri Queuille, headed a ministry that lasted longer than a year.

Both ideological and structural issues split the Radicals during the Fourth Republic. Should they cooperate with de Gaulle or work with the non-Communist parties on their left? Could Pierre Mendès-France reform their party structure and turn the Radicals into a disciplined national party? In his whirlwind attack on France's major problems during his premiership in 1954–55, Mendès-France ended the disastrous involvement in Indochina and strengthened the country's economic situation. Toppled from office by the withdrawal of the support of the right-wing Radicals, his group subsequently displaced the conservative party leaders and secured a seal of approval for a leftist emphasis in economic policy that recalled the early roots of Radicalism and heralded the possibility of an alliance with the Socialists. After the 1956 election, Mendès-France led the Radicals into a coalition with the Socialists (thereby reestablishing an anticlerical left—the Republican Front—for the only time in the history of the Fourth Republic). But the choice of Socialist Guy Mollet as premier weakened Mendès-France's hold on his own party, and in 1957 he resigned as leader of the Radicals. He had failed to break the local machines or to institute discipline among the party's parliamentary members. Moreover, the old members had been alienated, and the new ones he had attracted failed to remain constant. Thus the party suffered a striking defeat in 1958, despite the return to the *arrondissement* electoral system that had once been the basis of their strength.

When François Mitterrand (whose party, the *Union Démocratique et Socialiste de la Résistance* [UDSR], along with the Radicals, was loosely associated with the *Rassemblement Démocratique*) unexpectedly emerged as de Gaulle's competitor in the second ballot for the presidency in December 1965, the Radicals were provided with an apparent opportunity to plan again a coordinating role. They entered into an alliance with the Socialists to form the *Fédération de la Gauche Démocrate et Socialiste* (FGDS). The Federation then reached still more to the left to make an electoral agreement with the Communist party under which all would mass their support on the second ballot behind the strongest candidate on the left. Fairly effective in the 1967 election, this agreement resulted in a very considerable increase in parliamentary seats for the FGDS. But in 1968, many voters, apparently antagonized by the association with the Communists, withdrew their support on the second ballot, and the Federation suffered a disastrous drop in seats from 118 to 57.

Servan-Schreiber's role in political life as the dominant figure in an independent Radical Socialist party raises more questions than it answers. His spectacular defeat of a Gaullist at Nancy, Lorraine, in mid-1970 indicated the popularity of his attack on overcentralization from Paris. His subsequent flamboyant and unsuccessful challenge to Chaban-Delmas in the latter's home constituency of Bordeaux proved a tactical mistake. In October 1971, however, Servan-Schreiber displaced Maurice Faure as president of his party and immediately began to search for electoral alliances for the parliamentary elections of 1973. He still hopes for a reinvigorated France under Radical-Socialist leadership, but the chances are slim.

THE SOCIALIST PARTY

Of all the parties lying between the Gaullists and the Communists, the Socialists occupy the most difficult position. They, too, claim to be Marxist, yet compared to the better organized and more militant Communists, they appear ineffective and lacking in consistent application of the principles they voice. In one respect, the Socialist dilemma is the same one faced by all opponents of Gaullism: What relation should they have with the Communists, the only other party capable of maintaining a major share of electoral support? But the Socialists face this dilemma in a particularly acute way, because their ideological heritage impels them toward a Communist alliance while a realistic appraisal makes them aware that such an alliance would expose them either to Communist domination or absorption.

In the multiparty system of the Fourth Republic, the Socialist party was able to play a key role in the National Assembly, despite its declining electoral support and dwindling membership. In the Fifth Republic they failed to do so, despite a succession of attempts. They tried to capture some Gaullist aura in 1958, then to flirt with rightists prior to the 1962 election, and subsequently entered into an informal and later into a formal second-ballot agreement with the Communists in 1967 and 1968, to combine behind the strongest candidate of the left. Their merger with the FGDS after Mitterrand's challenge to de Gaulle in 1965 brought equally unsatisfactory results. It was all too apparent that neither the leadership, nor the doctrine, nor the organization of the party had essentially changed, and that there was a diminishing response to all three. When the party agreed in November 1968 to dissolve and build a new socialist party, there was little agreement on what form it should take.

The most controversial issue has been that of alignment. Gaston Defferre, mayor of Marseilles and unsuccessful contender in the 1969 presidential contest, favored a broad federation of all opposition parties except the Communists. He argued that the long-range, practical objectives of such an alignment were more important than an ideological commitment to socialism, and therefore that links should be forged with the center. Guy Mollet blocked any move toward such a federation during his twenty-two years of unchallenged dominance as secretary general. The reconstituted Socialist party received a blow in 1970 when its new leader, Alain Savary, who sought to be the candidate of a united opposition against Chaban-Delmas in Bordeaux, was pushed aside by Servan-Schreiber's personal candidacy. In June 1971, Savary's party merged with François Mitterrand's Convention of Independent Republicans taking the name Socialist and electing Mitterrand as first secretary. The new party will issue its program in 1972. In the meantime, Mitterrand has successfully attracted worker support with his criticisms of government wage and price policies. At the same time, although Mitterrand believes that an alliance with the Communists is the only hope of defeating the Gaullists electorally, he is critical of their attitudes to concrete French problems as well as to the more sensitive issue of political trials in Czechoslovakia.

While perhaps one-sixth of the working class still votes Socialist, the basic membership of the party has long been composed of locally elected politicians. Indeed, by 1965 it appeared that more than half its approximately 70,000 paid-up members were mayors—of whom there were 33 in towns of 30,000 or more inhabitants and 8 in cities of over 100,000—and municipal councilors (claimed by the party to number 40,029). Although always organized as a mass party, based theoretically on a section in every commune (in practice only about 8,000 sections in the 37,000 communes) that are grouped into departmental federations, more than half the vote in the 1967 party meeting came from the two federations of the Nord and Pas-de-Calais (Mollet's federation).

In 1958, one small group of Socialists had left the party over its support of de Gaulle and, subsequently joined by critics of Mollet, they formed the *Parti Socialiste Unifié* (PSU). The only national party to back the students wholeheartedly in the crisis of 1968, the PSU fought the ensuing election, with Pierre Mendès-France as its leader. By running more candidates than before, the party polled a higher total of votes; but none of its candidates were elected, and Mendès-France resigned. Later in the year, however, its leader, Michel Rocard, defeated Couve de Murville in a by-election, although the latter represented the Gaullists. An amalgam of old-line Marxists, revolutionary Catholics, and many who had lined the barricades in 1968, the PSU remains a thorn in the flesh of both Socialists and Communists because of its appeal to young intellectuals, especially in the universities, and to some trade unionists whom the other two parties would like to attract. The PSU's electoral future, however, appears limited.

THE COMMUNIST PARTY

The Communist party has long been unique among French parties in two significant ways: the stability of its substantial electoral support, rarely falling below one-sixth of the total number of votes cast and sometimes reaching one-quarter; and the traditional view of its militants that the party is "the model-in-miniature of the new society" whose paradigm is to be found in the Soviet Union. The first characteristic places the Communist party squarely within the representative system; the second characteristic suggests an ultimate intention to destroy that system. The question puzzling many close observers of Communist behavior under the Fifth Republic is whether its actions—its second ballot agreements with the FGDS in 1967 and 1968, its relative lack of obstructionism in the Assembly, its strenuous efforts on behalf of order during the crisis of 1968, and its assurance of Pompidou's victory in the 1969 presidential election by ordering its voters to abstain on the second ballot—indicate a profound and genuine reorientation of the party, as a noted French scholar, Professor Maurice Duverger believes, or whether these events are simply repetitions of the party's old efforts to capture control of the left and left-center without changing its own essential structure and beliefs.

Communist tactics in France have long been exceptionally opportunistic. On occasions, the party has promoted moderate policies aimed, not without success, at winning the support of small farmowners as well as the landless, and small businessmen as well as laborers. Although it tried to cripple the country with strikes from 1947 to 1950, it tried to end those called by the workers in 1968. While it has frequently—especially in 1962 and thereafter—approached the Socialists with proposals for common action, in 1969 it made impossible a victory by Poher, the candidate of the center and potentially of the left.

But certain special and distinctive characteristics of the party have remained unchanged. After a feeble statement "deploring" the Soviet invasion of Czechoslovakia, the party leadership returned to its previous unswerving support of the Soviet Union and went so far as to release to the new regime in Prague in 1969 the record of a secret conversation with Dubček that was subsequently used against him. In 1970, it expelled from the ranks of leadership several long-term prominent Communists, including Roger Garaudy, formerly hailed as the party's foremost Marxist thinker, and Charles Tillon, a seventy-three-year-old militant, who criticized the failure to take a strong stand against Soviet-led repression in Czechoslovakia. Garaudy's book, *Le Grand Tournant du Socialisme* (*Socialism's Great Turning Point*), published late in 1969, was violently condemned by the party leadership, which also turned its back on his eminently realistic assessment that the most significant group for party attention is no longer the old working class but the new cadres of young engineers, chemists, technical intellectuals, and students, whom older Communist doctrine had termed middle class, but who are often far more radical in their views and actions than are the bureaucrats of the French Communist party.

Indeed, that which calls itself the "true left" keeps its most biting strictures for the hidebound Communist party and for the trade unions as lackeys of the employers. Badly divided within and among themselves, the Trotskyites and Maoists continue to be convulsed by ideological debate. Alain Geismar's party, the *Gauche Prolétarienne* (Proletarian Left) was banned in 1970 ostensibly as the most dangerous of these splinter groups, probably in a Gaullist effort to discredit the whole extreme left, which rushed to express its solidarity with it. Paradoxically, the Communist leadership is hardly less anxious than the Gaullists to silence these radical gadflies that continue to assail their lack of an effective program and action on behalf of the working class.

In an interesting poll in December 1969 conducted by the French survey group *Sotres*, and published by *Le Figaro*, the majority doubted that the Communist party could ensure economic prosperity in France or would ensure greater social justice if it came to power. They rated the CGT higher than the Communist party, although they recognized that the decisions of this Communist-controlled trade union were motivated first by political considerations and only second by the interests of the workers. A substantial majority believed that

strikes did more harm than good because they damaged the economy. In another poll held in Paris and four provincial cities in August 1971, only a quarter felt that the party had become more independent of the Soviet Union. Half of those polled thought the Communist party would consider only its own interests if it were part of a governing coalition, and even more doubted that the party would ever relinquish political power if it once came into office.

Apparently unconcerned by such criticisms or prognostications, the thousands of bureaucrats and the inner core of leaders of the Communist party maintain its exclusiveness and keep their plans to themselves. With a membership of between three hundred thousand and three hundred fifty thousand, the party enrolls more than all the rest of French parties put together. Its discipline is much stricter than that of any other party except the UDR, whose paid membership is only between a quarter and a third as great. The Communist party commonly secures more than half the working-class vote, less probably because of ideological attachment than because of habit, prevalence of protest, and the historic appeal of the left. It is most strongly entrenched in the so-called red belt encircling Paris, where workers live in a ghettolike isolation that induces solidarity, and the party usually piles up 50 percent or more of the total vote behind Communist candidates. More surprising, the party also is well entrenched in some of the undeveloped rural areas, where its propaganda in support of small family farms has borne electoral fruit.

The organizational strength of the Communist party lies in its highly disciplined, hierarchical structure that gives supreme authority to those at the top. Its foundation is made up of cells of from three to eighty members. There are three types of cell: workplace, home, and rural. The workplace cells (comprising about one-fourth of the total number) are preferred for their effectiveness in developing class-consciousness and for being a potential basis for an underground organization. They are, however, difficult to organize in the face of employer opposition and shifting work schedules. The home cells are organized more loosely by streets or communes and thus have less revolutionary potentialities; the rural cells combine home and workplace.

The cells, each of which has its own bureau comprising a treasurer and secretary, are supposed to meet once a week or biweekly to consider national and international news in the light of party doctrine. Coordination is secured through the "section," which groups the cells in a large factory or in a particular area and "recommends" the party secretary whom a cell then "elects." The sections, in turn, are grouped into departmental federations, each of which has a secretariat of full-time, salaried officials. The federations, which have little contact with each other, send delegates to the national party congress that usually meets every three years and is technically the highest party authority. In fact, its role is educational: to present party orthodoxy to those present. Draft theses or motions may be circulated ahead of time and discussed vigorously in cell meetings, but there is no questioning or criticism at the congress itself.

Running true to form, the 1970 National Congress elected unanimously the slate of names presented to it for the central committee, enlarged in size from 95 to 107 to bring in more younger members and, as expected, omitting Garaudy's name. The central committee selects from its own members the fourteen-man Political Bureau that works on a day-to-day basis with the six-man secretariat headed by the secretary general. At this apex is the real source of power in the party. Quite unlike the British Labor party, the French Communist party Political Bureau and secretariat not only control the extraparliamentary organization but also instruct the party's parliamentary members on all important policy and organizational issues. Moreover, each Communist deputy must promise to resign if so requested by the head office, to which he also turns in his salary, receiving instead only a worker's pay.

The charges of ossification of the Communist party rest both on its failure to develop new policies and new adherents related to industrial modernization and on the long extended tenure in office of its top figures. Maurice Thorez had been secretary general for thirty-four years when he died in 1964. Although sixty-four-year-old Waldeck Rochet had been too ill for some

time for effective work, he was reelected as secretary general by the 1970 National Congress. At the same time, a new post was created, that of deputy secretary general, to which was named Georges Marchais, known for his close adherence to Soviet positions. Despite mistrust by many old-line Communists over his concealment of his nonparticipation in the Resistance during the war, Marchais is expected to be the next holder of the top position in the party. Despite an effort to present a more democratic appearance to the public by holding hundreds of open meetings throughout the country, the chances of basic change within the party in the foreseeable future appear slight.

POLITICAL CLUBS AND PRESSURE GROUPS

The relative immobility of the party system has dampened the enthusiasm for and diminished the role of the political clubs that, in the early years of the Fifth Republic, did a good deal to keep alive a spirit of questioning during the initial period of political apathy. Political clubs were found within all political groups from the extreme right to the left. Particularly attractive to the young, membership of the clubs numbered only in the hundreds. However, they sought to formulate coherent political programs and often enunciated distinctive ideological positions. The non-Communist left attracted the most active clubs. The Convention of Republic Institutions, whose overall organization backed Mitterrand's presidential candidacy in 1965, formed a part of the ill-fated FGDS, and it now has a small role in the efforts to develop a reinvigorated Socialist party.

Pressure groups, as we have already seen in Chapter 1, exist in all fields but are fragmented, often localized, and do not enjoy wide public approval. De Gaulle and Debré both criticized pressure groups severely as interfering intermediaries between people and government (a criticism de Gaulle also leveled at political parties). Candidates for local and parliamentary elections are regularly approached, however, by groups seeking endorsement of their special interests. In practice, the UNR-UDR has encouraged its candidates to be open to such activities in the interest of developing stronger local roots, and candidates of opposition parties also cultivate their local contacts. But the general lack of discipline among those parties lying between the UNR-UDR and the Communists makes all too apparent the particular spokesman for a special interest.

A most important problem is that the forums for effective decision-making in the Fifth Republic have shifted from the chambers to the executive and the administration. Thus it is no longer true, if it ever was, that the interests that French pressure groups articulate are effectively aggregated by the political parties through the process of analysis, comparison, and attempted reconciliation of divergent demands. Moreover, there have been decisive defeats of powerful lobbies like the pro-Algerian colonial lobby and business pressure groups that opposed ratification of the Schuman Plan for the European Coal and Steel Community (ECSC) in 1952 (see Chapter 8, Section 3). Thus the trend has been increasingly for pressure groups to seek their ends through influencing the executive, or working within the far-spreading system of advisory committees for special interests (see Chapter 6, Section 2), or through direct explosive action like recourse to the barricades.

CONCLUSION

It was common up to 1969 to assume that the party system of the Fifth Republic might change significantly after de Gaulle's masterful personality passed from the scene. There has as yet been no evidence that this has taken place. On the contrary, the UDR, already masterminded by Pompidou in the 1967 and 1968 elections, has retained its cohesion and discipline despite rumblings of discontent from its more liberal wing. The Communist party, the other serious contender for support and votes, has also shown no significant changes indicating that it plans to be a "party like all other parties" instead of retaining its exclusiveness. The reconstituted Socialist party under Mitterrand and the Radicals are both angling for support. But it seems likely that at least until the next election, probably in 1973, there will be no strikingly new developments. As the time approaches for the presidential election of 1976, however, whatever trends exist for simplification and consolidation of the party spectrum should be stimulated, perhaps even decisively, by the necessity of ultimately choosing between two candidates. Even here, however, change may be transitory.

3   VOTING AND ELECTIONS

The French national electorate maintains a high record of voting on national issues: between 68 and 85 percent turnout, despite the fact that during the first twelve years of the Fifth Republic it was called on to make significant decisions no less than eleven times—in four National Assembly elections (1958, 1962, 1967, 1968), two presidential elections (1965, 1969), and five referendums (1958, 1961, March 1962, October 1962, 1969). Moreover, since the voting system for both presidential elections and those for the National Assembly requires two ballots if the first runoff does not provide one candidate with more than 50 percent of the votes, most voters have gone to the polls a considerably larger number of times.

This high record of political participation is not new in France, for, apart from the post–

World War I election of 1919, voter turnout from 1885 to the Fifth Republic did not fall below 71 percent. In the last election of the Third Republic (1936), the turnout even rose to 84 percent, and in the last election in the Fourth Republic (1956) it was 83 percent. Although in general the less educated, less well-to-do, the youngest, the oldest, and nonemployed women have had lower voting averages, a more significant difference is between the better turnout in rural than in most urban constituencies and also in the north as compared to south of the Loire river. Contrary to the pattern in British and American elections, rural voters in France take a more intense interest in elections than do city dwellers, a consequence of the personalizing of local politics and an intimate knowledge of local candidates.

Rural electoral participation does a good deal (though not enough) to overcome the somewhat lower voting averages in the south of France.

The generally high voting averages in France seem contradictory to the considerable skepticism of the French electorate regarding its impact on the decision-making process. This skepticism arises in part from the fact that French electoral systems have been changed frequently in the past for partisan purposes. In the Fourth Republic, the MRP, the Socialists, and the Communists endorsed the proportional representation system used in the 1945 and 1946 elections because they judged correctly that to divide the seats in a large electoral district (commonly the *département*) according to the percentage of votes received would work to their advantage. In 1951, the system of *apparentements* (electoral alliances) was introduced to strengthen the center parties against the pressures from large parties on the right and the left—the RPF and the Communists. In 1958, to weaken the Communists and to aid the conservative parties, de Gaulle reintroduced the system characteristic of the Third Republic (except between 1919 and 1927)— the single-member district and two-ballot system.

More particularly, however, French voters naturally feel remote from the decisions ultimately reached by government. In the Third and Fourth Republics, the multiplicity of parties, the shifting pattern of government coalitions, and the not infrequent changes by deputies of their political alignments made it difficult to see any direct relation between the electoral process and legislative decisions. In the Fifth Republic, where the UNR-UDR has demonstrated the possibility of a majority party winning a French election, the National Assembly has been circumscribed in its political power. The referendums, which are supposed to provide voters with a direct means of affecting policy, were always intended as plebiscitary ratifications of de Gaulle's leadership. It is hardly surprising, therefore, that the greatest public interest and sense of vital participation has been evoked by direct voting in the presidential elections of 1965 and 1969. However controversial the device by which de Gaulle secured the radical change in the French constitutional system involved in the direct election of the president, there can be little question that it has introduced into French politics the most popular means of expressing the public will.

The most significant change in the French electorate is not that it is getting younger, for France's postwar population spurt will not affect the electorate until 1974–75. The most marked change is in the occupational make-up of the electorate. The number of shopkeepers, independent craftsmen, and farmers (all traditionally political moderates) has dropped, and by 1972 they will account for only 20 percent of the working population compared to 40 percent in 1954. The number of white-collar workers, of so-called middle executives, and of skilled workers has increased. Over all, France has become a country of wage earners totaling 76 percent in 1968 compared to 65 percent in 1954. In the light of the eruptions in the crisis of 1968, the psychological impact of youth cannot be overlooked in voting patterns, but this impact may be more negative than positive on the rapidly increasing cadres of the white-collar and skilled workers.

THE TWO-BALLOT SYSTEM

Used for the presidential elections, the two-ballot system provides a clear choice because only the two candidates who have received the largest number of votes in the first runoff are allowed to stand in the second round of voting. For elections to the National Assembly, the system established for the Fifth Republic permits more uncertainties. It is no longer permissible, as it was under the Third Republic, for new candidates to enter on the second ballot; moreover, any candidate who receives less than 10 percent (until November 1966, 5 percent) of the registered vote on the first ballot is not allowed to run in the second. Nonetheless, there can still be a spectrum of candidates offering themselves for the final vote. Much of interparty maneuvering focuses on whether each will continue to run its own candidate on the second ballot or whether it may withdraw him or her in the interests of massing votes behind the candidate of the right or the left with the greatest chance of winning.

It is the left and to a lesser degree the center that has faced the particular dilemma in the Fifth Republic of whether or not to try to mass its votes on the second ballot, as was fairly characteristic of party maneuvers of both left and right during the Third Republic. In 1958, when the Communists and left-wing non-Communist parties were sharply divided, neither yielded on the second ballot, except in a few places where the Communists did not oppose persons who had voted "no" in the referendum. The result was a disaster for the Communists who, because the left split its votes so widely, only gained ten seats with their 20 percent of the national vote. In 1962, the Socialists and Communists entered into an unwritten and not fully respected mutual withdrawal pact for the second ballot, which helped to increase the total of seats for both parties. In 1967, there was a more scrupulous adherence by the Communists and by Guy Mollet's section of the Socialists to the agreement to unite behind the candidate of either group who was best placed to win. But already this degree of alliance with the Communists had frightened voters of the center and probably had increased the already large support for the UNR and the extreme right.

The crisis of 1968 seriously impaired the left-center understanding Mitterrand seemed to achieve in his second ballot contest with de Gaulle in the presidential election of 1965. Thus the crisis divided the non-Communist opposition. Moreover, although the electoral agreement to mass support behind the leftist candidate most likely to win on the second ballot was adhered to scrupulously by the Communists in 1968, half a million voters in the electorate of the non-Communist left backed away from the Communist alliance. Partly for these reasons, but mainly because of the pervasive fear of the recent disorders, the UDR won the largest majority in French history, and for the first time it dominated the Assembly by itself.

This pattern of electoral returns demonstrates that while the electoral system probably has some effect on the results, the degree of solidarity in one of the broad groupings—left, left-center, or right—has considerably more. The French opposition is still dogged by its greatest problem: suspicion of the Communist party, which remains by far the largest vote-getter on the left. Without its participation in a sound working alliance, the left can never hope to rival the right; yet many among the non-Communist left fear that they will be swallowed up or perverted if they join in such a relationship. Such a dilemma appears insoluble. Servan-Schreiber believes the best chance of building a viable alternative to the UDR and its rightist allies is through an alliance of the center and non-Communist left. Mitterrand hopes for an alliance of the left committed to sufficiently moderate policies to gain majority support. It will be surprising if either of them is successful.

THE VOTER AND THE CANDIDATE

Regardless of changes in the electoral system, the conditions under which a person may vote and run as a candidate in France have remained approximately the same over the years. Candidates must be over twenty-three years old (voters over twenty-one), French by birth or naturalized for at least ten years (voters naturalized for five years), and free from any of the incapacities defined by law. These incapacities include such expected barriers as conviction for certain crimes. Since the days of General Boulanger, no one may run in more than one district. There is no positive residence qualification in France, a reflection of the concept that a deputy represents all French interests and not merely those of his constituency. This was one reason why Servan-Schreiber was able to run and be elected in Nancy, Lorraine, in 1969. But prefects and members of the judiciary may not run in districts where they have served until after a designated absence (between six months and three years, depending on the position).

The chief innovation of the Fifth Republic requires the nomination of a substitute to fill a member's seat in the chamber should the latter be selected as a minister or accept an incompatible position—for example, on the Constitutional Council or as a trade union official—or should he die. The position of the substitute is anomalous. He may choose whether or not to campaign, but in either case he has no financial responsibilities for the campaign. Since his name appears on the ballot along with that of the candidate, the voter is, in effect, selecting both, which may complicate his decision if he views the two candidates in different lights. Although the substitute only assumes a parliamentary seat if the member is unable to fulfill his own mandate, he is barred from opposing the member at the next election. On the other hand, when the substitute dies during the session, as did Premier Chaban-Delmas' replacement in mid-1970, the original member is permitted to run for reelection, as did Chaban-Delmas in Bordeaux, although, of course, his new substitute subsequently took his place in the Assembly.

Candidates must announce their candidacy at least twenty-one days before the first ballot and deposit one thousand francs (approximately two hundred dollars), which is only refundable if the candidate receives at least 10 percent of the registered votes in the first ballot.

Preparation for an election

As in any other democratic country, the first step toward fighting an election is to select the candidate. Major parties, like the Gaullists, Socialists, and Communists have little difficulty, but the Radicals and other loosely organized groups have had persistent trouble in choosing between the rival claims of would-be deputies.

Later the parties turn to propaganda, providing speakers, broadcasts, pamphlets, advice to candidates, and handouts to the press. The recognized legal forms of propaganda are posters to be displayed on official billboards and printing and mailing of election addresses. In an effort to equalize opportunities, the government pays these costs for any candidate who retains his deposit. But much else is done by the parties and candidates. Radio and television, particularly since the time of the 1965 presidential campaign (see Chapter 1, Section 5), play an increasingly important role, although still biased in favor of the government. Public meetings are common and fairly well attended. Individual canvassing is frowned on, and it is more common to work through influential local figures like mayors and interest groups. With rare exceptions, which include

Jean-Jacques Servan-Schreiber, French political parties and candidates do not engage in the kind of splashy electoral advertisements or gimmickry that often marks an American campaign.

Election expenses

Election expenses are not legally limited. One candidate is said to have spent nearly a quarter of a million dollars in getting himself elected through what the press called *"une campagne à l'américaine,"* but most local campaigns cost a great deal less, perhaps fifteen to thirty thousand dollars in Paris and half as much in the rest of the country. As campaigns have increasingly emphasized national leaders, the volume of propaganda from national headquarters has risen, although candidates use only that portion they feel is useful to them. Whereas broadcasting time, when secured, is free, the large parties, like the Gaullists and, for a while, the Christian Democrats, have spent huge sums of money on professional services supplied from Paris. Marginal constituencies are sometimes the scene of lavish expenditures by the contesting parties. Although most parties do not provide their candidates with funds, the Gaullists commonly underwrite about one thousand dollars of expenses for any candidate who requests it. There are also unofficial contributions by trade unions to Communists and Socialists. Professional and employers' groups, notably the *Confédération Nationale du Patronat Français* (CNPF), often support more than one party and may contribute to a left or center candidate if he seems likely to defeat a Communist. Thus the prevoting electoral scene remains mobile, although there is an increasing tendency toward emphasizing national political issues, themes, and allegiances.

ELECTIONS FOR
THE NATIONAL ASSEMBLY

The Fifth Republic's first two elections for the National Assembly, in 1958 and 1962, were held in the shadow of crucial referendums and can hardly be considered typical. The first followed shortly after the referendum on the constitution of the Fifth Republic and the second just after acceptance of de Gaulle's vital constitutional provision for direct election of the president. In neither instance could the electorate be expected to reject the president, whose molding of their constitutional framework they had so recently endorsed.

In November 1958, in addition to the UNR's successful campaign, fought on no more specific an issue than its complete loyalty to de Gaulle, the MRP, Guy Mollet's Socialists, a splinter group called the Autonomous Socialists, and, more reluctantly, Félix Gaillard's Radicals, supported de Gaulle's Algerian policy. Pierre Poujade's *Union de Défense des Commerçants et Artisans*, already a dying force, the Independents, and at the opposite end of the spectrum, the Communists, opposed de Gaulle and his Algerian policy. Thus, although the party spectrum numbered twelve parties or electoral coalitions, the dominant issue of the first ten years of the Fifth Republic—for or against de Gaulle—was apparent.

In November 1962, the swing to the Gaullists was even more noticeable. The referendum had already demonstrated that the Socialists, MRP, Independents, and Radicals had lost a considerable proportion of their supporters through their open opposition to it. The UNR also made capital out of the agreement between the Communists and Guy Mollet's Socialists to refrain from competing with each other on the second ballot. The extreme right virtually disappeared, and the MRP suffered substantially. Together with its moderate rightist allies, the UNR secured an unprecedented majority in the Assembly.

The March 1967 election for the National Assembly was more normal. It was held a year and a quarter after de Gaulle's successful but

General Elections, 1956–68
(Metropolitan France)

YEAR	COMMUNISTS	OTHER LEFT	PDM*	GAULLISTS	EXTREME RIGHT	NOT VOTING	REGISTERED VOTERS
Votes (millions) at First Ballot							
1956	5.5	6.5†	5.4	0.9	2.9	4.0	26.8
1958	3.9	4.5	7.8	3.6	0.7	6.2	27.2
1962	4.0	4.1	3.1	6.9	0.2	8.6	27.5
1965	—	7.7‡	4.2‡	10.5‡	1.3‡	4.3‡	28.4
1967	5.0	4.7	3.0	8.5	0.2	5.4	28.3
1968	4.4	4.5	2.7	10.1	0.03	5.6	28.2
Votes (millions) for Seats Fought at Second Ballot							
1958	3.8	3.3	6.1	5.2	0.2		
1962	3.2	3.4	2.0	6.4			
1967	4.0	4.7	1.3	8.0			
1968	3.0	3.1	1.2	7.0			
Seats						Total	
1956	145	162†	166	16	55	544	
1958	10	65	203	187		465	
1962	41	106	64	249		465	
1967	72	120	27	234		470	
1968	33	57	26	346		470	

* *Progrès et Démocratie Moderne*, Remnant of the MRP, the social-minded Catholic center party.
† Includes right-wing Radicals: 1 million votes, 32 deputies.
‡ Votes for presidential candidates.

Source: Adapted from David B. Goldey, "A Precarious Regime: The Events of May 1968," in Philip M. Williams, *French Politicians and Elections, 1951–1969* (Cambridge: Cambridge University Press, 1970), p. 273.

at the end hard-fought December 1965 campaign for president, in which François Mitterrand had run as the candidate of the left. The Gaullists and their allies retained their control of the National Assembly, but the newly formed FGDS and the Communists, benefitting from their mutual restraint in the second ballot, markedly increased their number of seats. For a brief time it looked as if the radical and moderate left and center might become an effective opposition to the Gaullists.

That hope disappeared with the crisis of 1968. Shortly before it broke, the FGDS and the Communists had agreed on a common platform that was presented to the public on February 23, 1968. Despite this achievement the document rested on shaky foundations, for the non-Communist left still feared domination by the better-organized Communists, and the latter feared that if Mitterrand secured power, he would form a center-based rather than left-oriented government. When the crisis erupted, neither the FGDS nor the Communists were prepared with alternative policies or a successor to de Gaulle. Moreover, the Communists and the CGT were well aware that the student revolutionaries might color the whole workers' movement with an insurrectionist tint that would effectively remove it from their control. Hence their efforts far from being revolutionary were directed toward keeping the nation-wide wildcat strikes within bounds. Nonetheless, the UDR, led by Pompidou, was able to harp on the violence and what they called Communist plots and to turn the May uprising into a huge electoral asset.

WHERE THE LEFT IS STRONG: NATIONAL ASSEMBLY ELECTION, JUNE 1968

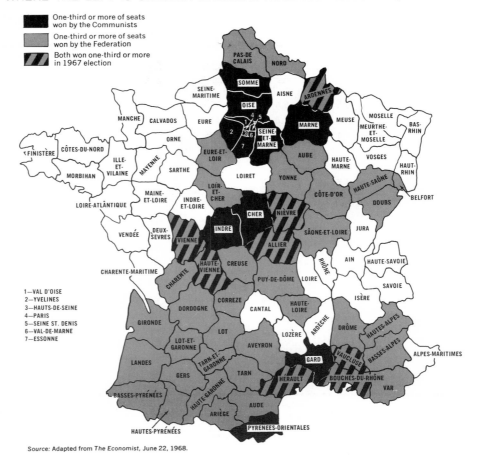

Source: Adapted from The Economist, June 22, 1968.

In France's long history no election has taken place so close to scenes of disorder. In 1958, de Gaulle had acceded to power in May, but the elections did not take place until November. In June 1968, the last great night on the Paris barricades was the eleventh to twelfth, and the first ballot was on June 23. The post office and railroad strikes did not end officially until June 6, the automatic telephone system still functioned inadequately, and the state radio and television network was half on strike, but candidacies had to be announced by Sunday, June 9. Taking refuge in a legal formality ruled by the Council of State, the electoral lists were not revised, preventing the 420,000 who had turned twenty-one years old after the end of February from registering to vote. Despite the increased youthfulness of France's population, the electorate that cast 78.58 valid votes, barely less than in 1967, was the oldest since World War I: 36 percent over age fifty-five, 19 percent over sixty-five, and only 8.5 percent under twenty-five.

The most significant results of the election were the detachment of voters from the old parties and the evidence that the Gaullists could poll a higher percentage of votes than the General himself. In terms both of strategy and of accepted leadership of the *Union pour la Défense de la République* (UDR, as the UNR was renamed), it was Pompidou's victory. His dismissal as premier by de Gaulle on July 10, 1968, did not change any of these facts, as was proved the following year by de Gaulle's defeat in the April referendum and Pompidou's victory in the presidential election that followed de Gaulle's resignation.

In June 1968, the UDR's most striking advances were among the peasantry, especially the most rural, small shopkeepers, and among those in parts of the industrial north, Paris itself, and in the so-called red south around Toulouse and Montpellier. Thus the UDR now represents much of the most backward as well as most modern sectors of France. But along with the most diversified support received by any political party in France's history is the fact that it included a preponderance of older age groups. Since France possesses a transitional economy that is still suffering from the effects of the prolonged 1968 strike and has half a million unemployed, the question of how to

THE GOVERNMENT'S VICTORY: 1968 ELECTION FOR NATIONAL ASSEMBLY

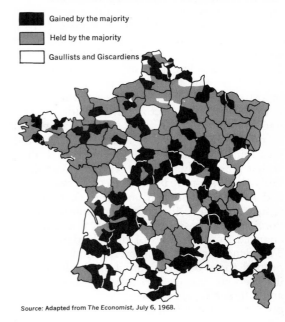

- Gained by the majority
- Held by the majority
- Gaullists and Giscardiens

Source: Adapted from *The Economist*, July 6, 1968.

appeal to the young, still dissatisfied groups in the population remains open.

ELECTIONS FOR THE SENATE

Quite unlike the National Assembly, elections for the Senate have not reflected the growing Gaullist majority throughout France. This situation, which has led the Senate into constant friction with the executive, is the result of the traditional system of electing the 255 senators for metropolitan France through a large electoral college of some 130,000 members among whom there is a high proportion of mayors and municipal councilors of small towns in predominantly rural areas. Only in the Assembly election of 1968 did the Gaullists begin to penetrate these areas of the country, which have been the least affected by modernization and are the most opposed to its impact.

A major dilemma that has always confronted France is how to devise a second chamber in a country dedicated to the principles of the sovereign people and universal franchise. If the second chamber is chosen by direct election, it is likely, as in the United States, to assume a large share of the decision-making function. But if it is chosen by indirect election and given a potential power of veto over the decisions of the directly elected representatives, it threatens to make the will of a minority superior to the popular will. Hence the Fourth Republic had left the second chamber—the Council of the Republic—virtually impotent in any clash with the National Assembly.

In devising the electoral system for the second chamber of the Fifth Republic, Debré had in mind a strong second chamber that would be a reinforcement for the executive in dealing with a potentially unstable National Assembly. Only the system of indirect election was specified in the constitution, and the electoral system, which left the small communes in so dominant a position, was left virtually unchanged from the days of the Third Republic. The Senate was given powers, however, well beyond those of the Council of the Republic: its consent is needed for a constitutional amendment (a reason why de Gaulle insisted on the unconstitutional expedient of a referendum on his controversial proposals in 1962 and 1969), and its initial lawmaking role is equivalent to that of the National Assembly except in matters of finance. In case of dispute, however, the executive can appoint a joint committee, and if this committee does not resolve the conflict, the executive decides which chamber's view is decisive. Thus, unlike the situation in the Third Republic, the Senate can, in practice, only temporarily block Assembly measures. But when the issue of the constitutionality of the 1962 referendum led to open conflict between de Gaulle and Gaston Monnerville, president of the Senate from 1947 to 1968, the Senate deliberately used its legislative power to slow down the passage of measures the executive wanted, and de Gaulle, in turn, snubbed the Senate by down-grading his representation to it.

For a long time before the referendum of 1969 in which de Gaulle sought unsuccessfully to change basically the powers and composition of the Senate, there had been discussion of merging that body with the able but impotent Economic and Social Council so as to create a semicorporative body representative of special interests as well as of local areas. As will be seen in the next section, this attempt foundered in the face of the effective opposition of local

notables. The Senate continues to be selected by local representatives voting (at home like the American electoral college) for party lists of candidates for the one-third of its members chosen every three years for nine year terms. The earlier pattern of party strength persisted in 1968 with the UDR in a weak minority position, and the RI, the non-Communist center, and the left in a majority. But the swing to the UDR in rural areas in the Assembly election of 1968 was reflected in the March 1970 elections for General Councils, an indication that the Senate's composition may change by 1974 to one closer to that of the National Assembly—if, in practice, the latter continues to be dominated by the UDR.

REFERENDUMS

Of the five referendums called by de Gaulle during his eleven years as president of the Fifth Republic, the first adopted the constitution of 1958, and the next two, in 1961 and 1962, prepared and endorsed in rather ambiguous terms the settlement of the Algerian war. While in each case the issue was one legitimately referred to a referendum, there is no doubt that primarily at issue in the minds of the voters was the necessity of maintaining de Gaulle's leadership of the country.

The two later referendums were far more controversial, since the issues should have been dealt with by constitutional amendment, as the Council of State pointed out. Yet in October 1962, when de Gaulle forced the country to vote by referendum on the introduction of the direct election of the president, he was still considered indispensable. In 1969, when he again laid his prestige and "indispensability" on the line in his effort to secure approval of two somewhat interrelated issues—regional deconcentration of authority and a fundamental reorganization of the Senate—his weakness at the time of the 1968 crisis and the availability of Pompidou as a successor, coupled with the association of a popular and an unpopular issue, led to de Gaulle's defeat and resignation.

There was thus more than the felt need for de Gaulle's leadership to differentiate between the referendums of 1962 and 1969. The public had already indicated in a poll in 1945 and again in 1961 its preference for direct election of the chief executive. In practice, the constitutional change has proved popular. Thus the referendum was approved, although the "old" parties campaigned against it in 1962, and the Senate leadership openly accused de Gaulle of violating the constitution (its opposition to the change may well have been a major reason why de Gaulle refused to use the amendment process in which the Senate has a decisive role). That the criticisms had their effect, however, was indicated by the fact that only 61.8 percent of the 77.2 percent of registered voters who exercised their franchise voted "yes," that is, only 46.4 percent of the registered voters.

In 1969, the issues were much more complicated. There is no doubt that, particularly after his obvious loss of public confidence in 1968, de Gaulle was seeking a national affirmation of support. But the issues were also ones on which he felt deeply. His concept of amalgamating the Senate, which was indirectly representative of local authorities, and the consultative Economic and Social Council, most of whose members were nominated by major interest groups, had already been suggested by him at Bayeux as early as June 1947. The Senate opposition to his October 1962 referendum added a further reason to weaken its power and that of the local *notables* who generally were anti-Gaullist. A 1965 article prepared at de Gaulle's request linked the composition of a new Senate to the twenty-one regions into which France had been divided in 1959–60 in the interests of economic planning. This type of regional organization was largely ineffective. By sending questionnaires on regional reform early in 1969 to a variety of social, economic, political, and cultural organizations throughout the country, the government stirred widespread discussion that stimulated considerable enthusiasm for change in this field. In fact, the change proposed was hardly likely to provide the decentralization so obviously desired and needed if the new Regional Councils were to work with the regional prefects, an arrangement that suggests the same comment as made to an earlier proposal for deconcentration: "It's the same hammer that strikes, but the handle has been shortened."

If regional reform evoked some enthusiasm, the same was not true of the proposal to change

the Senate. Moreover, this body proceeded to fight astutely and effectively for its existence. It elected a new president, Alain Poher, a Europeanist with no obvious record of anti-Gaullist domestic politics, who managed to restore relations with de Gaulle that had been broken since 1962. But no compromise could be secured on the powers and composition of the Senate, and Poher became one of the most effective opponents of the referendum, a fact that subsequently placed him in a good position to run for president of the Republic.

Almost immediately after the resounding Gaullist victory of June 1968, de Gaulle had set his advisers at working out the terms of the measures to be proposed at the referendum (even so it was described by a member of the Council of State as "the worst drafted bill it has ever considered"). Not until April 10, 1969, however, did de Gaulle announce that he would

THE 1969 REFERENDUM: PERCENTAGE OF NEGATIVE VOTES BY DEPARTMENTS

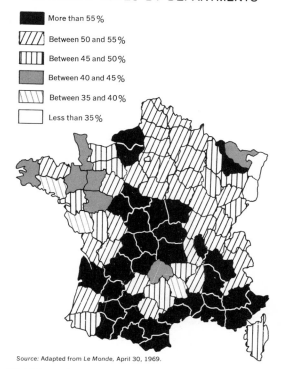

More than 55%

Between 50 and 55%

Between 45 and 50%

Between 40 and 45%

Between 35 and 40%

Less than 35%

Source: Adapted from Le Monde, April 30, 1969.

Official figures for the April 27 referendum indicated 28,656,494 registered voters: 5,565,475 (19.42 percent) abstained; 632,131 cast blank ballots. Of the remaining 22,458,838 voters, 53.17 percent were against the referendum and 46.82 for.

COMPARISON OF VOTES IN REFERENDUMS

The Overall Results of the 1958, 1962, and 1969 Referendums

| | | TOTAL | | | | "YES" AS PERCENTAGE OF | |
DATE	REGISTERED VOTERS	Total	Percent	YES	NO	Registered Voters	Turnout
1958	26,603,464	22,596,850	84.9	17,668,790	4,624,511	66.4	79.3
1962	27,582,113	21,301,816	77.2	12,809,363	7,932,695	46.4	61.8
1969	29,393,390	23,552,611	80.1	10,908,855	11,943,282	37.1	47.6

Source: Adapted from J. E. S. Hayward, "Presidential Suicide by Plebiscite: De Gaulle's Exit, April 1969," *Parliamentary Affairs,* 22 (4) (Fall 1969), p. 318.

The Regional Vote in the Referendums of 1962 and 1969

| | PERCENTAGE OF "NO" VOTES | | PERCENTAGE INCREASE |
REGION	1962	1969	1962–69
Paris	45.1	58.2	13.1
North			
Nord	38.2	52.7	14.5
Picardie	38.0	54.2	16.2
Haute-Normandie	37.3	55.5	18.2
Champagné	35.2	52.2	17.0
East			
Alsace	12.3	32.1	19.8
Lorraine	20.7	46.9	26.2
West			
Basse-Normandie	23.0	46.6	23.6
Bretagne	24.8	43.2	18.4
Pays de la Loire	27.2	44.2	17.0
Center			
Centre	40.9	54.2	13.3
Auvergne	41.2	54.9	13.7
Limousin	49.0	57.6	8.6
East-Center			
Bourgogne	40.8	54.3	13.5
Franche-Comté	29.9	51.0	21.1
Rhône-Alpes	39.6	55.6	16.0
Southeast			
Corse	44.4	45.9	1.5
Provence-Côte d'Azur	50.6	59.9	9.3
Languedoc	51.1	59.4	8.3
Southwest			
Midi-Pyrénées	49.1	56.0	6.9
Aquitaine	42.3	54.4	12.1
Poitou-Charente	37.3	52.2	14.9

Source: Adapted from J. E. S. Hayward, "Presidential Suicide by Plebiscite: De Gaulle's Exit, April 1969," *Parliamentary Affairs,* 22 (4) (Fall 1969), p. 318.

COMPARISON OF VOTES IN REFERENDUMS, 1958–69—*continued*

The Changing Composition of the "Yes" Vote in the 1962 and 1969 Referendums
(In Percentages)

I.F.O.P. POLL*	1962	1969†	DIFFERENCE
Total	63	52	—11
Sex: Men	57	46	—11
Women	70	60	—10
Age: 20–34	65	43	—22
35–49	60	52	—8
50–64	63	52	—11
65+	66	62	—4
Occupation: Farmers	71	62	—9
Shopkeepers, artisans, and industrialists	47	46	—1
Senior executives and professions	62	39	—23
White-collar employees	56	50	—6
Workers	61	45	—16
Unemployed	65	60	—5
Size of Commune: Rural	69	60	—9
Under 20,000 population	72	52	—20
20–100,000	57	54	—3
100,001+	60	47	—13
Paris	55	40	—15
Region: Paris	58	42	—16
Northwest	78	56	—22
Northeast	68	59	—9
Southwest	57	53	—4
Southeast	50	47	—3

* *L'Institut Français de l'Opinion Publique* (French Institute of Public Opinion).
† Based on cumulative results of April 1969 I.F.O.P. polls, excluding the final one, which showed a further 3 percent shift from "yes" to "no."

Source: Adapted from J. E. S. Hayward, "Presidential Suicide by Plebiscite: De Gaulle's Exit, April 1969," *Parliamentary Affairs*, 22 (4) (Fall 1969), p. 319. Based on a table published by A. Duhamel in *Le Monde*, April 1969, p. 4.

regard a "no" vote as reason to resign. Giscard d'Estaing was already leading his right-wing Gaullist Independent Republicans against the referendum, while the extraparliamentary and Senate wings of the center were heavily committed to its rejection, as were the Socialists, the Radicals, the Communists, and all the trade unions, the CGT, the left-wing Socialist-led CFDT, the FO, and the FEN. De Gaulle's threat was insufficient to turn the tide.

In a poll greater than that of 1962 (80.1 percent of registered voters in 1969 compared to 77.2 percent in 1962), the electorate rejected the proposals 53.17 percent to 46.82 percent. Even more significant was the fact that the "no" vote carried every *arrondissement* in Paris,

seventy-one *départements* of metropolitan France, sixteen of the twenty regions, and most of the big cities. The verdict was clear. The changing composition of the "yes" vote in the 1962 and 1969 referendums is shown above.

THE PRESIDENTIAL ELECTIONS

President de Gaulle resigned the morning after he lost the referendum of April 27, 1969. He had been elected in France's first direct election for the president on December 19, 1965, seven years after he had been chosen first president of the Fifth Republic by an electoral college of 81,764 members, which was only slightly different in composition from that which elects senators. In effect, he had been the chief executive since June 1, 1958, when the National Assembly had confirmed him as premier to rule by decree.

The contest for the 1965 election of the president had extended over more than two years, while the "old" parties sought to recoup themselves after their defeats in the referendum establishing direct election and the election that followed. The final stages of the 1965 election proved far more lively than ever expected and, to the general surprise, in the first ballot two of the six contestants—François Mitterrand, who secured solid support from the Socialists, Communists, and Radicals; and Jean Lecanuet, the MRP and center candidate, who had performed brilliantly on television—polled together a slightly higher percentage of the valid votes than de Gaulle himself received. Thus forced into a second ballot against Mitterrand, de Gaulle had won handily, but his 54.4 percent of the votes cast represented only 44.8 percent of registered voters.

In 1969, the campaign was necessarily very short. The constitution requires elections for a new president to take place between twenty and thirty-five days after the formal declaration of vacancy. On April 28, also in line with constitutional provisions, Alain Poher, president of the Senate, became acting president, and moved into what proved to be empty Elysée offices, for de Gaulle's staff had taken all the files with them. On April 29, Pompidou's candidacy was announced; on the same day, so was Gaston Defferre's, the anti-Communist, Socialist mayor of Marseilles, whose 1963–65 candidacy in the earlier presidential election had been so unsuccessful that he had withdrawn in June 1965. Defferre's move further complicated the effort of the Socialist party to turn itself into a "new Socialist party" at its founding congress less than a week later and made it doubly sure that the Communist party would not enter into any agreement on a joint candidate such as Mitterrand had been. With the non-Communist left in disarray, and the center too reduced in strength to pull together an alternative ma-

THE PRESIDENTIAL ELECTION DECEMBER 5 AND 19, 1965

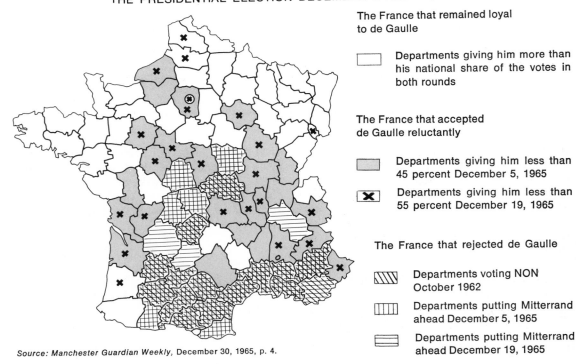

The France that remained loyal to de Gaulle

☐ Departments giving him more than his national share of the votes in both rounds

The France that accepted de Gaulle reluctantly

▨ Departments giving him less than 45 percent December 5, 1965

☒ Departments giving him less than 55 percent December 19, 1965

The France that rejected de Gaulle

▧ Departments voting NON October 1962

▥ Departments putting Mitterrand ahead December 5, 1965

▤ Departments putting Mitterrand ahead December 19, 1965

Source: Manchester Guardian Weekly, December 30, 1965, p. 4.

PRESIDENTIAL ELECTION, 1969

First Ballot Votes for Pompidou, June 1

- More than 50%
- Between 40 and 50%
- Between 30 and 40%

Second Ballot Votes for Pompidou, June 15

- More than 55%
- Between 50 and 55%
- Between 40 and 50%

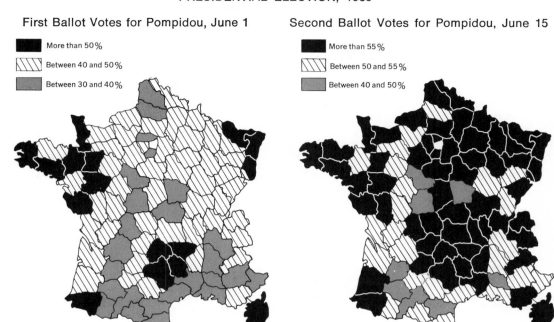

Source: Le Monde, June 4, 1969.

Source: Le Monde, June 18, 1969.

jority, the only two cohesive parties seemed the UDR and the Communists.

The UDR, which had tacitly accepted Pompidou as its leader in the crisis of 1968, remained united, partly also by what was once described as "the cohesive power of public plunder." Even Giscard d'Estaing somewhat reluctantly endorsed his rival. The Communists found themselves having to reestablish their control over their voters who, according to the polls, were showing a dangerous interest in the possible candidacy of Poher as having the best chance to defeat Pompidou. Finally the Communist party entered its own candidate, Jacques Duclos, its seventy-two-year-old secretary general, who proved a surprisingly effective candidate. Immediately after Duclos entered, Poher, emboldened by the polls, put forward his own candidacy, although without renouncing his office of acting president. Poher's move was too late to spur the left to reunify, and he proved a passive and colorless candidate. Nonetheless, he still had a chance to capture the largely

Where the Top Three Ran Strongest

- Pompidou more than 45%
- Poher more than 25%
- Duclos more than 25%

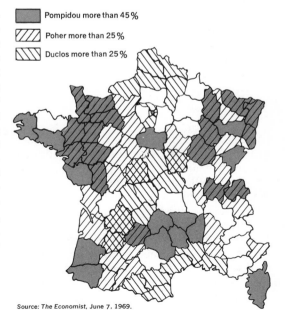

Source: The Economist, June 7, 1969.

Two Presidential Elections, 1965 and 1969
(Metropolitan France)

	Vote (millions)		Percentage of Vote		Percentage of Register	
	1965	1969	1965	1969	1965	1969
FIRST BALLOT						
Registered	28.2	28.8				
Not voting	4.2	6.3			15.0	21.8
Spoiled	0.2	0.3			0.9	1.0
Valid votes	23.8	23.2			84.2	77.2
De Gaulle	10.4		43.7		36.8	
Pompidou		9.8		43.9		33.9
Lecanuet	3.8		15.8		13.3	
Tixier	1.3		5.3		4.4	
Marcilhacy	0.4		1.7		1.5	
Poher		5.2		23.4		18.1
Mitterrand	7.7		32.2		27.1	
Duclos		4.8		21.5		16.6
Defferre		1.1		5.1		3.9
Rocard		0.8		3.7		2.8
Krivine		0.2		1.1		0.8
Barbu	0.3		1.2		1.0	
Ducatel		0.3		1.3		1.0
SECOND BALLOT						
Registered	28.2	28.8				
Not voting	4.4	8.9			15.5	30.9
Spoiled	0.7	1.3			2.4	4.5
Valid votes	23.2	18.6			82.2	64.5
De Gaulle	12.6		54.4		44.8	
Pompidou		10.7		57.6		37.2
Mitterrand	10.6		45.5		37.4	
Poher		7.9		42.4		27.4

Source: Adapted from David B. Goldey, "The French Presidential Elections of 1st and 15th June 1969," *Parliamentary Affairs*, 22 (4) (Fall 1969), p. 338.

uncommitted middle range of French voters. Pompidou, however, was conducting himself impressively, claiming credit for the good done under de Gaulle and, without censuring his predecessor, trying to separate himself from de Gaulle's obvious mistakes, a tightrope Hubert Humphrey had been less successful in walking.

The electoral law had been changed to permit those who had turned twenty-one since the annual revision of the electoral lists (estimated to be about 217,000) to register up to two weeks before the first ballot on June 1. But 60 percent of the electorate was over forty years old and 45 percent over age fifty.

Few had expected the first ballot to be decisive, and the greatest interest focused on which candidate would poll the second highest percentage of the votes and thus be in the second ballot with Pompidou. The race for second place was close. Poher, with most of the center votes and a substantial portion of those from the non-Communist left, managed to outstrip Duclos by just under 2 percent of the vote in a turnout of 78.18 percent of those registered, which was substantially lower than the record high of 84.99 percent in 1965. Pompidou was easily ahead with 43.96 percent of the vote, which was slightly higher than de Gaulle's percentage of the first ballot in 1965, although 3 percent lower in relation to registered voters.

While Duclos' votes did not place him on the second ballot, the Communists had acquired a major position of strength. In the first place they had clearly demonstrated their unaided dominance on the left. But beyond this their disciplined voters potentially held the electoral balance. If they supported Poher, Pompidou might be defeated, but this would mean a new election, fragmentation of parties, and a likely return to the instabilities of the Fourth Republic. Hence pressure was exerted on Poher to withdraw so that the second ballot could be a clear-cut contest between Pompidou and Duclos, the right and the left.

But Poher was determined to run and spent the two weeks between the elections in much more effective campaigning than he had engaged in previously. What threw the election to Pompidou was the Communist party's decision to call for abstention. A possibly revived center-left coalition under Poher was seen to be more dangerous to their future political role than another seven years of Gaullism; Duclos summed up the choice between Poher and Pompidou as between "cancer and scarlet fever." If Communist discipline held, the party would have demonstrated its indispensability for a change of regime.

In practice the poll in the second ballot fell to 69.04 percent (not quite as low as the 68.72 percent turnout in the November 1962 general election), but additionally spoiled and blank ballots numbered 4.5 percent, the highest in the Fifth Republic. Thus the percentage of valid votes to the register was only 64.52, a new low. Abstentions and spoiled ballots were highest in the Paris region, in the north, close to the Mediterranean, and west from Lyon to Limoges, but this evidence of Communist discipline did not extend to all the areas it customarily dominated. Abstentions were lower in the rural areas, where many voted for Poher, than in the towns. Although Poher increased his poll by a quarter, it is estimated that one-fifth of his original supporters abstained for fear that his victory might wreck the stability of the Fifth Republic.

The final result was 10.7 million for Pompidou (i.e., 57.6 percent of the cast vote, although only 37.2 percent of the registered voters) to 7.9 million votes for Poher (i.e., 42.4 percent of the cast vote and 27.4 percent of the registered voters). Both de Gaulle and Mitterrand had done better in 1965, with 12.6 million votes on the second ballot for de Gaulle (i.e., 54.4 percent of the poll and 44.8 percent of the registered voters) and 10.6 million votes for Mitterrand (i.e., 45.5 percent of cast votes and 37.4 percent of registered voters). What was particularly significant in Pompidou's victory, however, was that it demonstrated UDR influence in formerly Radical southern France, as well as in the industrial north and east and the largely Catholic west. More than ever the UDR had become a national party, and the transition had been made to a new and accepted leader.

4

The French parliament

1 THE ROLE OF PARLIAMENT

The most distinctive feature of the constitutional system of the Fifth Republic is its combination of parliamentary and presidential institutions. This combination, however, brings the working of France's constitutional system closer to those of Great Britain and the United States than was the relationship of executive and legislature in the Third and Fourth Republics. Under those regimes, the French parliament dominated the executive to a degree never known in either of the other two Western democracies. For nearly eighty years, no ministry dared to dissolve the French parliament, whereas the power of dissolution has always been in the hands of the British cabinet. In the United States, Congress can be a strong force limiting presidential action, although in recent years it has rarely initiated policies or tried to impose them on him. But in France it could truly be said during the Third and Fourth Republics that the ministry might propose but the chambers would dispose of policies. The fragmentation of parties, shifting alignments, and the consequent short tenure of office of most ministries underscored the dominance of the legislature.

De Gaulle had soon become frustrated by the dominant role of the National Assembly under the Fourth Republic and resigned as president. When he was called back to direct France at the time of the dangerous impasse over Algeria in 1958, he determined that the legislature would never again be allowed to cripple the executive. Although in presenting the constitution, Michel Debré, its drafter, declared that "the parliamentary regime is the only one suitable for France," the balance of power was radically changed by the limitations placed on the powers and the length of sessions of the legislature, and the greatly increased role allocated to the executive and particularly to the president—a role considerably enlarged by de Gaulle, especially during his early years as president. In any case, for the first time in French history, an organized majority, the UNR-UDR and its allies, underwrites in the National Assembly the policies demanded by the executive. Despite the abortive effort of the "old" parties in 1962 to reassert legislative power, the National Assembly in the Fifth Republic is more subordinated to executive wishes than is the British House of Commons or the American House of Representatives. Interestingly enough, despite the basic difference in their composition, it has been the Senate in France, as in the United States, that has persistently needled the executive, but the French Senate lacks the general public support arising out of direct election that underpins the coordinate authority of the American Senate.

THE COMPOSITION OF THE NATIONAL ASSEMBLY

The new balance in the constitutional system of the Fifth Republic belatedly reflects new social, economic, and political groups that came to prominence during the Resistance and post–World War II period. Until then, small farmers, businessmen, and local *notables* had arrogated to themselves the control of the national political machinery, which they manipulated so as to prevent any significant challenge to their entrenched positions. In World War II and thereafter, Socialist and Communist workers, Catholics with strong social consciences, the white-collar and skilled wage earners, and professional groups became increasingly important in political life and supported the rapid economic modernization that was the most constructive feature of the Fourth Republic.

During that regime, however, France was severely handicapped by the antidemocratic bias of the parties at both ends of the political spectrum—the Communists and the Poujadists—and by the persistent quarreling of Communists and Gaullists. Thus, although the Fourth Republic had many sound achievements to its credit in domestic and foreign affairs and in patching up a workable constitutional system, its ultimate lack of authority in dealing with the Algerian civil war discredited it beyond repair. Its achievements overlooked and its faults magnified, the Fourth Republic and its cabinet crises easily gave way to the executive dominance of the Fifth Republic. Yet the constitutional balance of the Fifth Republic, although tilted away from the legislature and toward the dual executive of cabinet and president, still includes principles of parliamentary government with the cabinet responsible to the National Assembly. An essential element in the stability of the Fifth Republic is the widespread support the electorate has given to the Gaullist parties and the large number of seats they hold in the National Assembly.

The 1968 election provided the UDR with more seats than any French party had ever had before—296 altogether, well over an absolute majority of the National Assembly's 487 seats (465 for metropolitan France, 10 for overseas departments, and 7 for those overseas territories that had not become independent states). Moreover, 54 Independent Republicans won seats as avowed allies of the UDR, while a number of others could be expected to vote on similar lines. Thus the executive could count on a huge majority in the house, an unprecedented situation in French parliamentary history. The

opposition, whose members were divided among themselves, consisted only of 34 Communists, 57 members from the shaky Federation of the Left, and 29 from the center—120 in all.

That the electorate viewed the parties in rather a different light is demonstrated by the percentages of votes they received in the first ballot. The UDR and associated RI candidates received 43.6 percent of the votes cast—a considerable increase over the 37.8 percent in the 1967 election but less than could be expected from the ultimate phenomenal increase of 108 seats. The Communist vote diminished from 22.5 to 20.03 percent, but again this seemed insufficient to explain the loss of 39 seats. The Federation of the Left won 16.5 percent of the votes, also only 2.4 percent less than in 1967 but resulting in a drop of 61 seats. The center similarly dropped 2.5 percent of its 1967 vote to 10.3 percent, resulting in a loss of 10 seats. Thus, as in other Fifth Republic elections, the electoral system had worked to the advantage of the more right-wing parties. More decisive, however, had been the increased spread of UDR support and the divisions among the left and center.

Characteristics of members of the National Assembly

The proportion of members of the National Assembly in the Fifth Republic who come from the middle class is higher than in most other Western parliaments, and many of these belong to the professions and public services or are skilled workers in industry or commerce. The French prize education, and almost all Assembly members have had secondary or more advanced education. Moreover, with the diminution in the number of Communist deputies, working-class representation has much diminished, so that manual laborers, clerks, subordinate officials, and elementary school teachers, who together numbered 177 in the 1946 National Assembly, only totaled 41 in 1958 (of these only 7 were working men). The percentage of deputies from these groups elected in France itself was only 9 in 1958 but rose to 17 in 1962 and to 19 in 1967. In the same period, however, the number of farmers in the Assembly became progressively smaller, ranging from 11.5 percent in 1958, to 9 percent in 1962, and 7 percent in 1967.

In contrast, the business and professional class became more prominent in the chamber. Engineers, managers, and businessmen increased their share of the representation to nearly 30 percent in 1958 and 1962 but it sank to 18.5 percent in 1967. Most striking is the pervasiveness of the professions—secondary school and university teachers, lawyers, doctors, journalists, high civil servants, army officers, priests—who together dominated the 1958 Assembly with 51 percent of its deputies and still maintained 46 and 43 percent respectively in the 1962 and 1967 Assemblies.

These occupational percentages follow party fortunes closely, for most working-class deputies are Communists, most teachers are Socialists, and most farmers are right-wing conservatives. The UNR-UDR has a high proportion of university graduates, higher in 1958 than in the British Conservative party. Many of their deputies also belong to newer technical fields rather than to more traditional law and letters, and there was a noticeable and steady drop from 1958 through 1967 in the number of lawyers elected.

The National Assembly elected in June 1968 is also dominated by industrial and commercial interests and the professions. Among its 487 members, there are 49 directors and general managers of plants (32 of them in the UDR) and 26 technicians (of whom 23 are UDR). Of the 17 engineers in the Assembly, 12 are UDR members. The 31 members in commerce are spread more evenly with 17 in the UDR, 4 each among the Socialists and Communists, and 3 each in the RI and the *Progrès et Démocratie Moderne* (PDM), the current form of the former MRP. There are 156 professionals (111 in the UDR) among whom the two largest groups are the 42 doctors (32 of them in the UDR) and 27 lawyers (19 in the UDR). Sixteen members of the *grands corps* (see Chapter 6, Section 5) became deputies, half of them in the UDR; 10 members of the prefectorial corps (see Chapter 6, Section 4), 6 of them in the UDR; and 9 members of the diplomatic corps (8 in the UDR). There is also a group of 32 in the Assembly who are associated with public enterprises, among whom 18 are members of the UDR. Secondary and technical school teachers also have substantial representation, numbering 28 in all, with the Socialists in the lead with 12 in this one category, while the UDR has 10. The three categories in which the Communists have higher representation than other parties are, not surprisingly, clerks (6 of 8), workingmen (10 of 12), and primary school teachers (6 of 8).

The most significant characteristic of members of the Assembly, however, is their local base as mayors or councilors. Already in the 1958 Assembly, nearly three-quarters of its members had been local councilors and almost two-thirds still were. Since the weakness of the Fifth Republic Assembly tended to downgrade the influence of the deputy in his local area, there was even more incentive to assume a strong local position as mayor, or in the new regional organizations. Members of the opposition, frustrated at their lack of power in Paris, were particularly prone to concentrate on municipal or regional activities and to treat their parliamentary duties on a very part-time basis. Although rules were introduced to prevent absenteeism by docking pay for sustained absence and by forbidding proxy voting (under which one deputy, known as the "postman," might cast votes for his whole party), Assembly members quickly developed an *esprit de corps* that nullified the effect of the rules. Indeed, the main result of the new provisions is that instead of stuffing ballots in a box, as in the Fourth and Third Republics, it is now necessary for some deputy to run and turn the key in the electronic voting machine each time the name of an absent deputy is called!

THE MEETING PLACE

In contrast to the rectangular chamber of the House of Commons, the National Assembly meets in a semicircular amphitheater in the Palais Bourbon, which has close-packed benches rising sharply one above another. Members of the ministry occupy special benches down front, where the representatives of committees may also sit when their topics are under consideration. In front of the auditorium is a high, ornate desk, approached by a flight of stairs on either side. Here sits the president of the Assembly, flanked by secretaries at lower desks. Immediately in front of the president's desk is a rostrum, the "tribune," from which deputies may address the Assembly.

Parties are commonly grouped on the curved benches according to the shade of their political views. The left is the prized position, and almost any kind of maneuver will be made to secure some of its prestige. Despite the obviously conservative character of most of the UNR deputies, that party (which first favored the British system of seating the government across from the opposition) refused in 1958 to sit on the extreme right (forcing the Independents to sit there) and was ultimately given a center position from which it overflowed into areas commonly occupied by parties more suitable to those positions. In 1962, the elimination of the extreme right, and a vast reduction in the strength of the Independents, forced the UNR into the section on the right of the chamber. In 1967 and 1968, the UNR-UDR covered much of the right. (The diagrams on page 286 indicate the relative strength of the major political groups following the elections of November 1946, June 1951, January 1956, November 1958, November 1962, March 1967, and June 1968. The diagrams, however, do not attempt to reproduce exactly the seating arrangements in the Assembly.)

The spirit of such an assembly differs fundamentally from that of the House of Commons. Instead of the sharp division between government and opposition—which forces every member of Parliament to take his position clearly on one side or the other, and which makes any deserting member extremely conspicuous—the French arrangement has been one of gradations from left to right. Under the weak party discipline of the Third Republic, and the changing party alignments, especially on the right, of the Fourth Republic, the instability of governments was sometimes attributed to the facility with which a member could shift to the left or the right and vote with his neighbors against his own party.

A more important consequence of the arrangement is the type of parliamentary oratory it permits. The French deputy who wishes to address his colleagues does not rise in his place, as in Great Britain, and speak in casual and conversational tones with courteous references to the honorable gentlemen on his right and left. He mounts the tribune, and often he orates. The speeches in the National Assembly frequently are more polished and brilliant than their Anglo-Saxon counterparts, but it is doubtful that they contribute as much to serious discussion and compromise. There is a great temptation to elicit cheers and applause from the close-packed benches and to impress or electrify an audience composed of connoisseurs of eloquence. The temptation is almost as great to provoke the fury of the opposition by the vigor of one's attack and the sharpness of one's taunts. Noble sentiments from the left are met with ironic laughter on the right; a particularly nasty taunt or insinuation provokes shouts of protest, and, in extreme instances in the past, deputies on one side of the auditorium have hurled themselves on their opponents, while attendants hastily intervened and the presiding officer suspended the session.

There has been a noticeable change under the Fifth Republic. Issues rarely rouse the kind of tension so prevalent in the Fourth Republic, simply because the Assembly now has so much less power. But two occasions on which the Palais Bourbon, the "House without Windows," regained its old passionate atmosphere were during the one successful motion of censure of the Fifth Republic, that of October 4, 1962, over de Gaulle's decision to use the referendum to test opinion on the direct election of the president, and during the motion of censure in April 1968 over the government's decision to allow commercials—only six minutes a day!—on the state-controlled ORTF. The first motion brought down the Pompidou government, but, as we have seen, it did not change the course of de Gaulle's policy. The second motion only failed by eight votes.

THE ORGANIZATION OF
THE NATIONAL ASSEMBLY

The president of the National Assembly

The president of the Assembly has certain new functions that increase his prestige and are intended to help him control the Assembly if control becomes a problem. He is one of those

SEATS IN THE FRENCH NATIONAL ASSEMBLY

After 1946 Elections

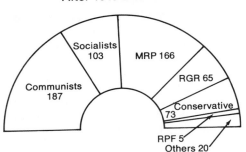

Communists 187 | Socialists 103 | MRP 166 | RGR 65 | Conservative 73 | RPF 5 | Others 20

After 1951 Elections

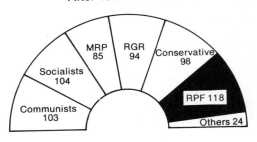

Communists 103 | Socialists 104 | MRP 85 | RGR 94 | Conservative 98 | RPF 118 | Others 24

After 1956 Elections

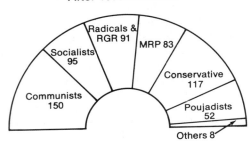

Communists 150 | Socialists 95 | Radicals & RGR 91 | MRP 83 | Conservative 117 | Poujadists 52 | Others 8

After 1958 Elections

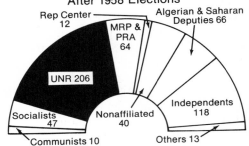

Rep Center 12 | MRP & PRA 64 | Algerian & Saharan Deputies 66 | UNR 206 | Socialists 47 | Communists 10 | Nonaffiliated 40 | Independents 118 | Others 13

After 1962 Elections

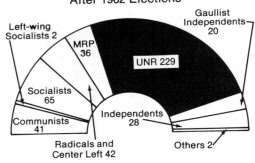

Gaullist Independents 20 | Left-wing Socialists 2 | MRP 36 | UNR 229 | Socialists 65 | Communists 41 | Radicals and Center Left 42 | Independents 28 | Others 2

After 1967 Elections

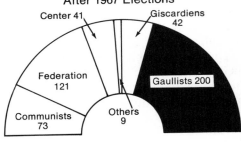

Center 41 | Giscardiens 42 | Federation 121 | Gaullists 200 | Communists 73 | Others 9

After 1968 Elections

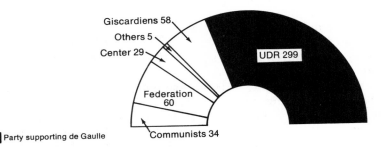

Giscardiens 58 | Others 5 | Center 29 | UDR 299 | Federation 60 | Communists 34

■ Party supporting de Gaulle

consulted by the president of the Republic in the event of an emergency. He chooses three of the nine members of the Constitutional Council. Moreover, he may submit to that body a private member's bill that he believes constitutional but that the government questions. Under the standing orders, he can call deputies to order and force the closure of debate. These powers are dependent, however, on practice, which, in the National Assembly, has characteristically developed out of action rather than rules. Since the Assembly exercises much less power in the Fifth Republic than it did in the Fourth, the president of the Assembly in practice now occupies a less important position than did his predecessor, who had to attempt to keep that all-powerful body in check through personal persuasion.

The groups

The basic units of organization within the Assembly are the parliamentary groups (*groupes*). In the Fifth Republic these are supposed to consist of at least thirty members (originally fourteen in the Fourth Republic although raised to twenty-eight in 1957). Their heads form the *Conférence des Présidents* (Presidents' Conference), which arranges for sittings and allocates time in the more important debates (a function performed by the Speaker in the House of Commons). The groups themselves make the appointments to committees and elect the officers of the chamber. These officers, known as the Bureau, consist of the president, six vice-presidents, fourteen secretaries, and three questors, who are jointly responsible for counting the votes, keeping the minutes, handling the accounts, and determining whether deputies' bills are admissible under the restrictions of Article 40 on financial legislation—that is, do not increase public expenditures or reduce revenues.

By enlarging the number of people required for a recognized group, the framers of the constitution had hoped to reduce the influence of the smaller parties, but, apart from the Communists (who were deliberately excluded from the Bureau after both the 1958 and 1962 elections but were provided with some representation after that of 1967), alliances have been used to bring numbers up to the required level. As the majority party, the UNR-UDR also organizes itself into working groups specializing in particular subjects to exert more leverage on relevant ministers.

2 THE NATIONAL ASSEMBLY IN ACTION

In relation to the traditional powers of the French lower chamber—making and supporting a government, criticizing and controlling that government, and shaping the laws—the National Assembly of the Fifth Republic has been placed under a severe handicap: it can overthrow a ministry but it cannot create one. The electorate determines the majority party, if there is one, and the president selects the premier, who is not necessarily the recognized leader of the majority party, as would be the case in Great Britain. Indeed, as we have seen, de Gaulle dismissed Pompidou almost immediately after the UDR, under the latter's direction, had won its spectacular electoral victory in 1968, and he replaced him by a not particularly popular or effective premier, Couve de Murville.

THE NATIONAL ASSEMBLY AND THE MINISTRY

It is customary for a new premier to present himself and his program to the Assembly, but Couve de Murville appears not to have done so, nor did Pompidou after he was renamed premier following the presidential elections of 1965. As a former president of the Assembly, Chaban-Delmas naturally did so after Pompidou named him premier, following the presidential election of 1969. The presentation of a program to the Assembly is an aid to securing its support, although the general compliance of the UDR deputies and their associates has long facilitated the passage of legislation about which the government feels strongly.

It is not true, however, that the Assembly,

or at least the majority UDR, has no influence on the ministry. Despite the limits on its sessions and timetable, limits that will be detailed shortly, the Assembly, or at least its majority Gaullists, benefited from Pompidou's efforts during his long period of office to do what Debré had not done, that is, to establish regular relations with the chamber and use tactics of conciliation rather than coercion. Where Debré had felt patronage to be demeaning and had resented criticism, Pompidou, without any parliamentary background, felt the necessity to create links with Assembly members, especially those from the majority party. He reversed Debré's policy of drawing ministers from the civil service and selected all but three from parliament itself.

Previously existing links thereafter led to numerous informal contacts between ministers and the parliamentary party. Pompidou himself held occasional lunches for its members. The government ceased to pressure the UNR to choose its own favorite candidate for chairman, and the latter, in turn, allowed the UNR deputies to select the vice-chairman. Moreover, UNR leaders reluctantly agreed during the second parliament of the Fifth Republic to a kind of regional "whip" system (not unlike the party whips in the British House of Commons and the American House of Representatives) that facilitates communication within their party. The whips consist of the twenty-two elected members of the UNR's *bureau politique*, who meet weekly with party leaders and keep in close touch with the government. Once a week the whole parliamentary party meets together and is often addressed by ministers or the premier. Since 1963, a junior minister responsible for relations with the Assembly meets regularly with the *bureau politique* and warns the government when party feelings are antagonistic. Thus, in practice, considerable interaction takes place between the majority party and the government in ways that bear some similarities to the relations between the Cabinet and its parliamentary party in the House of Commons.

There are notable limitations, however, on the National Assembly from which the House of Commons does not suffer. Instead of determining the length of sessions by the amount of business to be undertaken, the Assembly is restricted to two ordinary sessions a year: one for the budget, starting October 2, which, since an amendment of December 1963, can last eighty days, and the other, starting April 2, can last for ninety days. Moreover, these short periods are often interrupted by elections, and even when they are not, the five and a half months is often inadequate for handling government measures. Unlike the House of Commons, in which the opposition decides the business for twenty-eight days each session, the opposition in the French chamber has no time at all at its disposal. The government (not the Assembly itself as in Fourth and Third Republics) has primary determination of the timetable. Only time left free by the government, and the choice and duration of oral questions and debate on the one day a week reserved for them are controlled by the Presidents' Conference.

Parliament must meet under two special circumstances: on the second Tuesday after a general election for two weeks and, under Article 16, if the president assumes full powers in a national emergency. Otherwise special sessions can be called only to discuss a specific subject and can last only twelve days. Moreover, in March 1960, when 286 deputies requested a special session of the Assembly to deal with peasant grievances and agitation, de Gaulle arrogated to himself an unexpected right to refuse. While several special sessions have been called by the government, numerous requests from within the Assembly itself have always been refused.

The Assembly still retains the power, of course, to defeat legislation proposed by the government. The struggle over de Gaulle's plan for an independent French nuclear striking force demonstrated, however, that the government's threat to force a vote of confidence places it in a strong position in relation to the Assembly. Late in 1960, for example, Premier Debré twice answered strong criticism of the measure from the left and center, as well as motions of censure, with a demand for a vote of confidence. Although the deputies were frustrated and angry at being denied the chance to postpone or modify a measure with such far-reaching and possibly negative implications for France's European policy, they were unwilling to take the supreme step of overthrowing the ministry. Thus, in much the same way as a British prime minister is able to force through the House of Commons a particular measure that the House would not support on a free vote, the French premier under the Fifth Republic is able to dominate the once uncontrollable National Assembly.

In the debate on nuclear policy, the ministry and Assembly engaged in the kind of interaction characteristic of the parliamentary system in its classical form. The Assembly retained its right to withhold confidence, and the ministry forced the Assembly to declare for or against its continued life. But this classic expression of parliamentary action operates in a less traditional milieu in France than in Great Britain, and the Assembly is thus handicapped in maintaining executive responsibility under normal circumstances. The president of the Republic not only has the constitutional functions of supervision and arbitration between government and parliament, but, in practice, he also has assumed the right to intervene arbitrarily in the affairs of the Assembly. The ministry all too often abuses its dominant position unnecessarily. Moreover, because of French political history and the multiparty system, the traditional parliamentary devices for keeping a powerful executive alert and responsive to the criticism of private citizens and the community are only slowly developing in France, as we will see in considering the Assembly's work as a critic.

THE ASSEMBLY AS CRITIC

The two particular ways in which the deputies can criticize the government and check on its actions are through parliamentary questions and through a vote of censure. Unfortunately, in their efforts to prevent the unhappy experiences of earlier regimes in which cabinets were often forced to put even minor issues as votes of confidence, the framers of the constitution of the Fifth Republic have circumscribed legitimate means of keeping the government responsive. Most of the time, what concessions are made by the government are negotiated behind the scenes. Moreover, the deputies themselves have not been skillful in adapting the opportunities still open to them. Hence it is

only on rare occasions like those already mentioned or during the great debates on the 1965 plan and the withdrawal from NATO that the Assembly recovers its dynamism and public appeal.

Questions

The French have never used the parliamentary question with the same effect as the British, partly, at least, because under the Fourth Republic the question had little political significance. In contrast, the *interpellation*, which was a request to a minister for an explanation of his actions, had a great deal of political significance, since it always carried the threat that it might be followed by a condemnation of the minister and thus of the cabinet of which he was a member. By eliminating the *interpellation* and retaining only the parliamentary question, the Fifth Republic has drawn the sting from this procedure.

The British House of Commons sets aside the first period of each formal session for questions. These are commonly geared to topical issues and may range over the whole gamut of administration and policy (and thus serve as an important safeguard of civil liberties affected by governmental actions), and they are often framed in such a way as to embarrass the government. The French National Assembly, in contrast, reserves only Friday afternoons for questions, and the decision on whether and when they shall be debated is made by the Presidents' Conference, which is naturally dominated by the majority party and is less than enthusiastic about allowing ticklish issues to be raised at inconvenient moments. Thus while opposition deputies' questions are generally answered in due course, it has often been long after the impact of the information would have had a political effect. For instance, questions on wine-growers' grievances in May 1963 were nearly all answered *after* a significant by-election had been held in that area, and even in May, June, October, and November 1965, a Socialist deputy complained that his questions on the same subject had not yet been answered.

In April 1970, the National Assembly tried out a new procedure called "oral questions of immediate interest" that is closer to question time in the House of Commons. These oral questions are still restricted to Friday afternoons and must be tabled by noon the Wednesday before. The premier, himself, made a point of answering the first question, but his unusual demonstration of newly required brevity was promptly challenged as an inadequate answer by the questioner who was then cut short after the two minutes allowed for his reply. While oral questions "with debate" allow the questioner fifteen minutes to half an hour to reply to the minister's statement, and those without debate permit a five-minute reply, neither has been used effectively to air significant general issues on the British pattern. It remains to be seen whether the new procedure will become a useful means of keeping the government alert to public grievances and whether the customary verbosity of French deputies can be tailored to the new specifications.

Votes of confidence and censure

There are two occasions when the premier must seek a vote of confidence: once on his program when first appointed, and a few months later on his general policy. The government may also make the passage of a bill a matter of confidence; if so, the bill passes unless a censure motion is filed by one-tenth of the deputies within twenty-four hours and an absolute majority of the deputies (i.e., over 241) vote in support of censure. Opposition members can also introduce a motion of censure if one-tenth of the deputies sign it; after forty-eight hours it can be debated and voted on. Such a motion also requires an absolute majority of votes to pass. Signatories to a motion of censure are prohibited from proposing another in the same session unless in response to a government call for confidence on a bill.

Twenty votes of confidence and of censure took place in the Assembly between January 1959 and April 1968. Seven of these were normal votes of confidence; six were votes of censure following requests for confidence; seven were opposition calls for censure.[1] Only one of these votes was passed, that of October 1962 on the use of a referendum to introduce direct election of the president. The government then resigned, the referendum issue was approved, new elections were called, and Pompidou returned as premier with a stronger Gaullist majority than ever.

There is a basic difficulty in coupling strong opposition to a policy with the necessity of voting to overthrow the government, thereby causing new elections. Had the government permitted the chamber to vote on declarations of policy it made on its own initiative, the sentiment of the parties would have become easily apparent and the public alerted to the issue. But as early as 1958, such votes were forbidden. Debré even tried to prevent debates on such statements, and on those the government permitted, the process was too dull to elicit interest inside or outside the chamber. Pompidou permitted debate but no votes on his six declarations of policy, and in June 1962 the infuriated opposition walked out of the chamber in protest at being prevented from voting on the government's European policy.

It is thus apparent that the government can and usually does prevent a vote on its policies, apart from one that threatens its existence. It is only in the legislative process that the chamber is free to accept or reject government proposals, and it is in this sphere that the reform of procedures has been most satisfactory.

THE ASSEMBLY AS LEGISLATOR

While the Assembly has lost its former power of legislative self-determination, the new limits under which it operates have, in practice, made it a more efficient legislative body. The government can pass into law within a reasonable time the measures it wishes, and yet there is opportunity for criticism both in committee and on the floor of the chamber. By curbing the old flood of minor bills and those introduced by individual deputies, there is more chance to concentrate on important measures. The abuses of the legislative process through arbitrary or inefficient action by the government often overshadow the merits of the law-making system, but it has, in fact, brought into being a balance between executive and legislature that bears comparison with that in the House of Commons.

---

[1] Three of the opposition calls were concerned with agricultural policy, one with Algeria, one constitutional, one on the withdrawal from NATO, and one on introducing commercial advertising on television.

The background against which the new legislative balance was established was one of wholesale introduction of minor and major measures. There had also been endless conscientious consideration and sometimes drastic redrafting by committee *rapporteurs* of bills that might not even be debated on the floor. Moreover, major difficulties were experienced by cabinets in their effort to get vital legislation passed without wrecking amendments, leading all too often to the essential use of emergency procedures or, still more serious, to the downfall of the government. Thus legislative omnipotence often led to legislative incompetence and even impotence.

To curb these faults, parliament's legislative functions are now circumscribed by two major limitations: it cannot propose higher expenditures (a provision that American presidents would welcome!) or reduce revenue; and it can only legislate on matters that are specifically designated. The constitution differentiates between the "domain of law," to which parliament is restricted, and the "domain of regulations," within which parliament cannot interfere with the rules made by the government. The "domain of law" covers three fields: organic laws specified in the constitution, such as the budget; specific areas in which parliament may legislate in detail (through what are called "rules"), such as civil liberties, the electoral system, nationalization and denationalization of industries; and subjects like education, social security, and national defense, on which parliament can only deal with "fundamental principles." The "domain of regulations" covers everything else, but much of this falls into the sphere of minor bills such as those that once cluttered the legislative timetable.

The boundary between the two "domains" is guarded by the Constitutional Council, which, in practice, has tended to interpret the scope of parliamentary action in such a way as to give it more impact and meaning. Thus the council has insisted that in the areas where parliament can lay down rules, these must be important (e.g., it can determine qualifications for a proxy vote but must leave administrative procedures for claiming the proxy to the government). It has also insisted that where parliament can only lay down "fundamental principles," these may encompass such specific provisions as free choice of doctors under the medical-welfare scheme and that the administrative provisions for implementing "principles" must carry through their intention (e.g., social security benefits must be at an adequate level). The Council of State, which is the government's adviser on the drafting of measures, also has an influence in maintaining the boundary between the "domains" since, in its judicial capacity (see Chapter 7, Section 4), it can annul a decree on a subject it holds to be in the sphere of law. The government must also seek, although it is not bound by, the advice of the Council of State in acting in the "domain of regulations" if the effect is to override a law passed prior to the Fifth Republic; if the law was passed under the Fifth Republic, the regulation overriding it must secure the consent of the Constitutional Council. While parliament cannot refer a decree to the council for a ruling, its members can challenge it in the judicial section of the Council of State. Thus the government must also obey some limits, although the scales are tilted in its favor.

In the introduction of bills, the government has priority, and the number of private members' bills (i.e., introduced by an individual deputy) has dropped sharply from pre–Fifth Republic days. Sometimes the latter inspire government bills; not infrequently private members' bills still reflect local interests, such as legalizing cock-fighting, a favorite plea from the north. Favoritism toward bills proposed by UNR deputies has been charged by opposition parties, and not unfairly. But compared to British practice there is a fair amount of attention to private members' bills.

The committees

The committee stage is where the most obvious changes in form have been made. The nineteen specialized committees of the Fourth Republic, although proportionately representative of party strength, were dominated by special interests. Bills were often completely reshaped in committee, and, if they emerged, they were piloted through the chamber not by their author, whether deputy or government, but by the committee's *rapporteur*. To ensure that its measures are not obstructed by a committee, the government now has power to call up a measure to the floor (a procedure well beyond the power of the American executive and demanding greater than a simple majority of the relevant American chamber). Measures are usually thoroughly examined in committee stage, however, and the committee may insert amendments, although the chamber always debates the government's draft (but private members' bills on the committee draft).

In place of the nineteen specialist committees, the Assembly now has only six standing committees, to which members are allotted by proportional representation. Debré's preference was for thirty-member special *ad hoc* committees, but they proved too responsive to special interests to the government's discomfiture. Moreover, persistent absenteeism has tended to reduce the standing committees to a reasonable size of interested members, who are less susceptible to pressure groups.

The most serious criticisms of the legislative procedure result not from the new forms but from the government's abuse of its powers. Its management of the timetable has been exercised erratically, with relatively little business at the start of the sessions and overwhelming pressures toward the end. Moreover, far too often it demands a "package vote" on a bill (permitted under Article 44, paragraph 3), which means that controversial clauses cannot be singled out for amendment or exclusion since the measure must be voted as a whole. This practice, used often on the budget and on measures affecting agriculture, saves deputies in the majority party from embarrassing decisions over controversial sections, but it naturally infuriates the opposition.

3   THE SENATE

In social and political composition the Senate differs strikingly from the Assembly. With one-third of its members selected every three years for nine year terms by electoral colleges composed largely of local councilors, it is not surprising that it contains many more farmers and businessmen, fewer from the professions, and fewer still from among workers, clerks, and elementary school teachers than does the Assembly. It has remained the home of the Gaullists' political opponents from the traditional sector.

In determining the Senate's powers and competence, the framers of the Fifth Republic constitution had sought to prevent both the excessive power of the second chamber in the Third Republic and its impotence in the Fourth Republic; but above all they sought to facilitate the government's control of the legislative process. The Senate was provided with coordinate legislative power, in the expectation that it would work with the government to control an unruly Assembly. In practice, however, it has been the Assembly, with its Gaullist party majority, that supports the government, and it is the Senate that uses the opportunities available for reviewing and criticizing govern

ment measures. In either case, the government's position is strong, for it controls the *navette* (shuttle) of disputed bills between the two houses.

Should the government dislike a bill that goes to *navette*, it can simply keep it off the agenda or let the *navette* go on endlessly. If it so wishes, the government can take the following actions after the second reading of a bill (after one, if declared urgent): set up a conference committee of seven members from each house (in practice fourteen, since each member has a substitute who can speak but not vote unless the member is absent); if the committee reaches agreement, the government can submit it to parliament with such amendments as it approves; if the government disagrees with the committee's draft, it may ask the Assembly to make the decision. In case the government finds neither chamber compliant, it has the ultimate power of imposing its own will through a package vote coupled with a vote of confidence.

On the whole the conference procedure has worked well as long as the issue is not at the center of political controversy. Although the expectation was that the members of the com mittee chosen from each chamber would be proportionately representative of party strength, the Assembly drew heavily, if not exclusively, from the majority to counterbalance the strength of the opposition in the Senate. Nonetheless, compromises were often reached on nonsensitive matters. Even in controversial issues, when the Assembly was bound to get its way, Senate advice has sometimes been accept-able on technical or legal issues. Indeed, the bias of the Senate has often appealed to property-minded Gaullist deputies, and sometimes an apparent struggle between the Assembly and Senate was in fact a division between the views of a relatively conservative parliament and a reformist government. But whatever the basis of disagreement, the government will ultimately get the measure it wants.

4 THE BUDGET

The budget traditionally dominated the French legislative timetable and created the greatest problems for the relatively weak ministries of the past. Half the votes of confidence under the Fourth Republic were called in the effort to secure the revenue essential for carrying on the business of government. These long, drawn-out budget struggles pushed all other matters into the background where they received far too little attention. Thus in addition to being highly inefficient, the budgetary process under the Fourth Republic made it difficult to cope with other pressing problems that required legislation.

The Fifth Republic has streamlined budgetary procedures by giving the Assembly only forty days in which to vote on the government's proposals; thereafter the budget goes automatically to the Senate for two weeks. Differences are debated in conference committee. But if parliament does not vote the budget within seventy days, the government may bring it into effect by ordinance. Under any circumstances, the six-sevenths of the budget for "continuing services" must become law without change, and under Article 40 no deputy can propose increasing expenditures or lowering revenue in relation to the details of and total range of government budgetary proposals.

The net result of these provisions has been to make French budgetary procedures much more like those in Great Britain. The debates, often too rushed but still quite thorough, are used for detailed consideration of the policies and administration of ministries rather than for focusing on appropriations sought by particular interests (ex-servicemen, for example, still form a popular pressure group). Issues over which parliamentary questions have not elicited satisfactory answers are quite often brought up again in the budget hearing with more satisfactory results, since debate is less limited, the presence of the minister is assured, and a vote can be forced without resorting to the drastic procedure of censure. Amendments are proposed in both chambers and, not infrequently, with success, although the government can always insist on its own proposals. More effective are the informal behind-the-scenes negotiations or discussions in committee, where the government's prestige is not so much at stake as on the floor of the chamber.

As in the procedures for ordinary legislation, the inadequacies stem more from the government's abuse of its dominant position than from the system itself. Since transfers of credit from one ministry to another can be made without the finance committee's prior approval (a control introduced in 1956 but omitted from the Fifth Republic budgetary provisions), and since supplementals can be voted, detailed expenditures may end up quite differently from the amounts that were originally voted. Ministers also attach "riders" to the finance bill, much as deputies used to do, so as to take advantage of the simplified and rapid budgetary procedures. Thus by abusing its already very strong position, the government has not only assumed unnecessary expedients, but has also tended to discredit a constructive reform that, for the first time in France's history, both assures the passage of the budget each year before Christmas and a wide-ranging parliamentary scrutiny of government policies.

5

The French executive

The most striking feature of the Fifth Republic is the power and prestige of the president of the Republic. This is not only the dominant characteristic of the new regime, it also marks its sharpest contrast to the past.

The power of the executive has been a subject of perennial controversy in French politics. Generally speaking, the parties of the left have looked on a powerful executive as a threat to democratic institutions, while the parties of the right have seen in a strong executive the only hope for political order and authority. The constitution of the Fourth Republic represented a clear victory for the parties of the left, with authority concentrated in the National Assembly. The constitution of the Fifth Republic is oriented toward a powerful executive, including both the president, who like that of the United States is *not* responsible to the legislature, and the offices of the premier and ministry, which, as in the United Kingdom, *are* responsible to the legislature. But unlike British practice, the premier is *not* selected by the electorate (through returning his party with a majority in the House of Commons), nor by the Assembly, but by the president, who can also request his resignation at any moment.

The constitution of the Fifth Republic was intended, in Debré's view, to place the president in the position of an arbiter "to ensure the regular functioning of the public authorities" (Article 5). But the crisis situation in which the Fifth Republic came into being and de Gaulle's personality made such a role unrealistic. De Gaulle from the start envisaged himself as Rousseau's "guide" for France, who can iden-

tify the people's true, or general will (see Chapter 2, Section 4). He quickly assumed sole responsibility for foreign and military affairs, although there is no constitutional justification for excluding parliament from these areas. He moved steadily into the realm of decision-making in domestic affairs. Direct election of the president further sanctified his authority. Pompidou inherited in 1969 a wealth of precedents entrenching presidential dominance throughout the political structure, to which he, himself, as premier to de Gaulle, had greatly contributed.

Thus whatever the intention of the framers of the constitution, the balance between the dual executives is heavily weighted in favor of the president. The president can intervene directly in parliamentary organization and operations; he can appeal to the Constitutional Council if he feels that parliament has overstepped its constitutional boundaries. He has acquired the right of initiative in amending the constitution through the precedent of 1962 (which the Constitutional Council upheld once the referendum was over). Through Article 16, he can assume even wider emergency powers than the Weimar Republic possessed in its Article 48 (which Hitler used in coming to power). For while the president must consult with other organs of government before he uses Article 16, he is under no compulsion to follow their advice. With a guaranteed term of seven years, a centralized administration, and no federal division of powers, an acquiescent premier and ministry, and a curbed legislature, the French president possesses political powers that an American president might envy and that a British prime minister, regardless of the size of his majority, would never dream of using.

Why, one may ask, do the French, who have traditionally feared strong executive power, acquiesce in so substantial a concentration of authority in the hands of a single man? One explanation sometimes put forward is that since 1962, and more particularly since 1965 when the first direct election of the president took place, both the president and parliament embody that highest of all authority—popular sovereignty. In case of conflict between them, the president can appeal to the people through a referendum or call a new election; if parliament is dissolved, the new chambers are guaranteed a year of existence before another dissolution can take place. During that period parliament can, if it so desires, block government measures. Hence, say the proponents of the system, parliament, too, has a check on the president (although the outside observer may feel it takes rather a long and complex procedure to be effective). In practice, however, as we have seen, the adverse vote on the 1969 referendum led immediately to de Gaulle's resignation, thereby indicating that even France's most autocratic president had accepted the will of the people, expressed in a referendum, as an ultimate expression of popular sovereignty.

CONTRAST WITH THE PAST

How radically the position of the president has changed under the Fifth Republic is immediately apparent by contrasting it to the situation prior to 1958. Under the Third Republic the president of France had acted as something of a nonhereditary constitutional monarch. He was a dignified head of state, who could preside on ceremonial occasions, who stood above party, and who did not engage in partisan political activity. The rebuke given to Marshal MacMahon in 1877, and the forced resignation of President Millerand in 1924 for similar partisanship, were warnings enough against making independent decisions.

Such rebukes were seldom necessary. After the sad experience with Napoleon III, republicans were careful to see that no president should enjoy the prestige of popular election; and after the MacMahon crisis they took care to choose men who were colorless, reliably republican, and possessed of little popular appeal. Clemenceau's advice to Frenchmen to "vote for the most stupid" may have overstated the matter, but of all the presidents of the Third Republic only Poincaré could be considered a statesman of the first rank. Men of the prominence and ability of Clemenceau and Briand were regularly rejected.

Although the makers of the constitution of the Fourth Republic deliberately tried to reduce the power of the presidency, the office actually gained more power than it had had before and provided the president with considerably more opportunity to exert influence than has the British monarch. Whereas the British king ceased to attend cabinet meetings more than two centuries ago, the French president presided over the meetings of the Council of Ministers and had the right to participate in discussions (although he could not vote). This role was of some importance, since in practice the Council of Ministers discussed certain issues of policy instead of restricting itself to formal action, as it had under the Third Republic. Moreover, when for the first time records were made of these meetings, the president of the Republic (who was Vincent Auriol at that time) became their custodian. The president also had access to all important diplomatic papers, as was not always the case with his Third Republic predecessors.

1   THE FUNCTIONS OF THE PRESIDENT

Under the Fifth Republic, however, all these possibilities for exercising influence have been turned into positive sources of activity and power. The many formal offices the president holds have provided him with unparalleled opportunities for keeping himself informed on the course of policy in all public spheres and for directing it when he wishes to do so.

The most important of these formal functions is to preside over the Council of Ministers. In the first few years after de Gaulle succeeded to office in 1958, the Council of Ministers continued to act largely as a ratifying body for decisions reached jointly by the president and premier. As de Gaulle steadily increased the range of his decision-making, the council became a place where important issues were brought up for his ultimate verdict. But as de Gaulle disliked detailed administrative work, it was the premier's office, especially under Pompidou, that was responsible for reports and proposals on most subjects. These documents were then summarized along with ministerial proposals for de Gaulle's final consideration.

This rather lofty use of authority has now given way under Pompidou to more direct and personal supervision of all the business of government except a small domain in economic and social affairs that is left to the premier. Council meetings are businesslike and restricted to ministers directly concerned with matters under discussion. Decisions are made at the Elysée (presidential) Palace either in council or in private meetings. Where once de Gaulle had reigned, Pompidou now governs, in a style far closer to that of the American system than to that of the British.

Unlike American presidential nominations of top administrative personnel, which must be ratified by the Senate, the French president's power of appointment is very wide and needs no formal ratification. Whereas all French presidents have had a role in proposing premiers, only in the Fifth Republic has the president alone determined who the premier shall be. The acquiescence of the chambers in the leadership of Michel Debré, himself a parliamentarian and a believer in a "reformed" but functioning parliamentary system, was not surprising, particularly in the tense period succeeding 1958. But the measure of the chambers' docility was their acceptance of Pompidou (who had never been in parliament or even a member of a political party) and, even more striking, of Couve de Murville in 1968 after Pompidou's peremptory dismissal. (Technically a premier must be persuaded to tender his

resignation.) In comparison, Jacques Chaban-Delmas had had long experience as a minister before becoming Pompidou's first premier and had proved himself a skilled parliamentary conciliator.

The president also makes appointments to all state civilian and military posts, although the sheer magnitude of this task means that he must draw nominations from the premier and the Council of Ministers. The constitution specifically provided that the president appoint the members of the High Council of the Judiciary (a role shared under the Fourth Republic with the National Assembly, see Chapter 7, Section 2) as well as preside over it. The president also has the right of pardon, although a pardon is supposed to have the countersignature of the Minister of Justice.

All decrees passed by the Council of Ministers must be signed by the president to become valid, a further check on the parliamentary executive; so also must all laws, within fifteen days of being passed. It is conceivable that the president might refuse to sign a law, thereby exercising a "pocket veto," but as long as the Gaullist majority controls the Assembly, there will be no need for such tactics.

The roles most congenial to de Gaulle were the conduct of foreign affairs and command of the armed forces. The president is empowered to conduct international negotiations and to shape and sign treaties—roles into which de Gaulle entered with gusto and apparently without being restrained by the constitutional requirement that such actions should be countersigned by the premier. Pompidou has assumed no less decisive postures in foreign relations and has maintained a continuity of Gaullist policies, but without his predecessor's rhetoric.

THE PUBLIC PERSONALITY
OF THE PRESIDENT

In the end, however, the influence of the president, like that of any other chief executive in a nondictatorial state, rests not solely on his constitutional powers but on his ability to convince the country, or at least a sizeable proportion of its citizens, that he is acting in their best interests. De Gaulle possessed an unchallengeable position in this regard in the early years of the Fifth Republic, when finding a solution to the running sore of the Algerian civil war dominated all other issues. Aloof, magisterial, even ritualistic, de Gaulle's intense sense of destiny, and his identification of himself with France, were all-pervasive. As France returned to normal, his heroics became slightly boring. Even in 1965 his mystique was somewhat faded; in the crisis of 1968 it reasserted itself only after his lightning trip to the army in Germany and announcement of an election. In 1969, it was said that nothing became him so well as the speed and dignity with which he relinquished office. His shadow lingered for months after his retirement, but a year later the majority of Frenchmen maintained that although they were sorry de Gaulle had left office, they did not want him back.

The smoothness of the successions in 1969 was remarkable. Alain Poher, as president of the Senate, became acting president of the Republic and moved into the Elysée Palace. A grassroots politician from the center, Poher was the exact opposite of de Gaulle in bearing and attitudes. He promptly attacked the restrictions and inefficiency of the state-controlled radio and television, talked gravely about the abuses of power by the Gaullist regime, and acquired a remarkable, if temporary, popularity that carried him by a narrow margin into the second ballot for the presidency.

President Georges Pompidou is a different person from Premier Pompidou, who served under General Charles de Gaulle from 1962 to 1968, a longer period than that of any other French chief minister except Louis XIV's Colbert. Pompidou's peasant background in the Auvergne in central France, his brilliant academic record in literature and political science, his success as a stimulating teacher and as a constitutional lawyer in the civil service, his banking experience as chief director of the Rothschild family bank, and his appreciation of and familiarity with the arts and their practitioners have contributed to his durability as well as to his successful performance in both roles. But where Premier Pompidou was the perfect chief of staff, loyal and self-effacing until the grueling ordeal of the crisis of 1968, President Pompidou is the man who emerged

from that ordeal firmly in control of the Gaullist political forces, trusted by the unions as a tough but straightforward negotiator, and shrewd in his political judgments and leadership. Thus it was he who persuaded de Gaulle to give up his plan for a referendum and instead to call an election in 1968, and it was he who piloted the UDR to its impressive victory. In office as president, Pompidou has mingled Gaullist orthodoxy with decisive and well-timed moves like the devaluation of the franc while most Frenchmen were on holiday in August 1969. He has continued to be meticulous in his mastery of administrative and economic detail, using his phenomenal memory to supervise almost every aspect of policy. He has also shown flexibility in his relations with the press and television. It is less sure whether that same flexibility and some imaginative behavior will mark his relations with antagonistic groups like university students, small shopkeepers, and angry peasants, as well as his attitudes toward overcentralization and a too rigid social structure. Yet in the long run—and his term of office extends to 1976—it may well be his approach to these pressing issues that will prove most decisive for France in the seventies.

THE STAFF OF THE PRESIDENT

The effectiveness of all executive work is determined in large measure by the efficiency of the organization and the personnel that support the making and execution of decisions. De Gaulle's military background and experience, coupled with his wide-ranging concern for all aspects of public policy, domestic as well as foreign, led to a dramatic expansion of the presidential staff, which Pompidou has continued. Indeed, there has developed an administrative structure operating on behalf of the president that is parallel to and has sometimes been competitive with those of the government secretariat and of the civil service. Americans familiar with the White House organization find the French president's staff similar in many ways, although still much smaller.

The expansion of the presidential staff amply documents the revolution that has taken place in the presidential role. President Auriol's

Elysée staff in 1953 included only two political counselors—one prepared his papers for the relatively infrequent meetings of the Council of Ministers, and the other handled relations with the press—and twenty-one officers of professional rank. The moment de Gaulle assumed office in 1958, he appointed seventeen political counselors, of whom four were assigned to Community affairs. This latter group, enlarged by 1964 and moved to offices outside the Elysée Palace, has concentrated on France's relations with the former French-African territories.

De Gaulle's dislike of detailed administrative work meant that his staff mainly summarized reports, watched the progress of policy matters in which he was particularly interested, and developed position papers on pressing policy issues and on matters on which de Gaulle found ministerial action too slow. Pompidou, in contrast, remains his own chief of staff with a wealth of experience behind him in

effective delegation of work without losing ultimate control of the total picture in each area of concern.

The potential, and occasionally real, clash in early days between presidential staff and high civil servants was neutralized, and then virtually eliminated, by de Gaulle's and now Pompidou's practice of drawing presidential aides from among the civil servants themselves, either on a temporary or permanent basis. Only ten out of the seventeen political counselors in 1958 were high civil servants; by 1964, seventeen of the twenty top aides were. Virtually all now are.

The presidential staff has expanded not only in numbers but in influence. At the same time it has become closely intermeshed in attitudes and personnel with the higher civil service of the ministries. The end result has been to lessen administrative rivalries but, at the same time, to make and keep the presidency the dominant force throughout the administration.

2   THE PREMIER

From being the creature of the National Assembly of the Fourth Republic, subject to instant dismissal through the withdrawal of essential votes, the premier [1] in France has become the creature of the president of the Fifth Republic. This was certainly not the intention of the framer of the constitution of the Fifth Republic, Michel Debré, who became the Republic's first premier. Debré managed to combine an impressive loyalty to de Gaulle with an insistence on the rights (however circumscribed) of parliament and of himself as premier. He also fulfilled the more traditional role of the French premier, cajoling, threatening, and ultimately driving his program through the chambers. Pompidou's use of his office as premier was less spectacular, but this was largely because the Assembly possessed such a substantial Gaullist contingent after the election of

1962 that similar tactics could be replaced by more conciliatory ones carried on largely behind the scenes. Couve de Murville inherited an even larger Gaullist majority, which carried over to Chaban-Delmas. Thus while the person of the premier in the Fifth Republic is determined by the will of the president, the actual functioning of the office has been shaped by the development of a Gaullist majority in the National Assembly.

It is not new for the role of the French premier to be determined by the system within which he is working. Under the Third Republic, if anyone challenged the premier's status as *primus inter pares*, it was to insist that he was not even *primus*. His cabinet was likely to include several men not only of equal but of greater political stature, including the heads of other political parties and former premiers. Moreover, there was nothing to correspond to the British cabinet's loyalty to a party leader. The premier lacked the prestige that an American president and a British prime minister

[1] According to strict terminology, under the Fifth Republic the premier is prime minister; the older term *premier* has been retained, however, to avoid confusion with the British prime minister.

enjoy because, in contrast to them, he had not been elected to this office by the people and thus did not enjoy a popular mandate.

Those who drafted the constitution of the Fourth Republic intended to make the premier a real leader on the pattern of the British prime minister—an innovation, indeed. Formerly, the ministers had sent their bills directly to the Assembly; now they had to be signed by the premier before they could be presented. Under the Third Republic, ministers might call votes of confidence on their own initiative; now such votes could be called only by the premier, after full cabinet discussion. But while the drafters of the constitution of the Fourth Republic clearly hoped that these powers would give the premier genuine authority and prestige, the fact that they were exercised jointly with others (that is, with the appropriate minister or, in the case of high appointments, with the president), combined with the existence of the multiparty system, largely undercut this hope. Thus, except in the rare case of Mendès-France, it was the conciliators like Henri Queuille, René Pleven, and Antoine Pinay who were the most successful premiers, rather than dynamic individuals with programs of their own.

The same is true in the Fifth Republic but for a very different reason: the premier must work with a president who is far more powerful than himself. According to the constitution, the premier chooses his own ministers, formulates governmental policy in conjunction with them, presents it to the Assembly, or, in case the response is slow, carries it out through the government's independent powers (especially in finance). In practice, however, his activity has been limited to a joint formulation of policy with the president (in which the premier has played an increasingly subordinate role) and to managing the legislature so that it will accept the government's program.

THE PUBLIC PERSONALITY OF THE PREMIER

The premier must thus operate in a variety of different situations. He must satisfy the president, conciliate and manage the Assembly, work with a group of ministers, whom in prac-

tice, although not in theory, he chooses in conjunction with the president. When possible, he must also carve out an area of administration for his own domain. His success in combining effectively so many roles depends largely on his personality and skill.

The two most experienced parliamentarians to hold the office during the Fifth Republic have been Michel Debré and Jacques Chaban-Delmas. Debré's experience and tactics have already been described. Chaban-Delmas has also held many parliamentary offices. Minister several times during the Fourth Republic, he had been president of the National Assembly throughout the lifetime of the Fifth Republic until Pompidou chose him as his first premier. He fits perfectly Pompidou's description of the kind of man he wanted as premier: "A liberal personality, capable in his person of underlining my desire for national reconciliation." Although he had served as a Radical Socialist minister in the Fourth Republic, Chaban-Delmas is a genuine Gaullist, who had helped to prepare the way for de Gaulle's return to power in May 1958. Mayor of Bordeaux for twenty-four years, he demonstrated the strength of his support when challenged by Servan-Schreiber in the by-election in his constituency in September 1970. In the Assembly he is respected as a conciliator who gets on well with non-Gaullists as well as Gaullists.

Neither Pompidou nor Couve de Murville had had parliamentary experience before they became premier. But, as we have seen, Pompidou learned quickly, proved conciliatory in his relations with the Assembly, acquired a strong, and ultimately dominant position within the UNR-UDR, and handily won a seat in the Assembly on the first ballot in 1967. Couve de Murville, in contrast, a capable and experienced high civil servant who had served as de Gaulle's minister of Foreign Affairs throughout much of the Fifth Republic, was defeated in his first effort to win a parliamentary seat and showed little aptitude for the premiership he held so briefly from mid-July 1968 until Pompidou became president in 1969. Thus, as can be expected, the office of premier calls for genuine parliamentary skills. But to combine effective management of the cabinet and the Assembly with the necessary subservience to the president, who possesses the overriding power, calls for an almost superhuman combination of talents, so far exhibited most successfully by Pompidou himself.

THE PREMIER AND THE MINISTRY

By placing the choice of the premier in the hands of the president, the framers of the constitution of the Fifth Republic tried to underline the distinction between executive and legislature, but, as indicated above, parliamentary experience and tactics are clearly needed for effective execution of the premier's Assembly tasks. The same has proved true for the ministers. The constitution states that if he becomes a minister, a deputy must resign his seat for the legislative session (thereby handing it over to the substitute who runs on the same ticket with him). In the early days of the Fifth Republic, rather than coming from the Assembly, about one-third of the ministers were drawn from the high civil service, including the holders of such important "political" posts as Finance, Defense, Foreign Affairs, and Interior. But increasingly it was demonstrated that such persons carried very little weight in the Assembly and were thus handicapped in putting forward effectively the claims of their ministries. In 1967, all but two members of the ministry had been candidates in the previous election. Chaban-Delmas' ministry has an even stronger parliamentary flavor, with thirty-eight of its thirty-nine members current or former deputies, and one a senator. And while, as in previous cabinets, a number of these ministers or secretaries of state had formerly been high civil servants, this technocratic component has also shrunk.

The fact that deputies must resign their seats for the legislative session if they become ministers is one radical departure from British parliamentary procedure, where the constant interchanges in the body of the House of Commons are of the essence of the system. In further contrast, the French ministry is not chosen exclusively from the majority, despite the fact that for the first time in its parliamentary history, the Assembly now includes one. On the contrary, the practice of coalition ministries, made necessary by the multiparty fragmenta-

tion in the Third and Fourth Republics, has been carried on in the Fifth Republic. Indeed, in direct proportion to their voting strength in the Assembly, the centrists received the largest number of government posts under Chaban-Delmas and the Independent Republicans the next largest. The UDR, with 77.8 percent of the deputies, obtained only 71.6 percent of the cabinet posts and mourned the loss of six key ministries—Finance, Justice, Foreign Affairs, Interior, Agriculture, and Labor—handed over to others. The Gaullist right wing received many more posts than did the party's more liberal members, a fact resented by the latter. While some who had been negative on the 1969 referendum were included in the ministry, it was not surprising that no one who had actively opposed Pompidou in his presidential campaign secured a place.

In a normal cabinet, most members are in charge of a ministry. Others, the Ministers of State, have specific functions (for defense, cultural affairs, and relations with parliament under Chaban-Delmas, all held by Gaullists) in which they are assisted by small staffs. The third group, the Secretaries of State, correspond to American undersecretaries but, unlike them, participate in the working sessions of the cabinet.

The mixture of Gaullists and non-Gaullists in the cabinet has not been easy to guide harmoniously. In October 1969, the Gaullist Minister of Housing and Public Works made a public attack on Finance Minister Valéry Giscard d'Estaing for the formerly wavering policies of his wing of the RI. Moreover, it was not easy to convince Gaullists, with a primary allegiance to de Gaulle himself, that Pompidou and Chaban-Delmas were furthering the pure doctrines of Gaullism, particularly when the latter's policy statements have attacked the "blocks" in French society for whose continuation Gaullism could hardly avoid responsibility. With a team consisting largely of former ministers (among them an inflexible Gaullist, Michel Debré, as Minister of Defense), Chaban-Delmas has sometimes confronted problems akin to those of premiers in the Fourth Republic whose ministers seemed more entrenched than themselves. As long as the premier maintains the support of the president, however (which, in practice, means as long as he remains in office), he has the ultimate authority of the president behind him.

Sessions of the Council of the Cabinet, the name given to the meetings of the government that are held under the chairmanship of the premier, as contrasted to the Council of Ministers, which meets with the president in the chair, tend to concentrate on tactics rather than on policy decisions, particularly since it is apparent that the final word will be Pompidou's. Indeed, in contrast to the Third and, to a lesser degree, the Fourth Republic, the Council of Ministers has been the dominant decision-making body throughout the Fifth Republic, and the Council of the Cabinet has been a preparatory, rather than a policymaking organ.

THE GOVERNMENT SECRETARIAT

Adequate and efficient staff work is essential to effective government. But until the Fourth Republic, informality and *ad hoc* decisions and organization were characteristic of the operations of both the Council of Ministers and the cabinet. Under the Fourth Republic the embryonic secretariat established in 1935 was extended and minutes of council meetings were taken. In the Fifth Republic, a much more extensive expansion has taken place. The secretary general of the government, who has been the head of the secretariat since 1947, and his staff prepare and circulate the agenda of the Council of Ministers, check the preparation of bills and administrative regulations, prepare the minutes for the president, and report on decisions and their implementation.

The Secretariat General also performs something of a general coordinating role. The Planning Commissariat, the Atomic Energy Commissariat, and the offices of the Delegates General for scientific research and the development of the Paris region are associated, though somewhat indirectly, with the Secretariat General. Also attached, but with its own director general, is the division responsible for the management of the civil service. The School of National Administration (*École Nationale d'Administration*) and the Center for Advanced Administrative Study (*Centre des Hautes Études Administratives*) are also linked, but more tenuously, to the secretariat.

The Secretariat General, whose staff has changed little over the past years, forms the nucleus of the much larger office of the premier, coordinating a considerable part of its staff and assuming major responsibilities for some of its most important functions, like preparing for the premier's relations with parliament. That it has been paralleled by the secretariat of the president during the Fifth Republic has somewhat diminished the importance of its role in checking on and coordinating policies and providing the ultimate stamp of administrative approval. Sometimes, indeed, the two secretariats have supported opposing policies, but the president has the final word.

THE PREMIER AND THE ASSEMBLY

The constitution of the Fifth Republic strongly tilted the balance of power away from the legislature and in favor of the government. Thus, however diminished the importance of the premier vis-à-vis the president, there is no doubt that the premier and his government have become a great deal stronger than ever before in their relations with the Assembly.

Among the new rights accorded to the government by the Fifth Republic, as we have seen, are the right to the priority of government bills in the parliamentary timetable, the right to propose amendments to bills, and the right to open a general debate on a measure in either chamber. Thus deputies now hear the government's case on a bill before the *rapporteur* of the relevant committee can present his criticisms, and the debate takes place on the government's text, not on the text that emerges from committee. Moreover, the government has the right to reject amendments proposed from the floor after the committee stage and also to force the chamber to vote either on particular clauses of the bill or on the bill as a whole. The government can also spur a decision on a bill over which there is disagreement between the Senate and the Assembly. What the government cannot do, however, is to secure the passage of a bill (unless it is on finance) that the Assembly refuses to approve.

In finance the government has been given special powers to avoid the not uncommon situation of the past, that is, having the deadline for the budget go by before it was voted. As described above, the constitution provides a time limit for budgetary debates at the end of which the government can impose the budget by decree power if the Assembly has not voted it. The Fifth Republic also enforces the provision that deputies cannot propose measures involving increases in expenditures or decreases in revenue.

But more significant than the constitutional procedures that have strengthened the hands of the government is the fact that it has enjoyed majority support in the Assembly for its crucial policies—except over the direct election of the president, where the opposition clearly misread the temper of the public. As long as the Gaullists maintain a cohesive majority in the chamber, or the parties of the opposition fail to provide a unified front that offers a credible alternative, the premier and his ministers will be able to ensure the acceptance of the president's policies. Should the Gaullist majority split between its hardline and its liberal wings, however, and a new configuration of voting appear that shifts toward the center, the task of managing the Assembly would become a great deal more difficult. Moreover, the problems implicit in the existence of the dual executive would become greatly magnified.

THE PREMIER AND THE PRESIDENT

The accession of Pompidou to the office of president ushered in a new day in French politics. On the one hand, it could be said that his election is the first in which direct election received a fair trial as a means of legitimizing the vast powers of that office. Although de Gaulle was forced in 1965 into a more personal campaign than he had planned, it was almost inconceivable that he would be defeated. In 1969, the odds were not so decisively on Pompidou's side. Indeed, one of his genuine handicaps is that his victory in the second ballot was assured by the abstention of Communist voters.

Pompidou faces a still more serious problem: how to carry through the sometimes painful policies that France needs to break its logjams in so many fields and still maintain the cohesion of the broad spectrum of opinions that are to be found within the UDR. By dropping Faure, for example, from direction of the Ministry of Education, Pompidou incurred antagonism from the more liberal wing of the party; should his foreign policies run counter to Debré at the Ministry of Defense, he would have a serious threat from the right. Since Pompidou is the ultimate maker of policy, he inevitably is affected directly by any substantial split in the allegiance of the Gaullists.

The crucial link between presidential policymaking and Assembly support is the premier. Despite his lack of guaranteed tenure of office, the premier has a decisive role vis-à-vis the president if the Assembly becomes unruly. This possibility raises a basic question regarding the UDR: From whence comes its leadership? Pompidou clearly assumed such leadership during the 1968 crisis; he was just as clearly the party's candidate for president. On assuming that office, however, Pompidou announced that he would no longer belong to a party. But can a president whose ultimate support comes from a political party hand over its leadership to someone else? And if he does so, or if at least he depends on the skills of the other half of the dual executive to manage the key area of the legislature, can the president maintain his ultimate authority? In other words, can Pompidou find someone who will fit as comfortably together with him as he himself appears to have done with de Gaulle, particularly when Pompidou obviously takes a more detailed interest in the formulation and execution of policies in almost all fields than did de Gaulle? These are the overriding questions for the working of the dual executive in the seventies.

6

The French administration: national and local

1   THE CHARACTER OF THE FRENCH ADMINISTRATION

Despite the frequent changes of government in the past and the vagaries of the French parliamentary system, France has long exhibited a basic stability through its highly centralized administration, which, since the days of Napoleon, has dealt efficiently and, on the whole, justly with the manifold problems of public concern. The bureaucracy has reflected in its stratified, elitist structure many characteristics of French society: its dependence on recognized leadership as opposed to free-acting voluntarism, its prizing of theoretical and legal training, its relative rigidity. Far more of a technocracy than the British or American administrative structures, the French administration has long been regarded outside as well as inside France as a model of its kind. Yet in these days of stabilized executive leadership and, even more, of accelerated industrialism in France, it may be that the virtues of the French administration are at least in part turning into faults. In the absence of a steady stream of new talent from more varied strata of society, and by absorbing rather than encouraging locally inspired regional agencies, the bureaucracy remains somewhat remote from the ferment affecting France and stands as a bulwark of the overcentralization that has been one of the chief complaints of those seeking change throughout all of French life.

In one way the increased freedom of the executive from legislative supervision and control in the Fifth Republic has given the administration additional scope for action. Projects that had been shelved in the past because of the cabinet crises have been enacted. Newly extended rulemaking powers have been utilized for some major as well as minor matters. The reform of the court system (see Chapter 7, Section 3) and substantial changes in the social security system were outlined in detail by government technicians and brought into effect without ever going to the legislature. For this reason the Fifth Republic is often called "a civil service" or "administrative" state, or a "technocracy" or "enarchy" because of the pervasiveness of ENA graduates (see Section 4).

On the other hand, the civil service no longer finds itself in the position of being the major, or even the only, operating part of government, as happened at times in the Third and Fourth Republics. Overall policymaking is firmly in the hands of the president. Ministers in some areas are changed frequently, and in some cases even more frequently than used to be the case in earlier regimes when the tenure of some ministers was far longer than that of any particular cabinet. There is considerable in-fighting between ministries, and a great deal of executive shifting of bureaus from one ministry to another.

The civil service still complains of difficulties

in persuading politicians to support administrative projects and of lack of coordination between different branches of the service. What the administration most fears, however, is overlapping jurisdictions that threaten the cozy certainties of customary procedures and actions. Where American administrations may set up two or three competitive agencies, thereby entailing waste but sometimes producing creative ideas for change, the French shun such experimentation and tend instead to call for some superior body to provide still further centralization.

The major problem caused by the French administrative system, therefore, is that it tends to inhibit the changes needed by an increasingly mobile society. As we have seen with the education system, which parallels in many respects the characteristics of the administrative system, it is one thing for a new policy to be enunciated at the top and quite a different matter to have it permeate the structure. The gap between those who enunciate policy and those who are affected by it is commonly too wide for effective and creative interaction.

This is not to say that France is being governed without reference to special interests and pressure groups. Under the Third and Fourth Republics the establishment of numerous consultative committees was aimed at providing effective channels of influence for representative groups seeking special privileges and opportunities. So long as political parties were major factors in determining policy, interest groups divided their attention between these parties and the administration. As political parties and parliament became less important under the Fifth Republic, the interaction of pressure groups with the administration has become more pervasive.

Such efforts to influence governmental action hardly contribute to the genuine public interest, nor does the pressure exercised directly on administrative bureaus by particular groups that have not gone through the filter of a nationally organized political party. The tendency seems to be to pit special groups—farmers, railroad workers, even postal employees—against an administration that believes more in a "right answer" for every problem than in a British-type of compromise. In an expanding and prosperous economy, potential conflict—evidenced by angry protests, slowdowns, and strikes—tends to be neutralized, although, as we have seen, post-Algerian France has had many such outbursts. But all too often, particularly under Pompidou, the reaction to protest has been rigidity, even repression, rather than creativity.

THE PUBLIC SECTOR

The tasks placed on the French administration, both traditionally and now, have a strong collectivist flavor that helps to explain its pervasiveness. The state-wide administrative institutions that Napoleon consolidated have always undertaken certain social and economic activities aimed at national development. The common French expectation that the state mechanisms will provide and direct effective action on behalf of the public has been a powerful psychological factor in the expansion of the public sector into many economic and social areas, which in the United States are in private hands. To this French cultural characteristic was added during the periods of the Popular Front (1936–37) and the Liberation (1944–45) a strong socialist impulse that led to widespread nationalization projects. Still more distinctive than its nationalization and social welfare programs have been the character and impact of French national planning since World War II.

France, like some other Continental countries, has a number of long-established state monopolies: for example, the manufacture and sale of tobacco and matches. The state controls the production and distribution of fuel and power—electricity, gas, coal, and atomic energy—and has substantial interests in oil. The national government holds a dominant position in transportation—railroads, most airlines, and two shipping companies—but private interests compete both in air and sea transport as well as control most of the road transport. The state also engages in manufacturing: 45 percent of the aerospace industry is nationalized, while 55 percent is privately owned. The state owns about one-third of the motor industry (which was partly nationalized because of the Renault plant's collaborationist activities with the Nazis), naval shipyards, some subsidiary production of refrigerators, tractors, and motorcycles, and the production of most fertilizers. The state also controls agencies with 60 percent of all bank deposits and 40 percent of all insurance premiums.

Much of this control developed by spurts rather than systematically. Under the Third Republic, state intervention was usually prompted by the economic difficulties of private enterprise. The persistent deficits of the railroads, for example, led to their unification in 1937 under a *société d'économie mixte*, in which the government owned 51 percent of the capital. Broadcasting began in 1922 as a public enterprise, and television is also now a government monopoly. The manufacture of planes for maritime aviation was placed under a mixed corporation in 1933; in 1936 it was merged with the production for civil aviation under semiautonomous mixed companies.

France's postwar extensions of nationalization were more empirical than the British and also more varied. Although the British went further in nationalizing inland transport, they have nothing comparable to France's partial nationalization of credit and insurance. On the other hand, British public ownership is more monolithic than is the French—that is, in Great Britain nationalization commonly extends throughout a particular field, whereas in France it tends to be limited, except in coal mining, gas, and electricity, to the largest companies in that field. A further difference is that the punitive motive for nationalization, which led the French state to take over the Renault plants, the Gnôme et Rhône Airplane Motor Company, and collaborationist newspapers, did not exist at all in Great Britain. Finally, nationalization ceased in France after the airlines, the two largest maritime shipping companies, and the Paris transport system were brought under public control early in 1948. The bill to nationalize the steel industry was never brought to a vote.

Although it proved difficult at first to integrate private enterprise and the expanded public sector of the economy (which totaled about 20 percent of France's industrialized capacity, probably the highest percentage of any democratic country), the ultimate effect has been good. Massive investment in the public sector coupled with its early sloughing off of political influences have made it a pacesetter in modernization and productivity for the whole economy. Moreover, since French business and commerce have never been as hostile to government activities as is still true in parts of the American economy, a general spirit of cooperation has developed between public and private activities in the economy. Labor tends to be suspicious of both, although it turns to the state with its demands rather than depending on economic pressures.

ECONOMIC PLANNING

Although nationalization played a role in the recovery of France, the more decisive and long-range state contribution toward overcoming France's prewar stagnation and relatively low industrial capacity has come through France's own particular type of economic planning. Unlike the coercive and highly directive planning of the Soviet Union, French state planning operates by stimulating different segments of the economy toward accepted short-range targets for growth. Thus, French planning is commonly called *indicatif* rather than *dirigiste* —that is, it indicates and stimulates lines of development rather than forces them.

French planning has been characteristically flexible, dependent on financial incentives, stressing the quantity of production, and relevant to selected needs and goals. The emphasis of the first three plans—1946–53, 1954–57, 1958–61—was on modernization and equipment. The First Plan concentrated on a few basic industries: coal, electricity, transport, steel, cement, and agricultural machinery. The Second and Third plans placed special emphasis on adjusting the economy to participation in the Common Market and on increasing exports and raising domestic living standards. The Fourth and Fifth plans—1962–65 and 1966–70—have been more concerned with social and general economic development, particularly in backward regions. The Sixth Plan—1971–75—seeks further strengthening and modernizing of French industry to stand Common Market competition, and it also focuses on social needs, especially those of the aged, needy, and handicapped. In addition, it refers to the need to improve the quality of the environment.

2   THE ORGANIZATION OF THE PUBLIC ADMINISTRATION

The public administration in France is characterized by its unity, in contrast to the relative separateness of national and local government in Great Britain and the self-assertiveness of local government in the United States. The establishment of separate bodies in France is looked on as a delegation of state functions that should not impair the unity of all public services. Thus French ministries occupy a position of dominance unaffected by decentralizing particular functions to local bodies and public enterprises.

In general the expansion of services in France has led to the enlargement of the domain of the ministries. The nineteenth-century British theory of limited governmental responsibilities —laissez faire, or the public order state—never operated in France, nor has the British concentration of ministries in the capital city. In response to the monarchical and Napoleonic notion that government agencies operate their own services and are broadly responsible for the economic and social welfare of the community, French ministries have always maintained a network of regional and local branches and many functional agencies that keep the ministries in continuous and intimate contact with communities throughout the country.

The breadth of the functions of the ministries and the wide dispersal of their offices and staffs have made the problem of executive supervision particularly difficult, much more so than in Great Britain. Many of France's best civil servants, in fact, operate in supervisory roles. There is also a network of personal secretariats (*cabinets*) of ministers and of advisory committees. In a very real sense, therefore, there are two levels of national administration: the active level (consisting of the ministries), and the supervisory. Each plays an essential role in the functioning of the French public administration.

THE ACTIVE CENTRAL ADMINISTRATION: THE MINISTRIES

Contrary to what we might expect, the structure of ministries in France is far less coherent and uniform than in Great Britain. Ministries tend to be collections of units or services tied together very loosely under a single minister. Many of these units have long enjoyed considerable administrative autonomy and prestige of their own and have no intention of being dominated or submerged. Moreover, until the recent reorganization of regions, the external services of different ministries were not even planned according to uniform divisions. Thus any accurate description of the French national administration would have to be undertaken ministry by ministry.

Certain distinctive differences from the British administrative structure are, however, apparent. First, the British depend much more on semiautonomous local agencies and officials for the execution of national policies. In France, only a small proportion—less than 5 percent—of the central administration works in Paris; the rest are engaged in direct administration in the provinces. The direct external services provided by ministries are termed *déconcentration* as distinguished from decentralization, since the former involve field offices rather than separate local or corporate bodies. Administering through extensive field offices has always been characteristic of French ministries, whereas in Great Britain the practice was not introduced until after World War I and has never been extensive.

Second, technical personnel, in the broad sense of specialists, who are found in advisory roles in the British national administration, play a much more important role in France both in policymaking and in day-to-day administration. Indeed, there is in France no class of general administrator in the British sense, since all French administrators receive specialized training. Because administrative law is so highly developed and important in France, legal training of a broad character is part of the preparation of almost all administrators. It is also true, however, that many specialists in technical fields become general administrators at later stages of their careers.

Third, British ministries are more stable than French ministries. While both countries provide relatively permanent structures for foreign affairs, armed forces, and interior, there is a great deal more reshuffling in France of particular services from minister to minister—a process even more evident under the Fifth than under the Fourth Republic—than there is in Great Britain. Moreover, some French ministries have short lives—as had the Ministry of Information and the Ministry of Repatriation —or else their functions are transferred to the premier's office and then come under administrative agencies rather than ministers. This process is rather bewildering to the outsider but less so to those involved, since the bureaus tend to be virtually self-contained structures.

Fourth, French ministries only rarely are headed by an official comparable to the British permanent secretary of a department. The chiefs of *directions*, units roughly comparable to British departmental divisions, are directly responsible to the minister, a practice incompatible with a coordinating civil service head. Moreover, the very variety of functions within single ministries makes such coordination difficult. (The only two ministries with a secretary general—that is, the French equivalent of a permanent secretary—are those with a clear unity of purpose: Foreign Affairs and Telegraphs.) Finally, ministers find bureaucratic organization so stratified and rigid that they feel forced to entrust direction and stimulus to their own *cabinet* of personal aides.

THE SUPERVISORY ADMINISTRATION

The compartmentalization of the structure of French ministries has given rise to a highly important and diversified supervisory administration in France that has no obvious parallel in Great Britain. This supervisory administration consists of a personal secretariat, known as the cabinet, attached to each minister, and of the *grands corps*, the inspectorates, and the *Conseil d'État* (Council of State).

The ministerial cabinet

The minister's personal cabinet plays a particularly significant role in France, as in many Continental countries. Often called the minister's "eyes and ears," the members of his cabinet must share his political aims and yet also act as the administrative coordinators of his ministry. Originally, most cabinets were composed of political appointees, but increasingly they are staffed by members of the elite corps who possess political sensitivity. One member, at least, usually concentrates on the minister's behind-the-scenes parliamentary business (there is no French equivalent of the British parliamentary secretary who can speak for the minister on the floor of the house).

Cabinets are supposedly limited to ten members (except for those of the president, the premier, and the Ministers of Foreign Affairs, the Interior, and Finance) and their members are subject to most, although not all the rules of the civil service. Although their term of office in a ministry is commonly only that of a particular minister, members of a cabinet perform many of the functions of a British permanent secretary, acting as a brain trust and speeding along the minister's policy. Thus the overall working of the administration depends to a considerable degree on their tact and skill. Moreover, the combination of administrative and political skills that members of executive and ministerial cabinets display sometimes leads to high political office, and not infrequently to becoming junior ministers.

The inspectorates

Inspectorates exist side by side with public services and expand with their growth. They may be concerned with all activities in a ministry, or they may concentrate on a particular activity. They exist within virtually all the ministries, except those of Foreign Affairs and Justice. They are flexible instruments of supervision, composed entirely of civil servants, and their members provide a pool of experience at the disposal of ministers for special administrative or advisory functions.

The most important inspectorates are those of Finance. The Court of Accounts (*Cour des Comptes*) not only supervises the legality of public expenditure but also investigates whether public funds have been spent wisely and what standards of financial administration are used by public authorities. The Inspectorate of Finance not only audits all accounts but passes on the use of all funds by all ministries. Thus its members also possess wide powers of investigation that extend to any matter affecting public funds.

As in the case of members of ministerial cabinets, these supervisory positions combined with political experience may lead to high office. Chaban-Delmas began his career in the *Inspection des Finances*, and four members of his cabinet in 1969 had also served in the *Inspection*; also one had formerly been a member of the *Cour des Comptes* and two of the *Conseil d'État*.

The Council of State

Although technically the Council of State does not have direct responsibilities for administrative coordination and control, it is a body of confidential and trusted advisers that gives technical advice to ministries on the drafting of legislation (which in consequence is unusually well polished) and also aids the executive in planning and preparing its legislative program. It has been traditionally responsible for checking the form and character of governmental decrees, and its role in this regard has been spelled out under the Fifth Republic. Article 38 of the constitution, which legalizes "special powers" under which the government can issue *décrets-lois* in matters normally within the sphere of legislation, also specifies that these ordinances must be examined by the Council of State.

By any standard the Council of State is a remarkable institution, without parallel in Great Britain or the United States. Set up originally by Napoleon, its chief duties have always been those of planning, advising the executive, and resolving whatever difficulties may arise in the administrative field. Perhaps the most striking aspect of the Council of State

is that it is composed of interrelated parts: an administrative body, which has the most intimate knowledge of the legislative program of the Council of Ministers, and a judicial body, which forms the supreme administrative tribunal of the country (described in Chapter 7, Section 4). The prestige and authority of the Council of State rest on its independence in both its advisory and its judicial capacities.

The senior members of the Council of State are organized into five sections: four small administrative sections (of seven members each) that handle matters concerned with finance, interior, public works, and social affairs, respectively, and a fifth much larger judicial section. The administrative sections meet together in ordinary session once a week for regular review of bills, decrees, and other matters referred to them by a minister and once a month in plenary session for any special issues.

The junior members of the council, known as *auditeurs* (first and second class) and *maîtres des requêtes*, prepare reports for the consideration of the seventy *Conseillers d'État*. Promotion is from one grade to the next and is automatic after set periods of service. Particularly since the reforms of 1963, the organizational division between the council's administrative and judicial work has been bridged to enable each to have insight into the problems and policies of the other. Thus every *auditeur* (after three years of service) and every *maître des requêtes* serves both in the judicial section and in one administrative section; and one *conseiller* must be attached to each administrative section. Although the two roles are intermingled, they are kept rigidly separate in decision-making.

The legislative work of the Council of State has been more important under the Fifth Republic than ever before. The restrictions on the legislature's power to amend government bills put a heavy responsibility on the council to give these bills their correct legal form and to alert the president and the cabinet to unintended consequences or potential illegalities. The Council of State is also expected to guard against the impetuous use of decree powers and to restrain the executive from unconstitutional procedures, although restrictions were imposed in 1963 after it annulled ordinances setting up a military court under a law of April

13, 1962, passed by referendum. Nonetheless, the council remains the chief administrative restraint on executive action.

On all regulations of public administration—that is, the measures necessary to carry out a law—the Council of State must be consulted by the premier and his ministry, in which reside the rulemaking power in the Fifth Republic. Only in certain technical matters is the government forced to follow the advice of the Council of State, but in practice its advice is always influential. So too is the advice it gives ministries, on their request, concerning decrees, policy, and coordination. Although most of its work is necessarily unpublicized, the Council of State clearly enjoys general confidence and respect. It is the most distinctive and one of the most useful of French institutions.

Advisory committees of private interests

To institutionalize the interaction of private interests and the bureaucracy, advisory committees are attached to almost all, if not all, sections of the administration. Although the practice of having such advisory committees dates back to the days of the Revolution, there has been a luxuriant flowering of their presence since the two world wars. The Fifth Republic has affirmed its intention of reducing the number of such bodies but seems to have added more than it has disbanded. Henry Ehrmann estimates that at the national level there are some five hundred "Councils," twelve hundred "Committees," and three thousand "Commissions" that associate group representatives with members of the bureaucracy.[1]

What effect this maze of advisory bodies has on the working of the administration is probably determined largely by the degree of responsiveness or firmness shown by those whom the private interests seek to influence. What the French call "administrative pluralism" may further compartmentalize bureau programs by making them susceptible to special pressures. At their best, however, such interactions with private groups help to keep the bureaucracy aware of and sensitive to public needs.

At the apex of the representative structure is the Economic and Social Council (*Conseil*

Économique et Social), which, under a variety of names and statutes, has existed since 1924. Composed of representatives appointed by government or private interests, and including persons of eminence in cultural, social, and economic fields, the council under the Fifth Republic deliberates on all bills concerning economic and social matters, gives advice both early and late on the formulation of the Plan, and on other relevant matters prior to the drafting of bills. But although the debates and reports of the council are usually of high caliber, there is little evidence that they have an impact on policy. De Gaulle's plan for reconstituting the second chamber by making it representative of organized interest groups in social, economic, and cultural fields, such as now meet in the Economic and Social Council, would have brought fresh experience and skills into the legislative process. As we have seen (Chapter 3, Section 3), however, the 1969 referendum failed to secure adequate support for passage, partly at least because the notion of effective functional representation has no popular base in French public opinion.

Whatever the network of advisory committees of private interests may accomplish, therefore, does not include stimulating a process of creative coordination of public efforts to meet urgent national needs. Thus those seeking radical change in France's social and economic life quite naturally feel the necessity of using other, extraconstitutional, and often violent channels through which to impress the executive with the need for action.

THE ORGANIZATION FOR NATIONALIZED ENTERPRISES

Nationalization in France is not only broad in scope, it involves novel forms of representation. In addition to the more common public corporation is the *société d'économie mixte*, in which stock is held by private interests as well as by the state, and public money indirectly subsidizes private activity. This form has been used for railroads, airlines, and two major maritime shipping companies. Moreover, most nationalized enterprises (*établissements publics*) make wide use of special interest representation on their boards of directors, a practice that

[1] Henry Ehrmann, *Politics in France*, p. 184.

finds no parallel in British and American public corporations.

A still greater contrast with the use of the nationalized enterprise in the United Kingdom and United States is that the French agencies are looked on as a part of a unitary state machinery. Although most of these agencies are legal entities, capable of suing and being sued, are theoretically liable to taxation, and employ staffs that are not strictly subject to civil service rules (though they commonly enjoy comparable conditions of service), French nationalized enterprises are not financially autonomous. Their directors, who are appointed by the government, are often drawn from the civil service and have little, if any, more independence than does the chief of a division within a ministry. Moreover, the crucial decisions for the enterprises—on wages, prices, and investments, for example—are made by the responsible ministry.

Under the Fifth Republic, parliament plays no role in controlling their actions.

The fact that nationalized enterprises are subject to the central control of the administration places their boards in a relatively weak position. The tripartite representation of workers, consumers, and the state on the boards of these enterprises follows the formula of "industrialized nationalization" proposed by the CGT as early as 1918. Board members, unlike those in Britain, are unsalaried (except for the chairman) and the representatives of workers and consumers often outnumber those of the state. In addition, state enterprises also have advisory committees of special interests. But rather than being management agencies, the boards are at best advisory and supervisory. Like all other parts of the French administration, nationalized enterprises are encompassed within the ultimate unity of the system.

3 ECONOMIC PLANNING AND REGIONALISM

THE ORGANIZATION FOR ECONOMIC PLANNING

The great difference between French and Soviet planning is well illustrated by the contrast between the small, flexible staff of the French Planning Commissariat and the pervasive planning machinery of the Soviet state. Fewer than a hundred people form the Planning Commissariat, and many of these are clerical. Its dynamism comes from a relatively small group of very intelligent and, on the average, very young civil servants of varied backgrounds and skills who collaborate with government departments, leaving them all executive responsibility instead of trying to supersede them. Administratively attached to the premier's office, the Planning Commissariat has built up harmonious working relations with the Ministry of Finance, except when the latter's restrictions curb the development programs of which the planners are the formulators and subsequently the watchdogs. The Sixth Plan's ambitious social goals (e.g., for housing and hospitals, see Chapter 1) may

lead, however, to friction with the ministry's anti-inflationary drive.

Although the Planning Commissariat itself is small, those drawn into its preliminary work number as many as three thousand. This is because the members of a wide variety of specialized groups pool their experience and skills in line with the creative procedures laid down by the Commissariat's gifted first commissioner, Jean Monnet. While the plan is necessarily a government policy statement, those private as well as public sectors and enterprises with which a particular plan is concerned are drawn into the formulation process through specialized committees that attempt to estimate the potentialities and needs of particular sections of the economy. It is difficult to estimate with any exactitude the rate of potential growth, either of particular firms or of industries like aircraft, automotive, chemicals, electronics, pharmaceuticals. National planning for a country like France, which is part of the regionally organized Common Market, also presents special problems (see Chapter 8, Section 2). The process of preparing the plan has developed considerable interaction between public and private agencies, spread knowledge widely, not only of the character of specified segments of the economy but also of their interrelatedness, and identified production bottlenecks as well as areas whose stimulation can have a growth effect.

The annual state budget is the principal instrument for achieving implementation of the major goals of the plan. Each year when the budget is sent to parliament it is accompanied by a report on the economic trends of the preceding year, those expected for the coming year, and the relation of both to the targets set down in the plan. Although public interest in the plan has never been high, there is considerable educational value to these annual presentations, coupled with the extensive, systematic, and detailed data related to local growth targets once the overall growth options for the next five years have been determined.

Late in June 1970, after four days of debate, the National Assembly approved by 351 votes to 95 the broad outlines of the Sixth Plan, whose final version took nine months more to complete. The plan estimates, for each of the next five years, a GNP growth rate of 6 percent, an increase of 6 percent in individual consumption, 7.4 to 7.6 percent in social benefits, and 10 to 12 percent in investment for collective equipment. Thus it combines two of France's urgent needs: to further modernize France's industry to meet Common Market competition, a task to which the plan is principally directed; and to avoid social strife, to which all too little is directly allocated.

Whether these goals can be achieved while taxation remains near the present level, as is planned, remains to be seen. Increases in pay were matched by rises in taxation after the crisis of 1968 and amount to 34 percent of GNP, a higher burden than that carried by taxpayers as a whole in either Great Britain or Germany. French indirect taxation is proportionately much higher than that in Germany or the United States. France's chief innovation in indirect taxation, now widely copied in other countries, is the value added tax (VAT). The base of VAT is the total income originating from an enterprise and its profits without reference to the cost of the raw materials it uses.

The theory is that VAT is imposed on what a firm adds to the national income, and it is left to the individual firm to determine on what it shall be estimated. If the product is exported the tax is returnable, making it a means of subsidizing exports.

France's public expenditures are also higher in proportion to its GNP than those of any other country in the North Atlantic area. Investment in private industry still lags. There is also a significant lag in another crucial area for achieving France's social and economic objectives, the development of a genuine and effective regionalism.

REGIONALISM

Economic planning is intimately related to the units for which action is designed and within which it will be carried out, a fact that brought regionalism to the forefront of attention after World War II. Thus there has been a series of efforts to establish more rational units than the ninety-five departments into which France has historically been divided. But so far both local authorities and the national administration have placed blocks in the way of realizing this objective.

The need for effective regionalism in France is obvious. Paris is not only administratively dominant over the country, but, as we have seen (Chapter 1, Section 2), the city is also dominant in population, wealth, and cultural activities. With nearly one-quarter of the national income, and as the center of a spiderweb railroad system, Paris exerts a magnetic influence on industry, talent, and people from the peripheral areas of the country. Even one of France's most powerful industrial areas, the north, with its 4 million inhabitants and one-twelfth of France's GNP suffers from unemployment and a steady emigration to Paris, especially of the young. Comparatively poor areas like Brittany are even more seriously affected.

The original internal stimulus to organizing the departments into regions came not from the Planning Commissariat but from unofficial regional expansion committees that appeared first in 1950 in Brittany. They were recognized by government decree in 1954 and made fully official in 1961. Parallel to this progression went departmental inventories of regional resources and needs that, in turn, led to the establishment in 1960 of twenty-one (originally twenty-two) regions, including Paris, for all of which programs were drafted as part of the Fourth Plan.

In 1964, as the Fifth Plan was being prepared, each region was placed under a regional prefect, or superprefect (who also was prefect for the largest town in the area). A Regional Development Board (*Commission de Développement Économique Régionale*), known as CODER, was set up in each region to serve as

a channel through which special interests could make known their views and needs. Consisting of twenty to fifty members, half nominated by interest groups and one-quarter by the premier, while the remaining quarter was composed of traditional elected local leaders, mayors, and councilors, the CODER appeared to offer hope not only of maintaining effective voluntary participation in regional organization (on the model of national economic planning) but also of stimulating significant reforms in the cumbersome and overcentralized national administration.

Such hopes, however, have not been realized. The regions did not become a new level of government The regional prefects have been

DEPARTMENTS AND REGIONS

DEPARTMENT BOUNDARY

REGION BOUNDARY

the object of much jealousy from their fellow prefects, partly because of an ingrained expectation that all prefects are equal in relation to their overriding authority—the Minister of the Interior—and partly because of suspicion that the regional prefect will favor the economic development of his own local department over and above that of all others in his region. Moreover, the *notables* of the long-outdated tiny units of local administration have resisted efforts at consolidation and even look with suspicion on constructive programs of urban development that seek to foster the growth of cities, like Bordeaux, Marseilles, Lille, Lyons, and Strasbourg, to form some counterpoise to Paris. Any area with a population of over one hundred thousand can now secure, under a law of 1966, the status of an "urban community," which covers surrounding suburban areas and operates under a community council that has specific responsibilities in fields like town and development planning, housing, transportation, and roads.

The most serious block to genuine regionalism is the assimilative tendency of the national administration. The voluntary regional expansion committees, which had developed a national organization upholding their right to formulate regional priorities without administrative controls, had to give way in 1964 to the CODER. These committees then proved themselves incapable of challenging the regional prefect's direction of development in relation to national, rather than regional needs. De Gaulle's 1969 referendum, had it been approved, would have provided not only for a smaller number of regions, which might have had more chance to be effective economic units, but also for centralized control over the distributions of funds. Pompidou has spoken of the need to free local and regional administration from the strangle hold of Paris, but this would probably only occur if there were responsible local assemblies in each region, which would involve a division of popular sovereignty so far antithetical to French philosophy and experience. Thus although there is much agreement on the need for regional reform, there is as yet little consensus on its form and how to bring it about. In the meantime France continues with piecemeal efforts to meet one of the country's most serious problems, the stultifying effect of an overlarge and much overcentralized bureaucracy for which there is no effective countervailing force through local centers of power.

4 LOCAL GOVERNMENT

Like all other parts of the French administration, local government is an integral part of the hierarchy of national planning and operations despite the existence of a vast number of locally elected bodies. Thus local government in France has a different function and meaning from that which it has in Great Britain or the United States. In those countries, local government is prized because it encourages local participation in public affairs, roots many local decisions in local bodies with their own source of funds, and, so the theory runs, forms an important (some would say invaluable) counterbalance to the national government's control of so many aspects of life. Both in Great Britain and the United States many local services—including education, medical care, and public utilities—were first provided at the local level, although in Britain they were subsequently integrated into national systems.

In France, however, both the process and the assumptions run the other way. The French have always taken a broad view, as we have seen, of the scope of national responsibilities. Since the days of Napoleon, local representation and local responsibilities have been intermeshed with the integrated, national structure of administration.

French local government has alternated in practice between local control, prefectural control, and a balance between the two. The National Assemblies established a democratic and decentralized system of local government in 1789 and 1790. They set up elected councils in the *departments*,[2] and in the *communes*[3] (including cities, towns, and villages), and placed extensive powers in the hands of locally selected executives. Napoleon replaced this system with a highly centralized administrative hierarchy, headed in each department by a *prefect* who controlled the communes in the area as well as the department at large and was merely "advised" by appointed local bodies and officers.

Thereafter, continued efforts were made to increase local participation in deciding local affairs. Both the ninety-five departments and the more than thirty-seven thousand communes, the basic units of administration, ultimately won back the right to elect their own councils. Moreover, each communal council achieved the right to choose its own executive officer, the mayor, who was vested with considerable power. The characteristic feature of French local government, therefore, is the cooperative relationship between the prefect and the locally elected bodies. Since national politics, and national politicians, often have their base in local areas, the interaction between the prefect on the one hand, and the mayor on the other, is not so one-sided as the unity of the French administrative structure might lead one to expect. Indeed, there is considerable community of interest that acts as a strong brake

[2] The basic units of French local administration are the ninety-five departments, of which the original eighty-three were established in 1790 by the Constituent Assembly, the rest resulting from subsequent additions to French territory. They bear no relationship to earlier historical divisions (as do many English counties), since they were deliberately designed to stamp out local particularism. Each department was kept small enough so that any person could make the round trip from his home to its governing seat in the course of a single day with transport considerably slower than now exists. Departments vary markedly in population due to disparities in growth. Until 1968, for instance, the department of the Seine, including Paris and some of its suburbs, had more than five million inhabitants (divided among four departments in 1968), while Lozere, the smallest, had only eighty-two thousand. A surprising feature to a foreigner is that the departments have included not only areas in Continental France but also in overseas territories. The administrative subdivisions of Algeria long formed three of the departments. In 1946, Martinique, Guiana, Réunion, and Guadeloupe became departments as a mark of close assimilation, indeed "oneness," with metropolitan France.

[3] Most communes are rural, but they may be urban if they do not adopt the status of urban districts or communities.
There are two other units, the *arrondissement* and the *canton*, but they inspire little popular sentiment and lack important governmental functions.

on needed reform through promotion of regionalism and consolidation of local units. Moves in both these directions have so far been tentative. Regions, as we have seen, are not a recognized level of government in the sense that departments and communes are. Also, while 8,700 communes have recently associated to form urban districts (under a law of 1959), only 273 tiny communes have disappeared.

ORGANS AND FUNCTIONS

The close intermeshing of central and local administration in France is reflected not only in the pervasive authority of the prefect but also in the degree to which government departments carry on their functions through field offices in the local areas. Historically, national field offices operated locally before local administration acquired any measure of autonomy. Even now, a department general council only votes about one-quarter of what is spent in its area, most of it for roads, health, and assistance. Its president is still little more than a chairman, and for all practical purposes the department is run by state officials. Moreover, the relation between the prefect and departmental field offices is a matter of continuing conflict between the Ministry of the Interior and other ministries. Despite the 1953 decrees that sought to give the prefect more power, many government field offices in the department, including all those in technical fields, operate independently of him.

In the communes, the balance is a different one. Each commune elects a council, usually with a high degree of voter participation and independence of national politics, and each council elects a mayor. The mayor often has a long tenure of office and many hold a national position as a deputy. Indeed, as we have seen, deputies, particularly of opposition parties, are even more prone to seek local office under the Fifth Republic than before. In seeking favors for their local areas, mayors often appeal directly, therefore, to ministers as well as through the prefect. Moreover, communes have staffs of their own with which they can handle the ordinary business of their area, although, either through lack of ambition or because the job is technical, they quite often entrust it to a departmental field office.

In regard to functions and finance, there is to an American a curious arrangement. Communes *must* raise funds for school building, public health, police protection, fire control, and upkeep of minor roads; they *may* also provide such additional services as parks, playgrounds, nursery schools, municipal theaters, and opera houses. A high proportion of local expenditures are obligatory under national law, either as contributions toward national services or for mandatory local services. For other services the communes are supposed to raise adequate funds and may be sued if they fail to do so. But communes have no substantial source of revenue, like the property taxes or rates collected by American or English local governments, and must depend on a variety of small taxes, the income from public property and municipal enterprises, and national grants-in-aid covering about one-fifth of their total expenditures. Moreover, while the communal council votes the budget, a state official in each canton, the *percepteur*, pays it out. In very small communes, this official often in practice draws up the budget as well.

The overall control exercised in local areas by central government is called tutelage (*tutelle*) to distinguish it from direct administrative dominance. Tutelage means that local authorities must secure prior approval by national government agents before initiating any new program and that if a commune fails to include a mandatory item in its budget, or fails to balance its budget, the prefect, after due warning, can take direct action to rectify the omission. Thus, despite the political possibilities of by-passing some of the rigidities of national-local relations, the hold of the central administration is well entrenched.

The four most promising proposals for reforming French local government are as follows: to proceed energetically to regroup communes in suburbs and isolated areas; to provide expanding towns with some sources of revenue and more discretion in using it; to bring more flexibility into the state bureaucracy and stir up local officialdom so that it takes more initiative, instead of depending so much on national administrators; and to introduce democratic institutions into a revised regional organization that can provide a counterpoise to the presently overpowering centralized structure. Such a radical reorganization might have been possible after the sharp shock of the May 1968 outbursts, but failure to make creative use of this, and other such opportunities, has permitted old ideas, forms, alliances, and personnel to persist. Thus in a time of rapid economic and social change, and of far-reaching expectations among students and young administrators, the strait jacket of administrative centralization still imprisons official forms of action.

5 THE PUBLIC SERVICE

Despite the variety of regimes through which France has passed, the public service has always retained a strong sense of its own positive mission to provide administrative continuity under all circumstances and to stimulate and even direct economic advance. Its impulse is not toward socialist or revolutionary goals (despite the syndicalist sympathies within its lower ranks) but rather toward capitalist and nationalist advance.

In *The Bureaucratic Phenomenon*, Michel Crozier castigates the bureaucratic system of organization of French public administration as "certainly one of the most entrenched of such closed systems of social action that has existed in the modern world." [4] The pervasiveness of the national public service—so much greater than in Great Britain, where many tasks are performed by local officials (1,500,000 in the local government services in Great Britain, compared to 550,000 in France)—is combined with an exclusiveness that is reinforced by an intense dislike of outsiders and by self-confidence in its own capacities and high purpose. But along with its overall clannishness, the French civil service, particularly at the highest

[4] Michel Crozier, *The Bureaucratic Phenomenon*, p. 308.

ranks, is strongly affected by particularism and compartmentalization. The sharpest divisions are between the members of the *grands corps* and the rest of the civil administration, and between and within the *grands corps* themselves, over personalities and fundamental state policies (e.g., toward Algeria, the Common Market, administrative reorganization).

ORGANIZING THE CIVIL SERVICE

The general civil service code, passed in 1946, was intended to unify the whole service by providing uniform conditions for its management and organization under a single body. This code, somewhat modified by practice and regulation, has done a good deal, although not enough to blur the distinctions among different sections of the public service. The code is now assumed to apply to all civil servants except the judiciary, the military, and services or public corporations of an industrial or commercial character, where it applies only to those on salary.

Modeled on the organization of the British civil services, three other reforms were introduced following World War II. A civil service division (*Direction Générale de la Fonction Publique*), placed directly under the premier, was created in 1945 to provide a hoped-for but not very successful unity of direction. A school of administration, *École Nationale d'Administration* (ENA), was set up the same year to recruit for the administrative class (executive and clerical staffs are still recruited by each department) and to develop postentry training programs; and an overall structure established four general classes—A, B, C, and D—roughly equivalent to the British administrative, executive, clerical, and typist classes.

Despite these efforts to enforce uniformity throughout the civil service, the *grands corps* continue to maintain their distinctive position. Although in principle the highest posts are open to any civil administrator (in particular from the specially created nonspecialized corps), in practice they tend to remain the preserve of the members of the *grands corps*. These are looked on as a pool of talent, and they may be moved to any section of the administration in which they are needed. They

provide high standards of excellence because of their common training and ability but not the overall organizational unity aimed at by the reforms of 1944–46.

Recruiting and training the higher civil service

In recruiting higher civil servants, the French depend heavily on rigorous selection and training and on controlled experience provided through the ENA. This practice provides a different type of top administrator from those in Great Britain or the United States. In the former, the administrative branch recruits men and women of high intelligence and character and lets them learn on the job. In the United States, recruitment is based on special tests geared to academic capacity, or on experience. But the French recruit an elite group capable of passing stiff theoretical examinations and of demonstrating capacity to perform successfully in practical situations.

Both university graduates and civil servants from the executive class may apply to the ENA for entry, and competitiveness and impartiality govern the selection of the hundred accepted each year. Neither religion, sex, nor locality may be taken into account. Nor, since a ruling by the Council of State, may candidates be refused on ground of political affiliation since, in practice, this restriction would apply only to a connection with the Communist party. But the objective of drawing much of the higher civil service from a broader social base than was true when the *grandes écoles*, the *École Polytechnique*, and other university-level technological institutes were the sole route to particular parts of the service has not been realized. The French higher civil service, like the British, is still drawn predominantly from the middle and upper middle classes, with only a sprinkling from the lower middle class, and hardly any from the working class or farmers. Indeed, 60 percent of the trainees, and nearly 70 percent of the most successful are from the families of high civil servants, managers, and professional men. Not without reason, ENA graduates are often called the "new mandarins."

The three-year training course at the ENA includes both practical experience in a government department or a provincial prefecture, and academic training. The decisive point for the student's future career comes at the end of the second year, when a final examination determines where he or she will be assigned: a fortunate twenty or thirty to the *grands corps* (Council of State, Court of Accounts, Finance Inspectorate, and Foreign Service), and the rest to the general corps of civil administrators. Once the die has been cast, specialized experience and training are provided in the section to which the students have been assigned.

In the third year of training, the student also spends time in private industry. Not infrequently, high civil servants, including members of the *grands corps*, go into private employment in middle age when they can command higher salaries than in government service. Graduates of the renowned *grandes écoles* also still acquire high administrative positions in government, particularly in the nationalized industries, or in business. An important by-product of this situation is that the managers and directors of big business firms are likely to share common interests and assumptions with high civil servants, whereas in Great Britain top business executives have their natural contacts with members of the Conservative party.

Conditions of service

French civil servants enjoy far greater mobility both inside and outside the service than do their opposite numbers in Great Britain and the United States. They can move from one administrative section to another, and they may do so to secure promotion. They may take a post in a public corporation, a local authority, or an international organization without losing any of their rights, including their pension rights. They may also take leave and enter private employment without resigning, and they retain both their seniority and pension rights as of the moment of the change. Most surprising of all, and in contrast to the situation in Great Britain, a civil servant may go into politics either as a deputy or as a minister. Since there is no need to sever his connection with the service, the sharp distinction between civil servant and politician that the British maintain so carefully is blurred if not eliminated. This ability to move from public to private employment and back again, and from administrative to political roles and back again, reinforces the key position of the higher civil service in France.

Every French civil servant is formally responsible under the law for carrying out the duties of his particular office; he must obey the orders issued by his superiors; and he must adhere strictly to all laws and executive orders. The responsibility of maintaining strict professional discretion is also emphasized.

Side by side with the duties for which a French civil servant is legally responsible stand his guaranteed rights. He has protection by the government against suits for libel or attacks resulting from the performance of his duty, and he is protected by the long-existing right of a civil servant to take legal action over any violation of the personnel rules by a superior official or over an administrative decision that might harm the collective interests of civil servants. He is assured the right to receive a salary that is at least 120 percent of "the vital minimum," an officially endorsed subsistence wage. He receives family allowances and other social security benefits of generous character. Most important in the view of many civil servants are the rights of association and representation, including the right to form and join staff associations, and, since 1946, *syndicats*,[5] and also to have staff members on all administrative and technical commissions concerned with conditions of service.

UNIONS AND STRIKES
IN THE PUBLIC SERVICE

The most troublesome issue included in the definition of the status of civil servants has been that of membership in *syndicats*, or civil service unions. The *syndicats* are the outgrowth of staff associations that sometimes aimed at controlling the work of their particular minis-

---

[5] The French make a distinction between *le droit syndical*, which is the right to trade union organization for the defense of common economic interests, and *le droit d'association*, which is a less far-reaching right to form an association with other persons for a common purpose. French civil servants have had the right of association for many years, but although *syndicats* of civil servants have long existed *de facto*, the right to organize into trade unions was not officially recognized until the Law on the Status of Civil Servants of October 1946.

tries (e.g., "The post office should be run by the postmen" was one slogan). There are now four major organizations—the General Federation of Civil Servants, the Postal Federation, the Teachers' Federation (primary and secondary), and the Federation of Public Utility Workers—that are more moderate. Their right to affiliate with organizations such as the CGT has not yet been resolved *de jure*, though there has long been *de facto* affiliation.

Tension has centered about the use of the strike as a means of staff pressure. According to syndicalist doctrine, organized workers should use sabotage and the general strike as steps toward the overthrow of the capitalist order. In a modified form this ideology has been popular among the members of government unions. Although strikes have been usually of restricted scope, a few serious incidents have antagonized public opinion. Moreover, the memory of the postal and railroad strikes of 1909 and 1910 (the latter crushed by calling the strikers into the army to break their own strike) has persisted ominously on both sides.

While prefects, public prosecutors, the police, and higher civil servants are forbidden to go on strike, and the services of key government departments and nationalized industries must be maintained at all times, civil service strikes are not uncommon. The retaliation meted out to those in the ORTF who participated in the 1968 strike (see Chapter 1, Section 5) suggests, however, a more punitive attitude to such action, particularly in times of crisis.

Commissions paritaires

The rank and file of the civil service have equal representation (*paritaire*) with their employers on the administrative and technical committees (*commissions paritaires*) that supervise the organization and functioning of the whole civil service. Although this machinery is not unlike that of the British Whitley Councils, the French system appears to give more weight to employee representatives.

The administrative committees, to which staff members are elected by their colleagues, consider recruitment, promotion, discipline, transfers, and other personnel questions. The technical committees, whose staff members are designated by the most representative of the unions, are concerned with practical problems of organization, efficiency, and reform that may be referred to them by the minister or by a union.

At the top of the system is the National Civil Service Council (*Conseil Supérieur de la Fonction Publique*), with twenty-eight members (fourteen from each side) chaired by the premier himself. The council hears appeals if the two sides do not agree; decisions are then taken by majority vote, with the premier holding the deciding vote. It also coordinates the work of the technical committees and advises the premier on administrative organization.

Neat as the system of consultation appears, neither side has been particularly helpful in making it work. Higher civil servants have tended to be uncommunicative about the reasons for their decisions, and the unions are lukewarm about participation and sometimes intransigent in their objectives.

The status of employees in nationalized enterprises

In general, labor in nationalized enterprises occupies a position midway between the civil service and workers in private industry; it has a more effective share in management than the latter and less limited union activity than the former. Most frequently, the rules governing recruitment, dismissal, and remuneration remain the same under nationalization as before. But special guarantees for union activity are provided by agreement (e.g., the union is guaranteed all material facilities, such as meeting halls, that it needs for pursuing its objects by legal means), and there is an absolute prohibition, embodied in law, against discrimination toward an employee because of union activity.

Particular rules govern conditions of work and conciliation machinery for each of the nationalized enterprises. For example, the Miners' Charter (which takes the place of the collective agreement in private industry) includes provisions regarding pay, holidays, hours of work, social security, and so forth. Moreover, it establishes joint disciplinary and conciliation committees at the local, district, regional, and national levels. The first two levels of committees are particularly concerned with the enforcement of the Charter, but all may examine complaints and attempt to settle individual and collective disputes. Labor is also skeptical about these procedures but participates half-heartedly.

LOCAL GOVERNMENT OFFICIALS

Since the national administration assumes so extensive and detailed a role in local areas, the scope for local officials in France is much less than in England. Nonetheless, they could often perform more actively in their own spheres than they do. Unfortunately the rules governing positions in local services are designed to provide security rather than to foster initiative or efficiency.

Since 1930, the national government has insisted that each local unit must either have its own merit system or accept the civil service rules designed for local administration by the Council of State. With the exception of a few executives at the top and the ordinary laborers at the bottom, all local officials are now selected by open, competitive examination. These tests stress general educational qualifications and, in consequence, there is less differentiation between officials in the higher ranks and those in the lower than is true in English local government. Since promotion and salary increases are rigidly regulated, however, there is all too little incentive for outstanding employees, many of whom leave the service.

EVALUATION OF
THE FRENCH CIVIL SERVICE

An evaluation of the French civil service depends both on the criteria and on the weight placed on administrative organization as a factor in performance. As far as ability, training, probity, and dedication to its responsibilities are concerned, the French service, and particularly its upper echelons, ranks very high indeed. If one's evaluation stresses cooperation, coordination, and participatory civic

culture, a much more negative result appears. The French civil service is still largely a caste, impatient of lay criticism, convinced of its own superior wisdom, and often hidebound regarding modes of action.

There are two opposing views regarding the role of the administration in the total structure of government. The one view believes the administration should work to preserve stability and to balance opposing forces within the community in such a way that they do not threaten the unity of the state. This view is held by many of the older high administrators, despite their own strongly held opinions on critical state issues. The other view, held most often by younger administrators, is that the civil service must be a positive agent for change in tune with mobile social and economic forces. Thus the service is divided within itself as to its basic role in the community. In the absence of effective parliamentary supervision, the executive and the administration itself must work out the answers.

The chances of a radical attack on administrative overcentralization and compartmentalization seem slim. Only the president could mobilize sufficient public support for effective and democratically organized regionalism and for a pattern of local government that provided more power and sources of funds to growing cities and a simplified, less diffuse structure for rural areas. And where de Gaulle failed, though at least partly because of inadequate preparation of public opinion, Pompidou must proceed with great caution.

The greatest likelihood is that the administration will continue to perform much as it has done in the past. Natural forces of economic growth will have their impact, but in the absence of persistent pressures for participation stemming from the community itself, the long-term rigidity of administrative processes and structure seems unlikely to crack. In many ways the French administration mirrors French civic culture: it seems unlikely that the one will change significantly before the other.

7

French
law
and
courts

1 FRENCH CIVIL LAW

Much of the world has done French law the honor of imitation. English common law spread only to those countries colonized by the British, but French civil law became the pattern for many continental European and Latin American countries. Even Ethiopia, when it decided to supersede local customs by a unified national body of law, turned to the codes of French civil law, which are the product of a similar need.

The legislators of the revolutionary period in France sought to bring about national unity by creating an integrated, uniform system of laws in place of the mosaic of national, regional, and local laws existing in prerevolutionary France. They also had a further reason for restating legal rules and principles: they were carrying out a great social and economic revolution. The antiquated land laws, the privileged position of the Church, the hunting rights of the nobility, were swept away in an early outburst of democratic fervor.

But to overhaul and systematize the legal rules affecting every aspect of life was a monumental task, subsequently undertaken by French jurists, often under the personal direction of Napoleon, whose administrative genius and, less fortunately, authoritarian views contributed to the final form of the codes. In 1804 the Civil Code appeared; in 1806, the Code of Civil Procedure; in 1807, the Commercial Code; in 1808, the Code of Criminal Procedure;

and in 1810, the Penal Code. Together, they formed the *Code Napoléon*, a comprehensive, systematized body of laws covering all cases likely to be brought to the courts. As revised, supplemented, and enlarged in response to changing conditions, the Napoleonic codes constitute the law of France today.[1]

CODE LAW

The characteristic feature of French law is its codified form. The requirements of the new society ushered in by revolution led to many new and advanced legal rules. But the principle of codification was not new. It had been embodied for centuries in the codes of Roman law. The Roman emphasis on centralized authority rather than on the interests of the individual fitted the new French nationalism, although it might seem to conflict with French individualism. The greatest influence on French law, however, was the practice of relating the rules on particular subjects to general principles of justice. The judges who developed the English common law cited specific precedents rather than abstract principles of right as the bases for their decisions, however much they might

[1] The Civil Code was thoroughly revised and reissued in 1904; a new Code of Criminal Procedure came into operation in 1959; the law of marriage settlement was reformed in 1961 and 1969; and numerous revisions have been made of the Commercial Code.

privately be influenced by the latter. The jurists who prepared the French codes, however, like those who had prepared the great Roman codes, often prefaced the legal rules on a given subject by a statement of the basic principles on which they rested.

The codes reduced and consolidated the laws to relatively small compass. The Civil Code, for example, deals with civil status, marriage and divorce, ownership, domicile, guardianship, contracts, wills, and so forth. It comprises 2,281 separate articles, each framed with a precision of language and clarity of expression so remarkable that one of France's greatest writers, Stendhal, is said to have read a few articles of the code every day as a lesson in style.

The articles of the codes and legislative enactments form the fundamental sources of reference for judges making a decision in any given case. This practice marks the fundamental distinction between "code law" and "case law." Even in interpreting a statute, judges in Great Britain and the United States refer to earlier decisions of other judges in similar cases. In France, however, earlier interpretations are less influential than the code.

Code law has two obvious advantages: easy accessibility and uniformity. English and American common law must be sought in hundreds of volumes of law records and digests. French civil law is embodied in a comparatively small number of books. The French have always maintained, however, that only professionals should interpret legal rules; they have no group comparable to the unpaid and untrained English justices of the peace. But where case law must be learned through long experience, code law is so much more accessible that anyone with legal training can make use of it. This fact has a direct influence on the size and character of the French judiciary, which included 4,105 members in 1970, with ages ranging from twenty-five to seventy-five (in contrast, the English judiciary—apart from the justices of the peace and magistrates—numbers only about a hundred, all of mature age). The large size of the French judiciary means that French justice can be decentralized to a degree that contrasts sharply with the centralization of the English court structure in London. No less of a contrast is that the French judiciary is part of the civil service.

2   THE JUDICIARY

English judges are drawn from the legal profession, and so far only from that section of it that has been "called to the bar," that is, the barristers—a fact that makes for close harmony between lawyers and judges. But in France a young man decides at the beginning of his career whether he will be a lawyer or a member of the judiciary, and in all likelihood he will remain in the role he has chosen.

To become a judge, a law graduate must succeed in the competitive examinations for entry to the specialized professional school set up in 1958, the *Centre National d'Études Judiciaires* (CNEJ), and satisfactorily complete its three-year course, which, like that of the ENA (see Chapter 6, Section 5), combines practical experience with academic studies. Designed like ENA to broaden the social base of candidates, the CNEJ has been little more successful. Lowering prestige of the judiciary

has meant, however, higher percentages from the middle class and of women.

Like the administrative cadres, the members of the judiciary hold themselves remote from French political life and the processes of business and industry. Products of highly legalistic training and schooled to adhere rigidly to texts, whether of the codes or of laws, French jurists pay much less attention in their professional work to social and economic trends than do judges in the United States. Yet as members of the bourgeoisie, most French jurists are inevitably, if often unconsciously, biased in the direction of middle-class standards and of stability.

At the same time, French jurists are far from satisfied with their conditions of service. Of all government departments, the Ministry of Justice is the only one whose budget constantly decreases. Judges even threatened in mid-1970 to desert their posts to dramatize the need for a higher budget for the administration of justice, for an increase in the number of jurists (while projections indicate a need for 250 new jurists every year for the next decade, the budget provides only for 170 a year from the CNEJ), and for higher salaries. Salary increases are now automatic, and, since 1946, promotions are no longer subject to political influence but are determined largely by the *Conseil Supérieur de la Magistrature* (High Council of the Judiciary), whose members are chosen by the president from a list submitted by the Court of Cassation, France's highest court. But French jurists receive very low salaries, a factor affecting the caliber of the service and inhibiting recruitment.

While in England and the United States judges serve only on the bench, members of the French judiciary are divided into two main categories: those who judge cases, known as *magistrats du siège* (that is, judges who sit on the bench); and state prosecutors, forming the *paquet* or *magistrature debout* (standing magistrates), who act on behalf of the state in criminal cases. Judges have security of tenure and cannot be disciplined by the government, but prosecutors have less independence since they are ultimately under the authority of the Minister of Justice.

3   THE REGULAR COURTS

Because they were fearful that the courts would try to interfere with the social and economic changes they were introducing, the National Assemblies of the early revolutionary period specifically forbade the judiciary to limit or encroach on the sphere of the administration. Although the constitutions of subsequent Republics have included no similar prohibition, the courts in France have never adopted the practice of judicial review, which is so significant in the United States. A separate structure, the administrative courts, deals with any case affecting an administrative official or in which the state is a party (except for criminal cases). Thus the regular courts deal only with disputes between individuals (civil cases) and those in which an individual is accused of a breach of public order (criminal cases).

THE HIERARCHY OF
THE REGULAR COURTS

In 1959, the Fifth Republic reorganized the system of regular, or "ordinary," courts. The major casualties of the change were the three thousand legally trained *juges de paix* (so different from English justices of the peace), who used to be found in almost every small canton and who concentrated on conciliation and minor civil cases. Modern transportation made such decentralization unnecessary, and the revised system reduced the total number of courts by four-fifths.

The basic structure now consists of a lower court in each *arrondissement* (Court of First Instance) and a higher one in each department (Court of Major Instance or Superior Court). More courts are provided for densely populated departments—172 for 95 departments.

At the department level, each court is divided into two sections, one for civil cases and one for criminal cases, but they are staffed by the same judges and use the same courthouse. The next level of courts is divided, but the Court of Cassation at the apex of the system hears appeals from both civil and criminal cases.

The French facilitate the right of appeal but at the same time limit and structure it. Unless a case involves very minor sums, there is always a right of appeal. In both civil and criminal cases, the Superior Courts have both original and appellate jurisdiction. Above this level, appeals are split between the Courts of Appeal, which deal mainly with civil cases, and the Courts of Assize, which have both original and appellate jurisdiction in criminal cases. Normally, when an Assize Court acts as a court of first instance, a jury is present—the only time it is used in the French court system.

The Court of Cassation at the top of the system does not rule on the facts of a case, as

Regular Court System of France

Court of Cassation: Supreme Court of Appeal (*Cour de cassation*)

83 judges who work through five sections: two civil (personal and family status, and property)
of fifteen members each; one commercial; one social; and one criminal
7 judges to a case (15 if a principle involved, and all members if a second appeal)

Reviews interpretations of *law* in civil and criminal cases.
If the *Cour de cassation* quashes judgment, it sends case to another court at same level as that from which case was originally referred. On second appeal gives authoritative interpretation that must be followed by lower court.

Appeal Courts (*Cours d'appel*)

Several sections including one on social laws
3 to 5 judges

Take appeals on matters of *fact* from civil and criminal courts and retry cases.
Prepare indictments for Assize Courts.

HIGHER COURTS

CIVIL CASES

CRIMINAL CASES

Assize Courts (*Cours d'assises*)

95 (one in each department)
3 judges and jury of nine (verdict of guilty
requires a majority of eight votes)

Original jurisdiction and appeals for most serious crimes, like manslaughter.

Civil Courts—Superior
(*Tribunaux de grande instance*)

172
3 or more judges

Cases involving substantial sums, personal or family status, or real property.
Unlimited jurisdiction (that is, can try any case no matter how serious).

Criminal Courts (*Tribunaux correctionnels*)

172
several judges

More serious offenses. Can impose prison sentences from two months to five years and levy fines from two hundred francs up.

LOCAL COURTS

Courts of First Instance
(*Tribunaux d'instance*)

455 (one for each arrondissement)
1 judge

Minor civil cases.
Conciliation functions.
Settle election disputes.
Judge also presides over police court, family and guardianship councils.

Police Courts
(*Tribunaux de police*)

455

Minor offenses. May impose penalties of one day to two months in prison and small fines.

SPECIAL COURTS

Six courts linked to the regular court system
by various appeal procedures

Channel of Appeal

lower Appeal Courts can, but only on the interpretation of law. Even then it does not render a final judgment but sends the case back to another court at the level it has been tried before. In the unusual circumstance of a second appeal, the Court of Cassation renders a mandatory judgment on the point of law involved, which must be accepted. While technically this power of the Court of Cassation (defined in a law of 1837) is limited to the particular case, the judgment naturally has wide effect.

The higher the place in the hierarchy of courts, the larger the number of judges assigned to the case. At the lowest level, cases are heard by a single judge, although there is a panel available at each center to see that cases are dealt with promptly. At the department level, each case is handled by three judges. The twenty-seven Appeal Courts have three to five judges to a case, and when the Courts of Assize use a jury, there are three judges and nine jurors, of which eight of the twelve must agree on the verdict. The Court of Cassation has eighty-three judges divided into five sections: two civil, one criminal, one social, and one commercial. A screening section decides what cases should be reviewed. If a second appeal becomes necessary, all the judges in the Court of Cassation compose the bench.

SPECIAL COURTS

The French have established a number of courts for special purposes that are linked to the regular court structure. The most important, but fortunately by far the least used of these special courts, is the Permanent Court of State Security, which has original jurisdiction in cases of subversion and from which appeal goes only to the Court of Cassation. The event giving rise to the Court of State Security was the attempted assassination of President de Gaulle by some army officers who were embittered by his policy toward Algeria. Although the referendum on direct election of the president called by de Gaulle in 1962 included a broad grant of power under which the court was established, the *Conseil d'État* annulled the decree setting it up on the ground that it was incompatible with the general principles of

criminal law. Parliament subsequently authorized the court, and the *Conseil d'État*'s action sparked its own reorganization of 1963. Fresh controversy and concern were caused, however, by the use of the Court of State Security in 1970 to consider charges against the Proletarian Left (see Chapter 1, Section 3).

The other special courts operate at the lowest levels to deal through conciliation or legal processes with disputes in prescribed areas. Industrial councils and commercial tribunals deal respectively with disputes between employers and employees over such issues as dismissals and between merchants over sales or bankruptcy. By holding formalities to a minimum, giving those concerned the right to select their own representatives to undertake the conciliation, and by being cheap and quick, these structures are justifiably popular. The three other special courts—Juvenile Courts, Social Security Commissions, and Courts of Farm Leases—have obvious jurisdictions, and each includes one professional judge. Appeals through the civil court hierarchy are limited to the more serious cases.

EVALUATION OF
THE FRENCH COURT SYSTEM

The structure of the French court system provides many advantages that are lacking in England. The fact that not only the lower and superior courts but also the appeal courts are decentralized brings them within easy reach. Further, convenience, speed, and cheapness are enhanced by permitting only one appeal on the facts of a case, instead of two or even three as is possible in England. (Although there are occasional long delays in the Court of Cassation, the costs of a review by the Court of Cassation are borne by the state.) Finally, the uniformity of the system means that the inhabitants of a southwestern city have exactly the same kinds of courts of original jurisdiction and appeal as the inhabitants of Paris. In England, in contrast, not only are the appeal courts centralized in London, but the county courts, despite their concurrent jurisdiction in lesser cases with the divisions of the High Court of Justice, hardly rank on a plane of equality with the High Court in personnel.

A general evaluation of the French court system, however, requires consideration of other questions. What is the atmosphere of the courts? Do they provide an opportunity for all aspects of a situation to be explored? Do the courts give private persons adequate protection in criminal cases in which the resources of the government are behind the prosecution? Do they provide speedy, effective means of settling disputes? And is justice, in practice, open to all on equal terms?

The sessions of a French civil court are likely to seem sober and even dull to an American, for information is often presented in writing rather than orally. Some French critics claim that the parties to a case often do not understand what is going on, and that the judges adopt a magisterial posture that assumes some divine wisdom to their decisions that neither the judicial personnel nor the verdicts justify. They also have evidence that not only the rich but also the cultured have a marked advantage, particularly in criminal cases.

A more common concern about criminal cases is that the scales are heavily tilted toward the authorities. France has no writ of habeas corpus, and although the initial period of time of detention is supposed not to exceed twenty-four hours, the authorities not infrequently invoke exceptional circumstances to justify the police holding a suspect a much longer time before charging. Once an accusation is made, the process is more controlled, although often

long and drawn out. Investigation of the evidence is by a court official, the *juge d'instruction*. The judge or judges who try the case may also examine witnesses (often out of court), question lawyers, and press proceedings in whatever direction they feel necessary to elucidate the facts. It is not true, as is often charged, that a person accused of a crime in France is considered guilty unless he can prove himself innocent. But, whereas English and American criminal procedures are mainly motivated by fear that an innocent person may be convicted, French criminal procedures seem directed by concern lest a guilty person escape.

Late in 1969, French public opinion was roused by the suicide of a young school teacher, Gabrielle Russier, who had fallen in love with a teen-age student, was charged with "seduction" of a minor, went through the agony of long investigations, and finally killed herself when the prosecution demanded a heavier sentence on appeal. Reforms were subsequently announced replacing the much criticized practice of preventive detention by putting people awaiting trial "under court supervision," that is, restricting them to a certain area and adjusting bond to include staggered salary withholdings for those incapable of posting the full amount. Indemnification is also provided for cases of unjustified detention. These long overdue reforms make it more likely that the requirements of due process will be strictly observed.

4 THE ADMINISTRATIVE COURTS

Side by side with the hierarchy of the regular courts in France exists a second hierarchy, the administrative courts, which operate to keep the agents of the state within their grants of power and to give individual Frenchmen a remedy against arbitrary administrative decisions. Nothing exactly like the French administrative court system exists in England or the United States, although in both countries there is an increasing amount of administrative adjudication. Most Englishmen and Americans still feel that the best safeguard of justice is to have one law for everyone, rather than to have

separate courts for examining the acts of officials. But the vast increase in the functions and powers of the administration in every modern state increasingly raises the question of whether the highly flexible, inexpensive, and all-encompassing jurisdiction of the French administrative courts do not, in fact, provide a better protection of individuals from administrative arbitrariness than the much more cumbersome practice in England or the United States of bringing suit against officials through the regular courts.

Administrative courts (which are concerned

only with civil cases) exist on both the local and national level in France. Since 1953, the twenty-eight *Tribunaux Administratifs* have not only considered cases arising out of charges and claims against local administrations but also almost all the first-instance work transacted up to then by the Council of State (*Conseil d'État*). At the national level, the French administrative court system is headed by the Council of State, which we have already considered in its role as an advisory organ and administrative agency, and which is one of France's most remarkable institutions.

The French administrative courts can annul decisions or rulings that they decide are outside the grant of power or are otherwise invalid, but they do not substitute their own decisions or rulings. In other words, they act as a check on the administration's use of its authority, but they do not direct the administration along any specific lines. Moreover, the damages awarded by the administrative courts are paid by the government, not by the erring official. An individual can also institute a case against a public officer in the ordinary civil or criminal courts, but it is more difficult to secure damages than in Great Britain or the United States, where the doctrine of personal liability for abuse of power is much more strongly entrenched than in France.

The general distinction between cases that go to the regular courts and those that go to the administrative courts is drawn from the type and manner of activities, rather than from the legal status of the body involved. Thus where public agencies act like private undertakings—for example, nationalized industries—disputes go to the regular courts. Where semipublic committees have power to regulate industries, however, and impose penalties for violation of their decisions—that is, where they have powers that private bodies do not have—their actions are subject to review by the administrative courts.

Any controversy about whether a case belongs in the ordinary courts or in the administrative courts is settled by the *Tribunal des Conflits* (Court of Conflicts), which is composed of four members of the Council of State and four members of the Court of Cassation. In the rare case of a deadlock, the Minister of Justice casts the deciding vote.

THE LOWER ADMINISTRATIVE COURTS

With the reform of 1953, the Administrative Tribunals became the principal forum of administrative justice. They acquired new jurisdiction, importance, and status, leading to higher salaries and the guarantee of three places reserved in the Council of State for recruitment from their ranks. Except for a prescribed proportion of senior posts filled by civil servants with long administrative experience, members of the Administrative Tribunals are recruited from the ENA, and like other members of the administration (but unlike the judges of the civil and criminal courts) do not enjoy the status of irremovability.

The procedure in the Administrative Tribunals is simple and straightforward. Appeals may be mailed and need include only a small fee, an official form on which the complaint is described, and the necessary supporting documents. While petitioners may be represented by counsel in public session, this is not necessary. The court (unlike a regular court) makes the investigation itself, rather like the ombudsman and his staff in other countries.

In addition to the *general* administrative tribunals, there are some forty different types of *specialized* administrative courts. The most important of these is the Court of Accounts, the supreme audit agency, whose supervisory functions have already been described (Chapter 6, Section 2). Most of the other administrative tribunals are the disciplinary organs of professional groups (apart from bodies controlling the legal profession, which come under the civil courts). Over all these specialized jurisdictions the Council of State exercises supervision through cassation, that is, it cannot decide the merit of a decision but can only quash a verdict for illegality or procedural error and then send the case back to another body on the original level for retrial. Rather than establish a larger number of specialized tribunals, the French prefer to provide for consultation with affected parties as in most of the lower special courts.

THE COUNCIL OF STATE

The Council of State, as we have already seen, is one of the most prestigious institutions in

France. Recruited mainly from the most out-standing students of the ENA, its 250 members form a visible and justly renowned elite. About 150 of these serve in the five sections into which the council is divided, and 100 are on "detached" service throughout the high ranks of many ministries and in ministerial cabinets. The prestige of its members is at least as high as that of the other *grands corps*, and they come from the same strata of society.

Side by side with the 50 members serving principally in the four administrative sections are the 100 who serve chiefly in the *Section du Contentieux* (judicial section). This latter section is divided into nine subsections, of which two normally combine to consider a case. Should the case be particularly important, all the councilors of the *Section du Contentieux* may form the tribunal, and they may even be reinforced by members of the administrative sections.

To have administrative officials check other administrative officials might seem to make administrators judges in their own cases and so destroy the safeguards that the system is in-tended to provide. But the French believe that the more knowledge the members dealing with judicial matters have of administrative prob-lems, the sounder their decisions will be. Thus deliberate efforts were made in the reform of 1963 to bring the administrative and judicial sides of the Council of State closer together. Members can move from one section to an-other, as we have seen, either through promo-tion or desire; nine members of the judicial section participate in the work of the full ad-visory body that counsels the government on bills and decrees; two judicial members are on the standing committee that gives advice on urgent bills and regulations; and, conversely, the administrative sections elect several of their members to sit on the judicial section. Thus the judicial section has an awareness and an understanding of current developments in the political and administrative spheres that no member of the judiciary in Britain or the United States can match, and no member of the administration can dispute.

The procedures of the Council of State are similar to those of the Administrative Tribunals except that legal representation is normal; in-deed, they are very like those followed by such independent regulatory commissions in the United States as the Federal Trade Commis-sion. The practice may be compared to that of a criminal court, except that the roles are re-versed: the government official or agency is on trial on a charge made by a private citizen. At the level of the Council of State the investiga-tion is made by nonjudicial members, *auditeurs* and *maîtres des requêtes*, who are serving their apprenticeships. When presenting the issues of the case, following detailed investigation, the *maître des requêtes* is known as the *commis-saire du gouvernement*, but he is an impartial examiner and his conclusions (usually, though not always, accepted) often condemn officials or agencies.

If a plaintiff's claim is upheld, he pays no costs; if it is denied, he pays only a nominal amount. Although a claim for money damages may make special court and registration fees necessary, the total cost of proceedings is too small to deter anyone who has a reasonable claim.

One question that does arise is how the coun-cil's judgments are enforced on a possibly reluctant administration. The council has no power to order execution of its judgment, so the ultimate effect depends on its prestige and the compliance of the administrative agency found at fault. The reforms of 1963 specified that on government request a *rapporteur* must be appointed to explain the judgment and advise on how it can be executed. If a successful plaintiff notifies the council of difficulty in securing execution of the judgment, a *rap-porteur* may be appointed; but the ultimate sanction at the disposal of the council is to note the administrative noncompliance in its annual report. Moreover, this report is not made public. It appears, however, that on the whole the judgments of the administrative courts are respected.

EVALUATION OF
THE ADMINISTRATIVE COURTS

In their book *French Administrative Law*, L. Nelville Brown and J. F. Garner attribute the success of the French administrative courts to five factors: the composition and functions of the Council of State; the flexibility of the council's case law; the simplicity of the remedies available; the special procedures; and the uniform character of the substantive law they apply. The faults are slowness—commonly eighteen months at either level, although procedures can be rapid if there is an emergency—and difficulty of enforcement. But, in general, administrative units comply if they can find a reasonable means of so doing. Sometimes a judgment like replacing a dismissed official after a two- or three-year period requires considerable adjustments in the career structure of the whole department. The effects of such judgments, however, extend beyond the particular case and generally have an influence throughout the whole structure.

There can be no question that a Frenchman can more easily secure redress for abuse of power than can an Englishman or an American. But it is also true that neither Englishmen nor Americans face such a serious problem in connection with official liability as do the French, since both in England and the United States administration is far more decentralized than in France, and in both countries local units of government have long been liable for damages in many instances where the central government is not. Moreover, both the American federal government and the British government now permit suit against the state in torts, so that in most cases the Anglo-Saxon can now secure relatively the same pecuniary redress for the results of official mistakes as can the Frenchman. Under present conditions, the main difference between the Anglo-Saxon and Continental systems in matters of financial redress is that in Great Britain and the United States the unexpected consequences to someone else of an act in line of duty are not usually indemnified by the government as they are in France (e.g., bystanders injured by bullets fired by a policeman pursuing a suspect are not recompensed by the state in the United States or Great Britain, but they are in France).

Advocates of the Anglo-Saxon system maintain that while the French system provides greater protection against pecuniary loss by individuals, the Anglo-Saxon system provides a stricter adherence to law. They believe that the very fact that the ordinary courts deal with cases affecting the administration side by side with other cases means that government officials are kept aware of the necessity of adhering to the regular laws of the land. They point out, too, that the Anglo-Saxon notion of personal liability for abuse of power, regardless of whether the act is committed under orders or not, places the weight of personal responsibility directly on every official and prevents him from "passing the buck" to his superior.

It has been the proud boast of the Anglo-Saxon system that this tradition that every person, whether government official or not, is subject to the common rules of the law of the land, preserves liberty under the law in a way that no other system can match. With the all-pervasiveness of the modern administrative bureaucracy, it seems open to question, however, whether some special instrumentalities are not needed in Great Britain and the United States to buttress their present systems by providing formal, inexpensive, and speedy investigations into charges of official arbitrariness or abuse of power. It is obvious that it is not the administrative court system as such, but the high standards of integrity and independence of the French Council of State that have made it such an effective guardian of the public interest and of individual liberties. It seems not too much to anticipate that if Great Britain or the United States were to set up a comparable administrative body, it would operate under the same high standards by which the *Conseil d'Etat* acts to check the French administration from abuse or excess of power.

8

France
and
the
world

In recent years, France has played a significant role in international affairs. It has taken the lead in the movement for Western European integration; it has exploited its worldwide cultural influence and strategic geographical position; and it has asserted, particularly under President de Gaulle, independent lines of foreign policy within and outside Europe that reflect France's own interests and views. Thus despite the devastation and humiliation of World War II and the subsequent loss of virtually all its empire, France has regained a distinctive voice in world affairs. In so doing, it has provided a striking illustration that the art of statesmanship plays a significant role in international affairs.

1 FROM COMMUNITY TO AFRICAN INDEPENDENCE

When de Gaulle assumed power in 1958, France had suffered a series of humiliating defeats and withdrawals from former colonial territories, notably Indochina, Morocco, and Tunisia, and was engaged in an exhausting struggle in Algeria. Moreover, the units of its empire in West Africa and Madagascar were pressing for further self-government.

De Gaulle himself had included representatives from French Africa in the Constituent Assemblies that drafted the constitution of the Fourth Republic. But despite the efforts of the native representatives and the parties of the left to extend full self-government to the various units of a federated empire, the 1946 constitution included three types of political arrangements for the African colonies that in the end proved mutually exclusive. Following the assimilative principle so strong in France's earlier relations with its empire, the African colonies sent representatives to the French parliament throughout the Fourth Republic, as Algeria and the old colonies (Martinique, Guadeloupe, Réunion, and French Guiana) had long done. In a quasi-federal move, a new structure, the French Union, was established, whose Assembly was composed of an equal number of representatives from overseas territories and from France. The third, and ultimately the most significant, feature was to provide each colony with a local representative body. Strong and skillful pressure by the African deputies in the National Assembly led to the 1956 *loi cadre*. This measure permitted local legislatures, elected by universal franchise and directed by local African leaders, to exercise limited autonomy by the time the Fourth Republic collapsed in 1958.

THE COMMUNITY

The constitution of the Fifth Republic acknowledged the right of the African territories to choose secession and independence but also offered political, economic, and cultural association with France within a new form of association, the Community. Each member state of the Community was recognized as self-governing; in general, their internal pattern of institutions was like that in France, although commonly they had only one party. But highly important matters were reserved to the Community: foreign policy, defense, currency, common economic and financial policy, the disposition of strategic raw materials, and (except by special agreement) control of higher education, the courts, and the general organization of interstate and foreign transportation and telecommunication. These latter subjects were to be managed by a number of institutions established by and said to be common to all members of the Community,[1] but in practice executive and French control predominated. Not surprisingly, the original form of the Community was short-lived, although all former French territories in Africa, except Guinea, originally voted to become members.

Under pressure from Senegal and Soudan, temporarily united in the short-lived Mali Federation, de Gaulle reluctantly agreed in 1960 that membership in the Community did not prevent separate United Nations membership, like that enjoyed by the individual members of the British Commonwealth of Nations. At this point, however, Félix Houphouët-Boigny of the Ivory Coast, formerly the strongest advocate of the Community and probably responsible for its form, suddenly decided to seize the nationalist initiative by renouncing his country's links with the Community and applying immediately for United Nations

membership. Although an attenuated Community continues to exist in name, France's relations with each of its former African territories are now effectually determined by separate bilateral agreements.

FRENCH RELATIONS WITH AFRICA

Despite this development, France maintains strong ties with its former territories in sub-Saharan Africa. The aid it extends to them is greater in proportion to its national income (and used to be greater in extent) than that provided for Africa by Great Britain, the United States, or the Soviet Union. Aid includes the salaries for French teachers overseas (nearly one-half the total aid bill), general assistance, financing specific projects, and subsidies to maintain a high price for such African crops as coffee and cotton. France retains tight control over most of their currencies, however, through the franc zone.

All former African Community members[2]—and also the Congo (Kinshasa), Rwanda, Burundi, the Somali Republic, and, on a more limited basis, Kenya, Tanzania, and Uganda—became associate members of the Common Market. When Great Britain joins the Common Market, the status of associate membership will be extended to other African members of the Commonwealth. The Common Market's European Development Fund also aids the Associated States, and France has had a major share in determining how this money would be used. It continues to prefer bilateral programs.

The teachers, technicians, and administrators who have served, or continue to serve, in France's former African colonies, have been important in maintaining French influence in these countries. In their first years of independence it was common to have French civil servants playing a more decisive role in decision-making than did their African ministers. Many of the French administrators and technicians

[1] These institutions were as follows: the president, who was also the president of the French Republic in whose election the overseas departments and territories shared; the Executive Council, composed of the French premier, the heads of government of the member states, and the ministers responsible for the common affairs of the Community; the Senate, composed of delegates from the legislative assemblies of France and the other member states, whose numbers were determined both by population and responsibilities in the Community; and a Court of Arbitration, to settle disputes among members of the Community.

[2] They also developed their own purely African organization, known successively as the Brazzaville group, organized in 1961, the *Union Africaine et Malgache de Coopération Économique* (UAMCE), and now the *Organisation Commune Africaine et Malgache* (OCAM). Inside this grouping, the Ivory Coast and four weaker territories—Upper Volta, Togo, Dahomey, and Niger—associate in the Council of the Entente.

have now been withdrawn; so, too, have most of the French army units in Africa, which, on occasions, had played a decisive role in keeping friendly regimes in office. But the number of French teachers serving abroad—more than thirty thousand—has increased. Five thousand teach in former French African countries; twelve thousand in Algeria, and twelve thousand in Morocco, Tunisia, Asia, and Oceania. More than one and a half million students are enrolled in the more than fifteen hundred French teaching establishments abroad, and many of them take French as well as local examinations. The universities in former French African territories are still part of the French university system. Over forty thousand foreign students are studying in France. Thus the French continue to capitalize on the spread of their language and the high esteem for their culture.

Not all is well, however, with French relations in Africa. The death in 1970 of Foreign Legion soldiers fighting to maintain an unpopular regime in Chad awakened a storm of protest in France itself against continued military involvement in Africa. The complicated overlapping machinery managing French financial aid is criticized in Africa as unimaginative, ambivalent in objectives, and dilatory in fulfilling technical commitments. Moreover, tension developed early in 1971 over the holdings of French oil companies in Algeria. The Algerian war had ended in 1962 with the grant of independence to that territory, and Algeria and France had henceforth enjoyed a special relationship that enabled hundreds of thousands of Algerians to continue to earn their livelihood in France even though almost all the million French *colons* (settlers) had fled to there from Algeria. But there had never been cordiality from the side of the Algerians. In February 1971, after a short effort at negotiations, their government took over majority control of all French oil interests in Algeria and nationalized French assets in natural gas and gas pipe lines. This situation led to severe strain between the two countries. At the same time, the Algerian press encouraged the feelings of frustration felt by many young French-educated Africans at the continued French role in their national life and economy, which was termed "new and devious forms of the former colonial economic exploitation." Such changes of atmosphere may well lead to diminished French influence within the African continent.

2 FRENCH POLICIES IN EUROPE

Although the French still devote considerable attention to their relations with their former empire, their preponderant concern, inevitably, is with their position within Europe. And while economic cooperation and growth are of high priority in their European policies, security is still more so. The search for security has been mainly concerned with the means of restraining Germany, which had invaded France three times in three-quarters of a century. Failing at the end of the war to secure either partition or control of West Germany, France has developed the much more constructive policy of integrating it with itself in a network of economic associations based on a degree of Franco-German cooperation that would have seemed impossible in the past.

Postwar military arrangements for security have proved less satisfying to France. Although Great Britain agreed on March 4, 1947, to a fifty-year alliance with France to guarantee joint action in case of German aggression, France under de Gaulle was then seeking broader alignments, notably through its twenty-year defensive agreement with the Soviet Union of December 1944. But disappointed in its overly optimistic expectations of Soviet backing for a voice in the decisive Yalta Conference and thus perhaps securing again its old role in Europe of mediator between East and West, France reluctantly turned back to the latter. It accepted participation and, at least initially, an active role in NATO, despite the organization's American commander in chief. Faced with American insistence on strengthening NATO by rearming West Germany,

France's statesmen proposed, but its political divisions destroyed in 1954, the imaginative approach of a European Defense Community, which would have established a supranational European Army with French, German, Dutch, Belgian, Luxembourg, and Italian units. But when Great Britain's Conservative government unexpectedly offered the far-reaching military commitments of Western European Union, France agreed in October 1954 to permit the newly sovereign and rearmed West Germany to enter NATO.

Nonetheless, de Gaulle after 1958, and particularly after 1962 when the Algerian situation had been settled, found the strategic conception on which NATO had been founded too static, particularly after the Soviet Union possessed a nuclear threat. He was also irked by American predominance in the alliance. Fearing another war fought on French territory or, at the least, bombs dropped on it during a Soviet-American conflict, de Gaulle ejected American forces and NATO headquarters from French soil and pressed forward the development of France's own nuclear *force de frappe,* aimed at repelling danger well beyond France's borders. He hoped these policies would enhance French influence in Eastern Europe and the Third World, but the effect was less than he had anticipated. Moreover, by 1966 it was apparent that it was the economic integration of Western Europe that most attracted the French people and offered France the best dividends.

3 ORGANIZING WESTERN EUROPEAN INTEGRATION

From 1951 on, the French have promoted a series of supranational organizations to develop economic arrangements within Western Europe. These organizations, starting with the European Coal and Steel Community (ECSC), which was established on July 25, 1952, have created economic bonds between their six members—France, West Germany, Italy, Belgium, Holland, and Luxembourg—that are unprecedented in the history of Europe and offer a model of regional cooperation. Their underlying principle has been to move slowly but steadily toward the elimination of customs barriers between the Six and to do so by constant negotiation and adjustment. There is also an explicit commitment in the agreements to seek to cushion the shock of change and to relieve regional disparities. These latter purposes, however, have been more difficult to achieve.

In the background of these negotiations and occasionally aiding them is the eighteen-member Council of Europe, established in 1949 and operating quietly in Strasbourg. The functions of the council are not directed toward making policy, but to developing a sense of community among European countries outside the iron curtain. The council has a Secretariat, a Committee of Ministers who represent the participating governments, and a Consultative Assembly whose members are drawn from all sections of political opinion—except the Communists—in the parliaments of member countries. Frenchmen have been among the staunchest adherents of the Council of Europe.

The Communities, of course, represent a more structured and positive drive toward integration. The first of these Communities set the pattern by selecting for the original common free trade market a particularly important segment of the economy, coal and iron production (the basis of French and West German military and industrial strength and therefore of particular importance in France's strategic thinking). The second of the Communities was Euratom, under which was placed an atomic energy pool and coordination of nuclear research. Euratom came into existence at the same time as the third and by far the most important of the Communities, the European Economic Community (EEC), or Common Market, established by the Treaty of Rome on January 1, 1958.

The British declined to be included in any of these arrangements at the time that they were established. They also proposed, as an alternative to the Common Market, a wider European free trade market and also one that would include the Commonwealth, but these proposals were rejected by the members of the nascent EEC, the more sharply because they were obviously designed to place Great Britain rather than France at the center of the arrangements. The British then organized in 1959 largely as a bargaining counter a much less promising grouping of the so-called Seven, which included Norway, Sweden, Denmark, Austria, Switzerland, and Portugal. From 1961 on, however, Britain has sought entry, first under a Conservative and subsequently under a Labor government, into the increasingly prosperous Common Market. Despite two vetoes on its membership by General de Gaulle in 1963 and again in 1967, the British effort to negotiate satisfactory terms for entry into all three Communities was begun again by the Conservatives in 1970, and this time with more success.

The organization of the Coal and Steel Community will be described in some detail as the most complete and ultimately the nucleus of all three Communities. Established under a common authority and therefore not subject to the direction of any one government (although France has successfully asserted its right to a *liberum veto* on certain Common Market proposals), the Coal and Steel Community placed under supranational control the production of the two key resources of an area as important strategically as industrially: the rich coal and iron triangle of Western Europe that, in an area only half the size of Alabama, includes Lorraine, the Saar, the Ruhr, and the Rhineland.

The supranational political structure of the European Coal and Steel Community was as complex as it was novel. The executive body was the High Authority, made up of nine members (selected by general agreement of the six governments), who were chosen not to represent particular countries or industries but "for their general competence," and who served six-year staggered terms. The High Authority's decisions were by majority vote. It appears to have had unlimited power to gather information, to prevent the growth of private cartels, and to prohibit and break up mergers that violated the nondiscriminatory aims of the treaty. It had considerable power in other areas affecting production. In practice, however, it

worked with the consent of its member governments rather than by issuing orders to them.

An elaborate structure of checks and balances to the power of the High Authority was provided through four other organs: the Council of Ministers, the Assembly, the European Court of Justice, and the Consultative Committee. The Council of Ministers was the link between the governments and the High Authority; it consisted of one member from each government, and its approval was needed for High Authority action in certain spheres defined by the treaty, notably the development of industry and the regulation of foreign trade. The Assembly (subsequently enlarged into the European parliament, in which France, Germany, and Italy each had thirty-six members, Belgium and Holland each fourteen, and Luxembourg six) was an advisory body that met annually to consider the High Authority's general report. It had the supreme but untapped power of being able to force the resignation of the Authority by a two-thirds vote. The court, composed of seven judges appointed for six-year terms by the governments acting jointly, was the final tribunal in all disputes between the Authority and governments or firms. It could order and restrain action by the High Authority insofar as empowered by the treaty. The Consultative Committee appointed by the council gave producers, workers, and consumers equal representation and provided advice on production programs and the "re-adaptation" of industry and labor to the new conditions of a larger market and more efficient organization of production.

The purpose of this elaborate machinery was to supervise the tariff-free internal trade and common external tariff in coal and steel of the Six. A further purpose was to establish conditions that would progressively "ensure the most rational distribution of production at the highest possible level of productivity" while "safeguarding continuity of employment" and "avoiding the creation of fundamental and persistent disturbances in the economies of member states," to quote the Treaty of Paris, the basic document. The High Authority, through its power to institute studies and to provide financial support from its own resources, underwritten by contributions from the members of the Community, concentrated on aiding the "readaptation" and "reconversion" of local activities, which were made necessary by the impact of the Common Market. This aid was particularly directed to retraining and rehousing workers and to stimulating existing or new industries to absorb those workers who became superfluous through mergers or closing of inefficient enterprises. After 1960, expenditures on reconverting enterprises outstripped aid to workers for their readaptation to new jobs. Moreover, up to the mid-1960s, workers could be transferred to mines that offered better employment possibilities. These opportunities lessened markedly thereafter because of technological innovations in steel production and worsening of market possibilities for coal. The High Authority has tried, therefore, to stimulate new employment in distressed areas, a policy considerably more effective after the three Community executives were merged in 1967.

The second of the specialized functional agencies, Euratom, so quickly captured the public imagination that in July 1956, within a month of the drafting of the treaty, the French National Assembly approved joining the atomic energy pool, which was established in 1958. Euratom spreads the cost of nuclear research among a number of countries that could not afford it singly. But its importance is in the long run rather than immediately, since the high costs of production of atomic energy handicap it in competition with other types of fuel while Euratom itself faces stiff competition from the nuclear developments of Western Europe's private engineering industries.

By far the most significant and far-reaching of all Western European arrangements is the Common Market, which came into existence along with Euratom on January 1, 1958. The Common Market agreement ultimately aims to extend to the whole economy the principles that had been operating for coal and steel. The abolition of general restrictions on trade has naturally been more gradual than those on coal and steel, but through extensive and often hard-fought negotiations the Six have moved far toward a common external tariff and the abolition of all internal trade barriers. During the sixties, the hardest-fought negotiations were over establishing common agricul-

tural prices,[3] the area that will also present great difficulties for the British. In the seventies, the focus is likely to be on monetary matters. The French drew back indignantly in December 1970 from the implications of a Commission proposal for an economic and monetary union, which would necessarily involve a greater transfer of national decision-making to the supranational body than the French were there prepared to make. Yet the West German decision in mid-1971 to let the mark float, followed by President Nixon's comparable action for the dollar late in August 1971, forced a general rethinking of currency standards and may encourage moves toward a common European currency.

As already suggested, the institutions of the European Economic Community followed the pattern of and built upon the existing organs of the European Coal and Steel Community. Until the three executives were formally merged in 1967, the EEC had its own Council of Ministers to make policy decisions and Commission to serve as the permanent executive. It shared both the Court of Justice and the assembly of the ECSC, enlarged as indicated, and renamed the European parliament. The Commission had its headquarters in Brussels, the secretariat of the parliament in Luxembourg, and the assembly itself meets in the same building in Strasbourg as does the Council of Europe. Although the Treaty of Rome only required one meeting a year, the assembly generally meets for five-day sessions up to ten times a year. Its members are appointed by the respective governments, but they sit in party, not in national groupings.

The assembly only possesses advisory and supervisory functions, except for the one decisive but unexercised power to dismiss the whole Commission. It discusses the Commission's annual general report on its activities and reviews its budget, although without power to force conformity to the amendments it may suggest. The assembly has about a dozen specialist committees that study particular ques-

[3] For a case study of how the basic agreement in agricultural policy was reached, see Michel G. Duerr, "The Common Market: Farmers and Foreign Policy: An Agricultural Agreement for Europe," *Politics in Europe: Five Cases in European Government*, ed. by Gwendolen M. Carter and Alan F. Westin (New York, Harcourt Brace Jovanovich, Inc., 1965).

tions, and its Economic and Financial Committee, in particular, has issued significant reports, although, again, the assembly has no power to force conformity to its proposals. The assembly also probes the work of the Commission through written questions of which over five hundred were asked in 1970.

Although the Treaty of Rome included an article that stated, "the Assembly shall draw up proposals for elections by direct universal suffrage in accordance with a uniform procedure in all member states," the Council of Ministers has so far blocked this development, which would inevitably provide the assembly with a degree of popular support that it now almost wholly lacks. In 1969, British Prime Minister Wilson, whose application for entry to the Common Market had been blocked in 1967 by de Gaulle's second veto, joined with the Italian government in a joint request for "an elected parliament." De Gaulle and Pompidou have both been unwilling to go so far, and Prime Minister Heath has only suggested an indirect form of election through national legislatures in place of the current method of appointment of the European assembly members. The issue of some degree of effective popular control over the Commission is likely to become more pressing, however, as the latter acquires more financial resources and thus a greater say in policies affecting EEC members.[4]

Up to British entry, the evolution of the European Economic Commission was somewhat uneven. The Community was not set up with a single integrated institutional framework, and it has developed its institutions on a relatively *ad hoc* basis. Thus only the agricultural common policies acquired a full institutional setup.

The most effective results from the Treaty of Rome have been to lower and finally do away with internal tariffs between the Six. National tariffs on industrial products from other members of the Common Market had already been reduced by 1966 to one-fifth their 1957 level and had disappeared by 1967. Agricultural products, over which the hardest and most prolonged bargaining took place, were also freed from internal tariffs after the 1966 agreement, which artificially subsidized market prices for farm products (thereby easing the French problem of agricultural surpluses) and raised the external tariff high enough to prevent the competition of lower-priced food from outside countries. Since more expensive food has been one of the major, if not the major, argument against British entry into the Common Market, it is worth noting that while negotiations were in progress in February 1971, the European Commission proposed yet higher prices for cereals, milk, and beef, which would raise the annual expenditures of the Community Farm Support Fund to about $2,580 million.

Much less effective have been the positive regional policies that the Commission has been able to sponsor. It spent its first five years in building up information on the dimensions of the total region comprised by the Six and of its economically backward areas. On the basis of these facts the Commission began to call for active policies to secure more balance between undeveloped (largely agricultural) regions, industrial regions in decline, prosperous urban concentrations, and frontier areas. The particular imbalance the Commission highlighted was between the high-powered industrial areas of northeast France, especially near Paris, the Rhineland, and northern Italy on the one hand, and the undeveloped, peripheral areas of western France, West Germany's eastern frontier zone, and southern Italy on the other. Although the Commission called for adaptation of obsolete structures throughout the region comprised by the Six as a necessary concomitant to freer flow of goods between them, the implementation was left to national planning. From 1963 to 1967, the Commission concentrated on studying how best to coordinate national policies en route to developing more specifically common regional policies, an approach that suffered from the absence of agreed common goals. This period was marked in any case by a relative standstill in EEC development, due first to the veto on British

<hr />

[4] So far none of the other three European parliamentary institutions has more than advisory powers. The least known and least well organized is the NATO conference of parliamentarians, a semiofficial group that discusses defense questions. The Assembly of Western European Union, whose members are appointed by national governments, discusses defense matters in its meetings twice a year in Paris and makes recommendations to the Council of Ministers. The Council of Europe, which meets three times a year in Strasbourg, can discuss anything except defense issues.

entry of January 1963 and subsequently to the French withdrawal from the Council of Ministers in 1965 over a deadlock on Commission proposals for enlarging its functions and financial support and increasing the role of the European parliament at Strasbourg. Not until 1967, when the three executives of the Communities were merged, did renewed interest in their potentialities stimulate some advances.

The high point of this progress came in January 1970 with agreements on financing the Community budget, which offered the possibility of some surplus funds for supporting regional developments over and above those required by agricultural policy and financed through the Community Farm Support Fund. The Commission's rather disappointing financial resources, operational by 1964–65, were the European Investment Bank (established in 1959 for development purposes), the European Social Fund (whose objectives, as defined by the Rome treaty, were to increase "the availability of employment and the geographical and occupational mobility of workers"), and the European Agricultural Guidance and Guarantee Fund (founded in April 1962 and restricted to aiding production and marketing of agricultural products). None of these funds had enabled the Commission to take creative measures on its own but only to participate in national projects like the reconversion of the Italian shipbuilding and sulphur industries. Yet, as the Commission pointed out in a 1969 proposal, until the levels of development in different regions throughout the Six were moved closer to each other, a major block remains to integrating their economies.

The functioning of the institutional framework of the three Communities in regard to development aid has so far only been an auxiliary source of support for what remain relatively unharmonized national programs and policies. To summarize the situations among the Six: Holland and Belgium face the least serious regional economic problems, since Holland has a more equitable spread of incomes even than Great Britain, while Belgium, except for its serious linguistic-political split, could fairly easily adjust to the drift of investment and workers from the declining coal mines of the French-speaking east to the largely Flemish-speaking industrial areas near Antwerp. West Germany's most serious continuing regional problem, that of West Berlin, is also a political one. Italy suffers the greatest regional imbalances—the income of its southern provinces is barely half to a third that of its booming industrialized northern sector. There is little indication that this gap is closing, despite substantial incentives to private investment in the southern area. While this aid does not begin to compare with the development assistance provided by Great Britain for its depressed areas in the north, a good deal of the strain on Italy's southern tier has been relieved by substantial migration of Italian workers to other Community countries, particularly to West Germany.

France has the greatest variety of regional problems of any European country: declining coal and textile industries (creating more problems than in Belgium or West Germany because the labor is local and not foreign workers); depopulation in remote rural areas like the *Massif Central* in south-central France; agricultural decline in Brittany, intensifying its sense of cultural separatism; and lack of development in the southwest and Corsica. The Fourth Plan set regional targets for reorganizing and modernizing backward parts of the economy, but these have been largely unfulfilled despite government incentives to industry. On the whole, the government strategy up to 1966 when the economy was prosperous and expanding was to concentrate on growth points rather than on assistance to depressed areas. Since then, the worsening general economic situation plus the sharp decline in the coal industry has forced the government to pay greater attention to depressed areas. President de Gaulle's rejected 1969 referendum proposal would have established greater regional autonomy. This may still be possible, but at least more aid is being extended to the southwest and to Brittany, accompanied by curbs on industrial expansion in the Paris region to prevent still more imbalance.

It is clear from this brief survey that the major focus of development incentives and assistance within the Six continues to rest largely with the individual countries. No conflict has arisen from this fact because none of the Six has poured development aid into a depressed area to a degree that could conceivably offer dangerous competition to developments in the others. Current British development aid to its northern depressed areas can easily fit into this pattern.

The political implications of the Communities have so far been played down by French leaders. De Gaulle was clearly opposed to any obviously supranational political body, and Pompidou has come out firmly on the same line. Yet as an empiricist, he would no doubt be willing to move step by step toward some more political arrangements if they seemed feasible. In the meantime he remains committed to the freer trade aspects of the Common Market and to British participation in planning its future.

4 INTERNATIONAL RELATIONS

Whatever develops in Western Europe, that area cannot free itself from the awareness that there are still two superpowers—the United States and the Soviet Union—whose relations to each other and to Western Europe inevitably have an impact on the latter. Under President Pompidou, however, there has been considerable change in France's attitude to the United States from what it was under de Gaulle. Pompidou feels that there is now a more equitable balance of power between the United States and the Soviet Union than in the period when de Gaulle was so antagonistic to what he saw as overwhelming American power in Europe. Pompidou believes the Soviet Union is satisfied with the territorial extent of its control in Eastern Europe and harbors no ambitions to expand into Western Europe. But although he also watches for conclusive evidence that the Russians are ready for coexistence, Pompidou retains the same attitude as de Gaulle toward the NATO alliance and equally refuses to link France's atomic strike force with that of the United States.

Although there are still divergencies of attitude between France and the United States, there is also no direct rivalry in the other area in which France maintains primary interest: Mediterranean Africa. In the Middle East, France continues its embargo on arms to Israel and feels that American policy is coming closer to its own. It is less antagonistic over Vietnam since it appears to believe in American disengagement from that area in which France itself suffered such deep humiliation. It was critical of the 10 percent surcharge on foreign imports included in President Nixon's emergency measures of August 1971 and has been less flexible than its Common Market partners in seeking generally acceptable currency levels. In general, however, it can be said that France under Pompidou has developed a mildly pro-American position, the more so as the Soviet Union expands its Eurasian influence and its naval and air penetration of the Indian Ocean. In other words, the stronger the Soviet Union becomes as a world power, the more likely it seems to be that France will tend to throw what international political influence it has into the balance on the side of the United States. At all times, however, French interests per se must be expected to predominate.

Conclusion

France's future developments remain uncertain. On the one hand, the youthfulness of its population, its economic growth, and the continuity of political leadership since 1958 indicate a striking degree of prosperity and stability in a country marked in the past by a declining birth rate, a stagnant economy, and cabinet instability. Both nationally and internationally, France has regained the confidence and stature that enable it to play a distinctive and influential role on the world stage. Yet it is still true that France is marked internally by deep divisions between right and left, that each side mistrusts the leaders of the other side, that the structure of government of the Fifth Republic, like those of earlier French constitutional systems, does not make it easy to establish clear-cut responsibility for political decisions, and that the ordinary Frenchman still feels little sense of participation in or influence on the vast official hierarchy that ultimately controls his activities. Thus below the surface, and occasionally shattering its calm, are dissensions and outbursts whose short- and long-term effects are difficult to calculate.

In the sixties, the biggest question hanging over France politically was what would happen when de Gaulle retired or died. In the event, the transition to Pompidou was made with remarkable ease. The crisis of 1968 undermined the prestige of the founder of the Fifth Republic but not the constitutional system itself. The electoral success that marked the repudiation of the student-led revolt was an endorsement of Pompidou as much or more than of de Gaulle. Moreover, it was due to Pompidou, and indirectly to the abortive 1968 revolt, that the declining Gaullist party received its new lease on life. Although de Gaulle attempted to relegate his ablest supporter to relative obscurity by replacing him as premier by the ineffective Couve de Murville, Pompidou continued to conduct himself like de Gaulle's obvious successor. De Gaulle further undercut his own base of political support through the 1969 referendum with its attack on the Senate, the stronghold of an entrenched local as well as national political class. When the referendum failed and de Gaulle resigned, Pompidou was ready to take the opportunity to inherit his position and to wield his own type of power. That it would be a less personal and more organizational influence was certain; that it would be less effective was anticipated, incorrectly as it turned out.

Since he became president in 1969, Pompidou has maintained a firm hand on the machinery of government and has encouraged the police to deal sternly with evidences of disaffection. The latter symptoms of discontent continue, particularly among the students who are far from satisfied with the meager changes that have been instituted in the highly centralized system of education. The dock workers, 98 percent of whom belong to the Communist-dominated *Confédération Générale du Travail*, held their eleventh twenty-four-hour strike in six months in March 1971. Secondary school teachers and others have also held short strikes to publicize their grievances. The extended strike of Renault auto workers in May 1971 and the demonstration commemorating the hundredth anniversary of the Paris Commune are symptomatic of the sporadic activities of the revolutionary New Left. But there has been no repetition of the nation-wide outbursts of 1968, less because of any fundamental changes in the overcentralized system than because of frustration at the lack of results from that massive demonstration of opposition to policies and governmental impersonality, a phenomenon that should be well understood in the United States.

French political polarity continues. The municipal elections of March 1971 could be seen as victories for both right and left. The UDR and its allies won two important towns, Toulouse and Narbonne, from the Socialists in the southwest, a region traditionally hostile to the government majority. Moreover, they achieved an absolute majority in the relatively powerless city council of Paris. The UDR itself won majorities in nine more towns, but lost six. The Communists not only gained control of six more towns, they also lost none. Moreover, although orthodox socialists did not do well (nor did the centrists), left-wing unity under Communist leadership performed effectively. But if the Communists could feel satisfied with this degree of opposition solidarity, so could the UDR, for nothing seems so likely to continue its hold on political power in the next national election as the existence of an effective opposition under Communist domination.

Economically, France appeared to be doing well in the first years of the seventies, although it, like most other countries, remains dogged by persistent inflation. But with almost 20 percent of its exports to Common Market countries still in agricultural products, its 1971 trade surplus seemed none too sure. Industrial activity was increasing, but there were still marked discrepancies between production levels in different areas of the country, a predictable basis for continued discontent. Thus the continuation of stringent controls can be anticipated for the special purpose of shielding France from the worst of inflationary pressures.

Looking both forward and backward, it becomes apparent that despite the possibilities of political or economic difficulties, there is little likelihood of a repetition of the crises that overthrew the Third and Fourth Republics. France has a better international milieu in the seventies within which to work out its problems than has been the case since before World War I. Franco-German cooperation has removed the fear of territorial aggression that haunted France between the wars. France has freed itself of colonial and dependency connections that might threaten to embroil it outside its immediate borders as did its relations with Indochina and Algeria. The bitterness tainting Franco-American relations in the sixties appears to have faded with Pompidou's more conciliatory attitude. After twice rejecting British applications, France opened the door of the Common Market to the United Kingdom in mid-1971. Currency and agricultural problems remain to complicate France's relations with both the United States and the United Kingdom, but they can be tackled in a generally more harmonious atmosphere than existed under de Gaulle—although in large measure because de Gaulle restored French self-confidence and international prestige. Despite its internal strains, France has much to build on.

III The
government
of
Germany

Introduction

The government of Germany presents some complex and formidable problems to the student of comparative government. The terminology itself makes one pause: Should we not rather talk about "The Governments of the Two Germanies"? or, at least, "The Governments of Germany"? In the case of most other nations the subject matter of the inquiry, at least, is clear; in the case of Germany it is elusive. What is "Germany" today? Is it a nation, partitioned, to be sure, and presently under two different regimes, but somehow still one unit (nationally, ethnically, politically, even legally)? How do Germans themselves feel about this? Did they ever agree on what constituted, or ought to constitute, their country? As we shall see, there always was considerable disagreement and confusion about this "existential" question, so that the very problem of the subject matter of this section has to be discussed at length.

This is also one reason why, in contrast to many other countries, the German government must be traced deep into the past, and historical data (or "longitudinal analysis," as the now fashionable term goes) must be paid considerable attention. Germany is a country where everything, even that which elsewhere is taken for granted—the national unit itself—seems to be perennially in flux. If we have decided to still call this a study on "The Government of Germany," we are conscious of the ambiguity. The trend is toward the stabilization of partition and the emergence of two (and with West Berlin, possibly even three!) separate political entities on the way toward being recognized and recognizing each other as separate structures. Perhaps the next edition of this book will discuss Germany under a new title. However, predictions are unprofitable—in politics generally and in German affairs even more so. The reader is cautioned to remember not only the provisional character of things German, but also that frequently it is the provisional that endures.

1

German people and politics

1 THE GERMAN PROBLEM

Germany is the one major foreign power that has been most troublesome and most problematic to the world and to itself throughout recent history. In two world wars, Germany was the major enemy of all or most of the other big powers. Defeat in the second spelled loss of national identity, with the nation split into two political units with diametrically opposed political systems: the Communist-controlled German Democratic Republic and the Western-oriented German Federal Republic. The "Germany question"—that is, the issue of partition and reunification—is one of the few world problems over which a nuclear holocaust might involve the entire globe. Even short of such a holocaust, many Germans tremble lest a contest between East and West be fought over the German issue on German soil, with Germans fighting Germans.

Many people, however, are less than enthusiastic about the reunification of all the Germans. West Germany alone today ranks among the leading countries economically (third in world trade and fourth in industrial production), and it has risen to the status of the second strongest military power on the European continent. East Germany ranks eighth in world trade and is the second industrial power in the Communist world. What, then, might it mean for the world if the two were reunited?

The rapid rise, especially of West Germany, has been almost miraculous. But such radical transformation is not new for Germany. Frequent and extreme changes have swung Germany from fragmentation and disunity (until 1871) to unification (after 1871), to the extreme of centralization, under Hitler, and back to disunity today. In foreign affairs, Germany has swung from impotence to commanding power; internally, from authoritarianism to democracy and back to totalitarian tyranny; spiritually and culturally, from the greatness of Kant, Goethe, and Beethoven to the moral abyss of the Nazi "annihilation camp." No wonder that to the world Germans have alternately appeared as good and bad in the extreme; even a more temperate judgment is likely to be called anti-German by some and pro-German by others. Whoever seeks to understand the Germans, rather than to idealize or to condemn them, appears biased to some.

Opinions about democracy's chances of survival in Germany are equally diverse. To some observers there is only one answer. Germans, they say, have been and always will be a prey to some sort of authoritarianism: old-style Prussian conservatism, more recent fascist-type totalitarianism, Communist control as presently exercised in East Germany, or a neo-Nazism that has reappeared in West Germany. Others believe that democracy is by now firmly settled in the nation's Western section. The truth cannot be gained from preconceived ideas, but only from a study of those historical, geographical, and political forces that have shaped the present Germany. They show that Germany, politically as well as geographically, stands midway between the Western countries, with their longer and firmer traditions of democracy, and Russia, with its almost complete lack of any democratic traditions. Western influence has been strong enough to give Germany ideas, movements, and sometimes institutions that were basically democratic. But—and this has been the tragedy of the Germans—such forces did not in the past prove strong enough to prevail against authoritarian counterforces. This does not preclude their victory in the future. It is precisely the touch-and-go of democratic chances in West Germany that renders developments there so interesting to students of government and politics.

2   THE LAND AND THE PEOPLE

THE LAND

Germany is located in the heart of Europe and is bounded, roughly, by the Alps in the south, by the North Sea and the Baltic Sea in the north, by France and the Low Countries in the west, and in the east by whatever Slavic countries existed or now exist as political units. The vagueness of this description attests to the difficulty of defining Germany geographically. The map of Germany in different historic periods shows that until about a hundred years ago *Germany* was simply a geographical expression for the many territorial units into which the country was fragmented politically. After its unification in 1871, Germany reached from beyond the Rhine River in the west to far beyond the Vistula River in the east and was, with over 200,000 square miles, one of the largest countries in Europe; in addition, it held colonial possessions in Africa and the Pacific Ocean. These it lost in 1919 when defeated in World War I; but even more important were its territorial losses at home. In the west, Alsace-Lorraine, gained from France in 1871, was lost again, and in the east much territory was ceded to newly established Poland, leaving one province, East Prussia, geographically detached from the main part of the country. Reaction came with a vengeance: Hitler, at the height of his power, not only controlled most of the European continent politically but actually incorporated into Germany vast areas, including Austria, Bohemia, and most of Poland.

Present territory and population

Today's map is different again. After the surrender in 1945, the victorious powers agreed that pending a peace treaty all territories east of the rivers Oder and Neisse should be administered by Poland, except for the northern half of East Prussia, which would be administered by the Soviet Union. These territories now constitute integral parts of those countries.

In the present, German territory has shrunk to about the smallest in Germany's entire history. Between the two world wars Germany comprised over 180,000 square miles, somewhat more than California. Today it comprises 136,-000 square miles (about the size of Montana), divided between East and West Germany in the relation of about one to two. Within this rump Germany, however, there live more people than inhabited the former, larger Germany. This is due to the westward shift not only of Germany's boundaries but also of its population. Most Germans formerly living in the detached territories of the East, as well as the ethnically German populations of such countries as Czechoslovakia, Poland, and Hungary, were forced into Germany as "expellees," altogether some 12 million. Thus, in contrast to Britain's and France's approximately 50 million inhabitants each, there is a solid bloc of Germans approaching 80 million in the heart of Europe. Close to 60 million of these live in West Germany, 17 million in the East (including 1 million in East Berlin), and the rest (about 2 million) in West Berlin.

Commercial position and resources

Geography has had a profound impact on German economic and political developments. When the main trade lanes went through central Europe, Germany's location and system of rivers favored its economic development; but when the trade lanes shifted to the Atlantic during the age of overseas discoveries, Germany was left stranded in what became an "underdeveloped" area. This retarded the emergence of a German middle class. The advent of the industrial age, however, enabled Germany to become a great workshop, especially for the industrially less-developed eastern and southeastern regions of Europe which exchanged their agricultural surpluses for German industrial products. Germany's industrialization was rendered possible by one major resource, coal, found in abundance in what became Germany's industrial heart, the valley of the Ruhr River (tributary of the Rhine in western Germany).

But like Britain, and unlike the United States and the Soviet Union, Germany has not been self-sufficient in most other basic resources, including agricultural products. While the climate is as temperate as that of France, the soil is in the main less fertile. Even when Germany still possessed its breadbasket east of the Elbe River, it had to import food. In addition, it had to import such basic industrial raw materials as rubber, cotton, oil, and ores. For a while, it is true, the possession of Lorraine (from 1871 to 1918) enabled Germany's heavy industry to draw from within its own frontiers both iron ore (from Lorraine) and coal (from the Ruhr, the Saar, and Upper Silesia). Steel mills arose near the coal fields, and many different industries were developed around Berlin and in such regions as the upper Rhine and Saxony. Germany's compactness, the absence of high mountain barriers, and its extensive river system made possible a complex system of transportation by rail, water (canals connecting the main rivers), and highway.

But for Germany, as for Britain, it was, and still is, "export or die." The loss of the terri-

tories east of the Oder and Neisse meant the loss of the only region that had yielded a food surplus for the rest of Germany. Furthermore, dwindling trade between Eastern and Western Europe has deprived West Germany and its industry of important markets (only recently has there been a resumption of trade with the East). While industry in East Germany is increasingly integrated with the economy of the Soviet bloc, for which it has become a major workshop, West Germany has had to compete for markets with the main Western powers— which it has done with such success that it now ranks third behind the United States and Japan and before Britain, in volume of world trade. Its exports account for 20 percent of its GNP (as against about 5 percent in the United States).

Thus, to the political miracle of West Germany's return to status and power among the nations must be added the economic miracle of a recovery and prosperity without equal in Western Europe. Credit for this must be given to an ingrained German urge to work and to an undaunted determination to rebuild what had been destroyed by Nazism and war. Workers, for instance, restrained their wage demands in order to enable industry to compete in the world market. It is true, however, that Germans often forget the assistance lent them by others, especially by the United States, which poured billions into the German recovery effort. It must also be remembered that circumstances —paradoxically, those very circumstances that in the beginning seemed most adverse—aided recovery. Physical destruction, which necessitated rebuilding from scratch, provided Germany with an up-to-date, modern plant. Until the late fifties, demilitarization made it possible to concentrate on the manufacture of civilian goods, and the influx of expellees and refugees provided a much needed labor supply.

Strategic position and sectionalism

Politically, Germany's central location and open boundaries have been both an opportunity and a temptation. In contrast to England, with its protected island position, Germany has been either a battleground for others—when weak—or a center from which to expand and

GERMANY

DENMARK

BALTIC SEA

NORTH SEA

SCHLESWIG-HOLSTEIN

Kiel

Kiel Canal

Hamburg

Stettin

Bremen

POLAND

R. Elbe

R. Oder

LOWER   SAXONY

GERMAN

Berlin

DEMOCRATIC

NETHERLANDS

Hannover

R. Weser

R. Neisse

HARZ

REPUBLIC

R. Rhine

NORTH RHINE-
WESTPHALIA

Düsseldorf

Kassel

FEDERAL REPUBLIC

Cologne

ERZGEBIRGE

BELGIUM

Bonn ★

H E S S E

R. Mosel

OF GERMANY

Wiesbaden

Frankfurt

Prague

LUX.

Mainz

CZECHOSLOVAKIA

RHINELAND-
PALATINATE

R. Main

SAAR

Nürnberg

Saarbrücken

R. Rhine

Karlsruhe

B A V A R I A

Stuttgart

R. Danube

BADEN-
WÜRTTEMBERG

FRANCE

BLACK
FOREST

R. Danube

Munich

AUSTRIA

ALPS

SWITZERLAND

ALPS

● LAND CAPITALS   ★ CAPITALS

0   MILES   100

conquer—when strong. As with France and other Continental countries, open land frontiers made it necessary for the country to defend itself; this necessity led to the establishment of the modern state with its standing armies and permanent bureaucracies. In contrast to France, however, Germany's boundaries, except for the sea in the north and the Alps in the south, have been ill defined. This absence of natural frontiers has favored both foreign invasions and aggressive nationalism. Traditionally, German expansion was directed eastward (*Drang nach Osten*), but, as the wars of 1870, 1914, and 1939 showed, this did not preclude aggression toward the west.

If there were geographical causes for German expansionism, geography had also something to do with the opposite political phenomenon, sectionalism. The geography of Germany is diversified. Between the plains in the north and the Alps in the south, more than half of German territory is uplands, crisscrossed by rivers, valleys, hills, and mountain ranges. In the absence of early political unification (such as France was blessed with), regional variation slowed down the process of unification of the numerous, often thousand-year-old subnationalities (*Stämme*), which in the course of history developed their own political ambitions. "Particularism" (as the Germans call this kind of sectionalism) has been as important as nationalism, and its existence has given rise to the recurring problem of German federalism—the problem of how to create *e pluribus unum*.

THE PEOPLE: NATIONALITY

"Volk" and race

Germans may be defined as those German-speaking people who do not claim allegiance to another nation. This is a problematic definition. As a nation the Germans are perhaps more difficult to identify than most other peoples. The German term for nation, *Volk*, is much too vague.[1] Race was made the criterion

of nationhood by the Nazis and other racist Germans. But there are no genuine European races in the sense of subraces of the Caucasian race that can be distinguished by origin and physical characteristics. Physically, Germans are much less uniform than the usual stereotype suggests. The blond, tall, blue-eyed type, though more prevalent than the shorter, dark-haired, brown- or gray-eyed type in areas of northwestern Germany, yields to the latter in many other regions of the country.

One problem, which German racists turned into a race problem, hardly exists any longer: that of the German Jews. Prior to Hitler Jews comprised about 1 percent of the population (600,000) and, because of their tendency to adapt themselves through intermarriage as well as in customs and habits, they were on the way toward extinction by assimilation and intermarriage. The Nazis, considering them a dangerous group of alien race, eliminated them through enforced emigration and physical extermination. Today only some twenty thousand Jews live in Germany.

"Volk" and language

If we cannot define Germans by race, can we define them by language? Again we run into difficulties. For, while almost all inhabitants of what is Germany today speak one common language, not all German-speaking people in the world consider themselves Germans. Most Austrians or German-speaking Swiss, for example, do not consider themselves German in any more than a vague sense of cultural affinity. This reflects an historical process of continual "loss of national substance." Of the Germanic tribes that spread over Europe during the migrations of the fifth and sixth centuries A.D., many founded new nations (such as England) while others disappeared in non-Germanic populations. Those that remained in Germany started a countermovement toward the east where, as far west as the Elbe River, Slavs had settled. They colonized goodly portions of eastern and southeastern Europe, generally settling in mixture with the non-German populations. In what we today call Poland or Bohemia or

---

[1] *Volk* may refer to an organized community, in the sense of "nation," or "people" (as in "the American people"). Or it may have the political connotation of "the masses" as opposed to ruling minorities (as in *Volkssouveränität*: popular sovereignty). Or it may signify in a social sense "the lower strata" or "the common people" (as in the term *Volkswagen*, for "the car of the common man").

the Baltic countries, Germans emerged as a ruling minority, with the original inhabitants as subject populations. There, of course, they have now disappeared. In the west and south, on the other hand, groups that were originally German, such as the Franks (who founded France), the Swiss, and the Dutch, separated culturally and politically from Germany, while the German character of others—the Austrians, for example—became uncertain.

Hence, in contrast to France and Britain, where early political unification created the nation, and to Italy, where political unification came late but where the language was an effective defining agent, Germans could never agree as to what constituted the German *Volk*. This uncertainty contributed to the difficulty of political unification. When unification was finally achieved, in 1871, it was on the basis of what was called the "Little Germany" solution, which left outside the *Reich* (the name of the new political unit), many who considered themselves or were considered by Reich Germans to be national or racial Germans. No identity of Volk and Reich was achieved. On the other hand, the newly established Reich contained non-German national minorities, such as French in Alsace-Lorraine, Poles in the eastern provinces, and Danes in northern Schleswig, which created serious internal and foreign political problems. Between the two world wars, following the cession of Alsace-Lorraine to France and the eastern territories to Poland, few national minorities remained inside Germany; in Germany today there are hardly any, except for the Danes in Schleswig.

With the integration of Germans formerly living beyond the Reich frontiers, and with the recognition that Austrians are not Germans, the nation for the first time can be defined more clearly as one contiguous bloc—the inhabitants of West and East Germany. But their partition involves a danger that they may eventually disintegrate into two not only politically but socially and culturally different nations.

The Germans today

In its population trends Germany has shown the characteristic effects of industrialization, urbanization, and modern hygiene. While in 1800 about 25 million inhabitants of what

later became Germany faced 27 million Frenchmen, by 1900 the relation was 56 million to 39, a deeply disturbing fact to such French statesmen as Georges Clemenceau, who spoke of "20 million Germans too many." Yet even after the territorial losses incurred through World War I, Germany did not have the population density of Britain or Belgium. Today, despite the loss of over 3 million lives in World War II, there are, because of the influx of expellees and refugees, about 500 persons per square mile, or about the same as in Britain. Expellees are mostly concentrated in West Germany, where they have, in the main, been well integrated into the economy and society. But the issue of their lost homelands still poses political problems with which we shall have to deal below.

War and its subsequent upheavals have had a profound impact on German age and sex distribution. Immediately after the war (1946) there were about 1,300 women for every 1,000 men; in the age group twenty-five to forty there were 1,640 for every 1,000. Since then the disproportion has been reduced, but in 1969 there still were 1,106 women for 1,000 men in West Germany, and 1,179 for 1,000 in the East, with the extra women now in the age group over forty. Also, in both parts of Germany the population tends toward superannuation, and the birth rates are low and declining (by 1970, they had fallen below the minimum necessary to keep the population constant).

Within the German nation, the component subgroups are extremely diversified. Such major groups as Franks, Saxons, and Swabians divide into an indefinite number of subgroups. German popular dialects differ to such an extent that a German from the north speaking Low German and a German from the south speaking the Bavarian dialect can hardly understand each other. The common bond is the standard language taught by the schools and largely used in daily life. It is also the written language, which was established by Luther's translation of the Bible. Thus Germans, though religiously split because of Luther, owe to him a linguistic uniformity that has substantially contributed to national integration.

Germans also differ culturally, in customs and habits, and in temperament. Even contrasts between neighboring groups, such as the lighthearted and easy-going Rhinelanders and the heavy, stolid, brooding Westphalians, are striking. But the boundaries of the major German *Stämme* rarely coincide with those of the traditional political units in Germany (such as Prussia, Bavaria, and Württemberg). While the *Stämme* were medieval in origin, the political units were established later through conquest, marriage, and dynastic rule. Contrary to common opinion, the typical Prussian was found only in some parts of Prussia, and even the typical Bavarian only in south Bavaria. The picture is further complicated by the addition to the indigenous populations of the expellees and refugees, themselves divided into Silesians, East Prussians, and so forth. This makes for occasional friction. Yet, like urbanization, it tends to result in greater uniformity through mixture. Also, increasing mobility of people tends to attenuate *Stämme* distinctions.

THE PEOPLE: RELIGION

The impact of religious differences on German society and politics has been very strong. While the other major nations of Europe are denominationally more or less uniform, religion splits the German nation. This split has been more divisive in its effects than, say, in the United States, because it was compounded by the territorial split of Germany during the Reformation and Counter Reformation. It was agreed at the Peace of Augsburg (1555) and reconfirmed at the Peace of Westphalia (1648) that the rulers of the German principalities should independently determine the religion of their subjects, and as a result the conflict between Protestants and Catholics went through the heart of Germany. Even today, after many shifts of population, this division is still largely territorial, with the north and east predominantly Protestant, and the south and west Catholic. In the southwest, however, early subdivisions tend to confuse religious lines. In Württemberg and Hesse, for example, there are more Protestants than Catholics, and even in strongly Catholic Bavaria there are some predominantly Protestant areas. In the unified Reich of 1871, Protestants outnumbered Catholics by two to one. Today, the loss of the eastern territories and the split of the remain-

der into East and West has left West Germany with the two denominations in the relation of about one to one (Protestants having a slight edge), while East Germany is almost entirely Protestant (over 15 of 17 million).

This religious division has affected German society and politics because of the intimate connection between church and state. In some Catholic regions prior to the nineteenth century, bishops and archbishops were often simultaneously the spiritual leaders in their regions and the worldly rulers of corresponding "church principalities." In Protestant states individual rulers became the highest church authorities. Luther himself agreed to the state's having authority over church affairs in return for the princes' protection of Protestantism. This meant subjection to secular authority. Church organization became almost indistinguishable from state organization; in the eyes of the ordinary citizen, the Lutheran pastor became one of the persons representing state authority, the more so since the pastor received his salary through state subsidies granted to the churches. Thus Protestantism became a pillar of secular power, which throve, as in tsarist Russia, on the alliance of throne and altar. The basically conservative influence of Protestantism in Germany was strengthened by the absence of Nonconformists. The partnership of church and state left antiauthoritarian groups, middle class or labor, liberal or socialist, without religious backing. Many were thus driven into antireligious attitudes. Marx, a German, considered religion to be the "opium of the people," a mere ideology to keep the masses subservient. Numbers of non-Marxist Germans came to think similarly. Germans divided into (largely conservative) churchgoers and (largely socialist or liberal) nonbelievers.

The Catholic Church was basically as favorable to authoritarian tendencies as was Protestantism. After 1871, to be sure, it was driven to oppose the Prussian-dominated and thus basically Protestant new German state. Since Catholics were in a minority, and concentrated in certain regions, the Church developed what came to be known as "political Catholicism": a party (the Center party) to defend its interests, a press, and Christian trade unions. To retain its hold over the Catholic population, the clergy had to become politically active.

Until recently, Catholics were advised in sermons on election day how to cast their vote. The discontinuance of this practice clearly had some connection with the 1969 losses of the main "Christian" party in West Germany, the Christian Democratic Union (CDU), especially in Catholic areas, and the corresponding gains of its main competitor, the Social Democratic party (SPD). The resumption of this practice in a Bavarian election in 1970 probably had something to do with the gains of the Christian Social Union (CSU), the Bavarian affiliate of the CDU. Catholicism continues to struggle for the maintenance of a system under which primary schools in many regions divide into those of Catholic character and those of Protestant character, a system that is increasingly replaced by nondenominational education. Finally, the churches, Catholic as well as Protestant, have always depended on state subsidies. The intimate connection between church and state is apparent from the fact that this subsidization proceeds through taxation: a 10 percent church tax is added to the income tax of each German who has not officially given up church membership (which is acquired automatically by birth). For these reasons, Catholicism has had as much interest as Protestantism in participating in public affairs. This sometimes has caused Protestants to suspect that Catholicism had a pernicious, Vatican-directed influence over German affairs, while Catholics, on their part, would suspect Protestants of discriminating against them in civil service personnel policies or otherwise.

This mutual suspicion may, in part, be owing to the social differentiation between members of the two religions. By and large, Catholics are under-represented among the upper classes and high-status professions; proportionally, more of them live in rural and small-town regions, are farmers, miners, and lack higher education. Their income, on the average, is lower, their share in elite influence and decision-making less than that of Protestants. Whatever the reasons (which may be historical —such as the traditional Protestant domination of Prussia—or may be owing to the Protestant "spirit of capitalist enterprise" alleged by Max Weber, or even, as some have maintained, to the institution of celibacy, which has prevented

Catholic intelligentsia, in contrast to the contributions of the Protestant parsonage, from adding to Catholic leadership), social inequality has been an important factor in the religious cleavage in Germany and in its effects. For example, the fact that in Catholic industrial areas (such as the Ruhr) most Catholics are workers, while the managerial class is Protestant, has produced a typical "cross-cutting cleavage" in the political attitude of those whose social standing would lead them to vote "socialist" while their religious affiliation would induce many of them to vote "Christian."

On the other hand, and especially among Protestants, the historically close association of church and state, as well as the general secular trends of industrial societies, has caused a good deal of religious indifference. Nominally, about 95 percent of Germans in the West are members of a church, but many nominal Protestants tend to be unreligious, especially among Protestant workers. The hold of the Catholic Church over its members is greater. The promotion of social reform by important Catholic groups accounts for the continuing influence of the Church on workers professing Catholicism. However, in both churches the number of those officially relinquishing their affiliation has of late been significantly rising.

In contrast to the trend toward religious indifference, a striking new phenomenon in German Protestantism has been the rise of a small but elite group of "nonconformists." Drawing its inspiration from the stand taken by Protestants who resisted Nazism, it radically questions domestic as well as certain foreign policies and thus breaks with the tradition of German churches to permit the nation's politics to go unchallenged. Also, for the first time in the history of German Protestantism, the different churches (Lutheran, Reformed, etc.) in the different regions have joined in a kind of federal organization, the Evangelical Church in Germany (EKD); however, this could be had only at the price of disaffiliating from Protestantism in East Germany, where the churches were merged into a unit of their own under the pressure of the regime. German Catholicism, on the other hand, in contrast to the reformist and sometimes almost "revolutionary" developments in neighboring countries (such as the Netherlands), has remained conservative, in the main, especially among the hierarchy.

THE PEOPLE: SOCIAL STRUCTURE

The presentation of a clear picture of German society is difficult. The East and the West of Germany grow ever farther apart in their social structure. East Germany has assumed the features of a Communist state, with its social structure more and more patterned after that of the Soviet Union. In West Germany no such radical transformation of society has occurred. There is still the familiar picture of workers and industrialists, traders and peasants, all competing for social and political influence through established institutions and channels, through trade unions, professional associations, organizations of businessmen, political parties, and above all through the bureaucracy. Postwar developments have modified this picture slightly. Thus there was initially the turmoil created by the influx of the expellee millions, but as prosperity rose, most of them were assimilated and integrated into the West German economy and society; today there are only a few who consider themselves outcasts or "have-nots" in their new environment. Another group, rather, can be considered an "underclass" in present-day West Germany: the foreign workers, mostly from the Mediterranean countries, whose number has fluctuated with economic booms and busts but which at peaks has surpassed 2 million. Many of them have brought their families and thus tend to become part of the permanent population. But Germans, although needing them, are inclined to consider them an alien element; for some they emerge as a kind of ersatz-Jew, on whom it is permissible to vent hatred and resentment. Like the blacks in the United States, they are first to be fired; and, beyond this job insecurity, they are disadvantaged by the state's failure to provide adequate schooling for their children and exploited by the high rents charged for inadequate housing.

There are other pockets of poverty, for instance among the war-injured, the elderly, or those who lost their savings during the postwar inflation and failed to recoup their losses subsequently. The present inflation (there is no unemployment, but an increasing danger of inflation comparable to that in the United States) may prove politically explosive in a Germany with memories of two ruinous inflations (one after each world war). But by and large a prosperous system was able to indemnify those who for various reasons through the vagaries of Nazi rule, war, and postwar turmoil had lost out; most of them, including the expellees, formed or joined pressure groups that proved to be very efficient in winning assistance and benefits from the government.

German society has long been noted for its continuity, even rigidity. No change by revolution, as in France, has ever interrupted its steady development. Until about a hundred years ago, in contrast with Britain, Germany had been a predominantly agrarian country. It had played a relatively small part in the growth of commerce and trade in the West generally since the beginning of the modern age. Up to about 1850 the typical German social relationship, at least in the north and east, was still the feudal or half-feudal one of master and serf, of a noble landowner and an economically and socially dependent peasant; in the cities, handicraft, controlled by closed guilds, prevailed.

Then Germany became rapidly and thoroughly industrialized. As late as 1880, almost half of its gainfully employed people were in agriculture. After World War I, however, workers comprised half of those gainfully employed, while those in agriculture totaled less than a third. A tremendous migration from country to city took place in a brief period of time. New industrial centers developed rapidly. Today, one-third of West Germany's population lives in cities with over a hundred thousand inhabitants. Less than 10 percent of gainfully employed West Germans still work on the land; almost 50 percent work in industry, while close to 40 percent are engaged in service industries (somewhat less than half of them in commerce and transportation, over half of them in public or other services). The number of self-employed "independents" (comprising farmers, independent businessmen, artisans, and professionals) has declined steadily, while the number of white-collar employees and similar salaried persons has risen sharply, so that over four-fifths of the working population now consists of wage or salary earners. These are the characteristic features of the "third industrial revolution." The agricultural sector has been steadily declining, and the industrial sector has begun to decline proportionally to the rise of the service sector, both public and private. Not included in the above figures are the large numbers of recipients of retirement and other pensions and similar fixed income. Thus Germany, like other industrialized nations, consists of people increasingly dependent

Changes in Population, Occupation, and Income Distribution for the Reich and Federal Republic

	REICH			FEDERAL REPUBLIC	

Percentages of population in communities below 2,000 and over 100,000:

Communities	1871	1910	1939	1950	1967
−2,000	63.9	40.0	30.1	27.6	20.7
+100,000	4.8	21.3	31.6	30.1	32.5

Percentages of persons occupied in (a) agriculture and forestry, (b) industry, (c) service sector (commerce, transportation, public and private services):

1882			1925			1950			1967		
A	B	C	A	B	C	A	B	C	A	B	C
42	36	22	31	42	27	22	45	33	10	47	43

Percentages of working persons by status: (a) self-employed, (b) workers (including domestic workers), (c) white-collar and civil service employees:

1895			1925			1950			1967		
A	B	C	A	B	C	A	B	C	A	B	C
37	58	5	33	50	17	28	51	21	19	48	33

Percentage distribution of income between (a) upper 10 percent, (b) middle 40 percent, (c) lower 50 percent of income recipients:

1913			1928			1936			1950			1961		
A	B	C	A	B	C	A	B	C	A	B	C	A	B	C
40	36	24	37	38	25	39	43	18	34	46	20	38	40	22

Source: Adapted from Dieter Petzina, "Materialien zum sozialen und wirtschaftlichen Wandel in Deutschland seit dem Ende des 19. Jahrhunderts," *Vierteljahrshefte fuer Zeitgeschichte*, 17 (3) (July 1969), pp. 308ff.

Comparison in percentages of occupational structure of the Federal Republic and Democratic Republic, 1968

PERSONS WORKING IN:	FEDERAL REPUBLIC	DEMOCRATIC REPUBLIC
Agriculture	10.0	13.1
Industry	47.4	48.6
Commerce and transportation	17.8	16.9
Services	24.8	21.3

Source: *Bericht der Bundesregierung und Materialien zur Lage der Nation 1971* (Bonn, Bundesministerium fuer innerdeutsche Beziehungen, 1971), p. 79.

both economically and socially on jobs or similar security rather than private initiative.

Another feature of German society is its very unequal distribution of property and income. While average income and living standards have been rising for all classes in the postwar period, they still are significantly lower for workers than for white-collar employees and many of the self-employed. Relative income distribution among upper, middle, and lower income groups has varied little from the pre–World War I to post–World War II periods. Similar inequality is revealed by comparing on the one hand the proportional shares of total wages and salaries and on the other of profits and income from independent work, which in 1950 was 58 to 42 percent and in 1968, 65 to 35 percent (in view of the proportional rise in the number of wage and salary earners, the former should have risen to 69 percent).

Many of these features are shared by West Germany with most other capitalist and industrial societies. But there are some characteristics that distinguish Germany from, say, the United States, a country that was industrialized at the same time and with the same thoroughness. Germany's lower classes never had much opportunity to rise socially. The Marxist terms *bourgeoisie* and *proletariat* fitted Germany better than other industrialized countries: once born into either class one stayed there, and strong class consciousness prevailed.

These German characteristics can perhaps be further elucidated by applying the concept of "modernization" and asking in what respect and to what extent Germany constitutes a modernized society. If modernity implies not only scientifically based industrialization, efficiently run big government, and centralized administration, but also equality of opportunity and the disappearance of privilege based on birth, status, or class, German developments have been characterized by a pervasive conflict between modernizing and pre- or antimodern tendencies. The typical German contrast has been between modernization in science, technology, industry, and administration, and premodernity in social structure (classes, castes), education (reflecting class structure), governing elites, military, and, partly, attitude structure; in the latter sphere, a spirit of enlightenment and innovation, underlying splendid achievements in science and technology, strangely contrasts with romanticism and antienlightenment attitudes. For a long time, the premodern, "feudal" rule of an aristocracy aided by a "caste" of state officials was superimposed on the evolving industrial system; the attempt to replace it by a modern, Western-type democratic system failed, and, after the demise of the antimodern Nazi interlude (which, paradoxically, had created certain bases of modernization through its promotion of "rational" business structures and its physical destruction of portions of the German nobility), postwar "restoration" preserved in the Federal Republic much of the previous social rigidity. It is indeed remarkable that, despite the upheavals of the last half-century—inflation and depression, Nazi rule and war economy, influx of millions of refugees, and partition of the nation—Germans in the West were able to preserve a traditional social structure without basic changes. There is, to be sure, a bit more social mobility for individuals, and the working class has adopted middle-class habits of living, but, overall, the division of status and class is still prevalent. A coalition of bureaucracy, business, and peasantry, with labor in only half-hearted opposition, has been instrumental in lending West Germany its markedly conservative character. It is only very recently that countertendencies have become more noticeable, especially in the political radicalism of part of the new generation. Before studying how this, and especially how the discrepancy between modern and nonmodern features, is reflected in the German "political culture," we shall briefly survey the institutional characteristics of three areas that are basic for developments in the social system: education, labor, and business.

3   PROBLEMS OF EDUCATION

THE TRADITIONAL SYSTEM

No influence has been more important in maintaining the traditional class structure than the peculiar German system of education. It has divided Germans into two sharply defined groups: the educated (*Gebildete*) and those who have had no chance at more than a grade-school education. *Bildung* (inadequately translated as *education* or *culture*) has been the property of an elite, small as compared with the masses of the *Ungebildete*. Membership in this elite was attained not on the basis of selection of talent through equal opportunity but through the educational monopoly enjoyed by those financially able and, according to tradition and social status, obliged to send their children through the special institutions for higher education: the *Gymnasiums* (high schools) and the universities. The latter, in contrast to those in the United States, are not colleges for general education—which one is supposed to have acquired at the Gymnasium—but graduate institutions of specialized learning. The Gymnasium at an early point branched off from the grade or "people's school" (*Volksschule*, now usually called *Grundschule*, primary school), which, providing elementary training, was the only school that most German children attended. They stayed there until the age of fourteen, while the selected few were sent at about the age of ten to Gymnasium. Those finishing school at age fourteen would have to attend "vocational school" (*Berufsschule*) until age eighteen, but this school, supposed to train one for a job in trade or industry, was (and is) part-time and perfunctory. On the other hand, the minority, after attending Gymnasium for about nine years, would pass a final examination (*Abiturienten* examination), entitling them to enroll in a university. Thus the fate of a German child was determined at an early age and almost irrevocably.

It is true that occasionally parents of lower status through great sacrifice managed to give their children a higher education. This was par-

ticularly true of lower- and middle-rank officials eager to see their sons climb to higher rank; but it was a rare occurrence for a child of a worker or peasant. On the other hand, the connection between money and the prestige enjoyed through *Bildung* was by no means automatic. Higher education had been demanding; and *Akademiker* (university graduates, enjoying, among the *Gebildete*, especially high prestige) have traditionally filled the higher positions in administration, justice, education, and the professions, positions with generally lower income but higher social prestige than business. Thus even within the middle class there were multitudinous distinctions of higher or lower ranking, the ranks being indicated by a wealth of titles, indications of status or occupation, and similar outward signs of social stratification.

The traditional dual system of education was undemocratic not only in that it gave a small elite nearly exclusive access to the leading positions in state and society, but also in that it instilled into Germans generally the attitudes of authority and submission. The structure of the German family (with the father dominant) has often been held responsible for the authoritarian atmosphere in which the typical German has been raised. But it was more likely the typical social institutions the young German came to know—the schools, the army, factory, or shop—which chiefly created this atmosphere. The German family did not remain authoritarian any longer than the family in other European countries; it ceased to be so after World War I. But in the schools the authoritarian spirit by and large continued to prevail: the student remained in awe of the teacher and professor. Since nearly all schools and universities in Germany are state institutions, the pupil encountered state authority at a tender age in the person of the teacher (usually male) at the *Volksschule*. Teachers belong to the state officialdom, and education thus never was a matter of cooperation between local community and school. There were, and are, no school boards or PTA's to alleviate this rigid system.

TRENDS TOWARD EDUCATIONAL REFORM

While a complete transformation of the traditional educational system has occurred in East Germany (see Chapter 7, Section 7), at best only increased efforts toward reforming the system have occurred in West Germany. True, democratization of German society through educational reform had been a major goal of the occupying powers in the postwar period, but nothing had come of it. Even denazification had been a failure; most of those who had been teachers under the Nazis were allowed to continue. Many of them were nationalist-conservative rather than Nazi. They tended to avoid discussion of the Nazi past and continued the traditional, apolitical type of instruction. Hence the postwar German youth, who was receptive to new ideas that would fill the void left by Nazism, became "pragmatic" and throughout the fifties remained so, interested in career advancement rather than in general affairs, including political matters. Even the school texts remained apolitical, providing premodern, even preindustrial, material. For the most part, this is still true, although recently some modern textbooks dealing with the present, real world have appeared.

Since the middle sixties, this conservative apathy has given way to reformist zeal. The reformist trend began with a pragmatic problem-solving approach, continued with a mixed pragmatic-political tendency, and ended up with a full-fledged, partly radical movement for change. The pragmatic stage was initiated when scientists and statisticians showed that West Germany could not expect to stay in the ranks of first-rate industrial nations if it failed to train a vastly increased number of scientists, engineers, doctors, and so forth. Most impressive was the fact that in East Germany a proportionally higher number of students received technological training at universities. The threat of not having enough skilled people to meet the demands of a highly industrialized society led to increased governmental involvement with higher education. A number of new universities were, and are being, established for increasing numbers of students who are aided by government grants. A Council on Scientific Matters (*Wissenschaftsrat*) and a Council on Education (*Bildungsrat*) were created to advise

government on what to do and how to plan for the future. The central (federal) government, by constitutional amendment, was given jurisdiction in areas previously reserved to the states (*Länder*), which, under the social-liberal coalition government of Willy Brandt, has been used for long-range, centralized financial planning and coordination of reform, especially of higher studies.

The second area of reform has been at the opposite pole: primary education, and particularly with regard to a special German problem, that of the relation of the churches to education. As we mentioned earlier, German primary education has been characterized by strong church influence. Although there are no private denominational schools in Germany (all schools, with the exception of a handful of high schools, are run by the state), religious influence has been strong in those regions where primary public schools are established separately as Catholic or Protestant, according to the faith of pupils and teachers (*Bekenntnisschulen*). This meant standards were lowered in areas where, due to the small size of the denomination or, in rural areas, the small size of the population, there are only one- or two-grade schools; it also meant perpetuating the religious split of Germans by rooting it early in the mind of the child. But the Catholic Church, in particular, defended the system, because it proved instrumental in holding German Catholicism together as a strongly integrated group.

During the last decade, however, the trend has been in the direction of the other type of primary school: the nondenominational school (*Simultanschule*), where pupils of all faiths (or of no faith) are taught together, separating only for religious instruction. Since the decision of which type of school to have is left to the *Länder*, the issue became a political one, with the Christian Democrats advocating separate schools, the *Bekenntnisschulen*, and the socialists and liberals favoring the *Simultanschulen*. By now, most states have come out, or are in the process of coming out, for reform. Even in Bavaria and North Rhine-Westphalia, predominantly Catholic areas where the confessional schools were strongly entrenched, the mixed-faith schools are gradually being introduced. It is perhaps typical of the reformist trend that last-ditch resistance has come only from the hierarchy and not from Catholic parents. Opinion polls in the late sixties showed that large majorities (including Catholics) were in favor of nondenominational education (non-Catholics, 74 to 19 percent; Catholics, 61 to 31 percent). If this reform is carried through, one doctrinal issue that has traditionally divided Germans will have been resolved.

However, this still leaves the main issue unsolved: the undemocratic and elitist dual system of education. Although Gymnasium attendance has increased slightly, it is still a low 15 percent of the total school population. In part the low enrollment reflects the financial inability of lower-class parents to support their children through long years of higher education. But attitudinal studies point to further reasons, some deeply rooted in the traditional social structure. Lower-class parents are reluctant to send their children into a strange environment in which they feel they do not "belong"; they lack information on what education means, with a corresponding failure to plan their children's careers. This accounts, in part, for the low percentage of workers' children among university students (5 percent), whereas the previously high figure (about 50 percent) of children of academically trained parents, public officials, and professionals has gone down a bit in favor of the children whose parents lacked academic training, especially white-collar

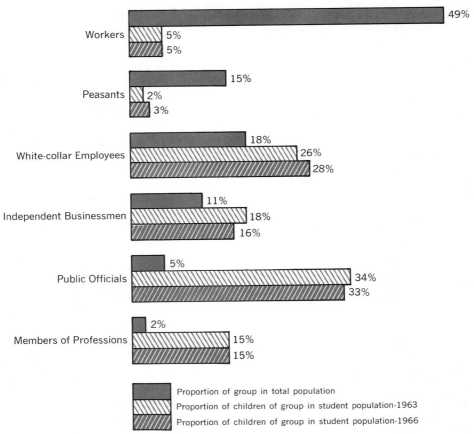

Social Background of West German University Students (1963)

Legend:
- Proportion of group in total population
- Proportion of children of group in student population-1963
- Proportion of children of group in student population-1966

Workers: 49%, 5%, 5%
Peasants: 15%, 2%, 3%
White-collar Employees: 18%, 26%, 28%
Independent Businessmen: 11%, 18%, 16%
Public Officials: 5%, 34%, 33%
Members of Professions: 2%, 15%, 15%

Source: Gewerkschaftliche Rundschau (September 1965), p. 545, and Jahrbuch der Öffentlichen Meinung (1967), p. 353.

employees (see chart on page 356). Thus, the barrier is slightly broken by the middle-status groups but not by the lower ones.

Suggestions to improve matters have ranged from opening the universities to more "outsiders" (e.g., persons who, while working, prepare themselves for study through evening courses), to extending the duration of *Volksschule* attendance by several years, while reducing the length of Gymnasium study correspondingly, and beyond this, to the "radical" proposal to replace the dual system by one of "comprehensive schools" (*Gesamtschulen*) on the American plan, where all students would attend one and the same system through what is now Gymnasium, allowing all who qualify to enter graduate study. The latter solution is favored by an increasing number of Germans, and not only among the leftists and lower strata. But it would imply a vast financial effort and could probably be introduced only gradually, in view of the unavailability of teachers and facilities for the big influx of children who would be going at least through high school. In addition, many Germans (and not only "reactionary" ones) are anxious lest the traditionally high German standards of advanced education (with complaints about qualitative deterioration already heard) might be watered down by mass education. Thus the difficulties in the path of a genuine reform providing equal

opportunity to the talented and loosening the oligarchic social structure of Germany are still great. Not to solve the educational and social problems at least over the next couple of decades, however, would constitute moral and political failure.

One area of reform, where success at least is beckoning, is the organization and structure of the universities themselves. The traditional system, where the head of an institute or the full professor ruled supreme not only over students but also over instructors, assistants, and so forth, is yielding almost everywhere to a variety of systems, some of which go far in the direction of student participation. The new system, although here and there taken advantage of by extremists, promises to give Germany the modernized higher instruction without which no "developed" country can remain in a foremost position.

If modernization is in time accompanied by educational democratization, it would eliminate what strikes the American most sharply when he meets Germans—their almost instinctive observation of the barriers between high and low, between educated and uneducated; it might gradually generate that feeling of being on an equal footing with everybody else, which a society without educational monopoly, such as the American, has created despite marked distinctions in wealth and income.

4   LABOR IN GERMAN SOCIETY

German labor, in both its status and its politics, reflects the rigidity of German society. The educational monopoly of the middle class and the absence of an economic frontier in Germany prevented social mobility of the American type and froze labor at the lower level of society as a distinct "class." Consequently, German labor developed class consciousness and a *political* labor movement with a political party (Social Democratic, or SPD), long dominated by the Marxist brand of socialist ideology, and trade unions, which, unlike those in America, have not limited themselves to industrial activities but have tried (more in the British manner) to achieve gains for labor through

influencing legislation and administration. Although (unlike British labor) German labor was not strong enough to put a program of socialization into practice, it has been able—and is now satisfied—to make significant advances through labor legislation and social reform.

GERMAN TRADE UNIONS

Most of labor's advances are due to the strong organization of its different branches and sectors in a by now largely unified trade union movement. In the past, German trade unions had been split; they were tied up with different political parties, chiefly the SPD and the (Catholic) Center party. After the literally "shattering" experience of the Nazi interlude, however, they reestablished themselves as one overall—and officially apolitical—German Trade Union Federation (DGB). Thus drawing support from both the SPD and the left wing of the CDU (Communist influence being negligible), they are required to be neutral in party issues, but it is no secret that in many respects the DGB is closer to the Social Democrats.

German trade unions have traditionally represented a large proportion of labor. The DGB alone has over six and a half million members and is, together with the American AFL-CIO and the British TUC, one of the three largest and most powerful union federations of the world. If one adds some non-DGB-affiliated unions, about 8 million out of 29 million West German workers and employees are organized. Within the DGB, about 78 percent of the membership are workers, 13 percent salaried employees, and 9 percent officials. Employees are split, with about half of the white-collar employees having a separate, non-DGB-affiliated union; officials are likewise organized in large numbers in a separate organization (the German Civil Service Association, DBB). seven hundred thousand of them, as against a hundred thousand in the DGB-affiliated public services union. This reflects the split in attitudes between members of the labor force in the higher strata and the workers. Even workers are unevenly organized, from miners (over 80 percent organized) down to agricultural laborers.

Among the DGB's sixteen federations, organized according to industries, the Big Five represent metal workers (with close to one-third of total union membership), chemical, construction workers, those in public services, and miners. German unions traditionally have followed uniform policies rather than trying, individually or locally, to gain favors for this or that group of labor. But it has been the federations, rather than the central organization or regional and local subdivisions that have set the pace. When unions bargain collectively, their opposite numbers usually are not single employers but employers' organizations for an entire industry. They, in turn, are organized in one overall Union of Employers' Associations, so that two huge organizations of "social partners" face each other. Industrial relations, like other fields in Germany, are less a grass-roots affair than one of arranging and organizing from the top.

German unions have been free from bossism (in the American sense); there has been no racketeering, and there are no prohibitive initiation fees. There is no closed shop; benefits gained by unions are in many cases extended to all workers in the respective industry. Wildcat strikes have been rare, and strikes organized by unions are disciplined. The unions employ thousands of paid functionaries and control large funds, used in part for educational purposes, including the training of a labor elite of union leaders, labor directors, works council leaders, and so forth—thus offering young workers one way of rising socially outside the established German educational pattern.

LABOR DEMANDS, CODETERMINATION

But once the unions became wealthy and powerful (running, among other enterprises, one of West Germany's largest banks) and developed professional, career staffs of their own, they became part of an "establishment," which some younger workers (and even some trade union leaders, especially in the "leftist" metal workers union) suspect of being more interested in its own "vested" interests than in promoting more far-reaching labor demands. In former times the demands of a socialist-oriented labor movement included socialization, in particular the nationalization of key industries. But this aim, which had a chance for realization in the immediate postwar period, was lost when the occupation powers delayed decisions until Konrad Adenauer took over at Bonn. Since then, trade unions, instead, have pressed for the introduction of a system in which labor gets a share in management ("codetermination").

Codetermination had its origin in the older institution, the works councils (shop or factory committees) established in the Weimar period. These councils, which continue to exist, are elected by workers and employees in all larger enterprises (whether union members or not, and usually on the basis of party lists) and have as their main function participation in matters affecting workers directly, such as adoption of safety rules, dismissals, individual grievances, and similar "in-plant" matters. Codetermination means extending such participation to general matters of management, at least in questions affecting workers and management alike, such as changes in the nature of the enterprise, mergers, and shutdowns. Following the pattern set by the Military Government (MG) for the temporary trusteeship management of the Ruhr industries, federal legislation first gave labor a codetermination right in the larger coal and steel enterprises and then, in somewhat different form, in the other larger corporations in the Republic. But labor is represented only on the supervisory boards of coal and steel on a fifty-fifty basis, on those of other joint stock companies by only one-third. In coal and steel companies it also sends a "labor director" as one of three members to the management board, or board of directors (the other members being the production and the business manager).

While labor expected a new type of economy and society from this innovation, and management was apprehensive of losing its control over the direction of industrial affairs, experience has shown that neither these fears nor labor's expectations were justified. Labor representatives bring the interests of workers or trade unions to bear on matters concerning labor more or less directly, and this has generally had a beneficial influence on labor-management relations. Beyond this, however, employers have remained masters in their own house. In the words of one American observer, Clark Kerr, codetermination in West Germany has proved to be "a sheep in wolf's clothing."

Although labor directors or labor representatives on the board of trustees are not instrumental in matters of price policies or investments or even in preventing mergers, cartels, or other restraints of trade, and although opinion polls have shown that most workers know little about the details of codetermination and are cynical about its effects, extension of the system under which unions are represented equally with management on the supervisory boards of *all* larger enterprises is now one of labor's chief demands. By 1971, attempts to broaden codetermination still faced an uncertain fate. Actually, it is likely that other matters will assume more urgency.

German labor, which had been modest in its demands during decades of postwar reconstruction, of late has started to ask for a larger share in the affluence that, as we have seen, has benefited the upper classes more than the lower. Various suggestions for having labor share in the profits and property of the corporations are in the offing. And with the main political arm of labor, the SPD, now in government and thus in the classical dilemma of a labor party, which has to consider the "commonweal" and not only the interests of one social group, it will be more and more up to the unions to see to it that labor's interests are promoted at the top government level. Indeed, ever since the SPD adopted a more moderate program over a decade ago, many among labor have been looking toward the unions as a kind of ersatz party to advance more leftist aims. Thus the unions may be faced with not only more conflict with government but, internally, with more conflict between the tendency to be part of a conservative establishment and an increasing demand for more reforms, if not revolution.

SOCIAL SECURITY

But German labor, although traditionally the lower class in German society, has hardly ever been revolutionary in attitudes and demands. It is this that has given German society its customary stability. One reason has been social security, which had been granted to those not sharing in property and wealth.

Germany was one of the first industrial countries to institute progressive labor legislation and social insurance. A comprehensive system of social insurance was adopted already in the nineteenth century. This system reflected a traditional German concern for the social welfare of the masses not otherwise admitted to political or social standing. Compulsory health insurance was introduced in 1883, accident insurance (workmen's compensation) in 1885; disability and old-age insurance followed in 1891; unemployment insurance was added after World War I; and family allowances for each child after the first, after World War II. While the German system has not been so all-inclusive as the British cradle-to-grave system, it now comes very close to it. Four out of five West

Germans are covered by public health insurance (which also provides for pay during prolonged illness). Old-age and disability insurance now covers many groups besides workers and low-income employees; pensions may reach 75 percent of the worker's last earnings and have been made adaptable to a rise in prices ("dynamic pensions"). With modern economies forever beset by inflation, this seems to be the socially decent thing to do, and it is being imitated by other nations. Yet pensions paid to certain groups (for example, war disabled and war widows) are still much too low.

The system functions on the basis of rights acquired through contributions, amounting by now close to 30 percent of wages shared equally by employers and employees. As in France, it is administered on a functionally and geographically decentralized basis, with local and regional funds for the different branches and boards on which employers and employees are represented. With the state contributing about one-third of its cost, about 16 percent of the West German GNP is spent for social security; one-fifth of the total public expenditures (federal, state, and local) goes into it.

Since its inception this system has been one of the most constant of German institutions. In its main features it is taken for granted by most Germans, despite the heavy financial burden it involves. Some maintain that the system has made the German too security-minded and

that facilities such as the manifold benefits under health insurance have been taken advantage of; but it is hardly contested that public health has benefited, and even the average doctor, who first objected that the system destroyed the personal relationship between doctor and patient, gave up his opposition when, in financially difficult periods, he survived only owing to his *Kassenpraxis* (fees paid him for treatment of insurance cases; fees, by the way, that are fixed by law). The problem of how to prevent abuses is, of course, a difficult one. In Britain, doctors (in addition to a small salary) are paid according to the number of patients treated, with the danger that they may want to treat as many as possible as little as possible. In Germany they receive fees for each individual service rendered, with the danger of superfluous treatments and prescriptions. This problem has now been attacked through direct, though small, charges for certain services.

It may be that the social insurance system strengthens a German tendency to rely on others. But it is difficult to see how the average German worker or employee, who cannot manage to save much from his earnings, could be self-reliant. The alternative to insurance would at best be reliance on charity or welfare. Insurance, with its contributions from the insured and its benefits thus earned by right, at least creates more self-respect than either of these alternatives.

5 BUSINESS AND AGRICULTURE

It would be a mistake to consider all those not in the working class as belonging to one big, overall, uniform, "middle class." While, after industrialization, other countries, such as Britain, more or less integrated their "premodern" classes (such as the aristocracy) into one huge business class, in Germany the "old upper classes" continued to rule politically and to set standards socially, and even after their political and social decline, a largely self-perpetuating higher bureaucracy has continued to play this role as a distinct "caste," since its role in government and administration is predominant (see Chapter 5). For a long time the military

was also a pronouncedly separate group. But despite the fragmentation of the elites, what may be called the genuine middle class, that of business (in trade, banking, industry, etc.), has played—now more than ever before—a tremendous role in the rather rigid social order of Germany. While in other countries the new industrial order has often introduced considerable social fluidity (social mobility, circulation of elites, etc.), Germany managed to integrate the new economic phenomena into an already established and rigidly fixed system in which new and old classes had their assigned place. Within that system, business and agriculture, in particular, grouped themselves into huge, effective, special interest organizations, jealously defending their status. As a counterpart to labor and its organizations, they are now the chief alternate part of a rigid social stratification.

BUSINESS: THE TRADITIONAL SYSTEM

Germany never had that broad basis of rising democracy, a large independent middle class of small and middle businessmen. Small and middle-size businesses were disadvantaged through the early rise of giant corporations, interconnected through cartel arrangements, which accompanied the sudden jump from precapitalist conditions to full-fledged capitalism in the second half of the nineteenth century. Small business was further disadvantaged as a consequence of such events as the currency inflation of the twenties, the depression of the thirties, and Hitler's total war of the forties. Big enterprises have dominated German economic life for a century, and the restraint of free-market competition by them became the rule. Thus in 1939 six big corporations controlled 95 percent of the Ruhr's steel production and two-thirds of its coal through "captive mines"; the huge I. G. Farben combine had a near monopoly of German chemical production. The result was not mass production for mass consumption but high prices for fewer buyers, a vested interest in armaments production, with a concomitant support of aggressive policies and a fear of political, social, and economic reform. From its beginnings big business in Germany backed antidemocratic forces and used its economic power for a political defense of the business status quo. Government generally supported the big business structure. No inheritance taxes, or very low ones, kept large fortunes concentrated in a few families; cartels remained largely undisturbed, and the state assisted big industry through subsidies.

POSTWAR DEVELOPMENTS IN INDUSTRY

While privately owned business has disappeared in East Germany (on this, and the corresponding fate of agriculture, see Chapter 7), West Germany has largely retained, and in part

even strengthened, the essentially oligarchic structure of business inherited from the past. Allied occupation policies did not affect its roots; although the Allies tried to decentralize industry by splitting up giant holdings, the long-term result has been the opposite: deconcentration yielded to reconcentration. In banking, the traditional Big Three are again predominant; so are Thyssen, Krupp, and two others in steel. In 1969, all Ruhr coal mines (twenty-nine enterprises in all), which had run into economic trouble, were merged into one huge company, Ruhrkohle AG (with a guarantee by government of its considerable debt). The corporations that had previously owned the mines thus got rid of no longer profitable holdings. Consolidation through merger has accelerated during the last few years, with favorable tax laws aiding such mergers. The result has been oligopoly in most areas, an ever tighter control over the economy by ever fewer corporations, and their rising influence in political affairs.[2]

The relation among these leading enterprises has not been characterized by free competition. On the contrary, their position has been further strengthened by the formation of cartels. Decartelization, which the occupying powers had at first ordered, quickly yielded to recartelization. However, the attempt to control cartels has continued, albeit without notable effect. A law prohibiting cartels was enacted in 1957 (after endless wrangling in the Bundestag, in which the then Minister of Economics, Ludwig Erhard, was pitted against big industry and a large portion of his own CDU party), but the outcome has been meager. Numerous qualifications and provisions allowing for exceptions have permitted the Federal Cartel Office to judge in favor of cartels rather than combat them, and there have been few decisions outlawing cartel arrangements. An attempt to

[2] The oligopolistic character of the West German economy can be seen from the fact that fifteen giant enterprises (all in industry) accounted in 1970 for about one-fifth of the total GNP. The fifteen were as follows: the three "Big" ones in automobile manufacture (Volkswagen, biggest of all German enterprises, Daimler-Benz, Opel); three in chemical (the former I. G. Farben monopoly now divided into three: Bayer, Hoechst, BASF); two in electrical (the two dominating ones: Siemens and AEG); four in steel and tube (Thyssen, Krupp, Kloeckner, Mannesmann); coal (now the one, consolidated Ruhrkohle AG); and two in power (RWE, Veba). (See *Frankfurter Allgemeine Zeitung*, August 29, 1970.)

strengthen the law in 1968 was a dismal failure. Thus it was not surprising that the so far boldest venture in postwar West German cartelization, that of an almost complete cartel of the steel industry, extending to the setting of prices and almost everything else, did not encounter legal difficulties. The ordinary courts have assisted rather than resisted the process.

Small wonder, then, that the influence of business organizations on government has been strong. Trade and industry as an interest group are centrally organized in nation-wide peak associations, the most important of which is the Federation of German Industry (BDI). Its thirty-nine member associations represent the main business activities; since voting for its organs is according to size of payroll, it is controlled by big business. One-half of its presidium members represent big business; of fifty-eight enterprises represented in its executive, twenty-one were big ones, of which three were twice, and one even three times, represented. As in the case of other special interest organizations (for example, farmers and artisans), influence is exercised in the legislative field through much direct representation of business organizations in parliament and the strong influence of such deputies in the respective committees. In addition, and even more important, pressures operate through direct contacts in the executive from the highest level (which now, with increasing integration of the German economy into the Common Market, is found at Brussels as well as Bonn) down to the ministerial departments. Everything here is organized in expert, streamlined, and centralized fashion. Thus, like labor, the bureaucracy, and agriculture, business as an interest group makes itself felt as one power bloc, leaving little leeway for the formulation and expression of local and individual trends and ideas. The individual businessman devotes himself to his own affairs; he leaves public promotion of his interests to others— the professionals in his associations—just as he leaves politics to professional politicians.

POSTWAR DEVELOPMENTS IN AGRICULTURE

The absence of significant changes in economic structure and policies has been particularly striking in agriculture, where the Allies made a considerable effort to achieve long overdue reforms. An alliance of vested interests and bureaucracy wrecked land reform—in the sense of cutting up larger estates into smaller holdings—in the West. Instead of social reform, the trend has been in the opposite direction, toward mechanization. The number of farms and people working in agriculture has dropped steadily and sharply. Still, owing to poorer soil, this has not lowered the production costs of German agriculture sufficiently to enable it to compete with more effective neighboring countries, especially the other members of the Common Market (EEC). Through its efficient interest organization, it has continued to demand and receive the protection and subsidies traditionally extended to it in the past. Free-market principles do not apply to German agriculture, nor do they apply to EEC agriculture as a whole, for which, in 1966, a complicated system was devised to maintain high prices for all member countries. The ensuing overproduction can be combatted (if one omits the obvious, but probably utopian, solution of using it for aid to the underproducing parts of the world) only by something like the Mansholt Plan, under which the number of farms and farmers would be drastically cut. For West Germany it would mean that by 1980 about half of the land presently used for farming would no longer be so used, and the number of those working on the land would be cut further by at least one-half. Although German farmers, understandably, are opposing the plan, something along this line seems likely to be adopted in the future. This way German agriculture, long premodern in ownership as well as production, would join the modernized sector of German economy and society.

6 GERMANY'S POLITICAL CULTURE

Over the last decade or so it has become the fashion among political scientists to speak of a nation's "political culture" in the sense of its peoples' basic attitudes toward government and their behavior patterns in politics. This is usually done with the aid of detailed and minute opinion and attitude surveys intended to yield reliable pictures of group and national trends and characteristics. While polls and "survey research" are an old story in the United States, they came somewhat belatedly to Germany. However, the Federal Republic is now as thoroughly "surveyed" as any country. But before using some of the data for studying German political culture, we believe that a caveat is due. Although survey research may, indeed, yield valuable insight, its evaluation requires that the results be placed in their historical context, especially in the case of a country like Germany, where the impact of the past has been stronger and longer-lasting than in more future-oriented countries.[3]

For example: a recent poll indicated that, while fifty-five of every hundred Germans have never met a Jew, fifty-four said they would never marry a Jew. What does this prove about the causes of and the trends in German anti-Semitism? This anti-Semitism can be understood only historically—that is, we must know that German Jews, since their emancipation during the nineteenth century, found themselves constituting a "liberal" minority outside the authoritarian-conservative mainstream of German thought and attitudes. Many Germans thus tended to consider the Jews "elements of decomposition" and, through the educational establishment, handed on this distrust from one generation to the other.

Or, according to a recent study of national attitude patterns, a majority of Germans, in contrast to Americans, British, and Italians, do not believe that, as citizens, they can do much about social or political ills, expecting remedy rather from the action of public officials. Germany, according to the authors of this study, thus presents "an authoritarian subject culture, which involves imparting legitimacy to authority and bureaucracy, but not to political parties and competitive elections."[4] Again, this finding simply reflects historical experience—in this case, the tradition of the *Rechtsstaat*. Unless we understand this tradition, we cannot assess the depth and stability of present attitude patterns and trends.

But this raises another problem. Making history responsible for the emergence of so-called national traits precludes our considering them as innate, or immutable, or applicable to all members of the nation. National characteristics—that is, the image a nation presents to the outside world—change. The English, now thought of as stolid, phlegmatic, "muddling through," were regarded in the seventeenth century as turbulent and excitable. This reputation they lost to the French in the eighteenth century, at a time when the Germans acquired the reputation of being the nation of poets and thinkers, living politically in the clouds. A hundred years later the Germans had become, in the view of many, aggressive people, chiefly interested in material goods, efficiency, and power.

If the Germans changed radically during the nineteenth century, one reason may be that they achieved unity and power through "blood and iron" rather than as the result of a popular

---

[3] A word should, perhaps, be said about the sources used here and in the following. As we just have pointed out, West Germans by now belong to the "most polled" of all people. There is an abundance of institutes engaging in "opinion research" (*Meinungsforschung*), some "independent" (that is, private survey organizations), others affiliated with industry or trade unions, still others with universities. Some make their findings freely available, others only to subscribers of their publications, but the more important results are published in the press or else in book form (e.g., the *Jahrbuch der öffentlichen Meinung*, published every couple of years by the Allensbach institute). There are very few scholarly studies in the English language that have analyzed such data per se (one of them is the article by Kendell Baker listed in the bibliography). In the following, polling data and other results of opinion research published by the respective institutes or in the West German press have been used unless a specific source is referred to.

[4] G. A. Almond and S. Verba, *The Civic Culture* (Boston, Little, Brown, 1965), pp. 112, 173.

movement. A history of disunity and disorder produced a high evaluation of order. When Bismarck's strong-arm methods overcame political disorder, the ideal of order became coupled with that of authority. An ordered but free society seemed a contradiction in terms. An ordered society must be established and ruled by those who know best, rather than by discussion and argument on the part of the many. For every foreseeable situation there should be a rule, duly set by some authority with power to enforce it, and obeyed faithfully by the subjects. Unused to taking the initiative to settle a public problem in an unregulated situation, many Germans instinctively look for somebody to do it for them. This authority need not be legitimate or traditional. It was surprisingly easy for the Allies in 1945 to command the obedience of Germans once they had laid down regulations in due form. But it had to be done by them.

This authoritarian inclination has never extended to all, nor has it meant absence of discussion and criticism, grumbling about abuses, complaint against authorities, and so forth. Often, however, it has resulted in a reluctance to stand up and defend one's rights, an inability to take the initiative in changing inherited rules and patterns, unfamiliarity with the liberal-democratic values and procedures of accommodation and compromise. No German Dreyfus affair established the primacy of individual liberty over *raison d'état*. Democratic attitudes in Germany failed to acquire the natural, spontaneous character that they have to some extent gained in other Western countries.

To what extent does this apply today? Has not democracy taken some root, at least in West Germany, by now? As we have emphasized, nations do change in and through history. Has not postwar history brought about some change? Attitude studies provide us with some material for judgment; but, as we shall see, the data are somewhat contradictory.

A considerable amount of data shows that Almond and Verba's "authoritarian subject culture" still prevails in many respects. One poll revealed that a majority (55 percent) believes one cannot trust most people, while 28 percent believe one can; another poll indicated that a majority (60 percent) considers life a task, a duty, while only 30 percent look at life as something to be enjoyed. Coming to the more specifically political issues, a majority (in 1969, 69 percent) saw the task of political opposition not in criticizing the government but in aiding it in its task, revealing a consensus ideology not easily agreeable with democratic-parliamentary procedures: 51 percent (with 30 percent against and 19 percent undecided) affirmed that "all we need is a couple of good politicians at the top; parties and their programs matter less." In a similar vein, 61 percent (versus 27 percent) prefer "the best man at the top" to decide, rather than that "several people" decide by agreement among themselves. As late as 1969, 60 percent (with 19 percent against and 21 percent undecided) backed this statement: "Generally speaking one can trust the government and be sure that it will do the right thing for us." A bare majority (51 percent, with 32 against) believed that there was any use trying to do something against an arbitrary act of an official. Polls reveal that white-collar employees, even those with low income, enjoy higher social prestige than workers; by the same token, *Akademiker* enjoy special prestige as compared with nonacademically trained people of equal income. In one 1970 poll, professors ranked first, then came governmental ministers, bishops, big-corporation managers, "princes," generals; other military officers, however, ranked low, as low as politicians. Other polls still reveal reactionary, premodern, or Nazi-type attitudes: in 1967, exactly half (50 percent versus 31 percent) were for reintroduction of capital punishment (abolished by the Bonn Constitution in 1949). Sixty percent in 1965 and 46 percent in 1969 were against prosecuting Nazi murderers any longer. Asked which day should be commemorated as a "national holiday," only 8 percent advocated the twentieth of July (the day of the attempt on Hitler's life by anti-Nazi Resistance), with most others in favor of celebrating "those who fell in war" or the seventeenth of June (the rising of East Germans against the regime in 1953).

It is not always clear, however, what meaning to attach to survey results; for instance, 34 percent of those polled said they were ready actively to resist a neo-Nazi attempt to take over, while 35 percent said they were opposed to such a takeover but would not take action, and 14 percent were uninterested. In a Lower Saxony poll, 60 percent held political demonstrations admissible, with 25 percent opposed (and 30 percent opposed in the case of student demonstrations). Is 60 percent encouraging or too little? One could judge only by comparison with other countries. In one poll, Germans proved not too different from Americans: asked about the admissibility of anti-Vietnam demonstrations by Germans in the Federal Republic, 24 percent were for, 51 percent against, and 25 percent undecided; this compared with American figures in 1966 concerning the right of citizens to demonstrate against the Vietnam war of 35 percent for, 52 percent against, and 7 percent undecided. In respect to military service, 7 percent of males polled said they would like to be soldiers, 38 percent considered it a "necessary duty," and 24 percent disliked it.

But there are other figures that indicate a change in attitudes, sometimes considerable, over the years of the Federal Republic (FRG). A 1969 poll on what should be the goals of education yielded as much as 45 percent for "independence and self-reliance" (versus only 28 percent in 1954), while "obedience and submission" polled only 19 percent (versus 28 percent in 1954). The question, "Which German has done most for Germany?" yielded radically differing answers in 1952, 1963, and 1967, respectively: 1952: Adenauer, 3 percent; Bismarck, 36; Hitler, 9; Frederick the Great, 7; in 1963: Adenauer, 28 percent; Bismarck, 21; Hitler, 5; Frederick the Great, 4; and in 1967: Adenauer, 60 percent (this was right after his death); Bismarck, 17; Hitler, 2; Frederick the Great, 1. Answers to the question whether Hitler, had he not led Germany into war, would have to be considered a great statesman: in 1955: yes, 48 percent; no, 36; in 1967: yes, 32 percent; no, 52. To the question, "Who was responsible for the outbreak of the war in 1939?" in 1951: Germany, 32 percent; other countries, 24; both sides, 18; in 1967: Germany, 62 percent; the others, 8; both sides, 8 (similarly, "treason and sabotage" were seen as causes of Germany's loss of the war by 23 percent in 1952 and by only 10 percent in 1967). Different remembrance of conditions because of lapse of time explains changed assessments in answers to questions like this: "When did Germany fare best?"

	1951	1963
Today	2%	62%
1933–39	42%	10%
1920–33	7%	5%
Before 1914	45%	16%

Clearly, there is a change of generations at work here; is it also a change in basic attitudes?

The problem of "political socialization," that is, the acquisition by the members of a political community, especially the young, of political values and behavior patterns, has always been a difficult one in Germany. We have already referred to the role of the schools, teachers, and textbooks in transmitting basically conservative attitude patterns to the young. The role of formal education in political socialization has been particularly strong because of the tradition of thorough study and the role of the teacher or professor as authority figure. But the impact of the family and of less formal channels of information (or indoctrination), such as news media, has been in the same conservative direction. Perhaps one should not call it "political" socialization, because in the main it was a pattern of apolitical values that was stressed and instilled: the values of *Innerlichkeit* (one's inner self) and of the "higher" things of culture, by which one played down or ignored socio-economic as well as psychological realities; a flight into an idealized past (ancient cultures and their literature, the classics, etc.), while one accepted as the only politically positive values those of state authority and a stereotyped nationalism. Thus it is not too surprising that surveys revealed through the sixties a discouraging absence of even elementary information on things political among the young and a widespread acceptance of authoritarian ideas and attitude patterns, despite lip service to democratic stereotypes.

Nothing, therefore, has been more striking than the sudden and seemingly radical change of attitudes of the young since the late sixties, variously referred to as "revolt of the youth," "student extremism," and so forth. To be sure, this is part of a global phenomenon, where German events do not differ from those in other developed countries. Thus a study by Ronald Inglehart comparing attitudes of young and old in the Common Market countries showed a generally "progressive" pattern among those sixteen to twenty-one years old in all six countries, as opposed to the uniformly conservative attitudes of the older generation. This seems to indicate a global revolt of the young against their being manipulated by an overdeveloped, technologically advanced society, which has proven itself increasingly unable to solve the ever more urgent problems of the environment, social welfare, and so forth. In Germany, moreover, it seems to signal a long-overdue revulsion of the postwar generation against parents who participated in Nazism and the war it provoked; it is perhaps no coincidence that the German "revolt" began when those born in and after 1945 attained the ages of seventeen to twenty years. But it is easy to oversimplify and overgeneralize. Let us look at some data.

A study by Hans Weiler of "dissent toleration" among West German youths (data collected in the fall of 1969) revealed (1) a relatively high level of such toleration (i.e., toleration of avowed atheists, antidemocrats, etc.), (2) a steep increase in toleration from grades nine to thirteen (fifteen- to nineteen-year-olds), (3) a much higher degree of toleration among Gymnasium students than those attending *Volksschule* or vocational school, (4) a higher degree among SPD and FDP (liberal, Free Democratic party) supporters than among those backing the CDU. But, may not toleration of "antidemocrats" betray sympathy with antidemocrats instead of a liberal-democratic attitude? Another study, by K. L. Baker, using data collected in 1967 in the Cologne area, indicated that it reflected an antiauthoritarian attitude.[5] In this study students rejected, as "objects unworthy of pride," war, Hitler, persecution of Jews, even being a German. Here too, the more "radical" attitude was adopted by the high school students, while those attending vocational school (i.e., young workers) were more conservative (e.g., "pride in being a German": Gymnasium students 5 percent, vocational students 14.9; pride in "nothing": Gymnasium students 12.6 percent, the others 1.2).

These figures attest to a significant split among the young, signaling a reversal of traditional attitudes. Previously, the only major group in Germany that would deviate from the conservative-authoritarian pattern was the working class. Workers, with their Marxist-socialist subculture, transmitted their own reformist-liberal or even revolutionary values to the young and thus produced at least a minority among them who became "deviant"; on the other hand, middle-class youth, with very few exceptions even among students, grew into the "establishment" pattern transmitted to them. Now the picture seems to be reversed: as in other countries, the young workers turn conservative, while the children of the "affluent" turn radical. In countries like the United States, liberal-democratic attitudes have traditionally correlated to the degree of education; in Germany, this is a new phenomenon. Even here, though, some caution is due. First of all, even among students, the proportion of "radicals" to either conservatives or "apoliticals" is that of a minority to a majority (although the radicals often manage to control student organizations and even educational institutions); second, there is a question whether "radicalism" signifies liberal-democratic attitudes or instead a new authoritarianism of the left or, even, the right. Evidence, so far, is inconclusive or contradictory. But the conclusion that something radically new has happened in regard to the standards of German political culture seems justified.

7 GERMAN POLITICAL IDEAS

Because of the impact ideologies have on the political culture of a nation, it behooves us to survey briefly the history of political ideas in Germany. The most important single fact is that the ideas of the ruling elite have had a

[5] Kendell L. Baker, "Political Alienation and the German Youth," *Comparative Political Studies*. Another (so far unpublished) study by the same author and using the same sample reveals a much higher proportion of youngsters

"being confident of their ability to influence the political process" than did the Almond and Verba study of ten years before.

greater effect on *all* groups than those of the masses or outsiders. Since Germans outside the elite (including many intellectuals) seldom had a chance to put their ideas into practice, they tended to become extremists. Kept from being radical in action, some German thinkers tended to be so in thought. Revolutions other nations made in the realm of action, Germans performed in the realm of philosophy. This way, theory, often remote from the daily political scene, easily assumed a metaphysical and abstract character. Prior to this century, few Germans (Lessing, Heine, and Nietzsche being notable exceptions) had the sense of analytical criticism—psychological when referring to persons, social when referring to institutions—that distinguished Latin and Anglo-Saxon cultures. To the average German, intellectual criticism seemed, and still seems, something "negative," a threat to entrenched patterns of belief. Thus, as in the 1920s, the term *Links-Intellektueller* (leftist intellectual—as if intellectuals by definition had to be leftist) has become a term of opprobrium again; especially now, since student radicalism, the anti-intellectuals are on the march.

GERMAN LIBERALISM

Early liberalism

In England all major schools of political thought are to some extent liberal, and liberal ideas predominate in the important classes and parties. In France, too, liberal-democratic thought has been the strongest ideological force in the last two hundred years. There was a time in Germany, also, at the end of the eighteenth century, when an entire generation was imbued with the ideals of the Enlightenment. German philosophers, such as Kant and the young Fichte, and poets, such as Schiller and Hölderlin, greeted the French Revolution with enthusiasm. Wilhelm von Humboldt (1767–1835), in his *Thoughts Concerning the Limits of State Action* (1792) saw the government's only legitimate function as the preservation of internal order and defense against foreign attack. In Humboldt's work the accent was on individual freedom, in Immanuel Kant's (1724–1804) it was on ordered freedom under law.

Regarding international relations, Kant, in *On Perpetual Peace* (1795), boldly proposed what at his time must have seemed a utopian idea, a world federation of republican commonwealths. He was more cautious in his ideas on internal government, emphasizing the necessity of order and the citizen's duties toward society. Even more important for the development of subsequent German thought, however, was his emphasis on man's rigorous obligations under the moral law. The concept of moral duty later served Kantian philosophers (and the elite they influenced) to impress on Germans that obedience to the law as such meant the fulfillment of ethical imperatives.

Kant's foremost disciple, J. G. Fichte (1762–1814), started out as an anarchist follower of the principles of the French Revolution, but ended as an ultranationalist who proclaimed the unique historical mission of the German people, and as a champion of a planned economy in a strong welfare state. This latter turn he shared with the majority of his compatriots, who, under the impact of the Napoleonic conquests, began to regard the Rights of Man as an alien ideology serving the French to deprive Germans of their freedom and independence.

Liberalism and romanticism

Liberal-democratic ideas continued to be influential in one aspect of German life between 1815 and 1870: the German movement for national unification. Here, however, they took the peculiar form of political romanticism, an ideology that influenced many other movements, including authoritarian ones. Romanticism is the reaction to rationalism. It rejects universal principles and worships, instead, the unique and diversified. In Germany romanticism, in one of its implications, meant anarchistic individualism. Thus, for Friedrich Nietzsche (1844–1900) it meant the glorification of the "will to power" of the strong individual who fights both that "coldest of all monsters," the state, and the slave-morality of the masses protected by the state.

Because of this extremism, individualist romanticism either remained politically ineffective or was exploited for its own different ends by subsequent political movements (such as the Nazis' exploitation of Nietzsche's ideas). *Politi-*

cal romanticism, on the other hand, insisting that uniqueness resides in collective entities, such as nationalities, rather than in individuals, became one of the main strands of German political thought. To an earlier representative of this thinking, J. G. Herder (1744–1803), all nationalities, each with its peculiar character and historical mission, were still equal in their rich variety; to subsequent German nationalists, however, the German nation assumed superiority over the others. Fichte has already been mentioned in this connection. In the German liberal-national movement the predominance of this thought meant that the "atomistic" individualism of the natural rights doctrine was rejected in favor of group supremacy over the individual. Germany was to be a democracy, but the individual was to be subordinated to the community and its will.

The Rechtsstaat

Although the liberal-national movement was defeated, its ideals did contribute to German constitutionalism and the putting into practice of the idea of the Rechtsstaat. A Rechtsstaat (a state where authority is bound by general rules of law), rather than guaranteeing the *political* rights of the people, guaranteed the citizen's legal security against executive arbitrariness. Its German promoters advocated above all the establishment of independent courts to protect the citizen against governmental encroachment. The establishment of the authoritarian Rechtsstaat in the nineteenth century sealed the alliance between a German middle class that obtained legal security and a ruling group that retained political power.

Germany and laissez faire

As French revolutionary social and political ideas came to appear alien to Germans, so in the field of economics did English laissez-faire liberalism, chiefly because the German fledgling industry needed protection. Friedrich List (1789–1846) opposed Adam Smith and advocated protective tariffs, state intervention for the protection of industries, and a long-range political direction of economic developments. The idea of state intervention in the economy

through subsidies, high tariffs, cartel arrangements, and similar restrictions of free enterprise remained strong in Germany long after German industry had outgrown its infancy. Here, too, liberalism remained ineffective unless adulterated with statism. One of the intellectual fathers of Nazism, Arthur Moeller van den Bruck (1876–1925), expressed a more general German feeling when he said that a genuine German political movement might partake of all kinds of political ideas, even socialism and democracy, but not of liberalism; the latter was only for wealthy "have" nations that could afford such a luxury.

GERMAN SOCIALISM

Marx and his friend and collaborator, Friedrich Engels (1820–95), were Germans, and socialism gained the allegiance of the German working class in the form of Marxism. That Marxism prevailed, rather than socialist reformism or gradualism of the Fabian type, was due to the failure of the ruling groups in Germany to integrate the rising industrial proletariat. It long remained an outcast group. Consequently, a doctrine that preached hostility to all existing institutions and predicted a workers' kingdom to come appealed to German workers. A competing socialism, such as that of Ferdinand Lassalle (1825–64), which expected emancipation to result from a remodeling of the existing state structure through parliamentary democracy had less appeal.

To Marx, there was no place for genuine freedom in any historic society; real freedom would come only after the great "leap" that would establish the classless society in which state and government would wither away. Any general theory of democracy in presocialist society was to him a mere subterfuge to cover up the control of society by capitalist rulers and vested interests.

Such negativism remained characteristic of German socialism even when, toward the end of the nineteenth century, certain social reforms gave German labor some stake in society, and even when, after 1918, German socialists obtained a share in government. Despite all theoretical discussions within German socialism, and despite the actual split of the movement into two major political factions (Social Democrats and Communists), its basic attitude remained doctrinaire, even where in practice it became "reformist." Only recently, since about 1960, have the West German Social Democrats turned reformist in theory, too, which provoked an ultradoctrinaire backlash on the left (see Chapter 3), while the Marxist doctrine as developed by Lenin now constitutes the theoretical basis of the East German state.

GERMAN CONSERVATISM

Legitimism

German conservatism existed in attitude long before its formulation in theory. Lutheran obedience to the established authority became the basis of Prussian authoritarianism. When the latter was increasingly attacked by nineteenth-century liberalism and socialism, Friedrich Julius Stahl (1802–61) fashioned its theoretical defense. All authority derives from God, he declared, and the divine-right monarchy is bound by its own laws alone, not by any constitutions, institutions, or majorities. "Authority, not majority" was to be the right principle of legitimate government. But in this legitimism lay the main weakness of the theory. In a Germany still split into territorial monarchies, legitimism could not solve the problem of unification. It was hostile, or at best indifferent, to nationalism. Bismarck, when unifying Germany by the use of Prussian armed force against the other established monarchies, destroyed legitimism in practice. German conservatism now assumed the form of nationalist authoritarianism, born when national liberalism dropped its liberalism, and legitimist conservatism its legitimism.

Hegel

To this new conservatism the great German philosopher Georg Friedrich Hegel (1770–1831) contributed decisive ideas. His views on internal government may be called the conservative reaction to the ideas of the French Revolution. Hegel, in agreement with political romanticism, rejected all "absolute" principles, such as natural rights and individual freedom. Such principles are to be thought of merely as historical incidents in a larger pattern of evolution. Evolution, it is true, according to Hegel means the unfolding of the "world spirit" toward eventual freedom. But this freedom was not the freedom that liberal democrats or rationalist enlightenment philosophers had in mind. To Hegel the French Revolution embodied merely an extreme that was opposed to the antithetical extreme of absolute despotism. In Hegel's dialectic philosophy, opposite extremes, that is, forces and counterforces, always result in a subsequent "synthesis." He found the synthesis of absolute freedom and absolute despotism in an authoritarian Rechtsstaat, where there prevails neither liberal license nor reactionary compulsion, but the ordered rule of an hereditary monarchy, aided by the estates, or major classes, and carried out by expert servants of the state, the officials. Such a state regulates class and group conflicts in the interests of all. Only a strong state can offer an abode to the highest manifestations of man: the arts, religion, and philosophy.

The state was also the highest political institution externally. Between conflicting claims of nations, only history passes judgment. Power, and ultimately war, decides which nation at a given period shall be the chosen instrument of the world spirit. Before its might all others legitimately perish.

The idea of the strong state exercised a tremendous influence in a Germany unified by force and trying to play its role as a world power. In the new Empire of 1871, German jurists and historians (such as Heinrich von Treitschke, 1834–96) fashioned the theory of the state as personified will and power. The concept of the state as a separate entity is as natural to a German as that of inalienable rights and freedoms of the individual is to an American.

Hegelianism has been responsible for yet another tendency of German political thought: to put social and political ideas and phenomena into the larger context of historical development. Everything in human affairs, according to this view, is part of one great historical process that determines all particular developments. Marx, in this respect, was Hegel's direct descendant. This tendency toward a uniform *Weltanschauung*, an overall world view or philosophy, easily leads to dogmatism. Different *Weltanschauungen* divide individuals, groups, parties, and movements more profoundly than do conflicting interests. The German habit of supporting such philosophies, added to religious, economic, and similar divisions, has been a handicap in the development of democracy, which calls for adjustment and compromise.

The German idea of the state

Out of this pattern of thought there developed under the Empire what may be called the dominant ideology of its elite—an ideology that also spread to large groups of the middle classes. According to the "German idea of the state," the type of state and society developed in Prussia-Germany is superior to Western liberal democracy because in the former "the best" rule with a sense of responsibility toward the many; social welfare is assured through efficient government by the expert; there is power enough to defend the community against threats from abroad, self-centered interest groups, and subversive forces; and, finally, all this serves to stimulate the higher cultural values of the arts, science, and philosophy.

Compared with this ideal of *Kulturstaat*, Western political systems appeared defective. In them, the community, a prey to individual or group egoism, is doomed to disintegrate. Where parliament is supreme, national interests become matters for bargaining, and factions haggle over the affairs of state. But the abyss between Germany and the West was even deeper; it was, according to this ideology, the abyss between *Kultur* and "mere" civilization. Kultur is concerned with the higher values of religion and truth, arts and poetry, and with the state as their protector; civilization is concerned only with the satisfaction of material wants, with technology and industry. German Kultur is idealistic; Western civilization utilitarian. This feeling of superiority carried Germany into its two "wars against the West"; it needed only slight alteration to emerge as Hitlerism.

TWENTIETH-CENTURY GERMAN POLITICAL THOUGHT

When the powerful state of the Hohenzollerns fell before Western strength, traditional authoritarianism was temporarily discredited. But no single strong political philosophy took its place during the period of the Weimar Republic. It was a period of great intellectual ferment. Besides Marxism and Catholic social thought, a large variety of doctrines emerged. Some tried to provide theoretical support for the new democracy. Thus Hugo Preuss (1860–1925), one of the makers of the Weimar Constitution, tried to fashion a kind of democratic pluralism out of Otto von Gierke's (1841–1921) *Genossenschafts-Theorie* (theory of associations, or corporations). Political life, in this theory, is not to be regulated from above, but is to be self-regulated by existing organic groups, the state resulting from the integration of such groupings into one nation. In Hans Kelsen's (b. 1881) "Pure Theory of Law," the state became identified with the existing legal system. To this concept of the state as pure law, Carl Schmitt (b. 1888), perhaps the most original, certainly the most versatile of twentieth-century German political philosophers, opposed that of the state as the vessel of power politics. Schmitt's theory proclaims as sovereign not the people, not the individual, not the state as such, but the one or the few who control the state in periods of emergency—for all politics, internal and external, is warfare, a friend-foe relationship. This theory revealed real though often hidden power relationships in a state and among states. But if less legalistic and more realistic than other theories, it also served those antidemocratic forces that put an end to Weimar democracy under the cloak of emergency powers.

This diversity of theories left Germans without generally accepted standards for belief and action. The feeling of uncertainty about what to believe contributed to the rise of a new, dogmatic creed to which large masses flocked: Nazism. This doctrine, as well as Nazi practice, will be discussed in Chapter 2. After the breakdown of Nazism, the way was again open to free thought, at least in the Western part of

Germany. But a significant new theory has not appeared. Instead, a spirit of pragmatism prevailed and led to a trend toward political moderation that has been noticeable in the area of thought, too: socialists, where they have not dropped Marxist doctrine altogether, are mildly reformist; rightists are, in the main, less nationalistic, less authoritarian-minded, open to new ideas, such as that of European federalism, and economically more liberal (at least, theoretically) in advocating a socially oriented free-market system (*soziale Marktwirtschaft*). This trend has brought German political thought more in line with Western trends; the introduction into West Germany of the American, empirical version of "political science" has strengthened this tendency. But among the many who are outside the circle of intellectuals and academics, this process of "Westernization" frequently remains on the level of lip service and pretense, leaving the "political culture" largely authoritarian. And even among

academics there are two nonmoderate trends noticeable at opposite ends of the spectrum: the one resuming the authoritarian Hegelian-Schmittian tradition, the other reviving the sophisticated neo-Marxism that flourished in the immediate pre-Nazi period (Frankfurt school of critical dialectic, Theodor Adorno, Max Horkheimer, and Juergen Habermas). Of such sophistication, it is true, there is little in the political thought of the "New Left," those mostly younger scholars who are trying to provide the rebellious youth, and especially the radical students, with a theory. In the main, it has been *Vulgär-Marxismus*, that oversimplified and crude version of Marxism of which Marx is supposed to have said "Moi, je ne suis pas Marxiste." In addition to some strands of anarchism, this doctrinairism is perhaps the peculiarly German element in a youth movement that elsewhere has produced more untraditional, original, and exciting types of thought.

8 ORGANS OF PUBLIC OPINION

It is a commonplace that democracy is based on an informed citizenry who in turn depend on the freedom of the communication media. The traditional task of free media—scrutinizing and criticizing the government—becomes imperative in a traditionally authoritarian country like Germany. In countries with "genuine" democratic political cultures like Britain, that job is performed, among others, by the parliamentary Opposition; in the German political culture, that function of parliament is minimized to this day, although, in practice, it has from time to time been noticeable and effective. There then remain only the organs of public opinion. But here we run into a problem that is not limited to Germany: those organs that assume increasing importance as *mass* media are limited in number, and control is therefore in the hands of a few people possessing more money. The worst system, from the viewpoint of free discussion of issues, free information, and ensuing formation of "public" opinion, of course, is the system controlled

centrally by government or by one dominant party (as was the case under Nazism and is now the case in the one-party state of East Germany). But the freer systems of countries like the Federal Republic are beset with the hardly less serious problems of media control by money, consolidation of press enterprises, and others. How has Germany coped with these problems?

EARLIER DEVELOPMENTS

In the past, German organs of opinion fulfilled their task up to a point. Opinion, even under the Hohenzollern regime, was not made exclusively from above. On the contrary, a wealth of different views could be expressed by a varied press. But the press hardly voiced an independent public opinion. It was rather the mouthpiece of established groups and parties with their rigid doctrines and fixed policies. An "opinion" press, it made little distinction between reporting and editorializing. Also, many newspapers, especially the chains formed in the provinces, came under the control of business interests. And of the more than four thousand dailies (1932), many were simply without full editorial staffs. Local diversity thus tended to vanish under the impact of opinion-making by large established interests. This system continued into the post–World War I period. People read the paper that voiced their line and confirmed their views. In a large city, for example, one was likely to find the official Social Democratic paper, the official Communist paper, the Center party paper, and later in the 1920s a Nazi paper. In addition —and probably with the largest circulation of all—would be a paper that claimed to be apolitical (or nonpartisan) but in reality was rightist-nationalist and an organ for business interests. The biggest chain was controlled by the leader of the rightist German Nationalist party, Alfred Hugenberg. There were, indeed, a couple of well-known liberal newspapers of high standards, but they were usually to the left of general opinion and, as elections showed, without much influence on political attitudes despite their nation-wide circulation. It was characteristically the other way around in France, where the big Paris press was to the right of public opinion. The German press was not openly corrupt, although the influence of special interests, through ownership and financial control, advertising and party connection, was strong.

THE PRESS IN WEST GERMANY

After twelve years of control of public opinion by the Nazis, the Germans in 1945 awoke with a burning desire for information in place of indoctrination. This gave the Allies a chance to try reorientation. Outside the Soviet zone, where Germans got a new type of indoctrination, they were quite successful in this respect. They avoided censorship but selected anti-Nazis as licensees of newspapers; these persons, in the main, proved to be free from party-political and doctrinal bonds. The new press adopted certain foreign features to make newspapers more genuinely free and representative, such as letters to the editor and more criticism of public authorities. In distinguishing reporting from editorializing, they provided a more objective kind of factual information. These factors have by now been generally accepted by the West German press, which, since the termination of licensing in 1949, has been free from regulation. It has been flourishing, but certain serious problems have also arisen.

Germans have ample opportunity to be well informed and to compare a variety of opinions. West Germany stands high in regard to circulation as well as per capita ratio of newspapers. There are over 500 dailies with a circulation of over 20 million, which compares favorably with Great Britain and France. But only some 150 have a complete editorial setup of their own. They are widespread regionally, and in place of the Berlin papers—which, for obvious reasons, no longer circulate nationally—some excellent ones have supraregional distribution. They form the "elite press," written for and read by the relatively small readership of leaders in business and administration, education and the professions. Among them is, for example, the *Frankfurter Allgemeine Zeitung*, which, though politically conservative, is independent in its editorials and remarkable for both opinion and coverage. There is, in the same city, its more leftist competitor, the *Frankfurter Rundschau*. Most larger cities have independent daily papers (West Berlin has 7). In addition, there are several weeklies of considerable quality, such as *Die Zeit* (Hamburg, liberal), perhaps the outstanding German paper today, *Rheinischer Merkur* (Cologne, conservative Catholic), *Christ und Welt* (now: *Deutsche Zeitung*, Stuttgart, Protestant), and *Welt der Arbeit* (Düsseldorf, organ of the German Trade Union Federation). In a class by itself is the Hamburg weekly *Der Spiegel*, patterned after *Time* magazine. Though it is often accused of sensationalism, it acts as a kind of private investigation committee and keeps the government on its toes by uncovering unsavory conditions, such as corruption in high places (on the *Spiegel* affair, see Chapter 2).

Among encouraging phenomena are also the small but influential quality periodicals (usually monthlies), such as *Frankfurter Hefte* (progressive Catholic), which stresses cultural and philosophical topics and is read by the cultural elite. There are also political cabarets, which provide needed criticism and biting humor in what is frequently a stodgy political atmosphere.

But there are discouraging trends, too. The impact of the more serious press has been impaired by the steady rise of tabloids and illustrated newspapers—about a hundred of them, with a circulation of 35 million. One of them, *Bild-Zeitung*, sensational even by American standards, providing chiefly sports, sex, crime information, and the like, sells 4.8 million copies daily to an estimated one-fourth of the adult population, 37 percent of whom read no other paper. This kind of paper thus provides "information" to the largest number of the people, workers, and the lower middle class.

The other big problem is that of concentration. In particular, the newspaper empire controlled by one man has reappeared. Axel Springer, now by far the biggest German press lord, owns serious papers, like *Die Welt*, and tabloids, like *Bild-Zeitung*, alike (besides many weeklies and monthlies appealing to women, young people, etc.). He controls over 30 percent of the weekday and about 80 percent of the Sunday circulation of newspapers. The total circulation of the Springer press is estimated at about 13 million. Yet the government, which had set up a commission to investigate the concentration trends in the press, has concluded that it has not yet reached the point where regulation is warranted. No wonder that the Springer concern has been the butt of sometimes violent demonstrations by students and others who feel that opinion is being manipulated in an intolerable fashion.

The problem is considered serious since the Springer empire is characterized by more or less hidden bias. When *Die Welt*, for example, came under Springer's control, it changed from a vivid, critical paper to a conservative, nationalistic one. Even aside from Springer, most of the press is either apolitical or conservative. To be sure, the trend away from the compartmentalized, dogmatic party press of Weimar and earlier periods toward nonpartisan, independent newspapers has been all to the good, particularly inasmuch as extremist, radically leftist or rightist publications have all but disappeared. (Some remnants of rightist radicalism persist in the press of the expellee groups and self-styled soldiers' or veterans'

organs and now of the neo-Nazi NPD, National Democratic party.) Only a few papers today are sponsored directly by or admit being close to a particular political party. But such independence hardly means what it does to an American who (admittedly with a more diffuse party system) is used to seeing his paper backing now one party and now the other, or even backing candidates of different parties during the same election. In Germany it usually means agreement with one party, or at least one "political orientation" (*Richtung*), and, in fact, as we have noted, the orientation is to the conservative right. It adds up to a system through which "political socialization" is still performed in traditional fashion and with the traditional conservative-authoritarian value standards (although terms like "democracy" never fail to be used, or misused), a system in which only a handful of organs, more popular (like *Der Spiegel*) or more esoteric (like *Die Zeit*), fulfill the function of critical enlightenment.

Radio and television

Thus not as many shades of opinion as one might wish find expression, and government can afford to be less sensitive to public opinion than it might be with a more politically varied and critical press. Since the chief reading matter of the average West German is the sports or crime page of a tabloid, the impact of those media, which in Germany as elsewhere tend to overshadow the printed word—namely radio and television—is all the more crucial. German broadcasting, since its inception, has been less an outlet for public opinion or mere entertainment than a vehicle of culture, providing its audience with generally high-standard (although not necessarily high-brow) programs. Radio stations, which now also operate television, are under public ownership but are organized independently from government as public corporations on a regional or *land* level. They are managed by mixed boards that are supposed to constitute a cross-section of society at large, with representatives of political parties, churches, educational institutions, trade unions, and other occupational groups. Radio and television are thus free from advertising (with the exception of short consecutive periods of time for commercials, which never interrupt a program) and from the ensuing bane of "lowest-common-denominator" entertainment based on rating, in return for which the German listener pays a few DM's monthly fee.[6] There now are about 250 television sets per 1,000 inhabitants. Most of the upkeep of radio and television, of course, comes from public subsidies. In return, the stations have to give free time to political leaders during election campaigns (which solves part of the problem of campaign financing) as well as generally to political parties, churches, and other agencies of different *Weltanschauungen.*

Until 1960, television shared a single network with the regional radio stations. In the early sixties Adenauer, aware of the political potentialities inherent in the control of a television channel and perhaps inspired by the de Gaulle example in France, tried to create a second-channel network, which was to be under the auspices of the federal government. Upon application by some *Länder,* the Federal Constitutional Court declared the plan unconstitutional as an invasion of the states' right to deal exclusively with these matters. Thereupon the second network was set up by the *Länder,* which operate it jointly.

As in other West European systems, avoid-

[6] 2.50 DM per radio set, 6 DM per television set.

ance of private ownership and management of radio and television has not meant their control by either government or political parties. The autonomy of the respective organizations and the participation of a large number of social groups in their management has so far prevented such a result. On the other hand, as compared with the corresponding American media, discussion of public and political issues has been generally less lively. But to the extent there is such discussion, it has frequently been more critical, more varied, and less accommodating than discussion of issues by the mass press. This has led to charges of being too "controversial" and to corresponding pressures, but the networks have withstood them so far. Thus the German seriously interested in forming his political opinion can find here occasional stimulation.

On the whole, however, the media in Germany, while highly successful instrumentalities of mass education, devoting themselves to sponsoring music, theater, the arts, and so forth, have been less successful as instruments of public opinion. Thus the West German communication media have not yet played the role so vital in the older democracies: that of a fourth estate that checks public authority by constituting the "voice of the people."

2

The German political heritage

1 HISTORY OF A DISUNITED NATION

"The legacy of German history is profoundly ambiguous. . . . It includes memories that counsel fear of remaining weak in a world of ruthless foreign interests, but it is also rich in memories of suffering and defeat following upon reckless bids for world power. It is rich in memories of success in fields requiring economic, technical and scientific performance; but it lacks memories of sustained political gains following upon peaceful development of democratic and constitutional practice. Dictatorship and war are remembered as terrible failures; but democracy and peaceful international relations are not at all widely remembered as successes." [1]

Almond and Verba's comparative-attitude study reveals that Germans follow political affairs at least as regularly as the Americans and British and are as well informed about government and politics. Yet few of them (7 percent, as against 46 percent in the United Kingdom and 85 percent in the United States!) take pride in their political or governmental institutions. This suggests, in the words of the authors, "alienation from the political system," an "interesting combination of high exposure and attentiveness to the political system, along with an absence of pride in it." [2] These findings are perhaps not too surprising in view of the still somewhat provisional character of the present German political units. But they reflect also something deeper, something that distinguishes Germany most strikingly from other major powers: the absence of any well-established pattern of governmental institutions and political processes that can be used as a model for organizing the present and planning the future. The absence of such a clear image has meant not that historical experience is less important to the Germans, but rather that the Germans, not sure of themselves, tend to be influenced, either in imitation or in rejection, by the varying pattern of their past. It is particularly necessary, therefore, to understand German history, and particularly its recent phases, if one is to understand present attitudes and practices.

THE HOLY ROMAN EMPIRE

For almost a thousand years (roughly from 800 to 1800) Germany was an empire claiming to be the successor to the Roman Empire and, as such, claiming supremacy over

[1] Karl W. Deutsch and Lewis J. Edinger, *Germany Rejoins the Powers* (Stanford, Stanford University Press, 1959), p. 17.

[2] G. A. Almond and S. Verba, *The Civic Culture*, pp. 64, 68.

Western Christianity. Yet the old Empire was never able to achieve the unification of Christendom. While its western portion developed into what we call today a nation-state (France), its eastern portion did not. It came to be called the "Holy Roman Empire of Germanic Nationality," but the emphasis was on empire, not on nationality, and it continued to aspire to European leadership throughout the Middle Ages.

This universalism had much to do with the subsequent failure of Germans to become a unified nation. The emperors' claim was contested by the pope and by the rulers of other European countries, with the result that the emperors became involved in unending and futile struggles outside Germany and were forced to grant ever more concessions to their powerful German vassals. Thus they lost their hold over Germany, which disintegrated into numerous territories. The liberties granted to the nobles led to the emergence of the higher lords as rulers of territorial states.

The territorial states

In England and France, medieval feudalism eventually gave way to a unified state that absorbed the feudal powers. In Germany, feudalism destroyed the old unity, so that public power had to be established separately in each of the territorial units where the higher lords now ruled. Thus the modern state, with its centralized state machinery, its triad of powers (standing army, bureaucracy, and taxation) and its triad of functions (lawmaking, administration, and justice) emerged in Germany separately in each of a number of units, which ranged all the way from large European powers (Hapsburg-Austria, and later Prussia) to middle-sized principalities (such as Bavaria, Saxony, Hanover) and to petty secular or ecclesiastical entities. The dream of universal rule had led to fragmentation.

The old Empire, to be sure, continued to exist into the Napoleonic age, but its control over territorial rulers was nominal. The office of emperor continued to be based on election, with the right to elect vested in the rulers of some of the main territorial states, the so-called electors. In practice, it became hereditary in the Hapsburg dynasty. The emperor was powerful only because of his Austrian possessions. As emperor he had to share whatever power he had with the imperial diet (*Reichstag*), an assembly in which the German "estates" (electors, other princes, and free cities), jealous of their individual sovereignties, were perennially incapable of common action. The Treaty of Westphalia (1648), terminating a war in which German princes, allied with outside countries, had fought each other bitterly and disastrously for thirty years, confirmed the estates' legal sovereignty.

Religious split, economic backwardness

The Treaty of Westphalia also put the final seal on another German catastrophe. To the territorial cleavage was added the religious split. Germany, home of the Lutheran Reformation, had been unable to gain religious unity. Since each ruler determined the religion of his territory, Austria and parts of southern and western Germany remained Catholic, while most of northern Germany, including Brandenburg-Prussia, became Protestant. Religious schism intensified contrasts. Lutheranism, stressing obedience to worldly authority, facilitated the rise of an efficient but austere absolutism in Protestant regions, especially in Prussia, while Catholic regions often developed a less rigid rule. Religion, of course, does not account for everything. Thus the peculiar social-economic system of Germany east of the Elbe River, with its large estates owned by the nobility (the Junker class), which held its peasants in hereditary serfdom, contributed to authoritarian developments in Prussia. These contrasted sharply with the more relaxed, enlightened atmosphere in Rhenish archbishoprics, or southern "free" cities, or the cosmopolitanism of the Austrians.

There was yet another cause of backwardness. In the sixteenth century, owing to the shift of European trade routes from the Continent to the Atlantic, the rise of a strong and prosperous German middle class that had begun in the later Middle Ages was suddenly arrested, and the German economy remained chiefly agricultural up to the nineteenth century. This retrogression was reflected in the realm of culture. Early in the sixteenth century the works of artists like Albrecht Dürer and Hans Holbein still reflected the sturdy and solid culture of the late medieval German city. There followed a period of barrenness that lasted until long after the Thirty Years' War (1618–48), when another generation began to put its dreams into sublime music and metaphysics (Bach, Leibniz). Only toward the end of the eighteenth century did German culture have a general—and splendid —revival.

THE RISE OF PRUSSIA

Thus political life in Germany came to center in the territorial states. And it was largely due to the rise of one of them, Prussia, that unification was eventually achieved. The rise of Prussia is one of the miracles of modern history. The Electorate of Brandenburg, named the Kingdom of Prussia in 1701, was remote from the centers of Germany and looked toward the Slavic East on the Baltic Sea. Who could have foreseen that it would become the most powerful of the German states and founder of the new Reich?

The Hohenzollerns

Unlike other German states, Prussia was in a way an artificial unit; it lacked *Stämme* unity and cultural tradition, a stable economic basis, and even geographical coherence. Its main territory was in the northeast, but other bits were scattered over the rest of Germany. Its rise was almost exclusively the work of its ruling dynasty, the Hohenzollerns, who built Prussia upon the sandy soil of eastern Germany by sheer will, energy, tyranny, and conquest. Frederick William, the "Great Elector" (1640–88), first in an almost uninterrupted hundred and fifty years' succession of brilliantly gifted rulers, defeated the feudal lords in his territory and then put them to work in his administration. King Frederick William I (1713–40) built up the Prussian army as the foremost part of the state. Finally Frederick II, the Great (1740–86), in a series of diplomatic maneuvers and wars that rendered him famous for ruthlessness even in an age of Machiavellian power politics, established Prussia as one of the recognized great powers of Europe.

Militarism

These achievements paralleled what Richelieu, Mazarin, and Louis XIV did for France, and, as in France, much of the administrative structure then established is still recognizable today. But Prussia's political climate was entirely its own. Lacking the wealth and the skilled and dense population of other European nations, it could maintain itself only by armed force and an effective, thoroughly economical organization of state affairs. The army always came first. Militarism meant not only a strong army but the dominance of the military spirit, with the principles of discipline, hierarchy, and blind obedience invading nonmilitary fields. It meant that military affairs remained exempt from civilian control even when other affairs came under the control of parliament and parties. The Prussian officer became the symbol of social prestige, the German counterpart of the English gentleman or the successful businessman in the United States.

Prussian administration

In administration, too, Prussia developed its own climate. While in France and other countries the nobility flocked to the court, Spartan Prussia could afford no class of noble drones. The Prussian nobles formed the backbone of a bureaucracy whose capacity for hard work, efficiency, and discipline was unique among the countries of the *ancien régime*. Prussia's kings considered themselves "first servants of the state," a phrase which Frederick the Great opposed to Louis XIV's "L'État, c'est moi." Glaring differences between rich and poor, capital and countryside, and the privileges of nobles living in luxury at the expense of peasant and burgher, made France ripe for revolution. In Prussia the rustic life style of rulers and Junkers (nobles) rendered more bearable the low living standard of the commoners. And the ruling groups, particularly the state officials, developed some sense of responsibility for their inferiors. There was to be no arbitrariness in the management of the affairs of state. Codified laws told the subjects what to expect, and law courts were established to protect them in whatever rights they were granted. Still, even though this was the beginning of the Rechtsstaat, everything remained based on the authoritarian principle of command and obedience. The few who by birth and ability were destined to rule did so efficiently, but no glimmer of freedom or political initiative penetrated the garrison-state.

On this Prussian spirit was patterned much that lasted in its effects on German life and institutions. The family was authoritarian; pupils were in awe of their teachers. In rural areas, the Junker landowner held public (police) powers over those living on his estate; in business, the head of the firm became the master; even in trade unions and political parties, which were formed in opposition to the regime, functionaries dominated the members. The state official became the model of management to such an extent that the very term *official (Beamter)* is still applied in Germany in fields of private management, for example, "banking officials."

Thus the rising middle classes in Prussia-Germany did not, as in other countries, replace the feudal-authoritarian pattern of life with a liberal-equalitarian one.

THE FIRST DEFEAT OF LIBERALISM

Up to the time of the French Revolution, internal developments in Germany paralleled those in most other Continental countries. Not so in the nineteenth century: no liberal middle class arose to replace authoritarian rule with a democratic system. In this, German developments paralleled those in Russia, except that Russia never knew a strong movement for liberal democracy. Germany did. The tragedy of her political history was that the liberal movement was unable to defeat its opponents. Instead, it was itself three times beaten.

Frustration of early reforms

The first defeat of liberalism occurred after a beginning of reform had been made in Prussia during the Napoleonic era. Defeat of Prussia at Napoleon's hands had shown up the weakness of her authoritarian rigidity. Therefore, more farsighted leaders, foremost among them Freiherr vom Stein (1757–1831), conceived the idea to modernize state and society by building up democracy from below, locally at first, and then

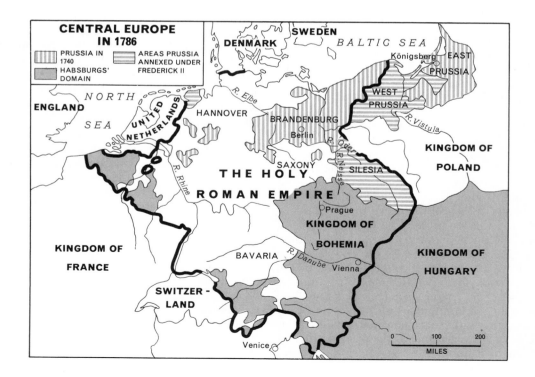

regionally and nationally, so as to give Germans a feeling of participation in public affairs. Thus the Prussian serfs were freed, Jews emancipated, and some measure of self-government was introduced in the cities. But the spirit of reform vanished after victory over Napoleon had been achieved (1813–14). The Prussians had fulfilled their duty on the battlefield, but the rulers forgot their word. A promised Prussian constitution never materialized. Reaction restored full rule from above. And while the peasant retained his legal freedom, he did not get land—any more than did the American black after his emancipation, or the Russian serf after 1861. There developed that contradiction between legal freedom and economic bondage that Karl Marx was quick to note and apply to his analysis of bourgeois society. The free but landless peasant migrated to the factories of the new industrial cities, where he was exploited to such an extent that the state had to intervene. It did so when, owing to the declining health of the urban proletariat, military conscription no longer yielded sufficient numbers of draftees. The king needed soldiers and factory legislation was passed. In Prussia even social policies had a military foundation.

Frustration of early nationalism

Thus liberal hopes were dashed temporarily. So were national aspirations for unification. German nationalism, particularly among German middle-class youth, had emerged in reaction to Napoleonic rule. Stein and others had the vision of a federated Germany built on a liberal-democratic foundation. Napoleon himself had unwittingly created a precondition for national unification. At the time of his conquests, many of the smaller territorial states, including all the ecclesiastical principalities, had been consolidated into a number of larger units, and existing larger states had acquired new territory. Prussia at the Congress of Vienna (1815) got Rhineland and Westphalia in western Germany—an area including the potentially rich Ruhr. But reaction after 1815 prevented unification. The dynasties, and the nobles and officials allied with them, stood for the maintenance of the sovereign independence of the states. Instead of a unified Germany, a German Confederation (*Deutscher Bund*) was formed.

It was a loose federation of German states without jurisdiction over inhabitants of member units. Its only organ, the federal diet, was not a representative body of the German people but an assembly of delegates from member states, a permanent conference of ambassadors that proved as incapable of action as had the diet of the defunct Holy Roman Empire. In practice it was chiefly used to suppress the liberal-national movement wherever it lifted its head.

THE SECOND DEFEAT OF LIBERALISM

The growth of national liberalism was not to be stopped, however, by suppression. With the beginnings of industrialization, agrarian Germany gradually modernized itself. The new industrial middle class demanded a share in government and clamored for national unity, especially since the many internal boundaries hampered trade. Economic unification of much of Germany was attained with the establishment, under Prussian leadership, of a customs union (*Zollverein*) in 1834. When a revolutionary tide swept Europe in 1848, Germany at last seemed ready to join the trend toward constitutionalism and democracy. The failure of the Revolution of 1848 was, instead, the second disaster of German liberalism.

The failure of 1848

At first, the revolutionary movement swept everything before it. The princes were forced to promise constitutions and to agree to the convening of an all-German constituent assembly. Issuing from universal manhood elections, it was Germany's first modern representative body. In its composition it was typical of German liberalism, which was a movement of the educated classes rather than of the masses. In St. Paul's Church in Frankfurt where the assembly convened, professors, poets, and intellectuals were as plentiful as lawyers are on Capitol Hill. With German thoroughness they began drafting a constitution. Instead of concentrating on setting up some kind of central government capable of resisting counter-revolutionary tendencies, they labored long over a catalog of fundamental rights. While they quarreled over whether or not Germany should include Austria, whether it should be a monarchy or a republic, unitary or federalist, the old powers acted. Armies and officialdom had in the main remained loyal to the dynasties. With their help the princes crushed liberal and democratic forces in Vienna, Berlin, and elsewhere. The king of Prussia, to whom the title of emperor had finally been offered at Frankfurt, refused to accept a "crown of mud." Thereupon, the Frankfurt parliament was dissolved. The middle classes, frightened by the specter of social revolution (although at that time socialist and similar movements were still quite weak in Germany), gave in without further resistance. Those who could not reconcile themselves to a new era of reaction emigrated to the United States. As in a later period of oppression, Germany lost to other countries the cream of its freedom-loving elite.

THE THIRD DEFEAT OF LIBERALISM AND THE FOUNDING OF THE EMPIRE

Before the unity that German liberals had been unable to achieve was finally established through "blood and iron," liberalism had another chance. Its failure has influenced the character of German government and politics ever since.

The Prussian Constitution

Among reforms that had survived 1848 were written constitutions, of which the Prussian Constitution of 1849–50 was one. This document reflected the peculiar German type of constitutionalism that has been mentioned before. It issued not from popular sovereignty but from the Crown, which retained executive power; and while there was to be a parliament, that body had no control over the cabinet, which was responsible only to the Crown. An upper house was composed of Junkers, appointed officials, and other dignitaries; a lower house represented the people, but in peculiar fashion: it was elected on the basis of a three-class system under which the handful of voters who paid the highest third of taxes elected one-third of the deputies, those who paid the second third again elected one-third, and the rest,

about 85 percent of all voters, the remaining third. This system was devised to perpetuate the rule of the land-owning nobility allied with the wealthy upper bourgeoisie.

The "Prussian conflict"

Still, the system offered an opening wedge for constitutionalism of the Western type. The test came when, during the European heyday of liberalism in the 1860s, a liberal majority was elected to the lower house in Prussia. This majority decided to establish once and for all its share in government power by rejecting a budget proposed by the conservative cabinet. Significantly, the issue was over appropriations for military service and the organization of the army. It thus affected one of the sacred principles of old Prussianism: the primacy of military affairs and their exemption from civil control. For a fleeting moment it looked as if this conflict between Crown and parliament might be solved as it had been in England in a similar situation two hundred years earlier. King William, unable to find a prime minister ready to fight it out with parliament, was on the point of abdicating when he found his man in the person of Bismarck.

Bismarck

Otto von Bismarck (1815–98) was that rare man who can weigh the real forces in politics and use them in a realistic fashion without regard to personal or political prejudices or predilections. A Junker, he stood for authoritarianism. But, unlike his fellow nobles, divine right of kings, legitimism, and similar dogmas meant nothing to him; only power, not principles, counted. While his fellow nobles stood for Prussian sovereignty against German unity, Bismarck realized that unity must inevitably come. If so, why not under Prussian hegemony? While others might hesitate to resort to force, scheming, and disregard of the law, Bismarck had no such scruples. He took up the fight for the authority of the Crown, ignored the rejection of the budget, and enforced the cabinet's fiscal program, all in violation of the constitution. He had judged the situation correctly: officials continued to serve, the people continued to pay taxes and obey the laws, and thus the cause of parliament was lost. "Might made right," and this quite literally, for when Bismarck had concluded the struggle victoriously, he permitted parliament to give retroactive sanction to his actions.

Unification

Bismarck now proceeded to forge German unity on the same iron basis on which he had reaffirmed authoritarianism. This meant fighting it out with the one power that opposed German unity under Prussian hegemony: Austria. The polarization of power in the German Confederation in two superpowers that dominated the smaller states could, in his view, be overcome only by armed contest. Once more disregarding a charter (this time that of the German Confederation), he took up the battle with its entire membership, and again might made right: after Austria's defeat (1866), a number of German states (Hanover, Hesse-Kassel, and others) were incorporated into Prussia. With the rest of the states in North Germany, Prussia now founded what amounted to a genuinely federal (not merely confederate) unit, the North German Federation. Its constitution foreshadowed that of the second Empire. This Empire (*Deutsches Reich*) was soon established through the accession of the South German states to the North German Federation at the conclusion of the war against France (1870–71). German unity was finally achieved.

These events had a lasting impact on Germans. To many they seemed to prove the inherent weakness of popular forces and the invincibility of the established powers of army and state: force is what counts in history; without its use the cherished aim of national unity could not have been achieved. In exchange for unity, the German middle class reconciled itself to a continued lack of domestic freedom. Democracy now appeared as a mirage that for a while had misled Germans but in the long run had been unable to seduce them. The black-red-gold flag of the old liberal movement and of 1848 was remembered at best as a symbol of a romantic dream. Its place was taken by the black-white-red (in which the black-white of Prussia predominated) of the new German Empire. In the words of Golo Mann (Thomas Mann's historian-son), the Empire's "origin was violent, its constitution jerry-built, its society garrulous, its government cesaristic, with Power and Success its new Gods." [3]

2 GERMANY AS AN EMPIRE (1871–1918)

There are eras in the history of nations that particularly affect the character of their lives, of their societies, and of their political institutions. For the Germans such a period began when they achieved unity in 1871. The period between 1871 and 1918 constitutes a great divide. It was during those five decades that Western nations moved toward liberal democracy, but Germany maintained and reinforced the authoritarian status quo. While Britain and France consolidated a pattern against which any antidemocratic tendencies and movements had to struggle, in Germany a pattern was set against which democracy had to struggle. This is what hampered Weimar democracy and still has some impact on Bonn. There is nothing to the stereotype that Germans are authoritarian by nature, but many were made so under and by the Empire. Hence its importance for subsequent German developments.

BISMARCK'S CONSTITUTION

The new Reich was genuinely federal, and not a loose confederation. There were central Reich organs and powers, and Reich laws were directly binding upon each citizen. But the structure differed from democratic federalism in that sovereignty, instead of residing in the people, rested with the princes of the member states, who were represented in the primary federal organ, the Federal Council (*Bundesrat*). Being federal, the Empire could not be a one-man autocracy. The emperor (*Kaiser*), sym-

[3] Golo Mann, "The First Partition," *Die Zeit* (July 1, 1966).

bol of the Reich's unity, was checked by the Bundesrat, and also by its only democratic-representative institution, the Federal Diet (*Reichstag*). Thus the constitution blended contrasting elements: federalism and hegemony, federalism and authoritarianism, and, lastly, authoritarianism and some measure of democracy.

The Reich and the member states

States' rights were strong. Most internal affairs remained under state jurisdiction, with the Reich's powers restricted to foreign affairs and certain economic matters. And even where the Reich had jurisdiction to legislate uniformly (for example, in civil, commercial, and criminal law), there was established a principle that to this day has been a peculiar feature of German government: the member states, generally, are in charge of the administration and execution of federal laws. Federal legislation thus does not usually require the establishment, as it does in the United States, of corresponding federal administration. To the citizen of

the Empire, therefore, *state* still meant primarily the member state and its bureaucracy. But the tendency toward centralization, which characterizes modern federalism everywhere, developed in the Empire too. Financially the Reich, which at first depended on contributions from the states, grew gradually more independent, and this was the basis for more independence in everything.

But the increase in Reich powers meant little as long as Prussia played a dominant role in Reich affairs. The main body through which Prussian influence was exercised was the Bundesrat. This council was not a representative assembly with delegates elected by people or parliaments of member states (as, for example, the United States Senate), but consisted of delegates—usually high government officials—appointed and instructed by the executives of the member states (as it does to this day at Bonn). The votes of the twenty-five states were weighted, with Prussia having seventeen out of fifty-eight. Since Prussia could usually count on votes from smaller states, it held a strong position. Most important, it could block con-

stitutional amendments, since fourteen votes sufficed to defeat an amendment. The council shared lawmaking power with the Reichstag.

The Reich executive

In the field of executive power, Prussia's influence was exercised through the kaiser. Since the Prussian king was automatically the kaiser, whatever powers he lacked as kaiser he could indirectly exercise as king of the dominant state. As kaiser, for example, he had no share in Reich legislation, but he could influence legislation through the Prussian votes in the Bundesrat. His other powers included foreign affairs, command of the armed forces, and appointing the Reich chancellor.

The relation between kaiser and chancellor depended on their respective personalities. While theoretically the chancellor was the creature of the kaiser, who could appoint and dismiss him regardless of parties, majorities, or any other influences, as long as Bismarck was at the helm Kaiser William I submitted to the political dominance of the chancellor. The relation changed with the advent of William II (1888–1918). This capricious and egotistic monarch preferred pliable administrators of his personal regime.

The chancellor headed no cabinet of the British or French type but was rather chief of a number of secretaries (ministers) who headed executive departments. His position thus resembled the relationship between an American president and his department heads, but with one crucial difference: the president's mandate issues from the electorate, while the chancellor's mandate issued solely from his monarch. The chancellor invariably was a high nobleman, officer, or official. The Reich bureaucracy, over which he presided, was staffed largely with Prussians. No party leaders, and very few representatives of other than the noble and official classes, could expect appointment to higher office. The Reich as well as Prussia was thus ruled by conservative forces.

Parliament and parties

At face value, parliament (the Reichstag) was a strangely democratic island in an authoritarian environment. It was exceptional in Germany (and in most of Europe, for that matter) in that it was based on universal manhood suffrage. Bismarck probably desired a strong popular symbol of German unity against any particularist or secessionist tendencies on the part of princes and member states. Also, he may have hoped that universal suffrage might turn out in favor of conservatives rather than liberals, since the Junkers controlled the rural vote.

The trouble was that the Reichstag's influ-

Reichstag Election Results Under the Empire

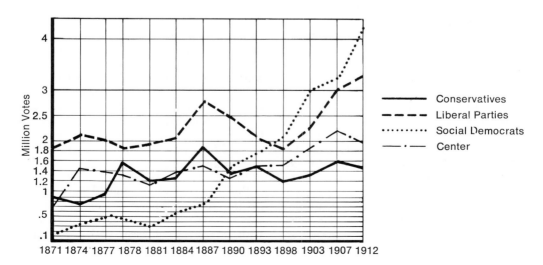

ence was chiefly negative. It had no power over the executive, and criticism and opposition were therefore pointless. It did have authority, with Bundesrat concurrence, to enact federal laws and pass the federal budget; to this extent, even a Bismarck had to have parliamentary majorities. Yet the chancellor's position remained vastly different from that of a parliamentary prime minister. His mandate continued to issue from the monarch. In only one instance did an adverse vote induce a chancellor to resign, and that failed to become a precedent. To get the laws he wanted passed, the chancellor manipulated the parties and their leaders. His task was made easier because the parties, lacking true governmental responsibilities, had little incentive to organize themselves into stable majorities or minorities in support of, or in opposition to, the government. Party leaders themselves could never hope to be called into responsible executive positions. To win them over, handouts would usually turn the trick, and if worse came to worst, the Reichstag could be dissolved. Debates at times were furious, but usually futile. Under this system Germans had no chance to learn the ways of responsible government.

THE RULERS

The success of a modern government may be measured by its ability to integrate economic and social classes into a nation. By this token the Empire was not a success. True, there was that admirable efficiency (the inheritance from Prussia) with which everything was organized and which lent it an appearance of strength and stability. But the Empire failed to integrate the forces that rose during its sway.

While at the time of its foundation the Reich was still more rural than urban, more small-town than big-city, more heavily based on handicrafts and small factories than giant enterprises, it rapidly changed into one of the world's foremost industrial, trading, banking, urbanized countries. Heavy industry based on coal and steel, and chemical, electrical, machinery, textile, and optical factories changed the countryside; and the rise of the industrial classes, managers, white-collar employees, and, above all,

industrial workers changed the social landscape. The class of big landowners (Junkers) lost proportionally in economic weight. But it did not lose its social and political power. That it could maintain that power into the industrial age was due to an arrangement under which the old powers retained political control, while the middle classes accepted the established authoritarian government in return for protection and promotion of their economic interests.

The National Liberals

This arrangement was the work of Bismarck. After their defeat in the Prussian conflict, the middle classes in the main gave up the idea of constitutional reform. A split occurred in the political party that represented these classes, the Liberal party. Its majority became the National Liberal party, while an uncompromising left minority established itself as the Progressive party but subsequently failed to attain any large voting strength or influence. (It was this group, however, that guarded the tradition of 1848 and carried its ideas over into the Weimar period.) The National Liberals, on the other hand, represented that combination of economic enterprise and submission to established authority that became typical of German businessmen.

These National Liberals no longer had much in common with the liberal nationalists of the early nineteenth century. Nationalism had then aimed at unification; it now turned expansionist, imperialist, aggressive, and even racist. The earlier political liberalism had been crushed. Bismarck thus could base the first decade of his rule on collaboration with a chastened neoliberalism. It had adopted his political framework and now assisted him in his battle against political Catholicism and socialism. Its reward was legislation that guaranteed legal security and freedom from executive interference in business activities.

Imperialism

But here difficulties loomed. Increasing competition from grain-producing countries overseas threatened German agriculture and therewith the economic basis of the Junkers. The

Junkers clamored for protection. When the National Liberals refused to yield to this demand, Bismarck, as suddenly as he had previously dropped conservative in favor of liberal backing, dissolved his liberal alignment in favor of renewed collaboration with conservatives. And again he split his adversaries: with protection for agriculture he combined protection for heavy industry. This alliance of Junkers and steel led to liberal-conservative reconciliation on the basis of high tariffs. Even trading interests were assuaged by the new imperialism, economic and political, which became the landmark of William II's era. William's naval program satisfied imperialists as well as the armament interests that thrived on navy orders.

The chief dangers of this system arose in foreign affairs. German imperialism was clumsy in its diplomatic aspects; its emphasis on prestige and its aggressive temper antagonized major powers. The cautious and moderate policy that Bismarck had inaugurated after 1871 gave way to William II's swaggering foreign policy, which was backed by a nationalist middle class, providing it with the vicarious satisfaction of political ambitions unsatisfied at home. Organizations such as the Pan-German League, which specialized in mass agitation for imperialism and colonialism, were largely middle class in character and membership.

Infeudation of the middle class

Internal political control was maintained by the authoritarian classes—the Junkers and their allies—partly through the Conservative party, partly, and more importantly, through a process of elite formation that may be called the infeudation of the upper middle class. The Conservative party, backed by nobility, army, officialdom, Protestant clergy, and part of the peasantry and of the middle classes, was merely the parliamentary arm of the ruling groups; it was grudgingly organized after 1848, when it appeared that nonconservatives had become politically vocal. Since the agrarian Junkers became numerically insignificant in the new industrial society, it was essential to draw from other classes, particularly the upper middle classes, those who would assist the nobles in

ruling Germany through the army and the higher bureaucracy. To qualify, a nonnoble had to be imbued with the standards and prejudices of the old classes through a long process of "education to be a gentleman." He would first go through higher education at the Gymnasium and then enter a university, joining one of the select fraternities. Equipped with a dueling scar, a commission as a reserve officer, and legal training, he would be ready for apprenticeship in administration or a similar field. To top it off, there might follow marriage into one of the old families. Promotion would likewise depend on these factors. At each step care was taken that only the right persons were selected. Catholics and Jews were seldom admitted, and none with unorthodox opinions. Prussians and Protestants were preferred.

THE RULED

The proletariat

This pattern deeply split German society. The average German during the Empire was prosperous, and the living standard of all classes was rising. The paternal state took care to provide some measure of security for those in distress. As we have seen (Chapter 1) a comprehensive system of social security was devised by Bismarck to prevent social unrest. But it was a grudging paternalism. There was no question of admitting the lower classes to social equality, let alone to political power. The rising tide of the proletariat filled the ruling classes with fear, which was answered by sullen hostility on the part of the workers. Most of them joined the socialist movement through the (Marxist) Social Democratic party (SPD). Bismarck's attempt to suppress it only strengthened it. Driven underground, it now had its martyrs and it reemerged into legality stronger than before. But, although it maintained an attitude of total opposition to the existing regime, its revolutionary doctrine slowly assumed the character of a "Sunday" creed, which was paid lip service at meetings and in publications. On workdays, however, Socialists were more interested in improving the worker's living standard through trade unions. The worker turned reformist, but socially and politically he remained an outcast.

Other outcast groups

Others besides the workers were forced into passivity or hostility. There were the tenants and agricultural workers on the eastern estates, many of them Catholic Poles, whose nationality and religion were two more reasons for discrimination. The Poles as well as the similarly Catholic inhabitants of Alsace-Lorraine were viewed with distrust. German Catholicism, a minority in the Reich, felt threatened and organized itself in the Center party. To Bismarck this seemed dangerous for the unity of the Reich. Backed by the National Liberals (who feared clericalism), he tried to destroy political Catholicism, but the Church and its organizations survived this culture struggle (*Kulturkampf*, as the anti-Catholics called it) as successfully as the Socialists survived Bismarck's anti-Socialist policies. Still, Catholics continued to be discriminated against in administrative appointments, and the interests of Catholic member states and regions were often neglected.

Toward the end of the Hohenzollern era, many Germans became aware of the cracks in German society and apprehensive of the danger of an adventurous foreign policy. As long as criticism was voiced by leftists, the ruling class could safely let them complain, since it controlled the main instruments of opinion, the schools and the universities. But criticism became more ominous when it was voiced by professors, such as Germany's great sociologist Max Weber (1864–1920), or by owners of big industrial combines, such as the industrialist and author Walther Rathenau (1867–1922). Such people realized the two-pronged danger inherent in foreign adventures and internal authoritarianism, and questioned whether it would be possible to steer the state through stormy waters while at the same time rejecting participation by the majority of the people. Toward the end of the era, responsible people began to think of constitutional reforms, especially the introduction of parliamentary government. It came in the final stages of World War I, but then it was too late.

3   GERMANY AS A REPUBLIC (1918–33)

Bonn is not Weimar, the title of a book on present West Germany, points up the connection between the first German experiment in democracy and the current one. While it is true that the latter has tried to distinguish itself from the former by avoiding its mistakes, it is also true that much in the present situation can be traced back to the earlier one. The Weimar period provided the only experience on which present German democracy could build. Moreover, many problems that confronted the first German republic still seem to confront nations trying to solve burning questions of our time, such as capitalism versus socialism, or how to defend democracy against its adversaries without destroying freedom itself. To analyze the Weimar system, assess its merits, and account for its failure is still of more than historical concern.

EMERGENCE AND CHARACTER OF THE WEIMAR SYSTEM

In November 1918, under the impact of defeat in World War I, William II and the other princes abdicated, and a group of socialist leaders (right- and left-wing Social Democrats) proclaimed a republic and set up a provisional government. Following general elections a constituent assembly adopted the Weimar Constitution in the summer of 1919.

The choice of the Thuringian town of Weimar (from which came the unofficial name of the republic) as meeting place of the assembly pointed up the difficulties as well as the hopes of the fledgling republic. The capital, Berlin, was found unsuitable for drafting a constitution because it was in the throes of bitter street fights between leftist radicals and their op-

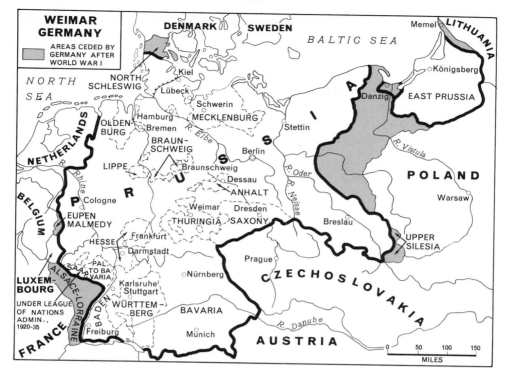

WEIMAR GERMANY

AREAS CEDED BY GERMANY AFTER WORLD WAR I

ponents, with the former opposed to constitution-making by parliamentary procedure. Weimar, the town where Goethe and Schiller had lived, was chosen in hopes that a new spirit, symbolizing Germany's cultural heritage, might henceforth replace the spirit of Potsdam, residence of the Prussian kings.

The fulfillment of this hope presented a difficult task indeed. German democrats were faced from the start with a military defeat, a severe peace treaty (the Treaty of Versailles, 1919), a deep social and political division of the German people, and ensuing internal disorder. They had to contend with Germany's isolation in foreign affairs, the vindictive attitude of her former enemies, a heavy financial burden caused by reparations, and an ensuing currency inflation that further increased internal dissatisfaction. Even more burdensome was the legacy of authoritarianism. The old powers at first seemed discredited. But after a short time the memory of the previous regime's shortcomings faded, while the glories of the past continued to be recalled. They were contrasted with present miseries, which, instead of being attributed to the failure of the previous regime, came to be blamed on the new one. German democracy thus was burdened both with the psychological handicap of being born of defeat in war and with economic conditions that compared unfavorably with those prevailing under the Empire. It was exposed from the outset to merciless attacks from both the left and the right.

The difficulties of those Germans who supported Weimar should be kept in mind by those who would censure them for their eventual failure. At least they made an effort. It was not, as has been sneeringly said, a "Republic without Republicans." And it would not seem that the experiment was doomed from the beginning. The Republic was heir to an important trend in German history, the trend that led from the freedom movements of the Napoleonic age to 1848. Dormant under the Empire, this liberal trend now emerged as the untried alternative to a system found wanting. As in the case of France's Third Republic, there was no reason to believe that Germany might not have grown, under favorable circumstances, into habits of democratic government. But bad luck seemed to stalk it from its inception.

Democracy or proletarian dictatorship?

The Weimar system was not based on revolutionary action. The so-called revolution of 1918 meant simply the disappearance of the old powers (emperors, princes, and their governments) without much pressure from the German masses. The old administrative machinery with most of its incumbents remained. Even the generals remained. There was left a political void now filled by the Republic. But what kind of republic? Here the first problem arose. Revolutionary socialists, who formed the radical wing of the Social Democratic party and soon split away from it as Communists, wanted a proletarian dictatorship exercised by the councils of workers and soldiers, which had sprung up in Germany in the fall of 1918 and that they hoped to control. The failure of uprisings they staged in the winter of 1918–19, however, showed that they did not carry with them the majority of workers, let alone the German people. The defeat of leftist radicalism opened the way for the second alternative: the establishment of a democratic republic.

Unfortunately for the future of German democracy, the Communists had been the only active revolutionary group. To beat them the Social Democrats had called upon generals and reactionary nationalist groups armed by the generals. Perhaps there was no alternative, since the republican masses were unarmed; yet the Social Democrats might have tried to arm these masses. In any event, it was a bad omen for democratic government that it owed its birth to the intervention of its rightist enemies.

Framing the constitution

For the time being, however, the way was clear for the framing of a constitution. The constitution, adopted by the Constituent Assembly at Weimar in 1919, was the work of three parties that together had obtained a large majority at its election: the Social Democrats, the Center party, and the Democratic party, heir to the Empire's Progressives and now the rallying point of the middle classes fearful of leftist radicalism. This election was important for two reasons. First, neither the radical left (the Independent Socialists, a split-off from the Social Democrats) nor the antirepublican rightists (chiefly the Conservatives, under their new label of German Nationalists) made a good showing. Second, the two socialist groups together (Social Democrats and Independents) failed to attain a majority. (The newly formed Communist party had boycotted the election.) Consequently, Germany's new structure had to be devised by a coalition of socialists and nonsocialists, workers and middle class.

The underlying compromise

Bismarck's Reich had been founded on an understanding between the authoritarian forces, which would go on ruling politically, and the upper middle class, which obtained freedom in the economic sphere. In similar fashion Weimar was based on a compromise, this time between the working class, as represented by Social Democrats and trade union leaders, and the middle class, acting through leading industrialists. The basis of agreement was the acceptance of the new, parliamentary-democratic framework of government. But it was an uneasy, and to some extent ambiguous, compromise. To the Social Democrats, for instance, a formal agreement between industrial and trade union leaders that had established the trade unions as equal partners in collective bargaining constituted the minimum from which to start in the direction of socialism. But to the industrialists this agreement seemed to be the maximum concession. Would they be ready to accept in good faith a vote nationalizing industries?

In addition, the tenuous compromise was endangered from the outside. Communist opposition from the left forced the Social Democrats to stress full socialism as their final aim. This, in turn, frightened the middle class; portions of it now joined the opposition from the right, which from the outset had been hostile to the new constitutional pattern. The Weimar system thus became endangered from the right as well as the left. It was on this shaky and narrowing foundation that the constitution rested.

The constitution as such was one of the

most progressive of its time. It provided for procedures and institutions of direct and of representative democracy, and its liberal orientation was emphasized by its elaborate code of civil and political liberties. It established progressive standards for social and economic policies. Its main shortcoming was its eclecticism; its makers seem to have hoped for the best of all possible worlds. There were borrowings from the United States, Britain, and France, but they failed to blend. Instead of a simple parliamentary system, for example, there was a counterweight to parliament in the office of an independent president, but without clear indication as to whether the cabinet was to be responsible to parliament or to the president.

WEIMAR FEDERALISM: REICH AND LÄNDER

First on the agenda at Weimar was the problem of Germany's territorial organization. What was to become of the member states? The age-old particularistic traditions and interests prevented any dismemberment of Prussia or absorption of all states into a unitary state; the federal structure of the Reich was maintained. But in contrast to the Bismarck Constitution, the central government emerged with strong powers. There remained hardly a field in which the Reich (this term denoting central government, as contrasted to that of the states, now called Länder, or, in the singular, Land) could not legislate if it so desired. To the Länder there chiefly remained administration of the federal laws. But even here new Reich administrations with their own bureaucracies were set up.

The federal constitution, moreover, prescribed that the internal structure of the Land governments would be republican and parliamentary. This did not mean, however, that Länder policies were always in agreement with Reich policies. Their political differentiation, rather than any pronounced sectional differences, made the Länder politically important during the Weimar period. Thus Prussia, in direct contrast to her Empire temper, became the stronghold of the moderate left, while Bavaria turned to the right.

A strengthening of central power also re-sulted from the abolition of Prussian hegemony. There was no longer a strong, Prussian-dominated army. What remained of the army was Reich-controlled. There was no emperor through whom Prussia could exercise influence, nor was there a Bundesrat in which Prussia ruled. In the financial sphere, where the old Reich had been dependent on the states, the Länder now became dependent on the Reich, with its own sources of income. The Reich government also possessed strong powers of supervision and enforcement. Its power to resort to sanctions against a recalcitrant Land was much used, and abused, whenever a Land government became too radically leftist. In cases of "rightist deviation" one was inclined to use milder methods.

A federal council (Reichsrat) was the organ through which Länder interests were to be safeguarded on the Reich level. Like its predecessor, the Bundesrat, the Reichsrat was composed of delegates instructed by the Länder governments. Since government in the Länder was now parliamentary, the delegates represented governing parties rather than the states as such. Yet, in practice, they acted chiefly as bureaucrats trying to bring Reich interests into accordance with those of the Länder.

PARLIAMENT AND ITS POWERS

The old Reich had placed sovereignty in the princes, under Prussian leadership. The Weimar Constitution placed sovereignty in the people. But how in a modern, large-scale nation are the people to exercise sovereignty? The classical European system is that of government by assembly: a representative body, issuing from a general election, acts as the sole mandatary of the people; all other organs of government must be under its control.

A mixed system

The French have always been inclined toward government by assembly. The Germans feared it would mean government by parties and party bosses and therefore sought a compromise. This can be seen most clearly in the way in which they tried to solve the problem of the relation between parliament and executive. This relationship had seen three or four basic types of development in the West: the American presidential system of separation of powers; the British system of government responsible to Parliament, but with the cabinet having the power to dissolve Parliament; the classical French parliamentary system in which the cabinet did *not* have the actual power to dissolve parliament; and the Swiss system, under which the executive always follows the instructions of parliament and does not resign even in case of disagreement. Weimar chiefly followed the British system: the cabinet was to be responsible to the Reichstag, which, in turn, could be dissolved by the executive. In contrast to Britain, however, such parliamentarism in Germany, with its many parties, involved the danger of cabinet instability of the French type. The Weimar Constitution therefore sought to render the executive strong and, to some extent, independent of the Reichstag; this constituted an American admixture. Certain devices of direct democracy were taken from the Swiss system, under which the people, through plebiscites, participate in legislation. In contrast to Swiss practice, this device was chiefly used for purposes of demagoguery on the part of extremist movements.

Reichstag and proportional representation

Despite these restrictions, the Reichstag was the keystone of the arch. In it the will of the people was to be reflected from the broadest basis of election. Women were now given the right to vote. The voting age was lowered from twenty-five to twenty. And, most important of all, election was by proportional representation, with each group of voters given an equal chance of being represented according to its voting strength at the polls. Each 60,000 votes elected one candidate from lists submitted by the parties in large election districts; each party got as many seats as resulted from dividing its number of votes by 60,000.

This system has been attacked by some as a main cause for the decline of the Republic. It is true that its virtue of representing relative party strength and political opinion more fairly than do other systems was offset by its faults in favoring party bureaucracy—which made up

the lists of candidates—and making it easier for splinter groups to get representation in parliament. But even under the single-member-district system of the Empire, Germans had voted for party rather than for individual candidates, and the system had produced about as many (and about the same) major parties as appeared under Weimar. Proportional representation can hardly be held responsible for customs deeply rooted in German history.

The Reichstag had comprehensive powers. It made the laws, adopted the budget, consented to treaties, and made continuance in office of the cabinet and each minister dependent on its confidence. But its power was not unlimited. It was checked slightly by the devices of direct democracy, somewhat more by the powers of the Reichsrat, and most of all by those of the president (and of the cabinet when availing itself of presidential powers).

THE EXECUTIVE

The cabinet

The position of the Weimar executive (the Reich president and the Reich government, consisting of the Reich chancellor and cabinet ministers) did not seem to deviate much from the established pattern of parliamentarism. Chancellor and ministers were responsible to the Reichstag. The president's powers included representation of the Reich in foreign affairs, supreme command of the armed forces, and appointment (and dismissal) of chancellor, ministers, and other high officials. But all presidential actions needed the countersignature of the chancellor or a minister. Since these persons in turn were responsible to parliament, presidential measures supposedly were within the range of parliamentary control.

Actually, during much of the Republic's life the system functioned as it was supposed to. The president generally deferred to the cabinet. The cabinet depended on coalitions of parties that had a majority in the Reichstag. As in France, the cabinet tended to be an alliance rather than a coherent unit, and to fall through internal dissensions more often than through outright defeat by parliamentary opposition. Cabinets usually did not last long; but in personnel and composition the new cabinet often resembled the preceding one. The chancellor was no longer the autocrat as in imperial times; his main concern was to keep the coalition going.

Parties and bureaucracy

Real decisions were made in the party caucuses. The party bureaucracy was now in possession of the key political positions. Unlike their British counterparts, those staffing the ministries were recruited, not from and through parliament as a school for political leadership, but usually from the ranks of party functionaries or related interest groups, such as trade unions and employers' associations directly. It was, by and large, honest government, but colorless, without much vision and thus unable to inspire enthusiasm. Moreover, it owed much of its efficiency to the permanent officialdom working under it. Inexpert ministers were generally dependent upon the established civil service, where a conservative or even reactionary outlook still prevailed. With certain exceptions (the Prussian police was one) the bureaucracy was not democratized. The government did not wish to impair the efficiency of the bureaucracy, even for the sake of reform. This reluctance prevented the Weimar Republic, as it did the Western Allies a generation later, from establishing a firm democratic basis for government and administration.

The presidency

The manner in which, under this half-parliamentary, half-bureaucratic system, political authoritarianism eventually reemerged is chiefly the story of the role played by the Weimar presidency. Even during the period of constitutional normalcy, until 1930, the president enjoyed considerable influence. Thus, although the small professional army (*Reichswehr*), which the Treaty of Versailles allowed Germany, was supposedly under the civilian control of cabinet ministers responsible to parliament, in practice defense ministers, backed by the president as supreme commander, evaded parliamentary supervision.

Two constitutional provisions contributed to this development. One was that the president should be elected by direct popular vote and for a period longer than that of the Reichstag (seven, as against four, years); the other concerned his emergency powers. Popular election meant giving the president a mandate independent from that of the Reichstag. This was hazardous in a country where the executive had traditionally represented antidemocratic groups. While in the United States the president often represents the commonweal as opposed to special interests entrenched in Congress, in Germany the election of a president, as, in 1925, of Paul von Hindenburg (1847–1934), a World War I general, could appear as a victory of conservative forces. Already prior to 1930, certain incidents made clear the difference between his attitude and that of a head of state in Britain. For instance, when the left initiated a popular vote on the expropriation of the former princes' holdings, Hindenburg expressed his opposition in an open letter. Compare this public intervention in a political issue with British custom, under which the king may not even marry without the consent of the cabinet.

Article 48 and presidential dictatorship

Many critics believe that Article 48 of the Weimar Constitution, which provided the president with emergency powers, opened the way for dictatorship. This article was in fact used in the late years of the Republic to sidetrack parliamentary government. But the existence of an emergency provision meant less than the circumstances that invited its misuse. Article 48 was even designed to prevent such misuse. Every emergency measure was to be communicated immediately to the Reichstag, which had the power to revoke it; it was to be a temporary suspension of ordinary constitutional processes in order to save the constitution as such.

But Article 48 was too broadly interpreted from the outset. Instead of being used as a safety valve, it served as an easy way out of ordinary difficulties. Economic or financial "emergencies" were construed as sufficient reasons to issue decrees. The time came when the president failed to obtain parliamentary approval for such measures. According to the constitution he should then have yielded to the Reichstag. But the power of dissolution provided him with a way out. If he found a chancellor ready to back him and defy the Reichstag (shades of William I and Bismarck!), he might dissolve it and call for general elections, instead of canceling his emergency measures. What if the election failed to provide him with a majority? Could he keep his chancellor in office and dissolve the newly elected Reichstag again? This obviously would mean flouting the will of the people and the sense of the constitution, but that is what happened at the final stages of the Weimar Republic.

BASIC RIGHTS

The constitution contained an elaborate catalog of "fundamental rights and duties" that was meant to protect individuals and groups against the state.

But the traditional political rights and freedoms, although specified in the constitution, were not protected, as they are in the United States, against infraction by law. Ordinary legislation, whether by the federal government or the *Länder*, could define, limit, or even suspend these rights. While in normal times these rights were respected, as they had already been to some extent under the Empire, there was little guarantee that they would be respected during the abnormal times that came to be more and more normal.

In addition there was a catalog of so-called social rights that was intended to solve some of the chief problems with which the Republic was faced: socialism versus private capitalism, secularism versus church influence, large estates versus land reform. However, the constitution was drafted by a coalition of opposed interests whose compromises had the effect of deferring critical decisions.

Thus, in the economic field, the federal level of government was accorded the right to nationalize industries, and the workers were assured the right to participate in the regulation not only of labor conditions but of general economic issues. On the other hand, private property was guaranteed against expropriation without full compensation. In practice, there was no nationalization of industries, but rather private capitalism with some admixture of social reform; no workers' participation in planning or regulation of economic affairs, although some participation in the regulation of labor conditions through factory councils. There was no agrarian reform, no breakup or control of cartels, and no curtailment of the privileges of the bureaucracy, the army, the recognized churches. Not much had been changed; basic conflicts remained.

SOCIAL AND POLITICAL FORCES

During the more peaceful middle period of the Republic it seemed as if these conflicts might yet be solved gradually. In a period of prosperity (1924–30), important sections of the population shared the fruits of a revived economy. The system of the middle 1920s was based on favors to industry, big landowners, and industrial workers alike. Big-business profits (based in part on price fixing by powerful combines) went hand in hand with an improvement of labor conditions through collective bargaining. But the lower middle classes, the professionals, the small savers, who had lost their holdings during the galloping inflation of 1920–23, were neglected. Their savings had enabled them to live better than the workers and to give their children a higher education. Now they were on the financial level of the proletariat, but they refused to consider themselves proletarians. They became hostile and frustrated, as did many small peasants, small businessmen, artisans, and shopkeepers.

Another inheritance from the years of postwar turmoil was nationalist activism. The defeat of the Communists in 1918–19 was credited to rightist action, rather than to the feeble Republic. Subsequently, the nationalist extremists, posing as guardians of the national interest, organized vigilantes, tried republican statesmen and others in kangaroo courts, and assassinated them. In ensuing court trials the judiciary often made a mockery of justice by letting rightist "patriotism" stand above the law.

THE CONSTITUTIONAL CRISIS

What little social and political harmony there was under Weimar ended abruptly when depression struck Germany at the end of 1929. Industrialists refused to let the state intervene in order to provide employment. Even at the height of depression the orthodoxy of the balanced budget was preserved. By 1932 there were 10 million unemployed in a nation of 65 million.

The economic crisis created a political and constitutional crisis. In the face of mounting radicalism on the right (Nazis) and on the left (Communists), the upper middle classes turned right, believing that the way to cope with communism was by repression rather than by social reform. Denouncing even moderate progressives as "red," they felt that only authoritarian government could preserve the existing system of property. They hoped to rule with the help of bureaucracy and the military; instead they opened the gates to Nazi totalitarianism. Hindenburg, dismissing a Social Democratic chancellor who still commanded a majority, and appointing a Center party leader of conservative leanings (Heinrich Brüning) in his stead, inaugurated the system of presidential government (1930). But the election of 1930 showed that the masses in distress were no longer under the control of these authoritarians; they had turned to more radical movements. Nazi representation rose from 12 to 107, that of Communists from 54 to 77. Yet there still existed ample opportunity to form a common front against these two extreme groups. Only after the July election of 1932 did Nazis and Communists combined have a so-called negative majority that could have stalled the parliamentary machinery. But the conservatives were unwilling to join forces with the republicans. The conservatives now ruled by decree, on the basis of Article 48, and the Social Democrats, still (with 143 deputies) the strongest party, backed them as the lesser evil.

Thus Chancellor Brüning, even as late as 1932, had some kind of majority, although he refused to consider the Reichstag the source of his authority. His authority, according to the new doctrine of the presidential system, lay in the confidence of the president. But when he was unable to persuade the Nazis to join the authoritarian regime, he was suddenly dismissed by Hindenburg, and a Junker, Franz von Papen, was appointed. His "cabinet of barons" had not the slightest chance of majority backing in parliament. There followed the tragicomedy of repeated dissolutions and new elections, with the monarchist-feudal group temporarily in the saddle, trying to ward off revolution from left and right. The extremists now organized themselves as states within the state, as "movements" with their own doctrines and loyalties and their own paramilitary formations, complete with emblems, slogans, uniforms: to the right the Nazis, with brown shirts and swastika; to the left the Communists' "red front" organizations and hammer and sickle. On the defensive were the conservative nationalists, with a Steel Helmet veterans' organization and the imperial black-white-red flag symbol; and, belatedly and timidly, the Social Democrats and other republicans with their Reich Banner organization featuring, for once, the black-red-gold Weimar colors.

In the face of this pluralism the state was ever less able to control the antagonistic forces. An atmosphere of civil war prevailed. In the daily clashes between the armed gangs, the Nazis, usually the attackers, were openly favored by the authorities. The only force potentially still siding with the republican left was the Prussian police. The Papen cabinet, deposing the legitimate Prussian government with the help of Article 48, got control of this last bulwark of democracy. This outrage might have aroused the non-Nazi and non-Communist masses, but their leaders instead appealed to the Constitutional Court. Industrialists, Junkers, generals, and officials, on their part, while at all times ready to fight Communists and republicans, were not ready to defend their own rule against the Nazi tide. They induced Hindenburg to dismiss the chancellor who had succeeded Papen and to appoint Adolf Hitler. The thirtieth of January 1933, a day as fateful for Germany as it was for the world, marked the end of Weimar. It was not, as the conservatives hoped, a return to Potsdam. No place name of German glory, cultural or military, can be associated with the new era that was to come: the emblem of shame invoked by Dachau and Auschwitz.

THE DOWNFALL OF THE REGIME: THE QUESTION OF RESPONSIBILITIES

Structural shortcomings

In dealing with causes and responsibilities for Weimar's failure one must distinguish between the more technical-structural shortcomings of the Weimar government and the underlying political, social, and economic factors. Among the former the unresolved relationship between parliamentary and presidential authority was perhaps the major one. This division of authority was not harmful so long as the forces and interests behind both were broadly identical, that is, until 1930. It led to disaster when this identity ceased. In the ensuing conflict, the executive, which had the backing of the military, prevailed. Even the Nazis succeeded only when power was handed over to them by the president.

The decline of the Weimar system has been attributed to a number of additional structural shortcomings, but in a curiously contradictory fashion. It is alleged, for instance, that too much or too little attention was given to civil rights and liberties; that political parties were too powerful, or that the executive—chiefly through Article 48—enjoyed too much power. But these criticisms will not really bear scrutiny. If it is charged that the Weimar Constitution granted too much liberty to political enemies of the regime, we find that in reality it was the unwillingness rather than any constitutional inability of the Republic to defend itself that helped the Nazis to rise to power. It knew how to defend itself effectively against its leftist enemies. And if it is charged that Article 48 was responsible for the establishment of authoritarian government after 1930, it would be legalistic indeed to assume that antidemocratic forces would not have found ways to gain power even in the absence of such a provision.

Political responsibilities

Real responsibility would seem to lie rather with certain social groups and political forces, and especially with their leaders. With the masses inclined to follow their leaders, much depended on the emergence of democratic leadership, but in the main the cultural, intellectual, political, and economic elite were either self-seeking or filled with a generally authoritarian doctrinairism. This was true regardless of party affiliation.

Communists

The Communists were chiefly responsible for splitting what might have been a strong democratic labor movement. Their insistence on control made cooperation with them impossible. Their utopianism consistently mistook "the fourth month of revolutionary pregnancy for the ninth." Their illusion of having the support of the masses led them to denounce all others as fascists, particularly the Social Democrats. Not even at the height of the depression were they strong enough to take over, but they *were* strong enough to provoke, in real fascism, "the counter-revolution against the revolution that never took place." Charging democracy as veiled fascism, unwilling to join forces with antifascists even after 1930, the Communists in effect helped to usher in that real fascism whose difference from democracy they noticed when it was too late.

Socialists

The moderate socialists, the trade union heads, and so forth, sinned rather through omission. By and large they were honestly devoted to democratic principles. But they were not leaders. Their lack of militancy, their timidity and legalism were striking. Theirs was the main responsibility for the failure to insist on basic social reforms when the progressive tide was still high. Then, they might have inaugurated reforms of the cartel system, broken up the Junker estates, democratized the civil service, Reichswehr, school system, and judiciary. Moreover, they lacked a vision that could command the allegiance of the young generation. They also lacked a sense of what the struggle for power demands, the readiness to take calculated risks. They were not traitors, as the Communists charged, but self-betrayed.

Catholics

Catholic leaders had similar shortcomings. In the initial period, under the influence of their workers' groups, they developed some progressive zeal, but later they became representatives of an interest party like others, although the interest was religious-cultural rather than economic. Democracy for them was an instrument rather than an aim, discarded when its value as a tool became doubtful. Then, political Catholicism fell back into the authoritarian groove. It is true that a courageous minority resisted this trend, but in vain: eventually political Catholicism helped vote Hitler into total power, thereby committing political suicide.

Conservatives

Outside the Communist, socialist, and Catholic elites, most of the German leadership under Weimar remained reactionary. The more liberal and progressive leaders of the middle classes soon became officers without an army. Many of those who had joined the liberal-democratic camp deserted it, longing for the good old prewar days and despising the less glamorous Republic. This elite had a great responsibility as social and intellectual leaders of the middle classes, as teachers and professors, pastors and journalists. By ridiculing the new system, they stifled incipient republican enthusiasm. They advertised patriotism as they understood it: a mixture of old-fashioned authoritarianism, defense of vested interest, and nationalism. But their own reactionary credo was revealed as weak when most of them failed to live up to it and became followers of the Nazis. Much in the Nazis' success was owing to the support by Conservatives. Among all those who contributed to the downfall of Weimar, this German elite's was perhaps the gravest guilt.

Foreign powers

Although it cannot provide Germans with an alibi, the responsibility of foreign powers cannot be denied. Revengefulness prevented them from encouraging the fledgling Republic and its democratic forces when there was still time; blindness and plain cowardice induced them to appease and to yield when totalitarianism was in the saddle. Their intransigence kept the Republic in isolation and denied it the success in foreign policy without which it could not gain prestige at home. When a few concessions were made toward the end of the period, it was too little and too late. The nationalism of the victors had provoked that of the vanquished; Aristide Briand and Gustav Stresemann, working for German-French reconciliation in the 1920s, could not make up for the revengefulness of the crucial first period. The names of foreign statesmen can unfortunately not be left out from the list of the gravediggers of Weimar.

It is true that much of what has been said about Germany applies to other countries, and yet they did not produce a Hitler. They too were struck by an economic depression; and the split in the working class, the drab and sometimes sordid ways of party politics, the authoritarian tendencies of the middle classes, the failure of the intelligentsia to provide progressive leadership—all these were not confined to Weimar Germany. Why, then, did Germany, and not France, for instance, produce Nazism? The factors mentioned above may account for the weakness and failure of German democracy; they do not explain the rise of a totalitarian movement. At most, they provided a basis on which such a movement *could* rise. That it *did* arise was due to something in addition: the emergence of a genius (an evil one, to be sure), who knew how to fashion a new creed and a mass movement under his leadership.

4 GERMANY AS A DICTATORSHIP

THE NAZI MOVEMENT: ITS CHARACTER AND ITS RISE

Even today it is difficult to approach the topic of National Socialism without emotion. Too profoundly has the fate of the world been influenced by the rise of this movement and by the war it provoked. Neither can it be considered a dead issue. Fascism, of which Nazism was merely the German form, is still one possible alternative to democracy (the other one, of course, being communism). And to many Germans these twelve short years still constitute "the undigested past," as it is sometimes referred to. Much depends on how they will eventually come to terms with this greatest transgression in their history.

Adolf Hitler

Adolf Hitler (1889–1945) rose from complete obscurity to head the German state. The son of an Austrian petty official, he failed every chance of gaining access to a normal occupation. After he had dropped out of high school, a Vienna art school refused to accept him. To the end of his days Hitler was convinced that he had the talent and the temperament of an artist; this conviction led him to despise the "better," educated people who had entered upon civil careers through normal channels, as well as to distrust the expert, who could set his knowledge against Hitler's intuition.

In his youth, without education, degree, or training, Hitler sank down into the underworld of beggars, vagrants, and criminals, working occasionally but not regularly, envying those who did, and thus accumulating a tremendous store of hatred and frustration.

Hitler managed to identify his impulses with the cause of a group that, in his imagination, was also victimized: the Germans as a nation or a race. In Austria, in particular, he saw them outnumbered by non-German nationalities and Jews. In the Reich they seemed threatened by foreign enemies intent on destroying German might. To him, as to many others, World War I was the way out of individual frustration. He enlisted in the German army; his life was now merged with a cause. But the defeat of Germany threw him into what became paranoia. He would not admit that his cause had been defeated in honest battle. In his eyes the frontline soldier had been "stabbed in the back" by Jews and Marxists. Since this was a world that did not appeal to Hitler, he had to change it; eventually, he had even to repeat the war, as would the boy who does not want his first defeat to count. He decided to enter politics.

At that time the disordered state of German affairs offered many a chance to become political adventurers. Innumerable "folkish" groups were founded, many engaging in terroristic activities, all clothed in some mystical nationalist or racist philosophy, all quarreling endlessly among themselves about fine points of their doctrine. Hitler joined one of them. He discovered his gift as an orator. Unlike most leaders in the Weimar period, he knew how to stir the people's imagination and enthusiasm. He soon became the leader of the National Socialist German Workers party, or NSDAP, which he used as a launching pad for his political ambitions. In contrast to minor rabble-rousers, he combined persistence with an ability to learn from experience. He would not make the same mistake twice. Defeated in his attempt to attain power by uprising (his "beer hall Putsch" in Munich, 1923), he realized the uselessness of frontal attack on established authorities. From now on his movement would pretend to be legal. Employing entirely novel tactics, he would capture the state from within, through the organization of a movement with a political religion.

Organization and rise of the movement

The story of Nazism's rise is still of prime importance because it is thus far the only instance in which a totalitarian movement gained power in a long-drawn-out battle with the existing regime. Nazism, indeed, battled Weimar throughout the entire existence of the Republic.

The very fact that most leaders and groups in Germany failed to take it seriously added to its strength.

From 1924 to 1930, the period of normalcy when other ultranationalist groups were vanishing, Hitler devoted his efforts to building up the cadre of an organization by reorganizing the NSDAP on the basis of authoritarianism. He established the program of the party as incontestable dogma; he established himself as the infallible leader; he disciplined the rank and file; he selected a group of henchmen who accepted his leadership unconditionally, weeding out those who showed independence of mind or personal ambition. Democratic principles, such as voting, election of party functionaries, and accountability to the membership, were outlawed in favor of the "leadership principle." A hierarchy of rank was established, each member deriving his status ultimately from Hitler. Special formations were set up, such as the paramilitary Storm Troopers (SA), groups of brown-shirted, high-booted hoodlums who were to engage in brawls and street fighting in order to capture the attention of the public and to demoralize other groups. Finally, he established the doctrine of the movement—the "ideology" that was to be promulgated in intensive propaganda campaigns.

The Nazi doctrine

Many political religions of our time offer explanations and values to those lost in mass society and despairing of understanding their condition. But Nazi doctrine did not even begin as an attempt to explain the world in rational terms. In Hitler's rambling and ranting *Mein Kampf* and in Alfred Rosenberg's book frankly titled *Myth of the Twentieth Century*, the doctrine was meant to be irrational myth, with racism, social Darwinism, and political romanticism its chief ingredients.

It may seem wasted effort to present details of so crude and fantastic a doctrine. Yet one should know the source of the intoxication that enabled human beings to commit, with apparent good conscience, crimes unequaled in history.

According to this myth, history is the struggle for survival and domination on the part of races. There are higher and lower races. Only the former, by subjugating the latter, are able to create culture. All civilizations have been created by one superior racial group variously referred to as Nordic, Aryan, or Germanic. Greek and Roman civilizations were founded by tribes of Nordic stock. Aryan Vikings founded Russia; Franks, France; Saxons, England. But the culture-creating minority is ever threatened with degeneration, especially through racial mixture with the masses of inferior breed whom they enslave. Germany itself scattered its forces. Its nobles degenerated; they imitated foreign ways and neglected the interest of the German racial community.

Subsequently the Germans encountered an even greater danger. The deadly enemy of all superior races, according to the Nazi myth, is a racial group sometimes characterized as a counterrace, the Jews, who are bent on destroying the inner strength of nations in order eventually to establish their own rule over the world. In this conspiratorial scheme they proceed with diabolic cunning. To soften up organized communities, they preach individual rights and liberties; they advocate formal democracy with its rule of the numbers, behind which looms their own rule. For, liberal democracy means either plutocracy, that is, "Jewish" economic exploitation of the Aryan, or Jewish Marxism, which divides by preaching class struggle and results in Bolshevism, the victory of the "Jewish-led" proletarian masses. In either case it is World Jewry that triumphs.

Germany, as Hitler saw it in the 1920s, was the country on which Jewry was concentrating. Acting through plutocratic capitalism ("Wall Street") *and* Marxist socialism ("Moscow"), it was attacking what remained of inner strength in the German people, utilizing liberalism, pacifism, internationalism, humanitarianism, even political Catholicism, as disintegrating influences. But counterforces must needs reassert themselves. Led by a savior, so Hitler predicted, Germany would establish its Third Reich. This Third Reich would be "a people's community," led by an elite for which the welfare of the whole would be the guiding principle. All power would be in the hands of a leader acting as trustee of the community.

All this would be in preparation for the Nazis' ultimate goal: to reestablish Germany as a world power with a world mission. They would revive the spirit and instruments of war,

that is, militarism and armed forces. Regained military might would enable Nazi Germany to throw off the fetters of Versailles and to unite all racial Germans, such as the Austrians, in a Greater Germany. Then Germany would turn east to acquire "living space" in those "vast open spaces." Before turning east, however, it would have to settle accounts with its hereditary enemy, France, the country that had always tried to prevent Germany from rising to greatness. After the defeat of the degenerate West, Germany would subdue eastern barbarism and in this way eliminate Bolshevism. Eventually, it was ordained to become master of the world.

This doctrine appealed to many Germans. It gave them a sense of belonging to a community and the hope of becoming leaders in a group destined to rule; a sense of a task to be fulfilled not only in sordid self-interest but for coming generations; a sense of challenge and adventure, and particularly the German joy of marching again in uniform. It would resolve their worries and give life a new meaning. It is obvious, too, that the doctrine fitted in with many a pre-Nazi ideal: authority and strong leadership; the rule of the best in the common interest; the idea of the *Volk* as the basic political unit, and of its mission in the world.

Nazi propaganda

If the Nazi doctrine were all that Hitler had produced, he would now be as little known as any peddler of hate and prejudice. But he knew how to use his doctrine in order to build up what really counted—his movement. His was an early experiment in political mass propaganda, with all its now well-known implements: terror, violence, and brainwashing—in short, psychological civil warfare.

Nazi propaganda, unlike that of the ordinary Weimar parties, was continuous, bombarding the people not just at election time, but day in and day out. The masses were showered with symbols: colors, display of flags, uniforms, insignia, the playing of anthems, the singing of songs, slogans endlessly repeated, an elaborate ritual. The tension was never relaxed.

Besides being incessant, Hitler's propaganda was primitive and emotional in its appeal to the instincts and sentiments of the masses. It made full use of stereotypes and prejudices. It was a concentrated offensive against one enemy in whom all evil and guilt was embodied. The attention of the masses was not distracted by multiple goals or multiple reasons. The Jew was *the* enemy. He was held responsible for everything adverse: for defeat in war and the peace terms, for reparations and runaway inflation, for depression and plutocratic exploitation, for the class struggle and national disunity.

Hitler discovered that the lie, if only big enough and repeated often enough, was a potent weapon, since facts are usually not able to keep up with it. Nazis might be proved libelous in solemn trial, but some of the slander would always stick, and the trial itself would serve them as a political forum. Thus they spread fear and terror, disrupted existing bonds and loyalties, and sowed confusion among non-Nazis. Many secretly joined the Nazi party as a means of political insurance. The Nazis managed to plant spies in government agencies, to emerge, once the party was in the saddle, as the framework of the Nazi government. They thus inaugurated what was to become known as fifth-column tactics, the tactics of boring from within, of forming a state within the state.

In contrast to the efforts of other parties, Nazi propaganda was devised to appeal not to one particular group but to all "racial comrades." To do this it had to be vague in order to bridge the great issues that divided the Germans. As one student of fascism has put it, "To be grandly vague is the shortest road to power, for a meaningless noise is that which divides us least." Nazi propaganda rejected plutocratic capitalism as well as Marxist socialism and stood for "genuine" national socialism. Under it the commonweal would prevail over private interest, but "legitimate" private initiative would not be destroyed and everybody would get his due. Parliamentary democracy as well as reactionary conservatism, republicanism as well as monarchism, were rejected in favor of the "ennobled democracy" of a people's community led by its elite.

Nazis were most successful with social groups that were frustrated by failure and unsophisticated enough to fall for high-sounding generalities: the small shopkeeper, losing ground in the competition with department and chain stores (the latter frequently Jewish-owned); the unsuccessful lawyer, resenting the success of Jewish (or other) colleagues; university graduates unable to find employment commensurate with their social status (the "academic proletariat"); small farmers, resenting exploitation at the hands of grain and cattle dealers (frequently Jewish); young people who throughout the depression had never had a job.

Nazi propaganda, however, was not equally

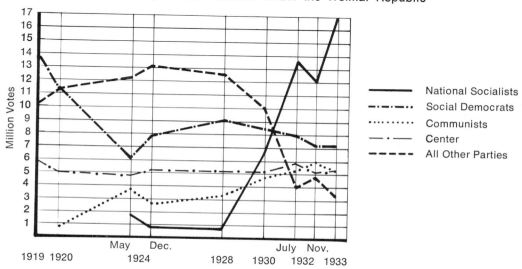

Reichstag Election Results Under the Weimar Republic

effective with other groups. Two major groups withstood it best: the proletariat and the Catholics. Election figures prior to 1933 show that Socialists and Communists combined steadily maintained about 35 percent of the vote. Depression merely meant that Socialists lost and Communists gained. The Center party similarly withstood the Nazi onslaught, maintaining a steady 15 percent. The masses supporting Nazism belonged to the non-Catholic middle classes, whose parties, between 1930 and 1933, were practically wiped out. In addition, many young new voters voted Nazi. So did the habitual nonvoter, who, under the frenzy whipped up by Nazi propaganda, now went to the polls.

Besides the masses, it was important for Hitler to obtain the backing of the upper classes, especially those groups that alone were able to hand over state power to him. Gradually, the rising tide of his movement persuaded important elements in the ruling groups, some industrialists, generals, officials, that his movement was the wave of the future and that they had to give him a share in power in order to maintain their own interests. Hitler now obtained financial subsidies from Ruhr industrialists. It was these groups that eventually persuaded Hindenburg to appoint Hitler chancellor. He neither had to gain a majority at the polls nor use force in order to obtain power. The national revolution, as the Nazis called their access to power, was neither national nor a revolution. It was victory by default.

Consolidation of power

What followed was a lesson in how to consolidate power. The real revolution occurred only after the formation of the Hitler cabinet. In this cabinet the Nazis were still a minority, and the Junkers thought it possible to keep them prisoners of the majority. They were to be cruelly disillusioned. Hitler and his chief henchmen, Göring and Goebbels, using the strategic positions of which they had foolishly been put in command (such as the Prussian police and the agencies of propaganda), now prepared for a final election by terror and intimidation. An emergency decree gave them the power to suppress opposition meetings and publications, arrest opposition leaders, and put them into pro-

tective custody (Göring's new invention, soon to be known under the less reassuring name of concentration camps). Shrewd enough to proceed step by step, the Nazis first turned against the extreme left in order not to frighten the moderates, who were to be dealt with later.

Despite all this, the election (in March 1933) failed to produce the hoped-for Nazi majority; even with their conservative allies the Nazis did not get the two-thirds majority that Hitler needed to formalize his rule through constitutional amendment. But Göring, in his dual capacity of president of the Reichstag and chief of police, took care of everything. He excluded the elected Communist delegates from the Reichstag session. Still, outside help was needed. Partly through intimidation and partly through promises (to be forgotten as soon as the vote was taken), the Center party, along with some liberal groups, was induced to vote for the Enabling Act of March 24, 1933. Only the Social Democrats opposed the Act. It concentrated all power in the executive (cabinet), which could now legislate by simple decree and even amend the constitution. The Reichstag and the parties had written their own death warrants. To be sure, the Act contained certain restrictions, for example, a guarantee of the existence of Reichstag, Reichsrat, and presidency. But who was now to protest if these limitations were disregarded?

They were. After the emasculation of parliament the real revolution started. But it was a strange revolution. Afterward no political institution resembled any previous one, and yet everything was achieved "peacefully" through a process of what was called *Gleichschaltung* (coordination, synchronization). The ever present threat of force, with the constant narcotic of propaganda, sufficed to stifle any idea of resisting. Thus, the *Länder* were coordinated, that is, provided with Nazi governments; so were the municipalities and other units of administration. All elected bodies in states, cities, and provinces were suspended. The civil service was purged of "politically unreliable" officials. Press, schools, universities, and the professions were coordinated; cultural and economic organizations and all other associations were put under the control of trusted Nazis. Labor was brought under control through the outlawing of the free trade unions. The political parties were outlawed one by one, proceeding from left to right, including those of the Nazis' own partners in the cabinet.

Except for the army, the circles around Hindenburg, and the churches, power was concentrated in Hitler's hands by July 1933. The revolution thereupon was declared officially terminated, to the dismay of a leftist wing in the party (particularly the SA leadership), which had expected more thoroughgoing action against plutocratic capitalists. Again taking the initiative, Hitler forestalled unrest by his blood-purge of June 30, 1934. Acting as prosecutor, judge, and executioner, he killed off the radicals in his party and used the occasion to liquidate those outside the party suspected of conservative-reactionary opposition. By thus eliminating potential centers of resistance, he served notice on any and all that he was in earnest. Army, bureaucracy, big business, whoever might still have hesitated, now conformed. Thereafter no public purges were necessary. When Hindenburg, by this time senile and completely isolated, died on August 2, 1934, Hitler put the final touch to his rule: he merged the presidency with the chancellorship, and thereby assumed whatever powers had remained with the president. The main impact was felt by the army. With soldiers and officers taking an oath of loyalty to Hitler as supreme commander, resistance from these quarters could henceforth be only scattered.

STATE AND SOCIETY UNDER NAZISM

Totalitarianism means concentration of political power in one man or group and the use of such power for the complete control of society. The Nazis maintained totalitarian control in five connected ways: (1) *by concentration of power*, that is, through organizing government in such a way as to allow no limitations on the power of the executive, remnants of autonomies, or similar checks; (2) *by atomization of society*, that is, through dissolving existing groups so as to isolate individuals; (3) *by coordination of the individual*, that is, by then reorganizing these individuals in new groups established and controlled by the regime; (4) *by organizing and applying a system of terror* to maintain this control; and (5) *by*

propaganda, that is, by maintaining a monopoly of information for the control of opinion and for indoctrination.

CONCENTRATION OF POWER

The leadership principle

In the absence of any real limitations of power, totalitarian government is structurally simple. The Nazis did not even bother with the semblance of a constitutional document. The only constitutional principle in the Nazi state was the leadership principle, which meant that the will of the Führer (now Hitler's official title) was the highest law and the ultimate source of authority. Below the Führer, assignment and delimitation of jurisdictions were always provisional and revocable. The Reich cabinet ceased to function as a body. Ministers, appointed and dismissed by, and exclusively responsible to, the Führer, became mere technical advisors, while decisions were made elsewhere, either by Hitler himself or by trusted lieutenants, usually high party leaders. After the Enabling Act most legislation occurred by decree, but it could also take other forms, such as the so-called Führer edict, a law issued by Hitler alone and sometimes not even made public.

There were some democratic trappings. "Elections" to a one-party Reichstag from a single list of candidates yielded the customary 99 percent majorities; so did so-called plebiscites. The Nazi Reichstag passed hardly any statutes, but rather served as an audience for Hitler's speeches, as did the annual party congress at Nuremberg. All this was to demonstrate to Germans and the world that the regime enjoyed the "enthusiastic backing of the people."

Centralization

Every totalitarian state tends in practice to be centralized, outward appearance notwithstanding, for it cannot afford to grant autonomy to subdivisions that might become centers of emerging opposition. Thus the Nazis abolished the federal structure of the Reich, which became a unitary state. The *Länder* became mere administrative districts under the direction of

Hitler-appointed governors. But there was little left for the governors to direct, since most government functions were now handled by Reich ministries. Prussia was for all practical purposes abolished, its administration being merged with that of the Reich, while the other *Länder* at least retained their boundaries. On the local level, mayors and other officials were appointed and dismissed by the Reich Minister of the Interior, and municipal councils were appointive and advisory only.

Bureaucracy and party

The Nazis were faced with a personnel problem with which all revolutionary regimes are confronted: whether to continue to utilize an existing, tested, and experienced but politically preregime bureaucracy, or to build up a new service from reliable but inexperienced followers. The Bolsheviks eventually chose the second alternative, as did the present rulers of East Germany. The Nazis, however, were in a hurry. Preparation for the war that Hitler wanted was the overriding consideration; in order to put Germany on a war footing, the Nazis needed the services of the existing bureaucracy. But they took no chances. After an initial purge, they put the remaining officials on notice. The sword of dismissal hung constantly over the heads of officials who depended on their jobs for their livelihood. Since they were specialists trained for this and no other profession, few dared not to conform.

Still, the old bureaucracy did not merge completely with the party appointees. A dual system continued, with older professional civil servants and new Nazi appointees working together with varying degrees of friction, although all were equally under the control of the top echelon of the party. Key posts in the state were frequently held by important party leaders. This way the party elite was in control of the bureaucracy. On the other hand, the lower-level party organizations were not permitted on their own to interfere with the state administration. Both state machinery and party organization were thus separately kept under the control of the Nazi elite, which ruled supreme, using for its purpose now the state and now the party.

Underneath Hitler, however, even this top group remained unorganized and ever changing. Unlike Stalin and Mussolini, Hitler avoided institutionalization of authority even at the top —and with good reason, as was demonstrated by Mussolini's experience with his own Fascist Grand Council, which voted for Mussolini's dismissal in 1943. Nazi rule is a unique example of how an unorganized but strongly led gang can subdue a modern nation.

ATOMIZATION OF SOCIETY

If concentration of power and rule from above constituted the only criterion of totalitarian government, it would not, in principle, be different from other types of authoritarian rule with which history abounds. But while traditional authoritarianism was never entirely unrestricted by tradition, precedent, and customs, modern totalitarianism molds everything. Society becomes the product of policy; it is created and not creative. Existing groups and institutions are dissolved in a process that may be called the atomization of society. Totalitarianism exploits the fears and anxieties that go with freedom and individualism in order to enslave the individual. Severed from previous relationships, the citizen becomes dependent on the new regime. Thus many Germans traded liberty in return for jobs under the Nazi armament program and for a stake in the glorious future that Nazism promised.

Eugenic policies

The racial policies of the regime illustrate the extent to which the individual was rendered helpless. Extermination of non-Aryans was only one side of this picture. The other side was purification of the "Aryan" race itself. Laws providing for sterilization and even castration of certain categories of people inaugurated a program of destruction of those found weak or obnoxious or merely useless. There were no guarantees against abuse; the individual was delivered to the tender mercies of those in power. This policy culminated in a Führer edict (kept secret and communicated only to those directly in charge of its execution) for the "mercy killing" of inmates of asylums. How many thousands of "pure Aryan" Germans were thus put to death will never be known.

The family

The way in which the family was attacked can serve as another illustration of "atomization." It was the task of schools and Nazi youth organizations to see to it that neither family nor Church exercised non-Nazi influence on the youthful mind. No unsupervised leisure was allowed. Informing—telling on parents by children, on teachers by pupils, on priests by members of the congregation—was not a dishonorable act but a sacred duty. The corruption of moral standards that ensued can easily be imagined.

The churches

Next to the family it was the churches that, with their own creed, seemed dangerous competitors for allegiance. With its glorification of non-Christian standards, of violence and other bellicose virtues, Nazism was in essence pagan. But the Nazis did not try to destroy the established churches outright. If by countenancing the outward forms of religion they could obtain essential allegiance from the churches, this would constitute a greater victory for the regime than suppression.

The Nazis were never able to overcome completely the resistance of the churches. But the nature and extent of this resistance have sometimes been exaggerated. In the Protestant churches it was a minority of preachers and lay members who organized the so-called Confessional church, the majority complied with the regime, and another minority even became active Nazis, organizing themselves as "German Christians." In the Catholic Church, because of its authoritarian structure, there was no such split. But the spirit of resistance could not be translated into action as long as the Vatican encouraged collaboration with the regime. The conclusion of a Concordat with the Holy See, in 1933, was Hitler's first triumph in foreign policy. The Church subsequently protested Hitler's systematic violation of its rights and interests, but neither the Confessional church nor Catholicism opposed Nazism—or the war it provoked—as a political system, although

they did oppose policies that were irreconcilable with religious doctrine.[4] Their opposition thus was not a matter of total principle. Yet they had their martyrs, and their defiance was a banner around which noncompliance could rally.

Army and nobility

Army circles and the nobility offered another example of resistance to total atomization. Authoritarian though the philosophy of these groups had always been, it was a philosophy that still respected certain moral standards. Nazism restored status to them and revived the spirit of militarism. But their ultimate ideals differed. Fighting, to the Junker, still meant fighting for some cause—defense of the fatherland, of throne, or of altar. The Nazis' ideal was conquest, of power for power's sake; in this battle, man was to become a morally insensible robot ready to commit any deed covered by "superior order."

When this became apparent, some officers and Junkers who were still imbued with their own standards of honor attempted to resist. But since they had allowed Hitler to assume complete control of the armed forces, resistance could only be carried on underground. The backbone of the resistance was broken by the blood-purge in 1934 and a subsequent purge in February 1938. We know now that a plan to overthrow the regime late in 1938 had to be postponed when the Western powers appeased Hitler in the Munich Agreement of September 1938 and thereby raised his prestige to its pinnacle. Not until the final stage of the war, when its loss was apparent, could a new attempt (July 1944) be undertaken. Its failure meant that even before postwar developments destroyed it economically, Junkerdom lost its best members to the Nazi executioner.[5]

[4] Discussion of Rolf Hochhuth's play, *The Deputy,* and its indictment of Pope Pius XII's failure to speak out against the extermination of European Jewry on the whole has not disproved the justice of condemning an inactivity that prevailed whenever groups or interests outside the Church were involved.

[5] This is not meant to imply that some Junkers (and some priests) were the only "resisters" to the regime. On the contrary, what has since been dubbed the Resistance comprised a broad front, from army officers on the right, to officials and businessmen, to workers, trade unionists, so-

COORDINATION OF THE INDIVIDUAL

Party and party organizations

The atomization of society and the isolation of the individual were only means to an end—the total control of the individual through groupings established by the regime. All organizations under Nazism became either controlling or controlled groups, and no individual or group was allowed to remain outside such organized control. This is what the much heralded "corporative" or "estates" structure of fascism (in Italy as well as in Germany) amounted to. It was not self-organization of the respective interests and groups, not pluralism, but merely a façade for totalitarian control. The main instrument for such supervision was the party itself, with its proliferation of affiliated and supervised party organizations. Frequently there were two organizations, controlling and controlled, for one and the same group or occupation. Thus, the Hitler Youth, an organization for every boy and girl, contained a select group, the *Stamm* (core) Hitler Youth, which was to be trained in special schools to become the future Nazi elite. As a result the party itself changed its character. The active "movement" of pre-1933 days was turned into an instrument as thoroughly manipulated as any other instrument of Nazi rulership. Only at its top level did it shade off into the realm of actual rulership.

Labor under Nazism

How did the main economic and social groups fare under Nazism? Was it continued rule of capitalism, or was it the rule of a group hostile to private property, "brown bolshevism"? To begin with, labor was deprived of

cialists and Communists. However, the Resistance remained scattered, a matter of individual persons rather than of organized groups. The latter-day claim of many Germans to have been members of the Resistance, if only passive ones, raises the problem of "collaboration," that is, at what point continuing in one's job, presumably to prevent worse things, turns into sharing responsibility and guilt. Neither in the German case, nor in that of French and other collaborators, nor in that of Stalinism, has a clear solution been found. However, it is likely that in most cases the genuineness of resistance was demonstrated by the claimant's exile, imprisonment, or death.

any influence or autonomy. Its trade unions were suppressed, together with the political parties that had represented its interests; strikes were forbidden; advocacy of workers' demands, unless voiced by official party spokesmen, was interpreted as advocacy of class struggle and was considered subversive. The Nazi-sponsored Labor Front was a front to conceal actual Nazi control. Since it included employers, it was not supposed to represent labor interests, and even less to participate in the regulation of labor conditions.

As for these, the status of the workingman was one of regimentation. The state determined his wages, hours, and where and in what kind of occupation he was to work. But his job was secure in an economy with labor shortages. The average worker, comparing this situation with depression conditions, preferred job security to freedom plus unemployment. Although passively and often grumblingly, the German worker collaborated—an attitude not very surprising in a full-employment economy that promised subsequent participation in the spoils of an entire continent. Longer hours, worsening living conditions, and scarcity of consumers' goods appeared as an investment that would pay off—cannons in order to get butter. Only when the cannons failed to procure the butter did the masses turn away from the regime. But one should not forget those workers—in particular, former socialists, Communists, trade unionists—who took up the underground fight against the regime, with many becoming martyrs of the Resistance.

The peasantry

Like the worker, the farmer was regimented; he was told what to plant and how much, what to deliver to the food authorities and at what price. Nazi agriculture was planned, although not collectivized. Under conditions of food shortage and rationing, the farmer was in a better bargaining position than the worker, and the regime treated him more gingerly. But there was no question of his belonging to, or being represented in, the ruling elite. Nazi Germany was as little a peasant's state as it was a worker's. Was it then the rule of the capitalists?

Business and middle classes

Nazism did not destroy capitalism as a system; it did not nationalize property. On the contrary, it made the owner "leader of the enterprise." He could now manage his affairs without fear of strikes or labor unrest. Nazism had released him from the fear of Communism and the necessity of dealing with organized labor as partner; it permitted high profits, strengthened cartel agreements, gave business a chance to profit from Aryanization of Jewish property and, subsequently, from the exploitation of conquered countries. This, however, was only one side of the picture. The other side was regimentation. The "leader of the enterprise" was told what wages he had to pay, how many hours his workers had to work, even which workers he might hire. Almost everything concerning management, from the allocation of raw materials and credit to the determination of what to produce or sell and at what price, was dictated to him. The Nazi economy was a regimented war economy even before the war started.

Under this system, ironically enough, those who fared worst were the small businessman, the artisan, the small shopkeeper or trader—in short, the groups that had flocked to Nazism at its rise in the hope of economic salvation. They were sacrificed in favor of more efficient (and more influential) big business.

Big business fared well, despite controls. It shared in handsome profits and was permitted somewhat greater influence over the management of its own affairs: its representatives in the estates (organs of "business self-administration") exercised more actual influence than did those other groups. They also had easier access to the highest leadership group. Big business profited from the destruction of small enterprise and the exploitation of cheap foreign and concentration-camp labor. Yet it operated in a system that gave it no influence over such crucial political decisions as the preparation for, and waging of, aggressive wars. It was, moreover, threatened by increasing state competition, as in the field of steel and chemical production, and it did not enjoy legal security. A system that can put anybody it dislikes into a concentration camp and that can confiscate property for any or no reason is scarcely the rule of "monopoly capitalism," even if it leaves monopolies temporarily intact and refrains from using the secret police against businessmen as long as they behave. The Nazi elite spared big business for the same reason it hesitated to destroy other forces, like the bureaucracy and the Junkers: it needed them for all-out war. What would have happened if Germany had won the war must remain an open question.

ORGANIZATION OF THE TERROR

To some extent all organized society rests on compulsion. What distinguishes totalitarianism from free society is that terror is institutionalized. The individual is under the permanent threat of forceful action against his possessions, his liberty, his life. When such organized violence is applied unpredictably, when its practitioners are free from supervision, there emerges the characteristic police-state atmosphere of pervasive fear that leaves the individual with a sense of utter helplessness. This modern terror is distinguished from coercion under despotism in three ways: (1) Its existence is never admitted. Officially, one lives in a genuinely free society, and anybody who dares intimate that terror exists is branded as subversive and is himself taken care of by the secret police. (2) It is systematized, that is, all institutions of state and regime are ultimately at its service. (3) It performs scientifically, using the refinements of modern psychology and other sciences for its purposes.

Nazi law

The law, under this system, ceases to consist of general rules defining rights and obligations and becomes pure command and coercion. As Nazi jurists put it, "Law is what is useful for the people," usefulness to be defined by the Nazis. Principles of ex post facto law and punishment by analogy were applied by judges who had lost their independence. Yet the Nazis found that many among the old judiciary could not entirely escape the Rechtsstaat spirit in which they had been trained. Hence Hitler's resentment against the judges, whom he accused of formalism. He established special courts, staffed with Nazi judges, picked from Nazi formations, and put them in charge of political crimes or the application of racial and eugenic legislation. This practice explains the blood-justice of the People's Court at Berlin and similar terror institutions.

The Gestapo

But even special courts failed to be satisfactory as the main instrument of terror. They might, although rarely, acquit an accused. The regime needed an institution that was entirely free from remnants of formalism; it created it in the form of the Secret State Police, or Gestapo. The Gestapo was an agency with unlimited power over any individual and any group, against whose actions and decisions there was no appeal to courts or any other authority. Gestapo authorities could arrest anybody without a warrant and detain him indefinitely without further trial in their concentration camps. They could, and did, arrest a person just acquitted by a court because they still deemed him dangerous. They supervised the citizen in his daily life, watched his movements, tapped his wires, read his correspondence, overheard his conversation. With the help of the Security Service (SD), a vast network of voluntary informers, they scrutinized everybody's attitudes. No one could trust anyone else. Formation of opposition groups in this way was either prevented or nipped in the bud.

The Gestapo was closely linked with the party's SS (Protective Formation, as it was euphemistically called), which had emerged from the SA to become the backbone of the regime's terror machinery. Both SS and Gestapo were headed by Heinrich Himmler, a cold-blooded fanatic, next to Hitler the most powerful figure of the regime and later the most execrated name in all Nazi-dominated Europe. SS members, selected for fanatical devotion and capacity to inflict utmost cruelty if so ordered, staffed the Gestapo, guarded the concentration camps, and later formed the most frightful organization of all, the *Einsatzgruppen*, or Special Task Formations, which followed the German armies all over Europe to hunt out and exterminate en masse Jews, Communists, and other marked groups.

In the concentration camp a new type of society spread over Europe. Paradoxically, it was the only institution with some self-government under Nazism. Internal management was usually left to one group of inmates, the ordinary criminals, whom the Nazis placed in the camps, along with vagrants and homosexuals, to be able to brand the political inmates, too, as criminals and perverts. Medical and other sadistic experiments performed on camp inmates were Nazi contributions to the study of how humans function under inhuman stress. Another contribution was the technique of mass extermination in gas chambers. It was no minor achievement, after all, to have "processed," within a few years, millions for the "final solution," requiring, as it did, the coordination of many thousands for the job of collecting, transporting, and killing the victims.

In the "ordinary" camps, meanwhile, the population, toward the end of the war, came to include many of the elite of Europe, from nationalists to Communists, from Catholics to Jehovah's Witnesses, officers and pacifists, Germans and non-Germans. Most of them perished, and many survivors were physically and mentally broken. From this loss Europe has long suffered.

What rendered the Nazi terror so frightful was its cold-blooded planning. Even what appeared as spontaneous mob violence (for example, the synagogue burnings of November 1938) was carefully planned. Of perhaps more lasting importance, however, was the legalization of terror by bureaucratic procedure. Here the German tradition of obedience to authority paid dividends. Since all participants acted under orders, they all felt that their actions were legal—the judge inflicting the death penalty upon one who refused to inform; the police official assembling Jews for deportation; doctors and nurses obeying the decree for mercy killing; managers of firms starving slave laborers or delivering incineration furnaces according to specification. The problem of how to treat such actions and their perpetrators was to become a legal and moral headache of post-Nazi regimes, and especially, post-Nazi Germany (see Chapter 6).

Jewish persecution

Jewish persecution offers the prime example of how this bureaucratized terror worked. Without it even the Nazis might not have managed to kill 6 million "non-Aryans" within three or four years. The Nazis shrewdly started with "mild" measures: first exclusion of Jews from professions, then gradual destruction of their economic life, finally their deportation to Auschwitz and other annihilation camps in Eastern Europe where they were either worked or gassed to death.

Besides satisfying its racist aims, this policy served the regime politically. It intimidated opponents, and it made allies of anti-Semites abroad who became the basis for fifth columns. It served as precedent for subsequent more general destruction of the rule of law. It was one (and almost the only) implementation of the original Nazi program, and this satisfied its earlier followers. In its confiscatory stage it appeared anticapitalist, but it also lined the pockets of those who could profit from Aryanization. It bound all participants in a common guilt with the Nazis and thus made jumping off the bandwagon more difficult. It would be wrong, however, to assume that it made all Germans Jew-haters. Some turned philo-Semitic under the impact of what they saw or learned, and even helped heroically. But the mass looked the other way, and many did not hesitate to profit. Like the Empress Maria Theresa at the partition of Poland, they wept but took.

Passivity and conformity were the main effects of the terror on the bulk of the population. If the average citizen did not "mix in things that did not concern him," he had a good chance of never being involved with the Gestapo. One should therefore not overestimate the impact of the terror on everyday life. The regime was satisfied if people knew in a vague and general way what threatened nonconformists. In this way resisters were isolated from their people even spiritually. It was different in occupied Europe, where the Nazis were the common enemy of resisters and the general population alike. For a German resister to work for freedom was to work for defeat of his country; this was the cruel dilemma into which Nazism had forced the decent German.

PROPAGANDA AND THE CONTROL OF MEN'S MINDS

Terror is one support of totalitarian power; the other is the organization of total allegiance or, at least, total conformity. While in pre-totalitarian societies, including the authoritarian ones, thought and opinion are to some extent spontaneous, totalitarianism strives to manipulate even this most intimate and personal realm. It monopolizes all channels of information and opinion and uses them for indoctrination.

The propaganda machine

This effort required: (1) the control not only of the traditional channels of communication but of everything that had any connection with thought, ideology, and opinion; (2) the distortion of information, research, and learning into indoctrination. Joseph Goebbels, as head of the Ministry of Propaganda, controlled not only press and radio but all cultural activities: the theater, films, music, the arts, and literature. Recalcitrants or suspects were condemned to economic death. Control extended into the schools, with their coordinated teaching staffs and Nazified curriculums and texts; into the universities; into the youth organizations.

Control of culture

Thought control drew an iron curtain around the German people, cutting them off from all information detrimental to the regime. Newspapers, magazines, radio, all voiced the same line. Thought control further meant the suppression of anything opposed to the official ideals. History was rewritten and retaught in accordance with racist doctrine; philosophy outlawed "liberalist" theories and "Judaized" thinkers; law repudiated the "formalistic" spirit of Roman law; art was purged of modern tendencies; literature was confined to writings extolling nationalism, militarism, heroism, and obedience. Nowhere else, perhaps, was the stultifying effect of conformity more apparent than in the cultural realm. Creative minds left Germany or withdrew into internal exile. The burning of books was the natural companion piece to the concentration camp.

Effects of indoctrination

While the anticultural action of the Nazis alienated an intellectual and cultural elite, the average German cared little as long as the regime provided bread and circuses. But indifference did not mean that indoctrination was a complete success. Nazi ideology penetrated German minds to a lesser extent than is commonly believed. The older generation was, for the most part, too deeply committed to pre-Nazi views to be easily won over. Even the youth upon whose conversion the regime was banking emerged less Nazified than might have been expected. An overdose of indoctrination resulted in widespread skepticism or indifference, which, while in one way facilitating the task of post-Nazi reeducation, also left a dangerous legacy of cynicism.

Thought control was more successful in the sphere of information proper, in the distortion and suppression of news. There was throughout the period of Nazism much grumbling; the political joke flourished (often tolerated by the regime as a relatively innocuous outlet); but correct information did not reach the masses. Gradually even what at first had been recognized as lie and distortion sank in. After the surrender in 1945, foreigners were amazed to find even genuine anti-Nazis believing that "the war had been forced upon us" because "the Poles started it." Totalitarianism may be unable to instill permanent enthusiasm but may well succeed in planting a distorted picture of the world.

SOME CONCLUSIONS

Nazism failed internally and externally. It boasted that it had replaced the confusion and inefficiency of parliamentary democracy with simple and efficient rule, but this was a myth. In actual fact, government, in becoming an ever more complex muddle of administrations, agencies, and jurisdictions, of party, state,

estates, and armed services, became a maze in which the citizen was lost. Never before had there been so much red tape. Connections meant everything, not to mention outright corruption and favoritism on an unprecedented scale. Moreover, the seemingly monolithic state was not able to eliminate pressures and influences working at cross purposes. Interests that in democracies operate in the open were active backstage. While the ultimate decision was always Hitler's, he usually avoided taking sides, preferring to play off one faction against the other. Conflicts were thus solved through temporary arrangement and compromise (as they are in the despised democracies).

In one respect only could the regime claim success of a sort: the Führer's personal control remained unimpaired to the end. Struggle over succession, with the pretenders jockeying for his favor, caused some strains. Hitler vacillated. He first designated Göring and then demoted him. Himmler, next in line, also incurred his wrath, and the last days of the crumbling regime saw a dark horse, Admiral Dönitz, nominated successor. But this also demonstrated that the dictator's power remained unaffected. Not even his most powerful lieutenants dared to oppose him openly. And unless such rule is broken by the disintegration of the entire leadership structure (as in Italy in 1943), it cannot be overthrown from within. This was demonstrated by the fate of the German Resistance. As a result the end of Nazism came only with military defeat and Hitler's death in his Berlin bunker (May 1, 1945).

This defeat sealed the failure of Nazi foreign policy. Nazism was unique in its singleness of purpose, with domination its objective and war its chosen means. Thus its fall through defeat in war was most fitting. But one should not forget how close it was to success (in 1940) and what its victory would have implied. Whatever form its hegemony would have finally assumed, its temporary New Order of Europe (1939–45) made it abundantly clear that to the doom of liberty for individuals and groups there would have been added the doom of independent nations; to inequality within Germany itself would have been added international inequality with the rule of Germany as a hegemonic nation and the enslavement of all others. Perhaps there might have been some gradation, with some groups or countries given preference, but there would have been loss of liberty and extinction of ancient values for all. When some people, such as Charles Lindbergh, assert that "in a broader sense" we lost the war because in effect it destroyed Western culture, one must remember that Nazi victory, with or without war, would have spelled the end of civilization in an even more drastic sense.

5 POSTWAR RECONSTRUCTION

GERMANY IN DEFEAT

The effect of the collapse of the Nazi regime in 1945 was more fundamental than that of Germany's defeat in World War I. Utmost concentration of totalitarian power suddenly gave way to virtual anarchy. The victors of World War II were thus faced with the collapse of an entire regime; their task was not merely restoring what had temporarily broken down but endowing a nation with a new type of society and public life.

This required temporary assumption of authority by the Allies themselves. Upon Germany's unconditional surrender in May 1945, the Allies allowed the territory east of the Oder-Neisse line to be placed under Polish administration, except for the northern half of East Prussia, which was turned over to the Soviet Union. The remainder of Germany was divided into zones of occupation, with the Russians in eastern Germany from the Oder and Neisse to and partly beyond the Elbe; the British in the Northwest; the Americans in the South; and the French with territory adjacent to France and carved out of the British and American areas. The zonal lines between East and West, which had been drawn up well be-

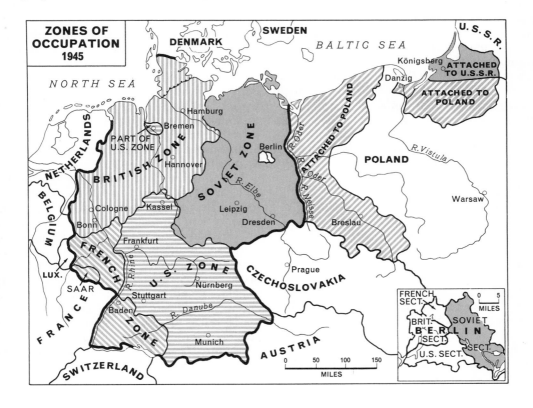

fore the surrender, have by now turned into the political boundary dividing the two Germanies and therewith the two power blocs. If Western leaders are sometimes blamed for having granted the Soviets too much, it must not be forgotten that no one, when the zonal boundaries were drawn up, could be sure that at the time of surrender Russian troops would not be on the Rhine, instead of the Elbe.

The Allies then assumed "supreme authority with respect to Germany." This assumption of power, they further declared, was not meant to "effect the annexation of Germany," but, on the contrary, to prepare for eventual restoration of democratic government in a unified Germany. But the attempt to exercise joint authority through an Allied Control Authority soon had to be given up. For some time sovereignty then devolved upon the occupying powers separately in their zones, and there were four Germanies instead of one—not counting the city of Berlin, which had been exempted from the zones. This process of disintegration was succeeded by one of integration of the three Western zones, coupled with gradual restoration of German autonomy. The establishment of two German Republics came by 1949: the Federal Republic of Germany (*Bundesrepublik Deutschland*, FRG), comprising the three Western zones, and the German Democratic Republic (*Deutsche Demokratische Republik*, DDR) in the Soviet zone, with Berlin (similarly divided into Western and Soviet-controlled parts) formally attached to neither unit. How to fashion one out of two— that is, how to reunify Germany—has remained an unsolved problem to this day.

FAILURE TO ESTABLISH GERMAN UNITY

The Potsdam program

The inability of the former Allies to restore German unity is explained by the estrangement between the Western powers and the Soviet Union and the ensuing cold war. Toward the end of World War II there was a good deal of agreement among the Big Three (Stalin, Roosevelt, Churchill) about the future of Germany. Early ideas of partitioning Germany into several independent states had been

rejected in favor of German unity. The Allies had further agreed not to destroy German industry; the ill-famed Morgenthau Plan for rendering Germany more or less an agricultural country had been shelved before the end of the war. The Big Three at Potsdam (July–August 1945) decided to treat Germany as an economic unit, with common policies for the different zones. Eventually it was to have its own government. In order to make sure that it would be democratic, a gradual process of political reconstruction was to begin at the local level and proceed to the restoration of indigenous government at higher levels, but provision was made for the immediate establishment of central German agencies in fields such as economics, finance, and transportation.

Divergent Allied approaches

Why did this program fail? The basic reason lay in the Allies' dissimilar conceptions of German reconstruction, which, in turn, went back to their disagreement about the nature of Nazism. To the Soviets, Nazism had been the natural outgrowth of capitalist developments; a non-Nazi Germany, therefore, had to be a noncapitalist Germany, and the transformation of bourgeois society into a socialist one was considered a prerequisite of German democratization. To the French, Nazism had simply been another form of age-old German aggressiveness, and any strong new Germany seemed to foreshadow more of the same. Their aim, therefore, was to keep Germany as decentralized as possible and to forestall reunification as long as possible.

The Americans and British, in contrast, had no clear-cut interpretation of Nazism and therefore no clear-cut occupation policy. The British Labor government which had come into power in 1945 had some ideas about backing democratic socialism in Germany, and Americans were, to some extent, convinced that Germans needed capitalism plus liberal-democratic reorientation and reeducation. In actual practice, however, administration was put ahead of policy in order to provide Germans as soon as possible with a functioning government.

Disunity began with the Allies' failure, chiefly because of French objections, to establish the central German administrative agencies envisaged at Potsdam. But it is likely that mutual distrust would have driven the Allies apart in any event. Inter-Allied negotiations on German unification showed that questions of detail might well have been solved. Much-advertised differences over the political structure of a future German government (which came to the fore at the four-power conference at Moscow in 1947) in reality did not reveal fundamental disagreement. Major points of dispute, such as the federal or unitary structure of government, were close to being solved by compromise, when the conference broke down because of the political rift between the Allies. Willingness to come to terms had diminished, since each side came to believe that the presence of its own respective Germany in its own sphere was more vital to its security than the restoration of German unity. Thus East and West were led into different paths of reconstruction.

THE FAILURE OF DEMOCRATIC REORIENTATION

The success of reconstruction depended upon something more basic—a German reorientation that first of all presupposed repudiation of the Nazi past. Any nation in whose name deeds such as the Nazi crimes were committed must cleanse itself of the past. A sound political community cannot be rebuilt if the most horrid crimes and their perpetrators remain unpunished. The theory of the collective guilt of the German people, which was current around 1945, was nonsense, if only because it would have involved all Germans in a common guilt that, eventually, would have meant absolving them all alike. But forgiveness for all was equally impossible. The elimination of active Nazis and their major collaborators from public life was necessary, not for reasons of revenge but as a measure of precaution in building up a new society and government.

Denazification

In order thus to reconstruct German public life, the Allies initiated a comprehensive program of denazification. In the East, it was in-

strumental in building up a new, undemocratic system (see Chapter 8). In the West it was a prerequisite of democratization. The failure of this effort had considerable impact on German society and government.

The most consistent effort at denazification was made in the American zone. It may therefore serve as an illustration. What happened, and why the venture failed, can perhaps be best understood by asking what might have been done. First of all, denazification, if it was to be part of a process of reconstruction, had to be preventive, not punitive—that is, its purpose had to be not trial and punishment (on the war crimes trials see Chapter 6), but elimination from positions of influence of persons dangerous to democratic reconstruction. Second, such elimination should have been limited to those who could be expected to sabotage efforts at reconstruction if remaining in or readmitted to positions of influence in administration, industry, education, and the like. It should have stopped short of the common Nazi followers who had joined the party or its organizations without taking an active part in its policies. We can now see that it would have been a practicable although by no means easy job for Allies cooperating with Germans thus to denazify by sifting the basic local setups (such as a local police office, a school, a broadcasting setup) individually and to weed out locally known real Nazis as well as to see to it that none entered or reentered subsequently.

Instead, occupation authorities undertook to sift, question, categorize, and judge an entire nation, which would have proved technically impossible even where political motives did not enter. In view of the "universe of motivations" upon which Germans had acted during the twelve years of the regime, what were to be the standards for dividing them into non- or anti-Nazis, major offenders, lesser offenders, followers? How could a few lay members of the German local boards established for that purpose hope to delve into the life history of hundreds or thousands of persons, most of them not locally known? (Most active Nazis had shifted from place to place and zone to zone, and many of them, especially those from the East, had falsified their questionnaires.) The investigation would have been difficult even where pressure and intimidation did not occur; and indeed pressures could hardly fail to develop where a majority of people were incriminated. A handful of nonincriminated Germans could hardly be expected to resist them, especially since the Military Government (MG) failed to back them up.

The addition of punitive measures increased a tendency to sympathize with the victims of denazification. Insignificant though most of the penalties were (low fines that were paid in worthless currency), they gave credence to those who charged punishment of mere political error. In the shuffle, the main issue—that of preventing real Nazis from entering public life—was lost sight of. When procedures bogged down, wholesale amnesties and whitewashing of practically all nonamnestied persons closed the operation. Seen in perspective, there had been initial indiscriminate indictment and in many cases indiscriminate internment, followed by indiscriminate release, indiscriminate acquittal, and, finally, indiscriminate reinstatement. As came to light in many subsequent cases, no confidence could be had that even all major Nazis had been caught in the proceedings. Thus the effects (such as suspension from office) were temporary at best, and practically ceased at the time when the new administrative machinery of West Germany was established.

Reeducation

The failure of denazification affected German reorientation beyond the sphere of staffing agencies and filling positions; it rendered the Allied objective of reeducating Germans for democracy more difficult, since to many Germans democracy became thus identified with something imported or imposed from abroad. As under Weimar, democracy had to establish itself in an environment of defeat, guilt, and distrust of foreign countries. In addition, there was partition; misery, increased by the refugee millions; vast destruction; and, as a legacy of Nazism, skepticism with regard to any creed old or new. Democracy became suspected of being just another propaganda slogan, this time used by the occupying powers for their own purposes.

Allied inconsistencies contributed to the growth of such cynicism. At first they tended to treat all Germans, Nazis, non-Nazis, and anti-Nazis, as bad, charging them all with collective guilt, taking or condoning stringent measures that operated against all alike, such as the dismantling of factories or the expulsion of ethnic Germans from their homes into a rump Germany under conditions of terrible hardship. This approach was gradually reversed to an equally unwarranted leniency, regarding Germans as decent fellows all. Anti-Nazis were then put on the defensive; they were suspected of radicalism or even communism when they advocated mild reforms, while former Nazis recommended themselves as reliable anti-Communists.

Given these circumstances, it is surprising that democratic attitudes developed at all in West Germany. At the time of defeat, revulsion against the Nazi regime and all it had stood for had been general; and this was coupled with a yearning for freedom and a political new beginning. Allied efforts did help here and there. Thus the German press, free although licensed, stimulated democratic orientation. While most people in the immediate postwar years were passive and bewildered, an active minority embraced democratic values. This meant that for a long time Germans became deeply divided in basic attitudes, with a minority devoted to democratic reconstruction and a majority betraying an absence of political commitment, and often a pronounced cynicism or opportunism.

The split continued into the 1950s. It revealed itself most forcibly in reactions to what had happened. To the "minority German" recent history began not, as it did for the majority, in 1945 but in 1933. He was ready to admit the responsibility of all Germans for what had happened under Nazism and was concerned about remedies; he possessed firm moral views, abhorring totalitarianism, whether of the right or of the left. The "majority German," although neither Nazi nor neo-Nazi—thus attesting to the relatively slight impact made by Nazi doctrine and propaganda as such —failed to be impressed by the reprehensible character of Nazism; he was inclined, for instance, to deny that what the trials of Nazi criminals had revealed had really happened.

He developed the habit of repressing what he disliked to remember.

In this way most Germans tended to become pragmatic, with at best a "show-me" attitude. In certain respects this caution was not unfavorable to reorientation: ultranationalism, militarism, foreign-policy adventurism, were rejected by the majority as well as the minority; while with the latter this rejection was a matter of principle, with the others it reflected the experience of a lost war and also a fear of endangering present prosperity.

These attitudes could still be observed in the 1960s. But the split was diminishing; it remained noticeable chiefly in the now aging generation that had lived under Weimar and Nazism. The younger generations had experienced Nazism only as children, if at all; thus, about half of all Germans alive were not directly involved in the Nazi crimes. Most of the youth are generally free from bias and ready to judge the merits of past systems objectively. They have turned from apathy and cynicism to a critical questioning and a moral condemnation of their elders for their behavior under Nazism and after. Moreover, to many young people much of this is by now ancient history. As we have seen, they have turned toward a scrutiny of the system they grew up in (namely, that of the Bonn Republic); their new criticism of democracy, however, derives not from old authoritarianism but rather from more radically conceived democratic alternatives.

But through the 1950s, and to some extent even to this day, the postwar ambiguities in basic attitudes were behind much that happened in that period. There were attitude shifts from neutralism and pacifism to assertiveness, from criticism of government policy to defense of authoritarianism. There had also been an inclination to ridicule anything liberal and democratic. Perhaps most unsettling, there had been a tendency to admit unreconstructed Nazis to positions of power. Even some of the staunch anti-Nazis, such as Adenauer, proved insensitive to the moral and political risks of employing such persons in high posts. Meanwhile, those who had sprung into the breach and filled positions under the Military Government after surrender were vilified and ostracized. Many Germans still have the readily observable habit of making Yalta and Potsdam, that is, the Allies, responsible for everything adverse, and they still exhibit a tendency to forgive even those revealed as participants in Nazism's worst crimes. It is one thing to forgive after judgment and repentance; it is quite another thing when forgiveness is claimed as a right by those who have failed even to admit guilt or error. These issues remained largely unresolved during the period of reconstruction, and they have returned to plague the German conscience. Submerged ultrarightest and even Nazi-type prejudices could thus, under stress, reemerge. We have already mentioned the emergence of a neo-Nazi political party in the 1960s. More recently, and perhaps even more ominously, we have seen among the workers a semifascist, "populist" type of "backlash" against student radicalism, hippie-ism, and similar phenomena, which the Nazis would have labeled "Jewish bolshevist." One should not make too much of this, but one cannot ignore it either.

GOVERNMENTAL RECONSTRUCTION IN THE TRANSITION PERIOD (1945–49)

The result of the territorial split and the failure of reorientation was a new totalitarian system in the Eastern zone and a democracy with some authoritarian features in West Germany.

Revival of political life

Revival of the processes and institutions of political democracy started at an early point in all four zones. In agreement with the Potsdam program, elections were held, first for town and city councils, then for *Land* diets, in which parties all claiming to be democratic, from rightist Liberals to Communists, participated. Officials and cabinets, initially appointed by the Military Government, were made responsible to such councils and diets, and government was organized in the *Länder* on the basis of constitutions adopted in more or less orthodox fashion.

This democratization, however, was more a form (or, at best, a promise) than a reality.

High voting figures made Allied officers assume that Germans now underwrote the processes of democracy. In reality, Germans, hungry and miserable, simply did what they thought would please the occupiers and thus produce higher calorie rations. Moreover, local and regional autonomy meant little, since the reconstruction of the war-torn country required large-scale planning and central policy decisions. What affected the average German most vitally, such as rationing and price controls, food delivery quotas, and the amount of permitted industrial production, remained outside German jurisdiction. Such matters were handled for entire zones, and even where the Allies used Germans on the zonal level, they were agents of the occupying power, not responsible administrators.

It is now clear that the introduction of formal democracy might better have been postponed until the Allies were ready to hand over genuine policymaking powers to Germans. Instead, MG divested itself of exactly those responsibilities that the Germans proved unready or unable to assume (such as denazification, or civil service and educational reforms), while they were *not* put in charge of the more technical tasks (economic administration and so forth) that they were able to perform. In the Soviet zone, on the other hand, basic social and economic reforms *were* inaugurated by the conqueror's fiat but were not followed by anything approximating genuine self-government.

Economic integration in the West

Faced with the impossibility of all-German unification, the Western Allies decided at least to unify their three zones. Economic preceded political integration. While the French balked, Americans and British merged their two zones economically in 1947. German bizonal agencies were fashioned into something resembling responsible government. There were an Economic Council, elected directly from *Land* diets and with legislative powers; a second chamber, representing *Länder* interests; and responsible heads of departments. In organization this foreshadowed the present Bonn government. In substance, it contributed little to democratization. Major jurisdictions were still reserved to the Allies, and even where Ger-

mans *did* have a free hand, actual power rested with the bureaucracy that staffed the new agencies, rather than with the people and their representatives. These officials considered efficient administration vastly more important for German reconstruction than control by parties and diets.

Establishment of Eastern and Western governments

Establishment of the present political German units of government—the Federal Republic of Germany and the German Democratic Republic—followed in 1949. In this the Western Allies took the initiative. The Soviets made it a rule always to trail the West by one step so as to shift responsibility for splitting Germany to the West and to appear as defenders of German unity.

The Western Allies had the more arduous task of first agreeing among themselves and then with the Germans. But the result was genuine self-government. In the Soviet zone, Germans were ostensibly left free to draft a constitution, but it was a foregone conclusion that the Socialist Unity party (SED) would act as the Soviet agent. The result was a puppet state, externally Soviet satellite and internally as pseudodemocratic as any other people's republic of the time. In the West the Germans eventually became fully sovereign, and the framework in which government operates is that of constitutionalism and democracy.

Thus there emerged two major units and two minor ones—West and East Berlin, a Germany in miniature. The boundaries are those of 1945, except that the Saar region, which was detached from Germany by the French after the war and set up with an autonomous government, was reunited with West Germany in 1957. The territory east of the Oder-Neisse line remains incorporated into Poland and the Soviet Union, a condition that even West Germans by now have come to recognize as permanent (see Chapter 8). The question as to what all this constitutes legally seems as unanswerable as is the much-debated legal question of whether Germany, or one of its present units, is identical with the prewar Reich. The legal confusion is but a reflection of actual disarray.

WEST GERMAN CONSTITUTION
AND GOVERNMENT

Drafting of the Bonn Constitution

Constitution-making in West Germany [6] started with an agreement reached by six Western countries (United States, United Kingdom, France, Belgium, Netherlands, Luxembourg) in London on June 1, 1948. This agreement set the goal ("that the German people in the different states . . . establish for themselves the political organization and institutions which will enable them to assume . . . governmental responsibilities"); prescribed procedures ("the minister-presidents will be authorized to convene a constituent assembly in order to prepare a constitution for the approval of the participating states"); broadly defined the limits within which the constitution-makers must work ("a federal form of government which adequately protects the rights of the respective states, and which at the same time provides for adequate central authority and which guarantees the rights and freedoms of the individual"); and put limits to future German autonomy through reservations concerning disarmament and the Ruhr. A further limitation, not mentioned in the London instrument, was contained in an Occupation Statute, which reserved important powers to the Allies.

The limitations concerning disarmament became largely pointless when integration of West Germany into the North Atlantic defense system shifted the accent toward rearming.[7] As for the Ruhr, an International Ruhr Authority, whose main function was to allocate Ruhr coal and steel to Germany and other countries, was soon superseded by the organization for pooling the coal and steel resources of Western Europe.

To avoid the impression of taking irrevocable steps toward splitting Germany, the minister-presidents of the eleven *Länder*—opposed to calling a "constituent assembly," to final popular ratification of the constitution, and even to the term *constitution* itself—called a Parlia-

[6] On the East see Chapter 7.

[7] Certain limitations persist, however, such as the vital prohibition on production of ABC (atomic, biological, chemical) weapons.

mentary Council of sixty-five members, chosen by the *Land* diets on the basis of *Länder* population and proportional strength of parties in the diets. The constitution was to be called Basic Law (*Grundgesetz*) and ratification was to be by at least two-thirds of all *Land* diets. The result was in fact a full-fledged constitution, with the lack of direct popular participation in its preparation and adoption made up for by the subsequent election of the first West German parliament.

This Bonn Constitution (so called from the present capital of the Federal Republic) is the result of compromise between the Allies and the German parties. With both, the main issue was that of federalism, that is, states' rights versus centralism. Surprisingly, other basic issues, such as the type of parliamentary system to be set up, powers of the executive, and guarantees and restrictions of civil liberties, received relatively scant attention, although in these fields there are important innovations. Regarding federalism, the French and the Bavarian particularists favored a loose federation of autonomous states; the British and the Americans believed such a solution unworkable, and there was indeed, with the exception of Bavaria, no strong feeling for it in Germany.

Thus the loose federation idea was ruled out, and the issue was narrowed to the question of the second chamber, the Bundesrat, which was to safeguard *Länder* influence in the central government. The Social Democrats wanted it to be elected by the *people* in the *Länder* (as senators are in the United States), but the more authoritarian Christian Democrats wanted it to be a body of delegates appointed by the governments of the *Länder* (as under the Hohenzollern and Weimar systems). The Socialists wanted it to have a suspensive veto only, while the Christian Democrats wanted it to have equal powers with the other chamber, the Bundestag. Eventually the Socialists conceded the bureaucratic type of council, while the Christian Democrats agreed to the suspensive veto.

Adoption of the draft constitution

With this problem out of the way, adoption of the draft constitution proceeded smoothly. The final vote was fifty-three to twelve, the minority comprising some Bavarians and a few representatives of smaller parties, among them the Communists. Social Democrats and Christian Democrats were able to agree on a constitution because workers as well as middle classes realized that German sovereignty on a non-Communist basis could be attained only through adoption of a democratic-parliamentary structure of government. The Basic Law was then approved by the three military governors and ratified by the *Land* diets, with all but the Bavarian diet voting for it. It was promulgated on May 23, 1949.

Elections for the Bundestag, the first free German election of a central parliament in seventeen years, were held on August 14, 1949. The two parties chiefly responsible for the Basic Law, Christian Democrats and Social Democrats, emerged as victors; their opponents, rightists as well as Communists, were soundly defeated. Although, strictly speaking, this was not a vote on the new constitution, politically it meant confirmation. Bundestag and Bundesrat then convened, and with the election of a federal president and a federal chancellor and the formation of a cabinet, the new government had started functioning by the end of September 1949.

Allied reservations

Allied approval of the constitution had been accompanied by reservations contained in an Occupation Statute promulgated by the three Allied military governors. Certain fields, such as demilitarization and security of the Allied occupation forces, were reserved to the Allies; in the fields left to the Germans, the Allies reserved the right to veto agreements between the federal government and foreign countries, and, in exceptional cases, to repeal any other German law; finally, the Allies reserved the right to resume "full authority" when "essential to security or to preserve democratic government in Germany or in pursuance of the international obligations of their governments." Ultimate authority thus still rested with the Allies. They exercised it through a civilian Allied High Commission, into which MG was transformed.

Subsequently, these restrictions of German autonomy were abolished step by step, and West Germany became fully independent in 1955 with the coming into effect of the London and Paris agreements of 1954. These, constituting an extraordinarily complicated network of treaties, protocols, and similar understandings of the Western powers with West Germany, terminated an occupation regime still based on unconditional surrender.[8] The old regime was replaced with a regime under which the Western powers' rights in Germany, and with respect to Germany, are retained with the consent of the Germans. This refers above all to the continued stationing of foreign troops on German territory. In domestic affairs the Germans were set completely free. Rule over a vanquished nation yielded to partnership.

The structure of the Bonn government

The structure of the Republic thus established will be analyzed in detail in subsequent chapters. Here we present only an overall sketch of its chief characteristics. Bonn is seemingly federal, liberal, and democratic. But Bonn federalism is tempered by strong central controls, and its democracy is balanced by authoritarian features. These are chiefly connected with the chancellorship. In contrast to Weimar, the president is weak. He now is not popularly elected, and he does not have his own powers of dissolution or emergency. The chancellor has emerged as the strong man. He cannot easily be deposed by the Bundestag, for, in order to avoid executive instability and frequent cabinet crises, the Bonn Constitution provides for the so-called constructive vote of nonconfidence—a vote which to be effective requires that a majority of the legal membership of the Bundestag simultaneously elect a successor to the chancellorship. Thus the opposition must agree on a new cabinet before the overthrow of the old one. Once elected at the beginning of the legislative period, a chancellor may thus be fairly sure of staying in office for the duration of a four-year term. This comes close to a Swiss version of parliamentary regimes, according to which the executive, once it has been established by the diet, continues to stay in office for the remainder of the parliamentary period. In countries with a firm parliamentary

---

[8] With the exception of Berlin, where, in principle if not in practice, the "four-power status" continues to this day (see Chapter 7).

Structure of the West German Federal Government
According to the Constitution of 1949

EXECUTIVE

President

Elected for five-year term by federal convention consisting of members of diet and equal number of members elected by *Land* diets.

All acts must be countersigned by chancellor or a federal minister.

Appoints and dismisses ministers on proposal of chancellor, nominates chancellor.

Promulgates laws, ratifies treaties, appoints federal officials.

Federal Cabinet

Chancellor

Nominated by president, elected by diet.

Selects ministers, may request their dismissal.

Determines general policy.

May propose dissolution of diet if diet refuses confidence.

Ministers

Appointed and dismissed by president on proposal of chancellor.

Responsible for direction of their departments.

Cabinet may request president to declare state of legislative emergency. Submits bills to diet.

LEGISLATIVE

Diet
(Bundestag)

Elected by people of the Republic for four-year term.

Passes federal laws, including constitutional amendments.

Elects chancellor.

May express nonconfidence in chancellor, but only by electing a successor at the same time.

May be dissolved within twenty-one days after it has refused to vote confidence in the chancellor, unless it elects a new chancellor.

Federal Council
(Bundesrat)

Members appointed and recalled freely by *Land* governments; each *Land* has from three to five votes.

Initiates bills, scrutinizes government bills; suspensive veto over laws. Approval of constitutional amendments and of certain financial laws.

Right to approve declaration, by president, of state of legislative emergency; in this case, its approval of bills replaces that of diet.

JUDICIAL

Supreme Court

Reviews decisions of lower courts, original criminal jurisdiction in treason trials.

Judges selected by federal Justice Minister and a committee composed of *Land* Ministers of Justice and equal number of members elected by diet.

Constitutional Court

Decides on constitutionality of federal laws, on compatibility of federal and state law, other constitutional conflicts between federal government and *Länder*, complaints about violation of basic rights of individuals, outlawry of antidemocratic parties, impeachment of president and other cases.

Consists of members of Supreme Court and other law-trained members, half of them elected by diet, the other half by Federal Council.

Other Highest Courts

(Special Courts)

---

tradition, like Switzerland, the executive can be relied upon to follow the directives of the assembly. In Germany, with her authoritarian tradition, there is a danger that it will overshadow parliament. Also, the Bonn Constitution permits the chancellor to appoint and dismiss ministers freely, and there is no provision for voting nonconfidence in ministers. Possibly the effort to avoid executive instability has shifted the weight too much to the executive side. At any rate, it enabled Chancellor Adenauer to rule West Germany for fourteen years on a paternalistic pattern. Since his demise, the executive has been weaker at times (e.g., under Chancellor Erhard) and predominant at other times (e.g., under the "grand coalition").

In other respects, the Bonn system tries to strike an interesting balance between liberal principles and protection of state authority. Nazi experience produced a strong desire for guarantees of political liberty and personal security. Weimar experience, on the other hand, called for safeguards against misuse of liberty for antidemocratic ends. As a result, the constitution goes far in defining rights and protects some against suspension by statutes or even by constitutional amendment. On the other hand, there are provisions that permit far-reaching infringement of these rights—for example, those that allow the outlawing of parties that are hostile to "the liberal-democratic order" or seek "to jeopardize the existence of the Republic."

On the whole, a valiant effort has been made in West Germany to lay the foundations of a working constitutional order. While demo-cratic forces still face some threats, there is at least a live and open issue as to how to win out. And in contrast to the closed system in the East, elections, votes in parliaments, competition among parties and among wings within parties are meaningful and relevant. In short, there is active political life; and democracy, while still frail, has begun to grow and to form a pattern that, given time, may develop into a genuine civic culture.

6   THE FEDERAL REPUBLIC OF GERMANY, 1949–71: A BRIEF OVERVIEW

We shall limit our discussion of the past twenty-some years to the Federal Republic, reserving the Eastern part of divided Germany to Chapter 7. A more detailed description of West Germany's governmental institutions and its political forces and processes will be found in subsequent chapters; this section will be confined to an outline of the historical development of the FRG's political system.

ADENAUER AND THE PERIOD OF "RESTORATION"

In the summer of 1970, an opinion poll of "world leaders" on what they considered "the best governed nation in the world" showed West Germany in the fourth place (ranking behind Switzerland, Great Britain, and Sweden, in that order).[9] Although the question was couched in terms so vague and general that it almost appears meaningless (what is meant by "best governed"?), the rank-ordering of West Germany is yet significant because it confirms a general impression, widely held within Germany and abroad, as to the solid, stable, and sound nature of the post-1949 system. And indeed, if one glances at what happened—or failed to happen—in West Germany in the fifties and sixties, it strikes one on the whole as the history of quiet achievement, quite unlike the preceding periods of German history that have been outlined before, and also unlike what happened in such a near-by country as

France during the same decades. This achievement has occurred despite national partition, the advent of the nuclear age, East-West polarization, and similarly disturbing events. We shall see that underlying this "quietism" there has emerged more recently a widespread malaise, not only regarding the political system but in respect to public life in general. This malaise has begun to pervade almost all "overdeveloped" industrial societies. As far as West Germany is concerned, the chief cause for the stability of the present system was the tremendous need Germans felt for making up for lost opportunities—during Nazism, the war, Weimar, and so forth (*Nachholbedarf*, the need to catch up, as they called it).

"Im Anfang war Adenauer" (in the beginning was Adenauer). Thus a German author begins his treatise on the first federal chancellor's foreign policy. One might begin a description of the FRG's entire history, foreign *and* domestic, this way. Konrad Adenauer (1876–1967), elected chancellor in September 1949 by a one-vote majority of the Bundestag (his own vote, as he unashamedly used to point out), became indeed more than a mere governmental and political leader. He became a kind of father figure for the nation, giving it—or rather that portion of it that had rallied together in the West—a feeling of identity and of new tasks to be accomplished. A nation was to be rebuilt upon the shambles of a shattered Reich, and after the demise of a discredited Führer. Adenauer was fully conscious of the greatness of his task, indeed so well that he remained in office as a perennial fixture of the new establishment,

[9] *New York Times*, August 13, 1970.

far beyond the period of reconstruction and into a time when the system he had inaugurated clearly needed new policies and new leadership to cope with the policies. Initially, however, he was the rallying point for all those who wanted nothing more, or less, than "law and order." Adenauer gave it to them in the form of the traditional German *Rechtsstaat* (state where law prevails) and of an order that turned out to be the restoration of what the German middle classes had come to consider the ideal pattern of life and politics: security of person and property for the enterprising, with each class in its set place, but with each citizen, whether rich or poor, lowly or high, guaranteed some social security. The entire system was rendered effective through majority consensus expressed in general elections and through a functioning party system.

The period of Adenauer's regime, therefore, could well be called an era of "restoration" (as the Social Democrats, perennial opposition throughout this period, called it), and the state he fashioned could be labeled a "CDU-state," after the name of the party he created (or which, although he did not create it single-handedly, he managed to control and preside over as a more or less benevolent despot). Adenauer has often been compared to Bismarck. There is, of course, the parallel of two leaders, each presiding over the establishment of a "new Germany"; but there the similarity ends. Bismarck, "blood and iron" power politician, defender of the old feudal classes and, as such, determined to modernize the Reich under the continued leadership of these classes, was almost the opposite, both personally and politically, of a chancellor who had spent his mature life as a middle-class Prussian official, wedded to the bourgeois ideal of a nonadventurous foreign and domestic policy. Personally, it is true, Adenauer, like Bismarck, was an authoritarian, but of the more bureaucratic type where the expert official (or politician) "who knows best" is in control, not the monarch or Junker who rules by right of birth. In the end, as in Bismarck's case, it was his tragedy not to perceive anyone who "knew well enough" to be groomed for successorship, and this led to the crisis of his system in the sixties.

But at first Adenauer put his imprint on the new state as no one else could. Germans are wont to refer to the immediate postwar period as "the year zero." It is true that in 1945 one had to start from scratch, but most of this, as we have seen, was done for the Germans by the occupying powers. Theirs was already a conservative or, rather, "restorative" policy. It allowed for the reestablishment of economic capitalism. The decisive step of currency reform had already been taken in 1948 by the Allies, a step that gave the West German economy a stable monetary basis and, by and large, permitted the propertied classes to retain, or regain, their possessions. As we have also seen, efforts toward reform, through denazification, "reeducation," decartelization, failed. It was on this basis, and not by starting from scratch, that the Adenauer regime began to rebuild the new framework of government and politics of the FRG.

THE ATTAINMENT OF INTERNATIONAL STATUS

When, shortly after Adenauer's death, Germans were asked what they considered his greatest achievements, most mentioned foreign policy rather than the domestic sphere. German foreign policy problems will be taken up in a separate chapter (see Chapter 8). Here we shall examine only Adenauer's early foreign policy decisions and their impact upon the subsequent development of the FRG. It was Adenauer who decided that, if at least part of Germany was to reemerge in the form of a liberal-democratic polity and avoid being swallowed by "expansionist" Communism, it had to ally itself firmly with the West. Thus, at the risk of losing whatever opportunities remained for restoring some degree of unity to East and West Germany, and over the violent protest of the opposition, he embarked on the policy that made the FRG an integral part of the Western alliance. West Germany became a member of NATO, an initiator of Western European economic integration, and an advocate of political rapprochement with France. Adenauer sought a special relationship with the "protecting power," the United States, and, again disregarding the opposition of what seemed a majority desire for neutralism and pacifism, pushed through the rearmament demanded by his

Western allies. His "Europeanism" was more in agreement with public attitudes and inclinations at the time. It initially envisaged not only economic integration of European nations, but the eventual replacement of sovereign nations by a supranational, federal organization.

The result of Adenauer's policies was the rapid rise of the Federal Republic to international status, the reacceptance, so to speak, of Germany by and into the world. The ostracism by the West of the other regime set up on German soil, the DDR, and the corresponding exclusion of 17 million Germans from what at least in the Western world was considered the only legitimate Germany, was the price paid for this rise and this integration. For the ruling forces in the Federal Republic it seemed a price worth paying for having gained reentrance into the community of nations.

THE DOMESTIC FRAMEWORK
OF THE "CDU-STATE"

It was on the basis of regained international status and the corresponding economic upsurge (the "economic miracle," as the sudden and steep rise in production, living standards, exports, etc. was referred to) that the domestic political system began to evolve within the framework of the Bonn Constitution. Simultaneous with the foreign policy steps that resulted in the "sovereignty" obtained through the Paris Conventions of 1954–55, a series of statutory enactments of fundamental importance created the domestic structure of West Germany, providing for the restoration of institutions and processes that had been abrogated or distorted by Nazi totalitarianism. Some of these affected industry and labor, others, public administration and the educational system, and still others the structure and freedom of the mass media and, eventually, the organization of the new military establishment. There was also legislation that implemented the constitution itself: a federal election law, a law on the new constitutional court, and so forth. It was a legislative program that, in the main, restored the social framework that had preceded the totalitarian interlude. It was indeed the restoration of a bureaucratic class system, since there was no basic reform of the dual and unequal

education, and the regime perpetuated an officialdom that chiefly originated from the middle classes as well as favored, by and large, the interests of big business. The working class was excluded from government where it really counted, that is, at the federal level (the SPD was limited to influence in some *Länder* and municipalities).

But economic growth permitted giving a share in the affluence (although a disproportionately small one) to the workers. Beyond this, and quite generally, affluence also made it possible to satisfy a number of groups, which otherwise might have become disgruntled, through a policy of handouts. Subsidies of one sort or another were granted to those who had been damaged through bombings or otherwise suffered from the effects of the war; to the expellees from the Eastern territories; to the victims of Nazi racial or political persecution (indeed, Adenauer's policy in this respect, which included a reparations agreement with Israel, also paid foreign policy dividends by rehabilitating Germany morally abroad). An able policy of combining indemnification for losses and providing jobs to the nearly 10 million expellees, who might have become radicalized through their dissatisfaction, resulted in their full integration into the West German economy. They actually provided a labor force without which the economic miracle could not have been achieved. After a while, only some of the older expellees remained irreconcilable. Without this integration, a later policy of *détente* toward the East would not have been possible. One had learned from contrary Weimar experience not to neglect important strata of society.

A "handout" policy also was characteristic of more specific legislation, for example, in respect to taxes or social security benefits, which used to precede general elections. It was "bribery" of the voters on a grand scale, but it paid dividends to Adenauer and the coalitions he formed for his more general policies. In this way he was able to maintain his control and prestige throughout the fifties.

Coalitions of "his" party with more or less manipulated, smaller middle-class parties in the Bundestag were for the chancellor only means of seeing his policies through. His behavior toward his own party was another equally high-handed means of achieving his ends. The party's more leftist wing, representing Catholic workers and other "small people," was banished to a political limbo (from which it would occasionally raise its voice in favor of socially progressive legislation). As in foreign affairs, where Adenauer acted himself as chief spokesman and negotiator, he would directly negotiate major policies in domestic affairs with the top representatives of the special interests, overriding or disregarding ministers, party leaders, and parliament. In his relationship to the interests, such as industry or agriculture, he used one against the other, much as he played off the coalition parties against one another or the political leaders within his own party. Although a loyal member of the Catholic Church, he was not obligated to the clergy either. Once, when his good friend Cardinal Frings, archbishop of his native Cologne, was a bit too insistent in regard to some piece of legislation, Adenauer is said to have told him: "I don't ask you to say 'yes' to it, only 'amen.'" It is true that the influence of the churches, both Protestant and Catholic, was pronounced in the "CDU-state," but this, too, merely reflected the restorative nature of the system. Church influence had always been strong in education, culture, and related matters. Religion was one of the traditionalist forces that reemerged after the Nazi interlude to shape postwar Germany jointly with reestablished business, officialdom, and soon thereafter, the military.

THE DECLINE OF ADENAUER'S REGIME

The prime of Adenauer's "chancellor democracy," a semiauthoritarian system, was reached in the middle fifties. In 1957, for the first time in German parliamentary history, one party (Adenauer's, of course) obtained an absolute majority of the vote in the Bundestag election. Adenauer was safely in control. Although he permitted small, conservative parties to join his government, he could feel perfectly secure. Political extremism was dormant (another first in German political history), at least for the time being. Communism was torpid because it could not avoid being identified with the oppressive regime in East Germany. Nazism lay quiescent because it was held responsible for

a disastrous war and its consequences. Moreover, although there were still a number of smaller "third" parties (most of them representing regional or conservative interests and thus competing with the CDU), they were soon to vanish; by 1961, only the FDP managed to retain representation in the Bundestag. It seemed that Germany was on the way to a two-party system or, since the SPD seemed doomed to perennial, rather ineffective opposition, toward a kind of "one-and-a-half-party system," where the CDU, under Adenauer, would be permanently in control.

But what one German observer has called the "sleepy fifties" were drawing to an end. The end was ushered in by the great reversal of the opposition SPD at the turn of the decade, which can still be seen as a result of the quietism of the times. This party, in its Godesberg Program of 1959, gave up its residual Marxist socialism and decided to turn into a reformist party similar to the British Labor party; it decided to represent labor *within* the established system of competitive capitalism and to appeal to larger middle-class strata as a genuine "people's party" (or "catchall party," to use Otto Kirchheimer's felicitous phrase for deideologized, pragmatic, mass parties). At the same time, it rejuvenated its overaged leadership by calling upon Willy Brandt, youthful mayor of beleaguered Berlin, as standardbearer of the party. The only major opposition party thus drew closer to the Adenauer system (even accepting its Western orientation, including rearmament). However, this also meant that it started to become a serious competitor to the other "catchall" party, the CDU.

About this time, Adenauer's prestige began to wane. His chief handiwork, the Federal Republic, was taken for granted, and dissatisfaction with the petrified "CDU-state" under his authoritarian leadership started to grow. In August 1961 when the Berlin Wall was erected Adenauer took little notice, while Brandt and the SPD made themselves spokesmen for national protest. The effect of this event could be seen in the general election that followed shortly. The CDU lost its absolute majority, while not only the SPD but Adenauer's major ally, the FDP, gained. The *Spiegel* affair of 1962 followed soon after and may be considered the true turning point from the first to the second period of Bonn. *Der Spiegel* is a weekly noted for its outspoken criticism of the regime and high regime figures. The affair reflected the harsh and high-handed way in which the Adenauer cabinet, spuriously claiming the paper's betrayal of military secrets, engaged in arbitrary arrests, seizures, and similar violations of constitutional rights. The uproar, not only among the opposition but the public at large, indicated the fact that times were changing. Executive arbitrariness was no longer taken quietly. Parliament became the mouthpiece of protest, before which the executive had to account for its actions. Severe criticism, some of it voiced even by the coalition parties, especially the FDP, compelled Adenauer to drop the aide chiefly involved, Defense Minister Franz Josef Strauss. It also meant that Adenauer himself now had finally to realize (or, if he did not, most Germans did) that at age eighty-seven he had overstayed his welcome. He resigned from the chancellorship in 1963 (still, however, tenaciously holding onto the party leadership for two more years, causing mischief among the CDU leadership through plotting and machinations). Economics Minister Ludwig Erhard, architect of the currency reform of 1948 and thus identified in the public mind with the postwar "economic miracle," became his successor. For most CDU members, indeed, for most West Germans, he seemed the natural choice, although Adenauer had warned of his lack of talent outside economics. Adenauer's assessment proved correct. Erhard turned out to be a weak and vacillating leader, lost among competing and feuding Adenauer lieutenants and also lost in the maze of domestic and foreign problems that suddenly besieged him and the Federal Republic.

ERHARD AND THE CRISIS OF 1966

Chief among these problems, ironically for Erhard, were economic and financial ones. In 1966, for the first time in the postwar era, a severe recession struck West Germany. Workers, especially miners, became restive. There was growing disagreement in the coalition, especially between leading CDU members and the FDP, on how to cope with a huge budget

deficit. A smashing SPD victory in the *Land* containing the biggest industrial area (North Rhine-Westphalia) was politically more ominous. Even more disturbing to *all* established parties was the sudden rise of the National Democrats (NPD), a coalition of previously divided and feuding radical rightist and neo-Nazi groups under a common party label. In two *Land* elections (Hesse and Bavaria) the NPD gained about 8 percent of the vote and therewith access to state diets. Many in and outside Germany feared a replay of Weimar, a Nazi-type threat to Bonn democracy.

All this led to the first political—and partly constitutional—crisis of the Bonn regime. In the fall of 1966 the leadership of the CDU disintegrated, with almost every leader vying for position in the cabinet arrangements that were expected to succeed Erhard's. The FDP withdrew from Erhard's coalition, leaving him to preside over a minority cabinet. The SPD clamored for new elections. But new elections, according to the constitution, could only be had if the chancellor asked for a vote of confidence, was defeated in such a vote, and could then persuade the federal president to dissolve the Bundestag. Erhard refused to play this game. Only reluctantly did he agree to resign. Who and what was to succeed him? It was the SPD who was faced with the chief dilemma. It could decide to stay in opposition, leaving a discredited CDU leadership to try to revamp its coalition with the FDP or to rule as a minority (which eventually would compel new elections anyway). The SPD might also try to form a "small coalition" of its own with the FDP, but on the basis of a razor-thin majority in parliament. Or the SPD might form a big, or "grand" coalition with the CDU. The latter, in order to salvage at least some of its unity and its accustomed power positions, was ready for the last solution. For the SPD it meant not only giving up its position as chief critic of the regime but entering as junior partner into an alliance with the very party they had always criticized as chiefly responsible for the policies of that regime. They thereby risked their image as well as the support of forces among labor that were more socialist or otherwise socially committed (especially among the young and some of the more leftist trade unions). They also risked weakening the very foundation of a political system that depends on meaningful political alternatives expressed by government and opposition. But they decided to run these risks.

With the two major political forces now jointly in government, the role of opposition was left to a rather insignificant FDP in parliament, with other critics forced into "extra-parliamentary opposition" (they were not long in organizing themselves into a leftist APO—German abbreviation for opposition outside parliament—a curious and only loosely joined band of left socialists, pacifists, Communists, student radicals, and others). But the "grand coalition" gave the SPD, for the first time in forty years, access to the "commando heights" of power; most importantly, it presented its leaders with a chance to prove themselves to the people at large as "governmental timber."

THE "GRAND COALITION"

The rule by "party cartel" lasted for three years. It did have the predictable effect of rendering politics rather lifeless; government was carried on from on high, without much more than mechanical participation by parliament. Whatever was decided by the leaders of the two parties in cabinet was sure to be endorsed by the huge CDU-SPD majority in the Bundestag. Moreover, at the top level a kind of inner cabinet, consisting of CDU Chancellor Kurt Georg Kiesinger, Vice-Chancellor Willy Brandt, and a few other leaders, more or less monopolized the true decision-making process by frequently meeting in seclusion at Kiesinger's vacation resort, Kressbronn. *Der Spiegel*, as always alert to irony, overstated only slightly when it called the Kressbronn circle "the only politbureau in the world which consists of two parties." But in other respects the "grand coalition" was a success. The SPD did not attain—it hardly tried to—any significant part of its program, moderate though their objectives had become after Godesberg. But the economic recession was overcome through the intimate and friendly cooperation of SPD Economics Minister Karl Schiller and, of all persons, Franz Josef Strauss, who had reentered the Bonn executive as Minister of Finance. And, as the election of 1969 showed, the SPD proved correct in expecting to become "respectable" in the eyes of considerable portions of the middle classes, while not losing support among labor.

The election results of fall 1969 and the ensuing formation of an SPD-FDP coalition under Brandt as chancellor were foreshadowed by what happened in the spring of that year, anent the election of a new federal president. In each ten-year period from 1949 on, this officer, holding a largely ceremonial position but in his personal habitus and political affiliation symbolic of the established regime, had been a member of the ruling circle. The first occupant of the position was a highly cultivated, liberal, FDP man, the second, less fortunately, a rather commonplace CDU leader hand-picked by Adenauer. In 1969, the SPD candidate Gustav Heinemann, a genuine democrat, an outspoken anti-Nazi, and a man with new ideas, was elected president with the aid of the FDP, which this way indicated its hope to reenter government in alliance with the SPD. To do this convincingly, the FDP had to get rid of its reputation for vacillation and unreliability, which its constant alternation from government to opposition had gained it in the past. It did so by embarking upon a "left" course with determination, thereby antagonizing its conservative right wing and losing almost half of its support in the election; yet it managed to get the minimum 5 percent of the vote required for representation in the Bundestag. The curious result was the formation of a "small coalition" of the SPD, which for the first time had obtained a vote close to that of the still largest CDU (42.7 percent as against 46.1 percent), and the much reduced FDP (from 9.5 percent to 5.8 percent), which thus was able to emerge again as government party and even obtain important posts, such as that of Foreign Minister. This arrangement, unfamiliar, perhaps, to the American voter, is not unusual in multiparty systems, where a small group may hold the balance of power between two major parties. Thus the previously reigning party was excluded from power. The CDU, bitterly but vainly complaining of "disregard of the voters' will," for the first time found itself in opposition.

THE BRANDT-SCHEEL GOVERNMENT
AND ITS PROBLEMS

Brandt and his team lost no time in developing a bold new approach to foreign policy. This policy, in particular, called for a reorientation of policy toward the East (chief program point in the new orientation of the FDP and its leader, now Foreign Minister, Walter Scheel). The meaning and implications of this venture will be discussed in Chapter 8. By the end of 1970, the concentration on foreign affairs had not left much time and energy to be spent on domestic affairs, where policies were pretty much continued as they had evolved under the "grand coalition." The big question is, What has been the impact of the new government upon the political regime that had held forth over the twenty years preceding it? In one respect the effect undoubtedly has been a healthy one. After many years there was again a vigorous and powerful opposition, determined to keep the government on its toes and supplant it on the first occasion with a meaningful alternative. This has meant the revival of the give and take characteristic of a genuine parliamentary regime, with parliament regaining its role of a debating and decision-making organ of government. In another, and deeper, respect, however, the answer is not so clear.

When discussing "reeducation," we remarked upon a new pragmatic attitude of the generations that grew up in the postwar period and knew the history of Weimar and Nazism only from books. Thus, directly familiar only with the Bonn system, many young people (and by no means only the noisier extremists) have developed a strong distaste for the ingrained class structure and authoritarianism of traditional German society. Like their contemporaries in other countries, they demand participatory democracy in all public institutions: government bureaus and administrative offices, political parties, factories and other enterprises, schools and universities. Having no race problem and not being involved in a foreign war, their chief objectives therefore lie in the areas of domestic policy.

But the SPD, the traditional instrument for novel policy, is in a quandary. Its program would seem to point in the direction of progress and reform, but the attitudes of much of its leadership (and partly even of its members) are as traditional-authoritarian as those of any other group, and this is reflected in its intraparty organization as well as its determined opposition to its own, intraparty, leftists. Moreover, much of its more recent support, accounting for its gains at the polls, comes from white-collar and even managerial and civil service strata, people who have come to trust it *not* to disturb the established system. Others, it is true, have turned to the SPD because that party seems to them to stand for "modernization." Modernization requires, among other things, more equality of opportunity for broader strata of the economically *and* educationally underprivileged, because only this way can a technologically advanced industrial country remain competitive. Thus at least some of the demands of the democratic left and the more enlightened strata of the middle classes coincide. If the challenges confronting the FRG in the seventies are met at least in this minimally reformist fashion, West Germany may yet acquire a face quite different from the one Adenauer and his generation conveyed upon it at its inception.

3

West German parties and elections

1 HISTORICAL ANTECEDENTS

On the face of it, West Germany has a party system that functions the same way as those of the traditionally democratic Western countries. It is a system in which well-organized and clearly identified parties perform the functions of articulating and aggregating the interests and desires of the people at large and of their major groupings. The parties thus serve as the classical intermediaries between the "people" and the governments: they represent the people in parliament after regularly occurring elections, send their leaders into the executive branch of government, challenge unpopular government actions, and offer alternative programs to those proposed by the government.

As we shall see in this and the following chapters, the foregoing description is by now largely true of the present West German political scene. But, in order to perceive how stable this system is, we have, again, to return to German history, which accounts for some of the serious obstacles in the development of a sound and efficient party system. While in the Western democracies, parties have long embodied the chief political forces that carry on government, in Germany, up to the postwar period, parties have usually been on the periphery rather than at the center of political life. Even today this fact continues in the attitudes reflected in the political culture of Germany.

The average German hesitates to identify himself with a political party. According to polls taken in the 1960s, over 80 percent of those polled declared that they were unwilling to become formal members of a party (this finding is supported by the relatively low membership figures of the major parties). As late as 1969, only 29 percent identified themselves with a particular party; 60 percent expressed disgust with the idea of becoming politicians, who (together with journalists and advertising agents) ranked lowest in peoples' estimation of professions. Only 4 percent of adult Germans said they participated "in some form of" political activity. Even among students, only 12 percent said they were members of either a party or a political student organization, while 41 percent declared they were against political activities. Even more disappointing were the results of a poll made of students (to be sure, taken in a mostly rural and small-town region), where over half of those attending Volksschule came out in favor of a one-party system, with less than half, but still a considerable portion, of Gymnasium students also doing so.

By the same token a German, when asked what party he belongs to, is likely to say that he is "above party." At the same time, however, he will admit to having close ties to one of the general philosophies, or world views, that underlie party programs. Thus the German has tended to be doctrinaire, with his opinion on all manner of specific problems determined by what the respective liberal, or socialist, or nationalist, or Catholic doctrine, to which he *and* his party adhere, has to say about the question. Thus he is partisan in his general attitudes. This explains why what appear to outsiders as minor issues have often been fought over in Germany as if they were matters of life and death. Only recently has there been some attenuation of this doctrinairism. At the same time, the German is inclined to deplore "party wrangling" in diets and assemblies, that is, he is skeptical of the role assigned to parties in public life.

Distrust of political parties and doctrinaire attitudes both have their roots in the German past. Parties arose in Germany after the state, with its authoritarian government, had long been in existence. In Britain and the United States parties were a part, and an essential part, of the state from the very beginning of modern government; in France they conquered the state. In Prussia-Germany they were imposed, like constitutions and parliaments, upon the preexisting and stable organization of a bureaucratic-militaristic state. The essential business of state continued to be done without or despite them. Until 1918, the parties could be left to bicker among themselves while government stability was guaranteed by rule from above. When responsibility to govern was suddenly thrust upon the parties, they were inexperienced, divided, unable to cooperate. Hence the failure of Weimar.

Germany's multiparty system was the result not of a peculiar election system but of Germany's authoritarian heritage, its lack of religious homogeneity, its regional diversity, and its deferred national unification. Different political movements originated in different parts of what later became Germany: democratic chiefly in the southwest, conservative mostly in the Prussian northeast, political Catholicism primarily in the Rhine region and Bavaria. Some of the resulting parties remained sectional parties, vestiges of which still survive. At the same time, classes, and the economic interests they represented, organized themselves as parties; and since they were not integrated into the state until after World War I they too tended to split into numerous groups, often representing petty special interests. Thus the average party remained a combination of "church" and pressure group. In the United States, pressures work chiefly from the outside on parties and their leaders and deputies; in Germany, such interests as labor or farmers have tended to organize themselves as political parties, trying to conceal their character behind an idealistic doctrine. In this they used to resemble French parties. But German parties, reflecting their society, have been more like centralized machines, without their members at large having much influence over organization and formulation of policies.

While this recalls the British system, in Germany there has more often been group leadership than individual leadership. Forceful leaders, such as Adenauer, have been infrequent in German party life. Local bosses in the American sense have also been the exception. Since the most important positions in public life were in the hands of a permanent bureaucracy, the politician had little by way of spoils to distribute. His own job as a politician, even if he managed to be elected to some assembly, was unimportant before 1918 and continued to be regarded so under Weimar. This accounts for the failure of German party life to attract the forceful, ambitious, and broad-minded, and for the prevalence of the mediocre, elderly, and bureaucratic-minded to this day.

Until recently, then, the German party system could be compared with the systems of the three main Western democracies as follows:

(1) It was a more-than-one-party system; that is, in common with the American, British, and French systems it was (except for the Nazi period) a system of genuine, freely organized, freely functioning, and competing parties.

(2) It was a more-than-two-party system; that is, like the French, and unlike the American and the British, the German party system did not produce two major parties that dominated the scene and alternated in government.

(3) It was a system without agreement on fundamental issues; that is, again like the French and unlike the American and British, German parties failed to agree on the essentials of a constitution. Fundamental problems of how to organize state and government remained party issues, and there was a tendency toward the formation of radical and extremist parties.

(4) German parties, unlike those of the United States, and like those of France and Britain, represented specific social classes, reflecting specific interests, and having definite doctrines.

(5) German parties were centralized; like the British and unlike the other two, they were not grassroots parties but were dominated by, and were integral parts of, a central machine and its bureaucracy.

Nothing is more indicative of genuine change in German political life and, possibly, even in German behavior patterns, than the changes that have taken place in regard to most of these points in the postwar period. The German party system now tends to resemble more the British, and even the American, system than the French. First of all, two major parties have tended to dominate the political scene, and since these two parties are moderate, there is today in West Germany a great deal of agreement on constitutional essentials. In addition, we discern a trend toward more forceful party leadership and even an increase in popular interest and participation. Doctrinairism is subsiding in favor of a more pragmatic approach to political issues. The heightened "prestige" of parties is reflected in the fact that the Bonn Constitution, in contrast to previous German constitutions, recognizes their existence and role. Article 21 provides that antidemocratic parties can be outlawed by the Federal Constitutional Court (see Chapter 6, Section 2), and the Law on Parties (1967) regulates their organizational structure in some detail, making sure that intraparty affairs are handled in a way that is at least minimally democratic. By the same token, however, parties are in danger of becoming ever more "institutionalized" and, in the eyes of the common man, considered as part of the "establishment" instead of as instruments of the people. That the parties are now state-subsidized cannot but strengthen that impression. And if one remembers that the emergence of some of the new features of the system was due to somewhat fortuitous circumstances (emergence of one strong party leader in the person of Konrad Adenauer, for instance, or long-lasting prosperity and the impact of partition) the optimism raised by the new developments should be restrained by caution.

2 THE PRESENT PARTY SYSTEM

POSTWAR REESTABLISHMENT OF PARTIES

The political reconstruction of Germany required the reorganization of political parties. But giving the Germans a free hand involved the risk that Nazis might revive their shattered organization. The solution resorted to by the four occupation powers was the licensing of a limited number of parties, with the Soviets taking the lead in their zone.

After importing exiled German Communists from Moscow and thus giving the Communist party (CP) a head start, the Soviet MG allowed the Social Democrats (SPD) to organize themselves; then, still expecting early German unification on an initial basis of "bourgeois" democracy, they licensed two middle-class parties, the Christian Democratic Union (CDU) and the Liberal Democratic party (LDP). This gave them the jump on the Western powers, which wanted the new parties in their zones to grow from the grassroots.

But the new parties in the Western zones failed to do so. Germans fell back into the habit of forming centrally organized parties. Surviving Weimar leaders filled the void and organized the four new licensed parties on the pattern they had known. The masses, dazed and apathetic, took little interest. Only when full domestic autonomy was granted did more popular interest assert itself.

PARTY TRENDS

The initial party trend was to the left. The Nazis and their rightist collaborators were discredited, more so than even the monarchists had been after 1918. The Communists, their brief defection of 1939–41 (the period of the

Stalin-Hitler pact) forgotten, had gained prestige as antifascist resisters. The German worker seemed ready to back up the cooperation of all socialists. But the Soviets squandered this store of good will; their behavior in the Soviet zone destroyed the chance of genuine labor collaboration. Outside their zone the Communist vote declined rapidly. In Rhineland-Westphalia, for example, an area that includes the traditional Communist stronghold of the Ruhr, it went down from 13.7 percent in 1946 to a mere 3.8 percent in 1954. In the last Bundestag election in which they took part (1953), the Communists attained hardly more than 2 percent of the vote. After their recent reappearance as the German Communist party (DKP), they have fared even worse at the polls. Thus West Germany contrasts strikingly with France and Italy, where the Communists emerged after the war as the stronger workers' party. In West Germany, the moderate socialists (SPD) have consistently enjoyed the support of the major portion of labor and in this way became one of two major parties.

The other major innovation in the German political landscape has been the emergence of one strong middle-class party, the Christian Democratic, which now controls the other large bloc of votes. While this picture was perhaps somewhat deceptive in the beginning, since the parties that might have appealed to antidemocratic voters were not allowed to exist, it has since become clear that the trend has genuinely been one toward moderation. With the end of licensing in 1950, there was at first a proliferation of other parties, including ultranationalist ones that enjoyed some regional success. But with the economic and foreign policy successes of the Adenauer government, the party system consolidated itself on the basis of two dominant parties.

This development raises three major questions. First, is radicalism dead? Second, does West Germany now have, or is it approaching, a genuine two-party system? Third, what can be said about the future of, and the relationships between, the two major parties?

Leftist extremism, in the form of communism, can be discounted as long as German partition and the resulting Communist control of East Germany endure. Communism had been strong in Weimar Germany because it appeared to a considerable segment of the working class as a genuine socialist movement. Since 1945, however, German communism has become identified with Soviet control of the East. Thus one could doubt the wisdom of the suppression (by verdict of the Constitutional Court, in 1956) of the Communist party as an "antidemocratic party." Its chances as a secret organization, aided and subsidized from the East, hardly diminished during this period of illegality, while in union and factory elections, where Communists frequently ran as nonpartisan representatives of labor, they were from time to time endorsed by politically non-Communist workers. It was therefore probably good policy to permit tacitly the Communist party, under a slightly changed name, to reorganize itself in 1968. It merely showed up its continuing insignificance in voter appeal. Even the alliance of the new DKP with some other leftist splinters gave that group less than one percent of the vote in the general election of 1969. Student radicalism has not helped. The left is deeply split, with only a minority backing the Moscow (and East Berlin) oriented Communists; others follow the Maoist or Trotskyite line, and still others are "antiauthoritarian" anarchists (in turn divided into nonviolent pacifists and advocates of violence). There does not seem to be much future in leftist radicalism in West Germany at this point.

Rightist radicalism is less easily discounted. True, the general climate of antiadventurism and moderation is genuine, but its roots have been largely pragmatic, if not opportunistic. As we have seen, a genuine reorientation toward democratic values has not been demonstrated by a majority of the people, and the continuance of moderation thus seems to be predicated upon continued prosperity on the one hand, and continuation of *détente* on the other. How shaky the basis of moderation still is can be seen from the fact that, when the economic boom was briefly interrupted by recession in the middle sixties, a newly formed radically rightist party, the National Democratic party (NPD), which just prior to recession had obtained a mere 2 percent of the vote, surged to an average of 8 percent shortly thereafter; even in the 1969 election it reached, with 4.3 percent of the vote, almost the required

5 percent to give it representation in the Bundestag.

The emergence of the NPD shows that there is still a reservoir of dissatisfaction that expresses itself as rightist radicalism among economically disfavored groups or when the economy shows signs of failing to provide general prosperity. There is more to the problem of rightist extremism than is revealed by voting and membership figures. In the main, the German mind is not yet steadily moderate, let alone democratic. When we were discussing democratic reorientation, we discovered a strong tendency to repress the Nazi past and to apologize for it; later on, we shall encounter the sometimes strongly nationalist orientation of nonparty political associations. Frequently, a strange medley of contradictory attitudes characterizes the West German political atmosphere. In 1961, about two-thirds of those Germans polled came out for severe punishment of Eichmann; in 1965 two-thirds said that they opposed further prosecution of Nazi murderers. Often, a pronounced nationalism that is as strongly anti-Western (especially anti-American and frequently anti-British) as it is anti-Russian comes to the fore despite the nation's official Western orientation. Violent and sometimes irrational anticommunism seems to have taken the place of former anti-Semitism; more recently, leftist students, or "the bearded ones,"

serve as scapegoats. Dreams of greatness and a hankering for strong, one-man leadership alternate with moderation and respect for individual rights and constitutional order.

In view of this ambivalence, much will depend on the development of more stable convictions among the supporters of the major parties as well as the strength of democratic leadership. Whenever conditions have seemed unfavorable for a separate rightist party, neo-Nazis and other rightists have been inclined to flock back to established parties that seemed to them to offer opportunities for influence or infiltration; this happened in the fifties chiefly in regard to the FDP. Now, with this party having turned left, the CDU, and especially its Bavarian affiliate, the CSU (Christian Social Union), seem to offer such chances, and certain leaders (such as Franz Josef Strauss of the CSU) have from time to time spoken of a great rightist rally against the "treacherous," Communist-leaning left (by which he chiefly meant the SPD). While neo-Nazism was long discredited by those who remembered Nazism only too well, by now the Nazi past is no longer part of the "experience" of half of the people, some of whom might become easy prey to a new, or new-old rightist myth. Rightist radicalism thus still bears watching.

Is there a trend toward a two-party system? There seems to be. The combined vote of the

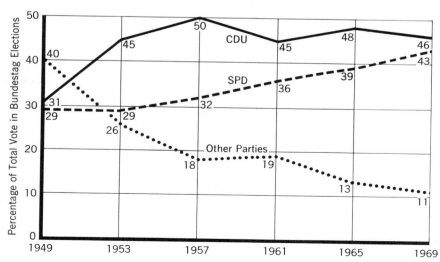

Evolution of a Two-Party System in West Germany, 1949–69

two major parties has risen steadily, from 60 percent in the first Bundestag election in 1949 to close to 90 percent in 1969. However, if by a two-party system one means that two parties alternate in office, with the one enjoying an absolute majority forming the government and the other the opposition, Germany does not yet have such a system. The Christian Democrats, who so far have always gained a relative majority, have never commanded more than 50 percent of the vote, with the one exception of 1957. Consequently, they (or, in 1969, the SPD) had to form a coalition with third parties, or with one third party, in order to gain the backing of a parliamentary majority. The third party in such circumstances holds the balance of power and wields an influence quite out of proportion to its relatively small voting base. Its influence on the composition of the cabinet

and, possibly, even the choice of chancellor, may thus become decisive.

For many years the FDP enjoyed this favorable position. It was deprived of it only from 1966–69, when the two major groups got together to form a government of the "grand coalition." But such a system, while constituting the acme of two-party *control*, can hardly compare to the classical two-party *system* (with one major group in office and the other one in opposition). Its danger lies in the vanishing of *any* opposition as well as the difficulty of agreeing on common policies. Not surprisingly, therefore, the experiment was given up in 1969 with the formation of another coalition consisting of one major and one "third" party. While this latter party, the FDP, has been declining, it is too early to anticipate its complete disappearance and therewith the

Three German Elections
(Empire, Weimar, Bonn)

	1912	1928		1949
		All Germ.	W. Germ.	W. Germ.
SPD (Social Democratic party)	34.8	29.8	26.9	29.2
CP (Communist party)		10.6	8.6	5.7
Center*	16.4	15.2	23.3	34.1
Liberals†	13.6	8.7	8.9 ⎫	11.9
Democrats‡	12.3	4.8	4.6 ⎭	
Conservatives§	12.2	14.2	9.5	
Others	10.7	16.7	18.2	19.1

* 1928: Including Bavarian People's party; 1949: CDU, CSU, Center party.
† 1928: German People's party; 1949: FDP.
‡ 1912: Progressive party; 1949: FDP.
§ 1928: German Nationalists.

Bundestag Elections 1949–69

	1949	1953	1957	1961	1965	1969
CDU-CSU	31	45.2	50.2	45.4	47.6	46.1
SPD	29.2	28.8	31.8	36.2	39.3	42.7
FDP	11.9	9.5	7.7	12.8	9.5	5.8
Bloc (BHE)*		5.9	4.6 ⎫	2.8		
DP*	4	3.3	3.4 ⎭			
CP	5.7	2.2				
Others	18.2	5.1	2.3	2.8	3.6†	5.4‡

* 1961: All-German party (GDP).
† NPD share 2.1.
‡ NPD share 4.3; ADF share 0.6. The ADF (Action Community for Democratic Progress) was an *ad hoc* coalition of extreme left groups, including the DKP.

emergence of a genuine two-party system. Also, third parties cannot be counted out on the subnational, especially the regional, level of government. In the past, there were several smaller parties with regionally concentrated strength, with relatively high voter support in their respective *Land*. Such regional parties have now disappeared, but the FDP has remained, and the NPD has become, significant in a couple of *Länder*. The West German system may well become a genuine two-party system in the future; it is not yet one.

Thirdly, can we distinguish significant party trends in relation to the two major parties themselves? Elaborate studies have been made of the results of the 1969 Bundestag election, and some of the findings are, perhaps, significant. To summarize: The SPD seems to be emerging as the party of "modernity," to which flock more of those who belong to the "modern" sectors of the society and the economy (e.g., the "tertiary," service sector concentrated in the big cities), while the CDU assumes increasingly the coloration of the party of the older and less modern groups (such as independent businessmen, small town and rural people, pensioners); in 1969 it avoided defeat chiefly because the conservative wing of the FDP, whose leadership had shifted to the left, voted CDU (indicating that that part of the FDP had basically always been CDU-inclined, voting FDP only to stem the CDU's clericalism and similar tendencies). Without that shift, the gains of the SPD at the expense of the CDU would have loomed even larger. These gains were primarily among white-collar employees and public officials (of the em-

ployees, 22 percent voted SPD in 1961, 28 percent in 1965, 45 percent in 1961; of officials, 28, 27, and 38 percent, respectively). The CDU vote among these groups decreased correspondingly but rose among independent self-employed (46, 50, and 52 percent); it also lost among farmers, although it is still strongly represented there (from 73 percent in 1965 to 59 percent in 1969); but these losses chiefly benefited the NPD. There was no increase in the SPD backing by skilled workers, but it was strong in those Catholic urban agglomerations (especially in the big cities of the Rhine-Ruhr area) that had been strongholds of the CDU. It was particularly strong among younger female age groups, especially women working in the professions or otherwise from the more highly educated class, and strong among young (new) voters, while the older women (those over age forty-five) still backed the CDU. Thus the SPD, while still strongly backed by the workers, moved into the "new" middle class; the CDU, on the other hand, emerged with somewhat larger worker support than it had before (every third, instead of, as formerly, every fourth CDU voter was a worker).

Taken at face value, these trends seem to bode well for the SPD, ill for the CDU. After all, the "third" sector is growing, also numerically; new young voters join the electorate, while the older voters die off. But the question is, How stable is the trend? Particularly with the SPD now, for the first time, leading the federal government, will it prove to have "government timber" and be able to deliver the goods? Usually, between elections, voters' disappointments make many turn to the opposi-

Party Gains and Losses in *Land* Elections, 1969–70
(As Compared with Voting Figures Obtained at Bundestag Election, 1969)*

LÄNDER	CDU-CSU	SPD	FDP	ELIGIBLE VOTERS
Hamburg	−1.2	+0.7	+0.8	1,381,000
North Rhine-Westphalia	+2.7	−0.7	+0.1	11,875,000
Lower Saxony	+0.5	+2.4	−1.2	5,085,000
Saarland	+1.8	+0.9	−2.3	783,000
Hesse	+1.3	−2.3	+3.4	3,835,000
Bavaria	+2.0	−1.3	+1.4	7,265,000

* *Land* elections in 1971 have shown a trend more favorable to the CDU and less favorable to the two Bonn coalition parties, with the CDU winning absolute majorities in Rhineland-Palatinate and Schleswig-Holstein, and the SPD gaining slightly at the expense of the FDP.

Source: Adapted from *Frankfurter Allgemeine Zeitung*, November 25, 1970.

GEOGRAPHY OF THE 1969 BUNDESTAG ELECTION

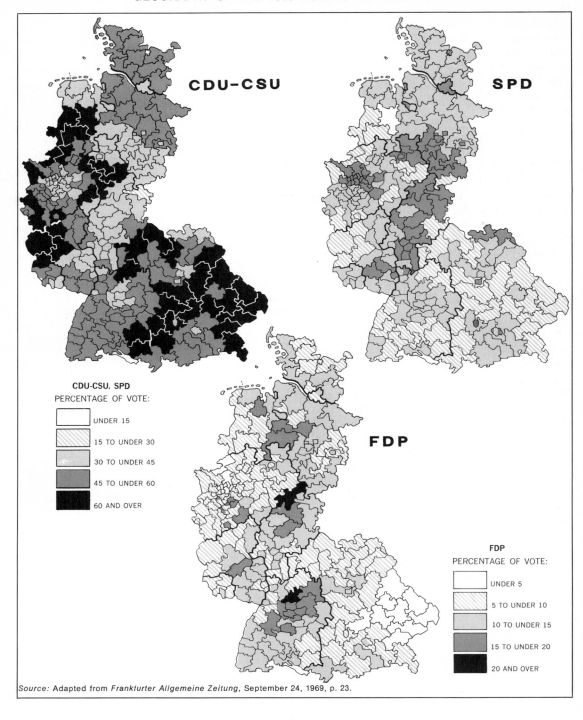

CDU-CSU

SPD

FDP

CDU-CSU, SPD
PERCENTAGE OF VOTE:

UNDER 15

15 TO UNDER 30

30 TO UNDER 45

45 TO UNDER 60

60 AND OVER

FDP
PERCENTAGE OF VOTE:

UNDER 5

5 TO UNDER 10

10 TO UNDER 15

15 TO UNDER 20

20 AND OVER

Source: Adapted from *Frankfurter Allgemeine Zeitung,* September 24, 1969, p. 23.

tion. In *Land* elections since 1969, however, such a reaction has not become visible: SPD returns have been varied, with some but not important losses; the CDU has made gains, but, again, not very important ones, while the FDP had some losses, and the NPD lost significantly. CDU gains were chiefly at the expense of the NPD; SPD gains at the expense of the FDP, to which many normally SPD voters had "lent" their vote in 1969 to keep that newly "leftist" group above the 5 percent level. What makes predictions especially difficult is the fact that the average German voter no longer seems so beholden to "his" party as he used to be: there has been

more shifting of votes than before, with Catholics, as noted previously, given the liberty to vote for other than "Christian" parties, with women less conservative than before, with upper-class people not hesitating to vote SPD, and so forth. In cases where parties formerly could rely on their regional strongholds, they can no longer be as confident (see chart on election geography). Vote-splitting (which in West Germany means splitting one's two votes between the district and the list candidates) has become more widespread (about 10 percent of the electorate split their vote in 1969). Thus one would seem to need a weatherman to know which way the wind is blowing.

3 THE PARTIES AND THEIR POLICIES

We turn now to a consideration of the individual parties, beginning with the party that dominated the federal government for twenty years and is still, numerically, the strongest in the country.

CHRISTIAN DEMOCRATIC (CHRISTIAN SOCIAL) UNION (CDU-CSU)

Background and development

For the first time in the history of German parties there has emerged a nonsocialist party that rallies the largest proportion of nonsocialist Germans, especially the middle classes but also a significant number of workers. And since the Christian Democratic party was *the* government party in West Germany from the inception of the Federal Republic to the end of 1966 (and even after that furnished the chancellor to the "grand coalition" for three more years), its policy has had a decisive bearing on domestic as well as foreign policies. What kind of party is it?

The answer is not easy. Despite its initially forceful leadership, it has been and is many things to different people. Successor to at least portions of all the pre-Nazi rightist and centrist parties, it combines elements and trends of all of them. Most important, perhaps, is the her-

itage of the old Center party, the party of the Catholics, which cut through all class lines and in program and policies reflected a merger of different social groups and economic interests. But the party is now more broadly Christian, that is, it joins Protestants and Catholics in its ranks. After World War II, large segments of European nonsocialists, liberated from or disillusioned with totalitarianism and unwilling to join rightist parties discredited by collaboration with fascism, favored a progressive movement based on Christian principles. Some of these nonsocialists genuinely embraced antitotalitarianism and democratic-social, if not socialist, ideals; others felt that this seemed to be the only effective way of stemming a more leftist flood. Hence the MRP in France and the Christian Democrats in Italy and Germany. Thus the CDU also fell heir to the former Conservatives (under Weimar, the German Nationalists, the representatives of the "old" ruling groups and classes) and in part, at least, also to various liberal parties (the National Liberals, later the German People's party, which chiefly represented big business, and the Progressives, later German Democrats, which represented lower-middle- and middle-middle-class elements). It is hard to state which force is dominant in this coalition of divergent forces. To a degree the party has succeeded in striking a balance, but over twenty-five years a trend can also be discerned that goes from more leftist beginnings toward a rightist and, in the socio-economic sense, conservative orientation. But while it thus has assumed the place of an antisocialist, conservative, middle-class party, it cannot be completely identified with traditional German rightist parties, since it accepts the liberal-democratic constitutional framework and stands for moderation in foreign policy.

Structure and organization

The CDU was the last among the postwar parties to organize itself on an interzonal level. Its affiliate, the Christian Social Union (CSU) in Bavaria, still remains organizationally separate. The CSU is the successor to a Bavarian Catholic party, which during Weimar had split away from the Center party, being more agrarian-conservative and states' rights minded than the latter. This is still so. Representing the native Bavarian peasant and middle classes, the CSU is under strongly conservative leadership and often experiences clerical influence. Although it forms a single parliamentary group (in Germany called a "fraction"; see Chapter 4) with the CDU in the Bundestag, it sometimes operates as if it were a separate party. Its present chairman, Franz Josef Strauss, has powerfully asserted its independence. Its, or rather his, chief organ, *Bayernkurier*, often voices stridently nationalist-authoritarian opinions.

The CDU, on the other hand, though in theory it embraces states' rights principles, in practice has long been under more centralized leadership. True, the statutes of the party provide for local and regional organization, but there is little apparatus of full-time party functionaries; it operates chiefly through honorary, part-time functionaries, who are sometimes little interested in party activities or efforts to increase party membership. On the top level there is a party congress of some five hundred and fifty members (representing the regional districts in proportion to CDU membership there and last Bundestag voting figures); a somewhat smaller "little party congress" (*Ausschuss*) of over a hundred; a party executive of thirty, which includes the highest-level

leadership; and the presidium, elected by the congress and headed by the party chairman and a party manager. Since 1967, the number of presidium members has been between nine and eleven; it includes the party's chairman, five deputy chairmen, and a manager. Until March 1966, the chairman had been Konrad Adenauer, one of the few forceful leaders ever produced in Germany, who could not be prevailed upon to give up his chairmanship even when, in 1963, he surrendered the chancellorship he had held for fourteen years. We have described his impact on West Germany as such before (see Chapter 2). As far as his party is concerned, so long as he was chancellor, none of the party bodies or their leaders could, or cared to, challenge this one real center of power. Under him there was dissension, rivalry, jockeying for successorship; all this was ably exploited by *Der Alte*, and talk of revolt or constitutionalization would regularly fizzle out after a while. When Erhard succeeded to the chancellorship, factionalism and a good deal of infighting developed, which Erhard tried in vain to overcome. His successor, Kurt Georg Kiesinger, managed to rally the support of his competitors as long as he presided over the "grand coalition" cabinet as chancellor, but since 1969, as leader of the opposition, he has had to compete with other leading figures, especially upcoming younger ones, such as ambitious Rainer Barzel, chairman of the CDU-CSU Bundestag fraction.

Membership and policies

The CDU, like other middle-class parties in Germany, is distinguished from the SPD in that fewer of its followers are actually members who take an active part in party affairs. As against eight hundred and forty thousand SPD members, there are about three hundred and fifty thousand members of the CDU (and some one hundred thousand CSU members), constituting less than 3 percent, as against 6 in the SPD, of those who vote for it. Thus the main problem is not to run the party—something that is done primarily by small groups of volunteers aided by party functionaries—but to maintain the allegiance of the different groups on whose support the party depends at election

Composition of Parties

	CDU-CSU	SPD	FDP
Men	41%	56%	49%
Women	59	44	51
21 to 29 years	21	22	17
30 to 44 years	26	33	29
45 to 59 years	30	27	31
60 and over	23	18	23
Grammar-school education	74	88	56
High-school education	26	12	44
Workers	37	67	21
White-collar employees	26	18	30
Officials	10	5	11
Businessmen	13	5	23
Professionals	2	1	4
Farmers	12	4	11
Monthly income below 400 DM	14	10	9
400 to 599	25	31	20
600 to 799	26	36	23
800 to 999	18	15	21
1,000 to 1,499	13	7	18
1,500 and over	4	1	9
Protestants	40	63	69
Catholics	58	31	26
Others	2	6	5

flicting interests: (1) Catholics and Protestants; (2) religious people and those who are more secular in orientation; (3) industrialists and other big business interests, as against the employees and particularly the workers in the party; and (4) the sectional balance between the party's two traditional strongholds, the primarily big-city area of the Rhine and the Ruhr, and the more rural and small-town Bavaria (controlled by the formally separate CSU).

The relatively broad range of support for the CDU, in contrast to the SPD and the FDP, is shown in the table at the left, which also reveals the proportion of the parties' supporters in regard to age groups, sex, education, and the like. These groups backed CDU, SPD, and FDP in the percentages listed (each percentage group adding up to one hundred) in the middle sixties. Since then, as noted above, support has somewhat shifted (especially as far as the FDP is concerned), but the figures are still broadly indicative.

The CDU's diversity of backing has not led to confusion in policies. Adenauer saw to that. He represented the conservative wing of the party, and his rule reflected the victory of this wing over the left. The left wing is chiefly composed of the workers' wing of political Catholicism and its trade union arm, the former Christian trade unions (now absorbed into the overall trade union organization, the DGB, see Chapter 1). The stronghold of this group is in the Ruhr, but its weakness is apparent in its failure to have even part of its program implemented. The wishes of this wing had been reflected in a platform of 1947, the so-called Ahlen program, which had gone so far as to advocate nationalization of coal and steel, participation of workers in the management of private industry, and dissolution of cartels and monopolies. But the actual policies of the party have favored protection of private property, free enterprise, and restraint of unions. These policies enjoy the backing of major portions of Ruhr industry, the civil service (the federal civil service was originally established on the basis of Adenauer's patronage), and large parts of the peasantry and the lower middle class.

The party's left wing is now primarily represented through its "social policy committees"

time. (The pattern is reversed in the SPD, whose followers can be better relied upon to troop to the polls.)

Who are these groups? First of all, Catholics, who make up about 50 percent of the total West German population, but amount to about 60 percent of those voting CDU, and about 70 percent of the party membership. This has not meant, however, that the party is predominantly Catholic in outlook or policies. While clerical influence has been noticeable here and there, there is a studious attempt to maintain "parity" between Catholics and Protestants in staffing party and state positions and in other personnel questions. Intraparty tension between socio-economic groups and interests has at times been greater than that between the two religious portions of the party. Indeed, the party represents a delicate balance among four distinct sets of potentially conof CDU workers and employees on different party levels. The party's organization of about one hundred thousand younger members (the Young Union) likewise tends to more progressive policies. But the left wing has been without forceful leadership, and on the whole the influence of the "big" interests has prevailed in questions of economic and similar policy. There has been tension from time to time, for example, over cartel legislation in the fifties, between the party's then economic leader, Ludwig Erhard, an old-fashioned economic "liberal," and Ruhr industry. On the whole, however, the spirit of big business has prevailed. In spite of this, prosperity enabled the CDU leadership to maintain its support by salary and wage earners. Its early foreign policy successes as well as Adenauer's forceful leadership contributed to its general success.

One of the party's most significant achievements has been its ability to obtain the backing of many Protestants, especially in the Protestant north. While for many Catholics the CDU is still the former Center party in a new guise, Protestants rally to it as to a more or less conservative middle-class party. While its Catholic element is more prominent in leadership and promotion, the Protestant vote is sufficient to make it broadly representative of a middle class to which have been restored profits, prosperity, status, and authoritarian values. Even today, nothing symbolizes better its general stand than its chief slogan in the 1957 election: "No experiments!" Even in as late as a 1968 poll, in which "readiness to take political risks" was tested against a "no experiments" policy, the latter was backed by 72 percent of CDU supporters (with only 16 percent "prorisk"), while the overall proportion was 53 percent to 33.

Prospects

The future of the CDU as one of the two major West German parties seems to depend on two things: policy orientation and leadership. As for policy, the question is whether the CDU program and policies will continue to satisfy a sufficient number of supporters to enable it to remain a "people's party," drawing support from all the major groups. In the past it has been successful in combining the representation of upper middle class, especially business, interests with an appeal to a broad strata of the lower middle classes and workers. As we have seen, however, recent trends have endangered its hold over considerable portions of white-collar employees, officials, new voters, women (at least the younger ones), and so forth.[1] The general increase in the number of salaried people (as distinguished from independents) in the modern economy means that more and more people (up to the higher management level) are now interested in job security, social insurance, salary levels, and similar issues, which many feel are better safeguarded through the SPD. Recent polls have revealed that voters considered the SPD, rather than the CDU, more competent in two chief domestic areas, socio-economic and education, and in one foreign policy area—relations to the "East," while the CDU was preferred only for its policy toward the West. These findings would indicate that the CDU's future lies in "modernizing" its policies to compete effectively with the SPD for the crucial modernizing sector of the population. Its dilemma is that this way it might antagonize the "non-modern" strata still loyal to it, who might conceivably flock to the NPD or potential other rightist groups. In this situation, its "Berlin Program" of 1968, finalized and rendered even more conservative at a party congress in 1971, was still orthodox in both foreign policy and such domestic issues as extension of co-determination (with parity for workers and employees on the boards, advocated by its left wing, decisively rejected).

Also, its traditional leadership would not easily preside over a drastic reorientation of policy. This leads to the second factor that will bear on the party's future. While under Adenauer it suffered from excessive control by one man, it has now faced the opposite danger of dissension for many years. This danger has been particularly grave since the formation of a government from which it has been excluded for the first time in its history. From the vantage point of the chancellorship it could still rally all party forces with at least a mini-

[1] *Land* elections in 1970 and 1971 revealed that the age group eighteen to twenty-one, newly admitted to the polls, disproportionally preferred SPD and, especially, FDP, thus further discomfiting the CDU.

mum of effectiveness. The fact that it lost control of the government, itself, created dissension among the leadership, many being inclined to blame its formal leader, Kiesinger. And while the leadership has since tried to bury disunion through an especially strident and violent opposition against the foreign policy of the Brandt government, it has not been able to rally the party behind one man, or a unified group, and a consistently positive policy. Feuding, stalling for position, mutual harassment, and incrimination are on the agenda again. Younger leaders, such as Barzel and "regional" chieftain Helmut Kohl, of Rhine-Palatinate, or Gerhard Stoltenberg, of Schleswig-Holstein, are eager to take over, with Strauss always in the background.[2] Will they be unorthodox, "progressive," modern enough to lead the party as one unit into the future? Much will depend on how well, or badly, its chief opposite number, the SPD, will live up to its claim to be "the wave of the future."

THE SOCIAL DEMOCRATIC PARTY (SPD)

Background and development

While the CDU is a new phenomenon in the history of German parties and politics, the SPD can look back on a hundred years' continuous development as *the* party of the German worker and at times the strongest and potentially most powerful party of all. Even at a time when communism was a competitor, democratic socialism never lost the support of a majority of the working people. Its sustained strength, from the time when it emerged triumphant from Bismarck's antisocialist fight to the end of the Weimar period, and from 1945 on-

ward when it again emerged from illegality, is thus hardly surprising. Its technically unsurpassed organization, the discipline and devotion of its members, its press, youth, and women's groups, and its close contact with free trade unions were envied and imitated by many other socialist parties. Yet it has had until recently little impact on German developments. When, after its long period of outsider status under the Empire, it at long last seemed to hold a commanding position (under Weimar), it failed even to preserve the constitutional framework of the new republican regime. And in the postwar period it was until 1966 condemned to play, in the main, the role of an impotent and frustrated opposition.

It is relatively easy to see why the SPD failed in the past. Under the Empire, when even moderately liberal groups were excluded from government, its role could only be negative, and its attitude reflected the radicalism of its founders, Marx and Engels. The German proletariat, denied recognition by the ruling classes, developed a kind of "socialist subculture" of its own. But, gradually, the SPD veered toward a revisionism that held that the aims of socialism could and should be attained through democratic processes. When, in 1918, this opportunity seemed to have come, the SPD missed it, even in the moderate sense of laying the foundations of genuine political democracy. The causes of this failure—chiefly, the split of the workers' movement, the absence of imaginative leadership, the strength of authoritarian and reactionary forces—have been analyzed above (see Chapter 2).

After 1945 these causes were no longer present. The workers, like all others in Germany, were united in their stand against communism. Initially, at least, there was forceful leadership, and reactionary forces were unable to endanger the liberal-democratic framework of the new constitution, so that the path toward the realization of the party's aims seemed open. Its lack of success for twenty more years may in part be explained by more "accidental" circumstances of an adverse nature: the separation of East Germany, a traditional SPD stronghold; the rise of an equally strong party as a competitor; and the emergence of strong leadership in that party. But another part of the

---

[2] By the fall of 1971, the choice had narrowed down to the following alternative: Since Kiesinger declared himself out of the running, the CDU would either select Barzel as both party chairman *and* "chancellor candidate" (to lead the party in the election campaign of 1973) or separate the two positions, in which case the Party Congress was likely to elect Kohl party chairman and designate Gerhard Schroeder, the party's foremost foreign policy expert, chancellor candidate. On October 4, 1971, Rainer Barzel was elected party chairman and designated chancellor candidate by the CDU Party Congress at Saarbruecken. His election foreshadowed a more nationalistic-conservative orientation than would have been the case if the more progressive Helmut Kohl had been elected (with the less "cold warrior" Schroeder as candidate for the chancellorship).

explanation lies in the party's own structure and policy.

Structure and organization

Traditionally, the SPD has been the prototype of the strongly centralized German party, with a party machine that managed to control the membership at large. In contrast to the more rightist, middle-class parties, more of its followers are actual members of the party and take an active interest in its policies and debates. But the party machine (traditionally consisting of paid party functionaries, employees of such party enterprises as the party press, Social Democratic trade union officials, and Social Democratic holders of government positions) has always formed a self-perpetuating party elite. The machine has manipulated the elected party organs through devices well known to students of American political organization; thus the party executive has usually been the vantage point from which the leadership has controlled the party at large.

The party machine has traditionally been organized so as to place control of party affairs and policies in an executive that consists of both honorary and full-time paid members (about thirty-five in all). In 1962 a presidium of ten emerged as the top-level group, within which, in turn, the chairman and two deputy chairmen form the pinnacle. Since 1968, the internal affairs of the party are seen to by a party manager. The executive has preponderant influence over the nomination of candidates for elections, controls the party's extensive properties and enterprises, appoints the permanent staff, and prepares the agenda of the party's "representative" body, the biannual convention, over whose deliberations it exercises great influence. A party council of delegates from the party's regional districts advises the executive. The convention, with some three-fourths of its roughly four hundred delegates representing the districts in proportion to their membership (the rest comprising members of the executive and other functionaries), is theoretically the highest organ. But the weight of the "apparatus" of the paid functionaries is felt everywhere, including the local and regional organizations, which are particularly important in view of the SPD's control of many states and by now most big cities.

For a time during the postwar period leadership was personal rather than oligarchic. In Kurt Schumacher the party for once had a chairman who, through his magnetic personality and his ability to appeal to the masses, held uncontested rule. But after Schumacher's untimely death in 1952, the SPD reverted to group rule and the party chairman became again part of the machine. Erich Ollenhauer, well-meaning and honest but colorless and uninspiring, was no match for Adenauer in the 1950s. Then came a change that had a good deal to do with the change in the party's fortunes. In 1961, Ollenhauer was forced to abandon his role as candidate for chancellor to a new standard-bearer, the young, vigorous, and popular mayor of West Berlin, Willy Brandt, who rallied a group of strong leaders around himself, and soon thereafter, upon Ollenhauer's death, became chairman of the party. The new leadership included Herbert Wehner, a former Communist who, in the SPD, had moved far to the right, had been instrumental in formulating the party's new reformist policy and now became the chief advocate of a coalition with the CDU, which, so he believed, would create the image of a party able to govern; Helmut Schmidt, who became the party's expert on defense and military affairs; and Karl Schiller, an economic expert, who substituted Keynesian "anticyclical" economic and financial policies for those of Erhard's laissez-faire policies when he entered the cabinet of the "grand coalition." This was done with such success that by 1969 he had become by far the most popular of SPD leaders among the electorate. As a group, therefore, the SPD leadership proved to have a stronger appeal to the 1969 electorate than did that of the CDU. But strong, unified leadership alone could hardly have led the party out of the doldrums without a change in program and policies.

Policies and programs

One of the reasons for the party's postwar lack of success was that Schumacher, in attempting to give it a new orientation free from its partly discredited tradition, based his new policy on wrong assumptions. One was in regard to nationalism. Socialism had been traditionally internationalist, which often earned it the undeserved stigma of being unpatriotic or even treasonable. The neonationalism of the postwar period with which the party appealed to the patriotic feelings of the German masses came exactly at a time when these masses, disillusioned with old-fashioned nationalism, were ready for some kind of supranationalist European regionalism, as advocated by Adenauer. Moreover, with West Germany's rise to international stature, the party's criticism of the Adenauer regime as being remiss in regard to German national interests had little impact. Its orientation being necessarily Western, its differences with the CDU in the foreign field had to be over matters of detail, and even here Soviet policy, when turning against such SPD-backed proposals as reunification through neutralization, pulled the rug from under the party.

In the domestic field, too, the party's policy failed when Schumacher's other assumption, namely that Adenauer's free-market economy would fail in the absence of effective government controls, proved wrong. For most people, including many workers, the first order of business in the first ten to fifteen years of the postwar period was reconstruction and higher living standards, and they thus were genuinely weary of "experiments." But by 1960 the postwar period had come to an end. Both domestically and in foreign affairs, prestige and prosperity had been regained, and the slogans of the Adenauer regime as well as its policies (emphasis on the "cold war," favors to big business, and hostility to social reforms) seemed to many even outside the "proletariat" no longer in tune with the times. The time had come for a party like the SPD to try to get out of the "desert," where it seemed condemned to control forever an insufficient 30 to 40 percent of the vote, to transform itself into a more broadly based "people's party," and this way eventually to assume political control.

Its turn to the right was signaled by the party's adoption of its first new "basic program" in thirty-five years. The Godesberg Program of 1959 turned decisively away from Marxist principles. What it proclaims in relation to the churches, namely that "socialism is not a substitute for religion," applies to the new attitude in a general sense. Nothing could be more expressive of its shift from a past in which socialism was the quasi-religious creed of proletarian masses. Now the party has become pragmatic. In economics the emphasis is on "market economy," that is, freedom of enterprise and freedom of competition. Planning and transfer of properties to public ownership are not ruled out but are considered policies of last resort rather than major policy objectives. Policy is "New Dealish" rather than socialist: control of overly powerful economic interests and of cartels, promotion of small business, and, of course, of labor's wage and similar interests. The formulation "competition so far as possible, planning so far as necessary" puts the accent neatly. The SPD had become the German version of the British Labor party, a reformist party, mildly to the left of its conservative chief competitor and ready to battle for the "middle ground." It prepared for the battle, strangely but successfully, by entering into a government coalition with its opponent, and as minor partner at that. But, as we have seen, Wehner's calculation proved correct. Three years of sharing in government had what has been called the "Wehner effect" of convincing portions of the middle class, especially the "new" strata of the tertiary sector, that the SPD had turned definitely away from its youthful sin of "atheistic socialism." Although not gaining a majority, not even a relative one, at the polls, it gained enough to form with the FDP a coalition government in which, for the first time, it acquired the chancellorship and a majority. What use has it made of its opportunity, and what are its prospects for the future?

Prospects

"We are a reformist, not a revolutionary party; a people's party, not a class party." Thus spoke Helmut Schmidt at the first party convention held after the formation of the Brandt government. He had to defend the policies of the new, SPD-led government against somewhat violent attacks on the part of the "Jusos," the party's youth organization,[3] which accused the leadership of what it had been accused whenever it had been in control (in the twenties, for instance, or, more recently, when the SPD had become the government party in states): timidity, lack of bold initiatives, allowing itself to be tied to formal rules and procedures, or dominated by the permanent bureaucracy. The response always was that those representing the SPD in government were not free to do what they wanted but were restrained by coalition partners—in this instance, the FDP. Thus, they explained, they could not, for the time being, promote one of the party's chief policy demands, the extension of codetermination to all corporations with parity of trade union and shareholders' representatives.

It may be true that in many respects the SPD leadership has been hampered this way. But after two years at the helm of the West German ship of state, one cannot avoid the impression that it has done less, perhaps, than might have been achieved, or at least tried, particularly in domestic affairs. In foreign policy, the government has been more bold and innovative (see Chapter 8), aided, to be sure, by the even bolder approach to these questions by the FDP. However, the domestic record of the government has been meager, especially for a reformist party that still claims to represent the "underdog" and to try to work for his economic and social improvement. In Germany two reforms, in particular, are overdue, and one would expect Social Democrats to give them top priority: one, to counter those authoritarian tendencies that still loom large, whether in the spirit, composition, and activities of the bureaucracy (including the judiciary), or in the military, or elsewhere. Second, to work for an educational reform that would at long last do away with the class system of education. SPD ministers have been trying to get certain reforms legislated, in the field of criminal law, for example, or in providing funds necessary for enlargement of uni-

versity studies or new research facilities for science; in foreign aid, especially technical assistance, the SPD has been progressive. But the basic areas have hardly been touched.

Another area of innovation is not restricted to Germany alone but is shared by all other industrialized nations: protection of the human environment against the encroachments of an exploding technological civilization (preservation, or restoration, of pure air, water, and soil, the planning of viable urban agglomerations, of transportation, and so forth). These demand putting interest in the public sector of the economy before interest in the private sector—a task uniquely befitting a social reform party less influenced by the special interests opposed to such measures (or, at least, less opposed to the appropriation of the necessary funds).

As a "people's party," the SPD has been characterized by a broadening spectrum of attitudes and wings. This spectrum ranges all the way from a conservatism hardly distinguishable from that of the CDU, which in the SPD is represented by leaders such as Schiller and Schmidt, through the center, which is now represented by Wehner and Brandt, to the ideologically socialist and partly revolutionary leftwingers, consisting of "Juso" members, socialist students, intellectuals, and some workers and union leaders. One of the anomalies of the situation is that the left wing of the CDU is now left of the right wing of the SPD. The left wing of the SPD is without influence on top party leadership and its policies, and by 1971 the tension between the left and the leadership had become pronounced, with the latter telling the "radicals" to shut up or get out.

While the young socialists have thus encountered the iron resistance of the leadership, the trade unions, some of which (as for instance, the metal workers union) have advocated more boldness and thus have become a kind of *Ersatzpartei* for those West Germans who are left of the official SPD line, find themselves in that half-support, half-opposition role typical of trade unions when a moderately reformist labor party is in control. The party, to be sure, is in a dilemma. If it wants to establish itself safely as a "people's party" and make further inroads into the domain of the middle-class parties, especially the CDU, it cannot af-

---

[3] In similar vein, Brandt, to an interviewer's question "What change does it represent for Germany to have a Socialist Government?" replied: "Let me say first that I am a Social Democrat and not a Socialist." The "Jusos," of course, want the party to be a "socialist" one, that is, a party aiming at "basic transformation," not mere "reform," of "the system."

ford to alienate those still rather conservative strata to which it wants to appeal. But might not such an overcautious approach in the long run alienate at least portions of those who used to be its chief support and still support it as the party of democratic progress, the workers? SPD leaders may feel that the workers have nowhere else to go, and the experience of the "grand coalition," which did not lose them workers' votes, seems to confirm this. However, workers might not only turn left but, conceivably, right; there are populist-fascist inclinations among workers that have come to the fore in their turning against student radicals, hippies, foreigners (as have American "hardhats" or British dock workers against colored immigrants). Indeed, animosity of German workers against foreign workers has been noticeable, too. Workers' support of the rightist NPD has not been inconsiderable. Among the "Jusos," whose leftist opposition became increasingly strident, not workers but students and intellectuals are the vocal and controlling elements. It would be strange, indeed, if the SPD, a party trying to represent increasingly broad strata of the population, would become so colorless as no longer to stand for what it professes to stand for above all: economic, social, and general progress, and fulfillment of the needs of the masses.

THE FREE DEMOCRATIC PARTY (FDP)

In many respects the FDP is a paradox. The trend toward a true two-party system, which we have noticed, threatens the very existence of the FDP, and it may be dead, at least as a significant force on the national level, by the time this book appears in print. But in 1969, despite severe losses at the polls, it still managed to move from a seemingly hopeless position in ineffectual opposition to that of influential partner in the federal government. Frequently but prematurely discounted, it has often managed to reassert itself as indispensable "holder of the balance" between the two major parties. Backed by rather diverse strata of the population that often represent different and even mutually contradictory policies, the party has tried to straddle the political space from right of the CDU to left of it and, more re-

cently, left of the SPD. Under these circumstances, what kind of party is the FDP, and what can it expect to be in the future?

Background and policies

In the postwar period the FDP established itself as successor to both previous liberal parties (National Liberals and Progressives in the Empire, Democrats and People's party in Weimar). It rallied those among the middle classes who, although strongly antisocialist and therefore fearful of the then still radical-looking SPD, favored an undiluted free enterprise system without concessions to state planning or even further social welfare steps (of which it suspected the CDU). What further distinguished it from the CDU was its stand for separation of church and state and the extension of the system of interdenominational schools; also, in contrast to the CDU, it was progressive in cultural matters, such as freedom of arts and literature from clerical or other influences, reform of criminal law, and so forth. It thus combined economic conservatism with progressivism in cultural and related areas.

But from the beginning the party was not homogeneous. It used to be supported by portions of big business and also by many in the middle ranks of the middle class, in particular smaller independents, tradesmen, artisans, members of the professions, in short, the strata of society traditionally threatened by and opposed to organized and concentrated big business. Part of its backing came from Protestants fearful of clericalism, who otherwise might have backed the CDU but wanted in a more liberal party an instrument to block or balance those CDU trends. In the fifties the party also was the rallying ground for nationalists (including former Nazis) who objected to Adenauer's Europeanism and his dependence on Western, especially American, policies, suspecting him of having given up a policy of reunification. But there were (and are now increasingly) those who hope for rapprochement with the "separated brethren" in the East by recognizing the DDR. To complicate matters, the party was supported by different groups in different regions: big business in the Ruhr, export trade in the Hanseatic cities of the north, the more enlightened burghers in southwest Germany (traditional stronghold of German liberalism), and also conservative farmers and small-town people in areas such as northern Hesse. Thus the party, in its backing as well as its policies, reflected reactionary as well as progressive tendencies.

As time went on, this discrepancy was increasingly felt in its policies. At first firmly settled as part of the Adenauer group (to which it presented, in the person of Theodor Heuss, Bonn's first and genuinely democratic federal president), it broke with the CDU as its coalition partner several times, only subsequently to enter government again. This created an impression of unreliability and fickleness not only in the major parties but in the electorate at large, where its support gradually decreased. Of course, liberalism in Germany has shared its decline since pre–World War I days with other countries. From a prewar 25 percent, the combined vote of liberal parties sank to about 15 percent under Weimar, and that of the FDP decreased (with ups and downs) from an initial 12 percent to barely over 5 percent in 1969. This led to a good deal of feuding in and over party leadership. When reduced to the status of lone opposition during the "grand coalition," it made the decision (believed suicidal by many outside and inside the party) of decisively turning left, thereby risking the loss (as happened in the 1969 election) of most of its conservative big business, and part of its smaller, middle-class backing. However, it retained (or gained) the support of the more progressive and enlightened voters, especially among the young (some of whom now even turned socialist). In short, the FDP transformed itself into "radical liberals." As we have seen in Chapter 2, the party ratified this decision by supporting the SPD candidate for the presidency, Heinemann, in the spring of 1969, thereby convincing the SPD of its reliability as a partner in an SPD-FDP combination, but also showing its traditional supporters where the new wind was blowing. While FDP voters had often split their vote (giving their first vote not to the FDP but to another party's district candidate), most had cast that vote for the CDU candidate, but in 1969 those still voting for the FDP list now cast that district vote for the SPD man (first vote among FDP second voters: 1965, 35 percent CDU, 8 percent SPD; 1969, 16 percent CDU, 34 per-

cent SPD). As a result the FDP has been able to play a prominent role at Bonn, especially through placing its chairman, Walter Scheel (who had been the chief force behind the party's policy change), as Foreign Minister in the Brandt government. On the other hand, the party, also as a consequence, has faced the danger of disintegration. Many conservatives, under the leadership of former party chairman Erich Mende, have left the party. Some, like Mende, joined the CDU, others tried to form a separate group under the label of "national liberals" (organizing, in 1971, a new political party, the "German Union"). While the latter is not likely to survive as a significant force, the secession threatens to reduce the FDP's already diminished strength on all levels, local, in states such as North Rhine-Westphalia (where it had already, prior to 1969, been in a "social-liberal" coalition), and nationally, where the coalition by now is based on a flimsy majority of six. Thus the fate of the FDP may well determine the future of West German politics in general.

THE NATIONAL DEMOCRATIC PARTY (NPD)

No event in recent German politics, perhaps, has roused the attention of the world as much as the emergence of an apparently Nazi-type party on the West German political scene. Many Germans have complained that the importance of the event was being exaggerated. What, so they ask, does less than 5 percent of the national vote (not enough to let the NPD enter the Bundestag) or even 8 or 9 percent in state elections mean, as compared with, say, the 15 percent a comparable group obtained in the United States? This, of course, overlooks the fateful role rightist radicalism has played in German history and the strong roots it still has in German authoritarian tradition and society. It would be foolish to forget that in the twenties, before the onset of the Great Depression, Hitler's party obtained less than the NPD's recent voting figures. But is it correct to consider the NPD "neo-Nazi"? Who are its leaders, who are its supporters, what have been its policies?

When the party was founded in 1964, it constituted a coalition of former Nazis (who, up to then, had been leaders of a variety of feuding and competing rightist splinter groups) and of conservative nationalists (many of the latter coming from one of the smaller conservative parties, the German party [DP], which had been a coalition partner of the CDU but had by then declined). Very soon the Nazis managed to occupy the new party's key positions and to control its finances. Three-fourths of its top leaders (but not party chairman Adolf von Thadden, a conservative without former Nazi affiliation), two-thirds of its district functionaries, a majority of its diet members, close to half of the lower functionaries, and one-third of its members are past members of the NSDAP or were Nazi functionaries. If the party leadership can legitimately be characterized as neo-Nazi, the social composition of its supporters is less so. While at first, besides former Nazis, its chief support came from those groups, such as the lower middle classes, farmers, and so forth, that had formed the mass backing of the Nazis, the party has since gained support from strata that, in the main, had been inaccessible to the Hitler movement, such as Catholics and workers. On the other hand, even this support has come mainly from regions in decline (e.g., rural and small-town areas in economic distress, where the young have migrated to the cities), and, in the case of workers, chiefly from those who are non-unionized. In general, the younger age groups and women are underrepresented. The age groups most strongly represented are drawn from among those who in 1945 were twenty-four to thirty-nine years old (thus showing that Nazi education and indoctrination did have some aftereffects). The NPD also is strongest in regions that used to be early Nazi strongholds, such as northern Hesse and the Palatinate. As mentioned before, economic recession (even though a mild one) drove voting figures up sharply. Surveys have shown that "experience of, or the fear of, a loss or change in social status and economic well-being" [4] accounts for a person's turning neo-Nazi. The NPD is a party of protest and resentment.

What has the party been telling its supporters? First of all, it has to be cautious in its pronouncements, especially those directed to-ward a more general audience (such as in election campaigns), since it must avoid falling under the constitutional ban of antidemocratic groups. In its statements, the leadership thus has voiced moderately conservative and nationalistic views, shunning Nazi trappings. In its internal propaganda, however—for example in its chief paper, *Deutsche Nachrichten*, read mainly by its members and with about the same circulation as the number of its members (which, in 1969, was about forty thousand but has since declined)—there has been less restraint. Its ideology (as expounded by party "philosopher" Ernst Anrich, an old Nazi "intellectual") is practically the same as that of the Nazis. It is virulently anti-Semitic and anti-Communist and also anti-American and generally xenophobic; foreign workers ("defiling German womanhood") and *Gammler* (the German version of hippies) are likewise objects of its phobia. Military leaders under the Nazis, as well as Nazi leaders condemned in post-Nazi trials, are glorified by the party or play the role of martyrs. Its program demands the end of such trials and the restoration of the honor of German World War soldiery; the end of payments of "reparations" to Jews, Israel, other foreign powers, and of aid to racially inferior countries. In foreign affairs the NPD is as anti-Western as it is anti-Communist, demanding the restoration of Germany's "equal rights." Domestically it condemns inefficiency of parliamentary government and corruption of established parties.

If, as Marx has said, history sometimes repeats a tragedy in the form of a farce, the way in which "little Adolf" (von Thadden) has so far led his party, in comparison to the role of the big Adolf, can hardly even aspire to being called farcical, because it has been so ineffective. NPD deputies have hardly ever been heard of in the diets to which they were elected. No major measure, however obstructive, has been promoted by them. Such absence of forceful leadership and action seems all to the good. But we should not forget that, basically, there is a considerable reservoir of discontent and emotionalism waiting to be tapped. Under favorable circumstances, such as economic decline, a party like the NPD could rally broad support, drawn from former rightist FDP members, as well as from the major parties (according to one investigation, among NPD voters there were at one point 23 percent former CDU-CSU voters, 26 percent former SPD voters, 7 percent former FDP voters, and 23 percent former nonvoters). It thus depends on the major parties, through their policies and actions in coping with the great tasks facing a modern nation, to prevent a second German relapse into barbarism.[5]

MINOR PARTIES AND NONPARTY ASSOCIATIONS OF A POLITICAL CHARACTER

Not much needs to be said about other parties because there are hardly any left. Germany, as we have seen, was traditionally a multiparty country. In the postwar period a large number had sprung up after the licensing of four parties had ended. But most of these were regional parties or represented particular socio-economic interests. There was the Hanoverian "German party" (DP), expressing the strongly conservative sectional attitudes of Lower Saxony farmers and burghers; there was the Bavaria party (BP), fighting Bonn "centralism" and all "alien," that is, non-Bavarian influences in that particularly "states'-rights"-oriented *Land*. Their demise reflects the lessening pull of sectionalism, the intermingling of an increasingly uniform (and nomadic) people. The chief "interest" party was that of the expellees, the All-German Bloc (BHE), which for years exerted powerful influence in and on government. BHE's very success led to its disappearance. The expellees became thoroughly integrated into the West German economy. And legislation enacted under BHE prodding provided so well for indemnification of those who had lost possessions, that most expellees no longer have a particular axe to grind. Only some, who still are not adjusted emotionally or

---

[5] Since 1969, the NPD has fared badly. In *Land* elections it did not even attain the minimum voting percentage to be represented in the respective state diets, with the CDU (or CSU) picking up most of the vote that previously had gone to the NPD. In 1971, its membership, which at one time had reached a figure of over forty thousand, was reported down to little more than twenty thousand. But this hardly proves more than that when times are better malcontents return to the party of second choice. It would be premature to write the NPD (or a similar party) off for good.

politically, keep the issue alive through nonparty associations.

There remains the German Communist party (DKP). We have seen above how communism fared in the postwar period in West Germany and why the recently established (or reestablished) party is unlikely to gain much importance in the foreseeable future. In organization and program it merely imitates the "Big Brother," which in this instance is the Socialist Unity Party (SED) of the DDR. This in itself limits its appeal. In addition, it is hampered by the splintering of the extreme left. For the election of 1969, the DKP set up an organization to run candidates (ADF, or Action for Democratic Progress) with some other groups only with great difficulty, and the result was meager; other left groups, ideologically opposed to any participation in elections, opposed even this get-together. Still, by 1971 the party reportedly had about thirty thousand members.

More significant are political associations of a nonparty nature. Such associations have often been more influential in German political life than parties proper. Especially the ones on the right have frequently been party substitutes for those Germans who wanted to stand above the "ever-wrangling interest parties." The Nazi party grew out of the racist "combat associations" of the post–World War I period. The post–World War II decades have witnessed a crop of veterans' organizations, former Waffen-SS members' associations, and the like, trying to pose as self-appointed guardians of the German national interest or honor. Their mouthpiece is a particularly vicious and strident publication, *Deutsche Nationalzeitung*, a weekly with a circulation of over one hundred thousand. It never ceases stirring up nationalist emotionalism.

Equally vituperative, and often more influential, are some of the nonparty organizations of refugees and expellees, which, organized according to origin (Silesians, East Prussians, etc.), still attract members from these ethnic groups. Most of them belong to the associations for nostalgic reasons, or to retain and periodically renew personal contacts with old friends, but the leadership has been more political, trying to perpetuate an insistence on the expellee's "right to the homeland" (which, in their view, comprises also the Sudeten area of Czechoslovakia) and to intimidate the major parties into unyielding policies in regard to the Oder-Neisse line, "lost territories," and so forth. Those refusing to be so intimidated are denounced as "politicians of renunciation," on the pattern of rightist defamation of Weimar statesmen. The effect has long been felt in the West German policy toward the East. Combined with the attacks by the present opposition (especially, the CSU) on the new policies of the Brandt government, this intimidation may still prove effective. By the end of 1970 a vicious terror organization, Action Resistance (*Aktion Widerstand*), had sprung up, indicting the government's Eastern policy as treason to the German Volk and trying to intimidate its members and supporters with slogans ("*Brandt an die Wand*"—Brandt to the gallows), reminding one ominously of similar groups and tactics during the twenties. Groups like these seemed to absorb those members of a declining NPD who were too radical and activist to join any of the established parties.

On the left, APO (German abbreviation for "Extra-Parliamentary Opposition") has not been one organized political association but rather a "movement," a composite of several leftist groups and organizations, united for certain purposes and actions but more often than not quarreling among each other concerning goals and methods. Its core has been student organizations that originated as branch organizations of the various parties but proved indigestible to the respective "parent parties" when turning to the left. Thus, the SPD's Socialist Student Association, *Sozialistischer Deutscher Studentenbund* (SDS), was already disowned by the SPD in the early sixties; the party then tried to substitute another association for it, the Social Democratic University Association (SHB), which in due time proved equally intractable; so it has been with the formerly FDP-affiliated student group, and even the one affiliated with the CDU is far to the left of the party. Thus these groups are castoffs of their parent organizations, results of the right turn of the SPD, the nonexistence of a strong party left of it, and, above all, the joining of the two major parties in "grand coalition" exactly at a time when the radical

wave was swelling, leaving no room for meaningful left opposition in parliaments or elections —or so it seemed from 1966 to 1969.

Beginning with the "Easter marches" and similar pacifist, "antiatomic" demonstrations of the early sixties, APO activities have for the most part been peaceful protest actions, ranging from street rallies to rock-throwing or window-smashing, but rarely assuming the form of life-endangering violence. Objects of their protest have ranged from world issues to local matters; from Vietnam to increased street-car fares. Above all, students have protested on behalf of university reform. *Umfunktionieren* (taking over in order to control for one's own purposes) meetings, lecture courses, or similar gatherings has been one of the inventions of APO. We have already seen that in regard to reform of university structures and teaching systems there has been quite some advance (occasionally going too far in the direction of "student power"). Generally speaking, however, with the constituents of APO so widely disagreeing on final objectives, the movement has declined. It was not even able to do what the French students accomplished, a general strike of workers; instead workers turned against it. The movement has provoked the inevitable backlash. While police repression has been relatively mild, the opprobrium radical students have gained among the public at large has been severe, uncovering latent fascist streaks in numerous Germans. One scholar reports: "Not infrequently one hears the statement, 'Under Hitler people like you would have been put into the gas ovens.'"

As we mentioned before, leftist radicalism could serve a useful, even necessary, function if it could free itself from negativism and join forces with those, in and outside the parliamentary system, who advocate "participatory democracy." But for this the movement would need allies within the "establishment," whether in the bureaucracy or the military, the corporations, or, indeed, the parties themselves. Radical-democratic youth, students and others, could be the "salt in the soup," insisting on reforms of the social environment, which has been neglected, and the protection of a natural environment that is being despoiled. After all, it is they, not the older generation, who will have to live with both environments longest.

4 ELECTIONS

THE PRESENT ELECTION SYSTEM

Germans, with their traditional multigroup system, have usually considered elections as means to have the comparative strength of the different political groups reflected in representative bodies, rather than as a way to form a stable government. This accounts for their attachment to proportional representation (PR). In the Empire, Reichstag elections had been single-member district elections, with runoff votes in case the first vote failed to give one candidate an absolute majority. Since socialists were usually isolated in the runoff vote, they came to advocate PR as a progressive principle and introduced it into the Weimar system. There, as we have seen, it was blamed, perhaps unjustly, for the weaknesses of Weimar parliamentarianism; as a result, after 1945 a mixed system was adopted for Bundestag and most regional elections, aimed at combining the advantages of PR (just representation of the various opinion groups) with those of the single-member system (more personal relation between voters and candidates and lessened party domination of elections). With slight variations in detail, the system works so that half of the deputies are elected from single-member districts by simple majority, the other half from *Land* lists set up by the parties. Each voter thus has two votes: one cast for a candidate in his district, a second for a party list. "List candidates" are elected in such a way that the overall composition of parliament reflects the results of the second vote in proportion to the strength of the different parties. However—and this constitutes the other most important innovation of the system—a party must obtain at least 5 percent of the overall list vote or win at least three district seats in order to be represented in the Bundestag (there are variations of this clause in some of the *Länder*).

This system has been a success. Its main effects have been as follows: (1) It has personalized PR somewhat by giving the voter a chance to cast one vote for an individual candidate. While the majority still votes a "straight ticket"—that is, for the district candidate belonging to "their" party—we have seen that sophisticated vote-splitting, especially by supporters of small parties like FDP and NPD (where district candidates have practically no chance to obtain a majority), has grown in importance. Also, "micro" election analyses have shown that the personality of the district candidate frequently plays a larger role than one had thought. (2) One main disadvantage of PR, splintering of the vote among too many small parties, has been avoided. As we have seen, the 5 percent clause has by now eliminated from the Bundestag all but the two major parties and the FDP. It may yet lead to the emergence of a genuine two-party system, a system that the opponents of PR used to consider possible only under a pure single-member district system. (3) The present system involves an intricate game of jockeying for position on the lists. These lists are made up by the regional party organizations, which determine who is placed on the respective party's list and in what place. A candidate running in a district can simultaneously be on the list, so that, in case he fails in his district, he may still enter parliament if he is in a safe, that is, forward, place on the list. The list, in turn, makes sure that the party's representation is a rounded one, with representatives from the major groups (pressure and others) backing the party, experts in certain fields, some women (who usually are not run in districts), and those national leaders of the party who might be defeated, or do not care to run, locally. In a way, this makes the system more representative than it would be if all were elected from districts.

On the other hand, the lists give party bureaucracies a chance to make many deputies creatures of the machines. In the districts it is not so much the central machines and the larger pressure groups that influence selections, but rather local groups. Still, the individual voter, who is not usually a party member, or even the ordinary party member, has little influence over nominations. Although nominations must be made by conventions of party delegates elected by party members in the districts, this is a far cry from direct primaries. In practice, regional party functionaries and interest groups do the determining, with the central party organization having an important voice though no veto. Occasionally, however, and especially in the case of the SPD, there has been genuine competition over nominations. Candidates may be selected from outside the districts, which, of course, enhances party control even more.

Despite its comparatively happy results, there have been those who advocate the replacement of this system by a system of undiluted plurality voting, based on the British or American pattern. Such an election reform was on the agenda of the "grand coalition" and would, of course, have been the death verdict for the only opposition party at the time, the FDP, as, probably, of any third party in the future. But the SPD hesitated, being afraid that the plurality system might in practice stabilize the control of one party, the CDU, instead of inaugurating a genuine system of two-party alternation. There was reason for such fear, since in previous Bundestag elections the SPD had always obtained fewer district majorities than the CDU-CSU (e.g., in 1949, 96 as against the CDU's 115; 1957, 46 versus 194; 1965, 95 versus 153). But in 1969, the SPD had the better of the CDU (127 as against 121). Thus the chances may be more equal now. But it seems doubtful whether the benefits of a new system could outweigh such drawbacks as the likelihood that Germany would be divided into one-party regions, with the CDU becoming a rural and small-town party and the SPD a big-city party, both with correspondingly narrowed interests and representation. Also, numbers of voters might become politically homeless, the more radical among them driven into resentment or futile "extraparliamentary opposition." Quite generally, the political landscape would become ever more colorless, with the two parties tending to offer that choice between "tweedledee" and "tweedledum," which is the bane of American politics. On the other hand, there would be more stability, more clear-cut government (no bothersome coalitions any more), and the likelihood of continued moderation.

Campaigns and procedures

On the whole, elections in Germany are carried out efficiently, and corruption, open or undercover, is not widespread, although there is little official regulation of electoral ethics. A usually high voting participation (around 80 percent) is facilitated by the absence of complicating procedures. No special registration is required; the authorities keep permanent lists of those entitled to vote; and rules for absentee voting are easy. There are no literacy tests or property qualifications, and residence requirements are liberal. Elections take place on Sundays, with ample time for everybody to vote. The voting age, until recently twenty-one, is now eighteen, and women have been admitted since 1919. Women's suffrage in Germany has generally strengthened the Catholic and conservative parties as against the left; paradoxically—since the socialists had always advocated women's suffrage—the CDU owes its superiority over the SPD to the female vote. Even now, with the SPD making inroads into the younger Catholic vote, that of women over age forty-five is still benefiting the CDU (and even more the Bavarian CSU). The lowering of the voting age, on the other hand, has so far been to the advantage of the SPD (and of the FDP).

Lately, in addition to the more traditional means of campaigning through posters, ads in newspapers, and the like, radio and especially television have become very prominent. Here, the public character of the media has saved the parties from the traditional American difficulty of "purchasing time." It's all free, and the free-for-all has been regulated by law in a way that combines the principles of equal time and proportionality to previous voting strength; in other words, the big ones are a bit "more equal" than the others when it comes to assigning time.

PROBLEMS OF POLITICAL FINANCE

Nevertheless, the problem of financing parties and elections has become a serious one in Germany as elsewhere. Democracy is in danger of turning into plutocracy if wealth is permitted to influence party policies and to determine nominations and election results.

The somewhat dramatic story of how West Germans have tried to solve the problem, therefore, may be instructive for others.

It started in the fifties, when government parties, especially the CDU and FDP, profited from an organized financing of their expenses by the interests backing them, in particular, industry. "Promoters' associations" of employers were set up to centralize fund raising by assessing individual enterprises and channeling the money to the nonsocialist parties according to an agreed-upon allocation. Tax exemption of such contributions meant that much of this financing was paid by the taxpayer. In 1958, however, the Constitutional Court outlawed such deductions as in violation of the "equality principle" of the constitution.

The fact that money from industry and similar large contributors now proved less easy to come by led to new developments. In the sixties, the parties represented in the Bundestag began to vote themselves direct annual state subsidies. These payments, officially for "educational" activities of the parties, were allocated according to their proportional strength. They increased each year and, by 1966, amounted to about 60 million DM. In that year, however, upon application by one *Land* and several of the nonbenefiting smaller parties, the Constitutional Court declared the practice unconstitutional. According to the judgment, such subsidizing of parties tended to render them dependent upon the state, endangering their existence as free instrumentalities of the popular will. But the prohibition was declared to affect only the overall activities of the parties (e.g., their organizational expenditures), thus leaving reimbursement of the costs of election campaigns legal (with the proviso that *all* groups participating in the campaign were to share in the benefits according to a reasonable key).

The proviso proved broad enough to solve the parties' major financial headaches. Now, on the basis of DM 2.50 for each party voter in federal elections (distributed among parties receiving at least 0.5 percent of the vote—the Constitutional Court, in still another decision, having determined that the originally legislated figure of 2.5 percent was too onerous for small groups), and between DM 1.50 and 2.50 in

Land elections, the parties, altogether, are subsidized to an amount about equal to the 60 million DM received previously.

But, despite free television, campaign and other expenditures are still high and have a tendency to get higher with every election. Overall expenditures for a year with a federal and some *Land* elections (1969) were estimated at over 200 million DM (with over 100 million for the federal election, and 70 million general operating costs). Parties thus still depend for over half of their expenditures on membership dues, voluntary contributions, and other income. A somewhat "nonparticipatory" attitude of middle-class party members, in contrast to SPD members (who, as we have seen, are more numerous), accounts for the fact that the CDU-CSU gets less than half the amount from membership fees than does the SPD.[6] It still therefore relies more on individual "big" contributors. One reason that the Law on Parties was so long delayed lay in a CDU refusal to agree to SPD demands that individual sources of party funds be revealed. In 1968, a compromise was found, under which names and amounts given must be revealed in cases of individual donors giving more than DM 20,000 per year, and of "legal persons," that is, corporations and such, with annual contributions of over DM 200,000. Again, the Constitutional Court intervened and declared the lower amount mandatory for corporations also. Whether publicity will have a restraining effect remains to be seen. Some Germans, interested in parties independent from government and business influence alike, have suggested tax-deductibility of a limited amount for individual annual contributions, but this has not yet been acted upon.

---

[6] Figures published for 1969 (a Bundestag election year) in the *Federal Gazette* (December 10, 1970) were as follows, in million DM:

	Income from Membership Dues	Income from Contributions
SPD	20.6	11.6
CDU-CSU	9.0	21.1
FDP	1.3	4.3
NPD	0.7	1.4

In addition, of course, there were the reimbursements of campaign expenditures from federal and state budgets, income from party enterprises and assets, and so forth. German law requires that campaign expenses be recorded and filed.

5 EFFECTIVENESS OF THE GERMAN PARTY SYSTEM

Germans have long regarded political parties as divisive forces interfering with the legitimate tasks of government, an attitude that often rendered parties ineffective and allowed the executive to function outside their orbit. Rule by a party elite over the party as such, and the ensuing lack of influence by members or voters on party policies and management, contributed to the traditionally low prestige of parties. Experience with Nazi propaganda caused many Germans to feel that political promises and avowed political ideals are mere decoys set by self-centered and self-perpetuating politicians. Polls still reveal a good deal of distrust. For example, many Germans feel that election campaigns are not necessary and refuse to reveal their party preference.

In other respects, as we have seen, there has been improvement. With the emergence of two major moderate parties, more Germans have come to think in terms of political alternation, compromise, and cooperation, instead of thinking primarily in terms of the doctrines, victories, and defeats of one or another political "movement." Yet, to the majority, parties are still identified with party leaders, and the leaders are considered as belonging to *die da oben*, those on top and in control, over whom the people at large have little influence. This is partly the parties' fault. Parties, even in their own self-image and behavior patterns, tend to be remote from the people, part of the official establishment that runs the nation. What might give the people more influence and render them more interested? A change in party organization might help—for example, by making membership less formal and more easy to obtain, as in the United States. At present, besides those few who are genuinely interested, most of the people who join parties do so because they expect rewards (for instance, candidates for office, or officials in search of promotion). Above all, there is need for more intraparty discussion of issues and interparty debate about policies. Here, the growing similarity of the two major parties, each desiring to become a "people's party" appealing to all strata, has had an inhibiting effect. One need not advocate a return to narrow doctrinairism to wish for more lively debate based on legitimate differences in principles and approaches.

In the absence of such revitalization, the role of parties is likely to remain small when decisions are made about the tasks to be performed by the inevitably expanding government of the future. The scientific and technological revolution will impose on Germany, as on other advanced nations, dimensions of planning (of environment, population, of science itself) unheard of so far. If these decisions are not made democratically by rejuvenated parties, they will be made autocratically by the traditional alliance of *die da oben*—that is, by bureaucratized and institutionalized parties in alliance with an administrative and scientific elite remote from the people. Only if and when more Germans realize that in a democracy the people must take the initiative in making parties and public life more expressive of popular desires will German parties implement democracy.

4

West
German
parliament

The meeting place of a representative assembly may be an index to its national importance. While Britain has the magnificent neo-Gothic structure of Westminster Palace, resurrected from World War II ruins in its old image, and while France has the classic Palais Bourbon in the very heart of Paris, the German assembly presently deserving the name of parliament still is housed in a sober office building at the "Federal Capital Village" of Bonn. No traditions surround it. The pompous Reichstag building in Berlin—like the diet it housed, more façade than substance—still stands as a burned-out symbol of Nazi incendiarism. Popular sovereignty in Germany is still in search of substantiation.

1 DEVELOPMENT AND CHARACTER OF GERMAN PARLIAMENTARY INSTITUTIONS

GENERAL CHARACTERISTICS

The place of parliamentary institutions in the German government is difficult to define. These institutions have never had the power and prestige of parliaments in Western countries. But neither have they been (except during totalitarian regimes) the make-believe, pseudo-representative institutions often found outside Europe. Rather, German parliaments have expressed a middle condition reflecting a desire for genuine representative government continually thwarted by both authoritarian and antidemocratic tendencies.

The Reichstag of the Empire, as we have seen, was not recognized as the equal of "real government," the authoritarian executive. Even under Weimar, parliament was checked by a semi-independent executive and proved unable to function when an emergency arose. Parliament is now reduced to a sham in the DDR.

In West Germany, on the other hand, the Bundestag has emerged as a genuine representative institution. Bonn has given parliamentarism a second chance.

The German parliament has traditionally contained multiple political groups. They are seated in a semicircle (as in France), with governmental representatives facing the deputies from raised seats (not, as in Britain, sitting on the front bench of one of the two opposed sides of the house).[1] But, unlike France, the various parliamentary parties are separated from each other as organized groups. Consequently, there is no reorganization of party groups in parliament after an election. The parties are fixed once and for all, they move as separate armies into a new parliament, and

[1] In the interest of democracy, however, the government bench has now been lowered from four steps to one step above the deputies; possibly a symbol of changing relationships.

West German Legislative Bodies, 1969

BUNDESTAG*

SPD
224

CDU-CSU
242

FDP 30

BUNDESRAT†

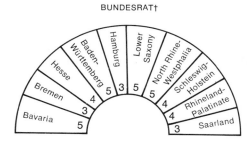

* Plus 22 nonvoting deputies from Berlin (13 SPD, 8 CDU, 1 FDP).

† In addition 4 nonvoting delegates for Berlin.

even an individual deputy's crossing from one party to another is rare.[2]

Unlike the practice in Britain and France, there is in the German parliament little genuine debate or brilliant oratory (although recent borrowings from certain Anglo-American features, such as rising to question an orator, have added a bit of spontaneity to debate). Since deputies usually speak not for themselves but present an (often compromise) attitude or decision of their party, this lack of spontaneity is not surprising. On the other hand, disorder and use of strong language have been frequent, reflecting lack of respect for the institution of parliament. Occasional television coverage of debates has not altered the widespread view of parliament as a place where interest groups wrangle and concern for the commonweal is lost. Many Germans still consider the existence of opposed and clashing views in parliament as something that is bad in itself.

Composition of parliament

The table on page 452 reveals the wide spread of social classes and interest groups represented in parliament. Certain features are characteristic. One is that specific groups and

occupations, though they send some direct representatives (farmers or entrepreneurs, for example), are also represented by the full-time officers of their respective interest organizations, such as the BDI (Federation of German Industry), farmers' associations, and so forth. Second, the relatively low number of "workers" indicates that they, too, are in the main represented by functionaries of their interest organization, the trade unions, and in addition by party functionaries and party journalists—persons who frequently have workers' backgrounds but have become professional politicians. Thus, the lower classes are in general represented by those who have risen in social status.

A large proportion of German deputies are representatives in a double sense: they represent both the people who elect them and the major classes and interests that strive to be represented in parliament. So it is not surprising that cross associations (Querverbindungen) of deputies from different parties but representing the same interest group frequently make common cause when their "cause" is at stake. (According to the slogan, "Farmers of all parties, unite! You have nothing to lose but your subsidies.") Also, such a system renders the lobby, so far as it affects deputies, less essential, since the chief interests are already represented by the deputies themselves. At Bonn, the lobby chiefly addresses itself to the executive—in particular, to the ministerial officials in charge of drafting bills. Indeed, government bills are quite regularly discussed with (if they have not been initiated by) officers or agents of the respective interest groups before they are approved by the cabinet for submission to parliament. But the lobby is active in the Bundestag,

[2] If it occurs when parties (or coalitions) are as closely balanced as they were after the formation of the Brandt government in 1969, defections or shifts of very few deputies may, of course, prove vital (or fatal). In 1970, a simulated offer by an FDP deputy to change his party for the CSU showed that the latter was ready to pay 400,-000 DM for the transaction—a first-rate political scandal. One result of this and similar occurrences was the adoption by the Bundestag of some "conflict-of-interest" regulations; they are not very far-reaching but provide at least for some accounting by deputies for income from outside activities other than their chief profession or occupation.

too, especially in hearings at committee stage. An effort to compel lobbyists to register with the Bundestag was defeated.

Another characteristic of German parliament has been the prevalence of public officials; in the 1969 Bundestag their number rose to one-third of the total membership. There is no incompatibility between belonging to the executive and being an elected representative in parliament. When elected, the official takes a leave of absence from his service, with part of his salary paid. Thus, when special group interests are at stake, no group is better represented. It also means that many laws are drafted by officials, enacted by officials on leave, and administered by officials.

In one respect, even nonofficial deputies have been assimilated to the status of civil servants: after a certain minimum service in parliament they are entitled to retirement pensions, and even their widows and young children are protected. Other features, similarly reflecting some characteristics of German society and political culture: about half of the deputies are *Akademiker* (i.e., university graduates), of whom, in turn, a majority (1969: 31 percent of the total membership) are either professors or at least have a doctoral degree;

Composition of the Bundestag
(In Percentages)

	CDU-CSU		SPD		FDP		ALL		FIRST BUNDESTAG
	1965	1969	1965	1969	1965	1969	1965	1969	1949–53
Executives and managers	8.4	8.8	5.5	7.6	12.0	6.5	7.5	8.1	0.7
Top entrepreneurs	4.4	5.2	0.9	1.3	8.0	9.7	3.3	3.7	
Independent businessmen	4.8	5.6	0.0	0.4	4.0	0.0	2.7	2.9	14.4
Functionaries of business organizations	4.8	4.4	0.5	0.8	4.0	6.5	2.9	2.9	
Handicraft (including professional organizations)	2.7	2.4	1.4	3.0	4.0	0.0	2.3	2.5	
Farmers (including farmers' organizations)	12.0	11.2	1.4	0.4	18.0	16.0	8.1	6.6	12.7
Workers and white-collar employees	5.6	7.2	12.0	10.9	2.0	3.2	8.1	8.7	6.3
Trade union officials	6.4	5.2	13.8	12.7	0.0	0.0	8.9	8.3	10.0
Party functionaries	2.7	2.8	11.6	9.7	10.0	12.9	7.1	6.6	13.4
Public officials and public employees	29.9	32.4	29.4	34.6	20.0	2.9	28.7	32.2	16.8
Professions (including clergy)	4.4	2.4	5.5	6.3	0.0	3.2	4.4	4.2	7.6
Attorneys and accountants	7.9	7.2	5.1	3.8	14.0	22.0	7.3	6.6	7.8
Journalists and publishers	4.0	4.0	9.7	7.2	4.0	6.5	6.4	5.6	8.5
Housewives	2.0	1.2	3.2	1.3	0.0	0.0	2.3	1.1	1.7

Source: Adapted from tables in *Berichte des deutschen Industrieinstituts,* 3 (6) (1969).

the share of women has declined, with only 32 (6.1 percent of the total) in the sixth Bundestag (1969).

THE ORGANIZATION OF THE BUNDESTAG

Fractions

The most important units in the Bundestag are the party groups called "fractions," each made up of the deputies of the same party. Thus, one speaks of the CDU-CSU fraction or the SPD fraction in a given Bundestag. Unless there is a subsequent schism or secession (something very rare in Germany), deputies belonging to the same party always constitute one single fraction, despite any political divergencies and wings that may exist within the party. In the case of the CDU-CSU, even two organizationally different parties have so far always formed one—the biggest—fraction in the Bundestag. The major reason for this cohesion is that fractions dominate parliamentary procedures, and fraction strength determines important rights. Fractions, for example, are represented in committees by members selected by them in proportion to their strength; time for debate is assigned to fraction spokesmen, often in proportion to fraction strength; only fractions may introduce legislative motions. They are represented on the Council of Elders (see below) according to their strength. If a group fails to attain, or loses, minimum fraction strength (according to Bonn standing orders, 5 percent of Bundestag membership), it loses its influence in the Bundestag.

Fractions now, especially those of the combined CDU-CSU and the SPD, are so large that they constitute parliaments in miniature. On many issues, therefore, they must first come to agreement among themselves; officially, they vote, but in practice the "experts," represented in the "working committees" of the party (which are set up corresponding to the various Bundestag committees), prevail—that is, the plenary party follows their suggestions. If conflict persists, the fraction leadership (executive committee, which also otherwise exercises tremendous influence in and over the fraction) usually prevails. Once a fraction has

made up its collective mind, strict party discipline is exercised, and the individual deputy is compelled to vote according to the line laid down. Otherwise he may be expelled from the party or lose party backing in subsequent elections. A study of voting in the Bundestag shows that over a given period fraction discipline was observed in the SPD in every case, in the CDU-CSU in nineteen out of twenty cases, in the FDP (here as in other matters less united) in nine out of ten.

Since campaign funds come from the party chest or from groups backing the party, for a deputy to disagree with the party over policies or program may mean the end of his political career. The professional politician in Germany —that is, one who devotes his career to politics—usually begins by running for election in a district, where he must be in the good graces of the local party. He then becomes a "back-bencher" in his fraction. From that lowly position he advances to "expert" status in some specialized area (labor affairs, agriculture, criminal law, or whatever); as such, he has to prove himself to parliament at large. If he does not specialize, he is nowhere. But if he is successful, he may advance to fraction and party leadership (and hence, possibly, into the government). He remains, however, beholden to his party. All this, though detrimental to individual initiative, makes for coherent party action. In contrast to an American voter, the German voter, though he often does not know *whom* he is voting for, at least knows *what* he is voting for.

Speaker and steering committee

The Bundestag elects its speaker (president) and his deputies, who preside over the sessions. The speaker has important disciplinary powers. He may, for instance, exclude a deputy for thirty session days. But the most important body in organizing procedures is the steering committee (Council of Elders). According to a recent overall revamping of the Bundestag standing rules (1969), it consists of the speaker, the two deputy speakers, and twenty-three members elected by the fractions. The chief objective of the reform was to enable the steering committee to program the activities of parliament better, that is, to plan its agenda ahead according to the subject matter to be considered. Legislative logjams due to the pressure of work have plagued the Bonn parliament as they have those in other countries. According to the new standing orders, a speaker is in principle limited to fifteen minutes per motion, but one speaker per fraction shall have forty-five minutes. In one respect the Bundestag now is perhaps the most modern of parliaments: electronic installation enables each deputy to vote by push button from his seat.

2   THE GERMAN PARLIAMENT IN ACTION

The German parliament, like other parliaments, reflects that modern trend in government under which actual lawmaking, formerly first among the functions of representative bodies, recedes in importance before the function of controlling and supervising the executive. But this latter function has always been precarious in Germany. The crucial question, of course, is how to combine effective supervision by parliament with stability of government. Under Weimar, while parliamentary supervision at first led to cabinet instability, the executive eventually emerged as the stronger power, destroying parliamentary control altogether.

THE BUNDESTAG AND THE EXECUTIVE UNDER THE BONN SYSTEM

Bundestag and executive

The makers of the Bonn Constitution, drawing on the Weimar experience, strengthened the executive without conferring important powers on the president. Strong executive power is vested in the chancellor. He is elected by the Bundestag, to be sure, but once elected he can be compelled to resign only by means of the so-called constructive vote of nonconfidence—that is, a vote by which the assembly simultaneously, and with a majority of its legal membership (as distinguished from a simple majority of those present), deposes one chancellor and elects his successor. This is intended to prevent a situation where opposition parties could join to overthrow a government without being able to form a new one. The chancellor's powers are further strengthened by the fact that he appoints and dismisses cabinet ministers independently of the Bundestag; the latter cannot, as is customary in most other parliamentary systems, oust the individual ministers. The chancellor, further, can ask the president to dissolve the Bundestag—though only when his demand for an expression of confidence has been rejected. His dissolution power is thus much more restricted than that of the British prime minister. It has so far never been exercised. The Bundestag cannot dissolve itself. Nor can it *compel* the chancellor to ask the president to dissolve it in order to have new elections (an inability that became crucial during the government crisis of 1966 [see Chapter 2]).

Questions and other means of control

In its supervisory functions, the Bundestag has at its disposal some techniques customary in Western parliamentary systems, such as a question hour and a chance to devote some time to discuss with representatives of the government "questions of general topical interest" (*Aktuelle Stunde*). A regular question period on the British pattern is, in principle, held at the beginning of each plenary meeting, but, although sometimes lively and revealing, it has failed to endow questions with the prestige that has rendered the British practice a check on the executive. Initiative and independence of the individual deputy are still inhibited in favor of party control. Although the number of questions has risen from less than one thousand in the first Bundestag period to over ten thousand during the fifth, the largest number, of course, has been answered in writing. A more lively give-and-take is usually had during *Aktuelle Stunde*, which, in contrast to the question hour, deals with matters of general concern and policy. But motions for such a discussion can only be made by fractions, not by individual deputies, and time is severely restricted (one hour, with no more than five minutes for each speaker).

Another means for supervision and control of the executive is through investigating committees. Their establishment is even provided for in the constitution. But they have not managed to play a significant role as a check on the executive. While the minority (opposition party) has the right to have such a committee established, once it has been established the majority party (or coalition) is in control and can direct (or hamper) proceedings. Thus, in the most conspicuous case so far, concerning alleged corruption in connection with defense orders, the (then) CDU majority managed to impede any clear discovery of what actually happened. It is therefore understandable that the number of such procedures has declined (from nine during the first Bundestag to two each in the fourth and the fifth). A recent attempt to convey powers of investigation to another committee, the one on petitions, hardly promises better results. This situation reflects the larger problem of how, in a system where the parliamentary majority party (or party coalition) is strongly controlled by the executive, parliament can effectively supervise this self-same executive.

There is one area, however, where the position of parliament as a supervising body has been strengthened: the military. When the West German armed forces were set up (see Chapter 5), concern with "Prussian" militarism and high-handedness led to the creation of the office of the Parliamentary Defense Commissioner (*Wehrbeauftragter*), a kind of ombudsman, appointed by the Bundestag, accountable only to the Bundestag, and with quasi-judicial powers to investigate complaints on the part of members of the armed forces. Although the Bundestag has not always been lucky in the selection of the commissioner, the practice is an important experiment in a country where the idea of unquestioning military discipline is supposed to be replaced by a more democratic, "citizens-in-arms" kind of spirit, giving due consideration to individual rights and human dignity.

LAWMAKING

Ordinary laws

In regard to legislative procedure, Germany stands between Britain, with its cabinet control, and the former French system, with parliament in full control. In the federal government since 1871, and in the member states since 1918, the executive has had no direct powers over lawmaking, not even veto powers. But the trend toward increased influence of the executive over lawmaking is found in Germany as elsewhere. It appeared especially early in Germany, because of the traditional authority of the expert, and, particularly, because of the role played by the ministerial bureaucracy in the preparation of bills. To a higher degree than elsewhere, the drafting, processing, and execution of laws in Germany have been carried out by the bureaucracy. Consequently, the chief efforts of interest and pressure groups have centered on the bureaucracy.

Although bills may originate in the Bundestag as well as in the cabinet, most of them are drafted in the ministries by expert officials. Of some thirty-five hundred bills initiated between 1949 and 1969, over two thousand were cabinet bills. Most of them were passed, while most of the diet-initiated bills were not (due to the fact that most of these originated with the opposition). Deputies are at a disadvantage because they lack the facilities and expert advice the departments possess; recently, it is true, some service has become available to legislators: each now has a right to a government-paid assistant (although, owing to low salary, more of the clerical than of the expert type), and the working committees of the fractions can make use of the services of a kind of legislative reference setup. The rules of the ministries, on the other hand, permit consulting interest organizations even prior to the drafting of the bills. As we have mentioned, this is one of the most valuable channels of access and influence available to the organizations. In order to prevent the worst abuses, the amended standing orders of the Bundestag now provide that, when cabinet bills are made accessible to interest representatives before the cabinet passes on them, they shall be made accessible to the speaker of parliament also.

Under the Bonn system, bills prepared in a ministerial department go to the cabinet, which has to approve them, and from there to the Bundesrat. This body scrutinizes them thoroughly through committees staffed by high *Land* officials. In practice, informal contacts between these state officials and the federal officials in charge of drafting precede this formal intervention of the Bundesrat in the legislative process, especially in cases where the legislation affects the *Länder* and has to be carried out there; the effect, as one has called it, has been "control of bureaucracy by bureaucracy," a more effective check on executive power than that exercised by the Bundestag.

After this first action by the Bundesrat (on its subsequent actions, see below), the bill goes to the Bundestag. There follow the usual three readings, with the second one the most detailed. Prior to the second reading the bill goes to committee; this stage is by far the most vital one. In plenary session, often only one member of each party discusses the bill, and usually under time restrictions. In the committees, which are set up according to subject matter, the parties are represented by their respective experts, and it is here that important bills receive careful scrutiny.

Committees are organized after each new election and usually correspond in number and topic to the respective executive departments. Thus, in the present (sixth) Bundestag there are fourteen standing committees, plus a number of special ones (such as on budget, petitions, and reform of criminal law).[3] There is no seniority principle. Parties occupy chairmanships in an alternating way, so that the opposition gets some even on important committees. But fractions are represented according to their strength, so that the cabinet can count on majorities in each of them. The chairman cannot be compared in power to his American opposite number; he cannot, for example, pigeonhole a bill, it has to be reported out (although frequently there are long delays). Ordinarily committee meetings are private, and there are few hearings on the

American pattern; if there are, it is usually representatives of special interests who are heard. Thus, since the fractions also send their experts in the respective field into the committees, it is there that pressure groups and special interests have their prime chance to influence and shape legislation. In addition, ministerial officials regularly attend the meetings to steer their bills through. Their influence as experts in the matter at hand is generally very great. Often agreement in committee is easy, because members, although of different parties, for the most part represent the same interest. And usually, once a measure has cleared committee, it is ratified by parliament. It amounts to log-rolling on a grand scale, and it also means, as one German observer has put it, that legislation all too often is concerned with "schools, not children; courts, not those before the courts; railroads, not travelers; war, not war victims."

Financial legislation

In financial legislation the German system lies somewhere between the British, where the cabinet, and especially the Treasury, is in complete control, and the American, where Congress has traditionally exercised its discretion. In Germany there is a tradition of a comprehensive, well-prepared, and well-coordinated budget to be adopted annually in the form of a law dealing with both revenues and expenditures. Since the Finance Ministry is in charge of preparing the budget, the Finance Minister emerges as a very powerful figure. While this resembles the British system, there is more real debate and scrutiny of the budget bill in the Bundestag. The constitution provides that budget increases proposed by the Bundestag or Bundesrat require the consent of the government. This gives the government important powers, of which, however, it has made little use so far. The provisions that were inserted into the constitution under the "grand coalition" government in 1968–69 are more important. They were inserted at a time when Economics Minister Karl Schiller, in "concerted action" with employers and trade unions, inaugurated a policy of long-range planning intended to cope with business cycles and economic growth. In order to be able to engage

---

[3] The parliamentary reform of 1969 now permits also the formation of special committees (*Enquête* committees) composed of deputies and outside experts, to deal with more general matters. Thus there is now one dealing with general reform of the constitution.

in "medium-range" economic and financial policies, cabinet and parliament are authorized to provide for preparation of budgets several years ahead, as well as for coordination of budgeting among federation, *Länder*, and municipalities (see Chapter 5).

Constitutional amendment

Under the Hohenzollerns as well as Weimar, German constitutions were flexible rather than rigid. Constitutional amendments could be passed by way of ordinary legislation through the regular legislative agencies. Under Weimar, such amendments passed with a qualified majority of two-thirds of both houses, and a practice developed of passing statutes that deviated materially from constitutional provisions without bothering to amend the text of the constitution.

Under the Bonn Constitution, as under Weimar, constitutional amendments can be passed by concurring two-thirds majorities in both houses. This is why it is important for a chancellor to control not only a simple but a qualified majority, in the Bundesrat as well as in the Bundestag. However, the Weimar practice of indirect or silent deviation from constitutional provisions is now prohibited. Amendments must expressly alter or add to the text of the constitution, and certain constitutional provisions, such as those affecting the federal structure of government or certain basic rights, are exempted from any alteration whatsoever.

Decrees

Germany, a country where the bureaucracy is older than parliamentary institutions, has a long tradition of administrative legislation. When lawmaking became a function of parliament, this tradition was continued, with parliaments often passing mere "framework," or "skeleton" laws that were implemented by executive decrees or ordinances. This delegation of lawmaking power to the executive has become more and more common with the extension of executive functions into all fields. Germans distinguish such decrees from mere internal directives in that lawmaking decrees bear on the rights and duties of citizens. The Bonn Constitution specifies the cases in which "lawmaking decrees" require consent of the Bundesrat. As a check on the ordinance power of the executive, German courts have always claimed the right, whenever an individual case came up, to review such measures to see whether they kept within the limits set by the framework law; if they were found *ultra vires* they were not applied.

Legislative emergencies and emergency legislation

In the past, another type of decree proved more dangerous to German democratic institutions than executive decrees—emergency decrees. Experience with Article 48 under the Weimar system led the authors of the Bonn Constitution to omit corresponding powers in the new document. But a watered-down version of emergency legislation was nevertheless retained. In case the Bundestag refuses to vote confidence in the chancellor (without, however, expressing nonconfidence by voting for a successor) and the president (acting on the chancellor's advice) does not choose to dissolve the Bundestag, he may declare a "state of legislative emergency," after a bill declared to be urgent by the executive has been rejected by the Bundestag. The bill, as well as any other bill rejected within a period of six months after such declaration, then becomes law if it is approved by the Bundesrat. The Bundesrat, however, is not likely to be so different in political complexion as to be ready to play this game against a determined Bundestag. This fact, together with the time limit and a restriction that emergency legislation must not amend or suspend any part of the constitution, renders the application of this provision unlikely.

More ominous, and of much greater political importance, has been the enactment in 1968 of emergency legislation that by amending or adding to many articles of the constitution provides for a great variety of special powers invested in a number of governmental organs in cases of foreign war, threats of war, or grave domestic crisis (the terms used are "state of defense," "state of tension," and "internal state of emergency"). Drafts of the legislation, originally prepared by a CDU-controlled government, would have provided the executive with far-reaching powers in case of external or internal crises, including the suspension of basic rights and the use of the military and police. The legislation had to await the coming into existence of the "grand coalition" to pass in considerably watered-down form, since the SPD, whose consent was required for the constitutional amendments, refused to go along with such sweeping measures. Prior to enactment, there was violent opposition on the part of the APO, trade unions, and leftist groups in the SPD. As it now stands, the emergency legislation is extremely complex. Some of the new rules established immediately valid law. Thus, for example, a new version of Article 10 (dealing with secrecy of the mail, etc.) authorizes a number of intelligence agencies to read the mail and "bug" telephone conversations under broad, practically unrestricted circumstances. The individuals concerned need not be notified even if surveillance continues without results, and they are expressly excluded from bringing the matter to court. The Constitutional Court in 1970 confirmed the validity of this legislation, with the exception of the exclusion of subsequent notification.

But the bulk of the legislation deals with the three "states" mentioned above and applies only after a formal finding concerning war or "tension" has been made (in case of "internal"

tension, however, such a finding is not necessary). The finding is made either by two-thirds majorities of both houses of parliament or, in an emergency, by a joint parliamentary committee or the federal president (subject to subsequent revocation by the two chambers). The Joint Committee, which has broad powers, especially in case of war or "tension," consists of twenty-two members of the Bundestag (with proportional representation of the parties) and eleven members of the Bundesrat (one for each *Land*). A kind of miniature parliament thus is supposed to act in conjunction with the executive.

Emergency powers of this or a similar nature may be necessary in time of war, but their authorization for an undefined period of "international tension" or a state of internal "threat to the democratic order" is more questionable. It is especially doubtful whether a small parliamentary group can be relied upon to restrain dictatorially minded executive leaders. Germans are too easily inclined to accept an unrestrained executive and the excuse that crises justify the abrogation of constitutional safeguards. Once before, German democracy committed suicide by conferring all power on the executive through an Enabling Act. One must hope that the second German experiment in democracy will not be imperiled in similar fashion.

3   THE FEDERAL COUNCIL (BUNDESRAT)

BACKGROUND AND CHARACTER

Second chambers in modern times are usually one of two types: they may represent a special class or caste or they may represent the territorial units of a federally organized country. In Germany the second chamber, since 1871, has reflected the federal structure of the country. The German second chamber shares this function with corresponding bodies in other federal systems, such as the United States Senate and the Swiss Council of States. The chief difference between these and the Bundesrat is that the former represent the people of the member units, while the latter represents the units as

such, that is, their respective governments and administrations. While the non-German second chambers consist of representatives elected by the people of the states, the German second chamber has always consisted of delegates *appointed* by the *governments* of the states and acting under their instructions. On the other hand, while non-German second chambers usually are based on the idea of equality of member states and therefore contain equal numbers of representatives from each, representation in the German second chamber has been weighted according to the size and strength of the member units, although not in exact proportion to their populations.

This has meant that politically the function of the Bundesrat has been less the parliamentary one of representing the people vis-à-vis the government than that of being another part of government, in charge of coordinating lawmaking with the execution of the laws. German administration is noted for its peculiar device of having the member states administer most federal laws. The persons representing member-state governments in the council (essentially a bureaucratic group consisting of high state officials or *Land* ministers) have traditionally considered it their chief responsibility to coordinate central legislation with state execution and to see that no essential state interests are infringed upon by such legislation. To be sure, with *Land* ministers now attending Bundesrat meetings themselves, party political issues often come to the fore, thus bringing political constellations in the various *Länder* to bear upon politics at the central level.

COMPOSITION

The old Bundesrat was devised to perpetuate Prussian hegemony. The Weimar Reichsrat was devised to lessen Prussian influence. In West Germany today the problem of weighting voting strength has been facilitated by the demise of Prussia. But the *Länder* are still vastly different in size and population. The largest population is 17 million (North Rhine-Westphalia) and the smallest less than 1 million (Bremen). Consequently, the constitution allows those with more than 6 million, five Bundesrat votes; those with over 2 million, four votes; and the others three each. There are altogether forty-one voting members (plus four nonvoting members from Berlin). Each *Land* may send as many delegates as it has votes, but it must cast its votes as a bloc. It is thus the individual (*Land*) cabinets that have to decide how, in a specific issue before the Bundesrat, the votes of a *Land* shall be cast. This may require a vote in the cabinet, especially if it is a coalition cabinet, and thus the policies of the Bundesrat are determined by which parties control the individual *Land* governments. In this way the party-political situation in the various *Länder* affects government on the central level. Frequently, however, the vote of Bundesrat members reflects the economic and financial situation of their *Länder* rather than their party or religious affiliations. Until 1966, with the CDU in control on the federal level, the Bundesrat, always counting a number of SPD-led governments among its members, was that branch of government where opposition policy sometimes had an important influence on national affairs. Under the "grand coalition" it had very little. Since 1969, the opposition CDU-CSU has its chance. In the main, however, it has been the instrument through which *Land* bureaucracies defend state rights as well as the interests of the administration they serve, and Bundesrat opposition or vetoes are generally encountered only when there is fear that the measures under consideration may prove onerous to the *Länder*, especially financially.

THE POWERS OF THE COUNCIL

Constitutionally, the powers of the Bundesrat lie chiefly in the field of lawmaking. As we have seen, it acts at an early stage of the legislative process when it scrutinizes a cabinet bill before the bill goes to the Bundestag. It becomes active a second time after completion of the process in the Bundestag. When a bill has been adopted there, the Council in principle has a suspensive veto. (If the Bundesrat votes its objections by a simple majority, it can be overridden by a majority vote of the Bundestag; if the vote is by a two-thirds majority, a two-thirds vote of the diet is required.) In many cases, however, especially in financial legislation, the Bundesrat has more than a suspensive veto; it has to give its consent and thus becomes an equal partner with the Bundestag. The same applies to constitutional amendments (a two-thirds vote is necessary in each body). In practice, about half of all bills have required consent. In most instances, conflict between the two chambers is avoided by the employment of a procedure modeled on the American conference committee. This joint committee (so-called Mediation Committee) is composed of eleven members from each chamber, with the Bundesrat members free from instructions; in over 90 percent of the cases it has been successful in smoothing out differences. Since it is the

Council, in this last stage of lawmaking, that can threaten to veto or to withhold its consent, it has generally succeeded in having its views prevail or at least its compromises adopted. Thus the freedom of action of the real parliamentary body, the diet, is once more restricted in favor of an essentially bureaucratic body. The other most important function of the Council is to issue ordinances or approve executive decrees (in twenty years there were close to four thousand of them).

Within the Council itself, the weight of influence has tended to shift from the politicians to the bureaucrats, for, while *Land* ministers attend the plenary sessions, permanent officials of the respective *Land* ministries (for example, financial or economic experts) attend those of the Bundesrat committees. The full session in practice ratifies committee recommendations; there is little chance of altering them, since the ministers, as delegates of their governments, are bound by the respective *Land* governments' instructions, and the instructions (to vote for or against) are based on committee recommendations. Often, too, there has been little time between bills received by the Council and voting.

On the whole, the Bundesrat has proved an important and effective part of the government. But its role is more technical than public. It has nothing to do with such political affairs as electing the chancellor or criticizing the executive, and even in legislating it deals chiefly with the more technical aspects of the procedure. Consequently, its prestige, though considerable among those active in or concerned with government, is not significant with the public at large; indeed, it is hardly known there.

CONCLUSION

Present West German democracy has not yet found the happy medium between, on the one hand, party dominance over both parliament and executive and, on the other, executive irresponsibility. Party bureaucracies try to rule supreme through the Bundestag, while administrative bureaucracy uses the cabinet and, within the legislature, the Bundesrat, as levers for its control. In the struggle between these forces the strong position of the chancellor both constitutionally and, at least in the Adenauer era, through the impact of his personality, has long favored the nonparliamentary forces. The resulting cabinet stability prevented the extreme of parliamentary control that was the bane of the French system. But it entailed the opposite danger of dooming parliament to impotence or subservience. The chief government party, the CDU, at times appeared a mere appendage of the executive. Parliament would exert itself energetically only under exceptional circumstances and after prodding by public concern (as during the *Spiegel* case in 1962). Under the "grand coalition" it languished even more. Now, with a rather shaky coalition in power, and the strongest party in opposition, eager to overthrow the government at the first occasion, passivity has yielded to the other extreme. There is a lot of vituperation and mutual, rather emotional, recriminations. But this may be a passing phase. Generally, parliament has suffered from low public visibility, due to the absence of genuine, spontaneous debate, the give-and-take between a majority and its opposition, public hearings in committees, and so forth. Rather than forming an arena where controversial issues and conflicting policies are debated and decided, the German parliament views itself as a collegiate body, where, frequently, a spirit of camaraderie among experts and professional politicians prevails (to the extent of addressing each other as "Herr Kollege"). No wonder, therefore, that the general public is still little informed and little interested in parliament (50 percent not knowing they have a district deputy in the Bundestag, for instance, and 83 percent never having heard of his activities; only 11 percent knowing what the Bundesrat is for; and so on). While functioning well as part of the government, smoothly performing tasks such as lawmaking, as a political body the West German parliament has still to come into its own.

5

West German executive and administration

1 CENTRAL GOVERNMENT

A well-conducted government must have a system as well knit as any system of philosophy; all measures taken must be well considered, and finances, policy, and the army must move together toward the same purpose which is the strengthening of the State and of its power. Now, a system cannot emanate except from one mind; therefore it must issue from that of the King. . . .

These words from Frederick the Great's "Political Testament" set the theme that runs through the history of German political institutions: the ideal of service to the state and the idea that government must be streamlined under strong executive leadership. Whether such leadership has been vested in kings or emperors, presidents with broad powers, a fascist Führer, or an authoritarian chancellor, and whether the source of its authority was found in divine grace or in real or alleged popular consent, matters less than the fact that Germans have traditionally expected their fate to be determined by executive leadership rather than by representatives answerable to the popular will. Leadership until 1918 was in the hands of dynasties assisted by hereditary nobles and members of an infeudated middle class. After World War I, an attempt was made to entrust the state to representatives of the people. But a large proportion of the people had no faith that party leaders could fill the exalted place

vacated by kings; they chose as leader a general who considered himself the place-holder for the monarchy. Instead of a new William, however, they got Hitler, tyranny, and defeat. Since the downfall of the Nazi system there has been more readiness to try democracy again, and progress has been made on that path.

In Germany, the ideal of centralized, coordinated leadership has been affected by two counterforces: first, the desire of various social groups and classes to make their influence felt and have their interests represented in the executive; and second, the federal organization of Germany. It is against this complex background that the problems of the executive in the West German government must be viewed.

THE PRESIDENT

The Bonn Constitution, as has been shown, facilitates the emergence of a strong executive. But in contrast to Weimar, it is no longer the presidency from which executive controls are likely to derive. The federal president, unlike the Weimar president, is elected not by the people but by a joint parliamentary body called Federal Assembly, consisting of the members of the Bundestag and an equal number of members elected by the *Land* diets, in accordance with the proportional strength of their parties. While he has the customary representative functions of a head of state, he has little influence over actual government. Unlike the Weimar president, he cannot dismiss cabinet or chancellor, and he has no emergency powers of his own. Such acts as are formally his (for instance, appointment of federal officials, exercise of the right of pardon) must be countersigned by the chancellor or the respective minister. This applies to control of the armed forces as well. His one important power is the designation of a chancellor, but even here he can be overruled by the Bundestag. The question of whether he may *refuse* action proposed to him by the chancellor or the cabinet (for instance, appointment of a minister recommended by the chancellor) has so far not arisen. President Heuss, during his two five-year terms of office (1949–59), showed no tendency toward independent action. His successor, Heinrich Lübke (1959–69), occasionally showed inclinations toward more independence. For example, he claimed the right to pass on the prospective chancellor's candidates for posts in the cabinet when Erhard was to form his new government in 1965. The incumbent, Gustav Heinemann, has claimed the right to pass on the constitutionality of laws before promulgating them. He has also raised his voice in such "nonpartisan" concerns as environment protection or peace research, in a broadly progressive and humanitarian sense. But none of this has created something like the Weimar dichotomy of power at the top. The president is overshadowed by the chancellor.

CHANCELLOR AND CABINET

The government consists of the federal chancellor and the federal ministers, but the chancellor is supposed to be its moving power. A changing relationship between chancellor and cabinet reflects the history of German constitutional developments. In the Empire, the chancellor was the only leader, and heads of departments had no part in the formulation of policy. Under Weimar, the chancellor was to be responsible for the general lines of policy, while each minister, within these lines, was to direct his department independently.

While the provisions of the Bonn Constitution on the relation of the chancellor to cabinet and ministers are generally similar to those under Weimar, two significant differences have enabled the chancellor to emerge as more powerful in practice. The "constructive vote of nonconfidence" means that once elected by a Bundestag majority, he is fairly safe from dismissal during the legislative period, unless he loses the backing of his own party, or the coalition forming his majority disintegrates (in 1966, both happened to Erhard at one and the same time), or there is defection of deputies to the opposition (something that has threatened the Brandt-Scheel government since 1970).

Secondly, he is free to form and reform his cabinet, over whose composition the Bundestag has no control. If he is also a strong personality, his office comes close to possessing the authority of the Hohenzollern chancellorship; the danger of autocracy in such a case is undeniable. Adenauer frequently ignored his ministerial colleagues in laying down policies or taking major political steps, denying them a chance to offer their advice and assuming major responsibilities himself, especially in fields where he was particularly interested, such as foreign affairs. Furthermore, he established the practice of dealing directly with top interest representatives, for instance, with the head of the German industrialists' organization or the leader of the farmers. He made his own office, the Chancellery, into a major top-level agency under his trusted and close adviser, Hans Globke. This has now become institutionalized.

Adenauer's successor, Erhard, had less of a "power instinct," and thus was troubled by certain factors that troubled Adenauer only little. In coalition governments ministers who do not belong to the chancellor's party are in practice protected from the threat of dismissal by the chancellor so long as their party backs them, which meant that Erhard's control over FDP members of his cabinet was limited; factions in the chancellor's own party may back ministers belonging to a faction against a chancellor whose personality is less forceful than was Adenauer's. Erhard's successor, Kiesinger, presiding over a coalition of almost equal party strength (represented in the cabinet in the relation of ten to nine), confronted an even more difficult task of leadership and coordination, while Brandt, now heading a cabinet with a strong preponderance of his party, has to pay much attention to his coalition partner exactly because of its weakness and the danger of its disintegration.

RESPONSIBILITY TO PARLIAMENT

A genuine parliamentary system, in the sense of enforceable responsibility of the executive to parliament, existed in Germany only as long as the Weimar Constitution functioned. At present, a semiparliamentary system can be said to exist. The constructive vote of nonconfidence required to force a chancellor out of office makes such an occurrence unlikely, although not impossible. Individual ministers can no longer be forced to resign; thus they are responsible to the chancellor, not to the Bundestag. Although the constitution is silent on this point, this has become an established practice. Thus, on occasion, ministers belonging to parties that withdrew from the government coalition were kept in office despite their parties' protests. While in practice ministers now are always members of parliament, this means very little if parliament has no control over them once they become ministers. Under these conditions, cabinet stability is not as much a problem as is responsible government in the British sense.

Paradoxically, the influence of parliament may come into play more forcefully at a time when a newly elected Bundestag has not even convened—that is, during the coalition negotiations for the formation of a new cabinet. These negotiations have sometimes been long protracted, with smaller parties trying to lay down conditions. The chancellor has also to consider the pressures from the different wings and groups within his own party. So long as there is no party in control of an absolute majority, there cannot be, as there so often is in Britain, a predetermined government. Once it took Adenauer sixty-five days to form a cabinet (the period between election day and final cabinet formation has ranged from that high to a low of only twenty-four days in the case of the Brandt government).

MINISTERS AND BUREAUCRACY

The loose relation between ministers and parliament has strengthened the association of the political executive and the permanent bureaucracy. Before 1918, the government was entirely a committee of the bureaucracy. Most ministers arrived at their posts through an official career; they were administrators, not politicians.

Since democracy took over in Germany, the minister has had the dual function of representing his party and of directing his branch of administration. The art of ruling in any parliamentary system requires combining these apparently contradictory functions. But in Germany the minister has tended to be either an official who concerns himself chiefly with administrative tasks or a politician paying attention to party and group interests to the neglect of administration. The habit of making ministries the political caretakers of particular clienteles has gained ground at Bonn. Thus departments such as agriculture have been "infiltrated" by special interest groups. As in other countries, ministers often are top members of the respective social or economic group. But the position of the ministerial bureaucracy is particularly strong in Germany.

A German minister is more closely surrounded with bureaucrats than his French or British colleague. There is no cabinet of the individual ministers as in France. Unlike his British colleagues, a minister may be without much parliamentary experience. Thus the danger of his coming under the influence of his assistants is a real one, the more so because the ministries are staffed entirely with permanent civil servants except for political undersecretaries (in Germany called secretaries of state). There are now two undersecretaries in each Bonn department: one is the traditional head of the particular ministry's administrative machine (under whom officials with the title of "ministerial director" preside over the different sections). He may thus be compared to the British permanent secretary but yet is a political appointee, serving at the pleasure of the minister; so is the second "state secretary," a kind of junior minister whose chief function is to maintain liaison between the ministry and parliament. But his office is a more recent invention, and his tasks are not yet very clearly defined.

Beneath this three-headed political peak, however, it is the permanent bureaucracy that is in control of administration. This includes a lot of decision-making. Since the staff of the ministries was established pretty much from scratch in 1949, it is still strongly CDU-conservative oriented, and the civil service tenure system does not allow for rapid turnover.

The minister himself often is little exposed to popular contacts and influences. He usually keeps within the narrow circle of his party's leadership and the representatives of the chief interest groups with which his department or party are concerned. Popular forces that are thus not represented are, for the most part, only dimly perceived from the heights where ministers dwell. Popular scrutiny and criticism— through debate and questioning in parliament, discussion in the press, press conferences, or similar devices that in the West have helped to ensure democratic control—have, at least so far, seldom been used to full effect.

ORGANIZATION OF MINISTRIES

Ministries in Germany have always been organized functionally—that is, according to spheres of government and administration. The number of ministries varies slightly according to political requirements at the time of cabinet formation or reformation. There may be an occasional minister without portfolio, or a ministry may be established in order to provide some coalition party or pressure group with a portfolio. In 1969, Brandt took the bold step of reducing them from nineteen to fourteen— this way eliminating some "unnecessary" ones. Usually, therefore, a ministry is in charge of a well-defined major field of government. This is more efficient than the somewhat untidy practice in Britain and the United States (independent agencies, boards, etc.). On the other hand, Germany's federal structure has rendered the distribution of functions between federal and *Land* ministries a problem. Some central ministries are nothing but agencies for the preparation of federal legislation, without administrative machinery and executive powers of their own, these being lodged with the different *Länder* and their ministries. For example, the justice and interior ministries under both Weimar and Bonn have functioned mainly on the *Land* level; and the respective central ministries, which exist side by side with the *Land* ministries, have been chiefly in charge of drafting legislation.

In the Anglo-Saxon countries the administration with its executive activities is concentrated chiefly in the capital. In Germany, the state is more diffused throughout the country. There is hardly a town without a number of federal and state administrative offices or authorities side by side with municipal agencies; the bureaucracy thus permeates society. This decentralization of the executive keeps the central ministry offices, whether federal or *Land*, small and compact. The authority of a ministry (sometimes federal, usually state) reaches down directly to its local agencies in the remotest parts of the country; there is rarely confusion of authority or jurisdiction. Even autonomous institutions under the jurisdiction of a ministry—for instance, the federal railroads—enjoy little real autonomy in matters of policy or appointments.

Each individual branch of administration is not only strictly organized; it has little relationship to any other. Departmentalization, as in France, characterizes German administration, and there is little interdepartmental coordination, such as that provided by the Treasury in Britain. Recently, however, more attention has been paid to coordination of ministries and, in particular, to the long-range planning of legislation on the cabinet level. For this purpose, the Chancellery, under the chancellor himself, is headed by an official of ministerial rank, entrusted with the necessary administrative functions and authority. (Since 1969, the active, energetic, and ambitious Brandt confidant, Horst Ehmke, has occupied this position. Ehmke has organized a planning staff, with "delegates" from each ministry, to work out agendas for legislation, established priorities for projects, and so forth. He has also introduced management techniques, such as a computerized information exchange system.)

A word should perhaps be said about public enterprises in Germany. Although the scope of general public activities has traditionally been broader than in other Western countries, much of this activity is handled on the local level. The recent central planning activities of Britain under the Labor government and of France since the war have been absent from West Germany for over twenty years; even the SPD-led Brandt government has so far not moved in that direction. Important state or federal enterprises, such as the Volkswagen works or Lufthansa, have even partly been made private (with some effort to have shares more widely distributed among low-income groups than is the case in most purely private corporations). The two main exceptions, of course, are the postal service and the railroads.

The German postal administration, as in Britain and France, also provides telegraph and telephone services, the technical part of radio broadcasting and television, and certain financial services, such as a savings institution. It used to be organized under its own ministry but has now been merged with the transportation department, functioning as a semiautonomous agency (on the pattern of the similar recent American reform).

German railroads have been public enterprises since Bismarck's time, when it was found advisable to build up the Prusso-German railroad system to facilitate rapid mobilization. The railroads were enterprises of the member states until Weimar, at which time they were consolidated under one Reich Transport Ministry, then the largest single transport enterprise in the world. Now, of course, they are divided into the West's Bundesbahn and the still so-called Reichsbahn of the East. The German railroads, like other European rail systems, have proved that it is possible to combine efficient, modernized service with economical management. Thus, in contrast to the United States, they provide opportunities for mass transportation that limit, at least in part, the ecologically negative effects of the automobile.

THE MILITARY

When West Germany was remilitarized in the middle fifties, it was done, paradoxically, more because of the insistence of those very powers which had fought two world wars to defeat German militarism than because of West German inclinations. It was the East-West split, the cold war, Korea, and the formation of two opposed military blocs that accounted for the turnabout. Germans, at least for the time being, had become pacific, if not antimilitarist and even neutralist. Adenauer, to be sure, welcomed remilitarization as a means to reestablish Germany's prestige and status in world affairs. But many, and by no means only leftists, were fearful lest it meant revival of militarism and the reemergence of a military caste influential in the state again. This is why many advocated voluntary enlistment or the organization of the armed forces in the form of a militia on the Swiss pattern. Nothing came of this. However, care was taken to ensure that the "Prussian" military spirit was not revived and that civil control over the armed forces (Bundeswehr) was safeguarded.

The result, so far, has been positive, although with some qualifications. When the new officer corps was selected, a genuine effort was made to eliminate those who had closely collaborated with the Nazi regime. But most professional soldiers, and especially generals, are drawn from the top strata of society (although no longer preponderantly from the former nobility). So far the military has not become a separate caste again but is part of the overall German elite. Concern with civilian control of the military is reflected in the cautious manner in which the controls are distributed among various authorities: the president (certain appointive powers); the chancellor (command in case of war); the Defense Minister (command in peacetime); and the "ombudsman," the parliamentary Defense Commissioner, who deals with individual complaints by members of the armed forces.

While the system is based on conscription (eighteen months to be lowered to fifteen), the constitution guarantees the right of conscientious objectors to refuse military service and serve instead in civilian social-service projects. The right has been broadly defined in practice, and the number of objectors has grown (from an earlier annual three thousand to over fourteen thousand in 1969, and over twenty thousand in 1970, or 2 percent of the draftees); objection is possible also while being in service, and not only for "dogmatic" pacifists who object to all wars. One-third of the objectors are students (who constitute only 10 percent of overall draftees), reflecting student radicalism. But more than radicalism is reflected in the growing number of objectors. From the outset there has been a lack of enthusiasm for military service. There have been abuses, chiefly of recruits by noncommissioned officers, but a deeper reason lies in the general "pacification" of German society. It is not, or not yet, as often charged by the East, a society of "militarists and revanchists." The military has not regained the prestige it had in pre-World War II times. The armed forces have found it difficult, in competition with the civilian sector of the economy, to build up a professional officers staff—a far cry from the times when officers were at the pinnacle of society in terms of status and prestige. Officers are now considered—and most consider themselves—technicians, without the traditional *esprit de corps.*

Out of this has come a certain alienation between society at large and the armed forces. And this has led to resentment, especially among the professional soldiers. In part the resentment is based on low pay and poor working conditions, but in part it is also based on the realization that, in a nuclear age, the nonnuclear military establishment seems to be without a meaningful function. Dissatisfaction among the military, in turn, has been exploited by those, especially among older generals, who are still wedded to the authoritarian spirit of

discipline, unquestioning obedience, duties of soldiers without rights, and so forth. Among these groups there is particular resentment at the idea of the soldier as a "citizen in uniform" and of the propagation of this more democratic attitude through what is officially called "internal guidance" (*innere Fuehrung*), a kind of antiauthoritarian indoctrination. These groups have not refrained from voicing their views, and conflict has arisen from time to time. Interestingly, objections against the old-fashioned view have also come from younger officers. The official line has been forcefully stated by Defense Minister Helmut Schmidt in his White Paper on Defense, 1970, who said: "A democratic society sets up armed forces and assigns them their mission; it is not the mission of the forces to form or reform state and society. . . . Neither can the Bundeswehr be the custodian of a given image of history. The nation is the school of the army, and not vice versa." Against this a high general officer, since dismissed, called upon the "collective unconscious" to revere the flag as a symbol and be ready to die for it and indicted radical-individualistic tendencies of "anarchic youth." The issue is clearly joined. Figures (in 1969), according to which about 20 percent of the officers and other professionals in the armed forces incline toward the NPD, show conclusively that the spirit of authoritarianism is not yet dead. *Videant consules* lest polarization between military and radical youth ensue!

2   THE GERMAN CIVIL SERVICE

Asked for the most significant German contribution to modern government, a student of political institutions will probably answer: its civil service system. Asked to evaluate this contribution, however, the experts are likely to disagree. While some consider it a model for other countries, others hold it responsible in part for the authoritarian trend in Prussian and German affairs. There is some justification for both views. As a matter of fact, this German problem reflects a more general dilemma of modern government: whether it is possible

to combine efficiency with democracy. Election of officials and rotation in office are means to a democratic civil service, but they also may open the door to spoils and incompetence. Career officials selected according to merit and appointed by the executive may be efficient, but they may also become a caste impervious to popular control. The American civil service reflects, in the main, the merits and dangers of the first alternative; the German system reflects the merits and dangers of the second.

ORIGINS AND STRUCTURE

The German civil service system is centuries old. Frederick William I of Prussia first defined the status, and especially the duties, of Prussian officials. Examinations governed appointment to certain categories of office; and to train candidates, matching professorships were established at state universities. Lower positions in the service were generally filled with ex-soldiers. This system, while regulating recruitment and duties, lacked well-defined rights. These were subsequently incorporated into the sum total of rules and regulations that became known as the "well-established rights" of civil servants. They include guarantee of life tenure, salary, and pension rights, and the privilege of suing the state in the ordinary courts in case of financial claims. The Prussian model was imitated by the other German states, so that there was uniform practice. The Weimar Constitution put all these rights and privileges under constitutional protection. Since the Nazi interlude—which politicized the system but did not abolish it—Bonn reaffirmed the traditional system after attempts by the occupation powers to democratize it had failed.

Recruitment

As frequently happens in the history of social institutions, the Prusso-German civil service system has been improved upon by other countries that started by using it as their model, while in Germany itself the system kept its less progressive character. The recruitment of personnel, for example, has always been based on expert training and, to that extent, on merit, but it has also largely remained a caste system under which only the few had access to the service, particularly to its higher ranks. Recruitment has been geared to the educational system. Graduation from certain schools has been the chief requirement for admission to examinations, and since higher education in Germany has remained largely a class affair, selection for the higher service has been largely restricted to the sons of the upper classes.[1]

Admission to the higher ranks has been tied to particularly demanding qualifications. The traditional entrance requirement has been graduation from law school. Following an examination based on these studies, the prospective official has to undergo several years of in-service training. A successful second examination makes him eligible for appointment to the higher level of the service. It can easily be seen that only a lifetime career warrants such extended preparation; that only comparatively wealthy parents can give their children the opportunity; and that, once secured, a position will be anxiously guarded against competition from outside or from the lower ranks.

The service thus became a closed caste, with a large proportion of officials being sons of officials themselves. Advancement from one level to another usually required one generation, with the middle-rank officials trying, at great personal sacrifice, to give one son the education entitling him to enter the higher ranks. Social mobility thus has largely been confined to the caste itself. And while the original appointment is generally free from such considerations as religion or party affiliation, promotion, especially to the highest positions, is frequently based on such factors. Personal pull is also important. It has always been useful to know the right people, to belong to the right student corps, to have the right political and religious affiliation.

Status of officials

In return for a long and expensive training, the service has provided the German official

[1] The higher service in Germany may be compared to the administrative class of the British service, but the number of higher officials in Germany is much greater, amounting to about 10 percent of the total number of officials. In 1970, this total of West German officials (federal, state, and local) was about 1.4 million (out of a grand total of *all* public employees: civil servants, white-collar employees, and workers, of about 3 million, breaking down into 44 percent civil servants, 26 percent employees, and 30 percent workers). The number of federal public servants (including about 170,000 civilian employees of the armed forces but *not* those working in the railroad and postal services) amounted to some 300,000, that of state employees to about 1 million, that of the municipalities (including their wholly owned enterprises) to about 800,000, and that of railroad and postal employees to about 850,000. These numbers include many categories of public servants (especially of officials) who in other countries, such as the United States, would not be included (e.g., members of the judiciary or teachers of all levels).

with security and status. While salaries have always been relatively modest, they have been balanced by economic as well as social privileges. The official has lifetime tenure. This above all distinguishes him from the numerous employees and workers in the public services. He cannot be dismissed except for cause, and even then only by a judicial verdict in a special court, whose members are his peers. There is thus full guarantee against arbitrariness. A politically objectionable official, for instance, would not be promoted; he might be transferred to another office at equal rank and salary, but he could not be dismissed even if he affiliated with a party hostile to the state. Persons hostile to the state hardly ever infiltrated the service in monarchical times, but there were occasional Communists and, more frequently, National Socialists in Weimar times. So long as an official did not violate his official duties for political aims, he might belong to any party. Under Bonn, however, membership in certain organizations (most of them Communist) has been made incompatible with official status.

In addition to salary and life tenure, civil service privileges include an elaborate system of pensions. The official, usually retired at the age of sixty-five, receives a generous retirement pension, and there are pensions for surviving dependents. He is retired on pension in case of invalidism and is entitled to leave with pay during temporary illness. His salary is increased if he has dependent children. Since the service in Germany comprises such large groups as teachers and postal and railroad officials, a large proportion of the German people thus have security from the cradle to beyond the grave; on the other hand, since the official loses his pension rights if he resigns, the system ties him to his office and makes it easier for a determined regime (such as the Nazis' was) to compel political conformity.

As highly cherished as material benefits are benefits having to do with status and prestige. There is an elaborate system of ranks and titles with which the service is endowed. Minute and, to a foreigner, often petty distinctions and refinements form the basis not only of job classifications but of the social standing of the official, his family, and the entire caste. Thus titles may never be omitted in talking to an official—not only when a nonofficial addresses

an official, but even among the officials themselves. It is never, as in the United States, "Ed" and "Joe," not even, as in Britain or France, "Mister" or "Monsieur," but "Herr Rat" (councilor), or "Herr Oberfinanzsekretär." The civil servant's title is customarily extended to his wife ("Frau Rat" means that not the lady but her husband is a councilor) and is never omitted from his obituary. Such titles are imitated in occupations outside the bureaucracy (for instance in the professions, or among employees of larger private enterprises); titles and the prestige they involve still form the backbone of German social stratification.

Political and professional rights

With regard to the professional and political rights and activities of civil servants, the German system is about midway between the severely limited Anglo-American type, and the unlimited French. But to judge the implications of this statement, one has to keep in mind the caste character and conservative-authoritarian background of the German service. Thus the right of professional association in Germany would not usually mean formation of groups affiliated with other workers' organizations and, together with them, opposed to the state as employer. Although since 1918 German officials have been free to join any professional association, only in the public enterprises (chiefly the postal and railroad services) have a majority affiliated with the general trade unions. Most other officials have avoided affiliation with ordinary workers and employees and have formed separate interest organizations of their own. In contrast to many groups of French officialdom (for example, teachers), even lower-rank officials in Germany have no feeling of solidarity with workers and insist on their special status. Their associations, in particular the powerful and influential *Deutscher Beamtenbund* (DBB), lobby against any infraction of the traditional privileges of their members and have been chiefly instrumental in preventing postwar reforms.[2]

[2] While the DBB has about seven hundred and fifty thousand members, the trade union for workers employed in public service has fewer than one hundred thousand officials among its close to one million members. In the postal and railroad services, however, most officials are organized

In relations between agencies as employers and officials as employees, the right to strike has rarely been claimed and never been conceded. Until recently, Germans had nothing comparable to the British Whitley Councils; individual grievances were brought before the respective superior officer, to be handled under set regulations. A law for Personnel Representation now provides for personnel committees elected separately by officials, employees, and workers in the various agencies, which take part in the issuance of service regulations, the handling of individual grievances, and in certain cases matters of appointments and promotions, a step toward a less rigid and more humanely organized civil service.

Although the German official is likely to profess that he is above parties, he may belong to one and engage in political activities. The British and American occupiers of West Germany, with their own ideal of an apolitical civil service, tried to impose on Germans a system under which an official would not be permitted to engage in political activities and would resign when running for elective office. Germans disregarded the policy from the beginning, and, as we have seen, officials "on leave" abound in West German parliaments.

GERMANY AND OTHER SYSTEMS COMPARED

The difference between the German and a Western civil service system may be illustrated by contrasting the German official with his American counterpart, the government employee.[3] The American comes and goes; the German is there for life. He is not likely to be on loan from some business firm or other agency, or a "dollar-a-year man," or a consultant. An American agency chief has to spend half his time justifying the agency to the public and to appropriations committees; German agencies labor (or thrive) under the opposite

shortcoming of being practically unabolishable, and some continue long after their real functions have vanished. Most American offices function under the glaring, although intermittent and erratic, light of publicity and investigation; German offices are protected from political interruptions but also from healthful criticism. The American government worker's job and salary are always under the threat of the congressional "meat-ax"; the German's are more secure than any business executive's. The American works at his government job as at any other job, loyally but without special devotion; the German feels that his service is an honor involving special duties and an allegiance originally owed to the king and now to that mystical higher entity, the state.

The German civil service has often been called too authoritarian. But every bureaucracy in a modern state must be based on the hierarchical organization and discipline that guarantee the efficient carrying out of directives from the top level. The advantages of such a civil service have been a sense of duty, industriousness, and, by and large, expert knowledge and probity. But authoritarianism and bureaucratism have been equally present. Sense of duty has meant unquestioned loyalty to a central authority that could do no wrong. The service has been impartial to individuals but less so in regard to classes. Officialdom has consciously or unconsciously favored the upper classes from which most of its members have been drawn.

And in regard to the public at large, it has been haughty and supercilious. Morally, the tradition of unquestioning fulfillment of duties in the service of the state proved calamitous. While such an attitude may be a virtue in countries with stable and largely uncontested value systems (such as Britain and the United States), on the Continent, where no such common value standards exist, it implies either hidden partiality for one group and one philosophy or a readiness to serve with equal zeal any master whatever. It may then entail lending one's services to the execution of any, even the most atrocious, policy. Thus the service could be relied upon to put into practice with equal efficiency a lofty program of social welfare and a program of exterminating Jews. It has been authoritarian when left alone; resistant when

together with those of employee and worker status in the respective trade unions. Altogether there are about six hundred thousand officials in the DGB-affiliated trade unions.

[3] The following constitutes what Max Weber has called "ideal types," polar opposites, which practice merely approximates. Especially in the United States, the newer trend, of course, is toward a career service.

under democratic direction; and conformist when under the direction of a forceful though untraditional ruling group such as the Nazis.

As a bureaucracy the Prusso-German official-dom has lacked initiative and a sense of individual responsibility. Their predominantly legal training, in particular, produced officials "more useful in a static than a dynamic state; excellent interpreters of the past but not inventors of the ways and means of the future; more apt to explain than to evaluate; and inflexible in the power to make exceptions." [4] Their training became too bookish and too long, their career too specialized, their attitude too compartmentalized. It was to such office, and not, as in England, to politics and parliament, that the German elite was attracted. It was natural that a more authoritarian-minded and less independent and self-reliant type of man prevailed.

THE PRESENT CIVIL SERVICE

In 1945, the problem was twofold: first, what to do about those—probably a minority—who had penetrated the service as active and convinced Nazis; and second, how to "democratize" German bureaucracy in the more general sense.

Reform suggestions

The failure of denazification proved a great handicap to civil service reform. Since the denazified former officials could reclaim their positions by right, a considerable number of "unreconstructed" Nazis regained even sensitive positions. While this in itself was disturbing, an even longer-range effect was that a chance to make large numbers of positions available to more democratically minded officeholders was missed. The occupation authorities tried hard but futilely to convince Germans of the merit of measures designed to provide broader and more equal access to the service; to break down the traditional monopoly of the academically—and especially legally—trained officials who alone have access to the higher service; and to stimulate a spirit of independence and

[4] Herman Finer, *Theory and Practice of Modern Government,* rev. ed. (New York, Holt, 1949), p. 802.

initiative within the service as well as among Germans in general in their dealings with, and attitudes toward, authorities. In particular they suggested open competitions for vacancies; legal training to be required only for positions of strictly juristic character; special examinations to enable nonacademically trained lower officials to be promoted to the higher service; more persons with outside experience to be called into the service; and similar measures.

Failure of the reform program

The fate of these suggestions illustrates the difficulty of transplanting institutions from one country to another with fundamentally dissimilar traditions. The Germans simply procrastinated until the powers of the occupation authorities lapsed and then enacted legislation continuing, in the main, the traditional system with all its "established rights." Thus, while personnel committees have been established, they have been used to see to it that no outsiders are called into the service. Competition for vacancies means little, because of the strict qualifications that are required; the monopoly of the legally trained, in particular, is generally continued. From all this one may infer that Germans, as they see it, are disinclined to sacrifice efficiency for democratization. The problem is whether it is possible to *combine* efficiency and training with democratization. Civil service reform in Germany will have no real chance as long as higher training and education, which alone open the path to higher positions in the service, remain the monopoly of the upper classes. But educational reform, as we have seen, is still in a very early stage.

The new "functionary" type of official

In one respect, despite the restoration of the traditional bureaucracy, present West German officialdom significantly differs from the older pattern. The old-fashioned "Prussian" official with his conservative system of values and ideals has, in the main, disappeared. The typical German official no longer identifies himself with *any* philosophy, conservative or otherwise. He tends to be neither prodemocratic nor (on the average) neo-Nazi; he is not pro-

or neo- anything, but merely serves whoever happens to be in charge. He usually belongs to a party, since this promotes his career; he certainly belongs to a church. But all this takes place without real commitment. Thus, from a genuine estate with a *Weltanschauung* to defend against hostile parties and parliaments, German officialdom has turned into a group of functionaries. Sober and unromantic, the new official is primarily interested in his and his caste's security; warned by Nazi and post-Nazi experience, he avoids taking risks. He does as directed and shuns responsibilities. Thus he appears moderate. He rejects adventurism in foreign affairs and, by and large, backs the Bonn Constitution as well as the Bonn regime—which, after all, has put him into office, has reestablished the authority and the rights of his caste and has generally, so far, ensured peace and prosperity. In this way one obstacle that handicapped Weimar democracy—political opposition of the civil service—has been eliminated at Bonn. The trouble is that this very fact implies the permeation of Bonn democracy with bureaucratic authoritarianism. The present alliance of the Bonn Constitution with the Bonn bureaucracy has rendered Bonn bureaucratic rather than the bureaucracy democratic.

RECENT REFORM PROPOSALS

This picture may have to be revised in the future. In recent years there has been slight movement toward a thorough reform of public administration. Discussion of what to do about the traditional civil service system has by now reached the level of the officials' associations, of the legal profession, and even of government itself. More radical reformers, seeing no basic difference in the services performed by *Beamte* and nonofficial public employees, suggest wiping out the special status of the former in favor of one overall public service. Officials' income and salary rights should be regulated by labor contract through collective bargaining with the authorities as employers, like those of workers and employees in general. In many areas, especially where their functions are not basically different from those performed by workers in private sectors, officials should have the right to strike. There should be access to promotion from one level to another so that career advancement no longer depends on educational qualifications only but primarily on performance in office, thus ensuring that the entire service would be "permeable" to talent from below and outside. Titles should be simplified into mere descriptions of office and function, tenure should be granted only after lengthy periods of probation, and there should be codetermination on all levels and especially in the public economic enterprises. In short, the relation between public servant and the state should be that of jobholder to employer rather than the somewhat mystical "fealty" relationship traditionally invoked for the "servant of the state."

Such a transformation would be in accordance with the trends toward a modernized society. After all, what used to be special prerogatives of German officialdom—job security, pension rights, and so forth—are now being granted to the ordinary worker and employee in private enterprise, so that, with the exception of the special aura of "authority" surrounding the official, the two categories are drawing closer to each other anyway. Setting up an overall service would probably mean making *Beamte* of nonofficials rather than "pulling down" officials to nonofficial status. However, resistance on the part of many officials and of their prime organization, the DBB, has so far been strong, and the future of the reform proposals is doubtful.

3 STATE GOVERNMENT AND PROBLEMS OF FEDERALISM

France has been called "a republic at the top but an empire at the base." Germany, one might say, has been an empire at the top, with some democracy at the base. The German tendency toward an authoritarian centralism has been tempered by dispersion of power and some self-government in regions and local units. It is true that authoritarianism may prevail—and in Germany has prevailed—in small units of government as in large ones. It was one of the errors of the Potsdam program to assume that decentralization by itself would cause democratization. In Germany, regional (state) units often were strongholds of reaction, while more progressive movements and policies were frequently national.[5] Yet whatever tradition of democratic self-government there was in Germany developed in local units (cities) at a time when most other government was authoritarian.

It must be understood that German regional and local units are not only self-governing but also agents for higher authority. A mayor, for instance, is both a local and a state official, and in the relation between central and state government there has been a similar connection, with *Land* agencies in charge of executing uniform central laws. This meant that the central government had to have powers to supervise the execution of its laws by the states and has even meant granting the federal government enforcement powers against the states. To an American who thinks of states as sovereign, such a system will seem a far cry from genuine federalism. Still, there is a good deal to distinguish it from outright centralism, such as that enforced on the *Länder* (and lower units) during the Nazi period.

TERRITORIAL STRUCTURE

While the long history of German disunity produced that reactionary particularism under which vested regional interests, such as state bureaucracies, clung to their own interests and prerogatives, it has also meant an attractive variety of cultural life. Instead of one Paris or London, Germany has had a multitude of regional centers. To this cultural variety the German is sincerely attached. Something, he feels, would be lost if it should give way to the uniformity so predominant in modern civilization.

But while regionalism in Germany has had a real basis in popular sentiment, by the nineteenth century actual political units had largely

ceased to coincide with cultural and traditional regions. Prussia, in particular, constituted the major obstacle to a sounder regional organization of Germany. With the elimination of Prussia, the postwar structure of Germany might have become a rational one if the newly established *Länder* had not had to follow the boundaries of the occupation zones. These boundaries were carved out of German territory with supreme disregard for traditional regions and boundaries. Thus the *Länder*, with the exception of Bavaria, at first commanded little genuine attachment, and there was a strong movement toward reorganization. Following the consolidation of three *Länder* in the southwest, however, opposition subsided, and the "cake of custom" by now has endowed the ten-*Länder* structure with some kind of general recognition.[6] But the problem of their economic viability has not allowed reform wishes and plans for reorganization to die down. After the accession to power of the Brandt government, a committee of experts was established to work on proposals such as the reorganization of the present ten-*Länder* structure into five units. The *Länder* would be more equal in population and economic strength and better able to resist "federal encroachments" that now threaten the smaller, less viable states in particular. This reorganization would leave the three largest *Länder*, North Rhine-Westphalia, Bavaria, and Baden-

---

[5] In the following the term *regional* refers to that of state government, that is, the government of the *Länder*.

[6] Of the previously existing *Länder*, only Bavaria and the two city-states of Hamburg and Bremen coincide with present units. The former Prussian provinces were made *Länder*. These include Schleswig-Holstein, which also includes the former city-state Lübeck; Lower Saxony, made up of the old province of Hanover plus the former *Länder* of Braunschweig, Oldenburg, and Schaumburg-Lippe; North Rhine-Westphalia, formed out of the former province of Westphalia and the northern, industrially most important part of the former Rhine Province, as well as the former *Land* Lippe; and Hesse, comprising the former province Hesse-Nassau and most of the former *Land* Hesse. The remaining units are entirely new: Rhine-Palatinate, a merger of the southern portion of the former Rhine Province with some portions of Hesse and with the former Bavarian Palatinate; and Baden-Württemberg, the product of territorial reform, composed of the two old states Baden and Württemberg which, after 1945, were split into three units and, following two plebiscites in the area, consolidated into the present *Land* in 1951. In 1970, this consolidation was once more confirmed by a plebiscite held in former *Land* Baden. To these nine, the Saar was added as the tenth *Land* in 1957. West Berlin, often referred to as an eleventh *Land*, is in a special position (see Chapter 8). For a map, see p. 346.

Württemberg intact, while consolidating Lower Saxony with the two city-states of Hamburg and Bremen into one "northwest state," and Hesse, Rhine-Palatinate, and the Saar into a "middle-Rhine state." It is doubtful whether much will come of such plans in the foreseeable future. Much can be said for the reorganization from the viewpoint of economic rationality. But while regionalism in general has declined (with parties, pressure groups, industrial establishments, all at least nation-wide —if not extending to even larger areas such as all of Western Europe), it is also true that the entrenched power and the vested interests of the existing units (their governments, bureaucracies, etc.) will offer strong opposition. Even political parties, or their subdivisions, are opposed wherever reorganization would disturb existing party patterns or endanger existing party controls (such as the SPD's control in Hesse or in the city-states, and the CDU's control in Rhine-Palatinate).

STATES' RIGHTS AND POWERS

It is not only the territorial structure of the *Länder* that is problematic. The distribution of powers between central and regional governments is also uncertain and has indeed been one of the major problems of German federalism. In the Hohenzollern Empire, power still lay mostly with the member states. In the Weimar Republic there was a strong trend toward centralization, carried to the extreme of totalitarian centralism by the Nazis. After the downfall of Nazism there was, understandably enough, a particularist reaction, which led to a postwar policy in favor of states' rights. But economic and political forces proved stronger than wishes and theories. In Germany as in every modern society fundamental economic and social problems tend to become national problems calling for solution on a nation-wide basis—particularly where, as in Germany, parties, trade unions, industrial associations, and similar groups are national rather than regional, and where the aftereffects of two world wars required a pooling of national strength.

The Bonn Constitution, to be sure, gives the *Länder* strong powers of legislation (as long as the federal government does not exercise its concurrent jurisdiction) and administration in many fields, such as interior and police, justice, and education. But the *Länder* have so far made little use of their power to legislate; the federal level has preempted most fields. Even in the field of education, supposedly left to the *Länder*, there has been, as we have seen (Chapter 1, Section 3), increasing coordination on the national level, and Bonn has obtained additional constitutional rights there. But the crucial problem has been that of the financial viability of the *Länder* (and, increasingly, the local units for which they are responsible). The Bonn Constitution sought to guarantee the *Länder* a strong position in that respect. Income and corporation taxes, for instance, were in principle reserved to them. But the federal government, having assumed the large expenses arising from war, occupation, and rearmament, began to claim an ever larger "federal portion." And the industrially weaker states, in particular, suffered from insufficient tax receipts. Thus in 1969, still under the "grand coalition," new legislation provided for a system under which the national government and *Länder* share income and corporation taxes equally, with the *Länder* giving up their previously larger share while getting part of the lucrative turnover tax hitherto reserved to the federal government. There is also provision for a more equitable share by the "poorer" *Länder*, so that the previous system, under which they were subsidized by the wealthy *Länder*, could be dropped. On the whole, this constitutes an attempt at "cooperative federalism," which, if it succeeds in substituting partnership of the different levels of government for traditional rivalry, may well give a new lease on life to the West German federal structure.

LAND ORGANIZATION AND POLITICS

The *Länder* in West Germany have more control over their internal organization than they had under Weimar. They are free to adopt their own election systems, and their constitutions vary somewhat, especially in regard to the relation between parliament and executive. The *Land* executive usually includes such departments as Interior, Justice, Finance, Economics, Agriculture, Education and Culture, Labor and Welfare. Generally speaking, the federal ministries are mainly concerned with the preparation of laws,[7] and the corresponding state ministries with their administration and execution.

To some degree, politics in the *Länder* revolves around national issues. Indeed, there is a kind of built-in nationalization of *Land* politics because of the impact *Land* elections and the ensuing formation of *Land* cabinets have on the composition of the Bundesrat. A further characteristic of politics in the *Länder* has been the unpredictability of cabinet formation after an election has taken place with, in practice, all possible combinations: CDU and FDP, SPD and FDP, and "grand coalition" of CDU and SPD. In recent years, however, there have been fewer and fewer "grand coalitions" and CDU-FDP combinations, in favor of one-party governments. This reflects the trend toward a two-party system on the state level.

"Nationalization" of *Land* politics stands in contrast to the dwindling political functions of *Land* diets and cabinets. There is less actual lawmaking going on in the *Länder*. The chief legislative function of the *Land* diets is to enact the budget. But even here, most of the expenditures are fixed, with up to 50 percent being spent for personnel (since the main burden of administration proper is still with the *Länder*), and only about 10 percent remaining for discretionary purposes. Thus, in the face of quite different intentions, Bonn federalism has left the *Länder* with not much more than administrative-executive functions. There remains some autonomy, and thus variety, in educational, cultural, religious, and similar fields. But even here, in a growing number of increasingly important matters the *Länder*—sometimes jointly with federal agencies—have set up boards or similar organs for cooperation and coordination.

The dwindling political functions of the *Land* diets are reflected in a generally lower voting participation (75 to 80 percent as compared with 85 percent or over in federal elections) and in the lesser interest (and, consequently, representation) shown in them by industrialists or functionaries of industrialists' organizations or of trade unions. Instead, there are more "small people" in the *Land* diets and, above all, more officials. Among the latter, a large number represent counties or cities, thus indicating the stake local government has in state politics.

4   PROBLEMS OF LOCAL GOVERNMENT

German local, especially city, government has generally been both popular and efficient. But it has not escaped the centralist tendencies and, more recently, the social and ecological problems that complicate the tasks of self-government in other modern countries.

UNITS OF LOCAL GOVERNMENT

German local government, like the British and unlike the uniform French, is a bewildering maze. The basic local government unit is the *Kreis* (county—literally "circle"). Larger cities (without, however, any strict delimitation) are known as city counties, which means that, there, county and municipal governments coincide. Rural and small-town areas are rural counties, traditionally headed by an official called *Landrat*. This may be compared to the British distinction between county boroughs and administrative counties. But the average German rural counties are smaller than the British administrative counties, not to mention the large American counties. This makes it more difficult for them to discharge tasks requiring large-scale planning and financing. In Germany, therefore, many such functions are entrusted to special authorities of the state, which, under the supervision of ministries and separate from county administration proper,

---

[7] Separate federal administrations, in the main, are limited to foreign affairs and defense (plus the more autonomous postal and railroad administrations).

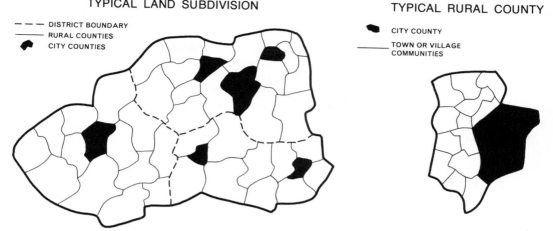

TYPICAL LAND SUBDIVISION

- – – – DISTRICT BOUNDARY
- ——— RURAL COUNTIES
- ⬛ CITY COUNTIES

TYPICAL RURAL COUNTY

- ⬛ CITY COUNTY
- ——— TOWN OR VILLAGE COMMUNITIES

function in the counties. In addition, there are town and village communities within the rural counties and between the county and state level (but only in the larger *Länder*) districts (*Regierungsbezirke*), which, however, are not units for self-government.

DEVELOPMENT OF LOCAL SELF-GOVERNMENT

It is in the individual municipalities, and especially in the cities, that the idea and practice of self-government took root in Germany. At the beginning of the nineteenth century Germany's liberal nobleman, Freiherr von Stein, remembering the medieval freedoms of German cities, hoped through urban self-government to teach the rising German middle classes to govern themselves in what he hoped would be a democratic nation of their own. This hope was not fulfilled nationally, but in the cities self-government began to flourish while state government was still authoritarian.

Municipal self-government was representative and autonomous, but only within certain limits. Representative institutions, until 1918, meant, not democratic government, but government by city patricians. This did give them administrative experience, however, which they could pass on to the lower classes when municipal government became genuinely democratic. The overlapping of state and local authority is also a part of this picture. Police affairs, for in-

stance, were handled by local authorities, such as mayors, in the name of the state, and the state generally reserved the right to confirm appointments. Consequently there developed a system of collaboration between officials and citizens beneficial to both. Officials taught expertness and stability and learned how to conduct themselves as responsible civil servants. Citizens learned the business of self-government in the numerous administrative committees established to help administer schools, hospitals, and other civic affairs. The state, while not having a right of direction, reserved powers of supervision which, however, were used sparingly.

Within this general pattern, there developed a great variety of local government systems under different types of charters. Somewhat as in the United States, and in contrast to the uniform systems of Britain and France, the states (and sometimes individual regions within states) developed their distinct patterns. Common to all of them, however, has been the close relationship between an elected council and the mayor (or mayor plus executive associates, a body called *Magistrat*). This system taught the heads of local administration to blend political responsibility with executive power—something not heretofore learned by Germans on the state or national level. This feature of German local government distinguished it from the British system with its all-powerful council and its unpolitical executive staff, the French system with its party-political, short-

Authorities and Lines of Local Government Supervision

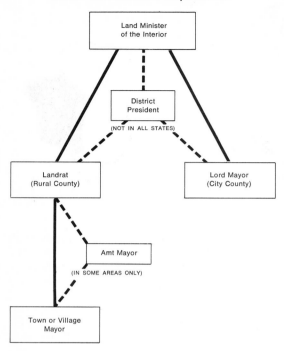

time mayor, and the American system with its separation-of-powers structure, its popularly elected mayors, its party patronage. In Germany the mayor was usually elected by the council but for a term exceeding that of the council (usually twelve years) and, although party affiliation played a role, from among trained and qualified experts. He was actually a professional civil servant, and with his long-term appointment was in a position to build up a staff of professional municipal officials to assist him.

POSTWAR CHANGES

There was no reason why after 1945 German local government could not have been rebuilt on the traditional pattern, but the Allies insisted on reforming it on the pattern of their own institutions. The questionable nature of such experiments is illustrated by what happened when the British introduced their system into their zone. They vested all power in a democratically elected council with its chair-

man as a mayor, and they conferred executive functions on a staff of apolitical civil servants headed by a director subordinated to the council. This was meant to revive grassroots democracy and to curb executive tyranny. But the resulting split between a largely ceremonial short-term mayor, as head of the council, and a long-term director, as chief of the administration, merely confused the Germans. In practice, they have converted the new system into their traditional one, with the director now almost indistinguishable from the previous mayor.

In the other former occupation zones preoccupation systems have generally been restored. Yet, as an overall result, there are now over a dozen different systems of local government, a diversity that even Germans consider excessive.

LOCAL ACTIVITIES

An American might marvel not only at the degree of municipal autonomy (considering that New York City, for example, cannot rearrange working hours of its police without a vote from Albany), but also at the wide range of activities in which German cities have for a long time engaged: economic and welfare services, public utilities, streetcars and buses, harbors, markets, slaughterhouses, pawnshops, swimming pools, parks, hospitals, housing developments, libraries, municipal theaters and opera houses, orchestras and concert halls, museums and art galleries, art schools, and sometimes universities. The few permanent opera houses in the United States find themselves in perpetual financial straits; performances of *Die Meistersinger* and *The Magic Flute* were given in the ruins of German cities in the winter of 1945–46. There are now over a hundred and fifty publicly owned and run theaters in some seventy West German cities, employing some twenty thousand persons. Many German municipalities have pioneered in city planning and public housing, and their record of rebuilding after 1945 was splendid. It is true that there were occasional scandals, but spoils and graft were generally small compared to that in many American cities.

More serious has been a tendency of the

state (federal or *Land* government) to burden the municipalities with so many mandatory tasks that less and less remains to local initiative. Such fields as welfare and housing have increasingly come under federal or state jurisdiction. With the increase in mandatory functions, cities have come more and more to rely on federal or state taxes turned over to them, or indeed on out-and-out subsidies. More recently, environmental problems (pollution, waste disposal, etc.) have added to their problems. Most larger cities are now controlled by the SPD, which, despite its generally conservative trend, has tried hard to cope with them in a socially progressive fashion. But increasing financial and other dependence on central authorities frustrates much of such effort, which, in turn, has led to rising demands (especially on the part of younger, more leftist city dwellers) for more "participatory democracy" on the part of the affected groups, or in the form of codetermination on the boards of the municipal enterprises.

Municipal enterprises in Germany are organized in a number of ways: directly under a municipal department; more frequently as a separate public institution with its own boards and budget; or as an ordinary corporation under municipal or public-private ownership. It has been local government, *in addition to* state government, that made Germany a welfare state; it has been local government *rather than* the state that has promoted public management of economic affairs in Germany. The cities have furnished most of the gas, water, and power supply for the German population, and most of the local transportation. In rural areas, the counties have engaged in similar activities. Receipts from municipal enterprises constitute one of the most important sources of income for local government.

Of late, with the urbanization of West Germany proceeding on what one may call an American pattern, and with some areas (particularly the Rhine-Ruhr region) resembling the megalopolitan American East or West Coast strips, problems of administrative-jurisdictional reform have come to the fore. Various plans in North Rhine-Westphalia envisage the abolition of many local, city, county, and district units and the establishment of entirely new, larger, and more effective entities. But political, bureaucratic, and other vested interests have so far prevented their realization. In other areas, similar to the United States (e.g., in the upper Rhine and Main industrial regions), such a reform would even have to involve consolidation across state boundaries. Eventually, something will have to be done by way of regional reform to cope with the ever more complex urban and ecological problems. Indeed, ecological problems (e.g., purification of the Rhine River and its tributaries) have become so large in scale that local or even regional units cannot tackle them alone. This is why the Brandt government has initiated a constitutional amendment procedure to give federal government powers to legislate in environmental matters (in addition, of course, international agreements will be necessary).

LOCAL OFFICIALDOM

Local officials resemble other public officials. They go through the same training and preparation for a career service, are divided into the same categories of higher, upper middle, middle, and lower, enjoy the same privileges and acquired rights, and are paid on comparable salary scales. They share with state officials status as a group apart from the general public, but the slightly freer atmosphere of local government makes them somewhat less authoritarian and exclusive. There is a good deal of interchange among civil servants of different local units. Since the individual units of local government have to select their staff from a restricted group, there is more genuine competition for jobs here than in the state service. Competitive hiring, to be sure, has frequently meant selection on the basis of political affiliation, religious denomination, and similar criteria, but these factors have not usually overridden knowledge and training. And the career status of most municipal employees has meant the absence, in the main, of that bane of American local government, patronage. Thus German local administration demonstrates one of the more attractive features of German government and politics.

6

West German
law and
administration
of justice

1 NATURE AND DEVELOPMENT OF THE GERMAN LEGAL SYSTEM

CHARACTER OF GERMAN LAW

In the Anglo-American tradition the two bulwarks of freedom against the authority of the state are parliament and the common law. On the Continent, however, law is less a bulwark than an expression of the will of the organized community or its ruling elite. At a time when English judges, armed with legal precedents and "right reason," protected the rights of the people from arbitrary authority, Continental jurists fashioned and codified the law as a body of rules for the ordered exercise of state authority over every subject. Judges and courts became a part of the state machinery thus established. In Germany, law is considered as state made, the court system as an integral part of the state organization, and judges, although enjoying independence, as state officials.

The German legal system thus resembles the French. First of all, it is code law, not case law. The statutory laws are supposed to provide a comprehensive source for the courts' findings. The German believes that it is one of the prerogatives of the state to regulate the citizen's activity through codified rules, and the prerogative of judges to see to it that these rules are correctly interpreted and applied. This attitude has produced an able but bureaucratic judiciary, controlling the public rather than protecting it

against state bureaucracy. This does not mean that law and administration of justice are felt to be arbitrary. The German feels secure and comfortable under rules that are elaborate enough to tell him how to act and behave. This is true above all for the class that presided over the drafting of the chief law codes. The independent small, middle, and even large businessman considers his civil law code (BGB), his commercial law code (HGB), and his code of civil procedures (ZPO) the "Magna Chartas" of his economic and civil rights. But, as in all class societies, these laws do not relieve social inequity. As Anatole France once remarked, "the law in its majesty forbids rich and poor equally to sleep under bridges." One might continue this thought and note that the law also forbids rich and poor equally to steal bread. Thus other codes, such as the more than one-hundred-year-old codes of criminal law (StGB) and criminal procedure (StPO), have in part been the embodiment of a repressive society. Only recently have long drawn-out efforts to liberalize them come closer to fruition.

EMERGENCE OF A UNIFIED
LEGAL SYSTEM

The history of German law reflects the country's political disunity. While Britain experienced early legal unification through precedents set by royal judges, and France, somewhat later, through uniform codes, German law remained splintered well into the period of the Hohenzollern Empire. It lacked uniformity although codes had been enacted in some principalities. Many regions had only the unwritten, so-called common law. This was basically Roman law as rediscovered in the late middle ages and subsequently adapted to modern conditions by practice and custom.

The reception of Roman law into Germany had served three purposes. It helped the rulers of the rising sovereign states to eliminate the remnants of feudal public powers. It made the feudal owner master of the estate and the peasant a mere tenant or laborer, thus destroying the medieval remnants of free peasantry. Finally, Roman law made the worker a mere party to a labor contract and thus destroyed traditional status relationships and the ensuing obligations of the employer. Roman law, in short, made the ruler sovereign, the Junker proprietor, and the employer master.

This law became the basis for nation-wide codification when the Reich was established in 1871 with federal power to legislate uniformly in fields such as civil and criminal law and procedure. Technically the resulting codes were so accomplished that even the Nazis, inveighing against their "alien" Roman features, did not see fit to abolish them. Revision of some of their harsher features after 1871 was accomplished only through enacting statutes for the regulation of special fields, such as labor law, rent law, the law relating to matters of taxation or to social insurance, and so forth. While in the DDR the old system is being abolished or revamped completely, basic reform in West Germany has begun only recently.

2 GERMAN COURTS

Despite its federal structure West Germany does not have two parallel sets of courts, as has the United States with its federal and state systems. It has a single integrated system, with state courts on the lower levels and federal at the top. Although most courts thus belong to different member states, the system is rather uniform, because courts and procedures (like the bulk of applicable substantive law) are regulated by federal codes. Judgments and legal instruments are recognized and executable throughout the nation. There are, for instance, no stricter and easier divorce laws in one part of Germany than in another, no problem of nonrecognition of divorce decrees, and no need to extradite fugitives from one state to another.

SPECIAL COURTS

On the other hand, German regular courts do not have the overall jurisdiction entrusted to courts in Britain and the United States. They rule in civil and criminal cases, while several sets of special courts deal with such matters as labor relations, suits against and among public authorities, and claims against social insurance institutions.[1] Thus labor courts, with their own local and appeal courts and a high court of legal review, decide lawsuits between employers and employees and cases arising out of collective labor agreements. They are staffed with learned judges sitting with lay assessors selected from and by employers and employees, and procedures are simplified, speedy, and inexpensive. Like France, Germany has a separate system of administrative tribunals that possesses guarantees of judicial independence and, by and large, has given fair protection against executive arbitrariness. The bulk of claims against public authorities, as well as suits between them, are handled by these tribunals. Judgment is rendered against the state and not against individual officials, thus giving better protection not only to the civil servant acting in his official capacity but to the

[1] The jurisdiction of the regular courts now, however, extends to one area not usually covered by the regular courts in other countries. Jurisdiction over members of the armed forces has been vested in the regular courts rather than in courts-martial—an encouraging expression of civilian supremacy.

damaged citizen, too. The jurisdiction of German administrative courts has generally not been as broad as in France, where almost anyone can file a petition in the public interest, but it has now been broadened to include all cases where a person's rights are affected by an act of public authority. Legal unity is provided through a federal Supreme Administrative Court.

REGULAR COURTS

The regular court system for civil and criminal cases has remained basically unchanged since its establishment under the Hohenzollerns. There are four levels of courts: local courts, district courts, appeal courts, and the Federal Supreme Court, successor to the Reich Supreme Court, which watched over German legal unity before 1945. Plans to transform the four-level system into three levels (which, in practice, would mean abolishing most of the scattered local courts) had not yet materialized by 1971.

Local courts

Local courts are found in all larger and many smaller cities and towns. In the smaller towns there is often only one judge, who takes care of civil and criminal as well as probate and similar noncontentious matters (there is no one comparable to lay justices of the peace on the British or French pattern). In larger places a local court has several judges who divide the different categories of cases. They act as single judges in minor civil and criminal cases and in probate and similar matters. In somewhat more important criminal cases the judge is joined by two lay assessors who are chosen by lot from among the local inhabitants.

District courts

District courts, which exist in all larger centers, are courts of primary jurisdiction as well as of review of local court judgments. They are staffed with a larger number of judges, who divide into sections (chambers) for different types of cases, and who always sit as collegiate bodies voting by majority. Their composition

and jurisdiction appear in the chart on page 481. In contrast to Britain, to appeal in Germany means to take up a case anew and to consider the facts as well as the law. The assize courts deal with particularly grave crimes, such as murder, and have nothing in common with jury trial. The lay members of the assize courts sit, decide, and vote *jointly* with the learned judges—a system that usually gives preponderance in the procedures to the latter.

Appeal courts

It is appropriate to use *appeal courts* to translate the German name of the next court level because, except for certain rare cases, they lack original jurisdiction. As in district courts, there are civil and criminal sections, here called *senates*. Criminal senates decide upon points of law only. The court may confirm a sentence, quash it, or order retrial by the lower court. It never tries the case itself.

The Supreme Court

The chief function of the Federal Supreme Court at Karlsruhe is to ensure uniformity of legal interpretation, which was especially necessary after years of legal confusion from 1945 to 1950. Besides deciding points of law in civil and criminal cases coming up to it from lower courts, however, it is also a court of first and last resort in political criminal cases (treason, subversion, etc.), where it has often dealt with East German agents and their Communist collaborators.

The Supreme Court consists of civil and criminal senates. All appeal court judgments involving sums above a stated value, as well as all cases in certain defined categories, such as divorce cases, are reviewable by this court. Unlike the United States Supreme Court, the highest German court cannot select the cases to be reviewed.

THE FEDERAL CONSTITUTIONAL COURT

This court constitutes a departure from the traditional German system. It is considered not part of the general court system but a separate top governmental institution on a par

Regular Court System of West Germany

FEDERAL COURT

Supreme Court
Main function is to ensure uniformity of legal interpretation
Cannot select cases to be reviewed

CIVIL SECTIONS	CRIMINAL SECTIONS	
5 judges	5 judges Original jurisdiction	5 judges Revision

CIVIL CASES

Courts of Appeal
3 judges
Lack original jurisdiction
Review district court judgments where district court had original jurisdiction

CRIMINAL CASES

Courts of Appeal
3 judges
Lack original jurisdiction
Decide upon points of law in cases of local court sentences appealed to the district court

LAND COURTS

District Courts
Decide in all matters outside the jurisdiction of local courts and on appeals against local court judgments

SECTIONS FOR APPEALS 3 judges	SECTIONS FOR ORIGINAL JURISDICTION 3 judges

Local Courts
1 judge
Minor civil cases

District Courts
Courts of primary jurisdiction and of review of local court judgments

SMALL CHAMBER 1 judge 2 lay assessors For lesser cases	LARGE CHAMBER 3 judges 2 assessors For appeals against local verdicts
LARGE CHAMBER 3 judges 2 assessors Original jurisdiction	ASSIZE COURT 3 judges 6 assessors For grave crimes such as murder

Local Courts	
1 judge Minor criminal cases	1 judge 2 lay assessors More important criminal cases

with the two other branches, the executive and parliament. In this it reflects the American system and, indeed, its establishment was due to American influence when the Bonn Constitution was drafted. Since coming into existence, in 1951, it has made ample use of its numerous and varied powers and by now enjoys fairly high prestige, perhaps the highest among the various West German governmental institutions, thus contributing an amount of legitimacy to Bonn democracy in general.

Among its most significant powers—likewise an innovation in Germany—is that of judicial review. Traditionally, German courts had no such power. While the French reject judicial review as an infraction of the people's sovereign lawmaking authority (and the English reject it as an infraction of the supremacy of parliament), Germans used to regard it as conflicting with the authority of the law-giving state. But, again at American suggestion, it was incorporated into the Bonn Constitution. In contrast to the American system, however, it is the separate constitutional court (not, as in the United States, one overall supreme court) upon which this jurisdiction was conferred, and it has it at the exclusion of the ordinary courts. It decides cases in which ordinary courts have doubts about the constitutionality of a law, or upon application by a cabinet (federal or *Land*) or a Bundestag minority of at least one-third of the legal membership. At first, misgivings were voiced by progressives who recalled that in the 1920s the courts had tried to check social legislation by assuming review power (producing a situation somewhat similar to that presented by the anti-New Deal United States Supreme Court of the mid-1930s). Ministerial officials, on their part, feared that review power would interfere with efficient lawmaking (understandably so, since they themselves were the chief drafters of bills).

Both fears have proved without substance. The court has acted with circumspection and frequently in a spirit of progressivism, and this is true also of the exercise of its other powers, which are substantial. It decides in cases of constitutional conflicts between federal and *Land* governments or among *Länder*, and also in cases of conflicts between the highest federal organs themselves. It may outlaw parties as antidemocratic (as it did in the case of a neo-

Nazi group and in that of the Communist party). Above all, it acts in cases of "constitutional complaint": any person claiming to have been deprived of a constitutional right by a public authority may appeal to it directly. About nine-tenths of the cases decided by the court originate in this fashion.[2] All this has meant broad protection of the basic individual and group rights amply provided for in the constitution. For instance, in regard to the constitutionally protected "equality before the law" provision, the court established the equal right of both parents in the care and education of their children; it compelled new legislation providing for equal rights of illegitimate children. Some other important decisions have been mentioned in their proper places.

The court's success and prestige may in part be due to its composition and method of selection. In contrast to most German courts, its members are elected by parliament, and the majority of its judges are drawn from outside the career judiciary. There are two separate panels, or "senates," of eight judges each. All members must be trained in the law, and while some of them are selected from among the judges of the other federal high courts, most of them are drawn from among professors and lawyers. This diversity of background may be the reason for the general spirit of liberality found in the court today. Since 1971, by an amendment of the Constitutional Court Act, all are appointed for one term of twelve years; the amendment further gave dissenting judges the right to publish dissenting opinions.

Half of the membership of the court is elected by the Bundesrat, voting by a two-thirds majority, the other half by a special committee of twelve electors set up by the Bundestag fractions, voting likewise by qualified majority (a minimum of nine out of twelve). In this manner no one party or party coalition can alone determine the composition of the court. In practice there have been CDU and SPD "quotas," with other party (or nonparty) affiliations rare.

---

[2] For example, in 1969, 1,592 out of 1,721 cases decided by the court were constitutional complaints, appealed directly to the court, despite the fact that the court can dismiss such complaints in preliminary procedures as "obviously unfounded"—a power conferred upon it when it appeared it was being swamped.

3 THE GERMAN JUDICIARY

JUDGES, PROSECUTORS, JUDICIAL ADMINISTRATION

The German judge is part of a bureaucratic structure. When he acts, the state acts through him. The judge remains anonymous even when he renders his judgment. He announces, for instance, that "the court" will take such and such a motion under advisement, and, with the exception mentioned above, no dissenting opinions are made public.

The anonymity and formalism of the judge are the result of his training and the influence of his administrative superiors. Ordinarily—that is, in all *Länder* judiciaries—he is appointed and promoted by *Land* Ministers of Justice.[3] He is, to be sure, independent so far as his judicial decisions are concerned. The chief guarantees of his independence are his life tenure (which means irremovability except for cause) and his protection against being transferred against his will from one post to another. Like other high officials, future judges have to undergo specialized studies and training at universities and in-service training in courts. After the second examination, opening the way to judicial position, they must decide whether to enter the bar as practicing lawyers, or to choose the state service. Unlike British judges but like the French, German judges are not drawn from the bar but devote themselves from the outset to an official career. This not only shuts them off from the wider views that dealing with clients gives to the attorney, but also makes them conscious of being part of a specialized bureaucratic machine. Their large number (over twelve thousand in about a thousand courts) contributes to this feeling.

Prosecution is a separate operation within the machine of the administration of justice. Judges and prosecutors usually specialize. Thus both judge and prosecutor tend to become bureaucratic, bookish, and authoritarian-minded. This tendency is intensified by the influence of their superiors. Both hierarchies, courts as well as prosecutors, are under the ultimate supervision of Justice Ministers. In the judiciary, as in other bureaucracies, conformity and industry provide an assured road to success. The judge knows that if he continually renders decisions not liked by his superiors or decisions that are frequently appealed and reversed, or if he generally behaves individualistically and "uncooperatively," he can hardly expect promotion. The German judge is free of the pressure exerted upon an elected judge by public opinion, parties, and politicians—perhaps too free, for the drawback of the German appointive system lies in the influence exercised by the group, or caste, to which the judge belongs. His prestige consists in being a member of this group and depends on the rank he holds in it. Caste is strengthened by in-breeding: each fourth judge in West Germany is the son of a judge or a lawyer, each second the son of an official. It is not surprising that a recent sociological analysis of the judiciary found as its characteristics "identification with state authority," "distance from social reality," "conformism and preference for formalistic regulation rather than innovation," and "high valuation of personal security"; this was true for the oncoming generation (in contrast to many other young professionals) also. It bodes none too well for future basic reforms of the legal system.

ADVANTAGES AND DISADVANTAGES OF THE LEGAL SYSTEM: ATTEMPTS AT REFORM

It is sometimes said that in England and the United States, but not on the Continent, the judge is "king." We have seen that in some respects this assertion is valid. But in another sense a French or German judge dominates proceedings and trials to a much greater extent

---

[3] The relatively small number of federal judges in the federal high courts are chosen in a procedure whereby a selection committee of the Bundestag acts jointly with the *Land* ministers (e.g., Ministers of Justice in case of members of the Federal Supreme Court, Ministers of Labor in case of judges of the Supreme Labor Court, etc.).

than his Anglo-American brethren ever do. For, while the British and the Americans look upon a lawsuit, and particularly a criminal trial, as a kind of duel in which the parties fight it out and the judge is a mere umpire to uphold the rules of the game, in Germany (as in France) the judge himself is entrusted with finding the truth, and the parties, attorneys, and prosecutors are simply aides in his investigation. In this sense, the law emerging from judicial proceedings is judge-made in Germany, while in Britain and the United States it is largely attorney-made.

The Continental system has its advantages and its disadvantages. Highly formalized rules of evidence provide better protection for the defendant in Britain and the United States, but the lesser degree of formalism on the Continent permits more thorough investigation and avoids that abuse of formalities that often makes American trials "judicial circuses." In Germany there is little cross-examination of witnesses; the presiding judge examines them. He admits and excludes evidence. There is no truth in the persistent myth that the defendant is presumed guilty; he is presumed to be innocent unless the prosecution proves his guilt. But the defense (defendant as well as defense lawyer) has a difficult stand against the machinery of justice. The prosecution—as well as the police in preliminary proceedings, and the court itself—is less bound by formal rules. Preliminary proceedings are often long and drawn out, and release of defendants from arrest on bail is very rare.

On the other hand, there is little police brutality, and the curious discrepancy, known to American criminal procedure, between a meticulously fair court trial and an arbitrary and brutal investigation by the police is unknown. Arrest must be confirmed by a judge not later than the end of the following day, and detention prior to trial has to be reviewed periodically. Nevertheless, overly long periods of detention have been common, and a recent reform has therefore defined stricter prerequisites for such detention; it has also specified additional rights for defendant and counsel. No defendant is sworn in as witness in his own case, although of course he has the right to be heard. A defendant acquitted as innocent can claim indemnification for pretrial detention. The death penalty has been abolished in the Federal Republic. This has benefited many Nazi murderers. Few German prisons are as progressive as some of the best in the United States, but on the other hand the cruel methods of punishment as well as the almost medieval conditions of detention found in other American prisons are not often found there, although overcrowding in antiquated buildings is frequent.

The German legal system is less weighted in favor of the rich than is the Anglo-American one. Appeals and revisions in civil cases, to be sure, often depend on a minimum money value of the case. But general costs are not high, mainly because, in civil cases, attorneys' fees are fixed at specific rates by statute. Impecunious parties or defendants are entitled to free proceedings (including the cost of witnesses and experts, in that case borne by the state) and the services of a court-appointed and state-paid lawyer. Justice in Germany thus is relatively inexpensive; it is, moreover, accessible, generally fair, and not overly complicated. But it has been authoritarian, and so is much of the substantive law, in addition to being anachronistic. Hence there are increasing calls for reform.

But reform has been protracted, slow, and in small quantities. We can mention here only two areas as examples. The divorce law has been based on the principle of guilt, of one or both parties, with the well-known drawbacks of either deception in procedures and advantage for the wealthy, or continuation of "sick" marriages. Intended reform introduces the principle of "objective decay" (*Zerruettung*), but the problem of support after divorce, in particular, has so far proved difficult to solve. Penal law, an object of reform proposals for decades, has similarly suffered from procrastination, but some headway is noticeable. Reform legislation in criminal law and procedure, begun in the sixties, proceeds in stages, to be accomplished by final revision of the codes of criminal law and procedure in 1973. Among accomplished reforms are substitution of fines for short prison terms (the fines to be scaled according to the resources of the violator); no distinction any longer between sentencing to ordinary prisons and to institutions at which hard labor was served; more provision for probation. In substantive law, reforms include: elimination of antiquated offenses such as "dueling" or "blasphemy," of many sexual crimes (including homosexuality among consenting adults and adultery), of pornography, in most cases; decreased penalties (but not freedom from punishment) for abortion. Following the *Spiegel* case, overly broad definitions of treason were narrowed and related "political crimes" thus made more reasonable and less "treasonable." An overdue gun law was enacted, as was a law making private wiretapping (but not that on the part of authorities, as we have seen) a punishable offense. The problem of how and to what extent to prosecute participants in mass demonstrations involving violence has posed particularly difficult questions. Recent liberal legislation tries to protect the right to demonstrate as one of the few remaining ways for the "people," and especially a radical opposition, to affirm controversial views against an "establishment" which controls most channels of communication and opinion. But the difficulty in drawing the line between "legitimate" expressions of unpopular views and "illegal" ways of presenting them is reflected in somewhat vague and complex rules.

4   THE LEGAL AFTERMATH OF NAZISM AND PROTECTION OF RIGHTS AND LIBERTIES

Perhaps no nation and no judiciary ever confronted legal problems as complex as those left to post-Nazi Germany as a legacy of the Nazi system. Unheard-of crimes had been committed, rights despoiled, new vested interests created in their stead. Many of these actions, moreover, had been carried out under statutes and regulations appearing in the form of law. Should all this now be left alone? Or should all of it be investigated, prosecuted, revamped? What was to be done about actions that the Nazis had made racial or political crimes and for which sentences had been passed? What, on the other hand, about acts that under the laws of the regime were not crimes, indeed may even have been legal duties, but that now appeared eminently punishable? What about Aryanized property of which Jews had been despoiled? What (to refer to a few particular cases) about the German soldier who, when all seemed over in 1945, deserted and went home? What about the judge who condemned him to death?

WAR CRIMES AND CRIMES AGAINST HUMANITY

What, above all, about the enormous crimes committed in and outside of Germany, which were later to be known as war crimes or crimes against humanity (such as extermination of Jews and other groups, medical experiments on living persons amounting to torture, maltreatment of slave labor), whose perpetrators the Allies had vowed to "pursue to the uttermost ends of the earth" to bring them to justice?

Germans were at first spared the trouble of worrying about these problems; the Allies took it upon themselves to deal with them before the Nuremberg International Military Tribunal as well as in courts set up by individual occupiers in their zones. Some groups of major war criminals were tried in this way by the Allies and sentenced (many of them later to be pardoned). The Allies also enacted a number of laws dealing with such problems as restitution of despoiled property. But this still left to Germany the prosecution of all but the somewhat haphazardly selected cases dealt with by the Allied tribunals.

COMING TO TERMS WITH THE PAST

Through nothing else might Germany have more truly purged itself than by the prosecution of such crimes. But the majority of Germans, as we have seen, failed to come to grips with the problem of what they refer to as their "undigested (or unresolved) past." This is perhaps revealed most poignantly in their attitude toward their own Resistance: while some have come to recognize the Resistance fighters as heroes who under most trying conditions fulfilled their patriotic duty, many still see them as traitors and their persecutors as people who "merely did their duty." [4] And the long drawn-out history of West Germany's attempts to cope with the problem of Nazi criminality reveals similar hesitation and confusion.

Here the failure of denazification, which reopened judicial positions to former Nazis, has borne the bitter fruit of biased or weak justice. Hardly anything was done to purge the judiciary itself, which during World War II had twenty-six thousand death verdicts to its account (as contrasted with less than three hundred in World War I).[5] For over ten years, prosecution lagged; it was often a matter of sheer coincidence when crimes and criminals were detected. Even then prosecution and trial often turned out to be a farce.[6] For a number of years Germans seemed to have solved the problem by ignoring it. But in the late 1950s (when many major war criminals were found among returnees from Soviet detention camps), the government decided to act. A central office was set up to collect evidence systematically (often abroad and among widely scattered witnesses) and coordinate the prosecution of the major crimes that could still be detected. A number of trials began, the most spectacular being the Auschwitz trial held at Frankfurt (at least in terms of the number of murders for which the defendants were indicted, which amounted to millions). These trials revealed not only what had long been known—the planned Hitlerite extermination of millions—but also that the "final solution" of the Jewish question as well as similar actions had been accompanied by excesses surpassing even a Dantesque imagination.[7]

But then one ran into new difficulties. While most countries do not have a statute of limitations for murder, the German penal code provided for twenty years' limitation, which would have made murder committed before 1945 unindictable in 1965. Twice, therefore, the Bundestag had to enact extensions (one in 1965, for four years, the other, in 1969, for thirty years calculated from 1949, i.e., to 1979); it did this with difficulty, with many in the CSU and also in the CDU and the (then still rightist) FDP opposed. In addition, "mere" accomplices to murder, to whom a lower limitation applied, were no longer punishable at all. Strangely, those responsible for the overall planning of actions, that is, top Gestapo officials who had organized them from their vantage point at Berlin, are considered "accomplices" and are not being tried (thus creating the same discrepancy between treatment of those who give the order and those who execute it, as has become observable in the American Vietnam cases). And the trials themselves have become more and more perfunctory. During the ten years from 1959 to 1969, in over one thousand trials, fewer than one hundred of those accused received life sentences, and fewer than three hundred limited terms. In a big trial, with several accused, one would usually be convicted, while the others were acquitted, often because there were few surviving witnesses and their testimony often was

---

[4] For some polling figures see Chapter 1, Section 6.

[5] As late as 1969, a judge of the Nazi "People's Court" who was found to have passed some two hundred and thirty death sentences (for such "crimes" as having criticized Nazis or told an anti-Nazi joke) was acquitted by an obviously "friendly" judge.

[6] A particularly tragic case may be cited here as an example of the conditions described above. In the last days of the war, a few members of the Hitler Youth, children of fourteen or fifteen years who had been hastily armed without any training, were disarmed and sent home by the enraged inhabitants of a village through which they were passing. Discovering this "crime," an SS court-martial without further formality condemned to death the village mayor as well as another inhabitant, both of whom had courageously stepped forth and assumed responsibility. When one member of the "court" (the local Nazi leader) refused to sign the verdict, he was likewise condemned, and the three were put to the gallows on the spot, the population being forbidden to take the corpses down.
  The trial of the guilty court members extended over eight years; it consisted of a series of acquittals by the assize courts, reversals of these verdicts by higher courts, and retrials by the assize courts. The final result of this tragicomedy was that one of the two lesser defendants was finally acquitted, the other got a light prison term, while the chief defendant died of natural causes during the last stages of the trial.

[7] The annals of humanity, or rather, inhumanity, should record such actions as the killing of newborn babies by smashing their heads against walls, or the way in which the commandant of the annihilation camp Treblinka used to kill inmates: he trained his dog, which he called Mensch (human being), to tear off human genitals; he would urge the dog on by shouting: "Mensch, get those dogs."

not considered credible because of the lapse of time. "Base motives," which must be proved to convict for first degree murder, were frequently not found. Increasingly, defendants have been found "too sick to stand trial," and an increasing number of the few actually convicted have been released for medical reasons.

None of the accused ever voiced regret. Most felt that being brought to trial so long after the event was unfair. Many Germans seem to agree with them, calling the continued prosecution of Nazi criminality "national masochism." If one considers Vietnam, or what happened (or failed to happen) after the crimes of the Stalin era were uncovered in the Soviet Union, one cannot, perhaps, expect too much by way of moral (and legal) expurgation from nations whose "very own" are discovered to be morally reprehensible. But in the case of Germany it was, after all, a new regime, and a people claiming to have broken with the darkest period of its past, that has been in charge. Many, it is true, have expressed shame and disgust, especially among the young, to whom their elders had described what happened as "atrocity tales" or, in any event, "gross exaggerations." Thus the soul of Germany has still not come to peace with itself.

PROTECTION OF CIVIL LIBERTIES

A more welcome legacy of the Nazi period has been the greater awareness on the part of many Germans of the importance of individual rights, civil liberties, and their protection. The wholesale destruction of liberty under the Nazi regime, and the sense of utter insecurity it created, engendered a marked appreciation for the blessings of personal freedom and privacy. Traditionally, in contrast to Britain and France, the law in Germany has been not so much an instrument for the defense of individual freedom as one to maintain order and enforce individual duties. True, there has generally been less unofficial interference with liberties and the area of privacy by pressure groups, such as has frequently developed in the United States (for instance, unofficial religious or political censorship of the press, theater, movies, and their employees). Public authorities in Germany, on the other hand, have been notoriously negligent in respecting such freedoms.

In this respect the postwar expansion of administrative jurisdiction and the liberal attitude of the Constitutional Court have added importantly to the protection of liberties. So have constitutional provisions, which, in contrast to the Weimar Constitution, give certain basic rights immediate applicability instead of leaving them as mere programmatic statements of aims. Thus the very first articles of the Bonn Constitution protect "the dignity of man" and the "free development of his personality." These somewhat vague formulations have been used from time to time to preserve privacy by protecting personal secrets and private correspondence, by guaranteeing the right not to have one's name or picture used in films or literature without permission, and by prohibiting wiretapping. It is, of course, difficult to draw the line between the right of privacy and freedom of opinion, for example, the right of the press to report freely on public figures. This dilemma can be as difficult as it is to delimit freedom of expression through demonstrative acts from violation of, say, property rights through nonviolent resistance (sit-ins, etc.). Further rights, which show progressive tendencies of the constitution, include the right of asylum for persons entering West Germany as political persecutees; the right of conscientious objection to military service; nondiscrimination not only in regard to sex but also in regard to race, religion, and political opinion; and prohibitions against mental or physical ill treatment of persons arrested or detained. As one can see, many of these provisions reflect the adverse experience of Nazi totalitarianism.

German authorities still tend to disregard such rights, especially in recent years, when student unrest, APO actions, and so forth have put their patience to the test. The authorities have been tempted to react in a lawless fashion to restore "law and order." But as the *Spiegel* affair had already shown in the early 1960s, the German public is less amenable than it once was to abuse by official arbitrariness. And through the jurisdiction of courts, in particular the Federal Constitutional Court, there now exists a corpus of case law in reference to all imaginable rights and liberties, their definition, and the ways of their protection. What is lacking, in the main, is an institutionalized procedure for criticism and control, whether through the official government institutions (where the office of the parliamentary Defense Commissioner is an exception) or through such more private and "grassroots" institutions as a German civil liberties union. These may grow up in time, since the basic requirement, public awareness, exists.

7

Berlin and the DDR
(German
Democratic
Republic)

1 THE GOVERNMENT OF BERLIN

The status of Germany's former capital mirrors not only that of the partitioned country but that of a world divided, a world whose problems—as is indicated by the term "Berlin crisis"—have frequently centered on this area where East and West have met so closely in the postwar period. Although its present fragmented, cut-off position contrasts sharply with its glorious past, the more than 3 million inhabitants of Berlin have adjusted to a "life lived dangerously" in surprising fashion. What is Berlin's present status? How did it emerge? What of the future?

EMERGENCE OF ITS PRESENT STATUS

It has been said that Berlin today offers "one of the strangest governmental phenomena of our times." Although it is no longer the German capital, one portion is headquarters of the government of one of Germany's two present units; ruled by two separate indigenous administrations and physically partitioned by a fortified wall, it is also under the authority of occupation powers; and its two portions are partly but not quite integrated into the two Germanies.

When the Allies, in September 1944, agreed on the zonal division of Germany, the area of Greater Berlin was exempted from the zones;

it was to be occupied by the Allies and administered by them jointly through an inter-Allied *Kommandatura*. In the summer of 1945, the four powers occupied their respective four "sectors" of the city and established patterns for their common rule. Under four-power rule, on the basis of a "preliminary constitution" issued by the Allies in 1946, Germans began to participate in government. But a major political problem, foreshadowing the subsequent split, arose even at this early stage. When the Soviets tried to force the two left parties to merge into one Communist-controlled "Socialist Unity Party" (SED), the Berlin SPD resisted the merger. (SPD membership in the three Western sectors—in the Eastern sector the vote was forbidden—voted against it by over 80 percent.) In the first all-Berlin vote, in October 1946, the SPD received 49 percent of the vote, the SED only 20 percent. A diet and a magistrate, the latter SPD-controlled, began to function and ruled Berlin for two years. In 1948, the diet was forcibly prevented (Soviet military police intervened in favor of Communist rioters) from meeting at its location in the Soviet sector and was shifted, with the remainder of the administration, to the Western sectors. After the failure of the Soviets to amalgamate the city by blockading it (the blockade was rendered ineffective by an American-British airlift), the split of Berlin into East and West was completed. West Berlin has operated since September 1, 1950 (on the East, see below) under a constitution patterned on Bonn parliamentarianism. West Berlin is organized like a *Land:* it has a diet, elected for four years; a cabinet, called "senate" (thirteen members headed by a "governing mayor"), responsible to the diet; administrative departments headed by senators; and twelve subdivisions called "districts," each with its separate organizational structure.

GOVERNMENT OF WEST BERLIN

Politically, West Berlin has been controlled by the SPD, which since 1958 has held an absolute majority.[1] Until 1971, when the party decided to form a government alone, it had always ruled in coalition with other parties (at first with the CDU and FDP, then with the CDU, and from 1963 to 1971 with the FDP). Under able and forceful mayors, from Ernst Reuter through Willy Brandt to incumbent Klaus Schütz, the West Berlin government has been both popular and effective.

However, the original West German idea to have West Berlin incorporated into the Federal Republic as a full-fledged *Land* was thwarted by the Western Allies, who, although not interested in maintaining occupation rights per se, insisted on at least formal continuation of Berlin's occupation status. A change of that status might have given the Soviets a pretext to abrogate the Western rights of free access to West Berlin through the Soviet zone. Thus the tripartite Allied *Kommandatura* is still in ultimate control, although its actual powers have been gradually shifted to the Germans. In 1955, the year when sovereignty was granted to Bonn, a "Berlin Declaration" by the three Western commandants, while reserving cer-

tain ultimate rights, granted West Berlin "the greatest possible degree of self-government compatible with the city's special situation." Thus, day-to-day government and administration are entirely German. However, the Allies reserve the right to control the police, if necessary, or to nullify legislation in conflict with Allied rights. And although they have granted Bonn the right to represent West Berlin internationally, they still review international agreements concluded by Bonn that are to apply to West Berlin.

Actually, legislation by the West Berlin government proceeds in close alignment with Bonn federal legislation: whenever a "Berlin clause" (that is, a clause declaring a statute to be applicable to Berlin also) is included in a federal law, the West Berlin legislature merely enacts a covering law stipulating the validity of this statute for West Berlin. At Bonn itself, the semi-inclusion of West Berlin in the Federal Republic is symbolized by the presence of twenty-two members from Berlin in the Bundestag and of four members in the Bundesrat. On Allied insistence, these representatives have no voting rights in plenary session, but they do vote in committees; on the other hand, the Bundestag members are not directly elected by the Berlin people but are selected by the Berlin diet in accordance with fraction strength. Also, West German high courts (with the exception of the Constitutional Court) have extended their jurisdiction to West Berlin, and a few even have their seat there, as have some other Bonn agencies.

West Berlin's economic ties to West Germany are as strong as its political ones. The city could hardly have survived without first American and then West German financial and similar aid. Financial aid, in the form of direct subsidies, tax relief, and the like, continues to the tune of over 2 billion DM annually. Almost all of its supplies come from the West by rail, road, or waterway; most of its exports go to the West;[2] its currency, of course, is the West German mark (DM). Within Berlin, on the other hand, there was until the summer of 1961 a strange but strong

---

[1] Election figures show the continued strength of the SPD and the insignificance of the Communist party, which, even after August 1961, was allowed, under the four-power status, to participate in West Berlin elections under the SED (since 1969, SEW, Socialist Unity Party of West Berlin) label.

	1948	1950	1954	1958	1963	1967	1971
SPD	64.5%	44.7%	44.6%	52.6%	61.9%	56.9%	50.4%
CDU	19.4	24.6	30.3	37.7	28.8	32.9	38.2
FDP	16.1	23.0	12.8	3.8	7.9	7.1	8.5
SED			2.7	1.9	1.4	2.0	2.3

[2] West Berlin, although comprising only part of Berlin's former industrial capacity, is still one of Germany's major industrial cities, with, for example, about 40 percent of West German electrical production.

symbiosis of West and East; thousands of Berliners commuted daily between their residences in East Berlin and their working places in the West and vice versa. Most means of communication and transportation operated on a city-wide basis.

On August 13, 1961, the East German regime built the wall that severed all communication between the city's two sections and thereby cut off East Berlin and the DDR (for whose inhabitants West Berlin had served as an escape hatch) completely from the West. This action was followed by Soviet demands to terminate Berlin's occupation status and render West Berlin a special, third German unit without ties to West Germany and with a "free city" status; access to it would be guaranteed, but control of the access lines was to devolve on the DDR. Refusal by the Western powers to yield any of their rights led to recurrent crises and East-West "confrontations." Finally in March 1970, four-power negotiations began in Berlin after an eleven-year interruption of contacts with a view to settle the "Berlin problem" once and for all. Before describing these and their results, we must briefly turn to East Berlin to see what happened to that section of the city after the split of 1948.

EAST BERLIN GOVERNMENT

The East Berlin government on the surface appears to be very similar to that of West Berlin in its close coordination with, but not complete inclusion in, its respective German unit, the DDR. Politically and economically East Berlin is of course completely communized and, as the seat of the DDR government, is East Germany's chief showcase. The East, nevertheless, has been as anxious as the West to observe the formalities of East Berlin's four-power status. East German statutes, for instance, do not automatically extend to East Berlin, and, like their West Berlin counterparts, the East Berlin members of the East German People's Chamber are not popularly elected (although now they seem to have full voting rights—perhaps a signal that one would not object to granting similar rights to West Berlin representatives at Bonn). In the organization of the government after the rupture

in 1948, SED members of the old diet were simply supplemented with members from Eastern-style mass organizations (trade unions, etc.), and the new "diet" in turn organized a "provisional democratic magistrate." Subsequently, in 1953, a "Provisional Organic Law for Greater Berlin," the present basis of East Berlin government, provided for an elected diet, magistrate, city districts, and a mayor. In practice, East Berlin functions as another district of the DDR. In regard to budget, economic planning, and enterprises, and in almost every other respect it is treated as an integral part of the Democratic Republic.

A NEW SETTLEMENT FOR WEST BERLIN

It is understandable how embarrassing the existence of West Berlin deep in Eastern territory must have been for the East, and especially for the rulers of the DDR. West Berlin served as a symbol of political freedom and economic prosperity and, until August 1961, as the chief escape route for those who wanted to flee from the DDR or East Berlin. Although West Berlin no longer fulfills that function, it continued to discomfit the world of the East, being heard (through the voice of its radio) and seen (through television). This is why the East—and Walter Ulbricht in particular—has long insisted that West Berlin constituted a "special political entity" located "on the territory of the DDR." The idea, of course, was to include it eventually in the DDR. While there was no legal justification for Ulbricht's claim that West Berlin's location on East German territory makes it part of the DDR, its legal and actual status has indeed been abnormal. Legally, it is true, West Berlin forms an enclave that has never come under the sovereignty of the surrounding unit, and its status could not legally be changed by mere fiat of the DDR or the Soviet Union, singly or jointly; nor could they abrogate Western access rights unilaterally. On the other hand, the position of the West has been none too clear either. No formal agreements had been concluded concerning West German access and transit rights, and only very informal, vague agreements governed even the rights of the Western Allies in respect to military traffic. Thus, in fact, most of the access and transit has been based on sufferance by DDR authorities (on whom the Soviets had conveyed the right to check persons and goods entering or leaving DDR territory years ago), and the means of harassment they possessed were uncomfortably varied, as frequent incidents have proved over the years. This situation, in turn, affected the life of the city itself. Despite aid and subsidization, its economy has suffered, with West German industry loath to invest. Its population is aging; young people have been attracted to the West or, at least, no new blood is attracted to Berlin. There was an increasing danger that the city's position of independence might, in the long run, become untenable.

There was thus a vital interest on the part of West Germany and her Western allies in a settlement that would put the future of West Berlin as an independent, Western-oriented, Western-type unit on a firmer basis. Since, by early 1970, the East, or at least the Soviet Union, seemed to be ready to remove the Berlin issue as a continuing threat to *détente*, negotiations could begin. They could only be based on a *quid pro quo*. The West would have liked, of course, to make *all* of Berlin the object of an agreement, but it soon appeared that East Berlin could as little be supposed to be detached from the DDR again as could West Berlin be supposed to be integrated with the DDR. "Reunification" here seems to be as unobtainable, at least for the time being, as overall German reunification is at this point. The interest of the West, therefore, concentrated on a firm commitment on the part of both the DDR and the Soviet Union not to interfere with access and transit rights to and from West Berlin (with detailed guarantees of undisturbed air, road, rail, and similar traffic, transportation, and communication) and to recognize the status of the city as independent from the DDR, including its manifold ties with the FRG. To obtain this, the West was ready to reconfirm the continued occupation status of West Berlin, which would preclude its political integration with West Germany and require Bonn's foregoing certain actions in West Berlin that had become customary over the years but had always been protested by the East as "provocative," such as holding presidential elections

there. To the West, what counted was the continued viability of a West Berlin independent from the East. For that, unhampered Western economic and financial ties seemed more important than insistence on a more or less symbolic political or governmental "presence" there. It was on this basis that four-power negotiations, extending over seventeen months, terminated in the "Quadripartite Agreement on Berlin" of September 1971.

Politically, the Agreement implies the East's recognition of West Berlin's continued status as a Western island within the East, a status that the DDR had never been ready to concede. Briefly, and chiefly, its rather complex text provides for the following: there shall be unimpeded and facilitated access and transit traffic between the city and West Germany; goods shall pass by road, rail, or waterway with only seals and documents inspected, persons in trains and buses with mere formal identification, and those using individual vehicles without paying fees or tolls (an annual lump sum, instead, to be paid by the FRG to the DDR for the use of the access routes and facilities); details to be agreed upon by the respective German authorities.

West Berlin's basic status continues: the West reconfirms its occupation rights and responsibilities and recognizes that the city is not a constituent part of the FRG, while the East recognizes the essential economic, cultural, legal, and other ties between the city and West Germany. These ties will be "maintained and developed," while, however, no "constitutional or official acts" (such as the convening of the Federal Assembly for the election of a federal president or sessions of the Bundestag or Bundesrat) will be performed there. This is spelled out in every detail (e.g., single committees may meet there in matters concerning Berlin, and single Bundestag fractions too, but not simultaneously).

Internationally, Bonn may continue to represent West Berlin. Treaties concluded by the FRG may be extended to Berlin and—something so far never conceded—Bonn's consular services will be available to West Berliners abroad; they may travel to Eastern countries on West German passports or identification papers stating that they are West Berlin residents. In return, the Soviet Union will be permitted to open a consulate and a trading office in West Berlin, with a view to increasing commercial activities there (details are spelled out down to the number of persons allowed to serve in such agencies).

Communication between West Berlin and the DDR shall be "improved"; this means that West Berliners shall be permitted to visit East Berlin and the rest of the DDR, with additional crossing points to be opened, but nothing is said about East Germans traveling West, so that the wall remains impenetrable to them. Telephonic and similar communications are to be improved. Again, details are to be spelled out by the Germans themselves.

Perhaps most important in an overall sense: the four powers agree that, "irrespective of differences in legal views the situation which has developed in the area shall not be changed unilaterally." There shall be no use or threat of force; disputes are to be settled peacefully through consultation. This means a Soviet commitment to *détente*; implicitly they will see to it that the DDR will also behave.

The Agreement was to enter into force only upon the conclusion, by the Germans, of the implementing agreements referred to in the Four Power Agreement (such as one on the details of transit and access). In the fall of 1971, when these inter-German negotiations were to begin, the DDR seemed to stall (claiming, for example, that certain agreements were to be made, not with the FRG but with the West Berlin Senate separately). It appeared unlikely, however, that the Soviets, apparently much interested in a speedy settlement of the Berlin issue because of other foreign-political objectives that depended on this settlement (see Chapter 8), would permit the DDR to torpedo the arrangement. Another question was whether Brandt would be able to see it through at Bonn in view of the rather violent opposition to his *détente* policy (also see Chapter 8). West Berliners, at any rate, although generally made wiser by past history and wary of agreements with the East, considered the arrangement as favorable (an opinion poll of September 1971, revealing about 80 percent of them as considering it satisfactory, with half of those who had intended to leave the city now inclined to stay).

From the vantage point of late 1971, it was too early to say whether the new Berlin arrangement (actually the first after World War II had left the city in an utterly uncertain state) would prove a success. What could be stated was that the agreements, if and when in force and observed, would eliminate a major crisis area in world relations. For West Berliners it would mean, in Brandt's words, that henceforth "they will be able to live and work in security."

2 THE ESTABLISHMENT OF COMMUNIST CONTROL IN THE SOVIET ZONE

Imagine that after a disastrous defeat the United States was divided along the Mississippi, with the land west of the Rockies detached and its population expelled into one of the two remaining sections. Imagine further that a totalitarian regime was set up by an occupation power in one portion, while the other one was allowed to continue its traditional way of life. This, by and large, is what happened to Germany in the late 1940s. And since partition by now has lasted a quarter of a century, the new system has gone far in making East Germany a separate nation different from the West not only in its economic, social, and political institutions but in its general way of life.

The transformation that East Germany has undergone is, in some ways, more profound than even the one that Nazism wrought on Germany. The Nazi regime, while subordinating everything to its power, did not affect certain basic institutions, such as private property in landed estates and industries or the bureaucracy as such. Communism, by contrast, proceeded to transform class lines and society radically. It wiped out the Prussian Junkers and divided their estates among the peasants; it destroyed the property-owning middle class and nationalized industrial and business enterprises; it replaced the old, authoritarian officialdom with public employees supposed to serve a society of "toilers and peasants." Initially, there was a good deal that was progressive in these measures: smallholders with too little land, as well as the landless agricultural proletariat and expellee settlers, got land; banking and industrial combines were deprived of their political influence; reactionary and Nazi officials were purged; war criminals were brought to justice. But no totalitarian regime does such things for their own sake; it builds on them its own control. If agrarian reform created a new class of smallholders, it did so only to absorb them subsequently through collectivization. If workers are no longer exploited by private employers, they are deprived of the right of collective bargaining and of the weapon of the strike and are forced to fulfill the norms of the plan set by the regime. If Nazi criminals were rightly convicted, trials were also used to eliminate "class enemies"; if denazification effectively purged Nazis from office, it also served to expropriate the middle classes. Application for membership in the dominant party, on the other hand, would buy forgiveness for a dubious past. A regime with a monopoly of political power could be lenient and allow former Nazis to hold or regain positions, as long as the regime controlled these positions.

Thus, the changes that have occurred resulted not from the free play of social forces but from the policies of the one group in political control, the leaders of the Socialist Unity party (SED), acting under the guidance of Soviet Communists. A new class, which absorbed many formerly independent businessmen, artisans, and members of the professions, performs essential clerical, technical, and administrative functions for the state administration, public enterprises, and the party organizations. In return for these indispensable services, it enjoys social and economic privileges placing it above the other classes; it does not yet share in the elite's political power.

This political elite, which originally gained control under the leadership of Ulbricht and the supervision of the Soviet occupation power, still holds the key positions in party and government and guards them jealously. And the way this group exercises control might still be called totalitarian and discussed under the headings used to describe Nazism. As under the Nazis, there is "coordination" of all pre-existing social groups, only now under new management, with organizations such as trade unions, farmers' associations, and youth groups converted into SED-controlled "mass organizations"; there is "atomization" of the individual through the attempt to weaken the influence of family, church, and religion; there is an established machinery of repression; and there is an all-pervasive propaganda that tries to engage the allegiance of the masses, this time with a *Weltanschauung* not racist but instead materialist. the doctrine of Marxism-Leninism.

Having said this, however, one must qualify the statement. It is no longer correct to hold the common Western view that East Germany is oppressed by a small minority supported by Soviet tanks, the military might that crushed the hopes of the East German workers in 1953 when they rose against the regime. Twenty years have brought about considerable change, not only in economic factors, such as living standards, but also in the attitudes of the people. We shall return to this matter at the conclusion of this chapter. For our present purpose it is sufficient to note that the picture of totalitarian oppression fully applies to the first half of the period, when the regime felt completely lacking in support from the majority and devoted its chief efforts to establish controls and prevent violent resistance. But beginning with the early 1960s, the regime could start to be more relaxed. Although this, too, is little known in the West, there has been an "economic miracle" in East Germany also. At the end of the war, 45 percent of its industrial capacity was destroyed (compared with 20 percent destruction in West Germany), and much of what had remained was "evacuated" to (i.e., stolen by) the Soviet Union. Today, in contrast, the DDR, with 17 million inhabitants, has surpassed in industrial production the Germany of 1936 with its 60 million people and constitutes one of the foremost industrial countries of the world. Its people could not forever remain in sullen opposition, and many took pride in such achievements. The majority, with increasing prosperity, has at least turned "apolitical," which, in respect to the regime, means passive compliance. The regime, in turn, could thus afford to place less reliance upon terroristic controls. It has, moreover, been flexible enough to engage in modern, "scientific" technological and economic management, thus creating the impression of being "up to date" and attracting those among the young who are technologically and scientifically oriented. This has also meant that East Germans, in general, no longer uncritically favor rejoining the West. Most, in all likelihood, would no longer run away even if they could. Inasmuch as they think about it at all, they would favor a "third way" between their own totalitarian Communism and Western capitalist liberalism. If ever there should come a chance for reunification, not only the changed institutions and structures of East Germany but also the changed attitudes of its people would have to be taken into consideration.

ESTABLISHMENT OF THE GERMAN DEMOCRATIC REPUBLIC (DDR)

Initial political measures in the Soviet zone seemed democratic. Political parties were allowed to reorganize, and free elections to local assemblies were held. But democratization was abruptly halted when the Soviets realized that the Communists were unable to gain control this way. Their chief competitors, the Social Democrats, thereupon were forced to merge "voluntarily" with the Communists in a Socialist Unity party (SED). As the Berlin elections of 1946 showed, this shotgun marriage failed to convert the bulk of Social Democrats, but it destroyed them as a separate party in the Soviet zone. The two "bourgeois" parties, Christian Democrats and Liberals, at first profited from this, gaining even among workers and peasants, but they did not profit for long. They were gradually transformed into mere appendages of the SED, which itself was turned into an apparatus strictly controlled by its Communist leaders. Under the so-called bloc principle, the parties would informally agree on presenting to the public a unanimous antifascist front before voting in diets or making any other decisions. "Unanimity" invariably meant that SED policy was accepted by the others. They were corralled into such conformity by purges in which the more independent leaders were replaced by puppets.

Under such conditions, constitution-making meant little. With the SED in control of procedures, it could act in pseudodemocratic fashion. A People's Congress of handpicked delegates in 1947 drafted a constitution primarily based on an earlier SED draft. In accordance with the Soviet policy of trailing the West by one step, formal adoption of the draft was delayed until 1949 when a new slate of Congress delegates was submitted to East German voters for "democratic confirmation." Then occurred the only accident in an otherwise smooth procedure: a surprisingly high percentage of voters (38 percent) failed to endorse this list. Thereafter the regime dispensed with further democratic trimmings. The Congress proclaimed that the constitution was now in force (October 7, 1949) and allowed a smaller group from its midst, the People's Council, to establish itself as the first People's Chamber, or parliament, under the new constitution. This body in turn formed a cabinet and, in conjunction with a Chamber of States (issuing

DISTRICTS OF EAST GERMANY
—— DISTRICT BOUNDARIES
- - - OLD LAND BOUNDARIES
● SEATS OF DISTRICT ADMINISTRATIONS

BALTIC SEA

FEDERAL REPUBLIC OF GERMANY

POLAND

CZECHOSLOVAKIA

ROSTOCK
SCHWERIN
NEUBRANDENBURG
MADGE-BURG
BERLIN
FRANKFURT
POTSDAM
HALLE
COTTBUS
ERFURT
LEIPZIG
DRESDEN
SUHL
GERA
CHEMNITZ

R. Elbe
R. Oder
R. Neisse

GERMAN DEMOCRATIC REPUBLIC

0   50   100
MILES

from existing *Land* diets), elected a president.

A year later the provisional parliament was replaced by the election of a definitive one (October 15, 1950). This election violated even the new constitution's own provisions, which prescribed elections by different parties under the system of proportional representation. Instead, the voter was presented with a single list of candidates. They were from different parties, to be sure, but the SED was careful to secure a majority for itself and its mass organizations on this list, while the CDU and the LDP together were allotted less than one-third. All the voter had to do was to confirm the list; no competing slate was admitted. Since voters were "urged" to vote openly, the none-too-surprising result was endorsement by 99.7 percent of the valid vote. Subsequent elections have all been single-slate affairs, yielding similar results.

3 CONSTITUTIONAL FRAMEWORK OF THE DDR

While the Bonn Constitution, despite some undemocratic undercurrents, provides "rules of the game" allowing for a genuine interplay of social and political forces, the Eastern constitutional framework is more a façade behind which government proceeds according to its own rules. Actually, East Germany has functioned under two constitutions: the one of 1949 (whose adoption we have described above) was replaced by the one presently in force, promulgated on April 8, 1968. The two are significantly different. The 1949 constitution, upon its face, was liberal, democratic, and federal. This apparently reflected a hope the East still nursed that reunification might be achieved soon under a constitution that would be acceptable to the West. Thus it was in some ways patterned on the Weimar Constitution. It included a long list of liberal-democratic basic rights (including the right to strike, to freely travel abroad, etc.). It provided for popular elections by proportional representation and extended the principle of PR even to the cabinet, in which all parties were to be represented according to their strength in the People's Chamber. In reality, this simply served to strengthen the SED, since in this way the opposition (if any) was compelled to participate in government and, under the bloc principle, obliged to toe the SED line, with non-SED groups rendered prisoners of the "state party." There was also to be a Western-style parliamentarianism, with the government responsible to parliament, but since the SED from the outset was in complete control of both, conflict between the two was unthinkable.

The 1949 constitution had followed the Weimar pattern also by establishing *Länder* as federal subdivisions, to participate in government on the central level through a Chamber of States. But this federal structure was changed as early as 1952 in favor of a centralized system: the five *Länder* were replaced by fourteen districts, which are mere subdivisions of the central government. Other changes, still under the old constitution, followed. In 1960, the presidency (whose power had been negligible) was abolished in favor of a Council of State (*Staatsrat*), a body that assumed top executive power and whose chairman, at least as long as it was Ulbricht, wielded that power. The new constitution ratified these changes. Ulbricht, at an SED party convention in 1967, had declared that the time had come to draft "a more timely constitution." Obviously, by this date all hope to use the 1949 document for reunification had vanished and the government wanted now to give symbolic confirmation to the separate and independent existence of the Democratic Republic. Outwardly, it proceeded more democratically than in 1949: a committee of parliament prepared a draft, which was presented to the people for discussion. This so-called *Volksaussprache* took place in the early months of 1968. That this was not an entirely meaningless procedure was proved by the insertion of a few substantive changes (thus, a provision giving the churches certain rights), on which the "discussant" people had apparently insisted. After adoption by the chamber the draft was referred to a referendum (April 6, 1968), which resulted in a 94.5 percent majority for the new constitution.[3]

The details of the constitution will be dealt with in the sections that follow. Generally, it can be characterized as having a double function: to formulate the reality of government structure and practice as they had developed over two decades, and to place all this in the ideological setting of the Marxist-Leninist doctrine, this way lending the document the character of exhortation, propaganda, and formulation of ultimate aims. Thus, the very first article defines the DDR as "a socialist state of German nationality" and "the political organization of the working people in town and countryside who, under the leadership of the workers' class and its Marxist-Leninist party, put socialism into practice." All power, ostensibly, is in the elected chamber, which, in turn, elects all other top organs of the state, but there is no longer any question of proportional representation or executive responsibility to parliament. Nor do we find, among the rights of citizens, the right to strike or to leave the country (Article 32 guarantees the right "freely to move within the territory of the DDR"!). Indeed, emphasis on "socialist" economic and social principles (e.g., right to a job or to an education) overshadows individual rights and freedoms, which may be limited or suspended by simple law and, like the corresponding rights of the Stalin Constitution in the Soviet Union, are qualified by being exercisable only "in agreement with the principles and aims of the constitution." Thus, there is still more appearance than reality to some of the rights guaranteed by the constitution. Rather than study in detail the provisions of a partly ceremonial constitution, it is best to investigate the actual powers and functions of government.

Finally, the external "sovereignty," granted the DDR at an early point, although not spurious, is also not entirely the same as in the case of the Federal Republic. As early as 1949, the newly established DDR was granted some international autonomy, including the right to have a Foreign Office, establish diplomatic relations with other countries, and conclude international treaties. The Moscow Treaty of September 1955 confirmed complete formal sovereignty, and an agreement of March 1957 transformed, as in the West, military occupation into rights of stationing troops.[4] Actually, of course, there was, and still is, a good deal of Soviet control. But it is not (if it ever was) a simple command-obedience relationship. In the post-Stalin era, coordination has been chiefly through meetings of the DDR and Soviet party leadership or through multilateral meetings of the bloc Communist parties. Soviet influence can be seen on two levels in particular: on the bloc level (e.g., in East European-Soviet economic planning) and in connection with the "Germany question" and the problems of Berlin, where Soviet influence has frequently served to moderate the more intransigent attitudes of the Ulbricht regime (most recently in connection with the *Ostpolitik* of Chancellor Brandt's government, see below, Chapter 8). The regime, in its domestic policies, has usually followed Soviet lines (e.g., in 1958, anent Khrushchev's policy of decentralizing economic administration, or, in 1963 and afterward, copying "Libermanism"[5] in regard to freer economic policies). On the other hand, it has more recently also gone ahead with its own new ventures and occasionally even served as a model for the other Communist countries, including the Soviet Union (e.g., in introducing cybernetics and similar modern management techniques for the direction of the economy and society). The limits of such "independent" action, however, are clear; they were set, for all to see, by the Brezhnev Doctrine in 1968.[6]

[4] A clause in this agreement provided, however, that the Soviet military may assume full governmental control "in the event of a threat to the security of the forces." There are twenty Soviet divisions, about two hundred and fifty thousand men, stationed in the DDR, in addition to close to two hundred thousand men of the indigenous NVA (National People's Army), which is integrated with the Warsaw Pact setup. The NVA is thoroughly indoctrinated, with about three-fourths of the officers members of the SED.

[5] Liberman is a Soviet economist who first advocated the introduction of some principles of competition and profit into Soviet economy, suggestions subsequently adopted officially.

[6] The doctrine, the official justification for the invasion and occupation of Czechoslovakia by joint military action of the bloc under Soviet leadership, states that such action is called for whenever socialism is threatened in one of the countries belonging to the Warsaw Pact.

[3] Under Eastern conditions, the figure is surprisingly low. While People's Chamber and similar elections invariably yield 99 percent majorities, the "no" vote here amounted to up to 10 percent in some of the industrial cities.

4   THE RULING PARTY

Power in the DDR, as in all Communist-ruled countries, is concentrated at the top level of the ruling party. This party in East Germany is officially known as the Socialist Unity party (SED), the outgrowth of the enforced merger in 1946 of the Communist and Socialist parties. At first an attempt was made to have parity in leadership between Communists and Social Democrats and to have as broad a mass base as possible. But when it appeared that the SED was unable to attract the rank and file of Social Democrats, parity was dropped, and the SED was transformed into an organization in which all key positions are held by Communists and the line of authority runs from top to bottom.

This self-styled "party of a new type" resembles in everything its big brother, the CPSU, whose statutes and programs those of the SED (1954, 1963) have copied faithfully. As in the Soviet Union, it is a kind of secular order, with members carefully selected for loyalty and discipline. Acceptance is preceded by a one-year period of initiation, or candidacy. Membership (in 1970, close to 2 million) represents about 15 percent of the electorate, which, compared with membership figures in free systems, seems high. But there is much pressure for membership, many come from the youth organizations, and many join for opportunistic reasons, so that probably not more than 10 percent of this membership, that is, a little over 1 percent of the population, consists of active and loyal supporters, on whose backing the regime can rely. To sift the large body of the membership, periodic "exchanges of membership cards" are arranged, an action during which members found unreliable are eliminated.

From the outset, efforts were made to have in the party of the "workers' and peasants' state" as many workers and peasants as possible, but this has not quite succeeded. Functionaries and other members of the so-called intelligentsia dominated it from the beginning, and they are numerically strong to this day, despite constant efforts to infuse "new blood"

into the party. Thus in 1966, according to official statistics, workers constituted less than half of the membership (45.6 percent), peasants 6.4 percent, white-collar employees 28.4 percent (of which 12.3 percent belonged to the intelligentsia), and "others" 19.6 percent. In many cases present functionaries were counted as "workers" on the basis of their social origin.

STRUCTURE

In its organizational hierarchy, the elected party bodies, such as the Party Congress (which used to meet every four years but, since 1971, meets every five years, in order to coincide with the adoptions of the five-year economic plans), hold little power; they are convened to give the leadership a platform to propagandize doctrine and policies and to legitimize, through "elections of officers," the latters' standing and functions. The decisive controls are with three top bodies, the Central Committee, its Politbureau, and its Secretariat. The Central Committee is a body of about a hundred and thirty members plus fifty candidate members; officially elected by the Party Congress, it is supposed in its composition to reflect society at large; it meets about once every three months, but it lacks the power to initiate decisions. The Politbureau is the real policy making top organ of the party. The number of members has varied, but is usually around twenty (in 1971, there were sixteen full members plus seven candidate members). It meets frequently (at least once a week). It controls the corresponding party bureaus on the district and local levels. The Secretariat is a large body staffed with about two thousand full-time party functionaries, organized in about twenty sections that parallel the ministries and other chief state agencies. They are headed by party secretaries (in 1971, after Ulbricht's ouster, nine), most of whom are simultaneously members of the Politbureau, which indicates their power and influence.

On the lowest level the party is organized in party groups or cells, which consist of from eight to a dozen members working in a shop or enterprise or agricultural collective; there are close to one hundred thousand cells. While these units are without influence over party policy, they are important to the party. They spread the gospel through the laity and also convey to higher party levels what the people at large are saying and feeling. In party terminology, they are the link between the "advance guard" and its base, the "masses."

The Central Committee of the SED has established two top educational institutions, the party university "Karl Marx," and an Institute for Social Sciences, to train the upcoming elite in the social and political sciences as interpreted by the party. Most of the younger leaders are graduates of these institutions. Regarding party finances, membership fees are staggered from 0.5 to 3 percent of the member's income; other revenues come from party enterprises and similar sources; much of the party budget is spent on "educational" and agitation purposes.

As for actual leadership, the SED is, perhaps, unique among the ruling Communist parties in that its top level and, in particular, Walter Ulbricht, first party secretary and Politbureau chief until his resignation in May 1971, have ruled uninterruptedly throughout the entire postwar period, with most members surviving storms, crises, and purges. Ulbricht, a compliant Communist party hack in the twenties, and, during the Nazi period, a "Moscow Communist" (i.e., a German Communist who went to the Soviet Union rather than a Western country at that time), enjoyed Kremlin backing from the outset and thus was able to remain the uncontested leader. Under him, one could distinguish two major groups of top leaders: one consisting of the old party leaders who came in with Ulbricht and are doctrinally committed to communism as an ideology and a movement; the other made up of younger men of the managerial type, experts in various fields who have risen through party, state, or managerial ranks and been taken onto the top level. One leading (Western) student of the DDR has called the first group the "strategic clique," the other the "institutionalized counter-elite." But this is misleading, because, so far, conflict between the two has been avoided in the main. The old guard, while

still jealously protecting its political position, has been open to innovation in regard to persons as well as policies, and thus the newcomers have not become politically hostile. Ulbricht, in particular, proved flexible in these matters despite his ideological dogmatism. There developed, of course, differences of attitudes and opinions among "hardliners" and more "liberal" leaders with respect to the various fields of policies and strategies. But Ulbricht, adroitly playing off one faction against another and shuffling his aides from one position to another, managed to preserve essential unity and to keep himself in control.

In the spring of 1971, after a quarter of a century of holding power (a record among leaders of Communist regimes), Ulbricht resigned from his post as party leader. While the background of his resignation is still not entirely clear, enough is known (or can be inferred from the rude way in which he has since been treated, or ignored) to assume that it was not, as it appeared at first, an example of a peaceful, in other words, planned and voluntary, transfer of power. It seems that Ulbricht's resignation was forced upon him for two major reasons: one, and probably foremost, his obstinacy in defending what he perceived as the "national interest" of the DDR. This created obstacles to a Soviet policy intent on coming to terms with the West on matters such as Berlin (see below, Chapter 8). In the past, Ulbricht had enjoyed great prestige with communist leaders abroad (he was one of the few who had still known Lenin personally!) and had often been able to convince Soviet leaders of the correctness of his line. However, this time he failed, and Moscow proved ready to enforce the desired change in policies and controls upon the DDR. The second major cause seems to have been in the domestic area: after his fall, Ulbricht was censured by his successors for wrong economic emphases, especially for an alleged neglect of the consumer sector in favor of "ostentatious" projects, such as vast government building complexes. Related to this, perhaps, was widespread disgust with the "personality cult" that had surrounded Ulbricht in his era. This can be surmised from his successors' new emphasis on "collective leadership," which was to replace Ulbricht's one-man control.

But whether such a "collective" would now

be in control remained to be seen. Certainly one man, or perhaps two or three, have emerged as "more equal than others" in the top collective bodies of party and government. Ulbricht's successor to the position of first party secretary (i.e., party chief) and other important posts, Erich Honecker, had long been heir apparent. A typical apparatchik, he had been the most prominent among the hardliners in the party leadership, opposing the leader of the more moderate faction, Prime Minister Willi Stoph. Whether Honecker would prove flexible enough to cope with questions of policy and leadership in the manner Ulbricht had frequently been capable of was not sure from his initial appointments to, and reshufflings of, party and government offices. Something like a triumvirate (perhaps a temporary one, as transition to complete one-man control) had emerged by late 1971, with Stoph groomed for the (perhaps now less important) position as chairman of the Council of State, and Horst Sindermann as successor to Stoph in the position of government chief (i.e., prime minister). Sindermann, long viewed as an up-and-coming younger leader, had been regional SED chief (in District Halle) and had not been closely affiliated with any party faction. But the future orientation of the party, and even its continued unity, seemed to depend chiefly on Honecker as "first among equals." The question was whether he would prove able and willing to give the "liberals" and the technocrats some chance, at least by playing them off against the doctrinaires (a group to which he himself had long belonged).

PROGRAM AND POLICIES

As noted earlier, the party is officially recognized in the new, 1968 constitution as "leader of the working class," and its function defined as "making socialism a reality." In undertaking this promise, the SED, in program and policies, has usually followed the Soviet line in all its sinuous details, echoing it in such different fields as foreign policy (peace propaganda, anti-imperialism, etc.) and the arts ("social realism"). There have been difficulties from time to time, especially in regard to "thaw" and "liberalization." Whenever there were such tendencies in the Soviet Union,

the SED was reluctant to follow suit. In the fifties, in particular, when mutual fear between rulers and ruled still characterized the DDR, Ulbricht was afraid to make concessions. Members of the party were purged when they seemed to perceive a new light after de-Stalinization in Moscow. Thus, in the area of free expression in opinion or culture there was no "thaw," and in this respect the regime continued to be "Stalinist." To some extent, it can be said to be so to this day. In another area, however, namely that of science, technology, and economic planning and management, the party "liberalized" its policies even before that of the CPSU. Also, in foreign policy, when it was a matter of its own, specific interests (such as DDR relations to West Germany, or in the Berlin question), the party leadership has not hesitated to put its own views over and against those of the Soviets, thus more than once proving quite a nuisance to Moscow policy. As we have just seen, it is likely that Ulbricht's "recalcitrance" in matters of these policies eventually cost him his job.

NATIONAL FRONT AND PUPPET PARTIES

All one-party regimes try to establish a façade of unity, with the people rallying around the aims and ideals of the "leading" party, but some, as the SED-led DDR, also permit additional parties to exist officially. This serves a double purpose: it allows the regime to show that all the different groups these parties supposedly represent are united behind the regime and its policies, and it enables people and groups who would not affiliate directly with the ruling party to have a means, however spurious, of participating in the "people's democracy."

Thus, at an early point, the SED formed a National Front of parties and other groups in the Republic. The National Front is in charge of making up the lists of candidates submitted to the electorate at election times. In addition to the original East Zone CDU and LDP, two more parties were subsequently added, a Democratic Farmers' party, to attract farmers, and a National Democratic party, to attract former Nazis. These two parties are complete dummies, but the CDU and LDP are also puppets subservient to the regime (in part even financed by it), serving only to gain control of groups that otherwise might not be controlled so easily. Initially more independent leaders either left East Germany or were purged; present leaders are pliable instruments in the hands of the ruling group. This "hegemonic" party system, where one party is in control of other parties, resembles that of Poland, while it contrasts with the "monoparty" system of the Soviet Union.

More important than controlling or organizing parties was the effort to coordinate the major social groups and interests through the establishment of so-called mass organizations; all of these are controlled by the SED through occupancy of key positions. Three main ones are these: in the field of agriculture, the peasants' Mutual Aid Organizations; in labor, the workers' and employees' Free Trade Unions; and for youth, the Free German Youth (FDJ). Thus the SED rules not only the state, but all social activity.

5 GOVERNMENT AND ADMINISTRATION

CENTRALISM

East German government is characterized by, first, complete centralism; second, preponderance of the executive over every other branch of government; and third, the pervading control of the SED. Centralism is reflected in the concentration of governmental power and authority in the central government. The districts are mere administrative subdivisions without discretion of their own. Below them there are local and county units. All have elected diets and executive "councils" composed of partly full-time, partly honorary members elected by the diets. The councils are considered "organs of state power" and are under control from the central level. Thus, although the councils are supposed to be under the dual control of the respective diet as well as of the next higher executive body (for example, a county council is under the district council; a district council is under the central ministry), the latter has the power to issue binding instructions to the councils. Hence it is the decisive element. There are about a hundred thousand members of diets on the various levels—that is, about one for every hundred adult inhabitants; their function is, as in the Soviet Union, "educational."

There is little room for local discretion. There are no legislative functions. Local and regional budgets are integral parts of the overall state budget, although small amounts (similar to the so-called directors' funds in enterprises) are left to the disposal of local authorities. It is to this streamlining from above that Ulbricht referred in his statement: "When we push that little button, the last village must report back within five minutes: Order executed."

AN EXECUTIVE-CONTROLLED PARLIAMENT

It is in the field of elections and parliament that the purely formal character of some governmental institutions reveals itself most clearly. Constitutionally, parliament controls the cabinet and other executive agencies and is supposed to be the sole lawmaker. Actually, it is a rubber stamp, whose eight fractions (five parties and three mass organizations) are coordinated through the bloc principle. When it meets, it functions more as a forum for government declarations than as a legislature. Even when it enacts statutes, its proceedings are usually distinguished by the absence of opposition, disagreement, criticism, or even debate. Only recently have committees been established and begun to function to some degree. But it still happens that deputies get draft bills only when the meeting begins.

Party functionaries and members of the Communist intelligentsia abound among the 434 deputies (to whom may be added 66 East Berlin members designated by the East Berlin diet). According to an official breakdown, the chamber elected in 1967 consisted of 251 workers, 41 farmers, 48 artisans and small businessmen, 56 employees, 27 intelligentsia, and 11 others. But here, again, social origin rather than present occupation seems to account for the large number of "workers."

Elections are held every four years and are by unity lists on which the groups constituting the National Front are represented according to a key giving the SED and the SED-controlled mass organization invariably a majority. This is the only list for which a vote can be validly cast, and it is thus not surprising that the nominees are elected by the notorious majorities of some 99 percent. A particle of choice is present since 1965 in the practice of putting more nominees on the lists than seats to be filled, so that the voter can strike out a few unwanted candidates. There is here a slight beginning of a more liberal election system.

Thus, elections are chiefly opportunities for rallying the people behind one or the other slogan for one or another of the forever changing "points of concentration" for which the propaganda machine is mobilized (for example, to raise agricultural productivity). The importance attached to elections is reflected in Ulbricht's statement: "We vote for one unity list because we are all united—that's why." To raise unity from a level of sullen apathy is the objective of all of the regime's mobilization efforts: elections, National Front, stooge parties, and "operative brigades" formed for any imaginable purpose.

A PARTY-CONTROLLED EXECUTIVE

The original executive consisted of a largely ceremonial president and a cabinet headed by a minister-president. Following the death of the first and only president (Wilhelm Pieck) in 1960, the presidency was abolished and replaced by a twenty-four-member Council of State, elected for four years by the People's Chamber. Besides ceremonial functions, it possesses powers to issue decrees with force of law and to lay down basic lines of policy, in particular for defense and security. Ulbricht, who assumed its chairmanship, had here another vantage point for control. After his downfall as party chief, in 1971, it looked as if he would soon have to give up that post also.

The center of the more ordinary governmental activity is the cabinet, or rather, an inner cabinet called the Presidium of the cabinet.

This consists of the premier and a number of deputy premiers as well as other ministers, altogether fifteen. SED leaders make up a majority. Actual policy is made or coordinated at the Presidium level. The cabinet at large (there were, in 1969, thirty-nine ministers) never meets as a body; the Presidium meets regularly.

SED control of government is exercised in two ways: first, important measures for which the government is formally responsible are actually initiated and worked out at the top level of the party. Thus, decrees or draft laws may originate with the Politbureau; they are then dealt with in detail in the respective department of the Central Committee; thence they go to the ministry in charge, which makes the official draft and submits it to the cabinet. Or, press directives come from the propaganda (Agitprop) section of the SED Secretariat to the press office of the minister-president.

The second means of control is through party leaders who simultaneously hold important government positions. There is now far-reaching personal identity between party and state leadership. Ulbricht, who was a mere deputy premier until he assumed the chairmanship of the Council of State in 1960, was head of party and state until he renounced the party leadership. Likewise, the premiership, which until 1964 was in the hands of a former, "coordinated" Social Democrat, has since been held by an SED man, Willi Stoph. The majority of the Presidium consists of Politbureau members. And there were, in 1969, twenty-five Central Committee members among the thirty-nine members of the cabinet, and nine in the Council of State.

In addition to the ministries there exist a number of top independent agencies whose chiefs usually have cabinet rank but whose main importance is in bringing party influence to bear on government and administration. Among these, a Workers' and Peasants' Inspectorate is charged with supervising the execution of laws on all levels, and with eliminating bottlenecks, preventing "sabotage," enforcing "discipline," and otherwise seeing that the economy functions properly. There is above all the State Planning Commission, replica of the Soviet Gosplan, which is in charge of all planning activities for the planned economy, and in particular of working out Five- or, occasionally, Seven-Year Plans; it is divided into departments, each of which is in charge of a major field. Major planning principles and policies derive either from SED leadership or, directly or indirectly, from the Soviet or Comecon level. Thus, here as elsewhere, actual lines of authority go downward rather than upward, and from party to government.

ADMINISTRATION AND CIVIL SERVICE

In the DDR the age-old problem of the German civil service has found a radical solution: the traditional service has simply been reformed out of existence. In order to do away with officialdom as a caste, public office was no longer to be differentiated from ordinary employment. This meant the abolition of the system of acquired rights and privileges: of guarantees of lifetime service, a separate pensions system, and so forth. All public officials now have the status of workers and employees. They have ordinary employment contracts, are under the general social security system (under which, instead of retirement pensions, they receive much lower old-age "rents"), and are affiliated with the general trade unions. In order to replace those, particularly in the higher ranks, who had fled or had been purged, rapid training courses were initially set up for candi-dates selected according to social origin and political progressivism. Since then the Walter Ulbricht Academy for Political and Legal Sciences has been in charge of training the elite of what in the West would be called the higher civil service. It is, of course, trained in the spirit of proletarian socialism.

But the problem of the cadres, that is, of having a loyal, reliable, and technically capable staff, continues to bother the regime. Replacement of the pre-Communist intelligentsia by the regime-trained new intelligentsia proceeded gradually, and many years after the beginning of the regime, it had still to be satisfied with an administrative staff hardly more than half proletarian in origin. Selection for appointment and promotion is exceedingly thorough. Files, supplemented by personal interviews, contain data on the private lives and the political attitudes and performances of the personnel. These files form the basis for any action of the personnel offices, which are invariably staffed with reliable SED members. In addition, duplicates of the files go to the corresponding cadre sections of the party, whose consent is required for appointments. It is the public employees' duty to behave even in their private lives according to prescribed standards, to report on "unreliable" colleagues, and so forth. They are, of course, dismissible at any time for reasons of unreliability. Whether the system has created more than passive collaborators—excepting the few loyal followers—seems doubtful.

6   ADMINISTRATION OF JUSTICE

LAW AND "SOCIALIST LEGALITY"

Since communism uses law chiefly to revamp society, it can be presented as a means for fighting the class enemy and building socialism. Serving to safeguard and enforce the varying policies of the regime, it is, as one observer has put it, "the respectable twin brother of terror." Actually, the regime has tried to dispense with terror whenever possible by substituting for it that engineering of consent—or at least an appearance of consent—that is also visible in connection with elections and opera-tive brigades. There have been fewer show trials and similar open methods of legal intimidation than in some other Communist countries, even in the early period. And in the wake of de-Stalinization, emphasis was placed on avoiding arbitrariness in law enforcement and on applying the laws on the statute books without discrimination. But socialist legality, as this more liberal attitude was called, then yielded again to what is now considered the true view of law enforcement: observance and interpretation of all law in the light of the party line. An intended liberalization of the law of criminal procedure, that touchstone of liberalism, was given up, and punitive laws, especially in the field of political and economic crimes, were made even more severe.

Only after the erection of the Berlin Wall did the regime apparently feel sufficiently at ease to enact a Law on Administration of Justice, which contains certain legal guarantees for an accused. It also transferred to a somewhat less autocratic body, the Supreme Court, some of the powers of supervision over the judiciary that the Minister of Justice had held previously. Further, instead of state courts, so-called conflict commissions, elected in enterprises but actually selected by the official trade union organization, were put in charge not only of labor conflicts but also, increasingly, of minor criminal cases in general. And informal "comradely courts," on the Soviet model, have been set up in neighborhoods to deal with relatively minor law infractions in an allegedly less legalistic and more "social" manner, paying attention to social background, social damage, and the like. It may be asked whether handing law enforcement over to such "social organs of jurisdiction," instead of lessening fear, does not actually create more of a police-state atmosphere; especially when legal sanctions are replaced with "educational" measures (reprimand, obligation to apologize, and so forth) which may imply social ostracism.

In the 1960s, such piecemeal legislation yielded to an attempt to replace the—until then valid—German law codes with an overall codification of the chief legal fields on the basis of "socialism." This began with the enactment of a code of family law in 1965, which liberalized divorce and provided for more equality among the marriage partners, and it was followed by a new penal law code in 1968. The new criminal law shares with other Communist legal systems features such as extremely harsh standards for "political crimes," which are broadly defined and in many cases allow for capital punishment. But, on the other hand, it deals more leniently with "ordinary" crimes and in some areas, such as sexual offenses, eliminates certain acts as punishable crimes altogether (thus paralleling recent reforms in the Federal Republic, see Chapter 6, Section

3). There are now on the agenda a new civil law code and a code on civil procedure. Together with such earlier legislation as one on education and schools and one on labor law, the present legal reform reflects growing estrangement from the system of law still valid in West Germany and the regime's intention of setting the DDR apart as a separate entity. The creation of a separate DDR citizenship (Citizenship Law of February 1967) points in the same direction. Thus reunification has in practice been dropped as an objective, and political partition is being accompanied by legal disunity.

JUDICIARY AND COURTS

"Judges of a new type," so-called people's judges, have replaced the former judiciary. They are trained not only in the technical details of the law, but also in the principles of Marxism-Leninism and their "social" application. Upon nomination by the Justice Ministry, judges are elected by diets for four years, but they can be recalled for "serious violation of their duties."

Thus judicial independence is limited. Besides elimination of lifetime tenure, coordination is achieved through the criticism of judgments by higher courts, official indication in official journals of how laws are expected to be applied, inspectors sent down to the local level, and, even, official directives issued by the ministry to judges. The prosecutor's penalty demands are practically binding upon courts, and any objective attitude is condemned as a serious deviatior

The court system consists of three levels: county courts, district courts, and a Supreme Court; in criminal cases the prosecution can freely determine which court shall hear a case. There is only one appeal (none where the Supreme Court has original jurisdiction); but even after a judgment has become *res judicata*, the Supreme Court, on its own or the prosecutor general's initiative, may quash it as contradicting the principles and policies of the regime. Lay assessors are selected according to political standards. Attorneys are organized in lawyers' cooperatives, which assign cases and clients; however, their influence has been declining. Execution of penalties (prison system, etc.) is under police administration.

Prosecutor general

The power of the prosecutor goes far beyond what prosecution ordinarily implies. The prosecutor general of the Republic, who is the head of a centralized state agency of prosecution, is not subordinated to the Ministry of Justice, and has cabinet rank; he resembles the public prosecutor of the Soviet Union in that he is supposed to watch over the proper execution of the laws, not only in the case of ordinary citizens but also on the part of any and all government agencies (including the ministries), all enterprises, and all their officers and employees. He and the members of his staff, whom he freely appoints and dismisses, thus exercise universal, police-type surveillance.

Secret police

In this matter of surveillance the prosecutor general seems to be in direct competition with another institution—the State Security Service (SSD)—which, like the Nazi Gestapo, is a separate police agency with a staff of its own and far-reaching powers. Whether the prosecutor general or the SSD acts in individual cases seems to depend on secret regulations that may themselves be the result of a behind-the-scenes tug-of-war for power and influence.

Before 1953, the SSD, under one of the regime's most powerful figures, had high status in the governmental structure. Subsequently, it was downgraded and no longer plays an independent political role. However, it remains the chief agency combatting political offenses. The sphere of its activity is apparent from the fact that, although their number has been slowly declining, there are still several thousand persons in prison for political crimes. Its estimated fifteen thousand officials maintain a network of informers that numbers about a hundred thousand; frequently persons are pressed into such service through blackmail and intimidation, or in return for freedom from prosecution in cases where they have come under suspicion. On the whole, however, it can be said that in recent years the influence of the police has receded. As one observer has commented, "Terror and repression have largely been replaced by pressure, persuasion, and incentive." This holds for other areas of government and society too.

7   ECONOMIC, SOCIAL, AND CULTURAL PROBLEMS

With the social and economic revolution that was inaugurated in the zone in 1945, the economic and social rule of the two traditional ruling groups in East Germany, the landowning Junkers and the upper middle class (industrialists and bankers), came to an end. It has been replaced by a planned economy, with economic and social controls exercised by the political ruling group; this was achieved through collectivization of agriculture and nationalization of trade and industry. Perhaps even more significant is the increasingly tight integration of the East German economy into the economic system of the Eastern bloc. Thus, by 1970, of a 30 billion Eastmark volume of international trade (imports and exports), 23 billion were with East bloc countries (13 billion of these with the Soviet Union).[7]

AGRICULTURE

The most dramatic of these transformations was land collectivization through a quickly launched, all-out campaign in the spring of 1960. But there had been previous revolutions

[7] Most of the statistical data and figures in the sections that follow are taken from a comprehensive recent report by the Federal Ministry for Intra-German Relations, *Bericht der Bundesregierung und Materialien zur Lage der Nation 1971* (Bonn, 1971). This report compares the conditions in the two parts of Germany in a manner that is as detailed as it is objective.

in the countryside. The first had distributed the large estates to smallholders and the landless. But farms allotted to peasants were generally so small as to make farmers dependent upon the state, with the latter's control exercised through compulsory delivery quotas and state-owned machine tractor stations. Then, in a first wave of collectivization in the early 1950s, the regime turned against the wealthier peasants, forcing many to flee to the West and consolidating their possessions in agricultural production cooperatives (LPG's), kolkhozes on the Soviet pattern. A new wave began in 1958, which by the end of 1959 had resulted in collectivizing about 50 percent of the land. We do not know what caused the regime, thereupon, to force a policy that had been supposed to extend over years to near 100 percent completion within a few weeks. We know only the method. While there was no law compelling anybody to sign up, there was total mobilization of party workers, police, and other activists who descended in "brigades" on the countryside and relentlessly worked on each farmer until, worn out and intimidated, he saw no other way than to capitulate.

"Socialism in the countryside" was virtually achieved by 1960. Today, 95 percent of the arable land is used by collectivized enterprises, and only 10,000 out of about 1 million people working on the land (i.e., 1 percent) are still independent farmers owning their private land; these, however, account for several percent of the farm product.

In 1960, collectivization had not yet reached the stage where the cattle and the farm implements are, in addition to the land, also commonly owned. This so-called Type III stage (where farmers may privately own only a few pigs and chickens) has now been extended to a majority of units and farmers. Moreover, the LPG's are being integrated into ever larger units, resembling more and more rural factories where farmers are mere wage-earning laborers; they are paid in "work units." All this has led to problems well known to collectivized agricultural systems in other countries, particularly the Soviet Union: lack of initiative and overbureaucratization have hampered agricultural production and made shortages endemic.[8]

On the other hand, technology has meant advance, and mechanization has made East German agriculture not only more efficient than that of the earlier Junker estates but, relatively speaking, also more efficient than that of the other Communist countries, including the Soviet Union's. It has also meant that the number of those working in the countryside has sharply declined (from about 2 million in 1950 to less than 1 million in 1970), reflecting a general trend in modernized countries, East and West.

INDUSTRY

Industry is completely planned and almost completely nationalized. At first, major enterprises were taken over directly by the Soviets and run as "Soviet corporations"; they were subsequently turned over to German ownership and management. This renationalization, however, has not prevented a growing coordination of the East German economy with that of the rest of the Soviet bloc.

East Germany, which was a victim of Soviet economic exploitation during the immediate postwar period, has since been transformed into one of the most important industrial units in the Communist world; as an industrial power it ranks eighth or ninth in the world, second (after the Soviet Union) in Comecon. It stands second in intrabloc trade and is the bloc's most important exporter of machinery. It further specializes in shipbuilding, tools, chemicals, and other products. It has become one of the heaviest Eastern traders with the underdeveloped world. Its economic growth, though initially behind that of West Germany (which was aided by Marshall Plan help while the East was squeezed by the Russians), has lately been as spectacular as that of West Germany. And the living standard of its people, although still lagging behind West Germany's, has been rising.

While big industry has by now become completely nationalized, private ownership survives in some smaller craft and retail-trade estab-

---

[8] Shortages of consumers' goods have periodically plagued the citizens of the DDR. In one story, a Leipzig man arrives home unexpectedly at noon to interrupt a tender scene between his wife and a strange man. Livid with rage, the husband roars at his wife: "How can you be wasting your time here when the grocer has lemons for sale?"

lishments; but even there it is declining. Under a system of enforced state participation (a government "partnership" with the private owner) enterprises are taken over by the government upon the death of the owner. Handicraft is being collectivized in artisans' cooperatives. By 1970, only 3 percent of those working were still "independent," accounting for 6 percent of the overall economic product.

Nationalized enterprises are organized as separate entities with separate budgets. Appointed directors, assisted by trade union-controlled boards, are responsible for their management and, especially, for the fulfillment of plan quotas. Since 1963, as in the other Eastern bloc economies, East Germany has tried, through a "New Economic System of Planning and Management" (NÖS), to reduce red tape and increase efficiency by giving plant managers more discretion in production, by permitting them to set prices calculated on the basis of actual production costs and market conditions, and by allowing for a certain amount of interfactory competition. More lately, overall planning has been based on long-range, scientific prognosis (with use of systems analysis and other ultramodern techniques), automation has been introduced, and science is further encouraged. With this development, the weight and influence of the technological and managerial elite, as against that of the ideological-political leadership, has been rising.[9]

LABOR

The fact that workers were in the forefront of the revolt in 1953 illustrates the paradox of a socialist regime that has not managed to command the allegiance of an appreciable part of the proletariat. This is the more remarkable in view of the improvement in living standards. Although wages and salaries in terms of purchasing power are still below the level of West Germany, there are many compensations, including low-rent (though still crowded) hous-

ing, free medical services for everybody, free education, including higher education accessible to all, and retirement and disability pensions comparable to those of West Germany.[10] For certain types of work, especially that done by engineers, managers, functionaries, and outstanding (that is, politically deserving) intellectuals, salaries are much above the average.

But it is a managed system. Labor lacks means to defend its interests. Strikes are outlawed, works councils abolished, and work standards ("technically justified work norms") prescribed; often piece wages compel workers to work hard and long hours. While in the Federal Republic 44 percent of the population are in the working force, 51 percent work in the DDR. Many of them are women and persons over sixty-five years of age. In the DDR, 46 percent of those working, as against 37 percent in the FRG, are women, but only 8 percent of them are in leading positions; of those over age sixty-five, 32 percent, as against 24 percent, still work in the DDR.

The Free Trade Association (FDGB) is the workers' only organization, but it is not really theirs. It is an SED-controlled, strictly centralized mass organization, with membership practically compulsory in all larger enterprises. Its chief purpose is to organize workers so as "to reach and surpass the norms of the planned economy." Similar to Soviet Union trade unions, the FDGB has some additional functions: one, to manage and control a social insurance system; and two, to supervise the observation of labor laws. It also organizes vacation and other free-time activities of workers and employees (owning and running resort hotels, etc.). The social insurance system, which has been set up as one huge, centralized system, comprises all the formerly separate branches of social insurance; it covers over 95 percent of the population, including public employees and students. It is financed by automatic deductions of 10 percent of all wages earned, a figure somewhat lower than the West German rates. There is no unemployment. On the contrary, increasing labor shortages, due partly still to the massive flight West (up to 1961) and partly to low birth rates, confront the East German

---

[9] However, in one of the swings of the pendulum that are characteristic of all Communist regimes, the ideology of the Economic System of Socialism (NÖS having been renamed ÖSS) puts the emphasis now on central guidance and role of the party again. Under Honecker's leadership this is likely to remain so.

[10] Of a total of 60 billion Eastmark public expenditures, 26 billion were for social security, health, and education (1969).

economy with one of its primary problems. Thus the status and attitude of the masses are ambiguous: driven and manipulated by what many still consider an oppressive regime, they nevertheless get some sense of security and even some sense of pride from the economic consequences of their work. To stimulate the latter feeling at the expense of the former is the aim of the regime's efforts in the fields of propaganda and indoctrination.

EDUCATION AND CULTURE

The system is still totalitarian in that all cultural activity entails propaganda and indoctrination. The basis of the unceasing effort to indoctrinate and propagandize is dialectical materialism, the theoretical foundation of Marxist-Leninist doctrine. This effort comprises, retroactively, Germany's entire past. The German cultural inheritance, including classical literature and idealistic philosophy, is reinterpreted, and its creators and creations are either admitted as "humanistic" forerunners of socialism or else disregarded. Theater, music, literature, arts are all under the direction of the Culture Ministry and thus coordinated. But intellectuals, writers, and artists who put themselves into the service of the new culture are not only well provided for materially but are extolled and honored, and this official promotion of culture cannot fail to make some impression even on the noncoordinated among a culture-minded people like the Germans.

Like culture, information and communication in all media—press, radio, television, film—are means of propaganda and indoctrination. Daily directives are handed out by the press office of the minister-president, and the official East German news agency is the only source of news reports. Therefore, he who reads *Neues Deutschland* (the central organ of the SED) has read them all (except for local news). People are forbidden to read the West German press or to listen to any but the official broadcasting programs. But communication between the two worlds is not cut off completely, especially as far as radio and television are concerned. On the other hand, there still is less interchange of ideas and persons than has developed of late between other Eastern countries and the West.

Incompleteness of control can also be seen in the relation of the regime to religion. Its basic hostility is clear from its antireligious philosophy and is expressed in harassment of churches, clergymen, and those lay people who cling to more active church membership. Religious instruction has of course been eliminated from the schools and can be given only in private. Children insisting on communion or confirmation do this at some risk to their future careers. Thus it is not surprising that over 90 percent of all children participate in a Communist "youth consecration," which the regime has created as a competing institution, as it has also established special "socialist" rituals and ceremonies for births, weddings, burials, and so forth. Financially, the churches are dependent on assessments of members, payments of which cannot be enforced; membership itself has dropped sharply, especially among men; by the middle sixties it stood at about two-thirds of the population and in the big cities had dropped to below one-half. Still, the churches have so far managed to survive. As under Nazism, and, to some extent, under the Soviet system, they remain the only recognized institutions not fully incorporated into the system and thus the only ones able to continue some doctrinal independence. Until 1969, the Protestants (who constitute the large majority of East German Christians) were even able to maintain an organizational link with their West German brethren through the federation of the "Evangelical Church in Germany" (EKD), but they then were compelled to break off that tie.

Winning over the young generation and using the gifted among them as a reservoir for the future elite has been a major objective of the regime. A considerable amount of effort and money has been expended on this goal. The educational system of the DDR shows appealingly progressive and repulsive features all in one. In its structure it provides free mass education on all levels in the place of the former class system. It is a one-track system of schools, from the kindergartens (provided for over half of all children between ages three and six, thus releasing their mothers, 71 percent of whom are working) to universities (with a percentage of students proportionally higher than in West Germany). After "basic school" (*Grundschule*) there follow ten years "poly-technical" schooling for all, extended to twelve years for those selected for university study. In the earlier period there was a kind of class system in reverse, with children of workers and peasants preferred and those of "bourgeois" background discriminated against. Under the impact of the growing demand for qualified people in the higher ranks of the economy and administration, this discrimination was dropped. Now the percentage of students of "proletarian" origin has declined to about one-third, while the offspring of the "intelligentsia" contributes almost as many. Study is tuition-free, and over 90 percent of the students receive "pay" for their living expenses in the form of stipends (which are also available for the last four years of preuniversity school for those needing financial aid). And a kind of "women's liberation" may be perceived in the fact that a much higher proportion of girls are admitted to higher study, and thus may become doctors or other professionals, than is the case in the FRG.

To establish close contact between theory (learning) and practice, children in the upper grades at school have to attend work in a factory or on a farm one day a week. While this may be all to the good, the almost exclusive focus of "polytechnical" education on training "polytechnical" man for the practical occupations and professions needed by the regime's economy, with its emphasis on science, math, and technical preparation for work, means neglect of general culture and humanities and of the development of the children's own personalities. They are groomed to become cogs in the technological machine. Thus the number of students graduating from engineering and related fields was triple that of those in the Federal Republic (29.7 percent of all students versus 9.8), while those in the cultural areas (language, art, music, etc.) accounted, in the DDR, for only 4.5 percent, as against 10.3 percent in the FRG. In addition, of course, there is indoctrination, with Marxist "civics" repeated at each grade, until it comes out of the children's ears. All things Russian and Soviet are stressed to achieve clear separation from the Western world of culture (with Rus-

sian language compulsory at high school). Another way of getting hold of the young ones' minds, of course, is their participation in the official youth organizations (Pioneers and FDJ). While the regime does not attempt to destroy the family (there are even children allowances, increasing with the number of children), the state competes with the family in regard to influencing minds and attitudes.

How successful has the regime been in this respect? Judging from the difficulties the regime has broadcast from time to time (e.g., indicting groups of youths for hooliganism or as "degenerate beats," or complaining of cynicism and lack of political involvement), one might conclude that youth is dissatisfied or, at least, not thoroughly controlled. But it seems that the majority are more or less opportunistic, interested in passing exams and adjusting themselves to the formal requirements of political organization and activity. And since desirable positions are open to the young more readily than in other countries, many are bribed into compliance and some even into sincere devotion to what appears to them an altruistic goal in life (building up socialism, etc.). It is significant that there has been no revolt over issues of university reform (not to mention more political issues) of the type that has characterized many other countries (including Eastern ones) in recent years. Apparently this was not due to fear of repression but to a kind of reform from above which the regime, anticipating student unrest, shrewdly provided for on its own, with more student participation in university administration, and so forth (but, of course, minus participation in more political decisions). Occasionally the regime polls students (with anonymity protected) about political attitudes and, in what is referred to as "socialist self-criticism," publicizes the results. These, in 1970, showed an officially admitted "propensity toward Social Democratism," that is, a third way outside Communism and capitalism—a socialism minus the coercive aspects of Communism.[11] Thus, while many of the

[11] A banner shown by some West German socialists anent the meeting of the two Willies, Willy Brandt and Willi Stoph, at Kassel in May 1970, perhaps is indicative of the yearnings of these East German youths also. It read: "Willy: more socialism—Willi: more democracy."

young (and of the people in general) probably hate the autocratic features of the regime, this by no means implies support of the way of life and the institutions of West Germany. It is doubtful whether they would give up a planned economy and nationalized industries for free enterprise and privately owned corporations, or free education for class-based education. These factors should not be overlooked by those in the West who still look toward reunification of the two Germanies sometime in the future.

CONCLUSION

What of the future? With Germany the birthplace of "scientific socialism," it is likely that Communism looks upon the contest between a Communist and a non-Communist Germany with particular interest, perhaps perceiving an historical mission in the DDR's building what a conference of Communist parties once called "the outpost of socialism in Western Europe." While it is unlikely—barring war or conquest—that Communism will succeed in West Germany, it may well succeed, given time, in establishing in East Germany a unit so deeply alienated from the West that it would emerge as an entirely different country. Many East Germans may even now be so alienated: we must not forget that all those below the age of forty to forty-five have never experienced liberal democracy or any other Western way of life; even the oldest among these grew up under Nazism and then, almost without break, have lived under Communism.

If the regime manages to solve the problem of recruiting and training an elite, not hostile, but devoted to the job that is required for a planned economy and society, it may well succeed even after the "founders" have gone. The DDR has developed from a satellite ruled by stooges of a foreign power into a junior partner of the Soviet Union. Economically, it has attained the highest living standard in the East (including the Soviet's). As to modernity, it has managed to combine scientific and technological innovation with political centralization and ideological unity. As one of its leaders has been able to boast: "We are not only ideologically sound but correctly programmed." The progress made is well summed up by a critical Western observer, who says: "By the late 1960's, East Germany had transformed itself from one of the most war-ravaged societies into the most ideologically and economically advanced science-oriented Communist state. After a fifty-year lapse, the combination of Prussian discipline, German scientific efficiency, and Leninist-Stalinist ideology has thus again made German communism a model for its Eastern neighbors." [12]

Thus economically flourishing and expanding, its Communism may come to seem more and more "natural" to a majority of its inhabitants. Today, it is still a system of accommodation, with many East Germans still resentful of bureaucracy, indoctrination, the remnants of repression, and, above all, of imprisonment, of being unable to come and go where they like. But they are adjusting to the notion of the DDR as "our republic" and not merely something transitory. Time seems to have by-passed the chances of early reunification. This realization is reflected not only in the foreign policy of the DDR but increasingly in the attitudes and policies of West Germany, too.

[12] Zbigniew Brzezinski, *Between Two Ages—America's Role in the Technetronic Age* (New York, Viking, 1970), p. 171.

8

World politics
and the
German problem

Our chapter dealing with Germany and the world cannot bear the title "German Foreign Policy" for the simple reason that there are two Germanies with two sets of foreign policies that have often been diametrically opposed to each other. But not to deal with foreign policy problems in a study of German government and politics would be almost ludicrous, so interwoven have foreign policy issues been with domestic policy in both parts of Germany ever since 1945, indeed, with the destiny of each individual German, who can hardly distinguish what is "domestic" and what "external" in German affairs. Thus an equal number of Germans answered in opposite ways when asked whether they considered the issue of reunification a matter of domestic or foreign policy.

For a hundred years now, Germany has stood in the center of world politics. Geographically, because it is located in the heart of the continent from which, since it contained most of the world powers, international politics has radiated. Politically, because, for most of these hundred years, Germany's foreign policy has been among the most dynamic of all nations'. Even after the center of world politics shifted, so to speak, to the peripheries, to the United States and Eurasia, Germany emerged as one of the three or four most crucial crisis areas on the globe. It was in the heart of defeated Germany that East and West met at the conclusion of World War II. It was over the German question that they split and became involved in a cold war that, at times, threatened to degenerate into a nuclear holocaust. And it is in

Germany that, at this moment, the question whether confrontation will finally yield to cooperation, is being decided. History records few comebacks as staggering and as swift as that of both Germanies in the postwar period—a comeback especially significant if one recalls how deep Germany's fall had been and how determined the victors had seemed never to allow her to rise again. But there are also few examples of a stalemate so deep and so protracted as the one that developed over the German question during that period. Then, suddenly at the end of 1969, everything seemed to get in flux. That which had been missed in 1945 and over which the stalemate and the continuing crisis had developed, a peace settlement with clear decisions concerning the status of Germany or the Germanies, recognized boundary lines, and so forth, now seemed in the offing. Suddenly, there were negotiations by all concerned parties about all outstanding issues: the Federal Republic and the Soviet Union on the European status quo (especially the territorial one), culminating in the Moscow Treaty of August 12, 1970; the Federal Republic and Poland on the Eastern (formerly German) territories and boundaries, leading to the Warsaw Treaty of December 1970; four-power negotiations on the status of Berlin; and even the two Germanies themselves on the relations between the two parts of the divided nation. By 1971 it was too early to predict their outcome. How far would the United States go in supporting these policies? Would domestic West German opposition inhibit them or even bring its initiators to fall? Would Soviet and DDR leadership prove ready to go all the way toward *détente?*

It is on these and related questions that the following discussion will center. For reasons of space we cannot trace in detail the historical phases of German foreign policy (to which brief references have been made in Chapter 2) nor can we deal with the innumerable problems of foreign policy that do not directly touch upon the "Germany question," that is, the question of the two Germanies, their relationship, their relations to East and West, and the problem of status quo versus revision (in particular, reunification). For the world at large, and the two superpowers in particular, this core question looms largest among all the various problems with which Germans in both parts of the divided country are concerned.

1   BACKGROUND AND FOREIGN POLICY "ORIENTATION"

The present German identity problem—whether there are or should be one or two countries, and if one, in what sense and within what confines—is foreshadowed in Germany's past. In contrast to the British, French, and Russians, with their long history as nation-states, Germans have not even always been sure they should, or could, form a political unit. Centuries-old disunity drove some of them (including Goethe) to the pessimistic conclusion that they were incapable of ruling themselves as a nation. What would be the form and role of their state? Should it be a nation-state like others, or a Reich—with its mystical connotation of a larger unity of several nationalities—with a European "mission"? The medieval Empire was meant to integrate all Western Christian nations, but it was feeble; its modern revival, since 1871, turned out to be intent on power politics and hegemony. The pendulum of attitudes had often swung from utopian idealism (cosmopolitanism around 1800, pacifism after World War I, Europeanism after World War II) to cynical realism (*Realpolitik*). Few Germans had learned the more modest but also more difficult job of living as good neighbors among equals. True, such an attitude was rendered difficult by Germany's belated unification as well as by her geographical location between an East that had never known political liberties, and the liberal-democratic West. Germans have been periodically attracted and repelled by these poles, oscillating between authoritarianism and democracy, romanticism and enlightenment, pragmatism and mysticism. This oscillation has been reflected in Germany's foreign policy orientation.

In actual foreign policies, this meant oscillating between an "Eastern" and a "Western orientation." When, in the late 1940s, Adenauer lined up "his" Germany with the West, and Ulbricht "his" with the East, these were only somewhat extreme repetitions of what had happened time and again since Bismarck founded the modern Reich. Even prior to that, the Prussian Junkers had seen in the autocratic regime of the tsars the backbone of order in Europe and thus in Eastern orientation an ultimate protection against the liberal West. After 1871, this orientation was translated into Germany's alliance with Russia. But to Bismarck's distress, William II abandoned the "wire to St. Petersburg" and did not replace it with a Western lineup. At that time anything but enmity toward France (a republic that to Germans seemed always to be tottering at the brink of "anarchy") was unthinkable to the German ruling classes. Since England was alienated by German colonial imperialism and naval competition, enmity toward the West and disengagement from the East meant for Germany "going it alone," paranoic obsession with being "encircled," a two-front World War I, and, eventually, defeat. In the Weimar period the leading republican parties and personalities (including Gustav Stresemann) leaned toward the Western victor nations, in hopes of regaining status and Eastern territory through peaceful revision of the Versailles status quo. But an Eastern orientation, despite the transformation of Russian monarchical autocracy into Bolshevism, was advocated by influential rightist circles, including leading Reichswehr generals and diplomats who hoped to find in Russia the lever with which to raise defeated Germany against a hostile West. Even among the Nazis a geopolitical school of thought dreamed of a huge Eurasian bloc, formed by Germany, Russia, and Japan, that would efface the Western empires. Hitler, however—repeating William's mistake on a grand scale—turned against West *and* East, hoping to destroy the former before finishing off the latter, and managed to destroy not only German power but the nation's very existence as a political unit.

When, after the fall of Nazism, the two present Germanies emerged, their "orientation" was less a matter of choice than of necessity. Both being creations of their respective occupying powers, their policies, even their chances of obtaining independence, depended very much on submitting to the policy lines and objectives of the blocs into which they were integrated, and especially the countries leading these blocs. In the case of the DDR, this meant satellite status throughout the 1950s and even now little leeway in following the general lines of Soviet foreign policy. In the case of West Germany, "sovereignty" seems to imply a much larger sphere of discretion. This situation has been due not only to the much greater weight a rearmed Federal Republic possesses in the world balance of power, but also to the fact that West Germany had to deal not only with one superpower but, despite the preponderance of the United States in the alliance, with several powers with sometimes divergent interests.

To assess their consequences and discuss possible alternatives, these Eastern and Western alignments must be seen in their connection with the power balance of the world at the time, in particular, the balance between the two superpowers as they emerged from World War II. Indeed, present partition follows almost exactly the line of deepest military penetration of Western and Soviet armies into Germany at the time of capitulation; inasmuch as it deviates from this (there was some penetration of American forces into what later became part of the Soviet zone), partition was based on pre-surrender agreements in turn based on what the powers expected to possess at the moment hostilities would cease. Thus, by and large, what East and West had been

able to conquer for themselves became the basis for postwar distribution of power and influence among the emerging two power blocs. To be sure, the original intention was to divide Germany only temporarily and restore central German government at an early point on the basis of the Potsdam principles. But since the powers were unable to agree on how to reestablish a Germany that would be neither pawn of the West nor puppet of the East, the line dividing the Western zones of occupation from the Soviet zone (and that separating the Western sectors of Berlin from the Soviet sector), remained the boundaries of their respective spheres of influence. East and West came to consider their vital interests tied up with control of their portions of Germany, and the cold war, with its mutual suspicions, rendered each side ever more anxious to preserve its sphere of influence and domination in Central Europe.

We have dealt in Chapter 2 (see Sections 4 and 5) with the events that led up to the establishment of the Federal Republic in 1949 and, beyond that, to the granting of full sovereignty through the Paris agreements of 1955 as well as West Germany's alignment with and integration into the West (military integration into Western European Union and NATO, economic integration first into the Schuman Plan iron and steel community, subsequently transformed into the European Communities of Common Market, Euratom, and so forth, and general cultural lineup with Western Europe through the Council of Europe). There had never been a stronger Western orientation in German history. We have seen, further, how this orientation was tied up with the emergence, internally, of a unit that is politically democratic (with some authoritarian remnants) and economically capitalist. In view of the radical transformation of that part of Germany which had fallen into the sphere of the Soviets, protection of West Germany seemed vital to most of its people, and thus the foreign policy of Adenauer was, in its main lines, approved. The idea of merging national identities in a larger Europe which in time would form a supranational entity, especially appealed to many Germans who had seen ultranationalism lead to war and defeat and national identity vanish into partition. There was some opposition, to be sure. As pointed out before (see Chapter 3, Section 3), the SPD, indicting Adenauer as the "chancellor of the Allies," resented West Germany's integration into what looked at that time like a predominantly conservative-Catholic Western Europe and was fearful that it meant giving up all hopes and chances of eventual reunification. They thus advocated neutralism, more or less vaguely defined as the nonalignment of both Germanies with either bloc. In addition, they also favored establishment of a demilitarized (or, at least, militarily "thinned out") area in Central Europe, and, after reunification, a policy of political nonalignment on the part of the new central German government. Besides the SPD, certain groups in the churches (especially among Protestants) and outside them, pacifists and others, also supported neutralism, fearful, as they were, of the effects of rearmament on a temporarily antimilitaristic population. Nationalists, on the other hand, resented loss of national independence and the prospect of becoming new Hessians for yesterday's enemy. We have seen how such apprehensions led to a very careful buildup of the new armed forces and an attempt to imbue its members with a spirit of "citizens-in-arms" type of democracy (see Chapter 5, Section 1). By and large, however, all this opposition came to naught vis-à-vis the compelling force of a policy that supplied not only renewed status and prestige but material well-being and prosperity unequaled in modern German history. One particular bonus of Western alignment was unique: the burial of the age-old enmity with France (culminating in the Franco-German "friendship treaty" of January 1963). Thus in the early 1960s, the future seemed to bode well for Germans. A united Europe to replace obsolete nation-states seemed in the offing, signaling a significant change in attitudes, particularly in a country whose middle classes for so long had rejected any nonhegemonial regionalism in favor of German nationalism. Strategically, West Germany seemed protected as an intrinsic part of a strong alliance system in which she was the strongest European power in terms of conventional forces and armaments and in which she could avoid the dangers of militarism through full integration in a higher setup. Culturally and in internal affairs, finally, she seemed to be gradually accepting Western-style liberal democracy. In short, West Germany seemed to have emerged as a powerful and respected member of international society.

2   THE REUNIFICATION PROBLEM AND FOREIGN POLICY STALEMATE

This pleasing picture overlooked one thing: this prosperous and apparently secure Germany in the West, which claimed to represent and speak for *all* Germans (*Alleinvertretungsanspruch*), as long as Germans in the East were not allowed to freely express their will, left in limbo 17 million Germans in the DDR, and West Germany's alignment with one part of the world could only deepen the chasm separating it from the other. Partition, the outgrowth of the cold war, in turn added to the latter's vigor; any time an East German trying to escape the DDR died in the barbed wire surrounding that country, each time East German authorities harassed traffic on the Autobahn to Berlin, each time East and West clashed over some Soviet "ultimatum" concerning the status of that city, the peace of the world was at the mercy of an incident. The German problem remained unsolved, reunification moved ever farther away.

In the face of this situation, original Western policy (promoted most vigorously by Adenauer and United States Secretary of State John Foster Dulles, but officially shared by the British and French, too) revealed its futility. What had that policy been? Its main assumptions can, perhaps, be summarized as follows: (1) East and West constitute two hostile camps, because (2) the East, by its very nature (with its Communist aim of world conquest) is and must remain expansionist. (3) The West, therefore, must be strong, especially militarily, in order to contain and then roll back the opponent. (4) The West has a chance to do so because it will become stronger, while the East, with its totalitarian terror system, will be weakened by internal crises and the absence of that freedom that is necessary for scientific-technological advance, especially in armaments.

Thus, "building positions of strength" and then "negotiating from strength," so Adenauer and Dulles hoped, would compel the Soviets eventually to make concessions; in the face of overwhelming Western power they would have to yield control over much of Eastern Europe, including East Germany. West German alignment with the West would open the way toward reunification and, conceivably, even the restoration of the frontiers of 1937.

But just as the Communists' assumption that the West would "inevitably" decay through economic crises proved wrong, the West was mistaken in its basic assumptions concerning Communism and the Soviets. Rather than proving expansionist, the Soviets adopted a policy of maintaining the spheres created at the end of the war. On the other hand, sputnik and, especially, their development of nuclear power—making them *the* other superpower—proved that totalitarian structure does not preclude technological prowess. This meant that the Western objectives, and in particular German reunification, had become unobtainable, unless one was ready to risk nuclear war. From now on the forever repeated aim of "unification through free elections," like that of "rollback" and "liberation" of satellite nations, partook more and more of the nature of mere cold war rhetoric. Reluctantly, the West became convinced that display of force could be used for mutual deterrence only and not for achieving a change in the existing balance of power. This realization, logically, implied mutual recognition of the two spheres of influence in Europe, and therewith of the line dividing Germany. But the road from such tacit admission (acted upon when the West abstained from interference at the time of the Hungarian revolution, or at the erection of the Berlin Wall) to actual acceptance proved a long and tortuous one. For the time being, there prevailed a policy of nonrecognition of a *de facto* situation still considered illegal. Although negotiating sub rosa with DDR authorities on such issues as interzonal trade, Bonn refused to establish any more formal ties. Official terminology forbade even the use of the word DDR, which remained the "Soviet Zone of Occupation," or, subsequently, "the other part of Germany"; if Eastern terms were referred to at all, they must at all times be put between quotation marks or prefaced with an "alleged" (for example, the alleged, or self-styled, "DDR"). If this sounds childish, there was more practical significance in the so-called Hallstein Doctrine, under which Bonn refused to have, or would break off, diplomatic relations with any country (except the Soviet Union) that recognized the East German regime. That policy hardly paid off; it merely embittered Bonn's relations with countries such as the Arab nations. It did not prevent them from dealing with the DDR through trade missions or consulates and, increasingly, from establishing official ties. Still, it was a partly successful joint Western attempt to isolate the DDR, which was not allowed, for instance, to be represented in most international organizations.

The policy of intransigence also meant that, repeatedly, chances of narrowing the gap between the two Germanies were missed, or at least remained unexplored. One chance that was missed might even have terminated at reunification: several times in the early 1950s the Soviets intimated that they might permit free elections in East Germany (which, of course, would have meant yielding their control) in return for some neutralization plan under which the West would withdraw from "its" Germany. Historians will long debate whether such a deal was possible, but the point is that the possibility was not even explored. Adenauer preferred to rely on NATO and rearmament and rejected these approaches out of hand. Thereupon, the Soviets shifted their emphasis to building up East Germany as an economic workshop and military bastion of the Eastern bloc. Still, up into the early 1960s, their line was that, while there were two German states which should be recognized as equal and independent, the two German governments should try to solve the reunification problem by establishing a kind of all-German confederacy, with a council or councils on which East and West Germans would be represented "by parity." Clearly, this would have given Ulbricht what he wanted most—recognition—and this is why Bonn never accepted it. But, again, a chance at a closer relationship was possibly missed.

When, later in the sixties, the idea of some form of official relationship with the DDR was no longer taboo at Bonn, East Berlin, now stronger and more self-assured, rejected the idea of confederation or any closer relation, insisting on complete separateness as long as West Germany was a "state with a different social system." A policy of "little steps" toward rapprochement with the East—such as improving economic and cultural relations with the DDR, or establishing diplomatic relations with other East European countries—had long been ad-

vocated by SPD and FDP leaders. This policy had even been inaugurated prior to the "grand coalition" by CDU Foreign Minister Schroeder and then been continued by Brandt as his successor in 1966. But now the shoe was on the other foot. Suspecting that these policies were dictated less by a desire for *détente* than by an effort to isolate the DDR among its Eastern bloc neighbors (and, for a while, the West actually had nourished such intentions), Ulbricht established a kind of "Hallstein Doctrine" in reverse. He tried to convince Moscow and the other Eastern capitals that they should refuse any closer relations with Bonn as long as Bonn denied him full recognition. Thus the little steps proved either too little or to be going in the wrong direction. The stalemate continued.

3   A NEW APPROACH

What accounts for the break in the stalemate that occurred at the start of the new decade? Toward the end of the 1960s, there were indications in the policies of the major powers that a change was coming. A policy of working toward a *détente*, instead of the rigid cold war posture of the 1950s, could be discerned in American statements and plans since the Kennedy administration took over, replacing strategies of "massive retaliation" with plans for a "flexible response" and suggestions for balanced forces in Europe. At the same time, France, under de Gaulle, inaugurated her own policy of rapprochement with the East, which, at one point, even involved official recognition of the Oder-Neisse line as the definitive Polish-German boundary. The idea of a reunited and thus even more powerful Germany had never appealed to European countries that had been past victims of German power. France's policy weakened NATO and thus attenuated the rigid bloc confrontation that had prevailed earlier. Changed Western policies in the German question could be seen as early as 1966. At that time, Britain, France, the United States, and West Germany, anent a NATO Council meeting, called not only for the removal of "barriers to freer and

more friendly reciprocal exchanges between countries of different social and economic systems" but also for moves to "develop human, economic, and cultural contacts between the two parts of Germany." The Soviets, in turn, had by now turned inward upon themselves; they became increasingly preoccupied with their domestic affairs, while, abroad, besides their concern with the bloc, they became involved with the new threat that developed at their Eastern flank in the form of Maoism. Except, perhaps, for the long pull, the Soviets were now chiefly interested in maintaining and stabilizing the status quo in Europe as it had issued from their profitable expansion into Eastern Europe through and after the war. While unwilling to give up any of their gains, they were now willing to forego ideas of further expansion and, for the time being, to accept even a Western-integrated Federal Republic of Germany as a fact of life. But was the Federal Republic, for its part, ready to accept the European status quo, including the partition of Germany?

The change in attitude of the Germans in the Federal Republic was significant. Up to the middle sixties, reunification ranked as by far the most important issue with them, surpassing any domestic or other foreign policy matters; partition was "intolerable," never to be forgotten over the more pressing problems of the day. The opposition shared that basic sentiment with the ruling regime, which it even accused of not paying enough attention to it. By 1967 or thereabout, this attitude had changed. While in 1963, 42 percent of those polled about what they considered the most important political problem facing Germans had mentioned reunification, only 19 percent did so in 1967, while problems of prices and salaries, which had been mentioned by 20 percent in 1963, reached 62 percent in 1967. During the 1969 election campaign, problems of educational policy and social welfare ranked at the top of concern, with reunification way down; instead, over 60 percent ranked *détente* as the most important foreign policy problem. This seems to indicate that the attitude change was caused by two factors: a heightened sense of security (e.g., Russia was seen as a threat to the FRG by 66 percent in 1952, by only 38 percent in 1966), and a growing concern with internal matters (partly based on the recession that interrupted the economic miracle in the middle sixties). Attitudes vary, of course, in respect to party political orientation, age groups (with the younger ones even less interested in unification than older age groups), and so forth, but the trend is unmistakable. It is not limited to reunification; it is really the issue of overall *détente* and improved relations with the East. Thus in 1969, over three-fourths rejected war as a possible means for solving foreign policy problems, with a large part doing so as a matter of principle (only NPD sympathizers rooting for war in significant numbers). This reflects the general trend toward moderation we have observed before.

Attitudes concerning other issues reveal the same tendency. While in 1951 almost every West German rejected the idea of accepting the Oder-Neisse boundary (80 percent versus 8 percent), almost half were resigned to it in 1967 (47 percent as against 34 percent). In 1968, therefore, Brandt, for the first time, could come out for such recognition in a statement before an SPD party convention. This trend enabled the government, which he now heads, to inaugurate the negotiations with the East; in the summer of 1970, 79 percent of polled West Germans considered it desirable (with only 8 percent opposed). In 1968, Brandt had said: "German policy today is based on the assumption that overcoming the division of Germany will be a long process whose duration no one can predict." [1] By 1970 it looked as if a majority in the FRG no longer considered the two Germanies as "provisional" units (with a poll showing about four-fifths in agreement with the Moscow Treaty, which perpetuates not only the exterior but also the intra-German boundaries).

OSTPOLITIK: PROPOSALS AND NEGOTIATIONS

What, then, about this whole complex of negotiations, treaties, new approaches? If both sides are now agreed on the acceptance of the status quo in Europe, existing units, boundaries, and so forth, why all the commotion? It is important to realize that the present status still leaves a large number of unsolved issues and concerns. What bothers the parties to these issues most? West Germany has been bothered most by the uncertain status of Berlin and of the access rights on which the city's survival depends. This is also important to the West in general, since, as we have seen, peace is threatened by the most trivial incident imaginable (the "tailgate" type of incident as one might call it, from an incident that involved the question of how many inches the tailgates of trucks carrying American soldiers from West Germany to Berlin had to be lowered for inspection). Equally bothersome is the isolation of West Berlin from East Berlin and quite generally the isolation of the people in East Germany from the West. What bothers the East most is that the West, and West Germany in particular, until recently seemed still not ready to officially recognize the "Eastern" results of World War II and, in particular, the diplomatic isolation, the "outlawry," of the DDR. Thus to both sides the existing situation, despite the tacit delimitation of spheres between East and West, appeared as a shaky one, based on shaky arrangements with many ambiguities.

[1] Willy Brandt, "German Policy Toward the East," *Foreign Affairs* (April 1968), p. 481.

An East-West package deal?

About 1970, it seemed that these mutual dissatisfactions and complaints could form the basis for a grand overall package deal, under which, by way of mutual concessions, the interests of all concerned might be taken care of. The Western part of the deal (in part already initiated through recent policy changes and arrangements) would include the following in particular: (1) West German recognition of the DDR and normalization of relations with its government; this would imply dropping of the Hallstein Doctrine (or whatever remains of it) and opening the way for other nations to fully recognize the DDR, enabling it to enter international agencies (including, together with the FRG, the UN); (2) West German recognition of the Oder-Neisse line (as now almost accomplished); (3) West German declaration that the Munich Pact of 1938 is invalid from the beginning (inaugurating normal relationships with Czechoslovakia); (4) West German abstention from actions in West Berlin considered "provocative" by the East (such as holding presidential elections or parliamentary sessions there); (5) West German renunciation forever of nuclear ambitions through ratification of the Non-Proliferation Treaty (NPT).

The Eastern part of the deal would include: (1) official Soviet and DDR recognition of West Berlin as an entity with a special status with guaranteed independence from control or interference by the DDR; (2) conclusion of an agreement or agreements between the Soviet Union and the DDR, on the one side, and on the other, the United States, the United Kingdom, France, and the FRG concerning access and transit rights to West Berlin, with guarantees of undisturbed air, road, rail, and similar transportation, traffic, and communications; (3) a declaration by the DDR that it will initiate free movement of persons between East Berlin and the DDR, on the one hand, and West Berlin and the FRG, on the other hand, at least part of such restoration to be put into effect immediately; (4) Soviet readiness not to interfere with the resumption of diplomatic relations and the development of economic and cultural ties between West Germany and the Eastern bloc countries.

A good deal of the above is in the process of being accomplished, but in a piecemeal way and with final success still in the balance. The Moscow Treaty between the FRG and the Soviet Union, whose core—Article 3—contains West Germany's recognition of the existing European frontiers (including the Oder-Neisse line and "the frontier between the Federal Republic of Germany and the German Democratic Republic") as well as of "the territorial integrity of all States in Europe within their present frontiers," [2] will be ratified by Bonn only after a satisfactory settlement on Berlin has been reached. Thus Western concessions are tied up with Eastern ones; the new "peace settlement" of Europe can only be based on mutuality. On the face of it, the treaty seems to imply full recognition of the DDR. But implication is not enough. The DDR and FRG themselves must formally agree on that, and here difficulties still loom.

The closer West Germany came to recognition in terminology as well as action ("summit meetings" of Brandt and Stoph have taken place twice so far), the more demanding Ulbricht became, until he demanded "full recog-

---

[2] The controlling portions of Article 3 read as follows:

[*The Federal Republic of Germany and the Union of Soviet Socialist Republics*] *undertake to respect without restriction the territorial integrity of all States in Europe within their present frontiers; they declare that they have no territorial claims against anybody nor will assert such claims in the future; they regard today and shall in future regard the frontiers of all States in Europe as inviolable such as they are on the date of signature of the present Treaty, including the Oder-Neisse line which forms the western frontier of the People's Republic of Poland and the frontier between the Federal Republic of Germany and the German Democratic Republic.*

Correspondingly, Article 1 of the Warsaw Treaty between the FRG and Poland reads:

(1) *The Federal Republic of Germany and the People's Republic of Poland state in mutual agreement that the existing boundary line the course of which is laid down in Chapter IX of the Decisions of the Potsdam Conference of 2 August 1945 as running from the Baltic Sea immediately west of Swinemuende, and thence along the Oder River to the confluence of the western Neisse River and along the western Neisse to the Czechoslovak frontier, shall constitute the western State frontier of the People's Republic of Poland. (2) They reaffirm the inviolability of their existing frontiers now and in the future and undertake to respect each other's territorial integrity without restriction. (3) They declare that they have no territorial claims whatsoever against each other and that they will not assert such claims in the future.*

According to present Bonn policies, ratification of the Warsaw Treaty will similarly await conclusion of a Berlin settlement.

nition of the DDR as a sovereign state in the sense of international law." West Germans, on the other hand, although prepared to conclude treaties that are "binding under international law" with the DDR, have refused to go that far. It is completely semantic again, but political reasons loom behind the semantic surface. For Ulbricht, the Moscow Treaty, with its rapprochement between the Soviets and the so far suspected "revanchist," militaristic, and therefore dangerous Federal Republic, must have conjured up the fear of being replaced by the FRG as the "foremost Germany," even in Eastern eyes. This is a bitter pill for the DDR leaders, and they may want to avoid an intra-German rapprochement altogether at this point. West Germans, on the other hand, seem still hampered by remnants of that legalism that is the hallmark of all "nonrecognition" policies, whether they apply to China or to the Baltic republics. Once the nonrecognized fact has become long-established and there is no prospect of its change any more, the policy becomes illusory. Under such policies, the Free City of Danzig would still have legal status; indeed, all of Germany would still constitute conquered four-power territory under the Allied Control Council, pending an overall German peace treaty.

In the Moscow and Warsaw treaties, West Germany has gone as far as to recognize the loss of territory east of the Oder-Neisse line. Bonn's reluctance to fully recognize the DDR and its present regime seems based on a fear that this would confer "legitimacy" on the East German government and destroy whatever chances remain for eventual unification. However, recognition of a state or government should not be confused with approval of its policies; indeed, in the case of the DDR, rather than adding strength to its present government, normalization of relations might well strengthen those forces that strive for alleviation of harsh conditions and permit (or compel) the present leadership to initiate the freedom of movement of persons. And as for eventual reunification, there have been examples before of sovereign states merging or federating, including those Germanic states that merged into the Reich in 1871. Such a possibility is officially referred to in a letter by Bonn Foreign Minister Scheel that was appended to the Moscow Treaty and in which (without the Soviet Union taking exception) he states that "this Treaty does not conflict with the political objective of the Federal Republic of Germany to work for a state of peace in Europe in which the German nation will recover its unity in free self-determination." As for the objection that through this treaty Germany gives up claims that are rightfully hers, Brandt said: "Nothing is lost with this treaty that was not gambled away long ago by a criminal regime." [3] Here we find acceptance of the fact that Germany lost the war and readiness to draw the conclusions from it, but the razor-thin majority that the Brandt government has in the Bundestag (which has to give its consent to ratification), and the violent opposition it has encountered on the part of the CDU-CSU and others (with Strauss bemoaning a "sellout" and "give-away," and expellee organizations charging "treason" and "appeasement") may account for the hesitancy to go all the way.

If the chief interest of Moscow lies now in establishing normal relations with Bonn and, especially, in utilizing West Germany's vast economic and technological capacities, it cannot well object to other East European countries doing the same. Thus closer or more normal ties between Bonn and these countries can be expected as part of overall *détente* policies. This would be most significant in the case of Czechoslovakia. Czechoslovakia is, besides Poland, the only Communist-controlled country sharing borders with Germany, and it, too, suffered from German expansionism. Bonn has repeatedly declared that it considers the Munich Pact "no longer valid." Prague wants it considered null and void from the outset. Bonn objects that nullity *ab initio* might render Sudeten Germans liable to prosecution in Czechoslovakia for having committed treason (since in that case they would have remained Czechoslovak citizens after 1938). But problems like these could certainly be settled by agreement if both sides show good will. Normalization of West German relations with the remainder of Eastern Europe (i.e., Hungary and Bulgaria—those with Rumania having al-

[3] Television address, December 7, 1970, in *The Treaty Between the Federal Republic of Germany and the People's Republic of Poland* (Bonn, 1971), pp. 21–22.

ready been established) might follow. Moscow might still be apprehensive of close ties between these countries and West Germany. Indeed, Moscow may generally fear a consequent far-reaching Western influence in Eastern Europe and, after its experience with the abortive "Prague spring" of 1968, suspicion might be warranted or at least understandable. But Moscow has made it brutally clear to the governments of these countries how far they can go. As long as they remain in the fold politically, it would seem that fears of the consequences of economic and similar penetration are unfounded.

Strangely, what appeared as the greatest stumbling block in the way of an overall *détente* —the means by which to find a mutually agreeable settlement of the Berlin problem, or problems—seemed about to be removed by late 1971. The Berlin question was so complex not only because of the many conflicting claims and interests and the "face" involved in many positions taken over twenty-five years, but also because so many different parties were vitally concerned with the issue—the four powers, still claiming "occupation" rights; the two Germanies; even West Berlin as a separate entity. There was, therefore, great scepticism in regard to success when four-power negotiations started early in 1970. But it turned out that the West's (and, in particular, Bonn's) insistence on a Berlin solution as a precondition of finalizing the Moscow and Warsaw agreements was good diplomacy. Moscow proved so vitally interested in having these agreements come into force (which might then open the way to further East-West negotiations, such as "mutual balanced force reductions" and the convening of a "European security conference" much desired by the Soviets) that they were ready to make far-reaching concessions on Berlin. We have spelled out the details of the Four Power Agreement on Berlin of September 3, 1971 in the section on Berlin (see Chapter 7, Section 1). What it amounted to was granting what in the "East-West package deal" outlined above were indicated as "Eastern concessions." While the Western powers, in that agreement, reconfirmed West Berlin's status as still under occupation and thus not a constituent part of the FRG, the Soviets admitted the actual Western ties and Western orientation of the

city, which are not to be interfered with by the East. Access and transit are to be improved and guaranteed against harassment and interference (by the DDR). And a beginning is to be made in regard to free movement of persons by at least opening the wall to West Berliners, although not the other way around.

As we have seen (Chapter 7, Section 4) Moscow, in opening the way toward these agreements, met with such resistance on the part of the DDR regime that Ulbricht had to be removed to make way to a more amenable leadership. But even this new leadership proved recalcitrant when, after the conclusion of the Four Power Agreement, it was called upon by the agreement to negotiate the implementing details with the other Germans. The DDR had always insisted that West Berlin constituted a "special entity," and it now insisted on negotiating the agreements on access, transit, visits to East Berlin, and other Berlin problems not only with the Bonn authorities but, also and separately, with those of West Berlin. This attitude stalled the intra-German talks, but it seemed unlikely that the Soviets would permit the entire settlement to founder on such stalling. Sooner or later, so it appeared, Moscow's influence over East Berlin would prove sufficiently strong to move "its" Germany in the desired direction. As we shall see below, a more serious obstacle to a Berlin arrangement appeared in the form of the strong opposition developing in West Germany against it as part and parcel of the Brandt-Scheel government's policy of *détente*. Although most of the Berlin arrangement was clearly favorable to Western claims and interests, the opposition selected relatively minor concessions (such as granting the Soviets the right to open a consulate in West Berlin) or unobtainable proposals (abolition of the Wall and reuniting East Berlin with West Berlin) as bases of its attack. Since Bonn is no longer subject to Western pressure the way East Berlin is to Moscow's, the fate of the new Berlin arrangement, and therewith of overall *détente*, was still in the balance.

Ratification by the FRG of the nuclear Non-Proliferation Treaty, which it has signed already, is somewhat outside the problems of territory and boundaries, but it is easy to see its connection with general *détente*. The Soviets consider it an essential element in a new settlement.

Actually, it would not be much of a concession, since West Germany, by the treaties of 1955, is already committed not to produce ABC weapons; it is thus a question of not obtaining them from a nuclear power. But some German nationalists (most vocally Strauss) have been dreaming of a federated Europe not bound by NPT restrictions and thus entitled to its own nuclear establishment. No power, including Western powers, can be happy about Germans, directly or indirectly, getting their fingers on the nuclear trigger. And Germany, of all countries, can least afford to have such ambitions. For the Soviets, German nuclear arms would mean what Chinese nuclear weapons mean to the United States. There was a time in the sixties when Americans, to stave off eventual German demands for independent nuclear status, proposed nuclear sharing (a multilateral force, MLF). But it turned out that Germans, in their majority, were not interested in it. They realized that, whatever protection is possible through deterrence, they already had in the "big" deterrent of the United States. To create a small one in addition seemed as pointless as France's *force de frappe*. Through definitely foregoing ambitions of this kind, that is, by assisting arms control, Germans could make a contribution not only to regional but to world-wide *détente*. Brandt once said: "Germany is an economic giant but a political pigmy." It is through political policies such as those inaugurated by himself, not through adventurous military ones, that Germany can regain political stature, too.[4]

Such stature would be strengthened by the entrance of both Germanies into the United Nations, a step that would naturally result from the success of the various negotiations now in progress. Indeed, admission procedures might well be tied up with the conclusion of such agreements, and, in particular, the ones on Berlin. Since present conditions there constitute a clear "threat to the peace," agreement on Berlin could be considered proof of the "peace-loving" nature of the two applicants (as required by Article 4 of the UN Charter). Some West Germans feel that membership of the two Germanies would burden the organization with yet another world problem, and that there would be a constant flow of accusations by the DDR against the FRG. As to the first, one might ask what is a peace organization for if not to confront major world problems? As for the second, Bonn might welcome an opportunity to discuss and disprove in open forum the accusations it considers unfounded. The UN itself, so often left out in major world crises (such as Vietnam), would gain in universality of membership and in chances to play a useful role in the settlement of issues that might arise in the future in Central Europe. And Germans, this way, might have another chance to fortify world peace.

OSTPOLITIK: CHANCES AND PROBLEMS

At this point, *Ostpolitik* (policies toward the East) seems to be endangered both from within and without. From within the FRG, because the hold of the present coalition government is shaky, and the opposition is eager to overthrow it on exactly these foreign policy issues. Yet it is doubtful whether even a CDU-led government could undo all that has been begun. As we have seen, opinion in West Germany favors *détente*, and disgruntled, cold-war, rightist groups are vocal but numerically small. Difficulties from the outside might develop in Washington, where signs of hesitancy and even distrust have appeared. Withdrawal of American support would constitute a strange turnabout: where previously Bonn was forever fearful lest Washington's policy of *détente* lead to a deal between the United States and the Soviet Union at the expense of Germany (i.e., that Washington would forget Germany's interests in reunification), now some Americans suspect the Germans of going too far in the direction of *détente* with the East, hence forgetting their ties with the West. Sometimes this fear is couched in terms of a new "Rapallo."[5] The fear is of a "deal" in which

---

[4] Progress in the area of arms control might also enable the powers to reduce their military establishments in Europe, thus not only reducing tension but lessening their financial burdens. This would facilitate solving the problem of "fair shares" in contributing to these burdens, a problem that has led to acrimony between the United States and its Western European allies, including the FRG.

[5] The term *Rapallo* has long been used (or misused) as shorthand for a German-Russian deal betraying the West. The original Rapallo agreement (1922) was no such thing: it provided for establishment of diplomatic relations

the Soviets would release "their" Germany from control in return for the FRG's withdrawal from NATO and other ties with the West and a political, if not military alignment with the Soviet Union. Such a radical break with Western orientation cannot be expected from any of the presently leading parties or groups in West Germany; and one can hardly imagine the Soviets engaging in a "deal" of this sort. It might beckon to them as a way to get rid of a Western "imperialist" bloc, which they still consider a threat, but, by the same token, it would destroy their hold over their own bloc members. And they must have learned from a similar deal, dateline 1939, that alignment with a "Greater Germany" can backfire. Even if the Soviets should expect a nonaligned (or allied) Germany to turn eventually Communist, they must fear a Communist big power at their left flank as much as they fear it now already at their right.

As for the American objectors (prominent among them are persons like Dean Acheson and former American High Commissioners in Germany John McCloy and Lucius Clay), it is difficult, indeed, to understand their doubts. One might almost think they wished to continue the old Adenauer-Dulles cold-war approach. If so, as in the fifties, it would be a strange coalition of Western "cold warriors" and intransigents in the East (Ulbricht or now his successor) that opposes *détente*. Or is it distrust of a more independent West German stance on the part of those who were used to German compliance with Washington that prompts these people to opposition? Perhaps they resent seeing "unreliable socialists" taking the place of their trusted Strausses and Kiesingers. Sometimes (in the United States as well as West Germany) the charge is made that Brandt's commitments toward the East violated the principle of *do ut des*, of give-and-take in diplomatic affairs. But even if the acceptance by Germany of the territorial status quo is considered a "give," there are "takes" in a settlement on Berlin, in economic opportunities in the East, and even such specific advantages as

between the Soviet Union and Germany and implied a certain assertion of independence on the part of the Germans but no realignment. In this respect it might be compared with the establishment of Bonn-Moscow relations by Adenauer in 1955.

the repatriation of remaining ethnic Germans in Poland, which actually has already begun.

Actually, *Ostpolitik* implies more than a mere political recognition of the facts and realities of the postwar European power balance; it implies a moral-political change in attitudes that should be profoundly welcomed by those who want a stable, moderate, and peaceful Germany in the center of Europe.

If Germans are now ready to sacrifice the idea of reunification (and of regaining lost territory) on the altar of *détente* and peaceful coexistence, this would eliminate the one area in Europe where "revisionism" has still been virulent and apt to generate recurring crises. It involves, then, more than symbolic reconciliation with former enemies. It means that a country, which so often had disturbed the peace of the world, now would be contributing to world peace rather than endangering it. As Brandt put it in the television address referred to before: "We have the courage to turn over a new page of history. This should benefit above all the younger generation, which has grown up in peace and without sharing the responsibility for the past, but which must nevertheless share in bearing the consequences of the war, since no one can run away from the history of his country." And the gesture of his taking along to Warsaw, as witnesses of his signing the treaty with Poland, such persons as Klaus von Bismarck, great-grandson of the Iron Chancellor, and Germany's great novelist Günter Grass, born in the Eastern territories, was to show that "a new page of history" was indeed being turned, and that the "other Germany," more liberal and peaceful, which so often had been defeated, was coming to the fore. Over the long pull, it might lead to liberalization even in East Germany, if and when withdrawal into resentful isolation proves counterproductive. In that event, the late philosopher Karl Jaspers' suggestion that a separate but liberalized East Germany might not be more intolerable than a separate Austria might yet prove to the point.

What does *Ostpolitik* mean in relation to the West? We have seen that it does not imply reorientation or realignment. West Germany cannot and does not want to forego its political, economic, and strategic ties with the

United States and the Western European countries. On the contrary, a Germany resigned to the status quo and no longer threatening war over boundaries, territories, access to Berlin, and so forth is liable to be a more stable partner than one bent on revision. A country like France, for instance, itself interested in European stability and *détente*, has welcomed the new policy, endorsing, in the words of its Foreign Minister, Maurice Schumann, "the grand design of the Federal Republic." Some fear that the idea and the chances of European integration might suffer from West Germany's devoting so much interest to the East. So far the opposite is true. Now that de Gaulle is gone, Bonn has even been able actively to promote Britain's entry into EEC and has been instrumental in getting plans adopted that develop the economic integration of the present Six even further. It is different, perhaps, in regard to "Europeanism" as an ideology and the idea of eventual political federation of Europe, but this has no relation to *Ostpolitik*. Already prior to that, indeed, for about a decade, Europeanism as an idea and a movement had been declining, and this in all European countries. While opinion polls and similar studies yield majorities as large as ever in favor of it, this seems more to reflect a payment of lip service that an expression of genuine feeling. One finds the strongest commitment among those who grew up in the fifties, while younger people care little. If one regrets this, one probably should blame the French more than the Germans for having missed that opportunity in the first postwar decade.

4 GERMANY AND THE WORLD

Germans, looking out toward the world and their role in world affairs, find themselves at a turning point. For a long time, throughout what one may call the postwar period, they were bewildered. Accustomed to being in the center of world politics and world interest, they suddenly found themselves without even a political center of their own. They were now at the mercy of powers that threatened each other and what remained of Germany, making both Germanies, which the powers had resurrected from the ruins, "penetrated systems" dependent on foreign powers for protection and without much of their own role to play. Some Germans looked backward toward big power status and dreamed of a replay. Others, especially in the West, hoped for amalgamation with other European nations in a higher, supranational political environment. For most, existing political units, whether FRG or DDR, still seemed "provisional."

Most Germans, too, hoped for reunification within a foreseeable future. That dream is also over. But every nation needs a sense of role fulfillment. Germans stand in particular need of it because their history never provided them with a consistent national goal. If, in the absence of hope that they may at least be reunited as a nation some time, they are not to fall prey to prolonged frustration and become a source of unrest again, they must be given alternatives that will strengthen their self-confidence.

Their plight is not unique. During the postwar period, Britain and France had to go through the pangs of being reduced from first-rank "world powers" to lower rank countries. Such nations may experience crises and unrest before finding compensation in different roles. Both these countries found substitute goals, such as building a modernized economy and society, that reconciled their people to loss of empire and power. Germans, perhaps more than others when frustrated, are threatened by radicalism, leftist as of late but even more so rightist. At this turning point, therefore, its leaders must strain all the more to give them worthwhile goals.

We have mentioned most of the goals that seem practicable now. We have mentioned previously the vast environmental problems that technology poses for the developed countries: the problems of urban agglomerations, of clean air and water, of conservation of resources, and of preservation of landscape and cultural-historical heritage. Added to the great social problems facing these countries—providing opportunity for all, elimination of class structures, and so forth—environment problems may well provide Germans with meaningful tasks for generations. In some of these respects, Germans have in the past shown more sense of responsibility than others; resuming that tradition, they may furnish a model for others.

Even such apparently domestic goals, however, can for the most part no longer be pursued in isolation. The pollution problem, for one, disregards boundaries. This points to a further role Germans can play. Instead of engaging in power politics—a game they lost repeatedly—they may want to support that which will save the world, if anything can: international cooperation. And here, the new turn in attitudes and policies that began in the late sixties points in the right direction. We have mentioned one area, arms control, where ratification of the NPT would encourage further efforts, especially on the part of the superpowers, to meet that most disastrous problem of mankind, the nuclear armament race. Any progress in disarmament, of course, bolsters political *détente*, and vice versa. In another area where disaster looms, that of the underdeveloped, starving, and yet restless majority of the people of the world, Germans have already begun taking over increased responsibilities through technical, financial, and economic assistance. In the still relatively small development program of the Communist bloc, the DDR plays a prominent role. And the Federal Republic, through gradually enhanced efforts over a couple of years, by 1970 had attained second place in actual dollar figures (immediately after the United States, whose contribution has actually been declining, and overtaking France, which had been among the top foreign aid countries); in terms of percentages of GNP, it had even surpassed the United States and, together with a few other countries, among them France, had topped the 1 percent the United Nations has established as the minimum the developed countries have to contribute to offer any hope to the underdeveloped. Long-range budget planning has enabled the Federal Republic to project annual increases of 9 percent and 18 percent for capital outlay and technical aid respectively, for 1970–74. But it is not only money that is involved. Germans, by a strange quirk of fate, having had to relinquish their colonies after World War I, are considered "noncolonialists" by Africans and others; their aid raises less suspicion and involves fewer political complications than that of other Western powers. Helping underdeveloped peoples seems in any event to have become the new version of the welfare state idea, with the "external" proletariat taking over the position held in former times by the internal proletariat. Germans, who in the best periods of their past have led the world in social consciousness and responsible welfare policies, might thus atone for the afflictions caused in their worst.

There remains the most "political" of role functions to be played by Germany in the international arena. These are the ones discussed at length in this chapter under the heading of "*Ostpolitik*." As we have seen, this is a policy that renounces revisionist goals and, by accepting existing boundaries and existing territorial and political arrangements, forms the basis of European *détente*. By the same token, however, it implies something even broader. Inasmuch as the chief threat to the world is the split that divides East and West, overcoming this split in one major part of the world would vitally contribute to the peace of the world at large. Although overcoming this split involves sacrifices by Germans as a nation, their function as bridge-builders between the two worlds would be a sacrifice that would benefit the interest of the people and the peace of the world.

Conclusion

Inspired, perhaps, by American presidents and their perennial proclamations of "New Deals," "Great Societies," and the like, West German Chancellor Ludwig Erhard once set for Germans the national goal of establishing a "Formed Society" (*formierte Gesellschaft*; in English better rendered as "structured society"). One should, perhaps, be glad to see Germans aim at a "formed" rather than a "uniformed" society. Yet the suggestion was not as innocuous as it may have sounded. It seemed to indicate a desire to achieve a society in which people do not form one colorless mass but a society in which they are clearly divided into groups with their own significant purpose and status, higher and lower, elites and others. Now it is true—as the German sociologist Ralf Dahrendorf has pointed out—that in contrast to a past when Germans were controlled by one class- and purpose-conscious feudal elite, present West German elites have been less coherent, less purposeful, even less conscious of being at the top. And this, in view of the traditional German habit of looking toward *die da oben* for standards and guidance, has created problems. Lacking the father figure who, for a decade and a half, gave them the assurance of being cared for, there has been abroad a feeling of directionlessness and even *anomie*, which, as we have seen, is particularly poignant in matters of national image and foreign policy goals.

But in terms of liberal-democratic prospects, such weakening of the elites—even though it may make some Germans feel uncomfortable—should not be considered as entirely unfortunate. The "structured society" that Erhard put up as a goal in fact has long existed in Germany, although in the undesirable form of the traditional division of Germans through their class system of education. And, since traditional authoritarian patterns of behavior are still extant, somewhat less emphasis on structure and more on social mobility, on "circulation of the elites," would seem to be called for. Such an emphasis would benefit democratic strivings. It would reduce the hold of authoritarian executives and officials on weak or inefficient parliaments. It would eliminate the caste character of the civil service (which is still overwhelmingly upper and middle class in origin, with 50 percent of *Beamte* coming from *Beamten* families!). It would reduce the strong bureaucratic tendencies in most organizations, including the major political parties. In short, it would alleviate the rigid class and status lines of German society. West German society might thus distinguish itself from the "structured" society of the East, which, although it is no longer based on educational monopoly and economic privilege, is a rigid society under the control of a coherent and self-assured political-cum-managerial elite.

Of late there have been stirrings. We have seen that even in the controlled East, the old guard in control has had to admit young blood less doctrinally oriented and, with its technological pragmatism, perhaps less authoritarian-minded. And in the West the younger generation, in particular, has demonstrated its unwillingness to cope with traditional, "establishment" authoritarianism. This transitional state is apparent in the area of liberties, freedom, and tolerance. Polls and attitude studies reveal a peculiar mixture of old and new, authoritarian and more liberal patterns. Thus the young and more highly educated are liable to be more tolerant of dissent, and so forth, but conservatism and intolerance still pervade the older and less educated ones (penetrating even the working class). While the *Spiegel* case and similar incidents, with the public reaction they provoked, reveal an encouraging trend toward a sense of what true liberal democracy means and requires, public reaction to the emergence of left radicalism (or even to such apolitical although unorthodox phenomena as the life style and hair style of "those *Gammler*," the hippies) has betrayed less tolerance.

We find a similar discrepancy in regard to interest and involvement in public issues. Over much of the postwar period there was decrease, a trend toward depoliticization and privatization. In view of previous doctrinal divisions, this may have had its wholesome aspects, but it also involved a waning of political discourse and of meaningful debate between prevailing thought and opposition. As a result, minorities were driven outside the established channels and procedures to form extraparliamentary groups and devices (such as APO). Pragmatism, if it turns apolitical, threatens the lifeblood of democratic life—a lively and sustained concern with vital public issues; polarization and radicalization exacerbate and often make futile their discussion.

But not everything in German social and political life and institutions has been negative. The foregoing chapters have outlined what amounts to a mixture of assets and liabilities. We have just mentioned liabilities. Among the assets we would list a capable, well-organized, and uncorrupt administration; a still flourishing, diversified local administration with a tradition of self-government; a system of social security that by and large has prevented distress; and an educational system of quality.

In addition, there is hope in the younger generation. Even now the heritage of the past still hangs heavily over the German people. Some of the older Germans must continue to bear responsibility for its abominations, and the fact that others, although they were not directly involved, still try to cover up the past, adds to the nation's burden. But it is encouraging to see younger people question their elders severely, and it would be unfair to condemn them for the sins of their fathers. Many young Germans reveal attitudes that were uncommon in the German past, such as openness to new ideas and untried ways of life. Some go to extremes, others are pragmatic, and while this may lead some into egocentrism or sectarianism, it may render others readier to experiment with more democratic devices in public life. Hopefully, they may give another chance to Germany's humanitarian, liberal, and democratic potentialities, which have so often been stifled in the past.

Moderation and pragmatism make it possible to imagine a development in which the assets could be used to Westernize German public life without sacrificing what is valuable and sometimes unique in the German tradition. Doctrinal splits might be moderated into useful debates between government and opposition; rule-mindedness and authority-consciousness might be tempered by reasonableness; and class and caste exclusiveness might yield to preference according to merit. Experience with postwar occupation policies and experiments has shown that such developments, especially democratization, must remain basically a German task; these processes do not lend themselves to imposition from abroad. But foreign experience can furnish models by which to orient oneself, as West Germans have done successfully in a variety of cases (such as judicial review and jurisdiction of a constitutional court, the military ombudsman, and others).

Foreigners (and frequently the Germans themselves) have had three dominant though widely contrasting impressions of Germany: the Germany that is *Gemütlichkeit*, a certain homely way of life, often appealing to Americans who do not have it but who would like to have time for it; second, the Germany that means know-how and efficiency, appealing or disturbing to Americans, depending on how such skills have been used; and third, the Germany that is music, poetry, philosophy, a mainspring of culture and thought.

But Germany is not only beer gardens and pigs' knuckles with sauerkraut; nor is it only the Volkswagen and I. G. Farben, the Prussian general staff and the SS; neither can it be reduced to Schiller and Beethoven, Kant and Luther. A nation is not summed up so easily.

And this is good, for even if Germany is a land of contrast and contradiction, that is better than if it were a country where all contrast and dissension were buried under enforced silence or conformity. The latter have been imposed on the Eastern portion of the country. If Germany in its main, Western portion should succeed in developing peacefully an open, free, and self-governing society, it will have gone far toward proving that democracy has a chance even under the most adverse conditions.

IV The government of the Soviet Union

Introduction

Since World War II the United States and the Soviet Union have been the two great world rivals in power, influence, and achievement. Soviet and American space exploits are heralded and compared. Soviet military potential forms the most frequently used argument for the buildup of American arms. The expansion and contraction of Soviet spheres of influence are major determinants of American foreign policies. How accurate are the assessments of Soviet strength and purpose on which these American policies are based?

It has been a common expectation that industrialization and the impact of industrial organization, growing affluence, and persistent international involvement would profoundly modify the working of the Soviet system in ways that would bring it closer to the functioning of our own. Although such surface evidences as dress, modes of life, and perhaps even aspirations have become more similar, there is little evidence that economic development has basically modified the working of the Soviet political system. In other words, there is no decisive evidence that there is a one-to-one correlation between the stage and character of economic growth and the proc-esses of political decision-making and the exercise of power. More important molding factors are the circumstances that created the system in the first place; the degree to which the former social system persisted, or was erased; the groups that shared in the creation of new institutions; and the ways in which they and others have seized and maintained power.

The chapters that follow are concerned with these factors. They describe the formative Soviet ideologies, historical circumstances, institutional frameworks, dynamic forces, and social groups that have created the policies that are so important for the United States. In addition to its political significance, the Soviet Union provides an absorbing study of the type of political system, communist totalitarianism, that is the polar opposite of democracy. By studying the evolution and characteristics of the Soviet Union, we not only learn about a system that differs widely in crucial respects from our own, but we can gain insight into a whole range of communist systems now found in many parts of the world. In the constantly interacting world of today, it is vital that we acquire such insight.

1

Soviet
ideology
and
history

1 CONTINUITY AND CHANGE IN SOVIET IDEOLOGY

By any standard, the Soviet Union has had a striking and paradoxical history during the past half-century. Born out of revolution and civil war, its regime has demonstrated a remarkable capacity to resist internal pressures and external aggression. Largely composed of peasants when the revolution occurred, it has become the world's second strongest industrial power, with agriculture its weakest point. Flaunting a banner of liberation from tsarist autocracy, the Soviet regime has used violence, cruelty, and oppression toward its own people during crucial but extended periods. The public adulation of Stalin, who dominated the country far longer than any other Communist leader, was rivaled only by the virulence of the attack on his character and actions after his death. Essentially conservative in its internal policies, the Soviet Union used force to crush growing liberalism in Czechoslovakia. Far outstripped in revolutionary fervor by China, the Soviet Union still loses no opportunity to extend its influence in the outside world and to destabilize the Western alliance and particularly the dominant position of the United States.

A study of the development of the Soviet Union naturally seeks to learn whether its policies have any clear underpinning of theory or whether they have been chiefly molded by circumstance. Was the massive concentration on heavy industry in the 1930s under the Five-Year Plans a response to Marxist-Leninist concepts or a preparation to meet the Nazi attack? Was the post-Stalin "thaw" the result of Khrushchev's leadership or a step toward some long-range goal? Is the current bureaucratic regime aiding purposes foreseen in theory, or is it responding to patterns already established by a highly centralized and hierarchical structure? Are Soviet foreign policies an extension of historic imperial aims or part of a grand Communist strategy? Or are these alternatives too sharply posed, whereas in practice doctrine and empiricism have gone hand in hand?

THE SOVIET UNION AND THE WORLD

The answers we give to these questions will affect the perspective within which we interpret current Soviet statements and actions. They may help us foresee the likely course of development in the Soviet Union's internal and external policies. And those policies are, of course, of vital significance to the United States, Great Britain, France, and Germany, not only because the Soviet Union is one of the world's great powers but also because of its influence on and relations with that very considerable proportion of the world that has accepted, in one form or another, a Communist ideology.

Since all Communist countries, and particularly the Soviet Union, avow their allegiance to the ideas of Marx and Lenin, it is essential to begin our study of the people and policies of the Soviet Union with an analysis of those ideas. We must also consider the ideas of the former Soviet leaders, Stalin and Khrushchev, and of the present ones, Brezhnev and Kosygin. Much of the conflict within the Communist world focuses—in words, if not always in reality—on interpretations of the Communist ideology and the rival claims of leaders and countries that they are correctly interpreting and promoting its true meaning. Much of the anxiety outside the Communist world is caused by fear of the implications of ideology for action, or its use as a cloak for national expansionism or for the subversion of other countries. It is essential, therefore, to have some knowledge of the doctrine.

THE IDEAS OF KARL MARX

Any brief description of a doctrine as comprehensive and complex as that of Karl Marx (1818–83) [1] inevitably suffers from oversimplification and incompleteness. It is possible, however, to sketch out several leading ideas.

Historical materialism

The first of these is the theory of historical materialism. According to Marx's own description in the Introduction to the *Critique of Political Economy* (1859), "the mode of production of the material life determines the general character of the social, political, and spiritual processes of life. It is not the consciousness of men which determines their existence, but, on the contrary, their social existence determines their consciousness."

In simpler terms, this statement means that the most important determinant of the character of any society is the economic factor: the

way in which men produce and distribute wealth. Its assumption is that the actions of individuals and groups can generally be accounted for by their material interests; and, more than this, that political and religious ideas, concepts of justice and morality, forms of government, the customs of society, even art and philosophy, are largely determined by the forces of production and by property relationships. Only by understanding the economic conditions essential to production can one understand the law, politics, art, religion, and philosophy of a society.

For some periods this theory is not particularly satisfactory, but in the nineteenth century it seemed to explain an obvious phenomenon. At that time the industrial revolution was transforming the way of life of all Western Europe; it would be hard to name any aspect of human existence or thought that was not affected by the change. The rise of an industrial middle class went hand in hand with the extension of the suffrage and the expansion of political democracy. The growth of the cities, the tremendous increase in productive power, and the shift from farm to factory meant that vast masses of people were leading lives utterly different from those of their parents and grandparents. With the increase in education needed for an industrialized society, the reading public grew and culture became "popularized," while the machine provided both new means of artistic creation and new ideas of the beautiful and efficient. Even religious attitudes underwent fundamental changes as the machine gave man greater control over his world and turned his mind from the supernatural.

Marx pointed out that as new forms of production appear in response to man's efforts to satisfy his needs, they conflict with existing property relationships. The ultimate result is a social revolution powered by class consciousness and conscious mass action to transform the institutions of society. The setting for such social revolution is the conflict between new productive forces (such as those of the industrial revolution) and an earlier system of production relations. The immediate stimulus creating the will to revolution on the part of the proletariat is the awareness that capitalists "exploit" workers through appropriating the

---

[1] Although Marx was born in Germany, most of his adult life was spent abroad, first in Belgium and France and eventually, for the last thirty years, in England, where the consequences of the industrial revolution were more apparent than in any other country. The *Communist Manifesto,* which he and Friedrich Engels published in 1848, became the platform of the First International, of which Marx was a leader during the last two decades of his life (while he was writing his monumental book, *Capital*).

profit made in selling the products of their labor, that is, by keeping the surplus value.

Surplus value

Marx's theory of surplus value has been used to explain the existence of great differences in income and, in particular, the fact that those who work hardest often receive small incomes and that others who work not at all receive very large ones. This theory was related to the *labor theory of value*, which taught that the value of any commodity for which there is a demand depends on the amount of labor required to produce it. Those things that are difficult to procure or manufacture are expensive; those that can be acquired without work are cheap or valueless. But although value is determined by the amount of labor, those who labor do not receive payment equal to the sale of the goods they produce. On the contrary, as Marx pointed out, the capitalists and the landlords (the *bourgeoisie*) who employ workers in their factories and on their farms keep the difference for themselves, that is, the surplus value, between the wages they pay, which equals the value of the labor provided, and what the employers are able to obtain in the market for the products.

Moreover, according to an *iron law of wages*, propertyless workers (the *proletariat*) are paid as little as possible. Marx declared, "The average price of wage labor is the minimum wage, that is, that quantum of the means of subsistence that is absolutely requisite to keep the laborer in bare existence as a laborer." As a result, the bourgeoisie accumulate more and more wealth (the *concentration of wealth*), while the proletariat become increasingly wretched (the *growing misery of the masses*).

Marx saw an "inevitable" contradiction between the unlimited expansion of the capacity to produce goods and the limited expansion of the demand for the goods produced, which was related in his view to the "reserve army" of impoverished unemployed existing in England at the time he was writing there. Faced with "epidemics of overproduction," the owners of the means of production acquire, through the use of economic or military force, foreign markets in which to sell their goods. In addition, less efficient employers are driven out of business by their competitors, and they themselves become part of the proletariat, which is suffering relative pauperization. In time, in Marx's words, "the proletariat not only increases in number; it becomes concentrated in greater masses, its strength grows and it feels that strength more." He envisaged the proletariat ultimately using this strength to overthrow the bourgeoisie, to "expropriate the expropriators," to destroy the existing social system and to eliminate the injustices of surplus value by abolishing private ownership of the instruments of production.

Class war

These concepts are inevitably related to Marx's key doctrine of class war. All history, he stated, is the history of warfare between classes, and it is the class struggle that is the bearer of change. Although in earlier times there were many different classes, in modern times the pattern has become simpler. In advanced countries, the slave and the serf have disappeared, and the nobility and the small property owner have vanished or lost their power. Increasingly, there are only two classes of any significance, the bourgeoisie and the proletariat. Warfare between them is inevitable; the ultimate triumph of the proletariat is certain. But it is the task of the Communists, who are "the most advanced and resolute section of the working-class parties in every country" and who have "over the proletariat the advantage of clearly understanding the line of march"—that is, the workings of the process of historical materialism—to educate, guide, and lead the proletariat and to prepare it for the violent seizure of political power.

Oddly enough in the light of subsequent events, Marx was essentially negative in his attitude toward the peasantry. He believed it was a dying class, condemned to disappear in the polarized society of the future. In any case, he saw the peasantry as basically a reactionary class, incapable, due to its dispersion, individualism, and attachment to private property, of acquiring a high degree of socialist consciousness. Thus he considered it necessary to depend on the proletariat to seize control of the state, "the organized power of one class for oppressing another." "The Communists disdain," wrote Marx and Engels in the closing lines of the *Communist Manifesto*, "to conceal their views and aims. They openly declare that their ends can be attained only by the forcible overthrow of all existing social conditions. Let the ruling classes tremble at a Communist revolution. The proletarians have nothing to lose but their chains. They have a world to win."

The tactics of revolution

Marx and Engels were thus concerned not only to interpret the world around them but to change it. Their economic and social analysis was directed primarily toward determining when the final revolutionary assault could be made. Thus their "scientific" approach to social development was matched by a sternly realistic evaluation of strategy in relation to immediate circumstances. "The world commercial crisis of 1847 was the real cause of the February and March revolutions," wrote Engels. "A new revolution is possible only as a consequence of a new crisis." Thus economic crisis, revolution, and war were seen as essentially interrelated, while apt timing was the major key to successful action. Moreover, in their view, developments in any single state were indissolubly interconnected with world politics, and military tactics thus became part of revolutionary strategy.

Aware that the revolutions of 1848 had been defeated through armies recruited from the peasants, Marx and Engels saw a need to prevent that group from thwarting social revolution, particularly if there was to be a revolution in Russia, a possibility to which Marx gave increasing attention in his later years. The nation in arms through compulsory military service "surpasses general franchise as a democratic agency," declared Engels in 1891. "By 1900 the army, once the most Prussian, the most reactionary element of the country, will be socialist in its majority as inescapably as fate." In the short run, this statement underestimated the power of the army to mold its members rather than be molded by them; in the days of the Soviet Civil War, however, it seemed prophetic.

The withering away of the state

Marx was less explicit about what would follow the triumph of the revolution. At first, the socialist society would bear "in every respect, economic, moral and intellectual," the marks of the capitalist society from whose womb it had issued. Thus each individual producer would be paid in proportion to the amount of work he did. Only in a higher phase of Communist society—"after labor has become not only a means of life but also the primary necessity of life," and when the forces of production had increased and there was universal abundance—would the final Communist ideal be achieved: "from each according to his abilities, to each according to his needs."

During the early postrevolutionary period, that is, during the "dictatorship of the proletariat," the power of the state would be used to destroy the bourgeoisie. As the task of liquidating the bourgeoisie proceeded, the "government over persons" would be progressively replaced by the "administration of things," and the state as an instrument of coercion would "wither away." In the new society all would share in the products of the toil of all and there would be plenty and prosperity for everyone.

THE REVISIONISTS

In the late nineteenth and early twentieth centuries, many of Marx's contemporaries or followers suggested modifications in his doctrine. While it was true that the rural middle class, by which Marx understood the peasantry, was drastically declining in size and importance with the advance of industrialization, he had failed to predict the development and centrality of a new urban middle class in the social structure of industrial countries. Moreover, the workers, by using their new power to vote (the suffrage had been severely restricted when Marx first wrote) and their power to organize in unions and cooperatives, had greatly improved their bargaining position and their material prosperity. In many countries of Western Europe, members of other classes helped in the enactment of social legislation: protection of women and children in industry, compensation for accidents, protection against dangerous machinery and unhealthful working conditions, limitations on minimum wages and maximum hours of work, and insurance against illness, unemployment, and old age. Marx himself had suggested that in advanced democratic countries, such as England, the United States, and Holland, the transition to a socialist society might come peacefully. Many socialist party leaders, such as Eduard Bernstein, were deeply interested in winning higher wages and better working conditions. Increasingly, they aimed to win a majority of the seats in Parliament and to introduce socialism through peaceful legislation rather than to prepare for revolution.[2]

THE IDEAS OF LENIN

It was against this moderate or evolutionary tendency in socialist thought that Nikolai Lenin revolted. He was born in Russia in 1870 and belonged, somewhat paradoxically, to an intellectual middle-class family. His father was a civil servant, an inspector of primary schools, while his mother belonged to the lesser gentry. His older brother, whom Lenin adored, took part in a plot to assassinate the tsar and was executed in 1887. In part from this experience, and in part out of the failure of the moderates

---

[2] The words *socialism* and *communism* are subject to some terminological confusion. At the time that Marx and Engels published the *Communist Manifesto* (1848), there were many different forms and prophets of socialism, and the word *communist* was used to distinguish Marxist socialists from others. Later in the nineteenth century, Marxism came to be the predominant form of socialist thought and, generally speaking, to be a socialist was to be a Marxist. The word *communist* returned to general use with the revolution in Russia. Up to that time the more radical wing of Russian Socialists had used the name Bolsheviks (derived from the Russian word for majority) in contrast to the more moderate Mensheviks (minority). Lenin, however, was eager to have a name more expressive of the doctrinal content of Bolshevik beliefs, and in 1918 the party officially adopted the name *Communist*. Lenin insisted that those parties in any country throughout the world that affiliated with the Russian Communists in the Third International must also adopt the name *Communist*.

In the Soviet Union the words are also used to mark the distinction between the first stage of communism (which is called *socialism*) and the second and higher stage (which is called *communism*).

Thus the words are used in a double sense: to mark a distinction between political parties, and to mark a distinction between different stages in the development of a Communist society.

to achieve decisive change, Lenin could draw the practical lesson that a successful revolutionary movement must be based not on individual acts of terrorism nor on parliamentary pressures, but on the combined and disciplined efforts of an elite that should dominate and direct the masses. He became active in the Marxist movement in Russia, suffering both imprisonment and exile to Siberia; but from 1900 to 1917 he spent most of his life abroad, devoting himself to building a revolutionary movement.

The party: the instrument of revolution

The restoration of violent revolution to a central place in Marxism, the need for highly disciplined organization, and the ability to transmit his own enthusiasm for single-purpose action are at the heart of Lenin's work. He bitterly attacked those Marxists and Socialists who were not revolutionary. In the Socialist periodical *Iskra* (the Spark), published after 1900 by Russians in exile, he insisted over and over again that the impetus for revolution could not come from a mass organization that inevitably would include the lukewarm and waste its time debating, voting, and compromising. It could be provided only by a small organization of professional revolutionaries, dedicated to absolute obedience and relentless action. Ties of friendship and individual rights must not stand in the way of the success of revolutionary action.

Lenin foresaw that the masses would not instinctively follow the lead of the Bolsheviks. On the contrary, he declared, "The history of all countries shows that the working class, exclusively by its own efforts, is able to develop only trade union consciousness." Thus, "Our task . . . is . . . to *divert* the labor movement from its spontaneous, trade unionist striving to go under the wing of the bourgeoisie, and to bring it under the wing of revolutionary Social-Democracy."

Ripeness for revolution

But if violent revolution was Lenin's aim, for what kind of revolution was Russia ripe? Orthodox Marxists believed that proletarian revolutions could occur only in highly industrialized countries where the majority of the people belonged to a class-conscious working class and where a bourgeois revolution (such as the French Revolution) had already taken place. The evolutionary-minded Mensheviks preached, therefore, that the first step toward ultimate socialism was to aid liberal bourgeois forces in their opposition to autocracy. Trotsky, the most brilliant of the revolutionaries and originally a Menshevik, felt, in contrast, that the Russian middle class was too weak to carry through the cultural and political tasks that the bourgeoisie performed in Western Europe; thus he insisted, and in 1917 Lenin accepted the view, that the bourgeois revolution in Russia could be promoted by the proletariat and that there could then be a direct transition to socialism and the proletariat dictatorship.

The alliance of proletariat and peasants

While Lenin was convinced that the proletariat would have to carry the burden of the bourgeois revolution in Russia, he formulated the more striking and significant notion that the necessary mass base for action could be provided by temporarily combining the numerically weak proletariat with the peasants. He recognized that the peasants possessed an enormous revolutionary potential for the destruction of the old order and he believed, therefore, that "the revolutionary-democratic dictatorship of the proletariat and the peasantry" could carry through "the democratic revolution." But he had limited faith that a worker-peasant alliance could build socialism, and thus he felt that immediately after the democratic revolution, the proletariat should ally itself with the landless peasantry (the only section of that class believed to have true socialist consciousness) to undertake the socialist revolution. Thus the small Russian industrial proletariat, led by the highly disciplined elite party, was to be the driving force in both revolutions. The concept was strategically brilliant and adaptable to the Russian situation.

Imperialism

Lenin also believed, however, that the ultimate success of the socialist revolution in Russia was tied to Communist victory in developed Western states. He declared in 1905 that "the *European-Socialist* proletariat" would have to come to the support of a revolution in Russia if socialism were to triumph. World War I seemed to offer the right opportunity. Bitterly disappointed when he found that far from uniting in proletarian comradeship, European socialists supported their national leaders at the outbreak of what was dubbed a capitalist war, Lenin reexamined the state of world politics in his *Imperialism, the Highest Stage of Capitalism*. In this book he argued that the fusion of banking and industrial capital had brought industrialized countries into the stage of monopoly capitalism. This stage was characterized by larger and larger monopolist units within these countries, by the increasing control of financial capital, and by the export of capital into other areas. Since there were no longer opportunities for free expansion and development of colonial and quasi-colonial empires, which served as places for profitable investment, as sources of raw materials, and as outlets for goods, the tension between existing empires inevitably led to rivalries, he declared, out of which wars were bound to grow.

Lenin explained the lack of revolutionary fervor of the proletariat in the advanced countries by the fact that the labor leaders had been bought off with improved standards of living at the expense of the exploited colonial peoples. He still believed that they could be fired to see their own overriding socialist interest if a break in the worldwide chain of capitalism took place. Russia, with its nascent modernized industrialism, was the "weakest link" in international capitalism, and by breaking that link Lenin hoped to provide the spark to ignite the proletarian revolution in England and France. The proletariat, urged Lenin, should do its best to "turn the imperialist war into a civil war." In 1917, events in Russia seemed a response to his challenge.

The state and revolution

During the summer of that year while the Bolsheviks were preparing for the seizure of power (which actually took place in November or, according to the old Russian calendar, October), Lenin found time to develop his ideas on the nature of the revolution and of the society that would succeed it in an unfinished book, *The State and Revolution*. Here he challenged those moderate and reformist Socialists who, like the members of the British Labor party, believed that democratic states could introduce socialism peacefully and gradually. At the same time, he contradicted Marx on the possibility that England could make the transition without violence. Progress, he wrote, "does not march along a simple, smooth, and direct path to 'greater and greater democracy.' . . . No, progressive development—that is, towards Communism—marches through the dictatorship of the proletariat. . . ." Parliaments provided no real path to power. "The actual work of the State is done behind the scenes and is carried out by the departments, the chancelleries and the staffs. Parliament itself is given up to talk for the special purpose of fooling the 'common people.'" Only by forcefully seizing control of the instruments of state power—the bureaucracy (the civil service), the army, and police force—could the proletariat triumph.

But Lenin maintained that once these instruments were captured, the revolutionary proletariat could not simply use them for its own purposes but must build its own state machinery. In this key respect, Lenin also differed fundamentally from the evolutionary socialists. Much of the controversy about the role and nature of modern bureaucracy has revolved around this issue.

The functions of the new state machinery were to be both coercive and constructive. Concerning the dictatorship of the proletariat, Lenin wrote in *The State and Revolution*:

> [It] will produce a series of restrictions of liberty in the case of oppressors, exploiters, and capitalists. We must crush them in order to free humanity from wage-slavery; and resistance must be broken by force. It is clear that where there is suppression there must also be violence, and there cannot be liberty or democracy. . . . The proletariat needs the State, the centralized organization of force and violence, both for the purpose of crushing the resistance of the exploiters and for the purpose of guiding the great mass of the population—the peasantry, the

lower middle class, the semi-proletariat—in the work of economic Socialist reconstruction.

As these purposes were achieved, however, the coercive apparatus of the state would become less and less necessary and could progressively wither away.

The first stage: socialism

Lenin distinguished between two stages in the withering away of the state. During the first stage, known as *socialism*, there would be certain resemblances to bourgeois society. The public responsibilities of the state must be carried out, but Lenin indicated that "the specific 'bossing' methods of the State can and must begin to be replaced—immediately, within twenty-four hours—by the simple functions of managers and clerks—functions which are now already quite within the capacity of the average townsman and can well be performed for a working man's wage." A certain amount of bourgeois law would be retained, and he warned that there would be "the *strictest* control, *by society and by the state*, of the quantity of labor and the quantity of consumption," since much of what was produced would have to be used, not for the immediate gratification of human wants but for the expansion of the industrial plant.

"The first phase of Communism," Lenin wrote, "still cannot produce justice and equality; differences, and unjust differences, in wealth will still exist, but the *exploitation* by one man of many will have become impossible, because it will be impossible to seize as private property the *means of production*, the factories, machines, land, and so on." While it would still be necessary for the state to act as an apparatus of suppression, the old standing, professional armed forces and police would be supplanted by the armed masses of the working class: "The majority of the nation *itself* suppresses its oppressors" and, he continued, "in this sense the State begins to disappear."

The second stage: communism

The second stage in the withering away of the coercive aspect of the state, Lenin envisaged as a far freer one. It would begin when socialism had been achieved, that is, when the hostile classes had been destroyed and productive property fully socialized. As this stage advanced, it would be accompanied by such great prosperity that it would no longer be necessary to calculate consumption carefully and to reward each person in proportion to his work. Instead there would be more than enough to reward everyone, not in accordance with his work (as under socialism) but in accordance with his needs.

THE INFLUENCE OF IDEOLOGY

These salient points in Lenin's most quoted work are outlined because of the powerful influence of what is commonly called Marxism-Leninism. Moreover, the fact that Lenin was the "living prophet of Communism" made him the key power figure in the party. But it is important to recognize that in his actions Lenin was inhibited neither by classical Marxism nor by what he himself had written. The Russian Revolution, in practice, bore little resemblance to Lenin's specifications. His genius lay in utilizing unexpected opportunities, not in following a systematic revolutionary plan. Lenin was already aware by 1917 that World War I had made the liberal-socialist expectations of the prewar period unrealistic and thus much of classical Marxism no longer viable. The Bolsheviks under Lenin achieved their successful domination after the revolution in large part because their opponents failed to grasp this fact. Moreover, the opponents of the Bolsheviks did not believe that such a small party could and, in the light of its Marxist commitment, would impose its will on the vast population of what Lenin himself called after the revolution "the freest country in the world." In practice, once the Bolshevik domination was achieved, Lenin and his successors, particularly Stalin, moved pragmatically to forge the character of the modern Soviet state.

This is not to say, however, that ideology became and remained unimportant. The goals of Marx's philosophical analyses and of Lenin's own writings remained to haunt Soviet leadership and even that of Lenin himself. Differing interpretations of Marxism-Leninism have focused and sharpened controversy at the highest

level. Trotsky, Zinoviev, and later Bukharin tried repeatedly to stem the tide of development in the Soviet state by appealing to Marxist-Leninist orthodoxy, but their efforts failed. Nevertheless, ideology still provides a basis for protests against official policies and a stimulus to revolutionary efforts outside the Soviet Union. Moreover, however different their goals may be from their actions, the Russian Communist party and the Soviet state have continued to invoke Marxist-Leninist philosophy as the ultimate ideological foundation for all communist political activity. By extension, this philosophy must also underlie all social and natural science. Thus students of the Soviet Union must attempt to thread their way between a realistic analysis of Soviet policies and actions reflected in events and the ideology and terminology used to justify them, and they must also attempt to differentiate between those situations in which there is some effective interaction between policies and ideology and those in which the two have little or no relation to each other.

LENIN'S SUCCESSOR: STALIN

After the death of Lenin in January 1924, which followed a series of strokes that had virtually incapacitated him, there was a struggle to determine who would succeed him as the living prophet of communism and thus mold the course of Soviet development. In the ensuing struggle for power between Joseph Stalin and Leon Trotsky (the two most famous of the revolutionary leaders after Lenin), Trotsky urged pushing forward the socialist revolution both at home and abroad, while Stalin supported concentration on the home situation, that is, "socialism in one country."

Lenin himself had hoped that the revolution would be international, although he recognized that it could occur, and had occurred, in only one country. But Lenin's position contained ambiguities that made it possible for both Trotsky and Stalin to invoke his writings as support for their opposing views on whether socialism could ultimately triumph in a single country as backward as Russia. Within a comparatively short time, it became clear that victory would rest ultimately with Joseph Stalin, because as secretary general of the Communist party of the Soviet Union, and thus in a position to manipulate that vast bureaucratic structure, he had succeeded in becoming the key power figure of the country.

Although Stalin had written on the problem of nationalities, he was in no sense a political theorist but a calculating and forceful administrator and a man of action. His role was to determine the practical policies to be followed in a country where Communists already held power. Stalin insisted on industrialization, collectivization of agriculture, and, above all, on his own undisputed control within the Soviet Union. By imposing harsh sacrifices on the population, Stalin forced a concentration on heavy industry that kept living standards low, was immensely wasteful, but ultimately produced an impressive, if lopsided, industrial structure. His theoretical justification for building the secret police into an all-pervasive, coercive force under his own control—and for crushing internal opposition through mass terror—was the doctrine that progress in the construction of socialism led to a "sharpening of the class struggle." He also justified the holocaust of the "Great Purge" that destroyed millions of persons by associating the slightest challenge to his authority with "capitalist encirclement," the view that outside powers not only threatened to attack the Soviet Union but fomented subversion within it.

To many old-line Bolsheviks, Stalin's abandonment of internationalism, his view that conditions had to get worse before they got better, and his fostering of personal adulation ran counter to what they had expected and fought for. The sacrifice of consumer goods to the needs of heavy industry, the growth of widely differing pay levels, social discrimination and stratification, authoritarianism, and the widespread use of terror became hallmarks of Stalin's reign. Indeed it is difficult to deny that Stalin's policies were chiefly motivated by his drive to establish and maintain undisputed power and to mold the Soviet Union into a society in which agriculture was sacrificed to industrialization, creativity to conformity, and popular participation to his own will and the wills of the few he trusted.

Although the accepted doctrine of the period continued to be called Marxism-Leninism,

the focus of policies had shifted to the current hard realities of autocracy and the relentless drive of the Five-Year Plans. It has been argued that Lenin and Stalin worked out the empirical consequences of the Marxist theory of the class struggle. Zbigniew Brzezinski has said that "Stalin consummated the marriage of Marxism-Leninism and Soviet (particularly Russian) nationalism." [3] It can equally well be asserted that Stalin's policies owed nothing to Marx's apocalyptic vision of the future and little to Lenin's designs. But for Stalin, as with all Soviet leaders, the conception of a monolithic party carrying on historic tasks, however fallacious in fact, was a significant factor in justifying the autocracy and totalitarianism he enforced in the Soviet state.

STALIN'S SUCCESSOR: KHRUSHCHEV

Stalin's death in 1953 opened a struggle for succession (as had Lenin's in an earlier period). Yet for all the shifts in power before Nikita Khrushchev emerged by 1957 as leader (which he was to remain until his abrupt ouster from power in 1964), the transition was far smoother than after Lenin's death. Khrushchev at first endorsed Stalin's emphasis on heavy industry, but by 1957 he had adopted a proconsumer policy. His strongest commitment, however, was to the power of the party *apparat* as the safeguard of the elite and the party as a whole against a recurrence of Stalinist terror.

Immediately after Stalin's death, the dominance of the secret police was broken and mass terror was eliminated. Law was gradually liberalized, and a greater emphasis was placed on "socialist legality" (see Chapter 7, Section 1). But the most startling manifestation of a new line after Stalin's death was Khrushchev's famous "secret" speech at the Twentieth Party Congress, February 1956. The two particular targets in Khrushchev's attack on Stalin and Stalinism were the "cult of the individual" and Stalin's arbitrariness toward party organs and high party functionaries after 1934 when he turned against the party. By vilifying Stalin for his arbitrariness and blaming him for the evils of the past, Khrushchev sought to legit-

[3] Zbigniew Brzezinski, "The Soviet Past and Future," *Encounter* (March 1970), p. 7.

imize his own authority and to clear the way for new approaches.

Khrushchev rejected Stalin's notion that progress in the construction of socialism led to the sharpening of the class struggle. In a general internal "thaw," Khrushchev sought to substitute "social organization" and social pressures for coercive state measures. He produced a deceptively simple conception that substituted society for the state. In 1961 he held out the enticing prospect that the technical and material bases for the transition to communism would be completed by 1980 and that the coercive aspects of the state would then wither away. Interestingly, this notion aroused little response.

In the realm of foreign policy, Khrushchev is associated on the one hand with the creation of crises over Berlin and the placing of Soviet missiles in Cuba, and on the other with the doctrine of "peaceful coexistence," interpreted by him to mean continued competition for influence and a continued ideological struggle but the exclusion of war as a means of promoting that competition. This basic idea of peaceful coexistence was not, in fact, new. Lenin called it "parallel existence" and believed it essential for the survival of the Soviet state. Triumphing over the Trotskyite plea for a revolutionary strategy, Stalin told the Fifteenth Congress, in December 1927, that "our relations with the capitalist countries are based on the assumption that the coexistence of two opposite systems is possible. Practice has fully confirmed this." What was distinctive about Khrushchev was that he used the doctrine of "peaceful coexistence" to open the iron curtain by encouraging tourism, cultural exchanges, and trade expansion.

Khrushchev also turned "neutralism" into a doctrine of positive advantage to the Soviet Union. In replacing the former concept of "he who is not with me is against me" by the open-ended "he who is not against me shall be counted for me," Khrushchev created a much more complex and useful (to the Soviet Union) picture of the world. In this scheme of things, numerous states—from Sweden to Yugoslavia, through the Middle East and Africa to India and Indonesia—that were not specifically aligned with the West were included in what

was called "the camp of peace." Inside this camp of peace was the "anti-imperialist camp" and still further inside was—and is—the "socialist camp" of Eastern European associates.

Regarding Stalin's pre–World War II doctrine of capitalist encirclement, which suggested a defensive attitude against overwhelming outside powers, Khrushchev once commented with perception, "At present it is not known who encircles whom." His own references to "hostile blocs" correctly evaluated the powerful position of the Soviet Union in the post–World War II period.

Despite Khrushchev's emphasis on the dominance of the professional party bureaucracy within the elite, his own reorganization of the party in November 1962 into two separate hierarchies—one charged with practical economic leadership in industry and the other in the rural sector—divided it institutionally and thus impaired its unity. As an unexpected consequence, the government bureaucracy reassumed some of its former integrative functions, thereby restoring much of the institutional balance existing under Stalin but minus the balancer. Without ideological sophistication, personal charisma, great technical capacity, or, most decisively, the powerful, personally controlled police machine that formed the core of Stalin's power, Khrushchev tried to make up for these lacks with crash programs, whirlwind tours, uninhibited outbursts, and calls for fresh intensity of effort. By the time he had been replaced by leaders, to whom flamboyance was distasteful, orderliness essential, and a more defined division between party apparatus and government bureaucracy desirable, Khrushchev had become, in Brzezinski's words, "an anachronism in the new political context he himself had helped to create." [4]

KHRUSHCHEV'S SUCCESSORS: BREZHNEV AND KOSYGIN

Leonid Brezhnev and Aleksei Kosygin, who took over from Khrushchev, represent a new type of political leader in the Soviet Union, whose most formative experiences are not of

[4] Brzezinski, "The Soviet Political System: Transformation or Degeneration," *Problems of Communism* (January–February 1966), p. 4.

the period of the revolution but of Stalin, of the turmoil of the purges, and of World War II. Their objective is stability and control; they are used to working together, and the smooth functioning of their complicated bureaucratic structure is more important than originality or ideological fervor.

Although they have continued Khrushchev's major allocation policies, his successors have established their own distinctive emphasis and approaches. They have sharpened the division between party and state bureaucracies, introduced a limited rehabilitation of Stalin, promoted repressive measures against dissident authors and other intellectuals, and enforced bureaucratic centralization, although in a context of far-reaching economic reform. The character of these and other policies and their effects will be spelled out in detail in the sections that follow.

SOME PRELIMINARY CONCLUSIONS

Questions raised at the start of this section were these: Does the course of policies in the Soviet Union show any clear line of continuity or has it been chiefly molded by circumstance? If the former, how influential has been the ideological base to which all Soviet leaders have avowed their allegiance? Some preliminary answers can now be attempted. Some aspects of Marxism and Leninism have been discarded, the latter even by their own author. Lenin subsequently called a "fairy tale" his own notion in *The State and Revolution* that the tasks of government could be performed by anyone. More fundamentally, it is apparent that far from reflecting Marx's historical materialism, which taught that politics are the reflection of the stage of economic development, the development of the Soviet Union is an outstanding example of economic growth being the result of political organization and drive.

Lenin's abiding contribution was to mate an adapted Marxism to the autocratic Russian tradition. Lenin's concept of an elite party to which the individual was subordinate provided the basis for Stalin's ultimate victory and the ideological basis for crushing opposition and serious intellectual deviations from the norms upheld by those in power. As the leadership of the Communist party of the Soviet Union changed from a diverse collection of cosmopolitan intellectuals to a bureaucratic apparatus in control of a following of predominantly Russian peasants, it did not give up its ideological commitment but tended to interpret this commitment in terms that were almost identical with those that national interest dictated. This is as much the case with the Brezhnev Doctrine (see Chapter 8, Section 2), used to justify the invasion of Czechoslovakia, as it was for Stalin's "socialism in one state." In this broad sense of dogmatic autocracy, there has been striking continuity despite appalling dislocations.

Its ideological doctrine has provided a twofold advantage for the Soviet Union. It embodies an integrative perspective capable of skillful manipulation in the hands of those in power, and it contains an ethical idealism appealing both inside and outside the country. It can also be said that it has in no degree inhibited opportunism, and, if anything, has aided the practices of autocracy by justifying repression of opposition.

Looking ahead, Brzezinski has suggested five possible alternative paths of future Soviet political development: petrification, pluralist evolution, technological adaptation, fundamentalism, and political disintegration.[5] His own view is that the most likely course is some combination of petrification, that is, retention of political control without innovations, with technological adaptations that will stress scientific expertise in the party rather than its traditional bureaucratic dogmatism. At the same time, Brzezinski does not rule out the possibility that internal decay and ineffective handling of Soviet dilemmas in preserving internal unity, fostering economic growth, and coping with external strains in its relations with the United States might lead to a revival of ideological fervor. These are possibilities to which we can return after a backward look at the Soviet political heritage and a more complete analysis of the character and policies of the Soviet state.

[5] Brzezinski, "Soviet Past and Future," p. 7.

2 HISTORICAL INFLUENCES

No aspect of Russian history has been more marked than the persistent tradition of absolutism in government, the recurrent use of revolutionary violence to solve political problems, and the lack of experience with democratic institutions and constitutional procedures. The domination of the country by the Tartars for two and a half centuries effectively halted whatever native development there might have been toward self-government and cut Russia off from any liberating influences from the West. The princes of Moscow first established their power through the favor of their Tartar rulers. The almost constant warfare through which they enhanced their power increased the need for leadership and a concentration of autocratic power at the same time as it maintained the barrier against Western influence.

No Russian sovereign was ever subject to effective constitutional limitations. Until the nineteenth century even the most powerful subject lived in danger of arbitrary arrest, imprisonment, and execution; and even during the nineteenth century the tsar's police and censors kept the closest guard against any symptom of political liberalism.

The people, it is true, were not always completely docile. From the sixteenth century on there were frequent peasant revolts, some of which covered great areas and threatened the state itself. But the first serious revolt against autocratic authority, the famous Decembrist uprising of December 1825, was the work of a small group of enlightened army officers who had been converted to the liberalism of Western Europe. They had no popular following, and their revolt was easily suppressed. More significant were the intellectual ferment among the intelligentsia throughout the nineteenth century and the efforts by some of them, especially the populist-minded Narodniks, to improve the condition of the peasants by working among them. It was not until late in the nineteenth century that the slowly growing urban middle class, which provided the impetus

for parliamentary democracy in the West, sought liberal reform, and then rather for the sake of trade and profit than for liberty as such. The landed nobility maintained their social and political support of tsarism.

There had been times when it seemed possible that representative institutions of a sort might develop. Ivan the Terrible in 1550 had established a national assembly, the Zemsky Sobor. At first it could consider only those questions submitted to it; but later, during the "Time of Troubles" (1584–1613), a period of almost constant disorder and civil war, its power grew. It elected Boris Godunov tsar, and in 1613 it chose the first Romanov as tsar. Yet its powers and method of procedure were never clearly worked out, and its authority declined. No Sobors were held from 1654 to 1682, and after 1698 Peter the Great and his successors summoned no Sobors at all.[6]

Another possible source of popular participation in government appeared in 1864 when there was a reorganization of the institutions of local government. The provincial and district

[6] After the death of Peter the Great in 1725, there was no clear succession to the throne, because Peter, like Ivan the Terrible (1533–84), had slain his heir. Peter's second wife, Catherine (who had been a Lithuanian servant girl and who had no personal right to the throne), seized power by force and held it until her death in 1727. The crown then passed to Peter's young grandson, Peter II (1727–30); then to Peter's niece, Anne (1730–40); then to Anne's infant grand-nephew, Ivan VI (1740–41), who was dethroned and later murdered in prison by Peter's daughter Elizabeth (1741–62). Elizabeth's nephew Peter III, a German prince, was dethroned by his wife, Catherine the Great (1762–96) and, like Ivan VI, was killed in prison. Catherine's son and successor, Paul (1796–1801), an unbalanced eccentric, was strangled by his own officials. Alexander I (1801–25), who had at first been influenced by liberal ideas, ended in the camp of reaction from which his brother and successor, Nicholas I (1825–55), never emerged. Nicholas I's son, Alexander II (1855–81), a conservative but no tyrant, introduced important reforms, notably the freeing of the serfs in 1861. For a time there was hope of a more liberal government. An attempt at assassination in 1866, however, precipitated a period of reaction and another (and successful) attempt in 1881 ended his regime. The next tsar, Alexander III (1881–94), ruled as an autocrat, and his successor, the last of the tsars, Nicholas II (1894–1917), followed a wavering course strongly marked by autocracy.

councils (*zemstvos*) were elected popularly, although the voters were divided into three classes and the peasants chose their representatives indirectly. Control rested in the hands of the gentry, many of whom were progressive in their political and social ideas. The powers of the *zemstvos* were never very clearly defined, however, and, particularly under Alexander III (1881–94), their activities were severely restricted. In 1890, election by the peasantry was almost completely eliminated.

The Duma

What appeared to be the most promising foundation for popular government was the Duma. Under the pressure of revolutionary agitation occasioned by the unsuccessful war against Japan, the tsar in the "October Manifesto" of 1905 agreed to the establishment of a popular assembly, the Duma, which was chosen by universal suffrage. Several political parties participated in the elections, the two most prominent being the Octobrists, a conservative party that took its name from the Manifesto; and the Constitutional Democrats or "Cadets," who represented the progressive middle class and desired a constitutional government patterned after those in Western Europe. The Socialist Revolutionaries, a radical peasant party, and the Mensheviks, who were revolutionary in temper but objected to Lenin's methods, both officially boycotted the election. The Bolsheviks also refused to take part.

The Duma was balanced in its authority by an upper chamber, the Council of State (first established in 1825), one-half of whose members were nominated by the tsar himself; there was accordingly no danger that legislation distasteful to the ruler would be passed. Moreover, when the first Duma, which was overwhelmingly liberal in composition, engaged in conflict with the tsar's ministers (who were responsible only to the ruler), it was dissolved just ten weeks after its first meeting (1906). An ensuing appeal by some two hundred of its members for widespread passive resistance had no effect. The second Duma (1907) was somewhat more radical than the first, and it too was dissolved. Before new elections were held, however, the tsar arbitrarily changed the entire basis of representation. He disenfranchised large areas of the country, reduced sharply the representation of the peasants, and increased that of the big landowners and the wealthier inhabitants of the cities. Thus the third Duma (1907–12), despite the Bolsheviks' participation in this and the succeeding election, was much more conservative and much less representative than its predecessors.

The failure of the imperial regime to keep the promises granted during the 1905 Revolution, the fact that the emancipation of 1861 had left the peasantry with inadequate landholdings, especially in the face of a rapidly increasing population, and the lack of intermediary independent social institutions that could serve as countervailing forces to the overpowering centralization of authority are among the reasons why revolution succeeded in 1917. The "underdevelopment of society and overdevelopment of the state" characterized prerevolutionary Russia. But there were also special features of strain to be exploited: the land hunger of the peasants; the radicalism caused by the existence of large-scale industry, in which more than one-third of all Russian workers were employed, without the social, cultural, and legal conditions characteristic of advanced industrialism; disgust at Rasputin's influence over the weak and stupid tsar and tsarina whose belief in his magical powers brought him vast political influence; and the incredible inefficiency and corruption that contributed to Russia's disastrous participation in World War I.

When strikes broke out in March 1917 because of the lack of bread and high cost of living, the tsarist government was unable to cope with them. The tsar abdicated, and authority passed to a provisional government appointed by the Duma, and to the workers' and soldiers' councils (soviets), which had sprung up spontaneously. But even when Prince Lvov was replaced by Alexander Kerensky, a moderate Socialist Revolutionary, the provisional government could not free itself from the old official class and administrative machine. It alienated the peasants by refusing to legalize land seizures. Kerensky also refused to cooperate with even the proliberal elements in the army and tried to keep Russia in the war despite the widespread clamor for peace.

THE COMMUNIST SEIZURE OF POWER

It was Lenin's great achievement that he saw the opportunity provided by such a situation. In an effort to weaken Russian resistance in the war, the Germans brought Lenin and other Bolsheviks back from exile in a sealed train in April 1917. The March to November period was characterized by a sharing of authority between the provisional government and the soviets, the Bolsheviks playing for popularity among the latter with slogans like "Peace, Land, and Bread" and "All Power to the Soviets." An attempt by rightists, under the leadership of General Kornilov, to overthrow the government in the summer of 1917 upset the balance. Although the central core of the Bolsheviks consisted only of between five and ten thousand, one-third of them intellectuals, and although their total numbers were no more than twenty-three thousand, they now confronted a weakened right and center. Lenin saw the chance for a *coup d'état* to overthrow the "bourgeois" democratic republic. The Bolshevik coup in November [7] triumphed with the same ease as had the earlier revolution.

Almost at once the Bolsheviks faced the test of a nation-wide election for the Constituent Assembly, the most truly popular body in the history of Russia. The Bolsheviks received only 25 percent of the votes, while the more democratic parties had 62 percent. In the "supplementary revolution" of January 5, 1918, Lenin dissolved the assembly in what he acknowledged was a "frank and complete liquidation of formal democracy in the name of the revolutionary dictatorship." He established a one-party regime later in 1918. Civil war ensued.

Every party within Russia was soon engaged in active struggle against the Communist regime. The "Red" terror by the Cheka (the secret police) was matched by the "White" terror of the counter-revolutionaries. The British, French, Japanese, and American governments supported "White" armies, although ineffectually, in the hope of reestablishing a second front against Germany (the Bolsheviks had made peace in the spring of 1918 by the Treaty of Brest-Litovsk). But by 1921 the Communists had defeated all the counter-revolutionary forces. In the process they had been forged into what Robert Conquest calls "a hardened and experienced machine in which loyalty to the organization came before any other consideration." [8]

During the period of the Civil War, means of production, land, banks, and industrial plants were nationalized, private trade was forbidden, and farmers' produce above immediate needs was confiscated. These drastic measures were not only opposed bitterly by the peasants, the trade unions, and the moderate parties, but they also failed to produce urgently needed supplies and goods. Millions died in the great famine of 1921. Lenin felt forced to ask for external aid and to introduce the economic retreat known as the New Economic Policy (NEP), which restored a freer market for both peasants and workers.

This admission that the earlier policies had been at least partly wrong encouraged the opposition at both party and popular levels. But Lenin was no less determined to crush such opposition than he had been to win the Civil War. Peasant uprisings were beaten down, and the wave of strikes and demonstrations in February 1921, followed in March by the Soviet Union's last great popular uprising, the Kronstadt Rebellion of workers and sailors that demanded "soviets without Communists," were dealt with mercilessly. The Menshevik party and the Social Revolutionaries were crushed, the latter through the trial of their leaders in 1922. No group was to be allowed to challenge the dominance of the Communist party. Moreover, the party itself was already being transformed into a bureaucracy in which, as the Stalin period demonstrated, manipulation could be more effective than argument.

THE SOVIET UNION UNDER STALIN

The Stalin period built on the past but so molded and conditioned the country and its people that it created the character of the Soviet Union as we know it. The material impact is clearly visible. The Five-Year Plans, which vastly distorted the growth of the econ-

---

[7] By the old calendar, the revolutions were in February and October, but the Bolsheviks soon adopted the same calendar as the West.

[8] Robert Conquest, *The Great Terror: The History of the Great Moscow Purge Trials*, p. 5.

omy by giving absolute priority to those sectors of heavy industry producing for the military and for heavy industry itself, kept consumption levels low. The inevitable corollary to this type of rapid industrialization was compulsory collectivization of agriculture aimed at securing adequate farm products to feed the workers without providing consumer goods in return. When the peasants refused to produce more than enough for their own use, that food was seized, thereby creating one of the world's greatest famines, and the only one deliberately manmade. Through famine, exile, and brutal force, most of those peasants who survived were grouped into collective and state farms, which still characterize Soviet agriculture although their production has never reached the desired levels.

No less significant for the character of the Soviet Union was the political transformation carried out through Stalin's purges, which culminated in the appalling outburst of mass terror without regard to individual guilt known as the "Great Purge" or "Great Terror," 1937–38. Through these purges not only were potentially hostile elements destroyed or sent to forced labor camps but also many loyal Stalinists, as we shall see. Robert Conquest's careful evaluation of the numbers involved suggests there were 5 million in jail or camps by January 1937 and a further 7 million arrested between January 1937 and December 1938, of whom 1 million were executed and 2 million died in the camps. Late in 1938, there were 9 million in captivity, 1 million in prison, and 8 million in camps.[9] The carnage was particularly heavy among the minority nationalities, as in the Ukraine. But the elements most strikingly decimated in terms of the future development of the country were the Communist party and the military.

Prior to 1934, all those openly opposed to Stalin had been eliminated from leading roles in the party. Step by step, Stalin had triumphed first over the so-called left opposition (Leon Trotsky, Gregory Zinoviev, and Lev Kamenev) and then over his erstwhile supporters, the right opposition (Nikolai Bukharin, Aleksei Rykov, and Mikhail Tomsky). But the purge between 1934 and 1939, set off by the planned

murder of Sergei Kirov, head of the party in Leningrad (almost certainly engineered by Stalin), eliminated virtually all the Stalinists themselves and thus placed Stalin in a unique position of dominance. Less than 2 percent of the delegates of the Seventeenth Party Congress of 1934 held positions in the Eighteenth Congress in 1939. Many of the most famous old Bolsheviks had perished, some after "confessions" in the public trials that puzzled many Western observers. These confessions reflected not only inquisitorial methods but also the ironic dilemma of those who had themselves sacrificed others to the overriding will of the party. The Communist party emerged as a new organization whose original cadres had perished and which was now composed of men dedicated to Stalin himself and to his methods. They had been forged by the experience of the purges, as their predecessors had been forged by the Civil War and subsequently by the battle of collectivization.

Proportionately, the element hardest hit by the purges was the military, a fact with grave implications for the war years ahead. Robert Conquest cites a Soviet source to enumerate almost unbelievable losses through the purges:[10] all 11 vice-commissars of Defense; 75 out of 80 members of the Supreme Military Soviet; 3 of the 5 marshals; 14 out of 16 Army commanders, Class I and II; all 8 admirals, Class I and II; 60 of the 67 Corps commanders; 136 of the 199 Divisional commanders; 221 of the 397 Brigade commanders; and about half the officer corps, that is, some 35,000 either shot or imprisoned. Almost all those with field experience were liquidated. A not surprising consequence was the poor performance of Soviet forces in the Finnish war of 1939–40 and the inability of the poorly led, although numerically larger and technically well equipped, Soviet army to stem the Nazi attack in June 1941.

Chiefly responsible for the inadequacies and unpreparedness of most Soviet military leaders in command posts at the outbreak of the Nazi offensive, however, was the extraordinary refusal of Stalin himself to accept the possibility that the pledges of the Nazi-Soviet Pact of 1939 were worthless and that Hitler might turn his forces against his erstwhile ally once he had

---

[9] Conquest, *The Great Terror*, p. 532.

[10] Conquest, *The Great Terror*, p. 485.

subdued the Low Countries and France. Stalin had done well through the pact. He had partitioned Poland with the Nazis and extended Soviet boundaries to include the three Baltic states and Bessarabia. Although the Finnish war had been a near fiasco, it had ended with the Soviet frontiers pushed farther away from Leningrad. Stalin also had designs on the Balkans, which were thwarted by Hitler whose forces overran Yugoslavia and Greece in the spring of 1941. Even then, and despite British and American warnings and Soviet intelligence regarding the massing of Nazi troops, Stalin trusted that the pact would keep his country safe. Thus, much of the Soviet air force was destroyed on the ground on June 22, 1941, when the Nazis attacked in force. Army units broke under the attack; Stalin's response was to have the commanders shot. Mass desertions took place, and some units joined the German army. The mirage of military preparedness and Soviet invulnerability so carefully fostered by the party left both the army and the people psychologically unprepared for war within their own territory and particularly for the lightning attack that carried the Nazi forces deep into Soviet territory. The vast area occupied by Nazi forces, including nearly half of European Russia, held 80 million people. More than 20 million in all lost their lives in the war. Vast dislocations of population and devastation followed the course of the fighting.

As the war proceeded, military talent came to the fore by sheer demonstration of success. Despite disastrous retreats, some coordination of forces was achieved under Marshal Zhukov, the ablest of those in high military office when the attack came. The system of dual (military and party) command gave way to undivided authority for military decisions in the hands of the commander, with party indoctrination left to the deputy commander for political affairs—a situation still in existence. The heroic defense of Leningrad lasting throughout 880 days of siege prevented the full control of western European Russia on which Hitler had counted. Allied aid was substantial, and the Allied landings in France in June 1944 confronted Hitler with the two-front war he had sought so long to avoid. In 1945, Soviet troops at last moved out of their own territory to sweep across Eastern Europe and ultimately into Berlin. This victory at the end, coupled with the arts of propaganda and Western sympathies, was long to conceal the appalling disaster of June 22, 1941, and its aftermath.

Despite the national concentration on what was called "The Great Patriotic War" and a few signs of relaxation, as, for example, in relations with the Russian Orthodox Church, the secret police (NKVD) continued their pervasive activities even within Leningrad during its siege. Prisoners in NKVD camps were shot as Nazi forces advanced, for fear they might join the army. Some old grudges were settled, and army and other leaders were shot while war was raging.

The end of the war brought no relaxation but rather an intensification of pressures to assert party primacy again in every aspect of life. In 1946–47, Jews, army officers, and many others were arrested. In Eastern Europe the old Soviet pattern of show trials and confessions took place even though Traicho Kostov, secretary of the Central Committee of the Bulgarian Communist party, proved their worthlessness by retracting his "confession" in open court in December 1949. There is also evidence that new purges and possible trials were planned by Stalin just before his death. In any event, the numbers in forced labor camps had mounted, and the deaths in them were vastly extended by the famine of 1947. Since releases were rare, the total of those in the camps performing heavy physical labor under supervision of the Ministry of Internal Affairs (MVD, the renamed NKVD) was probably as high at Stalin's death as ever before.

The impact of such systematic repression was to produce a population that was on the whole obedient and silent. Control was fully extended throughout the country, including the collective farms. Planning procedures had become regularized; substantial and steady increases in heavy industrial production were established. Just as the brutal punishment of failure in the military had finally concentrated command in some outstanding figures, so had the ruthless responses to inability to meet quotas in the industrial sphere. But the price had been incredibly high. Even cautious Soviet commentators and, more outspokenly, Khrushchev himself have agreed that it could have been achieved better by more evolutionary means and with far less cost.

THE SOVIET UNION AFTER STALIN

In his "secret" speech of 1956, Khrushchev raised doubts regarding the source of Kirov's murder, and he spoke openly of prolonged tortures suffered by old Bolsheviks and Communist leaders at the hands of the secret police and of the uncertainties suffered by anyone, no matter what his position, as to whether he would get out alive after entering Stalin's presence. Most striking, Khrushchev repaid some of the debt to the army by indicating Stalin's responsibility for Russian unpreparedness when the Nazis struck. But, necessary as Khrushchev felt this repudiation of Stalin to be, its effect was to raise general doubts regarding the wisdom of all past party policies and particularly of those who had so obviously been closely associated with Stalin and were now in office. Intellectuals rapidly took advantage of this precedent of criticism. Sections of the military had a vested interest in keeping Stalin's culpability to the fore. But the failure of efforts to trace a line in party orthodoxy direct from Leninism to the current holders of power led to a swing back to more repression in the interests of a redefined ideological orthodoxy. This repression struck hard at writers and artists, although they clung to their new freedom of expression. Rumors of plans to rehabilitate Stalin emerge from time to time. The interplay of forces within and outside the Soviet Union, which will be analyzed in more detail in the rest of the study, is still at work in molding the Soviet Union of the seventies.

3   THE SOVIET CONSTITUTION

Among the determining factors in Soviet politics, although of very minor importance compared to the will of the party, is the constitution that Stalin promulgated in 1936 [11] in the midst of the period of purges. This constitution differs sharply, except in form, from the constitutions that exist in Western countries. These latter constitutions provide the framework within which take place the processes of lawmaking and the interaction of political institutions. But the constitution of the Soviet Union does little to restrict the operations of political power. Thus its immensely detailed provisions confuse rather than clarify an understanding of Soviet governmental processes and the workings of power. Admittedly, much of the formal structure of institutions does exist, but the way in which these institutions operate is vastly different from the impression provided by the constitutional text. The Soviet constitution describes what is, in fact, a façade behind and through which operates the Communist party, the supreme locus of power, and the rights it guarantees are subject to the interpretation and current objectives of the regime.

This is not to say, however, that the constitution has no significance. By openly affirming the existence of a governmental structure, of federalism, and, particularly, of rights belonging to all Soviet citizens, the constitution provides a visible norm to which those working for change may point (see Chapter 2, Section 3). That the existence of the liberal provisions of the Soviet constitution has also served to cloak the reality of dictatorial rule and repression does not wholly overshadow the potential benefits of the public affirmation of rights embodied in its provisions.

In form the Soviet government looks quite like that of a Western European democracy. There is a national legislature, the Supreme Soviet, which is made up of two chambers: the Soviet of the Union, which contains one deputy for every three hundred thousand of the population, and the Soviet of Nationalities, in which the various union republics, autonomous republics, autonomous regions, and national

[11] A commission to produce a new constitution has been meeting for some years.

Theoretical Structure of the Soviet National Government

USSR SUPREME SOVIET

Soviet of the Union	Soviet of Nationalities
Elected by citizens of the USSR on the basis of one deputy for every 300,000 inhabitants.	Elected by citizens of the USSR voting by federal subdivisions.

Elected for a four-year term.

Exercises exclusive legislative power.

Elects the Presidium.

Appoints the Council of Ministers and holds it responsible.

Amends the constitution by a two-thirds vote.

Supreme Court

Elected by the Supreme Soviet for a five-year term. Supervises the judicial activities of all judicial organs of the USSR and the union republics.

Public Prosecutor

Procurator general

Appointed by the Supreme Soviet for a seven-year term.

Ensures the strict observance of the law by all ministries, officials, and citizens of the USSR.

Presidium

The chairman of the Presidium of the Supreme Soviet is nominal head of state

Convenes sessions of the Supreme Soviet.

Issues decrees.

Interprets laws.

Dissolves the Supreme Soviet in case of persistent disagreement between the two chambers.

In intervals between sessions of the Supreme Soviet, subject to subsequent confirmation, releases and appoints ministers of the USSR on the recommendation of the chairman of the Council of Ministers.

In intervals between sessions of the Supreme Soviet, proclaims a state of war in case of attack or to carry out treaty obligations.

Annuls decisions and orders of the Council of Ministers which do not conform to law.

Appoints and removes high military and diplomatic officials.

Ratifies and denounces treaties.

Orders mobilization and proclaims martial law.

Council of Ministers

The chairman of the Council of Ministers is the premier of the USSR

Responsible and accountable to the Supreme Soviet.

Coordinates and directs the work of the ministries and other administrative bodies.

Ensures execution of the national economic plan and the state budget.

Ensures the maintenance of public order and the protection of the interests of the state and the rights of its citizens.

Directs the conduct of foreign policy.

Directs the general organization of the armed forces.

Ministers

(All-Union and Union Republic) and chairman of state committees

Direct state administration within their jurisdiction.

Issue orders and instructions in pursuance of laws in operation and decisions and orders of the Council of Ministers.

areas receive representation. In the intervals between meetings of the Supreme Soviet, a smaller group of its members known as the Presidium, which technically is responsible and accountable to the Supreme Soviet, performs many of its duties.

Executive and administrative power are said to be vested in a Council of Ministers, which operates somewhat similarly to the British Cabinet or the French Council of Ministers. Technically, the council is responsible to the Supreme Soviet or, in the intervals between meetings, to the Presidium. But in practice, as we shall see (Chapter 5), there is an interlocking directorate between the Council of Ministers and the top organs of the Communist party, which is the locus of power.

THE FEDERAL SYSTEM

There is also a federal system that at first glance looks like the one in the United States except that it is much more complicated and seems designed to reflect the multinational character of the Soviet Union. Thus there are fifteen union republics [12] and, as further subdivisions for particular nationalities, seventeen autonomous republics, nine autonomous regions, and ten national areas. But one of the union republics, the Russian Soviet Federative Socialist Republic (RSFSR), contains more than half the total population, almost three-quarters of the country's territory and all the national areas. Moreover, although in form union republics have certain rights and powers that are greater than those of the American states—the theoretical right to secede and to conduct foreign policy (on which rests the claim of the Ukraine and Byelorussia to have separate representation in the United Nations) —in practice, federalism in the Soviet Union is a matter of administrative units, not of a division of powers.

[12] The Russian Soviet Federative Socialist Republic (which itself contains more than a hundred nationalities), the Ukrainian, the Byelorussian (or White Russian), the Azerbaijan, the Georgian, the Armenian, the Turkmen, the Uzbek, the Tadjik, the Kazakh, the Kirghiz, the Moldavian, the Lithuanian, the Latvian, and the Estonian Soviet Socialist Republics. The Karelo-Finnish Republic was abolished in 1956.

THE BILL OF RIGHTS AND DUTIES

No section of the Soviet constitution has attracted more attention than its Bill of Rights. These rights include the customary ones specified by modern constitutions—freedom of speech, assembly, press, organization, and religious worship (also, uniquely, of antireligious propaganda)—and freedom from arbitrary arrest. The inviolability of the home and the privacy of correspondence are guaranteed; so are equal rights for both sexes and no discrimination because of racial or national origin. More unusual are certain social rights clearly intended to be by-products of developments in the Soviet state. The "right to work," for example, is said to be ensured by "the socialist organization of the national economy, the steady growth of the productive forces of Soviet society, the elimination of the possibility of economic crises, and the abolition of unemployment."

Although no individual right is protected by the courts against the interests of the regime, the equal rights of women are normally enforceable in court. But the right to work, for example, is not enforceable in court. It remains a declaration of aspiration, and probably of expectation, once the Soviet state has achieved the necessary level of growth.

Side by side with the statement of rights goes a listing of duties that forms a further innovation in such documents. It is said to be the citizen's duty "to abide by the constitution" and "to observe the laws" as well as "to maintain labor discipline, honestly to perform public duties, and to respect the rules of socialist intercourse." There is a special duty to safeguard "public, socialist property." The last clause of the document affirms "the sacred duty" to defend the country and describes treason as "the most heinous of crimes," to be punished with "all the severity of the law"—that is, by the death penalty.

EVALUATION

It is clear that except in form the Soviet constitution differs radically from any Western constitution, whether the latter is formulated in a single written document or, as in Great Britain, in a medley of laws that enunciate accepted principles and practices. Whatever the specific provisions, the underlying significance of a Western constitution, whether written or technically unwritten, is that it embodies certain rules that limit and direct governmental and party authorities. In the Soviet Union the process works quite the other way. Moreover, in Western countries on the whole and, it may be said, particularly in Great Britain, there is a very keen public sensitivity regarding any violation of rights. Such a sentiment has been slow to develop in the Soviet Union for obvious reasons, but there are indications that some Soviet intellectuals are now beginning to enunciate a type of constitutionalism based on the specified guarantees of the Soviet constitution. These tentative and so far unsuccessful efforts seek to turn the Soviet constitution into a genuine protector for at least the right of freedom of expression instead of being a document whose interpretation in any public matter is subject to the will of the ruling regime.

2

Soviet land, people, and society

1 THE LAND AND RESOURCES

The country in which the first Communist state was established is the largest in the world. Its population of 241,748,000 (according to the 1970 census) is spread over one-sixth of the earth's land surface, an area of 8.5 million square miles (the area of the United States is a little more than 3 million square miles). From the Carpathian Mountains and the Baltic Sea on the western boundary to the Pacific Ocean on the eastern, the distance is as great as that from San Francisco to London. It is an area that includes both Arctic ice and the deserts of central Asia.

The natural resources of the Soviet Union are extremely rich and diversified. Official publications (which, in certain instances, represent rather optimistic estimates) claim for the Soviet Union first place in resources of iron ore, natural gas, oil, manganese, water power, and timber; and second place in coal, lead, nickel, and zinc. Thus, in contrast to Great Britain, the Soviet Union's great problem has not been to obtain raw materials but to exploit the resources it has in areas, particularly in Siberia, that are handicapped by harsh climate and distance from industrial centers.

Although it is common to speak of European and Asiatic Russia, the country is, in fact, a geographic unit. The Ural Mountains, which are often called the boundary between the two continents, are no more of a division than are the Rockies in the United States. A central theme of Russian, as of American, history was long the movement of population to the frontier (in Russia, to the north and east) and the progressive, if somewhat sporadic, expansion of Russian power over lands sparsely populated by less developed peoples. To the west, however, Russia has bordered on nations both populous and highly civilized; and on this frontier, where there is a lack of natural boundaries and natural defenses, there have been invasions by Napoleon and by Nazi forces. Whereas the United States has been protected by the Atlantic and Pacific, Great Britain by the Channel, and France (except for the northeast frontier) by mountains and the sea, the western boundaries of the Soviet Union are a great plain, without any physical obstacle to stand as a bulwark against the rest of Europe. The result has been anxiety and suspicion that can only be compared to the French preoccupation with protecting their northeastern boundary.

Although the Soviet Union is physically a unit, its tremendous size has created serious problems in communications. The rivers of European Russia, and particularly the famous "water road" of the Dnieper, the Neva, and the Dvina, which stretches from the Black Sea to the Baltic, form an important means of transportation, but the links between European Russia and the Pacific depend largely on manmade facilities. Like the United States, and in contrast to Great Britain, the Soviet Union has had to develop land communications in order to make full use of the resources of its great

THE UNION OF SOVIET SOCIALIST REPUBLICS

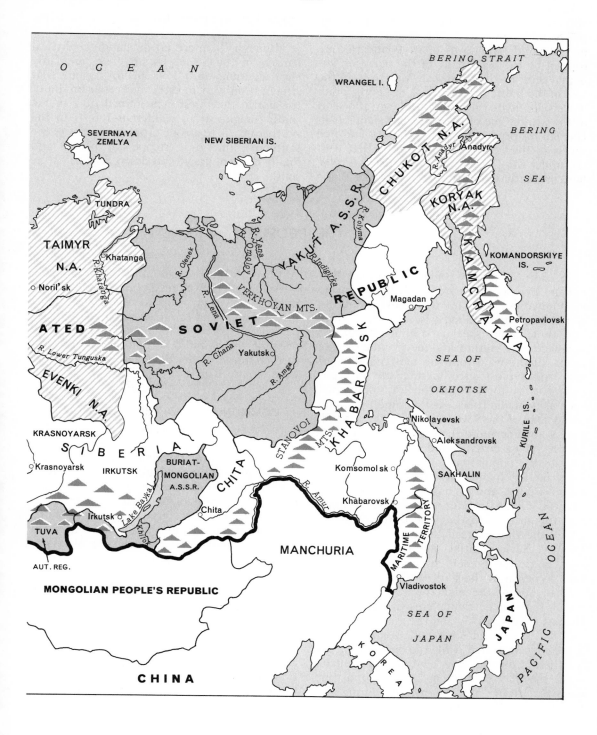

OCEAN

BERING STRAIT

WRANGEL I.

BERING

SEVERNAYA
ZEMLYA

NEW SIBERIAN IS.

CHUKOT N.A.

Anadyr

R. Anadyr

SEA

TUNDRA

KORYAK
N.A.

KOMANDORSKIYE
IS.

TAIMYR
N.A.

Khatanga

R. Khatanga

R. Olenek

R. Yana

R. Omoloy

YAKUT A.S.S.R.

R. Kolyma

R. Indigirka

KAMCHATKA

Noril'sk

VERKHOYAN MTS.

REPUBLIC

Magadan

Petropavlovsk

ATED

SOVIET

R. Lower Tunguska

R. Lena

R. Chana

Yakutsk

R. Amga

KHABAROVSK

SEA OF

OKHOTSK

EVENKI
N.A.

STANOVOI

MTS.

Nikolayevsk

KURILE IS.

KRASNOYARSK

Aleksandrovsk

SIBERIA

IRKUTSK

BURIAT-
MONGOLIAN
A.S.S.R.

CHITA

Komsomol'sk

SAKHALIN

Krasnoyarsk

Lake Baykal

R. Amur

Khabarovsk

Irkutsk

R. Khilok

Chita

MARITIME

TERRITORY

TUVA

MANCHURIA

OCEAN

AUT. REG.

JAPAN

MONGOLIAN PEOPLE'S REPUBLIC

Vladivostok

SEA OF

JAPAN

PACIFIC

KOREA

CHINA

empire. The sea is of little assistance. While the country has one of the longest coastlines in the world (two-thirds of its boundaries are formed by the sea), many of the ports are ice-bound most or all of the year. Moreover, in the case of the Baltic and the Black Sea ports, other powers dominate the outlets to the great oceans of the world. One of the persistent elements in Russian history has been the effort to find free access to the sea. It is characteristic that Russia, under the Communists as under the tsars, has constantly striven for control of the Baltic Sea and of the straits that lead from the Black Sea.

Although there are no outstanding physical barriers in the Soviet Union, there are fairly clear divisions into four major regions that stretch from west to east: the frozen tundra of the north; the forest area immediately to the south (ranging from coniferous forests in the northern parts to a zone of mixed forests in the southern); the great steppe (or plain); and finally the semidesert and desert regions of the south.

2   THE PEOPLE

In contrast to such countries as Great Britain and France, which are largely homogeneous in population, the Union of Soviet Socialist Republics contains almost two hundred different ethnic groups speaking a hundred and fifty languages. In culture and development, they range all the way from the most highly civilized and sophisticated, particularly in European Russia, to some of the least developed, such as nomadic tribes. At the same time, only about sixty of the Soviet Union's diverse ethnic groups include more than a few thousands of people; only a dozen include as much as 1 percent of the population.

By far the highest percentage of the population is Slav, and among the Slavs the Russians or "Great Russians" heavily predominate, not only in numbers but also in the degree to which they have spread throughout the whole country. Soviet officials are concerned, however, as are the French, at the declining birth rate. Whereas at the start of the century, Russia had one of the highest birth rates in the world, the average annual growth rate between the last census in 1959 and the most recent one in 1970 was only 1.4 percent. A cause of still more concern is that while the birth rate in the Southern Caucasus and central Asia remains high, the Slav component of the population decreased from 75 to 70 percent during this period, and the proportion of the politically dominant Great Russians declined from 55 to 53.4 percent of the population. Moreover, although more than half the Soviet population still lives in the Russian and western republics —the Ukraine, Byelorussia, and the Baltic republics—the population of the Uzbek, Tadjik, Turkmen, and Kazakh republics jumped 40 percent, in part due to migration from other parts of the country, a trend that suggests a further tilting of the demographic balance toward Asiatic Russia.

COMMUNISM AND THE NATIONALITY PROBLEM

It is ironic that the first country in which communism triumphed inherited so extreme a nationality problem. According to Marxist thought the workingman has no fatherland, and the course of history moves inevitably toward larger, more homogeneous units until the final achievement of a worldwide "proletarian" society. Yet Lenin found himself forced in 1913 to recognize that national aspirations and opposition to tsarist centralization had to be reckoned with if his revolutionary plans were to succeed.

Lenin's attempted resolution of the problem was to assert the right of "self-determination" as an exception to his general thesis of centralization. But while theoretically accepting the right to secession, he maintained in fact, both in his speeches and in his policy, that for nationalities to secede or even claim self-determination of their own status within the Communist state was tantamount to bourgeois counter-revolution. Stalin's *Report on the National Question* (1918) declared that "the principle of self-determination must be an instrument in the struggle for socialism and must be subordinated to the principles of socialism." The practical answer to the upsurge of independence by the nationalities on the west of Moscow was to send the Red Armies to subdue its manifestations and to force most of the provinces of the former tsarist empire—including the highly self-conscious Ukraine—into the Union. While constitutionally, as we have seen, each constituent republic has the ultimate right "freely" to secede, it is as dangerous to attempt to claim this right now as it was then. The overall pervasive control of the Communist party and central government nullify any such possibility.

The most drastic evidence that central control is unrestrained by nationality divisions came in World War II when four autonomous socialist republics—the Crimean Tartars, the Kalmucks, the Chechen-Ingush, and the Volga Germans—were erased from the map and their populations scattered and decimated. While inhabitants of the first three republics committed genuine acts of disloyalty through collaboration with the Nazis, the Volga-German region was liquidated without evidence of actual crime. Moreover, in 1944 the Meskhetians, a national group of about two hundred thousand people, were deported en masse (a fact unknown in the West until 1968), not for any act of collaboration but apparently to remove them from an area that might be reached by the enemy. Held under secret police control until 1956, they are still not permitted to return to their original homelands. Minor acts of restitution for the other groups were finally instituted under Khrushchev and his successors.

Nationality policies carried on inside the centralized Soviet structure exhibit a distinctive combination of cultural autonomy and political subordination. Separate languages have provided the most outstanding evidence of minority self-expression. Despite the attraction of political prestige and position through Russification, the major nationalities —the Ukrainians, Byelorussians, Georgians, and Turkic peoples of central Asia—were found by the census returns of 1959 to have even increased their overwhelming use of their native languages.

The 1970 census returns show that all nationality groups in central Asia continue to adhere firmly to their native languages. In general, local languages are used in the media and in lower levels of education (in the Baltic republic also for higher education) and in teachers' colleges and literature institutes. It is also true, however, that Hebrew and other cultural appurtenances of Soviet Jews have been officially banned and that, despite passionate opposition, Soviet Muslims have been forced to replace their religiously sanctioned Arabic script first by the Latin and then by the Cyrillic script. Still more socially disruptive, leading to bitter struggle and great loss of life, was the imposition of collectivization in the early 1930s on seminomadic peoples of central Asia, notably the Kazakh.

In general, opportunities for education, training, social mobility, and choice of residence are as open to the minorities as to the majority Russians. The spread of literacy among previously backward groups has been spectacular, and the number of educational institutions established in the minority areas is impressive. Libraries, theaters, movies, medical clinics, radio and television stations, clubs, newspapers, and so forth, have been established in proportionately the same ratio to population as in the RSFSR. Thus, except for Soviet Jews, minorities have received relative equality in treatment in training, social benefits, and economic opportunities. Power stations, factories, and towns have been established throughout much of the country in a process that is steadily increasing the industrialization and urbanization of the Soviet population.

It is in the political sphere that the national self-determination guaranteed by the constitution has been most obviously subordinated to unity largely under Great Russian direction. On the face of things, the minority nationalities have full equality, including separate political units in which many offices are regularly held by local persons, and the right to hold national public office. Photographs of the delegates to the Supreme Soviet often make a point of showing the great variety of racial types composing that body. But from the beginning, the self-government of the nationality units has been largely illusory because most of the important jobs of government are held by Great

Russians and, still more decisive, because the all-important Communist party controls radiate from Moscow. The Soviet slogan "national in form but socialist in content" sums up the situation. While the achievement of formal equality may provide some satisfaction for those nationalities that suffered under the tsars from overt discrimination, the lack of effective power has created tensions that are similar to those formerly exhibited by the intelligentsia in colonial areas.

RELIGION

Another significant area of strain and partial adjustment has been in the relation of the Soviet regime to organized religion, both as a social institution and as the visible expression of belief. In the years before the revolution of October 1917, the great majority of the Russian people were adherents of the Russian Orthodox church. Other religions, in particular Roman Catholicism, which was allied with the Greek Catholic church of the Ukraine, were persecuted by tsarist officials eager to "Russify" the country as a whole. The tsar himself directly controlled the Orthodox church, and it proved a docile instrument in support of his policy and power.

The Marxist-Leninist view, however, is that religion is an "illusion" born out of men's ignorance of the true factors controlling their existence, and that it is used by their exploiters to keep them content with the status quo. Thus the Soviet regime dedicated itself to eradicating "religious prejudice" by preaching "scientific atheism," by excluding religious teaching from the schools, and by seeking complete separation of church and state.

The situation of virtual warfare that developed between the Soviet state and the Russian Orthodox church during the period prior to World War II was the result not only of Marxist-Leninist doctrine, however, but also of anxiety by Soviet leaders over the great secular and political power of the church and its open opposition to the regime. By 1923, the secular power of the church had been broken, but as opposition to forcible collectivization coalesced around local priests, Soviet leaders remained fearful of the effect of Orthodox church

influence. Only after its major demonstration of patriotic loyalty in World War II did Stalin feel secure in state-church relations, a situation leading to the formal *modus vivendi* signed in 1943. The church agreed to place both its remaining organization and its personnel under party supervision; in return it was permitted to carry on its purely sacramental functions virtually unhampered, to train priests, and to issue religious publications for its own members. After 1958, however, there was a fresh wave of repression, and in 1965 and 1967 petitions by priests protested unwarranted encroachments by state officials in areas of church affairs, such as calling assemblies and electing bishops, that fall under canon law.

The number of Russian Orthodox churches has been substantially reduced over the years, but such services as are held are generally well attended, especially during festival periods. Moreover, there has recently been a growing number of appeals to reopen churches, and there is increased use in everyday life of religious objects like wedding rings, crosses, and ikons, which suggests a more open affirmation of religious symbolism. Informed estimates suggest that between a fifth and a fourth of the Soviet people, that is between 50 and 64 million, still follow some religious practices, and that these include a considerable number of the young.

Even the degree of toleration extended to the adherents of the Russian Orthodox church has been largely absent in the attitude of the Soviet regime toward "cosmopolitan" influences, such as those of the Roman Catholic Church. During the war the powerful Greek Catholic Uniate church in the Western Ukraine was forcibly detached from its allegiance to the Vatican and crushed as an independent force. Members of an unofficial protest movement that took shape in 1961 inside the structure of the Evangelical Christians and Baptists (ECB), the chief Protestant denominations, have suffered severe repression, including the forcible removal of their children.

The greatest pressures to conformity have been exerted, as already suggested, on those groups where a separate sense of nationality and a distinctive religion reinforce each other, that is, on Muslims and Jews. Muslims in the Soviet Union increased in number from 24 to nearly 35 million between 1959 and 1970, striking testimony to their high birth rate. But they have suffered intense Russification: their literature and language have been drastically modified by Russian forms; they retain only one training center for their mullahs (priests); and Muslim law has been superseded by Islamic law. Moreover, in central Asia, where two-thirds of the Muslims are found, millions of Russians direct industrial development and dominate the character of life.

The 2.15 million Jews reported in the 1970 Soviet census (a number below the common outside estimate of 3 million) is the second largest Jewish community in the world. Jews are so designated on their identity documents but are not granted the corresponding rights and cultural opportunities as a separate nationality. Subject to intense cultural and antireligious pressures after the early 1930s, Jews lived in a state of terror from the "anticosmopolitan" drive in 1948 until Stalin's death in 1953. Virtually all their cultural institutions had already been abolished by the end of 1948; organized Jewish religious observances met constant harassment; Hebrew cannot be taught; and the one Yiddish publication still permitted has a precarious existence. At one point Russification appeared to have gained so great an influence among the Jewish population of the Soviet Union that distinctive Jewish cultural forms might have died away. But there is now a marked and open revival of interest in Jewish culture, particularly among the young. Many Jews petition for permission to migrate to Israel (once again a potential basis for prosecution), but others who fully accept their roles as Soviet citizens assert their Jewish heritage.

Most striking evidence of a new spirit is the growing association between those struggling for realization of the freedom of conscience, which is one of the paper guarantees of the Soviet constitution, and the intellectuals, whose appeals are similarly couched in terms of rights that the Soviet regime professes to uphold. Although the Russian intelligentsia have long rejected the church, the writings of outstanding literary figures like Dostoevsky and Pasternak, in the past, and of contemporary creative authors like Aleksandr Solzhenitsyn, Andrei Siniavsky, and Joseph Brodsky are infused with religious values. Moreover, considerable publicity regarding religious dissent appears in some of the underground publications. Thus, in a measure, religious persecution is proving counterproductive.

SOCIAL STRUCTURE

The vast changes in Soviet society over the past half century stem, as already indicated, from the interaction of three powerful factors: the objectives of the power elite; the new institutional forms and forces resulting from the revolution and the forceful efforts of Soviet leaders to implement their programs; and the social structure and prevailing mores that they inherited. The violence of the changes forced in the early period of the seizure of power, lasting roughly up to 1924, destroyed major institutional features of the previously existing order. The succeeding period up to 1936 wrought still more fundamental changes through the brutal collectivization of agriculture (still the least satisfactory area of Soviet experimentation) and the massive concentration on heavy industry. But since 1936, by which time the main features of the new social order had been built, Soviet regimes have favored measures stabilizing basic social relations, such as the family, that contribute to its purposes. Antireligious campaigns erupt from time to time, as from 1959 to 1964, but the major objectives of Soviet leaders over the past thirty-five years appear to be to produce conforming, hard-working citizens in a social order that corresponds to the needs of industrialization and urbanization.

How far change has gone in the latter respect can easily be seen by comparing the current situation with the 17 percent of the population that comprised the urban population in 1913, which consisted mainly of white-collar employees and manual workers. While the rural population is still proportionately far higher than in industrialized Western countries, some 56 percent of the people now live in towns. Nearly 1.5 million move from country to town every year, a slightly higher percentage than the rural birth rate. In 1959, at the last census prior to that of 1970, there were only three cities with over a million inhabitants—Moscow, Leningrad, and Kiev. By 1970, Moscow had over 7 million people, Leningrad just under 4 million, Kiev 1.6 million, and seven more cities had reached the million mark—Tashkent, Baku, Kharkov, Gorki, Novosibirsk, Kuybyshev, and Sverdlovsk. Minsk, the capital of Byelorussia, was approaching that level. Moreover, mushrooming towns are scattered throughout the country, most of them related to specific projects such as power stations or automobile manufacture. These developments and massive industrialization provide the setting within which the Soviet regime has experimented with particular policies aimed at ideological or practical goals.

The family and the position of women

In no area of social relation has Soviet policy changed so fundamentally as in regard to the family. Originally, the regime followed Engels' view that the family would cease to be an economic unit in society, that housekeeping would become a social industry, and that the care and education of children would be a state responsibility. Legal and free abortion and divorce by mail were instituted up to 1936. At that point the regime reversed itself and despite vigorous opposition, especially by urban women, severely restricted both abortion and divorce. In 1955, abortion on the woman's request was again legalized if certain specified procedures were followed; otherwise it remained a crime. In the mid-1960s, the liberalizing of divorce procedures was under consideration. Nonetheless, the family as an institution has been firmly reinstituted as the main pillar of Soviet society.

At the same time, women have sought new opportunities outside the family, or they have been forced into employment to supplement the meager earnings of their husbands or to fill particular needs of the Soviet state, such as in industry or to provide 75 percent of the vast number of doctors and dentists needed to operate and supervise the state health system. By the eve of World War II, women constituted 38 percent of the total labor force and 40 percent of all specialists. Their advance in training kept pace with these responsibilities, and between 1928 and 1938 the proportion of women in the universities increased from 28 to 43 percent and from 37 to 51 percent in the special-

ized secondary schools. Moreover, since women are paid directly for their labor on collective farms, the system has enhanced their position in rural society.

The 1970 census disclosed the fact that women strikingly outnumber men in numbers —130 million to 111 million—and that the disparity, because of wartime losses, is greatest among those over age forty. These proportions help to explain the steady rise in the use of female labor throughout the economy. But women must also look after their households, stand in lines for food and other shopping, and cope with chores like dishwashing and laundry without the benefit of mechanical aids. For them, the Bolshevik promise of emancipation has meant far more social mobility but also staggering burdens as they cope with their multiple roles.

Education

In education, major changes of emphasis and direction have also taken place.[1] Originally, education was seen as the great liberating force through which all individuals could be developed into the knowledgeable, self-operating citizens who would participate at every level in the building of Soviet society. Progressive education and experimentation were encouraged in the vast and impressive spread of schools throughout the country and in the programs of mass literacy. In its acceptance and implementation of the principle of universal free education, the Soviet Union rivaled the United States.

In the 1930s, however, Stalinists largely replaced the goal of self-fulfillment through general education by vocational training directed toward meeting the demands of the industrial state. Literacy remained essential to transmit the basic conceptions of political ideology and to provide mass training for industrial work. Higher education now focused on the preparation of specialists to meet the needs of rapidly

---

[1] The educational experience and the system of schools that the Bolsheviks inherited were not inconsiderable. Catherine the Great had sponsored a handful of unrelated schools of which one was for women. Tsarist universities were centers of liberalism for the relatively small numbers who attended, and during periods of repression their students worked for radical reform. But before the Soviet period, education touched only a minute proportion of the peasants.

expanding industry, and admission was regulated by nation-wide competitive examinations and fees. In 1940, this process reached a peak when the regime simultaneously introduced tuition fees for the last three years of secondary education and an annual labor draft of a million youths between the ages of fourteen and seventeen for training and service as industrial workers, partly to meet industry's urgent needs and partly to get rural youth off the farms. The youths were subject to a year at hard labor if they deserted from a labor reserve school or were guilty of a serious violation of labor discipline while in training. After graduation they were obliged to work for four years in an enterprise selected by the state.

In March 1955, however, the post-Stalin regime abolished the drafting of youth for labor training and service; six months later it did away with the fees for secondary and higher education. The amended constitution of January 1, 1965, guarantees "universal compulsory eight-year education" and makes provision for "a system of state living allowances." Grants are made on the basis of academic record and material need and are for one term only but subject to renewal. (Approximately 80 percent of students in higher educational institutions receive stipends.) Graduates of secondary specialized and college-level professional schools must still work for three years after graduation in places to which they have been assigned. For lower level jobs it has been left to the Komsomol (see Chapter 3, Section 4) to direct volunteers to labor-deficit areas through a variety of incentives.

The restraint on social mobility through imposing tuition fees for higher education, from 1940 to 1955, had minimal effect in urban areas, while peasants rarely achieved even seventh-grade levels in any case. More important in the drive for higher education appears to be the cultural factor that members of the intelligentsia make more effort to advance their children through academic channels where stipends are not granted but from which entrance to higher educational institutions is direct if basic requirements are met. By the latest figures available (the regime has ceased to publish them), between 60 and 70 percent of students in post-secondary schools in 1958 in the city of Moscow were of professional, semiprofessional,

or white-collar origin, although throughout the country at large only 17 percent of the population was estimated to belong to these groups.

These factors interact with the practice of the regime after 1940 of increasingly drawing its managerial personnel from those who had acquired advanced secondary and higher education. Thus in place of the striking mobility of industrial personnel in the initial period of rapid industrialization of the thirties, there are only relatively rare instances now in which a particular individual moves upward from the status of worker to manager. The 1959 census indicated that 90 percent or more of virtually all important posts in the country were held by those with advanced education. Nearly all newly appointed managers are university trained, and those in the universities come overwhelmingly from professional and white-collar families.

Social stratification

This high degree of social stratification found in higher education and in the allocation of significant posts in the regime is clearly related to the Soviet emphasis on modern, large-scale production and to the leveling-off period in industrial development. Those in high and well-rewarded positions reached them through legitimate means and naturally wish to assure the best possible opportunities for their children. That the situation is contrary to Lenin's expectations is clear. Lenin anticipated a continuation of inequality of reward, as we have seen, but much less differentiation in returns. What is surprising to an American is not that those at the top receive rich returns and can afford to provide special opportunities for their children but that so high a proportion of the people of the Soviet Union exist at so low a standard of living because of the limited supply of consumer goods and general necessities of life. It is this latter fact that accentuates the rigidity of social stratification in the Soviet Union.

In 1936, in introducing the new constitution, Stalin declared that there were two major classes in Soviet society—the working class and the peasantry—and a third group, the intelligentsia, which he called a stratum of the working class. All three groups were said to be "equal in rights," and the social, economic, and political distances between them were said to be diminishing. In fact, the opposite process was in progress, due largely to pressures generated by Stalin himself. As early as 1931, high labor turnover and low productivity under the First Five-Year Plan led Stalin to attack wage equality and to insist on "a system of pay which gives each worker his due according to his qualifications." Step by step he introduced those devices for increasing output that had been stigmatized as the most despicable features of capitalism: payment for piecework, wide differences in the wages of the skilled and unskilled, and bonuses for managers who ground more production out of their workers.

By 1940, the Soviet Union possessed an elaborately stratified system, in which Alex Inkeles differentiated ten major social-class groups.[2] He identified four subunits of the intelligentsia: the small powerful ruling elite; the superior intelligentsia, drawn from the same official groups, scientists and artists plus some technical specialists; the general intelligentsia, made up of professional groups, middle-level bureaucracy, managers of small enterprises, and so forth; and the white-collar group, ranging all the way from petty bureaucrats to office workers. The working class he divided into three groups: the working class "aristocracy," that is, the most highly productive, including so-called Stakhanovites, who compete for high individual production levels; the rank-and-file workers; and the disadvantaged, numbering perhaps one-quarter of the total, whose low levels of skills kept them permanently from advancing. The peasants, although more homogeneous, he divided into the well-to-do and the average peasants. Below all these was the residual group in the forced labor camps.

Inkeles points out, however, that although these divisions correspond to the stratification within the three major groups identified by Stalin, their rank order within the system as a whole was somewhat different. He placed the first three categories of the intelligentsia in that order, followed by the working class "aristocracy" and then the white-collar group. Below these first five he ranks in descending order the well-to-do peasants, average workers, average peasants, disadvantaged workers, and forced labor. This general rank order, determined largely by occupation, skill, income, and share in power, appears to have persisted.

It is clear that these groups intermesh and that the boundaries between them are far from rigid. Nonetheless, they have been sufficiently differentiated to develop characteristic life styles, to evidence group consciousness, and to establish separate patterns of association. They represent the new shifts of population resulting from the enormous expansion of the economy under the Five-Year Plans, which thrust vast groups into new roles. The number of workers and employees virtually doubled during the first decade of the plans; the intelligentsia nearly quadrupled between 1926 and 1937 and increased by 1.6 percent between 1937 and 1956. In the earlier period the number of managers of large- and small-scale enterprises increased 4.6 percent, engineers and architects 7.9 percent, and scientific workers, including professors, 5.9 percent. In 1938 alone, 6.5 million people received initial and refresher courses in industry and allied fields, and in 1937 and 1938 more than a million were trained for skilled and responsible jobs in agriculture. This unprecedented mobility in a virtually open-class system gave place during the war years to a stabilization that intensified the major lines of demarcation developed by that time. Recognition of status and contribution through monetary rewards had the greater effect because of the Soviet tax system in which 60 percent is collected through the turnover tax levied primarily on consumption goods and included in the purchase price. There are only minor increases in taxation rates for higher incomes, and the inheritance tax was abolished in the 1940s.

However much the prestige and relative economic position of the intelligentsia has risen, however, only that section of it that possesses top political power actually rules in the Soviet Union. Indeed, the ruling elite watches with constant wariness the possibility that others of the intelligentsia, with their indispensibility for the functioning of modern society, might present a challenge to the authority of the regime's leaders. Hence the latter also bring into roles of authority in the Communist party members from other groups in the social struc-

[2] Alex Inkeles, *Social Change in Soviet Russia*, pp. 150–74.

ture, the working class "aristocracy," peasants, and lower level white-collar workers. But this process does not represent an attack on the social system itself but only an insurance for the political authority of the ruling elite. It is well to remember that the centralization of political authority in the hands of a relatively small, closely knit elite is the one feature of the Soviet system that has never changed.

The military

Within Soviet society the only group that could conceivably challenge the power position of the leaders of the Communist party is the military. Since the military possesses the instruments for organized violence against either internal or external adversaries, it necessarily offers a potential challenge to the party's elite. That, in practice, the military has not posed such a threat to the political leadership reflects its own general satisfaction with the maintenance of orderly government and the degree to which the regime has responded to the military's own basic professional interests and needs. Thus the situation in the Soviet Union

tends to confirm the view that, as in other societies, the military is an essentially conservative organization that favors stable and firm rule over an orderly society in which its own distinctive position and role is recognized and supported.

This analysis is not intended to suggest that the military forms a unified community under monolithic direction. Its members represent many different interests, needs, and attitudes, as is true of other elements in society. But in the face of any threat to the interests of the military as a group there has been a striking coalescence behind a common front. This front has narrow and self-concerned interests, not those of broad social and economic change. Nor has the military exhibited any particular political acumen in the rare situations of party dissent, when its influence expanded. Thus, despite the vast and indeed growing importance of the functions and expertise of the Soviet military in a time of continuing international tension and advances in weaponry, there appears no current likelihood that it will provide any internal challenge to the effective control of the Communist party elite.

3 MASS COMMUNICATION AND PERSUASION

In their molding of society, Soviet leaders use a far-reaching paraphernalia of laws and administrative regulations, backed up, where deemed necessary, by the exercise of force against persons and institutions that appear to challenge their power position or the policies they decree. Behind these means to induce change or maintain stability, however, lie elaborate mechanisms working constantly to shape the opinions of the Soviet people. In the West, public opinion is studied to ascertain the desires and inclinations of the community; in the Soviet Union, public opinion is studied to determine what techniques of persuasion or coercion may be necessary to bring the populace to the necessary state of support for the party's policies. For the Leninist view of the party as the general staff of the proletarian army recognizes that no staff can achieve its purposes without the obedience, or at least the acquies-

cence, of the mass of its followers, in this case the people. To mobilize popular support for its programs, the Soviet regime extends its control over all media of communication.

There is thus a fundamental difference between Western and Soviet views of the responsibilities of the media and of authors and artists. In the United States and Great Britain, it is presumed that news should be based on fact, that different approaches to current issues should be encouraged, and that government policy and speeches are subject to criticism. It is accepted that writers and artists express their own inner urges—or produce what they think will sell. Scientists and other researchers are expected to publicize the results of their work and to let their theories and conclusions compete in the open.

Neither these attitudes nor the assumption that a balanced view requires exposure to different opinions and sources of information is acceptable in the Soviet Union. An orthodox Communist maintains that truth and morality are relative to the interests of a society. Thus he views all forms of expression in a capitalist society as reflections of capitalist ideas. Equally, he holds that all means of communication in a Communist society should deliberately contribute to its basic purposes. And since the direction of Soviet endeavors is in the hands of party leaders, all media of communication are expected to contribute in their own ways to the goals enunciated by those leaders.

There have been periods in Soviet history, notably under Stalin, when a dead and deadly uniformity infused most media. Even then it was possible by very careful examination to detect certain trends of opinion on particular issues. In times when leadership was not settled, however, as between 1953 and 1957—that is, between Stalin's death and Khrushchev's emergence as paramount leader—different publications reflected different approaches to matters at issue between rival groups. Thus the Soviet's two most prominent newspapers, *Izvestia* and *Pravda*, participated in the heavy-light industry debate between Khrushchev and Georgi Malenkov during the succession struggle after Stalin's death. In general, moreover, Khrushchev encouraged a livelier presentation of news and a freer literary expression. Even before he was ousted from office in 1964, however, a greater emphasis on orthodoxy had emerged. It has been pressed harder by his successors. Thus behind the alternations of "freeze" and "thaw" lies the will of the party.

In part the work of directing public opinion is the negative task of preventing the publication of "wrong" ideas. For this purpose there is a government censorship office (*Glavlit*) that must give its approval to all material distributed inside the USSR or sent outside the country. Far more important, however, is the work of spreading "right" ideas; and this task falls preeminently to the Communist party's Department of Propaganda and Agitation (*Agitprop*), which unifies and directs equivalent sections in every party unit in the country in their task of explaining policy decisions and mobilizing support for them. In response to directives, government agencies directly under the Council of Ministers of the USSR appoint newspaper editors, supervise their editorial policy, determine what films may be produced and exhibited, criticize the work of authors and artists, and direct hundreds of thousands of "agitators" or "political enlightenment workers" in their work of molding public opinion.

PROPAGANDA AND AGITATION

The Communists differentiate between propaganda and agitation. Communist *propaganda* is said to be the "intense elucidation of the teachings of Marx, Engels, Lenin" and of the history of the Bolshevik party and its tasks. Through this elucidation in schools and universities, training courses, and constant planned discussions, party and government officials, directors of industries, and intellectuals are "armed" with knowledge of the "laws" that govern the development of society and political conflicts. After 1956, Khrushchev's pragmatic line led to an equal emphasis on economics and technology.

Agitation, in contrast, is the process of explaining to the masses the government's decision and policies and of mobilizing their efforts to carry these out. Thus, while propaganda is directed chiefly at the more advanced strata in Communist society, agitation is aimed at the great mass of the people.

A colossal number of persons are engaged in the incessant propaganda and agitation that pervade every aspect of Soviet life. Between 1946 and 1956, some fifty-five thousand party workers were trained for these purposes in republic and regional party three-year schools and forty thousand more by correspondence, while at the top level Higher Party Schools trained some twenty-eight hundred individuals and over six thousand more by correspondence. Since three-quarters of all "responsible party workers," down to the district level, had been trained by 1956, the emphasis in a limited number of successor four-year interregional schools was shifted as indicated to economic and technical matters. The required two-year course in the political schools for all Communists, particularly new members, was continued, as were the seminars on Marxist-Leninist philosophy and the history of the Communist party, but a new program of two-year evening schools on economics became extremely popular. This system of party schools was supplemented by a vast program of popular lectures carried on by the All-Union Society for the Dissemination of Political and Scientific Information for those persons neither purposive nor educated enough for the party schools and yet above the level of the great mass of the Soviet population, who are approached through oral agitation.

Oral agitation, the regime's unique system of bringing its messages through face-to-face contacts, is carried on by 2 million, or during special campaigns, by as many as 3 million part-time, unpaid "volunteers," selected mainly from party ranks. Constantly at work to explain in the simplest terms the reasons for the party's decisions or shifts in emphasis and to make clear where individual workers fit into the overall Soviet plan, agitators hold brief but frequent sessions of ten to fifteen persons in every shop and farm and even in homes. Inkeles concludes that the party's utilization of the Bolshevik agitator is "probably one of the most effective of all instruments of mass communication." [3]

Nonetheless, the agitator's role carries little prestige or appeal. Because the agitator must answer criticisms and questions and also must urge his comrades to harder and harder efforts, he often serves as a target for hostility that might otherwise be directed toward the regime's leaders. He is also expected to provide a rough testing of public reactions for the party hierarchy above him. Thus the agitator finds himself under pressures both from below and from above.

THE MASS MEDIA

The press

By the 1960s, many Soviet commentators were suggesting that improved levels of education made oral agitation outdated and that there should be concentration on the mass media. Lenin early characterized the press as "a collective propagandist, agitator and organizer," and Stalin called it a "driving belt" between the party and the people. Thus daily

and weekly newspapers, magazines, wall newspapers, posters, electric signs, public loudspeakers, all pour out what party leaders wish the people to hear. The flood of propaganda is all-pervasive and quite possibly numbing.

Since the government has a full monopoly over publishing and news-gathering agencies, it is easy to alter the interpretation of events, to withhold information, or to publicize an event or view throughout the country. Nonetheless, the extraordinarily large number of newspapers in the Soviet Union, between seven thousand and eight thousand, including collective farm papers, provide some variety in news and interpretations. There are three main types of publication: organs of the Communist party, including papers published by regional, provincial, and city party committees; organs of government; and specialized papers reflecting the interests of every organized group in Soviet society. Approximately half the papers are printed in languages other than Russian.

The most important of all Soviet newspapers is the Communist party's *Pravda* (Truth); each republic and most of the urban centers has its own newspaper, which is carefully patterned on (although not always named after) the Moscow model. The latter's principal editorial is wired or radioed daily to all other papers in the country. Thus, despite the fact that the USSR is a much larger country than the United States, *Pravda* provides nation-wide guidance on the handling of news.

The leading government publication is *Izvestia*, which carries the texts of laws and decrees as well as a wide range of news. *Pravda* and *Izvestia* have their own foreign correspondents; other publications are supplied by Tass, the government news agency, or by Novosti, the second Soviet "wire service." Individual ministries also have newspapers and magazines of their own; the Red Army, for example, publishes *Red Star*, and the Ministry of Agriculture's daily is said to have a circulation of a million. The trade union paper *Trud* (Labor) is particularly important, since it must supervise all trade union papers at lower levels. In 1966 there were 132 newspapers for youth, headed by *Komsomolskaya Pravda*, with a circulation of nearly 7 million.

While party and government policies are above criticism, this is far from true of the ad-

[3] Inkeles, *Social Change in Soviet Russia*, p. 275.

ministration of policies or the administrators themselves, at least at lower levels. One of the activities of newspapers is to use thousands of worker and peasant correspondents throughout the country to investigate instances cited by their readers of slackness, inefficiency, discourtesy, and stupidity on the part of administrators, factory directors, and public servants generally. The Soviet institution of "self-criticism" (*samokritika*) through letters to the editor, helps to drain off frustrations and provides another source of insight into public opinion and the inadequacies of the lesser bureaucracy. With all its limitations, it is one of the more substantial links between the masses of people and the top party leaders; at the same time, it provides some encouragement for the ordinary citizen to look at authority with critical eyes and to indulge in a type of freedom of speech.

Radio and television

Widely regarded as the supreme media of mass communication, radio and television, like the press, are directed by the party and the government. Radio is highly centralized with Radio Moscow broadcasting four simultaneous programs that are relayed through the country. By 1965, the Soviet Union shared first place with France in Europe with a ratio of one radio to every three persons. (The United States averages more than one set per person.) Fifty percent of radio program receivers were still wired receivers, although the proportion had declined from the 75 percent in the 1950s. Wired receivers transmit only one program and provide the regime with special advantages: they cannot be used for listening to foreign broadcasts like the Voice of America; they permit contact during air raids, since they cannot be used as a guide by hostile airplanes; and their programs can be precisely tailored to the message the regime wishes to transmit to a particular group.

Television is now exploited nearly as fully as the press and radio since its propaganda potential has been realized. The film industry is looked on as a useful instrument and its productivity is substantial, despite the restraints exercised by the Ministry of Culture (which is responsible to the party's Central Committee), by the Department of Propaganda and Agita-

tion, and by a special Arts Council that supervises the ideological correctness of all movies. Thus the overriding ulterior purposes of indoctrination and persuasion have not prevented creative work in this medium.

ARTISTIC AND INTELLECTUAL EXPRESSION OF DISSENT

In the battle to mold men's minds, theater, novels, poetry, painting, and even music have been used, in addition to the mass media, as weapons for indoctrination and for stimulating more productive efforts. Notable examples are the dreary "construction novels" of the Stalin era, in which farm workers should only make love to their tractors. Behind such sterility lay the use of mass terror in the 1930s against all who represented dissent to any degree, an artistic devastation most fully carried out in the wholesale liquidation of writers, artists, scholars, and critics in the Ukraine, but which also decimated and intimidated intellectuals throughout the Soviet Union.

Khrushchev's "secret" speech to the Twentieth Party Congress, attacking Stalin's arbitrariness, opened a new period of intellectual questioning and realistic works. In 1962, through the personal intervention of Khrushchev himself, Aleksandr Solzhenitsyn's *One Day in the Life of Ivan Denisovich* appeared—not only a masterpiece of prose, but the first unvarnished account of a Stalin concentration camp to be published legally. An ensuing flood of such first-hand accounts were written—and not published. To cite Sidney Monas: "Publication became much freer, yet not altogether free. The formulas of socialist realism were torn to shreds; yet the basic idea of an *organized* literature remained." [4] Within these bounds, experimentation continued and the party became increasingly concerned.

In February 1966, a new climax was reached with the trial of Andrei Siniavsky and Yuli Daniel, whose creative writings, under the pen names of Abram Tertz and Nikolai Arzhak, had for years been smuggled out and published in the West. Accused of "anti-Soviet propa-

---

[4] Sidney Monas, "Engineers or Martyrs: Dissent and the Intelligentsia," *In Quest of Justice: Protest and Dissent in the Soviet Union Today,* ed. by Abraham Brumberg, p. 17.

ganda and agitation," under Article 70 of the Criminal Code, the accused were browbeaten in court in a way all too reminiscent of the days of Stalin. But unlike the victims of those trials, whose association with the regime's repressions undercut their own defenses, Siniavsky and Daniel pleaded not guilty, defended themselves courageously and effectively on literary grounds, and appealed to provisions of the constitution to defend their rights. Strikingly, their harsh sentences followed by the clamping down of censorship did not silence protest but intensified it. Demonstrations in Moscow in 1967 against this curbing of intellectual freedom and against the notorious Article 70 linked the right to literary expressions to political freedom and the rule of law and led to further arrests of young writers, trials and forced-labor sentences. In January 1968, another "rigged" trial and sentencing of well-known figures like Alexander Ginzburg, who had long been involved in "underground" literary publications (*Samizdat*), created a much wider storm of open protest. Despite harsh punishments, including confinement in mental institutions, well-publicized protests continue, and official retaliation is meted out.

Soviet intellectuals have chosen many different paths in the past few years in their struggle for intellectual freedom. Alexander Tvardovsky, from 1950 to 1954 and again from 1958 to 1970, when he was forced to resign, edited the Soviet Union's most progressive journal, *Novy Mir* (New World). Not only was he the first to publish Solzhenitsyn's *Ivan Denisovich*, but he also sought persistently, although unsuccessfully, to be allowed to print that author's *Cancer Ward* and *The First Circle*, which finally appeared only in the West. Solzhenitsyn, it should be noted, was ousted from the Soviet Union of Writers the year before he received the Nobel Prize for literature in 1970. *Samizdat* (do-it-yourself) manuscripts, produced and distributed in secret, contain protests against oppression, discrimination, and persecution, almost all of them signed by the author's name, and also much excellent fiction and memoirs. The novelist Anatoly Kutnetsov, finally defected to England. In contrast, the writer Andrei Amalrik rejects such a move. He prizes his personal integrity above safety and spoke openly in an interview he knew was to be shown on American television against restrictions on intellectual freedom. After eighteen months' exile in Siberia on a charge of "parasitism," he wrote *Involuntary Journey to Siberia* and *Will the Soviet Union Survive Until 1984?* In the latter book, Amalrik sees bureaucratic inflexibility as unable to cope with international challenges from Eastern Europe and from China and with internal demands by non-Russian nationalities. Amalrik is now serving a three-year sentence in one of the most dreaded forced-labor camps near the Arctic Circle for spreading "anti-Soviet fabrications." Another brilliant young dissident writer, Vladimir K. Bukovsky, was detained for months in 1971 in the Serbsky Psychiatric Institute after sending abroad an open letter charging Soviet officials with using mental institutions to detain nonconformist intellectuals.

What leads to this continued, and indeed expanding, outpouring of creativity and of protests against restrictions on intellectual freedom? Partly it is the need for individual expression, but beyond this it is the urge to bring about a society in which such expression can flourish. Basic in the modern wave of protests is the vast gap they point out between the paper guarantees of the Soviet constitution and the reality of repression. The constitution guarantees freedom of speech, as we have seen, but cases in the Soviet Union are officially decided "on the basis of law in conformity with socialist consciousness." In practice, therefore, it is the Communist party's ideological interpretation of the facts and implications of the case that are decisive in the judgments. By appealing to an implicit constitutionalism, these protests against the limits on individual freedom of expression strike at the primacy of the party's control of thought, and the party strikes back.

History

No field is more rigorously controlled than is the writing of history, particularly the history of the Communist party. Up to 1931, historians had been relatively free to use facts as they knew them, as long as their general bias was pro-Bolshevik. But in 1931, Stalin made a formal attack on "archive rats" who based their writing on objective material rather than on the version of history acceptable to the party. In 1938, the *Short Course on the History of the All-Union Communist Party* (Bolsheviks) appeared with visible marks of Stalin's imprint and a striking lack of relation to what had occurred.

Khrushchev's exposé on Stalin in his "secret" speech, in February 1956, appeared to open new possibilities for historians, particularly his open attack on Stalin's gross misjudgment of Hitler's intentions on the eve of the Nazi attack and on Stalin's military blunders (see Chapter 1, Section 2). Alexander Nekrich, an outstanding Soviet historian and member of the Academy of Science as well as of the Communist party, took advantage of this new openness to write a cautious but essentially valid history of what happened at the time of the Nazi attack. It was published under the title of *June 22, 1941*, in the summer of 1965, and was at first praised widely but later subject to a storm of criticism. In July 1967, Nekrich was expelled from the party and bitterly attacked personally. Although he continues to work at the Institute of History and has published a few articles and reviews, his fate stands as a warning that whatever the movement of the pendulum, which began to swing back again to a limited rehabilitation of Stalin as early as 1962 and more decisively after the fall of Khrushchev, the party demands that the work of historians support the current party interpretations of events.

Science

Science is often looked at as the branch of learning that is the most direct outcome of research and therefore the most independent in its conclusions. But in the Soviet state there may also be a party orthodoxy in regard to scientific conclusions. This fact is abundantly clear from the genetics controversy in which a party fiat endorsed a particular scientific position to the ultimate detriment of Soviet agriculture.

In this genetics controversy the party overthrew the almost universally accepted Mendelian theory of heredity in favor of an older, pseudoscientific Michurian concept, upheld by the Soviet scientist T. D. Lysenko, that characteristics are inherited through a cumulative process. In favor throughout Stalin's lifetime, Lysenko's crop rotation system, which pro-

moted the use of feed grasses rather than grain, was employed by Khrushchev, although with increasing skepticism, in his drive to open up virgin lands in the Soviet east. Demoted in April 1956, Lysenko subsequently returned to a position of some prominence, from which he was only finally removed in 1965 after Khrushchev's downfall. In mid-1965, Soviet biologists joined in Mendel's centenary celebrations and vowed to redouble their efforts to make up for the time lost through following Lysenko's concepts.

A curious corollary to the Lysenko controversy, however, has been the continued refusal of the post-Khrushchev leadership to permit the publication of a history of the case by Zhores Medvedev, a prominent Soviet biologist. Finally Medvedev permitted publication abroad, and the book was issued in 1969 in the United States.[5] In June 1970, although declared by Soviet psychiatrists to be of sound mind, Medvedev was forcibly lodged for nineteen days in an insane asylum, presumably as a warning against publicizing earlier Soviet mistakes, and he was released only after sustained protests by prominent Soviet scientists. Late in 1971, Medvedev's journal, *A Question of Madness*, which describes his ordeal, was published in the United States.

Soviet space exploits from Sputnik to Lunokhod (the moon space vehicle) have given Soviet science an enviable reputation. In fact, however, the achievements in aviation, rocketry, atomic energy, and space exploration have been matched in few other areas of scientific research. No Russian scientist since Pavlov has produced a major new scientific theory, although there are many whose applied science has produced outstanding results. We know that there exists an academy research system that revolves around the two-hundred-year-old Academy of Science, an industrial research system, and a higher education research system, but we know relatively little about scientific research priorities and how they are supported by the regime. Exchanges, both through personal contact and in writing between Soviet and foreign scientists, take place on a wide variety of subjects, from the processes for iron and

[5] Zhores Medvedev, *The Rise and Fall of T. D. Lysenko*, tr. by Michael I. Lerner.

steel to space platforms, but with what effect it is again difficult to evaluate. On the whole, secrecy is more pervasive in Soviet science than in the Soviet economy.

Scientists have not been omitted from the groups expected to lend themselves to the ideological purposes of the regime. In a sharp rebuke to the Lebedev Institute of Physics in November 1970, the Communist party's Central Committee emphasized "the necessity of systematically waging propaganda among scientists for the Marxist-Leninist understanding of contemporary political, socio-economic, and philosophical problems, and for uncompromising attitudes towards the ideological conceptions of anti-communism and revisionism." Shortly after, Andrei Sakharov, a member of the Soviet Academy of Sciences and the leading Soviet physicist, sometimes known as "the father of the Soviet H-bomb," who had openly defended both Medvedev and the mathematician R. Pimenov earlier in the year, made an unprecedented announcement that he and two younger colleagues had established a private committee to study the "theoretical aspects of the problem of defense of human rights." Sakharov emphasized that the committee would act "in conformity with the laws of the state" by refusing membership to persons belonging to a political party or social organizations involved in the running of the political apparatus or to those who might use it either to criticize the government or as a political tool. Such an association is clearly valid under the Soviet constitution. Yet one remembers that even distinguished scientists have not been immune in the past from harsh punishments for what were looked on as ideological deviations.

CONFORMITY THROUGH COERCION

The ultimate goal for orthodox Communists is to have all members of the state internalize prescribed objectives and values so that they think and act instinctively in acceptable ways. The continuous pressures of mass communication are highly persuasive methods for creating such responses but not, it is apparent, infallible ones. Thus the desired transformation of human beings must be induced also by coercive institutions. These institutions are law and terror.

When a Communist regime has seized central power, it almost inevitably uses terror to eliminate its most dangerous adversaries and to deter others from attacking it. To use terror at the so-called mobilization stage is less common. Both uses occurred in the Soviet Union and, in effect, the latter was even more violent than the former. The "Red" Terror, unleashed against opponents inside Russia, aimed at the political survival of the relatively small Bolshevik group that had seized power. The shift away from terror toward the end of the Civil War was dictated by fear of its impact on popular support. Wholesale terror flared again during the mobilization stage of collectivizing agriculture and directing all energies to industrialization. It was also a by-product of Stalin's own insistence on monolithic authority, the extermination of all subgroup autonomy, and the suppression of all those whose loyalties were not narrowly and acceptably focused on him. In these appalling holocausts the secret, or political, police acted not only as pretrial investigators but also as judges and executioners.

Mass terror against whole groups, regardless of individual guilt, ended with the Stalin era. Punishment of those considered guilty of infractions of rules, however irrational, continues. Punishments consist, as is well known, not only of prison terms or execution but also of forced labor, exile to barren areas, or confinement in mental institutions.

The Committee of State Security (KGB), which in 1954 succeeded the earlier organizations of political police—the Cheka, GPU, OGPU, NKVD, MVD (Ministry of Internal Affairs), and MGB (Ministry of State Security) —is subordinate to the party, as its predecessors under Beria and Stalin were not. Since the KGB was placed under A. N. Shelepin in 1958, it has been headed by a political rather than police figure and won back its fuller representation on the Central Committee. The present head, Yury V. Andropov, denied during the fiftieth anniversary celebrations of the organization in December 1967 that the KGB is some kind of "secret police," although little is known about its recruitment, terms of service, or operations. It is, at least, a vast intelligence organization employing more than seven hundred thousand men and women in external espionage—dramatically exposed late in 1971 through the defection of a KGB spy, Oleg Lyalin, to Great Britain—and internal surveillance. It manages the Soviet border guards, maintains its own internal security forces, and has close links with the Soviet police force. It also operates special sections in the armed forces, administrative, industrial, and agricultural bodies, and educational institutions. Its controls over daily life are underpinned by the fact that all citizens over age sixteen residing outside of collective farm areas must possess internal passports, which require additional certification to assure residence.

The KGB undertakes the crucially important pretrial investigation in any case with political connotations. The investigation of so-called economic crimes affecting the operation of the planned economy (for which the death penalty was introduced in 1961) also falls to the KGB. These investigations take place in secret and, as detailed in the Chornovil document by an official of the Young Communist League regarding the 1967 interrogations of Ukrainian intellectuals, embody many of the same processes of intimidation used under Stalin. Thus the legal barriers erected against political police arbitrariness after the Stalin era are only very partially effective. Indeed, it would appear that the regime continues to feel the necessity for its own security of an elaborate internal detection and investigation apparatus.

It also appears that there is a network of concentration camps for dissenters, of which the most specific information is on the Mordovian complex, southeast of Moscow. Anatoly Marchenko, in his book *My Testimony*, described camp conditions as "legalized lawlessness, plus legalized hunger, plus legalized forced labor." Seven prisoners, of whom Alexander Ginzburg and Yury Galanskov are the best

known, smuggled out to the West (together with portrait sketches made in late 1969 by one of them, Yury Ivanov) a description of "camp 17a," in the Mordovian swamps, where twenty thousand prisoners were detained. It reported "forced labor and cruel exploitation." Three of the other signatories belonged to the All-Russian Social-Christian Union for the Liberation of the People, founded in 1964 and consisting mainly of young staff and graduates of Leningrad University. Searches for the whereabouts of five hundred or so detained Soviet Baptists have disclosed camps in many parts of the country. The exact location of 202 camps is said to have been established and estimates made that there are perhaps 1,000 camps, with a total of a million prisoners.[6]

The extent of dissent, and such forcible handling of its manifestations, is startling in a period of relatively stable collective leadership at the top. It gives credence to reports of nationality ferment and youth disillusionment as well as intellectual dissent. While the official reaction does not bear resemblance to the mass terror and rigged trials of the Stalinist period, it discloses a much less stable social structure than could have been expected more than fifty years after the establishment of the Soviet regime. Although the regime itself is clearly not threatened by the noteworthy persistence of protests and dissent, it is still open to question whether its response to them will be gradual change along the lines they suggest, or tightened repression.

[6] See *Ferment in the Ukraine,* ed. by Michael Browne (New York, Macmillan, 1971). Ginzburg, whose smuggled tape-recorded message was heard on American television in mid-1970, was subsequently transferred to Vladimir prison, one hundred miles east of Moscow. Galanskov, in a personal message smuggled out of "camp 17a," also appealed to Western sources to "publicize arbitrariness and acts of cruel coercion by Soviet official personnel and thus *force* the state bodies and officials to take quick action," a suggestion that external publicity and pressure could have a beneficial effect.

3

The Communist party

1 THE PARTY IN THE PREREVOLUTIONARY PERIOD

Judged by the standards of British and French party systems, the party structure of the Soviet Union is novel and perplexing. To understand it the foreigner must rid himself of almost every preconception about the purpose, the form, and even the spirit of party activity; it would, in fact, be far better if some word other than *party* could be used to designate the Communist organization.

The differences between the Communist party and Western parties are the response to a different kind of purpose. The general purpose of Western political parties is to aggregate interests and to articulate lines of policy. Their immediate purpose is to become governing groups through winning elections and to conduct themselves in office constructively and in such a way as to succeed in being returned to office at the next electoral test. The parties that are not successful in the election strive to demonstrate by their criticism and alternative policies that they should form the next government. There is constant interaction, therefore, between parties and interest groups, which increases in intensity as election dates grow closer.

Such a situation is as remote from political organization in the Soviet Union as it was from tsarist Russia. The tsarist regime had no intention of permitting its political opponents to win control of the government peacefully and responded harshly to even the type of criticism

voiced in the Duma. Lenin, in any case, saw no hope through "reformist" parties, like the British Labor party, that planned to win power and to institute changes through peaceful, democratic, parliamentary means. What he preached, as we have seen, was a party of professional revolutionaries who were ready to devote to their work not their "spare evenings" but "the whole of their lives." If autocracy was to be overthrown, he maintained, it could only be through a highly disciplined and centralized organization, functioning in secret where necessary and directing trade unions and all other mass organizations of workers in a unified struggle for power.

Marxism had envisaged the Communist party as the party of the working class, but Lenin insisted, in his most decisive addition to Marxism, that the party was the *vanguard* of the proletariat, not necessarily consisting wholly or even predominantly of the working class but rather of those with an understanding of Marxism. Police repression in 1907 drove out many who had joined the revolutionary parties during and after the 1905 Revolution, and others abandoned the radical camp because the reforms provided them with the opportunities they sought. But although the Bolsheviks were thereby reduced again to a hard core of several thousand members, the party was never composed exclusively of full-time revolutionaries. While leadership inside the country tended to be in the hands of those working underground, there was always a group of Bolsheviks who furthered the work of the party in legal trade union and other institutions, even including the Duma. Moreover, the party was so rent by factionalism in the pre-1917 period that Lenin himself was often reduced to a sense of helplessness. The Bolsheviks only succeeded in their 1917 *coup d'état* because they were at least better organized than any other party and because of the power vacuum that followed the collapse of tsarist authority.

2 THE PARTY IN THE POSTREVOLUTIONARY PERIOD

The party that emerged from the Civil War had been confirmed in its purposes by the intensity of the struggle. It also grew rapidly between 1919 and 1921 to total three-quarters of a million members. As a result, there developed a three-fold division of membership: (1) the full-time party officials; (2) the party members who hold leading offices in government, trade unions, the military, and other organizations; and (3) the rank-and-file members in factories, offices, educational institutions, and elsewhere. Basically, this division has persisted to the present.

The full-time officials of the party Secretariat, and the pervasive bureaucracy they direct, provide continuous leadership and administration through and within the party. It should be noted, however, that some of the key figures in the party, including Lenin—in the past—and Kosygin—in the present—are not full-time party officials but hold offices in government and elsewhere that guarantee them seats on the top deliberative and executive organs of the party, the Central Committee and the Politburo. This second category of the tripartite division mentioned above thus participates in the exercise of supreme power. It also fulfills another and essential role of linking the rank-and-file of their own particular organizations with the full-time officials. The special responsibilities of the rank-and-file party members are to interpret to others in their organization and to the masses the orthodoxy handed down by the party leaders, to stimulate to desired efforts those with whom they are in contact, and to integrate them along approved channels. While the top-ranking, full-time party officials exercise preponderant power, the leading members of the second group of party leaders perform significant triple roles: sharing in the top decision-making, leading the party fractions within their own organizations, and directing the latter as a whole in the special functions for which they are responsible.

THE MULTIPLICITY OF PARTY FUNCTIONS

No Western political party begins to fulfill the multiplicity of functions that the Communist party is expected to perform. T. H. Rigby outlines four functions commonly indicated by Soviet sources:

1. supplying leading cadres for all social organisms, governmental and otherwise;
2. giving guiding directions derived from basic party doctrines and current party priorities on all important matters requiring decision in governmental and nongovernmental bodies;
3. systematically checking up on how these directions are carried out;
4. "mobilizing the masses" for the successful fulfillment of these directions.[1]

In addition, the party is responsible for elite recruitment, popular indoctrination, socialization, and politicization, providing communication in both directions between the regime and the people, securing compliance with regime policies, and including a pool of skilled manpower at the complete disposal of the regime.

Since these functions appear to be so all-encompassing, it is worth noting what the party does *not* do: the maintenance of internal order; external defense; certain aspects of rule and policy application; and, apart from its own newspapers, much of mass media communication. Internal order falls to the political and

[1] T. H. Rigby, *Communist Party Membership in the U.S.S.R., 1917–1967,* pp. 11–12.

internal police, the security service, forced-labor camps, procuracy, and courts. External defense is handled by the military, intelligence and counterintelligence, and the foreign ministry. Rule and policy applications are the functions of the state and industrial administrations, trade unions, cooperatives, and comparable bodies. The party has a crucial role, however, in regard to staffing, guiding, supervising, and ultimately dominating all these agencies.

The political police and the military forces are potentially the most threatening contenders for supreme power. Stalin crushed the military in the "Great Purge" of 1937–38 and after the war instituted yet another purge of smaller dimensions. Stalin used the political, or secret, police, however, to decimate and fragment the party in the interests of his own undisputed dictatorship and totalitarian control. While neither the military nor the political police now appears to threaten party domination, no party leader can be unaware of their inevitable power. That the only two nonparty elites that currently are close to having a large proportion of party members in the top and middle ranks are the armed forces and the police is a reflection of this fact.[2]

THE EVOLUTION OF THE COMMUNIST PARTY

The Communist party evolved only painfully and by degrees into the instrument described in the last section. When the Bolsheviks seized power they had neither devised a concrete program of social change nor an institutional structure. The Civil War led to an insistence on discipline and coercion, forceful requisition of supplies, power by the Cheka (political police), bureaucratization of the soviets and the party, and the concentration of decision-making in the hands of the central party leadership that has remained the key feature of the Soviet political structure. Both in the country and within the party these developments created frustration among those who had looked forward to self-assertion in their own spheres of life. Strikes, revolts, the Kronstadt mutiny bore witness to external dissatisfaction,

as we have seen, while within the party the Democratic Centralists and the Workers' Opposition emerged as self-conscious factions that challenged and even overthrew Central Committee decisions. In response in March 1921 the Tenth Congress condemned "anarcho-syndicalism" and "factionalism" and provided for expulsion of Communists who promoted "platforms" at variance with official policies. About one-third of the party membership was dropped in the purge of 1921, and more restrictive recruitment rules were adopted. This precedent of action against "factionalism" was to serve the Politburo and Stalin (who became secretary general of the Central Committee Secretariat in 1922) in their subsequent outmaneuvering and ejecting of critics and opponents, first from the left and then from the right (see Chapter 1, Section 2). The transition from the collective leadership inherent in the Politburo, within which Lenin usually had ascendancy through his unparalleled prestige, to the personal dictatorship of Stalin through his control of the party bureaucracy was a gradual one. Following Lenin's death in January 1924, Stalin cautiously added his own followers to key party organs until they became a majority of the Politburo by December 1927. By 1930, almost all its members were personally committed to Stalin. In the meantime, mass recruitment had gone hand in hand with purges of existing members and the advance of new recruits to responsible positions, under the control of Stalin's machine. The 1929–30 purge, which expelled 11 percent of current members, struck hard at those suspected of opposition to Stalin's policies of collectivization and industrialization and left vacant a wealth of party, trade union, administrative, and managerial jobs for Stalin's new working-class recruits. It formed a watershed in the Stalinization of the Soviet bureaucracy.

The 1930s provided a strikingly different and far more decisive development for the Communist party. The party had been used in the period of collectivization and the First Five-Year Plan as "a hammer with which Stalin beat Soviet society into a completely new shape."[3] Now the violence it had turned on society was

[2] Rigby, *Communist Party Membership in the U.S.S.R.*, p. 453.

[3] Rigby, *Communist Party Membership in the U.S.S.R.*, p. 197.

turned back on itself. In the purges that culminated in the "Great Purge" of 1937–38, the proletarianization of the 1920s gave way to the dominance of the "intelligentsia" and white-collar workers. Between 1933 and 1939, there was a 50 percent turnover in party membership; by the latter date only one party member in five survived from the 1920s. Whereas up to 1937, the purges had been turned against those whose loyalty to Stalin was suspect, in 1937–38 it was the Stalinists themselves who were destroyed. Their replacements were of the new type. Rigby estimates that between 1939 and 1941 less than 20 percent of the recruits to the party were workers, under 10 percent were peasants, and over 70 percent were intelligentsia and white-collar workers.[4] Proportionately, the greatest advances were made, and for the first time, among professional and technical personnel.

The Communist party emerged from the rigors of the struggle against Nazi Germany with some 6 million members, only one-third of whom predated the invasion. Some of these members had worked in occupied territories, others had been displaced by the fighting and now returned to their localities, while those enlisted during military service numbered about 40 percent of the total. Stalin's response to their disparate character was to reinstitute harsh controls and political police terror. Recruits were more rigorously investigated prior to acceptance, with the emphasis on enrolling professionals and white-collar skilled workers, and between 1950 and 1953 one hundred thousand expulsions a year rivaled the level of the 1921–22 and 1929–30 purges. For the first time, a substantial proportion of collective farms, five out of six, achieved a party organization, partly because demobilization brought young peasants back into them and partly because of the reorganization that drastically reduced their number. Yet, despite these developments, the party basically still suffered by the time of Stalin's death in March 1953 from an outworn political and administrative leadership, recruited in the 1930s, that hampered the rise to power of the younger, better-educated generation of Communists at lower levels of the organization.

[4] Rigby, *Communist Party Membership in the U.S.S.R.*, p. 225.

The decisive changes in the post-Stalin period were not in the roles of the party, which remained essentially those outlined above, but that the personal dictatorship was not reestablished, and the political police were brought under party control instead of being an arbitrary instrument for scourging the party in the interests of personal rule. Although Khrushchev acquired a marked ascendancy after 1957, it was of a very different kind from that of Stalin, since he always operated with sharply limited personal power.

Within the party, Khrushchev urged reducing the scale of expulsions and accelerating admissions, leading to a larger absolute expansion in numbers than in any other period of the party's history and resulting in a total of over 12 million members by 1965. The sharp turn away from recruitment of worker and peasant members, reflected in dropping the preferential admission procedures for workers at the Eighteenth Congress in 1939 and in eliminating the words "vanguard of the working class" in the 1952 Nineteenth Congress amendments of the party rules, was reversed, especially up to 1960–61. Whereas in 1955 nearly 50 percent of new recruits to the party were from the intelligentsia, professionals, and white-collar workers, 30 percent from industrial workers, and 20 percent from collective farms, in 1960 the proportions were only just over 35 percent from the intelligentsia and over 40 percent workers. The percent from collective farms remained about constant. From 1961, the emphasis shifted again to general recruiting of all those working "in the field of material production."

In the post-Khrushchev period, recruitment has been curtailed in the interests of more careful selection and consolidation. Brezhnev reiterated to the Twenty-third Congress, in March 1966, Lenin's view that it was better to keep out of the party ten who work than to let in one chatterbox! Party rules were changed to require a two-thirds majority in a primary party organization to approve admission, five years standing (instead of three) for those recommending the candidate, and Komsomol membership for those up to age twenty-three (previously from eighteen to twenty), a suggestion that youth training had been found inadequate. Disciplinary rules governing expulsion were also tightened.

3 PARTY MEMBERSHIP AND CHARACTERISTICS

Membership in the Communist party means accepting the right of the party to make major decisions affecting the character of life and training. The party can determine the type of work undertaken by its members and where it is carried on. It is said that the member "does not have the right to move from place to place at his own discretion or change his work as he thinks best. He can do this only with the permission of the Party organization." [5] This control over the movements and career of a party member is maintained by keeping his registration card on file in his local party office, from which it can be transferred to another location only with the permission of both jurisdictions. Local party organs have the right not only to try to restrain movement if they feel it will impair local production but also to dismiss managerial personnel if found inefficient or lacking in initiative. Communist party membership, therefore, entails both responsibilities and power and heavy commitments.

Historically, the most striking fact about Communist party membership has been its lack of stability. For the most part, recent recruits to the party have formed the majority of its members. This trend is most marked in its first twenty-five years in power. Only 90,000 of the 430,000 party members of 1920 survived in 1939. Only about 15 percent of the party members of the 1920s were still there at the end of World War II. Greater stability is apparent in the postwar period up to 1956 and with some fluctuations also thereafter. Although large-scale recruiting led between 1957 and 1967 to a decline from 45 to 21 percent in the proportion of party members of ten- to twenty-years standing, those of twenty- to thirty-year standing increased from 7 to 16 percent.[6] Prospects for the future are for much greater stability among its 13 million members, with particularly strong representa-

tion among those with twenty to thirty years' experience in the party.

The relation of this recent trend to the party's persistent efforts to recruit young people remains to be seen. In the 1920s, a considerable proportion of party members were under age thirty. The purges of the late 1930s, which principally struck at older party members, and subsequent wartime recruitment, shifted the balance once more to younger members. Those in their thirties again heavily outnumbered older age groups after Khrushchev's recruiting drive, thereby introducing the new cadres so badly needed at Stalin's death. Moreover, a considerable number of Communists were by that time reaching retirement age, which helped break up the bottlenecks to promotion. These bottlenecks have been one of the liabilities resulting from alternate periods of mass recruitment and membership stability and may have some relation to the history of purges. Although half the nearly 7 million candidates admitted between 1956 and 1963 came from the Komsomol, the age structure of the Communist party is now closer to that of Soviet adults as a whole than ever before. If the current leadership keeps recruitment levels low, the representation of those in their twenties may slip below the national average.

Ideologically, the Soviet Union is committed to the equality of sexes, but despite the marked advance of women in many spheres (see Chapter 2, Section 2), they have always remained a tiny minority in top administrative and managerial fields and, probably largely in consequence, have never formed more than about 20 percent of total party membership. One woman, Y. A. Furtseva, was an alternate member of the Central Committee from 1952 to 1956 and a full member thereafter. She became an alternate member of the party Presidium from 1956 to 1957 and a full member from 1957 to 1961. But otherwise women have tended to occupy relatively low posts in the party.[7]

---

[5] Jerry F. Hough, *The Soviet Prefects: The Local Party Organs in Industrial Decision-Making*, pp. 114–15.

[6] Rigby, *Communist Party Membership in the U.S.S.R.*, pp. 352–53.

[7] Women have held some important state offices. Furtseva was Minister of Culture from 1960 on, and Yadgar S.

The representation of the non-Russian nationalities in the Communist party is distinctly uneven. Persistently low levels of membership in the border areas, especially among Estonians, Latvians, and Turkmen, evidence continued resentment at Great Russian dominance. The low levels in central Asia reflect both the cultural distinctiveness and lack of urbanization of those minorities. The overall position of non-Slavs in the party has, in fact, worsened over the years. Rigby estimates that whereas they formed 22.6 percent of the population and 19.1 percent of party membership in 1927, in 1965 their 23.7 percent of the population was represented only by 18.9 percent of party membership.[8] More significant in terms of influence within the highly centralized Communist party are the low levels of representation of non-Slavs at the top decision-making levels and even the low proportions of indigenous nationalities in the local party organizations in their areas. Only in Georgia and Armenia have the local nationalities maintained a clear majority in their local party organizations. The Ukraine, Byelorussia, and Uzbekistan have regained and probably can maintain such a majority; it now also exists in the Baltic states and Turkmenia, although their indigenous majority is more precarious. Elsewhere in nationality areas, with very few exceptions, the Russian component of the local party is numerically as well as politically dominant.

The number and position of Jews within the party is distinctive, particularly in relation to the extreme pressures to which they have been subject within Soviet society. Proportionately, Jews, like some other minorities persecuted by the tsarist regime, originally provided a much more substantial proportion of those in leadership roles than their numbers in the population would suggest. They appear also to have maintained their representation in party ranks, although at a reduced level, even though their position in the top ranks of the party worsened dramatically from the 1930s on. The explanation for the continuation of proportionately high party membership appears to be the

consistent emphasis on townsmen in the party and the steadily increasing importance of educational qualifications, both characteristic of the Jewish population.

The steadily increasing educational qualifications of party members, a natural by-product of industrialization and modernity, confronts the party with its most serious problem of national representativeness. The official characterization of the party is now that it includes "the *best* representatives of the working class, the kolkhoz peasantry [collective farmers] and the Soviet intelligentsia." Clearly this includes all those holding high offices in every sphere of life. But it is equally clear that if one takes the proportion of workers, collective farmers, and white-collar intelligentsia in the country at large and compares it with the proportions in the party, a worker has twice as good a chance of entering the party as has a collective farmer, but a member of the intelligentsia has five to six times the chance of a worker. In the early 1960s, the likelihood that a party member had higher education was five times greater than that of an average citizen, and the chance that he had completed secondary school was two and a half times as great. Although the Soviet population as a whole has moved steadily toward literacy, one-third of the adult population had not completed four years of primary school as late as 1959, whereas only one party member in thirty had less than seven years schooling. By 1966, over 15 percent of the party members had achieved higher education and about 35 percent had secondary education. It should be noted also that about 30 percent of all those with higher education employed in the national economy have been in the party since World War II. The representational dilemma posed by these statistics is how to retain the party's incidence of the highly trained, who are crucial to the working of the planned economy and its social institutions, without losing its roots in the great mass of the population.

While it is to be expected that persons in responsible government posts will be party members, the rule is not universal, apart from the top levels. Chairmen and deputy chairmen of the executive committees of soviets at all levels are party members, as are ministers and dep-

---

Nasriddinova, president of the Uzbek Republic, was selected chairman of the Soviet of Nationalities in 1970 (see Chapter 4).

[8] Rigby, *Communist Party Membership in the U.S.S.R.*, p. 391.

uty ministers in republic governments. Nonparty members staff considerable numbers of junior government posts, however, and probably sometimes reach the middle levels. The internal security police, as already indicated, is completely saturated with party members at the operational level; so are the courts from the regional level up (except for the half million lay assessors, who are half party and half nonparty; see Chapter 7, Section 2). Public prosecutors and their assistants and staff are virtually all party members. Thus the two chief means of maintaining order and obedience are decisively manned with party personnel.

From the early 1930s, there has been a marked growth of party membership among the managers and specialists of enterprises to match that of the superior industrial administration. At the same time, the one party conference devoted exclusively to industrial problems in 1941 took the stand that has persisted to this day: good work and conscientiousness are more important in leading industrial posts than is party membership. Only directorships of plants, factories, trusts, and so forth, are reserved for party members, although a substantial proportion of managerial personnel appears also to be in the party. For those below this level, it seems to be immaterial whether they are party members or not.

The weakest point of party representation has always been in agriculture. Not until the sixties could the chief executive position in the collective farms, the kolkhoz chairmanship, be restricted to party members. In the late 1950s, as the training, skill, organization, and powers of the farm executives became more comparable to those in industry, party membership began to spread quite quickly among lower kolkhoz officials, while perhaps two-fifths of agricultural specialists were party members. Executives of the state farms and machine tractor stations (until the stations were abolished in 1958) have invariably been party members.

As far as professional fields are concerned, in 1964 over 40 percent of all engineers were party members and 25 percent of the teachers held membership, as did a slightly smaller proportion of the doctors. All editors are party members and possibly most journalists, but otherwise few professional groups in the Soviet Union appear to contain a majority of party members. Just over half the members of the Union of Soviet Writers were Communists in 1967, but the latitude allowed to favored non-Communist writers and artists appears now to be constricting. In this area, as in science, the party as well as the individuals concerned have felt the tension of deciding between the claims of creativity and the norms enunciated by the party's highest authorities.

Scholars, no less than artists and scientists, are watched carefully for orthodoxy and have been increasingly brought into the party since the 1930s. The largest proportion of party members are found, predictably, in the social sciences and philosophy, the lowest probably in art and medicine. Taking together all senior scholars and doctoral candidates in 1965, just about one-half were party members. Moreover, their influence within the party appears to have grown significantly between 1955 and 1965. Although they do not number more than one in forty of all party members, they relate to other professional and cultural cadres in the party, thereby maximizing the effect of this most rapidly growing segment both of Soviet society and of party membership.

By the mid-1960s, one Soviet citizen in twelve was a Communist party member. (In 1970, Brezhnev put the proportion at nearly one in eleven.) The party itself formed a particular kind of elite that supervised and coordinated all other elites. Where the party remained weakest was within nonelite groups at the lower levels of industry and, more particularly, in agriculture. If, as it claimed, the party includes "the *best*" of each of the three main strata of Soviet society—workers, peasants, and intelligentsia—it is permeated far more by the last group than by either of the other two. The party that Marxism originally envisaged as representing the working class has become the forceful instrument of the intelligentsia.

4 THE PARTY ORGANIZATION

The traditional description of the organization of the Communist party as a pyramid, in which information flows from below up and orders flow from above down, is vastly oversimplified and misleading. It is true that the official theory is that of *democratic centralism*, according to which there is freedom of discussion within the party until a policy is adopted but absolute obedience to that policy once it has been adopted. This theory also includes strict party discipline, subordination of the minority to the majority, and the absolutely binding character of the decisions of higher bodies on lower bodies. But, in practice, every level of the party organization has its own particular responsibilities that involve interaction with all nonparty bodies to which it relates.

Usually it is only when there are genuine difficulties in resolving differences over policy or its results that the matter is officially referred to the next level of the party. In general, local party organs are in relatively strong positions vis-à-vis state administrators at the territorial level or below, but above these levels administrators are in a stronger position and may also wield their own influence downward to the detriment of the local party organs. Above the territorial level, party organizations also interact with the other organizations on their own levels, providing another series of interrelations that extend all the way through to the Politburo itself.

It should be kept constantly in mind that the Communist party is to varying degrees a part of every organization in the country. This fact is the corollary to the degree of permeation of different groups in the country by the party membership. The structure and functioning of party organization in the Soviet Union is not directed solely, therefore, as are Western political parties, toward elections and a role in the legislature. Communist party members are leaders, stimulators, and also participants in all the day-to-day as well as long-range planning and reviewing activities of a modern state.

PRIMARY PARTY ORGANIZATIONS

This interaction is most clearly evident at the lowest level of party organization, in the more than three hundred and fifty thousand primary party organizations. According to the party rules, these organizations

> . . . are set up in mills, factories, state farms, machine and tractor stations and other economic establishments, in collective farms, units of the Red Army and Navy, in villages, offices, educational establishments, etc., where there are not less than three Party members.

The tasks of the primary party organizations in relation to the place of work are partly ideological, particularly where there is a relatively new group of workers. Since the First Five-Year Plan, however, ideology has gone hand in hand with efforts through agitation (see Chapter 2, Section 3) to stimulate "socialist competition" aimed at increasing production within and between plants. By mid-1965, 30 million workers were involved in such competition.[9]

The place where friction is most likely to develop in an enterprise is in the relation between the full-time, paid secretary of the primary party organization and the manager of the plant. The ideological work within the plant is clearly directed by the secretary, but the party organization also has responsibilities —known as *pravo kontrolia*—for checking the overall performance of the enterprise and, moreover, for participating in the process of policymaking. Since the manager and his most effective subordinates will also be party members, they will form most of the party's executive organ, the bureau, but the latter also includes the secretary, who is supposedly independent of the manager. What happens when the manager and secretary disagree? As far as day-to-day decisions in the plant are concerned, it is clear that the manager has the authority. As far as stimulating greater efforts by the workers, the primary party organization may be urged

[9] Hough, *Soviet Prefects*, p. 131.

from above to provide a more effective example to the nonparty workers in the plant. But when it comes to actual disagreements on production matters, the secretary's powers are limited to persuasion and an appeal to a higher party organ. At the same time, the manager is held responsible for submitting all relevant information on plant performance to the secretary. Moreover, the workers may describe defects and bring complaints to the secretary. Rather than clearly defining the scope of authority of manager and secretary, the Soviet regime prefers to put the responsibility on both of them to make their efforts contribute cooperatively to the overriding objective of maximum efficiency in production.

The relationship between managers and secretaries within Soviet enterprises illustrates most clearly the Soviet view that effective organization does *not* consist of clear lines of command within distinct spheres of competence but rather of overlapping jurisdictions to provide many-sided evaluations of the situation. Contrary to the general view, the managers of enterprises generally have very considerable discretion to develop policies they consider appropriate both to particular circumstances and to the targets they are expected to meet. Yet party supervision and stimulation are characteristic features of the whole Soviet system. While it appears that those whom George Fischer calls the dual executives,[10] that is, those with both technical and political skills and experience, are increasingly assuming top roles in the Communist party, something of the same advantages are secured by placing the burden of consultation and coordination squarely on the manager and party secretary themselves to find ways to reconcile and thus unite their two approaches.

LOCAL PARTY ORGANIZATIONS

A local party organization exists in each administrative area into which the country is divided: in each rural and urban district (*raion*), city, region (*oblast*), and republic. (An area described as an autonomous republic or as a territory (*krai*) is, in fact, equivalent to a region

[10] George Fischer, *The Soviet System and Modern Society.*

(*oblast*) but contains a particular nationality.) Nearly all the regions and equivalent divisions are concentrated inside the larger republics, that is, the RSFSR, Ukraine, Byelorussia, and Kazakhstan, and they vary widely in size, as do republics themselves. Small towns and villages in the countryside are under the jurisdiction of the rural district; large towns and cities are administered separately and come directly under the appropriate region, if there is one, or otherwise directly under the republic. Since 1962, medium-size cities seem to be included in the latter group. The rule is that wherever there is a defined area, it will have both a governmental and a party organization.

The ideological work of the lower levels of local party organs is in part to supervise local mass media, such as theaters, movies, and the press, to see that they maintain approved standards contributing, as their directions state, to "the forming of a scientific world-view based on Marxism-Leninism." The local party organizations also help the primary ones by arranging for visits of propagandists, establishing training facilities, and maintaining some coordination in the themes considered appropriate to that particular area. Thus the local party organizations assume overall responsibilities for political socialization and, of course, for the maintenance of political stability.

Above all, however, local party organizations act at each level, and particularly at the regional level, as coordinating agencies. This is why Hough calls them "the Soviet prefects," that is, the organs that, as in France, act as the agents of the central administration (in the Soviet case, the central organs of the Communist party) in coordinating the network of other agencies within their area, in particular those dealing with economic development.

Since there are such layers of administration all the way from local districts or towns through to the All-Union level, there is undoubtedly some overlapping also in the planning and supervision of economic development. Party theory, as we have seen, states unequivocally "the unconditional binding nature of the decisions of the higher organs for the lower," and there is no question that lower organs are subordinate to those above them. But in practice it appears that Communist and Soviet officials do not worry if there is some overlapping in the supervision provided particular enterprises or lack of clear-cut spheres within which a particular local party agency operates. The managers of the enterprises themselves may well be irritated by numerous, apparently uncoordinated checks on their activities, but, in general, lack of coordination appears to be more of a theoretical than a practical possibility. Moreover, the Soviet Union encourages more checking rather than less, believing that it is better to cover the same situation two or three times than to risk having it overlooked.

Local party organizations have their own congress (or conference, if below the republic level), central committee (or committee), bureau, secretariat, and first secretary, on the model of the All-Union institutions. From the point of view of functions and significance, these local party institutions are also comparable to those at the top level. The *party congress*, or conference, which meets once every two years in each region and every four years in each republic, is a major platform for enunciating policies and, regardless of what the rules say, is *not* the forum for making them. The *central committee*, or committee "elected" to form the supreme party organ until the next congress, commonly includes a cross section of the most important groups in the area, including party and state officials, directors of enterprises, and some ordinary workers and farmers,[11] but its plenary sessions, which must be held three times a year, are mainly concerned with reiterations of policies already adopted. The preparatory review of some special aspect of the area's life and the informal discussions during its sessions may, however, be of some special use. It is, however, the *bureau*, the executive organ whose members the committee technically "selects," that, along with the secretariat,

is the real seat of power. While the bureau contains the top governmental officials of the area, it is dominated by the full-time party officials. Hough describes a typical nine-man republic bureau as consisting of five party secretaries, the chairman of the council of ministers, the presidium of the supreme soviet, the peoples' control committee, and the first deputy chairman of the council of ministers.[12] Bureaus on lower levels have more or less similar membership.

Within the bureau the first secretary is far more than the first among equals; one emigré described him as "a small scale God and Tsar." Indeed the bureau exists less as a working unit than as a means to enable other secretaries, each of whom has responsibility for a separate sphere of activity, to keep the actions and policies of the first secretary under review. The latter are key members of the centrally controlled hierarchy. All first secretaries, including those at city and district levels, are appointed by the central party organization. Moreover, republic and regional first secretaries hold important positions at the All-Union level. All republic first secretaries were elected full members of the All-Union Central Committee in 1966, and almost all the RSFSR regional first secretaries and twenty-one from non-Russian regions became either full or candidate members. Even more significant, nine of the eleven voting members of the 1967 Politburo were republic or regional first secretaries.

The relation between party officials at these higher levels and the administrators of huge industrial enterprises is not unlike the interaction at the lower level. From the time of the "Great Purge" there has been increased recruitment of party members, as we have seen, from among those with technical and scientific training. Advancement in party ranks has often gone to those who can discuss complicated industrial questions with the managers of major industrial enterprises. The latter were inevitably more specialized in their own domains than would be most party officials whose responsibilities necessarily extend also to agriculture or urban life, depending on the area. Thus, whereas city and district secretaries used to be

---

[11] The 1966 Ukrainian Central Committee, for example, had 127 full members, of whom 42 were party officials, including 6 republic secretaries and the heads of four departments—agriculture, heavy industry, organizational work, and propaganda-agitation—the first secretaries of the 25 regions, second secretary of Kiev region, first secretaries of the two main cities, Kiev and Krivoi Rog, and 6 secretaries of rural districts. In addition, the committee included 33 state administrators, the directors of a number of important enterprises, 6 collective farm chairmen, the chairmen of the trade union council and the Komsomol organization, 6 research directors, 1 educator, 2 writers, 6 military officers, 11 workers, and 7 farmers. (Hough, *Soviet Prefects*, pp. 321–24.)

[12] Hough, *Soviet Prefects*, p. 14.

appointed directly from the ranks of the enterprise managers, this is rare since 1965, since they were found insufficiently experienced for nonindustrial duties. But in heavily industrialized areas, the regional bureau has often contained persons with diversified industrial specializations who can interact with industrial administrators on their own terms. Moreover, the number of regional first secretaries with advanced technical training was sharply increased with the establishment of the regional economic councils (*sovnarkhozes*), which administered industry and much of construction between 1957 and 1964.

In November 1962, Khrushchev reorganized the party into two separate hierarchies: one for industry and the other for agriculture (see Chapter 2, Section 2). This division did not survive his ouster, but there was very little change in party personnel, especially in industry. Nor was there any change in the general level of technical competence demanded of these party functionaries. Thus advice on planning, investment, and technical matters inevitably has much weight with industrial administrators, although the latter can be expected usually to hold their own through their still more specialized technical competence as well as experience.

ALL-UNION PARTY ORGANS

Whatever the structure and functions of local party organs, there is no question that the focus of decision-making and power is at the top of the party hierarchy—the party organs of the USSR as a whole, which are themselves tightly integrated and directed by the small knot of leaders in the Politburo and Secretariat. Indeed, throughout much of the history of the Communist party there has been one figure who has dominated all, as under Stalin, or, as after 1957 under Khrushchev, much of the policymaking functions. The collective leadership of Brezhnev and Kosygin and the Politburo as a whole since 1964 is much more rare than is the dominance of one man, and many observers have been expecting the simpler form to reemerge again.

Technically, the supreme organ at the All-Union level is the Party Congress; the congress elects the Central Committee; the Central Committee chooses the Politburo and the Secretariat. In practice, control operates in reverse. An apt comparison is between the party and an army. The full-time professionals are the generals; the functional specialists are the officers' corps; and the secretaries of party units are the noncommissioned officers. Above them is the general staff, the Politburo, and the commander in chief, the First or (as now) General Secretary.

There are two other top party organs of some significance: the Central Auditing Commission, appointed by the congress, and the Party Control Committee, appointed by the Central Committee. The former has general supervisory responsibilities regarding the relation of party activities and expenditures. (No accounts have been published since the revolution, but the 1956 congress was told that 73 percent of funds come from party dues—local party organs must transmit 10 percent of their income to the Central Committee—and the rest from party enterprises like publishing.) The Party Control Committee enforces party discipline at the All-Union level, since the tradition established in 1922 places responsibility for adjudicating conflicts on the leaders of the hierarchy within which the conflict arises. The Party-State Control Committee, established by Khrushchev in 1962 and directed by A. N. Shelepin, a former head of the security police who had been appointed to the party Secretariat, was abolished in December 1965, and the right to discipline party members reverted to the responsible party organ. The earlier Organization Bureau was abolished in 1952. There is provision for a party conference to be convened annually between the meetings of the Party Congress, but no party conference has been held since 1941.

THE PARTY CONGRESS

According to party rules, the Party Congress is the supreme organ of the party: it should determine the tactical line of the party on issues of current concern, revise and amend the program and rules of the party, hear and act on the reports of the Central Committee and

Central Leadership Structure of the Communist Party

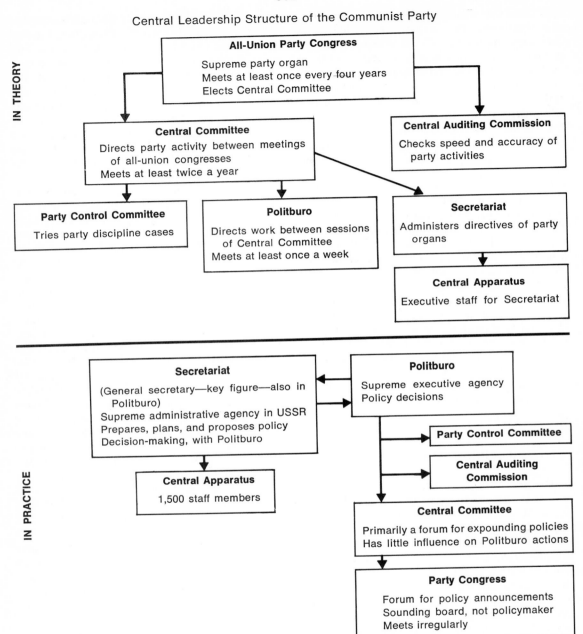

other central party organs, and elect the members of the next Central Committee, which is supposed to be the policymaking body between meetings of the Party Congress. In practice, however, the Party Congress is little more than a sounding board, used by party leaders to enunciate their policies and to give them publicity. The members of a Party Congress are chosen in accordance with norms laid down by the Central Committee and naturally consist of supporters of the leaders in power. Its size fluctuates widely. In 1956, fewer than fourteen hundred voting delegates were selected; in 1961, there were over three times as many; in 1966, there were five thousand delegates; and in 1971, approximately the same number. Moreover, meetings of the Party Congress have been very irregular, with one thirteen-year lapse under Stalin and two five-year lapses within the last decade.

This irregularity was not the case at first. From the time of the revolution until 1925, meetings were held annually. Thereafter, the interval between meetings grew progressively longer: two years between 1925 to 1927, a three-year lapse until 1930, a four-year interval until 1934, five years until 1939, and then the thirteen-year lapse until October 1952, shortly before Stalin's death. Since then there have been five congresses: the regular Twentieth Party Congress in February 1956, the Extraordinary Twenty-first Party Congress in January–February 1959, the Twenty-second Party Congress in October 1961, the Twenty-third Party Congress in March–April 1966, and the Twenty-fourth Party Congress in March–April 1971. Henceforth, the congress is to meet every five years.

The particular importance of modern party congresses is that they provide opportunities for those inside and outside the country to gain insight into new lines of policy or emphasis. Those few congresses that follow changes of leadership, notably those in 1956 and 1966, are watched with special attention. Khrushchev's "secret" speech attacking Stalin's policies was unprecedented, and despite its wide publicity abroad it has still not been released publicly in the Soviet Union itself. Nothing comparable followed Khrushchev's own ouster from power in 1964, not only because the break was far less sharp but also because the reverberations of Khrushchev's disclosures had shaken the party's authority to an unexpected and disturbing degree, and the objective of the new leaders was to reestablish traditional forms and policies, not to suggest new ones.

THE CENTRAL COMMITTEE

Like the Party Congress, the Central Committee usually has far less power, or even influence, than the party rules suggest. At the same time, membership in the Central Committee provides prestige, visibility, access to information, and latent power.[13] The members include the holders of top offices in administration, the foreign service, the military, and, above all, the party. In times of uncertain leadership, the Central Committee may play an important role in decision-making, but normally, consisting as it does largely of persons who hold particular offices, the membership of the Central Committee is strongly affected by the top leadership's power of appointment. Although 44 percent of the members of the 1956 Central Committee—40 full members and 71 candidates—were new, the percentage of incumbents was higher, in fact, than at any previous congress since 1930. The much heralded "rejuvenation" of the elite in 1961, reflected in the election of new members to the Central Committee, was achieved largely through expanding the membership of that body from 225 in 1956 to 330 members and candidates in 1961. Nonetheless, by 1964, when a few additional replacements had been made, Khrushchev had appointed nearly 100 of the 175 full members of the Central Committee—73 in the party apparatus, 14 military members, and 12 personal supporters. Since a two-thirds vote in the committee (in which full and candidate members and those of the Central Revision Commission participate) is necessary for a vital decision like the expulsion of a member, Khrushchev felt comfortably secure in his top party position. In the actual event, however, his own close colleagues turned against him, and the Central Committee, when appraised of the situation, ratified his ouster from power.

In Stalin's later years, the Central Committee met only rarely. Khrushchev, however, used the Central Committee on at least two occasions to review issues over which the party Presidium (Politburo) lacked its customary unanimity. The first occasion was in 1955, when V. M. Molotov disagreed sharply with other members of the Presidium over policy toward Yugoslavia. Molotov was overridden also in the Central Committee. The second resulted from the much more serious clash in June 1957

---

13 Severyn Bialer, "The Soviet Political Elite: Concept, Sample, Case Study," unpublished doctoral dissertation in political science, Columbia University, 1966, cited by Fischer, *Soviet System and Modern Society*, pp. 119–21.

between Khrushchev and what was called the antiparty group. Khrushchev was outvoted in the Presidium but hastily assembled the members of the Central Committee, with the aid of the army, and won the customary unanimous vote that follows discussion. His opponents—Malenkov, Molotov, Lazar Kaganovich, and Dmitri Shepilov—were expelled from the Central Committee, and these four, along with M. Z. Saburov and M. G. Pervukhin, were also expelled from the Presidium. Following these events, Khrushchev acquired the top position in the country.

In the far smoother transition from Khrushchev to Brezhnev and Kosygin in 1964, Khrushchev and his supporters, including those in the army, were unaware of plans for his ouster. Indeed, some key figures, including Khrushchev himself, were out of Moscow when the decision on his ouster was made. When the members of the Central Committee met, Khrushchev's successors had already triumphed.

According to a new party rule adopted at the Twenty-second Congress, not less than one-quarter of the members of the Central Committee were to be "renewed" at each congress; this rule was rescinded by the Twenty-third Congress. In practice, the collective leadership has maintained an unprecedented stability in Central Committee membership.

Among the 360 members of the Central Committee elected in 1966 (195 regular voting members and the rest candidate members), there was a marked predominance of those recruited into the party between 1938 and the end of the war; very few—only 39—of the postwar generation of party members were elected. The average age of the 1966 Central Committee members was fifty-six, and their average length of service in the party was twenty-nine years. Nearly 25 percent of the members were over sixty, and an equal percentage had served on the Central Committee under Stalin.

In 1971, the Twenty-fourth Party Congress reelected just over three-quarters of the voting members of the former Central Committee. Forty-five members were not reelected; some because of ill-health, others because they were out of favor. By enlarging the number of voting members to 241 (candidate members were reduced from 165 to 155 in number) 88 newcomers were introduced into the Central Committee, enough to form nearly a third of its voting members. Fifty of the new voting members were included almost automatically because of having assumed regional party posts or key ministerial posts (some of which are receiving special attention under more consumer-oriented economic policies). The other 38 were promoted from candidate, that is, nonvoting status, and included several of Brezhnev's close aides.

THE POLITBURO

The Politburo is the ultimate center of power within the Communist party. It makes the most important decisions on policies and appointments. The greatest freedom of discussion occurs within its ranks, but the greatest secrecy cloaks the number of its meetings and the character of its discussions. Apart from the open split in 1957 and Khrushchev's successful recourse to the Central Committee to override the Presidium majority against him, the latter body has long presented a solid front to the rest of the party, which neither resists nor rejects its decisions. In this one respect, at least, top party leaders heed Stalin's warning: "We must never forget we are a *ruling* Party. We must not forget that any open expression of our differences may reduce our influence in the country—to say nothing of the effect it may have abroad."

Since Khrushchev's ouster, collective leadership appears to have operated quite smoothly, more so than between 1953 and 1957 and at least as well as in the early days of the Soviet regime. No single figure combines party and state offices as Khrushchev came to do as First Secretary of the party, Chairman of the Council of Ministers, Chairman of the Presidium, Chairman of the RSFSR Bureau (subsequently abolished) and commander in chief of the Armed Forces. The eleven full members of the Politburo announced at the Twenty-third Party Congress in 1966 represented almost equally the party professionals and the state administrators. This group included only four new members since Khrushchev's ouster in 1964. In April 1971, the Twenty-fourth Party Congress increased the Politburo membership to fifteen, without removing any of the existing members.

Three of the new full members—V. V. Grishin, D. A. Kunayev, and V. V. Scherbitsky—were previously candidate members, and one, F. D. Kulakov, was brought in from the Secretariat. Of these four additional members, three hold party offices and one a state post.

Such information as we have of the workings of the present collective leadership suggests that issues are considered carefully and decisions deferred unless a majority can be secured. One by-product is that there have been major delays in formulating decisions, for example, on the Five-Year Plans and a new collective farm charter, and there also have been some quite fundamental switches in policy as, for example, in the allocation of funds to the military and agriculture.

Prime responsibilities for party affairs and supervision of policy execution have fallen to party secretaries Brezhnev, M. A. Suslov, and A. P. Kirilenko, while Kosygin is the specialist on economic planning and management. N. V. Podgorny, also considered to be among those with outstanding personal influence, was shifted from the Secretariat, although not from the Politburo, late in 1965 and became Soviet President (see Chapter 5, Section 6), from which office he developed a role in the supervision of state economic agencies. These five men, all of whom are in their early or late sixties, are said to constitute the inner circle of the Politburo. They were the first five listed by Brezhnev in his April 9, 1971, announcement of the full members of the Politburo, following the Twenty-fourth Party Congress (see chart on page 584). Some observers believe, however, that the inner ring of power inside the Soviet leadership is now composed of the four men who combine full Politburo and Secretariat membership—Brezhnev, Suslov, Kirilenko, and Kulakov—who were listed in that order in the April 1971 announcement of the Secretariat members.

In 1967, the inner circle of the Politburo consolidated its position of power by transferring the ambitious and more youthful Shelepin (age fifty-two in 1970) from the Secretariat to the Trade Union Council. This shift was made despite the fact that he had been involved in planning Khrushchev's ouster, although Shelepin was head of the Party-State Control Committee when the ouster took place. Shelepin

retained his position on the Politburo, and he, Scherbitsky, and Kulakov are presently its most youthful members. The 1971 additions to the Politburo brought the average age down to sixty, but no full or candidate member belonged to the postwar generation of party members, and the youngest was fifty-three.

Two potentially important Politburo additions since Khrushchev's dismissal are D. F. Ustinov, who became a member of the Secretariat and candidate member of the Politburo in March 1965, and Y. V. Andropov, who became a candidate member of the Politburo in June 1967. The former has long been the top technical expert on the defense industry; the latter had shortly before become chairman of the KGB (security service, see Chapter 2, Section 3). If, as appears to be the case, the Politburo represents genuine collective leadership, then this assortment of individuals implies effective cooperation of the top figures of the major power centers in the country: party, industry, and political police. Despite known differences of opinion over priorities in the allocation of resources, reforms in economic management, attitudes toward Stalin and Stalinism, and the relation between state and party organs (issues that will be discussed in more detail later; see Chapter 5), policies still appear to be the result of collective consideration and decision.

THE SECRETARIAT

The most important body in the Soviet Union for preparing plans and proposing policy is the Secretariat of the Central Committee. It ranks second only to the Politburo in making decisions, and the six secretaries—Brezhnev, Kirilenko, Suslov, P. N. Demichev, Ustinov, and Kulakov (since April 1971)—who are Politburo members, provide the interlocking relations between the two bodies.

Although the secretaries are formally elected by the Central Committee in plenary session, the latter's action is merely *pro forma* approval of a list already prepared by the top leaders. In the post-Stalin period, the number of secretaries has varied between three (February to July, 1955) and ten (December 1957 to 1960). In 1961 there were five: F. R. Kozlov, O. V. Kuusinen, N. A. Mukhitdinov, and Suslov, working un-

Members of the April 1971 Politburo and Secretariat

MEMBERS *		YEAR OF BIRTH	CATEGORY OF EXPERIENCE BY FISCHER SCALE †
Politburo			
Members			
Brezhnev, L. I.	June 1957	1906	T
	(Candidate member: October 1952– March 1964; February 1956–June 1957)		
Podgorny, N. V.	May 1960	1903	T
Kosygin, A. N.	May 1960	1904	—
Suslov, M. A.	July 1955	1902	O
Kirilenko, A. P.	April 1962	1906	HE
Pel'she, A. Y.	April 1966	1899	O
Mazurov, K. T.	March 1965	1914	O
Polyansky, D. S.	May 1960	1917	HE
Shelest, P. Y.	November 1964	1908	DE
Voronov, G. I.	October 1961	1910	—
Shelepin, A. N.	November 1964	1918	O
Grishin, V. V.	April 1971	1914	O
	(Candidate member: January 1961– April 1971)		
Kunayev, D. A.	April 1971	1912	T
	(Candidate member: April 1966– April 1971)		
Scherbitsky, V. V.	April 1971	1918	—
	(Candidate member: December 1965–April 1971)		
Kulakov, F. D.	April 1971	1918	T
Candidate Members (attend meetings but have no vote)			
Andropov, Y. V.	June 1967	1914	O
Demichev, P. N.	November 1964	1918	HE
Masherov, P. M.	April 1966	1918	O
Mzhavanadze, V. P.	June 1957	1902	O
Rashidov, S. R.	October 1961	1917	O
Ustinov, D. F.	March 1965	1908	T
Secretariat			
Brezhnev, L. I. (General Secretary)	October 1964	1906	T
	(Secretariat: October 1952–May 1960; June 1963–October 1964)		
Suslov, M. A.	March 1947	1902	O
Kirilenko, A. P.	April 1966	1906	HE
Kulakov, F. D.	September 1965	1918	T
Ustinov, D. F.	March 1965	1908	T
Demichev, P. N.	October 1961	1918	HE
Kapitonov, I. V.	December 1965	1915	HE
Ponomarev, B. N.	October 1961	1905	O
Katushev, K. F.	April 1968	1927	DE
Solomentsev, M. S.	April 1966	1913	DE
Party Control Committee Pel'she, A. Y. (Chairman)		1899	O
Central Auditing Commission Sizov, F. (Chairman)		1903	T

* Listed in the order given in Brezhnev's final speech to the Party Congress.
† The following symbols are used by Fischer in *The Soviet System and Modern Society* (see below):
T Technician   O Official   DE Dual executive
— Not rated in Fischer Scale   HE Hybrid executive
Source: Adapted from George Fischer, *The Soviet System and Modern Society.*

der Khrushchev—a number increased to nine after the Twenty-second Party Congress. (Mukhitdinov lost his post here and in the Party Presidium.) In 1971, there were ten. While arrangements seem fairly flexible, the allocation of responsibilities in December 1959 when there were also ten secretaries suggests the major groupings: general supervision over the administrative staff of the Secretariat; foreign Communist parties; party and personnel matters; industry, transport, and political work in military organizations; culture, education, youth, and women's affairs; agriculture; central Asian and Muslim affairs; and ideology, propaganda, and agitation.

Administrative staffs

In supervising all activities in these varied fields, the Secretariat depends on administrative staffs, which, not surprisingly, are organized very much like a government. The most important of these staffs is the Apparatus of the Central Committee, which assists all the top central agencies but is directly responsible to the Secretariat. Its fifteen hundred experienced and particularly trustworthy Communists are responsible for overseeing all spheres of Soviet life; they have active field staffs, wide sources of information, and considerable authority.

Although shifts in organization are not infrequent, the work of the Apparatus makes certain divisions essential. Schapiro lists twenty-one departments known to exist in 1968 but cautions that there may be more. The five departments primarily concerned with administration are as follows: administration of affairs (i.e., office management); general (coordinating the work of the Politburo); administration organs (i.e., in relation to security organs, army, procurators, and judicial service); chief political administration of the Army and Navy (a joint department with the armed forces); and organizational party work (which is responsible for the appointments—technically, elections of officials in the party Apparatus, Komsomol, and trade unions, for membership cards, cadres, organization, and rules questions, and for supervising the work of the Apparatus). One department deals with agriculture and seven with industry: construction, chemical industry, defense industries, food industries, machine build-

ing, light and heavy industry, transport, and communications. Planning and financial organs and trade and public services each have their own department. Three departments are allocated respectively to science and educational establishments, culture, and propaganda. The remaining three relate to activities outside the country: international, personnel abroad, and relations with Communist parties of other socialist countries. Schapiro also lists the Party Control Commission and the Ideological Commission as under the Secretariat.[14]

The Central Apparatus makes use of promising young Communists as functional specialists, but it is not a direct career channel to higher positions. Apart from the secretaries, fewer than ten of its members were on the 1966 Central Committee. But the role of the Central Apparatus is of marked importance and pervasiveness as the listing above indicates.

Naturally, there are also apparatuses at the lower party levels. But the apparatuses form only some, although the most important, of the many administrative agencies of the party, composed of full-time paid officials. In 1939, there were probably about 194,000 such officials, stretching all the way from the lowest to the highest party levels, that is, about 1 official to every 12 party members, and candidates.[15] In 1958, after considerable reductions in staff, the numbers of paid secretaries were estimated as 2,250 in the Central Apparatus and republics; 9,000 in the regional committees; 200,000 in the city and district committees; and 29,000 full-time secretaries of primary organizations. Together, these officials total 240,250, which probably remains the approximate size of the full-time Apparatus today, a much smaller proportion of the total party membership of over 13 million than in the earlier period.

THE RISE OF THE DUAL EXECUTIVE

In his searching analysis of the skills currently demanded of the top party leaders in this period of "modernity," George Fischer first

[14] Leonard Schapiro, *The Communist Party of the Soviet Union*, 2nd rev. ed., p. 654.

[15] Schapiro, *Communist Party of the Soviet Union*, p. 449.

differentiates them from those of the "specialists in persuasion" in the early period of nation-building and the "specialists in coercion" of the Stalin period of rapid industrialization. Fischer then examines the career patterns of 360 top party executives from 1958 through 1962. These top officials included all USSR secretaries and heads of major party departments, first and second secretaries for the fourteen republics other than the RSFSR, which has no separate party organization, the first secretaries of the republic capitals, including Moscow and Leningrad, and the first secretaries of provinces and comparable units. Two-thirds of the number belonged to the last mentioned group. His sample (for which he drew his information from the "Who's Who" for the Supreme Soviet of 1958 and 1962) includes almost all the chief executive and administrative officials of the party in that period, a group whose character appears to have changed little in the succeeding years (see Chapter 5, Section 3).

Fischer's general findings are that 44 percent of his sample fall into the simple category of official—that is, one who has had neither technical training nor extensive work in the economy—but that the remaining 56 percent have had some considerable experience of one or the other or both before assuming a top party post.[16] This latter group he divides into the "dual executive," that is, one who has had prior technical and party work within the economy; "technician," with prior extensive technical but not party work within the economy; and "hybrid executive," with prior technical training but no extensive technical work in the economy. In his extensive sample, Fischer found 16 percent dual executives, 29 percent technicians, and 11 percent hybrid executives. His evidence suggests that while those he calls dual executives tend to move more frequently and thus to hold their top party jobs for shorter periods of time than those in the other categories, there is a perceptible trend, already indicated in the description of lower party organs, toward greater use of dual executives in top party offices.

Fischer's analysis of the social origin and nationality of the 360 top party figures points up the very high percentage of posts at the All-Union level held by Russians (84 percent in 1958 and 92 percent in 1962) [17] but a more surprising figure of only 45 percent both in 1958 and 1962 of those in top posts below the All-Union level. But on closer examination his data reveal an ethnic division of functions on the lower levels, with the Russians occupying the posts that unite political and economic responsibilities, and the minority nationalities, especially in the less developed areas, filling more purely political roles. This division appears to confirm not only the dominance of Russian party officials but also the importance of the dual executive type of experience.

Fischer's data also suggest, although less decisively, that social mobility still operates within the Soviet party system, since a considerable proportion of those whose careers he examined had fathers who began life as workers or as peasants. But education is increasingly more important. While older officeholders, particularly those with largely political responsibilities, still include a high percentage without education beyond secondary school, all those with a closer relation to the economy have higher education, some with training in agronomy and even more in engineering. A later study of the top central and provincial officeholders elected to the Central Committee confirms the emphasis on specialist training and experience prior to assuming these offices.[18]

The general conclusions that emerge from Fischer's study are that in an era in which there is likely to be more industrialization, more higher education, continued dominance of those of Russian origin, and few if any substantial changes in the role and structure of the ruling group, there is a steadily increasing need to recruit persons who combine in themselves the political and economic training and experience that a modern state demands. Since the Soviet system assumes the primacy of the state and thus of the party over the economy—in contrast to the Western model, in which the economy is dominated by the private business sector—there is considerably more reason to seek such dual skills instead of having them separated. Fischer believes he has identified such a

---

[16] Fischer, *The Soviet System and Modern Society*, p. 39.

[17] Fischer, *The Soviet System and Modern Society*, p. 74.

[18] Michael P. Gehlen, "The Soviet Apparatchiki," *Political Leadership in Eastern Europe and the Soviet Union*, ed. by R. Barry Farrell.

trend, and, if he is correct, this may well prove one of the strongest bulwarks of the Soviet monistic system.

YOUTH ORGANIZATIONS

The Communist party has a special concern for securing the loyalty of young people, and a graduated series of nonspecialized youth organizations—the Little Octobrists, Young Pioneers, and the Komsomol, or All-Union Leninist Communist League of Youth—associate a high proportion of those between the ages of eight and twenty-eight with party programs and discipline.

In the early days of the regime, the Komsomol concentrated on recruiting working-class and poor peasant youth and included only a small proportion of politically active members. Since the party was also recruiting actively for members in their teens and early twenties, there was considerable overlap. In the mid-1920s, Stalin and Trotsky vied for the allegiance of youth, particularly students, and the "Stalinization" of the Komsomol by 1932 led to one-eighth of all party members being simultaneously in the Komsomol. Unintentionally, the Komsomol became an early channel for white-collar recruitment to the party, a process curbed in the late 1920s but of particular importance after the purges as the party dropped its proletarian emphasis in favor of the intelligentsia.

In 1939, it was decided that only those occupying leading roles in the Komsomol could simultaneously be party members. In 1949, party membership became obligatory for city and district Komsomol secretaries (apart from a few exceptions permitted after 1954). These latter developments reflected two significant changes in the youth organization. In the first place, its membership had swelled from about 5 percent of the relevant age groups in 1926 to 20 percent in 1949, with most young people in the towns enrolled. The corollary was that instead of forming the vanguard of the most alert

and purposeful youth groups in society, the Komsomol was turned into an instrument for control of Soviet youth. It thus lost its independent prestige and authority and became yet another "driving belt" of the party.

In the Octobrists, for children ages seven through nine, political education begins. From ages ten through fourteen almost all urban young people are in the Pioneers, where political indoctrination is more intense. The Pioneers provide many organized activities, and "socially useful" work is encouraged, sometimes to the detriment of formal education. At fourteen, young people can become members of the Komsomol, where numbers are increasingly an object. From a wartime high of 15 million, membership had dropped to between 8 and 9 million in 1948, but an all-out enrollment drive raised the figure to 16 million in 1952, 18 million in 1958, and 23 million in 1966. Altogether by that year, more than 53 million children and young adults were members of Communist youth organizations.

In his speech to the Twenty-third Party Congress in March 1966, Brezhnev declared:

> It cannot be regarded as correct that of the two and a half million communists aged up to 30 only 270,000 are working in the komsomol. Young communists must be drawn more actively into work in komsomol organizations, this being treated as a most important party assignment.

This assertion marked a reversal of the trend of the previous years when, in the interest of encouraging more independence, there had been a partial disengagement of Komsomol officials and activists from their party identification. The new line may well reflect the party's concern with the visible restlessness of Soviet youth and their obvious attraction to Western cultural styles. It may be difficult to stimulate much response, however, in the light of lower party recruitment levels and the noticeable lack of enthusiasm among young party members for Komsomol assignments.

5 EVALUATION OF THE SOVIET PARTY SYSTEM

The Soviet party system must be evaluated in terms of its own purposes, not those of Western party systems. It is obviously not intended to give the people a "meaningful and adequate choice, both of policies and of leaders," which is a major criterion used to evaluate the latter. The process of elections in the Soviet Union, described in the next chapter, permits only minimal choice between candidates, selected or at least approved by the Communist party, while the structure of the soviets through to the Supreme Soviet has little if any effect on the policies determined through the party itself. Moreover, within the Communist party the proclaimed process of "election of all leading Party bodies, from the highest to the lowest," which is part of democratic centralism as outlined in Article 18 of the 1939 Party Regulations, has no reality. All top party secretaries at every level, as we have seen, are appointed by the central organs of the party, whose domination over ultimate policymaking is undisputed.

But there are certain respects in which criteria used in relation to Western party systems have some relevance to the Communist party system. There is no doubt that the party is an effective instrument for carrying out policy, although, in contrast, the policy is not one that has been submitted to voters but is either determined through personal dictatorship, as under Stalin, or hammered out at the top level through the current interactions of collective leadership. It would be a mistake, also, to suggest that there is no popular participation in the Communist party structure. In fact, the participation is constant at every level and a key feature of the system. From the moment when a candidate for membership is voted into party ranks, he is expected to demonstrate through his activities on behalf of party purposes his dedication to the official ideology as interpreted by party leaders and to implement its current form in whatever aspect of the economy or society he relates to. "Self-criticism" is very much a part of this activity, as is "socialist competition." Although the participation is of a very special type, it is, in fact, much more constant and purposeful than is the participation by the members of any Western party.

To evaluate the Soviet party system in its own terms, as representing "the best" of the whole people, is to identify several problems, however, in this highly organized system. The top leadership of the party is composed almost exclusively of older members drawn from the late Stalin period, is predominantly male (only 2 of the 360 top officials whose careers Fischer examined were women), and is heavily overrepresented in key positions by those of Russian origin. Its alternations between heavy recruitment and contraction can lead to expectations of promotion that may be frustrated by lack of openings in the hierarchy and may distort the age level of members to the disadvantage of the younger generation whose experience is gained during the post-Stalin period. Above all, the party's emphasis on education, particularly of a technical and scientific type, may bring it out of touch with the great mass of the population at the worker and peasant levels. Thus it is possible that the very emphasis on effectiveness, particularly in relation to the direction of the economy, may hamper the party in its role as an early warning system to detect threatening popular dissatisfaction. While it appears that coercion can curb the independence of writers, despite their persistence, the toppling of an apparently well-entrenched leader, Gomulka, in Poland in December 1970, following riots that were brought on by a sharp rise in consumer prices, is a warning that in the end the unrepresented masses may seek their own route to change.

One further question has been raised regarding the size and representativeness of the Communist party. At the present time, the party includes over 13 million members, that is, about one-eleventh of the adult population. How much larger can it get and still retain its distinctiveness? This question must have influenced the post-Khrushchev leadership in its decision to reduce recruitment. So a certain dilemma remains that need never be faced by Western political parties: Can the representativeness that requires constant recruiting of the young be combined with the kind of discipline, sense of purpose, and subservience to the will of top party leaders that stamp the ruling party in a monistic state?

4

The soviets

1 THE NATURE OF THE SOVIETS

Side by side with the pyramid of Communist party organizations in the USSR, and largely controlled by them is a pyramid of governmental organizations known as the soviets—beginning with local soviets, which are roughly the equivalent of town or village councils in the United States, and culminating in a Supreme Soviet, which corresponds roughly to the United States Congress or the British Parliament.

Originally, however, the system of soviets was intended to be something quite different. It was regarded as an outstanding achievement of the November Revolution of 1917 that the soviets were substituted for legislative assemblies of the traditional type. According to Lenin and his followers, parliaments in Western countries were simply show windows to delude the masses. The representatives chosen by the people might talk to their hearts' content, but behind the scenes real power rested in the hands not of the parliamentary talkers but of the bureaucracy, the army, and the police force. Lenin could quote Marx to the effect that what was needed was "not a parliamentary but a working corporation, legislative and executive, at one and the same time." The masses, if they were to rule, must be the executive as well as the legislature. "Our aim," Lenin wrote, "is to draw *the whole of the poor* into the practical work of administration." The soviets were the instrument by which this objective was to be realized.

The word *soviet* in Russian is simply the word for council. It acquired special signifi-cance, however, during the Revolution of 1905 when councils or soviets of workers' deputies sprang up spontaneously in many Russian cities and provided the leadership for the revolutionary movement. These were organizations of the workers themselves, and to Lenin they suggested both a pattern for future revolutionary action and a type of organization through which the mass of the workers might participate directly in political life. Moreover, the experience with the soviets of 1905 had captured the popular imagination. In spite of their suppression, the memory of their leadership persisted; and when the March Revolution of 1917 occurred, it was only natural for soviets of workers' and soldiers' deputies to be formed throughout the country.

Lenin, upon his return to Russia in April, vigorously supported this type of organization. "The Soviet of Workers' Deputies is the *only possible* form of revolutionary government," he told his followers. "To return to a parliamentary republic from the Soviet of Workers' Deputies would be a retrograde step." There must be "not a parliamentary republic . . . but a republic of soviets of Workers', Agricultural Laborers' or Peasants' Deputies throughout the country, from top to bottom." The slogan of the Communists, as we have seen, was "All Power to the Soviets."

In part, Lenin's enthusiasm for the soviets resulted from tactical considerations. As the elections for the Constituent Assembly proved, the Bolsheviks could not hope to win control of a popularly elected parliament chosen by all classes of the population. But they could hope to win control of the soviets, since these were composed predominantly of the urban working class where the Bolsheviks had their greatest strength. By the time of the November Revolution the Bolsheviks had succeeded in winning majorities in the important soviets in Moscow and in Petrograd, of which the latter became the instrument of the seizure of power. They also won control of the All-Russian Congress of Workers' and Soldiers' Deputies, which was made up of deputies from these and other local soviets. Thus they had powerful centers of influence from which to operate.

In particular, however, the soviets were hailed by Lenin as a special instrument, immensely superior to bourgeois parliamentarism for drawing "in the freest, broadest, and most energetic manner, all the masses into the work of government. . . . It is a power that is open to all, that does everything in sight of the masses, that is accessible to the masses, that springs directly from the masses; it is the direct organ of the masses and of their will."

THE SOVIETS BEFORE 1936

Almost immediately, however, the Bolsheviks faced the problem that has remained at the heart of their relations with the masses: how to win popular support and at the same time maintain party control. Concentration of authority in the period of War Communism meant similar concentration within the soviets also. Lower soviets were made responsible to higher ones; power came to be exercised by executive committees rather than by the members of the soviets as a whole. But it was still more significant that the Eighth Party Congress in 1919 decreed that party fractions under strict party discipline should be set up within each soviet with the aim of unifying and subordinating the whole structure of the soviets to the single will of the party. "The Russian Communist Party must win for itself undivided political mastery in the soviets," it declared, "and practical control over all their work."

While party membership in the soviets themselves rarely rose above 50 percent, even in the cities, party members and candidates formed between 70 and 90 percent of their executive committees by the end of 1919. As these committees grew larger, power passed to their inner group, the presidium, which became virtual party monopolies.

Centralization of control led directly to a loss of mass support for the soviets, evidenced most forcefully by the abortive Kronstadt Rebellion of 1921, with its slogan of "Soviets without Communists." Despite some relaxation of administrative controls during the 1920s, the soviets never regained their initial position as popular agencies. They provided no adequate contact between the party and the masses during the tense period of collectivization of agriculture. "The soviet organs of the proletarian dictatorship which ought to be in the center and provide the leadership of every revolutionary undertaking," it was declared in 1930, "drag at the tail of this vast movement of social change."

Thereafter the party embarked on a more active policy of stimulating, as well as leading, the soviets. Great emphasis was placed on getting the maximum number of people to vote in elections for the soviets; at least a minimum number of questions were required from the floor at soviet meetings. At the same time, party and administrative controls were tightened so that the soviets became a major "driving belt" between the party and the people, and, to a degree, an extension of the party administrative structure.

Although mass participation was one of the major purposes of the structure of the soviets, there were formal limitations on elections for the higher soviets until 1936. Election to the All-Union Congress of Soviets, "the supreme authority of the USSR," was indirect—that is, delegates were chosen as representatives of town and village soviets. Elections were also unequal: the town soviets sent one deputy for every twenty-five thousand voters, while the village soviets were limited to one deputy for every one hundred and twenty-five thousand inhabitants. Voting was public, by a show of hands, and class enemies (clergymen, employers of labor, those who engaged in trade or lived on their incomes, and former members of the tsarist police) were not allowed to vote. In addition, the Congress of Soviets met for only a few days every two or more years, a practice that left little opportunity for even nominal participation in government by these indirectly chosen representatives of the masses. In the long intervals between meetings of the congress, power was delegated to a Central Executive Committee that had two chambers, a Union Council and a Council of Nationalities. This body was supposed to meet three times in the interval between congresses.

THE CONSTITUTION OF 1936

The new constitution of 1936 introduced drastic changes in the form of elections and organs. Stalin explained these changes by saying that the socialist system had now been unshakably established in all spheres of the national economy. The capitalist, landlord, and kulak classes had disappeared, and there was now a new collective farm peasantry.

Under this constitution suffrage has become universal. With the exception of the insane and of criminals, who are deprived of electoral rights, every citizen over eighteen years old, regardless of social origin or past activities, is guaranteed the right to vote. Each vote counts equally—urban areas no longer have any advantage over rural ones. Moreover, the voting for deputies is both secret and direct, despite the fact that since the Civil War all elections to the soviets have been uncontested, with the selection of candidates closely controlled by the party. To emphasize participation through voting, elections are held every two years, but at different times, for local soviets and republic soviets and every four years for the Supreme

Soviet, with those for the latter being, of course, the most important.

The Supreme Soviet consists of two chambers, a Soviet of the Union and a Soviet of Nationalities, the former representing the country by population and the latter giving special representation to federal areas. Both are elected at the same time, most recently in June 1970. All other soviets are unicameral.

The extent of party membership in the soviets since World War II has differed substantially at different levels. At the lowest levels, more attention is paid to the role of the soviets in linking the masses to the system and less is paid to the largely symbolic legitimation of authority that forms the chief role of higher organs. Thus nonparty representation is commonly a little over 50 percent at the village and urban district levels, whereas it diminishes steadily at the higher levels. Nonparty members also made up 30 percent of village soviet executive committees in 1967, representation that decreased sharply until it was only 3 percent at the regional level. Party representation in the local soviets of different republics used to vary widely (from 11.6 percent in Lithuania in 1947–48 to 52.6 percent in Armenia) but achieved more equal levels by 1967: the lowest, Estonia, with 38.6 percent; the highest, Azerbaidzhan, with just over 50 percent; and the RSFSR midway with 46.1 percent. In the supreme soviets of the union republics, the percentages of party membership were naturally higher, varying in 1967 from 63.9 percent in Latvia, to 77.9 percent in Azerbaidzhan, to 67.2 percent in the RSFSR. Party membership in the Supreme Soviet in 1966 was approximately 75 percent in each of the two houses.[1]

2   SOVIET ELECTIONS

Despite the implication of choice in the guarantees of the Soviet constitution for universal, direct, equal, and secret suffrage, regardless of race, religion, or sex, the right to vote in the USSR, in practice, is the right either to vote for the only candidate on the ballot or to cross out his name and vote for no one at all. Whereas the citizen in a liberal democracy can choose

positively between alternatives, candidates, and programs, the Soviet voter can express only general approval or, by inference, disapproval of how the country is being run.

Before the name is placed on the ballot, however, a selection has been made by the

[1] T. H. Rigby, *Communist Party Membership in the U.S.S.R., 1917–1967*, pp. 471–80.

electoral commission from among the many candidates who have been nominated by the party itself or by organizations that are controlled by the party. Top leaders have often been nominated for election in several districts (Brezhnev in more than forty in 1966) with one chosen shortly before the election. The practice was dropped in 1970. Naturally, less illustrious candidates who are finally registered have, in effect, been selected by the party, although they are not necessarily members of the party.

The end result in the Supreme Soviet is a fair cross section of the population: in 1962, the largest representation was of party career officials (224), government administrators (220), industrial workers (310), agricultural labor and collective farm peasants (220), and collective farm chairmen and state farm directors (118). The military, scientists, artists and writers, teachers, and physicians included between 47 and 60 members each. Nationality representatives provide a colorful spectacle. Men from Uzbekistan and Kirghiz with Mongol features and silver-embroidered black skullcaps and women deputies from the Ukraine with flowered kerchiefs around their dark hair mingle with fair-haired Estonians and swarthy Armenians. The basis of choice is not, however, to obtain a majority of people who will be able to discuss legislation wisely, since they will have no opportunity to do so in any case. The selection of deputies for the Supreme Soviet is chiefly an encouragement to themselves or to others of their kind; and their presence in that body—like the Supreme Soviet itself—is largely symbolic.

THE ELECTORAL CAMPAIGN

But despite the fact that there is never any doubt as to who will win each election and that the results do not affect the government in any way, there is a vast amount of activity before the voting takes place. Speeches of prominent leaders are broadcast and reprinted in millions of pamphlets. Campaign headquarters are set up in the voting precincts, replete with literature and lectures and entertainment. Organizations designate official campaigners to head their activities, to arrange meetings, and to direct the work of thousands of other campaigners who carry on a house-to-house canvass. These canvassers explain the structure of the government, the nature of its program, the technicalities of the election laws—and, of course, they get out the vote. On election day cars carry invalids to the polls, and precincts are set up on trains, ships, at airports, on touring voting trucks, in hospitals, and in homes for the aged so that everyone may vote. Altogether it is not an exaggeration to say, in the words of the *Soviet Information Bulletin*, "No country of the world has known such election activity on the part of the voters as is manifested in the Soviet Union." Moreover, no other country has such an incredibly high poll—99.8 percent, it was announced in 1970. In fact, it takes great courage not only to vote against a candidate,[2] but not to vote at all.

If one asks why such apparently unnecessary activity is undertaken, the answer is that it serves very well the general purposes of the Soviet state. Elections provide an admirable opportunity for rousing popular enthusiasm and giving the people an outlet. The speeches of the candidates explain the purposes of the government. The voters see and hear the most important officials of the party and state. Mass meetings and mass propaganda are directed toward building a fresh loyalty to and confidence in the party and its leaders. The people are made to feel that their support is important and that the government is concerned with their approval. The elite receives reassurance of its support. Thus the campaign is, in part, an education for the voter and, in part, a device for demonstrating solidarity and devotion.

[2] On rare occasions a candidate does not obtain the necessary absolute majority of those entitled to vote. The election is then declared invalid, and fresh nominations are made. The total number of negative votes reported officially for recent Soviet of the Union elections was 247,897 in 1954; 580,641 in 1958; and 746,563 in 1962. In the same years it was 187,357; 363,736; and 464,115 for the Soviet of Nationalities.

3   THE SUPREME SOVIET

The auditorium in which the Supreme Soviet meets (for the two chambers often sit together to elect officials, to listen to speeches, or to discuss proposals), like the rooms in which the British House of Commons and the French National Assembly meet, indicates something of the spirit in which the work is done. In the House of Commons, the rows of benches facing each other imply that there will always be two opposing groups, while the smallness of the chamber makes it easy to carry on discussion and to engage in a running debate marked by easy and informal participation from all parts of the room. In the French National Assembly, the fanlike arrangement of the amphitheater encourages the deputies to range themselves from left to right according to their political ideas. But the auditorium in which the Supreme Soviet meets allows no such differentiation. It is a large hall with many rows of desks and chairs. There is no sweep from left to right as in France; and there are no distinctive places for supporters or opponents of the government as in Great Britain. The members constitute a solid mass, as is appropriate in a country in which there is but one party and in which all delegates are assumed to be supporters of the government. Moreover, the delegates sit as an audience, ready to listen to and applaud the statements made by their leaders from the platform, not as an active group of legislators who may rise informally in their places to catch the eye of the presiding officer and take part in the debate.

That their function is to listen rather than debate is apparent from the infrequency and brevity of the meetings. There are usually only two sessions each year. More significant is the fact that the sessions never last longer than twelve days, while the average period is five days. The British, American, French, and German legislatures, in contrast, sit about two hundred days a year and then can barely get through their work.

In the Soviet Union, however, deputies are expected to spend most of their time in their home districts, carrying on their regular occu-pations. Their function is not to explain the ideas of the people at home to the government, or to keep a careful check on what the government does, but to carry back to their neighbors the information they have received and, hope-fully, to communicate to them something of the enthusiasm aroused in them by participation in the Soviet pageant.

ORGANIZATION AND PROCEDURE

The Supreme Soviet is elected for four years, as we have seen, both houses at the same time. The Soviet of the Union has one member for each 300,000 of the population; the Soviet of Nationalities has 25 for each union republic, 11 for each autonomous republic, 5 for each autonomous region, and 1 for each national area. The total number of deputies in 1970 was 1,517 (767 in the Soviet of the Union and 750 in the Soviet of Nationalities). Much of the time the two houses meet together, but this is optional. Laws are passed by a simple majority in each house and constitutional amendments by a two-thirds majority. Elaborate provisions exist in case the houses disagree, but, of course, they never do.

The first order of business is to ratify the slates of candidates for office that have been prepared by the central organs of the party. Each house has its own chairman (in 1970, a new one in each case: Aleksei P. Shitikov, party chief of a Far East region, in the Soviet of the Union; and a woman, President Yadgar S. Nasriddinova of the Uzbek Republic, in the So-viet of Nationalities) and four deputy chair-men. Thereafter, the Supreme Soviet approves the thirty-three man Presidium, which holds office until the next Supreme Soviet is elected. Moreover, at the beginning of the sessions of a Supreme Soviet, the Council of Ministers of the USSR tenders its resignation, but, natu-rally, the proposed slate of names is approved.

Since August 1966, there have also been ten standing committees: for legislative proposals, for foreign affairs, as before, for mandates, and seven for economic questions, including the plan and budget. These committees are working bodies and undertake what scrutiny is made of government policies. Each committee has between thirty-one and fifty-one members. The Plan and Budget Committee is the largest. But since the scrutiny of the 1966–70 plan did not take place until December 1966 and of the 1971–75 plan until the end of 1971, it is questionable how much influence such parliamentary review can have, despite the protests that gave rise to this tentative effort at control (see Chapter 6, Section 3).

In the course of its brief sessions, the Supreme Soviet takes up pending legislation and the budget, hears a report on the activities and plans of the government for which special publicity is desired, and cheers its leaders enthusiastically. The greatest part of its very limited allotment of time is reserved for the budget; its provisions are explained by both the Minister of Finance and the members of the Supreme Soviet's own budgetary committee, who have somewhat more information at their command than the other members of the Supreme Soviet. When one realizes, however, that the Soviet budget takes in the entire economic life of the country, it is apparent that giving it the greatest proportion of time means only that the deputies are allowed a rapid (and not very revealing) look at the most important developments in store for their country. Moreover, the only criticisms that are ever uttered within the Supreme Soviet are about the workings of certain ministries that have not fulfilled their quotas or have an unusually high cost of production, and these criticisms quite obviously emanate from the government itself.

Education and inspiration

One of the obvious purposes of the meetings of the Supreme Soviet is to inspire the delegates and to educate both them and their constitu-

ents. In addition to impressing those who attend from afar, the sessions provide an excellent forum from which the party leaders can address not only the delegates but the entire country. The press and the radio report faithfully and at length the speeches, the plans, and the discussion. During meetings of the Supreme Soviet the attention of the whole country is centered upon it, and certain of the plans and purposes of the government in this way become familiar to the entire nation.

Education in this sense, of course, is very different from the education at which Western parliaments aim. It is like Her Majesty's "Gracious Speech" in Great Britain—with the discussion and debate cut off. It is not "education" in that the public is informed of a particular program through the clash—in debate—of its pros and cons. Rather it is a set of authoritative pronouncements that aim at publicizing the details of a program to which all citizens are expected to give joyful and unanimous support.

THE PRESIDIUM

If the Supreme Soviet does not perform the lawmaking function in the Soviet Union, what body does? Its Presidium,[3] which functions as a collective executive under a chairman who serves as the nominal head of state, may exercise all the powers of the Supreme Soviet. Far more, in fact, is put into effect through the edicts and decrees of the Presidium than through the relatively small number of laws passed so perfunctorily by the Supreme Soviet. Yet, if one looks more deeply, it is clear that the Presidium, like the Supreme Soviet, is in turn subordinate to other agencies: the Council of Ministers and, still more, the Politburo and Secretariat.

[3] The Presidium has thirty-three members: fifteen vice-chairmen, who are the chairmen of the Supreme Soviets of the fifteen constituent republics; sixteen other members; and the secretary and chairman.

5

Soviet political leadership

1 THE STABILITY OF SOVIET LEADERSHIP

The most striking and probably the most significant characteristic of Soviet political leadership has been its stability. This may be a startling statement in the light of Stalin's "great purges" and, until recently, the continuous changes in party membership that have commonly made the number of recruits greater than that of full members. But these changes at the lower levels, coupled with the vast holocaust of the late 1930s, tend to conceal the fact that top political leadership in the Soviet Union has changed remarkably infrequently and, since Stalin shaped the character of the country, only in ways that have ameliorated the harshest features of the system: nationality deportations, mass terror, arbitrary imprisonment, and forced labor. Compared to the United States, United Kingdom, and France, the Soviet Union has had an incredibly small number of top leaders in its more than fifty years of existence.

The most significant example of this stability is that in the whole course of Soviet history only three men have held the top office in the ruling Communist party: Stalin, Khrushchev, and Brezhnev.[1] There has been no change in nineteen out of twenty members of the most important organ of the country, the Politburo,

since Khrushchev's ouster, except to raise three of the candidate members to full membership in April 1971. Moreover, as the chart in Chapter 3, Section 4, demonstrates, about one-half of its total membership held their positions well before 1964. There have only been eight premiers, including Kosygin, four of whom are alive today. Of the seven heads of state, including Podgorny, five are still alive and members of the Central Committee. Moreover, a very considerable number of those holding ministerial posts have occupied them for remarkably long periods of time: the Minister of the Food Industry since 1938; the ministers of Nonferrous Metallurgy and of Fisheries since 1940; D. F. Ustinov, who is now a member of both the Politburo and the Secretariat, has dealt with the sensitive area of the defense industries since 1941; the Minister of Heavy Machine Building since 1945; the ministers of Transport and of Communications since 1948; and there are others whose service has been continuous from the Stalin period. Andrei Gromyko was first appointed an ambassador in 1943 and Foreign Secretary in 1957. Timor Szamuely also points out that at the highly important territorial and regional levels of the RSFSR, the seventy-six first secretaries had held their posts in 1969 for an average of six years, that is, antedating the Khrushchev dismissal.[2]

---

[1] Lenin, as chairman of the Council of People's Commissars, dominated the party as well as the government machinery, but the party had not reached its full power during his active life. Malenkov's ten days in the top party office in 1953 were too temporary to rank.

[2] Timor Szamuely, "Five Years After Khrushchev," *Survey* (Summer 1969), pp. 51–69.

Succession in the Soviet Leadership Since 1917

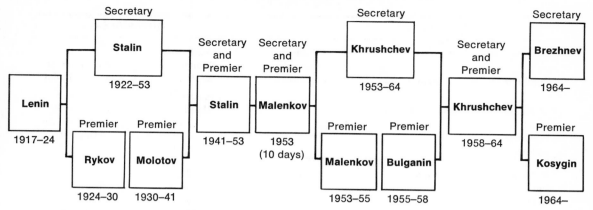

The title assumed by the key member of the Secretariat has varied from Secretary-General to First Secretary to General Secretary but the significance of the office noted on the chart simply as Secretary has remained constant.

This degree of stability within a complex but highly monistic system indicates a remarkable correspondence between leadership and structure. Lenin's role, while indispensable for his period, was unique. Under Stalin, and to a much lesser extent under Khrushchev after 1957, the structure reached its apex in personal leadership. Since 1964, collective leadership has operated in a somewhat cumbersome but, on the whole, effective manner in reaching decisions and providing overall direction for the regime.

2   THE INTERLOCKING DIRECTORATE OF PARTY AND STATE

The Politburo, already described in Chapter 3, includes not only party but also government leaders and, in addition, the head of the security service and the head of the organization of trade unions, which provides an important "driving belt" of the party that will be described in Chapter 6. The Politburo is indisputably the key organ in the country. It provides the supreme example of interlocking directorates of party, state, and society. That we know less about its actual operations than those of the party and state organs subject to its top leadership is in the nature of supreme policy-making.

While the Politburo hammers out decisions on policy, these are implemented through the mechanisms of the party, as already described, and of the government. Within the Soviet government, the most important agency for planning and coordinating policy and for formulating and implementing the structure of laws that legitimate action is the Council of Minis-

ters. Although in theory the council is "elected" by the Supreme Soviet, the latter gives automatic approval, as we have seen, to whatever list of members is decided upon by the top leaders. And while it is quite clear that the Supreme Soviet will accept any decision made by the Council of Ministers, it is equally clear that the council is too large a body for effective discussions and decision-making. Its nearly a hundred members include fifty-five ministers, fourteen heads of departments at ministerial level, and fifteen chairmen of councils of ministers of the constituent republics. Thus, in turn, it accepts the overall coordination and direction of its own Presidium, which consists officially of its chairman, Kosygin, its two first deputy chairmen, K. T. Mazurov and D. S. Polyansky—all three of whom are among the fifteen full members of the Politburo—and the nine deputy chairmen. Along with the host of others who are in charge of different aspects of the economy, these latter figures head vast ad-

Interlocking Directorate of Party and Government Since the Twenty-fourth Party Congress
(MARCH–APRIL 1971)

PARTY			GOVERNMENT	
Politburo *	Secretariat	Party Control Committee	Presidium of Council of Ministers	Presidium of Supreme Soviet †
			Premier and Chairman	Chairman (Ceremonial Head of State)
Full Members	General Secretary			
Brezhnev	Brezhnev			Podgorny
Podgorny				
Kosygin			Kosygin	
Suslov	Suslov			
Kirilenko	Kirilenko			
Pel'she		Chairman Pel'she	First Deputy Premiers	
Mazurov			Mazurov	
Polyansky			Polyansky	
Shelest				
Voronov	Kapitonov			
Shelepin	Ponomarev			
Grishin	Katushev			
Kunayev	Solomentsev			
Scherbitsky				
Kulakov	Kulakov			
Candidate Members				
Andropov				
Demichev	Demichev			
Masherov				
Mzhavanadze				
Rashidov				
Ustinov	Ustinov			

* The first five have formed, since October 1964, what has been called the inner cabinet of the Politburo. The order of the full members of the Politburo is as given by Brezhnev in his final speech to the Congress.

† All members and candidate members of the Politburo are either officials or deputies of the Supreme Soviet.

ministrative structures and interact through these structures with the parallel organization of the party.

Some of the difficulties of these interactions between party and state organs at every level have already been suggested in Chapter 3. The background to the current situation is suggestive. In the period before World War II, the parallel structure on the government side, which acted as a coordinator for the whole economy up to the mid-1930s, was the Supreme Economic Council, attached to the Council of People's Commissars and chaired by V. M. Molotov. Thereafter, its responsibilities were divided among separate industrial ministries. The party Secretariat under Malenkov and A. A. Andreev

had responsibilities for the whole economy, and probably only Stalin's overall decision-making kept these structures from bitter conflict. During the war such divisions and competitions were abolished, and the State Committee of Defense, directly under Stalin himself, undertook complete, unified authority over all organizations of the country: state, party, and military. After the war this committee was in turn abolished, but Stalin remained Chairman of the Council of People's Commissars (renamed Council of Ministers in 1946) as well as General Secretary of the party. With his personal power enforced through both structures and through the political police, Stalin tended to downgrade the party, to emphasize the ministerial bureaucracy, and to issue legislative enactments through the Council of Ministers. Friction and considerable slackness marked the lower levels of the party and government structures, both of which tended to await decision from above.

In 1948, Malenkov resumed control of the party Apparatus. Its subsequent reorganization established a number of departments for different branches of industry, which, with modifications (and a slight hiatus during Khrushchev's reorganizations of 1962–64), have continued to form an important part of the central Apparatus. The rapid recovery of heavy industry in the next few years may be attributed in considerable measure to the forceful party direction exercised through these mechanisms. Agriculture was a different story. Efforts to increase party control were furthered by the machine tractor stations and subsequently by the amalgamation of collective farms into a smaller number of larger units, in which party units could more easily be organized. But production levels remained unsatisfactory.

At the 1952 All-Union Congress, a radical change was instituted in the top organs of power. The Politburo and Orgburo (previously concerned with party organization) were abolished and replaced by a greatly enlarged Presidium of twenty-five full members and eleven candidate members who, between them, included the top personnel of both party and state: ten secretaries and a number of region and republic party leaders, along with thirteen vice-chairmen of the Council of Ministers and the ministers of State Security and Foreign Affairs. So large was the new group that a smaller but secret bureau was set up whose existence was only revealed after Stalin's death, and whose membership has never been announced.

After Stalin's death it became common practice to legislate by joint decree of the Central Committee and the Council of Ministers. But in practice the authority of the latter body steadily diminished as party control was strengthened. While the business of administration was largely left to the state machinery, coordination and control were firmly in the hands of the party bureaucracy. In April 1958, after his successful ouster of Malenkov and others from the Presidium (see Chapter 3, Section 4), Khru-

shchev formally assumed the top position in the government machinery and added the title of premier to that of First Secretary. It placed a seal on his policy of asserting party primacy.

Already in 1957, Khrushchev had replaced the ministerial system by the *sovnarkhozes* (councils of national economy). His motives appear to have been three-fold: to improve the efficiency of industrial direction; to weaken the influence of the "antiparty" group, over which he triumphed the following year; and to strengthen his own supporters in the territorial party organization by extending their power. But the first and third of these objectives proved incompatible. By setting up a *sovnarkhoz* in almost every oblast of the RSFSR and Ukraine, Khrushchev had designated too small an economic unit for efficiency, while the party secretaries of these units were too inexperienced to direct industry. Moreover, combining the handling of industry and agriculture (still the most unsatisfactory section of the economy) proved unsatisfactory. Coupled with the pressing need to bring younger party members into positions of authority, these disturbing effects of the 1957 reorganization gave rise in 1961 and 1962 to further reorganizations of both industrial direction and party control.

The hundred-odd *sovnarkhozes* were replaced in 1961 by thirty-one, each remaining under an industrial director, and single overall councils were approved late in 1962 to further their supervision. The more significant reorganization, however, was the bifurcation in 1962 of the party apparatus at all levels except the very top into industrial and agricultural branches. The immediate result at the oblast level (where the party committee is known as obkom) was to double the number of obkom first secretaries in the sixty-one oblasts where this division took place. Thus, while the number of *sovnarkhozes* was much diminished, the number of obkoms was considerably increased, resulting in a situation in which there was an average of nearly five first secretaries, two of them industrial obkom first secretaries, to each *sovnarkhoz* director. Moreover, the great majority of the industrial first secretaries were new, for only fifteen of the former first secretaries became secretaries of industrial obkoms. All except one of these latter secretaries had received training in technical higher schools, commonly as engineers.

By so enlarging the number of obkom first secretaries, Khrushchev was enabled to bring into important party roles at the obkom level a large number of younger men, without dismissing those already in these posts. The first secretaries of the nineteen obkoms that were not divided remained in their positions. Of those whose obkoms were divided, the forty who had more limited education but training and experience with party and farming became first secretaries of agricultural obkoms. The new entries, therefore, were mainly at the industrial level.

John A. Armstrong hypothesizes that Khrushchev planned a further reorganization that would have enlarged the area of the oblasts to correspond to that of the *sovnarkhozes*.[3] Such a development would have had the effect of removing a very considerable number of the "old" first secretaries who had become agricultural secretaries. It seems possible that fear of such a "purge" either caused or facilitated Khrushchev's removal in October 1964.[4] At least within two months of his removal the obkoms were reunified and, with few exceptions, under the original first secretaries. Ten months later, the *sovnarkhoz* system was replaced with central ministries. But the price of renewed party stability under Brezhnev and Kosygin

may well have been reduced industrial efficiency.

The post-Khrushchev leadership has been distinguished, as already emphasized, by a party-state duality within the Politburo that stretches down through the two hierarchies. In this dual system, the party maintains its primacy but in a less dominating fashion than in most earlier eras. Also, increasingly, as George Fischer has pointed out in *The Soviet System and Modern Society*, the mixture of political and technological training and experience of an increasing number of officials provides a new kind of interaction between those concerned with the operations of the economy and those who check and direct from outside, whether through state administrative channels or those of the party. Collective leadership at the top and constant interaction all the way down to the enterprise and local unit levels have a common purpose —the steady increase of production, particularly still in heavy and defense industries. Thus it appears that differences are over means rather than ends, and it is possible that the edges of personal rivalries are being at least blunted by the continuousness of discussions and the relative slowness of ultimate decision-making. Alternatively, it is possible, although less likely, that such slowness is giving rise to serious tensions among those eager to press ahead along new scientific and technological lines, or that the patient masses are becoming less so.

3   CAREER PATTERNS OF SOVIET LEADERS

The three outstanding leaders in the Soviet Union prior to 1964 were clearly Lenin, Stalin, and Khrushchev. Each had a distinctive career pattern that will be briefly mentioned as a background to the careers of contemporary leaders. Lenin, of course, acquired his importance before the Bolsheviks seized power; only for a short time was he the dominant figure in the direction of the Soviet Union. We have already seen the powerful influence he exercised —and still exercises—in ideology, strategy, and legend.

Stalin also began his career before the revolution. Although an active figure in the revolutionary movement after his expulsion from the theological seminary where he was a student, Stalin was far less well known when the Bolsheviks came to power than were many other leaders, like Trotsky. He acquired his ultimately dominant position, as we have seen, first through holding all the threads of party organization in his hands as Secretary General, and exploiting these bureaucratic possibilities,

[3] John A. Armstrong, "Party Bifurcation and Elite Interests," *Soviet Studies* (April 1966), pp. 424–27.

[4] Jeremy R. Azrael believes the original bifurcation in 1962 had "dealt the entire party apparat a potentially crippling blow." (*Managerial Power and Soviet Politics,* p. 146.)

and thereafter by using the most ruthless methods of control both to shape the Soviet Union into its modern form and to provide himself with unparalleled personal power.

Khrushchev did not join the Communists until after the Bolshevik Revolution, but he fought throughout the Civil War and subsequently enrolled in the Doniets Mining Technical School, one of the special workers' schools set up to train Communist cadres in "socialist construction." Immediately on his graduation, Khrushchev became party secretary in the Doniets Basin and a delegate to the All-Ukrainian and All-Union Party congresses (the latter was the scene of the bitter struggle over Stalin's concentration of power that ended in the latter's triumph). In 1929, Khrushchev was brought to Moscow, where his rise was meteoric. From being first secretary to one of the ten Moscow districts in 1931, he moved by stages to become a full member of the Politburo by 1939. In the meantime he had returned to the Ukraine in January 1938 to direct the purge of most of its top party and government officials. He remained party head of the Ukraine for a decade (from 1944 to 1947 he was also head of the Ukrainian government), directed the political assimilation of the western Ukraine when the Red Army invaded east Poland following the Soviet-German Pact of 1939, and headed the "purification" of the Ukraine after the Nazi forces were driven out. In this area he ruthlessly exercised a type of power possessed by no one else in the country except Stalin and Lavrenti Beria, head of the secret police.

In 1949, Khrushchev returned to Moscow as first secretary of the Moscow region and, still more important, as one of the secretaries of the Central Committee, with special responsibilities for agriculture. From this time on, Khrushchev's chief rival for power in the party was Malenkov, a rivalry not settled until the latter was expelled from the Presidium and Central Committee in June 1957. Only then was Khrushchev's own top position assured, although he had become head of the Secretariat in 1953.

The transition to the new leaders in 1964 was both much quicker and much smoother, involving none of the open rivalries for power that marked the period from 1953 to 1957. Since, as far as one can tell, the leadership has been genuinely collective, it is necessary to indicate some aspects of career patterns for more than the top figures generally singled out—Brezhnev and Kosygin. Since these two head respectively the party and the government hierarchies, however, their career patterns will be the first to be described.

Leonid Brezhnev has had an unusually long but interrupted career in top party positions. He was in the central Secretariat from 1952 to May 1960 (when he was shifted to Chairman of the Presidium of the Supreme Soviet) and then continuously from June 1963. He also became a candidate member of the Party Presidium in 1952, was dropped in 1953 after Stalin's death but reestablished in February 1956, and became a full member in June 1957. Immediately on Khrushchev's ouster, Brezhnev became First (now General) Secretary of the party. Trained in a metallurgical institute in the Ukraine, where he was born in 1906 of Russian parents, Brezhnev began work as an engineer in 1935 in an iron and steel works and is thus one of the technically trained members of the Politburo. His first post was as early as 1937 when he became deputy chairman of a city soviet. After several years as party official in the Ukraine, where his work attracted Khrushchev's favorable notice, Brezhnev became republic first secretary in Moldavia. From there he moved to Moscow for a fairly rapid if irregular rise to the top party office.

Alexei N. Kosygin, who is two years older than Brezhnev, has had still wider experience, although less in party posts. A graduate of the Leningrad Textile Institute in 1935, he became both director of a factory and member of a district party bureau in 1937. A year later he became head of the industrial-transport section of the party in Leningrad and mayor the same year. Premier of the RSFSR from 1943 to 1946, he became a candidate member of the Politburo in 1946 and a full member in 1948. He was then returned to candidate membership from 1952 to 1953 and again in 1957. His substantial service in economic ministries included the post of USSR Minister of Light Industry. In March 1959, he became head of the Gosplan (State Planning Commission). In May 1960, Kosygin became a full member of the Presidium; and in 1964, after Khrushchev's ouster, head of the government hierarchy.

Among current leaders, Kosygin possesses unparalleled administrative and economic expertise.

A third important Soviet leader, Nikolai Podgorny, left the Secretariat in 1965 to become titular head of the Soviet Union, that is, President, or, more accurately, Chairman of the Presidium of the Supreme Soviet. Podgorny was considered by some authorities to be Brezhnev's rival in 1963 as Khrushchev's ultimate successor and remains one of the key figures in the Politburo. A year older than Kosygin, Podgorny, like Brezhnev, was a product of Khrushchev's Ukrainian party machine. Deputy commissar for the Ukrainian food industry from 1939 to 1940, he returned to that post after four years in the same field in Moscow and, subsequently, from 1946 to 1950 acted as representative in Moscow for the Ukrainian government. From then on he rose quickly in party offices from first secretary of Kharkov province in 1950 to second secretary of the Ukraine in 1953 and first secretary in 1957. Candidate member of the Presidium in May 1958, he became a full member in May 1960. Podgorny also became a secretary of the Central Committee in June 1963 but, as we have seen, only for a brief time. He had early experience as an engineer in Ukrainian sugar factories from 1931 to 1937 and has claimed a role in economic management since becoming president.

Yet another significant figure is Mikhail Suslov, who has been a member of the Secretariat since March 1947, longer than any other person. In that same year he helped Stalin to set up the Comintern (an organization directed by Moscow to stimulate and coordinate international communism). In the Secretariat, Suslov has always been concerned with ideology, propaganda, and agitation, both as head of the Agit-prop Department and of *Pravda*. He is a pillar of orthodoxy. He studied at the Moscow Institute of National Economy and the Industrial Institute and assumed a leading role in the brutal purges of Caucasian nationalists, the deportation of the Karachai nation for collaboration with the Germans, and the ruthless reimposition of Soviet rule in Lithuania at the end of the war. He was briefly a member of the Presidium from October 1952 to March 1953, but there was a gap until he became a full member in July 1955. Apparently one of Khrushchev's major opponents at a much earlier date, Suslov presented the main indictment against him in October 1964 in the Central Committee. Although in 1971, at age sixty-nine, he is the second oldest member of the Politburo (Pel'she is seventy-two), Suslov is still a figure to reckon with inside the collective leadership.

The fifth figure generally indicated as in the inner councils of the Politburo is A. P. Kirilenko, another man who served in Khrushchev's Ukrainian machine and one whose career has paralleled that of Brezhnev to a striking degree. Born in the same year, they both joined the party in 1931, received engineering training and experience in their twenties, and were plummeted into party activities in their thirties as a result of Stalin's purge in their area. Both undertook party work in the army during the fighting in World War II and then returned to party offices. The two served together (with Brezhnev the senior) as first and second secretaries in a Ukrainian region until both became first secretaries in different regions in 1947. When Brezhnev went to Moldavia and subsequently to Moscow, however, he moved ahead of Kirilenko, who stayed as a regional first secretary until 1955, then was moved by Khrushchev to the Urals and became a candidate member of the Presidium in 1957 and a full member in 1960. Ousted from the latter in 1961, Kirilenko regained his ground in 1962 when he became Khrushchev's deputy in the Russian Bureau of the Central Committee and again a full member of the Presidium.

What is obviously common to four of these five men is that they served their apprenticeships in Khrushchev's Ukrainian machine, and that their advancement owed him much. These facts did not stand in the way of their quiet putsch against him. Another common feature for all of them is their age, ranging from sixty-five to sixty-nine in 1971. This latter fact leads many commentators to single out also the younger members of the Politburo—Shelepin, Polyansky, and Mazurov—all of whom are in their fifties.

Dmitri Polyansky is an ethnic Ukrainian, who worked in its party machine after graduating from the Kharkov Agricultural Institute. From 1939 to 1940, he worked in the Komsomol, then in the provincial apparatus, and from 1945 to 1949 he was in charge of the personnel department in the Central Committee. Subsequently, he was progressively first secretary of two regional committees and one territorial committee. In 1958, he was appointed head of the government of the Russian Republic and then a member of the USSR government. Polyansky was thirty-eight when he first entered the Central Committee in 1956 but rose rapidly to become a full member of the Presidium in 1960, at the same time as Kosygin and Podgorny. He has been a consistent advocate of more capital investment in agriculture and is generally popular with the masses, especially the farmers, and with the Apparatus.

Kiril Mazurov, an ethnic Byelorussian, shares with Polyansky the role of First Deputy Chairman of the Council of Ministers immediately under Kosygin. Mazurov graduated from a road engineering institute (spending three years thereafter as a road engineer) and was trained by correspondence at the Moscow Higher Party School. He is thought to be one of the subgroup, including Shelepin, Pel'she, Voronov, and Suslov, least skilled in production matters. From age twenty-four he served as a party official, and during much of the war he was with partisans behind the German lines. From 1953 to 1956, he held the top government office in Byelorussia, and from 1956 to 1965 was that republic's first secretary. He became a candidate member of the Presidium in 1957 when Khrushchev ousted the antiparty group and a full member of the Politburo in 1965.

The largest number of questions have been raised regarding Alexander Shelepin, whom many observers have picked as ultimately the most likely top person in the party. He too was born in the Ukraine but is Russian, studied at the Moscow Institute of History, Philosophy and Literature (the only Politburo member to have a primarily nontechnical higher education), saw service in the Soviet-Finnish war, and was assigned in 1940 to work in the Komsomol. Here he rose quickly with Stalin's approval to become a secretary of its central committee from 1943 to 1952 and subsequently first secretary until 1956. In 1954, he helped to mobilize nearly half a million Komsomol members to settle in the virgin lands of central Asia, one of Khrushchev's high priority projects.

Thereafter, his rise in central offices was meteoric. In 1956, Shelepin became head of the party organs department of the Central Committee, a post with high potential for power, and two years later head of the KGB, the security service. In October 1961, he became one of the secretaries; in the autumn of 1962 he became head of Khrushchev's powerful new Party-State Control Committee, and subsequently he was appointed vice-premier, the only man other than Khrushchev himself to hold high rank in both party and state at the USSR level. Contrary to expectations, however, Shelepin did not acquire Politburo membership until October 1964, immediately after Khrushchev's ouster (in which he is believed to have played a key role). Shelepin suffered what were considered career setbacks when the Party-State Control Committee was disbanded in 1965 and even more when he was relieved of his post in the Secretariat in July 1967 and appointed head of the All-Union Central Council of Trade Unions. But Shelepin retains his position in the Politburo, where he is said to favor tough policies both at home and abroad.

Of the three other full members of the Politburo, up to April 1971, A. Yuri Pel'she, first secretary of Latvia since 1959 and head of the Party Control Committee, is a party veteran but is too old to be considered for more than his experience and Baltic representation. Pyotr Y. Shelest, who did not get into the Central Committee until 1961, is an ethnic Ukrainian with a plant-engineer's experience who rose rapidly from being a regional second secretary in 1957 to become Podgorny's successor as first secretary in the Ukraine in 1963 and a candidate member of the Presidium. From this rank he was elevated to be a full member in November 1964. His number of speeches to party plenums was second only to those of Brezhnev from the fall of Khrushchev to July 15, 1968.[5] Genadi Voronov, born in the Urals and a graduate of an industrial institute in Tomsk in Siberia (with earlier work experience as an electrician) and of the Institute of Marxism-Leninism in Novosibirsk, served as party official in Siberia and the Far East until appointed Deputy Minister of Agriculture by Khrushchev in 1955,

[5] Frederick C. Barghoorn, "Trends in Top Political Leadership in USSR," *Political Leadership in Eastern Europe and the Soviet Union,* ed. by R. Barry Farrell, p. 69.

with particular responsibilities for the latter's project of settling and developing virgin lands. From 1957 to 1961, he was first secretary for the Orenburg regional party committee, from where Khrushchev brought him to Moscow as a candidate and, almost immediately, a full member of the Presidium. He subsequently also became first vice-chairman of the bureau of the RSFSR and premier of the Russian Federal Republic, a post he still holds. His age falls between those of the younger and the older Politburo members, and his long party experience makes him a useful Politburo member.

The four additions to the full members of the Politburo include three former candidate members and one, F. D. Kulakov, who came direct from the Secretariat. V. V. Grishin, who became a full member of the Politburo in April 1971, after being a candidate member since January 1961, had been a full member of the Central Committee since 1952 and formerly chairman of the Central Council of Trade Unions. He is head of the Moscow city party organization. V. V. Scherbitsky and D. A. Kunayev, also formerly candidate members, had both received promotion under Brezhnev when they were serving in the Ukraine and Kazakhstan, respectively. Scherbitsky was prime minister of the Ukraine and Kunayev was first secretary of the party in Kazakhstan when they became full members of the Politburo. F. D. Kulakov has had particular responsibility for agriculture within the Secretariat. He took a correspondence degree in agriculture, and he served previously as party secretary in agricultural regions and as Deputy Minister of Agriculture.

Two candidate members of the Politburo are on the Secretariat: P. N. Demichev, who added the former office in November 1964 to the latter which he had acquired in October 1961; and D. F. Ustinov, who acquired both posts in March 1965. Trained as a chemical engineer, Demichev is looked on as an ideological specialist and liaison with the intellectual and artistic community. Ustinov, who is also a trained engineer with much of his experience in the munitions industry, has had most of his other experience in government rather than the party.

The four members of the Secretariat, apart from those serving in the Politburo—that is,

apart from Brezhnev, Kirilenko, Suslov, Kulakov, Demichev, and Ustinov—are also close to the administrative levers of power. Apart from B. N. Ponomarev, said to be "an ideological, foreign affairs, and historical specialist" [6] who is one year older than Brezhnev, those not in the Politburo are, on the average, younger, ranging from M. S. Solomentsev (fifty-eight in 1971) to K. F. Katushev (forty-four in 1971). M. S. Solomentsev, with his extensive experience as party secretary and as an engineer, is the chief heavy industry specialist on the Secretariat and the embodiment of Fischer's dual executive (see Chapter 3, Section 4). Barghoorn pays particular attention to K. F. Katushev because of his youth in a group otherwise exclusively in their fifties and sixties. Ethnically Russian, he is a graduate of Gorki Polytechnic Institute, with experience in the construction industry and subsequently as party secretary first in industrial plants and then as first secretary of the Gorki city party committee. Katushev thus qualifies as a dual or at least hybrid executive. Sponsored by Brezhnev, he achieved the Central Committee in 1966 and the Secretariat in 1968. He has been reported as concerned with Eastern European affairs, but his particular field of competence is the production of passenger automobiles, said to be a new line of leadership concern.

There are various other ways of grouping these men. All five secretaries who are not in the Politburo as full or candidate members appear to be Russian. Six of the full members of the Politburo—Brezhnev, Kirilenko, Kosygin, Shelepin, Voronov, and Grishin—are also Russian, as are three of the candidate members: Demichev, Ustinov, and Y. V. Andropov, head of the KGB. Non-Russians figure quite largely, although only rarely, as perhaps with Pel'she, can they be thought of as nationality representatives. Podgorny, Polyansky, Shelest, and V. V. Scherbitsky are Ukrainian; Mazurov, Byelorussian; Pel'she, Latvian; D. A. Kunayev, Kazakh; S. R. Rashidov, Uzbek; and V. P. Mzhavanadze, Georgian.

Fischer lists among his 360 executives [7] all

[6] Barghoorn, "Trends in Top Political Leadership in USSR," *Political Leadership in Eastern Europe and the Soviet Union*, p. 82.

[7] George Fischer, *The Soviet System and Modern Society*, pp. 185–92.

those mentioned above except Kosygin, Voronov, Scherbitsky, and Katushev. Only two—Solomentsev and Shelest—or possibly three, with Katushev, fall directly into his dual executive category. Four are in the hybrid executive group: Kirilenko, Polyansky, Demichev, and I. V. Kapitonov. Brezhnev himself, and Podgorny, Kunayev, Ustinov, and Kulakov are in the technician category; Mazurov, Pel'she, Shelepin, Suslov, Grishin, P. M. Masherov, Mzhavanadze, Rashidov, and Ponomarev are in the list of officials. Thus the latter category decisively predominates on the overall count, but it is more significant that in the Secretariat only the two oldest—Suslov and Ponomarev—rank as officials, one—or possibly two, with Katushev—rank as dual executives, three as hybrid executives, and three as technicians.

4   POLITICAL SUCCESSION IN THE USSR

Characteristic of states like the USSR that do not operate in accordance with fixed constitutional rules is the lack of an assured mechanism for transferring authority from one ruler, or set of rulers, to another. Thus the succession may give rise, as after the deaths of Lenin and Stalin, to a period of crisis in which there is no assurance that the men who appear likely to become the next possessors of supreme power will do so. Thus Trotsky was outmaneuvered by Stalin, and Malenkov by Khrushchev, but only after substantial periods of infighting. The succession after Khrushchev was, in contrast, remarkably smooth, since by far the major portion of those in high roles under his aegis continued in office, merely replacing his predominant power with their own collective weight.

Aiding the transition in 1964, of course, was the fact that despite his bombastic appearances, Khrushchev never approached the authority of either Lenin or Stalin and, in practice, was always limited in the power he was able to exercise. Thus the shift to the Politburo and collective leadership was far less of a radical change in the exercise of top authority than was the transition from Stalin's personal power to the limited spheres of action within which any single leader has been able to operate since his death. Even if Brezhnev (or someone else) emerges decisively as much more than the first among equals, it is hardly to be expected that, without a vast resurgence of political police activity on his behalf, his authority will be uncircumscribed. Barring the other possibility of an all-out war, no other man seems likely to acquire the power that flowed from Lenin's ideological primacy or Stalin's personal ruthlessness in the period in which the Soviet Union was forcibly shaped into its present form.

That some fortunes will rise and fall is inevitable. Much was made of the fact that in September 1970 the powerful, ruthless, and ambitious first secretary of Leningrad, Vassili S. Tolstikov, one of Fischer's dual executives, was posted to Peking as ambassador, thereby removing the man believed by some observers to be Brezhnev's most formidable rival. Kremlinologists watch closely the order of precedence at official functions and count the number of speeches made by particular leaders. But it would be surprising if the most decisive contests for influence and determination of policies were not carried on in secret or if we learn the results only when some laconic announcement is made or, as in October 1964, when the immense photograph of the most prominent figure is quietly removed from the streets.

5   ISSUES DIVIDING THE TOP LEADERSHIP

However successful the top Soviet leadership has been in maintaining the forms of collective leadership since Khrushchev's removal, it has long been apparent that there are serious differences of opinion on significant issues, as there had been in the Politburo under Khrushchev. It is commonly believed that these differences led to the postponement of the Twenty-fourth Party Congress from 1970 to the end of March 1971 and to the associated delay in announcing the details of the Five-Year Plan for 1971–75. These differences appear to revolve around the following issues: priorities in the allocation of resources; economic reforms; the issue of Stalin and Stalinism; and the relation of party and state organs.[8]

Since Khrushchev's ouster, there have been changes in all these fields. His division of the party Apparatus into industrial and agricultural cadres had met complaints from both sides: from the older party stalwarts who feared the competition of younger, more technologically trained party officials, and from the state, which feared the dominance of such expert party officials. By November 1964, the change had been abolished. The post-Khrushchev leadership also moved, as we have seen, to a limited rehabilitation of Stalin and adopted some of the features of Stalinism in the harsh treatment of intellectuals. Khrushchev's organization of economic planning and management was in general reversed in the interests of bureaucratic centralization. The Soviet Union's humiliating backdown over the missile bases in Cuba led to renewed concentration on military power at the expense of the limited emphasis Khrushchev had encouraged for consumption goods.

Yet despite these apparently agreed changes, divisions over policies continued. In 1967, Polyansky publicly attacked the decision to cut back state investment in agriculture below the levels specified in the 1966–70 plan. In the same year, Kosygin, followed naturally by the government organ, *Izvestia*, pressed for more allocation of investment for consumer goods in the 1971–75 plan, while Brezhnev, supported by the military, emphasized the continued needs of heavy industry. The decline in industrial growth in recent years has also led to differences of opinion on whether output should continue to be directed by quotas, or whether prices calculated on the basis of scarcities would not be a more effective stimulus, or, even more important, whether there should be a freer sale of goods regulated by Soviet-style profits.

Debate on a new model Kolkhoz Charter also evidenced differences of opinion. Proponents of a Khrushchev-favored plan advocated assigning land and machinery for long periods of time to small teams, called "links," whose remuneration would be based on unit productivity—a plan experimented with successfully in several places. Opponents feared it might transform the kolkhozes into family-type farms. Despite Voronov's strong support, the plan ultimately was watered down from the original draft to omit the provision for long-term assignments. Proposals to establish a nation-wide kolkhoz authority with decision-making powers or, on a lesser scale, to permit kolkhozes to form "associations and unions" that might bargain over crop delivery quotas elicited only a minor provision whereby a network of kolkhoz chairmen and agricultural specialists would be permitted to make recommendations to the government. That agricultural problems ultimately forced some drastic changes, however, appeared in July 1970 when Brezhnev announced substantial increases in prices to be paid farmers for dairy and meat products (not to be passed on to consumers) and increased capital investment in 1971–75 to almost double that in 1966–70. He also added a defense of the private agricultural production on the small plots of Soviet farmers, which, in practice, produce a high proportion of Soviet consumer needs for meat, milk, and vegetables.

What position to take in regard to Stalin seems still undecided within the Politburo. It appears to be less an issue in itself than a prob-

---

[8] Sidney I. Ploss, "Politics in the Kremlin," *Problems of Communism* (May–June 1970), pp. 1–14.

lem related to the tenor of particular policies. Exposés of the brutalities and excesses of the Stalin period by some writers seem condemned as derogatory to the Soviet Union itself. The harsh reactions to intellectuals who are stamped as dissidents may well be chiefly motivated, however, by fear of focusing known discontents among youth and nationality groups.

In the light of the more or less equal representation of top party and state figures in the Politburo, the issue of party versus state, which is ever present in the Soviet Union, may well be the most fundamental. Complaints have been made by party officials against over-assertive state managers; equally, there have been warnings against "immoderate worship" of the authority of first secretaries.[9] Brezhnev can be expected to stress party authority; Kosygin and Podgorny that of state authorities. It remains to be seen whether the balance tilts in one direction or the other, or remains even.

The monistic system of the Soviet Union throws a far greater number of basic decisions into the hands of a relatively small number of persons than happens in any Western system. The absence of any open organized opposition to challenge these decisions and to publicize mistakes not only walls off the power elite from the masses but also adds the danger that information and views may be based on too limited a sample. To maintain a workable balance within so centralized a system requires great self-restraint on the part of its leaders, flexibility, and an ability to use the efforts of others in a way that contributes to their advantage as well as that of those at the top.

The qualities needed by leaders in the Soviet Union are thus very different from those demanded of Western leaders. They do not need personal charisma or the gifts of winning popularity or convincing public opinion, for their decisive actions are not taken in public, and their reputations can be created by the arts of propaganda. But far more than Western leaders, those in the Soviet Union need understanding of economic processes and of how to maintain their lines of control throughout party and state bureaucracies, the security forces, and the army. Centralization of authority may be simpler on paper, but in practice in a complex, modern system it means an overwhelming number of converging issues, pressures, and possibilities for the top leadership to consider.

6 TITULAR LEADERSHIP

Every political system must make provision for a wide series of ceremonial actions, either through the chief executive, as in the United States, or through an office like the British monarchy, that take much of the burden of ceremony off the shoulders of the top political figure. In the Soviet Union, the office that used to be looked on chiefly as of ceremonial importance is that of the Chairman of the Presidium of the Supreme Soviet, sometimes called the President.

The first holders of this office, Iakov Mikhailovich Sverdlov, Mikhail Kalinen (a sympathetic family figure), Nikolai Shvernik (former head of the Soviet trade unions), and the aged and respected Marshal Voroshilov, could be thought to have acquired this office as a reward for long service. Another figure who fit this pattern was Anastas I. Mikoyan, a veteran political figure who survived long in more significant offices and crowned his career from 1964 to 1965 with this one.

Much more surprising, however, were the appointments to the office of chairman of Brezhnev (thought at the time to be a demotion) and Podgorny in December 1965. It is apparent, therefore, that the office is now regarded as a suitable one for a highly placed political figure, from which he can reach out to operate in whatever field he most desires. At the same time, the office ranks with the top ceremonial positions in other countries. Thus it provides certain useful opportunities for high-level contacts, at the same time that the office receives its own chief distinction from the importance of the particular person who occupies it.

---

[9] Ploss, "Politics in the Kremlin," p. 13.

6

Administration
in the
USSR:
planning and controls

Administration in the Soviet Union has two major purposes that interact with each other: the chief purpose is to preserve the integrity and cohesiveness of centralized political control; the secondary purpose is to promote economic growth, measured primarily in terms of heavy industry directed to its own and to military needs. These two purposes are complementary, since political control of the economy is the vital means of maintaining the centralized monistic system of the Soviet Union, whereas a strong economy is vital to the Soviet Union's position in the world.

The Soviet Union's planned development of its economy is not an outgrowth of Marxist ideology.[1] Nor is Soviet planning a pattern followed exactly by other "socialist" states or by developing societies. It is natural, of course, that the forms and techniques of economic planning in Great Britain and in France are

radically different from those in the Soviet Union, chiefly because of the duality of political and economic structures in the capitalist countries. But the difference is also because in these countries economic planning represents a late stage in governmental activity, superimposed on existing governmental machinery in the effort to counteract some of the distortions of capitalist expansion in a mature economy and to make that economy serve more directly the social needs of the community. It is more surprising to find that countries in Eastern Europe, notably Yugoslavia, but also those within the Soviet bloc, as well as most other developing countries, have modified the Soviet model of economic planning to find other, more flexible means to urge forward their economic growth and maturity.

Although, as we shall indicate, there are unique features to the Soviet Union's administrative planning for economic growth, it is worth noting that, as Alexander Gerschenkron suggests in his book of essays on economic backwardness in historical perspective, there seems a general pattern to the introduction of industrialization in a country suffering from lack of economic development. The more backward the economy, he feels, the more likely it is to start with a spectacular spurt of manufacturing; to stress bigness of plant and enterprise in its industrialization; to concentrate on production rather than consumer goods with a consequent lowering of the consumption levels of the populace; to use coercion to enforce the

[1] Marx wrote against the anarchy of production under capitalism, but he said little about production and distribution under socialism. He had no conception of a group of planners molding economic life in any way comparable to the USSR's State Planning Commission. On the contrary, Marx had faith that society would be gradually transformed by a semideterministic "series of historic processes." When a socialist society was achieved, he believed it would be "organized as a conscious and systematic association" within which the producers themselves "would regulate the exchange of products and place it under their common control instead of allowing it to rule over them as a blind force." But this was no more than a vague idea that once the workers were in control they would organize themselves for the purposes of production and distribution and that they would know instinctively how to undertake these tasks. Marx's utopian "stateless society" is the antithesis of planning.

supply of capital and skills to the nascent industries; and to underplay agricultural productivity as the base for an expanding industrial
market.[2] All these factors are clearly reflected
in Soviet development, despite the fact that
large-scale industry already had a substantial
foothold in Russia before the Bolsheviks seized
power.

The drastic measures of War Communism,
the first Five-Year Plans, and the collectivization of agriculture resulted, however, from the
particular circumstances with which the ruling
groups in the Soviet Union were confronted.
While it was not inevitable that the measures
went to such extremes, with disastrous consequences for large sections of the Russian people—notably the peasants—the basic programs
were probably essential to enable the regime
to maintain its political and economic dominance.

1   THE DEVELOPMENT OF ECONOMIC PLANNING

Drastic measures of nationalization of all resources in the country were taken almost immediately after the Bolsheviks seized power.
Officially, the draconian program was justified
as the means of ending economic inequalities,
but in fact it resulted from the desperate state
of the national economy with its breakdown of
production, collapse of transportation links,
rampant inflation, and burgeoning black market.
The Civil War threw the country into still
worse chaos, leading to the period known as
War Communism, in which the government,
beset by "war and ruin," as Lenin acknowledged, resorted to barter and seizure of produce
despite bitter resistance by the peasants. To the
ravages of civil war, accentuated by foreign intervention and blockade, was added conflict between country and city, the former hoarding
its food, the latter seeking by force to extract
it. By 1921, at the end of the Civil War, industrial production had dropped to 13 percent of
pre-1914 levels, and agriculture was utterly disrupted.

Faced with economic ruin, Lenin made the
compromise known as the New Economic Policy, which stamped the period from 1921 to
1928. Requisitioning of surplus grain ceased,
and peasants were allowed to sell it in a free
competitive market. Heavy industry was retained under centralized state administration
but managed on a commercial basis. Apart from
the approximately 10 percent of industrial enterprises considered vital to the national economy, the rest were given administrative and financial independence or leased to foreign interests. A stabilized currency was instituted in
1923. But at no time was foreign trade freed
from strict government control. Moreover, the
Communist party had not abrogated its overall
national control. Its efforts to establish goals
for the economy (see Section 3), and the prevailing confusion within the mixed economy,
kept up constant tension over policies.

As long as the rebuilding of prewar industry
was the focus of development and the supply
of consumer goods adequate, the potential conflict between the demands of industry and of
agriculture was in abeyance. But as industry demanded larger investment to increase output,
the crucial issue of where to secure the additional funds moved to the fore. At the same
time, the peasants found inadequate supplies
for their purchasing power and reduced their
marketing of grain. The ensuing economic crisis
was still more a political crisis. Failure to provide adequate food for the towns, and the growing, if diffused, power of the peasants challenged the dominant decision-making of the
Soviet regime. It was under the pressure of this
threat, Gerschenkron believes, that Stalin "embarked upon the gamble of the First Five-Year
Plan"[3] (1928).

In the event, what began as limited collectivization catapulted into all-out conflict between the party and the peasants, who were
stubbornly determined to keep the lands they
had seized during the revolution. In the struggle, the peasants lost their land and millions

[2] Alexander Gerschenkron, *Economic Backwardness in Historical Perspective: A Book of Essays*, pp. 353–54.

[3] Gerschenkron, *Economic Backwardness in Historical Perspective*, p. 145.

of them lost their lives. Nearly complete collectivization was achieved. Henceforth, agricultural output could be secured through "compulsory deliveries" without providing a return in consumer goods. In consequence, what might have been a temporary expedient to balance industry and agriculture was turned into a series of Five-Year Plans that launched the country on an intensive and extended period of industrial development. Rigorous controls coupled with modern technology directed to a comparatively limited segment of the economy—heavy industry producing for its own needs and those of the military—achieved spectacular results in developing the national economic power base that Stalin sought. Thus the Soviet Union moved into the ranks of industrial powers. Moreover, the regime had subordinated the only group, the peasants, that might conceivably have forced it to change its policies. Instead the thirties became the period of vast and violent purges, of mass terror, and of the progressive extension of political and ultimately personal control by Stalin over all groups in society, including those involved in the economic process.

2 THE CHARACTER OF SOVIET ECONOMIC PLANNING

The distinctive feature of Soviet economic planning is that central authorities determine the targets for economic units and the means for attaining them. This process means that decisions on production, distribution, and investment are made administratively and passed down through the hierarchy to the individual enterprises. Growth rates are fixed arbitrarily and plans drawn up to achieve them. Estimates generally presuppose favorable conditions.

Under Stalin, economic planning operated in relation to changing goals, which he enunciated, and with relatively little, although increasing, regard to available resources and their distribution. Then, as now, the plan was considered the criterion of performance. Failure to achieve its levels could be a signal for harsh punishment in the Stalin period. Competition for scarce resources often distorted production. It has remained true that standards of measurement for particular products have sometimes led to absurd results, as when measuring the output of nails by weight led to gross exaggeration in their size. In the post-Stalin period, the greater complexity of the economy, coupled with the removal of mass terror, has made for more rational evaluations. It still appears that the retention of centralized administrative planning of economic growth is an inefficient system for maximizing the use of the country's productive resources and meeting the needs of its people. But from the point of view of central political control, it serves its purpose extremely well.

A useful concept for analyzing Soviet economic development is that of "uneven development." The Soviet Union startled the world when it launched the first Sputnik; its space program has remained spectacular. Yet there is still no good Soviet razor blade! To an American there is an extraordinary gap between achievements in an intricate and sophisticated mechanical area and the shoddiness of most Soviet consumer production. This situation has led one economist to characterize the Soviet Union as both the most developed backward country and the most backward developed country. Its massive production, particularly in steel, electric power, machinery, and oil, has brought the Soviet Union into second place in the world in industrial output. This achievement commonly overshadows the vast disparities in its different areas of production.

Soviet agriculture remains backward partly because of inadequate investment, partly for lack of incentives, and partly because of poor organization—three factors that have interacted in different ways at different times. The strongest evidence of the drag that collectivism imposes on agricultural production is that the private plots of the peasants, which represent only about 3 percent of the cultivated land, produce from one- to two-thirds of the total Soviet supplies of vegetables, fruit, eggs, butter, and milk.

Moreover, since the late 1950s, the Soviet Union's rates of growth have slowed considerably, dropping to a level of 6 percent during most of 1961–65, as compared with 8.2 percent in the previous five years. This fact appears to result from the overconcentration on heavy industry in the Stalin period, with its consequent neglect of basic infrastructure investments. As long as growth could be maintained by massive infusions of manpower and capital into selected fields, and as long as the Soviet Union's rich resource base provided the raw materials for its economic autarky, both the process and the economic institutions supporting it could remain virtually unchanged. But as the supply of resources became somewhat scarcer by the mid-1950s, the rate of growth began to suffer from the lack of a well-balanced infrastructure. The nuclear age brought spiraling costs, the inflexibility of the Stalinist system made it difficult to accommodate the traditional coal and steel industrial base to the new technology of modern industry. At the same time, relaxation of Stalinist controls permitted economic institutions to seek more of their own goals without improving overall economic efficiency. Part of the motivation for Khrushchev's dismissal was the need to seek new methods of economic planning and administration, as indicated by the economic reforms Kosygin announced in October 1965. The fact that their implementation has been hesitant is probably a reflection of the differences in approach to economic decisions within the collective leadership described in the last chapter.

No country has paid as high a price for its industrialization as has the Soviet Union. No other major economy, in a historical period in which per capita income was comparable to that of the Soviet Union from 1928 to 1937, has directed as high a proportion of its gross national product—one-fourth—to industrial production. In the middle of the nineteenth century, the British economy absorbed one-eighth of the GNP for this purpose; the German economy, one-seventh. In the 1870s and 1880s, the United States, with a higher per capita income than the USSR in 1928, poured one-fifth of its GNP into industrialization. The high percentage in the Soviet Union is the more striking—and drained the consumption levels of the Soviet people still more severely—because it drew entirely from domestic sources, whereas most other countries, and particularly the United States, were able to draw on capital inflows from external sources.

Soviet economic development is most often criticized outside the country because of the sacrifices it has imposed on the standards of living of the Soviet people. It is not necessarily a disadvantage to the regime, however, to keep consumption levels relatively low, except as these may impair incentives to work and the total balance of the economy. Gerschenkron suggests that "plentiful supplies of consumer goods produce a climate of relaxation among the populace which is not congenial to dictatorships." [4] The particular spurs to changes in planning are to improve efficiency in production and in control. The problem for current Soviet leaders in determining what type of organization is most likely to produce both objectives is that they suggest different answers: decentralization for more efficient production but centralization for more effective control. The post-Khrushchev leaders are still striving to straighten out the overlapping and conflicting jurisdictions resulting from Khrushchev's bureaucratic improvisations. At the same time they must seek an improved mixture of centralized and decentralized decision-making that will better harness local knowledge and initiative to the basic program decreed by the central authorities.

3   THE STRUCTURE OF ADMINISTRATION

Given the preponderance of attention by the Soviet regime to the issues of economic development and political control, it is perhaps not surprising that there are two parallel structures of administration in the Soviet Union, one of them belonging to the party and the other to

[4] Gerschenkron, *Economic Backwardness in Historical Perspective*, pp. 267–68.

the government. Many departments of the Secretariat of the party's Central Committee are exclusively concerned with economic matters, while a number of others, like those for science and education and for Army and Navy general administration, have multiple functions that have economic effects. These departments have their prototypes at lower territorial levels, as already described, where they interact, as at the center, with the bureaucratic agencies of the government.

These latter state agencies are coordinated, at least technically, by the Council of Ministers, in which all economic fields are directly represented. These fields each have their ministries, either "all-union" or "union republic." The former directly administer all enterprises in their fields throughout the Soviet Union; the latter direct the work of corresponding ministries at the union-republic level. The difference is largely one of internal administrative organization and method of exercising control and does not represent any guaranteed division of responsibilities. Republic ministries without union counterparts also exist in certain fields such as local industry.

A series of administrative reorganizations have attempted in recent years to cope with the manifold problems of planning, coordination, and direction of the economy. In 1953, after Stalin's death, there was a fusion of ministries; in 1957, economic management was reorganized under 104 regional *sovnarkhozes* (councils of the national economy), which were subsequently reduced to 31 (see Chapter 5, Section 2). Along with this consolidation, Khrushchev sought reconcentration of economic organization through Central Committee approval in November 1962 of a new All-Russian Council of the National Economy and a single interrepublic *sovnarkhoz* for the central Asian republics. Within a year of Khrushchev's ouster, however, the *sovnarkhozes* were abolished and the industrial ministries reestablished. The description that follows is of the most recent period.

The USSR Council of Ministers in 1966 after the post-Khrushchev leaders had restored the industrial ministries included, in addition to the Chairman (Kosygin): two first vice-chairmen and nine vice-chairmen, the heads of twenty-two All-Union ministries and of twenty-

five Union-Republic ministries, the chairmen of the fifteen republic councils of ministers, of nine autonomous state committees, and of five other state committees and agencies under the direct control of the Council—notably the State Bank, the Central Statistical Administration, the Union for Sale of Agricultural Produce, and the Committees for National Control and State Security. The Committee on the State Plan, or Gosplan, is one of the autonomous state committees. It acts as an expert adviser, but is subject to conflicting pressures from the party and the government, on the one hand, and the ministries and republics on the other. The final decisions about allocation of resources are made at the highest levels, either by one of the first vice-chairmen of the Council of Ministers or by the Politburo itself.

ADMINISTRATION OF INDUSTRY

The reestablishment of the industrial ministries following the reforms of October 2, 1965, was intended to consolidate the functions that had been exercised by a series of agencies: state committees, Gosplan, and Gosstroi (the USSR State Building Committee), and USSR *Sovnarkhoz*. The industrial ministries are supposed to supervise the fulfillment of plans, direct production, cope with problems of technological innovation, see that the supply of materials and equipment is adequate, supervise financial arrangements, and watch over employment and wages. Funds allocated for the supply of materials and equipment now go direct to the ministries that manage them. The industrial ministries have also been placed in direct control of the scientific research institutes in their respective fields. It is apparent, therefore, that the industrial ministries have secured a wide measure of power, including power in planning in their own particular spheres.

Side by side with greater centralization of control in the industrial ministries has gone a move for greater autonomy for individual enterprises, coupled with extension of the rights of enterprise managers and more share in management for the workers. Although authorized by the Central Committee in November 1962, the regulation embodying these provisions was not adopted by the Council of Ministers until

October 1965. The objective is to free the enterprises not only from excessive detail in their planned goals but also from interference in day-to-day operations. In practice, however, enterprises are not guaranteed protection against being assigned goals that are unrealistic. The volume of working capital is determined by higher authorities and can only be changed if the production plan is altered. Only within the limits allowed by the higher authority does the enterprise management have full freedom to act. It appears, therefore, that regardless of the new regulation there is no genuine autonomy for individual enterprises, for the latter remain responsible for carrying on their productive activity "under the direction of the agency above it and in conformity with the national plan."

This is not to say, however, that there has been no experimentation in administration within the industrial system. One particular experiment that was started in July 1964 was to establish "direct links" between seller and buyer or, in other words, production in response to specific orders rather than to plan. The first attempt was to link clothing factories with retail stores. But even here there was careful limitation of the arrangements to particular factories and particular stores, and complications resulted from the failure of associated textile mills to provide adequate supplies of fabrics in time. Moreover, as the system has been extended, initial privileges have been replaced by restrictions.

Although the Kosygin reforms stressed flexibility, changes have been hesitant and slow. They can be characterized better as continuous adjustments of methods of planning and management than any kind of radical change. It is apparent that Soviet leaders have still not made up their minds to countenance change in the established system of centralized authority in planning and of using the plan as the criterion of performance. Unless and until they do so the current rigidities will continue.

ADMINISTRATION OF AGRICULTURE

The administration of agriculture is considerably more complex than that in industry, and results have been consistently unsatisfactory. There are two types of organization imposed by the Soviet regime: the *kolkhozes*, or collective farms, and the *sovkhozes*, or state farms. On a collective farm peasants work public land with machinery owned cooperatively. The state farm, in contrast, is state-operated with hired labor under a single director, or more recently a state farm council, and run like an industrial enterprise.

Until the early 1950s, the collective farms, into which the peasants had been forced in the period of collectivization, were by far the predominant form of organization for agriculture. Thereafter, especially under Khrushchev, the number of state farms increased rapidly. Many were established in the virgin lands development and weaker collective farms were absorbed into state farms. In addition, many of those remaining were grouped into larger units. Between 1950 and 1959, the number of collective farms dropped from 254,000 to 67,700; between 1959 and 1964, the number dropped to 38,829. Instead of including 18,800,000 families in 1959, that is, an average of 276 families per farm, the collective farms only included 16,200,000 families in 1964, that is, an average of 411 families per farm. In this latter period the number of state farms grew from 6,002, with a work force of 3,835,000, to 9,175 state farms, employing more than 7,000,000. Throughout this period, however, there was sharp controversy at top levels about the respective merits of the two forms of agricultural organization and their needs, and the post-Khrushchev leaders have slowed, although not stopped, the process of transformation of collective farms into state farms. It appears, therefore, that both forms will continue and that, as in industry, the efforts to stimulate better output will proceed within the established framework of centralized planning.

The collective farm is commonly organized as an *artel*, in which some possessions are owned by the whole group and some by individual households. Since the mid-1930s, an individual household has been allowed to own its own house, a garden plot, varying in size by region and averaging less than an acre (estimated in 1967 to produce almost one-third of total agricultural output), hand tools such as a spade, and some animals, such as a cow and a few pigs, goats, sheep, and poultry. Individual surpluses and, after state-imposed delivery quotas have been met, those of the collective farm may be sold on the local market.

The work of the collective farm is apportioned in terms of an artificial unit called a "labor day," which is related to the amount of skill needed on a particular job. (Tractor drivers earn three to five labor days for one day of work, while ordinary chores yield only one-half labor day.) Each member of a household must provide a minimum number of labor days, which may total over one hundred and fifty. At the end of each month, the total number of labor days contributed to the farm is divided into the farm's collective net income—that is, after all its expenses have been paid—and each individual is credited with his share in accordance with the number of labor days he has contributed. This time-accounting basis is not only difficult to administer equitably but also patently inefficient.

In theory, the members of the collective farm "alone are the masters of their own farm"; according to the charter, they manage it through a general assembly that elects a chairman, an executive board, and a control committee. But few, if any, collective farms are now without party cadres, and a major effort has been made to strengthen the latter through party specialists. This has been particularly the case since the wholesale transfer of mechanized equipment from the state-run, party-controlled machine tractor stations to the collective farms. Moreover, the number of trained agricultural scientists in leading positions on collective farms has also noticeably increased. At the same time, collective farms, like state farms, remain subject to the planning powers of both party and government.

The post-Khrushchev leaders have introduced a little more flexibility into the collective farm setup. One improvement is that instead of having to divide the allowable returns of the collective farm (i.e., the amount it has earned through production over the quota, minus the cost of whatever machinery and so forth it has been given), there is now a guaranteed minimum monthly payment on the same level as state farmers doing the same work in the same region. Another sign of flexibility has been the still somewhat controversial "link" system of permitting mechanized brigades from different collective farms to work together. Additionally,

substantially greater funds are being poured into agriculture.

The state farms, which now supply between 40 and 50 percent of state purchases of some important commodities, have also benefitted by innovations under the Kosygin reforms. Always heavily favored in relation to the collective farms in capital investments, allocation of machinery and fertilizer, and technical innovations, the state farms have also run chronic deficits in the past due to excessive costs. The post-Khrushchev leadership has quietly subdivided some of the largest state farms, instituted increased prices for farm products (increases extended also to the collective farms), and has replaced the director by a state farm council, composed of specialists and workers with general management responsibilities and some discretion to decide on commodities for production where factors of supply and demand are favorable.

Some of these changes clearly bring the functioning of collective and state farms closer together. On the whole, collective farms appear to have cost the government less for production and to remain efficient means of securing produce from the peasantry. Neither the state nor the collective farms have been distinguished for agricultural innovations, except that the state farms pioneered the widespread use of artificial insemination among certain types of animals, a practice subsequently taken up and improved by the West. In neither type of farm is labor productivity high.

Regardless of adjustments, the essential features of the agricultural system remain unchanged. Neither the collective farm nor the state farm can determine its own plan. In agriculture, as in industry, the advantages of political control through centralized administrative planning (i.e., control both of the peasants and of the supply of food) override the potential economic advantages of greater production stimulated by profit.

THE ADMINISTRATION OF
FOREIGN TRADE

The Soviet attitude to foreign trade has been decisively influenced from the beginning by ideology. Lenin was determined to prevent outside countries from interfering with the economic experimentation being tried in the Soviet Union and clung to his cumbersome system of state trading despite frequent criticisms from his colleagues. Lenin envisaged the importation of critical items needed to revive economic life after the Civil War as a temporary measure. Even when it became imperative during the New Economic Policy to draw outside skills into the Soviet milieu, he insisted that such arrangements should be purely contractual so they could be terminated by the regime's own action. Stalin's preferred approach to using foreign skills was through short-term technical assistance contracts, in which specific Western firms would send engineers and skilled workmen to help build basic industries in the Soviet Union that would free the country from its dependence on foreign goods. Between 1928 and 1933, the United States alone provided the Soviet Union with about two thousand technical experts. But at no time was the Soviet foreign trade monopoly relaxed. Although in this period the Soviet Union became the world's leading importer of machinery and equipment, the goal remained technological and for economic self-sufficiency.

The massive economic assistance extended to the Soviet Union during World War II by the Western allies made no appreciable difference to its postwar attitude on foreign trade with these countries. The extension of Communist rule into Eastern Europe, however, provided both a greatly enlarged political domain and an approved area for its economic activity. Trade with Communist China was similarly fostered. By the time of Stalin's death in 1953, 60 percent of the Soviet Union's foreign trade was with Communist-controlled Eastern Europe (as compared with 1.5 percent with the same countries in 1938), and 18 percent with

China (to which only 4 percent had gone in 1938).[5]

As the post-Stalin leadership, notably Khrushchev, became aware that the Soviet Union had been slipping behind in technological fields due to its economic isolationism, the trend was somewhat reversed. Once more complete industrial plants were imported from the West; patents were purchased with hard currency. But Khrushchev remained basically committed to intrabloc trade, both because of its political and economic by-products and because of the belief it would weaken the Western countries to exclude them from trading with that area.

In few fields have attitudes changed more noticeably under the post-Khrushchev leadership than in foreign trade. A more openly critical examination of intrabloc trade disclosed the heavy drain on Soviet resources in raw materials, minerals, and fuels exported to Eastern European countries and the overpricing of the machinery and consumer goods the Soviet Union was receiving in return, especially from Czechoslovakia and East Germany. Moreover, there were complaints from Eastern European countries that the demands for specific products for the Soviet market were distorting their own economic development. Within the Soviet Union, Kosygin is the particular advocate of broader international trade that reaches out beyond the Communist-controlled countries and developing states to what the directives for the Eighth Five-Year Plan (1966–70) termed "the industrially developed capitalist countries." While there is no question of giving up the foreign trade monopoly through which the bureaucracy of party and government determine the degree and character of exchanges, the notion of economic autarky within Communist-controlled boundaries has been discarded as out of date.

4 THE PROCESS OF PLANNING

While centralized planning is all-pervasive in the Soviet system, its formulation and execution are far from clear-cut and simple. In general, planning procedures may be differentiated between *indicative planning*, in which central

authorities propose goals but do not require specific ways of implementing them; *flexible planning*, in which implementation is through

[5] Leon M. Herman, "The Promise of Economic Self-Sufficiency Under Soviet Socialism," *The Development of the*

monetary provisions like price; and *administrative planning*, in which there is authoritative allocation of specific goals throughout the economy. The Soviet Union has concentrated on centralized administrative planning, but it uses a variety of means to achieve its purposes: authoritarian allocation of resources; some monetary and fiscal tools to influence demand; and occasionally some flexibility in the relation of supply and demand.

For the brief period of the New Economic Policy, the Soviet Union experimented with indicative planning. With characteristic insight, Lenin picked electricity as the key to the transformation of the national economy. A great plan of work to develop electric power throughout the whole country was important, he declared, not only economically but also psychologically. It "must be given at once, in a graphic, popular form, in order to captivate the masses by a clear and brilliant prospect (absolutely scientific in principle)," he wrote. "To work! and in ten to twenty years' time all Russia—industrial and agricultural—will be electrified!"

The State Commission for the Electrification of Russia (Goelro) was appointed in 1920 and expanded in February 1921 into the State Planning Commission (Gosplan). The task at this time was beyond either the skill or the resources of the country; the commission's door even bore the notice, "Please knock, the electric bell does not work." But the idea of planning was strongly held and work had begun.

During the next few years transition was made from a series of projects, such as Lenin envisioned, to a centrally directed plan for an integrated national economy. In 1925, "control figures" were introduced that laid down the goals for industrial production in many fields. And a start was made with authoritative allocation of resources.

The era of the Five-Year Plans was introduced, as we have seen, in the highly coercive period from 1928 to 1932 that almost paralleled the intense nationalization of productive activity and authoritative allocation of resources of the Civil War and of the Soviet participation in World War II. In all these three periods, the exercise of centralized power took the place of planning.

What may be called operational plans began to have effect from 1933 on, except for the hiatus of the 1941–45 war. The Five-Year Plans and longer-range plans [6] are drawn up on the basis of current information and trends and are subject, therefore, to constant revision. More accurate allocations are made in annual and quarterly plans, which reach down to the enterprise level. Yet at the same time, certain aspects of these plans always fail to fit with other features of the directed economy, emergencies develop, and there is continuous bargaining for supplies. Low priority sectors, such as agriculture and consumer goods, have almost always been sacrificed when competition for scarce resources became intense. Even official Soviet calculations, which are generally higher than those of Western estimates, show only 74 percent of the Second Five-Year Plan (1933–37) for agriculture fulfilled by 1937, and 67.6 percent of the Seven-Year Plan (1959–65) by 1965; the percentage fulfilled for consumer goods, 85.4 percent by 1937, and 97 percent by 1965; whereas in both periods industrial production went above 100 percent of planned growth.[7] As far as accuracy in plan fulfillment of selected products was concerned, however, Eugène Zaleski estimates that there was wide variation and concludes that there has not been very much overall improvement between the earlier and later plans.[8]

Two major difficulties in plan fulfillment

[6] The published versions have varied in size. The First Five-Year Plan was printed in four volumes, the Second in two volumes, the Third in one volume of 238 pages, and the Fourth presented in a very condensed form as a pamphlet of 96 pages. Little specific publicity was given to the Fifth Five-Year Plan, but the Sixth Five-Year Plan was presented in great detail to the Twentieth Party Congress, February 1956. Khrushchev's Seven-Year Plan for 1959–65, which superseded the Sixth Five-Year Plan, was described in detail to the Extraordinary Twenty-first Congress, January–February 1959. An initial draft of directives for the Eighth Five-Year Plan was published preceding the Twenty-third Congress and approved by it—as usual, unanimously—after some brief but pointed suggestions from the congress floor. An abbreviated Ninth Five-Year Plan for 1971–75 was published in mid-February 1971, approved by the Central Committee on March 24, and subsequently by the Party Congress.

[7] Eugène Zaleski, "Planning for Industrial Growth," *Development of the Soviet Economy*, ed. by Treml and Farrell, pp. 62–64.

[8] Zaleski, "Planning for Industrial Growth," p. 66.

Soviet Economy: Plan and Performance, ed. by Vladimir G. Treml and Robert Farrell, p. 230.

have been the detailed arbitrary provisions imposed on enterprises from above and the frequent changes made during even the annual plans. Moreover, the measures provided to check fulfillment of planned targets have often been unsatisfactory in producing desirable goods. Kosygin's reforms, announced in October 1965, aimed at introducing more flexibility into the system through a reduction in the number of products subject to central planning and supplies. So far the process has not gone far enough to warrant any conclusions. It is suggestive, however, that most items of basic production of the Eighth Five-Year Plan (1966–70) fell short of their original objectives, and that the planned growth figure for 1971 of 6.1 percent is considerably lower than the 7.6 percent for 1970. This decrease is at least partly the stage of economic maturity reached by the Soviet Union, but some experts feel it is also the continued effect of overcentralized administrative planning.

THE STRUCTURE FOR PLANNING

The special agency responsible for economic planning is the Gosplan, now known as the Committee on the State Plan and one of the Autonomous State Committees of the Council of Ministers. While its powers have varied from time to time, it has generally retained direction of two basic spheres—overall, long-range planning and the annual and quarterly current planning—but usually not the other necessary functions of planning: planning of supplies and statistical checks on the fulfillment of the plan. The latter, in practice, is kept in separate hands by the regime to serve as a check on both plans and performance.

There are major difficulties in combining responsibilities for both long-range plans and annual and quarterly plans in the same body, for the latter almost inevitably take precedence over the former. Nonetheless, a 1963 decree confirmed Gosplan's control over both spheres, in which it is to set wholesale and retail prices for industrial and agricultural products and is to determine consumption norms for fuel, raw materials, and use of equipment. Its work is divided, however, into two stages: the first is the preparation of forecasts and the study of

proposed directives; only the second stage is concerned with compulsory provisions prepared in conjunction with involved agencies and approved by the government before being put into effect. The republic gosplans prepare and submit plans for the ministries in their own areas, and can make suggestions for the preparation of plans by USSR ministries. At all times, however, defense industries are outside any republic jurisdiction.

The number of persons involved in these intricate and detailed calculations is inevitably very large indeed. In 1958, for example, there were 323 scientific bodies subordinated to the USSR and regional gosplans and the Economic Council. Of their 19,000 scientific workers, 16,000 came directly under the jurisdiction of the gosplans. In 1962, the Moscow section of the USSR Gosplan had a staff of 2,700 persons.[9] Preparation of the budget for the United States or the United Kingdom is a monumental task, but it pales in comparison with the calculations confronting planning authorities in the Soviet Union.

It remains to be pointed out that Gosplan shares its planning responsibilities and power with many other agencies: both USSR and republic ministries, which are in particularly strategic positions to influence the formulation and the carrying out of plans; the Budget and Plan Committee of the Supreme Soviet; the republic councils of ministers, which according to Kosygin's October 1965 speech were to have new responsibilities for planning, investment, employment, and wage policies; the Gosstroi, or USSR State Building Committee, established in 1962, which deals with construction and plans for model projects, in as far as these have not been placed under relevant state committees and ministries; and, of course, the top government and party organs. Thus, despite the special position accorded Gosplan in the planning process, it can hardly be said that there is an integral or unified administrative planning agency.

Although retaining its faith in overall administrative direction of the economy, or what may be called a command economy, as its alternative to a market economy, the Soviet

[9] Eugène Zaleski, *Planning Reforms in the Soviet Union, 1962–1966: An Analysis of Recent Trends in Economic Organization and Management*, p. 39.

Union has clearly never developed what it considers wholly satisfactory arrangements for planning. The more complex and mature its economy becomes, the more difficult it is to enforce comprehensive planning. Once again one can only wait to see whether the greater flexibility suggested by Kosygin in October 1965, but apparently circumscribed since then by numerous restrictions and interacting jurisdictions, will result in any substantial modifications in what have been the basic characteristics of the planned economy since the introduction of the Five-Year Plans.

THE BUDGET

The Soviet financial system and the annual Soviet budget are of major importance in the working of the planned economy. All funds must go through the State Bank, while all statistical data (except on the party) are collected and processed by the Central Statistical Administration. It may seem strange that the Soviet Union depends so greatly on finance when production is according to plan rather than profits. In fact, although its use is very different from that in a capitalist country, finance is no less important. The plan is translated into financial terms that are used as a detailed check on its operations. Moreover, monetary incentives are widely used to stimulate output, while deliberately inflated prices curb consumption. Thus finance is rarely an independent factor and is chiefly an agency of control.

Few facts indicate so graphically the enormous growth of state power and activity as the sharp rise from the 23 billion rubles devoted to government expenditures in 1931 to 174 billion in 1940, 642 billion in 1958, and 82 (new) billion in 1962 (the equivalent of 820 billion old rubles). These expenditures include, of course, a wide variety of industrial and cultural activities that are undertaken in the United States by private sources. The Soviet budget for 1962, for example, appropriated 36.2 billion rubles for the national economy, 28.9 billion for social and cultural services (that is, education, social welfare, and public health), and 12.7 billion for military defense. (The proportion for military expenditures went up sub-stantially in subsequent years.) These totals include the expenditures for all levels of government—local, regional, and union republic as well as national—making the scope of the budget as complicated as its total is vast.

Enterprise budgeting

Up to the time of Kosygin's reforms, enterprises did not pay any interest on the capital assigned them, and the taxes they paid on profits bore no relation to their level of productive capital. Kosygin proposed that his reform of wholesale prices be coupled with rental charges for the use of productive capital. These charges, together with the taxes on profits, were to become the major source of national budgetary income. Each enterprise has its individual rental charge fixed by its ministry, with the average being 6 percent, but different rates are accorded different types of use (e.g., lower rates for technological innovations or new construction). Gosplan also has an important voice in the granting of credits. Thus the new system is neither more uniform nor simplified but is intended to provide more incentive for efficient production.

Before these changes, incentive payments were made primarily from what was called the enterprise fund made up of 1 to 6 percent of the planned profits and 30 to 60 percent of any profits in excess of the plan (profits are written into the plan but there can also be additional profits when the planned targets are exceeded). This fund was compulsorily divided between at least two-fifths spent on communal construction and repairs, not more than two-fifths on workers' bonuses for health and vacations, and one-fifth on new technology. But since many enterprises had either no enterprise fund or a very small one, most bonuses in practice were paid out of the wage fund. There are now three separate funds: wage funds, those for material incentives, and those for social and cultural welfare. These are financed through enterprise-wide norms for profits that are expected to rise as the plan is filled or overfulfilled.

Individual taxes

The government, of course, can price goods at any level it wants so long as revenue meets the total cost of production plus sums adequate for replacements and further capital expansion. The sources of revenue open to it are the profits (in bookkeeping) of state enterprises (23.9 billion rubles in 1962, about 18 percent of revenue) and collective farms, and the direct and indirect taxes on individuals. By far the most important source of revenue, amounting generally to well over one-third of the total, is the *turnover* or *general sales tax* placed on certain types of goods, mostly consumer goods. This is levied every time a producer or distributor sells a product—that is, when it goes from one enterprise to another in the course of production as well as when it is sold to the consumer; thus it vastly increases the cost of a product.

From 60 to 70 percent of the final retail price of such necessities as meat, butter, and soap may represent taxes—which means that the basic economic price may have been tripled. The prices of sugar, salt, and cigarettes are still more inflated by tax. This form of taxation is most convenient for the government because the retail outlets are turned into tax collectors, and since this share of the cost is not listed separately, as it is in the United States, the public does not even realize why the goods are so expensive. Direct taxes, such as income taxes, on which the British and American governments depend so greatly, play a small role for the Soviet government and this particular means of revenue collection may even be abolished as a propaganda measure. The turnover tax, of course, takes a very much higher proportion of the income of the poor than of the rich and is a major device for keeping consumption levels down.

5   ADMINISTRATION AT THE LOCAL LEVEL

The functions of local government are as extensive and varied as those of Soviet government as a whole. Some of these functions, like traffic control, keeping public records, care of parks, and provision of local services, are similar to those in any modern country. In addition, local government in the Soviet Union maintains such public facilities as hospitals, schools, stores for retail distribution, markets, and repair shops. Local soviets also function as draft boards, recruiting those liable for military service. They are also charged with local construction and small industry.

Local soviets lack adequate powers and resources, however, to handle these manifold tasks effectively. All units, in practice, are the agents of the centralized bureaucracy. Moreover, large industrial units often dominate the local communities in their areas, turning them virtually into company towns and usurping local government functions in road and bridge building, housing, and other services to meet their own needs. Vying with other comparable local units for a share of the resources doled out by higher agencies, competing with large-scale industry, and subject to sometimes conflicting orders from above, local administrations have retained little if any of the prestige and power they possessed in the early period of local autonomy.

In mid-March 1971, prior to the opening of the Twenty-fourth Party Congress, the Central Committee announced that government organs at the national and republic levels had been ordered to draw up legislation to strengthen the power of city and district soviets and to allocate new sources of taxation to them. Three specific measures have been decreed whose impact will only be determined in practice. One decree stated that urban and district soviets are to receive direct taxes from economic enterprises located in their areas, the amounts to be determined by the national and republic councils of ministers. Under the second decree, soviets are to take direct control of a sizeable proportion of the housing and other amenities presently controlled by factories and other semiautonomous organizations and used by them as an incentive and to help stabilize the work force. The soviets, it is said, are also to exercise closer control over the building of such amenities. The third decree requires legislation regularizing the rights and obligations of the soviets, which are broadly defined as looking after the welfare of the population but include furthering agricultural production in rural areas.

Should these measures be fully implemented, they would put an unprecedented degree of power in the hands of the soviets and also the funds to underwrite that power. Since, however, the announcement of the new program went side by side with trenchant criticisms of the current working of the soviets and an appeal to local party organs to exercise greater control over the choice of people to serve on the soviets, the effect of the decrees is likely to be minimized. Moreover, the functions proposed by the decrees challenge established powers of the economic bureaucracy. Thus although their application might introduce some new ideas and useful practices, they seem likely to receive considerable opposition and would also add to the overlapping jurisdictions and, indeed, confusion still complicating the working of the administrative system.

The units of local government within a union republic have no guaranteed spheres of power but are used by the party and government to organize structures. The nationality divisions—the autonomous republics, autonomous regions, and national areas, of which the latter exist only inside the RSFSR—serve chiefly, as we have seen, to give the appearance of respect for nationality differences. The largest administrative division, the *krai* (territory), also found only in the RSFSR, covers too much area to be particularly useful. The *oblasts* (regions) are too small to be the key economic units that Khrushchev tried to make them. At the foot of the scale are the *raions* (districts), which are both urban and rural subdivisions.

In form, of course, every administrative unit operates under the direction of the soviet for its area. The members of these soviets are elected directly by local voters for periods of two years. As in national elections, there is only one candidate at the time of election, but the percentage of nonparty candidates is far higher. In the RSFSR, industrial workers and collective farmers form over 50 percent of deputies in the local soviets; in other union republics they may form over 80 percent of the members. This fact suggests that the primary

function of the soviets is to recruit the energies of large numbers of persons.

This function helps to explain why the soviets have always had so many members. Such cities as Moscow and Leningrad have approximately a thousand deputies; even a hamlet of a thousand people has nine members, and slightly larger ones may have twenty-five. Moreover, the sections into which the soviets are divided to deal with areas such as public health, education, local industry, and finance are also large. A section works alongside the administrative department in its field, both aiding and checking its work. But as an English authority once wrote, "The section recommends, advises, complains, and even demands. The *presidium* decides." Local departments also are subordinate to the relevant union ministries. Thus popular action is combined with retention of full power in executive hands.

The participation of a large number of people in public service has a good effect in itself. This can be seen also with the "activists," who are organized by the soviets to give help in local services in their spare time. Some of this activity results from public spirit that is not difficult to rouse over matters of immediate concern to the community; some of it may be to attract attention that may lead to a job as an administrator or full-time agitator. In either case it helps to get necessary work done and to associate people with the purposes of the state.

But there is another advantage to the regime in the elaborate structure of soviets. It provides an outlet for grievances and thus a means for learning about administrative incompetence, or even concentrations of power. Even with all the listening posts provided by party members, the soviets may sometimes provide additional insights into the operations of local administration that may be extremely useful to higher authorities.

As far as the exercise of power goes, the soviets are controlled by their own executives, and behind these again are the real governors: the central administration and the party. A parallel may still be drawn, in fact, between the classic pattern of colonial rule and the operations of Soviet local government. The soviets are not unlike colonial assemblies in the period when they were allowed to talk but were given little share in political power. The Soviet central

POLITICAL SUBDIVISIONS OF THE USSR

	UNION REPUBLICS OTHER THAN RSFSR
	AUTONOMOUS REPUBLICS WITHIN RSFSR
	NATIONAL AREAS
	RSFSR
---	BOUNDARIES OF REGIONS, TERRITORIES, AND AUTONOMOUS REPUBLICS
★	CAPITALS OF UNION REPUBLICS

BARENTS   SEA

NENETS

YAMALO-NENETS

KOMI A.S.S.R.

RUSSIAN SOCIALIST

FEDERATED SOVIET REPUBLIC

Murmansk

Archangel

SWEDEN

FINLAND

KARELO-FINNISH A.S.S.R.

BALTIC SEA

Helsinki

Tallinn

ESTONIAN S.S.R.

Leningrad

Petrozavodsk

KOMI-PERMYAK

Vologda

Perm

Novgorod

Kirov

Sverdlovsk

Riga

LATVIAN S.S.R.

Pskov

UDMURT A.S.S.R.

LITHUANIAN S.S.R.

Velikie Luki

Kalinin

Yaroslavl

Kostroma

Vilna

Smolensk

Moscow

Vladimir

Ivanovo

MARI A.S.S.R.

Kazan

Chelyabinsk

Kalinin-grad

Gorky

CHUVASH A.S.S.R.

TATAR A.S.S.R.

Ufa

POLAND

Minsk

BYELORUSSIAN S.S.R.

Kaluga

Tula

Ryazan

MORDOVIAN A.S.S.R.

BASHKIR A.S.S.R.

Briansk

Orel

Ulianovsk

Penza

Kuibyshev

Orenburg

Lvov

Kiev

Kursk

Tambov

Saratov

Kharkov

Voronezh

KAZAKH S.S.R.

UKRAINIAN S.S.R.

Volgograd

MOLDAVIAN S.S.R.

Dnepropetrovsk

Kishinev

Odessa

Rostov

Astrakhan

CASPIAN SEA

UZBEK S.S.R.

RUMANIA

CRIMEA

Simferopol

Krasnodar

Stavropol

1. ADIGEI A.R.
2. CHERKESS A.R.
3. KABARDIN A.S.S.R.
4. N. OSETIN A.S.S.R.
5. S. OSETIN A.R.
6. NAGORNO-KARABAKH A.R.

BULGARIA

BLACK SEA

Grozny

DAGESTAN A.S.S.R.

ABKHAZIAN A.S.S.R.

GEORGIAN S.S.R.

ADZHAR A.S.S.R.

Tiflis

TURKEY

ARMENIAN S.S.R.

AZERBAYDZHAN S.S.R.

Erivan

Baku

TURKMEN S.S.R.

NAKHICHEVAN A.S.S.R.

IRAN

0   100   200   300

MILES

government and party correspond to the imperial authority that retained all the threads of power in its own hands. The analogy is most apt in Soviet central Asia, where administration is mainly carried on by Russians who have little contact with or sympathy for the local inhabitants; but in essence it is applicable to all Soviet local administration.

6   THE WORKERS

The most colossal and in some ways the most decisive task in building the planned economy has been the mass recruitment of its workers. Probably three out of every four who were working in industry or administration by 1940 had been drawn into the system since the First Five-Year Plan.

The great majority of these workers came from the peasantry, always a source of supply for labor and increasingly released after 1930 through the collectivization of the farms. From 1917 to 1962 the proportion of the peasantry in the population dropped from four-fifths to one-fourth.

High turnover and low discipline were the not surprising results of absorbing such huge masses of unskilled labor. There was so much demand for labor by different industries that it was nearly always easy to secure alternative employment. Out of this situation arose the present system, which still makes use of piecework and incentive payments and of such disciplinary devices as labor books.

LABOR CONSCRIPTION

To ensure a constant supply of trained labor, the government in 1940 for the first time instituted labor conscription. In that year it organized the so-called Free Labor Force, or State Labor Reserves, by ordering an annual draft of eight hundred thousand to a million boys between the ages of fourteen and seventeen. Only students qualifying for higher education were exempt. As revised in 1947, the draft also included girls and provided that boys between fourteen and seventeen and girls of fifteen and sixteen should go to railway and trade schools for two years to train as skilled workers. Fourteen- to eighteen-year-olds of both sexes had to serve in factory plant schools for three to six months before being drafted into less skilled trades.

This compulsory drafting was replaced in March 1955 by voluntary recruitment. Nevertheless, during 1955–56 more than two-thirds of the young workers sent to the eastern regions to open up new lands had a one- to three-year period of labor conscription known as *orgnabor*. Otherwise, organized recruiting in the villages for industrial and building purposes is now for volunteers.

LABOR INCENTIVES

The Soviet government's greatest concern remains the relatively low productivity, which means that it currently takes three Soviet workers to produce the same unit of output as one American worker. Standards are set for most work, such as bricklaying or even typing, and additional percentages are paid for output beyond the standard. By 1938, only 16 percent of all workers and employees received ordinary time-wages; the rest were on piecework or received bonuses in addition to basic wages. Thus the "piece-wage," which Marx had declared to be "the form of wages most in harmony with the capitalist mode of production," was adopted by the Stalin regime as typically socialist.

The post-Stalin leaders have somewhat modified the essential characteristics of the system. They have simplified the piecework system by reducing the vast number of different categories by which pay rates are estimated. They have established minimum wages and have lessened the difference in the wage rates of the skilled and unskilled—chiefly through increasing production norms, which, in effect, means reducing the advantage of the skilled. Workers must still have a labor book, a passport, and police permission to settle in any major city. Since January 1, 1960, however, they can change their jobs without losing their sick-pay or temporary disability benefits and can retain their record of "uninterrupted service" if they start a new job within a month.

Thus definite efforts are being made to improve the conditions of the workers—efforts that have the more effect because they stand against the background of the stringent restrictions and punitive incentives of the Stalinist regime in the war and postwar periods. Although conditions remain hard by Western standards, post-Stalin leaders are obviously determined to make the workers feel that the regime is aware of their interests. This is evidenced by strikingly cheap bread and by low rents, though housing itself remains poor and scarce. Thus Soviet leaders are trying to depend as greatly as possible on persuasion rather than coercion.

TRADE UNIONS

Naturally the concept of collective bargaining and the role of trade unions have been transformed within the Soviet state from what we know in the West. Trade unions were legal under the tsarist government, although often persecuted under trumped-up charges, but collective bargaining was virtually unknown in Russia until 1917. It disappeared again with the decree of June 17, 1920, which established state control over all wages. Although a measure of bargaining freedom appeared again under the NEP, it was soon apparent that the traditional concepts of trade unionism ill became the movement toward total economic control. To the trade union leaders it remained important for workers to secure shorter hours and higher wages, but to the government what was important was that the workers should contribute their energies to the country as a whole.

Equally important in creating conflict was the fact that once the Workers' Opposition (see Chapter 3, Section 2) had been suppressed in 1921, the trade unions remained the only organized force capable of competing with the party. The old leaders of the trade unions were therefore replaced by more docile officials. After June 1929 it was officially stated

that the collective agreement was "to cease serving the immediate interests of the wage earners and become an instrument of rapid industrialization"; and after 1934, collective agreements were not renewed. When they were reintroduced quietly in February 1947, it was soon apparent that the move had little significance.

In recent years, some efforts have been made to broaden the responsibilities of labor unions. A decree of January 31, 1957, gave the unions a share in the settlement of labor disputes, which can never come, however, to the point of a strike or lock-out. A further decree of July 15, 1958, authorized the unions within enterprises to participate in the formulation of enterprise plans. In 1966, trade union representatives were assured a share with enterprise managers in the more flexible system of allocating bonuses and deciding their size. Requests for greater autonomy in regard to wages and work conditions are likely if management can increasingly exercise its own initiative in the distribution of profits. Trade union members have been urged to criticize management when appropriate and without clearing their remarks through higher authorities, another example of encouraging "popular participation." At the same time, the chief purpose of the unions—to increase or improve production—and their close association with the party are reflected in the high salaries of top trade union leaders and their prominent position at party congresses.

SOCIAL SERVICES

One unusual function for the trade unions, however, is the administration of much of the social welfare system. Every factory and place of work has a social insurance council set up by the local trade union committee. Unpaid "insurance delegates" supervise the rest homes and generally check on workers' needs and performances. Except for health services and old-age pensions (which are administered by the Ministry of Social Assistance), the Soviet social security system operates under the overall direction of the All-Union Central Trade Union Council.

The Soviet Union provides almost all the social services that are also fairly common in Western countries: children's aid, disability and maternity benefits, survivors' insurance for needy dependents of deceased workers, old-age pensions, socialized medicine, and, in addition, rest homes, sanitariums (and travel expenses to reach them), and funeral expenses. The one major omission since 1930 is unemployment insurance, which is said to be unnecessary because of full employment. Since wages are low, however, the lack of unemployment aid provides managers with substantial control over their workers.

In other ways, Soviet social services differ from such systems in other parts of the world. They are looked on as part of the worker's real wages. Moreover, special benefits are accorded those who perform specially arduous tasks or those considered of special value to the regime. Thus social security is a positive labor incentive. Moreover, since workers do not contribute to the system except through their trade union fees, they cannot claim benefits as of right. Benefits are usually higher the longer a worker serves in a particular enterprise, another incentive to labor stability.

Since paid absence from work in industry requires a medical certificate, there is a very large number of doctors (mostly women) to provide the necessary checks authorizing sick leave or treatment in hospitals. Dentists, specialists, and hospitals are also under state control and financed by the state budget. Medicines, however, must generally be paid for by the recipient.

It is difficult to evaluate the position of workers in the Soviet Union in relation to those in other countries. Their rates of pay are low in comparison with those in the United States, but this is hardly a fair comparison despite the massive industrial development in the Soviet Union. Soviet levels of workers' pay and care probably correspond more to the less advanced parts of Italy. Their standard of living is still not sufficient to enable them to enjoy the luxury of the "climate of relaxation," which Gerschenkron finds so uncongenial to dictatorship.

7   THE MANAGERS

In the Soviet Union there is clearly no such distinction between the government official and the businessman as is familiar to Americans. Every industrial or business manager in the Soviet Union, as well as each of his workers, is a state employee. Every enterprise is as much a part of the government service as is a department in a ministry. Thus to describe the personnel of the public service in the Soviet Union is to describe the work of almost everyone in the country.

Since the energies of the Soviet Union are concentrated to such a vast extent upon industrial production, it is hardly surprising that the outstanding "public servants" in the country are the industrial managers. The distinctive characteristic of a manager is that, within the limits of the plan, he is entrusted with the operations of his own particular part of the public economy. A minister is considered to be a manager just as much as is the head of a factory, the difference in their work being one of scope rather than of kind.

As a result, there is much less difficulty in moving from a position as manager of an enterprise to an important position in a ministry than would be the case in the United States, Great Britain, France, or Germany. Former factory managers now occupy many of the highest administrative posts both in the Soviet government and in the Communist party.[10] Since the party and the government direct industry, governmental, industrial, and some high-ranking party posts require many of the same qualifications: technical knowledge of industry, efficiency in handling work and people, and commitment to the purposes of the

[10] There are, of course, other types of positions, such as those in the diplomatic service, which are of very different character and hence require different training and experience. But the men in these positions are far fewer and of a less clearly defined type than those in industrial management.

regime. Increasingly, as George Fischer's study shows (see Chapter 3, Section 4), this commitment leads to experience also as party officials within the economic structure: the dual executives.

THE BOURGEOIS SPECIALISTS

Not surprisingly, Russian industrial specialists and engineers were not supporters of the Bolshevik coup, but as early as April 1919 their original opposition gave way to what Jeremy Azrael calls "conscientious collaboration and active cooperation." [11] Lenin's imaginative 1920 plan for the electrification of the country was prepared by a group of specialists who ultimately formed the nucleus of Gosplan. The support of technical specialists may have been induced partly by relatively high rates of pay but more directly by the regime's stern curbing of the "anarcho-syndicalism" of management by workers' councils that had seized many of the factories. The problem was rather within the party itself, and there was sharp disagreement before Lenin succeeded at the Ninth Party Congress in 1920 in securing approval of one-man authority in industrial management. In practice, bourgeois specialists directed almost all industrial development in the Soviet Union until 1928, but despite continued party apprehensions they had relatively slight political impact, even on the formulation of general economic strategy. Throughout, many strategic policymaking posts in the economic structure at middle and lower levels, and all those at the top, were filled by trusted Bolsheviks, the "red directors," while the system of competing bureaucracies, which characterizes the Soviet system, had already made its appearance.

Although convinced of the value of central planning and rapid industrial growth, the specialists of bourgeois origin almost all opposed the forced industrialization of the Five-Year Plans and collectivization of agriculture as irrationally distorting economic growth. Stalin's answer was to force them to become open adherents of his system if they were to retain

[11] Jeremy R. Azrael, *Managerial Power and Soviet Politics,* p. 29.

their positions. The accompanying invitation to enter the party in large numbers met a widespread response that demonstrated their willingness to conform to these new demands. They survived the substantial purges of technicians from 1928 to 1932, which were justified by trumped-up charges of "wreckage" designed to divert mass hostility caused by the hardships resulting from Stalinist policies, and even the "Great Purge" itself, thereby demonstrating both their usefulness and degree of conformity.

THE "RED DIRECTORS"

The "red directors" fared less well. Despite their high posts, their position had long been paradoxical. Their overriding commitment to economic advance made them a more or less cohesive group inside the party that occasionally threatened, as with their initial attraction to Trotsky, to bring them into conflict with the more political party apparatus. Convinced of Stalin's commitment to industrialization, they opposed the irrationally high targets, lack of needed resources, and above all the undercutting of their managerial and operational authority during the First Five-Year Plan. Azrael thinks there is a possibility that the "red directors," with the support of Sergei Kirov (see Chapter 1, Section 2), may have been involved at the Seventeenth Party Congress in 1934 in forcing the successful reduction of the targets for the Second Five-Year Plan, with a veiled threat of otherwise seeking Stalin's resignation. Whether or not this was the case, the "red directors," who had in practice served Stalin so well, were high on the list of liquidation from December 1934, when Kirov was murdered, through the "Great Purge" of 1937 and 1938.

THE "RED SPECIALISTS"

The "red directors" were replaced by the "red specialists," the new technical and professional elite brought into the party in such numbers at the end of the 1930s. Unlike the "red directors," Stalin had no fear that this new group might question his decisions, the more so because first the war and then more economic rationality in the Five-Year Plans removed spurs to doing so. In practice, as we have seen (Chapter 5, Section 2), Stalin transferred many policymaking functions from the top party machinery to the state bureaucracy after World War II. Although the party and, in particular, the political police did not lose their preeminence, managerial specialists achieved a greater influence and there was more enterprise autonomy.

POST-STALIN DEVELOPMENTS

In the immediate post-Stalin period, managerial support went to Malenkov, a factor, but only one, in Khrushchev's sharp criticisms of the industrial establishment that preceded the basic overhaul of the whole system of economic administration. The liquidation of the ministries in favor of regional economic councils followed. The almost universal opposition of the managerial group to this development was caused not only by the blow to its position and power but also by the considerable irrationality of the scheme of organization, which they felt threatened the progress of technological innovation and industrial specialization. But whatever their inadequacies, Khrushchev's plans for stirring up the managerial elite had their justification in the complacency, overindulgence, and, in many instances, lack of adequate training existing within the economic bureaucracy.

By purging the industrial establishment, Khrushchev sought to remove those who were associated with his "antiparty" rivals over whom he triumphed in 1958. His next move was to develop technical specialists who would be dependent only on himself. By 1962, Azrael points out, the "young, literate people" Khrushchev had been pushing ahead since 1957 were ready to be placed in positions of authority.[12] By bifurcating the party Apparat into industrial and agricultural wings, Khrushchev made new places for a number of these younger men. Moreover, by consolidating the *sovnarkhozes* from the original more than a hundred into thirty-one in 1961 and by seeking approval

of the Central Committee in November 1962 for coordinating the All-Russian and central Asian *sovnarkhozes*, Khrushchev moved to recentralize the economic bureaucracy.

We do not know his ultimate plans. Was he following "a policy of reducing the authority of the party apparat relative to that of the state bureaucracy," as Azrael suggests? Was he planning to expand the size and thus reduce the number of the oblasts to match the reduced number of *sovnarkhozes*, thereby threatening the positions of the older Obkom first secretaries, as Armstrong hypothesizes (see Chapter 5, Section 2)? Whatever Khrushchev had in mind, it is clear that some of the top party figures believed their positions were threatened. Coupled with the failure of some of Khrushchev's cherished projects, their suspicions led to the carefully planned conspiracy that resulted in Khrushchev's deposition.

The post-Khrushchev leadership has reversed the trends that might have threatened party primacy but without downgrading the managerial elite. Through Kosygin, the first representative of the managerial group to become premier, and Ustinov, the economic bureaucracy has ready access to policy formation. The ministries have been reestablished. There has been cautious experimentation at lower levels and open discussion of the need to place more emphasis on consumer goods and of possibilities of introducing more dependence on price mechanisms. The younger managers may well favor the latter developments.

Typical members of the emerging managerial elite, as described by Azrael in 1966, are in their thirties or forties, with first-class technical training, a sound grasp of technological processes, and commitment to technical innovations.[13] Many are also alleged to have "a persuasive or consultative managerial style," whether gained through party experience or the interplay with party officials is not suggested. The model is not entirely a technocratic one but certainly not a liberal-democratic one, for it includes the notion of superiority and even a self-perpetuating elite. To those who look for change in the Soviet Union through its ever growing economic complexity and maturity and the impact of these younger technologically sophis-

---

[12] Azrael, *Managerial Power and Soviet Politics*, p. 144.

[13] Azrael, *Managerial Power and Soviet Politics*, p. 153.

ticated experts, it is important also to stress the relative political weakness of the latter in a system geared to party dominance and overall centralized planning. In addition, one must note their commitment to the Soviet system, which provides them with almost everything they could want: superior equipment, economic rewards, and social prestige.

CONCLUSION

The interaction between party officials and the managerial structure extends throughout the economic process. Relatively stabilized since Khrushchev's ouster, it is never entirely so, for the goals of the two are discernibly different, even though economic expansion, particularly in heavy industry, is a common objective. Managers and administrative personnel seek stability not only because they want to safeguard their own positions but also because the production process operates more smoothly under such conditions. The party, by its very nature, is constantly seeking to mold society closer to what the current regime sees as its most desirable form.

Throughout the history of the Soviet Union, there have been disputes within the party, as there are today within the top leadership, about objectives and ways to achieve them. There is a constant ferment, which only occasionally achieves publicity. In this ferment, the economic bureaucracy has both special influence and special problems. It has direct representation at the Council of Ministers and Politburo levels. Its expertise gives its advice a particular impact. But the demands placed on the economic bureaucracy are not infrequently impossible to meet. Moreover, changing directives from the highest levels on the prime objectives for industry and the means to pursue them complicate the industrial task. At the lowest levels, as pointed out in Chapter 3, Section 4, there is a constant interaction between party personnel and enterprise management, which has stimulated a variety of informal adjustive mechanisms. This interplay extends in varying degrees throughout the system. On occasions, the economic bureaucracy is used to achieve the purposes of others; more often it appears to maintain its own basic purposes through its own skills and indispensability. Industrial development is the touchstone of Soviet achievements as well as the basis of Soviet strength. Yet economic purposes can never be viewed in the Soviet Union as apart from the overriding purposes of those in power. Here as elsewhere, the primacy of politics remains the cardinal feature of the Soviet regime.

7

Soviet
law
and
courts

1   SOVIET LAW

Both the Soviet constitution and individual statutes and decrees abound with the phrase "according to the law." But the Soviet conception of the nature and function of law differs sharply from that held by Western democratic states. The latter look on law as a body of rules, equally binding upon private persons and government officials, administered by independent courts, and amendable only by regular and accepted political processes. Moreover, in countries such as the United States and Great Britain, which have a common law system, rules of law are modified by judicial decisions, based on precedents and justified by logical legal argument. In the Soviet Union, however, the specific criterion for deciding a case is "on the basis of law in conformity with socialist legal consciousness."

Increasingly, there is a serious effort to handle cases in accordance with specific laws that have been duly promulgated and to provide judges and lawyers with legal training. Increasingly, also, intellectuals have challenged coercive actions on the ground of their "illegality" and to some degree with success. Moreover, there is a marked difference between areas, like economic disputes, where the rule of law is applied more consistently (e.g., through the system of *arbitrazh*) and those where the political elite sees a possible threat to its authority. In cases

of particular public interest, the judge is likely to turn to the sole source of interpretation of the ideological purpose of the law: the party. Moreover, the security service, or political police, still operates in what in a Western country would be termed extralegal ways. Thus law in the Soviet Union is not an impartial standard by which acts of individuals and government agents can alike be judged, nor has it that degree of certainty that makes it the bulwark of liberties in Western countries.

The characteristic notions of Soviet law have developed out of the prerevolutionary Russian legal tradition and also out of Marxist ideology. But law in the Soviet Union today is far more important than Marx and Engels ever conceived it would be.

MARX'S CONCEPTION OF LAW

The views of Marx and Engels arose naturally out of their reaction to the societies within which they lived. Both men were highly critical of the laws that existed in bourgeois states. When other writers maintained that the laws governing society were the reflection of principles of universal justice, Engels replied that "the jurist imagines he is operating with *a priori* principles, whereas they are really only economic reflexes." The law of the bourgeois state, declares the *Communist Manifesto,* "is but the will of your class made into law for all, a will whose essential character and direction are determined by the economic conditions of existence of your class."

Both Marx and Engels were equally critical of the way in which laws were administered in bourgeois states. Marx, like some contemporary liberal critics, considered that the notion of equality before the law was a cloak for actual inequality, because of the cost of legal proceedings and because he believed that judges were predisposed to the interests of property.

Marx's criticism of existing states and existing laws led him to believe that the ultimate goal was a society where coercion would be unnecessary. In the advanced stages of socialist society, the absence of economic exploitation would leave everyone free to act according to his own interest, which would be the interest of the whole group. Thus the oppressive functions of the state would "wither away" as people began voluntarily to perform the acts they had previously been forced to perform. Laws would therefore become unnecessary, Marx and Engels believed, and fixed rules governing conduct would be replaced by the power of public opinion.

LENIN'S VIEWS ON LAW

Lenin had already made some modifications in Marx's views on law before the revolution took place. He foresaw that there would be a long period between the crushing of the bourgeoisie and the achievement of a prosperous communist society, and, in the interval, he believed it would be necessary to retain some bourgeois law. He felt, too, that although most crimes in bourgeois society resulted from economic conditions that would be removed when communism was achieved, there would still be individual excesses in the intervening period of the socialist state. Hence, he believed that coercive law would be necessary throughout this period to enforce labor discipline, to regulate the unequal distribution of the products of society, and to curb individual excesses.

THE EVOLUTION OF LAW IN THE SOVIET UNION

The period of War Communism, 1917–21

When the revolution broke out in 1917, Lenin pressed for "revolutionary legality"—that is, that the organs of the new regime should not act arbitrarily but observe the rules that the government adopted. But the rapidity of the changes, the circumstances of civil war, and the great decentralization of activity meant that law quickly lost the elements of predictability and uniformity. All prerevolutionary courts were abolished en bloc, and punishments inflicted by the new People's Courts were determined "by the circumstances of the case" and by "the Socialist consciousness of justice." The rules enforced were a blend of party programs, individual interpretations of socialist needs, and existing laws, of which only those passed by the Soviet government were officially binding. Criminal offenses were dealt with by the Cheka (secret police) and by revolutionary tribunals, which acted without regard for legal processes. Thus there was little, if any, machinery for protection of private rights.

This period, 1917 to 1921, saw the establishment of certain important principles of the Soviet state: its exclusive ownership of basic economic resources (land, water, industry, etc.), the monopoly by the government of major economic activities (banking, insurance, foreign trade), and ultimate governmental authority over such private property as was still permitted. But economic conditions were still too chaotic to be reduced to law except in the broadest terms.

In regard to the personal relations of citizens, some decisive steps were taken, such as the civil registration of marriage and the divorce law.[1] The effective changes in the period have been called those of a "great bourgeois revolution with the principles of 1793 adapted to twenti-

---

[1] In 1944, divorce ceased to be a matter of right and became dependent on a court ruling; moreover, only children born of a registered marriage now have rights to inheritance. Whereas originally there was total confiscation of the estate of a deceased person, inheritance of savings and personal possessions is now permitted without restriction; wills have binding force, except that minors cannot be disinherited.

eth-century conditions." Some of the more radical of these measures (free abortion, for example) did not long survive.

The period of the New Economic Policy (1921–28) saw the organization of the new court system and the promulgation of basic codes of law. The People's Courts, with one judge and two assessors, regularized the use of nonprofessionals in the lower courts. Superior courts were set up with power to review the decisions of lower courts. All courts were dependent, however, on the state organs that passed the laws; and the chief result of establishing superior courts was to secure greater central control of local jurisdiction.

The Civil Code issued in 1922 was patterned to some extent on the most advanced of Western European codes, the German and Swiss, but shaped by the "revolutionary consciousness" of the period of War Communism. The first article of the Civil Code declared that "civil rights shall be protected by law except in instances where they are exercised in contradiction with their social-economic purpose." Thus social purposes were elevated far above any individual rights.

A similar disregard of individual rights appeared in the extensive use of the rule of analogy, which nullified the Western principle of "no penalty without a law" under which ex post facto laws (that is, laws with retroactive effect) are forbidden. The rule of analogy, as used in the Soviet Union, until it was eliminated in the 1960 RSFSR criminal code, meant that any act that a judge considered to be similar to a punishable action was *ipso facto* a crime. Under this rule, acts were punished that had been committed under legal orders in the prerevolutionary period. Moreover, current crimes and penalties were determined according to particular circumstances, to the views of the judges, and to the relation of the act to the policy of the regime. Thus a member of the Communist party might be punished more severely for a breach of labor discipline than an ordinary citizen, just because he was a member of the ruling group.

Despite this use of law as a flexible instrument for the purposes of the regime, the tendency under the New Economic Policy was toward codification of law and a more systematic organization of the courts. With the steady advance of socialization, however, the questions Marx had raised became more pressing. Had law a place in a socialist society from which capitalist elements had been eliminated? And if so, what character would it assume?

The First Five-Year Plans, 1928–37

The first Five-Year Plans provided part of the answer to these questions. They constituted the second great revolution in the history of the Soviet Union, a revolution caused by massive industrialization forced by the coercive pressures of the Soviet government. This process was defined to some degree in laws and decrees.

Rights exercised under the NEP were withdrawn or abolished by decree. Similarly, the conditions under which the new collectivized agriculture was to function (for example, the organization of the collective farms and the distribution of their products) were prescribed by decree.

But if one looks beyond the mere matter of form, it is clear that such violent, ruthless, and radical changes as were involved in the collectivization of agriculture were revolutionary in character. Even official apologists admitted that the legal system had been broken in order to meet this problem of revolutionary transition.

Not surprisingly, some Soviet theorists were now convinced that, since capitalist elements were being eliminated from the Soviet state under the Five-Year Plans, there would no longer be any need for law and judicial proceedings. In other words, law as an essentially bourgeois institution would "wither away."

But this view soon lost official favor. The more changes there were to make, the greater was the emphasis on legal rules backed by coercive penalties. Even when the new economic forms in agriculture took definite shape and social relations arising out of nationalized industry and collectivized agriculture became more stable, there was no change in official attitude and policy. Law was declared to be the instrument of organization of the socialist society. Like the state, law became accepted officially as normal in the socialist stage of development.

LAW IN THE SOCIALIST STAGE OF DEVELOPMENT

Soviet laws and procedures, as exemplified by the 1936 constitution and subsequent laws, decrees, and practices, are a curious mixture of Western concepts and distinctive Soviet features. The Soviet constitution, as we have seen, includes two types of rights: those that are enforceable in court, such as the equal rights of women, and those that are an objective of public policy but are not enforceable, such as the right to work. A striking recent development, as we saw in the section on intellectual dissent (Chapter 2, Section 3), is the appeal to provisions of the constitution for freer expression of opinions.

The immediate post-Stalin trend was to liberalize and rationalize (although not even now fully to codify) the vastly complex and numerous provisions of Soviet law. Penalties were reduced for a variety of acts considered crimes under Stalin, and secret police boards, which, like military courts, had been permitted to use summary procedures, were abolished. In 1958, military tribunals were restricted in their jurisdiction over civilians to cases of espionage or complicity in military crimes. The 1960 RSFSR criminal code, which marks a high point in this process, eliminated the category "counter-revolutionary crimes," although it was replaced by two other vague formulations: "especially dangerous crimes against the state," and "other crimes against the state."

Khrushchev favored extended use of public pressure to achieve labor discipline. His "antiparasite" laws were administered through special neighborhood courts empowered to deal with "unsocialist behaviour" through penalties of two to five years hard labor. Indignation inside and outside the Soviet Union at the sentencing in this manner in 1964 of Joseph Brodsky (perhaps the most distinguished of Soviet poets) to five years labor on a state farm led not only to a review and remission of the sentence but to the quiet downgrading of "antiparasite" activity. The "antiparasite" laws were ultimately replaced in 1970 with a new criminal regulation that forces people to engage in "socially useful work" or face the possibility of a year in prison or in a labor camp.

As far as minor offenses are concerned, the Soviet system has sometimes proved itself humane and enlightened. The three "accidental" causes of crime generally recognized—alcoholism, overcrowding through the housing crisis, and "excessive leniency of parents to their children"—are often weighed carefully and taken into account in determining penalties. Outsiders would add to the causes of crime low salaries, prohibition on private enterprise, and heavy responsibilities for plan fulfillment that encourage falsification of accounts. But these factors are inherent in the system so far, and the Soviet answer to them is further education and control.

"Economic" crimes are regarded in practice as particularly serious. In 1961 and 1962, the death penalty was established for taking bribes, for speculation, and subsequently for the "criminally" wrongful use of agricultural material or for distortion of accounts regarding plan fulfillment. Disturbingly, these decrees, which have broad wording, have not all been published.

In general it appears that the post-Khrushchev leaders, impatient with the continuation of criminal activity in the Soviet Union, have encouraged two developments in the character and administration of law. The first is to bring most of the processes that were carried on through the community (e.g., the "antiparasite" provisions) under the jurisdiction of the regular court system. The second is to tighten the administration of justice.

In 1966, a national police ministry was set up, now given the title of the Ministry for Internal Affairs, with centralized control over police and penal bodies. The special boards of the older Federal Ministry of the Interior (MVD) had been abolished in 1953 when the power of the political police was curbed, and the ministry itself was replaced in 1960 with analogous ministries in the fifteen constituent republics. In September 1970, it was announced that dissatisfaction with the way the Soviet judicial system was being run by the procurator general's office and the Supreme Court had led to the reestablishment of the USSR Ministry of Justice. This ministry, which had played a role in the staged purge trials of the thirties, had been abolished in 1956 as part of the general reform of the legal system. The republic ministries of justice, which had been renamed "ministries for the preservation of public order," have resumed their original names. An avowed purpose of the new Ministry of Justice is to strengthen measures against infractions of law and labor discipline that affect the country's economic performance. The ministry may also have a role in the projected standardization and codification of the maze of laws throughout the country.

The greatest amount of adverse publicity regarding the Soviet judicial system has naturally been the trials and sentencing of distinguished authors and other intellectual dissidents through processes that appeared strongly slanted. The basic charge against Siniavsky, Daniel, and others has been that their writings or actions have an "anti-Soviet character." Penalties have ranged from forced labor in Siberia to confinement in a lunatic asylum or a psychiatric hospital prison.

Andrei Amalrik, author of *Involuntary Journey to Siberia* and *Will the USSR Survive to 1984?*, who has twice been sentenced to forced labor, makes a distinction between cases in which a person is convicted by lower organs and manifestly without cause, and those in which the objective is to make an example of the accused. In the former, as with Joseph Brodsky and his own first sentence, a review by a higher court and reduction of sentence are relatively common. In those cases, however, where authorities are making an example of what they oppose, they publicize the case with reports in the press, as with Siniavsky, Daniel, and Ginzburg, and there is no hope of a review of sentence and probably not of a return to Moscow.[2]

In a very different situation—the trials in December 1970 of Jews accused of plotting to hijack an airplane to flee to Finland or Sweden and thence to Israel—the original death sentence for "treason" imposed on two of the defendants was commuted to imprisonment on appeal to the Supreme Court. In this case worldwide publicity and appeals are believed to have had their effect, although the final punishments of four to fifteen years in prison sound incredibly severe for an offense in which there was no actual stealing and one, as Sakharov, the physicist, pointed out, which had been caused by the restrictions placed on the legal right of Jews to leave the country. This appeal is yet another attempt to ameliorate the harshness of provisions and punishments by reference to the "guarantees" of the Soviet constitution and laws.

Because it has taken all spheres of life under its control, the socialist state depends even more heavily than the capitalist state on positive law. Yet the ceaseless efforts of the Communist party to mold the character of Soviet men and women to fit the overriding purposes of the regime mean that ultimately law retains its revolutionary purpose. On the whole this purpose is well known by the Soviet people through the channels of the party and the state. In such a perspective, law and the courts take a secondary position as molding influences. Yet it is clear that the regime looks on them as significant factors in its overall control and direction of life. Moreover, law and the courts play both an educational and a political socialization role. But only when, or if, it is deemed desirable to establish known and fixed legal frameworks within which not only the ordinary processes of life but also the party and state agencies operate will genuine legal stability be established in the Soviet Union.

2   THE JUDICIARY AND THE COURTS

The administration of law, like the work of local organs of state power, combines widespread popular participation at the lower levels with central control. People in Soviet towns and villages share in the decision of cases in informal gatherings and in the courts to a degree far exceeding the participation of Americans and Englishmen in judicial action through the jury system. At no level, however, does the Soviet court system possess the independence from party and political control that characterizes the court systems in Western countries.

[2] Andrei Amalrik, "I Want to Be Understood Correctly," *Survey* (Winter–Spring 1970), p. 105.

Outside the judicial structure, informal comradely courts can be set up in industries, educational institutions, apartment buildings, and so forth, wherever a collective exceeds fifty persons. The forerunners of the comradely courts, from 1919 to 1923 and 1928 to 1940, were concerned almost entirely with enforcing labor discipline. After 1940, severe labor measures made them superfluous. Revived under Khrushchev, comradely courts can impose minor penalties for "wrong behavior"—for example, falsehood or rudeness in housing disputes. Their work is looked on as educative rather than coercive.

All major and more serious minor crimes and disputes between citizens are dealt with by the regular courts. The lowest of these, the People's Courts, each has a judge (elected for five years) and two lay assessors (one chosen from within and one from outside of the party for two-year terms but only serving ten consecutive days a year). These courts also have a highly informal procedure, a characteristic feature of lower Soviet courts from the beginning. Witnesses interrupt each other and shout lustily when passions are running high. Decisions, which are reached by majority vote of the bench, are argued over like those of football games. Since these courts deal with simple, everyday matters, they have considerable independence in practice, despite the fact that all Soviet courts are subject to supervision and review from above.

Not surprisingly, there is much less of this liveliness and sense of popular participation in the higher courts at the regional, territorial, and union-republic levels, in the Supreme Court of the USSR, or in special tribunals, all of which are replete with party members. Most of these courts also use one judge and two lay assessors (chosen for five-year terms) if the case comes to them for its first trial; otherwise there are three or more judges. Above the level of the People's Courts, however, the election of members of the bench is, at least technically, by the appropriate soviet, including the Supreme Soviet. The nomination of judges since 1948 has been reserved to the Communist party and related organizations and, as in other elections, only one slate of candidates is presented for election. Judges are technically subject to recall and, in practice, may be dismissed by the party or the relevant Ministry of Justice, although this is much less common than in the earlier years of the Soviet Union.

The Supreme Court consists of a president, two deputy presidents, and nine justices, elected by the Supreme Soviet and the presidents of the fifteen supreme courts of individual republics. As a court of original jurisdiction for the most serious civil and criminal cases, it generally meets in plenary session. In the reorganization of 1957, its appellate jurisdiction, generally exercised by three justices, was restricted to the review of cases where the decision of a union republic court appeared to violate all-union law, or the rights of another republic. This scope has now been increased and cases can be brought—as with the Leningrad hijacking case—on an appeal transmitted by the USSR procurator general or the president of the USSR Supreme Court. Constitutionally, decisions by the Supreme Court can be reviewed by the Presidium of the Supreme Soviet.

JUDGES AND LAWYERS

The Soviet Union accepted only gradually the notion that judges need legal training, but by 1967 some 85 percent of judges had received higher legal education. This training involves five years of specialized legal courses in the Faculty of Law but almost no interdisciplinary study. Field work in government institutions such as lower courts or soviets is a requirement both during the school year and during summer vacation. Students receive a stipend, related to the grades they receive, and can be assigned to specific employment after graduation.

The position of lawyers has been more equivocal than that of judges. Since the Five-Year Plans, each region has had its own college of attorneys who are established in cities and districts. On payment of a fixed fee, a plaintiff or defendant will be assigned a lawyer, or occasionally may be allowed to pick his own. The lawyer's compensation comes directly from the center and, as it is paid out of the fees received, remains very low. Although it is illegal to receive additional recompense from clients, it is not uncommon. Most of the work of Soviet lawyers deals with housing and family disputes, but when it impinges on issues where the community is said to have an interest, party officials

Structure of Soviet Courts

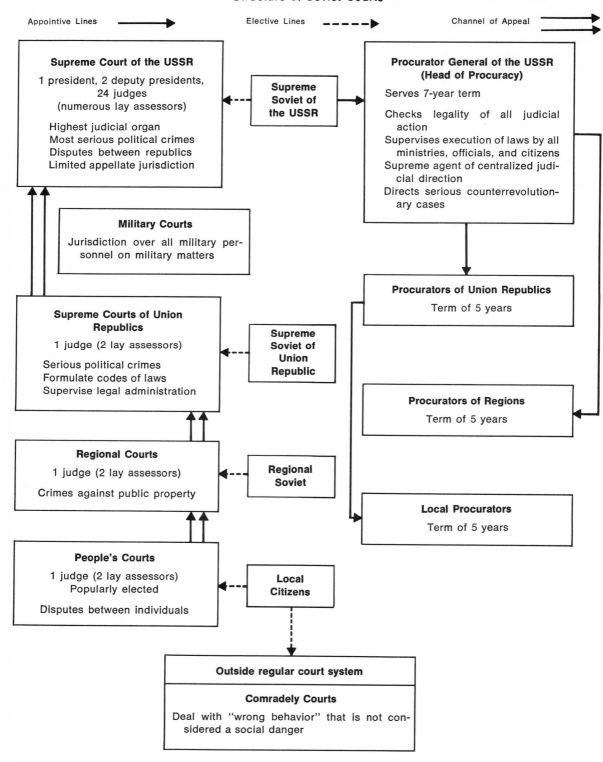

Appointive Lines ➡   Elective Lines ┄┄▶   Channel of Appeal ➡➡

Supreme Court of the USSR

1 president, 2 deputy presidents,
24 judges
(numerous lay assessors)

Highest judicial organ
Most serious political crimes
Disputes between republics
Limited appellate jurisdiction

Supreme Soviet of the USSR

Procurator General of the USSR (Head of Procuracy)

Serves 7-year term

Checks legality of all judicial action
Supervises execution of laws by all ministries, officials, and citizens
Supreme agent of centralized judicial direction
Directs serious counterrevolutionary cases

Military Courts

Jurisdiction over all military personnel on military matters

Supreme Courts of Union Republics

1 judge (2 lay assessors)

Serious political crimes
Formulate codes of laws
Supervise legal administration

Supreme Soviet of Union Republic

Procurators of Union Republics

Term of 5 years

Regional Courts

1 judge (2 lay assessors)

Crimes against public property

Regional Soviet

Procurators of Regions

Term of 5 years

People's Courts

1 judge (2 lay assessors)
Popularly elected

Disputes between individuals

Local Citizens

Local Procurators

Term of 5 years

Outside regular court system

Comradely Courts

Deal with "wrong behavior" that is not considered a social danger are both watchful and distrustful. Thus lawyers face the strain of balancing individual and community interests, a likely explanation of why by 1968 there were only thirteen thousand lawyers practicing in the whole country.

THE OFFICE OF THE PROCURATOR GENERAL

The office of the procurator general is of the utmost importance in the Soviet judicial system. It fulfills two functions: the expected one of charging criminal offenders and prosecuting them in court; and the more surprising but more significant function of supervising what Article 113 of the constitution details as "the strict execution of the laws by all ministries and institutions subordinated to them, as well as by officials and citizens of the USSR generally." In this latter regard, its work has been compared favorably with that of the ombudsman and, in practice, the procurator general examines administrative abuses on a far wider scale. He investigates thousands of complaints every year.

The procurator general is always a high-ranking member of the Communist party, since the office is a crucial place from which to supervise and control the economic bureaucracy. Technically appointed by the Supreme Soviet for a term of seven years, the procurator general appoints the procurators for the republics, territories, and regions, and confirms the appointments for those at the area, district, and city levels. Moreover, this entire structure is subject to his authority and not to the relevant administrative division in which the lower levels of the procuracy function. Procurators are responsible for reviewing all orders and regulations passed by governmental organs, and may insist they be referred to higher organs for review. They can appoint the pretrial investigators in major criminal cases, enter any lawsuit at any time on either side, and move to reopen a case, although the courts make the final judgments. They can also review the legality of actions by the state security agencies and police, subject to the ultimate will of the party. Thus in a system that is governed by an autocratic central authority that has not hesitated on occasion to crush human rights, there exists in the procuracy a system of supervision and review that can correct abuses of such rights by ordinary administrative officials.

3 EVALUATION OF THE SOVIET LEGAL SYSTEM

Law and the courts are highly important in the socialist society, for they provide the chief means through which conduct is regulated in every field. Moreover, as is obvious, this involves a much wider range of activities than in the United States or Great Britain. Law, enforced by coercive action, can be a spur to the laborer as well as a deterrent to the thief.

It is not the national control by the state of the economy but rather the attitude of the governing group that ultimately determines the characteristic features of Soviet courts. The present Soviet government has moved away from arbitrary action, but it has not yet firmly established the guarantee of the rule of law that exists in democratic states: the principle that the state machinery, in general, and the judiciary, in particular, are bound at all times to respect and uphold the law. The procuracy does a great deal to check the abuses of administrators. Minor officials are prosecuted for negligence or "overzealous" action; workers appeal penalties and are sometimes upheld. But if an issue of political loyalty is raised, it overrides every other consideration.

The courts in the Soviet Union accept the notion that the rules of law are relative to the circumstances and aims of the socialist state at a given time. The basic policies of the leaders of the state cannot be challenged. Yet since Stalin's death mass terror has been eliminated, and the laws and procedures have been reformed. Thus there still remains a constant tension between the desire to make law a fixed and certain norm and the determination to retain the ultimately unrestricted power of the regime.

8

The
Soviet Union
and
foreign affairs

The outstanding feature of international relations since the end of World War II has been the existence of only two superpowers in the world: the United States and the Soviet Union. The predominance of both countries rests on their industrial strength and their strategic position, the one dominating the Americas and the other holding the central place in the Eurasian land mass. Although each has a long history of expanding influence, only since World War II have the interests of the two countries begun to touch all over the world. Neither country, moreover, had been accustomed to taking a leading part in international relations, since the United States pursued an isolationist policy during most of the interwar period, while the Soviet Union was excluded from international society because of its political unorthodoxy. Thus both were relatively unprepared for the positions of leadership forced on them by the outcome of the war.

The dominance of two powers that are so far apart ideologically has vastly complicated the problem of world peace. The United States, as the last powerful representative of nineteenth-century liberal capitalism, is the leading defender of that free enterprise of which the Soviet Union is the most vigorous opponent. And although both countries proclaim their devotion to democracy, the senses in which they use the word are so different as to constitute an added provocation.

The problems arising from the difference in the political and economic aims of the two countries are complicated by fear and suspicion on both sides. Americans have long seen a dual drive behind Soviet policy: the ambition of an imperialist power seeking to extend its political influence and control far beyond its own boundaries; and the efforts of what is still the most powerful Communist state to use international communism as a means of disrupting the capitalist world. From its side, the Soviet Union pictures the United States as the leader of the imperialist world, dominated by finance-capital and the military-industrial complex and dedicated to crushing communism. Although Soviet leaders no longer claim that war between the United States and the Soviet Union is inevitable, they maintain that this is because the Soviet Union has become too strong to be attacked with impunity. Thus coexistence is possible on the military although not on the ideological level. Moreover, its form tends to change with each thrust and counterthrust from these major centers of power.

International politics have become more complicated, of course, with the emergence of China as a major competitive force in international communism, the recovery and economic advance of Western Europe, and the participation in international affairs of so many newly independent states in Asia and Africa. Only the most significant developments in and for Soviet policy will be indicated in the sections that follow. These developments demonstrate, however, that despite the complexity of the international interactions of the sixties and early seventies, Soviet-American relations remain crucial to both sides.

1 POSTWAR POLICIES UP TO 1964

Three developments in 1949 changed the configuration of postwar international relations. The first was the formation of the North Atlantic Treaty Organization (NATO) with its unified command and joint army. NATO was expected to provide adequate protection against any aggressive tendencies by the Soviet Union, but it postulated the latter's prenuclear period. In the very year of NATO's formation, however, the Soviet Union detonated its first atomic bomb, thereby breaking the American atomic monopoly. The third development complicating the international picture was the final victory of the Chinese Communists in their drive to control all of mainland China. Thus two new factors conditioned future Soviet policies. The Soviet Union had successfully staved off any possibility of Western intervention in its satellites in Eastern Europe during the time of its greatest weakness from 1946 to 1950. But at the same time there was emerging on its eastern flank a fellow Communist country that was not long to remain a satellite.

Within Europe, the American commitment to stay in Germany and defend Western Europe was less a matter of concern to the Soviet Union than was the fear of West Germany's rearmament. Already by 1950, the risky Berlin blockade, which sought to discourage the formation of a unified West Germany, had been given up, and the Federal Republic not only had become politically stable but also had emerged as a major industrial power. But continued French opposition to West Germany's participation in NATO held it up until 1954. The view that a rearmed West Germany was a potential threat to the Soviet position was reflected in the move by the Soviet Union in that year to establish a formal counterorganization to NATO, the Warsaw Pact, under which the Soviet Union could continue to station its troops in certain Eastern European countries.

In the Far East, where the United States had taken no active steps to counter the successful Chinese Communist drive on the mainland, the Soviet Union urged the North Koreans to invade South Korea in 1950. But this stratagem to free that part of the Asian mainland from a regime dependent on the United States backfired with the United Nations' effort, organized by the American government. Moreover, prudence then determined the Soviet leaders to turn over to the Chinese the protection of North Korea against a thrust across the 38th Parallel. Not only did the Soviet Union lose its former satellite, North Korea, to the Chinese Communists, but the latter ceased, in practice if not at once in form, to be a satellite group and emerged as their own masters. Still more decisive in this regard was the death of Stalin in March 1953, for never again would a single figure dominate both the foreign policy of the Soviet Union and that of the Communist world.

With the uncertainty over succession within the Kremlin, the new Soviet leaders adopted a conciliatory posture in international affairs. They exchanged ambassadors with Yugoslavia and Greece and renounced Soviet territorial claims in Turkey. They also encouraged a "thaw" in the satellites, the abolition of mass terror, and the type of collective leadership they were themselves uneasily experiencing. The results were mixed: some of the satellites went to extremes, in the Soviet view, in their de-Stalinization; others, like Rakosi in Hungary, hardly changed. The subsequent shock of Khrushchev's "secret" speech in 1956 denouncing Stalin's misdeeds had still greater impact, however, in the satellites than within the Soviet Union. The fostering of a new cordiality with Marshal Tito of Yugoslavia provided a favored model to be held up to Eastern European regimes. But ferment in Poland and the 1956 open outbreak in Hungary, mercilessly crushed by Soviet troops and leading to a flood of refugees into Austria and beyond, unveiled the depths of opposition in the satellites. For the Soviet Union, the 1956 Anglo-French debacle over Egypt came only in the nick of time to divert world attention from the disturbances in Eastern Europe and to provide a new arena, the Middle East, in which Soviet influence would henceforth play an increasingly important role.

Khrushchev's success in 1957 in turning the tables on the antiparty group that sought his dismissal (see Chapter 3, Section 4) placed him in a dominant yet somewhat insecure position at the head of the Soviet regime. Hence his unpredictable alternations in external policies between overtures of friendship to the United States and open challenges in Berlin, the Middle East, Africa, and Cuba. The technical successes of the Soviet Union in exploding a hydrogen bomb in 1953 and placing a Sputnik in orbit in 1957 provided a basis of strength from which to operate internationally. Yet fear that China, then about to embark on the "great leap forward," might secure its own nuclear weapons, counseled support for programs limiting their proliferation. From that year on, Soviet foreign policy increasingly had to operate within the triangular relations of three powers: the United States, China, and itself.

Part of the challenge offered by China was its threat to the ideological leadership of the Soviet Union within the Communist world. Whether spurred by this concern, or encouraged by the obvious disarray of the Western entente after the Suez debacle, or seeking a sparkling success to bolster his position at home, Khrushchev decided to create a new Berlin crisis. Adam Ulam suggests that Khrushchev was angling to prevent West Germany from securing atomic weapons by holding out to the Americans an expectation that he could then dissuade the Chinese from attempting to develop them.[1] At one stroke, therefore, the Soviet Union would have been freed of its two greatest potential threats. But the West refused to panic over Berlin, and Khrushchev finally withdrew the ultimatum in return for Eisenhower's promise to hold a summit meeting (which, in the event, proved abortive). The attempt to persuade the Chinese to renounce developing a nuclear deterrent led, however, to bitter Soviet-Chinese controversy. Although the Soviet Union never lived up to its 1957 pledge to provide Communist China with atomic information and a specimen bomb, the Chinese were not deflected from their determination to

develop such a weapon. Temporarily mollified by the 1959 agreement to provide vast quantities of Soviet heavy industrial goods, services, and training for the Chinese, the relations between the two countries progressively deteriorated from this time on. Thus despite the grandness of Khrushchev's design, it soon collapsed into ruins.

In its place came confrontation with both the United States and China between 1960 and 1964. Twice in 1960 in Communist gatherings, in the latter of which eighty-one Communist parties were represented at Moscow, Khrushchev and the Chinese Communists clashed dramatically in exchanges that only became known publically at a later date. Khrushchev was accused harshly of being soft on capitalism. But the Chinese, who were still dependent on Soviet economic help—all Soviet advisers had been withdrawn from China as a threat between the two meetings—yielded to the pleas to maintain outward unity. The most violent public denunciations of the Soviet Union and exaltations of China for its true Marxism-Leninism were thereafter voiced by China's tiny satellite in the Balkans, Albania. But when Khrushchev attacked Albania at the Twenty-second Congress in 1961, the Chinese came openly to its defense with counterblasts at the Soviet Union. The split between the Soviet Union and Communist China was no longer a secret.

Khrushchev could still hope desperately and futilely that the Soviet Union's chief adversary inside the Communist camp, China, would not develop a nuclear capability. Still more significant, however, was the Soviet Union's relation with its chief "capitalist" adversary, the United States. Associated with this relation was the changing status of West Germany, which opened up the possibility that a nuclear capability might be developed in the center of Europe. Thus Khrushchev sought a German peace treaty to perpetuate the division of that country and to limit Germany's arms capability.

The Cuban missile venture, September to October 1962, appears to have been a sudden and bold initiative aimed at setting the United States off balance, redressing with a single stroke the Soviet Union's strategic inferiority to

[1] Adam B. Ulam, *Expansion and Coexistence: The History of Soviet Foreign Policy 1917–67*, pp. 622–27.

that country, and providing an effective lever with which to exert pressure on the West to concede the Soviet demands on Berlin.[2] When the Soviet Union yielded to the American ultimatum to withdraw the missiles and dismantle the launching pads, another "grand design" had collapsed. In the process the Soviet Union suffered a humiliating retreat, and Khrushchev's own prestige and position within the Soviet Union were weakened sufficiently to have contributed to his ouster in October 1964.

After the Cuban missile crisis had been resolved, both the United States and the Soviet Union achieved minor successes in their approaches to limiting the spread of nuclear weapons. The American proposal for a multilateral nuclear force in NATO, through which the United States had hoped to satisfy French and German aspirations without adding to the "nuclear club," was abandoned. But on July 25, 1963, the United States, Soviet Union, and Great Britain agreed not to test nuclear weapons in the atmosphere, in outer space, or under the water. Underground testing was exempted,

however, because of lack of agreement on inspection.

For both the Soviet Union and the United States, the agreement was a poor substitute for a nonproliferation treaty that covered China and France (the latter refused even to sign the test ban). Moreover, the Soviet Union failed to secure the nonaggression pact between NATO and the Warsaw Pact countries that it favored in order to provide formal recognition by the West of the East German Democratic Republic and the Potsdam agreement on Poland's territorial gains.

Had all been going well internally, Khrushchev's foreign affairs mishaps might have been overlooked by other Soviet leaders, but the combination of personal unpredictability, a lagging agriculture, increasing intellectual dissent at home, and open Chinese affronts proved too much. On October 14, 1964, Khrushchev was eased out of office and more cautious and conservative figures, Brezhnev and Kosygin, took over as the most prominent of a working collective leadership.

2 FOREIGN POLICY AFTER KHRUSHCHEV

The new Soviet leaders inherited the uncertain triangular balance between their own country, the United States, and China, a balance that was made still more sensitive on all sides by deeper and deeper involvement by the United States in Vietnam. The Soviet Union, as "the" leader of Communist states, could not remain aloof from North Vietnam's needs and thus sent massive war materiel; the Chinese suspected the Soviet Union of doing so to gain influence in "their" area and to use it in bargaining with the United States.[3] Both China and the Soviet Union had also harbored suspicions in this period that the other was seeking to embroil its Communist rival in war with the United States. In fact, the Soviet Union has gained much from American entanglement

in Vietnam: the weakening of the morale and unity of the United States; disillusionment of its allies at its blundering policies; the absorption of so much of its military power. More positively, most Communist countries appear to have applauded the kind of aid the Soviet Union has provided North Vietnam in contrast to the Chinese refusal to join in its fighting. Moreover, at home, Soviet leaders have found it useful to document their theme of American imperialism with the spectacle of its embroilment in Southeast Asia.

Vietnam, however, is only one point (albeit a very important one) at which Soviet interests impinge on those of China and of the United States. The Soviet Union remains vitally involved with the Communist-controlled countries of Eastern Europe and with international communism. Moreover, West Germany is still a major focus of its attention as it is for the United States and the rest of Western Europe.

[2] Ulam, *Expansion and Coexistence*, pp. 649–78. See also Carl A. Linden, *Khrushchev and the Soviet Leadership, 1957–1964*, pp. 146–58.

[3] Ulam, *Expansion and Coexistence*, p. 705.

SOVIET EXPANSION
IN THE EAST
SINCE 1939

USSR IN 1939
AREAS ANNEXED BY USSR
SINCE 1939
COMMUNIST, IN ALLIANCE
WITH USSR
COMMUNIST, NOT ALLIED
TO USSR

ARCTIC   SEA

BERING STRAIT

SIBERIA

SOVIET   UNION

SAKHALIN

KURILE IS.

TANNU TUVA

Irkutsk

Harbin

Vladivostok

Ulan Bator

JAPAN

MONGOLIAN

Mukden

NORTH
KOREA

PEOPLE'S REPUBLIC

Peking

Seoul

Tokyo

Port Arthur

SOUTH
KOREA

PAKISTAN

C H I N A

Nanking

Shanghai

TIBET

OKINAWA

NEPAL

BHUTAN

Chungking

TAIWAN

SIKKIM

PAKI-
STAN

Canton

INDIA

Hong Kong

BURMA

PHILIPPINES

L
A
O
S

N. VIETNAM

THAILAND

CAM-
BODIA

S. VIETNAM

0   200   400   600
MILES

SOVIET EXPANSION IN THE WEST
SINCE 1939

- USSR IN 1939
- AREAS ANNEXED BY USSR SINCE 1939
- COMMUNIST, IN ALLIANCE WITH USSR
- COMMUNIST, NOT ALLIED TO USSR
- BOUNDARIES OF 1939

Petsamo

N O R W A Y

S W E D E N

F I N L A N D

Porkkalla

Leningrad

Tallinn

B A L T I C

S E A

ESTONIA

S O V I E T

Moscow

LATVIA

Riga

NORTH SEA

DENMARK

LITHUANIA

Kaunas

Königsberg

U N I O N

Minsk

NETH.

FEDERAL

GERMAN

Berlin

DEMO-
CRATIC

Warsaw

P O L A N D

BELG.

REPUBLIC

REPUBLIC

Kiev

LUX.

OF GERMANY

Prague

Lwow

F R A N C E

C Z E C H O S L O V A K I A

SWITZ.

A U S T R I A

BESSARABIA

Budapest

BUKOVINA

HUNGARY

Odessa

R U M A N I A

I T A L Y

Y U G O S L A V I A

Belgrade

Bucharest

BLACK SEA

B U L G A R I A

ALBANIA

Sofia

GREECE

T U R K E Y

0   100   200   300
MILES

It seems wise, therefore, to drop the chronological approach at this point and to deal with each one of these areas of Soviet concern separately before returning to some general conclusions.

RELATIONS WITH CHINA

The Sino-Soviet split colors every aspect of Soviet foreign policy. Since the fiasco of the Cuban missile crisis, there could be no illusion that China would accept a relationship based on Soviet domination. Indeed, it had been steadily edging away from such a relationship since Stalin's death. Yet China's economic dependence on the Soviet Union plus the general desire to maintain a façade of Communist unity long kept the two giants from an open break, either politically or ideologically.

Each of the two has elements of strength not possessed by the other. Despite China's successful explosion of a nuclear device in 1964, it cannot begin to match the Soviet Union's industrial development. On the other hand, China's more than 700 million people dwarf the population of the Soviet Union. These factors may well be the most significant in the political confrontation of the two countries, particularly since Communist China has assumed its seat in the United Nations General Assembly and Security Council and welcomed President Nixon to Peking. Ideological purity also weighs heavily in the degree of acceptance by particular Communist states of the leadership of the one or the other within the Communist world, although proximity is necessarily also a powerful factor.

Each side has accused the other of deviating from "true" Marxism-Leninism and of lowering the prestige, as well as impairing the unity, of international communism. The Chinese still insist the root of trouble lies in the original denunciation of Stalin; Soviet leaders accuse the Chinese of dangerous deviation, such as the communes experiment and their left-wing dogmatism coupled with encouragement of revolutionary adventures. The Chinese maintain that Soviet leaders promote "a rich man's Communism," cautious and angling for accommodations with imperialist powers, while Soviet leaders see a racist theme in Chinese

activities in Africa, Asia, and Latin America. From the Soviet side, the unforgiveable sin is that the Chinese have been unwilling to subordinate their aims and policies to those of the "original" socialist state; from the side of the Chinese it is, presumably, the Soviet attempts to retain that relationship. That both countries espouse ideological Communism has in some sense bridged divisions that might otherwise have led to active conflict. Yet their differences in interpretation of dogma and in aims and policies have split the Communist world and, all too often for Soviet comfort, suggested alternative routes of development to different groups inside particular Communist countries.

If the Sino-Soviet relationship were the only one with which the Soviet Union had to cope, its task would not be so difficult. But not only the Chinese brand of communism but also the Yugoslav variant and, as Czechoslovakia under Dubček demonstrated, still more democratic forms of national communism appealed to the East European countries that had graduated from satellite status in the 1960s to being junior partners to their huge Communist neighbor. Moreover, West Germany, even without the nuclear deterrent, remained the forward post of the Western, particularly the American, stance in Europe. We turn, therefore, to these aspects of foreign policy, which the Soviet Union must balance against its nagging and sometimes almost threatening relationship with China.

RELATIONS WITH EASTERN EUROPE

The post-Stalin period has witnessed major changes in the relations of the Soviet Union with the Eastern European countries. The exploitation and overt domination of the Stalin period were at first modified and then, especially after 1956, abandoned. Indeed, so far did the change go that in the early 1960s Soviet leaders considered reversing the trend to make the bloc a closer knit economic unity. Comecon (the Council of Mutual Economic Assistance), which had been set up in 1949 in imitation of the European Recovery Program and until 1953 had been simply a device for milking the satellites, was now called on to centralize economic planning for Eastern Europe and the Soviet Union. But from June 1962 on, Rumania openly challenged the new Soviet effort to determine the scale and character of Eastern Europe's industrialism and its relations with the West. Yugoslavia had long maintained its independence in both regards, thereby drawing upon itself the focus of Soviet wrath with brief interludes of being feted under Khrushchev and his successors. But for Rumania to assert its economic independence so forcefully presented Soviet leaders with a dilemma, which they quietly shelved at the end of 1962 by dropping the plan.

Rumania's growing self-assertiveness, which steadily increased through 1965, was coupled, however, with continued membership in the Warsaw Pact. Earlier, the attempted withdrawal from the pact by Hungary had resulted in use of Soviet troops to curb its growing independence of action. In less developed and more hard-line Bulgaria, the apparent move away from centralized economic planning in 1965 and 1966 was reversed in mid-1968 to reassert Stalinist-type economic priorities and closer integration with the Soviet economy.

The focus of attention by 1967, however, was on Czechoslovakia. Its purge of security forces (including many Soviet agents), army and economic reforms, and evolutionary policies appeared not only to threaten the primacy of its party but also to make the country an uncertain base for Soviet strategic planning in case of pressures from the West. Walter Ulbricht, the intransigent leader of East Germany at that time, was particularly concerned with the developments in Czechoslovakia. Czech leaders were well aware of the tensions over their policies that were building up in Eastern Europe and the Soviet Union, but they were temporarily relieved by the Bratislava agreement with five other Warsaw Pact members in August 1967, which seemed to herald the withdrawal of the Soviet troops that were on "maneuvers" in their country. There is considerable evidence that Soviet inner circles were uncertain as to what policy to pursue, but the scales appear to have been tipped toward invasion by an alarming report from Ulbricht late in August 1967 suggesting there were secret negotiations between Prague and Bonn, coupled with moves toward neutralism by both

Czechoslovakia and Rumania.[4] In August 1968, troops of the Soviet Union and four of its Warsaw Pact allies (Rumania did not participate) invaded Czechoslovakia. Thus ended the liberal "Prague Spring" of that same year. The invasion and occupation inaugurated the wholesale purge within Czechoslovakia that has steadily transformed the character of its institutions, economy, and ways of life. Continued alienation of Czech intellectuals and even workers from the existing regime has contributed to continued severe internal repression and to the regime's complete dependence on Moscow.

This forceful reassertion of Soviet control over Czechoslovakia has had somewhat mixed results. It has increased the alienation of Soviet intellectuals and may well have caused some other better-concealed divisions within the Soviet Union. It was sharply criticized by the large Communist parties in France and in Italy and by many smaller, less important ones outside the immediate zone of Soviet influence. The crushing of liberalism and independent policies in Czechoslovakia has provided conclusive evidence, however, that the current Soviet regime will not permit wide deviations in structure or in actions by countries that it considers of high-strategic importance to itself. The Brezhnev Doctrine implies that the Soviet Union is the guardian of the "socialist" system and that therefore it has not only the right but also the duty to take forcible measures to prevent the defection of a unit from the socialist sphere into that of the "capitalist order."[5]

---

[4] Pavel Tigrid, "Czechoslovakia: A Post-Mortem, II," *Survey* (Winter–Spring 1970), p. 115.

[5] The "Brezhnev Doctrine," formulated by him at the Polish Party Congress in Warsaw on November 12, 1968, states:

> When the internal and external forces hostile to socialism seek to turn back the development of any Socialist country to restore the capitalist order, when a threat emerges to the cause of socialism in that country, a threat to the security of the Socialist Commonwealth as a whole, this is no longer a matter only for the people of the country in question, but it is also a common problem, which is a matter of concern for all Socialist countries.
>
> It goes without saying that such an action as military aid to a fraternal country to thwart the threat to the Socialist order is an extraordinary, enforced (that is, last resort) measure. It can be caused only by the direct actions of the enemies of socialism inside the country and beyond its boundaries—actions which

Nonetheless, the Soviet Union still confronts a certain dilemma in determining the boundaries of advisable interference by force in the affairs of Eastern European countries. In Hungary in 1956 and in Czechoslovakia in 1968 it has used force with what must be considered satisfactory results in terms of its own military security. It retains substantial numbers of troops in all Eastern European countries except Rumania, Yugoslavia, and Albania. But the Soviet Union must work through local leaders, and it is obviously much better off if it can gain its ultimate ends without resort to force. Hence Soviet leaders apparently watched the workers' strikes in Poland in December 1970, which toppled Gomulka from power, with apprehension but also with ultimate relief that the situation in that country has not become from their point of view more serious.

To protect its western flank, the Soviet Union seeks to associate its control of the countries of Eastern Europe with a *détente* with West Germany and the United States. Thus the Soviet Union greeted with satisfaction Chancellor Willy Brandt's formal acceptance late in 1970 of Poland's postwar boundaries and the German-Soviet treaty. Both agreements fulfill long-held Soviet objectives, while freer access to West Germany's industrial capacity is yet another advantage expected from the treaty. The latter was endorsed automatically by the Warsaw Pact countries but faced its most serious stumbling block in the still far from harmonious relations between East and West Germany. Protracted negotiations in 1971 between the four powers—the United States, Great Britain, France, and the Soviet Union—over the status of Berlin and freer access between the two parts of Germany only resulted in partial success because of East German reluctance. Whether the four power security pact that the Soviet Union favors would solve this situation is still uncertain.

The Soviet Union faces something of a

create a threat to the common interests of the Socialist camp.

It should be noted that the British Communist party promptly demanded that the new doctrine should be "speedily and officially repudiated," and the Italian party paper, *Unita,* declared that "it is not known what right they have to act as judges in such questions."

dilemma, in practice, in regard both to East Germany and to a *détente* with the West. East Germany holds a strategic position on the edge of the Soviet zone, and its regime has been the most unswerving in following the Soviet hard line. To force East Germany to develop much freer access with West Germany might be to open the floodgates to a movement of population and would at least lead to a far freer exchange of ideas. Yet it is apparent from the experience with Czechoslovakia that movements of people and of ideas are apt to weaken the control of local regimes. Indeed, there are centrifugal forces at work already within Eastern Europe, encouraged by the relative independence of action of Yugoslavia and Rumania and internal trends of public opinion. *Détente* with the West, particularly West Germany and the United States, strengthens these centrifugal tendencies and thus acts counter to the Soviet Union's centripetal pressures to maintain its dominance in Eastern Europe. The thirty Soviet divisions stationed in East Germany, Poland, and Hungary, with smaller numbers in Bulgaria, can maintain this dominance by force if necessary, but such a policy, added to the crushing of Czech liberalism, would be a further indication that party solidarity, political influence, economic pressures, and ideology no longer provide adequate cohesive bonds (which is probably now true).

RELATIONS WITH THE UNITED STATES

Looking back on Soviet-American relations since World War II, it is apparent that they have moved from the "cold war" era through periods of uncertainty into a general atmosphere of coexistence. In the current period the Soviet Union has lost much of its fear of American nuclear dominance and arms superiority because of its own vast advances in these fields. Thus it is once again cautiously considering disarmament—the SALT negotiations—at the same time that it probes persistently in many areas, and particularly in the Middle East, to expand its influence without precipitating an open break with the United States. In these latter policies, the Soviet Union is greatly aided by the American entanglement in the Southeast Asia morass and by open divisions in American opinion over foreign policy and American commitments abroad.

Soviet policy seeks to isolate the United States wherever possible both from its allies and from areas of the world in which American interests and activities are playing a significant role. Thus it seeks to edge the United States out of Southeast Asia, to limit its role in the Middle East, and to make it less important to Western Europe. Where feasible it inserts its own influence in place of American. At the same time, the Soviet Union recognizes the need to deal bilaterally with the United States as a superpower and therefore engages in joint, small-scale scientific investigations—for example, mutual use of each other's huge atom smashers and space data—that contribute to its own development.

It must be emphasized again that these Soviet policies carry their own dilemmas. One dilemma, of course, is that as the Soviet Union probes outward for increased political influence, it impinges on ever more sensitive areas of American engagement both in the Middle East and in central Europe. While it is British Conservative leaders, notably Prime Minister Heath himself, who are now most concerned over the increasing Soviet presence in the Indian Ocean, this too—if Soviet influence expands there—will impinge on American sensibilities. Current Soviet leaders are too wise to engage in such direct challenges as Khrushchev's Cuban venture. So far they have concentrated on, and been extremely successful in, expanding their concerns in areas adjacent to themselves, in particular the Middle East. Their efforts have been helped, of course, by the major American commitment in Southeast Asia. But even in a time when reducing foreign commitments seems the official theme of American foreign policy, there remain deep interests and significant alignments that few American leaders would dare to ignore.

3   OVERVIEW

In evaluating Soviet foreign policy, it is all too easy to assume that its regime can steer whatever course it wishes, and that it has been exceptionally successful over the years compared with policies pursued by the West and particularly by the United States. It is true that the Soviet regime can reach its decisions in secret (as it did over the invasion of Czechoslovakia) and act with relatively little concern for its own public opinion or, indeed, that of its more subservient neighbors. But even so cursory a review as has been presented here has indicated major miscalculations made by Soviet leaders, such as Stalin's extraordinary trust in the Nazi-Soviet Pact and consequent failure to prepare against the Nazi attack in 1941 (see Chapter 1, Section 2), the Berlin blockades, North Korea, the Congo, the Cuban missile crisis. Major achievements like consolidating Soviet control in Eastern Europe at the end of World War II, securing a divided Germany, and expanding influence in the Arab Middle East have been due more to early miscalcula-tions of postwar Soviet strength by the West, and subsequently to the Suez blunder, than to any particular brilliance on the part of Soviet strategists.

By bluffing, playing power politics, and engaging in realistic hard bargaining, Soviet leaders have scored in comparison with the more rigid, legalistic, and at times moralistic (e.g., over Suez) lines American foreign-policy makers have adopted. In the Middle East, and possibly in Nigeria (where the Soviet Union aided the federal government consistently during the civil war, while the United States maintained neutrality), the Soviet Union appears in a strong position vis-à-vis the West. But neither it nor the United States is in full control of situations in the Middle East, or Africa, let alone Asia. Indeed, we appear to be in a period when it is the "clients" rather than the superpowers that determine developments. And in the total milieu in which the Soviet Union must operate, there are conflicting interests and pressures that impinge at all times upon its policies.

The vast territorial expansion of the Communist world after World War II, looked on with such apprehension by most Americans and at first providing so genuine a source of strength to the Soviet Union, now leads to its greatest strains. On the one hand is China, which has become a political and ideological rival instead of a follower. The impact on international communism of the Sino-Soviet split has been to tear apart its ideological unity based on Soviet leadership and to demonstrate the disruptive force of alternative power bases within the Communist community.

The Communist countries on the opposite side of the Soviet Union provide a very different strategic problem and a counter ideological pull to that of China. Lying between Soviet boundaries and the West, they form a strategic zone of protection, reinforced in Hungary, Bulgaria, Poland, and East Germany by the Soviet troops already within their boundaries. With the example of Czechoslovakia in view, none of their regimes is likely to challenge Soviet political dominance, but there are persistent efforts, as in Hungary, to free their economic processes from centralized control, both internally and by the Soviet Union. With the examples of Yugoslavia and Rumania existing side by side with them, and the attraction of the more open societies and better conditions of life in their Western neighbors, particularly West Germany, it is small wonder that the populations in the conforming Eastern European countries exhibit restlessness from time to time, as in Poland in December and January, 1970–71. While their people would welcome *détente* with the West, the regimes, particularly in East Germany, fear it as they feared the impact of Czechoslovakian liberalization prior to the invasion. So these pulls and counterpulls also form part of the milieu within which Soviet foreign policy must operate.

Current Soviet leaders are cautious for good reasons. They have a superb strategic position stretching across the Eurasian land mass, but it opens them to pressures from both their east and their west, which tend to pull them in different directions. Their chief rival in economic capacity, the United States, is creating its own external and, to some degree, internal difficulties but without seriously impairing its vast pro-

ductive capacity. Although Soviet leaders appear to have a tight hand on their internal situation, the economic progress in their country is currently unsatisfactory. The tension between heavy industry and consumer needs remains; agricultural production is still far lower than desired; general production figures are below plan estimates. In place of the greater flexibility in economic organization that has tentatively been introduced, the likelihood now seems that there will be a tightening of party control at the expense of the economic bureaucracy. Perhaps above all, the problem of succession may rear its head again.

It is not inconceivable that Soviet shrewdness and American flexibility could devise a broad world settlement out of their mutual problems and needs. Neither superpower is any longer in its old position of unchallengeability within its own sphere. However maladroit and unsuccessful their execution, Khrushchev's "grand designs" sought by threats and bargaining to arrive at such a settlement. But the United States would have to bargain from strength, and this involves not only withdrawal from the conflict in Southeast Asia but also countering the trends toward isolationism that suggest that other involvements abroad are dangerous. Nothing, in fact, would be more dangerous for Americans than to encourage Soviet expansionism by default. A judicious policy of encouraging (and certainly not discouraging) interactions between West Germany and Eastern Europe, of aiding Yugoslavia and Rumania to the degree they desire such aid, and comparable policies elsewhere—in India, Indonesia, Africa, the Caribbean, and Latin America, for example—can aid the growth of independence in developing countries, whether under Communist influence or control or not. Such independence is more to American than to Soviet advantage.

But above all, American and Soviet policymakers need mutually to resolve their tensions in central Europe, the Middle East, and over armaments, as through the SALT talks. The former will be reduced if Willy Brandt's courageous initiatives come to fruition, perhaps through a four power pact. Moreover, Great Britain's membership in the Common Market will strengthen the political capacities of Western Europe. More evenhandedness in the Middle East might win back some Arab trust without undercutting Israeli confidence. In Asia the vast productive capacity of Japan may help to stabilize the area. The process of worldwide accommodation may well be a long and arduous one, but with perception, awareness of all the factors involved, and alertness to respond to opportunities it is not impossible.

Conclusion

The policies of the Soviet Union are still those that have the greatest impact on the United States. This is partly because of the extent and character of the Soviet Union's own power and influence, partly because it remains the key factor in the total Communist sphere, however divided in practice within itself that sphere may be, and partly because of the apparent unpredictability of its internal and external actions. It is beyond question that the Soviet Union seeks other goals, both internationally and for itself, than does the United States and that it uses different means to achieve these goals. Throughout this consideration of the Soviet Union's establishment, growth, and present characteristics, these differences have been stressed. But it is important at this point also to recall some of its similarities to the United States as we seek a balanced perspective on the Soviet Union.

Both the United States and the Soviet Union operate on a continental plane; both contain a variety of peoples with varied ethnic backgrounds; both are affected by stages of development in which differing economic opportunities and relations to the exercise of political power provide continued sources of internal tension; both have been and are still involved in rapid technological and industrial advances; both experience internal strains because of their international policies; both bear a relationship to European political systems, but each has evolved its own distinctive institutions and characteristic values; both regard themselves as the standard bearers of universally valid principles; and both have overwhelming pressures (although of different kinds) toward homogenized cultures, in comparison with the delicately balanced class interactions and patterns of culture in other Western European countries.

Despite surface manifestations of uniformity and a totality of political control from the top, Soviet society and political processes are no less complex than those of more easily examined Western states. The striking differences among the Communist systems of Eastern Europe, and between the Soviet Union and Commu-

nist China, reflect constant and pervasive internal interactions as well as the predispositions of their leaders. Thus easy generalizations regarding change or continuity in Soviet practices must now be questioned in the light of new factors and more searching inquiries.

Until Khrushchev's ouster, it was thought that only death or possibly resignation could lead to the replacement of the dominant figure in the Soviet Union. It is still a common expectation that the logic of Soviet organization leads to the domination of a single person, and that the spotlight on Leonid Brezhnev during the Twenty-fourth Party Congress in March–April 1971 and thereafter has heralded the fading of collective leadership. Yet there is also substantial evidence that a significant process of vertical decentralization within the Soviet system is engaging an increasing number of participants in the governmental process. Although the final decisions on policy continue to be made in a highly structured context of concentrated supreme control, there are many groups participating in the shaping of the intermediate level of life and organization that affects the decisions made at the top.

Moreover, the pressures on centralized policymaking facilities constantly increase with the growth and complexity of the Soviet industrial system. Since political power created the Soviet economic system, it would be illusory to expect that the relationship will be reversed, any more than that the economic characteristics of American society will be fundamentally changed by its political institutions. But inevitably there is an affecting interaction of the economic and political spheres of life, in response to new needs and demands, that leads to cautious experimentation; on the Soviet side, experimentation with the relaxation of certain controls and the encouragement of what is called "creative initiative," and on the American side, experimentation with wage and price controls and with the attempted curbing of the previously unlimited opportunities of industry to maximize production and profit at the expense of the environment.

The first section of the first chapter of this book ended with Zbigniew Brzezinski's list of possible alternative paths of future Soviet political development: petrification, pluralist evolution, technological adaptation, fundamentalism, and political disintegration. His own view, expressed in March 1970, was that there would be a combination of petrification, that is, retention of political control without innovation, and technological adaptations that would stress scientific expertise in the party rather than its traditional bureaucratic dogmatism. He also cited the possibility that there might be a degree of internal decay and ineffective handling of Soviet dilemmas in preserving internal unity, fostering economic growth, and coping with external strains in its relations with the United States that might lead to a revival of ideological fervor. So far there is no evidence of these latter developments, while there is considerable indication that the former evaluation is valid. The continuity in the personnel of the top leadership, the lack of striking innovation in the Ninth Five-Year Plan, despite its affirmation of more concern for consumer needs, the hesitation to press forward with more flexible and permissive economic management, suggest that the Soviet Union is in a period in which adaptations to circumstances are more likely than basic changes. Looking ahead, however, it is always well to keep in mind the difficulties in ascertaining the realities that lie behind the surface manifestations in the Soviet Union.

Conclusion

Having concluded our study of four major powers, we now return to the more general questions concerning modern political processes and governmental arrangements raised in the Introduction. We now can indicate, in a comparative vein, how these countries illustrate some of the fundamental problems of government, particularly the role and function of constitutions, whether federal arrangements still work, and the place of political movements, parties, and representative assemblies in the increasingly complex political systems of our day, especially vis-à-vis that Moloch that threatens to overwhelm them—the bureaucratic-administrative-executive "complex." In developing our analysis, we shall be constantly concerned with the factor that chiefly distinguishes liberal democracy from nondemocratic systems: limited government. Our discussion will proceed in three stages. First, we shall consider the means for keeping government limited and their effectiveness. Second, we shall examine the channels of political action—elections, political parties, and so forth—that are available to the people and how these operate under different systems. And, finally, we shall discuss the functions that political and administrative leadership fulfills in the maze of competing elites. Our tripartite analysis should provide an overview of the political process.

LIMITED GOVERNMENT AND POWER-LIMITING INSTITUTIONS

There are various ways in which government and those operating it can be kept in bounds. Constitutions may set the boundaries of political action and in this way define the spheres that are reserved to the private activities of individuals and groups. Government itself may be divided into branches and levels in which each has its own sphere of jurisdiction and thus is limited in its authority vis-à-vis the others. This may be done horizontally or vertically: horizontally, for instance, if an independent judiciary places limits on what executive power can do in the area of "rule-application"; vertically, if a federal level of government must respect what a state or local level is permitted to engage in.

CONSTITUTIONALISM: FUNCTIONS AND PROBLEMS

The primary function of constitutions is to define, and thereby to limit, public power. A constitutional framework provides that governmental powers shall be exercised in accordance with known procedures, and it protects certain areas of personal and group life from governmental interference.

Only in nontotalitarian countries do constitutions provide such limitations. Formal appearances notwithstanding, totalitarian regimes do not have them. Whatever rules exist there—and they may even be called "constitutions"—either lack assured political impact and meaning (as in

651

relation to parliamentary legislation or to individual liberties in the Soviet Union) or are forever provisional and changeable at the whim of the party or leader. Thus they lack the generality, reliability, and hence calculability that the rules of law can be expected to possess. Genuine constitutionalism is likewise absent where constitutions are forever made and remade, changed and abolished, so as to fit the political needs of the respective powerholders, as has happened in some developing countries and Latin American states.

Even regimes that we commonly call totalitarian, however, may show the beginnings of limitations that, in time, might develop into something like constitutionalism. It is problematic as to whether this is the case in regard to certain "rights" that have been more widely respected in the Soviet Union since the demise of Stalin (for example, a lower incidence of arbitrary arrest and detention). But in Poland a number of seats in parliament have been reserved, as if by customary law, to representatives of Catholicism, who are permitted genuine criticism, a practice that constitutes more restraint than does the presence of "stooge" parties in the East German People's Chamber.

What counts in nontotalitarian countries is not so much the existence of written constitutions as such but the degree to which there is adherence to known and established practices. The British constitution, as we have seen, is largely composed of custom. And even in the United States there are certain rules of prime importance (such as those referring to presidential nominations or to the organization and procedures in Congress) that are respected, although either customary or without constitutional force. What counts is whether there is a general consensus on the legitimacy of the political framework that the constitution embodies and specifies. Such consensus can be inferred from the agreement (usually unspoken and implied) of the major political parties and social groups on this framework and the relative unimportance of parties or other groups that want to abolish it *in toto*. The constitution, then, becomes the symbol of a nation's integration into one political unit. But this kind of legitimacy more often than not requires the development of ideas and attitude patterns over a considerable stretch of time.

As in Britain, and also the United States, the constitutional system then becomes a totality of rules and practices that is transmitted from generation to generation through the process of "socialization." The system is no longer questioned in its fundamental features.

No such underlying basic consensus has yet been achieved in France (where consequently, as we have seen, the constitutional framework frequently has been changed) or in Germany (where, despite more general consensus on the domestic constitutional framework in West Germany, the "existential" question of national identity is still unsolved). Whether the "opposition of principle," now noticeable on the part of those among the new generation who rally around forces like the New Left, will endanger the existing constitutional consensus may depend on how the consensual nations respond to the needs of "postindustrial" society.

There are thus wide variations in the origin, function, and strength of constitutions. These variations can be illustrated by the systems of rights and liberties and by the existence and type of constitutional jurisdiction their systems provide.

BASIC RIGHTS AND LIBERTIES TODAY

The "classical" type of fundamental rights and liberties, as embodied in the American Bill of Rights, has been criticized in this century as too individualistic and too little concerned with the needs of groups. Catalogs of social and economic rights—such as the right to education, to work, and to decent payment for work, and so forth—have been inserted not only in documents such as the Stalin constitution but also in modern democratic constitutions, for example, the Weimar Constitution of Germany and in the preamble to the constitution of the Fourth French Republic. These guarantees, as well as the classical rights, reflect an increasing concern with the needs and aspirations felt all over the world. Further evidence for the worldwide demand for "basic human rights" can be seen in the headway made by the UN's attempt to codify them into binding universal conventions. Indeed, the Declaration on Human Rights of 1948, which in the beginning was not considered legally binding, is increasingly being regarded as valid law, especially its anticolonialist stipulations. This view also serves to show that more and more needs assume the character of universal ones, not only in the "material" spheres of economic and ecological necessities but in the political and moral spheres as well.

The classical rights and freedoms, in particular, have gained new luster where people have had the bitter experience of losing them. Life under totalitarian lawlessness teaches people the importance of such guarantees as legal security in its most elementary sense of freedom from arbitrary arrest and detention. It is significant that the post-Nazi Bonn Constitution, while dropping most of the Weimar catalog of economic and social rights, gives the traditional bill of rights new emphasis.

There are also advances in the sphere of the classical freedoms themselves. In an age of mass society, we need to protect the right to nonconformity in areas that have not yet been invaded by the state or by other big organizations. Technological progress, for example in the area of electronic devices for invading privacy, makes protection imperative. Thus in the developed constitutional systems, there has been increasing concern with the rights of creative expression in the arts, in literature, and in the entertainment fields; with the right to be protected against the noise of one's environment; of audiences to refuse to become captive victims of advertising; and of citizens, in a shrinking and integrated world, to move freely not only within their own country but in the world abroad, that is, with the freedom to leave and reenter their country.

But the chief field of basic rights remains that of the classical bills of rights. Through these, from the time of "the mother of them all," the English Bill of Rights, there have been established not only the basic boundary lines of freedom but also a bridge between liberalism and democracy, since without guarantees of some fundamental political rights (for example, freedom of the press and of association), genuine democracy, in the sense of rule by the people, would be impossible.

In examining the present status of these rights and liberties in the major countries, let us start with the Soviet Union. Up to and through the Stalin era it would have been ludicrous to talk about protected rights in any meaningful sense, in view of the pervasive terror machinery of the regime. The famous Bill of Rights of the Stalin constitution was merely a device to cover up a dictatorship that, like most modern nondemocratic regimes, seemed unable to dispense with pseudodemocratic trappings. In the post-Stalin period, however, while there has not yet been evidence of meaningful freedom of opinion and genuine guarantees of political rights, it is difficult to imagine that a legally unchecked secret police could be reintroduced in a nation now accustomed to at least a minimal degree of security. In the area of social and economic rights, free education and free health services have prevailed since the beginning of the regime, so that they would seem for all intents and purposes irrevocable. These illustrations serve to show that even under dictatorship, lip-service and paper promises may turn into restraints on rulers who cannot afford to disregard the expectations of their people in a modernized or modernizing society.

The way in which rights and liberties are protected in the United States—their elaborate listing in federal and state constitutions, their protection not only against executive but also against legislative infringement, and their enforcement by effective independent courts—seems to lie at the opposite pole. But even here, reality does not always come up to potentialities. First of all, the enforcement machinery of the state—that is, the local and state police authorities—has often been woefully inadequate in the protection of individual and group rights and liberties. This has been true both in general and in regard to particular groups, such as blacks or those groups battling on their behalf. Indeed, on occasion—especially in the South—the police have even turned against those needing protection, and the courts have been unavailable or ineffective in the face of such abuse of power. Moreover, first under the impact of the cold war and more recently under that of racial conflict and other domestic unrest, erosion of liberties has taken place in various ways. The slogan of "law and order" has been used to secure enactment of laws that undermine constitutional law and order by permitting, for example, wiretapping on a large scale. Still more dangerous is the mobilization of extralegal social pressures for conformity or for mob action against dissenters. Not showing the flag, or wearing long hair and beards, may then become grounds for ostracism or worse. "Silent majorities" may be organized for the "backlash." When the danger is perceived as deriving primarily from the left, the backlash may degenerate into protofascism. These pressures show how dependent formal guarantees are on a sufficient strength of genuine liberalism.

Great Britain offers encouraging evidence of such strength. The preservation of traditional liberties in that country provides a prime illustration of the force of tradition and the prevailing spirit of a nation as contrasted with the impact of formal rules and institutions. Even though no higher law of a written constitution protects the basic rights of an Englishman, they are safely guarded through the application of the rule of law; and while Parliament, by legislation, or the Cabinet, by delegated power, clearly has the power to tamper with these rights, the danger is remote that they would do so more than temporarily, and then only during genuine emergencies. Despite the anticolored feeling exploited by Enoch Powell, the British remain so basically integrated as a nation of free men mutually tolerant and respectful of their differences that, in Churchill's words, they can "lump" the most unpleasant of such divergencies.

In contrast to the British, the French since the age of the Enlightenment and the Great Revolution have raised the battle cry of the "rights of man" rather than the rights of Frenchmen. But the trouble has been that it was the battle cry of only one group of Frenchmen in the perennial French conflict of opposing ideologies. Many a glorious legal and political battle has been fought over these rights and their protection, and some of them have been decisive for the liberal democratic development of the country—as witness the Dreyfus affair. But it can hardly be said that these rights are as safely anchored in France as they are in Britain. The French system is at its best in the protection of individual liberties it offers through its system of administrative jurisdiction, but these procedures protect personal rights, such as property rights, against an entrenched bureaucracy, rather than political freedoms. It would be gratifying to infer from the broad freedoms enjoyed in France by radical political movements a British-type agreement on "lumping it" in the interests of freedom and diversity. But recent violent outbursts leading to severe countermeasures indicate basic social divisions not conducive to such an attitude.

In Germany, as in France, liberalism has not been unsuccessful in the realm of personal security and property rights; these were clearly protected by that central European marriage of freedom and order known as the *Rechtsstaat.* But political rights prior to Weimar meant little. If the Weimar regime distinguished—and perhaps extinguished—itself through an overly broad grant of political freedoms, the Bonn Constitution is double-faced. It contains a strong catalog of basic rights and liberties, some of which are even "unamendable"; but it also puts limits on the exercise of political rights when used "in order to attack the liberal-democratic framework" of the constitution. Insertion of "emergency" provisions in the constitution in 1968, moreover, has seriously affected certain rights (such as secrecy of mail and telephone communication).

In this respect, one particular problem which democracies are confronted with is perhaps the most intricate: how to face organized activity of "state-hostile" groups and movements. Communism, of course, has been foremost among these, but there is also that of rightist, and, more recently, non-Communist leftist radicalism. The range of reactions to these groups has gone from outlawry to toleration. The dilemma is whether to grant freedom to those who would use it to destroy freedom for others, or whether to restrict freedom and thereby risk far-reaching curtailment of liberties in general. Nothing is more easy and more tempting than to use provisions supposedly directed against a specific group or movement, such as communism, for attacking any unwanted, nonconformist, or merely opposition group, party, or opinion. South Africa's Suppression of Communism Act, under which anybody advocating economic or social change can be charged with the offense of "statutory communism," constitutes one of the most glaring cases of such abuse. Such a policy can even threaten to transform a previously free system into a noxious "rightist" totalitarianism. Moreover, there is little evidence that a ban on the Communist party does much more than drive its activities underground. In few areas is it more necessary to combine restraint on the part of government with constant alertness by the governed if individual rights are to be safeguarded.

CONSTITUTIONAL JURISDICTION

Constitutional jurisdiction means court action to secure the observance of the rules of a constitution. It may be concerned not only with the protection of individual and group rights but also with keeping state action within constitutional limits. Thus it may attain political importance far beyond that of other judicial action.

Constitutional jurisdiction has been particularly important in countries with a federal structure in which the powers of member units are delimited in relation to those of the federal (national) government. It took a civil war in the United States to establish the principle that a judicial organ of the federal government, rather than an individual state (or states) is the final arbiter. As resistance to the Supreme Court's decision on school desegregation has shown, this principle has to be reestablished again and again. Ultimately, limitations of power that have significant social effects depend not only on judicial interpretation but also on persuading the most powerful forces in a community to accept the decisions that have been made.

Constitutional jurisdiction has assumed major importance in both West Germany and the United States. There are three chief areas in which courts may undertake to guarantee the functioning of a constitutional system. In the first place, the courts may act to keep in balance both the powers of, and the relations among, the organs of government, for example, the spheres of the legislature and executive, the rights of majorities and minorities in parliament, or the jurisdictions of the federal government and the member states. A second important sphere is the relation between ordinary legislation and the law of the constitution. The third relates to the individual or group

rights and liberties that a constitution protects. Thus constitutional jurisdiction may deal with any or all of the following: (a) "organ conflicts," that is, conflicts between the organs of the state or government; (b) judicial review of the constitutionality of laws; and/or (c) conflicts between the state and individuals or groups over whether there has been a violation of basic rights or liberties.

The new German system is perhaps most interesting in providing for legal settlement of organ conflicts. The idea of offering political groups and governmental authorities a chance to fight out constitutional conflicts in court was not entirely novel. Already under the German Empire (when the Bundesrat had jurisdiction) and later under Weimar (when a constitutional tribunal was established) provision had been made for the resolution of certain types of organ conflicts. But only now has full "juridification" of the system been attained, with the Bonn Constitution allotting to the federal Constitutional Court the power to decide even those conflicts that arise among the highest federal organs and agencies. This, for a country with strong authoritarian traditions, is an important new venture.

The American judicial system is not concerned with this particular aspect of organ conflicts, but it hears suits regarding encroachment by the executive or the legislature in the sphere of the other and, of course, also those concerning the territorial-federal division of power. In addition, American courts are concerned with the protection of rights and liberties. The distinctive function of the American judicial system, however, is judicial review, that is, the maintenance of the superiority of the Constitution over all state action, including ordinary lawmaking. This reflects an ingrained American feeling that the Constitution is the higher law, to be preserved against the changing and possibly transitory will of the people.

What about constitutional jurisdiction in other countries and systems? Totalitarian regimes, of course, cannot permit procedures for the effective limitation of power; they avoid even their outward appearance, asserting that to give courts powers of judicial review would hamstring the sovereign legislature. The French traditionally have believed that sovereignty rests inalienably in the people and in those on whom they bestow it. Their unitary system leaves no room for federal-state conflicts, and the courts have never assumed the right of judicial review of national legislation. The Constitutional Council, however, polices the boundaries between executive and legislative competence as defined in the 1958 constitution. Moreover, it would be strange, indeed, to have no institutional protection of individual rights in the very country of *les droits de l'homme et du citoyen*; and such protection does reside in the system of administrative jurisdiction.

The British system of parliamentary supremacy operates without judicial review or judicial settlement of organ conflicts. It is typically British in avoiding the institutionalization of protection. It relies instead on such general provisions and traditions as the rule of law, the independence of the judiciary, the recognition of implied restraints on state power, and the application of the rule of reason to any and all of the system's manifestations. And since constitutionalism is hardly anywhere more safely anchored than in that country, Britain again illustrates the fact that national tradition can be a more important safeguard of rights than constitutional procedures and institutional devices.

INDEPENDENCE OF THE JUDICIARY

Constitutional jurisdiction is not the only device for placing limits on governmental power. Independence of the judiciary constitutes another one. In contrast to police states, where the courts are looked on as instruments of the regime in carrying out its purposes, courts in constitutional systems are separate, independent agencies bound by their own rules of procedure and determining cases according to publicly known law.

It is through judicial independence (usually guaranteed by the appointment for life and the irremovability of judges) that Montesquieu's device for the limitation of power [1] has found

its last redoubt even in countries such as Great Britain and France, where little else remains of the separation of power. Under modern conditions of the welfare state and of government regulations, the separation between the lawmaking and the executive branches may no longer be as feasible or even as desirable as it used to be; but the separation of an independent judiciary from both seems to be the irreducible minimum required for an effective system of limitation of power. The more modern government interferes, administers, and regulates, the more urgent is the need to preserve a check on the way these activities affect individuals and groups. The helplessness of the individual in the absence of such control is all too obvious in systems where the judiciary is either dependent or powerless, whether they be modern totalitarian systems with their knock on the door in the dead of night or premodern ones with their *lettres de cachet*.

Strong as the feeling may be for judicial independence, there can still be problems. Equal justice under law must, after all, be dispensed by men. And men possess ideals and predilections, and even preconceived ideas and prejudices. An aging judiciary may be behind the times; a judiciary drawn from certain strata or classes may reflect class or caste bias. Moreover, the substantive law itself necessarily reflects class interest where there is class rule, economic interests where such interests prevail in a given society, religious interests where particular denominations or churches predominate. The remedy here is not a change in the judicial system but a change in the laws through democratic processes. As for class, personal, or any other bias of the judicial personnel, the remedy is not in rendering the judiciary more dependent but in bringing about reforms that render such shortcomings less likely—for example, selecting the German and even the British judiciary from a less narrow base, and protecting the American judiciary, especially in the states, from undue political pressures.

Further problems arise if courts are entrusted with overly political tasks. When, as in the United States, courts have to make decisions in such significant and controversial areas as free enterprise versus governmental regulation, or racial segregation versus integration, through

[1] Montesquieu was the first major political philosopher in modern times to stress separation of the branches of public power as a prime device for the restraint of such power. His ideas strongly influenced the fathers of the American Constitution.

the interpretation of broad terms such as "due process of law" or "equal protection of the laws," their decisions are bound to involve elements of policymaking. Many countries consider certain political issues (such as foreign policy decisions in American practice, or *actes de gouvernement* in France) to be nonjusticiable. Since decisions in such cases have to be made somewhere, however, it seems to be a matter of convenience whether ultimate control is given to a judicial body or to the more political part of the government.

The more encompassing the range of what is considered justiciable, however, the greater the danger that in a conflict involving basic issues of policy or fundamentally opposed forces in state and society, normative judgment will prove unenforceable. It is the crises of a regime or country that test the very bases of its institutions and put constitutionalism to its real test. Only a civil war, and not the Supreme Court, could solve the issues of slavery and of state sovereignty in the United States. And, as we have seen, the Constitutional Court of Weimar Germany was equally unable to enforce its verdict when antidemocratic forces undertook to destroy the last stronghold of Weimar democracy. Everything depends in such cases on whether judicial bodies are backed up by public determination sufficiently strong to uphold the rule of law in this broader sense.

DECENTRALIZATION OF POWER

A further way of limiting the authority of the central government is through decentralization of power. Providing local or larger geographical subdivisions of a country with important jurisdictions gives citizens additional spheres of participation in government and also restrains government through diversification. As elsewhere, however, the trend toward big and comprehensive government has tended to limit, if not eliminate, genuine autonomy and self-government at these lower levels, or render local and regional governments too big for such effective participation.

Traditionally, one of the counterweights against too much centralized government was

found in local self-government. It is often said, and with some justice, that the grassroots, the essential training ground of democracy, is to be found at the local level. It is there that people deal with problems of immediate and direct importance to themselves. Significantly, local government in Germany developed at a time when German state institutions were still authoritarian; again, after the German collapse at the end of World War II, self-government first reasserted itself at the local level. Local self-governing institutions have shown stubborn vitality in times of stress. They can also provide a healthy counterbalance to overcentralization by restraining the "apoplexy at the center and the anaemia at the extremities," both of which are dangers in the highly organized, bureaucratic state of today.

Even in countries with long traditions of local self-government, however, there is a marked trend toward centralized supervision, financing, and even control. In Great Britain, for instance, activities such as education and public health that used to be locally oriented are now organized nationally. Yet there is still a major difference between the functions and functioning of local government in Britain and the United States and those in France, where the prefect is the political agent of the central administration. The most serious evidence of decline in the vitality of local government is the lack of interest in local issues. In France, Britain, and Germany, for instance, local elections are increasingly looked on as trials of strength for the national parties, which interject national issues into local contests.

There is a further problem that may yet pose the gravest threat to meaningful local government: the trend not only toward urbanization but toward the formation of huge metropolitan areas, encompassing tens of millions of people and covering territory that overlaps local government areas or even the boundaries of higher political units. The problem then is, how to make even local issues meaningful to individuals who are mere atoms in huge communities and how to coordinate the affairs of a megalopolis whose government and administration are cut up among so many units. Genuinely "participatory democracy," in such circumstances, requires that sublocal groups and units be given a share in running their affairs (as has been recently experimented with in the United States in overly large school systems, welfare and poverty programs, and so forth). If democracy is to remain viable, such participation is essential. But it will have to assert itself in opposition to the trend toward concentration of decision-making at ever higher levels.

In our time, what is the importance of an intermediate level of government between local and national affairs, that is, federalism? Its role in nation-building can be seen easily. Neither the United States nor Germany could have been immediately established as full-fledged unitary structures from separate, independent units. Today, when large, noncohesive units under colonial administration gain independence, federalism may be the only, or the best, way to prevent their disintegration into separate linguistic or ethnic units. But what about federalism's continuing role once nations have been formed?

Of the major powers treated in this book, only two have even the appearance of federalism. In Germany it is comparatively strong, because the nation arose from formerly independent units, and some tradition of sectionalism has remained. In the Soviet Union, by contrast, as in any dictatorial regime, federalism is more apparent than real, since, as the Nazi experience also demonstrated, the concentration of power in one man or in a small ruling group heading a nation-wide single party stands in sharp contradiction to the limitation on central power that federalism involves. It then tends to become a mere administrative subdelegation of functions.

But even in such classical federal systems as the United States, Canada, Australia, Germany, and Switzerland, there is now a serious question of whether units below the national government that are not mere administrative subdivisions of that government can effectively carry out more than strictly local functions in a period when so many activities are necessarily nation-wide, if not even broader. In an age when ecological problems should compel even the largest nation-states to agree to international regulation, subnational units can hardly insist on separateness and "sovereignty." Where discharge of oil or waste at the coastline

threatens to pollute entire oceans, discharge of such matter into domestic waterways obviously concerns the nation and not only one or the other of its subdivisions. And only the nation commands the resources to finance large-scale tasks and programs.

In the face of this development, students of federalism have given much thought to its inherent constitutional and political problems. Should the federal or state sphere possess the unspecified residual powers? Should the administration of national laws be entrusted to national executive agencies, as in the United States, or left in the main to state bureaucracies under federal supervision, as in Germany and Switzerland? And how should the body be organized that represents the member states on the federal level? Should it be composed of representatives of the people in the states, on the American senatorial pattern, or, as in Germany, of delegates representing state governments?

But experience shows that however these problems are met technically, what really counts are underlying social trends and the viability of the member units. Thus, in the United States, terms such as *interstate commerce* were used to enhance central power at the expense of member units despite the vesting of residual powers in the latter. Member-state viability is determined today by two main factors: the financial and the political. Financial viability depends on the distribution of the chief financial resources, especially taxes. Even systems such as the German, which reserved most of the sources of income to the states, have ended by giving the federal government the major share of power and resources. In the United States, where there is free competition among levels of government in tapping resources, the balance has similarly shifted overwhelmingly to the national level.

Even more relevant to the survival of federalism is whether strong sentiments of regionalism exist or whether sectional interests, backed by regionally concentrated nationality, linguistic, or religious groups, seek protection from centralization through reinforcing states' rights. In contrast to the new countries of the world, federalism in the older systems seems to survive chiefly through the latter factor, sectional interest, rather than through true regionalist sentiment. Indeed, as distances shrink in the air age, as metropolitan areas cut through state lines and people move like latter-day nomads from place to place, such tradition-bound, regional sentiment tends to atrophy.

It is nevertheless true in the older federal countries that certain interests that by themselves have little to do with regionalism have tried to underpin federal divisions. Thus in Germany, national political parties find their control of state governments a vantage point from which to influence national policies. In the United States, mining, gas, oil, or similar interests, by their dominant position in particular states and a consequent influence on those states' senators in Washington, may become more strongly entrenched and thus ardent supporters of federalism. The American party system as such, of course, is still built on local and regional organization. But none of this evidences strong regional feelings among the people at large—feelings that do not in fact exist except for white sectionalism in the South. And, as in other industrialized countries, the interests and organizations of the chief social and economic groups (in labor, trade, and industry) are nation-wide and thus counteract whatever regional interests and sentiments remain.

Thus the outlook for federalism in the older systems is none too good. But this does not necessarily provide a danger for liberalism. It is far from sure that smaller units of government are more sensitive to the rights and liberties of individuals and groups than are larger ones. Moreover, against the pressure of nongovernmental power, such as that of "big business" or any other big interest group, central government sometimes provides more effective protection. Whether subnational autonomy and diversity are preserved or not depends, as William Riker has remarked, more on the political culture than on structural arrangements. Having studied paired countries, one federal and one unitary (such as Australia and New Zealand, Chile and Argentina, the United Kingdom and the United States), he observed: "In no pair of countries with a similar political culture is the federal member of the pair significantly more permissive to local and regional interests than the unitary member." [2] Federalism, thus, is another example of how relatively less important constitutional or legal arrangements may be compared with the underlying ways and traditions of political life.

CHANNELS OF POLITICAL ACTION

In the Introduction we posed questions about whether and how, in our modern mechanized society, popular control can be maintained through channels of political action. We also pointed out how dependent popular action is on certain preinstitutional requirements, such as the ability to secure accurate information and the freedom to express opinion. Under constitutionalism, we have considered to what extent these and other freedoms are still meaningful today and how they are safeguarded in different countries and systems. We now turn to the institutionalized means of political action: to elections, parties, and parliaments.

Such devices and institutions are essential in modern times because populations are generally too large and too dispersed for direct action.

The device of a plebiscite is occasionally used, as in Switzerland and France, and other forms of direct, "participatory" democracy are tried out on a sublocal, "community" level (as here and there in the United States). But, chiefly, modern government is representative government. This very fact raises a vast number of other questions: How are representatives to be chosen so that they will be responsible to their constituents? How can they make their influence effective on the executive? In other words, how can the vast variety of often opposing groups in a modern community be linked effectively with the process of government in such a

[2] William H. Riker, "Six Books in Search of a Subject or Does Federalism Exist and Does It Matter?" *Comparative Politics*, 2 (1) (October 1969), p. 142.

way that policymaking can be carried on speedily and decisively and yet with due regard to the consent of the governed?

TOTALITARIAN REGIMES

In the absence of direct democracy, "rule of the people" is more than make-believe only where the people at large have ways and means ("channels") open to them to exercise influence over what happens in government and politics. The unavailability of effective means creates the malaise typical of nondemocratic regimes. What, indeed, is the meaning of elections in which voters have a choice neither between candidates nor between programs? How can "party" be an instrument for exercising popular power or control if there exists only one party which in practice exercises power and control over the people? How can assemblies be "representative" where they are merely permitted to voice an occasional acclaim of members and policies of the ruling group?

To one raised in the Western tradition, the chief function of such institutions appears to be to create the illusion of popular control and consent where it does not exist. But we should not overlook the fact that at least in the ideology of communism things appear somewhat differently. For a regime whose leaders, for all we know, may be honestly convinced that socialism means the emancipation of mankind, restrictions of popular control may assume the character of necessary but temporary transition measures. During a period in which the vanguard must still lead, it cannot give free rein to deviating policies and opinions. But neither can it rule in a vacuum, since its doctrine is predicated on the assumption that what the vanguard does is merely the fulfillment of what history wills and that the masses, if enlightened, must of necessity will this same thing. Thus its objective for the masses of the people is universal education and "enlightenment." Election campaigns, the discussion of issues within the party, and debates in assemblies all have this function. In addition, however, they serve the purpose of engineering consent that also underlies the often frantic efforts of the regime to mobilize the masses in other fields of life. Indicative of the same purposes are calls to the

people to engage in criticism (within carefully defined limits) or to engage in discussion of problems close to "the basis," that is, in the enterprises, at the lowest level of administration, in neighborhood units, and the like. The term *close to the basis* itself reflects the yearning of a group that somehow feels that its basis for ruling is not democratically legitimate yet wants to be recognized in a more than make-believe way. Thus what appears to the outside observer to be phony and deceptive remains for the true believer something real, necessary, and vital—a means of maintaining contact between the masses and their vanguard.

These facts apply above all to the ruling "state-party." In the doctrinal sense, this party constitutes the primary embodiment of "historical reason" and therefore the "real" will of the (presumed) revolutionary majority of the people. Rather than comparing such a party to parties in nontotalitarian systems, it should be compared with the other chief organizations in totalitarian regimes. Significantly these are referred to as "mass organizations" and are supposedly the real representatives of the masses in the particular fields of industry (trade unions), agriculture, culture, or in men's, youth, or women's groups. Trade unions, under communism, are not considered to represent one group *against* another, as in the United States, but rather as organs for coordinating a common purpose. In a similar fashion, the party is not supposed to represent diverse groups but, rather, to see to it that one set of principles and one policy prevail throughout government and society. Thus it must operate on the principle of "democratic centralism": criticism may be offered in the early stages of a proposal, but once a decision has been made everyone must accept it. Thus, also, it must sift its membership carefully to ensure conformity to the doctrine and policy lines set by the leadership. The purge of deviators thus constitutes an inevitable feature of such regimes.

Yet liberal democrats may derive a slight measure of encouragement even from the purposes for which institutions like parties and elections are used under dictatorship. Ideas and institutions often have their own way of deceiving or betraying those who hold and use them. The use of elections and parliaments for "educational" purposes may turn out to be truly educational by telling people something about the ways of exercising genuine influence. Authoritarian rulers may eventually see fit to permit some measure of such influence. A constant urge to keep "close to the basis" may ultimately render leaders more amenable to the opinions, wishes, and needs of the masses than dictators ruling by terror and intimidation would be. Such "thawing" of regimes depends, of course, on so many other factors that expectations or predictions of liberalization are premature. But as the cases of Yugoslavia and, to some extent, of some of the former satellites have shown, such a development is not impossible.

ELECTIONS AND PARTIES IN LIBERAL DEMOCRACIES

Communist countries are not the only ones where elections are of doubtful significance. In many self-styled democracies among the developing nations, for instance, electoral procedures are merely means to provide the regime with the democratic façade it believes it needs to be an ally of a Western power, receive military or economic aid from the power, or deceive public opinion within and abroad. The constitutional trappings of a country like South Vietnam furnish a prime example. As one district chief there commented on the rigging of elections: "Elections are really quite simple. You can't expect most voters to know who is good and who is bad. Either they don't bother to come and vote, or else they choose their candidates at random. Far better to let us choose the candidates for them." [3]

[3] *New York Times,* July 15, 1970. In this connection, we would like to voice a warning in regard to the way political processes in developing countries are now frequently researched. The availability of ample election figures, figures on seat distribution and votes in "parliaments," and similar quantitative means seem to lead to a new type of "formalism" or "institutionalism" that fails to go below the surface. This is not to underestimate the large number of searching and perceptive studies that have been or are being undertaken. We still need, among others, however, comparative studies of systems of corruption and clientele relationships, of the uses of repression, detention, torture, for the maintenance of oftentimes feudal, military, or otherwise authoritarian controls. And we also need studies of the ways in which some regimes try to use pseudodemocratic institutions such as elections and parlia-

As for liberal democracies among the developed (and some of the developing) countries, elections and party systems certainly are more meaningful. Yet we should not forget the antidemocratic criticism of the type we referred to in the Introduction that is frequently leveled against these institutions. What about elections where the choice is only between two very similar programs? What about parties that are influenced or even controlled by special interests that finance their activities?

Electoral problems

There are also more technical questions referring, for example, to the procedural details of voting systems, which have serious political implications. For instance: Should elections be held in single-member districts where the decision is always clear, or in multimember constituencies, where the results, through proportional allocation of seats, more closely reflect the popular attitudes? Single-member districts have the advantage that there is a clear-cut contest and that usually one party emerges as the majority group capable of forming a stable government and carrying out a coherent program; they have the disadvantage of possibly disenfranchising the minority party or parties and of weighting power too much in favor of what may be only a relative majority representing less than 50 percent of the electorate. Proportional representation, on the other hand, while facilitating the effective voicing of a larger number of different opinions and lines of policy, may split the electorate, and therewith the legislature, into so many groups that stable and effective government becomes difficult. A combination of the two, providing for district *and* list votes but requiring a minimum of 5 percent of the total vote for any group to be represented in parliament, has proved quite satisfactory in West Germany, and something like this might constitute a relatively "ideal" solution.

There are other issues related to the aim of

ments for maintaining authoritarian controls. Finally, we continue to need studies of the resistance thus provoked, the ideologies and tactics of opposition and insurrectionist movements, and so forth. That such studies are difficult to secure is clear, but they are badly needed to balance too hasty generalizations drawn from official data and interviews.

equal representation. Mathematical equality can hardly be expected to prevail even under proportional representation. But to draw election districts in such a way that they contain markedly unequal numbers of voters or so that their boundaries contribute to the advantage of specific groups (gerrymandering) may make a mockery of democracy. Thus some American districts had not been redistricted for over a century so that the rural population was generally vastly overrepresented in Congress as well as in state legislatures to the disadvantage of urban dwellers. "Redistricting" has now begun to make representation more equitable in the House of Representatives and in the state chambers.

There are two still more fundamental problems concerning elections: the one regarding "real freedom of choice"; the other the influence of powerful "interests." Communist doctrine maintains that no real alternative is offered voters under capitalism, since a capitalist system permits only those candidates and parties supporting that system to compete. Thus, it asserts, there is no meaningful choice between American Republicans and Democrats, or British Conservatives and Laborites. To the non-Communist, however, there is a difference, and possibly a vital one, between the representatives of big business and of trade unions, of farmers and of urban people, of advocates of free enterprise and those of the welfare state, of black and white supremacists. What may from time to time be true, however, is that one or the other of these groups lacks the "equal opportunity" to compete, either because certain technical regulations work against it or because there is an atmosphere of fear or intimidation. Such an atmosphere can be not unlike that which prevails in totalitarian systems, be it for political reasons (for example, intimidation of black voters in the South) or for economic ones (employee voters in a company town).

Equally serious may be the overbearing influence of powerful vested interests, especially during a campaign, or even in the prior stage of nominating candidates (whether through primary elections or otherwise). Under modern conditions, an election is a vastly expensive business both for the candidates and the parties concerned. Those who can lavish huge

sums of money on press, radio, and television campaigns enjoy an undue advantage. If the subsidies come from a few special interest groups rather than from a large number of small contributors, there is a very real danger that candidates and parties will become beholden to these interests. And while here again we can hardly expect mathematical equality or proportionality for all groups, democracy suffers when there is too high a degree of inequality in this respect. It then remains exposed to charges that wealthy or other powerful interests are in control behind an egalitarian façade. Therefore there is urgency in devising systems of restraint: limitation of expenditures, equal and free time for debate over the mass media, state subsidies, tax exemption of contributions, and so forth, some of which have prevented the worst abuses in two of the countries we have dealt with (Britain and West Germany).

Political parties

This issue of finance in campaigns leads us to problems that concern political parties as such. Basic to the process of choice in an election is the role of parties in formulating issues, presenting candidates, and providing the chief means through which individual and group interests can organize to secure and exercise political power. One of the major problems of the mass party, which is the natural product of universal suffrage and of the need to appeal broadly to different groups, is that it tends to be highly organized with large numbers of often full-time and salaried functionaries, and, like all "big" organizations, to be controlled in an "oligarchic" manner by "bosses" or self-perpetuating party bureaucrats. This does not imply that the trend is always toward a nationwide centralism of such mass parties, as has been the case in Britain and Germany. In the United States, except at short periods during presidential campaigns, the parties tend to disintegrate into frequently feuding regional and local groupings. Even so, the oligarchic tendencies that are characteristic of modern party organizations are noticeable at the local, county, or state level.

This trend raises the problem of how the internal structure and operations of parties can be kept or made more democratic—that is, how to have meaningful interaction between party members, party supporters, and leaders. In this regard such technicalities as devising the right kind of intraparty regulations and arranging the nominations of candidates and elections of party officials in such a manner that there is free debate, open competition, and less behind-the-scene wirepulling can play as important a role as do primary elections, provisions for re-call, and so forth. But beyond these devices is the necessity of securing the active interest and participation of the people at large in party life. "Mass party" does not automatically imply either mass participation or mass membership; only where such active public concern and participation prevail is there hope of transform-ing parties from oligarchic or otherwise man-aged groups into genuinely democratic insti-tutions.

Besides the problems of intraparty democracy there are those involving the relations between parties, that is, what one usually refers to as a country's party *system*. The most frequently discussed question here is that of two-party (or two-major-parties) versus multiparty sys-tems. It is true that while one-party systems are the hallmark of totalitarianism, there are cases, especially in new states, where one ruling party is so organized as to allow for intraparty wings and groupings that provide chances of debate and give-and-take, but more frequently such a system prevents or stifles true democratic processes. These, generally, require plural party systems.

Two-party systems, especially where the two are strongly centralized, provide, as in Great Britain, for that "classical" contrast of, and alternation between, majority and opposition that is the heart of genuine parliamentary government. At the same time, this system may force the voter to support a party because it has a chance to be effective rather than because it reflects his point of view. If the two parties are strongly based on two chief social groups, it may also involve the rigid and possibly pro-tracted rule of one single powerful class, group, or interest to the exclusion of all others.

In a multiparty system, on the other hand, the process of compromise that may go on with-in the major parties in a two-party system is transferred to the floor of the assembly or to the rooms where party leaders meet to hammer out the composition and program of a coalition government. The advantages are the more genuine discretion and influence of small groups or party deputies in the assembly and of the assembly itself vis-à-vis the executive. The shortcomings are equally obvious: the likeli-hood of executive instability, the excessive in-fluence of often insignificant but strategically placed groups (such as the Free Democratic party [FDP] in West Germany or the religious parties in Israel), continuous "horse-trading," even over matters of principle, and the uncer-tainty for the voter in knowing whether the party for which he votes is going to form the central part of a government coalition or not (for example, a group gaining a relative major-ity may even find itself in opposition as in 1969 in West Germany).

The choice between the two systems is not, of course, a free one. Whether a two-party or multiparty system exists in a given country is usually a matter of historical development and of existing social, ethnic, racial, or ideological cleavages. Americans have a preference for two-party structures because their two main parties are really coalitions of many groups and inter-ests. This assimilative characteristic enables the parties to absorb the many cleavages existing in the United States and impels them toward moderation. The tendency toward moderation is reinforced by the need to appeal to all or most strata on a national level. This process now also applies to the two chief parties in Britain and the German Federal Republic. But where two major parties represent radically opposed groups or even doctrines, such as the extreme right and the radical left, or where, as is the case in France and Italy in relation to their respective Communist parties, two major parties are so opposed to each other that a coalition between them is unthinkable, such a two-major-parties system makes for feeble government or else for authoritarian tendencies. In such circumstances a system of three or even more parties more equal in size and more bal-anced in support may well be the lesser evil.

Mentioning moderation and extremism calls to mind the problem of party programs and party policies. The old charge, already referred to, that the major parties in a liberal democ-racy do not offer a real choice was based on the

Marxist assumption that in a bourgeois society political parties reflect the interests of the ruling class to the exclusion of the ruled. The rise of labor parties and similar groups disproved this interpretation. However, largely because of the increased share of workers in the affluence of modernized society, there has been of late a trend, especially in European parties, toward what Otto Kirchheimer called "catch-all" parties and away from those that constitute meaningful alternatives (even where they did not constitute an "opposition of principle" such as socialist, Communist, or fascist). Where the affluent society creates a broad middle class to which all major parties appeal, attitudes may become blurred, party distinctions may lose their color, and the role of the opposition may dwindle.

Doubtlessly such a situation lessens the internecine warfare of parties, especially doctrinally divided ones, and diminishes the concomitant threat of deeply dividing a nation, as in the Germany of the Weimar Republic, in the French Third and Fourth Republics, and in Italy today. But it also involves dangers: public interest in real issues, formerly promoted by parties that differed in meaningful ways, may be translated into "popularity contests" of the respective party leaders. Moreover, if all major parties concentrate their interest on a broad, more or less affluent majority, the minorities that are still economically or otherwise disadvantaged or simply have different ideas may find themselves without political advocates and will tend to be forgotten. Such has been the situation in the United States. As long as major groups, such as labor, were still economically disadvantaged or racially or ethnically discriminated against, political democracy meant that, sooner or later, they would form or find majorities that enacted the reforms that fulfilled their claims and wants. What was necessary was that an active *and* reform-minded president was backed by a strong reform movement controlling a majority in Congress; this constellation did not happen often but it did take place, for instance, under the New Deal. Many developed countries now have such "compact majorities." Where the majorities feel that the economic and social status quo satisfies their interests, democracy may turn out to have the function of merely stabilizing the

existing status and of preventing the further progress that the remaining minorities of the underprivileged may need. Society then petrifies, conjuring up the emergence of what Gunnar Myrdal has called the permanent "underclass" of the poor and/or racially discriminated who, in contrast even to the exploited but working proletariats of an earlier period, are excluded from the social mobility of an active economy and society.

This danger threatening democracy points up certain advantages in having at least minimally ideological parties, parties with a general liberal, progressive, or democratic-socialist *Weltanschauung*, that have a concern not only for the interests they represent but also for social justice and the needs and welfare of all. In contrast to the United States, this used to be the tradition of the European left. Unless such an attitude reasserts itself in the mass societies of our time, democracy may degenerate into a system in which a satisfied and therefore conservative majority, operating through its major parties, protects itself against change. Such a system could become as oppressive of minority groups and opinions, and even of the "public interest" where it differs from that of the majority, as any oligarchy of old.

THE ROLE OF PARLIAMENTS IN LIBERAL DEMOCRACIES

When popular movements in the nineteenth century raised the battle cry of representative government, the way in which "the people" were to be represented was primarily through delegates elected to an assembly patterned on the first modern representative body, the House of Commons. Parliament was to be in the center of democratic political action. But the operations of modern government have since largely disproved the belief of early liberalism, according to which the "truth" would emerge from a battle of wits and a competition of ideas in assembly; decisions and actions, particularly in lawmaking, would be based on this emerging truth. Although parliament is still an important center of political action in liberal democracies, it is no longer *the* main one (for big government has shifted more and more weight to the executive), nor do its debates sway the government's decisions the way earlier periods expected.

One reason for its decline, paradoxically, has been the victory of democracy. In many European countries—in England after the Glorious Revolution and in France as well as other countries in the nineteenth century—parliament had been the fighting force of the middle classes against authoritarian executives (the Crown, and so forth); as such, its members developed an independent spirit and a sense of their distinctive task, in legislation, budget-making, and criticism of the administration. But as authoritarian forces disappeared from the political scene the executive has been drawn from the majority party (or parties), which tends to feel under no obligation to embarrass an executive that represents the same political constituency as itself. If, as in Britain and West Germany, and even more markedly in France, the executive actually turns out to be more powerful than parliament, and if, as we have observed before, there is a trend for even the opposition to play a weaker role, parliament could be in danger of becoming a rubber stamp. In lawmaking, then, it takes second place to the initiating functions of the administration or of interest groups; in addition, the executive's decree-making and rule-making functions grow. And parliamentary debate, while occasionally approximating the idealized "contest for truth," more often turns out to be a contest among representatives of special interests or among the leaders of parties who keep the ordinary deputies under tight control.

There are, in fact, two extremes of parliamentary development into which the modern system of representative government may degenerate. At one end rigid party discipline, especially where the two-party system prevails, may render parliament ultimately subservient to the executive; this has been a possible by-product of the British parliamentary system. Even without strong party discipline or a two-party system, France's unique blend of presidential and parliamentary institutions in the Fifth Republic has assured the dominance of its dual executive. At the other end, especially where the cabinet is a weak coalition of several parties, it is possible to find parliament not only dominating the executive but also endlessly wrangling and thus causing that inefficiency, instability, and

log-rolling that discredited the systems of the French Third and Fourth Republics and of Weimar Germany. Moreover, under a system of separate powers, as in the United States, executive stability may be combined with a pattern of divided parties or interests in the legislature.

While, in contrast to the British Parliament, Congress and the state legislatures in the United States have effective power over the process of law- and budget-making, they also illustrate the difficulties of modern assemblies in regard to organization and procedures. To carry the crushing burden of modern parliamentary work loads requires labor-dividing procedures through devices such as committees, allocation of time for debate, and so on. But these devices may develop into a brake on action rather than as a spur to it (as in filibusters in the Senate, or the role of the Rules Committee in the House), or make laws reflect the power of entrenched groups rather than the majority will in the assembly. Bills may be stalled, pigeonholed, killed, amended, or compromised at so many way stations in their passage through the two houses (plus the conference committee) that Congress, rather than being a legislative body, turns into a legislation-preventing one. This happens most frequently when legislation disliked by some major interest group or powerful lobby is at stake. However, bills favored by such groups may pass like lightning, without even being debated by the majority voting for them.

Modern parliament must find a middle course between overriding the rights of individual deputies, or groups of them, and yielding too easily to their influence and demands. There is the danger of parliaments becoming either ineffective or the instruments of their most powerful members and the special interests behind them.

Still, under a system in which the separation of power is maintained, the assembly can serve better as a means to limit executive power than under the "fusion" system of most parliamentary regimes. A further means of checking power with power is bicameralism. This is indeed its chief advantage when there is no additional reason for having a second chamber, such as representing the member-units in a federal system. Even then, however, the second chamber is warranted only where there remains genuine sectional sentiment, which, as we have seen, is dwindling in modern federalism. The United States Senate today represents states' rights and interests hardly more than does the House. Occasionally, however, bicameralism serves a particular purpose as, for example, in West Germany, where the Federal Council successfully coordinates federal lawmaking with the administration of the laws in the states.

Despite all this criticism, a modern democratic assembly has an enduring value in certain areas. To expect any large and varied group of nonspecialized representatives to frame the laws of a complex society or to coordinate the government's far-flung activities is to impose a burden no assembly can be expected to bear. What a well-organized assembly can do—and do well—is to analyze, criticize, and judge the policies and proposals of the government; to voice the desires and anxieties of the mass of the citizens; to protect their liberties against abuse of power by the government; to educate public opinion through its debates; and, finally, to participate in the process of lawmaking to the extent this is still possible in an area that relies so much on the expert and the administrator.

In some ways the legislature is particularly suited to these tasks. Ideally, its members possess a kind of knowledge that the experts are not likely to have; they represent a range of experience in terms of class and geographical origin and have an intimate knowledge of their constituents that should make them exceptionally good judges of public opinion and of the acceptability and workability of laws. As protector of individual liberties against abuse of governmental power, the House of Commons is unexcelled; for educating the public on important issues its debates are remarkably effective, as is the opposition as critic of proposed legislation. Thus it is in its scrutinizing, supervising, and criticizing function that parliament, at its best, comes into its own.

POLITICAL LEADERSHIP

In the Introduction we emphasized that almost all trends in modern society—the growth in the functions of government, the oligarchic tendencies within any big organization, and especially the chronic crises in international affairs—have contributed to a disproportionate increase in the power of the executive. It is here, at the top level, rather than in legislatures or other institutions, that leadership now rests. This situation confronts democratic government with a twofold imperative: to see that such leadership provides strong, determined, and forceful direction to the community while at the same time remaining ultimately accountable to the people and responsive to the public interest.

Dictatorial or authoritarian regimes do not have this dilemma. Their all-too-forceful leadership considers itself responsible not to any institutionally expressed popular will but to a cause, or to the "welfare of the community" as interpreted solely by the leadership. Fascist doctrine states this frankly, while Communist theory proclaims responsibility to the masses whom the leaders are not supposed to leave too far behind. But in the absence of institutionalized criticism and control, who holds the vanguard to its task? Even though Stalin's rule was indicted as deviationist by his successors, there is little evidence that effective procedures for the enforcement of responsibility have since been devised or observed.

In democracies, on the other hand, the decisive constitutional rules and procedures—direct election of a chief executive or voting for a party whose leader then becomes head of the government—aim at providing responsible leadership through conferring a mandate limited in time. Democratic leadership means, in fact, power with a time limit. Although this leadership may possess, during its mandate, power that appears uncomfortably large and comprehensive—especially when it includes special "martial-law" powers to cope with emergencies—it is understood that it will periodically revert to the people.

Still, such leadership confronts two dangers of opposite kinds. One danger is that in order to be and stay responsible, the leaders look too anxiously for, and follow too closely, whatever appears to be the mood of the people or their representatives at the moment. Modern executive leadership must develop initiative as the most important motive power in government. If it is weak or pliant, leadership falls nowhere, or elsewhere. The opposite problem is illustrated by the dilemma that President Franklin Roosevelt faced when, with a largely isolationist public opinion, he realized that America had to intervene against Nazi fascism. Should he then, as a responsible leader, have yielded to the pressure of opinion against his own better judgment or should he have gone ahead? In doing the latter, he was accused of acting "dictatorially," but history showed that intervention was necessary to save the democratic forces in the world. Recent administrations faced a similar dilemma in Vietnam, this time, however, with history apparently showing that theirs had not been "the better judgment." Everything in such instances depends on whether a "broad" interpretation of the popular mandate is still in line with ultimate democratic objectives and the public or national interest. Thus democratic leadership requires not only initiative and broad powers but also a deep sense of responsibility to the basic purposes of the people.

SELECTION, SUCCESSION, ACCESS

The preceding discussion underlines the tremendous role of personality and therefore the problems of selection, succession, and access. Various nontotalitarian systems differ widely concerning the prerequisites for top leadership and the ways to achieve it. In parliamentary systems leaders usually go through a lengthy period of political apprenticeship in a party organization and parliament; in presidential systems this is not necessarily the case. The somewhat haphazard nominating system of the two major American parties provides no guarantee that the choice will fall on a man with previous experience and qualifications in the most decisive areas of statesmanship.

In regard to succession, however, it is dictatorship that faces the more serious problems.

In systems where law determines what happens in government, succession will proceed in prescribed ways. A system based on a unique and infallible leader is put to its greatest test with his demise or overthrow. Totalitarian leaders have been loath to designate successors in order not to endanger their own power while they still exercise it. A lack of clear designation, however, usually leads to strife among contestants. "Collective leadership," as events in the Soviet Union showed after Stalin's death and even after Khrushchev's ouster, is difficult to maintain, and it is generally the toughest and most ruthless who emerge as the fittest in this process of natural selection.

However great the trend is toward concentration of power at the top, and however strong the top leader may be, he must delegate work even of the most decisive nature in order to cope with his task. Moreover, all leaders inevitably listen to official and unofficial advisers. Hence, the vital problem of access to leadership. To whom does the chief executive listen? With whom does he associate both inside and outside the formal office structure? Where, and how, does he get his information? It is here that informal channels of access may prove as important as formal ones, or even more so. Unofficial aides or friends may turn out to wield vast, and often hidden, influence, and their existence may raise real problems for maintaining responsible leadership. Moreover, the very fact of a chief executive's limited time points up another problem. An appointment secretary, deciding whom the leader sees and for how long, may be more influential than top government aides.

Since for security and related reasons the top level of policymaking has necessarily to be conducted in secrecy, responsible democratic government depends greatly on whether and how the decision-makers are held to account for their decisions, especially by parliament and by the mouthpieces of public opinion. Internal checks may be provided by organizational means, such as the cabinet system. But where a cabinet decision is made by majority vote, it is likely to weaken the top leadership, as was the case with earlier French regimes. Cabinets that consist of party coalitions may provide the individual minister with much more independent authority than that enjoyed by a British

Cabinet minister, since in a multiparty system he is probably the representative of a party whose support is needed to keep the coalition together. Cabinet solidarity, however, may render even ministers subservient to the top leader—as witness the West German system under Adenauer. The British system has generally proved more successful at combining effective action with accountability, while in the American system where, "cabinets" or National Security Councils notwithstanding, "the buck always stops" at the president's desk, internal checks have often proved ineffective.

LEADERSHIP AND BUREAUCRACY

Under any circumstances, the top leadership must delegate some of its powers, and it is this fact that creates the political role of the bureaucracy, and in particular of that higher level of the service that participates in policymaking. And since the administration carries the responsibility of executing the laws and of seeing that they fulfill the purposes for which they were designed, the way in which the bureaucracy functions, and especially whether it considers itself responsible to the people as a genuine civil service, are decisive factors in the functioning of democratic government.

In modern government the civil service is supposed to implement impartially the directives of the government (cabinet, minister, and so forth); but in practice much depends on the history, the traditions, and the general structure of bureaucracy and administration in a given country. Where, as in Prussia-Germany, the officialdom antedates representative and democratic institutions, or where, as in the French Third and Fourth Republics, unstable government made the civil service the dominant permanent force in the state, its political influence is likely to surpass the limits of mere executive-administrative action. If its members are selected from specific classes or come to constitute a caste of their own, this type of bureaucracy may color a nation's entire government and politics, as has been not uncommon in some Continental European countries.

In the Anglo-American systems, on the other hand, the modern civil service was established in a more democratic environment that by and large avoided or eliminated special social selectivity. In England this has produced generally felicitous results; and in the United States the cross-fertilization between public service and other occupations, such as business, has had much to do with keeping the service free from any pronounced caste spirit. But the turnover among officeholders in the United States causes a good deal of inefficiency and waste of manpower. Moreover, lack of permanence, especially in the upper ranks of the service, may open the way to the corrupting influences of special interests. "Patronage"—that is, the system in which public office is used to reward often unqualified persons to whom party leaders are obligated politically or possibly financially (for example, for contributions to campaign funds), or to appoint those who, in turn, will be beholden to the person or party making the appointment for their jobs—was long the bane of the American system (as it is the bane of any genuine civil service system) and still occasionally leads to highly unsuitable appointments. Of course, the larger the number of "political" positions that are not under the merit system, the greater this danger. The removal of the American post office from this area of patronage has been a great advance.

There are thus two opposite dangers in regard to bureaucracy: one, that it becomes too strong a power in the state and develops attitudes of high-handedness and authoritarianism (often, this way, causing attitudes of submissiveness in the public over which it "rules"); the other danger is that it becomes too weak, too little organized as that "backbone" of government that, especially these days, is needed to resist and counter the pressures of the powerful nongovernmental interests. (Of course, both authoritarianism toward the public and submissiveness to private interests can go hand-in-hand—the worst of all possible worlds.) A system like the American, with many important political appointees and the constant exchange of persons between public service and business and similar outside professions, illustrates the second danger. The Pentagon official (or general) in charge of defense contracts, who sees himself already in the corporate position of his opposite number after resigning (or retiring from) his present one, may not wholeheartedly represent the public interest in negotiating a contract, and the corporation representative, knowing this, may want to exploit this weakness. The lawyer in the antitrust division of the justice department may already think of becoming an attorney for big corporations, where he then can apply what he has learned in government against the government. Can he be trusted to act forcefully as an official of the government? A wildlife official of the Department of the Interior, instead of protecting a species, is used to destroy its members systematically to clear them from ranch land; mine inspectors of the Department of Labor may fail to inspect thoroughly; and so forth.

To protect the weaker party (or natural environment, which is now the weaker party in its struggle with technology and human greed), the state needs a civil service with *esprit de corps*, a "civic" spirit of its own. This spirit, in countries where the "game of politics," with its concomitant corruption and inefficiency, has been part of the "political culture," requires entirely new attitudes. The public servant must rise in social prestige vis-à-vis the businessman; he must be given better remuneration and job security and, above all, a chance to rise in the hierarchy of officialdom to many of the high positions now reserved to political appointments. Compared with the United States, countries like Britain and Germany have an easier job in this respect. Whatever the shortcomings peculiar to their systems, there has developed more of a genuine public spirit there than elsewhere. That it is not impossible to change from one type of system to the other, however, is demonstrated by the fact that in Britain, too, corruption characterized its public life at an earlier period. But it takes an aware public and far-sighted leadership to have this change come about.

GOVERNMENT AND PRESSURE GROUPS

What we have just been saying already indicates the vital role of pressure groups in modern society and the vital problem, for government, of how to deal with them. Inevitably, in any open society, a large number of varied interest groups exercise pressure on government and politics whenever lawmaking or the application of law affects them. If a country's larger and smaller interest groups, themselves organized democratically, operate freely and compete with each other on an equal footing, this is not a danger to, but an expression of, democracy. But where these groups, especially mutually opposed ones (such as management and labor), do not balance each other—where big business prevails or (as from time to time in Scandinavian countries) organized labor or agricultural or even feudal interests prevail—pluralism, with its "countervailing" forces, yields to predominance. Even where influence groups balance each other, it should not be the task of the public power merely to register the compromises and deals of opposed interests. The public interest may well be different from such solutions. Management and labor, for example, might agree on wage increases in what appears to both sides to be their mutual interest, but such an agreement might yet run counter to the common good (in this instance, the interest of consumers) because of consequent price increases and inflationary effects on a nation's economy. Or, as frequently occurs now, various groups may agree on the exploitation of a resource that, because of the threat of its exhaustion or the pollution that it causes, is not in the public interest.

This is not to say that interest groups and their representatives should be excluded from the policymaking and administrative process altogether. Lobbying has its legitimate functions. Provided pressure groups are not permitted to usurp a political function, and that administrators remain mindful that they represent the national interest vis-à-vis such groups, the latter's specialized knowledge can serve as an important link between government and the people to whom it is responsible.

It is here that the type and attitude of leadership will be decisive. Especially in a country such as the United States, where the parties are the chief representatives of competing interests, the national mandate of the presidency is of utmost importance. If there is no integration of the plurality of groups and interests at this point, there will be none at all. Still, the American system, where interests, although working in and through parties, are not organized *as* parties, seems to be at an advantage compared with systems where coalition governments composed of representatives from interest parties have a hard time rising above a mere plundering of the commonwealth in their own favor.

The type of party and governmental systems determines to a large extent the degree of pressure-group influence and the way the pressures operate. Where, as in Great Britain or West Germany, or in France today, basic decisions are made at the top level of the executive rather than in parliament, lobbyists are more likely to besiege the executive and administration than members of parliament. Where, as previously in France and now in Italy, the legislature predominates at least in lawmaking, deputies bear the brunt. Under a separation of powers, as in the United States, pressures are likely to affect both branches equally. Moreover, the way in which parties represent particular interests has a bearing on how pressures will be applied and on their chances of success. Where, as in the United States, both parties appeal to all major strata, pressures operate on and within both parties, and it then is of particular importance which interests predominate in a lawmaker's constituency, how susceptible he is to influence, and so forth. Where, as in Britain, the two major parties still represent to a considerable

degree two distinct classes, in a way they function as interest groups themselves, as witness the number of trade unionists among Labor MP's or of businessmen among Conservatives. Where, as in Germany (and Japan), members of interest groups, such as industrialists or farmers, tend to leave the representation of their interests to professionals, one finds many officials of interest organizations serving as deputies in parliament. Such infiltration of parliament by the lobby tends to make it a social and economic council rather than a body representing the people.

The importance of forceful, disinterested, and responsible leadership in the democracies is thus obvious. It is heightened by two current developments. In the domestic sphere, the advent of the affluent society has shifted the urgency of governmental functions to the much neglected public sector of life. But since it is now a minority rather than, as in the past, a majority that is likely to be economically underprivileged and disadvantaged, it may be more difficult, though no less necessary, to marshal support for it in a framework of majority procedures. Internationally, the democracies are confronted with a somewhat comparable situation. Here the developed nations constitute the affluent few who must help the vast masses of the developing world. Democratic leadership, in both situations, must convince the people to act on behalf of the interests of others; if they fail to do so, the democracies will not only be defeated morally and politically by their chief opponents, but will also deny their own basic values.

DEMOCRACY IN THE MODERN WORLD

What is the outlook for democracy in a world beset with the threats of totalitarianism, the uncertainties of an emerging world of developing new nations, and its own trends toward oligarchism and an erosion of liberties? As we look over our list of weaknesses and shortcomings of liberal democracy, we may feel discouraged. Does it not add up to a deficient rather than efficient system, one in which professed ideals and promises are contradicted

more often than not by the facts? Has the ideal of a freely debating, freely deciding, and freely consenting "sovereign" people yielded, in practice, to the actuality of manipulated opinion-making, of parties and legislatures controlled by oligarchs or special interests, of administrations lording it over helpless citizens, and of leaders weak and thus easily influenced by private interests or so powerful that little distinguishes them from dictators?

Before we make a judgment, however, let us note that democratic theory has always been inclined to measure realities with the yardstick of ideals that have hardly been realizable. The belief of eighteenth-century Enlightenment and nineteenth-century Progressivism in a mankind that would come ever closer to a state of internal and external peace, a harmony of interests, and a community of the free and equal has yielded under the impact of the cruel experiences of our century to the more realistic insight that the ideal must forever remain unobtainable. Yet it can still serve as a guiding star for efforts to measure up to it. And this is where democracy has a value far beyond anything that nondemocratic belief systems and regimes can offer. As long as there remains the possibility of debate, the competition of opinion and policy groups, and changes of procedures and institutions, democracy will continue to be an open system in which experimentation is the means of remedying insufficiencies and providing reform. The very fact of criticism like ours points up this basic asset. And it has always been one of the greatest strengths of democracy that it possesses an abundant variety of devices that can be used to move closer to the ideal of free, representative, responsible, and efficient government. Electoral systems can be used for the worse, but also for the better. So can the procedures of legislatures, or systems for the recruitment of public officials. Novel institutions such as the public corporation can be invented to cope with problems of government ownership; or an institution like that of the ombudsman can be taken over for better protection against administrative arbitrariness.

Best of all, democracy allows people to learn from experience. Institutions that have proved successful in one country can be introduced in another. Each democracy is a laboratory for others. Here, it is true, we must again beware of overoptimism. Every country develops its institutions in terms of its own historical heritage, its social and economic framework, its own political culture and "way of life." We have seen that overambitious experiments in reeducation may fail. But we also can find successful imitation and adaptation as broad as that of the general parliamentary pattern and as specific as administrative courts and judicial review.

Thus democratic self-analysis is neither fair nor valid if it overlooks the successes and potentialities of democracy or if it is more critical of democratic than of totalitarian shortcomings. Revelations of Hitler and his "court" have disclosed a degree of folly of which no democracy has shown itself capable. Similarly, it would be hard to think of a more devastating indictment of Soviet leadership than the revelations about Stalin made by the Soviet's own top leadership. The greatest indictment of nondemocratic systems is that, in general, there is no way to change them except by force. There is a good deal of feeling abroad that democracies too have become so petrified and their "Establishments" so unresponsive to attempts to bring about change in peaceful and lawful ways that only revolt and violence remain as effective means for change. We do not believe that it has come to such a pass. If it ever should, democracy would have lost its *raison d'être*.

There remains one problem. The devices and institutions of democracy are operational. They deal with ways and means to achieve ends but leave open the question of the objective of government—that is, the type of community to be established by free discussion and consent. Even though the devices may be unimpeachably democratic, the people using them may be confused as to their ultimate aims. It is then that *anomie* and frustration may beset them. Certainly, the greatest strength of totalitarianism is its belief in a cause, and its attempt and frequent success in providing people with certain and appealing aims.

But there is no reason why democracy cannot also avoid emptiness. We have no shortage of worthwhile objectives, ranging all the way from ensuring peace and genuine peaceful coexistence to aiding the advance of the underdeveloped majority of the human race, and now, ever more urgently, the preservation of a human and livable environment for all on the "space-ship Earth."

It is especially in the area of advancing the underdeveloped South of the globe that the fate of liberal democracy is likely to be decided. Democracy flourishes best where there is a feeling of economic well-being and security. The absence of these economic requirements makes the fulfillment of democratic requirements, such as detached assessment of public affairs and consideration for the interests and rights of others, extremely difficult. The rising and rapidly multiplying masses of the world's South, the agricultural and subsistence proletariat of the present-day world, can hardly achieve the maturity liberal democracy requires without a rapid improvement in living standards; unless the poorer nations are helped in their present struggle to meet their aspirations, their governments, whether democratically inclined or not, are likely to fall prey to anarchy, radicalism, or militant forces, and the great powers may be pulled into the vortex. Coupled with the tasks still facing the democracies at home—such as wiping out their own areas of discrimination and poverty and coping with their environmental tasks—this external challenge is enough to provide them with objectives for the remainder of this century.

The democratic way of life is not an easy one, but its rewards are great. No form of government appears simpler than that of autocracy; yet history stands as a record of the abuse of power so concentrated. Democracy requires from its citizens political intelligence, experience, maturity, public spirit, and self-restraint; it also demands the exercise of ingenuity in finding solutions and developing the political machinery appropriate for a system that desires freedom and responsibility as well as efficiency. The great strength of democracy is that its way of life fosters and encourages these very qualities. It is in democracies that no one attitude or solution is orthodox, that diversity and experiment are considered natural and desirable. And as one looks at the great variety of devices that the democracies have developed for the realization of their aims, it would be rash to conclude that in imaginativeness, willingness to experiment, and social idealism the democracies yield in any way to other forms of government.

ABBREVIATIONS

FRANCE

CD *Centre démocrate* (Lecanuet's party drawn from MRP, moderate Conservatives, and right-wing Radicals, 1965)

CFDT *Confédération française démocratique du travail* (trade union federation formed 1964 from CFTC)

CFTC *Confédération française des travailleurs chrétiens* (majority changed name to CFDT, 1964; minority remain as small conservative Catholic trade union federation)

CGC *Confédération générale des cadres* (white-collar and supervisory staffs' union)

CGPF *Confédération générale de la production française* (employers' association formed in 1919, superseded by CNPF)

CGT *Confédération générale du travail* (largest trade union federation, Communist dominated)

CGT-FO *See* FO

CNEJ *Centre national d'études judiciares* (specialized professional law school set up in 1958)

CNIP *Centre national des indépendents et paysans* (loose conservative grouping formed in 1948 and joined in 1954 by remnants of the RPF after de Gaulle dissolved the latter. Reached its electoral peak in 1958 and had split into three groups by 1962.)

CNJA *Cercle national des jeunes agriculteurs* (formed by JAC to promote rural reform)

CNPF *Confédération nationale du patronat français* (main employers' organization)

CNR *Conseil national de la Résistance* (war-time organization led by Bidault, who revived the name for his pro-OAS front, 1962)

ECSC European Coal and Steel Community

EDC European Defense Community (rejected in French Assembly, 1954)

ENA *École nationale d'administration* (graduate school of public administration)

FEN *Fédération de l'éducation nationale* (main state teachers' organization)

FER *Fédération des étudiants révolutionnaires* (Trotskyite group, important in 1968 events)

FGDS *Fédération de la gauche démocrate et socialiste* (alliance of Socialists, Radicals, and political clubs born of Mitterrand's presidential campaign, 1965)

FLN *Front de libération nationale* (Algerian nationalists)

FNSEA *Fédération nationale des syndicats d'exploitants agricoles* (main peasant pressure group)

FO *CGT-Force-Ouvrière* (trade union federation, mainly in public sector, that split from CGT, 1947; vaguely Socialist in outlook)

ISA *Institut supérieur d'affaires* (graduate business school)

JAC *Jeunesse agricole chrétienne* (Catholic youth organization)

JCML *Jeunesses communistes marxistes-leninistes* (Maoist group important in 1968 events)

JCR *Jeunesses communistes révolutionnaires* (Trotskyite group important in 1968 events)

JEC *Jeunesses étudiantes chrétiennes* (Catholic students)

MRP *Mouvement républicain populaire* (Catholic party, merged into CD)

NATO North Atlantic Treaty Organization (military)

OAS *Organisation de l'armée secrète* (Algerian military and settlers' civil war organization; attempted terrorism in France, 1962)

ORTF *Office de radiodiffusion-télévision française* (the state broadcasting service)

PCF *Parti communiste français* (Communist party)

PDM *Progrès et démocratie moderne* (center party developing out of CD; Jacques Duhamel's party)

PRL *Parti républicain de la liberté* (right-wing party, 1946)

PSU *Parti socialiste unifié* (left-wing socialist party in Fifth Republic)

RDA *Rassemblement democratique Africain* (major preindependence political grouping in French-controlled Africa)

RGR *Rassemblement des gauches républicaines* (center group in Fourth Republic linking Radical party to its allies; became right-wing Radicals' party organization in 1956 election)

RI *Républicaines indépendents* (Conservative allies of Gaullists; Giscard d'Estaing's party)

RPF *Rassemblement du peuple français* (de Gaulle's party, 1947–53)

RS *Républicains sociaux* (Gaullist party after de Gaulle withdrew, 1953)

RTF *Radiodiffusion-télévision française* (old name of ORTF)

SFIO *Section française de l'Internationale ouvrière* (the Socialist party)

UDR *Union pour la défense de la République* (the Gaullist party, 1968)

UDSR *Union démocratique et socialiste de la Résistance* (small center party of Fourth Republic; Pleven's and Mitterrand's party)

UDT *Union démocratique du travail* (left Gaullist party, 1958–62)

UDVᵉ *Union démocratique de la Vᵉ Republique* (the Gaullist party, 1967)

UEC *Union des étudiants communistes* (Communist students)

UFD *Union des forces démocratiques* (small left-center party, 1958; included Mendès-France; merged into PSU)

UNEF *Union nationale des étudiants français* (the French national union of students)

UNR *Union pour la nouvelle République* (the Gaullist party, 1958; became UNR-UDT, 1962)

GERMANY

APO *Ausserparlamentarische Opposition* (Extraparliamentary Opposition)

BDI *Bund Deutscher Industrieller* (Federation of German Industry)

CDU *Christlich-Demokratische Union* (Christian Democratic Union)

CSU *Christlich-Soziale Union* (Christian Social Union)

DBB *Deutscher Beamtenbund* (German Civil Servants' Association)

DDR *Deutsche Demokratische Republik* (German Democratic Republic)

DGB *Deutscher Gewerkschaftsbund* (German Trade Union Federation)

DKP *Deutsche Kommunistische Partei* (German Communist Party)

FDGB *Freier Deutscher Gewerkschaftsbund* (German Free Trade Union Association)

FDP *Freie Demokratische Partei* (Free Democratic Party)

FRG *Bundesrepublik Deutschland* (Federal Republic of Germany)

NPD *Nationaldemokratische Partei Deutschlands* (National Democratic Party of Germany)

NSDAP *Nationalsozialistische Deutsche Arbeiterpartei* (National Socialist German Workers' Party)

SDS *Sozialistischer Deutscher Studentenbund* (Socialist German Students' Association)

SED *Sozialistische Einheitspartei Deutschlands* (Socialist Unity Party of Germany)

SPD *Sozialdemokratische Partei Deutschlands* (Social Democratic Party of Germany)

Bibliography

Prepared by

LOUISE W. HOLBORN

Radcliffe Institute, Cambridge, Mass.

The steady output of new books on many aspects of the governments and politics of the major foreign powers has made it necessary to cull with care those listed in the previous bibliographies. A high proportion of the books included in this bibliography were published from 1965 on; books that appeared earlier are not listed unless they are of particular importance. Articles have been included only when they form a major source of information on a particular subject.

For those who want a more detailed survey of earlier material, attention is drawn to the comprehensive bibliographies in earlier editions of *Major Foreign Powers*.

In keeping with the practice in earlier bibliographies, this compilation has been confined to publications in English. The wealth of material on foreign governments available in this language is a reflection of the vastly increased concern of the English-speaking world to understand the peoples and policies of other countries.

Except in rare instances, government publications are not included. They can be secured from the following information centers:

United States: Superintendent of Documents, Government Printing Office, Washington, D.C. 20025
United Kingdom of Great Britain: Pendragon House, Inc., 1093 Charter Avenue, Redwood City, Calif. 94063
France: French Embassy, Press and Information Services, 972 Fifth Avenue, New York, N.Y. 10021
Federal Republic of Germany: German Information Center, 410 Park Avenue, New York, N.Y. 10022
For USSR Material in English: Publishing House, Moscow, through Four Continent Book Co., 156 Fifth Avenue, New York, N.Y. 10010

ABBREVIATIONS

BBC: British Broadcasting Corporation, London.
Cmnd.: *Command Paper*, HMSO, London.
COI: Central Office of Information, London.
For. Lang. Pub.: Foreign Language Publications, Moscow.
Hansard: Hansard Society for Parliamentary Affairs, London.
HMSO: Her Majesty's Stationery Office, London.
Inst.: Institute.
Int.: International.
J: *Journal*.
Lib.: Library.
Lib. Cong.: Library of Congress, Washington, D.C.

LJ: *Law Journal*.
LR: *Law Review*.
MIT: Massachusetts Institute of Technology, Cambridge, Mass.
P: Press.
PEP: Political and Economic Planning, London.
Pbk.: Paperback.
Pub.: Publisher.
Publ.: Publication.
Pub. Aff.: Public Affairs Press, Washington, D.C.
Q: *Quarterly*.
R: *Review*.
Ref. Pamph.: Reference Pamphlet.
RIIA: Royal Institute of International Affairs, London.
Trans.: Translation.
TUC: Trade Union Congress.
U: University.
USGPO: United States Government Printing Office, Washington, D.C.

COMPARATIVE MATERIAL

1. Periodicals

AJCL: *American Journal of Comparative Law*, Ann Arbor, Mich., quarterly.
AJS: *American Journal of Sociology*, Chicago, bi-monthly.
APSR: *American Political Science Review*, Washington, D.C., quarterly.
Aussenpolitik [German Foreign Affairs Review], Hamburg, quarterly.
BJPS: *British Journal of Political Science*, Cambridge UP, quarterly.
BJS: *British Journal of Sociology*, London, quarterly.
CEH: *Central European History*, Emory UP, Atlanta, Ga., quarterly.
CG: *Comparative Government*.
CJEPS: *Canadian Journal of Economic and Political Science*, Toronto, quarterly.
Comp. Pol.: *Comparative Politics*, Chicago, quarterly.
CPF: *Comparative Political Finance*.
CPS: *Comparative Political Studies*, Beverly Hills, Calif.
CS: *Commonwealth Survey*, London, fortnightly.
CSSH: *Comparative Studies in Society and History*, The Hague, quarterly.
E: *The Economist*, London, weekly.
ESR: *European Studies Review*, U Lancaster, Macmillan, London, first issue, Jan. 1971.
FA: *Foreign Affairs*, New York, quarterly.
GFP: *German Foreign Policy*, Institute for Interna-

tional Relations, VEB Deutscher Verlag der Wissenschaften, Berlin, German Democratic Republic.

Gov. & Opp.: Government and Opposition, London, first issue, 1966, quarterly.

HLR: Harvard Law Review, Cambridge, Mass., monthly (Nov–June).

IA: International Affairs, London, monthly.

IC: International Conciliation, New York, monthly.

ICLQ: International and Comparative Law Quarterly, London.

IJ: International Journal, Toronto, quarterly.

IJP: International Journal of Politics, Journal of Translations from Worldwide Sources, New York, first issue, Winter 1969–70.

IO: International Organization, Boston, quarterly.

IPSA: International Political Science Abstracts, Oxford, quarterly.

ISSJ: International Social Science Journal, Paris, quarterly.

JCEA: Journal of Central European Affairs, Boulder, Colo., quarterly.

JCH: Journal of Contemporary History, London, quarterly.

JCPS: Journal of Commonwealth Political Studies, Leicester UP, monthly (Nov–June).

JHI: Journal of Historical Ideas.

JIA: Journal of International Affairs, Columbia U, New York.

JICJ: Journal of International Commission of Jurists, Geneva, monthly.

JMH: Journal of Modern History, Chicago, quarterly.

JP: The Journal of Politics, Gainesville, Fla., quarterly.

MJPS: Midwest Journal of Political Science, Wayne State UP, Detroit, quarterly.

Parl. Aff.: Parliamentary Affairs, London, quarterly.

The Parliamentarian, Journal of the Parliaments of the Commonwealth, ed. by Commonwealth Parliamentary Association, House of Parliament, quarterly.

PQ: Political Quarterly, London.

PS: Political Studies, Oxford, three issues annually.

PSQ: Political Science Quarterly, New York.

Pub. Ad.: Public Administration, London, quarterly.

Pub. Law: The Constitutional and Administrative Law of the Commonwealth, London, quarterly.

Race Today, Institute of Race Relations, London, monthly.

Round Table: The Commonwealth, London, quarterly.

SR: Social Research, New York, quarterly.

WP: World Politics, Princeton, N.J., quarterly.

WPQ: The Western Political Quarterly, Salt Lake City, Utah, quarterly.

WT: The World Today, London, monthly.

YLJ: Yale Law Journal, New Haven, Conn., monthly (Nov–June).

YR: Yale Review, New Haven, Conn., quarterly.

2. Books

Abraham, Henry J., *The Judicial Process, An Introductory Analysis of the Courts of the United States, England, and France*, 2nd ed., Oxford UP, 1968, 502 pp, pbk.

Agricultural Policies in Europe and the Soviet Union, Dept. of Agriculture, Economic Research Service, 1968, 59 pp.

Albinski, Henry S. and Lawrence K. Pettit, eds., *European Political Processes: Essays and Readings*, Allyn and Bacon, 1968, 448 pp, pbk.

Almond, Gabriel A. and James S. Coleman, eds., *The Politics of the Developing Areas*, Princeton UP, 1960, 591 pp.

———— and G. Bingham Powell, Sr., *Comparative Politics: A Developmental Approach*, Little, Brown, 1966, 348 pp.

———— and Sidney Verba, *The Civic Culture: Political Attitudes and Democracy in Five Nations*, Little, Brown, 1965, 379 pp, pbk.

Anderson, Charles W., Fred R. von der Mehden, and Crawford Young, *Issues of Political Development*, Prentice-Hall, 1967, 248 pp.

Andrews, William G., ed., *Constitutions and Constitutionalism*, 3rd ed., Van Nostrand, 1968, 240 pp, pbk.

————, ed., *European Politics II: The Dynamics of Change*, Van Nostrand Reinhold, 1969, 278 pp, pbk.

———— and Uri Ra'anan, eds., *The Politics of the Coup D'Etat: Five Case Studies*, Van Nostrand Reinhold, 1969, 153 pp, pbk.

Arendt, Hannah, *The Origins of Totalitarianism*, new rev. ed., Harcourt Brace Jovanovich, 1966, 526 pp.

Bachrach, P., *The Theory of Democratic Elitism: A Critique*, Little, Brown, 1967, 109 pp.

Barry, Brian, *Political Argument*, Humanities Press, 1965, 364 pp.

Bayley, David H., *Public Liberties in the New States*, Rand McNally, 1964, 152 pp, pbk.

Black, Cyril E., *The Dynamics of Modernization: A Study in Comparative History*, Harper, 1966, 207 pp.

Blondel, Jean, *Comparative Government: A Reader*, Doubleday, 1969, 270 pp, pbk.

————, *An Introduction to Comparative Government*, Praeger, 1970, 557 pp, pbk.

Bloom, Bridget, *Parliaments and Electoral Systems: A World Handbook*, Institute of Electoral Research, London, 1962, 128 pp.

Braibanti, Ralph, "Comparative Political Analytics Reconsidered," *JP*, Feb. 1968:25–65.

Brogan, Sir Denis W., *Worlds in Conflict*, Harper, 1967, 133 pp.

———— and Douglas V. Verney, *Political Patterns in Today's World*, 2nd ed., Harcourt Brace Jovanovich, 1968, 278 pp, pbk.

Bruce, Maurice, *The Coming of the Welfare State*, rev. ed., Schocken Books, 1966, 308 pp.

Bryce, Viscount James, *Modern Democracies*, Macmillan, 1924, 2 vols, 567 and 757 pp.

Brzezinski, Zbigniew and Samuel P. Huntington, *Political Power, USA/USSR: Similarities and Contrasts, Convergence or Evolution*, Viking, 1964, 461 pp.

Bunn, Ronald F. and William G. Andrews, eds., *Politics and Civil Liberties in Europe: Four Case Studies*, Van Nostrand, 1968, 221 pp, pbk.

Burin, Frederick S. and Kurt Shell, eds., *Politics, Law and Social Change: Selected Essays of Otto Kirchheimer*, Columbia UP, 1969, 483 pp.

Burns, Sir Alan, ed., *Parliament as an Export*, Allen & Unwin, London, 1966, 271 pp.

Butler, David E., ed., *Elections Abroad*, St. Martin's, 1959, 280 pp.

Campbell, Angus, P. E. Converse, W. E. Miller, and D. E. Stokes, *Elections and the Political Order*, John Wiley & Sons, 1966, 385 pp.

Campion, Lord and D. W. S. Lidderdale, *European Parliamentary Procedure: A Comparative Handbook*, Allen & Unwin, London, 1955, 270 pp.

Carter, Gwendolen M., ed., *National Unity and Regionalism in Eight African States*, Cornell UP, 1966, 565 pp.

———, ed., *Politics in Africa: Seven Cases*, Harcourt Brace Jovanovich, 1966, 283 pp, pbk.

——— and John H. Herz, *Government and Politics in the Twentieth Century*, rev. enl. ed., Praeger, 1965, 231 pp, pbk.

——— and Alan F. Westin, eds., *Politics in Europe: 5 Cases in European Government*, Harcourt Brace Jovanovich, 1965, 205 pp.

Castberg, Freda, *Freedom of Speech in the West: A Comparative Study of Public Law in France, the United States and Germany*, Allen & Unwin, London, 1961, 475 pp.

Castles, Francis G., *Pressure Groups and Political Culture: A Comparative Study*, Routledge, London, 1967, 112 pp.

Chapman, Brian, *The Profession of Government: The Public Service in Europe*, 3rd ed., Allen & Unwin, London, 1966, 352 pp.

Christoph, James B. and Bernard E. Brown, *Cases in Comparative Politics*, 2nd ed., Little, Brown, 1969, 301 pp, pbk.

Cole, George D. H., *A History of Socialist Thought*, St. Martin's, 5 vols: *The Forerunners, 1789–1850*, 1953, 345 pp; *Marxism and Anarchism, 1850–1890*, 1954, 481 pp; *The Second International, 1889–1914*, 1956, 1,042 pp; *Communism and Social Democracy, 1914–1931*, 1959, 940 pp; *Socialism and Fascism, 1931–1939*, 1960, 350 pp.

Coleman, James S., ed., *Studies in Political Development*, Princeton UP, 1965, 620 pp.

Curtis, Michael, *Comparative Government and Politics: An Introductory Essay in Political Science*, Harper, 1968, 266 pp.

Dahl, Robert A., *After the Revolution? Authority in a Good Society*, Yale UP, 1970, 172 pp, pbk.

———, ed., *Political Opposition in Western Democracies*, Yale UP, 1968, 458 pp, pbk.

———, *Polyarchy*, Yale UP, 1970, 200 pp.

David, René, *Major Legal Systems in the World Today: An Introduction to the Comparative Study of Law*, trans. John E. C. Brierley, Stevens, London, 1968, 203 pp, pbk.

Dawson, Richard E. and Kenneth Prewitt, *Political Socialization*, Little, Brown, 1969, 226 pp.

Denton, Geoffrey, Murray Forsyth, and Malcolm MacLennan, *Economic Planning and Policies in Britain, France and Germany*, Praeger, 1969, 424 pp.

Duchacek, Ivo D., *Comparative Federalism: The Territorial Dimension of Politics*, Holt, 1970, 370 pp.

Duverger, Maurice, *Political Parties: Their Organization and Activity in the Modern State*, trans. Barbara and Robert North, Wiley, 1954, 439 pp.

———, *The Political Role of Women*, UNESCO, Paris, 1955, 221 pp.

Edinger, Lewis J., ed., *Political Leadership in Industrialized Societies: Studies in Comparative Analysis*, Wiley, 1967, 376 pp, pbk.

Ehrmann, Henry W., ed., *Democracy in a Changing Society*, Praeger, 1964, 210 pp, pbk.

———, ed., *Interest Groups on Four Continents*, Pittsburgh UP, 1958, 316 pp.

Epstein, Leon D., *Political Parties in Western Democracies*, Praeger, 1967, 374 pp.

Fagen, Richard R., *Politics and Communication*, Little, Brown, 1966, 162 pp, pbk.

Fairlie, Henry, *The Life of Politics*, Basic, 1968, 271 pp.

Farrell, R. Barry, ed., *Approaches to Comparative and International Politics*, Northwestern UP, 1966, 368 pp.

Field, G. Lowell, *Comparative Political Development: The Precedent of the West*, Routledge, London, 1968, 247 pp.

Finer, Herman, *The Theory and Practice of Modern Government*, 4th ed., Methuen, London, 1961, 982 pp.

Finer, S. E., *Comparative Government*, Penguin, 1970, 615 pp.

———, *The Man on Horseback: The Role of the Military in Politics*, Pall Mall, London, 1962, 268 pp.

——— and Gabriel A. Almond, "Polemics in Comparative Politics," *Gov. & Opp.*, 5(1), Winter 1969–70: 3–40.

Fogarty, Michael P., *Christian Democracy in Western Europe, 1820–1953*, Notre Dame UP, 1957, 461 pp.

Francis-Williams, Baron Edward, *The Right to Know: The Rise of the World Press*, Longmans, London, 1969, 336 pp.

Fried, Robert C., *Comparative Political Institutions*, Macmillan, 1966, 152 pp, pbk.

Friedmann, Wolfgang and J. F. Garner, eds., *Government Enterprise: A Comparative Study*, Stevens, London, 1970, 351 pp.

Friedrich, Carl J., *Constitutional Government and Democracy*, 4th ed., Blaisdell, 1968, 728 pp.

———, *The Impact of American Constitutionalism Abroad*, Boston UP, 1968, 112 pp.

——— and Zbigniew K. Brzezinski, *Totalitarian Dictatorship and Autocracy*, 2nd rev. ed., Praeger, 1966, 427 pp, pbk.

Gellhorn, Walter, *Ombudsmen and Others: Citizens' Protectors in Nine Countries*, Harvard UP, 1966, 448 pp.

Gurr, Ted, *Why Men Rebel*, Princeton UP, 1970, 421 pp.

Heady, Ferrel, *Public Administration: A Comparative Perspective*, Prentice-Hall, 1966, 115 pp, pbk.

Heidenheimer, Arnold J., ed., *Political Corruption: Readings in Comparative Analysis*, Holt, 1970, 582 pp, pbk.

Hennig, Stanley and John Ander, eds., *European Political Parties*, Praeger, 1970, 565 pp.

Herz, John H., *International Politics in the Atomic Age*, Columbia UP, 1962, 360 pp, pbk.

———, *Political Realism and Political Idealism: A Study in Theories and Realities*, Chicago UP, 1951, 275 pp.

Hoch, Paul, *Academic Freedom in Action*, Sheed & Ward, London, 1970, 212 pp.

Holborn, Louise W., John H. Herz, and Gwendolen M. Carter, eds., *Documents of Major Foreign Powers: A Sourcebook on Great Britain, France, Germany and the Soviet Union*, Harcourt Brace Jovanovich, 1968, 381 pp, pbk.

Holt, Robert and John Turner, *The Political Basis of Economic Development: An Exploration in Comparative Political Analysis*, Van Nostrand, 1966, 410 pp, pbk.

Huntington, Samuel P., *Political Order in Changing Societies*, Yale UP, 1968, 488 pp.

Ionescu, G., *The Politics of the European Communist States*, Weidenfeld & Nicolson, London, 1967, 304 pp.

IPI Survey, *The Press in Authoritarian Countries*, Int Press Inst., Zurich, 1959, 201 pp.

Jacob, Charles E., *Policy and Bureaucrary*, Van Nostrand, 1965, 217 pp.

Jones, Roy E., *The Functional Analysis of Politics: An Introductory Discussion*, Humanities Press, 1967, 101 pp.

Kersell, John E., *Parliamentary Supervision of Delegated Legislation: The United Kingdom, Australia, New Zealand and Canada*, Stevens, London, 1960, 178 pp.

King, Edmund J., *Comparative Studies and Educational Decision*, Methuen, London, 1968, 182 pp.

Kirchheimer, Otto, *Political Justice: The Use of Legal Procedure for Political Ends*, Princeton UP, 1961, 452 pp.

Kolarz, Walter, *Communism and Colonialism*, St. Martin's, 1964, 147 pp.

La Palombara, Joseph, ed., *Bureaucracy and Political Development*, Princeton UP, 1963, 487 pp.

—— and Myron Weiner, eds., *Political Parties and Political Development*, Princeton UP, 1966, 495 pp.

Lerner, Daniel and Morton Gordon, *Euratlantica: The Changing Perspectives of the European Elites*, MIT Press, 1969, 416 pp.

Lindsay, Alexander D., *The Modern Democratic State*, Oxford UP, Vol 1, 1943, 286 pp.

Lipset, Seymour M., ed., *Party Systems and Voter Alignments: Cross National Perspectives*, Free Press, 1967, 554 pp.

London, Kurt, *The Making of Foreign Policy: East and West*, Lippincott, 1965, 368 pp, pbk.

Lorwin, Lewis L., *The International Labor Movement: History, Policies, Outlook*, Harper, 1953, 366 pp.

Mackenzie, W. J. M., *Free Elections*, Rinehart, 1958, 184 pp.

——, *Politics and Social Science*, Penguin, 1967, 424 pp.

Macridis, Roy C., ed., *Political Parties: Contemporary Trends and Ideas*, Harper, 1967, 268 pp, pbk.

—— and Bernard E. Brown, *Comparative Politics: Notes and Readings*, 3rd ed., Dorsey, 1968, 660 pp, pbk.

Marshall, Arthur H., *Local Government in the Modern World*, Athlone Press, London, 1965, 38 pp.

Mayer, J. de, *et al.*, *Elections in the Countries of the European Communities and in the United Kingdom*, De Tempel, Bruges, 1967, 378 pp.

Merkl, Peter H., *Modern Comparative Politics*, Holt, 1970, 416 pp, pbk.

Merkl, Peter H., *Political Continuity and Change*, Harper, 1967, 606 pp.

Miller, John D., *The Politics of the Third World*, Oxford UP, 1967, 126 pp, pbk.

Milnor, Andrew, *Elections and Political Stability*, Little, Brown, 1969, 224 pp, pbk.

Mitchell, Joan, *Groundwork to Economic Planning*, Secker and Warburg, London, 1966, 316 pp.

Mueller, Bernard, *Western Europe, Canada and the United States: A Statistical Handbook of the North Atlantic Area*, Twentieth Century, 1965, 239 pp.

Munger, Frank, ed., *Studies in Comparative Politics*, Crowell, 1967, 313 pp.

Neumann, Sigmund, ed., *Modern Political Parties: Approaches to Comparative Politics*, Chicago UP, 1956, 460 pp.

Nolte, Ernst, *Three Faces of Fascism: Action Française, Italian Fascism, National Socialism*, Holt, 1966, 561 pp, pbk.

Normanton, E. L., *The Accountability and Audit of Government*, Praeger, 1966, 470 pp.

Northedge, Frederick S., ed., *The Foreign Politics of the Powers*, Praeger, 1969, 299 pp, pbk.

Parry, Geraint, *Political Elites*, Praeger, 1969, 169 pp.

Peaslee, Amos J., *Constitutions of the Nations*, 4 vols, rev. 3rd ed., Nijhoff, The Hague, 1965, 2,752 pp.

Pesonen, Pertti, ed., *Scandinavian Political Studies: Vols 1 & 2*, Columbia UP, 1966, 341 pp.

Plamenatz, John, *On Alien Rule and Self-Government*, Longmans, London, 1960, 224 pp.

Political Handbook of the World, ed. Walter H. Mallory, Harper, publ. annually.

Preston, Nathaniel S., *Politics, Economics, and Power: Ideology and Practice Under Capitalism, Socialism, Communism, and Fascism*, Macmillan, 1967, 242 pp, pbk.

Pye, Lucien W., *Aspects of Political Development: An Analytic Study*, Little, Brown, 1966, 205 pp.

——, ed., *Communications and Political Development*, Princeton UP, 1963, 381 pp.

—— and Sidney Verba, *Political Culture and Political Development*, Princeton UP, 1965, 584 pp.

Radice, Giles, *Democratic Socialism*, Longmans, London, 1970, 164 pp.

Rae, Douglas W., *The Political Consequences of Electoral Laws*, Yale UP, 1967, 173 pp.

Rasmussen, Jorgen S., *The Process of Politics: A Comparative Approach*, Atherton, 1969, 225 pp, pbk.

Richardson, G. Henry, *Economic and Financial Aspects of Social Security: An International Survey*, Allen & Unwin, London, 1960, 270 pp.

Rogger, Hans and Eugen Weber, eds., *The European Right: A Historical Profile*, California UP, 1965, 589 pp.

Rokkan, S. and J. Meyriat, eds., *International Guide to Electoral Statistics*, Humanities Press, 1969, 351 pp.

Ross, Murray G., ed., *New Universities in the Modern World*, St. Martin's, 1966, 190 pp.

Rowat, Donald C., ed., *The Ombudsman: Citizen's Defender*, Allen & Unwin, London, 1965, 348 pp, pbk.

Sampson, Anthony, *The New Europeans: A Guide to the Workings, Institutions and Character of Contemporary Western Europe*, Hodder & Stoughton, London, 1968, 462 pp.

Schwartz, Bernard, ed., *The Code Napoleon and the Common-Law World*, New York UP, 1956, 448 pp.

Seidman, Harold, *Politics, Position and Power: The Dynamics of Federal Organization*, Oxford UP, 1970, 311 pp.

Sigmund, Paul E., ed., *The Ideologies of the Developing Nations*, rev. ed., Praeger, 1967, 428 pp.

Smith, Bruce L. R. and D. C. Hague, eds., *The Dilemma of Accountability in Modern Government*, Macmillan, 1971, 391 pp.

Stebbins, Richard P., ed., *Political Handbook and Atlas of the World*, Simon and Schuster, 1970.

Stewart, Michael, *Modern Forms of Government: A Comparative Study*, 3rd ed., Allen & Unwin, London, 1964, 284 pp.

Strauss, E., *The Ruling Servants: Bureaucracy in Russia, France and Britain*, Praeger, 1961, 308 pp.

Strong, C. F., *A History of Modern Political Constitutions: An Introduction to Comparative Study of Their History and Existing Form*, Capricorn, 1964, 389 pp, pbk.

Thompson, James D., ed., *Comparative Studies in Administration*, Pittsburgh UP, 1960, 224 pp.

Ulich, Robert, *The Education of Nations: A Comparison in Historical Perspective*, rev. ed., Harvard UP, 1967, 365 pp.

Walsh, Annmarie H., *The Urban Challenge to Government: An International Comparison of Thirteen Cities*, Praeger, 1969, 294 pp.

——, *Urban Government for the Paris Region*, Praeger, 1967, 217 pp.

Wheare, Kenneth C., *Federal Government*, 4th ed., Oxford UP, 1964, 266 pp, pbk.

——, *Legislatures*, 2nd ed., Oxford UP, 1968, 166 pp, pbk.

——, *Modern Constitutions*, 2nd ed., Oxford UP, 1966, 150 pp, pbk.

Wheeler-Bennett, John W., *A Wreath to Clio: Studies in British, American and German Affairs*, St. Martin's, 1967, 224 pp.

Willis, Roy F., *France, Germany, and the New Europe 1945-1967*, rev. ed., Stanford UP, 1968, 431 pp.

Wiseman, H. Victor, *Political Systems: Some Sociological Approaches*, Praeger, 1966, 254 pp, pbk.

Wolf-Phillips, Leslie, *Constitutions of Modern States*, Praeger, 1967, 274 pp, pbk.

Woolf, S. J., ed., *European Fascism*, Weidenfeld & Nicolson, London, 1968, 386 pp.

Zolberg, Aristide R., *Creating Political Order*, Rand McNally, 1966, 168 pp, pbk.

GREAT BRITAIN

GENERAL WORKS

Bailey, Sidney D., *British Parliamentary Democracy*, 3rd ed., Houghton, Mifflin, 1971, 281 pp, pbk.

Birch, A. H., *The British System of Government*, Allen & Unwin, London, 1967, 284 pp, pbk.

Booker, Christopher, *The Neophiliacs: A Study of the Revolution of English Life in the Fifties and Sixties*, Collins, London, 1969, 381 pp.

Brasher, N. H., *Studies in British Government*, 2nd ed., St. Martin's, 1971, 224 pp.

Bray, Jeremy, *Decision in Government*, Gollancz, London, 1970, 320 pp.

Britain 1971: An Official Handbook, HMSO, 1971, 522 pp. (annual)

Butler, David E. and J. Freeman, *British Political Facts, 1900-67*, 2nd ed., St. Martin's, 1968, 314 pp.

—— and Donald Stokes, *Political Change in Britain*, Penguin, 1971, 80 pp.

Calleo, David P., *Britain's Future*, Hodder & Stoughton, London, 1968, 252 pp.

Caves, Richard E. *et al.*, *Britain's Economic Prospects*, Brookings Inst., 1968, 510 pp.

Crick, Bernard, ed., *Essays on Reform, 1967: A Centenary Tribute*, Oxford UP, 1967, 222 pp.

——, "The 1970's in Retrospect," *Parl. Aff.*, 41(1), Jan–Mar. 1970:106–14.

—— and William A. Robson, *Protest and Discontent*, Penguin, 1970, 220 pp.

Crosland, Anthony, *A Social Democratic Britain*, Fabian Tract 404, London, 1970–71, 16 pp.

Fairlie, H., *The Life of Politics*, Methuen, London, 1968, 271 pp.

Great Britain Central Statistical Office: Social Trends No. 1, HMSO, 1970, 184 pp.

Hanson, A. H. and M. Walles, *Governing Britain*, Fontana, London, 1970, 304 pp, pbk.

Jay, Douglas, *After the Common Market: A Better Alternative for Britain*, Penguin, 1968, 126 pp.

Jennings, Sir Ivor, *The Queen's Government*, rev. ed., Pelican, 1967, 164 pp.

Jones, Grace, *The Political Structure*, Longmans, London, 1969, 110 pp, pbk.

Lapping, Brian, *The Labour Government 1964–1970*, Penguin, 1970, 219 pp.

Levin, Bernard, *The Pendulum Years: Britain and the Sixties*, Cape, London, 1970, 451 pp.

Mackintosh, John P., *The Government and Politics of Britain*, Hutchinson, London, 1970, 206 pp.

Mathiot, André, *The British Political System*, trans. Jennifer S. Hines, Stanford UP, 1967, 352 pp, pbk.

Moorhouse, Geoffrey, *Britain in the Sixties: The Other England*, Penguin, 1964, 189 pp.

Morrison, Lord of Lambeth, Herbert Stanley, *Government and Parliament: A Survey from the Inside*, 3rd ed., Oxford UP, 1964, 386 pp, pbk.

Nicholson, Edward M., *The System*, Hodder, London, 1967, 525 pp.

Oakley, R. and P. Rose, *The Political Year, 1970*, Pitman, London, 1970, 250 pp. (to be issued annually)

Pollard, Sidney and David W. Crossley, *The Wealth of Britain 1085–1966*, Batsford, London, 1968, 303 pp.

Popham, C. T., *Government in Britain*, Pergamon, London, 1969, 268 pp, pbk.

Punnett, Robert M., *British Government and Politics*, Heinemann, London, 1968, 488 pp.

Reynolds, E. E. and N. H. Brasher, *Britain in the Twentieth Century, 1900–1964*, Cambridge UP, 1966, 375 pp, pbk.

Robson, William A., *Politics and Government At Home and Abroad*, Allen & Unwin, London, 1967, 299 pp.

Rose, Richard, *People in Politics: Observations Across the Atlantic*, Faber, London, 1969, 251 pp.

———, ed., *Policy-Making in Britain: A Reader in Government*, Macmillan, 1969, 375 pp.

———, *Politics in England: An Interpretation*, Little, Brown, 1964, 266 pp, pbk.

———, ed., *Studies in British Politics: A Reader in Political Sociology*, 2nd rev. ed., Macmillan, London, 1969, 428 pp.

Sampson, Anthony, *The New Anatomy of Britain*, Hodder & Stoughton, London, 1971, 731 pp.

Stacey, Frank, *The Government of Modern Britain*, Oxford UP, 1968, 500 pp, pbk.

Stankiewicz, W. J., *Crisis in British Government: The Need for Reform*, Collier-Macmillan, London, 1967, 410 pp.

Stewart, Michael, *The British Approach to Politics*, 5th ed., Allen & Unwin, London, 1966, 310 pp, pbk.

Summerskill, Edith, *A Woman's World*, Heinemann, London, 1967, 258 pp.

Vig, Norman J., *Science and Technology in British Politics*, Pergamon, London, 1968, 190 pp.

Whitaker, Ben, ed., *A Radical Future*, Cape, London, 1967, 223 pp.

Wiseman, H. Victor, *Politics in Everyday Life*, Blackwell, Oxford, 1966, 222 pp.

Woodhouse, C. M., *Post-War Britain*, Bodley Head, London, 1966, 94 pp.

Wootton, Barbara, *In a World I Never Made*, Allen & Unwin, London, 1967, 283 pp.

Chapter 1. THE BRITISH PEOPLE AND THEIR POLITICS

1. LAND, PEOPLE, SOCIETY, AND ECONOMY

Adams, Walter, ed., *The Brain Drain*, Collier-Macmillan, 1968, 273 pp.

Benewick, Robert, *Political Violence and Public Order: A Study of British Fascism*, Penguin, 1969, 340 pp.

Bottomore, Thomas B., *Elites and Society*, Penguin, 1966, 160 pp.

Bruce, Maurice, *The Coming of the Welfare State*, 4th ed., Batsford, London, 1961, 374 pp.

Cairncross, Sir Alec, ed., *Britain's Economic Prospects Reconsidered*, Allen & Unwin, London, 1971, 244 pp, pbk.

Cole, George D. H. and Raymond Postgate, *The British Common People*, Barnes & Noble, 1961, 742 pp, pbk.

Coupland, Sir Reginald, *Welsh and Scottish Nationalism*, Collins, London, 1954, 448 pp.

Gilbert, Bentley B., *British Social Policy, 1914–1939*, Batsford, London, 1971, 343 pp.

Gregg, Pauline, *The Welfare State*, Harrap, London, 1967, 400 pp.

Guttsman, Wilhelm L., *The British Political Elite*, Basic Books, 1964, 398 pp.

———, ed., *The English Ruling Class: Readings in Politics and Society*, Weidenfeld & Nicolson, London, 1969, 310 pp.

Hackett, John W. and A. M. Hackett, *The British Economy: Problems and Prospects*, Allen & Unwin, London, 1967, 221 pp.

Harris, John S., *Government Patronage of the Arts in Great Britain*, Chicago UP, 1970, 341 pp.

Henderson, Patrick D., ed., *Economic Growth in Britain*, Weidenfeld & Nicolson, London, 1966, 296 pp.

Hutchinson, T. W., *Economics and Economic Policy in Britain, 1946–1966: Some Aspects of Their Interrelations*, Allen & Unwin, London, 1968, 307 pp.

Jackson, Brian, *Working Class Community: Some General Notions Raised by a Series of Studies in Northern England*, Routledge, London, 1968, 191 pp.

Jackson, J. A., ed., *Social Stratification*, Cambridge UP, 1968, 238 pp.

Kaufman, G., ed., *The Left: A Symposium (The Great Society* series), Blond, London, 1967, 184 pp, pbk.

Leach, Gerald, *The Brocrats*, Cape, London, 1970, 317 pp.

Lewis, Roy and Angus Maude, *The English Middle Classes*, Knopf, 1950, 386 pp.

Mabey, R., ed., *Class: A Symposium (The Great Society* series), Blond, London, 1967, 176 pp, pbk.

McGregor, O. R., Louis Blom-Cooper, and Colin Gibson, *Separated Spouses*, Duckworth, London, 1971, 281 pp.

MacNeil, Robert, *The People Machine*, Eyre & Spottiswoode, London, 1970, 364 pp.

Miller, S. M., *Social Class and Social Policy*, Basic Books, 1968, 336 pp.

Parkin, Frank, *Middle Class Radicalism*, Manchester UP, 1968, 207 pp.

"Protest and Discontent," special issue, *PQ*, 40(4), Oct–Dec. 1969.

Raynor, John, *The Middle Classes*, Longmans, London, 1969, 125 pp, pbk.

Roberts, Robert, *The Classic Slum*, Manchester UP, 1971, 219 pp.

Rose, Gordon, *The Working Class*, Longmans, London, 1968, 151 pp.

Schorr, Alvin, *Explorations in Social Policy*, Basic Books, 1968, 308 pp.

Seabrook, Jeremy, *The City Close-Up*, Penguin, 1971, 283 pp.

Shonfield, Andrew, *Modern Capitalism: The Changing Balance of Public and Private Power*, Oxford UP, 1969, 456 pp, pbk.

Stamp, Lawrence D., *The Land of Britain: Its Use and Misuse*, 3rd ed., Longmans, London, 1962, 546 pp.

——— and S. H. Beaver, *The British Isles: A Geographic and Economic Survey*, 5th ed., Longmans, London, 1964, 820 pp.

Thompson, E. P., *The Making of the English Working Class*, Pantheon, 1964, 845 pp.

Willmott, Peter and Michael Young, *Family and Class in a London Suburb*, Humanities Press, 1960, 187 pp.

2. NORTHERN IRELAND

DePoor, Liam, *Divided Ulster*, Penguin, 1970, 208 pp.

Devlin, Bernadette, *The Price of My Soul*, Deutsch/ Pan, London, 1969, 206 pp.

Hastings, Max, *Ulster 1969: The Fight for Civil Rights in Northern Ireland*, Gollancz, London, 1970, 203 pp.

Lawrence, R. J., *The Government of Northern Ireland: Public Finance and Public Services 1921–1964*, Clarendon Press, Oxford, 1965, 198 pp.

Rose, Richard, *Governing Without Consensus: An Irish Perspective*, Faber, London, 1971, 567 pp.

Wilson, Thomas, ed., *Ulster Under Home Rule: A Study of the Political and Economic Problems of Northern Ireland*, Oxford UP, 1956, 253 pp.

3. CHURCHES

Grubb, Sir Kenneth, *Crypts of Power*, Hodder, London, 1971.

Heubel, E. J., "Church and State in England: The Price of Establishment," *WPQ*, 18(3), Sept. 1965: 646–55.

Hill, Clifford S., *West Indian Migrants and the London Churches*, Oxford UP, 1963, 89 pp.

Hunter, Leslie S., *The English Church: A New Look*, Penguin, 1966, 176 pp.

Mayfield, Guy, *The Church of England: Its Members and Its Business*, 2nd ed., Oxford UP, 1963, 211 pp.

4. IMMIGRATION AND RACE RELATIONS

Ambalavaner, S., *Coloured Immigrants in Britain: Selected Bibliography*, 2nd ed., Inst. for Race Relations, London, 1968, 82 pp.

Banton, Michael, *Race Relations*, Tavistock, London, 1967, 434 pp.

———, *White and Coloured: The Behavior of British People Toward Coloured Immigrants*, Cape, London, 1959, 223 pp.

Brockway, Fenner and Norman Pannell, *Immigration: What Is the Answer? Two Opposing Views*, Routledge, London, 1965, 120 pp, pbk.

Davison, R. B., *Commonwealth Immigrants*, Oxford UP, 1964, 87 pp.

Deakin, Nicholas, ed., *Colour and the British Electorate, 1964: Six Case Studies*, Pall Mall, London, 1965, 172 pp.

Economic Issues in Immigration, Inst. of Economic Affairs, London, 1970, 180 pp.

Facts Paper on the United Kingdom, 1970–71, Inst. for Race Relations, London, 1970, 48 pp.

Foot, Paul, *Immigration and Race in British Politics*, Penguin Special, 1965, 254 pp.

Freedman, Maurice, ed., *A Minority in Britain: Social Studies of the Anglo-Jewish Community*, Mitchell, London, 1955, 304 pp.

Garrard, John A., *The English and Immigration, 1880–1910*, Oxford UP, 1971, 244 pp.

Glass, Ruth and Harold Pollins, *London's Newcomers: The West Indian Migrants*, Harvard UP, 1961, 278 pp.

Hepple, Bob, *Race, Jobs, and the Law in Britain*, Allen Lane, London, 1968, 256 pp.

Hill, Clifford, *Immigration and Integration*, Pergamon, 1970, 224 pp.

Hiro, Dilip, *Black British, White British*, Eyre & Spottiswoode, London, 1971.

Hooper, Richard, ed., *Colour in Britain*, BBC, London, 1965, 239 pp.

Huxley, Elspeth, *Back Street New Worlds: A Look at Immigrants in Britain*, Morrow, 1965, 190 pp.

Isaac, Julius, *British Postwar Migration*, Cambridge UP, 1955, 329 pp.

Jones, K. and A. D. Smith, *The Economic Impact of Commonwealth Immigration*, Cambridge UP, 1970, 186 pp.

Lewin, Julius, *The Struggle for Racial Equality*, Longmans, London, 1967, 191 pp.

Mandle, W. F., *Anti-Semitism and the British Union of Fascists*, Longmans, London 1968, 78 pp.

Patterson, Sheila, *Immigration and Race Relations in Britain, 1960–67*, Oxford UP, 1969, 460 pp.

Peach, Ceri, *West Indian Migration to Britain: A Social Geography*, Oxford UP, 1968, 122 pp.

Rose, Eliot J. B. *et al.*, *Colour and Citizenship: A Report on British Race Relations*, Oxford UP, 1969, 815 pp. (Updated and abridged by Nicholas Deakin, *Colour, Citizenship and British Society*, Panther, London, 1970)

Smithies, Billy and Peter Fiddick, *Enoch Powell on Immigration: An Analysis*, Sphere, London, 1969, 158 pp.

Steel, David M. S., *No Entry: The Background and Implications of the Commonwealth Immigrants Act 1968*, Hurst, London, 1969, 263 pp.

Zubaida, Sami, ed., *Race and Racialism*, Tavistock, London, 1970, 185 pp.

5. EDUCATION

Armytage, Walter H. G., *Four Hundred Years of English Education*, Cambridge UP, 1964, 353 pp, pbk.

Ashby, Sir Eric and Mary Anderson, *The Rise of the Student Estate in Britain*, Macmillan, 1970, 186 pp, pbk.

Avorn, Jerry L. *et al.*, *University in Revolt*, Macdonald, London, 1969, 307 pp.

Baron, George A., *A Bibliographical Guide to the English Educational System*, enl. ed., Athlone, London, 1960, 97 pp.

Beloff, Michael, *The Plateglass Universities*, Secker & Warburg, London, 1968, 208 pp.

Blackstone, Tessa, Kathleen Gales, Roger Hadley, and Wyn Lewis, *Students in Conflict*, Weidenfeld & Nicolson, London, 1970, 384 pp.

Butler, Lord, *The Education Act of 1944 and After*, Longmans, London, 1966, 24 pp.

Caine, Sir Sydney, *British Universities: Purpose and Prospects*, Bodley Head, London, 1969, 272 pp.

Cockburn, Alexander and Robin Blackburn, eds., *Student Power: Problems, Diagnosis, Action*, Penguin, 1969, 378 pp.

Crawley, Harriet, *A Degree of Defiance: Students in England and Europe Now*, Weidenfeld & Nicolson, London, 1969, 207 pp.

Crouch, Colin, *The Student Revolt*, Bodley Head, London, 1970, 251 pp.

Dent, Harold C., *British Education*, rev. ed., Longmans, London, 1966, 70 pp.

Dent, Harold C., *The Educational System of England and Wales*, London UP, 1961, 224 pp.

Dodd, H. W., L. M. Hacker, and L. Rogers, *Government Assistance to the Universities in Great Britain*, Columbia UP, 1952, 133 pp.

Douglas, James W. B., J. M. Ross, and H. R. Simpson, *All Our Future: A Longitudinal Study of Secondary Education*, Peter Davies, London, 1968, 255 pp.

Driver, Christopher, *The Exploding University*, Hodder & Stoughton, London, 1971.

15 to 18: Report of the Central Advisory Council for Education in England, The Crowther Report, 2 vols, HMSO, 1959 (reprinted 1962), 759 pp.

Gosden, P. H., *The Development of Educational Administration in England and Wales*, Blackwell, Oxford, 1966, 228 pp.

Half Our Future: Report of the Central Advisory Council for Education in England, The Newsom Report, HMSO, Aug. 1963, 299 pp.

Halsey, A. H. and Martin Trow, *The British Academics*, Faber, London, 1971, 560 pp.

Higher Education: Government Statement on the Robbins Report, Cmd. 2165, HMSO, 1963, 5 pp.

Higher Education: The Robbins Report, Cmd. 2154, HMSO, Oct. 1963, 335 pp.

House of Commons, *Report from the Select Committee on Education and Science*, Session 1968–69, *Student Relations*, HC 449, Vol. I–VII, HMSO, 1969, 201 pp. (With six volumes of evidence, etc.)

———, *Second Report from the Committee of Privileges*, Session 1968–69, *Events Attending Visit of Subcommittee B Appointed by the Select Committee on Education and Science to the U of Essex*, HC 308, HMSO, 1969, 44 pp.

Illingworth, Sir Charles, *University Statesman: Sir Hector Hetherington*, George Outram, Glasgow, 1971.

Kamm, Josephine, *Hope Deferred: Girls' Education in English History*, Methuen, London, 1964, 332 pp.

Kelly, Thomas, *A History of Adult Education in Great Britain*, Liverpool UP, 1962, 352 pp.

Kidd, Harry, *The Trouble at LSE: 1966–67*, Oxford UP, 1969, 199 pp.

Lester-Smith, William O., *Education in Great Britain*, 5th ed., Oxford UP, 1968, 167 pp.

Lowndes, G. A. N., *The British Educational System*, Hutchinson, London, 1960, 183 pp.

McGuigan, Gerald F. *et al.*, *Student Protest*, Methuen, Canada, 1968, 285 pp.

Manzer, Ronald A., *Teachers and Politics in England and Wales*, Manchester UP, 1970, 164 pp.

Mountford, Sir James F., *British Universities*, Oxford UP, 1966, 180 pp.

Nagel, Julian, ed., *Student Power*, Merlin Press, London, 1969, 235 pp.

Parkinson, Michael, *The Labour Party and the Reorganisation of Secondary Education, 1918–1965*, Routledge, London, 1970, 139 pp.

Partridge, John, *Middle School: The Secondary Modern School*, Gollancz, London, 1966, 176 pp.

Payne, George Louis, *Britain's Scientific and Technological Manpower*, Stanford UP, 1960, 466 pp.

Pedley, Robin, *The Comprehensive School*, Penguin, 1963, 222 pp.

Peterson, Paul E., "British Interest Group Theory Reexamined: The Politics of Comprehensive Education in Three British Cases," *Comp. Pol.*, 3(3), April 1971:381–402.

Robbins, Lord, *The University in the Modern World*, Macmillan, 1966, 170 pp.

Rudd, Ernest and Stephen Hatch, *Graduate Study and After*, Weidenfeld & Nicolson, London, 1968, 229 pp.

Spender, Stephen, *The Year of the Young Rebels*, Weidenfeld & Nicolson, London, 1969, 186 pp.

Students and Staff of the Hornsey College of Art, *The Hornsey Affair*, Penguin, 1969, 220 pp.

Wakeford, John, *The Cloistered Elite: A Sociological Analysis of the English Boarding School*, Macmillan, 1969, 269 pp.

Wilkinson, Rupert Hugh, *The Prefects: British Leadership and the Public School Tradition*, Oxford UP, 1963, 243 pp.

The Years of Crisis: Report of the Labour Party's Study Group on Higher Education, Transport House, 1963, 47 pp.

6. SOCIAL SERVICES

Abel-Smith, Brian and Kathleen Gales, *British Doctors at Home and Abroad*, Codicote, Herts, 1964, 64 pp.

The Beveridge Report: Social Insurance and Allied Services, Cmd. 6404, Macmillan, 1942, 249 pp.

Brain, Lord, *Medicine and Government*, Tavistock, London, 1967, 21 pp.

Brand, Jeanne L., *Doctors and the State: The British Medical Profession and Government Action in Public Health, 1870–1912*, Johns Hopkins UP, 1965, 307 pp.

Brown, Muriel, *Introduction to Social Administration in Great Britain*, Hutchinson, London, 1969, 208 pp, pbk.

Cartwright, Ann, *Human Relations and Hospital Care*, Routledge, London, 1964, 272 pp.

Eckstein, Harry, *The English Health Service: Its Origins, Structure and Achievements*, Harvard UP, 1959, 289 pp.

Farndale, W. A. J., *Trends in the National Health Service*, Pergamon, London, 1964, 423 pp.

Freeman, Hugh and W. A. J. Farndale, eds., *New Aspects of the Mental Health Services*, Pergamon, London, 1967, 776 pp.

"The Future of the Social Services," special issue, *PQ*, 40(1), Jan–Mar. 1969.

George, V. N., *Social Security: Beveridge and After*, Routledge, London, 1968, 258 pp.

Gilbert, Bentley, *British Social Policy*, Batsford, London, 1971, 343 pp.

———, *The Evolution of National Insurance in Great Britain: The Origins of the Welfare State*, Joseph, London, 1966, 498 pp.

Harris, Robert W., *National Health Insurance in Great Britain, 1911–1946*, Allen & Unwin, London, 1946, 224 pp.

Jefferys, Margot, *An Anatomy of Social Welfare Services*, Joseph, London, 1966, 371 pp.

Lindsey, Almont, *Socialized Medicine in England and Wales: The National Health Service, 1948–1961*, North Carolina UP, 1963, 561 pp.

Marmor, Theodor R., *The Politics of Medicare*, Routledge, 1970, 146 pp.

Marshall, T. H., *Social Policy*, 2nd ed., Hutchinson, London, 1970, 200 pp.

Morris, Mary, *Voluntary Work in the Welfare State*, Routledge, London, 1969, 279 pp.

National Health Service: The "Guillebaud" Report, Cmd. 9963, HMSO, 1956.

Owen, David, ed., *A Unified Health Service*, Pergamon, London, 1968, 148 pp.

Powell, Enoch, *A New Look at Medicine and Politics*, Pitman, London, 1966, 74 pp.

Robson, W. A., *The Future of the Social Services*, Pelican, 1970, 206 pp.

Rowntree, B. Seebohm and G. R. Lavers, *Poverty and the Welfare State*, Longmans, London, 1951, 104 pp.

Slack, Kathleen M., *Social Administration and the Citizen*, 2nd rev. ed., Joseph, 1969, 269 pp.

Stevens, Rosemary, *Medical Practice in Modern England: The Impact of Specialization and State Medicine*, Yale UP, 1966, 413 pp.

Strategy for Pensions, Cmnd. 4755, HMSO, 1971.

Titmuss, Richard M., *Commitment to Welfare*, Allen & Unwin, 1968, 272 pp.

Willcocks, Arthur J., *The Creation of the National Health Service: A Study of Pressure Groups and a Major Social Policy*, Humanities Press, 1967, 118 pp.

Williams, Lady Gertrude, *The Coming of the Welfare State*, Allen & Unwin, London, 1967, 120 pp.

Young, A. F., *Social Services in British Industry*, Routledge, London, 1968, 258 pp.

7. TRADE UNIONS AND INDUSTRIAL RELATIONS

Bain, G. S., *The Growth of White Collar Unionism*, Oxford UP, 1970, 233 pp.

Blackburn, Robin and A. Cockburn, eds., *The Incompatibles: Trade Union Militancy and the Consensus*, Penguin, 1967, 281 pp.

Brown, E. H. Phelps, *The Growth of British Industrial Relations*, Macmillan, 1960, 451 pp.

Citrine, Lord, *Men and Work: Autobiography*, Hutchinson, London, 1964, 384 pp.

Clegg, H. A., *The System of Industrial Relations in Great Britain*, Blackwell, Oxford, 1970, 484 pp.

Fay, Stephen, *Measure for Measure: Reforming the Trade Unions*, Chatto & Windus, London, 1970, 131 pp.

Flanders, Allan, *Trade Unions*, 7th rev. ed., Hutchinson, London, 1968, 212 pp, pbk.

Goldthorpe, John H. *et al.*, *The Affluent Worker in the Class Structure*, Cambridge UP, London, 1969, 246 pp, pbk.

Hobsbawn, Eric J., *Labouring Men: Studies in the History of Labour*, Weidenfeld & Nicolson, London, 1964, 401 pp.

Hughes, John, *The TUC: A Plan for the 1970's*, Fabian, London, 1969, 36 pp.

In Place of Strife: A Policy for Industrial Relations, Cmnd. 3888, HMSO, 1969.

Kilroy-Silk, Robert, "Legislating on Industrial Relations," *Parl. Aff.*, 22(3), Summer 1969:250–57.

Lowell, John and B. L. Roberts, *A Short History of the TUC*, Macmillan, 1968, 200 pp.

Paynter, Will, *British Trade Unions and the Problem of Change*, Allen & Unwin, London, 1970, 172 pp.

Pollard, Sidney, *Cooperatives at the Crossroads*, Fabian, London, 1965, 44 pp.

Report of the Royal Commission on Trade Unions and Employers' Associations 1965–68, Cmnd. 3623 (Donovan), HMSO, 1968.

Trades Union Congress, *Action on Donovan, Interim Statement by the TUC General Council Response to the Report of the Royal Commission on TU and Employment Associations*, TUC, London, 1968, 40 pp.

———, General Council, *Industrial Relations: Program for Action*, TUC, London, 1969.

Turner, Herbert A., *Is Britain Really Strike-Prone? A Review of the Incidence, Character and Costs of Industrial Conflict*, Cambridge UP, 1969, 48 pp.

Wigham, Eric L., *Trade Unions*, 2nd ed., Oxford UP, 1969, 189 pp.

Wilson, Charles, *Unilever, 1945–1965: Challenge and Response in the Post-War Industrial Revolution*, Cassell, London, 1968, 299 pp.

Zweig, Ferdynand, *The Worker in an Affluent Society: Family Life and Industry*, Heinemann, London, 1961, 268 pp.

8. PRESSURE GROUPS

Castles, F. G., *Pressure Groups and Political Culture: A Comparative Study*, Routledge, London, 1967, 112 pp, pbk.

Christoph, James B., *Capital Punishment and British Politics: The British Movement to Abolish the Death Penalty, 1955–1957*, Allen & Unwin, London, 1962, 202 pp.

Eckstein, Harry, *Pressure Group Politics: The Case of the British Medical Association*, Allen & Unwin, London, 1960, 168 pp.

Finer, S. E., *Anonymous Empire: A Study of the Lobby in Great Britain*, 2nd rev. ed., Pall Mall, London, 1966, 173 pp, pbk.

Howarth, Richard W., "The Political Strength of British Agriculture," *PS*, 17(4), Dec. 1969:458–69.

Moodie, G. C. and G. Studdert-Kennedy, *Opinions, Publics and Pressure Groups*, Allen & Unwin, London, 1970, 115 pp.

Potter, A. M., *Organised Groups in British National Politics*, Faber, London, 1961, 396 pp.

Roberts, G. K., *Political Parties and Pressure Groups in Britain*, Weidenfeld & Nicolson, London, 1970, 203 pp.

Self, Peter and Herbert J. Storing, *The State and the Farmer*, Allen & Unwin, London, 1962, 251 pp.

Stewart, J. D., *British Pressure Groups: Their Role in Relation to the House of Commons*, Oxford UP, 1958, 273 pp.

Swartz, Marvin, *The Union of Democratic Control in British Politics During the First World War*, Oxford UP, 1971, 281 pp.

Wilson, H. H., *Pressure Group: The Campaign for Commercial Television*, Secker & Warburg, London, 1961, 232 pp.

Wootton, Graham, *The Politics of Influence: British Ex-Servicemen, Cabinet Decisions and Cultural Change, 1917–1957*, Routledge, London, 1963, 301 pp.

9. PRESS, BROADCASTING, AND TELEVISION

Andrews, Sir Linton, *The Autobiography of a Journalist*, Benn, London, 1964, 262 pp.

Annual Reports and Accounts of the British Broadcasting Corporation, HMSO.

Annual Reports and Accounts of the Independent Television Authority, HMSO.

Ayerst, David, *Guardian: Biography of a Newspaper*, Collins, London, 1971, 702 pp.

BBC Handbook, BBC, London, published annually.

Blumler, Jay G. and Denis McQuail, *Television in Politics: Its Uses and Influence*, Faber, London, 1968, 379 pp.

Braddon, Russell, *Roy Thomson of Fleet Street*, Collins, London, 1965, 396 pp.

Briggs, Asa, *The History of Broadcasting in the United Kingdom*, Oxford UP, 3 vols: *The Birth of Broadcasting*, 1961, 415 pp; *The Golden Age of Wireless*, 1965, 688 pp; *The War of Words*, 1970, 784 pp.

The British Broadcasting Corporation Act, Cmnd. 9138 and Cmnd. 9196, HMSO, 1954.

Cudlipp, Hugh, *At Your Peril*, Weidenfeld & Nicolson, London, 1963, 400 pp.

The "D" Notice System, Cmnd. 3312, HMSO, 1967, 16 pp. (Government reply to the Radcliffe Report)

Francis-Williams, Baron, *Nothing So Strange*, Cassell, London, 1970, 354 pp.

Gannon, Franklin R., *The British Press and Germany, 1936–39*, Oxford UP, 1971, 328 pp.

General Council of the Press, *Annual Reports*, since Oct. 1954, The Council, London.

Greene, Sir Hugh, *The Third Floor Front: A View of Broadcasting in the Sixties*, Bodley Head, London, 1969, 144 pp.

Halloran, James, Philip Elliott, and Graham Murdock, *Demonstrations and Communication: A Case Study*, Penguin Special, 1970, 334 pp.

Hedley, Peter and C. Aynsley, *The "D" Notice Affair*, Joseph, London, 1968, 144 pp.

Hopkinson, Tom, ed., *Picture Post, 1938–50*, Penguin, 1970, 288 pp, pbk.

Howard, Peter, *Beaverbrook: A Study of Max the Unknown*, Hutchinson, London, 1964, 164 pp.

Independent Television Authority, *ITV, A Guide to Independent Television*, ITA, 1970, 241 pp.

King, Cecil H., *Strictly Personal: Some Memoirs of Cecil H. King*, Weidenfeld & Nicolson, London, 1969, 240 pp.

———, *With Malice Toward None: A War Diary*, Sidgwick & Jackson, London, 1970, 343 pp.

Levy, Herman P., *The Press Council: History Procedure and Cases*, Macmillan, 1967, 505 pp.

McLachlan, Donald, *In the Chair: Barrington-Ward of the Times*, Weidenfeld & Nicolson, London, 1971, 319 pp.

Report of the Broadcasting Committee, 1949 (Beveridge Committee), Cmnd. 8116, HMSO, 1951, 327 pp.

Report of the Royal Commission on the Press, 1947–1949, Cmnd. 7700, HMSO, 1949, 363 pp.

Robson, W. A., ed., *The Political Quarterly in the Thirties*, Penguin, 1971, 250 pp, pbk.

Seymour-Ure, Colin, *The Press, Politics and the Public: An Essay on the Role of the National Press in the British Political System*, Methuen, London, 1968, 328 pp.

Trenaman, Joseph and Denis McQuail, *Television and the Political Image: A Study of the Impact of Television on the 1959 General Election*, Methuen, London, 1961, 287 pp.

Tunstall, Jeremy, *The Westminster Lobby Correspondents: A Sociological Study of National Political Journalism*, Routledge, London, 1970, 142 pp.

Wedell, Eberhard G., *Broadcasting and Public Policy*, Joseph, London, 1968, 370 pp.

———, *Structures of Broadcasting: A Symposium*, Manchester UP, 1970, 108 pp.

Whale, John, *The Half-Shut Eye: Television and Politics in Britain and America*, Macmillan, 1969, 219 pp.

Wilson, Trevor, ed., *The Political Diaries of C. P. Scott 1911–1928*, Collins, London, 1970, 509 pp.

Windlesham, Lord David, *Communication and Political Power*, Cape, London, 1966, 288 pp.

Chapter 2. THE BRITISH POLITICAL HERITAGE

1. HISTORY AND CONSTITUTION

Amery, Leopold, *Thoughts on the Constitution*, 2nd ed., Oxford UP, 1964, 195 pp, pbk.

Anson, Sir William R., *Law and Custom of the Constitution*, 4th ed., 2 vols, Oxford UP, 1922–35, 404 pp.

Bagehot, Walter, *The English Constitution*, Cornell UP, 1966, 310 pp.

Birch, A. H., *Representative and Responsible Government*, Allen & Unwin, London, 1964, 252 pp.

Blake, Robert, *Disraeli*, St. Martin's, 1966, 819 pp.

Brose, Olive J., *Church and Parliament: The Reshaping of the Church of England, 1828–1960*, Stanford UP, 1959, 239 pp.

Churchill, Sir Winston S., *The Great Democracies: A History of the English-Speaking Peoples*, Dodd, Mead, 4 vols: *The Birth of Britain* (to 1485), 1956, 521 pp; *The New World* (1485–1688), 1956, 433 pp; *The Age of Revolution* (1688–1815), 1957, 402 pp; *The Great Democracies* (1815–1900), 1958, 403 pp.

Clark, Sir George, *English History: A Survey*, Clarendon Press, Oxford, 1971, 567 pp.

Clarke, P. F., *Lancashire and the New Liberalism*, Cambridge UP, 1971, 481 pp.

Critchley, Thomas A., *The Conquest of Violence: Order and Liberty in Britain*, Constable, London, 1970, 226 pp.

Dicey, Albert V., *Introduction to the Study of the Law of the Constitution*, 10th ed., Macmillan, 1959, 837 pp, 1961, 535 pp, pbk.

Gregory, Roy, *The Miners and British Politics, 1906–1914*, Oxford UP, 1968, 215 pp.

Harvey, Jack and L. Bather, *The British Constitution*, St. Martin's, 1964, 572 pp.

Jennings, Sir Ivor, *The British Constitution*, 5th rev. ed., Cambridge UP, 1966, 210 pp, pbk.

——, *Magna Carta and Its Influence in the World Today*, HMSO, 1965, 43 pp.

Kidd, Ronald, *British Liberty in Danger: An Introduction to the Study of Civil Rights*, Lawrence & Wishart, London, 1941, 270 pp.

Maitland, Frederic W., *The Constitutional History of England*, Macmillan, 1961, 548 pp, pbk.

Marshall, Geoffrey and Graeme C. Moodie, *Some Problems of the Constitution*, rev. ed., Hutchinson, London, 1961, 201 pp.

Pallister, Anne, *Magna Charta: The Heritage of Liberty*, Oxford UP, 1971, 131 pp.

Pollard, Sidney, intro., *The Sheffield Outrages*, Adams & Dart, London, 1971, 468 pp.

Sedgwick, Romney, *The House of Commons, 1715–1754*, HMSO, 1970, 2 vols: I. 633 pp; II. 571 pp.

Smellie, Kingsley, *Great Britain Since 1688*, Michigan UP, 1964, 488 pp.

Smith, F. B., *The Making of the Second Reform Bill*, Cambridge UP, 1966, 297 pp.

Street, Harry, *Civil Liberties*, Pelican, 1964, 316 pp.

Taylor, Alan J. P., *English History, 1914–1945*, Oxford UP, 1965, 736 pp.

Thomson, David, *England in the Nineteenth Century, 1815–1914*, rev. ed., Penguin, 1964, 251 pp.

——, *England in the Twentieth Century*, Penguin, 1965, 304 pp.

Trevelyan, George M., *Illustrated History of England*, Longmans, London, 1956, 758 pp.

Vile, M. J. C., *Constitutionalism and the Separation of Powers*, Oxford UP, 1967, 359 pp.

Vincent, John, *The Formation of the Liberal Party 1875 to 1868*, Constable, London, 1966, 281 pp.

Williams, Lord Francis, *A Pattern of Rulers*, Longmans, London, 1965, 272 pp.

Woodward, E. L., *History of England*, Methuen, London, 1948, 273 pp.

2. POLITICAL IDEAS

Anderson, Perry and Robin Blackburn, eds., *Towards Socialism*, Cornell UP, 1966, 397 pp.

Autobiography of John Stuart Mill, Dolphin, Oxford, 1962, 240 pp, pbk.

Bennett, George, ed., *The Concept of Empire: Burke to Attlee, 1774–1947*, Black, London, 1953, 434 pp.

Brinton, Crane, *English Political Thought in the Nineteenth Century*, Benn, London, 1933, 311 pp.

Cecil, Lord Hugh, *Conservatism*, Butterworth, London, 1912, 254 pp.

Coates, Ken, *The Crisis of British Socialism*, Spokesman, London, 1971.

Cobban, Alfred, *Edmund Burke and the Revolt Against the Eighteenth Century*, Allen & Unwin, London, 1960, 280 pp.

Cole, Margaret, *The Story of Fabian Socialism*, Stanford UP, 1962, 366 pp.

Davidson, W. L., *Political Thought in England, The Utilitarians from Bentham to J. S. Mill*, Oxford UP, 1947, 196 pp.

Fremantle, Anne, *This Little Band of Prophets: The British Fabians*, Mentor, 1960, 320 pp, pbk.

Gooch, G. P., *Political Thought in England: Bacon to Halifax*, Oxford UP, 1946, 108 pp.

Hearnshaw, F. J. C., *Conservatism in England: An Analytical, Historical and Political Survey*, Macmillan, 1935, 322 pp.

Hobhouse, Leonard T., *Liberalism*, Holt, 1911, 254 pp.

Hulse, James W., *Revolutionists in London: A Study of Five Unorthodox Socialists*, Oxford UP, London, 1970, 246 pp.

Kendall, Walter, *The Revolutionary Movement in Britain: 1900–21, The Origins of British Communism*, Weidenfeld & Nicolson, London, 1969, 465 pp.

Letwin, Shirley R., *The Pursuit of Certainty: David Hume, Jeremy Bentham, John Stuart Mill, Beatrice Webb*, Cambridge UP, 1965, 391 pp.

Lichtheim, George, *A Short History of Socialism*, Weidenfeld & Nicolson, London, 1970, 362 pp.

McDowell, R. R., *British Conservatism, 1832–1914*, Faber, London, 1960, 191 pp.

MacKenzie, Norman, *Socialism: A Short History*, Hutchinson, London, 1966, 192 pp, pbk.

Morris, C., *Political Thought in England: Tyndale to Hooker*, Oxford UP, 1953, 220 pp.

Plamenatz, J. P., *Consent, Freedom and Political Obligation*, 2nd ed., Oxford UP, 1968, 182 pp, pbk.

——, *The English Utilitarians*, Macmillan, 1949, 228 pp.

Thompson, Laurence, *The Enthusiasts*, Gollancz, London, 1971, 256 pp.

Tsuzuki, Chüshichi, *H. M. Hyndman and British Socialism*, Oxford UP, 1961, 304 pp.

Ulam, Adam B., *Philosophical Foundations of English Socialism*, Harvard UP, 1951, 173 pp.

Chapter 3. BRITISH PARTIES AND ELECTIONS

To obtain material on the British parties, the following addresses in the United Kingdom are useful:

Conservative Party: Conservative and Unionist Central Office, 32 Smith Square, Westminster, London, S.W. 1; Bow Group, 60 Berners Street, London, W. 1.

Labour Party: The Labour Party, Transport House, Smith Square, London, S.W. 1; Fabian Society, 11 Dartmouth Street, London, S.W. 1.

Liberal Party: The Liberal Party, 36 Smith Square, London, S.W. 1.

1. GENERAL

Beattie, Alan, ed., *English Party Politics and Society*, Vol. I: *1660–1906*, Vol. II: *1906–1970*, Weidenfeld & Nicolson, 1970, 219 pp, 638 pp, pbk.

Beer, Samuel H., *British Politics in the Collectivist Age*, Knopf, 1964, 384 pp.

Berry, David, *The Sociology of Grass Roots Politics: A Study of Party Membership*, St. Martin's, 1970, 155 pp.

Blondel, Jean, *Voters, Parties, and Leaders: The Social Fabric of British Politics*, Penguin, 1963, 272 pp, pbk.

Budge, Ian and D. W. Urwin, *Scottish Political Behaviour: A Case Study in British Homogeneity*, Barnes & Noble, 1966, 148 pp.

Bulmer-Thomas, Ivor, *The Growth of the British Party System*, Humanities Press, 1966, 2 vols: I, 344 pp; II, 328 pp.

———, *The Party System in Great Britain*, Macmillan, 1953, 328 pp.

Cross, Colin, *The Fascists in Britain*, St. Martin's, 1963, 214 pp.

Jackson, Robert J., *Rebels and Whips: An Analysis of Dissension, Discipline and Cohesion in British Political Parties Since 1945*, St. Martin's, 1968, 346 pp.

Jennings, Sir Ivor, *Party Politics*, Cambridge UP, 3 vols: *Appeal to the People*, 1960, 387 pp; *The Growth of Parties*, 1961, 404 pp; *The Stuff of Politics*, 1962, 504 pp.

King, Anthony, ed., *British Politics: People, Parties and Parliament*, Heath, 1966, 180 pp.

McKenzie, Robert T., *British Political Parties: The Distribution of Power Within the Conservative and Labour Parties*, 2nd ed., Praeger, 1963, 694 pp, pbk.

Mayhew, Christopher, *Party Games*, Hutchinson, London, 1969, 176 pp.

Pulzer, Peter G. J., *Political Representation and Elections: Parties and Voting in Great Britain*, Praeger, 1968, 168 pp.

Thayer, George, *The British Political Fringe*, Blond, London, 1965, 256 pp.

2. CONSERVATIVE PARTY

Birch, Nigel, *The Conservative Party*, Collins, London, 1949, 49 pp.

Blake, R., *The Conservative Party from Peel to Churchill*, Eyre & Spottiswoode, London, 1970, 317 pp.

Dickie, John, *The Uncommon Commoner: A Study of Sir Alec Douglas-Home*, Praeger, 1964, 224 pp.

Hailsham, Viscount (Quintin M. Hogg), *The Conservative Case*, Penguin, 1959, 176 pp.

Hoffman, J. D., *The Conservative Party in Opposition, 1945–51*, MacGibbon & Kee, London, 1964, 288 pp.

McKenzie, Robert and Allan Silver, *Angels in Marble: Working Class Conservatives in Urban England*, Heinemann, London, 1968, 295 pp.

Maude, A., *The Common Problem*, Constable, London, 1969, 307 pp.

Nordlinger, Eric A., *The Working Class Tories: Authority, Deference, and Stable Democracy*, California UP, 1967, 276 pp.

Petrie, Sir Charles, *The Carlton Club*, Eyre & Spottiswoode, London, 1955, 221 pp.

Raison, Timothy, *Why Conservative?* Penguin, 1964, 144 pp.

Roth, Andrew, *Enoch Powell: Tory Tribune*, Macdonald, London, 1970, 393 pp.

Sparrow, Gerald, *Rab, Study of a Statesman: The Career of Baron Butler of Saffron Walden*, Odhams, London, 1965, 253 pp.

Thomson, Neville, *Silent Minority*, Oxford UP, 1971, 256 pp.

Utley, T. E., *Enoch Powell: The Man and His Thinking*, Kimber, London, 1968, 190 pp.

White, Reginald James, ed., *The Conservative Tradition*, 2nd ed., Black, London, 1964, 256 pp.

3. LABOR PARTY

Abrams, Mark and Richard Rose, *Must Labour Lose?* Penguin, 1960, 127 pp.

Attlee, Clement Richard, 1st Earl, *The Labour Party in Perspective, and Twelve Years Later*, Longmans, London, 1949, 199 pp.

Bealey, Frank, ed., *The Social and Political Thought of the British Labour Party*, Weidenfeld & Nicolson, London, 1970, 233 pp.

Brand, Carl F., *The British Labour Party: A Short History*, Stanford UP, 1964, 340 pp.

Briggs, Asa and John Saville, eds., *Essays in Labour History, 1886–1923*, Macmillan, 1971, 368 pp.

Burgess, Tyrell, *Matters of Principle: Labour's Last Chance*, Penguin, 1968, 128 pp, pbk.

"Cassandra" (William Connor), *George Brown: A Profile*, Pergamon, London, 1964, 96 pp.

Collins, Henry and Chimer Abramsky, *Karl Marx and the British Labour Movement: Years of the First International*, Macmillan, 1965, 356 pp.

Cowling, Maurice, *The Impact of Labour, 1920–1924*, Cambridge UP, 1971, 579 pp.

Crosland, C. A. R., *The Conservative Enemy: A Programme of Radical Reform for the 1960's*, Cape, London, 1963, 251 pp.

Crossman, Richard H. S., ed., *New Fabian Essays*, republ. with new intro., Dent, London, 1970, 215 pp.

———, *The Politics of Socialism*, Atheneum, 1965, 252 pp.

Fabian Essays in Socialism, 6th ed., Allen & Unwin, London, 1962, 322 pp.

Gregory, Roy, *The Miners and British Politics: 1906–1914*, Oxford UP, 1969, 215 pp.

Hall, Peter Geoffrey, *Labour's New Frontiers*, Deutsche, London, 1964, 180 pp, pbk.

Harrison, Martin, *Trade Unions and the Labour Party Since 1945*, Wayne State UP, 1960, 360 pp.

Howard, Anthony and Richard West, *The Road to Number 10*, Macmillan, 1965, 317 pp.

Janosik, E. G., *Constituency Labour Parties in Britain*, Pall Mall, London, 1968, 222 pp.

Jay, Douglas, *Socialism in the New Society*, Longmans, London, 1962, 358 pp.

Jenkins, Roy, *The Labour Case*, Penguin, 1959, 146 pp.

Labour Party, *Bibliography of Labour Party Publications*, London, 1968, 95 pp.

Middlemas, Robert Keith, *The Clydesiders: A Left Wing Struggle for Parliamentary Power*, Hutchinson, London, 1965, 307 pp.

Miliband, Ralph, *Parliamentary Socialism: A Study in the Politics of the Labour Party*, Merlin, London, 1964, 356 pp, pbk.

Northcott, Jim, *Why Labour?* Penguin, 1964, 192 pp.

Phillips, Morgan, *Labour in the Sixties,* Labour Party, London, 1960, 24 pp.

Poirier, Philip P., *The Advent of the British Labour Party,* Columbia UP, 1958, 288 pp.

Rodgers, W. T., ed., *Hugh Gaitskell 1906–1963,* Thames & Hudson, London, 1964, 167 pp.

—— and Bernard Donoughue, *The People into Parliament: A Concise History of the Labour Movement in Britain,* Viking, 1966, 191 pp.

Tawney, R. H., *The Radical Tradition,* Allen & Unwin, London, 1964, 240 pp.

Towards Socialism: Essays, Fontana Lib., 1965, 397 pp, pbk.

Worsthorne, Peregrine, *The Socialist Myth,* Cassell, London, 1971, 256 pp.

Young, James D., "A Survey of Some Recent Literature on the Labour Movement," *PQ,* 39(2), Apr–June 1968:205–14.

4. LIBERAL PARTY

Butler, Jeffrey, *The Liberal Party and the Jameson Raid,* Oxford UP, 1968, 336 pp.

Cowie, Harry, *Why Liberal?* Penguin, 1964, 155 pp.

Cross, Colin, *The Liberals in Power, 1905–1914,* Barrie & Rockliff, London, 1963, 198 pp.

Douglas, Roy, *The History of the Liberal Party, 1895–1970,* Sidgwick and Jackson, London, 1971, 331 pp, pbk.

Foord, A. S., "Whigs into Liberals," *Gov. & Opp.,* 3(2), Spring 1968:243–48.

Fulford, Roger, *The Liberal Case,* Penguin, 1959, 175 pp.

Grimond, Joseph, *The Liberal Challenge: Democracy Through Participation,* Hollis & Carter, London, 1965, 320 pp.

Rasmussen, Jorgen S., *Retrenchment and Revival: A Study of the Contemporary British Liberal Party,* Arizona UP, 1964, 285 pp.

Vincent, John, *The Formation of the Liberal Party, 1857–1868,* Constable, 1966, 316 pp.

Watkins, Alan, *The Liberal Dilemma,* MacGibbon & Kee, London, 1966, 158 pp.

Watson, George, ed., *Radical Alternative: Essays in Liberalism by the Oxford Liberal Group,* Eyre & Spottiswoode, London, 1962, 190 pp.

Wilson, Trevor, *The Downfall of the Liberal Party, 1914–1935,* Cornell UP, 1966, 416 pp.

5. COMMUNIST PARTY

Darke, Bob, *The Communist Technique in Britain,* Penguin, 1952, 159 pp.

Gallacher, William, *The Case for Communism,* Penguin, 1949, 208 pp.

MacFarlane, L. J., *The British Communist Party: Its Origin and Development Until 1929,* MacGibbon & Kee, London, 1966, 338 pp.

Martin, Roderick, *Communism and the British Trade Union, 1924–1933: A Study of the National Minority Movement,* Clarendon Press, Oxford, 1969, 209 pp.

Newton, Kenneth, *The Sociology of British Communism,* Allen Lane, 1969, 214 pp.

Pelling, Henry, *The British Communist Party: A Historical Profile,* Macmillan, 1958, 204 pp.

Wood, Neal, *Communism and British Intellectuals,* Columbia UP, 1959, 256 pp.

6. ELECTIONS

Allen, A. J., *The English Voter,* English UP, London, 1964, 258 pp, pbk.

Bealey, Frank, J. Blondel, and W. P. McCann, *Constituency Politics: A Study of Newcastle-Under-Lyme,* Faber, London, 1965, 440 pp.

Benney, Mark *et al., How People Vote: A Study of Electoral Behaviour in Greenwich,* Routledge, London, 1956, 227 pp.

Birch, A. H., *Small-Town Politics, A Study of Political Life in Glossop,* Oxford UP, 1959, 199 pp.

Bonham, John, *The Middle Class Vote,* Faber, London, 1954, 210 pp.

Butler, David E., *The British General Election of 1951,* Macmillan, 1952, 288 pp.

——, *The British General Election of 1955,* Macmillan, 1956, 236 pp.

——, *The Electoral System in Britain Since 1918,* 2nd ed., Clarendon Press, Oxford, 1963, 232 pp.

—— and Anthony King, *The British General Election of 1964,* St. Martin's, 1965, 410 pp.

—— and Anthony King, *The British General Election of 1966,* St. Martin's, 1967, 320 pp.

—— and Michael Pinto-Duschinsky, *The British General Election of 1970,* St. Martin's, 1971, 493 pp.

—— and Richard Rose, *The British General Election of 1959,* St. Martin's, 1960, 203 pp.

—— and Donald Stokes, *Political Change in Britain: Factors Shaping Electoral Choice,* St. Martin's, 1969, 516 pp.

Campbell, Angus *et al., Elections and the Political Order,* Wiley, 1966, 385 pp.

Comfort, George O., *Professional Politicians: A Study of British Party Agents,* Pub. Aff., 1958, 69 pp.

Conclusions on Review of the Law Relating to Parliamentary Elections, Cmnd. 3717, HMSO, 1968. (Labor government proposals)

Conference on Electoral Law: Final Report, Cmnd. 3550, HMSO, 1968.

Craig, F. W. S., ed., *British General Election Manifestos 1918–1966,* Pol. Ref. Pubs., London, 1970, 303 pp.

——, comp. and ed., *British Parliamentary Election Results,* Vol. I. *1918–1949,* Pol. Ref. Pubs., London, 1969, 760 pp.

——, ed., *British Parliamentary Election Statistics 1918–1970,* Pol. Ref. Pubs., 1971, 110 pp.

Daudt, H., *Floating Voters and the Floating Vote: A Critical Analysis of American and English Election Studies,* Stenfert Kroise, N.V., Leyden, 1961, 171 pp.

Deakin, Nicholas and Jenny Bourne, "Powell, The Minorities, and the 1970 Election," *PQ,* 41(4), Oct–Dec. 1970:399–415.

Fletcher, Peter, "An Explanation of Variations in 'Turnout' in Local Elections," *PS,* 17(4), Dec. 1969: 495–502.

Fulford, R., *Votes for Women: The Story of a Struggle,* Faber, London, 1957, 343 pp.

Hanham, H. J., *Elections and Party Management*, Longmans, London, 1959, 485 pp.

Hodder-Williams, Richard, *Public Opinion Polls and British Politics*, Routledge, London, 1970, 103 pp.

Holt, Robert T. and John E. Turner, *Political Parties in Action: The Battle of Barons Court*, Collier-Macmillan, 1968, 311 pp.

Kavanagh, Dennis, *Constituency Electioneering in Britain*, Longmans, London, 1970, 118 pp.

Kinnear, Michael, *The British Voter: An Atlas and Survey Since 1885*, Cornell UP, 1968, 160 pp.

Leonard, R., *Elections in Britain*, Van Nostrand, 1968, 192 pp.

McCallum, Ronald B. and Alison Readman, *The British General Election of 1945*, Oxford UP, 1947, 311 pp.

McKie, David and Chris Cook, *Election '70*, The Guardian/Panther, London, 1971, 204 pp.

Martin, Laurence W., "The Bournemouth Affair: Britain's First Primary Election," *JP*, 22(4), Nov. 1960:654–81.

Milne, R. S. and H. C. MacKenzie, *Marginal Seat, 1955: A Study of Voting Behaviour in the Constituency of Bristol North-East at the General Election of 1955*, Hansard, London, 1958, 210 pp.

———, *Straight Fight: A Study of Voting Behaviour in the Constituency of Bristol North-East at the General Election of 1951*, Hansard, London, 1954, 174 pp.

Mitchell, Brian R. and Klaus Boehm, *British Parliamentary Election Results, 1950–1964*, Cambridge UP, 1966, 135 pp.

Nicholas, H. G., *The British General Election of 1950*, Macmillan, 1951, 353 pp.

1966 Census: General and Parliamentary Constituency Tables, HMSO, 1970.

O'Leary, Cornelius, *The Elimination of Corrupt Practices in British Elections, 1868–1911*, Oxford UP, 1962, 262 pp.

Paterson, P., *The Selectorate*, MacGibbon & Kee, London, 1967, 190 pp.

Ranney, Austin, *Pathways to Parliament: Candidate Selection in Britain*, Wisconsin UP, 1965, 298 pp.

Report of the Committee on the Age of Majority (Latey), *Cmnd. 3342*, HMSO, 1967.

Rose, Richard, *Influencing Voters: A Study of Campaign Rationality*, Faber, London, 1967, 288 pp.

———, ed., *The Polls and the 1970 Election*, Strathclyde UP, 1971, 67 pp.

Rush, Michael, *The Selection of Parliamentary Candidates*, Nelson, London, 1969, 307 pp.

Sharpe, Laurence J., ed., *Voting in Cities: The 1964 Borough Elections*, Macmillan, 1967, 356 pp.

Trenaman, Joseph and D. McQuail, *Television and the Political Image: A Study of the Impact of Television on the 1959 General Election*, Methuen, London, 1961, 287 pp.

Wood, J., *Powell and the 1970 Election*, Elliott Right Way Books, London, 1970, 125 pp.

Chapter 4. THE BRITISH PARLIAMENT

Abraham, L. A. and S. C. Hawtrey, *A Parliamentary Dictionary*, 2nd ed., Butterworth, London, 1965, 241 pp.

Adams, John Clarke, *The Quest for Democratic Law: The Role of Parliament in the Legislative Process*, Crowell, 1970, 241 pp.

Advisory Committees in British Government: A PEP Report, Allen & Unwin, London, 1960, 228 pp.

Aitken, Jonathan, *Officially Secret*, Weidenfeld & Nicolson, London, 1971.

Barker, Anthony and Michael Rush, *The Member of Parliament and His Information*, Allen & Unwin, London, 1970, 443 pp.

Berkeley, Humphry, *Crossing the Floor*, Allen & Unwin, London, 1971.

Birt, Phyllis and Harry Mitchell, comps., *Who Does What in Parliament?* Mitchell and Birt, London, 1971, 63 pp. (quarterly)

Bossom, Alfred C., Lord Bossom of Maidstone, *Our House: An Introduction to Parliamentary Procedure*, rev. ed., Barrie-Rockliff, London, 1965, 207 pp, pbk.

Boulton, C. J., "Recent Developments in House of Commons Procedure," *PA*, 23(1), Winter 1969–70: 61–71.

Bromhead, Peter A., *The House of Lords and Contemporary Politics, 1911–1957*, Routledge, London, 1958, 283 pp.

———, *Private Members' Bills in the British Parliament*, Routledge, London, 1956, 216 pp.

——— and Donald Shell, "The Lords and Their House," *PA*, 20(4), Autumn 1967:37–49.

Butt, Ronald, *The Power of Parliament*, Constable, London, 1967, 468 pp.

Campion, Lord, *An Introduction to the Procedure of the House of Commons*, 3rd ed., St. Martin's, 1958, 350 pp.

Cawthorne, Graham, *Mr. Speaker, Sir*, Cleaver-Hume, London, 1952, 164 pp.

Chester, D. N. and Nona Bowring, *Questions in Parliament*, Oxford UP, 1962, 335 pp.

Chubb, Basil, *The Control of Public Expenditure: Financial Committees of the House of Commons*, Oxford UP, 1952, 291 pp.

Cocks, Sir Barnett, ed., *Erskine May's Parliamentary Practice*, 18th ed., Butterworth, London, 1971, 1,108 pp.

Conference on the Reform of the Second Chamber, 1918 (The Bryce Report), *Cmnd. 9038*, HMSO, 1918.

Coombes, David, *The Member of Parliament and the Administration: The Case of the Select Committee on Nationalized Industries*, Allen & Unwin, London, 1966, 221 pp.

Crick, Bernard, *The Reform of Parliament*, rev. ed., Weidenfeld & Nicolson, London, 1968, 325 pp.

Denning, Lord, *The Profumo-Christine Keeler Affair: Report to Parliament*, Popular Lib., 1963, 174 pp, pbk.

Eaves, John, Jr., *Emergency Powers and the Parliamentary Watchdog: Parliament and the Executive in Great Britain, 1939–1951*, Hansard, London, 1957, 208 pp.

Finer, S. E., H. B. Bennington, and D. V. Bartholomew, *Backbench Opinion in the House of Commons, 1955–1959*, Pergamon, London, 1961, 219 pp.

Ford, P. and G. Ford, *A Breviate of Parliamentary Papers*, Blackwell, Oxford, 3 vols: *The Foundation of the Welfare State, 1900–1916*, 1957, 470 pp; *Inter-War Period, 1917–1939*, 1951, 571 pp; *War and Reconstruction, 1940–1954*, 1961, 515 pp.

Ford, P. and G. Ford, *A Guide to Parliamentary Papers: What They Are, How to Find Them, How to Use Them*, new ed., Blackwell, Oxford, 1956, 79 pp.

——, *Select List of British Parliamentary Papers, 1833–1899*, Blackwell, Oxford, 1953, 165 pp.

Frasure, Robert C., "Constituency, Racial Composition and the Attitudes of British MP's," *Comp. Pol.*, 3(2), Jan. 1971:201–10.

Friedmann, Karl A., "Commons, Complaints and the Ombudsman," *PA*, 21(1), Winter 1967–68:38–47.

Gordon, Strathearn, *Our Parliament*, 6th ed., Cassell, London, 1964, 256 pp.

Hanson, A. H., *Parliament and Public Ownership*, Cassell, London, 1961, 248 pp.

—— and Bernard Crick, eds., *The Commons in Transition*, Collins, London, 1970, 304 pp, pbk.

Hazlehurst, Cameron, *Politicians At War: July, 1914, to May, 1915*, Cape, London, 1971, 346 pp.

Heasman, D. J., "Parliamentary Paths to High Office," *Parl. Aff.*, 16(3), Summer 1963:315–30.

Herbert, Sir Alan P., *The Ayes Have It*, Methuen, London, 1937, 240 pp.

——, *Independent Member*, Doubleday, 1951, 363 pp.

Hill, Andrew and Anthony Wichelow, *What's Wrong with Parliament?* Penguin, 1964, 102 pp.

House of Commons, issued after each election, The Times, London.

House of Commons, *Select Committee on Broadcasting: First Report*, HC 146, HMSO, 1966, 184 pp.

House of Lords Reform, Cmnd. 3799, HMSO, 1968, 36 pp.

Howarth, Patrick, *Questions in the House: The History of a Unique British Institution*, Lane, London, 1956, 220 pp.

Humberstone, Thomas L., *University Representation*, Hutchinson, London, 1951, 128 pp.

Irving, Clive, Ron Hall, and Jeremy Wallington, *Scandal '63: A Study of the Profumo Affair*, Heinemann, London, 1963, 227 pp, pbk.

Jennings, Sir Ivor, *Parliament*, 2nd ed., Cambridge UP, 1959, 587 pp.

Johnson, Donald, *A Cassandra at Westminster*, Johnson, London, 1967, 239 pp.

Johnson, Nevil, *Parliament and Administration: The Estimates Committee, 1945–1965*, Allen & Unwin, London, 1967, 200 pp.

Justice, *The Citizen and the Administration: The Redress of Grievances* (The Whyatt Report), Stevens, London, 1961, 104 pp.

Kersell, John E., *Parliamentary Supervision of Delegated Legislation*, Stevens, London, 1960, 178 pp.

King, Horace M., *Before Hansard*, Dent, London, 1968, 114 pp.

——, *Parliament and Freedom*, new ed., Murray, London, 1962, 144 pp.

Laundy, Philip, *The Office of Speaker*, Cassell, London, 1964, 488 pp.

Lee, J. M., "Select Committees and the Constitution," *PQ*, 41(2), Apr–June 1970:182–94.

Lindsay, T. F., *Parliament From the Press Gallery*, Macmillan, 1967, 176 pp.

Mann, Jean, *Women in Parliament*, Odhams, London, 1962, 256 pp.

Manual of Procedure in Public Business, 8th ed., HMSO, 1951 (only official work on parliamentary procedure).

Marsden, Philip, *The Officers of the Commons, 1363–1965*, Barrie & Rockliff, London, 1966, 240 pp.

Menhennet, David and John Palmer, *Parliament in Perspective*, Bodley Head, London, 1967, 156 pp.

Morris, Alfred, ed., *The Growth of Parliamentary Scrutiny by Committee*, Pergamon, London, 1970, 156 pp.

Morrison, Lord of Lambeth, Herbert Stanley, *Government and Parliament: A Survey from the Inside*, 3rd ed., Oxford UP, 1964, 384 pp, pbk.

Palmer, John, *Government and Parliament in Britain: A Bibliography*, 2nd rev. ed. and enl., Hansard, London, 1964, 51 pp.

Parliamentary Commissioner for Administration, *Papers on Work since 1967*, HMSO, 1968.

Parliamentary Reforms, *A Survey of Suggested Reforms Covering the Period from 1933–1966*, 2nd ed., Cassell, London, 1968, 208 pp.

"Reforming the Commons by Members of the Study of Parliament Group," *Planning*, 31(491), Oct. 1965: 271–310.

Reid, Gordon, *The Politics of Financial Control: The Role of the House of Commons*, Hutchinson, London, 1966, 176 pp, pbk.

Richards, Peter G., *Honourable Members: A Study of the British Backbencher*, new ed., Faber, London, 1964, 294 pp.

——, *Parliament and Conscience*, Allen & Unwin, London, 1970, 229 pp.

——, *Parliament and Foreign Affairs*, Allen & Unwin, London, 1967, 191 pp.

Roth, Andrew, *The Business Background of MPs: Parliamentary Profiles*, Parl. Profile Serv., London, 1967, 412 pp.

——, *Can Parliament Decide—About Europe or About Anything?* Macdonald, London, 1971.

Rowat, Donald C., *The Ombudsman*, 2nd ed., Allen & Unwin, London, 1968, 384 pp, pbk.

Taylor, Eric, *The House of Commons at Work*, 7th ed., Penguin, 1967, 256 pp.

Walkland, S. A., *The Legislative Process in Great Britain*, Allen & Unwin, London, 1968, 109 pp, pbk.

Weston, Corime C., *English Constitutional Theory and the House of Lords*, Routledge, London, 1965, 304 pp.

Wheare, Kenneth C., *Government by Committee: An Essay on the British Constitution*, Oxford UP, 1955, 264 pp.

Winterton, Lord, *Orders of the Day*, Cassell, London, 1954, 369 pp.

Wiseman, H. V., *Parliament and the Executive: An Analysis with Readings*, Routledge, London, 1966, 271 pp, pbk.

Wymer, Norman G., *Behind the Scenes in Parliament*, Phoenix, London, 1966, 95 pp.

Young, Roland, *The British Parliament*, Faber, London, 1962, 259 pp.

Young, Wayland, *The Profumo Affair: Aspects of Conservatism*, Penguin, 1963, 117 pp.

Chapter 5. THE BRITISH CABINET, PRIME MINISTER, AND MONARCH

1. CABINET AND PRIME MINISTER

Alexander, Andrew and Alan Watkins, *The Making of the Prime Minister 1970*, Macdonald, London, 1970, 218 pp.

Attlee, Clement R., *As It Happened*, Heinemann, London, 1954, 227 pp.

Baldwin, A. W., *My Father: The True Story*, Essential, London, 1956, 360 pp.

Bardens, Dennis, *Portrait of a Statesman: The Personal Life Story of Sir Anthony Eden*, Phil. Lib., 1956, 326 pp.

Benemy, F. W. G., *The Elected Monarch: The Development of the Power of the Prime Minister*, Harrap, London, 1965, 284 pp.

Berkeley, Humphry, *The Power of the Prime Minister*, Allen & Unwin, London, 1968, 128 pp.

Brown, R. Douglas, *The Battle of Crichel Down*, Lane, London, 1955, 192 pp.

Bullock, Alan C., *The Life and Times of Ernest Bevin*, Heinemann, London, 2 vols: *Trade Union Leader 1881–1940*, 1960, 685 pp; Vol. II., 1967, 407 pp.

Butler, R. A., *The Art of the Possible: The Memoirs of Lord Butler*, Hamish Hamilton, London, 1971, 288 pp.

Campbell-Johnson, Alan, *Sir Anthony Eden: A Biography*, McGraw-Hill, 1955, 272 pp.

Carlton, David, *MacDonald versus Henderson*, Macmillan, 1970, 239 pp.

Carter, Byrum E., *The Office of Prime Minister*, Princeton UP, 1956, 364 pp.

Carter, Lady Violet Bonham, *Winston Churchill: An Intimate Portrait*, Harcourt Brace Jovanovich, 1965, 413 pp.

Churchill, Randolph S., *Winston S. Churchill*, Houghton, 2 vols with companion documents: *Youth: 1874–1900*, 1967, 614 pp, 2 companion volumes, 1967, 1,290 pp; *Young Statesman: 1901–1914*, 1967, 775 pp, 3 companion volumes, 1968, 2,159 pp.

Citrine, Walter, McLennan, 1st Baron Citrine, *Memoirs*, Hutchinson, London, 2 vols: *Men at Work*, 1964, 384 pp; *Two Careers*, 1967, 384 pp.

Cross, Colin, *The Eloquent Conventionalist: Philip Snowden*, Barrie & Rockliff, London, 1966, 366 pp.

Cross, J. A. and R. K. Alderman, *The Tactics of Resignation*, Routledge, London, 1967, 88 pp, pbk.

Daalder, Hans, *Cabinet Reform in Britain, 1914–1963*, Stanford UP, 1963, 381 pp.

Dalton, Hugh, *Memoirs*, Muller, London, 3 vols: *Call Back Yesterday, 1887–1931*, 1953, 330 pp; *The Fateful Years, 1931–1945*, 1957, 493 pp; *High Tide and After, 1945–1960*, 1962, 453 pp.

De'ath, Wilfred, *Barbara Castle: A Portrait from Life*, Clifton Books, Brighton, 1970, 126 pp.

Dilks, David, ed., *The Diaries of Sir Alexander Cadogan, 1938–1948*, Cassell, London, 1971.

Eden, Sir Anthony (Earl of Avon), *Memoirs*, Houghton Mifflin, 2 vols: *Full Circle: 1951–1957*, 1960, 676 pp; *The Reckoning*, 1965, 704 pp.

Ehrman, John, *Cabinet Government and War, 1890–1940*, Cambridge UP, 1958, 138 pp.

Feiling, Keith, *The Life of Neville Chamberlain*, Macmillan, 1946, 475 pp.

Foot, Paul, *The Politics of Harold Wilson*, Penguin, 1968, 347 pp, pbk.

Fry, Geoffrey K., "Thoughts on the Present State of the Convention of Ministerial Responsibility," PA, 23(1), Winter 1969–70:10–20.

George-Brown, Lord, *In My Way: The Political Memoirs*, Gollancz, London, 1971, 299 pp.

Gilbert, Martin, *Winston Churchill*, Vol. III. *1914–1916*, Heinemann, London, 1971, 1,025 pp.

Great Britain, Public Record Office, "The Records of the Cabinet Office to 1922," HMSO, 1966 (Public Record Office Handbook no. 11), 60 pp.

Halifax, Earl of, *Fullness of Days*, Collins, London, 1957, 319 pp.

Heath, Edward, *Old World, New Horizons: Britain, Europe, and the Atlantic Alliance*, Harvard UP, 1970, 128 pp.

Hughes, Emrys, *Macmillan: Portrait of a Politician*, Allen & Unwin, London, 1962, 256 pp.

Hutchinson, George, *Edward Heath: A Personal and Political Biography*, Longmans, London, 1970, 229 pp.

James, Robert R., *Churchill: A Study in Failure 1900–1939*, Weidenfeld & Nicolson, London, 1970, 387 pp.

———, *Roseberg*, Weidenfeld & Nicolson, London, 1963, 548 pp.

Jenkins, Peter, *The Battle of Downing Street*, Charles Knight, London, 1970, 185 pp, pbk.

Jenkins, Roy, *Asquith: Portrait of a Man and an Era*, Collins, London, 1964, 572 pp.

———, *Mr. Attlee*, Heinemann, London, 1948, 266 pp.

Jennings, Sir Ivor, *Cabinet Government*, 3rd ed., Cambridge UP, 1959, 587 pp.

Jones, Thomas, *A Diary with Letters, 1931–1950*, Oxford UP, 1954, 582 pp.

———, *Lloyd George*, Harvard UP, 1951, 330 pp.

———, *Whitehall Diary*, ed. Keith Middlemas, Oxford UP, 2 vols: I. *1916–1925*, 1969, 382 pp; II. *1926–1930*, 1969, 324 pp.

King, Anthony, ed., *The British Prime Minister: A Reader*, Macmillan, 1969, 221 pp.

King, Mark M., *Aneurin Bevin: Cautious Rebel*, Yoseloff, London, 1961, 316 pp.

Lowenstein, Karl, *British Cabinet Government*, trans. Roger Evans, Oxford UP, 1967, 396 pp, pbk.

Mackintosh, John P., *The British Cabinet*, 2nd ed., Methuen, London, 1968, 651 pp, pbk.

———, "The Prime Minister and the Cabinet," *Parl. Aff.*, 21(1), Winter 1967–68:53–68.

Macleod, Iain, *Neville Chamberlain*, Atheneum, 1962, 319 pp.

Macmillan, Harold, *Memoirs*, Harper, 4 vols: *Winds of Change 1914–1930*, 1966, 584 pp; *The Blast of War 1939–1945*, 1968, 623 pp; *Tides of Fortune 1945–1955*, 1969, 749 pp; *Riding the Storm 1956–1959*, 1971, 686 pp.

Middlemas, Keith and John Barnes, *Baldwin: A Biography*, Weidenfeld & Nicolson, London, 1969, 1,116 pp.

Morrison, Herbert, Lord of Lambeth, *An Autobiography*, Odhams, London, 1960, 336 pp.

Mosley, Richard K., *The Story of the Cabinet Office*, Routledge, London, 1969, 94 pp.

Nicolson, Sir Harold G., *Curzon: The Last Phase, 1919–1925*, Harcourt Brace Jovanovich, 1939, 416 pp.

Nicolson, Nigel, ed., *Harold Nicolson: Diaries and Letters*, Atheneum, London, 3 vols: I. *1930–1939*, 1966, 446 pp; II. *1939–1945*, 1967, 511 pp; III. *1945–1962*, 1968, 448 pp.

Noel, G. E., *Harold Wilson and the "New Britain," The Making of a Modern Prime Minister*, Gollancz, London, 1964, 143 pp.

Norwich, Alfred Duff Cooper, Viscount, *Old Men Forget: An Autobiography*, Hart-Davis, London, 1953, 399 pp.

Owen, Frank, *Tempestuous Journey: Lloyd George, His Life and Times*, McGraw-Hill, 1955, 756 pp.

Red, Bruce and Geoffrey Williams, *Dennis Healey and the Policies of Power*, Sidgwick & Jackson, London, 1971, 288 pp.

Report of the Machinery of Government Committee (Haldane), *Cmnd. 9230*, HMSO, 1918.

Robbins, Keith, *Sir Edward Grey: A Biography of Lord Grey of Fallodon*, Cassell, London, 1971, 438 pp.

Roskill, Stephen, *Hankey: Man of Secrets*, Vol. I. *1877–1918*, Collins, London, 1970, 672 pp.

Sampson, Anthony, *Macmillan: A Study in Ambiguity*, Penguin, 1968, 271 pp.

Shrimsley, Anthony, *The First Hundred Days of Harold Wilson*, Praeger, 1965, 162 pp.

Skidelsky, Robert, *Politicians and the Slump: The Labour Government of 1929–1931*, Humanities Press, 1967, 431 pp.

Smith, Dudley, *Harold Wilson: A Critical Biography*, Hale, London, 1964, 224 pp.

Smith, Leslie, *Harold Wilson: The Authentic Portrait*, Scribner's, 1965, 231 pp.

Southgate, Donald, *"The Most English Prime Minister," The Policies and Politics of Palmerston*, Macmillan, 1966, 647 pp.

Stevenson, Frances, *Lloyd George: A Diary*, Hutchinson, London, 1971, 338 pp.

Taylor, Alan J. P., ed., *Lloyd George: Twelve Essays*, Hamish Hamilton, London, 1971, 393 pp.

Turner, Duncan R., *The Shadow Cabinet in British Politics*, Routledge, London, 1969, 106 pp.

Walker, Patrick G., *The Cabinet*, Cape, London, 1970, 190 pp.

Williams, Sir Francis, *A Prime Minister Remembers: The War and Post-War Memoirs of the Rt. Hon. Earl Attlee*, Heinemann, London, 1961, 264 pp.

Wilson, Harold, *The Labour Government 1964–1970: A Personal Record*, Weidenfeld & Nicolson, London, 1971, 855 pp.

————, *The New Britain, Labour's Plan: Selected Speeches 1964*, Penguin, 1964, 134 pp.

————, *Purpose in Politics: Selected Speeches, 1956–1963*, Weidenfeld & Nicolson, London, 1964, 270 pp.

————, *The Relevance of British Socialism*, Weidenfeld & Nicolson, London, 1964, 115 pp.

Young, Kenneth, *Arthur James Balfour*, Bell, London, 1963, 542 pp.

————, *Churchill and Beaverbrook: A Study in Friendship and Politics*, Eyre & Spottiswoode, London, 1966, 349 pp.

————, *Sir Alec Douglas-Home*, Dent, London, 1970, 282 pp.

2. THE MONARCHY

Beaverbrook, Lord, *The Abdication of King Edward VIII*, ed. Allan J. P. Taylor, Hamilton, London, 1966, 122 pp.

Benemy, F. W. G., *The Queen Reigns, She Does Not Rule*, Harrap, London, 1963, 182 pp.

Boothroyd, Basil, *Philip*, Longmans, London, 1971, 238 pp.

Duncan, Andrew, *The Reality of Monarchy*, Heinemann, London, 1970, 387 pp.

Hardie, Frank, *The Political Influence of the British Monarchy, 1868–1952*, Batsford, London, 1970, 224 pp.

Magnus, Philip, *King Edward the Seventh*, Dutton, 1964, 528 pp.

Martin, Kingsley, *The Crown and the Establishment*, rev. ed., Penguin, 1965, 192 pp.

Morrah, Dermont, *The Work of the Queen*, Kimber, London, 1958, 191 pp.

Murray-Brown, Jeremy, ed., *The Monarchy and the Future*, Allen & Unwin, London, 1969, 227 pp.

Nicolson, Sir Harold G., *King George the Fifth: His Life and Reign*, Doubleday, 1953, 570 pp.

————, *Monarchy*, Weidenfeld & Nicolson, London, 1962, 335 pp.

Petrie, Sir Charles Alexander, *The Modern British Monarchy*, Eyre & Spottiswoode, London, 1961, 228 pp.

Pope-Hennessey, James, *Queen Mary*, Allen & Unwin, London, 1960, 685 pp.

Ratcliff, Edward C., *The Coronation Service of Her Majesty Queen Elizabeth II*, Cambridge UP, 1953, 79 pp.

Wheeler-Bennett, Sir John W., *King George VI: His Life and Reign*, Macmillan, 1958, 891 pp.

Chapter 6. THE BRITISH ADMINISTRATION: NATIONAL AND LOCAL

1. NATIONAL ADMINISTRATION AND ECONOMIC POLICY

Barnes, Robert J., *Central Government in Britain*, 2nd rev. ed., Butterworth, London, 1969, 169 pp.

Beer, Samuel H., *British Politics in the Collectivist Age*, Knopf, 1965, 384 pp.

————, *Treasury Control: The Coordination of Financial and Economic Policy in Great Britain*, 2nd ed., Oxford UP, 1957, 138 pp.

Beveridge, Sir William H., *Full Employment in a Free Society*, Norton, 1945, 429 pp.

Brandon, Henry, *In the Red: The Struggle for Sterling, 1964–66*, Deutsch, London, 1966, 125 pp.

Brittan, Samuel, *Government and the Economic Market Economy*, Hobart, London, 1971, 93 pp, pbk.

————, *Steering the Economy: The Role of the Treasury*, Secker & Warburg, London, 1969, 360 pp.

Brown, Rupert G. S., *The Administrative Process in Britain*, Methuen, London, 1970, 349 pp.

Chester, D. N. and F. M. G. Willson, eds., *The Organization of British Central Government 1914–1964*, 2nd rev. ed., Allen & Unwin, London, 1968, 521 pp.

Clarke, John J., *Outlines of Central Government, Including the Judicial System of England*, 14th ed., Pitman, London, 1965, 275 pp.

Coatman, John, *Police*, Oxford UP, 1959, 248 pp.

Control of Public Expenditure (Plowden Report), *Cmnd. 1432*, HMSO, June 9, 1961.

Critchley, T. A., A *History of Police in England and Wales 900–1966*, Constable, London, 1969, 347 pp.

Cullingworth, J. B., *Town and Country Planning in England and Wales*, 3rd rev. ed., Allen & Unwin, London, 1967, 341 pp.

Davis, William, *Three Years Hard Labour: The Road to Devaluation*, Deutsch, London, 1968, 224 pp.

Economic Survey, Cmnd., HMSO (annual since 1947).

Fedden, Robin, *The Continuing Purpose: A History of the National Trust, Its Aims and Work*, Longmans, London, 1968, 226 pp.

Gladden, Edgar N., *The Essentials of Public Administration*, 3rd ed., Staples, London, 1964, 288 pp.

———, *An Introduction to Public Administration*, 4th ed., 1966, 260 pp.

Hagen, Everett E. and S. F. T. White, *Great Britain: Quiet Revolution in Planning*, Syracuse UP, 1966, 180 pp.

Heap, Desmond, *An Outline of Planning Law*, 5th ed., Sweet & Maxwell, London, 1969, 299 pp.

Jay, the Rt. Hon. Douglas, M. P., "Government Control of the Economy: Defects in the Machinery," *PQ*, 39(2), Apr–June 1968:134–44.

Jewkes, John, *The New Ordeal by Planning: The Experience of the Forties and Sixties*, Macmillan, 1968, 240 pp.

Johnson, Franklyn A., *Defence by Committee: The British Committee of Imperial Defence, 1885–1959*, Oxford UP, 1960, 416 pp.

Lewis, W. Arthur, *Development Planning*, Allen & Unwin, London, 1966, 278 pp, pbk.

"The Machinery for Economic Planning," *Pub. Ad.*, 44, Spring 1966:1–72.

Marshall, G., *Police and Government*, Methuen, London, 1967, 168 pp, pbk.

Martin, J. P. and Gail Wilson, *The Police: A Study in Manpower*, Heinemann, London, 1969, 296 pp.

Meyers, P., *An Introduction to Public Administration*, Butterworth, London, 1971, 226 pp.

Peacock, Alan T. and Jack Wiseman, *The Growth of Public Expenditure in the United Kingdom*, Princeton UP, 1962, 244 pp.

Political and Economic Planning, *Advisory Committees in British Government*, Allen & Unwin, London, 1960, 228 pp.

Productivity, Prices and Incomes Policy in 1968 and 1969, Cmnd. 3590, HMSO, 1968.

Productivity, Prices and Incomes Policy after 1969, Cmnd. 4237, HMSO, 1969.

Robertson, James, *Reform of British Central Government*, Chatto & Windus, London, 1971.

Rosweare, Henry, *The Treasury: The Evolution of a British Institution*, Allen Lane, London, 1969, 406 pp.

Rowley, C. K., *The British Monopolies Commission*, Allen & Unwin, London, 1966, 394 pp.

Sabine, B. E. V., *British Budgets in Peace and War, 1932–1945*, Allen & Unwin, London, 1970, 336 pp.

Schaffer, F., *The New Town Story*, McGibbon & Kee, London, 1970, 342 pp.

Shonfield, Andrew, *British Economic Policy Since the War*, Penguin, 1958, 288 pp.

Williams, Alan, *Public Finance and Budgetary Policy*, Allen & Unwin, London, 1963, 283 pp, pbk.

Wiseman, H. Victor, *The Organisation of British Central Government, 1914–64*, 2nd ed., Allen & Unwin, London, 1968, 251 pp.

New Whitehall Series, under the auspices of the RIPA, studies of individual departments by senior civil servants, Allen & Unwin, London:

    The Colonial Office, Sir Charles Jeffries, 1956, 222 pp.

    The Department of Scientific and Industrial Research, Sir Harry Melville, 1962, 196 pp.

    The Foreign Office, Lord Strang, 1955, 226 pp.

    Her Majesty's Customs and Excise, Sir James Crombie, 1962, 208 pp.

    The Home Office, Sir Frank Newsam, 1954, 224 pp.

    The Inland Revenue, Alexander Johnston, 1965, 201 pp.

    The Ministry of Agriculture, Fisheries and Food, Sir John Winnifrith, 1962, 224 pp.

    The Ministry of Housing and Local Government, Evelyn Sharp, 1969, 253 pp.

    The Ministry of Labour and National Service, Sir Godfrey Ince, 1960, 215 pp.

    The Ministry of Pensions and National Insurance, Sir Geoffrey King, 1958, 163 pp.

    The Ministry of Transport and Civil Aviation, Sir Gilmour Jenkins, 1959, 231 pp.

    The Ministry of Works, Sir Harold Emmerson, 1956, 171 pp.

    The Scottish Office and Other Scottish Government Departments, Sir David Milne, 1957, 232 pp.

    The Treasury, Lord Bridges, 2nd ed., 1967, 248 pp.

2. PUBLIC ENTERPRISE AND INDUSTRIAL POLICY

Barry, Eldon E., *British Economic Policy Since 1951*, Penguin, 1971.

———, *Nationalization in British Politics: The Historical Background*, Stanford UP, 1965, 396 pp.

Broadway, Frank E., *State Intervention in British Industry, 1964–68*, Kaye & Ward, London, 1969, 191 pp.

Dow, J. C. R., *The Management of the British Economy, 1945–1960*, Cambridge UP, 1966, 462 pp.

Grove, J. W., *Government and Industry in Britain*, Longmans, London, 1962, 514 pp.

Hanson, A. H., *Parliament and Public Ownership*, 2nd ed., Cassell, London, 1962, 248 pp.

House of Commons, Select Committee on Nationalized Industries, Sess. 1967–68, Report: *Ministerial Control of the Nationalised Industries*, HC371-I, 235 pp; *Minutes of Evidence*, HC371-II, 730 pp; *Appendices and Index*, 267 pp; HMSO, 1968.

Jewkes, John, *Public and Private Enterprise*, Routledge, London, 1965, 94 pp.

Keeling, B. S. and A. E. G. Wright, *The Development of the Modern British Steel Industry*, Longmans, London, 1965, 210 pp.

Kelf-Cohen, Reuben, *Twenty Years of Nationalisation: The British Experience, 1947–1968*, Macmillan, 1969, 339 pp.

Moonman, Eric, *Reluctant Partnership: A Critical Study of the Relationship between Government and Industry*, Gollancz, London, 1971, 224 pp.

Nationalised Industry, Nos. 1–12, ed. G. R. Taylor, Acton Society, London, 1950–52.

Robson, William A., *Nationalized Industry and Public Ownership*, rev. ed., Allen & Unwin, London, 1962, 567 pp.

Shanks, Michael F., *The Innovators: The Economics of Technology*, Penguin, 1967, 294 pp.

——, ed., *Lessons of Public Enterprise*, Fabian, London, 1963, 314 pp.

Thornhill, W., *The Nationalized Industries*, Nelson, London, 1968, 248 pp.

Tivey, Leonard J., *Nationalization in British Industry*, Cape, London, 1966, 219 pp.

3. LOCAL GOVERNMENT

Birch, A. H., *Small-Town Politics*, Oxford UP, 1959, 199 pp.

Bulpitt, J. G., *Party Politics in English Local Government*, Longmans, London, 1967, 133 pp.

Burney, Elizabeth, *Housing on Trial: A Study of Immigrants in Local Government*, Oxford UP, 1967, 267 pp.

Buxton, R. J., *Local Government*, Penguin, 1970, 287 pp, pbk.

Clarke, John J., *Outlines of Local Government of the United Kingdom*, 20th ed., Pitman, London, 1969, 245 pp.

Clements, Roger V., *Local Notables and the City Council*, Macmillan, 1969, 207 pp.

Cullingworth, J. B., *Housing and Local Government*, Allen & Unwin, London, 1966, 275 pp.

Donnison, D. V., *The Government of Housing*, Penguin, 1967, 397 pp.

Griffith, J. A. G., *Central Departments and Local Authorities*, Allen & Unwin, London, 1966, 574 pp.

Hampton, William, *Democracy and Community*, Oxford UP, 1970, 349 pp.

Hart, Sir William O., *Introduction to the Law of Local Government and Administration*, 8th rev. ed., Butterworth, London, 1968, 784 pp.

Headrick, T. E., *The Town Clerk in English Local Government*, Allen & Unwin, London, 1962, 232 pp.

Jackson, Richard M., *The Machinery of Local Government*, Macmillan, 1968, 390 pp.

Jackson, William E., *Achievement: A Short History of the London County Council*, Longmans, London, 1965, 304 pp.

——, *Local Government in England and Wales*, 3rd ed., Pelican, 1963, 222 pp.

Jewell, R. E. C., *Central and Local Government*, Charles Knight, London, 1966, 295 pp.

Jones, G. W., *Borough Politics: A Study of the Wolverhampton Borough Council, 1888–1964*, Macmillan, 1969, 404 pp.

McCrone, Gavin, *Regional Policy in Britain*, Allen & Unwin, London, 1969, 277 pp.

Mackintosh, John P., *The Devolution of Power: Local Democracy, Regionalism, and Nationalism*, Penguin, 1968, 207 pp.

Redlich, Josef and Francis W. Hirst, *The History of Local Government in England*, ed. Brian Keith-Lucas, St. Martin's, 1970, 284 pp.

Rees, Joan B., *Government by Community*, Charles Knight, London, 1971, 256 pp.

Reform of Local Government in England (Labour Govt. proposals for reform), Cmnd. 4276, HMSO, 1970, 40 pp.

Report of Royal Commission on Local Government in England, 1966–1969 (Redcliffe-Maud), Cmnd. 4040, HMSO, 1969, 388 pp (short version, Cmnd. 4039).

Report of Royal Commission on Local Government in Greater London, Cmnd. 1164, HMSO, 1960.

Report of Royal Commission on Local Government in Scotland, 1966–1969 (Wheatley), Cmnd. 4150, HMSO, 1969, 320 pp (appendices 130 pp.).

Rhodes, Gerald, *The Government of London: The Struggle for Reform*, Weidenfeld & Nicolson, London, 1970, 320 pp.

—— and Sydney K. Ruth, *The Government of Greater London*, Allen & Unwin, London, 1970, 197 pp.

Richards, Peter G., *The New Local Government System*, Allen & Unwin, London, 1968, 192 pp.

Ripley, Brian J., *Administration in Local Authorities*, Butterworth, London, 1970, 157 pp, pbk.

Robson, William A., *Local Government in Crisis*, Allen & Unwin, London, 1966, 160 pp, pbk.

Salter, James A., 1st Baron Salter, *Slave of the Lamp*, Weidenfeld & Nicolson, London, 1967, 301 pp.

Smallwood, Frank, *Greater London: The Politics of Metropolitan Reform*, Bobbs-Merrill, 1965, 324 pp, pbk.

Smellie, K. B., *A History of Local Government*, 4th ed., Allen & Unwin, London, 1968, 176 pp.

Stanyer, Jeffrey, *County Government in England and Wales*, Routledge, London, 1967, 116 pp, pbk.

Steed, Michael, Bryan Keith-Lucas, and Peter Hall, *The Maud Report*, New Society Pub., 1969, 20 pp.

Townsend, Peter et al., *The Fifth Social Service*, Fabian Society, London, 1970, 160 pp, pbk.

Wiseman, H. Victor, *Local Government at Work: A Case Study of a County Borough*, Routledge, London, 1967, 116 pp, pbk.

——, ed., *Local Government in England 1958–69*, Routledge, London, 1970, 206 pp.

4. PUBLIC SERVICE

Abramovitz, Moses and Vera Eliasberg, *The Growth of Public Employment in Great Britain*, Princeton UP, 1957, 151 pp.

Balogh, Thomas, *The Civil Service: Whitehall Appraised*, Blond, London, 1967, 128 pp, pbk.

——, R. Opie, and H. Thomas, *The Civil Service: An Enquiry*, Blond, London, 1968, 141 pp.

Campbell, G. A., *The Civil Service in Britain*, 2nd ed., Duckworth, London, 1965, 256 pp.

Chapman, R. A., *The Higher Civil Service in Britain*, Constable, London, 1970, 194 pp.

Foot, M. R. D., *SOE in France*, HMSO, 1966, 578 pp.

Fry, Geoffrey K., "Some Weaknesses in the Fulton Report on the British Home Civil Service," *PS*, 17(4), Dec. 1969:484–94.

——, *Statesmen in Disguise: The Changing Role of the Administrative Class of the British Home Civil Service, 1853–1966*, Macmillan, 1969, 479 pp.

Gladden, Edgar N., *Civil Services in the United Kingdom, 1853–1970*, 3rd rev. ed., Frank Cass, 1967, 289 pp.

Heussler, Robert, *Yesterday's Rulers: The Making of the British Colonial Service*, Syracuse UP, 1963, 260 pp.

Hough, Richard, *First Sea Lord: An Authorized Biography of Admiral Lord Fisher*, Allen & Unwin, London, 1969, 372 pp.

Keeling, Desmond, "The Development of Central Training in the Civil Service, 1963–70," *Pub. Ad.*, 49, Spring 1971:51–72.

Kingsley, John D., *Representative Bureaucracy: An Interpretation of the British Civil Service*, Allen & Unwin, London, 1938, 218 pp.

Mallaby, Sir George, *From My Level: Unwritten Minutes*, Hutchinson, London, 1965, 222 pp.

Ministry of Agriculture and Fisheries, *Public Inquiry into the Disposal of Land at Crichel Down, Cmnd. 176*, HMSO, 1954, 33 pp.

Parris, Henry, *Constitutional Bureaucracy: The Development of British Central Administration Since the Eighteenth Century*, Allen & Unwin, London, 1969, 324 pp, pbk.

Report of the Committee on the Civil Service, 1966–68 (Fulton), *Cmnd. 3638*, HMSO, 1968, 3 vols: 1. 206 pp; 2. 115 pp; 3. (surveys and investigations), 465 pp.

Report of the Review Committee on Overseas Representation 1968–1969 (Duncan), *Cmnd. 4107*, HMSO, 1969, 204 pp.

Richards, Peter G., *Patronage in British Government*, Toronto UP, 1963, 285 pp.

Ridley, F. F., *Specialists and Generalists: A Comparative Study of the Professional Civil Servant at Home and Abroad*, Allen & Unwin, London, 1968, 213 pp.

Robinton, Madeline R., "The Lynskey Tribunal: The British Method of Dealing with Political Corruption," *PSQ*, 68(1), Mar. 1953:109–24.

Robson, William A., "The Fulton Report on the Civil Service," *PQ*, Oct–Dec. 1968:397–414.

Salter, Lord, *Memoirs of a Public Servant*, Faber, London, 1961, 355 pp.

Stack, Freida, "Civil Service Associations and the Whitley Report of 1917," *PQ*, 40(3), July–Sept. 1969:283–95.

Strong, Kenneth, *Intelligence At The Top: The Recollection of an Intelligence Officer*, Cassell, London, 1968, 284 pp.

Thomas, Hugh S., ed., *Crisis in the Civil Service*, Blond, London, 1968, 141 pp.

Walker, N., *Morale in the Civil Service, A Study of the Desk Worker*, Edinburgh UP, 1961, 302 pp.

Wilson, H. H., *The Problem of Internal Security in Great Britain, 1948–1953*, Doubleday, 1954, 86 pp.

Wright, Maurice, *Treasury Control of the Civil Service, 1854–1874*, Oxford UP, 1969, 441 pp.

Chapter 7. ENGLISH LAW AND COURTS

1. THE LAW

Allen, Sir Carleton Kemp, *Common and Statute Law in the Making*, 7th ed., Oxford UP, 1964, 649 pp.

Cross, Rupert and P. Asterley Jones, *An Introduction to the Criminal Law*, 6th rev. ed., Butterworth, London, 1968, 366 pp.

Dicey, Albert V., *Law and Public Opinion in England*, Macmillan, 1962, 600 pp, pbk.

Gatley, John C. C., *Libel and Slander*, 6th ed., rev. R. L. McEwen and P. S. C. Lewis, Sweet & Maxwell, London, 1967, 768 pp.

Geldart, William M., *Elements of English Law*, 7th ed., prepared D. C. M. Yardley, Oxford UP, 1966, 182 pp.

Giles, Francis T., *Criminal Law: A Short Introduction*, 3rd ed., Penguin, 1963, 300 pp.

Ginsberg, Morris, ed., *Law and Opinion in England in the Twentieth Century*, Stevens, London, 1959, 407 pp.

Jacobs, Francis, *Criminal Responsibility in English Law*, Weidenfeld & Nicolson, London, 1971, 224 pp.

Keeton, George W. and G. Schwarzenberger, eds., *Current Legal Problems*, Stevens, London (published annually).

Keir, D. L. and F. H. Lawson, *Cases in Constitutional Law*, 5th rev. ed., Oxford UP, 1967, 559 pp.

Street, Harry, *Freedom, the Individual and the Law*, 2nd ed., Penguin, 1967, 335 pp.

——, *Justice in the Welfare State*, Stevens, London, 1968, 130 pp, pbk.

Wade, E. C. S. and G. Godfrey Phillips, *Constitutional Law: An Outline of the Law and Practice of the Constitution, Including Central and Local Government and the Constitutional Relations of the British Commonwealth*, 8th ed., Longmans, London, 1967, 767 pp.

Yardley, David C. M., *Introduction to British Constitutional Law*, 3rd rev. ed., Butterworth, London, 1969, 157 pp.

2. JUDGES AND THE COURT SYSTEM

Abel-Smith, Brian and Robert Stevens, *In Search of Justice: Society and the Legal System*, Allen Lane, London, 1968, 384 pp.

——, *Lawyers and the Courts: A Sociological Study of the English Legal System, 1750–1965*, Heinemann, London, 1967, 518 pp.

Cornish, William R., *The Jury*, Allen Lane, London, 1968, 298 pp.

Devlin, Lord Patrick, *The Criminal Prosecution in England*, Yale UP, 1958, 150 pp.

——, *Trial by Jury*, Stevens, London, 1956, 187 pp.

Drewry, Gavin, "The House of Lords as a Final Court of Appeal," *BJS*, 19, Dec. 1968:445–52.

—— and Jenny Morgan, "Law Lords as Legislators," *Parl. Aff.*, 22(3), Summer 1969:226–39.

Edwards, J. L. J., *The Law Officers of the Crown: A Study of the Offices of Attorney-General and Solici-*

tor-General of England with an Account of the Office of the Director of Public Prosecutions of England, Sweet & Maxwell, London, 1964, 425 pp.

Fellman, David, The Defendant's Rights Under English Law, Wisconsin UP, 1966, 137 pp.

Giles, Francis T., The Juvenile Courts: Their Work and Problems, Allen & Unwin, London, 1946, 131 pp.

———, The Magistrate Courts: What They Do, How They Do It and Why, new ed., Stevens, London, 1963, 250 pp.

Hanbury, Harold G., English Courts of Law, 4th ed., Oxford UP, 1967, 152 pp.

Heuston, R. F. V., Lives of the Lord Chancellors, 1885–1940, Oxford UP, 1964, 632 pp.

Hyde, H. Montgomery, Lord Justice: The Life and Times of Lord Birkett of Ulverston, Random House, 1965, 683 pp.

Jackson, Richard M., The Machinery of Justice in England, 4th ed., Cambridge UP, 1964, 455 pp.

McClean, John D. and J. C. Wood, Criminal Justice and the Treatment of Offenders, Sweet & Maxwell, London, 1969, 327 pp.

Page, Leo, Justice of the Peace, 3rd ed., Faber, London, 1967, 278 pp.

Radcliffe, G. R. Y. and Geoffrey Cross, The English Legal System, 4th ed., Butterworth, London, 1964, 460 pp.

Watson, John, Which is the Justice? Allen & Unwin, London, 1969, 242 pp.

Williams, Glanville, The Proof of Guilt: A Study of the English Criminal Trial, Stevens, London, 1958, 326 pp.

Zander, Michael, Lawyers and the Public Interest, Weidenfeld & Nicolson, London, 1968, 342 pp.

3. ADMINISTRATIVE LAW AND TRIBUNALS

Allen, Sir Carleton Kemp, Law and Orders: An Inquiry into the Nature and Scope of Delegated Legislation and Executive Powers in England, 3rd ed., Stevens, London, 1965, 412 pp.

Garner, J. F., Administrative Law, 3rd ed., Butterworth, London, 1970, 473 pp.

Griffith, John A. G. and Harry Street, Principles of Administrative Law, 4th rev. ed., Pitman, London, 1967, 339 pp.

Phillips, O. Hood, Constitutional and Administrative Law, 4th rev. ed., Sweet & Maxwell, London, 1967, 865 pp.

———, Leading Cases in Constitutional and Administrative Law, 3rd rev. ed., Sweet & Maxwell, London, 1967, 452 pp.

Wade, Henry W. R., Administrative Law, 2nd rev. ed., Oxford UP, 1967, 338 pp.

Chapter 8. GREAT BRITAIN AND THE WORLD

1. EMPIRE TO COMMONWEALTH

Beloff, Max, Imperial Sunset, Vol. 1. Britain's Liberal Empire, 1897–1921, Methuen, London, 1969, 387 pp.

Clutterbuck, Richard, The Long Long War: The Emergency in Malaya, 1948–1960, Cassell, London, 1967, 220 pp.

Cohen, Sir Andrew, British Policy in Changing Africa, Northwestern UP, 1959, 116 pp.

Coupland, R., The Durham Report: An Abridged Version with an Introduction and Notes, Oxford UP, 1945, 186 pp.

Cross, Colin, The Fall of the British Empire, 1918–1968, Coward-McCann, London, 1969, 359 pp.

Elias, Taslim O., British Colonial Law, Stevens & Sons, London, 1962, 323 pp.

Furnivall, J. S., Colonial Policy and Practice, New York UP, 1956, 568 pp.

Goldsworthy, D. J., Colonial Issues in British Politics 1945–1961, Oxford UP, 1971, 425 pp.

Hancock, William K., Empire in the Changing World, Penguin, 1943, 186 pp.

Hollander, Barnett, Colonial Justice: The Unique Achievement of the Privy Council's Committee of Judges, Bowes & Bowes, London, 1961, 115 pp.

Jeffries, Sir Charles, The Transfer of Power: Problems of the Passage to Self-Government, Pall Mall, London, 1960, 148 pp.

Johnson, Franklyn A., Defence by Committee: The British Committee of Imperial Defence, 1885–1959, Oxford UP, 1960, 416 pp.

Jones, Arthur C., ed., New Fabian Colonial Essays, Hogarth, London, 1959, 271 pp.

Kirkman, W. P., Unscrambling an Empire: A Critique of British Colonial Policy, 1956–1966, Chatto & Windus, London, 1966, 214 pp.

Lee, J. M., Colonial Development and Good Government: A Study of the Ideas Expressed by the British Official Classes in Planning Decolonialization, 1939–1964, Oxford UP, 1967, 319 pp.

Morris, James, Pax-Britannica: The Climax of an Empire, Harcourt Brace Jovanovich, 1968, 544 pp.

Perham, Dame Margery, ed., Colonial Government: Annotated Reading List on British Colonial Government with Some General and Comparative Material upon Foreign Empires, Oxford UP, 1950, 80 pp.

———, The Colonial Reckoning: The End of Imperial Rule in Africa in the Light of British Experience, Knopf, 1962, 203 pp.

———, Colonial Sequence: 1930–1949, Methuen, London, 1967, 351 pp.

Young, Kenneth, Rhodesia and Independence: A Study in British Colonial Policy, 2nd rev. ed., Dent, London, 1969, 581 pp.

2. THE COMMONWEALTH OF NATIONS

Arnold, Guy, Towards Peace and a Multi-Racial Commonwealth, Chapman & Hall, London, 1964, 184 pp.

Ball, M. Margaret, The "Open" Commonwealth, Duke UP, 1971, 275 pp.

Beaton, Leonard, Commonwealth in a New Era: Pioneers of an Open World, Trade Policy Research Center, London, 1969, 32 pp.

Burns, Sir Alan, ed., Parliament as an Export, Allen & Unwin, London, 1966, 271 pp.

Caiden, G. E., The Commonwealth Bureaucracy, Melbourne UP, 1967, 445 pp.

Caradon, Lord, Race Relations in the British Commonwealth and The United Nations, Cambridge UP, 1967, 25 pp.

Carter, Gwendolen M., The British Commonwealth and International Security: The Role of the Dominions, 1919–1939, Ryerson, Toronto, 1947, 326 pp.

Carter, Gwendolen M., "The Commonwealth and the United Nations," *IO*, 4(2), May 1, 1950:247–60.

——, "The Expanding Commonwealth," *FA*, 35(1), Oct. 1956:131–43.

Commonwealth Prime Ministers' Meeting in London, 7–15 January 1969, Final Communiqué, Cmnd. 3919, HMSO, 1969, 15 pp.

The Commonwealth Relations Conference, 1959, Oxford UP, 1959, 64 pp.

Conservative Political Center, *Wind of Change: The Challenge of the Commonwealth*, London, 1960, 63 pp.

Eayrs, J., ed., *The Commonwealth and Suez: A Documentary Survey*, Oxford UP, 1964, 483 pp.

Hamilton, W. B., Kenneth Robinson, and C. D. W. Goodwin, eds., *A Decade of the Commonwealth 1955–1964*, Duke UP, 1966, 567 pp.

Hancock, William K., *Survey of British Commonwealth Affairs*, Oxford UP, 2 vols in 3 parts: *Problems of Nationality, 1918–1936*, 673 pp; *Problems of Economic Policy, 1918–1939, 1937–1942*, 324 and 355 pp.

Harvey, Heather J., *Consultation and Co-operation in The Commonwealth: A Handbook on Methods and Practice*, Oxford UP, 1951, 411 pp.

Mansergh, Nicholas, *The Commonwealth Experience*, Weidenfeld & Nicolson, London, 1969, 471 pp.

——, ed., *Documents and Speeches on British Commonwealth Affairs, 1931–1952*, 2 vols, Oxford UP, 1954, 604 and 690 pp; and *1952–1962*, 1963, 775 pp.

——, *Survey of British Commonwealth Affairs*, Oxford UP, 2 vols: *Problems of External Policy, 1931–1939*, 1952, 481 pp; *Problems of Wartime Co-operation and Post-war Change, 1939–1952*, 1958, 469 pp.

Marshall, Geoffrey, *Parliamentary Sovereignty and the Commonwealth*, Oxford UP, 1957, 277 pp.

Mazrui, Ali A., *The Anglo-African Commonwealth: Political Friction and Cultural Fusion*, Pergamon, London, 1967, 163 pp.

Mendelsohn, Ronald, *Social Security in the British Commonwealth*, Athlone, London, 1954, 390 pp.

Millar, Thomas B., *The Commonwealth and the United Nations*, Sydney UP, 1967, 237 pp.

——, "Empire into Commonwealth into History: A Review of Recent Writing on the Commonwealth," *IO*, 24(1), Winter 1970:93–99.

Miller, J. D. B., *Britain and the Old Dominions*, Chatto & Windus, London, 1966, 286 pp.

Soper, Tom, *Evolving Commonwealth*, Pergamon, London, 1966, 150 pp.

Symonds, Richard, *The British and their Successors: A Study in the Development of the Government Services in the New States*, Faber, London, 1966, 287 pp.

United Kingdom, *Colombo Plan for Cooperative Economic Development in South and Southeast Asia*, Annual Reports of the Consultative Committee, HMSO (annually since 1957).

Watts, Ronald L., *New Federations: Experiments in the Commonwealth*, Oxford UP, 1967, 419 pp.

Wheare, Kenneth C., *The Constitutional Structure of the Commonwealth*, Oxford UP, 1961, 201 pp.

——, *The Statute of Westminster and Dominion Status*, 5th ed., Oxford UP, 1953, 347 pp.

Wiseman, H. V., *Britain and the Commonwealth*, Allen & Unwin, London, 1966, 157 pp, pbk.

——, *The Cabinet in the Commonwealth: Post-War Developments in Africa, The West Indies, and South-East Asia*, Praeger, 1959, 364 pp.

3. BRITAIN AND EUROPE

Allen, Harry C., *The Anglo-American Predicament: the British Commonwealth, the United States and European Unity*, St. Martin's, 1960, 241 pp.

Birch, R. C., *Britain and Europe 1871–1939*, Pergamon, London, 1966, 313 pp.

Britain and the European Communities: An Economic Assessment, Cmnd. 4289, HMSO, 1970, 46 pp.

Camps, Miriam, *Britain and the European Community, 1955–1963*, Princeton UP, 1964, 547 pp.

Carter, W. Horsfall, *Speaking European: The Anglo-Continental Cleavage*, Allen & Unwin, London, 1966, 223 pp.

Coffey, Peter and John R. Presley, *European Monetary Integration*, Macmillan, 1971, 143 pp.

Cosgrove, Carol A., *A Reader's Guide to Britain and The European Communities*, RIIA, London, 1970, 106 pp.

Davidson, Ian, *Britain and the Making of Europe*, Macdonald, London, 1971.

Einzig, Paul, *The Case Against Joining the Common Market*, St. Martin's, 1971, 132 pp.

Gladwyn, Lord, *The European Idea*, Weidenfeld & Nicolson, London, 1966, 171 pp.

Kaiser, Karl and Roger Morgan, eds., *Britain and West Germany: Changing Societies and the Future of Foreign Policy*, Oxford UP, 1971, 294 pp.

Kitzinger, Uwe E., *Britain, Europe and Beyond*, Sijthoff, Leyden, 1965, 222 pp.

——, *The Second Try: Labour and the EEC*, Pergamon, London, 1969, 353 pp.

Lieber, Robert J., *British Politics and European Unity: Parties, Elites and Pressure Groups*, California UP, 1971, 317 pp.

Mally, Gerhard, *Britain and European Unity*, Hansard, London, 1966, 156 pp.

Mandel, Ernest, *Europe versus America? Contradictions of Imperialism*, NLB, London, 1970, 139 pp.

Marsh, John S. and Christopher Ritson, *Agricultural Policy and The Common Market*, RIIA, London, 1971, 199 pp.

Pfaltzgraff, Robert L., Jr., *Britain Faces Europe, 1957–1967*, Pennsylvania UP, 1969, 228 pp.

Pickles, William, *Britain and Europe: How Much Has Changed?* Blackwell, Oxford, 1967, 119 pp, pbk.

Pinder, John, *Britain and the Common Market*, Cresset, London, 1961, 134 pp.

The United Kingdom and European Communities, Cmnd. 4715, HMSO, July 7, 1971.

Watt, D. C., *Britain Looks to Germany: A Study of British Opinion and Policy Towards Germany since 1945*, Wolff, London, 1965, 164 pp.

4. INTERNATIONAL RELATIONS

Barker, A. J., *Suez, The Seven-Day War*, Faber, London, 1964, 223 pp.

Beloff, Max, *The Balance of Power*, Allen & Unwin, 1968, 73 pp.

Beloff, Max, *New Dimensions in Foreign Policy: A Study in British Administrative Experience, 1947–1959*, Macmillan, 1961, 208 pp.

Brown, Neville, *Arms without Empire: British Defense Role in the Modern World*, Penguin, 1967, 169 pp.

Busk, Douglas, *The Craft of Diplomacy: Mechanics and Development of National Representation Overseas*, Pall Mall, London, 1967, 293 pp.

Crosby, Gerda R., *Disarmament and Peace in British Politics, 1914–1919*, Harvard UP, 1957, 192 pp.

Epstein, Leon D., *British Politics in the Suez Crisis*, Illinois UP, 1964, 220 pp.

Fitzsimons, M. A., *The Foreign Policy of the British Labour Government, 1945–1951*, Notre Dame UP, 1953, 182 pp.

Fleming, Danna F., *The Cold War and Its Origins, 1917–1960*, 2 vols, Doubleday, 1961, 1,158 pp.

Gaitskell, Hugh, *The Challenge of Coexistence*, Harvard UP, 1957, 114 pp.

Glubb, John B., *Britain and the Arabs, 1908–1958*, Hodder & Stoughton, London, 1958, 496 pp.

Gordon, Michael R., *Conflict and Consensus in Labour's Foreign Policy, 1914–1965*, Stanford UP, 1969, 333 pp.

Great Britain Foreign Office: Documents on British Foreign Policy, 1919–1939, HMSO, London, First Series: 17 vols, 1919 to 1930, 1947–70; Series IA, 3 vols, 1925 to 1929, 1966–70; Second Series, 11 vols, 1930 to March 1938, 1946–70; Third Series, 10 vols, March 1938 to Sept. 1939, 1949–61.

Harvey, John, ed., *The Diplomatic Diaries of Oliver Harvey, 1937–1940*, Collins, London, 1970, 448 pp.

Hawley, Donald, *The Trucial States*, Allen & Unwin, London, 1971, 379 pp.

Hayter, Teresa, *Aid as Imperialism*, Penguin, 1971, 222 pp.

Higgins, Rosalyn, *The Administration of United Kingdom Foreign Policy through the United Nations*, ed. G. J. Mangone, Syracuse UP, 1966, 63 pp.

Luard, Evan, *Britain and China*, Chatto & Windus, London, 1962, 256 pp.

Maclean, Donald, *British Foreign Policy Since Suez*, Hodder & Stoughton, London, 1970, 343 pp.

Medlicott, W. N., *British Foreign Policy Since Versailles 1919–1963*, Methuen, London, 1968, 362 pp.

Meehan, Eugene J., *The British Left Wing and Foreign Policy: A Study of the Influence of Ideology*, Rutgers UP, 1961, 201 pp.

Moncrieff, Anthony, ed., *Suez: Ten Years After*, BBC, London, 1968, 160 pp.

Monroe, Elizabeth, *Britain's Moment in the Middle East, 1914–1956*, Johns Hopkins UP, 1963, 254 pp.

Moulton, James L., *Defence in a Changing World*, Eyre & Spottiswoode, London, 1964, 191 pp.

Naylor, John F., *Labour's International Policy: The Labour Party in the 1930s*, Weidenfeld & Nicolson, London, 1969, 388 pp.

Nicholas, H. G., *Britain and the United States*, Chatto & Windus, London, 1963, 180 pp.

Northedge, F. S., *British Foreign Policy: The Process of Readjustment, 1945–1961*, Allen & Unwin, London, 1962, 341 pp, pbk.

——, *The Troubled Giant: Britain Among the Great Powers, 1916–1939*, Bell, London, 1966, 657 pp.

Nutting, Anthony, *No End of a Lesson*, Constable, London, 1967, 206 pp.

Robertson, Terence, *Crisis: The Inside Story of the Suez Conspiracy*, Hutchinson, London, 1965, 349 pp.

Rosecrance, R. N., *Defense of the Realm: British Strategy in the Nuclear Epoch*, Columbia UP, 1968, 308 pp.

Steiner, Zara S., *The Foreign Office and Foreign Policy, 1898–1914*, Cambridge UP, 1970, 274 pp.

Thomas, H., *The Suez Affair*, Weidenfeld & Nicolson, London, 1967, 243 pp.

Vital, David, *The Making of British Foreign Policy*, Allen & Unwin, London, 1968, 119 pp, pbk.

Waltz, Kenneth N., *Foreign Policy and Democratic Politics: The American and British Experience*, Little, Brown, 1967, 352 pp.

Ward, Barbara and P. T. Bauer, *Two Views on Aid to Developing Countries*, Inst. of Economic Affairs, London, 1966, 58 pp.

Watkins, K. W., *Britain Divided: The Effect of the Spanish Civil War on British Political Opinion*, Nelson, London, 1963, 270 pp.

Watt, Donald Cameron, *Personalities and Policies: Studies in the Formulation of British Foreign Policy in the Twentieth Century*, Longmans, London, 1965, 277 pp.

Woodward, Llewellyn, *British Foreign Policy in the Second World War*, Vol. I, HMSO, 1970, 680 pp.

Younger, Kenneth, *Changing Perspectives in British Foreign Policy*, Oxford UP, 1965, 147 pp.

FRANCE

GENERAL WORKS

Avril, Pierre, *Politics in France*, trans. John Ross, Penguin, 1970, 303 pp.

Blondel, Jean and E. Drexel Godfrey, Jr., *The Government of France*, 3rd ed., Crowell, 1968, 230 pp, pbk.

Brinton, Clarence C., *The Americans and the French*, Harvard UP, 1968, 305 pp.

Brogan, Sir Denis W., *The Development of Modern France*, rev. ed., Hamish Hamilton, London, 1967, 775 pp.

Cairns, John C., *France*, Prentice-Hall, 1965, 180 pp, pbk.

Carroll, Joseph T., *The French: How They Live and Work*, Davis & Charles, London, 1968, 179 pp.

Ehrmann, Henry W., *Politics in France*, 2nd ed., Little, Brown, 1971, 344 pp, pbk.

Guérard, Albert L., *France: A Modern History*, Michigan UP, 1969, 616 pp.

Harvey, Donald J., *France Since the Revolution*, Collier-Macmillan, 1968, 366 pp.

Hoffman, Stanley H. *et al.*, *In Search of France*, Harper, 1965, 441 pp, pbk.

Jones, Howard M., *America and French Culture*, North Carolina UP, 1927, 615 pp.

Noonan, Lowell G., *France: The Politics of Continuity in Change*, Holt, 1970, 528 pp.

Nourissier, François, *The French*, trans. Adrienne Foulke, Knopf, 1968, 309 pp.

Pickles, Dorothy, *The Fifth French Republic: Institutions and Politics*, 3rd ed., Praeger, 1967, 261 pp.

Pierce, Roy, *French Politics and Political Institutions*, Harper, 1968, 275 pp, pbk.

Rudorff, Raymond, *The Myth of France*, Hamish Hamilton, London, 1970, 255 pp.

Sheahan, John, *An Introduction to the French Economy*, Merrill, 1969, 118 pp, pbk.

Thompson, I. B., *Modern France: A Social and Economic Geography*, Butterworth, London, 1970, 465 pp.

Thomson, David, *Democracy in France Since 1870*, 5th rev. ed., Oxford UP, 1969, 344 pp, pbk.

Wylie, Laurence and Armand Bégué, *Les Français*, Prentice-Hall, 1970, 444 pp.

Chapter 1. THE FRENCH PEOPLE AND THEIR POLITICS

1. GENERAL

Ardagh, John, *The New French Revolution: A Social and Economic Study of France, 1945–1968*, Harper, 1969, 501 pp.

Bosworth, William, *Catholicism and Crisis in Modern France: French Catholic Groups at the Threshold of the Fifth Republic*, Princeton UP, 1962, 408 pp.

Byrnes, Robert F., *Anti-Semitism in Modern France: The Prologue to the Dreyfus Affair*, 2nd ed., Fertig, 1969, 348 pp.

Camp, Wesley D., *Marriage and the Family in France Since the Revolution: An Essay in the History of Population*, Twayne, 1959, 203 pp.

Curtius, Ernst R., *The Civilization of France: An Introduction*, trans. Olive Wyon, Allen & Unwin, London, 1932, 247 pp.

Evans, Sir Emrys, *France: An Introductory Geography*, Praeger, 1966, 192 pp.

Flanner, Janet (Genêt), *Paris Journal*, ed. William Shawn, Atheneum, 2 vols: *1944–1965*, 1965, 615 pp; *1965–1971*, 1971, 438 pp.

Joll, James, *Intellectuals in Politics*, Weidenfeld & Nicolson, London, 1960, 217 pp.

Mendès-France, Pierre, *A Modern French Republic*, trans. Anne Carter, Hill & Wang, 1968, 205 pp.

Metraux, Rhoda and Margaret Mead, *Themes in French Culture: A Preface to a Study of French Community*, Stanford UP, 1954, 120 pp.

Peyre, Henri, *The Contemporary French Novel*, Oxford UP, 1955, 363 pp.

Schram, Stuart R., *Protestantism and Politics in France*, Corbiere & Jugain, Alençon, 1954, 288 pp.

Sieburg, Friedrich, *Who Are These French?* Macmillan, 1932, 303 pp.

Siegfried, André, *France: A Study in Nationality*, Yale UP, 1930, 122 pp.

2. VILLAGE SOCIETY

Anderson, Barbara G. and Robert T. Anderson, *Bus Stop From Paris*, Doubleday, 1966, 303 pp, pbk.

Morin, Edgar Plodémet, *The Red and the White:*

Report from a French Village, Pantheon, 1970, 263 pp.

Morin, Edgar Plodémet, *A Report from a French Village*, Allen Lane, London, 1971.

Wylie, Laurence, ed., *Chanzeaux: A Village in Anjou*, rev. ed., Harper, 1966, 383 pp.

———, *Village in the Vaucluse*, 2nd ed. enlarged, Harvard UP, 1964, 377 pp.

3. EDUCATION AND THE STUDENT REVOLT, 1968

Bourges, Hervé, comp., *The Student Revolt: The Activists Speak*, trans. B. R. Brewster, Hill & Wang, 1968, 144 pp.

Field, A. Belden, *Student Politics in France: A History of L'Union Nationale De France*, Basic Books, 1970, 198 pp.

Fraser, W. R., *Education and Society in Modern France*, Humanities Press, 1963, 140 pp.

Posner, Charles, ed., *Reflections on the Revolution in France: 1968*, Penguin, 1970, 40 pp, pbk.

Quattrocchi, Angelo and Tom Nairn, *The Beginning of the End: France, May 1968*, Panther, 1968, 175 pp.

Seale, Patrick and Maureen McConville, *Red Flag, Black Flag: French Revolution of 1968*, Putnam, 1968, 252 pp.

Servan-Schreiber, J. J., *The Spirit of May*, trans. Ronald Steel, McGraw-Hill, 1968, 116 pp, pbk.

Singer, Daniel, *Prelude to Revolution: France in May, 1968*, Cape, London, 1970, 447 pp.

Talbott, John E., *The Politics of Educational Reform in France, 1918–1940*, Princeton UP, 1969, 283 pp.

4. SOCIAL POLICY

Collins, Doreen, "The French Social Security Reform of 1967," *Pub. Ad.*, 47, Spring 1969:91–112.

Peterson, Wallace C., *The Welfare State in France*, Nebraska UP, 1960, 115 pp.

Social Security in France, Ministry of Labor and Social Security, Paris, 1965, 79 pp.

5. INTEREST GROUPS

Ambler, John S., *The French Army in Politics, 1945–1962*, Ohio State UP, 1966, 427 pp (as *Soldiers Against the State*, Anchor-Doubleday, 1968, 464 pp, pbk.).

Clark, James M., *Teachers and Politics in France: A Pressure Group Study of the Fédération de l'Education Nationale*, Syracuse UP, 1967, 197 pp.

Ehrmann, Henry W., "Bureaucracy and Interest Groups in the Decision-Making Process of the Fifth Republic," Festschrift für Ernst Fraenkel, Berlin, 1963.

———, *French Labor from Popular Front to Liberation*, Oxford UP, 1947, 342 pp.

———, "The French Trade Associations and the Ratification of the Schuman Plan," *WP*, 6(4), July 1954: 453–81.

———, *Organized Business in France*, Princeton UP, 1957, 514 pp.

Hamilton, Richard F., *Affluence and the French Worker in the Fourth Republic*, Princeton UP, 1967, 464 pp.

Kelly, George Armstrong, *Lost Soldiers: The French*

Army and Empire in Crisis, 1947–1962, MIT Press, 1965, 404 pp.

Lorwin, Val R., *The French Labor Movement in Post-war France*, Harvard UP, 1931, 346 pp.

Menard, Orville D., *The Army and the Fifth Republic*, Nebraska UP, 1967, 265 pp.

Wright, Gordon, *Rural Revolution in France: The Peasantry in the Twentieth Century*, Stanford UP, 1968, 271 pp, pbk.

Chapter 2. THE FRENCH POLITICAL HERITAGE

1. THE THIRD REPUBLIC AND BEFORE

Armstrong, Hamilton F., *Chronology of Failure: The Last Days of the French Republic*, Macmillan, 1940, 202 pp.

Barthélemy, Joseph, *The Government of France*, Allen & Unwin, London, 1924, 222 pp.

Brogan, Denis W., *France Under the Republic*, Harper, 1940, 744 pp.

Chapman, Guy, *The Dreyfus Case: A Reassessment*, Viking, 1955, 400 pp.

Cobban, Alfred, *Aspects of the French Revolution*, Braziller, 1968, 328 pp.

———, *The Decline of the Third Republic*, Chatto & Windus, London, 1960, 127 pp.

———, *A History of Modern France*, Penguin, 3 vols: *Old Regime and Revolution, 1715–1799*, 1957, 287 pp; *From the First Empire to the Fourth Republic, 1799–1945*, 1961, 287 pp; *France of the Republics, 1871–1962*, 1965, 272 pp.

———, *The Social Interpretation of the French Revolution*, Cambridge UP, 1964, 178 pp.

Colton, Joel, *Léon Blum: Humanist in Politics*, Knopf, 1966, 512 pp.

Darby, Louise E., *Léon Blum: Evolution of a Socialist*, Yoseloff, London, 1963, 447 pp.

De Tocqueville, Alexis, *The Old Regime and the French Revolution*, trans. Stuart Gilbert, Doubleday, 1955, 300 pp.

Edwards, Stewart, *The Paris Commune 1871*, Eyre & Spottiswoode, London, 1971, 417 pp.

Gooch, Robert K., *Parliamentary Government in France: Revolutionary Origins, 1789–1791*, Cornell UP, 1960, 253 pp.

Guérard, Albert L., *France, A Modern History*, Michigan UP, 1959, 563 pp.

Halasz, Nicholas, *Captain Dreyfus: The Story of a Mass Hysteria*, Simon and Schuster, 1956, 274 pp.

Horne, Alistair, *The Terrible Year: The Paris Commune 1871*, Macmillan, 1971, 172 pp.

Jackson, J. Hampden, ed., *A Short History of France from Early Times to 1958*, Cambridge UP, 1959, 222 pp.

Jellinek, Frank, *The Paris Commune of 1871*, rev. ed., Gollancz, London, 1971, 453 pp.

Johnson, Douglas, *France and the Dreyfus Affair*, Walker, 1966, 242 pp.

Joll, James, ed., *The Decline of the Third Republic*, Praeger, 1959, 127 pp.

Lefèbvre, Henri, *The Explosion: Marxism and the French Upheaval*, trans. Alfred Ehrenfeld, Monthly Review Press, 1969, 157 pp.

Lofts, Norah and Margery Weiner, *Eternal France: A History of France 1789–1944*, Doubleday, 1968, 326 pp.

Maurois, André, *A History of France*, rev. ed., Farrar, Straus, 1957, 598 pp; Grove, 1960, pbk.

Micaud, Charles A., *The French Right and Nazi Germany, 1933–1939*, Duke UP, 1943, 255 pp.

Paul-Boncour, Joseph, *Recollections of the Third Republic*, Vol. I, trans. George Marion, Jr., Speller, 1958, 269 pp.

Pinkney, David H., *Napoleon III and the Rebuilding of Paris*, Princeton UP, 1958, 245 pp.

Romier, Lucien, *A History of France*, trans. and completed A. L. Rowse, Macmillan, 1953, 487 pp.

Rudé, George, *The Crowd in the French Revolution*, Oxford UP, 1959, 267 pp.

Seignobos, Charles, *The Evolution of the French People*, Knopf, 1932, 382 pp.

Thomson, David, *France: Empire and Republic, 1850–1940, Historical Documents*, Harper, 1968, 383 pp, pbk.

Weber, Eugen, *Action Française: Royalism and Reaction in Twentieth-Century France*, Stanford UP, 1966, 594 pp.

———, *The Nationalist Revival in France, 1905–1914*, California UP, 1959, 237 pp.

Werth, Alexander, *France and Munich*, Harper, 1939, 447 pp.

———, *France in Ferment*, Harper, 1935, 309 pp.

———, *The Twilight of France, 1933–1940*, Harper, 1942, 368 pp.

Zeldin, Theodore, *The Political System of Napoleon III*, Macmillan, 1958, 196 pp.

2. THE VICHY REGIME AND THE FREE FRENCH

Aron, Robert, *De Gaulle Triumphant: The Liberation of France, August 1944–May 1945*, Putnam, 1964, 360 pp.

———, *France Reborn: The History of the Liberation, June 1944–May 1945*, trans. Humphrey Hare, Scribner's, 1964, 490 pp.

——— and George Elgey, *The Vichy Regime, 1940–1944*, trans. Humphrey Hare, Macmillan, 1958, 536 pp.

Beaufre, General André, *1940—The Fall of France*, Knopf, 1968, 215 pp.

Bidault, Georges, *Resistance*, Weidenfeld and Nicolson, London, 1967, 368 pp.

Cole, Hubert, *Laval: A Biography*, Putnam, 1963, 314 pp.

Hytier, Adrienne D., *Two Years of French Foreign Policy: Vichy 1940–1942*, Drosz, Geneva, 1958, 402 pp.

Laval, Pierre, *The Diary of Pierre Laval*, Scribner's, 1948, 240 pp.

Novick, Peter, *The Resistance Versus Vichy: The Purge of Collaborators in Liberated France*, Columbia UP, 1968, 245 pp.

Paxton, Robert O., *Parades and Politics at Vichy: The French Officer Corps Under Marshal Pétain*, Princeton UP, 1966, 432 pp.

Pickles, Dorothy M., *France Between the Republics*, Love & Malcolmson, London, 1946, 247 pp.

Reynaud, Paul, *In the Thick of the Fight, 1930–1945*,

trans. James L. Lambert, Cassell, London, 1955, 694 pp.

Shirer, William L., *The Collapse of the Third Republic: An Inquiry Into the Fall of France in 1940*, Simon and Schuster, 1969, 1,082 pp.

Spears, Edward, *Assignment to Catastrophe*, A. A. Wyn, 2 vols: *Prelude to Dunkirk, July 1939–May 1940*, 1954–55, 332 pp; *The Fall of France, June 1940*, 1954–55, 336 pp.

———, *Two Men Who Saved France: Pétain and De Gaulle*, Eyre & Spottiswoode, London, 1966, 222 pp.

Viorst, Milton, *Hostile Allies: FDR and Charles de Gaulle*, Macmillan, 1964, 280 pp.

Warner, Geoffrey, *Pierre Laval and the Eclipse of France*, Eyre & Spottiswoode, London, 1969, 461 pp.

White, Dorothy S., *Seeds of Discord: De Gaulle, Free France, and the Allies*, Syracuse UP, 1964, 471 pp.

3. THE FOURTH REPUBLIC

Duverger, Maurice, *The French Political System*, Chicago UP, 1958, 227 pp.

Goguel, François, *France Under the Fourth Republic*, Cornell UP, 1952, 198 pp.

Macrae, Duncan, *Parliament, Parties and Society in France, 1946–1958*, St. Martin's, 1967, 375 pp.

Matthews, Ronald, *The Death of the Fourth Republic*, Praeger, 1954, 318 pp.

Meisel, James J., *The Fall of the Republic: Military Revolt in France*, Michigan UP, 1963, 320 pp.

Pickles, Dorothy M., *French Politics: The First Years of the Fourth Republic*, Oxford UP, 1953, 302 pp.

Taylor, O. R., *The Fourth Republic of France: Constitution and Political Parties*, Oxford UP, 1951, 216 pp.

Werth, Alexander, *France, 1940–1956*, Holt, 1956, 764 pp.

Williams, Philip M., *Crisis and Compromise: Politics in the Fourth Republic*, Doubleday, 1966, 546 pp, pbk.

Wright, Gordon, *The Reshaping of French Democracy*, Reynal, 1948, 277 pp.

4. THE FIFTH REPUBLIC

Aron, Robert, *An Explanation of de Gaulle*, Harper, 1966, 202 pp, pbk.

Campbell, Peter and Brian Chapman, *The Constitution of the Fifth Republic: Translation and Commentary*, Blackwell, Oxford, 1958, 60 pp, pbk.

Charlot, Jean, *The Gaullist Phenomenon*, trans. Monica Charlot and Marianne Neighbor, Allen & Unwin, London, 1971, 205 pp, pbk.

The French Constitution Adopted by Referendum of Sept. 28, 1958 and Promulgated on Oct. 4, 1958, French text and English trans., French Embassy, Press and Information Division, 1958, 75 pp.

Friedrich, Carl Joachim, "The New French Constitution in Political and Historical Perspective," *HLR*, 72(5), Mar. 1959:801–37.

Harrison, Martin, "The Constitution of the Fifth Republic: A Commentary," *PS*, 7(1), Feb. 1959: 41–62.

Heinz, Grete and Agnes Peterson, comps., *The French Fifth Republic, Establishment and Consolidation 1958–1965: A Bibliography*, Hoover Inst., 1970, 170 pp.

Hoffman, Stanley H. and Nicholas Wahl, "The French Constitution," Part 1. "The Final Text and Its Prospects," Part 2. "The Initial Draft and Its Origin," *APSR*, 53(2), July 1959:332–82.

Kirchheimer, Otto, "France from the Fourth to the Fifth Republic," *SR*, 26(4), Winter 1958:379–414.

Maier, Charles S. and Dan S. White, eds., *The Thirteenth of May: The Advent of deG's Republic*, Oxford UP, 1968, 402 pp, pbk.

Werth, Alexander, *The de Gaulle Revolution*, Hale, London, 1960, 404 pp.

Williams, Philip M. and Martin Harrison, *Politics and Society in De Gaulle's Republic*, Longmans, 1971, 403 pp.

5. POLITICAL IDEAS

Becker, Carl L., *The Heavenly City of the Eighteenth Century Philosophers*, Yale UP, 1932, 168 pp.

Binion, Rudolph, *Defeated Leaders: The Political Fate of Callou, Jouvenal and Tardieu*, Columbia UP, 1960, 425 pp.

Broderick, Albert, *The French Institutionalists: Maurice Hauriou, Georges Renard, and Joseph T. Delos*, trans. Mary Welling, Harvard UP, 1970, 370 pp.

Buthman, William C., *The Rise of Integral Nationalism in France*, Columbia UP, 1939, 355 pp.

Caute, David, *Communism and the French Intellectuals 1914–1960*, Macmillan, 1964, 413 pp.

Charlton, D. G., *Positivist Thought in France During the Second Empire, 1852–1870*, Oxford UP, 1959, 251 pp.

Curtis, Michael, *Three Against the Third Republic: Lorel, Barres, and Maurras*, Princeton UP, 1959, 313 pp.

Elbow, Matthew H., *French Corporative Theory, 1789–1948: A Chapter in the History of Ideas*, Columbia UP, 1954, 222 pp.

Graham, B. D., *The French Socialists and Tripartisme, 1944–1947*, Toronto UP, 1965, 299 pp.

Hughes, H. Stuart, *The Obstructed Path: French Social Thought in the Years of Desperation, 1930–1960*, Harper, 1968, 304 pp.

Lichtheim, George, *Marxism in Modern France*, Columbia UP, 1966, 212 pp, pbk.

Manuel, Frank E., *The New World of Henri Saint-Simon*, Harvard UP, 1956, 423 pp.

Martin, Kingsley, *The Rise of French Liberal Thought: A Study of Political Ideas from Bayle to Condorcet*, 2nd ed., ed. J. P. Mayer, New York UP, 1954, 316 pp.

Micaud, Charles A., *Communism and the French Left*, Weidenfeld & Nicolson, London, 1963, 308 pp.

Muret, Charlotte, *French Royalist Doctrines Since the Revolution*, Columbia UP, 1933, 326 pp.

Pierce, Roy, *Contemporary Political Thought*, Oxford UP, 1966, 288 pp, pbk.

Soltau, Roger, *French Political Thought in the Nineteenth Century*, Yale UP, 1931, 500 pp.

Wilkinson, David, *Malraux: An Essay in Political Criticism*, Harvard UP, 1967, 224 pp.

Wilson, Stephen, "History and Traditionalism: Maurras and the Action Française," *JHI*, 29(3), July–Sept. 1968:365–80.

Chapter 3. FRENCH PARTIES AND ELECTIONS

Andrews, William G. and Uri Ra'anan, eds., *The Politics of the Coup d'État*, Van Nostrand, 1969, 153 pp, pbk.

Berger, Suzanne, Peter Gourevitch, Patrice Higonnet, and Karl Kaiser, "The Problems of Reform in France: The Political Ideas of Local Elites," *PSQ*, 84(3), Sept. 1969:436–60.

Blum, Léon, *For All Mankind*, Viking, 1946, 186 pp.

Brower, Daniel R., *The New Jacobins: The French Communist Party and the Popular Front*, Cornell UP, 1968, 296 pp.

Campbell, Peter, *French Electoral Systems and Elections Since 1789*, 2nd ed., Faber, London, 1965, 155 pp.

Caute, David, *Communism and the French Intellectuals 1914–1960*, Macmillan, 1964, 413 pp.

De Tarr, Francis, *The French Radical Party from Herriot to Mendès-France*, Oxford UP, 1961, 264 pp.

Einaudi, Mario and François Goguel, *Christian Democracy in Italy and France*, Notre Dame UP, 1952, 229 pp.

Fetjö, François, *The French Communist Party and the Crisis of International Communism*, MIT Press, 1968, 225 pp.

"The French General Election of March 1967," *Parl. Aff.*, 20(3), Summer 1967:205–46.

Godfrey, E. Drexel, Jr., *The Fate of the French Non-Communist Left*, Doubleday, 1955, 79 pp.

Goldey, David B., "The French Presidential Election of 1st and 15th June 1969," *Parl. Aff.*, 22(4), Autumn 1969:320–48.

Hamilton, Richard F., *Affluence and the French Worker in the Fourth Republic*, Princeton UP, 1967, 464 pp.

Hayward, J. E. S., "Presidential Suicide by Plebiscite: De Gaulle's Exit, April 1969," *Parl. Aff.*, 22(4), Autumn 1969:289–319.

Jackson, Robert J., "The Succession of Georges Pompidou: The French Presidential Election of 1969," *PQ*, 41(2), Apr–June 1970:156–68.

Larmour, Peter J., *The French Radical Party in the 1930's*, Stanford UP, 1964, 327 pp.

McHale, Vincent E., "Electoral Traditions and Opposition Building in France," *Comp. Pol.*, 3(4), July 1971:499–516.

Marcus, John T., *French Socialism in the Crisis Years, 1933–1936: Fascism and the French Left*, Praeger, 1958, 216 pp.

Noland, Aaron, *The Founding of the French Socialist Party, 1893–1905*, Harvard UP, 1956, 248 pp.

Osgood, Samuel M., *French Royalism Under the Third and Fourth Republics*, Nijhoff, The Hague, 1960, 228 pp.

Rémond, René, *The Right Wing in France, from 1815 to De Gaulle*, trans. James M. Laux, Pennsylvania UP, 1966, 425 pp.

Rosenthal, Howard, "The Electoral Politics of Gaullists in the Fourth French Republic: Ideology or Constituency Interest?" *APSR*, 63(2), June 1969:476–87.

Rossi, Angelo, *A Communist Party in Action: An Account of the Organization and Operations in France*, Yale UP, 1949, 301 pp.

Servan-Schreiber, Jean-Jacques, *The Radical Alternative*, Macdonald, London, 1970, 207 pp.

Simmons, Harvey G., "The French Socialist Opposition in 1969," *Gov. & Opp.*, 4(3), Summer 1969:294–307.

Thorez, Maurice, *France Today and the People's Front*, Int. Pub., 1936, 255 pp.

Tucker, William R., "The New Look of the Extreme Right in France," *WPQ*, Mar. 1968:86–97.

Williams, Philip M., *Wars, Plots and Scandals in Post-War France*, Cambridge UP, 1970, 232 pp.

—— with David Goldey and Martin Harrison, *French Politicians and Elections, 1951–1968*, Cambridge UP, 1970, 313 pp.

Wilson, Frank L., "The Club Phenomenon in France," *Comp. Pol.*, 3(4), July 1971:517–28.

——, *The French Democratic Left, 1963–1969: Towards a Modern Party System*, Stanford UP, 1971, 258 pp.

Wohl, Robert, *French Communism in the Making, 1914–1924*, Stanford UP, 1966, 530 pp.

Chapter 4. THE FRENCH PARLIAMENT

Gooch, Robert K., *The French Parliamentary Committee System*, Appleton-Century-Crofts, 1935, 259 pp.

Howard, John E., *Parliament and Foreign Policy in France*, Cresset, London, 1948, 172 pp.

King, Jere C., *Generals and Politicians: Conflict Between France's High Command, Parliament and Government*, California UP, 1951, 294 pp.

Leites, Nathan, *On the Game of Politics in France*, Stanford UP, 1959, 190 pp.

——, *The Rules of the Game in Paris*, trans. Derek Coltman, Chicago UP, 1969, 355 pp.

Lidderdale, D. W. S., *The Parliament of France*, Hansard, London, 1951, 296 pp.

Macrae, Duncan, *Parliament, Parties and Society in France, 1946–1958*, St. Martin's, 1967, 375 pp.

Mavrinac, Albert, *Organization and Procedure of the National Assembly of the Fifth French Republic*, Hansard, London, 1960, 39 pp.

Williams, Philip M., *The French Parliament: Politics in the Fifth Republic*, Praeger, 1968, 136 pp. (Same as *The French Parliament, 1958–1967*.)

Wood, David M., "Issue Dimensions in a Multi-Party System: The French National Assembly and European Unification," *MJPS*, (3), Aug. 1964:255–76.

——, "Majority vs. Opposition in the French National Assembly, 1956–1965: A Guttman Scale Analysis," *APSQ*, 62(1), Mar. 1968:88–109.

Chapter 5. THE FRENCH EXECUTIVE

Anderson, Malcolm, *Government in France: An Introduction to the Executive Power*, Pergamon, London, 1970, 219 pp, pbk.

Aron, Robert, *An Explanation of de Gaulle*, trans. Marianne Sinclair, Harper, 1966, 210 pp.

Crawley, A., *De Gaulle: A Biography*, Collins, London, 1969, 510 pp.

De Gaulle, Charles, *The Edge of the Sword*, Criterion, 1960, 128 pp.

————, *Major Addresses, Statements, and Press Conferences, May 19, 1958–January 31, 1964*, French Embassy, Public Information Division, 1964, 258 pp.

————, *Memoirs of Hope, 1958–62; Endeavour, 1962–*, trans. Terence Kilmartin, Weidenfeld & Nicolson, London, 1971, 392 pp.

————, *Speeches*, Oxford UP, 1944, 189 pp.

————, *War Memoirs*, Simon and Schuster, 1955–60, 5 vols: *Call to Honour, 1940–1942; Unity, 1942–1944; Salvation, 1944–1946; Unity, Documents, 1942–1944; Salvation, Documents, 1944–1946.*

De Lamothe, A. D., "Ministerial Cabinets in France," *Pub. Ad.*, 43, Winter 1965:365–81.

Funk, Arthur L., *Charles de Gaulle: The Crucial Years, 1943–1944*, Oklahoma UP, 1959, 336 pp.

Furniss, Edgar S., Jr., *De Gaulle and the French Army: An Appraisal of a Civil Military Crisis*, Twentieth Century Fund, 1964, 331 pp.

————, *The Office of the Premier in French Foreign Policy-Making: An Application of Decision-Making Analysis*, Princeton UP, 1954, 67 pp.

"Gaullism and After," *IA*, 23(2), Spring 1968:187–295.

Harrison, Martin, "The French Experience of Exceptional Powers, 1961," *JP*, 25(1), Feb. 1963:139–58.

Herriot, Edouard, *In Those Days Before the First World War*, trans. Adolphe de Milly, Old and New World Pub., 1952, 276 pp.

Hess, John L., *The Case for De Gaulle: An American Viewpoint*, Morrow, 1968, 154 pp.

Hoffman, Stanley and Inge Hoffman, "De Gaulle as Political Artist," in Dankwart Rustow, ed., *Philosophers and Kings*, Braziller, 1970, pp. 248–316.

Lacouture, Jean, *De Gaulle*, trans. Francis K. Price, Avon Books, 1968, 188 pp, pbk.

McCormick, Donald, *Mr. France: The Life and Times of France's Dynamic Postwar Premier*, Jarrolds, London, 1955, 240 pp.

Mauriac, François, *De Gaulle*, Doubleday, 1966, 229 pp.

Melnik, Constantin and Nathan Leites, *The House Without Windows: France Selects a President*, trans. Ralph Manheim, Row, Peterson, 1958, 358 pp.

Mendès-France, Pierre, *The Pursuit of Freedom: An Autobiography*, Longmans, London, 1956, 256 pp.

Pickles, William, "Special Powers in France, Article 16 in Practice," *Pub. Law*, Spring 1963:23–50.

Schoenbrun, David, *The Three Lives of Charles de Gaulle*, Atheneum, 1966, 373 pp.

Tournoux, J. R., *Pétain and De Gaulle*, trans. Oliver Coburn, Heinemann, London, 1966, 245 pp.

Viansson-Ponte, Pierre, *The King and His Court (Les Gaullistes)*, Houghton Mifflin, 1965, 250 pp.

Werth, Alexander, *De Gaulle: A Political Biography*, Penguin, 1966, 391 pp.

————, *Lost Statesman: The Strange Story of Pierre Mendès-France*, Abelard-Schuman, 1958, 428 pp.

Wright, Gordon, *Raymond Poincaré and the French Presidency*, Stanford UP, 1942, 271 pp.

Chapter 6. THE FRENCH ADMINISTRATION: NATIONAL AND LOCAL

1. NATIONAL AND REGIONAL ADMINISTRATION

Allen, Kelvin and M. C. Mackleman, *Regional Problems and Policies in Italy and France*, Allen & Unwin, London, 1970, 352 pp.

Baum, Warren C., *The French Economy and the State*, Princeton UP, 1958, 391 pp.

Cohen, Stephen, *Modern Capitalist Planning: The French Model*, Harvard UP, 1970, 310 pp.

Crozier, Michel, *The Bureaucratic Phenomenon*, Chicago UP, 1964, 320 pp.

Einaudi, Mario *et al.*, *Nationalization in France and Italy*, Cornell UP, 1955, 260 pp.

Gilpin, Robert, *France in the Age of the Scientific State*, Princeton UP, 1968, 474 pp.

Grégoire, Roger, *The French Civil Service*, trans. rev. ed., Int. Inst. Administrative Services, Brussels, 1965, 363 pp, pbk.

Hackett, John W. and Anne-Marie Hackett, *Economic Planning in France*, Harvard UP, 1963, 418 pp. (The Fourth Plan, 1961–1965)

Hansen, Niles M., *French Regional Planning*, Indiana UP, 1968, 319 pp.

Hayward, J. E. S., "From Functional Regionalism to Functional Representation in France: The Battle of Brittany," *PS*, 17(1), Mar. 1969:48–75.

————, *Private Interests and Public Policy: The Experience of the French*, Barnes & Noble, 1966, 115 pp, pbk. (The Economic and Social Council)

McArthur, John H. and Bruce R. Scott, *Industrial Planning France*, Harvard Business School, 1969, 592 pp.

Ridley, F. and J. Blondel, *Public Administration in France*, 2nd ed., Routledge, London, 1969, 391 pp.

Rindel, Margherita, *The Administrative Functions of the French Conseil d'Etat*, Weidenfeld & Nicolson, London, 1970, 320 pp.

Robson, William, ed., *The Civil Service in Britain and France*, Macmillan, 1965, 191 pp.

Sheahan, John B., *Promotion and Control of Industry in Postwar France*, Harvard UP, 1963, 301 pp.

Wilson, John S. G., *French Banking Structure and Credit Policy*, Harvard UP, 1957, 453 pp.

2. LOCAL ADMINISTRATION

Chapman, Brian, *Introduction to French Local Government*, Allen & Unwin, London, 1953, 328 pp.

Kesselman, Mark, *The Ambiguous Consensus: A Study of Local Government in France*, Knopf, 1967, 224 pp.

Walsh, Annmarie H., *Urban Government for the Paris Region*, Praeger, 1967, 217 pp.

Chapter 7. FRENCH LAW AND COURTS

1. CIVIL LAW AND COURTS

Amos, Sir Maurice Sheldon and F. P. Walton, *Introduction to French Law*, 3rd ed., Oxford UP, 1967, 412 pp.

David, René and Henry P. de Vries, *The French Legal System: An Introduction to Civil Law Systems*, Oceana, 1958, 152 pp.

Lewy, Claude *et al.*, *Essays on French Law*, Washington Law Society, 1958, 96 pp.

McPherson, William H. and Frederick Meyers, *The French Labor Courts: Judgment by Peers*, Illinois UP, 1966, 104 pp.

2. ADMINISTRATIVE LAW AND COURTS

Brown, L. Neville and J. F. Garner, *French Administrative Law*, Butterworth, London, 1967, 160 pp.

Drago, Roland, "Some Recent Reforms of the French Conseil d'Etat," *ICLQ*, 13(4), Oct. 1964:1,282–99.

Freedman, Charles E., *The Conseil d'État in Modern France*, Columbia UP, 1961, 205 pp.

Hamson, C. J., *Executive Discretion and Judicial Control: An Aspect of the French Conseil d'État*, Stevens, London, 1954, 222 pp.

Parris, Henry, "The Conseil d'Etat in the Fifth Republic," *Gov. & Opp.*, 2(1), Nov. 1966:89–104.

Schwartz, Bernard, *French Administrative Law and the Common-Law World*, New York UP, 1954, 367 pp.

Chapter 8. FRANCE AND THE WORLD

1. FROM COMMUNITY TO AFRICAN INDEPENDENCE

Andrews, William G., *French Politics and Algeria: The Process of Policy Formation 1954–1962*, Appleton-Century-Crofts, 1962, 217 pp, pbk.

Cady, John F., *The Roots of French Imperialism in Eastern Asia*, Cornell UP, 1956, 322 pp.

Delavignette, Robert, *Freedom and Authority in French West Africa*, Oxford UP, 1950, 152 pp.

Gordon, David C., *The Passing of French Algeria*, Oxford UP, 1966, 265 pp.

Hammer, Ellen J., *The Struggle for Indo-China*, Stanford UP, 1954, 342 pp.

Hayter, Teresa, *French Aid*, Overseas Development Inst., London, 1966, 230 pp.

Pickles, Dorothy, *Algeria and France: From Colonialism to Co-operation*, Methuen, London, 1963, 215 pp.

Robinson, Kenneth, "A Survey of the Background Material for the Study of Government in French Tropical Africa," *APSR*, 50(1), Mar. 1956:179–98.

Sulzberger, Cyrus L., *The Test: De Gaulle and Algeria*, Harcourt Brace Jovanovich, 1962, 228 pp.

Thompson, Virginia and Richard Adloff, *French Equatorial Africa*, Stanford UP, 1961, 595 pp.

——, *French West Africa*, Stanford UP, 1958, 626 pp.

Tillon, Germaine, *Algeria: The Realities*, Knopf, 1958, 128 pp.

2. FRENCH POLICIES IN EUROPE

Aron, Raymond and Daniel Lerner, eds., *France Defeats EDC: Studies in an International Controversy*, Praeger, 1957, 225 pp.

Beloff, Nora, *The General Says No: Britain's Exclusion from Europe*, Penguin, 1963, 181 pp.

Camps, Miriam, *What Kind of Europe? The Community Since de Gaulle's Veto*, Oxford UP, 1965, 140 pp, pbk.

Cowan, Laing G., *France and the Saar: 1680–1948*, Columbia UP, 1950, 247 pp.

Deniau, J. F., *The Common Market: Its Structure and Purpose*, Barrie-Rockliff, London, 1960, 143 pp.

Fisher, Sidney Nettleton, ed., *France and the European Community*, Ohio State UP, 1964, 176 pp.

Jordan, W. M. *Great Britain, France, and the German Problem, 1918–1939: A Study of Anglo-French Relations in the Making and Maintenance of the Versailles Settlement*, Oxford UP, 1944, 235 pp.

Kleiman, Robert, *Atlantic Crisis: American Diplomacy Confronts a Resurgent Europe*, Norton, 1964, 158 pp.

Lauret, René, *France and Germany: The Legacy of Charlemagne*, trans. Wells Chamberlin, Regnery, 1964, 272 pp.

Lindberg, Leon N. and Stuart A. Scheingold, *Europe's Would Be Policy: Patterns of Change in the European Community*, Prentice Hall, 1969, 256 pp.

Mayne, Richard, *The Recovery of Europe: From Devaluation to Unity*, Weidenfeld & Nicolson, London, 1970, 375 pp.

Robertson, A. H., *European Institutions, Integration, Unification*, 2nd ed., Stevens, London, 1966, 427 pp.

Serfaty, Simon, *France, De Gaulle, and Europe: The Policy of the Fourth and Fifth Republics Toward the Continent*, Johns Hopkins UP, 1968, 176 pp.

Willis, F. Roy, *France, Germany, and the New Europe, 1945–1967*, rev. ed., Stanford UP, 1968, 448 pp.

Wolfers, Arnold, *Britain and France Between Two Wars: Conflicting Strategies of Peace Since Versailles*, Harcourt Brace Jovanovich, 1940, 467 pp.

3. INTERNATIONAL RELATIONS

Blumenthal, Henry, *France and the United States: Their Diplomatic Relations*, North Carolina UP, 1969, 312 pp.

De Carmoy, Guy, *The Foreign Policies of France, 1944–1968*, trans. Elaine Halperin, Chicago UP, 1969, 510 pp.

DePorte, A. W., *De Gaulle's Foreign Policy: 1944–1946*, Harvard UP, 1968, 327 pp.

Grosser, Alfred, *French Foreign Policy under de Gaulle*, Little, Brown, 1967, 192 pp.

Kulski, W. W., *De Gaulle and the World: The Foreign Policy of the Fifth French Republic*, Syracuse UP, 1966, 428 pp.

Marcus, John T., *Neutralism and Nationalism in France*, Twayne, 1959, 207 pp.

Mendl, Wolf, *Deterrence and Persuasion: French Nuclear Policy in the Context of National Policy, 1945–1968*, Praeger, 1970, 256 pp.

Newhouse, John, *De Gaulle and the Anglo-Saxons*, Viking, 1970, 371 pp.

Reynaud, Paul, *The Foreign Policy of Charles de Gaulle: A Critical Assessment*, Odyssey Press, 1964, 160 pp.

Stanley, Timothy W., *NATO in Transition: The Future of the Atlantic Alliance*, Praeger, 1965, 417 pp.

GERMANY

Chapter 1. GERMAN PEOPLE AND POLITICS

1. LAND AND PEOPLE

Adler, H. G., *The Jews in Germany*, Notre Dame UP, 1969, 152 pp.

Arndt, Hans-Joachim, *West Germany: Politics of Non-Planning*, Syracuse UP, 1966, 162 pp.

Dahrendorf, Ralf, *Society and Democracy in Germany*, Doubleday, 1967, 482 pp.

Dill, Marshall, Jr., *Germany*, Michigan UP, 1964, 504 pp.

Janowitz, Morris, "Social Stratification and Mobility in West Germany," *AJS*, 64(1), July 1958:6–24.

Landauer, Carl, *Germany: Illusions and Dilemmas*, Harcourt Brace Jovanovich, 1969, 360 pp.

Noelle, Elizabeth and Erich P. Neumann, eds., *The Germans: Public Opinion Polls, 1947–1966*, Verlag für Demoskopie, Allensbach: Germany, 1967, 630 pp.

Schalk, Adolf, *The Germans*, Prentice Hall, 1971.

Schoenberg, Hans W., *Germans from the East: A Study of their Migration, Resettlement, and Subsequent Group History Since 1945*, Nijhoff, The Hague, 1970, 366 pp.

Veblen, Thorstein, *Imperial Germany and the Industrial Revolution*, Viking, 1939, 324 pp.

2. EDUCATION

"Education in Transition, The Schools in Germany," in J. F. Cramer and G. S. Brown, eds., *Contemporary Education*, Harcourt Brace Jovanovich, 1956, pp. 432–73.

Stahl, Walter, *Education for Democracy in West Germany*, Praeger, 1961, 356 pp.

3. LABOR AND SOCIAL SECURITY

Bunn, Ronald F., "Codetermination and the Federation of German Employers' Organizations," *MJPS*, 2(3), Aug. 1958:278–97.

Homze, Edward L., *Foreign Labor in Nazi Germany*, Princeton UP, 1967, 350 pp.

Huddleston, John, "Trade Unions in the German Federal Republic," *PQ*, 38(2), Apr–June 1967: 165–76.

Kirchheimer, Otto, "West German Trade Unions: Their Domestic and Foreign Policies," in Hans Speier and W. Phillips Davison, eds., *West German Leadership and Foreign Policy*, Row, Peterson, 1957, pp. 136–94.

Reich, Nathan, *Labor Relations in Republican Germany 1918–1933*, Oxford UP, 1938, 293 pp.

Schuchman, Abraham, *Codetermination: Labor's Middle Way in Germany*, Pub. Aff., 1957, 247 pp.

Spiro, Herbert J., *The Politics of German Codetermination*, Harvard UP, 1958, 180 pp.

Wunderlich, Frieda, *Farm Labor in Germany*, Princeton UP, 1961, 390 pp.

4. BUSINESS AND AGRICULTURE

Almond, Gabriel A., "The Politics of German Business," in Hans Speier and W. Phillips Davison, eds., *West German Leadership and Foreign Policy*, Row, Peterson, 1957, pp. 195–241.

Braunthal, Gerard, *The Federation of German Industry in Politics*, Cornell UP, 1965, 389 pp.

———, "The Struggle for Cartel Legislation," in James B. Christoph and Bernard E. Brown, eds., *Cases in Comparative Politics*, Little, Brown, 1969, pp. 187–206.

Erhard, Ludwig, *Prosperity Through Competition*, trans. and ed. Edith Temple Roberts and John B. Wood, Praeger, 1958, 272 pp.

Hartmann, Heinz, *Authority and Organization in German Management*, Princeton UP, 1959, 318 pp.

Hirsch-Weber, Wolfgang, "Some Remarks on Interest Groups in the German Federal Republic," in Henry W. Ehrmann, ed., *Interest Groups on Four Continents*, Pittsburgh UP, 1958, pp. 96–116.

Martin, James Stuart, *All Honorable Men*, Little, Brown, 1950, 326 pp.

Muhlen, Norbert, *The Incredible Krupps*, Holt, 1959, 308 pp.

5. POLITICAL THOUGHT AND POLITICAL CULTURE

Baker, Kendall L., "Political Alienation and the German Youth," *CPS*, 3(1), Apr. 1970:117–30.

Butz, Otto, *Modern German Political Theory*, Doubleday, 1955, 72 pp.

Hartmann, Heinz, "Institutional Immobility and Attitudinal Change in West Germany," *Comp. Pol.*, July 1970:579–692.

Klemperer, Klemens von, *Germany's New Conservatism: Its History and Dilemma in the Twentieth Century*, Princeton UP, 1957, 268 pp.

Krieger, Leonard, *The German Idea of Freedom: History of a Political Tradition*, Beacon, 1957, 540 pp.

Lebovics, Herman, *Social Conservatism and the Middle Classes in Germany, 1914–1933*, Princeton UP, 1969, 272 pp.

Megay, Edward N., "Anti-Pluralist Liberalism, The German Neoliberals," *PSQ*, 85(3), Sept. 1970:422–42.

Merritt, Richard L., "The Student Protest Movement in West Berlin," *Comp. Pol.*, 1(4), July 1969:516–33.

Mosse, George L., *The Crisis of German Ideology: The Intellectual Origins of the Third Reich*, New University Lib, 1964, 373 pp.

Schram, Glenn, "Ideology and Politics, The *Rechtsstaat* Idea in West Germany," *JP*, 33(1), Feb. 1971:133–57.

Sontheimer, Kurt, "Anti-Democratic Tendencies in Contemporary German Thought," *PQ*, 40(3), July–Sept. 1969:268–82.

Stern, Fritz, *The Politics of Cultural Despair: A Study in the Rise of the Germanic Ideology*, California UP, 1961, 367 pp.

Verba, Sidney, "The Remaking of Political Culture," in Lucian W. Pye and Sidney Verba, eds., *Political Culture and Political Development*, Princeton UP, 1965, pp. 130–70.

6. MEDIA

Davison, W. Phillips, "The Mass Media in West German Political Life," in Hans Speier and W.

Phillips Davison, eds., *West German Leadership and Foreign Policy*, Row, Peterson, 1957, pp. 242–81.

Fliess, Peter J., *Freedom of the Press in the German Republic, 1918–1933*, Louisiana State UP, 1955, 147 pp.

Mass Media in the Federal Republic of Germany, Inter Nationes, Bonn, 1971, 36 pp.

Chapter 2. THE GERMAN POLITICAL HERITAGE

1. GENERAL HISTORY

Balfour, Michael, *The Kaiser and His Times*, Houghton Mifflin, 1964, 524 pp.

Barraclough, G., *The Origins of Modern Germany*, 2nd ed., Blackwell, Oxford, 1949, 481 pp.

Bryce, James, *The Holy Roman Empire*, rev. ed., Macmillan, 1932, 575 pp.

Childs, David, *Germany Since 1918*, Harper, 1971, 208 pp.

Dill, Marshall, *Germany: A Modern History*, rev. ed., Michigan UP, 1961, 490 pp.

Eyck, Erich, *Bismarck and the German Empire*, Allen & Unwin, London, 1950, 327 pp.

Fischer, Fritz, *Germany's Aims in the First World War*, trans. from the German *Griff Nach der Weltmacht*, intr. Hajo Holborn and James Joll, Norton, 1967, 652 pp.

Flenley, Ralph, *Modern German History*, rev. ed., Dent, London, 1964, 491 pp.

Grosser, Alfred, *Germany in Our Time*, Pall Mall, London, 1971, 288 pp.

Holborn, Hajo, *A History of Modern Germany*, Knopf, 3 vols: *The Reformation*, 1959, 374 pp; *1648–1840*, 1964, 531 pp; *1840–1945*, 1969, 818 pp.

Holborn, Louise W., Gwendolen M. Carter, and John H. Herz, *German Constitutional Documents Since 1871: Selected Texts and Commentary*, Praeger, 1971, 243 pp, pbk.

Mann, Golo, *The History of Germany Since 1789*, trans. Marian Jackson, Praeger, 1970, 547 pp.

Pinson, Koppel S., *Modern Germany*, 2nd ed., Macmillan, 1966, 682 pp.

Ramm, Agatha, *Germany 1789–1919: A Political History*, Methuen, London, 1967, 517 pp.

Ritter, Gerhard, *The German Problem: Basic Questions of German Political Life, Past and Present*, Ohio State UP, 1966, 233 pp.

Simon, W. M., *Germany: A Brief History*, Random House, 1966, 358 pp.

Snyder, Louis L., *Basic History of Modern Germany*, Van Nostrand, 1957, 192 pp.

Taylor, Alan J. P., *The Course of German History*, rev. ed., Methuen, London, 1961, 271 pp.

2. WEIMAR REPUBLIC

Blachley, Frederick F. and Miriam E. Oatman, *The Government and Administration of Germany*, Johns Hopkins UP, 1928, 770 pp.

Brecht, Arnold, *Prelude to Silence: The End of the German Republic*, Oxford UP, 1944, 156 pp.

Carsten, Francis L., *The Reichswehr and Politics, 1918–1933*, Oxford UP, 1966, 435 pp.

Conway, John, ed., *The Path to Dictatorship 1918–1933: Ten Essays by German Scholars*, Anchor Doubleday, 1966, 217 pp, pbk.

Dorpalen, Andreas, *Hindenburg and the Weimar Republic*, Princeton UP, 1964, 506 pp.

Eyck, Erich, *A History of the Weimar Republic*, trans. H. P. Hanson and R. G. L. Waite, Harvard UP, 2 vols: *From the Collapse of the Empire to Hindenburg's Election*, 1962, 373 pp; *From the Locarno Conference to Hitler's Seizure of Power*, 1963, 535 pp.

Gay, Peter, *Weimar Culture: The Outsider as Insider*, Harper, 1969, 205 pp.

Hertzman, Lewis, *DNVP: Right-Wing Opposition in the Weimar Republic, 1918–1924*, Nebraska UP, 1964, 263 pp.

Hunt, Richard N., *German Social Democracy, 1918–1933*, Yale UP, 1964, 292 pp, pbk.

Rosenberg, Arthur, *A History of the German Republic*, Methuen, London, 1936, 350 pp.

Schorske, Carl E., *German Social Democracy, 1905–1917: The Development of the Great Schism*, Wiley, 1965, 358 pp.

Vermeil, Edmond, *Germany in the Twentieth Century: A Political and Cultural History of the Weimar Republic and the Third Reich*, trans. L. J. Ludovici, Praeger, 1956, 288 pp.

3. NAZI PERIOD

Allen, William S., *The Nazi Seizure of Power: The Experience of a Single German Town, 1930–1935*, Quadrangle Books, 1965, 345 pp.

Bracher, Karl D., *The German Dictatorship: The Origins, Structure, and Effects of National Socialism*, Praeger, 1971, 553 pp.

Bramsted, Ernest K., *Goebbels and National Socialist Propaganda, 1925–1945*, Michigan State UP, 1965, 488 pp.

Broszat, Martin, *German National Socialism, 1919–1945*, trans. Kurt Rosenbaum and Inge Boehm, ABC-Clio Press, 1966, 154 pp.

Bullock, Alan L. C., *Hitler: A Study in Tyranny*, rev. ed., Harper, 1970, 848 pp.

Conway, J. S., *The Nazi Persecution of the Churches, 1933–45*, Basic Books, 1968, 474 pp.

Davidson, Eugene, *The Trials of the Germans: Nuremberg, 1945–46*, Macmillan, 1966, 630 pp.

Delarue, Jacques, *The Gestapo*, Morrow, 1964, 384 pp.

Fest, Joachim C., *The Face of the Third Reich: Portraits of the Nazi Leadership*, trans. Michael Bullock, Pantheon, 1970, 402 pp.

Grunberger, Richard, *The 12-Year Reich: A Social History of Nazi Germany, 1933–1945*, Weidenfeld & Nicolson, London, 1971, 535 pp.

Hale, Orono J., *The Captive Press in the Third Reich*, Princeton UP, 1964, 353 pp.

Heiden, Konrad, *Der Fuehrer: Hitler's Rise to Power*, Houghton Mifflin, 1944, 788 pp.

Hilberg, Raul, *The Destruction of the European Jews*, Quadrangle Books, 1961, 790 pp.

Hitler, Adolf, *Hitler's Secret Book*, trans. Salvator Attanasia, Grove, 1961, 230 pp.

———, *Mein Kampf*, Reynal & Hitchcock, 1941, 1,003 pp.

International Military Tribunal, *The Trial of German Major War Criminals*, 15 vols, HMSO, 1946–47.

Krausnick, Helmut, *Anatomy of the SS State*, trans. Richard Barry, Walker, 1969, 614 pp.

Lewy, Guenter, *The Catholic Church and Nazi Germany*, McGraw-Hill, 1964, 416 pp.

Mosse, George L., *Nazi Culture: Intellectual, Cultural, and Social Life in the Third Reich*, Grosset & Dunlap, 1966, 386 pp.

Neumann, Franz L., *Behemoth: The Structure and Practice of National Socialism, 1933–1944*, 2nd ed., Harper, 1963, 649 pp.

Orlow, Dietrich, *The History of the Nazi Party: 1919–1933*, Vol. 1, Pittsburgh UP, 1969, 338 pp.

Prittie, Terence, *Germans Against Hitler*, Hutchinson, London, 1964, 292 pp.

Rauschning, Hermann, *The Voice of Destruction*, Putnam's, 1940, 295 pp.

Reitlinger, Gerald, *The Final Solution: The Attempts to Exterminate the Jews of Europe, 1938–1945*, new ed., Yoseloff, London, 1968, 668 pp.

Ritter, Gerhard, *The German Resistance*, trans. R. T. Clark, Praeger, 1959, 330 pp.

Rothfels, Hans, *The German Opposition to Hitler*, Wolff, London, 1961, 166 pp.

Schoenbaum, David, *Hitler's Social Revolution: Class and Status in Nazi Germany 1933–1939*, Doubleday, 1966, 336 pp.

Schweitzer, Arthur, *Big Business in the Third Reich*, Indiana UP, 1964, 739 pp.

Shirer, William L., *The Rise and Fall of the Third Reich: A History of Nazi Germany*, Simon and Schuster, 1960, 1,245 pp; Fawcett World Lib., 1962, pbk.

Speer, Albert, *Inside the Third Reich: Memoirs*, trans. Richard and Clara Winston, intro. Eugene Davidson, Macmillan, 1970, 596 pp.

Taylor, Telford, *Final Report on the Nuremberg War Crimes Trials*, USGPO, 1949, 346 pp.

Toynbee, Arnold and Veronica M. Toynbee, eds., *Survey of International Affairs: Hitler's Europe*, Oxford UP, 1954, 730 pp.

Trevor-Roper, Hugh R., ed., *Hitler's Secret Conversations, 1941–44*, Farrar, Straus, 1953, 597 pp.

Van Roon, Ger, *German Resistance to Hitler, Count von Moltke and the Kreisauer Circle*, trans. Peter Ludlov, Van Nostrand, 1971, 412 pp.

Von Schuschnigg, Kurt, *Brutal Takeover*, Atheneum, 1971.

Zeman, Z. A. B., *Nazi Propaganda*, Oxford UP, 1964, 226 pp.

4. POSTWAR PERIOD

Adenauer, Konrad, *Memoirs, 1945–1953*, trans. Beate Ruhm von Oppen, Regnery, 1966, 478 pp.

Balfour, Michael, *West Germany*, Praeger, 1968, 344 pp.

—— and John Mair, *Four Power Control in Germany and Austria, 1945–1946*, Oxford UP, 1956, 390 pp.

Boelling, Klaus, *Republic in Suspense: Politics, Parties, and Personalities in Postwar Germany*, Praeger, 1964, 276 pp.

Bunn, Ronald F., *German Politics and the Spiegel Affair: A Case Study of the Bonn System*, Louisiana State UP, 1968, 230 pp.

Clay, Lucius D., *Decision in Germany*, Doubleday, 1950, 522 pp.

Davidson, Eugene, *The Death and Life of Germany: An Account of the American Occupation*, Knopf, 1959, 422 pp.

Ebsworth, Raymond, *Restoring Democracy in Germany: The British Contribution*, Praeger, 1961, 215 pp.

Edinger, Lewis J., *Politics in Germany*, Little, Brown, 1968, 360 pp.

Epstein, Klaus, "Germany After Adenauer," *Headline Series*, No. 164, Apr. 1964, 63 pp.

Erler, Fritz, *Democracy in Germany*, Harvard UP, 1965, 150 pp, pbk.

Freymond, Jacques, *The Saar Conflict 1945–1955*, Praeger, 1960, 395 pp.

Friedrich, Carl J., Leonard Krieger, and Peter Merkl, in John D. Montgomery and Albert O. Hirschman, eds., "Military Occupation and Policy Change in Germany," *Public Policy*, 17:1–104.

Gimbel, John, *The American Occupation of Germany: Politics and the Military, 1945–1949*, Stanford UP, 1968, 335 pp.

——, *A German Community Under American Occupation: Marburg, 1945–52*, Stanford UP, 1961, 259 pp.

Golay, John F., *The Founding of the Federal Republic of Germany*, Chicago UP, 1958, 256 pp.

Grosser, Alfred, *The Colossus Again: Western Germany from Defeat to Rearmament*, Praeger, 1955, 249 pp.

——, *The Federal Republic of Germany*, Praeger, 1964, 150 pp, pbk.

Herz, John H., "The Fiasco of Denazification in Germany," *PSQ*, 43, 1948:569–94.

——, "The Formation of the Grand Coalition," in James B. Christoph and Bernard E. Brown, eds., *Cases in Comparative Politics*, Little, Brown, 1969, pp. 207–39.

—— (issue editor), Special Issue on the West German Election of 1969, *Comp. Pol.*, 2(4), July 1970.

Hiscocks, Richard, *The Adenauer Era*, Lippincott, 1966, 271 pp.

Kirchheimer, Otto and Constantine Menges, "A Free Press in a Democratic State? The Spiegel Case," in Gwendolen M. Carter and Alan F. Westin, eds., *Politics in Europe*, Harcourt Brace Jovanovich, 1965, pp. 87–138.

Leonhardt, Rudolf W., *This Germany: The Story Since the Third Reich*, N.Y. Graphic Society, 1964, 275 pp.

McInnis, Edgar, R. Hiscocks, and R. Spencer, *The Shaping of Postwar Germany*, Praeger, 1961, 195 pp.

Merkl, Peter H., "Coalition Politics in West Germany," in S. Groennings, ed., *The Study of Coalition Behavior*, Holt, 1970, pp. 13–42.

——, *Germany: Yesterday and Tomorrow*, Oxford UP, 1965, 366 pp.

——, *The Origin of the West German Republic*, Oxford UP, 1963, 269 pp.

Merritt, Richard L. and Anna J. Merritt, "West Germany Enters the Seventies," *Headline Series*, No. 205, Apr. 1971.

Montgomery, John D., *Forced to Be Free: The Arti-*

ficial Revolution in Germany and Japan, Chicago UP, 1957, 209 pp.

Oppen, Beate Ruhm von, ed., *Documents on Germany Under Occupation 1945–1954,* Oxford UP, 1955, 660 pp.

Plischke, Elmer, *Contemporary Governments in Germany,* 2nd ed., Houghton Mifflin, 1969, 237 pp, pbk.

"Potsdam After Twenty-Five Years," *IA,* 46(3), July 1970:441–74.

Romoser, George K., "Change in West German Politics after Erhard's Fall," in William G. Andrews, ed., *European Politics II: The Dynamics of Change,* Van Nostrand, 1969, pp. 177–240.

Schoenbaum, David, *The Spiegel Affair,* Doubleday, 1968, 239 pp.

Stahl, Walter, ed., *The Politics of Postwar Germany,* Praeger, 1963, 480 pp.

US Office of Military Government, *Documents on Germany, 1944–61,* USGPO, 1961, 833 pp.

Willis, F. Roy, *The French in Germany, 1945–1949,* Stanford UP, 1961, 308 pp.

Zink, Harold, *The United States in Germany, 1944–1955,* Van Nostrand, 1957, 374 pp.

Chapter 3. WEST GERMAN PARTIES AND ELECTIONS

Braunthal, Gerard, "The Free Democratic Party in West Germany," *WPQ,* 13(2), June 1960:332–48.

Chalmers, Douglas A., *The Social Democratic Party of Germany: From Working-Class Movement to Modern Political Party,* Yale UP, 1964, 258 pp, pbk.

Childs, David, *From Schumacher to Brandt: The Story of German Socialism, 1945–1965,* Pergamon, 1966, 194 pp.

Cromwell, Richard S., "Rightist Extremism in Postwar West Germany," *WPQ,* 17(2), June 1964:284–93.

Dittmer, Lowell, "The German NPD: A Psycho-Sociological Analysis of 'Neo-Nazism'," *Comp. Pol.,* 2(1), Oct. 1969:79–110.

Edinger, Lewis J., *Kurt Schumacher: A Study in Personality and Political Behavior,* Stanford UP, 1965, 390 pp.

———, "Political Change in Germany: The Federal Republic after the 1969 Election," *Comp. Pol.,* July 1970:549–78.

——— and Paul Luebke, "Grass-Roots Electoral Politics in the German Federal Republic," *Comp. Pol.,* 3(4), July 1971:463–98.

Frye, Charles E., "Parties and Pressure Groups in Weimar and Bonn," *WP,* 17(4), July 1965:635–55.

Heberle, Rudolph, "Analysis of a Neo-Fascist Party: The NPD," *Polity,* 3(1), Fall 1970:126–34.

Heidenheimer, Arnold J., *Adenauer and the CDU: The Rise of the Leader and the Integration of the Party,* Nijhoff, The Hague, 1960, 259 pp.

———, "German Party Finance: The CDU," *APSR,* 51, 1957:369–85.

Johnson, Nevil, "State Finance for Political Parties in Western Germany," *Parl. Aff.,* 18(3), Summer 1965:279–92.

Kaltefleiter, Werner, "The Impact of the Election of 1969 and the Formation of the New Government on

the German Party System," *Comp. Pol.,* July 1970:593–603.

Kitzinger, Uwe, *German Electoral Politics: A Study of the 1957 Campaign,* Oxford UP, 1960, 365 pp.

———, "The West German Electoral Law," *Parl. Aff.,* 11(2), Spring 1958:220–37.

Klingemann, Hans D. and Franz Urban Pappi, "The 1969 Bundestag Election in the Federal Republic of Germany: An Analysis of Voting Behavior," *Comp. Pol.,* July 1970:523–48.

Loewenberg, Gerhard, "The Remaking of the German Party System," *Polity,* 1(1), Fall 1968:96–113.

Nagle, John D., *Right Radicalism in the Federal Republic of Germany: The National Democratic Party,* California UP, 1970, 221 pp.

Pulzer, Peter G. J., "The German Party System in the Sixties," *PS,* 19(1), Mar. 1971:1–17.

Schellenger, H. Kent, "The German Social Democratic Party After World War II, The Conservatism of Power," *WPQ,* 19(2), June 1966:251–65.

Schleth, Uwe, "Germany," in Arnold J. Heidenheimer, ed., *Comparative Political Finance,* Heath, 1970, pp. 23–49.

Schneider, Carl J., "Political Parties and the German Basic Law of 1949," *WPQ,* 10(3), Sept. 1957:527–40.

Segal, David R., "Social Structural Bases of Political Partisanship in West Germany and the United States," in William J. Crotty, ed., *Public Opinion and Politics,* Holt, 1969, pp. 216–35.

Shell, Kurt L., "Extraparliamentary Opposition in Postwar Germany," *Comp. Pol.,* July 1970:563–80.

Stiefbold, R. P., "The Significance of Void Ballots in West German Elections," *APSR,* 59(2), June 1965:391–407.

Tauber, Kurt P., *Beyond Eagle and Swastika: German Nationalism Since 1945,* 2 vols, Wesleyan UP, 1967, 1,598 pp.

———, "Nationalism and Social Restoration: Fraternities in Postwar Germany," *PSQ,* 78(1), Mar. 1963:66–85.

Warnecke, Steven, "The Future of Rightist Extremism in West Germany," *Comp. Pol.,* July 1970:629–52.

Zohlnhoffer, Werner, "Party Identification in the Federal Republic of Germany and the United States," in Kurt L. Shell, ed., *The Democratic Political Process,* Ginn, 1969, pp. 148–58.

Chapter 4. WEST GERMAN PARLIAMENTARY INSTITUTIONS

Foster, Charles R. and George K. Romoser, "Parliamentary Reform in West Germany," *Parl. Aff.,* 21(1), Winter 1967–68:69–74.

Johnson, Nevil, "Questions in the Bundestag," *Parl. Aff.,* 16(1), Winter 1962:22–34.

King-Hall, Stephen and Richard K. Ullmann, *German Parliaments,* Praeger, 1954, 162 pp.

Kirchheimer, Otto, "Germany, The Vanishing Opposition," in Robert A. Dahl, ed., *Political Opposition in Western Democracies,* Yale UP, 1966, pp. 237–59.

Loewenberg, Gerhard, "The Influence of Parliamentary Behavior on Regime Stability," *Comp. Pol.,* 3(2), Jan. 1971:177–200.

Loewenberg, Gerhard, *Parliament in the German Political System*, Cornell UP, 1966, 464 pp.

Lohse, Egon, "West Germany's Military Ombudsman," in Donald C. Rowat, ed., *Ombudsman, Citizen's Defender*, Allen & Unwin, London, 1965, pp. 119–26.

Neunreither, Karlheinz, "Politics and Bureaucracy in the West German Bundesrat," APSR, 53(3), Sept. 1959:713–31.

Pinney, Edward L., *Federalism, Bureaucracy, and Party Politics in Western Germany: The Role of the Bundesrat*, North Carolina UP, 1963, 268 pp.

Preece, R. J. C., "Federal German Emergency Powers Legislation," *Parl. Aff.*, 12(2), Summer 1969:216–25.

Ridley, F., "The Parliamentary Commissioner for Military Affairs in the Federal Republic of Germany," PS, 12(1), Feb. 1964:1–20.

Rueckert, George L. and W. Crane, "CDU Deviance in the German Bundestag," JP, 24(3), Aug. 1962: 477–88.

Schweitzer, Carl C., "Emergency Powers in the Federal Republic of Germany," WPQ, 22, Mar. 1969: 112–21.

Trossmann, Hans, *The German Bundestag: Organization and Operation*, Neue Darmstaedter Verlagsanstalt, 1965, 156 pp, pbk.

Chapter 5. WEST GERMAN EXECUTIVE AND ADMINISTRATION

1. GOVERNMENT, MILITARY, AND CIVIL SERVICE

Bolesch, Hermann Otto and Hans Diter Leicht, *Willy Brandt: A Portrait of the German Chancellor*, Erdmann, Tübingen, 1971, 84 pp.

Brandt, Willy, *In Exile: Essays, Reflections, and Letters, 1933–1945*, Pennsylvania UP, 1971, 214 pp.

Gunlicks, Arthur B., "Intraparty Democracy in Western Germany: A Look at the Local Level," *Comp. Pol.*, 2(2), Jan. 1970:220–49.

Herz, John H., "Political Views of the West German Civil Service," in Hans Speier and W. Phillips Davison, *West German Leadership and Foreign Policy*, Row, Peterson, 1957, pp. 96–135.

Jacob, Herbert, *German Administration Since Bismarck: Central Authority Versus Local Autonomy*, Yale UP, 1963, 224 pp.

Merkl, Peter H., "Equilibrium, Structure of Interests and Leadership, and Adenauer's Survival as Chancellor," APSR, 56(3), Sept. 1962:634–50.

Neunreither, Karlheinz, "Federalism and the West German Bureaucracy," PS, 7(3), Oct. 1959:233–45.

Prittie, Terence, *Adenauer*, Stacey, London, 1971.

Rosenberg, Hans, *Bureaucracy, Aristocracy and Autocracy: The Prussian Experience, 1660–1815*, Harvard UP, 1958, 247 pp.

Schmidt, Helmut, *The Balance of Power*, trans. Edward Thomas, Kimber, London, 1971, 301 pp.

White Paper 1970 on the Security of the Federal Republic of Germany and on the State of the German Federal Armed Forces, Press and Information Office of the Federal Government: Published by the Federal Minister of Defense, Bonn, 1970, 212 pp.

Wighton, Charles, *Adenauer: A Critical Biography*, Coward-McCann, 1963, 389 pp.

2. STATE AND LOCAL GOVERNMENT

Braunthal, Gerard, "Federalism in Germany: The Broadcasting Controversy," JP, 24(3), Aug. 1962: 545–61.

Brecht, Arnold, *Federalism and Regionalism in Germany*, Oxford UP, 1945, 202 pp.

Chaput de Saintonge, R. A. A., *Public Administration in Germany: A Study in Regional and Local Administration in Land Rheinland-Pfalz*, Weidenfeld & Nicolson, London, 1961, 371 pp.

Culver, Lowell W., "Land Elections in West German Politics," WPQ, 19(2), June 1966:304–36.

Gunlicks, Arthur B., "Representative Role Perceptions Among Local Councilors in Western Germany," JP, 31(2), May, 1969:423–64.

Merkl, Peter H., "Executive-Legislative Federalism in West Germany," APSR, 53(3), Sept. 1959:732–41.

Wells, Roger H., *German Cities*, Princeton UP, 1932, 283 pp.

———, *The States in West-German Federalism: A Study in Federal-State Relations, 1949–1960*, Bookman, 1961, 148 pp.

Chapter 6. WEST GERMAN LAW AND ADMINISTRATION OF JUSTICE

Baade, Hans W., "Social Science Evidence and the Federal Constitutional Court of West Germany," JP, 23(3), Aug. 1961:421–61.

Cole, Taylor, "Three Constitutional Courts: A Comparison," APSR, 53(4), Dec. 1959:963–84.

"German Administrative Law with Special Reference to the Latest Developments in the System of Legal Protection," ICLQ, 2(3), July 1953:368–82.

Loewenstein, Karl, "Law and the Legislative Process in Occupied Germany," YLJ, 57, Mar–Apr. 1958: 724–60.

McWhinney, Edward, *Constitutionalism in Germany and the Federal Constitutional Court*, Sijthoff, Leyden, 1962, 71 pp.

———, "The German Federal Court and the Communist Party Decision," *Indiana LJ*, 32(3), Spring 1957:295–312.

Müller, Gebhard, "The Federal Constitutional Court of the Federal Republic of Germany," JICJ, 6(2), Winter 1965:191–218.

Naumann, Bernd, *Auschwitz: A Report on the Proceedings Against Robert Karl Ludwig Mulka and Others Before the Court at Frankfurt*, Praeger, 1966, 433 pp.

Reich, Donald R., "Court, Comity and Federalism in West Germany," MJPS, 7, Aug. 1963:197–228.

Rheinstein, Max, "Approach to German Law," *Indiana LJ*, 34(4), Summer 1959:546–58.

Rosenne, S., *Constitutionalism in Germany and the Federal Constitutional Court*, Oceana, 1962, 72 pp.

Rupp, Hans G., "The Federal Constitutional Court in Germany: Scope of its Jurisdiction and Procedure," *Notre Dame Lawyer*, 44(4), Apr. 1969:548–59.

———, "Judicial Review in the Federal Republic of Germany," AJCL, 9(1), 1960:29–47.

Schmertzing, Wolfgang P. von, trans. and ed., *Outlawing the Communist Party: A Case History*, Bookmailer, 1957, 227 pp.

Wunderlich, Frieda, *German Labor Courts*, North Carolina UP, 1946, 252 pp.

Chapter 7. BERLIN AND THE GERMAN DEMOCRATIC REPUBLIC (DDR)

1. BERLIN

Davison, W. Phillips, *The Berlin Blockade*, Princeton UP, 1958, 446 pp.

Galante, Pierre, *The Berlin Wall*, Doubleday, 1965, 277 pp.

Gottlieb, Manuel, *The German Peace Settlement and the Berlin Crisis*, Paine-Whitman, 1960, 275 pp.

Masur, Gerhard, *The Imperial Berlin*, Basic Books, 1970, 353 pp.

Plischke, Elmer, *Government and Politics of Contemporary Berlin*, Nijhoff, The Hague, 1963, 119 pp.

———, "Integrating Berlin and the Federal Republic of Germany," *JP*, 27, Feb. 1965:35–65.

Press and Information Office of the Federal Government, *The Quadripartite Agreement on Berlin of September 3, 1971*, Text and Documents, Wiesbaden, 1971, 119 pp.

Schlick, Jack M., *The Berlin Crisis, 1958–1962*, Pennsylvania UP, 1971.

Smith, Bruce L., "The Governance of Berlin," *IC*, 525, 1959, 230 pp.

Speier, Hans, *Divided Berlin: The Anatomy of Soviet Political Blackmail*, Praeger, 1961, 201 pp.

Von der Gablentz, O. M., ed., *Documents on the Status of Berlin, 1944 to 1959*, Oldenbourg, Munich, 1959, 240 pp.

Windsor, Philip, *City on Leave: A History of Berlin, 1945–1962*, Praeger, 1963, 275 pp.

2. DDR

Baylis, Thomas A., "Economic Reform as Ideology: East Germany's New Economic System," *Comp. Pol.*, 3(2), Jan. 1970:211–29.

Bendix, Reinhard, "Managerial Ideologies in the Soviet Orbit," in *Work and Authority in Industry*, Wiley, 1956, pp. 341–433.

Brant, Stefen, *The East German Uprising, 17th June 1953*, trans. and adapted Charles Wheeler, Praeger, 1955, 202 pp.

Childs, David, *East Germany*, Praeger, 1969, 286 pp.

———, "The Socialist Unity Party of East Germany," *PS*, 14(3), Oct. 1967:301–21.

The Constitution of the DDR, official trans., Staatsverlag der DDR, 1968, 18 pp.

Croan, Melvin, "After Ulbricht: The End of an Era?" *Survey*, 17(2), Spring 1971:74–92.

Dornberg, John, *The Other Germany*, Doubleday, 1968, 370 pp.

Forster, Thomas M., *The East German Army*, trans. A. Buzek, Allen & Unwin, London, 1968, 256 pp.

Friedrich, Carl J., ed., *The Soviet Zone of Germany*, Human Relations Area Files, 1956, 646 pp.

Grothe, Peter, *To Win the Minds of Men*, Pacific Books, 1958, 241 pp.

Hangen, Welles, *The Muted Revolution: East Germany's Challenge to Russia and the West*, Knopf, 1966, 231 pp.

Hanhardt, Arthur M., Jr., *The German Democratic Republic*, Johns Hopkins UP, 1968, 126 pp, pbk.

Hanhardt, Arthur M., Jr., "Political Socialization in the German Democratic Republic," *Societas, A Review of Social History*, 1(2), Spring 1971:101–21.

Herz, John H., "East Germany, Progress and Prospects," *SR*, 17(2), Summer 1960:139–56.

Hornsby, Lex, ed., *Profile of East Germany*, ABC, 1967, 115 pp.

Kirchheimer, Otto, *Political Justice*, Princeton UP, 1961:259–303.

Ludz, Peter C., *The German Democratic Republic from the Sixties to the Seventies*, Center for Int. Aff., Harvard UP, 1970, 97 pp.

Nettl, J. P., *The Eastern Zone and Soviet Policy in Germany, 1945–1950*, Oxford UP, 1951, 324 pp.

Shell, Kurt, "Totalitarianism in Retreat: The Example of the DDR," *WP*, 18(1), Oct. 1965:105–16.

Skilling, H. Gordon, *The Governments of Communist East Europe*, Crowell, 1966, 256 pp.

Smith, Jean E., *Germany Beyond the Wall: People, Politics, and Prosperity*, Little, Brown, 1969, 338 pp.

———, "The Red Prussianism of the German Democratic Republic," *PSQ*, 82(3), Sept. 1967:368–85.

Stern, Carola, *Ulbricht: A Political Biography*, Praeger, 1965, 231 pp.

Stolper, Wolfgang F. and Karl Roskamp, *The Structure of the East German Economy*, Harvard UP, 1960, 478 pp.

Ulbricht, Walter, *Whither Germany?* German Institute of Contemporary History, Berlin, 1966, 440 pp.

Von Harpe, Werner, comp., "Eastern Germany Under Polish Administration," trans. F. Kerkarn, in *Eastern Germany: A Handbook*, Vol. 3: *Economy*, The Göttingen Research Committee, Holzberg Verlag, Würzburg, 1960, pp. 203–35.

Wunderlich, Frieda, *Farmer and Farm Labor in the Soviet Zone of Germany*, Twayne, 1958, 162 pp.

Chapter 8. GERMANY AND THE WORLD

Aussenpolitik (German Foreign Affairs Review), Hamburg, quarterly.

Bathurst, M. E. and J. L. Simpson, *Germany and the North Atlantic Community: A Legal Survey*, Praeger, 1956, 217 pp.

Bracher, Karl D., "The Foreign Policy of the Federal Republic of Germany," in Joseph E. Black and Kenneth W. Thompson, *Foreign Policies in a World of Change*, Harper, 1963, pp. 115–47.

Brandt, Willy, "German Policy Toward the East," *FA*, 46(3), Apr. 1968:476–86.

———, *The Ordeal of Coexistence*, Harvard UP, 1963, 112 pp.

———, *A Peace Policy for Europe*, trans. Joel Carmichael, Holt, 1969, 225 pp.

Couwenberg, S. W., "The German Problem and European Security," *World Justice* (Louvain, Belgium), 12(3), Mar. 1971:309–22.

Craig, Gordon A., *From Bismarck to Adenauer: Aspects of German Statecraft*, rev. ed., Harper, 1965, 136 pp.

Czempiel, Ernst-Otto, "Foreign Policy Issues in the West German Federal Election of 1969," *Comp. Pol.*, July 1970:605–28.

Deutsch, Karl W. and Lewis J. Edinger, *Germany Rejoins the Powers: Mass Opinion, Interest Groups and Elites in Contemporary German Foreign Policy*, Stanford UP, 1959, 320 pp.

Deutsch, Karl W. and Lewis J. Edinger *et al.*, *France, Germany and the Western Alliance: A Study of Elite Attitudes on European Integration and World Politics*, Scribner's, 1967, 324 pp.

Freund, Gerald, *Germany Between Two Worlds*, Harcourt Brace Jovanovich, 1961, 296 pp.

Grosser, Alfred, "France and Germany: Divergent Outlooks," *FA*, 44(1), Oct. 1965:26–36.

Hanrieder, Wolfram F., *The Stable Crisis: Two Decades of German Foreign Policy*, Harper, 1970, 221 pp.

——, *West German Foreign Policy, 1949–1963: International Pressure and Domestic Response*, Stanford UP, 1967, 275 pp.

Hartmann, Frederick H., *Germany Between East and West: The Reunification Problem*, Prentice-Hall, 1965, 181 pp, pbk.

Holbik, Karel and Henry A. Myers, *Post-War Trade in Divided Germany: The Internal and International Issues*, Johns Hopkins UP, 1964, 138 pp.

——, *West German Foreign Aid, 1956–1966: Its Economic and Political Aspects*, Boston UP, 1969, 158 pp.

Holborn, Hajo, *Germany and Europe: Historical Essays*, Doubleday, 1970, 327 pp.

Kaiser, Karl, *German Foreign Policy in Transition: Bonn Between East and West*, Oxford UP, 1969, 153 pp.

Luza, Radomir, *The Transfer of the Sudeten Germans: A Study of Czech-German Relations, 1933–1962*, New York UP, 1964, 565 pp.

McGeehan, Robert, *The German Rearmament Question: American Diplomacy and European Defense After World War II*, Illinois UP, 1971, 296 pp.

Merkl, Peter H., "Politico-Cultural Restraints on West German Foreign Policy: Sense of Trust, Identity, and Agency," *CPS*, 3(4), Jan. 1971:443–67.

Meyer, Henry Cord, *Mitteleuropa in German Thought and Action, 1915–1945*, Nijhoff, The Hague, 1955, 378 pp.

Morgenthau, Hans J., "The Problem of Germany," in *Truth and Power*, Praeger, 1970, pp. 347–54.

Neal, Fred Warner, *War and Peace and Germany*, Norton, 1962, 166 pp.

Press and Information Office of the Federal Government, *The Treaty of August 12, 1970 between the Federal Republic of Germany and the Union of Soviet Socialist Republics*, Text and Documents, Wiesbaden, 1970, 204 pp.

——, *The Treaty between the Federal Republic of Germany and the People's Republic of Poland*, Text and Documents, Wiesbaden, 1971, 200 pp.

Rhode, Gotthold and Wolfgang Wagner, comps. and eds., *The Genesis of the Oder-Neisse Line: Sources and Documents*, Brentano, Stuttgart, 1959, 287 pp.

Richardson, James L., *Germany and the Atlantic Alliance: The Interaction of Strategy and Politics*, Harvard UP, 1966, 403 pp.

Schmidt, Helmut, "Germany and the Era of Negotiations," *FA*, 49(1), Oct. 1970:40–50.

Schroeder, Gerhard, "Germany Looks at Eastern Europe," *FA*, 44(1), Oct. 1965:15–25.

Snell, John L., *Wartime Origins of the East-West Dilemma over Germany*, Hauser, 1959, 268 pp.

Speier, Hans, *German Rearmament and Atomic War: The Views of German Military and Political Leaders*, Row, Peterson, 1957, 272 pp.

Strauss, Franz J., *Challenge and Response: A Programme for Europe*, Atheneum, London, 1970, 175 pp.

——, *The Grand Design: A European Solution to German Reunification*, Praeger, 1966, 105 pp.

Wagner, Wolfgang, *The Genesis of the Oder-Neisse Line: A Study in the Diplomatic Negotiations During World War II*, Brentano, Stuttgart, 1957, 167 pp.

Wahrhaftig, Samuel L., "The Development of German Foreign Policy Institutions," in Hans Speier and W. Phillips Davison, eds., *West German Leadership and Foreign Policy*, Row, Peterson, 1957, pp. 7–56.

White, John, *German Aid: A Survey of the Sources, Policy, and Structure of German Aid*, The Overseas Inst., London, 1965, 221 pp.

Willis, F. Roy, *France, Germany and the New Europe 1945–1963*, Stanford UP, 1965, 387 pp.

Windsor, Philip, *Germany and the Management of Détente*, Chatto & Windus, London, 1971, 207 pp.

SOVIET UNION

PERIODICALS

BIS-USSR, *Bulletin of the Inst. for the Study of the USSR*, Munich, monthly.

A Chronicle of Current Events, Uncensored Soviet Civil Rights Journal, since 1969, Amnesty Int. Publications, London, bimonthly.

The Current Digest of the Soviet Press, Joint Committee on Slavic Studies, New York, weekly.

Problems of Communism, USGPO, Washington, D.C., bimonthly.

Soviet Affairs, St. Antony's Papers, occasional, Oxford.

Soviet Documents (formerly *Current Soviet Documents*), a weekly information service, published by Crosscurrents, New York.

Soviet Law and Government: Journal of Translations from Soviet Sources, Int. Arts & Sciences Press, New York, quarterly.

Soviet Studies and Decisions, Journal of Translations from Soviet Sources, Int. Arts & Sciences Press, New York.

Survey: A Journal of East and West Studies, Oxford UP, quarterly.

GENERAL WORKS

The American Bibliography of Russian and East European Studies, Indiana UP, published annually since 1957.

The Anatomy of Terror: Khrushchev's Revelations About Stalin's Regime, intro. Nathaniel Weyl, Pub. Aff., 1956, 73 pp.

Andrews, William G., ed., *Soviet Political Institutions and Policies: Inside Views*, Van Nostrand, 1965, 411 pp, pbk.

Armstrong, John A., *Ideology, Politics and Government in the Soviet Union: An Introduction*, rev. ed., Praeger, 1967, 192 pp, pbk.

Barghoorn, Fredrick C., *Politics in the USSR: A Country Study*, Little, Brown, 1966, 418 pp, pbk.

Braham, Randolph L., ed., *Readings in Soviet Politics and Government*, Knopf, 1965, 615 pp, pbk.

Brzezinski, Zbigniew, ed., *Dilemmas of Change in Soviet Politics*, Columbia UP, 1969, 144 pp, pbk.

Churchward, L. G., *Contemporary Soviet Government*, Routledge, London, 1968, 366 pp.

Conquest, Robert, *Power and Policy in the USSR: The Study of Soviet Dynastics*, St. Martin's, 1961, 485 pp.

———, *Russia After Khrushchev*, Praeger, 1965, 267 pp.

Cornell, Richard A., *The Soviet Political System: A Book of Readings*, Prentice-Hall, 1970, 400 pp, pbk.

Crozier, Brian, *The Future of Communist Power*, Eyre & Spottiswoode, London, 1970, 247 pp.

Dallin, Alexander and Alan F. Westin, *Politics in the Soviet Union: 7 Cases*, Harcourt Brace Jovanovich, 1966, 320 pp, pbk.

Deutscher, Isaac, *Russia in Transition*, rev. ed., Grove, 1960, 265 pp, pbk.

Drachkovitch, Milorad M., ed., *Fifty Years of Communism in Russia*, Pennsylvania State UP, 1968, 316 pp.

Fainsod, Merle, *How Russia Is Ruled*, 2nd ed., Harvard UP, 1963, 684 pp.

"Fifty Years of Bolshevism," *IJ*, 22(4), Autumn 1967: 539–646.

Gripp, R. C., *Patterns of Soviet Politics*, rev. ed., Dorsey, 1970, 386 pp.

Hazard, John N., *The Soviet System of Government*, 4th ed., Chicago UP, 1968, 275 pp, pbk.

Hendel, Samuel and Randolph L. Braham, eds., *The U.S.S.R. After 50 Years: Promise and Reality*, Knopf, 1967, 299 pp, pbk.

Hindus, Maurice, *The Kremlin's Human Dilemma: Russia After Half A Century of Revolution*, Doubleday, 1967, 395 pp.

Horecky, Paul L., ed., *Russia and the Soviet Union: A Bibliographic Guide to Western Language Publications*, Chicago UP, 1965, 473 pp.

Johnson, Chalmers, ed., *Change in Communist Systems*, Stanford UP, 1970, 668 pp.

Kingsbury, Robert C. and Robert N. Taaffe, *An Atlas of Soviet Affairs*, Praeger, 1965, 150 pp.

Koestler, Arthur, *The Yogi and the Commissar*, Macmillan, 1945, 247 pp.

Kohler, Foy D., *Understanding the Russians: A Citizen's Primer*, Harper, 1970, 441 pp.

Kolarz, Walter, ed., *Books on Communism, Bibliography*, 2nd ed., Allen & Unwin, London, 1964, 453 pp.

Kulski, Wladyslaw W., *The Soviet Regime: Communism in Practice*, 4th rev. ed., Syracuse UP, 1963, 444 pp.

Lane, David, *Politics and Society in the USSR*, Weidenfeld & Nicolson, London, 1970, 616 pp.

McClosky, Herbert and John E. Turner, *The Soviet Dictatorship*, McGraw-Hill, 1960, 657 pp.

Maichel, Karol, *Guide to Russian Reference Books*, Vol. II. *History, Auxiliary Historical Sciences, Ethnography and Geography*, ed. J. S. G. Simmons, Stanford UP, 1964, 297 pp.

Meisel, James and Edward S. Kozers, *Materials for the Study of the Soviet System*, 2nd ed., Wahr, 1953, 613 pp.

Meyer, Alfred G., *The Soviet Political System: An Interpretation*, Random House, 1965, 494 pp.

Moore, Barrington, Jr., *Terror and Progress, USSR: Some Sources of Change and Stability in the Soviet Dictatorship*, Harvard UP, 1954, 261 pp.

Morath, Inge and Arthur Miller, *In Russia*, Viking, 1969, 240 pp.

Nettl, J. P., *The Soviet Achievement*, Harcourt Brace Jovanovich, 1968, 288 pp.

Pipes, Richard, ed., *Revolutionary Russia*, Harvard UP, 1968, 365 pp.

Randall, Francis B., *Stalin's Russia*, Free Press, 1965, 328 pp.

Raymond, Ellsworth, *The Soviet State*, Macmillan, 1968, 462 pp.

Reshetar, John S., Jr., *The Soviet Polity: Government and Politics in the USSR*, Dodd, Mead, 1971, 412 pp, pbk.

Riha, Thomas, ed., *Readings in Russian Civilization*, Chicago UP, 1964, 801 pp.

Salisbury, Harrison E., ed., *The Soviet Union: The Fifty Years*, New American Lib., 1968, 544 pp.

Schapiro, Leonard, *The Government and Politics of the Soviet Union*, 2nd ed., Random House, 1967, 176 pp.

Scott, Derek J. R., *Russian Political Institutions*, rev. ed., Praeger, 1966, 276 pp.

Seibert, Theodor, *Red Russia*, Allen & Unwin, London, 1932, 422 pp.

Shub, Anatole, *An Empire Loses Hope: The Return of Stalin's Ghost*, Norton, 1970, 474 pp.

———, *The New Russian Tragedy*, Norton, 1970, 128 pp.

Towster, Julian, *Political Power in the USSR: 1917–1947*, Oxford UP, 1948, 443 pp.

Webb, Sidney and Beatrice Webb, *Soviet Communism, A New Civilization?* 2 vols, Scribner's, 1936.

Werth, Alexander, *Russia: Hopes and Fears*, Simon and Schuster, 1969, 362 pp.

Whiting, Kenneth R., *The Soviet Union Today*, rev. ed., Praeger, 1966, 423 pp.

Chapter 1. SOVIET IDEOLOGY AND HISTORY

1. IDEOLOGY

Acton, H. B., *The Illusion of the Epoch: Marxism-Leninism as a Philosophical Creed*, Cohen & West, London, 1955, 278 pp.

Althussev, Louis, *For Marx*, trans. Ben Brewster, Allen Lane, London, 1970, 271 pp.

Anderson, Thornton, *Masters of Russian Marxism*, Appleton-Century-Crofts, 1964, 296 pp, pbk.

———, *Russian Political Thought: An Introduction*, Cornell UP, 1967, 444 pp.

Avineri, Shlomo, *The Social and Political Thought of Karl Marx*, Cambridge UP, 1968, 268 pp.

Balabanoff, Angelica, *Impressions of Lenin*, Michigan UP, 1964, 152 pp.

Baron, Samuel H., *Plekhanov: The Father of Russian Marxism*, Stanford UP, 1963, 400 pp.

Beer, Samuel, ed., *The Communist Manifesto with Selections from the Eighteenth Brumaire of Bonaparte and Capital*, Appleton-Century-Crofts, 1955, 96 pp.

Berdyaev, Nickolai A., *Russian Revolution*, Michigan UP, 1961, 91 pp, pbk.

Berlin, Isaiah, *Karl Marx, His Life and Environment*, 3rd ed., Oxford UP, 1963, 295 pp.

Brzezinski, Zbigniew K., *Ideology and Power in Soviet Politics*, rev. ed., Praeger, 1967, 291 pp.

Burkharin, Nikolai, *Historical Materialism*, Int. Pub., 1926, 318 pp.

Dan, Theodore (Fedor Ilich), *The Origins of Bolshevism*, Secker & Warburg, London, 1964, 469 pp.

Daniels, Robert V., ed., *A Documentary History of Communism*, 2 vols, Random House, 1960, 391 and 393 pp.

——, *Marxism and Communism: Essential Readings*, Random House, 1965, 178 pp.

DeGeorge, Richard T., *Patterns of Soviet Thought*, Michigan UP, 1970, 293 pp.

Deutscher, Isaac, ed., *The Age of Permanent Revolution: A Trotsky Anthology*, Dell Laurel, 1964, pbk.

Fischer, Louis, *The Life of Lenin*, Harper, 1964, 703 pp.

Haimson, Leopold H., *The Russian Marxists and the Origins of Bolshevism*, Harvard UP, 1955, 272 pp.

Hook, Sidney, *Marx and Marxists: The Ambiguous Legacy*, Van Nostrand, 1955, 254 pp.

Howe, Irving, ed., *The Basic Writings of Trotsky*, Random House, 1963, 427 pp.

Hunt, R. N. Carew, *The Theory and Practice of Communism*, Penguin, 1963, 315 pp, pbk.

Jacobs, Dan N., *The New Communisms*, Harper, 1969, 326 pp, pbk.

——, ed., *The New Communist Manifesto and Related Documents*, Row, Peterson, 1961, 217 pp.

Jaworskyj, Michael, ed. and trans., *Soviet Political Thought: An Anthology*, Johns Hopkins UP, 1967, 621 pp.

Kautsky, Karl, *Dictatorship of the Proletariat*, National Labour Press, Manchester, 1919, 149 pp.

Khrushchev, Nikita S., *The International Situation and Soviet Foreign Policy*, Crosscurrents, 1960, 36 pp.

——, *USSR Victory in Peaceful Competition with Capitalism*, Dutton, 1960, 784 pp.

Kuusinen, Otto V., ed., *Fundamentals of Marxism-Leninism*, 2nd ed., For. Lang. Pub., Moscow, 1963, 734 pp (official CPSU statement of Communist doctrine).

Labedz, Leopold, ed., *Revisionism: Essays on the History of Marxist Ideas*, Allen & Unwin, London, 1962, 404 pp.

—— and Walter S. Laqueur, eds., *The Future of Communist Society*, Praeger, 1961, 202 pp.

Lane, David, *The Roots of Russian Communism: A Social and Historical Study of Russian Social Democracy, 1898–1907*, Royal Van Gorcum & Co., Assen, Netherlands, 1969, 240 pp.

Lenin, Vladimir, *Letters*, ed. Elizabeth Hill and Doris Mudie, Harcourt Brace Jovanovich, 1937, 499 pp.

——, *Selected Works of V. I. Lenin*, 12 vols, Int. Pub., 1935–39.

——, *Selected Works of V. I. Lenin*, 3 vols, Int. Pub., 1968, 2,700 pp.

——, *What Is to Be Done?* ed. and intro. and notes S. V. Utechin, trans. S. V. Utechin and Patricia Utechin, Clarendon Press, Oxford, 1963, 213 pp.

Lewis, John, *Life and Teaching of Karl Marx*, Int. Pub., 1965, 286 pp, pbk.

Lindsay, Alexander D., *Karl Marx' Capital: An Introductory Essay*, Oxford UP, 1947, 128 pp.

Low, Alfred D., *Lenin on the Question of Nationality*, Bookman, 1958, 193 pp.

McLellan, David, ed. and trans., *Karl Marx: Early Texts*, Blackwell, Oxford, 1971, 223 pp, pbk.

——, *Marx before Marxism*, Macmillan, 1970, 241 pp.

——, ed., *Marx's Grundrisse*, Macmillan, 1971, 156 pp.

McNeal, Robert H., *Lenin, Stalin, Khrushchev*, Prentice-Hall, 1963, 2 vols: *Voices of Bolshevism*, 180 pp; *The Bolshevik Tradition*, 181 pp, pbk.

——, comp., *Stalin's Works: An Annotated Bibliography*, Hoover Inst., 1967, 197 pp, pbk.

Marcuse, Herbert, *Soviet Marxism, A Critical Analysis*, Columbia UP, 1958, 271 pp.

Marx, Karl, *Capital, the Communist Manifesto, and Other Writings*, Modern Lib., 1932, 429 pp.

——, F. Engels, and V. Lenin, *The Essential Left: Four Classic Texts on the Principles of Socialism*, Barnes & Noble, 1961, 254 pp, pbk.

Marx-Engels-Lenin Inst., *Joseph Stalin*, Int. Pub., 1949, 128 pp.

Mehring, Franz, *Karl Marx, The Story of His Life*, trans. Edward Fitzgerald, Michigan UP, 1962, 575 pp, pbk.

Meyer, Alfred G., *Communism*, 3rd ed., Random House, 1967, 256 pp, pbk.

——, *Leninism*, Praeger, 1962, 336 pp.

——, *Marxism, The Unity of Theory and Practice: A Critical Essay*, rev. with new intro., Harvard UP, 1970, 182 pp, pbk.

Plamenatz, John, *German Marxism and Russian Communism*, Longmans, London, 1954, 356 pp.

Sabine, George H., *Marxism*, Cornell UP, 1958, 60 pp.

Schapiro, Leonard and Peter Reddaway, eds., assisted by Paul Rosta, *Lenin. The Man, the Theorist, the Leader: A Reappraisal*, Praeger, 1967, 317 pp.

Shub, David, *Lenin, A Biography*, New American Lib., 1966, 496 pp, pbk.

Stalin, Joseph, *Collected Works*, For. Lang. Pub., Moscow, 1953.

——, *Economic Problems of Socialism in the U.S.S.R.*, Int. Pub., 1952, 71 pp.

——, *The Great Patriotic War of the Soviet Union*, Int. Pub., 1945, 167 pp.

——, *Leninism*, Int. Pub., 2 vols, 1928–33.

——, *Leninism, Selected Writings*, Int. Pub., 1942, 479 pp.

——, *Marxism and the National and Colonial Question*, Int. Pub., 1936, 304 pp.

Stalin, Joseph, *Selected Writings*, Int. Pub., 1945, 479 pp.

Tertz, Abram (pseud.), *On Socialist Realism*, Pantheon, 1961, 95 pp.

Trotsky, Leon, *The Case of Leon Trotsky*, Harper, 1937, 617 pp.

————, *Lenin*, Putnam-Capricorn, 1962, 216 pp, pbk.

————, *Lessons of October*, Pioneer, 1937, 125 pp.

————, *My Life*, Scribner's, 1930, 613 pp.

————, *The New Course*, Michigan UP, 1965, 265 pp.

————, *The Real Situation in Russia*, Harcourt Brace Jovanovich, 1928, 364 pp.

————, *The Revolution Betrayed*, Doubleday, 1937, 308 pp.

————, *Stalin*, Harper, 1946, 516 pp.

————, *Terrorism and Communism*, Michigan UP, 1961, 191 pp, pbk.

Tucker, Robert C., *The Marxian Revolutionary Idea*, Norton, 1969, 240 pp.

————, *The Soviet Political Mind: Studies in Stalinism and Post-Stalin Change*, Praeger, 1963, 251 pp, pbk.

Two Communist Manifestoes, Washington Center of Foreign Policy Research, 1961, 108 pp.

Ulam, Adam B., *The New Face of Soviet Totalitarianism: An Essay on the Sources of Influence of Marxism and Communism*, Harvard UP, 1963, 233 pp.

Utechin, S. V., *Russian Political Thought*, Praeger, 1963, 320 pp, pbk.

Wetter, Gustav A., *Dialectical Materialism: A Historical and Systematic Survey of Philosophy in the Soviet Union*, Praeger, 1959, 609 pp.

Wiles, P. J. D., *The Political Economy of Communism: A Critical Study of Communist Theory and Practice*, Harvard UP, 1963, 404 pp.

Wolfe, Bertram D., *Marxism: One Hundred Years in the Life of a Doctrine*, Dial Press, 1965, 404 pp.

2. HISTORY

Armstrong, John A., ed., *Soviet Partisans in World War II*, Wisconsin UP, 1964, 792 pp.

Black, C. E., ed., *Rewriting Russian History: Soviet Interpretations of Russia's Past*, Praeger, 1956, 420 pp.

Carr, Edward H., *The Bolshevik Revolution, 1917–1923*, 3 vols, Penguin, 1967.

————, *A History of Soviet Russia*, Macmillan, 6 vols: *The Bolshevik Revolution, 1917–1923*, 1951, 430 pp; *The Struggle for Power, 1923–1928*, 1952, 400 pp; *The Economic Order and Soviet Russia and the World*, 1953, 614 pp; *The Interregnum, 1923–1924*, 1954, 392 pp; *Socialism in One Country, 1924–1926*, 1958, 1960, and 1964, 557 pp, 557 pp, and 1,050 pp.

Conquest, Robert, *The Great Terror: Stalin's Purge of the Thirties*, Macmillan, 1968, 633 pp.

Daniels, Robert V., ed., *Documentary History of Communism*, 2 vols, Vintage, 1960, 321 and 393 pp, pbk.

Deutscher, Isaac, *Ironies of History*, Oxford UP, 1966, 278 pp.

————, *The Prophet Armed: Trotsky, 1879–1921*, Oxford UP, 1954, 540 pp.

————, *The Prophet Outcast: Trotsky, 1929–1940*, Oxford UP, 1963, 543 pp.

————, *The Prophet Unarmed: Trotsky, 1921–1929*, Oxford UP, 1959, 490 pp.

Deutscher, Isaac, *The Unfinished Revolution, Russia, 1917–1967*, Oxford UP, 1967, 115 pp.

Dmytryskya, Basil, *USSR: A Concise History*, Scribner's, 1965, 620 pp.

Ehrenburg, Ilya, *Men, Years, Life, The War, 1941–1945*, Vol. 5, MacGibbon & Kee, London, 1964, 198 pp.

Erickson, John, *The Soviet High Command: A Military Political History, 1918–1941*, St. Martin's, 1962, 889 pp.

Fainsod, Merle, *Smolensk Under Soviet Rule*, Harvard UP, 1958, 484 pp.

Grey, Ian, *The First Fifty Years: Soviet Russia 1917–1967*, Coward-McCann, 1967, 558 pp.

Hendel, Samuel, ed., *The Soviet Crucible, 1917–1967*, 3rd ed., Van Nostrand, 1967, 525 pp.

Hudson, G. F., *Fifty Years of Communism: Theory and Practice 1917–1967*, Watts, London, 1968, 234 pp.

Keep, J. L. H., *The Rise of Social Democracy in Russia*, Clarendon Press, Oxford, 1963, 334 pp.

Kennan, George, *Soviet-American Relations, 1917–1920*, Princeton UP, 2 vols: *Russia Leaves the War*, 1956, 544 pp; *The Decision to Intervene*, 1958, 524 pp.

Kerensky, Alexander, *The Crucifixion of Liberty*, Day, 1944, 406 pp.

Laqueur, Walter, *The Fate of the Revolution: Interpretations of Soviet History*, Weidenfeld & Nicolson, London, 1967, 224 pp.

Levin, Alfred, *The Second Duma*, Yale UP, 1940, 414 pp.

Lewin, Moshe, *Lenin's Last Struggle*, Faber, London, 1968, 193 pp.

————, *Russian Peasants and Soviet Power: A Study of Collectivization*, Northwestern UP, 1968, 539 pp.

Liebman, Marcel, *The Russian Revolution*, trans. Arnold J. Pomerans, Random House, 1970, 389 pp.

Maisky, Ivan, *Memoirs of a Soviet Ambassador: The War, 1939–43*, trans. A. Rothstein, Scribner's, 1968, 408 pp.

Mazour, Anatole G., *Modern Russian Historiography*, rev. enl. ed., Van Nostrand, 1958, 260 pp.

Pavlov, Dimitri, *Leningrad 1941: The Blockade*, Chicago UP, 1965, 186 pp.

Petrov, Vladimir, *"June 22, 1941": Soviet Historians and the German Invasion*, USCP, 1968, 322 pp.

Pipes, Richard, *The Formation of the Soviet Union: Communism and Nationalism, 1917–1923*, rev. ed., Harvard UP, 1964, 365 pp.

Salisbury, Harrison E., *The 900 Days: The Siege of Leningrad*, Harper, 1969, 635 pp.

Seton-Watson, Hugh, *The Decline of Imperial Russia, 1855–1914*, Praeger, 1953, 406 pp.

————, *The Pattern of Communistic Revolution: A Historical Analysis*, rev. enl. ed., Methuen, London, 1961, 432 pp.

Silverlight, John, *The Victors' Dilemma*, Barrie & Jenkins, London, 1970, 392 pp.

Toynbee, A. J., ed., *The Impact of the Russian Revolution 1917–1967*, Oxford UP, 1967, 357 pp.

Trotsky, Leon, *The History of the Russian Revolution*, 3 vols, Gollancz, London, 1965.

Trotsky, Leon, *The Russian Revolution*, condensed, Doubleday, 1959, 524 pp.

Vernadsky, George, *A History of Russia*, 4th ed., Yale UP, 1961, 512 pp, pbk.

Von Laue, Theodore H., *Why Lenin? Why Stalin? A Reappraisal of the Russian Revolution, 1900–1930*, Weidenfeld & Nicolson, London, 1966, 242 pp.

Von Rauch, Georg, *A History of Soviet Russia*, 5th rev. ed., Pall Mall, London, 1967, 530 pp.

Walkin, Jacob, *The Rise of Democracy in Pre-Revolutionary Russia*, Thames & Hudson, London, 1963, 320 pp.

Werth, Alexander, *Russia at War, 1941–1945*, Barrie & Rockliff, London, 1964, 1,100 pp.

Westwood, J. N., *Russia 1917–1964*, Harper, 1966, 208 pp.

Wolfe, Bertram D., *An Ideology in Power: Reflections on the Russian Revolution*, Allen & Unwin, London, 1970, 405 pp.

———, *Three Who Made a Revolution: A Biographical History*, Dial, 1964, 659 pp, pbk.

Zhukov, Grigori, *The Memoirs of Marshal Zhukov*, Cape, London, 1971, 711 pp.

Chapter 2. SOVIET LAND, PEOPLE, AND SOCIETY

1. LAND AND RESOURCES

Cole, J. P., *A Geography of the USSR*, Penguin, 1967, 326 pp, pbk.

——— and F. C. German, *A Geography of the USSR: The Background to a Planned Economy*, Butterworth, London, 1961, 290 pp.

Cressey, George B., *Soviet Potentials: A Geographic Appraisal*, Syracuse UP, 1962, 256 pp.

Gregory, James S., *Russian Land, Soviet People: A Geographical Approach to the USSR*, Pegasus, 1968, 947 pp.

Grossman, Gregory, *Soviet Statistics of Physical Output of Industrial Commodities*, Princeton UP, 1960, 151 pp.

Jorré, Georges, *The Soviet Union, The Land and Its People*, trans. and rev. E. D. Laborde, Longmans, London, 1961, 392 pp.

Kalb, Marvin, *The Volga: A Political Journey Through Russia*, Macmillan, 1967, 191 pp.

Kirby, E. Stuart, *The Soviet Far East*, Macmillan, 1971, 288 pp.

Krypton, Constantine, *The Northern Sea Route and the Economy of the Soviet North*, Praeger, 1956, 219 pp.

Murarka, Dev, *The Soviet Union*, Thames & Hudson, London, 1971, 240 pp.

St. George, George, *Siberia: The New Frontier*, Hodder & Stoughton, London, 1971, 374 pp.

Shabad, Theodore, *Twentieth Century Russia*, rev. ed., Rand McNally, 1964.

2. NATIONALITIES AND RELIGION

Armstrong, John A., *Ukrainian Nationalism, 1939–1945*, Columbia UP, 1955, 322 pp.

Baron, Salo W., *The Russian Jew under Tsars and Soviets*, Macmillan, 1964, 427 pp.

Bilinsky, Yaroslav, *The Second Soviet Republic, The Ukraine After World War II*, Rutgers UP, 1964, 539 pp.

Bourdeaux, Michael, *Religious Ferment in Russia: Protestant Opposition to Soviet Religious Policy*, St. Martin's, 1968, 255 pp.

——— with the assistance of Kathleen Matchett and Cornelia Gerstenmaier, *Religious Minorities in the Soviet Union (1960–1970)*, Minority Rights Group, London, 1970, 38 pp.

Braham, Randolph L., *Jews in the Communist World: A Bibliography, 1945–1960*, Bookman, 1961, 64 pp.

Ciszed, Walter J. and Daniel J. Flaherty, *With God in Russia*, Peter Davies, London, 1964, 302 pp.

Cong, Joel, *Fate and Future of Soviet Jewry: A Brief Summary and Analysis*, Board of Deputies of British Jews, London, 1966, 17 pp.

Conquest, Robert, *The Nation Killers: The Soviet Deportation of Nationalities*, Macmillan, 1970, 222 pp.

———, ed., *Soviet Nationalities Policy in Practice*, Praeger, 1967, 160 pp.

Curtiss, John S., *The Russian Church and the Soviet State, 1917–1950*, Little, Brown, 1953, 387 pp.

Daniels, Robert V., *The Conscience of the Revolution: Communist Opposition in Soviet Russia*, Harvard UP, 1960, 526 pp.

Fireside, Harvey, *Icon and Swastika: The Russian Orthodox Church Under Nazi and Soviet Control*, Harvard UP, 1970, 245 pp.

Fletcher, William C., *A Study in Survival: The Russian Orthodox Church, 1927–1943*, Macmillan, 1965, 169 pp.

——— and A. F. Stroves, eds., *Religion and the Search for New Ideals in the USSR*, Praeger, 1967, 143 pp.

Goldberg, B. Z., *The Jewish Problem in the Soviet Union*, Crown, 1961, 374 pp.

Goldhagen, Erich, ed., *Ethnic Minorities in the Soviet Union*, Praeger, 1968, 351 pp.

Hayward, Max and William C. Fletcher, eds., *Religion and the Soviet State: A Dilemma of Power*, Praeger, 1969, 200 pp.

Kochan, Lionel, ed., *The Jews in Soviet Russia Since 1917*, Oxford UP, 1970, 366 pp.

Kolarz, Walter, *Religion in the Soviet Union*, St. Martin's, 1961, 518 pp.

Marshall, Richard H., Jr., ed., *Aspects of Religion in the Soviet Union, 1917–1967*, Chicago UP, 1970, 489 pp.

Rakowska-Harmstone, Teresa, *Russia and Nationalism in Central Asia: The Case of Tadzhikistan*, Johns Hopkins UP, 1970, 352 pp.

Rubin, Ronald I., ed., *The Unredeemed: Anti-Semitism in the Soviet Union*, Quadrangle Books, 1968, 316 pp.

Schlesinger, Rudolf, ed., *The Nationalities Problem and Soviet Administration: Selected Readings on the Development of Soviet Nationalities Policies*, trans. W. W. Gottlieb, Routledge, London, 1956, 294 pp.

Scott, Richenda C., *Quakers in Russia*, Michael Joseph, London, 1964, 302 pp.

Szczesniak, Bolislaw, ed. and trans., *The Russian Revolution and Religion*, Notre Dame UP, 1960, 289 pp.

Taurulis, Albert N., *Soviet Policy Toward the Baltic States, 1918–1940*, Notre Dame UP, 1959, 276 pp.

3. SOCIAL STRUCTURE

Bauer, Raymond A., *Nine Soviet Portraits*, MIT Press, 1965, 187 pp, pbk.

Black, Cyril E., ed., *The Transformation of Russian Society: Aspects of Change Since 1861*, Harvard UP, 1960, 695 pp.

Dodge, Norton T., *Women in the Soviet Economy: Their Role in Economic, Scientific, and Technical Development*, Johns Hopkins UP, 1966, 331 pp.

Dunn, Stephen P. and Ethel Dunn, *The Peasants of Central Russia*, Holt, 1967, 139 pp.

Fischer, George, ed., *The Soviet System and Modern Society*, Atherton, 1968, 199 pp.

—— *et al.*, *Science and Ideology in Soviet Society*, Atherton, 1968, 176 pp.

Inkeles, Alex, *Social Change in Soviet Russia*, Harvard UP, 1968, 475 pp.

—— and Raymond A. Bauer, *The Soviet Citizen: Daily Life in a Totalitarian Society*, Harvard UP, 1959, 540 pp.

Kassof, Allen, ed., *Prospects for Soviet Society*, Praeger, 1968, 586 pp.

Kluckhohn, Clyde K. M., Raymond A. Bauer, and Alex Inkeles, *The Soviet System: Cultural, Psychological and Social Themes*, Harvard UP, 1956, 274 pp, pbk.

Kolarz, Walter, *The Peoples of the Soviet Far East*, Praeger, 1955, 194 pp.

——, *Russia and Her Colonies*, 3rd ed., Praeger, 1955, 350 pp.

Kolasky, John, *Two Years in the Soviet Ukraine*, Peter Martin, London, 1970, 264 pp.

Lorimer, Frank, *The Population of the Soviet Union: History and Prospects*, League of Nations, Geneva, 1946, 289 pp.

Mace, David and Vera Mace, *The Soviet Family*, Doubleday, 1963, 367 pp.

Mehnert, Klaus, *Soviet Man and His World*, trans. from German by Maurice Rosenbaum, Praeger, 1961, 310 pp.

Miller, Jack, *Life in Russia Today*, Putnam, 1969, 198 pp.

Observer, An, *Message from Moscow*, Knopf, 1969, 288 pp.

Sorlin, Pierre, *The Soviet People and Their Society: From 1917 to the Present*, trans. Daniel Weissbort, Pall Mall, London, 1970, 301 pp.

Taubman, William, *The View from Lenin Hills: An American Student's Report on Soviet Youth in Ferment*, Coward-McCann, 1967, 249 pp.

4. EDUCATION

Bereday, George Z. F. and Joan Pennar, eds., *The Politics of Soviet Education*, Praeger, 1960, 217 pp.

Bowen, James, *Soviet Education: Anton Makarenko and the Years of Experiment*, Wisconsin UP, 1965, 244 pp, pbk.

Bronfenbrenner, Urie, with the assistance of John C. Condry, Jr., *Two Worlds of Childhood*, Basic Books, 1971, 190 pp.

DeWitt, Nicholas, *Education and Professional Employment in the USSR*, Nat. Sci. Fdn., 1962, 856 pp.

——, *Soviet Professional Manpower: Its Education, Training and Supply*, Nat. Sci. Fdn., 1955, 400 pp.

Kline, George L., ed., *Soviet Education*, Columbia UP, 1957, 192 pp.

Kolasky, John, *Education in the Soviet Ukraine: A Study in Discrimination and Russification*, Peter Martin, London, 1968, 238 pp.

Korol, Alexander G., *Soviet Education for Science and Technology*, Wiley, 1957, 494 pp.

Meek, Dorothea L., ed. and trans., *Soviet Youth: Some Achievements and Problems*, Routledge, London, 1957, 251 pp.

Redl, Helen B., *Soviet Educators on Soviet Education*, Free Press, 1964, 252 pp.

Report of the Second Seminar on Education in the Soviet Union, Inst. of Int. Educ., 1959, 78 pp.

Simirenko, Alex, ed., *Social Thought in the Soviet Union*, Quadrangle Books, 1969, 439 pp.

——, ed., *Soviet Sociology: Historical Antecedents and Current Appraisals*, Quadrangle Books, 1966, 384 pp.

5. INTELLECTUALS AND THE CONTROL OF IDEAS

Aczel, Tamas and Tibor Meray, *The Revolt of the Mind*, Praeger, 1960, 449 pp.

Anatoli, A., *Babi Yar*, Cape, London, 1970, 478 pp.

Brumberg, Abraham, ed., *In Quest of Justice: Protest and Dissent in the Soviet Union Today*, Praeger, 1970, 460 pp.

Buzek, Antony, *How the Communist Press Works*, Praeger, 1964, 287 pp.

Conquest, Robert, *The Courage of Genius, The Pasternak Affair: A Documentary Report on its Literary and Political Significance*, Collins, London, 1961, 191 pp.

——, *The Politics of Ideas in the USSR*, Praeger, 1967, 175 pp.

Dudintsev, Vladimir, *Not by Bread Alone*, trans. Edith Bone, Dutton, 1957, 215 pp.

Ehrenburg, Ilya, *Post-War Years 1945–1954*, trans. Tatiana Shebunina, World Pub., 1967, 349 pp.

Gibian, George, *Interval of Freedom: Soviet Literature During the Thaw, 1954–1957*, Michigan UP, 1960, 180 pp.

Hare, Richard, *The Art and Artists of Russia*, Methuen, London, 1965, 295 pp.

Hayward, Max, ed. and trans., *On Trial: The Soviet State Versus "Abram Tertz" and "Nikolai Arzhak,"* Harper, 1966, 183 pp, pbk.

—— and Edward L. Crowley, eds., *Soviet Literature in the Sixties: An International Symposium*, Praeger, 1964, 264 pp.

Hopkins, Mark W., *Mass Media in the Soviet Union*, Pegasus, 1970, 384 pp.

Inkeles, Alex, *Public Opinion in Soviet Russia: A Study in Mass Persuasion*, Harvard UP, 1950, 379 pp.

Johnson, Priscilla, *Khrushchev and the Arts: The Politics of Soviet Culture, 1962–1964*, MIT Press, 1965, 300 pp.

Joravsky, David, *The Lysenko Affair*, Harvard UP, 1971, 459 pp.

Keep, John, ed., *Contemporary History in the Soviet Mirror*, Praeger, 1964, 331 pp.

Labedz, Leopold, *Solzhenitsyn: A Documentary Record*, Allen Lane, London, 1970, 198 pp.

Litvinov, Pavel, *Demonstration at Pushkin Square*, trans. Manya Harari, Harvill Press, London, 1969, 176 pp.

Maichel, Karol, *Soviet and Russian Newspapers at the Hoover Institution: A Catalogue*, Hoover Inst., 1966, 235 pp.

Mandelshtam, Nazdezhda, *Hope against Hope: A Memoir*, trans. Max Hayward, Collins, London, 1971, 438 pp.

Marchenko, Anatoly, *My Testimony*, Dutton, 1969, 415 pp.

Medvedev, Zhores, *The Rise and Fall of I. D. Lysenko*, trans. Michael I. Lerner, Columbia UP, 1969, 284 pp.

Mihajilov, Mahajlo, *Moscow Summer*, Farrar, Straus & Giroux, 1965, 220 pp.

Muchnic, Helen, *Russian Writers: Notes and Essays*, Random House, 1971, 462 pp.

Pasternak, Boris, *Dr. Zhivago*, trans. Max Hayward and Manya Harari, Pantheon, 1958, 558 pp.

Pipes, Richard, ed., *The Russian Intelligentsia*, Columbia UP, 1961, 234 pp.

Sholokhov, Mikhail A., *Harvest on the Don*, trans. H. C. Stevens, Putnam, 1960, 399 pp.

Stillman, Edmund, ed., *Bitter Harvest: The Intellectual Revolt Behind the Iron Curtain*, Praeger, 1959, 313 pp, pbk.

Tillett, Lowell R., *The Great Friendship: Soviet Historians on the Non-Russian Nationalities*, North Carolina UP, 1969, 480 pp.

Vucinich, Alexander, *The Soviet Academy of Sciences*, Stanford UP, 1956, 157 pp.

Zamyatin, Yevgeny, *A Soviet Heretic: Selected Essays*, ed. and trans. Mirra Ginsburg, Chicago UP, 1970, 322 pp.

6. SUPPRESSION OF OPPOSITION

Amal'rik, Andrei, *Involuntary Journey to Siberia*, trans. Manya Harari and Max Hayward, Harcourt Brace Jovanovich, 1970, 297 pp.

———, *Will the Soviet Union Survive Until 1984?* Harper, 1970, 93 pp.

Browne, Michael, ed., *Ferment in the Ukraine*, Macmillan, 1971, 267 pp.

Brzezinski, Zbigniew K., *The Permanent Purge: Politics in Soviet Totalitarianism*, Harvard UP, 1956, 256 pp.

Conquest, Robert, *The Nation Killers: The Soviet Deportation of Nationalities*, Macmillan, 1970, 222 pp.

———, ed., *The Soviet Police System*, Praeger, 1968, 103 pp.

Dallin, Alexander and G. Breslaurer, *Political Terror in Communist Systems*, Stanford UP, 1970, 172 pp.

Deriabin, Peter *et al.*, *The Secret World*, Doubleday, 1959, 334 pp.

Hingley, Ronald, *The Russian Secret Police: Muscovite, Imperial Russian and Soviet Political Security Operations, 1565–1970*, Hutchinson, London, 1970, 305 pp.

Koestler, Arthur, *Darkness at Noon*, Macmillan, 1941, 267 pp.

Leites, Nathan and Elsa Bernaut, *Ritual of Liquidation: The Case of the Moscow Trials*, Free Press, 1954, 515 pp.

Lipper, Elinor, *Eleven Years in Soviet Prison Camps*, Regnery, 1951, 310 pp.

Medvedev, Zhores A., *The Medvedev Papers: The Plight of Soviet Science Today*, trans. Vera Rich, St. Martins, 1971, 470 pp.

——— and Roy A. Medvedev, *A Question of Madness*, trans. Ellen de Kadt, Knopf, 1971, 224 pp.

Penkovsky, Oleg, *The Penkovsky Papers*, trans. Peter Deriabin, Doubleday, 1966, 411 pp.

Schapiro, Leonard, *Origin of the Communist Autocracy: Political Opposition in the Soviet State, First Phase, 1917–1922*, Harvard UP, 1955, 397 pp.

Solzhenitsyn, Aleksandr I., *Cancer Ward*, trans. Thomas P. Whitney, Farrar, Straus & Giroux, 1969, 560 pp.

———, *The First Circle*, Harper, 1968, 580 pp.

———, *One Day in the Life of Ivan Denisovich*, trans. Max Hayward and Ronald Hingley, Praeger, 1963, 210 pp.

Tucker, Robert C. and Stephen Cohen, eds., *The Great Purge Trial*, Grosset & Dunlap, 1965, 725 pp, pbk.

Wolin, Simon and Robert S. Slusser, eds., *The Soviet Secret Police*, Praeger, 1957, 408 pp.

Chapter 3. THE COMMUNIST PARTY

Armstrong, John A., "Party Bifurcation and Elite Interests," *Soviet Studies*, April, 1966:417–30.

———, *The Politics of Totalitarianism: The Communist Party of the Soviet Union from 1934 to the Present*, Random House, 1961, 458 pp.

———, *The Soviet Bureaucratic Elite: A Case Study of the Ukrainian Apparatus*, Praeger, 1959, 174 pp.

Avtorkhanov, A., *Stalin and the Communist Party*, Stevens, London, 1960, 379 pp.

Borys, Jurij, *The Russian Communist Party and the Sovietization of the Ukraine*, Norstedt & Sonel, Stockholm, 1960, 374 pp.

Brezhnev, Leonid, *Report of the Central Committee of the Communist Party of the Soviet Union at the Twenty-Fourth Congress of the CPSU, March 30, 1971*, Novosti Press, Moscow, 1971, 124 pp.

Embree, G. D., *The Soviet Union Between the 19th and 20th Party Congresses, 1952–1956*, Nijhoff, The Hague, 1959, 365 pp.

Farrell, R. Barry, ed., *Political Leadership in Eastern Europe and the Soviet Union*, Aldine, 1969, 359 pp.

Fischer, George, *The Soviet System and Modern Society*, Atherton, 1968, 199 pp.

Fischer, Ralph T., Jr., *Pattern for Soviet Youth: A Study of the Congresses of the Komsomol, 1918–1954*, Columbia UP, 1959, 452 pp.

Gehlen, Michael P. and Michael McBridge, "The Soviet Central Committee: An Elite Analysis," *APSR*, Dec. 1968:1,232–41.

Gruliow, Leo, ed., *Documentary Records* of the 19th, 20th, 21st, and 22nd CPSU Congresses, 4 vols, Praeger, 1953 and 1957, 270 and 247 pp; Columbia UP, 1960 and 1962, 230 and 248 pp.

History of the Communist Party of the Soviet Union (Bolsheviks), Short Course, ed. by a commission of the Central Committee of the CPSU, Int. Pub., 1939, 487 pp.

Hough, Jerry F., *The Soviet Prefects: The Local Party Organs in Industrial Decision-Making*, Harvard UP, 1969, 416 pp.

Jacobs, Daniel Norman, ed., *The New Communist Manifesto, and Related Documents*, Harper, 1962, 250 pp, pbk.

Kassof, Allen, *The Soviet Youth Program: Regimentation and Rebellion*, Harvard UP, 1965, 206 pp.

Khrushchev, Nikita S., *Report of the Central Committee of the Communist Party of the Soviet Union to the 20th Party Congress*, For. Lang. Pub., Moscow, 1956, 145 pp.

Kolkowitz, Roman, *The Soviet Military and the Communist Party*, Princeton UP, 1967, 448 pp.

Malenkov, G., *Report to the Nineteenth Party Congress on the Work of the Central Committee of the CPSU*, Collet's Holdings, London, 1952, 147 pp.

Meissner, Boris, ed., *The Communist Party of the Soviet Union*, Praeger, 1956, 276 pp.

Meyer, Frank S., *The Moulding of Communists: The Training of the Communist Cadre*, Harcourt Brace Jovanovich, 1961, 214 pp.

Mickiewicz, Ellen P., *Soviet Political Schools: The Communist Party Adult Instruction System*, Yale UP, 1967, 190 pp.

Our Friends Take the Floor: Speeches of Foreign Guests at the Twenty-Third Congress of the CPSU, Novosti Press, Moscow, 1966, 511 pp.

Pethybridge, Roger, *A Key to Soviet Politics: The Crisis of the "Anti-Party" Group*, Allen & Unwin, London, 1962, 207 pp.

Popov, Nikolai N., *Outline History of the Communist Party of the Soviet Union*, 2 vols, Int. Pub., 1934, 414 and 460 pp.

Programme of the Communist Party of the Soviet Union, Adopted by the Twenty-Second Congress of the CPSU, October 31, 1961, For. Lang. Pub., Moscow, 1961, 127 pp.

Reshetar, John S., Jr., *A Concise History of the Communist Party of the Soviet Union*, rev. ed., Praeger, 1964, 372 pp, pbk.

Rigby, T. H., *Communist Party Membership in the USSR, 1917–1967*, Princeton UP, 1968, 590 pp.

The Road to Communism: Documents of the Twenty-Second Congress of the Communist Party of the Soviet Union, October 17–31, 1961, For. Lang. Pub., Moscow, 1961, 633 pp.

Schapiro, Leonard, *The Communist Party of the Soviet Union*, rev. ed., Random House, 1971, 686 pp.

Schwartz, Harry, ed. with commentary, *Russia Enters the 1960's: A Documentary Report on the Twenty-Second Congress of the CPSU*, Lippincott, 1962, 278 pp.

Skilling, H. Gordon and Franklyn Griffiths, eds., *Interest Groups in Soviet Politics*, Princeton UP, 1971, 440 pp.

Triska, Jan R., ed., *Soviet Communist Programs and Rules: Official Texts of 1919, 1952, (1956), 1961*, Chandler, 1962, 196 pp, pbk.

Twenty-Third Congress of the CPSU, Novosti Press, Moscow, 1966, 439 pp.

Vladimirov, P., *The Twenty-Third Congress of the CPSU and the World Revolutionary Movement*, Novosti Press, Moscow, 1967, 39 pp.

Wolfe, Bertram D., *Khrushchev and Stalin's Ghost: The Text, Background and Meaning of Khrushchev's Secret Address*, Praeger, 1956, 322 pp.

Chapter 4. THE SOVIETS

Carson, George Barr, Jr., *Electoral Practices in the USSR*, Praeger, 1955, 151 pp.

Karpinsky, V., *The Social and State Structure of the USSR*, For. Lang. Pub., Moscow, 1952, 239 pp.

Mote, Max E., *Soviet Local and Republic Elections: A Description of the 1963 Elections in Leningrad Based on Official Documents, Press Accounts, and Private Interviews*, Stanford UP, 1965, 123 pp.

Chapter 5. SOVIET POLITICAL LEADERSHIP

Azrael, Jeremy R., *Managerial Power and Soviet Politics*, Harvard UP, 1968, 258 pp.

Crankshaw, Edward, *Khrushchev: A Career*, Viking, 1966, 311 pp.

Dallin, Alexander and Thomas B. Larson, eds., *Soviet Politics Since Khrushchev*, Prentice-Hall, 1968, 181 pp.

Deutscher, Isaac, *Stalin: A Political Biography*, 2nd ed., Oxford UP, 1967.

Ebon, Martin, *Malenkov: Stalin's Successor*, New York UP, 1953, 284 pp.

Farrell, R. Barry, ed., *Political Leadership in Eastern Europe and the Soviet Union*, Aldine, 1969, 359 pp.

Fischer, George, *The Soviet System and Modern Society*, Atherton, 1968, 199 pp.

Frankland, Mark, *Khrushchev*, Penguin, 1966, 213 pp.

Institute for the Study of the USSR, *Who's Who in the USSR*, 2nd ed., Scarecrow, 1965, 1,189 pp.

Juviler, Peter H. and Henry W. Morton, *Soviet Policy-Making: Studies of Communism in Transition*, Praeger, 1967, 274 pp.

Kellen, Konrad, *Khrushchev: A Political Portrait*, Praeger, 1961, 271 pp.

Khrushchev, Nikita, *Khrushchev Remembers*, ed. and trans. Strobe Talbott, Little, Brown, 1970, 639 pp.

Leonhard, Wolfgang, *The Kremlin Since Stalin*, trans. from German by Elizabeth Wiskemann and Marian Jackson, Praeger, 1962, 403 pp.

Linden, Carl A., *Khrushchev and the Soviet Leadership, 1957–1964*, Johns Hopkins UP, 1966, 270 pp, pbk.

Moore, Barrington, *Soviet Politics: The Dilemmas of Power; The Role of Ideas in Social Change*, Harvard UP, 1950, 503 pp.

Nicolaevsky, Boris, *Power and the Soviet Elite*, ed. Jane Zagoria, Praeger, 1965, 275 pp.

Payne, Robert, *The Rise and Fall of Stalin*, Simon and Schuster, 1965, 767 pp.

Randall, Francis B., *Stalin's Russia*, Free Press, 1965, 328 pp.

Rigby, T. H., ed., *Stalin*, Prentice-Hall, 1966, 182 pp.

Rush, Myron, *Political Succession in the USSR*, 2nd ed., Columbia UP, 1968, 281 pp, pbk.

Schueller, George K., *The Politburo*, Stanford UP, 1951, 79 pp.

Tatu, Michel, *Power in the Kremlin: From Khrushchev to Kosygin*, trans. Helen Katel, Viking, 1969, 570 pp.

Chapter 6. ADMINISTRATION IN THE USSR: PLANNING AND CONTROLS

1. THE PLANNED ECONOMY

Balinky, Alexander *et al.*, *Planning and the Market in the USSR: The 1960's*, Rutgers UP, 1967, 132 pp.

Bergson, Abram, *The Economics of Soviet Planning*, Yale UP, 1964, 394 pp, pbk.

——, *Planning and Productivity under Soviet Socialism*, Columbia UP, 1968, 95 pp.

Bernard, Philippe J., *Planning in the Soviet Union*, Pergamon, London, 1966, 309 pp.

Campbell, Robert W., *Soviet Economic Power: Its Organization, Growth and Challenge*, Houghton Mifflin, 1960, 209 pp, pbk.

Conklin, David W., *An Evaluation of the Soviet Profit Reforms with Special Reference to Agriculture*, Praeger, 1971, 210 pp.

Davies, R. W., *The Development of the Soviet Budgetary System*, Cambridge UP, 1959, 372 pp.

Degras, Jane, ed., *Soviet Planning*, Praeger, 1965, 224 pp.

Ellman, Michael, *Economic Reform in the Soviet Union*, PEP, London, 1969, pbk.

Erlich, Alexander, *The Soviet Industrialization Debate, 1924–1928*, Harvard UP, 1960, 214 pp.

Gerschenkron, Alexander, *Continuity in History and Other Essays*, Harvard UP, 1968, 534 pp.

——, *Economic Backwardness in Historical Perspective: A Book of Essays*, Harvard UP, 1962, 364 pp.

Goldman, Marshall I., *The Soviet Economy: Myth and Reality*, Prentice-Hall, 1968, 176 pp, pbk.

Grossman, Gregory, *Soviet Statistics of Physical Output of Industrial Commodities*, Princeton UP, 1960, 151 pp.

Hodgkins, Jordan A., *Soviet Power, Energy Resources, Production and Potentials*, Prentice-Hall, 1961, 190 pp.

Hodgman, Donald R., *Soviet Industrial Production, 1928–1951*, Harvard UP, 1954, 241 pp.

Holzman, Franklyn D., *Soviet Taxation: The Fiscal and Monetary Problems of a Planned Economy*, Harvard UP, 1955, 376 pp.

Jasny, Naum, *Soviet Industrialization, 1928–1952*, Chicago UP, 1961, 488 pp.

Kazakov, George, *The Soviet Peat Industry: A Descriptive Study*, Praeger, 1956, 245 pp.

Kosygin, Alexei N., *Directives of the Five-Year Economic Plan of the USSR for 1971–1975: Report to the Twenty-Fourth Congress of the CPSU, April 6, 1971*, Novosti Press, Moscow, 1971, 79 pp.

——, *Report on the Directives for the Five-Year Economic Development Plan of the USSR for 1966–1970: Delivered at the Twenty-Third Congress of the CPSU*, Novosti Press, Moscow, 1966, 110 pp.

Mazour, Anatole G., *Soviet Economic Development: Operation Outstrip 1921–1965*, Van Nostrand, 1967, 191 pp, pbk.

Miller, Margaret *et al.*, *Communist Economy Under Change: Studies in the Theory and Practice of Markets and Competition in Russia, Poland, and Yugoslavia*, Deutsche, London, 1963, 272 pp.

Nove, Alec, *Economic Rationality and Soviet Politics, or Was Stalin Really Necessary?* Praeger, 1964, 316 pp.

——, *The Soviet Economy: An Introduction*, 2nd ed., Praeger, 1969, 373 pp, pbk.

Nutter, G. Warren, *The Growth of Industrial Production in the Soviet Union*, Princeton UP, 1962, 733 pp.

Preobazhensky, E., *The New Economics*, trans. Brian Pearce, Oxford UP, 1965, 310 pp.

Schwartz, Harry G., *The Soviet Economy Since Stalin*, Lippincott, 1965, 256 pp, pbk.

Shaffer, Harry G., *The Soviet Economy: A Collection of Western and Soviet Views*, Appleton-Century-Crofts, 1964, 465 pp, pbk.

Sutton, Antony, *Western Technology and Soviet Economic Development, 1917–1930*, Hoover Inst., 1968, 381 pp.

Treml, Vladimir G. and Robert Farrell, eds., *The Development of the Soviet Economy: Plan and Performance*, Praeger, 1968, 296 pp.

Wiles, P. J. D., *The Political Economy of Communism*, Blackwell, Oxford, 1962, 404 pp.

Zaleski, Eugène, *Planning Reforms in the Soviet Union, 1962–1966: An Analysis of Recent Trends in Economic Organization and Management*, trans. M. Macandrew and G. Warren Nutter, North Carolina UP, 1967, 203 pp.

2. AGRICULTURAL POLICY

Belov, Fedor, *The History of a Soviet Collective Farm*, Praeger, 1955, 237 pp.

Conquest, Robert, ed., *Agricultural Workers in the USSR*, Praeger, 1969, 139 pp.

Dinerstein, Herbert S. and Leon Goure, *Two Studies in Soviet Controls: Communism and the Russian Peasant, and Moscow in Crisis*, Free Press, 1955, 254 pp.

Jasny, Naum, *The Socialized Agriculture of the USSR: Plans and Performance*, Stanford UP, 1949, 837 pp.

Karcz, Jerzy F. and V. P. Timoshenko, *Soviet Agricultural Policy, 1953–1962*, Stanford UP, 1964, 41 pp.

Laird, Roy D., *Collective Farming in Russia: A Political Study of the Soviet Kolkhozy*, Kansas UP, 1958, 176 pp.

——, ed., *Soviet Agriculture and Peasant Affairs*, Kansas UP, 1963, 335 pp.

—— and Edward L. Crowley, eds., *Soviet Agriculture: The Permanent Crisis*, Praeger, 1965, 209 pp.

—— and Betty A. Laird, *Soviet Communism and Agrarian Revolution*, Penguin, 1970, 158 pp, pbk.

Lewin, Moshe, *Russian Peasants and Soviet Power: A Study of Collectivization*, trans. Irene Nove, Northwestern UP, 1968, 539 pp.

Ploss, Sidney I., *Conflict and Decision-Making in Soviet Russia: A Case Study of Agricultural Policy, 1953–1963*, Princeton UP, 1965, 312 pp, pbk.

3. LOCAL ADMINISTRATION

Cattell, David T., *Leningrad: A Case Study of Soviet Urban Government*, Praeger, 1968, 171 pp.

4. LABOR, WELFARE, AND MANAGEMENT

Azrael, Jeremy R., *Managerial Power and Soviet Politics*, Harvard UP, 1966, 258 pp.

Barker, G. Russell, *Some Problems of Incentives and Labour Productivity in Soviet Industry*, Blackwell, Oxford, 1956, 130 pp.

Berliner, Joseph S., *Factory and Manager in the USSR*, Harvard UP, 1957, 386 pp.

Brown, Emily C., *Soviet Trade Unions and Labor Relations*, Harvard UP, 1966, 394 pp.

Chapman, Janet G., *Real Wages in Soviet Russia Since 1928*, Harvard UP, 1963, 395 pp.

Conquest, Robert, ed., *Industrial Workers in the USSR*, Praeger, 1967, 203 pp.

Field, Mark G., *Soviet Socialized Medicine: An Introduction*, Free Press, 1967, 231 pp.

Granick, David, *Management of the Industrial Firm in the USSR: A Study in Soviet Economic Planning*, Columbia UP, 1954, 346 pp.

———, *The Red Executive: A Study of the Organization Man in Russian Industry*, Doubleday, 1960, 336 pp.

McAuley, Mary, *Labour Disputes in Russia 1957–1965*, Oxford UP, 1969, 269 pp.

Madison, Bernice Q., *Social Welfare in the Soviet Union*, Stanford UP, 1968, 298 pp.

Miller, Margaret, *Rise of the Russian Consumer*, Inst. of Economic Affairs, London, 1965, 254 pp, pbk.

Organisation and Administration of Social Welfare Programmes: A Series of Country Studies, USSR, U.N. Department of Economics and Social Affairs, 1967, 78 pp.

Osborn, Robert J., *Soviet Social Policies, Welfare, Equality, and Community*, Dorsey Press, 1970.

Principal Current Soviet Labor Legislation: A Compilation of Documents, U.S. Dept. of Labor, 1962, 135 pp.

A Report on Social Security Administration in the Soviet Union, U.S. Social Security Administration, 1960, 157 pp.

A Report on Social Security Programs in the Soviet Union, U.S. Dept. of Health, Education, and Welfare, 1960, 157 pp.

Swianiewicz, S., *Forced Labour and Economic Development: An Enquiry into the Experience of Soviet Industrialization*, Oxford UP, 1965, 321 pp.

Chapter 7. SOVIET LAW AND COURTS

Berman, Harold J., *Justice in the USSR: An Interpretation of Soviet Law*, rev. ed., Harvard UP, 1963, 450 pp.

——— and John B. Quigley, Jr., eds., *Basic Laws on the Structure of the Soviet State*, Harvard UP, 1969, 325 pp, pbk.

——— and James W. Spindler, trans. and intro., *Soviet Criminal Law and Procedure: The RSFSR Codes*, Harvard UP, 1966, 501 pp.

Conquest, Robert, ed., *Justice and the Legal System in the USSR*, Praeger, 1968, 152 pp.

———, *The Soviet Police System*, Praeger, 1968, 103 pp.

Feifer, George, *Justice in Moscow*, Simon and Schuster, 1964, 353 pp.

Gsovski, Vladimir and Kazimierz Grzybowski, eds., *Government, Law and Courts in the Soviet Union and Eastern Europe*, 2 vols, Praeger, 1960, 2,067 pp.

Guins, George C., *Soviet Law and Soviet Society*, Nijhoff, The Hague, 1954, 457 pp.

Hazard, John N., *Law and Social Change in the USSR*, Carswell, Toronto, 1953, 310 pp.

———, *Settling Disputes in Soviet Society: The Formative Years of Legal Institutions*, Columbia UP, 1960, 534 pp.

———, ed., *Soviet Legal Philosophy*, Harvard UP, 1952, 520 pp.

———, Isaac Shapiro, and Peter B. Maggs, *The Soviet Legal System: Post-Stalin Contemporary Documentation and Historical Commentary*, 2nd ed., 1969, 667 pp.

Kelsen, Hans, *The Communist Theory of Law*, Praeger, 1955, 203 pp.

La Fave, Wayne, ed., *Law in the Soviet Society*, Illinois UP, 1965, 297 pp, pbk.

Lappena, Ivo, *Soviet Penal Policy*, Dufour, 1968, 251 pp.

Massell, Gregory, "Law as an Instrument of Revolutionary Transformation in a Traditional Milieu," *Law & Society Review*, 2, 1968: 179–228.

Morgan, Glenn G., *Soviet Administrative Legality: The Role of the Attorney General's Office*, Stanford UP, 1962, 281 pp.

Szirmai, Z., ed., *Law in Eastern Europe*, Vol. 3. *The Federal Criminal Law of the Soviet Union*, Sijthoff, Leyden, 1959, 157 pp.

Vyshinsky, Andrei Y., *The Law of the Soviet State*, Macmillan, 1948, 749 pp.

Chapter 8. THE SOVIET UNION AND FOREIGN AFFAIRS

1. SOVIET RELATIONS WITH OTHER COMMUNIST COUNTRIES

Bromke, Adam, *Poland's Politics: Idealism versus Realism*, Harvard UP, 1967, 316 pp.

Brown, J. F., *The New Eastern Europe: The Khrushchev Era and After*, Praeger, 1966, 306 pp.

Brzezinski, Zbigniew K., *The Soviet Bloc: Unity and Conflict*, rev. ed., Harvard UP, 1967, 575 pp.

Burks, R. V., *The Dynamics of Communism in Eastern Europe*, Princeton UP, 1961, 388 pp, pbk.

Byrnes, Robert F., ed., *The United States and Eastern Europe*, Prentice-Hall, 1967, 176 pp, pbk.

Chapman, Colin, *August 21st: The Rape of Czechoslovakia*, Cassell, London, 1968, 124 pp.

Clemens, Walter C., *The Arms Race and Sino-Soviet Relations*, Hoover Inst., 1969, 335 pp, pbk.

Clissold, Stephen, ed., *Soviet Relations with Latin America, 1918–1968: A Documentary Survey*, Oxford UP, 1970, 313 pp.

Clubb, O. Edmund, *China and Russia: The Great Game*, Columbia UP, 1971, 578 pp.

Cornell, Richard, "Comparative Analysis of Communist Movements," *JP*, 30(1), Feb. 1968:66–89.

Dedijer, Vladimir, *The Battle Stalin Lost: Memoirs of Yugoslavia 1948–1953*, Viking, 1971, 341 pp.

Gamarnikow, Michael, *Economic Reforms in Eastern Europe*, Wayne State UP, 1968, 206 pp.

Gittings, John, *Survey of the Sino-Soviet Dispute: A Commentary and Extracts from the Recent Polemics, 1963–1967*, Oxford UP, 1968, 410 pp.

Griffith, William E., ed., *Communism in Europe: Continuity, Change, and the Sino-Soviet Dispute*, Vol. 2, MIT Press, 1966, 439 pp.

———, *Sino-Soviet Relations, 1964–65*, MIT Press, 1968, 504 pp.

———, *The Sino-Soviet Rift*, MIT Press, 1964, 512 pp., pbk.

Hiscocks, Richard, *Poland, Bridge for the Abyss: An Interpretation of Developments in Postwar Poland*, Oxford UP, 1963, 359 pp.

Ionescu, Ghita, *The Politics of the European Communist States*, Weidenfeld & Nicolson, London, 1968, 304 pp.

Jamgotch, Nish, Jr., *Soviet-Eastern European Dialogue: International Relations of a New Type?* Hoover Inst., 1968, 165 pp, pbk.

Kaser, Michael, *Comecon: Integration Problems of the Planned Economies*, 2nd ed., Oxford UP, 1968, 279 pp.

Kertesz, Stephen D., ed., *East Central Europe and the World: Developments in the Post-Stalin Era*, Notre Dame UP, 1966, 350 pp.

Kusin, Vladimir V., *The Intellectual Origins of the Prague Spring*, Cambridge UP, 1971.

Macartney, C. A., *Hungary: A Short History*, Aldine, 1970, 262 pp.

Morrison, James F., *The Polish People's Republic*, Johns Hopkins UP, 1968, 160 pp, pbk.

Pelikan, Jiri, ed., *The Czechoslovak Political Trials, 1950–54*, Macdonald, London, 1971.

———, ed., *The Secrecy Vysocany Congress*, Penguin, 1971, 304 pp.

Pounds, Norman J. G., *Eastern Europe*, Aldine, 1969, 912 pp.

Remington, Robin A., ed., *Winter In Prague: Documents on Czechoslovak Communism in Crisis*, MIT Press, 1969, 480 pp.

Schwartz, Benjamin I., *Communism and China: Ideology in Flux*, Harvard UP, 1968, 254 pp.

Schwartz, Harry, *Prague's 200 Days: The Struggle for Democracy in Czechoslovakia*, Praeger, 1969, 274 pp.

Seton-Watson, Hugh, *Nationalism and Communism: Essays, 1946–1963*, Methuen, London, 1964, 288 pp.

Shawcross, William, *Dubcek*, Simon and Schuster, 1971, 317 pp.

Shoup, Paul, *Communism and the Yugoslav National Question*, Columbia UP, 1968, 308 pp.

Sirc, L., *Economic Devolution of Eastern Europe*, Longmans, London, 1969, 166 pp.

Skilling, H. Gordon, "Background to the Study of Opposition in Communist Eastern Europe," *Gov. & Opp.*, Summer 1968:294–324.

———, *Communism, National and International: Eastern Europe After Stalin*, Toronto UP, 1965, 168 pp, pbk.

Stehle, Hansjakob, *The Independent Satellite: Society and Politics in Poland Since 1945*, Praeger, 1965, 361 pp.

Sugar, P. F. and I. J. Lederer, eds., *Nationalism in Eastern Europe*, Washington UP, 1970, 465 pp.

Sviták, Ivan, *The Czechoslovak Experiment, 1968–1969*, Columbia UP, 1971, 243 pp.

Tarulis, Albert N., *Soviet Policy Toward the Baltic States, 1918–1940*, Notre Dame UP, 1959, 276 pp.

Tigrid, Pavel, *Why Dubzek Fell*, Macdonald, London, 1971.

Trevelyan, Lord Humphrey, *World Apart: China, 1953–55, USSR, 1962–65*, Macmillan, 1971.

Váli, Ferenc A., *Rift and Revolt in Hungary: Nationalism Versus Communism*, Harvard UP, 1961, 590 pp.

Weisskopf, Kurt, *The Agony of Czechoslovakia, 1938–1968*, Elek, London, 1968, 234 pp.

Wiles, P. J. D., *Communist International Economics*, Blackwell, Oxford, 1967, 580 pp.

Windsor, Philip and Adam Roberts, *Czechoslovakia 1968: Reform, Repression and Resistance*, Chatto & Windus, London, 1969, 208 pp, pbk.

Zaninovich, M. George, *The Development of Socialist Yugoslavia*, Johns Hopkins UP, 1968, 182 pp, pbk.

2. FOREIGN POLICY

Allard, Sven, *Russia and the Austrian State Treaty: A Case Study of Soviet Policy in Europe*, Pennsylvania State UP, 1970, 248 pp.

Barghoorn, Frederick C., *The Soviet Cultural Offensive: The Role of Cultural Diplomacy in Soviet Foreign Policy*, Princeton UP, 1960, 353 pp.

Beloff, Max, *The Foreign Policy of Soviet Russia, 1929–1941*, Oxford UP, 2 vols: 1929–1936, 1947, 261 pp; 1936–1941, 1949, 434 pp.

———, *Soviet Policy in the Far East, 1944–1951*, Oxford UP, 1954, 278 pp.

Berliner, Joseph S., *Soviet Economic Aid: The New Aid and Trade Policy in Underdeveloped Countries*, Praeger, 1958, 232 pp.

Bloomfield, Lincoln, Walter C. Clemens, and Franklyn Griffiths, *Khrushchev and the Arms Race: Soviet Interests in Arms Control and Disarmament, 1954–1964*, MIT Press, 1966, 338 pp.

Carr, Edward H., *German-Soviet Relations Between the Two World Wars, 1919–1939*, Johns Hopkins UP, 1951, 146 pp.

Clemens, Walter C., *Soviet Disarmament Policy, 1917–1963*, Stanford UP, 1965, 151 pp, pbk.

Dallin, Alexander, "Soviet Foreign Policy and Domestic Politics: A Framework for Analysis," *JIA*, 23(2) 1969:250–65.

———, *The Soviet Union at the United Nations: Inquiry into Soviet Motives and Objectives*, Praeger, 1962, 250 pp, pbk.

Deane, John R., *The Strange Alliance: The Story of Our Efforts at Wartime Co-operation with Russia*, Viking, 1947, 344 pp.

Degras, Jane, ed., *Soviet Documents on Foreign Policy*, Oxford UP, 3 vols: 1917–1924, 1951, 501 pp; 1925–1932, 1952, 560 pp; 1933–1941, 1953, 522 pp.

Dinerstein, Herbert S., *Fifty Years of Soviet Foreign Policy*, Johns Hopkins UP, 1968, 326 pp, pbk.

Embree, George D., ed., *The Soviet Union and the German Question, Sept. 1958–June 1961*, Nijhoff, The Hague, 1963, 331 pp.

Eudin, Xenia J. and Robert M. Slusser, *Soviet Foreign Policy, 1928–1934: Documents and Materials*, 2 vols, Pennsylvania State UP, 1966–67, 778 pp.

Fischer, Louis, *Russia, America and the World*, Harper, 1961, 244 pp.

Goldman, Marshall I., *Soviet Foreign Aid*, Praeger, 1967, 265 pp.

Gvishiani, Lyndmila A., *Soviet Russia and the U.S.A., 1917–1920*, 1970, 328 pp (Kosygin's daughter).

Harriman, W. Averell, *America and Russia in a Changing World: A Half Century of Personal Observation*, Doubleday, 1970, 218 pp.

Hayter, Sir William, *The Kremlin and the Embassy*, Macmillan, 1967.

Horelick, Arnold L. and Myron Rush, *Strategic Power and Soviet Foreign Policy*, Chicago UP, 1966, 225 pp.

Hurewitz, J. C., ed., *Soviet-American Rivalry in the Middle East*, Proceedings of the Academy of Political Science, 29(3), Praeger, 1969, 250 pp, pbk.

Jacobson, Harold Karan, *The USSR and the UN's Economic and Social Activities*, Notre Dame UP, 1963, 309 pp.

Jados, Stanley S., *Documents on Russian-American Relations: Washington to Eisenhower*, Catholic University of America Press, 1965, 416 pp.

Joy, Admiral C. Turner, *How the Communists Negotiate*, Macmillan, 1956, 178 pp.

Kennan, George F., *On Dealing with the Communist World*, Harper, 1964, 57 pp, pbk.

Laqueur, Walter, *Russia and Germany: A Century of Conflict*, Weidenfeld & Nicolson, London, 1965, 367 pp.

Larson, Thomas B., *Disarmament and Soviet Policy, 1964–1968*, Prentice-Hall, 1969, 280 pp.

Lederer, Ivo J., ed., *Russian Foreign Policy: Essays in Historical Perspective*, Yale UP, 1964, 620 pp.

Lenczowski, George, *Russia and the West in Iran, 1918–1948: A Study in Big-Power Rivalry*, Cornell UP, 1949, 393 pp.

Linden, Carl A., *Khrushchev and the Soviet Leadership, 1957–1964*, Johns Hopkins UP, 1966, 278 pp, pbk.

Morrison, David, *The USSR and Africa*, Oxford UP, 1964, 124 pp.

Pryor, Frederic L., *The Communist Foreign Trade Systems*, Allen & Unwin, London, 1963, 296 pp.

Rees, David, *The Age of Containment: The Cold War, 1945–1965*, St. Martin's, 1967, 156 pp, pbk.

Rubinstein, Alvin Z., ed., *The Foreign Policy of the Soviet Union*, 2nd ed., Random House, 1966, 478 pp, pbk.

————, *The Soviets in International Organizations: Changing Policy Towards Developing Countries, 1953–1963*, Princeton UP, 1964, 380 pp.

Schweisfurth, Theodor, "Moscow Doctrine as a Norm of International Law," *Aussenpolitik*, 22(1), Hamburg, 1971:85–101.

Shapiro, Leonard, *Soviet Treaty Series*, Georgetown UP, 2 vols: *1917–1929*, 1950, 406 pp; *1929–1939*, 1955, 257 pp.

Sharp, Samuel L., *Soviet Foreign Policy: A 50-Year Perspective*, Atherton, 1966.

Shulman, Marshall, *Beyond the Cold War*, Yale UP, 1966, 111 pp, pbk.

Stalin's Correspondence with Churchill, Attlee, Roosevelt and Truman, 1941–1945, 2 vols, Lawrence & Wishart, London, 1958, 401 and 302 pp.

Thornton, Thomas P., ed., *The Third World in Soviet Perspective: Studies by Soviet Writers on the Developing Areas*, Princeton UP, 1964, 355 pp.

Triska, Jan F. and Robert M. Slusser, *The Theory, Law and Policy of Soviet Treaties*, Stanford UP, 1962, 593 pp.

Ulam, Adam B., *Expansion and Coexistence: The History of Soviet Foreign Policy 1917–67*, Praeger, 1968, 775 pp.

————, *The Rivals: America and Russia Since World War II*, Viking, 1971, 405 pp.

Weeks, Albert L., *The Other Side of Coexistence*, Pitman, 1970, 304 pp.

Wesson, Robert G., *Soviet Foreign Policy in Perspective*, Dorsey, 1969, 472 pp.

Wilbur, Charles K., *The Soviet Model and Underdeveloped Countries*, North Carolina UP, 1969, 241 pp.

Zimmerman, William, *Soviet Perspectives on International Relations: 1956–1967*, Princeton UP, 1969, 336 pp.

3. ARMED FORCES

Erickson, John, *Soviet Military Power*, Royal United Service Inst., London, 1971.

Fairhall, David, *Russia Looks to the Sea*, Deutsch, London, 1971, 288 pp.

Garder, Michel, *A History of the Soviet Army*, Praeger, 1966, 226 pp.

Garthoff, Raymond L., *Soviet Military Policy: A Historical Analysis*, Praeger, 1966, 276 pp.

————, *Soviet Strategy in the Nuclear Age*, Praeger, 1962, 320 pp, pbk.

Joshua, Wynfred and Stephen P. Gilbert, *Arms for the Third World: Soviet Military Aid Diplomacy*, Johns Hopkins UP, 1969, 179 pp.

Kilmarx, Robert A., *A History of Soviet Air Power*, Faber, London, 1962, 366 pp.

Kintner, William R. and Harriet F. Scott, eds., *The Nuclear Revolution in Soviet Military Affairs*, Oklahoma UP, 1968, 420 pp.

Kolkowicz, Roman, *The Soviet Military and the Communist Party*, Princeton UP, 1967, 429 pp.

Milsom, John, *Russian Tanks 1900–1970*, Arms & Armour Press, London, 1970, 192 pp.

O'Ballance, Edgar, *The Red Army*, Faber, London, 1964, 237 pp.

Ra'anan, Uri, *The USSR Arms the Third World: Case Studies in Soviet Foreign Policy*, MIT Press, 1969, 256 pp.

Sokolovski, Marshal Vasilii Danilovich, ed., *Military Strategy: Soviet Doctrine and Concepts*, Praeger, 1963, 396 pp.

4. INTERNATIONAL COMMUNISM

Allen, Richard V., ed., *Yearbook on International Communist Affairs: 1969*, Hoover Inst., 1970, 1,165 pp.

Aspaturian, Vernon V., *The Soviet Union in the World Communist System*, Hoover Inst., 1966, 96 pp, pbk.

Braunthal, Julius, *History of the International*, trans. Henry Collins and Kenneth Mitchell, Praeger, 2 vols: *1864–1914*, 1967, 376 pp; *1914–1943*, 1967, 581 pp.

Cronyn, George W., *A Primer on Communism*, rev. ed., Dutton, 1962, 192 pp, pbk.

Degras, Jane, ed., *The Communist International, 1919–1943: Documents*, Oxford UP, 3 vols: *1919–1922*,

1956, 479 pp; *1923–1928*, 1960, 584 pp; *1929–1943*, 1965, 494 pp.

Drachkovitch, Milorad M., ed., *The Revolutionary Internationals, 1864–1943*, Stanford UP, 1966, 256 pp.

———, ed., *Yearbook on International Communist Affairs 1966*, Hoover Inst., 1967, 766 pp.

——— and Branko Lazitch, eds., *The Comintern: Historical Highlights*, Praeger, 1966, 430 pp.

Hammond, Thomas T., ed., *Soviet Foreign Relations and World Communism: A Selected, Annotated Bibliography of 7,000 Books in 30 Languages*, Princeton UP, 1965, 1,240 pp.

Labedz, Leopold, ed., *International Communism After Khrushchev*, MIT Press, 1965, 232 pp.

Lowenthal, Richard, *World Communism: The Disintegration of a Secular Faith*, Oxford UP, 1964, 296 pp.

Seton-Watson, Hugh, *From Lenin to Khrushchev: The History of World Communism*, rev. ed., Praeger, 1960, 447 pp, pbk.

Sworakowski, Witold S., *The Communist International and Its Front Organizations: Research Guide and Check List of Holdings in American and European Libraries*, Stanford UP, 1966, 493 pp.

World Communism: A Selected Annotated Bibliography, U.S. 88th Cong. 2nd Sess., Senate Doc. No. 69, 1964, 394 pp.

Index

A 2
B 3
C 4
D 5
E 6
F 7
G 8
H 9
I 0
J 1